lonely planet

England

David Else,
Oliver Berry, Fionn Davenport, Belinda Dixon,
Peter Dragicevich, Nana Luckham,
Etain O'Carroll, Neil Wilson

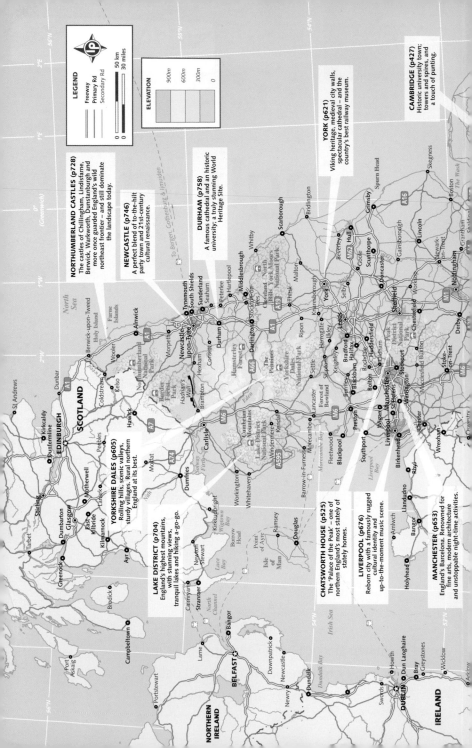

NORTHUMBERLAND CASTLES (p728)
The castles of Chillingham, Lindisfarne, Berwick, Warkworth, Dunstanburgh and more once guarded England's wild northeast frontier – and still dominate the landscape today.

NEWCASTLE (p746)
A perfect blend of to-the-hilt party town and 21st-century cultural renaissance.

DURHAM (p758)
A famous cathedral and an historic university; a truly stunning World Heritage Site.

YORK (p621)
Viking heritage, medieval city walls, spectacular cathedral – and the country's best railway museum.

CAMBRIDGE (p427)
Historic university town; towers and spires, and a touch of punting.

YORKSHIRE DALES (p605)
Rolling hills, scenic valleys, sturdy villages. Rural northern England at its best.

LAKE DISTRICT (p704)
England's highest mountains, with stunning views, tranquil lakes and hiking a-go-go.

CHATSWORTH HOUSE (p525)
The 'Palace of the Peak' – one of northern England's most stately of stately homes.

LIVERPOOL (p676)
Reborn city with a famously rugged cultural identity and up-to-the-moment music scene.

MANCHESTER (p653)
England's Barcelona. Renowned for fine arts, modern architecture and unstoppable night-time activities.

LEGEND

Freeway
Primary Rd
Secondary Rd

0   50 km
0   30 miles

ELEVATION

900m
600m
300m
0

NEWQUAY (p400)
England's surf capital: big waves, bleached hair, kombis – the lot.

THE COTSWOLDS (p244)
Classic rural scenery. Picture-postcard villages. Antique shops on every corner.

BRISTOL (p329)
A fierce mix of rich history and modern outlook, with a music scene to rival hip northern outposts.

DEVON & CORNWALL (p369)
England's wild west – rolling moors, lush farmland, beautiful bays and sandy beaches.

AVEBURY (p326)
England's largest stone circle, sometimes dubbed the 'other Stonehenge', it's even more mysterious and mystical.

BATH (p341)
Stylish and lively city, superb Georgian crescents, famous Roman ruins.

WINCHESTER (p278)
The ancient English capital of King Alfred the Great, now home to handsome historic buildings and a wondrous cathedral.

OXFORD (p222)
Ancient university, manicured colleges, evocative architecture – reeking of history.

BRIGHTON (p204)
Outrageously hip, delightfully camp and incessantly vibrant seaside resort.

CANTERBURY (p175)
Gorgeous medieval buildings; one of the finest cathedrals in Europe. History to die for.

LONDON (p91)
England's capital, Britain's cultural melting-pot. Europe's largest metropolis. The world in one city.

On the Road

DAVID ELSE Coordinating Author

Working on this and several previous editions of Lonely Planet's *England* guide, I've travelled the length and breadth of my homeland. This picture was taken near the top end of the country, at the iconic – and gigantic – *Angel of the North*. I'm the one on the right.

OLIVER BERRY I've hiked all over the world from Corsica to Canada, but for me there's still nowhere that quite compares with the Lakeland fells. Helvellyn and Scafell Pike get all the plaudits (and most of the visitors) – here I'm standing on top of one of the less-visited fells, Sergeant Man, after a long slog up from Easedale Tarn. You can just see the shimmer of Lake Windermere in the far background over my left shoulder.

FIONN DAVENPORT This picture was taken in the Liverpool Superstore…which I visited purely for research purposes. It was just before I got 'Liverpool FC 4Ever' tattooed on my heart. Not the skin above my heart. My actual heart.

NANA LUCKHAM The cycleway around Rutland Water is the best place in the country to rediscover cycling, so I took the opportunity to get back in the saddle after a 15-year break. It was a perfect English summer's day until, shortly after this picture was taken, it poured with rain and I got a puncture.

PETER DRAGICEVICH Alternative music, Camden and booze go together, but alternative music, Camden, drinking wine and lazing in the sun is a rarer combination. This photo was taken on a particularly blissful Sunday afternoon at Proud in the Camden Stables Market. There was a band playing inside, but the sun won out.

BELINDA DIXON I'm drinking in my favourite view. From Plymouth's Smeaton's Tower you see a historic harbour, a lively city and the wildernesses of Dartmoor. Which sums up what the west country has: a rich past, a vibrant present and a future full of exciting possibilities. It's a whole lot of fun way out west.

NEIL WILSON Think Scarborough and you think sandcastles on the beach, donkey rides, and fish and chips. But there's much more to the place than traditional seaside resort stuff – like an impressive medieval castle, a Roman lookout station (that's it I'm sitting on), and superb coastal hiking. Yorkshire's like that – there's a lot more to discover beyond the main attractions.

ETAIN O'CARROLL It's a privilege living in Oxford and being surrounded by such a wealth of history and architecture, but there's a whole other world behind those college walls. The divide between town and gown is very much alive and I always feel a bit like I'm on the outside looking in.

For full author biographies see p817.

England Highlights

Modern England is a tale of two countries. On one hand it's a place full of imposing castles and cathedrals, 'olde' local pubs, rolling hills and a general sense of history permeating the whole country. A visitor looking for this England won't be disappointed, but there's also a host of not-to-be-missed contemporary attractions to be enjoyed, from regenerated provincial cities with cool museums and cutting-edge architecture to the best in cuisine from around the globe. Sample a little of both worlds and you'll get a real taste of England in the 21st century.

ROCCO FAS

1 FISH & CHIPS

England's contributions to the culinary world may be limited, but for this simple and incredibly tasty meal. Nothing beats fresh fish and chips (p76), doused with salt and vinegar, and preferably eaten at the seaside *after* a ride on the roller coaster.

Caroline Sieg, Lonely Planet staff

BEAUTIFUL BATH

Soak like a centurion in the therapeutic waters or imagine yourself in a Jane Austen novel wandering the elegant Georgian streets – England's most attractive city (p341) allows you to indulge your inner history buff, and also has great shopping, eating and drinking options.

Belinda Dixon, author

JON DAVISON

2

LOSING YOUR HEAD IN HISTORY AT THE TOWER OF LONDON

Europe's best-preserved medieval fortress (p122) lives up to all expectations. You can wander around on your own to discover quieter corners or join one of the Beefeater tours for insights into the Tower's 1000-year history. But whatever you do don't miss the Crown Jewels, the Bloody Tower and the scaffold site with a list of the unfortunates who have died here.

Peter Dragicevich, author

RICHARD I'ANSON

3

GLENN BEANLAND

4

ST IVES BEACHES

All of the beaches around St Ives Bay (p416) in Cornwall are staggeringly beautiful and sandy. The fact that you can also reach them all by foot from one another makes them wonderfully accessible. If you're lucky and get sunny weather, I don't know another spot in Britain that can compare to Cornish beaches.

'envirosam' (online name), traveller

NICE CUP OF TEA

6

There may be something more civilised than an English tearoom (p81), but I haven't found it.

Maria Hudgins, traveller, Hampton, USA

5 PINT DOWN THE PUB

Whether it's a quick after-work drink or a celebration of whatever kind, the traditional pub (p82) is still the centre of socialising in England. And as well as making new friends over a pint, these days you can also often get decent pub grub to go with your drink.

Sally Schafer, Lonely Planet staff

7 NATIONAL PARKS

In such a small country it's amazing how many national parks they manage to fit in – 10 at last count. Stretching from the windswept wilds of Northumberland (p774) to the heavily populated but no less beautiful South Downs (p173), they originated in the 1950s and today are enjoyed by millions of visitors. Walking is the best way to appreciate their history and rural charm.

Imogen Hall, Lonely Planet staff

YORK & ITS AWE-INSPIRING MINSTER

'Too much history' was how a friend once described York (p621), but if the past is your thing then York will press all the right buttons. And there's plenty to do still, even if you're more interested in great shopping, old pubs and cool restaurants than in old stones and tales of yore.

**Clifton Wilkinson,
Lonely Planet staff**

CHRIS MELLOR

9

BARBARA VAN ZANTEN

8

MEDIEVAL SPLENDOUR IN A COTSWOLD VILLAGE

The villages and rolling hills of the Cotswolds (p240) present an irresistibly quaint image of a bygone England. The cottages, village greens and winding country lanes can all be enjoyed during the day, but spend the night and you can appreciate them without the crowds and also pamper yourself in some of the best boutique hotels in the country.

Etain O'Carroll, author

ANDERS BLOMQVIST

MAGICAL MYSTERY STONES

Stonehenge (p320) is a must-see, but crowds and high expectations can make it a bit disappointing, so once you've admired its ancient slabs head up the road to visit the much more atmospheric and mystical stone circle at Avebury (p326). You can even stay in style at a farm within the circle and enjoy views of the stones from your room.

Belinda Dixon, author

OXFORD & CAMBRIDGE

Oxford and Cambridge may have a long-standing rivalry but they both offer a highly educational look at student life over the last 800 years. In Oxford (p222) you're following in the footsteps of Tolkien, Lyra, CS Lewis and Inspector Morse; in Cambridge (p427) the top attractions are the beautiful colleges and the chance to punt on the river.

Etain O'Carroll, author

12

HOLGER

11

CASTLE-SPOTTING IN NORTHUMBERLAND

RUTH & MAX EASTHAM & PAOLI

When you're the border area between two warring nations, you're going to need some impressive fortresses, and Northumberland has plenty. With dramatic ruins like Dunstanburgh (p780) and still-lived-in splendours like Alnwick (p778), you can spend days visiting these castles and enjoying the equally dramatic countryside and coastline at the same time.

Fionn Davenport, author

13

SEASIDE FUN IN BRIGHTON

CHRISTER FREDRIK

It might be one of England's oldest seaside resorts, but Brighton (p204) still has plenty of life left in it. The pier and the beach are good fun during the day but it's in the evening, when the bars, restaurants and clubs start filling up, that the city truly recalls its Regency decadence.

Nana Luckham, author

ORIEN HARVEY

THE IMPERIAL WAR MUSEUM IN MANCHESTER

A dark but fascinating exploration of warfare housed in a stunning building that's as much a part of the museum's appeal as the displays within (p659).

Fionn Davenport, author

15

14

CANTERBURY & ITS CATHEDRAL

This is the most amazing and beautiful town (p175) in England, peaceful and not too crowded. Visit the cathedral, stroll down the shop-filled main street, then take a rest in one of the splendid parks. Magnificent!

Tijana Salaj, traveller, Osijek, Croatia

DAVID TOMLINSON

16

VISITING THE LAKE DISTRICT

The world-famous Lake District (p704) is pretty much a year-round destination, but a few periods have their own special attractions – autumn for the colours, spring for the daffodils and rhododendrons, and winter for real peace and quiet.

'robynsj123' (online name), traveller

LONDON TUBE MAP

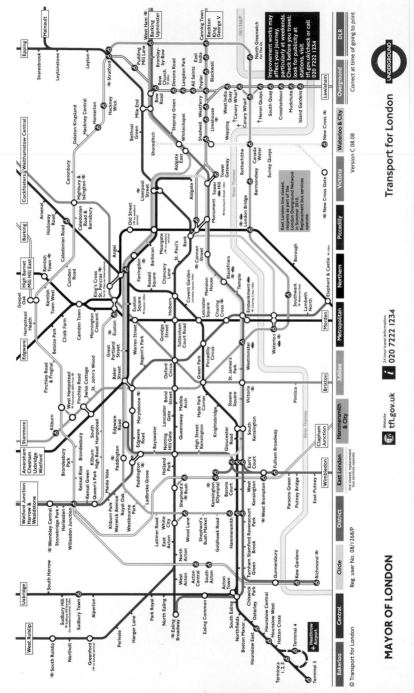

MAYOR OF LONDON

Reg. user No. 08/1268/P

Website tfl.gov.uk

24 hour travel information 020 7222 1234

Transport for London

UNDERGROUND

Version C 08.08   Correct at time of going to print

Bakerloo   Central   Circle   District   East London   Hammersmith & City   Jubilee   Metropolitan   Northern   Piccadilly   Victoria   Waterloo & City   Overground   DLR

Improvement works may affect your journey, particularly at weekends. Check before you travel: look for publicity at stations, visit tfl.gov.uk/check or call 020 7222 1234

East London line closed, reopens as part of the London Overground Network in Summer 2010. Replacement bus services operate

Contents

Regional Map Contents

The Northeast p745

Cumbria & the Lake District p703

Yorkshire pp586-7

The Northwest p652

The East Midlands p473

The West Midlands & the Marches p529

East Anglia p426

Oxford, the Cotswolds & Around p221

London pp96-7

Wessex p277

The Southeast p174

Devon & Cornwall p370

Destination England

Throughout its long history, it's been a green and pleasant land, a sceptred isle and a nation of shopkeepers. It's stood as a beacon of democracy and a bastion of ideological freedom, as well as a crucible of empire and a cradle of class oppression. The Magna Carta, the King James Bible and the welfare state were all dreamt up here, but then again so were beer bellies, Bovril and *Mr Bean*. It's a nation of tea-tippling eccentrics and train spotters, of dog lovers and footy fanatics, of punk rockers, gardeners, gnome collectors, celebrity wannabes, superstar chefs, free-wheeling city traders, pigeon fanciers, cricket bores and part-time Morris Dancers. To some it's Albion. To others it's Blighty. To many it's the most eccentric, extraordinary and downright incomprehensible place on earth. Welcome to England.

Few places can boast such a muddle of conflicting characters as this tiny country. It's a place where contradiction is soaked into the fabric of the landscape. For every green field and rolling dale, there's a flat fen or wind-battered stretch of coastline, and for every faded seaside resort, historic castle and thatch-topped village there's a gleaming new skyscraper, concrete office block or carbuncular car park to match.

It's a nation in thrall to its history but also addicted to a constant process of reinvention. Shiny new cappuccino bars, chain pubs and out-of-town shopping centres have plugged the gap left behind by closing post offices, country inns and village shops. Rural villages are filling up with second-homers and urban refugees, while the old smog-blackened cities of England's northern heartland are finding new leases of life as centres of cultural adventure and artistic innovation. But while change is rampant in some corners, others remain stubbornly resistant to progress: despite huge investment, the trains haven't improved that much, the National Health Service still doesn't work and England still can't string a few wins together at cricket (or football, or rugby, or tennis). Even the old North–South divide is still alive and well: ask any northerner what they think about having to foot the multi-million-pound bill for London to host the 2012 Olympics, and chances are the answer won't be all that complimentary.

After a decade of unprecedented growth, soaring house prices and booming profits, underpinned by some dubious financial wheezes in the City, it looks like England's financial bubble has finally popped. As we go to press in late 2008, the property market is in freefall, petrol prices had gone through the roof and unemployment, food prices and inflation are all on the rise. And no one – neither the cabbies nor the newspaper commentators, and certainly not the mandarins and spin-doctors in Whitehall – seems to have the foggiest idea where England is headed as the global downturn bites and the shadow of recession looms.

But beyond the dreaded return to boom-and-bust economics, there are deeper schisms at work. In the wake of continuing devolution of power from the central government to regionally elected assemblies in Scotland, Wales and Northern Ireland, England's own identity has become a subject of fierce debate. There's even the possibility that the centuries-old Union could be at risk of breaking up – with consequences not just for England's bank balance, but also for the nation's fundamental sense of self. This cuts to the heart of some profound questions about what the notion of Englishness means in a globalised, homogenised world, about the values, beliefs and institutions that bind the country together. Ever nervous about causing unnecessary conflict between the country's increasingly polarised

FAST FACTS

Population: 51 million

Size: 50,000 sq miles (130,000 sq km)

Inflation: 5.2%

Unemployment: 5.7%

Average number of cups of tea drunk per person per day: 3

Hours spent commuting per year: 139

Number of divorces granted per year: 132,500

Number of Jedis in official census: 390,000

Total number of televisions: 30,500,000

Average number of days when it rains: 1 in 3

communities – black and white, Muslim and Christian, North and South, town and country – England finds itself stuck in a kind of ideological limbo, with people wary of taking a stance that might be misinterpreted or misrepresented by the headline-hungry jackals of the British media.

This national process of soul-searching chimes in with a growing sense of unease about where English society is headed. A recent spate of stabbings and shootings coupled with the growing gang culture in many English cities, plus the continuing divisiveness of the wars in the Middle East and the fallout from the 7/7 tube bombings (committed by British-born extremists) all hint at the disaffection and disillusionment felt by many English communities. Even the most unbiased observer would have to admit that there's something slightly awry in a country that has more CCTV and speed cameras than anywhere else in Europe and where the nation's kids have been dubbed 'the unhappiest in the Western World' according to a recent Unicef poll.

It's perhaps unsurprising that record numbers of people are giving Blighty the boot in favour of pastures new. But others are opting to stay in England and go back to the land, quitting the cities for slower, greener, more sustainable lives in the countryside. Transition towns, organic farms, yurt campsites, rooftop wind-generators and grow-your-own vegetable patches are all the rage in England. In a world staring down the barrel of irreversible climate change, England's newfound eco-consciousness might have arrived in the nick of time.

So while there may be choppy waters ahead, if there's one thing this plucky little nation has proven down the centuries, it's resilience (so long as there's a nice hot mug of tea to hand, of course). More than 2000 years of history are packed into this pocket-sized island, and no matter what the future may hold, the true jewels in England's crown – its country houses, castles and chocolate-box villages, its landmark monuments and buzzing music scene, its sweeping countryside, revitalised cities and extraordinary coastline – remain as bright and untarnished as ever. The wars are still raging, the economy's looking dicey and the weather's as reliably awful as ever, but one thing's for certain – England hasn't had her day just yet.

Getting Started

If there were an international league table measuring sights per square acre, this proportionally challenged country would top the charts. England's diminutive dimensions might be a recurrent headache for its residents, but they're a boon for travellers: you're pretty much guaranteed to be no more than a day's journey from the next must-see sight, historic monument or landmark town.

But despite its small size, England doesn't always do its best to make travelling easy (spend a few days negotiating the public transport network and you'll see what we mean). So some pretrip planning is really worthwhile, allowing you to access cut-price hotel rates, cheap train fares and out-of-season deals that you won't find if you leave everything to the last minute. One thing's for sure – there's an English adventure to suit all tastes and budgets, whether that means camping under country skies, bunking down in a boutique B&B or splashing out on a swish metropolitan pad.

WHEN TO GO

There's more information about British weather (including average temperatures and rainfall) in the climate charts on p794.

When you travel will depend on the type of holiday you're looking for, but regardless of when you arrive, the good old British weather is bound to play a part in your plans. The English have long been preoccupied with the nation's weather, and things look set to become even more unpredictable thanks to climate change (just look at the devastating summer floods of 2007 for a sign of things to come). But despite the unpredictability, there are a few rules that underpin the seasons. Winters tend to be cold and wet, with the hottest and driest weather generally reserved for July and August. The shoulder seasons often produce the best weather: sunny spells jostle for space with sudden showers between March and May, while balmy 'Indian summers' often pitch up between September and October. Snow in England generally arrives either end of winter, especially in November and February.

All things considered, late April to September is the best period to travel. Summer sees England at its liveliest: holiday traffic increases substantially during the peak period between late July and August (when the schools are on holiday), especially in seaside areas, national parks and popular cities such as Oxford, Bath and York. Opening hours tend to be reduced between October and Easter, and some places shut down altogether for the winter. But in the big cities – especially London – you'll find plenty to do no matter when you travel.

COSTS & MONEY

There's no getting around it – England isn't cheap. Public transport, admission fees, restaurants and hotel rooms all tend towards the expensive end. A recent survey concluded that Britain's hotels were on average more expensive than those of any other European country. But that doesn't mean an English trip has to break the bank. Staying in B&Bs, prebooking your travel arrangements, and looking out for cheap (or free) attractions will bring your trip budget down to a reasonable level. And don't forget that you won't have to stump up a penny to enjoy England's best asset: its wonderful countryside and coastline. For those on less measly budgets, it's worth noting that restaurant and hotel standards have gone up a lot recently, and there's better value for money than even a few years ago.

In terms of costs, London occupies its own price bracket. Backpackers could scrape by for about £50 a day: £20 on a dorm bed, £10 on self-catering

---

DON'T LEAVE HOME WITHOUT...

Travelling in England is hardly a voyage into the wilderness, but there are a few essentials that are worth bringing along.

- a rain jacket (and a brolly!)
- comfy walking shoes, and maybe some sturdy boots for tackling the countryside trails
- a shoulder-bag or rucksack
- a travel adaptor
- an understanding of imperial measures
- a taste for warm beer
- an ironic sense of humour

---

supplies, £8 to £10 on admissions and £7 for a one-day travelcard. Anything under £80 for a double room could be considered budget accommodation. Upwards of £150 nudges into the top-end bracket. A decent cafe or bistro lunch can be had for between £10 and £15 per person, while dinner is more likely to approach £30 not including wine. Spend upwards of £50 and you should expect something special; shell out £100 and nothing less than celebrity chef standard will do.

Prices outside the capital city vary depending on where you're heading. Top hotels and restaurants in provincial cities such as Manchester, Newcastle, Bath and Bristol can be every bit as expensive as their London counterparts, but there's usually more latitude in the price ranges. The further you travel from the big cities, the more affordable things become. In general, budget travellers should manage on £30 a day including hostels and food; midrangers will travel comfortably on £100 per person, allowing £40 to £50 for B&Bs, £20 to £30 for food, and £20 on travel and admissions.

Travel costs can make a hefty hole in your budget if you don't book ahead – train fares can double or even triple if you buy on the day of travel. Long-distance buses (coaches) are substantially cheaper, often costing half as much as a comparable train fare. Car drivers should remember that petrol in England is heavily taxed; count on 15p to 20p a mile, plus £5 to £10 for parking, and £25 to £50 for a day's car hire.

Many national and municipal museums are free. Parents travelling with kids should keep a lookout for family tickets to sights and attractions, and family rooms in B&Bs. If you're staying in one area for a while, renting self-catering accommodation is by far the most cost-effective option.

HOW MUCH?

Double room in a B&B £60

The Times (newspaper) 60p

One-way train ticket from London to Manchester £115

Pot of tea £4

Pint of beer £3

TRAVELLING RESPONSIBLY

Eco-initiatives have cropped up all over the country, from transition towns and green B&Bs to yurt campsites and even Britain's first plastic bag–free town (Modbury in North Devon). While there's still a way to go, it's perfectly possible to travel around the country while keeping your carbon footprint to a minimum.

In a country as tiny as England there's no need to fly anywhere (using trains and buses is much greener, despite the challenges of timetables and pricey fares). There's also no need for a car in the main cities, although public transport is admittedly patchier in more rural areas. Cycling is worth considering (especially in the flatter and more pedal-friendly counties of the southeast); a huge investment in the **Sustrans** (www.sustrans.co.uk) cycle network has recently been announced, promising a great expansion in England's bike lanes over the next few years.

Food is one of the areas where England's setting the pace. There's been an explosion of interest in locally sourced food in recent years, and every restaurant worth its salt is keen to tout its green credentials. Farmers markets and small food shops are more likely to source their produce locally than the big supermarket chains. Keep your eyes peeled for ecofriendly accommodation, too; the UK has several green accreditation schemes, including the Green Business Award, given to businesses that can prove their commitment to sustainability.

Car Share (www.carshare.com) Catch a lift practically anywhere in England.

Enjoy England (www.enjoyengland.com) Search for 'green tourism' for information on ecotravel in England from the tourist board.

Environment Agency (www.environment-agency.co.uk) Advice from the UK's main environmental body.

Green England (www.green-england.co.uk) Searchable directory of ecofriendly businesses in England, from restaurants to clothes shops.

Green Tourism Business Scheme (www.green-business.co.uk) Accreditation for green businesses, with searchable listings for accommodation and attractions.

One Planet Future (www.wwf.org.uk/oneplanet/) WWF campaign for making Britain greener, with practical tips on ecotravel.

READING UP

What better way to get acquainted with England than by reading someone else's adventures? Here are some of our favourite books about English travel, along with a few tomes exploring the quirkier side of this sceptred isle.

Notes from a Small Island is a bestselling memoir by the American-born author Bill Bryson, based on trips around Britain in the 1970s and '80s. Employing Bryson's trademark fussy style and self-deprecating wit, it's incisive, observant and very funny.

In Search of England by HV Morton is one of the classic prewar English travelogues, written by a veteran *Daily Express* columnist in the 1920s. The language is old-fashioned, but it makes a fascinating companion to more modern texts.

Nigel Cawthorne's *The Strange Laws of Old England* explores lots of weird and wonderful laws on the English statute book. Required reading if you're planning on entering Parliament in a suit of armour or transporting corpses in a London cab.

In *England: 1000 Things You Need To Know,* Nicolas Hobbes examines lots of quintessentially English things, from the people, legends and events that have shaped the nation's history through to the origins of stilton, roast beef and the Royal Mail. Another investigation into 'Englishness' is *In Search of the English Eccentric* by Henry Hemming – a poised, perceptive and frequently hilarious exploration of some of the nation's eccentrics, including crop-circle makers, a man who thinks he's the reincarnation of King Arthur, and Captain Beany, who likes to spend his days bathing in baked beans.

Pies and Prejudice: In Search of the North is a whimsical journey through England's northerly counties by British radio DJ Stuart Maconie, a 'Northerner in exile', who returns to his roots to discover the truth about life Up North.

Paul Gogarty's *The Water Road* travels along England's canals between London and the Humber, Severn and Mersey, colloquially known as the 'Cut' or the 'Grand Cross'. It's a mix of historical account and modern-day travelogue; Gogarty relates a similar trip around English shores in *The Coast Road.*

TOP PICKS

MUST-SEE MOVIES

English cinema has had its ups and downs over the last century, but against all the odds home-grown directors are still carving out a niche for themselves. Here are a few key English movies. For a more in-depth overview, see p62.

- *Brief Encounter* (1945) David Lean
- *Kind Hearts and Coronets* (1949) Robert Hamer
- *This Sporting Life* (1963) Lindsay Anderson
- *The Wicker Man* (1973) Robin Hardy
- *Chariots of Fire* (1981) Hugh Hudson
- *Withnail & I* (1987) Bruce Robinson

- *Hope & Glory* (1987) John Boorman
- *Four Weddings and a Funeral* (1994) Mike Newell
- *Secrets & Lies* (1996) Mike Leigh
- *Shaun of the Dead* (2004) Edgar Wright
- *This Is England* (2006) Shane Meadows

RAVE READS

England has produced a formidable line-up of literary giants down the centuries. We've picked out a few tomes exploring various aspects of the complex English character. See p59 for more recommendations.

- *Sense and Sensibility* (1811) Jane Austen
- *Oliver Twist* (1838) Charles Dickens
- *Wuthering Heights* (1847) Emily Brontë
- *Sons and Lovers* (1913) DH Lawrence
- *The Road to Wigan Pier* (1937) George Orwell
- *Brighton Rock* (1938) Graham Greene
- *Cider with Rosie* (1959) Laurie Lee

- *London Fields* (1989) Martin Amis
- *The Remains of the Day* (1989) Kazuo Ishiguro
- *Last Orders* (1996) Graham Swift
- *White Teeth* (2000) Zadie Smith
- *Atonement* (2001) Ian McEwan
- *Small Island* (2004) Andrea Levy
- *Black Swan Green* (2006) David Mitchell

SOUNDS OF THE SUBURBS

Here's a (highly subjective) pick of some albums we think have played a key part in shaping the nation's musical landscape.

- *Sergeant Pepper's Lonely Hearts Club Band* (1967) – The Beatles
- *The Village Green Preservation Society* (1968) – The Kinks
- *Led Zeppelin IV* (1971) – Led Zeppelin
- *Exile On Main Street* (1972) – The Rolling Stones
- *Ziggy Stardust and the Spiders from Mars* (1972) – David Bowie
- *Never Mind The Bollocks* (1977) – The Sex Pistols

- *London Calling* (1979) – The Clash
- *The Queen Is Dead* (1986) – The Smiths
- *The Stone Roses* (1989) – The Stone Roses
- *Protection* (1994) – Massive Attack
- *Different Class* (1995) – Pulp
- *What's The Story Morning Glory* (1995) – Oasis
- *OK Computer* (1997) – Radiohead
- *Franz Ferdinand* (2004) – Franz Ferdinand
- *Whatever People Say I Am, That's What I'm Not* (2006) – Arctic Monkeys

INTERNET RESOURCES

Here are some top sites to check out before you hit the road.

BBC (www.bbc.co.uk) News and entertainment courtesy of the nation's much-loved broadcaster.

British Council (www.britishcouncil.org) National body dedicated to promoting British culture, arts and science.

eFestivals (www.efestivals.co.uk) Latest news, dates and gossip from the UK's top music festivals.

Enjoy England (www.enjoyengland.co.uk) England's official tourism website; accommodation, attractions, events and much more.

i-UK (www.i-uk.com) Information on living, working and visiting the UK.

Lonely Planet (lonelyplanet.com) Destination guides and travel tips from our own good selves.

National Rail (www.nationalrail.co.uk) Online resource for train timetables and fares.

Sustrans (www.sustrans.org.uk) Sustainable travel advice from England's largest green travel charity.

UK Tea Council (www.tea.co.uk) Everything you ever wanted to know about the nation's favourite tipple (including how to make the perfect brew).

Which (www.which.co.uk) Reviews ranging from travel insurance and consumer rights to sat nav and vacuum cleaners.

Events Calendar

FEBRUARY

JORVIK VIKING FESTIVAL mid-Feb
York becomes home to Horned helmets galore, plus mock invaders and longship races (p628).

MARCH

CRUFTS DOG SHOW early Mar
Coiffured canines strut their stuff in a bid to be awarded Best in Show at Birmingham's historic doggy gathering (p537).

UNIVERSITY BOAT RACE late Mar
Annual race (p135) down the Thames between rowing teams from Cambridge and Oxford Universities, an institution since 1856.

APRIL

GRAND NATIONAL 1st Sat in Apr
Half the country has a flutter on the Aintree horse race (p687), with a testing course and high jumps.

LONDON MARATHON early Apr
Super-fit athletes cover 26 miles 385 yards in just over two hours, while others dress up in daft costumes and take considerably longer (p136).

MAY

FA CUP FINAL early May
The highlight of the football season for over a century. Teams from all England's football divisions battle it out in a knock-out tournament, culminating in this heady spectacle (p54) at Wembley.

BRIGHTON FESTIVAL May
Lively three-week arts fest (p207), which takes over the streets of buzzy Brighton.

CHELSEA FLOWER SHOW late May
Top garden designers take away gold, silver and bronze medals at this Royal Horticultural Society flower show (p135), while the punters take away the plants in the last-day giveaway.

GLYNDEBOURNE late May-Aug
World-class opera in the pastoral surroundings of Glyndebourne House (p204) in East Sussex.

JUNE

THE COTSWOLDS OLIMPICKS early Jun
Welly-wanging, pole-climbing and shin-kicking are the key disciplines at this traditional Gloucestershire sports day (p245), held every year since 1612.

DERBY WEEK early Jun
Horse-racing, people-watching and clothes-spotting are on the agenda at this week-long race meeting (www.epsomderby.co.uk) in Epsom, Surrey.

DOWNLOAD FESTIVAL early Jun
Expect ear-splitting feedback and fists thrust aloft at this heavy-metal fest (www.downloadfestival.co.uk) in Donington Park, Derbyshire.

ISLE OF WIGHT FESTIVAL mid-Jun
Originally held at the height of the Summer of Love in 1968, this musical extravaganza (p295) was resurrected in 2002, and today it attracts top bands (especially from the indie and rock fraternities).

TROOPING THE COLOUR mid-Jun
Military bands and bear-skinned grenadiers march down London's Whitehall in this martial pageant (p136) to mark the monarch's birthday.

ROYAL ASCOT mid-Jun
It's hard to tell which matters more – the fashion or the fillies – at Berkshire's Royal Ascot (p273). Expect top hats, designer frocks and plenty of frantic betting.

WIMBLEDON LAWN TENNIS CHAMPIONSHIPS late Jun
Top grass-court tennis and tons of strawberries at the All England Club's annual tournament (p136). No sign of a British winner coming through any time soon, though.

GLASTONBURY FESTIVAL late Jun
England's favourite musical mudfest (p359), held (nearly) every year on Michael Eavis' dairy farm in Pilton, Somerset, and still a rite of passage for every self-respecting British teenager.

ROYAL REGATTA   late Jun/early Jul
Boats of every description take to the water for Henley's upper-crust river regatta (p238).

PRIDE   late Jun/early Jul
London's West End is home to one of Europe's biggest gay pride festivals (p137) – loud, proud and very definitely out.

JULY

INTERNATIONAL BIRDMAN COMPETITION   1st weekend of Jul
Competitors dressed as batmen, fairies and flying machines compete in an outlandish celebration of self-powered flight at West Sussex' Bognor Regis. The furthest flight takes the top £30,000 prize – so far no-one's got near the hallowed 100m goal.

HAMPTON COURT PALACE FLOWER SHOW   early Jul
Blooming spectacular flower show held in the stately surroundings of London's Hampton Court Palace (p133).

LATITUDE FESTIVAL   mid-Jul
Theatre, cabaret, art, literature and poetry readings, plus top names from the alternative music scene, feature at this small but fast-growing fest (p456) in Suffolk's Southwold.

WORLD SNAIL RACING CHAMPIONSHIPS   mid-Jul
Three hundred of the nation's sportiest snails gather for Congham's speedfest (p441). The prize? A tankard of lettuce leaves, of course.

COWES WEEK   late Jul
Yachting spectacular (p295) on the choppy seas around the Isle of Wight.

WOMAD   late Jul
Roots, jazz, and world music take centre stage at this former Malmesbury-based festival (www.womad.org).

BIG GREEN GATHERING   late Jul/early Aug
The UK's biggest eco-festival (p355), based in Cheddar, Somerset, showcases everything from sustainable living techniques to solar panels and composting toilets, and has recently spawned sister festivals in Ireland, Wales and Leeds.

TRUCK   late Jul
Independent music festival (www.thisistruck.com) in Steventon, Oxfordshire, with a loyal following, known for its eclectic acts.

AUGUST

NOTTING HILL CARNIVAL   late Aug
A multicultural Caribbean-style street carnival (p137) held on the streets of Notting Hill. No sign of Hugh Grant, thank heavens.

READING FESTIVAL   late Aug
England's second-oldest music fest (boxed text, p274) after Glastonbury. Poppier than it once was, but still a good bet for big-name bands.

LEEDS FESTIVAL   late Aug
Leeds' major music festival (p595) shares a line-up with Reading, its southern sister.

SEPTEMBER

BESTIVAL   early Sep
Quirky music festival (p295) with a different fancy dress theme every year, held each year at Robin Hill Country Park on the Isle of Wight.

WORLD GURNING CHAMPIONSHIPS   mid-Sep
Elastic-faced contestants come to Egremont, Cumbria, to contort their features in a bid to pull the most grotesque expression possible.

OCTOBER

HORSE OF THE YEAR SHOW   early Oct
Dressage and show-jumping (p537) at the NEC arena near Birmingham.

NOVEMBER

GUY FAWKES DAY   5 Nov
Bonfires and fireworks fill the country's skies in commemoration of England's original terrorist.

REMEMBRANCE DAY   11 Nov
Poppies are worn and wreaths are laid in commemoration of Britain's brave servicemen and women killed and injured in the line of duty.

WORLD'S BIGGEST LIAR CONTEST   mid-Nov
Fibbers from all walks of life go head-to-head in a battle of mendacity (p723) at Santon Bridge's Bridge Inn in Wasdale, Cumbria.

DECEMBER

NEW YEAR CELEBRATIONS   31 Dec
Fireworks and street parties light up the nation as the New Year rolls in.

Itineraries
CLASSIC ROUTES

THE FULL MONTY One Month / London to Cambridge

Kick off the grand tour in the nation's capital, **London** (p91), before heading down to buzzy **Brighton** (p204) and the picturesque **New Forest** (p289).

Cut inland to **Stonehenge** (p320) via the cathedral cities of **Winchester** (p278) and **Salisbury** (p315), then head west via Hardy's hometown, **Dorchester** (p305), en route to **Exeter** (p373) and wild **Dartmoor National Park** (p387). Head northwest via historic **Wells** (p351) en route to Georgian **Bath** (p341) and the southwest's big little city, **Bristol** (p329).

Then it's across the **Cotswolds** (p240) to England's original seat of learning, **Oxford** (p222), and Shakespeare central in **Stratford-upon-Avon** (p546), before journeying north via the **Peak District** (p512) to cultural **Liverpool** (p676). Detour via the scenic **Lake District** (p704) and follow **Hadrian's Wall** (p769) east to revitalised **Newcastle-upon-Tyne** (p746), with a swift side trip into wild **Northumberland** (p774). Then it's into the home stretch via **Durham Cathedral** (p758), the windswept **North York Moors** (p641) and the Viking city of **York** (p621) en route to journey's end in scholarly **Cambridge** (p427).

England's essentials wrapped up in one whistlestop package. It's a hefty journey of at least 1200 miles from start to finish: cut some sights if you're time-strapped, and allow room for a few unexpected detours to make the most of this classic English journey.

THE WILD SIDE   One Month / Northumberland to Land's End

'Our England is a garden that is full of stately views', wrote Rudyard Kipling, and who are we to argue? In honour of Mr Kipling and the countless other writers, poets and painters who have drawn inspiration from the English landscape, this north–south route strings together some of the stateliest views.

Start off in **Northumberland National Park** (p774), England's final frontier, dotted with fortified castles, breathtaking coastline and wind-lashed hilltops. Then it's west via the crumbling **Hadrian's Wall** (p769) to the radiant **Lake District** (p704), spiritual mecca for the Romantic poets, littered with dramatic hikes, cosy inns and the country's highest peak, **Scaféll Pike** (p729).

Travelling east from the Lakes carries you across 'England's backbone', the Pennine Hills. To the south lie the green hills and valleys of the **Yorkshire Dales** (p605), and to the east are the heather-clad **North York Moors** (p641), where humpbacked hills smack into the grey rollers of the North Sea.

Travelling south through the **Peak District** (p512) and Elgar's beloved **Malvern Hills** (p560) brings you to the southwest's doorstep. Savour the epic dimensions of Salisbury Plain, home to **Stonehenge** (p320) and archaeological interests, followed by the rolling fields and sandy coves of **Exmoor** (p361) or the stunning rust-red sweep of Lyme Bay and the **Jurassic Coast** (p305). Further west, the eerie granite tors of **Dartmoor** (p387) and **Bodmin Moor** (p404) offer some of England's most bleakly beautiful views, rivalled only by the gorse-clad cliff tops and sparkling bays of Cornwall's **North Coast** (p396). Last port of call on this scenic excursion is **Land's End** (p415), where the English mainland finally runs out of steam and plunges headlong into the restless Atlantic. Toodle-pip, England – next stop, America…

A top-to-bottom journey through England's most unforgettable landscapes, covering about 900 miles. The trip lasts around four weeks, or closer to six if you're a dedicated hiker or a real view junky – just don't forget to bring along that camera…

ENGLAND, MY ENGLAND   Three weeks / London to Cumbria

This journey through England's heart and soul starts in London, with a host of quintessential English sights: **Trafalgar Square** (p114), **Westminster Abbey** (p115), the **Tower of London** (p122), **St Paul's** (p122) and the Queen's city-centre pad, **Buckingham Palace** (p117). The gorgeous gardens at **Kew** (p133), **Eton College** (p271) and regal **Windsor Castle** (p269) are also must-see landmarks.

Beyond the capital you'll move into old England proper, especially around the market towns and sleepy villages of **Kent** (p173), **Hampshire** (p278) and **Hertfordshire** (p263). **Hatfield House** (p265) and **Canterbury Cathedral** (p175) jostle for top spot in the architectural stakes, while the southeast coastline hosts a string of classic seaside resorts, from **Whitstable** (p182) and **Margate** (p184) round to **Brighton** (p204) via the **White Cliffs of Dover** (p190).

Out to the west, the cities of **Winchester** (p278), **Salisbury** (p315) and **Bath** (p341) are crammed with landmark English architecture, while the picture-perfect idyllic **Cotswolds** (p240) conceal a host of pretty villages.

Nearby **Oxford** (p222) has been educating the country's elite for centuries, while **Stratford-upon-Avon** (p546) gave the world one Will Shakespeare. The surrounding countryside is littered with traditional English towns, including **Cirencester** (p248), **Wantage** (p239) and **Cheltenham** (p254), as well as the grand estate of **Blenheim Palace** (p236) and historic **Warwick Castle** (p544). Further north, you'll find the home of English pottery in **Stoke-on-Trent** (p553).

Detour via stately **Buxton** (p516) and **Chatsworth House** (p525) en route to another dazzling medieval cathedral in **Lincoln** (p490), before arriving in England's prettiest provincial city, **York** (p621). From here it's a scenic trundle across the rugged **Yorkshire Dales** (p605) via the **Settle–Carlisle railway** (p609) all the way into **Cumbria** (p701).

From the well-to-do south to the windswept north, this itinerary delves into contrasting sides of the national character, travelling via thatched villages, seaside resorts, historic cities and national parks. It's a trip of between 700 and 900 miles depending on your precise route.

ROADS LESS TRAVELLED

NORTHERN SOUL   Two Weeks / Leeds to Newcastle

If you're after a glimpse of where England's at, step outside the self-centred capital and take a spin round England's revitalised north.

Start in **Leeds** (p593), where textile factories and warehouses have been replaced by sleek shops, loft apartments and ritzy boutiques (especially around the restored Victoria Quarter, p599). Take time to explore Bradford's **National Media Museum** (p599) and Claphouse's **National Coal Mining Museum** (p601).

Jockeying with Leeds for the 'England's second city' title is **Manchester** (p653), famous for its music and all-conquering football team (sorry City, we're talking about United). Kip in style at the **Lowry** (p663) or the **Yang Sing Oriental Hotel** (p663) and visit the **Imperial War Museum North** (p659).

Nearby **Liverpool** (p676) has finally stepped out of The Beatles' shadow, reinventing itself as a cultural capital. Stroll its historic waterfront, **Albert Dock** (p680), down a pint at the shipshape **Philarmonic** (p686), indulge at fantastic **Hope Street Hotel** (p684) and check out the **Ropewalks** (p686) club scene.

Long tainted with the smudge of coal and steel, **Newcastle-upon-Tyne** (p746) has given up heavy industries in favour of art and architecture. Cross the wonderful **Millennium Bridge** (p748) to Gateshead and the **Baltic** (p751), a former grain factory turned cutting-edge art gallery, before catching a show at the Sir Norman Foster–designed **Sage Gateshead** concert hall (p755).

Conclude your tour with a visit to England's most popular piece of public art, the iron-winged **Angel of the North** (p757).

It's grim up north (so the saying goes), but this itinerary shows how much things have changed in England's upper half over the last decade. It's barely 100 miles from end to end, so you'll have ample time to explore off the beaten track.

THE EDGE OF ENGLAND   Two Weeks / Suffolk to Northumberland

England's popular national parks are certainly beautiful, but they're hardly a well-kept secret. If you like your landscapes a little less hectic, try this backwater route through England's less-travelled corners.

Start in sleepy **Suffolk** (p446), once a centre for the medieval wool industry, now a favourite getaway for painters, boaters and bird lovers. Quaint villages and stout market towns such as **Sudbury** (p449) and **Lavenham** (p449) dot the landscape, while along the coast there are bird reserves, shingly beaches and fishing ports such as **Aldeburgh** (p453) and **Southwold** (p455).

Things get quieter northwards into **Norfolk** (p456), especially around the misty fens and rivers of the **Broads** (p463), crammed with rare butterflies and birdlife, and the bogs and reed beds of the **Cley Marshes** (p465). For a flavour of the faded English seaside, dig out the crab net and head for **Cromer** (p464) and **Wells-next-the-Sea** (p465), or for something classier, try the beaches and boutique hideaways around **Holkham** (p466).

Across the border into Lincolnshire are the eerie, pan-flat **Fens** (p500), drained during the 17th century and now a haven for otters, red deer and all kinds of bird life, especially around the nature reserves at **Wicken Fen** (p500) and **Saltfleetby-Theddlethorpe** (p499).

Beyond the massive seabird colonies roosting at **Bempton Cliffs** (p621) are the breezy **North York Moors** (p641), which get far fewer visitors than the nearby Dales. Browse the scenic coastline from **Robin Hood's Bay** (p649) to **Whitby** (p646), before venturing inland to villages such as **Hutton-le-Hole** (p645) and **Coxwold** (p644), and the moody ruins of **Rievaulx Abbey** (p644). Round things off with a blustery stroll across the Cheviot Hills in the heart of **Northumberland National Park** (p774).

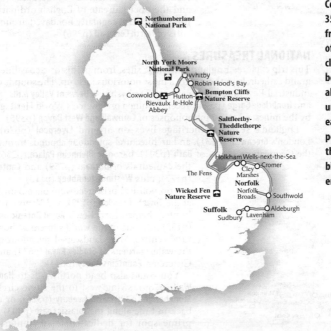

Covering around 350 to 450 miles from the flats of Suffolk to the cliffs of Northumberland, this trip along England's under-explored eastern edge is for people who like their landscapes big, wild and empty.

TAILORED TRIPS

ERUDITE ENGLAND

Literary landmarks are scattered across the English landscape. Open the book in London at the home of pioneering dictionary-maker, **Dr Samuel Johnson** (p124), before exploring the literary history of **Bloomsbury** (p120; see more about the Bloomsbury group in the boxed text, p201) and Dickensian **Clerkenwell** (p121). Pay your respects to some of the nation's most illustrious writers, interred in Poet's Corner in **Westminster Abbey** (p115). Round your tour off at Shakespeare's **Globe** (p126), a replica of the original theatre where many of the Bard's plays were premiered.

Outside the capital, the spires of **Oxford** (p222) inspired JRR Tolkien, CS Lewis and Philip Pullman, while Shakespearean connections continue at the Bard's birthplace, **Stratford-upon-Avon** (p546). The **Midlands** (p527) is classic DH Lawrence country, while Philip Larkin laboured at the university library in **Hull** (p615). Further north, Brontë fans flock to the south Pennines, especially **Haworth** (p602), and diehard Romantics follow in the footsteps of Wordsworth, Coleridge, de Quincey and co in the **Lake District** (p704).

West of London you'll find Jane Austen locations dotted around **Bath** (p341). Nearby **Dorset** (p297) doubled as Thomas Hardy's fictional Wessex, Arthur Conan Doyle set his classic *Hound of the Baskervilles* on **Dartmoor** (p387), and the poet laureate of English ordinariness, John Betjeman, regularly holidayed around the cliffs of **North Cornwall** (p396).

NATIONAL TREASURES

This trip explores England's heritage sites, from prehistoric coastlines and grand cathedrals to the nation's most notorious lock-up. The sounds of the Industrial Revolution echo around Derbyshire's **Derwent Valley Mills** (p511) and **Ironbridge Gorge** (p574), recently joined on Unesco's World Heritage List by the minestacks and pumphouses of **Cornwall and West Devon** (p395).

England's seafaring heritage lives on around **Liverpool** (p676) and London's **Greenwich** (p131), and architectural splendour abounds throughout the Georgian crescents of **Bath** (p341), baroque **Blenheim Palace** (p236) and the cathedrals of **Durham** (p759) and **Canterbury** (p177), plus **Westminster Abbey** (p115).

Top political prisoners were once banged up at the **Tower of London** (p122), and Victorian plant hunters helped turn Kew's **Royal Botanic Gardens** (p133) into one of the world's foremost horticultural centres. More landscaped splendour graces the water gardens of **Studley Royal** (p634) and the Cistercian **Fountains Abbey** (p634).

You could also head northwards to **Hadrian's Wall** (p769), swing west to the stone circles of **Stonehenge** (p320) and **Avebury** (p326), or travel back in time along the **Jurassic Coast** (p303) – the prime spot for dedicated fossil hunters and amateur archaeologists.

OFFBEAT BLIGHTY

If there's one thing the English are famous for, it's eccentricity; this trip picks out some of the country's more peculiar attractions.

Start out in Cornwall with a clamber through the enchanted **Men-an-tol stone** (p416) and a visit to extraordinary **Wayside Folk Museum** (p415) in Zennor. Browse voodoo poppets and magic skulls at the Boscastle's **Museum of Witchcraft** (p398), visit King Arthur's legendary birthplace, **Tintagel Castle** (p398) and participate in a 19th-century murder trial in **Bodmin** (p404).

In Devon, you could dine amongst Damien Hirst exhibits in **Ilfracombe** (p395) or go to Exeter to stay at a **converted eye hospital** (Hotel Barcelona, p376), wander around spooky underground **catacombs** (p375) and check out England's most extraordinary DIY project, the 16-sided cottage of **A La Ronde** (p378).

Over in Dorset, check out the nation's rudest piece of public art, the **Cerne Giant** (p307), and mix with bongo players, white witches and part-time druids in England's hippie capital, **Glastonbury** (p356), before discovering the nation's largest **stone circle** (p327) and the mysterious hummock of **Silbury Hill** (p328), both near Avebury.

In the Cotswolds, you could participate in the **Pooh Sticks World Championships** (p237), hurtle downhill in pursuit of a runaway block of Double Gloucester in Cranham's **cheese-rolling competition** (p253), and test your mettle in Chipping Campden's **Cotswold Olimpicks** (p245), with a spot of welly-wanging, pole-climbing or shin-kicking. Only in England...

GO SLOW

England is slowly waking up to the ecological agenda, and the southwest is doing its green bit better than anywhere else.

Start in the seaside town of **St Ives** (p416), which brims with ecofriendly B&Bs and local produce restaurants, including the fantastic **Primrose Valley Hotel** (p418). Then head (by public transport, or even cycling) to England's ecological flagship, the **Eden Project** (p406), with three space-age greenhouses (the world's largest) and pioneering environmental initiatives from recycled rainwater to wind generators and composting loos. Explore the coastline and beaches around **Padstow** (p399) and the north coast along the **Camel Cycle Trail** (p399), and book yourself a tepee in **Fowey** (p406).

Catch the scenic railway to England's original transition town, **Totnes** (p382), long-known for its hippie-ish vibe and eco-chic credentials. Wholefood restaurants and organic cafes line the town's cobbled streets, and you can sample fantastic home-grown produce at the **Riverford Field Kitchen** (p382) and Devon chardonnays at **Sharpham Vineyard** (p382). Ferries putter from Totnes to the harbour of **Dartmouth** (p380), from where you can hike the scenic estuary or catch a boat to Agatha Christie's house at **Greenway** (p380), now winning green tourism awards. Lastly, head north for some hiking and biking around **Dartmoor** (p387). And all without an automobile in sight...

History

England may be a small country on the edge of Europe, but it was never on the sidelines of history. For thousands of years, invaders and incomers have arrived, settled and made their mark. The result is England's fascinating mix of landscape, culture and language – a dynamic pattern that shaped the nation and continues to evolve today.

For many visitors, this rich historical legacy – everything from Stonehenge and Hadrian's Wall to Canterbury Cathedral and the Tower of London – is England's main attraction, so this chapter concentrates on high-profile events, and wherever possible mentions the historic locations you're likely to see on your travels. Even if you're no fan of dates and dynasties, we hope this overview will help you get the most from your trip.

EARLY DAYS

Probably built around 3000 BC, Stonehenge has stood on Salisbury Plain for more than 5000 years and is older than the Great Pyramids of Egypt.

Stone tools discovered near Lowestoft in Suffolk show that human habitation in England stretches back at least 700,000 years, although exact dates depend on your definition of 'human'. These early peoples were migrant hunter-gatherers, but by around 6000 years before our own time most had settled down, notably in open areas like Salisbury Plain in southern England. Alongside their fields they built burial mounds (today called barrows), but their most enduring legacies are the great stone circles of Avebury (p326) and Stonehenge (p320), still clearly visible today.

Move on a millennium or two and it's the Iron Age. Better tools meant trees could be felled and more land turned to farming. As landscapes altered, this was also a time of cultural change: Celtic arrivals absorbed the indigenous people, and the resulting Celtic-British population – sometimes called the 'Ancient Britons' – divided into about 20 different tribes, including the Cantiaci (in today's county of Kent), the Iceni (today's Norfolk) and the Brigantes (northwest England).

Notice the Latin-sounding names? That's because the tribal tags were handed out by the next arrivals on England's shores…

THREE IN ONE

The country of England (with Wales and Scotland) is *part of* the island of Great Britain. The words 'England' and 'Britain' are not synonymous, although visitors sometimes miss the distinction – as do a lot of English people (though never the Scottish or the Welsh). Getting a grip on this basic principle will ease your understanding of English history and culture, and make your travel here more enjoyable.

TIMELINE

4000 BC	c 500 BC	c 55 BC
Neolithic peoples migrate from continental Europe. They differ significantly from previous arrivals: instead of hunting and moving on, they settle in one place and start farming.	The Celts, a group originally from Central Europe, have by this time settled across much of the island of Britain, absorbing the indigenous people.	Relatively small groups of Roman invaders under the command of Emperor Julius Caesar make forays into southern England from the northern coast of continental Europe (today's France).

THE ROMAN ERA

Although there had been some earlier expeditionary campaigns, the main Roman invasion of England was in AD 43. These arrivals called their new-won province Britannia, and within a decade most of southern England was under Roman control. It wasn't a walkover though: some locals fought back, most famously the warrior-queen Boudica, who led a rebel army against Londinium, the Roman port on the present site of London.

Opposition was mostly sporadic, however, and no real threat to the legions' military might. By around AD 80 Britannia comprised much of today's England and Wales. And although it's tempting to imagine noble natives battling courageously against occupying forces, Roman control and stability was probably welcomed by the general population, tired of feuding chiefs and insecure tribal territories, allowing Roman settlement in England to continue for almost four centuries.

Intermarriage was common between locals and incomers (many from other parts of the empire – including modern-day Belgium, Spain and Syria – rather than Rome itself) so that a Romano-British population evolved, particularly in the towns, while indigenous Celtic-British culture remained in rural areas.

Along with stability and wealth, the Romans introduced another cultural facet: a new religion called Christianity, after it was recognised by Emperor Constantine in the 4th century. But by this time, although Romano-British culture was thriving in Britannia, back in its Mediterranean heartland the Empire was already in decline.

It was an untidy finale. The Romans were not driven out by the ancient Britons (after more than 300 years, Romano-British culture was so established there was nowhere for many to go 'home' to). In reality, Britannia was simply dumped by the rulers in Rome, and the colony slowly fizzled

The Year 1000 by Robert Lacey and Danny Danziger looks hard and deep at English life a millennium ago. Apparently it was cold and damp then, too.

LEGACY OF THE LEGIONS

To control their new territory, the Romans built garrisons across England. Many developed into towns, later called 'chesters', today remembered by names like Winchester, Manchester and, of course, Chester. ('Cester' was a variation – hence Cirencester, Bicester, Leicester etc.) The Romans are also well known for their roads, initially built so soldiers could march quickly from place to place, and later so that trade could develop. Wherever possible the roads were straight lines (because it was efficient, not – as the old joke goes – to stop Ancient Britons hiding round corners), and included Ermine Street between London and York, Watling Street between Kent and Wales, and the Fosse Way between Exeter and Lincoln. As you travel around England, you'll notice many modern highways still follow Roman roads. In a country better known for old lanes and turnpike routes winding through the landscape, these ruler-straight highways clearly stand out on the map.

AD 43	122	c 410
Emperor Claudius leads the first proper Roman invasion of England. His army wages a ruthless campaign, and the Romans control basically everywhere in southern England by AD 50.	Rather than conquer wild north British tribes, Emperor Hadrian settles for building a coast-to-coast barricade. For nearly 300 years, Hadrian's Wall marks the northernmost limit of the Roman Empire.	As the classical world's greatest Empire finally declines after more than three centuries of relative peace and prosperity, Roman rule ends in Britain with more of a whimper than a bang.

In the years after the invasion, the French-speaking Normans and the English-speaking Anglo-Saxon inhabitants kept pretty much to themselves. A strict hierarchy of class developed, known as the feudal system. At the top was the monarch, below that the nobles (barons, bishops, dukes and earls), then knights and lords, and at the bottom were peasants or 'serfs', the basis of a class system that to a certain extent still exists in England today.

Intermarriage was not completely unknown – Henry himself married a Saxon princess. Nonetheless, such unifying moves stood for nothing after Henry's death: a bitter struggle for succession followed, finally won by Henry II, who took the throne as the first king of the House of Plantagenet.

ROYAL & HOLY SQUABBLING

The fight to follow Henry I continued the English habit of competition for the throne, and introduced an equally enduring tendency of bickering between royalty and the Church. Things came to a head in 1170 when Henry II had 'turbulent priest' Thomas Becket murdered in Canterbury Cathedral (p177), still an important shrine today.

Perhaps the next king, Richard I, wanted to make amends for his forebears' unholy sentiments by fighting against Muslim 'infidels' in the Holy Land (today's Middle East). Unfortunately, he was too busy crusading to bother about governing England – although his bravery earned him the Richard the Lionheart sobriquet – and in his absence the country fell into disarray.

Richard was succeeded by his brother John, and things got even worse for the general population. According to legend, it was during this time that a nobleman called Robert of Loxley, better known as Robin Hood, hid in Sherwood Forest (p506) and engaged in a spot of wealth redistribution…

PLANTAGENET PROGRESS

By the early 13th century King John's erratic rule was too much for the powerful barons and they forced him to sign a document called the Magna Carta ('Great Charter') at Runnymede, near Windsor; you can still visit the site today (boxed text, p272). Intended as a set of handy ground rules, the Magna Carta became a fledgling bill of human rights and eventually led to the creation of Parliament – a body to rule the country, independent of the throne.

LOOKING SOUTH

The arrival of William the Conqueror was a seminal event, as it marked the end of England's century-old ties to the countries of northern Europe. Perspective turned to France and the Mediterranean, with massive cultural implications that last into our own time. In addition, the events capped an era of armed invasion. Since 1066, in the near-on thousand years to the present day, England has never again been successfully invaded by an overseas enemy.

1095	12th century	1215
The start of the First Crusade – a campaign of Christian European armies against the Muslim occupation of Jerusalem and the 'Holy Land'. A series of crusades continues until 1272.	Oxford University founded. There's evidence of teaching in the area since 1096, but King Henry II's 1167 ban on students attending the University of Paris solidified Oxford's importance.	King John signs the Magna Carta, presented to him by powerful barons, limiting the monarch's power for the first time in English history and an early step on the path towards constitutional rule.

The next king was Henry III, followed in 1272 by Edward I – a skilled ruler and ambitious general. During a busy 35-year reign, he was a firm believer in English nationalism and unashamedly expansionist, leading campaigns into Wales and Scotland, where his ruthless activities earned him the title 'Hammer of the Scots'.

Edward I was succeeded by Edward II, who lacked his forebear's military success – his favouring of friends over barons didn't help. He failed in the marriage department, too, and came to a grisly end when his wife, Isabella, and her lover, Roger Mortimer, had him murdered in Berkeley Castle (p252).

HOUSES OF LANCASTER & YORK

In 1399 the last of the Plantagenets, Richard II, was ousted by a powerful baron called Henry Bolingbroke, who became Henry IV – the first monarch of the House of Lancaster. He was followed, neatly, by Henry V, who decided it was time to finally end (or stir up) the Hundred Years' War, a long-standing conflict between England and France. Henry's defeat of France at the Battle of Agincourt and the patriotic speech he was given by Shakespeare in his namesake play ('cry God for Harry, England and St George') ensured his position among the most famous English monarchs.

Still keeping things neat, Henry V was followed by Henry VI. His main claim to fame was overseeing the building of great places of worship (King's College Chapel, p430, in Cambridge, Eton Chapel, p271, near Windsor), interspersed with great bouts of insanity.

When the Hundred Years' War finally ground to a halt in 1453, you'd have thought things would be calm for a while. But no. Just a few years later, a civil conflict dubbed the Wars of the Roses flared up.

Briefly it went like this: Henry VI of the House of Lancaster (whose emblem was a red rose) was challenged by Richard, Duke of York (proud holder of a white-rose flag). Henry was weak and it was almost a walkover for Richard, but Henry's wife, Margaret of Anjou, was made of sterner mettle and her forces defeated the challenger. But it didn't rest there. Richard's son Edward entered with an army, turned the tables, drove out Henry, and became King Edward IV – the first monarch of the House of York. (For a slightly longer Wars of the Roses overview, see p657.)

DARK DEEDS IN THE TOWER

Life was never easy for the guy at the top. Edward IV hardly had time to catch his breath before facing a challenger to his own throne. Enter scheming Richard Neville, Earl of Warwick, who liked to be billed as 'the kingmaker'. In 1470 he teamed up with the energetic Margaret of Anjou to shuttle Edward into exile and bring Henry VI to the throne. But a year later Edward IV came bouncing back; he killed Warwick, captured Margaret and had Henry snuffed out in the Tower of London (p122).

Shakespeare's *Henry V* was filmed most recently in 1989 – a superb epic, starring English cinema darling Kenneth Branagh as the eponymous king. Also worth catching is the earlier movie of the same name starring Laurence Olivier, made in 1944 as a patriotic rallying cry.

1337–1453	1348	1381
England battles against France in a long conflict known as Hundred Years' War. It was actually a series of small conflicts. And it lasted for more than a century, too...	The arrival of the Black Death. Commonly attributed to bubonic plague, the pandemic killed more than 1.5 million people, over a third of the country's population.	Richard II confronted by the Peasants' Revolt. This attempt by commoners to overthrow the feudal system is brutally suppressed, further injuring an already deeply divided country.

RULING THE ROOST

A glance at the story of England's ruling dynasties clearly shows that life is never dull for the person at the top. Despite immense power and privilege, the position of monarch (or, perhaps worse, *potential* monarch) probably ranks as one of history's least safe occupations. English kings to meet an untimely end include Harold (killed in battle), William II (assassinated), Charles I (beheaded by Republicans), Edward V (murdered by an uncle), Richard II (probably starved to death), John (too much eating and drinking), James II (deposed), Edward II (dispatched by his queen and her lover) and William III (died after his horse tripped over a molehill). As you visit the castles and battlefields of England, you may feel a touch of sympathy – but only a touch – for those all-powerful figures continually looking over their shoulders.

Although Edward IV's position seemed secure, he ruled for only a decade before being succeeded by his 12-year-old son, now Edward V. But the boy-king's reign was even shorter than his dad's. In 1483 he was mysteriously murdered, along with his brother, and once again the Tower of London was the scene of the crime.

With the 'little princes' dispatched, the throne was open for their dear old Uncle Richard. Whether he was the princes' killer remains the subject of debate, but his rule as Richard III was short-lived. Despite another famous Shakespearean sound bite ('A horse, a horse, my kingdom for a horse'), few tears were shed in 1485 when he was tumbled from the top job by a nobleman from Wales called Henry Tudor, who became King Henry VII.

MOVES TOWARDS UNITY

There hadn't been a Henry on the throne for a while, and the new incumbent harked back to the days of his namesakes with a skilful reign. Following the Wars of the Roses, Henry VII's Tudor neutrality was important. He also mended fences with his northern neighbours by marrying off his daughter to James IV of Scotland, thereby linking the Tudor and Stewart lines.

Elizabeth (1998), directed by Shekhar Kapur and starring Cate Blanchett, covers the early years of the Virgin Queen's rule – as she graduates from novice princess to commanding monarch – a time of forbidden love, unwanted suitors, intrigue and death.

Henry VII's successor, Henry VIII, is one of England's best-known monarchs, mainly thanks to his string of six wives – the result of a desperate quest for a male heir. In terms of historical importance, he is also known for his excommunication from the Roman Catholic Church and for breaking the Church of England from Rome, followed by the 'Dissolution' – the infamous closure or demolition of many monasteries (in reality more a blatant land grab than part of the struggle between church and state).

THE ELIZABETHAN AGE

Henry VIII was succeeded by his son Edward VI, then his daughter Mary I, but their reigns were short. So, unexpectedly, the third child, Elizabeth, came to the throne.

1459–71	1485	1509–47
The Wars of the Roses – an ongoing conflict between two competing dynasties: the Houses of Lancaster and York. The Yorkists are eventually successful, enabling King Edward IV to gain the throne.	Henry Tudor defeats Richard III at the Battle of Bosworth to become King Henry VII, establishing the Tudor dynasty and ending York-Lancaster rivalry for the throne.	The rule of Henry VIII. The Pope's disapproval of Henry's desire for divorce results in the Reformation. English authority is exerted over Wales; the Acts of Union (1536–43) formally tie the two countries.

As Elizabeth I, she inherited a nasty mess of religious strife and divided loyalties, but after an uncertain start she gained confidence and turned the country round. Refusing marriage, she borrowed biblical imagery and became known as the Virgin Queen – perhaps the first English monarch to create a cult image.

Highlights of her 45-year reign included the naval defeat of the Spanish Armada, the far-flung explorations of English seafarers Walter Raleigh and Francis Drake, the expansion of England's trading network, including the newly established colonies on the east coast of America – not to mention a cultural flourishing thanks to writers such as William Shakespeare and Christopher Marlowe.

Meanwhile, Elizabeth's cousin Mary (daughter of Scottish King James V, and a Catholic) had become Queen of Scotland. She'd spent her childhood in France and had married the French dauphin (crown prince), thereby becoming queen of France as well. Why stop at two? After her husband's death, Mary returned to Scotland, and from there ambitiously claimed the English throne as well – on the grounds that Elizabeth was illegitimate.

Mary's plans failed; she was imprisoned and forced to abdicate, but escaped to England and appealed to Elizabeth for help. This could have been a rookie error, or she might have been advised by courtiers with their own agenda. Either way, it was a bad move. Mary was – not surprisingly – seen as a security risk and imprisoned once again. In an uncharacteristic display of indecision, Elizabeth held Mary under arrest for 19 years – moving her frequently from house to house, so that today England has many stately homes (and even a few pubs) claiming 'Mary Queen of Scots slept here' – before finally ordering her execution.

> 'Elizabeth borrowed biblical imagery and became known as the Virgin Queen'

UNITED & DISUNITED BRITAIN

When Elizabeth died in 1603, despite a bountiful reign, the Virgin Queen had failed to provide was an heir. She was succeeded by her closest relative, the Scottish King James, the safely Protestant son of the murdered Mary. He became James I of England and VI of Scotland, the first English monarch of the House of Stuart (Mary's time in France had Gallicised the Stewart name). James did his best to sooth Catholic-Protestant tensions and united England, Wales and Scotland into one kingdom for the first time – another step towards British unity, at least on paper.

But the divide between king and Parliament continued to smoulder, and the power struggle worsened during the reign of Charles I, eventually degenerating into the English Civil War. The antiroyalist forces were led by Oliver Cromwell, a Puritan who preached against the excesses of the monarchy and established church, and his parliamentarian (or Roundhead) army was pitched against the king's forces (the Cavaliers) in a war that tore England apart – although for the last time in history. It ended with victory

1558–1603	1605	1644–49
The reign of Queen Elizabeth I, a period of boundless English optimism. Enter stage right playwright William Shakespeare. Exit due west navigators Walter Raleigh and Francis Drake.	King James' attempts to smooth religious relations are set back by an anti-Catholic outcry following the infamous Gunpowder Plot, a terrorist attempt to blow up Parliament led by Guy Fawkes.	English Civil War between the king's Cavaliers and Oliver Cromwell's Roundheads, establishing the Commonwealth of England.

for the Roundheads, the king executed, and England declared a republic – with Cromwell hailed as 'Protector'.

THE RETURN OF THE KING

By 1653 Cromwell was finding Parliament too restricting and assumed dictatorial powers, much to his supporters' dismay. On his death in 1658, he was followed half-heartedly by his son, but in 1660 Parliament decided to re-establish the monarchy – as republican alternatives were proving far worse.

Charles II (the exiled son of Charles I) came to the throne, and his rule – known as 'the Restoration' – saw scientific and cultural activity bursting forth after the straight-laced ethics of Cromwell's time. Exploration and expansion were also on the agenda. Backed by the army and navy (which had been modernised by Cromwell), colonies stretched down the American coast, while the East India Company set up headquarters in Bombay, laying foundations for what was to become the British Empire.

The next king, James II, had a harder time. Attempts to ease restrictive laws on Catholics ended with his defeat at the Battle of the Boyne by William III, the Protestant king of Holland, aka William of Orange. William was married to James' daughter Mary, but it didn't stop him doing the dirty on his father-in-law. William and Mary both had equal rights to the throne and their joint accession in 1688 was known as the Glorious Revolution. Lucky they were married or there might have been another civil war.

EMPIRE BUILDING

In 1694 Mary died, leaving just William as monarch. He died a few years later and was followed by his sister-in-law, Anne. During her reign, in 1707, the Act of Union was passed, linking the countries of England, Wales and Scotland under one Parliament – based in London – for the first time.

Anne died without an heir in 1714, marking the end of the Stuart line. The throne passed to distant (but still safely Protestant) German relatives – the House of Hanover. Meanwhile, the British Empire – which, despite its title, was predominantly an English entity – continued to grow in the Americas, as well as in Asia, while claims were made to Australia after James Cook's epic voyage in 1768.

THE INDUSTRIAL AGE

While the Empire expanded abroad, at home Britain had become the crucible of the Industrial Revolution. Steam power (patented by James Watt in 1781) and steam trains (launched by George Stephenson in 1830) transformed methods of production and transport, and the towns of the English Midlands became the first industrial cities.

The industrial growth led to Britain's first major period of internal migration, as vast numbers of people from the countryside came to the cities in

'in 1707, the Act of the Union was passed, linking the countries of England, Wales and Scotland under one Parliament'

1688	1721–42	1749
William of Orange and his wife Mary, daughter of King James II, jointly ascend the throne after William defeats his father-in-law in the Glorious Revolution.	Violent struggles for the throne are a thing of the past and the Hanoverian kings increasingly rely on Parliament to govern the country. Robert Walpole becomes Britain's first prime minister.	Author and magistrate Henry Fielding founds the Bow Street Runners, cited as London's first professional police force. A 1792 Act of Parliament allowed the Bow Street model to spread across England.

search of work. At the same time, medical advances improved life expectancy, creating a sharp population increase, so for many ordinary people the effects of Britain's economic blossoming were dislocation and poverty.

Nevertheless, by the time Queen Victoria took the throne in 1837, Britain's factories dominated world trade and its fleets dominated the oceans. The rest of the 19th century was seen as Britain's Golden Age (for some people, it still is) – a period of confidence not seen since the days of the last great queen, Elizabeth I.

In a final move of PR genius, the queen's chief spin doctor and most effective prime minister, Benjamin Disraeli, had Victoria crowned Empress of India. She'd never been to the subcontinent, but the British people simply loved the idea.

The times were optimistic, but it wasn't all tub-thumping jingoism. Disraeli and his successor William Gladstone also introduced social reforms to address the worst excesses of the Industrial Revolution. Education became universal, trade unions were legalised and the right to vote was extended to commoners. Well, to male commoners – women didn't get the vote for another few decades. Disraeli and Gladstone may have been enlightened gentlemen, but there *were* limits.

WORLD WAR I

When Queen Victoria died in 1901, it seemed that England's (and all of Britain's) energy fizzled out too, and the country entered a period of decline. Meanwhile, in continental Europe, other states were more active: the military powers of Russia, Austro-Hungary, Turkey and Germany were sabre-rattling in the Balkan states, a dispute that eventually culminated in WWI. When German forces entered Belgium, on their way to invade France, Britain and the Allied countries were drawn in, and the 'Great War' became a vicious conflict of stalemate and horrendous slaughter.

By the war's weary end in 1918 over a million Britons had died (not to mention millions more from many other countries) and there was hardly a street or village untouched by death, as the sobering lists of names on war memorials all over England still show. The conflict added 'trench warfare' to the dictionary, and further deepened the huge gulf between ruling and working classes.

When the soldiers who did return from WWI found the social order back home little changed, their disillusion helped create a new political force to upset the balance long enjoyed by the Liberal and Conservative parties: the Labour Party, representing the working class.

The Labour Party came to power for the first time, in coalition with the Liberals, in the 1923 election, with James Ramsay MacDonald as prime minister, but by the mid-1920s the Conservatives were back. The world economy was now in decline and industrial unrest had become widespread.

Birdsong by Sebastian Faulks is partly set in the trenches of WWI. Understated, perfectly paced and intensely moving, it tells of passion, fear, waste, incompetent generals and the poor bloody infantry.

1776–83	1799–1815	1837–1901
The American War of Independence is the British Empire's first major reverse, forcing England to withdraw – for a while, at least – from the world stage, a fact not missed by French ruler Napoleon.	The Napoleonic Wars. Napoleon threatens invasion on a weakened Britain, but his ambitions are curtailed by Nelson and Wellington at the famous battles of Trafalgar (1805) and Waterloo (1815) respectively.	The reign of Queen Victoria. The British Empire – 'the Empire where the sun never sets'– expands from Canada through Africa and India to Australia and New Zealand.

The Culture

THE NATIONAL PSYCHE

Everyone from Winston Churchill and George Orwell to broadcast journalist Jeremy Paxman has had a stab at defining the English character, but no one's ever managed to pin down any concrete definition of 'Englishness'. It's become increasingly important as devolution has gathered pace, but the notion of the national character remains slippery, especially since the terms England, Britain and UK are still used fairly interchangeably by foreigners and the English (our accents are English, we're British citizens but our passports belong to the UK).

Several centuries of cultural cherry-picking have given English culture a genuinely polyglot feel. The national language is peppered with ancient Latin, Anglo-Saxon, Celtic, French, Indian, Italian, German and Japanese. Factor in the global influence of TV and cinema, and the successive waves of immigration that have contributed to the multicultural melting pot of modern-day England, and you'll realise how hard it is to come up with any kind of overarching national character.

But peek beneath the surface and you'll find a few home truths about the English. While they're not quite as inhibited, reserved or unswervingly polite as you might expect, there's still a deep-seated respect for good manners, courtesy and tolerance, coupled with a belief in a rather vague notion of 'fairness' (though no one can quite define it, everyone instinctively seems to know when the boundary's been crossed). Unsurprisingly, people tend to be friendlier outside the big cities; trying to spark up a chat on the tube is likely to win you stares of incredulous horror, while you'll often find yourself having a natter if you're held up in a northern bus queue.

Which brings us to the question of good old English reserve. While the nation has become less inhibited about expressing their emotions, there's still some deep corner of the national psyche that involuntarily winces at the spectacle of *Jerry Springer*. There's nothing that the English like better than a good moan, but watch the collective cringe when someone starts complaining too loudly in a restaurant and you'll realise that English reserve hasn't disappeared just yet.

In general the English frown on displays of public exhibitionism or over-familiarity, but any city centre jaunt on a Saturday night will tell you that the old stereotype of a nation of buttoned-up, stiff-upper-lip intellectuals is definitely a thing of the past. The old 'no sex, please, we're British' adage hasn't entirely disappeared, either – displays of public nudity or gratuitous profanity prompt a generous round of tut-tutting and raising of eyebrows, and yet a recent survey suggested that Britain is actually the world's fastest-growing market for internet porn.

All of which goes to show what a contrary bunch the English are. They're deeply fond of championing their love of animals, their generosity towards charities and their liberal, progressive values, but ask them to abandon their imperial measurements, ditch their beloved pound or build something on green-belt land and they'll fight to the bitter end. And despite what the politicians say, the class system is still very much alive: recent studies have concluded that England has one of the widest wealth gaps and lowest levels of social mobility anywhere in the western world, and class-ridden epithets – chavs, toffs, townies, snobs, nimbies – are bandied about with relative abandon.

But if there's one thing that binds the eclectic English, it's their sense of humour. This is the nation that gave the world Spike Milligan and the Goons,

One of the more perceptive takes on the national character is *The English,* written by Jeremy Paxman, a BBC broadcaster known for his ferocious interviewing technique and razor-sharp wit.

Ever wondered about the origins of the world's first garden gnome, or the location of the world's largest bell foundry? Then you'll love Christopher Winn's *I Never Knew That About England,* a treasure trove of bizarre Blighty-themed facts.

Monty Python, the League of Gentlemen and Ali G. Being able to have a laugh at things (and more importantly, at themselves) has got the English through some seriously sticky patches. Heavily ironic, sharp and self-deprecating, the English sense of humour sails over the heads of many visitors, but until you get a handle on the English habit of 'taking the mickey', you'll be missing a crucial key for understanding what makes this peculiar little country tick.

LIFESTYLE

'An Englishman's home is his castle', runs the old saying – a reflection of the crucial importance the English place on owning a house. While many other European countries see no stigma in lifelong renting, in England owning a house is a crucial step towards health, wealth and happiness.

Unfortunately, actually trying to buy a house is unlikely to do your bank balance (or your blood pressure) any good. A decade of record price rises has placed the dreamt-of home well out of reach of most first-time buyers, with average homes outstripping average earnings by well over six times. In England, you'll need just under £200,000 to pick up the middle-of-the-road home, rising closer to £350,000 in London, or a million-plus in the most fashionable areas. But with the average national salary hovering around the £26,000 mark (£31,000 in London), most 'key workers' – including teachers, nurses, paramedics and bin collectors – find a hefty 25-year mortgage a depressing necessity if they ever want to be able to afford their own home.

So it's perhaps unsurprising that the English work the longest hours and spend more time commuting to work than practically anywhere in Europe. While their cousins across the Channel work an average of 40.3 hours, the UK working week comes in at a punishing 43.6 hours, topped only by workaholic nations such as Japan and the United States. But while the average English male slogs his guts out at work, at home he's a real couch potato: according to the Office of National Statistics, every week he spends over 56 hours asleep and 20 hours goggling in front of the TV, but just 23 minutes a day reading a book, and 13 minutes engaged in outdoor activity.

This marked lack of cardiovascular enthusiasm perhaps explains England's expanding waistlines. The UK has one of the fastest growing rates of obesity in the western world; at the last count, almost 25% of the population were classified as clinically obese, and almost two-thirds were considered overweight. Obesity is an especially serious problem among the nation's youngsters, but England's kids aren't quite the fattest in Europe just yet – the nation's girls and boys were recently placed fourth and sixth respectively in the European obesity league tables.

While the English are piling on the pounds, at least they're not smoking as much. Following the ban on smoking in enclosed public places that came into effect in 2007, there has been a 22% rise in the number of people successfully quitting the pernicious weed, and incidences of smoking-related illnesses and chronic heart disease have both taken a dip (although they're still among the UK's top killers).

But while they may be stubbing out their fags (that's cigarettes in England), the English don't seem all that keen on cutting back on the booze. Alcohol consumption and binge drinking have become major public-health issues. A 2005 survey revealed that 31% of men and 22% of women aged 16 to 24 were regularly exceeding the recommended daily dose of alcohol, while 22% of pupils in England aged 11 to 15 confessed to having drunk alcohol in the last week. The extension of licensing hours to promote a more European 'cafe culture' seems to have done little to change the nation's intractable drinking habits; many commentators have laid the blame on supermarkets and nightclubs selling cut-price booze and 'alcopops'.

If you're flummoxed by English imperial measurements, convert them to something that makes more sense at www .metric-conversions.org.

The average salary for a train driver in 2008 was £37,231, while library assistants earned just £10,749.

THE GREAT ENGLISH CUPPA

Nothing sums up the English more than their favourite tipple. Nationwide the English get through an astonishing 165 million cups of tea a day; 70% drink it on a regular basis, with an average daily consumption of three cups.

It's been popular since the 18th century, when the British East India Company established trading links with tea plantations on the Indian subcontinent. But in the early days it was far from a working-class drink; tea was considered a luxury commodity and heavily taxed, initially making it the preserve of upper-class coffee houses. Tea was one of the most important contrabands for Britain's smugglers – at one time around four-fifths of all the tea drunk in England had escaped official duty. But eventually – in part prompted by the infamous Boston Tea Party, which began as a protest against punitive British duties on tea, and helped light the fuse for the American War of Independence – the government relaxed duty restrictions, and tea steadily percolated down through the English classes. Tea-drinking quickly gained many devotees – Dr Samuel Johnson was a particularly staunch advocate – but not everyone was a fan. The Methodist preacher John Wesley swore that the drink induced 'paralytick disorders', licentiousness, intemperance and generally loose morals.

But within the space of a few decades, the English had taken tea firmly to their hearts. By the mid-19th century it was being drunk across all echelons of English society – several of Dickens' penurious characters warm themselves over a steaming tea kettle, while Jane Austen described the elaborate ritual of afternoon tea in high society. During the World Wars tea was rationed by the government to ensure a steady supply (in order to prevent widespread panic and moral collapse); George Orwell even published his 'eleven golden rules' for making the perfect cuppa in the *Evening Standard*. One of his more controversial suggestions – that the milk should be poured *after* the tea – remains a matter of heated debate among the English, with the 'tea after' and 'tea before' camps defending their positions with an intensity usually only reserved for discussing the merits of Marmite.

Ironically, one of the great modern innovations in tea-drinking was an American invention – the first tea bags were accidentally invented in 1908 by a New York tea merchant called Thomas Sullivan, who sent out samples to his customers in small silken bags. Today tea bags account for 96% off all the tea drunk in England.

Drinking isn't the nation's only vice. According to the recent Home Office figures, a quarter of 16 to 24 year olds admitted to using drugs in the last year; around 18% had smoked a joint, while 7% had taken cocaine. The government's flip-flopping on the classification of cannabis hasn't helped; having downgraded the drug from Class B to C, the decision was reversed in 2008, against the recommendations of government scientific advisers. But despite bad habits and ballooning waistlines, life expectancy in England continues to creep upwards: boys and girls born in the UK in 2007 could expect to live an average of 76.9 years and 81.3 years respectively, the highest figures so far recorded.

Though they're living longer, the English aren't statistically likely to pass away married to their childhood sweetheart; currently about one in three marriages in England ends in divorce. But while the divorce rate has rocketed, the social stigma that was once attached to 'living in sin' has long since fallen by the wayside. It's perfectly acceptable these days for unmarried couples to live together, and even have kids; around a third of couples choose to live together without tying the knot, and around 40% of children are born to unmarried parents. There's also been a major rise in people choosing to live on their own – around seven million people now live on their lonesome, nearly four times as many as in 1961. Gay and lesbian relationships have also steadily become more acceptable, especially since the implementation of the Civil Partnership Act in 2005.

POPULATION

In a country as small as England, population is a perennial topic. At last count, 50.76 million people lived in England, accounting for 83.8% of the UK's population. Since 2001 the population has grown by an average of 0.5% every year, helped by falling-infant mortality rates and increased life expectancy.

More recently, immigration has caused a record spike in England's population growth. According to the Office for National Statistics, the UK's population grew by 2.5% between 2001 and 2006, the fastest rate since the 1960s.

Over a quarter of England's population is crammed into the southeast, indicative of a general trend of north-to-south migration that's been in action since the late 19th century. But despite the spiralling cost of living and sky-high house prices down south, it's proved difficult to convince people to try out life up north: attempts to shift civil service and BBC jobs from London (several key departments of the BBC now operate from Manchester) have met with resistance from trade unions and employees.

Meanwhile, England's rural corners are booming. The southwest is the fastest growing of any of England's regions, with an increasing number of people quitting the city in search of a better quality of life. Good news for cash-strapped rural economies, where the traditional industries of farming, fishing and manufacturing are on the wane; not such good news for local residents struggling to get onto the housing ladder.

Over one in five people in the UK are currently employed in the financial-services sector, compared with about one in 10 in 1981.

SPORT

The English may have dreamt up many of the world's favourite sports – including cricket, tennis, rugby and football – but unfortunately the national teams aren't very good at playing (or at least winning) them. Despite a few standout success stories, including victories at the Rugby World Cup in 2004 and a long-awaited win against the Aussies in the 2005 Ashes series, England has a poor track record in most sporting tournaments, especially in football (the last major tournament win was the 1966 World Cup, a hallowed date that's enshrined in the brains of every self-respecting footy fan).

Cricket

Starched whites, village greens and the knick of ball on willow – what could be more English than a cricket match? Cricket's origins stretch back to the 14th century (Edward I played a bat-and-ball game known as *creag*, an early forerunner of cricket). During the colonial era, cricket spread throughout the Commonwealth: Australia, the Caribbean and the Indian subcontinent took to the game with gusto, and a century on Britain's former colonies still delight in giving the old country a good spanking on the cricket pitch.

To the uninitiated, cricket is a pretty impenetrable spectacle. Spread over one-day games or five-day 'test matches', and dominated by arcane terminology like googlies, outswingers, leg-byes and silly mid-offs, cricket

In 2007, the most popular boys' name in the UK was Jack, while the most popular girls' name was Grace.

QUEUING FOR ENGLAND

The English are notoriously addicted to queues – for buses, train tickets, or to pay at the supermarket. The order is sacrosanct and woe betide any foreigner who gets this wrong! Few things are more likely to spark an outburst of tutting – about as publicly cross as most English get – than pushing in at a queue.

One notable exception is the capital, where queue-jumping is pretty common – although it's worth remembering the accepted etiquette on the tube escalators, where it's polite to stand on the right-hand side so that people in a hurry can climb past on the left. You can expect rather more than a bit of furious tutting if you get in the way of a Londoner in a hurry.

THE ASHES

The historic test cricket series between England and Australia known as the Ashes has been played every other year since 1882 (bar a few interruptions during the World Wars). The contest's name dates back to the landmark test match of 1882, won (for the very first time) by the Australians. Defeat at the hands of the all-conquering Aussies is a depressingly familiar feeling for the modern-day English cricket fan, but at the time the Australians' win was a source of profound national shock: a mock-obituary in the *Sporting Times* lamented the death of English cricket and referred to the sport's ashes being taken to Australia.

According to cricketing legend, the name also refers to a 6in-high terracotta urn presented to the English captain Ivo Bligh (later Lord Darnley), purportedly containing the cremated ashes of a stump or bail used in the match. Since 1953 this hallowed relic has resided at the Marylebone Cricket Club (MCC) Museum at Lord's, and is a source of considerable controversy between the two nations. Having repeatedly won the tournament over recent decades, Australia feel they've earned the right to retain the Darnley Urn, while the English cricketing authorities are adamant that the urn should remain in the MCC Museum.

England's cricket team isn't doing much to ease the situation: after eight straight defeats, England won the Ashes in 2005, only to hand them straight back again after another humiliating 5-0 thrashing in 2007.

is tantamount to a religion for certain sectors of English society. One-day games and international tests are played at grounds including Lords in London, Edgbaston in Birmingham and Headingley in Leeds. Tickets cost from £30 to well over £200.

The County Championship pits the best county teams against each other. Tickets cost £15 to £25, and only the most crucial games tend to sell out. The new boy on the pitch is the Twenty20 Cup, in which each side is limited to a single innings and 20 overs, laying the emphasis on big batting scores rather than careful run-building. While many traditionalists think this crowd-pleasing new format is changing the character of the game, there's no doubting its popularity – most Twenty20 matches sell out.

Football (Soccer)

The English Premier League is up there with the big boys of European football (please don't call it soccer in front of the English), with some of the best players and richest clubs in the world – not to mention the recent European champions, Manchester United. The league's recent history has been dominated by the four top teams – Arsenal, Liverpool, Chelsea and Manchester United – all (with the notable exception of Arsenal) owned by multimillionaire foreigners, whose limitless transfer budgets have allowed the clubs to attract many of the world's best players.

A notch down in quality (and a hefty notch down in spending power) are England's other domestic leagues – the Championship, League One and League Two. The football season is the same for all divisions (August to May), but tickets for the Premier League are like gold dust – your chances of bagging a ticket are pretty much zilch unless you're a club member, so you're better off trying for a ticket at one of the lower-division games. Try the club websites or online agencies like www.ticketmaster.co.uk and www.myticketmarket.com.

One of the nation's great footballing spectacles is the annual FA Cup, a knock-out competition that has been in existence since 1871 and is contested every year by teams drawn from across the nation's professional leagues (meaning top-flight teams often find themselves playing against tiny teams from the lowliest echelons of English football).

For the latest low-down on everything relating to the national 11, consult the Football Association's website at www.thefa .com.

Rugby

A wit once said that football is a gentlemen's game played by hooligans and rugby is the reverse. Whatever the truth of the adage, rugby remains a popular sport, especially since England's historic World Cup win against Australia in 2004 (the national team unexpectedly reached the final in the 2008 World Cup, only to be beaten by South Africa).

There are two versions of rugby in England: Rugby Union, traditionally played in southern England, Wales and Scotland, and Rugby League, favoured in the north. Both trace their roots back to Rugby School, in Warwickshire, where in 1823 a young lad called William Webb Ellis, frustrated at booting a football around the pitch, picked up the ball and charged towards the opponents' goal, unwittingly spawning an entirely new sport. The Rugby World Cup is named the Webb Ellis trophy after this enterprising young tearaway.

League and Union in England are divided into several divisions. Top-flight union teams include Bath, Gloucester, Leicester and recent champions London Wasps. On the League side look out for the Wigan Warriors, Bradford Bulls, St Helens and 2008 Super League winners, Leeds Rhinos.

As well as the various club competitions, international matches include the Six Nations Championships, contested by England, Scotland, Wales, Ireland, France and Italy every spring.

Tennis

Tennis is a popular summertime sport, especially around the time of the All England Championships – otherwise known as **Wimbledon** (www.wimbledon.org) – held in the last week of June and first week of July. Famous for its impeccably trimmed grass courts, all-white dress code and historic champions, Wimbledon is also notorious for rain delays (during one famous episode, Cliff Richard crooned to the crowd on Centre Court during an extended bad-weather break). Stoppages are due to be a thing of the past after 2009 with the installation of a sliding roof on Centre Court, but there's little sign of an end to England's long wait for the next home-grown champion: the last British winner was Virginia Wade in 1977, and after the retirement of England's top player Tim Henman in 2007, the nation's hopes rest on up-and-coming Andy Murray (even though he's actually a Scot). The 2008 champion was Rafael Nadal, who ended a run of five straight victories for Swiss champion Roger Federer.

Demand for Wimbledon tickets is huge, but tickets are (unusually) allocated through a public ballot to ensure fairness. Around 6000 tickets are available each day (except the last four) for punters willing to brave the queues, but you'll need to be an early riser: dedicated fans start queuing before dawn.

Over 27 tonnes of strawberries and 7000L of cream are consumed every year during the two weeks of the Wimbledon Tennis Championships.

Horse Racing

The tradition of horse racing in England stretches back centuries. The most prestigious event is **Royal Ascot** (www.royalascot.co.uk) in mid-June, where the fashion is almost as important as the fillies. Other highlights include the Grand National steeplechase at Aintree in early April, and the Derby, run at Epsom on the first Saturday in June.

MULTICULTURALISM

Few topics stir up as fierce a debate in England as the issue of multiculturalism, but despite what you might read in the tabloids, Britain's always been a nation of immigrants. The island's original settlers, the Celts, were supplanted by successive waves of invaders, including the Angles and Saxons (from Germany), Vikings (from Denmark) and Romans (from Italy), and then the Normans (from France) in 1066. Throughout the Middle Ages, England was

---

WEB WOES

The BBC's online service, the **BBC iPlayer** (www.bbc.co.uk/iplayer), allows viewers to watch the last seven days of BBC TV and radio via the internet. Launched at Christmas 2007, the iPlayer's massive success took everyone (even the BBC bigwigs) by surprise. Within the space of a few months, the service accounted for 5% of the UK's total internet traffic, with exponential growth projected over the coming years. The service has led to heated wrangles between the BBC and the nation's internet service providers, who want the corporation to stump up some of the estimated £831m required to upgrade the network. So far the Beeb has shown no sign of budging, but with dire predictions about the net grinding to a halt under the influence of the iPlayer, it might only be a matter of time before they have to reach a deal.

Celebrity-obsessed England has plenty of gossipy rags dishing the dirt on the country's WAGs (Wives and Girlfriends, generally of football stars), Z-listers and soap stars: titles range from bottom-of-the-barrel *Heat* to high-society *Hello*. The late 1990s saw a brief flourish of 'lad's mags', epitomised by titles such as *Loaded, Nuts* and *Zoo*. One of England's other classic magazines, the *New Musical Express,* is still going strong after five decades of covering the country's shifting musical trends. It might not be the hallowed journal it once was, but it's still required reading for the nation's teens; it joined forces with long-term rival *Melody Maker* in 2000.

TV & Radio

Compared to many nations, the UK has a limited line-up of channels, but this is set to change with the switch-over from analogue to digital TV (the first all-digital signal was beamed to Whitehaven in Cumbria in 2007, with the wider UK due to follow suit by 2012).

Popularly referred to as the Beeb or Auntie, the **British Broadcasting Corporation** (BBC; www.bbc.co.uk) remains the top broadcaster. It's one of the few broadcasters that remains advertising-free: its services are financed by an annual licence fee paid by every UK household with a TV (blind people only get a 50% discount). The BBC has a deserved reputation for world-class TV, especially in news and current affairs, though many think the increasing reliance on reality TV and 'dumbed-down' programs has resulted in a decline in standards. The BBC has also been rapped over the knuckles for its London-centric focus: a stinging 2008 report concluded that the corporation failed to accurately reflect devolved modern Britain and must improve its regional coverage in future years.

The main BBC channels are BBC One and the more eccentric BBC Two, supplemented by digital channels BBC Three (aimed at under-25s), BBC Four (arts, history and documentaries) and the BBC News Channel. The BBC's main rivals are ITV and its subsidiary Channel Four, known for its provocative programming. The baby of the bunch is Five, launched in 1997, which is slowly shifting from cheap, trashy programming to more highbrow content. All the channels have digital counterparts: one of the most popular is ITV2; E4 grabs viewers with high-profile US shows and series; and Film4 specialises in cult films. Satellite broadcasting is dominated by Sky, part of the Murdoch-owned News International Corporation.

The main radio stations are provided by the BBC. Radios 1 to 5 are analogue and digital, but the others are digital-only, so you'll need a DAB receiver to hear them. Radio 1 is the main music station, playing everything from banging house to chart-topping pop. Older listeners graduate to Radio 2, known for its eclectic playlist and vintage line-up of DJs (most of whom got too long in the tooth for Radio 1). Radio 3 specialises in classical, jazz and world music, while Radio 4 (formerly the Home Service) is a very British blend of current affairs, comedy, documentaries and radio plays. Sport and chat dominate Radio 5 Live, Radio 6 broadcasts alternative music, Radio 7 is arts and classic comedy, while Radio 1 Xtra and the BBC Asian Network are aimed at Britain's black and Asian communities respectively.

Alongside the Beeb, you'll find lots of commercial stations, including poppy Virgin Radio and classical specialist Classic FM. To find the right spot on the dial, see p788.

RELIGION

The Church of England (C of E, or Anglican Church) was founded in the 16th century at the behest of Henry VIII (who wanted to marry his mistress Anne Boleyn but couldn't get the Pope's permission, so decided to form his own church instead). The church is overseen by the Archbishop of Canterbury, a position currently held by Dr Rowan Williams; it's traditionally seen as a conservative force in British society (hence its unofficial pseudonym, 'the Tory Party at prayer'), although it has recently moved towards a more liberal stance thanks to its decision to allow the ordination of women and gay bishops (a cause of much controversy in the wider Anglican community).

Though church attendance is falling across the country – only about one in 50 people now attend Sunday services – Christianity is by far the UK's dominant religion. At the last census, 35 million people described themselves as Christian, with around 10% describing themselves as Roman Catholic and the majority of the rest falling under the auspices of the Church of England. Around 15% of the English population have no religion, 3% are Muslims, followed by Hindus (1%), Sikhs (0.7%), Jews (0.5%) and Buddhists (0.3%) – plus around 390,000 Jedis (apparently even the official census isn't immune from the British sense of humour).

ARTS
Literature

England's literary heritage stretches back for over eight centuries. The nation's first literary giant was Geoffrey Chaucer, who strung together a series of fables, stories and morality tales in his medieval 'road movie' *The Canterbury Tales* (p180), published in 1387.

But it was during the late 16th century when English literature truly exploded onto the stage, thanks to a clutch of Elizabethan and Jacobean writers – like Christopher 'Kit' Marlowe, Ben Jonson, Thomas Kyd and a certain William Shakespeare – who forged new dramatic ground with their hard-hitting themes, poetic dialogue and often shocking subject matter, while English myths and fables informed Edmund Spenser's *The Faerie Queene*. Hot on their heels came the 17th-century metaphysical poets, including John Donne and Andrew Marvell, who used everyday objects as a springboard to explore deep philosophical conceits – a drop of dew as an allegory for the human soul, or the points of a compass to symbolise conjoined lovers.

Following the carnage of the Civil War, John Milton's *Paradise Lost* turned the tale of Adam and Eve into an epic poem, and John Bunyan's *Pilgrim's Progress* did the same for the everyday Christian struggle. On a rather more prosaic level, everyday London life provided the material for the wonderful *Diaries* of Samuel Pepys.

During the early 18th century, English literature took on a new political edge. Writers like Alexander Pope and Jonathan Swift delighted in attacking

Shameless has been one of the biggest hits for Channel 4 over the last few years, following the trials and tribulations of a deeply dysfunctional northern family and its alcoholic patriarch, Frank Gallagher.

WHITHER THE WEATHER?

It was Dr Johnson who noted that 'when two Englishmen meet, their first talk is of the weather'. Two centuries later, little has changed: weather is an enduring English obsession. According to the **UK Meteorological Office** (www.metoffice.gov.uk) – known to all as the Met Office – weather reports are the third-most watched TV broadcasts, and when BBC Radio 4 proposed cutting the late-night shipping forecast ('warning of gales in North Atlantic; Viking, Forties, good' etc) there was a huge outcry from listeners – most of whom never went anywhere near the sea.

This fascination with the weather is part of a long tradition, and ancient folklore is full of mantras for second-guessing the moods of the elements. Snow on St Dorothea's Day (6 February) means no heavier snowfall that year, while rain on St Swithin's Day (15 July) means it'll continue for the next 40 days. The slightest tinge of a pink cloud can cause locals to chant 'red sky at night, shepherd's delight' like a mantra.

But despite this obsession, the weather still keeps the English on their toes. A few weeks without rain and garden-hose bans are enacted; too much rain and rivers burst their banks, flooding low-lying towns. Similarly, a fall of snow (the amount that in Germany or Switzerland would be brushed off without a second thought) often brings English motorways to a standstill. The rail network is particularly susceptible to weather delay – trains have been cancelled for everything from leaves on the track to the wrong kind of snow.

---

the mores of contemporary society through their allegorical tales, while Daniel Defoe wrote the original desert-island story, *Robinson Crusoe*, a literary blockbuster since its publication in 1719.

As the Industrial Revolution took hold in the late 18th and early 19th centuries, a new generation of writers drew inspiration from the natural world and the human imagination (in many cases helped along by a healthy dose of laudanum). Keats, Shelley, Byron and Coleridge became the figureheads of the Romantic movement, alongside William Wordsworth, who composed much of his poetry wandering about the high hills of the Lake District (p704).

Gothic literature represented the Romantic flipside – the power of the imagination to create horror rather than joy. A favourite Gothic text is Mary Shelley's *Frankenstein*, a cautionary tale about the dangers of human ambition and perverted technology, and a meditation on a post-Enlightenment society facing up to a godless world.

As the 19th century dawned, many writers began to use the trials and tribulations of everyday English society as the basis for their novels. Jane Austen's exquisitely observed tales of class, society, love, friendship and buttoned-up passion are fascinating social documents of their day; later writers, including George Eliot and Elizabeth Gaskell, continued Austen's fascination with the minutiae of English society. The three Brontë sisters combined Gothic mystery and repressed sexuality with a good old-fashioned yarn; fans still flock to their Haworth home (p602) in the Yorkshire Dales.

As the Industrial Revolution steamed along, writers increasingly used their novels to comment on the social and political ills of Victorian society. Charles Dickens tackled practically all the prevailing issues of his day: from poverty and crime in *Oliver Twist* and the Byzantine English legal system *(Bleak House)* to the terrors of public-school education *(Nicholas Nickleby)*. Thomas Hardy continued the Dickensian tradition, examining the impact of war, industrialisation and social change on ordinary people in the fictionalised county of Wessex (largely based on his home in Dorset, p297). Other writers explored Britain's rapidly expanding frontiers, notably Rudyard Kipling, perhaps the classic chronicler of empire, in works such as *Kim, Gunga Din* and *The Jungle Book*.

England – and its literature – changed forever following the devastating carnage of WWI, which unpicked the stitches that had hitherto held British

For a taste of surreal humour, try two of England's funniest (and most successful) writers: Douglas Adams *(The Hitchhiker's Guide to the Galaxy)* and Terry Pratchett (the *Discworld* series). Pratchett was the best-selling author in the UK for the 1990s.

society together: class, government, aristocracy and empire. Patriotic poems such as Rupert Brooke's *The Soldier* ('If I should die, think only this of me…') gave way to excoriating dissections of the false glory of war in the work of Siegfried Sassoon and Wilfred Owen. Even Kipling recanted his unquestioning devotion to the English cause following the death of his only son, John, killed at the Battle of Loos in 1915. Kipling's devastating refrain 'If any question why we died/Tell them, because our fathers lied' has since become a mantra for the anti-war movement.

The ideological chaos and social disruption of the postwar period fed into the fractured narratives of modernism. Perhaps the greatest domestic writer of the interwar period is DH Lawrence, who charted changing Britain in novels including *Sons and Lovers, The Rainbow* and the controversial *Lady Chatterley's Lover,* for which the publishers were prosecuted in 1960 under the recently introduced Obscene Publications Act (they were found not guilty by showing the work was of 'literary merit'). Other writers ploughed a similar course: EM Forster's *A Passage to India* depicted the downfall of British colonial rule, while Evelyn Waugh explored moral, social and political disintegration in *A Handful of Dust, Vile Bodies* and *Brideshead Revisited.* The interwar period also spawned a generation of gifted poets – WH Auden, Stephen Spender, Louis MacNeice, Robert Graves – who collectively documented the crumbling pillars of British (and European) society.

The chaos of WWII led to a new wave of self-examination and paranoia. George Orwell made his name with semidocumentary novels such as *Down and Out in Paris and London* and *Coming Up for Air,* and later with classic books such as the antitotalitarian fable *Animal Farm* and *1984,* the novel that gave Big Brother to the wider world. The Cold War inspired other writers, too – notably Graham Greene, whose *Our Man in Havana* follows a hapless vacuum salesman turned secret spook, and Ian Fleming, who introduced the world to the sexed-up, licensed-to-kill secret agent James Bond (who first appeared in 1953's *Casino Royale*).

Several of the major novelists of the 1970s and '80s remain key figures in the English literary scene. Martin Amis was 24 when he published his debut, *The Rachel Papers,* in 1974, and has been getting up the noses of the establishment ever since. Meanwhile Ian McEwan debuted with *The Cement Garden* in 1978 and has found critical acclaim with finely observed studies of the English character such as *Enduring Love, Atonement* and *On Chesil Beach.* Kazuo Ishiguro penned perhaps the finest tale of English repression, *The Remains of The Day,* which follows the doomed love affair between a butler and his housekeeper.

The nature of multicultural Britain has provided a rich seam for contemporary novelists. Hanif Kurieshi sowed the seeds with his ground-breaking 1990 novel *The Buddha of Suburbia,* which examined the hopes and fears of a group of suburban Anglo-Asians in London. Multicultural themes have informed the work of Andrea Levy, Monica Ali, Hari Kunzru and Zadie Smith, who published her acclaimed debut *White Teeth* when she was 25, and has since followed with a string of literary best sellers, including *The Autograph Man* and *On Beauty.*

Other contemporary writers worth seeking out are Will Self, known for his surreal, satirical novels, including his most recent book, *Liver,* a typically imaginative tale that explores the livers of four London characters in various stages of disease, decay and disintegration; David Mitchell, whose multilayered, time-bending *Cloud Atlas* marked him out as a writer to watch; and Sarah Waters, a gifted novelist who often places lesbian issues at the core of her work, in books including *Tipping the Velvet* and *Night Watch.*

Brighton Rock by Graham Greene is a classic account of wayward English youth. For an even more shocking take, try Antony Burgess' novel *A Clockwork Orange,* filmed by Stanley Kubrick in 1971 and withdrawn in the UK by the director following a spate of copycat acts.

At the more popular end is the best-selling author Nick Hornby, who's carved out a niche chronicling the fragilities and insecurities of the English middle-class male in novels like *Fever Pitch* and *High Fidelity*. Louis de Bernières penned a best-selling tale of wartime love in *Captain Corelli's Mandolin,* but has struggled to match his earlier success, while Sebastian Faulks established himself with his wartime novels *Birdsong* and *Charlotte Gray,* and was recently chosen to write the first new James Bond novel in over 50 years to mark the centenary of Ian Fleming's birth (*Devil May Care* has since become one of the fastest-selling hardbacks ever published, shifting 44,093 copies in its first four days).

Money by Martin Amis is a freewheeling romp through the seedier side of 1980s capitalism, centring on the fat, unscrupulous and (occasionally) filthy rich businessman John Self.

But even James Bond can't hold a candle to the literary phenomenon that is the *Harry Potter* series, the magical adventures that have entertained millions of children (and a fair few adults too) over the last decade. JK Rowling's Potter series is the latest in a long line of English children's classics, stretching back to the works of Lewis Carroll (*Alice's Adventures in Wonderland*), E Nesbit (*The Railway Children, Five Children and It*), AA Milne (*Winnie-the-Pooh*), JRR Tolkien (*The Hobbit*), TH White (*The Once and Future King*) and CS Lewis (*The Chronicles of Narnia*), and continued by (Welsh-born but English-schooled) Roald Dahl and most recently Philip Pullman, with his controversial *His Dark Materials* trilogy.

Not all English books are quite so praiseworthy. The recent trend for scurrilous celebrity memoirs – penned by everyone from footballer Wayne Rooney to Tony Blair's wife, Cherie Blair – is a reminder of the increasing importance placed on marketing hype over literary merit in the modern book market. Whatever you make of their literary qualities, it's hard to argue with the figures – the British public buys them by the bucket load.

Cinema

England had a number of successful directors in the early days of cinema. Many famous directors cut their cinematic teeth in the silent-film industry – including Alfred Hitchcock, who directed *Blackmail*, one of the first English 'talkies' in 1929 (marketed as the first British 'all-talkie'), and went on to direct a string of films during the 1930s before migrating to Hollywood in the early 1940s.

During WWII, British films were dominated by patriotic stories designed to keep up morale on the Home Front: films like *Went the Day Well?* (1942), *In Which We Serve* (1942) and *We Dive at Dawn* (1943) are classics of the genre. The war years also marked the start of one of the great partnerships of British cinema, between the English writer-director Michael Powell and the Hungarian-born scriptwriter Emeric Pressburger. Jointly they produced some of the most enduring British films ever made, including *The Life and Death of Colonel Blimp* (1941), *A Matter of Life and Death* (1946) and *The Red Shoes* (1948).

Roald Dahl's autobiographical novel *Boy* explores the author's own early childhood, including his eye-wateringly excruciating experiences of English public-school discipline at Repton.

Following the hardships of the war, English audiences were in the mood for escape and entertainment. During the late 1940s and early '50s, the domestic film industry specialised in eccentric English comedies epitomised by the work of Ealing Studios: notable titles include *Whisky Galore!* (1949), *Kind Hearts and Coronets* (1949) and *The Titfield Thunderbolt* (1953). During this period the precocious young director David Lean directed a series of striking Dickens adaptations and the classic tale of buttoned-up English passion, *Brief Encounter* (1945), before graduating to Hollywood epics including *Lawrence of Arabia* and *Doctor Zhivago*. And in an England still struggling with rationing and food shortages, tales of heroic derring-do such as *The Dam Busters* (1955) and *Reach for The Sky* (1956) helped lighten the national mood.

HAMMER HORROR

The low-budget horror flicks produced by Hammer Film Productions are revered among horror fans across the globe. Founded in 1934, the company was best known for its string of horror flicks produced in the 1950s and '60s, starting with the science-fiction thriller *The Quatermass Xperiment* in 1955 and the landmark Hammer horror *The Curse of Frankenstein* (1957). The two stars of the latter – Peter Cushing as Dr Frankenstein and Christopher Lee as the Monster – would feature in many of Hammer's best films over the next 20 years.

Hammer produced some absolute classics of the horror genre, including a string of nine *Dracula* films (most of which star Lee as Dracula and Cushing as Van Helsing or his descendants) and six *Frankenstein* sequels. The studio launched the careers of several other notable actors (including Oliver Reed, who made his film debut in *The Curse of the Werewolf*, 1961) and inspired a legion of low-budget horror directors – Wes Craven, John Carpenter and Sam Raimi have all acknowledged Hammer films as an early influence. The studio even spawned its very own Carry On spoof, *Carry On Screaming* – the ultimate English seal of approval.

Find out all about the history of Hammer at www.hammerfilms.com.

In the late 1950s 'British New Wave' and 'Free Cinema' explored the gritty realities of British life in an intimate, semidocumentary style, borrowing techniques from the 'kitchen-sink' theatre of the '50s and the vérité style of the French New Wave. Lindsay Anderson and Tony Richardson crystallised the movement in films such as *This Sporting Life* (1961) and *A Taste of Honey* (1961). At the other end of the spectrum were the *Carry On* films, the cinematic equivalent of the smutty seaside postcard, packed with bawdy gags and a revolving troupe of actors including Barbara Windsor, Sid James and Kenneth Williams. The 1960s also saw the birth of another classic English hero: James Bond, adapted from the Ian Fleming novels and ironically played by a Scotsman, Sean Connery – the character was later given a Scottish heritage.

After a brief boom during the swinging '60s, English cinema entered troubled waters in the '70s. Dwindling production funds and increasing international competition meant that by the mid-1970s the only films being made in England were financed with foreign cash. Despite the hardships, new directors including Ken Russell, Nic Roeg, Ken Loach and Mike Hodges emerged, and the American director Stanley Kubrick produced some of his films in Britain, including *A Clockwork Orange* (1971).

But it wasn't until 1981, when David Puttnam's *Chariots of Fire* scooped four Oscars, that the British industry rediscovered its sense of self. The newly established Channel Four invested in edgy films such as *My Beautiful Laundrette* (1985), and exciting new talents including Neil Jordan, Mike Newell and American-born (and member of the Monty Python team) Terry Gilliam. Meanwhile, the British producing duo of Ismail Merchant and James Ivory played Hollywood at its own game with epic tales including *Heat and Dust* (1983) and *A Room With A View* (1986), riding on the success of Richard Attenborough's big-budget *Gandhi* (1982), which bagged eight Academy Awards.

The 1990s saw another minor renaissance in English films, ushered in by the massively successful *Four Weddings and a Funeral* (1994), introducing Hugh Grant in his trademark role as a bumbling, self-deprecating Englishman, a character type he reprised in subsequent hits including *Notting Hill, About a Boy* and *Love Actually*. All these films were co-financed by Working Title, a London-based production company which has become one of the big players of British cinema (and also unleashed Rowan Atkinson's hapless Mr Bean onto the global stage).

A survey by the UK Film Council concluded that Britain's film industry contributed £840.1m to the nation's coffers in 2006.

The British Film Institute (BFI; www.bfi.org.uk) is dedicated to promoting film and cinema in Britain, and publishes the monthly academic journal *Sight & Sound*.

English cinema refocused its attention on domestic issues in the late 1990s. *Brassed Off* (1996) related the trials of a struggling colliery band; the smash-hit *The Full Monty* (1997) followed a troupe of laid-off steel workers turned male strippers; and *Billy Elliott* (2000) charted the story of an aspiring young ballet dancer striving to escape the slag-heaps and boarded-up factories of the industrial north. Films including *East Is East* (1999) and *Bend it like Beckham* (2002) explored the tensions of modern multicultural Britain, while veteran British director Mike Leigh, known for his heavily improvised style, found success with *Life Is Sweet* (1991), *Naked* (1993) and the Palme d'Or winning *Secrets and Lies* (1996), in which an adopted black woman traces her white mother.

So far this decade, literary adaptations have continued to provide the richest seam of success. Following a disappointing big-screen version of the massive-selling *Captain Corelli's Mandolin* (2001), more recent literary hits include blockbuster adaptations of the *Bridget Jones* and *Harry Potter* books, as well as 2005's *The Constant Gardener* (based on a John Le Carré novel), and Ang Lee's interpretation of *Sense and Sensibility*, 2007's *The Last King of Scotland* (featuring Forest Whittaker as Ugandan dictator Idi Amin) and *Atonement* (2008), a big-budget adaptation of Ian McEwan's novel.

Biopics are also a perennial favourite: recent big-screen subjects include Ian Curtis from Joy Division (*Control*, 2007), Elizabeth I (*Elizabeth: The Golden Age*, 2007), Dylan Thomas (*The Edge of Love*, 2008) and even the Queen (in, erm, *The Queen*, 2006).

The Ladykillers (1955) is a classic Ealing comedy about a band of hapless bank robbers holed up in a London guest house, and features Alec Guinness sporting quite possibly the most outrageous set of false teeth ever committed to celluloid.

But life remains tough for the British filmmaker, especially those at the low-budget end. Many talented names – including Paul Greengrass, Stephen Daldry, Stephen Frears, Danny Boyle and Andrew Macdonald – often take better-paid work abroad in order to finance their British ventures. Genuinely British films about genuinely British subjects tend to struggle in an over-saturated marketplace: two of Britain's best directors, Shane Meadows (*Dead Man's Shoes, This is England*) and Michael Winterbottom (*9 Songs, 24 Hour Party People*) are both yet to score a big splash at the box office.

But while it's Hollywood money that keeps Britain's three main studios (Pinewood, Shepperton and Elstree) ticking over, Britain's small but dedicated cinematic community soldiers on. The comedy trio of Simon Pegg, Edgar Wright and Nick Frost have had worldwide success with their zombie homage *Shaun of The Dead* (2004) and its cop-flick follow-up, *Hot Fuzz* (2007), while music-video director Garth Jennings followed his adaptation of *The Hitchhiker's Guide to the Galaxy* (2005) with a low-budget tale of youthful friendship and shoestring moviemaking in *Son of Rambow* (2007).

The UK's biggest film magazine is *Empire* (www.empireonline .co.uk), but for less mainstream opinion check out *Little White Lies* (www .littlewhitelies.co.uk).

Veteran directors like Mike Leigh and Ken Loach are still going strong: Leigh's *Vera Drake* (2004), about a housewife turned backstreet abortionist in 1950s Britain, won the Golden Lion at the Venice Film Festival, while Loach's *The Wind that Shakes the Barley* (2006), a hard-hitting account of the Irish struggle for independence, scooped the Palme d'Or at Cannes. And there still seems to be life in even the oldest of English franchises: a tough, toned 21st-century James Bond appeared in 2006 courtesy of Daniel Craig and the blockbuster *Casino Royale*, followed by 2008's *Quantum of Solace*.

Television

If there's one thing the English excel at, it's the telly. Over the last 80-odd years of broadcasting, England has produced some of the world's finest programming, from classic comedy through to ground-breaking drama;

THE PLASTICINE MAN

One of the great success stories of English television and cinema has been Bristol-based animator Nick Park and the production company Aardman Animations, best known for the award-winning animations starring the man-and-dog duo Wallace and Gromit. This lovable pair first appeared in Park's graduation film, *A Grand Day Out* (1989), and went on to star in *The Wrong Trousers* (1993), *A Close Shave* (1995) and their feature debut, *Wallace & Gromit in The Curse of the Were-Rabbit* (2005). Known for their intricate plots, film homages and amazingly realistic animation, the Wallace and Gromit films scooped Nick Park four Oscars. Aardman Animations has also produced two successful animated features, *Chicken Run* (2000) and *Flushed Away* (2006), in partnership with Hollywood's DreamWorks studios.

---

many of the world's most popular formats have their origins in English broadcasting (including the phenomenon known as reality TV).

The BBC is famous for its news and natural-history programming, symbolised by landmark series such as *Planet Earth* and *The Blue Planet* (helmed by the reassuring presence of David Attenborough, a national institution on British screens since the 1970s). The big-budget costume drama is another Sunday-night staple; British viewers have been treated to adaptations of practically every Dickens, Austen and Thackeray novel in the canon over the last decade. More recently ITV has been making in-roads into costume-drama territory, notably with Jane Austen's *Persuasion*, *Mansfield Park* and *Northanger Abbey*. Both channels are also known for their long-running 'soaps' – *Eastenders* (BBC), *Emmerdale* and *Coronation Street* (both ITV), which have collectively been running on British screens for well over a century.

Reality TV has dominated many channels in recent years, although the popularity of shows such as *Big Brother* and *I'm a Celebrity – Get Me Out of Here!* seems to be on the wane. On the flipside, talent and variety are making a big comeback, with programs like *Strictly Come Dancing* and *Britain's Got Talent* being syndicated all over the world. Game shows are another big success story, with *Who Wants to be a Millionaire?* and *The Weakest Link* spawning countless foreign versions.

BBC2 and Channel 4 tend to produce edgier and more experimental content. Both channels are known for their documentaries – Channel 4 has a particular penchant for shocking subject matter (one of the channel's most controversial recent programs was *Autopsy*, which did exactly what it said on the label). Comedy is another strong point – the satirical news quiz *Have I Got News For You* is still going strong after 15 years, while classic British comedies such as *Monty Python, Steptoe & Son* and *Only Fools & Horses* have more recently been joined in comedy's hall of fame by cult hits *The Mighty Boosh, The League of Gentlemen, I'm Alan Partridge, Ali G, Spaced* and Ricky Gervais' double-whammy, *The Office* and *Extras*.

Britain's longest running soap is *Coronation Street*, which has charted everyday life in the fictional northern town of Weatherfield since 1960.

Music
POP & ROCK

England's been putting the world through its musical paces ever since a mop-haired four-piece from Liverpool tuned up their Rickenbackers and became 'bigger than Jesus', to quote John Lennon.

While some may claim that Elvis invented rock and roll, it was the Fab Four who transformed it into a global phenomenon, backed by The Rolling Stones, The Who, Cream, The Kinks and the other bands of the 'British Invasion'. Glam rock swaggered in to replace peace and love in the early seventies, with Marc Bolan and David Bowie donning spandex and glittery guitars in a variety of chameleonic guises, succeeded by art-rockers Roxy Music and anthemic pop-sters Queen and Elton John. Meanwhile Led Zeppelin laid down the blueprint for heavy metal and hard rock, and 1960s psychedelia morphed into the spacey noodlings of prog rock, epitomised by Pink Floyd, Genesis and Yes.

By the late 1970s the prog bands were looking out of touch in an England wracked by rampant unemployment, industrial unrest and the three-day week. Flicking a giant two fingers to the establishment, punk exploded onto the scene in the late '70s, summing up the general air of doom and gloom with nihilistic lyrics and short, sharp, three-chord tunes. The Sex Pistols produced one landmark album (*Never Mind the Bollocks, Here's the Sex Pistols*), a clutch of (mostly banned) singles, and a storm of controversy, ably assisted by other punk pioneers such as The Clash, The Damned, The Buzzcocks and The Stranglers.

While punk burned itself out in a blaze of squealing guitars and ear-splitting feedback, New Wave acts including The Jam and Elvis Costello took up the punk torch, blending spiky tunes and sharp lyrics into a poppier, more radio-friendly sound. A little later The Specials, Selecter and baggy-trousered rude boys Madness mixed punk, reggae and ska into Two Tone (a nod to the movement's cross-racial ethos).

The classic English youth movie is *Quadrophenia*, a visceral tale of Mods, Rockers, and pimped-up mopeds, with a top-notch soundtrack courtesy of The Who.

The big money and conspicuous consumption of Thatcherite Britain in the early 1980s bled over into the decade's pop scene. Big hair, shiny suits and shoulder pads became the uniform of New Romantics such as Spandau Ballet, Duran Duran and Culture Club, while the advent of synthesisers and processed beats led to the development of a new electronic sound in the music of Depeche Mode and Human League. But the glitz and glitter of '80s pop concealed a murky underbelly: bands like The Cure, Bauhaus, and Siouxsie and the Banshees were employing doom-laden lyrics and apocalyptically heavy riffs, while the rock heritage of Led Zeppelin inspired the birth of heavy-metal acts such as Iron Maiden, Judas Priest and Black Sabbath. The arch-priests of 'miserabilism', The Smiths – fronted by extravagantly quiffed wordsmith Morrissey – summed up the disaffection of mid-1980s England in classic albums such as *The Queen is Dead* and *Meat is Murder*.

The beats and bleeps of 1980s electronica fuelled the burgeoning dance-music scene of the early '90s. Pioneering artists such as New Order (risen from the ashes of Joy Division) and The Orb used synthesised sounds to inspire the soundtrack for the new, ecstasy-fuelled rave culture, centred on famous clubs like Manchester's Haçienda and London's Ministry of Sound. Subgenres such as trip-hop, drum and bass, jungle, house and big-beat cropped up in other UK cities, with key acts including Massive Attack, Portishead and the Chemical Brothers.

Manchester was also a focus for the burgeoning British 'indie' scene, driven by guitar-based bands such as The Charlatans, The Stone Roses, James, Happy Mondays and Manchester's most famous musical export, Oasis. In the late 1990s indie segued into Britpop, a catch-all term covering several bands including Oasis, Pulp, Supergrass and Blur, whose distinctively British music chimed with the country's new sense of optimism following the landslide election of New Labour in 1997 (Noel and Liam Gallagher were even invited for afternoon tea at Number Ten). But the phenomenon of 'Cool Britannia' was short-lived; by the millennium, most of Britpop's big acts had self-destructed. Damon Albarn later went on to create a new virtual band, Gorillaz, in partnership with cult cartoonist and illustrator Jamie Hewlett.

So where does that leave us in the noughties? In many ways, the era of MySpace, iTunes and file sharing has seen Britain's music scene become more diverse and divided than ever. Jazz, soul, R&B and hip-hop beats have fused into a new 'urban' sound (summed up by artists like Jamelia, The

Streets and Dizzee Rascal), while dance music continues to morph through new forms. On the pop side, singer-songwriters have made a comeback: Katie Mellua, Duffy and self-destructive songstress Amy Winehouse are flying the flag for the female artists, while Damien Rice, Ed Harcourt and ex-soldier James Blunt croon for the boys. The spirit of shoe-gazing British indie is alive and well thanks to Keane, Foals, Editors and world-conquering Coldplay; traces of punk and postpunk survive thanks to Franz Ferdinand, Razorlight, Babyshambles, Muse, Klaxons, Dirty Pretty Things and download phenomenon Arctic Monkeys; and the swagger of the Manchester sound still echoes through the music of Primal Scream, Kaiser Chiefs, Kasabian, Doves and The (reformed) Verve.

And as ever, alternative music continues to push the nation's musical boundaries: names to look out for include British Sea Power, The Ting Tings, Guillemots, Elbow, The Hoosiers and Young Knives, not to mention the most eclectic band at work in Britain today: Radiohead.

CLASSICAL MUSIC & OPERA
The country that gave us The Beatles and Oasis is also a hive of classical music, with several professional symphony orchestras, dozens of amateur orchestras and an active National Association of Youth Orchestras. Such enthusiasm is all the more remarkable given England's small number of well-known classical composers, especially compared with Austria, Germany and Italy.

Key figures include Henry Purcell, who flourished in the Restoration period and is still regarded as one of the finest English composers; Thomas Arne, best known for the patriotic anthem 'Rule, Britannia!'; Edward Elgar, famous for his 'Enigma Variations'; Gustav Holst, from Cheltenham, who wrote 'The Planets'; Vaughan Williams, whose 'A London Symphony' ends with chimes from Big Ben; and Benjamin Britten, perhaps the finest English composer of the last century, best known for 'The Young Person's Guide to the Orchestra' and the opera *Peter Grimes*. More recently, the works of Sirs Michael Tippett, Peter Maxwell Davies, John Tavener and Harrison Birtwhistle have found international fame, while the music of composer William Lloyd Webber has been brought to public attention by his sons, cellist Julian and composer Andrew.

Best-known of all English classical-music concert programs is The Proms (short for 'promenade' – people used to walk about, or stand, while they listened) – one of the world's greatest music festivals, held from mid-July to mid-September each year at the Royal Albert Hall in London and widely broadcast on radio and TV.

Architecture
With an architectural heritage stretching back for millennia, England's architecture is an obvious highlight. The country's oldest landmarks are the stone circles and megaliths left behind by neolithic (if not older) builders: dolmens, burial mounds and menhirs are dotted from Cornwall to Cumbria, but the most upstanding examples are the iconic stone rings of Stonehenge (p320) and Avebury (p327) in Wiltshire. Newer, but no less dramatic, are the chalk figures gracing many of England's hilltops. Some, such as the Uffington White Horse (p239), date from the Bronze Age, but most are more recent; the formidably endowed Cerne Abbas Giant (p307) is often thought to be an ancient pagan figure, but recent research suggests it was etched sometime in the 17th century.

During the Iron Age, hill forts were built to protect against seaborne raiders and inter-tribal conflict. A famous example is Maiden Castle (p307) in Dorset. Some of the rapists and pillagers even put down roots: York's

Some movies worth checking out to understand England's modern music scene: *Backbeat* (1994), a look at the early days of The Beatles; *Sid and Nancy* (1986), following The Sex Pistols bassist and his American girlfriend; *Velvet Goldmine* (1998), a tawdry glimpse of the glam-rock scene; and *24 Hour Party People* (2002), tracing the Manchester scene.

fascinating Jorvik (p626) is home to one of Europe's best-preserved Viking settlements.

Roman remains litter many cities, including Chester (p670), Exeter (p373) and St Albans (p263), as well as the lavish Roman holiday complex in Bath (p342). But the nation's most obvious Roman relic is the 73-mile sweep of Hadrian's Wall (p769), built in the 2nd century AD to stop marauding Pictish warriors (from modern Scotland) from plundering England's northern cities.

Once the political scene settled down following the coronation of Alfred I, England saw an explosion of architecture inspired by the two most pressing concerns of the day: worship and defence. Churches, abbeys, monasteries, minsters and feudal castles sprang up during the early Middle Ages, including many landmark cathedrals, such as York Minster (p622), Salisbury (p315) and Canterbury (p177). As for castles, you're spoilt for choice: the nation's strongholds range from the atmospheric ruins of Tintagel (p398) and Dunstanburgh (p780) and the feudal keeps of Lancaster (p692) and Bamburgh (p781) to the fortresses of Warwick (p544), Windsor (p269) and the Tower of London (p122).

London: A Biography by Peter Ackroyd is a fascinating and encyclopaedic overview of how a tiny harbour on the Thames turned into the nation's great metropolis.

While castles were excellent for keeping out the riff-raff, they were too draughty to make comfortable homes. Following the Civil War, the landed gentry developed a taste for fine 'country houses' designed by the most famous architects of the day. These grand country piles litter the English landscape: among the most extravagant are Holkham Hall (p466), Chatsworth House (p525) and Blenheim Palace (p236). All display the proportion, symmetry and architectural harmony so in vogue during the Georgian era over the 18th and 19th centuries, styles reflected in the fashionable houses of the era (most notably in Bath's stunning Royal Crescent, p344).

The Victorian era left perhaps the most enduring mark on the English landscape. Massive 'red-brick' terraces transformed the face of many English cities, built to accommodate the massive influx of workers needed to man the country's factories. Meanwhile the newly moneyed middle classes built street upon street of smart, solid, well-to-do town houses, and engineers embarked on an astonishing range of bridges, stations, museums, railways and public buildings, from the Clifton Suspension Bridge (p333) and the Natural History Museum (p128) to the Houses of Parliament (p116) and St Pancras Station (p130).

Many of the nation's major roads trace the course of old Roman thoroughfares.

The rush to reconstruct the nation's shattered cities after WWII left England with its fair share of postwar carbuncles. Entire terraces were swept away in favour of high-rise tower blocks, while the 'brutalist' architects of the 1950s and '60s fell head over heels for the cheap, efficient materials of steel and concrete, showing scant regard for the aesthetic appeal of the nation's cities. London's Southbank Centre (p164) is a typical example of brutalism; love it or loathe it, it certainly makes a statement.

Still stinging from the architectural misfires of the 1960s and '70s, the modern-day English remain a somewhat conservative bunch in terms of the houses they choose to inhabit. The traditional 'two rooms upstairs, two rooms downstairs' is still the ideal home for many people, and overly ambitious or experimental buildings (especially ones financed with public money) tend to receive rather short shrift. But as ever, the English are a contrary lot, and even the oddest buildings can find a place in their affections. London's Swiss Re building (aka 'the Gherkin') has journeyed from architectural eyesore to local landmark, and the disastrous Millennium Dome (now rebranded as the O2 arena, p132) has been transformed from a source of national embarrassment into one of the capital's leading live-music venues.

The last decade has seen many areas of England place a new importance on progressive, popular architecture as a part of wider regeneration: just look at Newcastle's Sage Gateshead (p755), Manchester's Imperial War Museum North (p659), Birmingham's Bullring (p540) and Cornwall's futuristic Eden Project (p406). Skyscrapers also seem to be all the rage in many of England's cities: Leeds, Manchester, Brighton and Birmingham have all announced plans for a rash of new 200m-plus buildings, while Liverpool has put forward proposals to reinvent its historic waterfront with over 50 high-rise towers. Top of the heap, however, is the London Bridge Tower (aka 'the Shard'), which, at 306m, is set to become one of Europe's tallest buildings when it's completed in around 2012. And the trend for ecofriendly homes looks set to become an increasingly important part of England's architectural landscape over the coming decades: the government recently announced plans for 10 new 'eco-towns' (designed to showcase environmentally friendly and sustainable construction principles) around England by 2020.

Painting & Sculpture

Until the 18th century, continental Europe – especially Holland, Spain, France and Italy – set the artistic agenda. The first artist with a truly English style and sensibility was arguably William Hogarth, whose riotous (and deeply rude) canvases exposed the vice and corruption of 18th-century London. His most celebrated work is *A Rake's Progress,* displayed today at Sir John Soane's Museum (p121) in London, kick-starting a long tradition of British caricatures that can be traced right through to the work of modern-day cartoonists such as Gerald Scarfe and Steve Bell.

While Hogarth was busy satirising society, other artists were hard at work showing it in its best light. The leading figures of 18th-century English portraiture are Sir Joshua Reynolds; his rival, Thomas Gainsborough; the Cumbrian-born George Romney; and George Stubbs, known for his intricate studies of animal anatomy (particularly horses). Most of these artists are represented at Tate Britain (p117) or the National Gallery (p115).

The English landscape was the main preserve of the 19th-century painters, especially John Constable, whose idyllic depictions of the Suffolk countryside are summed up in *The Haywain* (National Gallery, p115) and JMW Turner, who was fascinated by the effects of light and colour on English scenes. Turner's paintings became almost entirely abstract by the 1840s; though widely vilified, in many ways they were ahead of their time, prefiguring the Impressionist movement of the late 19th century. Meanwhile poet, painter and visionary William Blake occupied a world of his own, mixing fantastical landscapes and mythological scenes with motifs drawn from classical art, religious iconography and English legend.

While Turner was becoming more abstract, the Pre-Raphaelite movement harked back to the figurative style of classical Italian and Flemish art, tying in with the prevailing Victorian taste for English fables, myths and fairy tales. Key members of the movement included Dante Gabriel Rosetti, John Everett Millais, and William Holman Hunt, all represented at either Tate Britain (p117) or the Victoria & Albert Museum (p128).

In the tumultuous 20th century, English art became increasingly experimental. Francis Bacon placed Freudian psychoanalysis on the canvas in his portraits, while pioneering sculptors such as Henry Moore and Barbara Hepworth experimented with natural forms and all kinds of new materials. Some of Moore's work can be seen at the Yorkshire Sculpture Park (p601), and Hepworth is forever associated with St Ives (p416). Other artists including Patrick Heron and Terry Frost developed their own version of abstract expressionism, while amateur artist LS Lowry was setting his strange 'matchstick men' among the smokestacks and terraces of northern England.

BANANA is an acronym for 'Build absolutely nothing anywhere near anything (or anyone)' – a sly dig at the average English attitude to town planning.

The Institute of Contemporary Arts (ICA; www .ica.org.uk) in London is a great place to find out about the movers and shakers of contemporary British culture.

The mid-1950s and early '60s saw an explosion of English artists who plundered adverts, TV, music and pop culture for inspiration. The new pop-art movement was summed up by young artists such as Bradford-born David Hockney, who used bold colours and simple lines to depict his dachshunds and swimming pools, and Peter Blake, who designed the cut-up collage cover for the Beatles' landmark *Sergeant Pepper* album. The '60s also saw the rise of sculptor Anthony Caro, who held his first ground-breaking exhibition at the Whitechapel Art Gallery in 1963. Creating large abstract works in steel and bronze, he remains one of England's most influential sculptors.

But England had to wait a while for its next big splash. 'Britart' exploded onto the scene (thanks to advertising tycoon Charles Saatchi) through a series of provocative and playful exhibitions in the 1990s. The figureheads of the movement include Damien Hirst, famous for his pickled sharks, enbalmed cows and more recently a diamond-encrusted skull; Tracy Emin, whose work has ranged from confessional videos to a tent entitled *All The People I Have Ever Slept With*; and the Chapman Brothers, known for their deformed child mannequins (often featuring genitalia in inappropriate places).

Apart from Hirst, one of the few Britart graduates to find mainstream success is Rachel Whiteread, known for her resin casts of everyday objects. In 2008 she was one of five artists short-listed for the Angel of the South, a £2 million project to create a huge outdoor sculpture near Ebbsfleet in Kent to counterbalance the celebrated *Angel Of The North* (p757) created by Antony Gormley outside Gateshead in 1998. Whiteread's idea for the project was a plaster-cast of a house interior on an artificial hill; other ideas include a stack of 26 giant polyhedrons, a winged disc, a tower of cubes, and a massive horse, proposed by Mark Wallinger, winner of the 2007 Turner Prize. The winning design will be built in 2009.

Gormley is also busy on other projects – a recent major work, *Event Horizon,* placed 31 life-size bodies on top of prominent buildings around London (including Westminster Bridge and the Shell Building). But don't go looking for them – the sculptures were removed in September 2007.

One of England's other artistic exports is Banksy, the Bristol-based graffiti artist famous for his provocative murals and semi-secret identity – check out the boxed text on p335 for more.

Theatre & Dance

The nation's best-known theatrical name is, of course, William Shakespeare, whose plays were first performed in the 16th century, most of them at the Globe Theatre. Ground zero for the national poet is Stratford-upon-Avon (p546), and you can also catch the bard's plays at a replica of the original Globe (see p126) on London's South Bank.

Following the Civil War, the puritanical Oliver Cromwell closed the nation's theatres, but when Charles II returned from exile in 1660 he reopened the doors and encouraged many radical innovations, including actresses (female roles had previously been played by boys). Bawdy Restoration comedies satirised the upper classes and indulged in fabulously lewd jokes (William Wycherley's *The Country Wife* is a prime example). One of the leading actresses of the day, Nell Gwyn, became Charles II's mistress; England's first female playwright, Aphra Benn, also emerged during this period.

English drama entered a sharp decline during the 18th century, mainly due to the rise in operas and burlesque entertainment. It wasn't until the Victorian era that serious drama came back into fashion; during the mid-19th century classical plays competed for space on London's stages with a broad mix of melodramas, comic operas, vaudeville and music hall.

There's a wealth of fascinating information at your fingertips at the National Archives website (www.nationalarchives .gov.uk), where you can find everything from WWII spy records to celebrity death certificates.

WHAT A PANTOMIME

If any English tradition is guaranteed to bemuse outsiders, it's the pantomime. This over-the-top Christmas spectacle hits stages throughout the land throughout December and January, and traces its roots back to Celtic legends, medieval morality plays and the English music hall. The modern incarnation is usually based on a classic fairy tale and features a mix of saucy dialogue, comedy skits, song-and-dance routines and plenty of custard-pie humour, mixed in with topical gags for the grown-ups. Tradition dictates that the leading 'boy' is played by a woman, and the leading lady, or 'dame', played by a chap. B-list celebrities, struggling actors and soap stars famously make a small fortune hamming it up for the Christmas panto, and there are always a few staple routines that everyone knows and joins in ('Where's that dragon/wizard/pirate/lion?' – 'He's behind you!'). It's cheesy, daft and frequently rather surreal, but guaranteed to be great fun for the family. Oh, no it isn't! Oh, yes it is! Oh, no it isn't..!

The masters of the Victorian stage were Gilbert and Sullivan, who produced a string of comic operas including *HMS Pinafore, The Pirates of Penzance* and *The Mikado*. Of the Victorian and Edwardian dramatists, Oscar Wilde, George Bernard Shaw and Noel Coward are the most famous names; Scottish-born JM Barrie also found huge success with his classic children's fairy-tale *Peter Pan*, first performed as a London stage play in 1904.

The theatre soldiered on during the early 20th century, despite increasing competition from the cinema, but it wasn't until the 1950s that a new generation of English playwrights brought theatre back to life with a bang. The 'Angry Young Men', including John Osborne, Joe Orton and Terence Rattigan, railed against the injustices of mid-1950s Britain with a searing and confrontational new style of theatre, while playwright Harold Pinter developed his own unique dramatic voice, full of non sequiturs, pauses and dead ends (not to mention plenty of menace).

Other ground-breaking playwrights – Tom Stoppard *(Rosencrantz and Guildenstern are Dead)*, Peter Shaffer *(Amadeus)*, Michael Frayn *(Noises Off)* and Alan Ayckbourn *(The Norman Conquests)* – experimented with language and form during the 1960s and '70s, while new directors like Peter Hall and Peter Brook took new risks with dramatic staging. It was also a golden period for stage acting – the staid, declamatory style of performance of the past steadily gave way to a new, edgy realism in the performances of Laurence Olivier and Richard Burton, succeeded by actors such as Antony Sher, Judi Dench, Glenda Jackson and Ian McKellen.

Many of these actors remain big names, although they're perhaps better-known for their appearances in big-budget films across the pond. Other notable English actors – including Ralph Fiennes, Brenda Blethyn, Toby Stephens and Simon Callow – also juggle high-paying Hollywood roles with theatrical appearances on the English stage.

Interestingly, many major Hollywood stars have taken hefty pay cuts to tread the London boards – including Glenn Close, Nicole Kidman, Gwyneth Paltrow, Macaulay Culkin and Christian Slater. Kevin Spacey liked it so much he decided to take over a theatre. Since 2004 he's been in charge at London's Old Vic (p162), producing acclaimed (and sometimes not so acclaimed) productions, most recently Peter Hall's version of *Pygmalion* in 2008. Perhaps the most interesting film-star appearance on the London stage in recent years was Daniel Radcliffe – otherwise known as Harry Potter – who agreed to strip off in a recent production of Peter Shaffer's *Equus*.

Another notable to look out for in current English theatre is playwright Mark Ravenhill, who made his name with the provocatively titled

Withnail and I is one of the great cult British comedies. Directed by Bruce Robinson, it stars Paul McGann and Richard E Grant as a pair of hapless out-of-work actors on a disastrous holiday to Wales.

debut *Shopping and Fucking,* and has since penned a series of challenging productions, including a collection of 17 short plays about war, entitled *Shoot/Get Treasure/Repeat.* The controversial young female directors Katie Mitchell and Emma Rice are also names to watch. A storm of controversy broke out in 2007 when Rice's production of *A Matter of Life and Death* was panned by (mostly male) broadsheet critics, prompting the director of the National Theatre, Nicholas Hytner, to dub them 'dead white males'. Hytner had better luck with his own award-winning staging of Alan Bennett's *The History Boys.*

But if it's controversy you're looking for, you won't find it in the West End. London's theatreland is mostly the preserve of classic plays and big musicals (including *Mary Poppins, The Sound of Music* and all the Lloyd Webber canon). If you're after new or experimental work, you'll be better served at the capital's smaller theatres like the Donmar Warehouse (p162), the Battersea Arts Centre (p162) or the Royal Court (p162).

England also has a well-deserved reputation for cutting-edge dance. Major national companies – including the English National Ballet, the Royal Ballet and Rambert – produce top-quality productions, while leading names in the world of contemporary dance include DV8, CandoCo, Vincent Dance Theatre, Ballet Lorent, Protein Dance, the Ballet Boyz and the Richard Alston Dance Company, plus ground-breaking choreographers Michael Clark, Jasmin Vardimon, Lea Anderson and Matthew Bourne (best-known for his version of *Swan Lake* featuring all-male swans).

Food & Drink

Once upon a time, English food was highly regarded. In the later medieval period and 17th century, many people – especially the wealthy – ate a varied diet. Then along came the Industrial Revolution, with mass migration from the country to the city, and food quality took a nosedive – a legacy that means there's still no English equivalent for the phrase *bon appétit*.

But today the tide has turned once again. In 2005, food bible *Gourmet* magazine famously singled out London as having the best collection of restaurants in the world, and in the years since then the choice for food lovers – whatever their budget – has continued to improve, so it's now easy to find decent food in other cities, as well as country areas across England.

Having said that, a post-industrial culinary heritage of ready-sliced white bread, fatty meats and vegetables boiled to death, all washed down by tea with four sugars, remains firmly in place in many parts of the country. But wherever you travel, for each greasy spoon or fast-food joint, there's a local pub or restaurant serving up enticing home-grown specialities. Epicures can splash out big bucks on fine dining, while more impecunious visitors can enjoy tasty eating in England that definitely won't break the bank.

The infamous outbreaks of 'mad cow' disease in the late 1990s and foot-and-mouth disease in 2001 are history now, and British beef is once again exported to the world. An upside of the bad press was a massive surge in demand for organic food, and there's now a plethora of natural, unadulterated, chemical-free products available from producers or in shops, markets, cafes and restaurants across the country.

For locals and visitors, organic food usually means better food, but there are some anomalies: it seems impossible to buy English apples in some supermarkets during the autumn cropping season, although you can chose between 10 different varieties imported from New Zealand, Chile or South Africa.

Alongside the greater awareness of food's quality and provenance, there have been other changes to English food thanks to outside influences. For decades most towns have boasted Chinese and Indian restaurants, so a vindaloo or a chow mein is no longer considered 'exotic'; in fact, curry is the most popular takeaway food, outstripping even fish and chips.

As well as the food available in Indian restaurants (which in many cases are actually owned, run and staffed by Pakistanis or Bangladeshis), dishes from Japan, Korea, Thailand and other countries east of Suez have become available in more recent times too. From the other side of the world, there's been a growth in restaurants serving up South American, African or Caribbean cuisine. Closer to home, pasta, pizza and a wide range of Mediterranean dishes – from countries as diverse as Morocco and Greece – are commonplace, not only in smarter restaurants but also in everyday eateries.

Queen Elizabeth I reputedly had the kitchen at Hampton Court Palace moved because the smell of cooking food drifted into her bedroom and spoilt her clothes.

According to leading organic-food campaign group the Soil Association (www.soilassociation.org), more than 85% of people in Britain want pesticide-free food. For more info, see www.whyorganic.org.

WHERE THERE'S SMOKE

All restaurants and cafes in England are non-smoking throughout. Virtually all pubs have the same rule, which is why there's often a small crowd of smokers standing on the pavement outside. Some pubs provide specific outdoor smoking areas, ranging from a simple yard to elaborate gazebos with canvas walls and the full complement of lighting, heating, piped music and TV screens – where you'd never need to know you were 'outside' at all, apart from the pungent clouds of burning tobacco.

The overall effect of these foreign influences has been the introduction to 'traditional' English cuisine of new techniques (eg steaming), new condiments (eg chilli or soy sauce), new implements (eg woks) and even revolutionary ingredients (eg crisp, fresh vegetables). So now we have 'modern British cuisine', where even humble bangers and mash rise to new heights when handmade pork, apple and thyme-flavoured sausages are paired with lightly chopped fennel and new potatoes, and 'fusion' dishes where native ingredients get new flavours from adding, for example, Oriental spices. Perhaps the best example of fusion cuisine is chicken tikka masala, the UK's favourite 'Indian' dish created specifically for the British palate and unheard of in India itself.

But beware the hype. While some restaurants in England experiment with new ideas and are undeniably excellent, others are not. Only a few months after *Gourmet* magazine called the capital 'the best place in the world to eat right now,' one of the country's most respected food critics, the *Evening Standard*'s Fay Maschler, decried the domination of style over substance, and accused several top eateries of offering poor value for money. As any food fan will tell you, rather than forking out £30 in a restaurant for a 'modern European' concoction that tastes as though it came from a can, you're often better off spending £5 on a top-notch curry in Bradford or a homemade steak-and-ale pie in a country pub in Devon.

A pub? Yes. Not so many years ago your choice would be a ham or cheese roll, with pickled onions if you were lucky, but today many foreign visitors to England are surprised to learn that pub food is often a good-value option, whether you want a toasted sandwich or a three-course meal. Many pubs have upped the food quality to such a degree that a whole new genre of eatery – the gastropub – was born.

While some gastropubs have become almost restaurants in style (with formal decor, neat menus and uniformed table service) others have gone for a more relaxed atmosphere where you'll find mismatched cutlery, no tablecloths, waiters in T-shirts, and today's choices chalked up on a blackboard. And in true pub style, you order and pay at the bar, just as you do for your drinks. For visitors relaxing after a hard day doing the sights, nothing beats the luxury of a wholesome shepherd's pie washed down with a decent ale without the worry of guessing which fork to use.

Of course, there's more to food than eating out. The lavishly illustrated food sections in weekend newspapers and the bookshop shelves groaning under the weight of countless new cookery books all indicate that food is now officially fashionable. Feeding on this is the current phenomenon of so-called 'celebrity chefs', including Hugh Fernley-Whittingstall, who famously scored a £2 million deal with his publishers in early 2006, and Gordon Ramsay who featured in a list of Britain's richest self-made entrepreneurs a few months later. They are not alone; every night on a TV channel near you a star of the kitchen demonstrates imaginative and simple techniques for producing stylish, tasty and healthy food.

There's change afoot in the shops too. Supermarkets still dominate – four companies (Asda Wal-Mart, Morrisons, Sainsbury's, Tesco) account for around 80% of all grocery shopping – squeezing suppliers to sell at everlower prices, while forcing out old-fashioned butchers and bakers from high streets and neighbourhoods – but they're selling more organic food than ever before, and new labels show just how much fat, salt and sugar the foodstuffs contain.

Alongside these changes at the multiples there's an increase in the number of independent stores selling high-quality food, while the relatively new phenomenon of farmers markets create an opportunity for food producers to sell high-quality, locally sourced meat, veg, fruit, eggs, honey and so on direct to

Rick Stein is a TV chef, energetic restaurateur and good-food evangelist. His *Food Heroes* and *Food Heroes – Another Helping* books extol small-scale producers and top-notch local food, from organic veg to wild boar sausages.

Like meat, but not battery pens? Go to the Royal Society for the Prevention of Cruelty to Animals (www.rspca.org .uk) and follow links to Freedom Food.

THE PIG, THE WHOLE SHEEP & NOTHING BUT THE COW

One of the many trends enjoyed by modern British cuisine is the revival of 'nose to tail' cooking – that is, using the whole animal, not just the more obvious cuts such as chops and fillet steaks. This does not mean boiling or grilling a pig or sheep all in one go – although spit-roasts are popular. It means utilising the parts that may at first seem unappetising or, frankly, inedible. So as well as dishes involving liver, heart, chitterlings (intestines) and other offal, traditional delights such as bone marrow on toast or tripe (stomach) and onions once again grace the menus of fashionable restaurants. The movement is particularly spearheaded by chef Fergus Henderson at his St John restaurant in London (p154), and via his influential recipe book *Nose to Tail Eating: A Kind of British Cooking* and 2007's follow-up *Beyond Nose To Tail*.

---

the public. And not just in country towns where you might expect to see them, but in cities too: there's around 20 farmers markets in London alone.

But behind the scenes, and despite the growing availability of good food in shops, markets, pubs and restaurants, many English folk still have an odd attitude to eating at home. They love to sit on the sofa and *watch* TV food shows. Then, inspired, they rush out and buy all the TV-tie-in recipe books. Then on the way back, they pop into the supermarket and buy a stack of ready-made meals. Homemade food sounds great in theory, but in reality the recipe for dinner is more likely to be something like this: open freezer, take out package, bung in microwave, ping, eat.

In fact, more junk food and ready-made meals are consumed in the UK than in all the rest of the countries of Europe put together. So it's no surprise that the English are getting increasingly heavy, with over 60% of the adult population overweight and almost 25% obese. But despite the vast intakes, average nutrition rates are lower now than they were during 1950s post-war rationing.

So in summary, yes, as a local or a visitor you can definitely find great food in England. It's just that not all the English seem to like eating it.

For tasty details on the whereabouts of farmers markets see www .farmersmarkets.net.

STAPLES & SPECIALITIES

Although grazing on a steady supply of snacks is increasingly commonplace, the English culinary day is still punctuated by the three main meals of breakfast, lunch and dinner, also called – depending on social class and location – breakfast, dinner and tea.

Breakfast

Although most working people make do with toast or a bowl of cereal before dashing to the office or factory, visitors staying in B&Bs will undoubtedly encounter a phenomenon called the 'Full English Breakfast'. This usually consists of bacon, sausages, eggs, tomatoes, mushrooms, baked beans and fried bread. In northern England (if you're really lucky) you may get black pudding – see Regional Specialties, following. And just in case you thought this insufficient, it's still preceded by cereal, and followed by toast and marmalade.

If you don't feel like eating half a farmyard first thing in the morning it's OK to ask for just the egg and tomatoes, for example, while some B&Bs offer other alternatives such as kippers (smoked fish) or a 'continental breakfast' – which completely omits the cooked stuff and may even add something exotic such as croissants.

Lunch

One of the many great inventions that England gave the world is the sandwich. The word originates from Sandwich, a town in southeast England

---

VEGETARIANS & VEGANS

It's official, vegetarians are no longer weird. Many restaurants and pubs in England have at least one token vegetarian dish (another meat-free lasagne, anyone?), but better places offer much more imaginative choices. Vegans will find the going more tricky, except of course at dedicated vegie/vegan restaurants – and where possible we recommend good options throughout this book. For more ideas see www.happycow.com.

(p186). Slapping a slice of cheese or ham between two bits of bread may seem a simple concept, but no one apparently thought of it until the 18th century when the earl of Sandwich ordered his servants to bring cold meat between bread so he could keep working at his desk or, as some historians claim, keep playing cards late at night. Of course, he didn't really invent the idea – various cultures around the world had been doing it for millennia – but the name stuck and sandwiches became fashionable food for the aristocracy. Their popularity grew among the lower classes in the early days of the Industrial Revolution: labourers heading for mines and factories needed a handy way to carry their midday meal to work.

A favourite sandwich ingredient is Marmite, a dark and pungent yeast extract that generations of English kids have loved or hated. Either way, it's a passion that continues through adulthood. In 2006, when the manufacturer of Marmite moved from selling the stuff in a near-spherical glass jar to a (much more practical) plastic tube, much was the consternation across the land. Similar to the Australian icon, Vegemite (but not the same – oh no, sir!), it's also popular on toast at breakfast and especially great for late-night munchies.

Another English classic that perhaps epitomises English food more than any other – especially in pubs – is the ploughman's lunch. Basically it's bread and cheese, and although hearty yokels probably did carry such food to the fields (no doubt wrapped in a red spotted handkerchief) over many centuries, the meal is actually a modern phenomenon. It was invented in the 1960s by the marketing chief of the national cheese-makers' organisation as a way to boost consumption, neatly cashing in on public nostalgia and fondness for tradition – even if it was fake.

You can still find a basic ploughman's lunch offered in some pubs – and it undeniably goes well with a pint or two of local ale at lunchtime – but these days the meal has usually been smartened up to include butter, salad, pickle, pickled onion and dressings. At some pubs you get a selection of cheeses. You'll also find other variations, such as a farmer's lunch (bread and chicken), stockman's lunch (bread and ham), Frenchman's lunch (brie and baguette) and fisherman's lunch (you guessed it, with fish).

Dinner

For generations, a typical English dinner has been 'meat and two veg'. Dressed up as 'evening meal' or dressed down as 'cooked tea', there was little variation: the meat would be pork, beef or lamb, one of the veg would be potatoes and the other would inevitably be carrots, cabbage or cauliflower – just as inevitably cooked long and hard. Although tastes and diets are changing, this classic combination still graces the tables of many English families several times a week.

Traditionally, the beef is roasted beef (that's why the French call the English 'les rosbif'), although meat consumption – and British farming – took a dive in 2000 and 2001 following the outbreak of mad-cow and foot-and-mouth disease. These events were still most notoriously recalled in

---

NAME THAT PASTY

A favourite in southwest England is the Cornish pasty – originally a mix of cooked vegetables wrapped in pastry – now available everywhere in England, and often including meat varieties (much to the chagrin of the Cornish people). Invented long before Tupperware, the pasty was an all-in-one-lunch pack that tin miners carried underground and left on a ledge ready for mealtime. So pasties weren't mixed up, they were marked with their owners' initials – always at one end, so the miner could eat half and safely leave the rest to snack on later without it mistakenly disappearing into the mouth of a workmate. Before going back to the surface, the miners traditionally left the last few crumbs of the pasty as a gift for the spirits of the mine, known as 'knockers', to ensure a safe shift the next day.

2005 by France's President Jacques Chirac; joking with fellow leaders at an international conference, he quipped about the British, 'The only thing they have done for European agriculture is mad cow.' But despite Mr Chirac's derogatory comments, good-quality roasts from well-reared cattle grace menus once again.

And with the beef – especially at Sunday lunches – comes Yorkshire pudding. It's simply roast batter, but very tasty when properly cooked. Another classic English dish brings Yorkshire pudding and sausages together, with the delightful name of toad-in-the-hole.

Yorkshire pudding also turns up at dinner in another guise, especially in pubs and cafes in northern England, where menus may offer a big bowl-shaped Yorkshire pudding filled with meat stew, beans or vegetables. You can even find Yorkshire puddings filled with curry – a favourite multicultural crossover that says something about English society today.

But perhaps the best-known classic English meal is fish and chips, often bought from the 'chippie' as a takeaway wrapped in paper to enjoy at home – especially popular with families on a Friday night. Later in the evening, epicures may order their fish and chips 'open' to eat immediately while walking back from the pub. For visitors, English fish and chips can be an acquired taste. Sometimes the chips can be limp and soggy, and fish can be greasy and tasteless, especially once you get away from the sea, but in towns with salt in the air this classic deep-fried delight is always worth trying.

> In Yorkshire, the eponymous pudding is traditionally a *starter*, a reminder of days when food was scarce and the pudding was a pre-meal stomach-filler.

Regional Specialities

If fish is your thing, Yorkshire's coastal resorts are particularly famous for huge servings of cod – despite it becoming an endangered species, thanks to overfishing – while restaurants in Devon and Cornwall regularly conjure up prawns, lobster, oysters, mussels and scallops. Seafood you may encounter elsewhere on your travels includes Norfolk crab, Northumberland kippers, and jellied eels in London.

Meat-based treats in northern and central England include Cumberland sausage – a tasty mix of minced pork and herbs, so large it has to be spiralled to fit on your plate – and Melton Mowbray pork pies (motto: 'gracious goodness for over 100 years') – cooked ham compressed in a casing of pastry and always eaten cold, ideally with pickle. A legal victory in 2005 ensured that only pies made in the eponymous Midlands town could carry the Melton Mowbray moniker – in the same way that fizzy wine from other regions can't be called Champagne.

Another English speciality that enjoys the same protection is Stilton – a strong white cheese, either plain or in a blue vein variety. Only five dairies all of England – four in the Vale of Belvoir, and one in Derbyshire – are allowed to produce cheese with this name. Bizarrely, the cheese cannot be

---

SNACK BOX

Despite promotion, and general awareness, of the need for a healthy diet, items such as biscuits, chocolate and crisps still form a large part of the average English person's daily intake – as a stroll down the aisles in any supermarket will immediately show.

Among biscuits, 'international' favourites include bourbons and garibaldis, while home-grown iconic styles and brands include chocolate 'digestives' (a name originating from early advertising campaigns that claimed the biscuits had antacid properties) and HobNobs (famously lauded by comedian Peter Kay as 'the Marines of the biscuit world' because they don't fall apart when immersed – that is, when you dunk (dip) them in a cup of tea).

Moving onto chocolate bars, long-standing favourites include the well-known global brands such as the Mars Bar, KitKat, Twix and Snickers (in the UK still remembered fondly as the Marathon by anyone over 30). A firm favourite of the 1980s and 90s, the Wispa bar, was discontinued in 2003 but made a comeback in 2007 after a surprisingly well-supported 'Bring Back Wispa' internet campaign.

And then there are crisps – the thin fried slices of potato eaten cold from a packet, known to most other parts of the world as 'chips'. (But not in Britain, where chips are chunks of potato deep fried and eaten hot – often with fish – known elsewhere as 'fries'.) The main brands of crisp are Walkers, Golden Wonder and McCoy's, and the main flavours are ready salted, cheese and onion, and salt and vinegar. Others include smoky bacon, prawn cocktail and roast chicken. Kettle Chips are marketed as a more upmarket brand, with flavours such as sea salt and balsamic vinegar, and sour cream and chive.

Until the 1980s most British crisp manufacturers used the same colour packaging for the same flavours (ready salted was in a blue packet, cheese & onion in green, and so on). Then Walkers took the revolutionary step of packaging cheese & onion in blue, salt & vinegar in green and ready salted in red. The confusion was great, and the public controversy even greater, but the end result – bizarrely – was a massive gain in market share for Walkers, and the near disappearance of Golden Wonder. A concurrent series of clever – and occasionally controversial – TV adverts featuring footballer Gary Lineker helped a lot too.

Naturally, Walkers kept their colour scheme but many years later so-called 'instinctive' crisp buyers still get home from the shop with a flavour they weren't expecting.

---

made in the village of Stilton in Cambridgeshire, although this is where it was first sold – hence the name.

Perhaps less appealing is black pudding, effectively a large sausage made from ground meat, offal, fat and blood, and traditionally served for breakfast. It's known in other countries as 'blood sausage', but the English version has a high content of oatmeal so that it doesn't fall apart in the pan when fried.

Puddings

After the main course comes dessert or 'pudding'. A speciality is rhubarb, the juicy stem of a large-leafed garden plant, best eaten in a 'crumble' – fruit with a crunchy flour, butter and sugar topping – and served with custard or ice cream. For much of the 20th century, rhubarb was a very popular food, with overnight trains dubbed the 'rhubarb express' bringing tonnes of the stuff to London and the cities of the south from the main growing area in Yorkshire, between the towns of Leeds, Wakefield and Morely, known – inevitably – as the 'rhubarb triangle'. It fell out of fashion around the 1980s but is currently enjoying a renaissance in gourmet restaurants as well as humble kitchens.

Moving onto another sweet option, Bakewell pudding blundered into the recipe books around 1860 when a cook at the Rutland Arms Hotel in the Derbyshire town of Bakewell was making a strawberry tart, but mistakenly (some stories say drunkenly) spread the egg mixture on top of the jam instead of stirring it into the pastry. Especially in northern England, the

Bakewell pudding (pudding, mark you, not 'Bakewell tart' as it's sometimes erroneously called) features regularly on local dessert menus and is certainly worth sampling.

Other favourite English dishes from the same stable include sherry trifle (a classic from the same era – the 1970s – that gave us cheese cubes and tinned pineapple chunks on cocktail sticks), treacle sponge and bread-and-butter pudding. While key ingredients of most puddings are self-explanatory, they are perhaps not for another well-loved favourite, spotted dick, a suet pudding with currants. Plus sugar, of course. Most English puddings have loads of butter or sugar, preferably both. Light, subtle and healthy? Not on your life.

Then there's plum pudding, a dome-shaped cake with fruit, nuts and brandy or rum, traditionally eaten at Christmas, when it's called – surprise, surprise – Christmas pudding. This pudding is steamed (rather than baked), cut into slices, and served with brandy butter. It's eaten after the traditional Christmas lunch of roast turkey and brussels sprouts, and shortly before the traditional sleep on the sofa when the annual Queen's speech airs on TV. Watch out for coins inserted in the pudding by superstitious cooks – if you bite one it means good luck for the next year, but it may play havoc with your fillings.

And to polish of our tour de table, staying with the sweet stuff, a reminder that the international favourite banoffee pie (a delightfully sticky dessert made from bananas and toffee) is also an English invention, first developed in a pub in Sussex in southern England in the early 1970s. A plaque on the wall of the pub proudly commemorates this landmark culinary event.

DRINKS
Alcoholic

Among alcoholic drinks, England is probably best known for its beer. Typically ranging from dark brown to bright orange in colour, and generally served at room temperature, technically it's called ale and is more commonly called 'bitter'. This is to distinguish it from lager – the drink that most of the rest of the word calls 'beer' – which is generally yellow and served cold.

Well-known international brands such as Fosters, Carling and Budweiser are all available in England, but as you travel around the country, you should definitely try some native traditional beer, also known as real ale. But be ready! If you're used to the 'amber nectar' or 'king of beers', a local English brew may come as a shock – a warm, flat and expensive shock. This is partly to do with England's climate, and partly to do with the beer being served by hand pump rather than gas pressure. Most important, though, is the integral flavour: traditional English beer doesn't *need* to be chilled or

The Campaign for Real Ale promotes the understanding of traditional British beer. Look for endorsement stickers on pub windows, and for more info see www .camra.org.uk.

CLASSIC BREWS

For keen students of real ale, classic brewery names to look out for – and their beers to sample – as you travel around England include: Adnams (eastern England), Arkell's (south, southwest), Black Sheep (north), Fuller's (southeast), Greene King (eastern, central, south), Hardys & Hansons (central), Hook Norton (south, midlands), Jennings (northwest), Marston's (south, central, north), St Austell (west), Shepherd Neame (southeast), Timothy Taylor (north) and Wadworth (west). For more ideas, tipplers' favourite tomes include the annual *Good Beer Guide to Great Britain,* produced by the Campaign for Real Ale, which steers you to the best beers and the pubs that serve them, and the *Good Pub Guide,* which details thousands of fine establishments across the country. Look out too for the wonderful *300 Beers to Try Before you Die* by Roger Protz; unashamedly jumping on the current trend for lists, this homage to British beers (and a few from other countries) is educational and jolly good fun.

fizzed to make it palatable. In contrast, sample a pint of lager that's sat in its glass for an hour and you'll see it has very little actual taste.

Another key feature is that real ale must be looked after, usually meaning a willingness on the part of the pub manager or landlord to put in extra effort – often translating into extra effort on food, atmosphere, cleanliness and so on too. But the extra effort is why many pubs don't serve real ale, so beware of places where bar staff give the barrels as much care and attention as they give the condom machine in the toilets. There's honestly nothing worse than a bad pint of real ale.

If beer doesn't tickle your palate, try cider – available in sweet and dry varieties. In western parts of England, notably Herefordshire and the southwestern counties such as Devon and Somerset, you could try 'scrumpy', a very strong dry cider traditionally made from local apples. Many pubs serve it straight from the barrel.

On hot summer days, you could go for shandy – beer and lemonade mixed in equal quantities. You'll usually need to specify 'lager shandy' or 'bitter shandy'. It may seem an astonishing combination for outsiders, but it's very refreshing and of course not very strong. Another hybrid is 'snakebite', an equal mix of cider and lager, favoured by students as it's a cost-efficient way to get drunk – thanks to the lager's bubbles and the cider's strength – the very reason some pubs refuse to serve it.

Back to more sensible tipples, many visitors are surprised to learn that wine is produced in England, and has been since the time of the Romans. Today, more than 400 vineyards and wineries produce around two million bottles a year – many highly regarded and frequently winning major awards. English white sparkling wines have been a particular success story recently, many produced in the southeast of the country where the chalky soil and climatic conditions are similar to those of the Champagne region in France. At the 2005 International Wine and Spirit Competition, a wine called Ridgeview Marret Bloomsbury from the Ditchling Vineyard in East Sussex beat entrants from 55 other countries to win the accolade 'best sparkling wine in the world'. For more see p192.

Nonalcoholic

In England, a drink means any ingestible liquid, so if you're from overseas and a local asks 'would you like a drink?', don't automatically expect a gin and tonic. They may well mean a 'cuppa' – a cup of tea – England's best-known beverage. Tea is sometimes billed as the national drink, although coffee is equally popular these days; the Brits consume 165 million cups a day and the British coffee market is worth almost £700 million a year – but with the

---

THE OLDEST PUB IN ENGLAND?

Many drinkers are often surprised to learn that the word 'pub', short for 'public house', although apparently steeped in history, dates only from the 19th century. But places selling beer have been around for much longer, and the 'oldest pub in England' is a hotly contested title.

One of the country's oldest pubs, with the paperwork to prove it, is Ye Olde Trip to Jerusalem in Nottingham (p504), which was serving ale to departing crusaders in the 12th century.

Other contenders sniff that Ye Trip is a mere newcomer. A fine old hotel called the Eagle & Child in Stow-on-the-Wold (Gloucestershire, p247) claims to have been selling beer since around AD 950, while another pub called Ye Olde Fighting Cocks in St Albans (Hertfordshire, p265) apparently dates back to the 8th century – although the 13th is more likely.

But then back comes Ye Olde Trip with a counter-claim: one of its bars is a cave hollowed out of living rock, and that's more than a million years old.

prices some coffee shops charge, maybe that's not surprising. And a final word of warning – when you're ordering a coffee and the server says 'white or black', don't panic. It simply means 'do you want milk in it?'

WHERE TO EAT & DRINK

There's a huge choice of places to eat in England, and this section outlines just some of your options. For details on opening times, see p793. The tricky issue of tipping is covered on p798, while some pointers on restaurants' attitudes to kids are on p793.

Picnics & Self-catering

When shopping for food, as well as the more obvious chain stores and corner shops, markets can be a great place for bargains – everything from dented tins of tomatoes for 1p to home-baked cakes and organic goat's cheese. Farmers markets, mentioned earlier in this section, are always worth a browse; they're a great way for producers to sell good food direct to consumers; with both sides avoiding the grip of the supermarkets.

Cafes & Teashops

The traditional English cafe is nothing like its continental European namesake. For a start, asking for a brandy with your coffee may cause confusion, as most cafes in England don't serve alcohol. Most cafes are simply basic places serving simple meals suchs meat pie, beans on toast, baked potato or omelette with chips (costing around £3 to £4) and stuff like sandwiches, cakes and other snacks (£1 to £2). Quality varies enormously: some cafes definitely earn their 'greasy spoon' handle, while others are neat and clean.

Smarter cafes are called teashops, and you might pay a bit more for extras like twee decor and table service. Teashops are your best bet for sampling a 'cream tea' – a plate of scones, clotted cream and jam, served with a pot of tea. This is known as a Devonshire tea in some other English-speaking countries, but not in England (except of course in the county of Devon, where Devonshire cream tea is a well-known – and much-hyped – local speciality).

In country areas, many market towns and villages have cafes catering for tourists, walkers, cyclists and other outdoor types, and in summer they're open every day. Good cafes are a wonderful institution and always worth a stop during your travels.

As well as the traditional establishments, in most cities and towns you'll also find American-flavoured coffee shops – the inevitable Starbucks on every corner – and Euro-style cafe-bars, serving decent lattes and espressos, and offering bagels or ciabattas rather than beans on toast (you'll probably be able to get that brandy, too). Some of these modern places even have outdoor chairs and tables – rather brave considering the narrow pavements and inclement weather much of England enjoys.

Restaurants

London has scores of excellent restaurants that could hold their own in major cities worldwide, while places in Bath, Leeds and Manchester can give

Since the major coffee-shop chains arrived in Britain in the 1990s, around 80% of local cafes have closed.

Eggs, Bacon, Chips & Beans by Russell Davies showcases 50 of the UK's finest traditional cafes, with tongue-in-cheek taster's notes on their various versions of the traditional fry-up. The conversation continues at http://russelldavies.typepad.com.

EATING INTO THE FINANCES

Most of the Eating sections in the chapters throughout this book are divided into three price bands: budget (up to £8 per person for a main course with a drink), midrange (£8 to £16) and top end (over £16). For more guidance, see Costs on p20.

EARLY DOORS, LATE NIGHTS

Pubs in towns and country areas usually open daily, from 11am to 11pm Sunday to Thursday, sometimes to midnight or 1am Friday and Saturday. Most open all day, although some may shut from 3pm to 6pm. Throughout this book, we don't list pub opening and closing times unless they vary significantly from these hours.

In cities, some pubs open until midnight or later, but it's mostly bars and clubs that take advantage of new licensing laws ('the provision of late-night refreshment', as it's officially and charmingly called) to stay open to 1am, 2am or later. As every place is different, we list opening hours for all bars and clubs.

---

the capital a fair run for its money (actually, often for rather less money). We've taken great pleasure in seeking out some of the best and best-value restaurants in England, and have recommended a small selection throughout this book.

Prices vary considerably across the country, with a main course in a straightforward restaurant costing around £7 to £10 and rising to £15 or £20 at good-quality places. Utterly excellent food, service and surroundings can be enjoyed for £30 to £50 per person – although in London you can, if you want, pay double this.

Pubs & Bars

The difference between pubs and bars is sometimes vague, but generally bars are smarter, larger and louder than pubs, with a younger crowd. Drinks are more expensive too, unless there's a gallon-of-vodka-and-Red-Bull-for-a-fiver promotion – which there often is.

As well as beer, cider, wine and the other drinks mentioned earlier in this chapter, pubs and bars offer the usual choice of spirits, often served with a 'mixer', producing English favourites such as gin and tonic, rum and coke or vodka and lime. These drinks are served in measures called singles and doubles. A single is 35ml – just over one US fluid ounce. A double is of course 70ml – still disappointingly small when compared to measures in other countries. To add further to your disappointment, the vast array of cocktail options, as found in America, is generally restricted to more upmarket city bars in England.

And while we're serving out warnings, here are two more: First, if you see a pub calling itself a 'free house', it's simply a place that doesn't belong to a brewery or pub company, and thus is 'free' to sell any brand of beer. Unfortunately, it doesn't mean the beer is free of charge. Second, remember that drinks in English pubs are ordered and paid for at the bar. If the pub serves food, that's usually ordered and paid for at the bar as well. You can always spot the out-of-towners – they're the ones sitting forlornly at a empty table hoping to spot a waiter.

When it comes to gratuities, it's not usual to tip pub and bar staff, as it is, say, in America. However, if you're ordering a large round, or the service has been good all evening, you can say to the person behind the bar 'and one for yourself'. They may not have a drink, but they'll add the monetary equivalent to the total you pay and keep it as a tip.

Apart from good service, what makes a good pub? It's often surprisingly hard to pin down, but in our opinion the best pubs follow a remarkably simple formula: they offer a welcoming atmosphere, pleasant surroundings and, in villages where pubs have been the centre of the community for centuries, they often offer a sense of history (see the boxed text, p80). The best pubs also offer a good range of hand-pulled beer and a good menu of

ENGLAND'S TOP PICKS

Looking for something special? Here's our highly subjective selection of English eateries, ranging from temples of gastronomy to humble-but-excellent pubs, with other parameters – such as the finest food (obviously), the friendliest staff or simply the best view – thrown in for good measure.

Restaurant	Location	Go for...	Page
5 North St	Winchcombe	friendly service, good atmosphere, great food	p246
Al Frash	Birmingham	no frills decor and hearty balti	p538
Terre á Terre	Brighton	inventive, robust vegetarian fare, for vegetarians and carnivores alike	p209
Blake's Coffee House	Newcastle-upon-Tyne	Sunday morning cures all week long	p754
Bordeaux Quay	Bristol	high quality dishes, low food miles	p338
Cap'n Jaspers	Plymouth	funky feel of a local institution	p386
Daffodil	Cheltenham	modern food in a converted art-deco cinema	p258
Demuth's	Bath	fabulous, imaginative vegetarian cuisine	p349
Drunken Duck	Hawkshead	first-class Cumbrian cooking	p718
Engineer	London	gastropub eating with a hip vibe	p158
Fifteen	London	a touch of fame and a wide range of price options	p155
Lighthouse	Aldeburgh	welcoming atmosphere and top-notch international dining	p454
Magpie Cafe	Whitby	fantastic fish and chips (but crowds to match)	p649
Midsummer House	Cambridge	excellent French Mediterranean cuisine in a Victorian setting	p436
Modern	Manchester	amazing city views with food to match	p664
Mr Underhill's	Ludlow	Michelin-starred modern British menu	p583
Oldfields	Durham	seasonal menus featuring local and organic ingredients	p762
Olive Branch	Rutland	county pub vibe with dining that exceeds expectations	p490
Riverford Field Kitchen	Totnes	organic lunch including a tour of the farm	p382
Teza Indian Canteen	Carlisle	21st-century Indian cuisine	p740
Wheeler's Oyster Bar	Whitstable	fine seafood in historic surroundings	p183
Stone Trough Inn	York	valley views and gourmet pub grub	p632

snacks and meals (cooked on the premises, not shipped in by the truck-full and defrosted in the microwave). After months of painstaking research, this is the type of pub we recommend throughout this book but, of course, there are many more pubs in England than even we could sample, and nothing beats the fun of doing your own investigating. So, armed with the advice in this chapter, we urge you to get out there and tipple your taste buds.

FOOD GLOSSARY

aubergine – large purple-skinned vegetable; 'eggplant' in the USA and Australia

bangers – sausages (colloquial)
bap – a large, wide, flat, soft bread roll
bevvy – drink (originally from northern England)
bill – the total you need to pay after eating in a restaurant ('check' to Americans)
bitter – ale; a type of beer
black pudding – type of sausage made from dried blood and other ingredients
bun – bread roll, usually sweet, eg current bun, cream bun
BYO – bring your own (usually in the context of bringing your own drink to a restaurant)

caff – abbreviated form of cafe
candy floss – light sugar-based confectionery; called 'cotton candy' in the USA, 'fairy floss' in Australia

chips – sliced, deep-fried potatoes, eaten hot (what Americans call 'fries')
cider – beer made from apples
clotted cream – cream so heavy or rich that it's become almost solid (but not sour)
corkage – a small charge levied by the restaurant when you BYO (bring your own)
courgette – green vegetable ('zucchini' to Americans)
cream cracker – white unsalted savoury biscuit
cream tea – cup of tea and a scone loaded with jam and cream
crisps – thin slices of fried potato bought in a packet, eaten cold; called 'chips' or 'potato chips' in the USA and Australia
crumpet – circular piece of doughy bread, toasted before eating, usually covered with butter

double cream – heavy or thick cream
dram – whisky measure

fish fingers – strips of fish pieces covered in breadcrumbs, usually bought frozen, cooked by frying or grilling

greasy spoon – cheap cafe

ice lolly – flavoured ice on a stick; called 'popsicle' in the USA, 'icy pole' in Australia
icing – thick, sweet and solid covering on a cake; called 'frosting' in the USA

jam – fruit conserve often spread on bread
jelly – sweet desert of flavoured gelatine
joint – cut of meat used for roasting

kippers – salted and smoked fish, traditionally herring

pickle – a thick, vinegary vegetable-based condiment
Pimms – popular English spirit mixed with lemonade, mint and fresh fruit
pint – beer (as in 'let me buy you a pint')

salad cream – creamy vinegary salad dressing, much sharper than mayonnaise
scrumpy – a type of strong dry *cider* originally made in England's West Country; many pubs serve it straight from the barrel
shandy – beer and lemonade mixed together in equal quantities; when ordering, specify a bitter shandy or a lager shandy
shepherd's pie – two-layered oven dish with a ground beef and onion mixture on the bottom and mashed potato on the top – no pastry
single cream – light cream (to distinguish from *double cream* and *clotted cream*)
snakebite – equal mix of cider and lager; favoured by students as it reputedly gets you drunk quickly thanks to the lager's bubbles and the cider's strength
snug – usually a small separate room in a pub
squash – fruit drink concentrate mixed with water
stout – dark, full-bodied beer made from malt; Guinness is the most famous variety
swede – large root vegetable; sometimes called 'yellow turnip' or 'rutabaga' in the USA

tipple – an old-fashioned word for drink, often used ironically, eg 'Do you fancy a tipple?'; a tippler is a drinker
treacle – molasses or dark syrup

Environment

England is the largest of the three nations on the island of Britain, with Scotland to the north and Wales to the west. Further west lies the island of Ireland. Looking south, France is just 20 miles away across the strait known to the French as La Manche (the sleeve) and to the English – with characteristic modesty – as the English Channel.

THE LAND

England is not a place of geographical extremes – there are no Himalayas or Lake Baikals here – but even a relatively short journey can take you through a surprising mix of landscapes.

Southern England's countryside is gently undulating, with a few hilly areas like the Cotswolds, and farmland between the towns and cities. East Anglia is mainly low and flat, while the Southwest Peninsula has wild moors and rich pastures – hence Devon's world-famous cream – with a rugged coast and sheltered beaches that make it a favourite holiday destination.

In England's north, farmland remains interspersed with towns and cities, but the landscape is bumpier. A line of large hills called the Pennines (fondly tagged 'the backbone of England') runs from Derbyshire to the Scottish border, and includes the peaty plateaus of the Peak District, the delightful valleys of the Yorkshire Dales and the frequently windswept but ruggedly beautiful moors of Northumberland.

Perhaps England's best-known landscape is the Lake District, a small but spectacular cluster of hills and mountains in the northwest, where Scaféll Pike (a towering 978m) is England's highest peak.

WILDLIFE

For a small country, England has a diverse range of plants and animals. Many native species are hidden away, but there are some undoubted gems – from lowland woods carpeted in shimmering bluebells to stately herds of deer on the high moors – and taking the time to have a closer look will enhance your trip enormously.

Animals

In farmland areas, rabbits are everywhere, but if you're hiking through the countryside be on the lookout for brown hares, an increasingly rare species. They're related to rabbits but much larger. Males who battle for territory by boxing on their hind legs in early spring are, of course, as 'mad as a March hare'.

Although hare numbers are on the decline, down on the riverbank the once-rare otter is making a comeback, while in farmland the black-and-white striped badger is under threat from farmers who believe they transmit bovine tuberculosis to cattle. Conservationists say the case is far from proven and seem to have won the argument; mooted badger culls were abandoned by the government in July 2008.

Common birds of farmland and similar countryside (and urban gardens) include the robin, with its instantly recognisable red breast and cheerful whistle; the wren, whose loud trilling song belies its tiny size; and the yellowhammer, with a song that sounds like (if you use your imagination) 'a-little-bit-of-bread-and-no-cheese'. In open fields, the warbling cry of a skylark is another classic, but now threatened, sound of the English outdoors. A larger bird is the pheasant, originally introduced from Russia to the

Wildlife of Britain by George McGavin et al is subtitled 'the definitive visual guide'. Although too heavy to carry around, this beautiful photographic book is great for pretrip inspiration or post-trip memories.

For more in-depth information on the nation's flora and fauna, www .wildaboutbritain.co.uk Is an award-winning site that's comprehensive, accessible and interactive.

WILD READING

Is it a rabbit or a hare? A gull or a tern? Buttercup or cowslip? If you need to know a bit more about England's plant and animal kingdoms the following guidebooks are ideal for entry-level naturalists:

■ *Complete Guide to British Wildlife* by Paul Sterry is portable and highly recommended, covering mammals, birds, fish, plants, snakes, insects and even fungi, with brief descriptions and excellent photos.

■ If feathered friends are enough, the *Complete Guide to British Birds* by Paul Sterry combines clear photos and descriptions, plus when and where each species may be seen.

■ *Wildlife of the North Atlantic* by world-famous film-maker Tony Soper beautifully covers the animals seen from beach, boat and cliff top in the British Isles and beyond.

■ Collins Gem series includes handy little books on wildlife topics such as *Birds*, *Trees*, *Fish* and *Wild Flowers*.

Perhaps surprisingly, England's most wooded county is Surrey, despite its proximity to London. The soil is too poor for agriculture, and while woodland areas elsewhere in England were cleared, Surrey's trees got a stay of execution.

nobility's shooting estates, but now considered naturalised and commonly seen in farmland and moorland.

In woodland areas, mammals include the small white-spotted fallow deer and the even smaller roe deer. Woodland is full of birds too, but you'll hear them more than see them. Listen out for willow warblers (which have a warbling song with a descending cadence) and chiffchaffs (which, also not surprisingly, make a repetitive 'chiff chaff' noise).

If you hear rustling among the fallen leaves it might be a hedgehog – a cute-looking, spiny-backed insect eater – but it's an increasingly rare sound these days; conservationists say they'll be extinct in Britain by 2025, thanks to insecticides in farming, increased building in rural areas (hedgehogs are notoriously bad at crossing roads) and the changing nature of city parks that once made up the hedgehog's habitat.

In contrast, foxes are widespread and well adapted to a scavenging life in rural towns, and even city suburbs. A controversial law banning the hunting of foxes with dogs was introduced in 2005, but as this activity (a traditional country pursuit or savage blood sport, depending who you talk to) killed only a small proportion of the total fox population, opinion is still divided on whether the ban has had any impact on numbers.

Grey squirrels (introduced from North America) have also proved very adaptable, to the extent that native red squirrels are severely endangered because the greys eat all the food.

Britain's Best Wildlife by Mike Dilger is a 'Top 40' countdown of favourites compiled by experts and the public, with details on when and where to see the country's finest wildlife spectaculars.

Perhaps unexpectedly, England is home to herds of 'wild' ponies, notably in the New Forest, Exmoor and Dartmoor, but although these animals roam free they are privately owned and regularly managed. There's even a pocket of wild goats near Lynmouth in Devon, where they've apparently gambolled merrily for almost 1000 years.

On mountains and high moors – including the Lake District and Northumberland – the most visible mammal is the red deer. Males of the species grow their famous large antlers between April and July, and shed them again in February. Also on the high ground, well-known and easily recognised birds include the red grouse, which often hides in the heather until almost stepped on then flies away with a loud warning call, and the curlew, with it's stately long legs and elegant curved bill. Look hard, and you may see beautifully camouflaged golden plovers, while the spectacular aerial displays of lapwings are impossible to miss.

Down by the sea, mammals include seals – see boxed text, opposite – and in areas such as Norfolk and Northumberland boat trips to see their

---

SEA LIFE

Two seal species frequent English coasts: the larger grey seal, which is more often seen, and the misnamed common seal. Dolphins, porpoises, minke whales and basking sharks can also be seen off the western coasts, especially from about May to September when viewing conditions are better – although you may need to go with someone who knows where to look!

---

colonies are a popular attraction. Estuaries and mudflats are feeding grounds for numerous migrant wading birds; easily spotted are black-and-white oystercatchers with their long red bills, while flocks of small ringed plovers skitter along the sand.

On the coastal cliffs in early summer, particularly in Cornwall and Yorkshire, countless thousands of guillemots, razorbills, kittiwakes and other breeding seabirds fight for space on crowded rock ledges, and the air is thick with their sound. Even if you're not into bird spotting, this is one of England's finest wildlife spectacles.

Plants

In the chalky hill country of southern England and the limestone areas further north (such as the Peak District and Yorkshire Dales), the best place to see wildflowers are the fields that evade large-scale farming – many erupt with great profusions of cowslips and primroses in April and May.

For woodland flowers, the best time is also April and May, before the leaf canopy is fully developed so sunlight can reach plants such as bluebells – a beautiful and internationally rare species.

Another classic English plant is gorse: you can't miss the swaths of this spiky bush in heath areas like the New Forest. Legend says it's the season for kissing when gorse blooms. Luckily its vivid yellow flowers show year-round.

In contrast, the blooming season for heather is quite short, but no less dramatic; through August and September areas such as the North York Moors and Dartmoor are covered in a riot of purple.

> The latest edition of the ever-popular *Wildlife Walks* book, published by the Wildlife Trusts, suggests great days out on foot in 500 wildlife reserves across the country.

NATIONAL PARKS

Back in 1810, poet and outdoor-fan William Wordsworth suggested that the Lake District should be 'a sort of national property, in which every man has a right'. More than a century later this area is indeed a national park (although quite different from Wordsworth's vision), along with Dartmoor, Exmoor, the New Forest, Norfolk and Suffolk Broads, Northumberland, the North York Moors, the Peak District and the Yorkshire Dales. A new park, the South Downs, is in the process of being created.

It's an impressive total, covering 8% of England's land area, but the term 'national park' can cause confusion. First, they are not state-owned: nearly all land is private, belonging to farmers, private estates and conservation organisations. Second, they are *not* areas of wilderness as in many other countries; in England's national parks you'll see crop-fields in lower areas and grazing sheep on the uplands, as well as roads, railways and villages, and even towns, quarries and factories in some parks. It's a reminder of the balance that needs to be struck in this crowded country between protecting the natural environment and catering for the people who live in it.

Despite these apparent anomalies, national parks still contain vast tracts of mountain and moorland, with rolling downs, river valleys and other areas of quiet countryside, all ideal for long walks, easy rambles, cycle rides, sightseeing or just lounging around.

> To explore England's national parks from your computer, before putting on your boots and getting out there, an excellent portal site is www .nationalparks.gov.uk.

ENGLAND'S TOP NATIONAL PARKS

National Park	Features	Activities	Best Time to Visit	Page
Dartmoor	rolling hills, rocky tors and serene valleys: wild ponies, deer, peregrine falcons	walking, off-road cycling, horse riding	May-Jun (wild flowers in bloom)	p387
Exmoor	sweeping moors and craggy sea cliffs: red deer, wild ponies, horned sheep	horse riding, walking	Sep (heather in bloom)	p361
Lake District	majestic fells, rugged mountains and shimmering lakes: ospreys, red squirrels, golden eagles	water sports, walking, cycling, mountaineering, rock climbing	Sep-Oct (summer crowds have left and autumn colours abound)	p704
New Forest	woodlands and heath: wild ponies, otters, Dartford warbler, southern damselfly	walking, cycling, horse riding	Apr-Sep (lush vegetation, wild ponies grazing)	p289
Norfolk & Suffolk Broads	expansive shallow lakes, rivers and marshlands: water lilies, wildfowl, otters	walking, cycling, boating	Apr-May (birds most active)	p463
North York Moors	heather-clad hills, deep-green valleys, lonely farms and isolated villages: merlins, curlews and golden plovers	cycling, on- and off-road	Aug-Sep (heather flowering)	p641
Northumberland	wild rolling moors, heather and gorse: black grouse, red squirrels, Hadrian's Wall	walking, cycling, climbing	Apr-May (lambs) & Sep (heather flowering)	p774
Peak District	high moors, tranquil dales, limestone caves: kestrels, badgers, grouse	walking, cycling, hang-gliding, rock climbing	Apr-May (even more lambs)	p512
Yorkshire Dales	rugged hills and lush valleys, crossed by stone walls and dotted with monastic ruins	walking, cycling, climbing	Apr-May (you guessed it, when lambs outnumber visitors)	p605

ENVIRONMENTAL ISSUES

With England's long history of human occupation, it's not surprising that the country's appearance is almost totally the result of people's interaction with the environment. Since the earliest times (see the History chapter) people have been chopping down trees and creating fields for crops or animals, but the most dramatic changes in rural areas came after WWII in the late 1940s, continuing into the '50s and '60s, when a drive to be self-reliant in food meant new – intensive and large-scale – farming methods. The visible result: an ancient patchwork of small meadows became a landscape of vast prairies, as walls were demolished, woodlands felled, ponds filled, wetlands drained and, most notably, hedgerows ripped out.

In most cases the hedgerows were lines of dense bushes, shrubs and trees forming a network that stretched across the countryside, protecting fields from erosion, supporting a varied range of flowers, and providing shelter for numerous insects, birds and small mammals. But in the rush to improve farm yields, thousands of miles of hedgerows were destroyed in the postwar decades, and between the mid-1980s and the early 2000s another 25% disappeared.

Hedgerows have come to symbolise many other environmental issues in rural areas, and in recent years the destruction has abated, partly because farmers recognise their anti-erosion qualities, partly because they don't

Britain's new 'hedgerows' are the long strips of grass and bushes alongside motorways and major roads. Rarely trod by humans, they support rare flowers, thousands of insect species plus mice, shrews and other small mammals – so kestrels are often seen hovering nearby.

need to remove any more, and partly because they're encouraged to 'set aside' such areas as wildlife havens – although in 2008 set-aside land was again under threat as farmers sought to take advantage of soaring grain prices (but by harvest time, prices had dropped again). Nonetheless, subsidies from government or European agencies are now available to replant hedgerows. Ironic, when only 20 years ago there were subsidies to pull them out.

Of course, environmental issues are by no means exclusive to rural areas. In England's towns and cities, topics such as air and light pollution, levels of car use, public-transport provision and household-waste recycling are never far from the political agenda, although some might say they're not quite near enough to the top of the list. Over the past decade, the main political parties have lacked engagement with the issues, although the opposition Conservatives have made sustainability a major tenet – even changing their logo in 2006 to include a tree. Their Party leader David Cameron famously made a big deal about cycling to work, which looked good (and would have been fine if he'd emphasised the health benefits) until the press discovered his chauffer still drove his official car to Parliament, carrying a huge stack of paperwork and a change of clothes. On the other side of the political fence, the Labour government has also come in for criticism; for example, an independent scientific study released in 2007 reported that the UK's carbon dioxide emissions in 2020 may be a 17% reduction on current levels, significantly lower than the 30% target. The government has also been lampooned by critics for championing 'headline grabbing' environmental initiatives (such as the Green Homes Project information portal) on one hand, while approving motorway-widening and airport expansion on the other.

But perhaps the politicians are only representing public opinion. While numerous surveys show high proportions of respondents *saying* they care, a poll in mid-2008 revealed that only 1% of holidaymakers considered the environmental impact of flying as a priority when booking their trip.

Meanwhile, back in the country, in addition to hedgerow clearance, other farming techniques remain hot environmental issues: the use of pesticides, monocropping, intensive irrigation, and the 'battery' rearing of cows, sheep and other stock. The results of these unsustainable methods, say environmentalists, are rivers running dry, fish poisoned by run-off, and fields with one type of grass and not another plant to be seen. These 'green deserts' support no insects, so in turn some wild bird populations have dropped by an incredible 70%. This is not a case of wizened old peasants recalling the idyllic days of their forbears; you only have to be over about 30 in England to remember a countryside where birds such as skylarks or lapwings were visibly much more numerous.

England buries most of its rubbish in 'landfill sites' such as disused quarries and gravel pits. By 2015, say environmental campaigners, these will all be full. Options will then be more recycling, or more controversial methods such as incineration.

The Environment Agency is responsible for everything from clean air and flood warnings to boat permits and fishing licences. Find information at www.environment agency.gov.uk.

COMPARING COVERAGE

Statistics can be boring, but these essential measurements may be handy for planning or perspective as you travel around:

England: 50,000 sq miles
Britain: 88,500 sq miles
UK: 95,000 sq miles
British Isles: 123,000 sq miles

If you want some comparisons, France is about 212,000 sq miles, Texas 266,000 sq miles, Australia 2.7 million sq miles and the USA about 3.5 million sq miles.

But all is not lost. In the face of apparently overwhelming odds, England still boasts great biodiversity, and some of the best wildlife habitats are protected (to a greater or lesser extent) by the creation of national parks and similar areas, or private reserves owned by conservation campaign groups such as the **Wildlife Trusts** (www.wildlifetrusts.org), **Woodland Trust** (www.woodland-trust .org), **National Trust** (www.nationaltrust.org.uk) and the **Royal Society for the Protection of Birds** (www.rspb.org.uk). Many of these areas are open to the public – ideal spots for walking, bird watching or simply enjoying the peace and beauty of the countryside – and well worth a visit as you travel around the country.

London

Everyone comes to London with a preconception of the metropolis shaped by a multitude of books, movies, TV shows and songs. Whatever yours is, prepare to have it shattered by this endlessly fascinating, amorphous city.

Don't believe anyone who claims to know London – you could spend a lifetime exploring it and find that the slippery thing's gone and changed on you. One thing is constant: that great serpent of a river enfolding the city in its sinuous loops, linking London both to the green heart of England and the world. The Empire may be long gone but the engines of global capital continue to be stoked by the side of the Thames. This only adds to London's vibrant, finger-on-the-pulse persona. It's also what makes it the third-most expensive city in the world.

Those who call London grey are only telling part of the story. It's also surprisingly green and even a little wild. Deer still wander some of its parks, foxes roam the streets at night and the tenacity of the foliage leaves you in little doubt that a few years without human intervention would transform the whole place into Sleeping Beauty's castle.

But London's in no danger of slumbering anytime soon. From Roman times the world has come to London, put down roots and whinged about the weather. There is no place on earth that is more multicultural; any given street yields a rich harvest of languages. Those narrow streets are also steeped in history, art, architecture and popular culture. With endless reserves of cool, London is one of the world's great cities, if not the greatest.

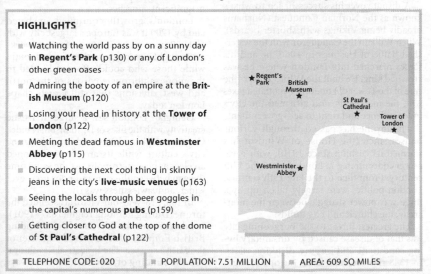

HIGHLIGHTS

- Watching the world pass by on a sunny day in **Regent's Park** (p130) or any of London's other green oases
- Admiring the booty of an empire at the **British Museum** (p120)
- Losing your head in history at the **Tower of London** (p122)
- Meeting the dead famous in **Westminster Abbey** (p115)
- Discovering the next cool thing in skinny jeans in the city's **live-music venues** (p163)
- Seeing the locals through beer goggles in the capital's numerous **pubs** (p159)
- Getting closer to God at the top of the dome of **St Paul's Cathedral** (p122)

★ Regent's Park
British Museum ★
St Paul's Cathedral ★
Tower of London ★
Westminister ★ Abbey

| ▪ TELEPHONE CODE: 020 | ▪ POPULATION: 7.51 MILLION | ▪ AREA: 609 SQ MILES |

HISTORY

London first came into being as a Celtic village near a ford across the River Thames, but it wasn't until after the Roman invasion, in the year 43, that the city really began to take off. The Romans enclosed their Londinium in walls that are still echoed in the shape of the City of London (the big 'C' City) today.

By the end of the 3rd century AD, Londinium was almost as multicultural as it is now, with 30,000 people of various ethnic groups and temples dedicated to a large number of cults. Internal strife and relentless barbarian attacks took their toll on the Romans who abandoned Britain in the 5th century, reducing the conurbation to a sparsely populated backwater.

The Saxons then moved in to the area, establishing farmsteads and villages. Their 'Lundenwic' prospered, becoming a large, well-organised town divided into 20 different wards. As the city grew in importance, it caught the eye of Danish Vikings who launched many invasions and razed the city in the 9th century. The Saxons held on until, finally beaten down in 1016, they were forced to accept the Danish leader Knut (Canute) as King of England, after which London replaced Winchester as its capital. In 1042 the throne reverted to the Saxon Edward the Confessor, whose main contribution to the city was the building of Westminster Abbey.

A dispute over his successor led to what's known as the Norman Conquest (Normans broadly being Vikings with shorter beards). When William the Conqueror won the watershed Battle of Hastings in 1066, he and his forces marched into London where he was crowned king. He built the White Tower (the core of the Tower of London), negotiated taxes with the merchants, and affirmed the city's independence and right to self-government.

The throne has passed through various houses since (the House of Windsor has warmed its cushion since 1910), with royal power concentrated in London from the 12th century. From then to the late 15th century, London politics were largely taken up by a three-way power struggle between the monarchy, the church and city guilds.

The greatest threat to the burgeoning city was that of disease caused by unsanitary living conditions and impure drinking water. In 1348 rats on ships from Europe brought the bubonic plague, which wiped out a third of London's population of 100,000 over the following year.

Violence became commonplace in the hard times that followed. In 1381, miscalculating or just disregarding the mood of the nation, the king tried to impose a poll tax on everyone in the realm. Tens of thousands of peasants marched on London. Several ministers were murdered and many buildings razed before the so-called Peasants' Revolt ran its course. The ringleaders were executed, but there was no more mention of a poll tax (until Margaret Thatcher, not heeding the lessons of history, tried to introduce it in the 1980s).

Despite these setbacks, London was consolidated as the seat of law and government in the kingdom during the 14th century. An uneasy political compromise was reached between the factions, and the city expanded rapidly in the 16th century under the House of Tudor.

The Great Plague struck in 1665 and by the time the winter cold arrested the epidemic 100,000 Londoners had perished. Just as the population considered a sigh of relief, another disaster struck.

The mother of all blazes, the Great Fire of 1666, virtually razed the place, destroying most of its medieval, Tudor and Jacobean architecture. One plus was that it created a blank canvas upon which master architect Sir Christopher Wren could build his magnificent churches.

London's growth continued unabated and by 1700 it was Europe's largest city with 600,000 people. An influx of foreign workers brought expansion to the east and south, while those who could afford it headed to the more salubrious environs of the north and west, divisions that still largely shape London today.

Georgian London saw a surge in artistic creativity with the likes of Dr Johnson, Handel, Gainsborough and Reynolds enriching the city's culture while its architects fashioned an elegant new metropolis. At the same time the gap between the rich and poor grew ever wider, and lawlessness was rife.

In 1837, 18-year-old Victoria ascended the throne. During her long reign (1837–1901), London became the fulcrum of the expanding British Empire, which covered a quarter of the earth's surface. The Industrial Revolution saw the building of new docks and railways (including the first underground line in 1863), while the Great Exhibition of 1851 showcased London to the world. The city's population mushroomed from just over two million to 6.6 million during Victoria's reign.

Road transport was revolutionised in the early 20th century when the first motor buses were introduced, replacing the horse-drawn versions that had trotted their trade since 1829.

Although London suffered relatively minor damage during WWI, it was devastated by the Luftwaffe in WWII when huge swathes of the centre and East End were flattened and 32,000 people were killed. Ugly housing and low-cost developments were hastily erected in postwar London, and immigrants from around the world flocked to the city and changed its character forever.

The last major disaster to beset the capital was the Great Smog on 6 December 1952, when a lethal combination of fog, smoke and pollution descended on the city and killed some 4000 people.

Prosperity gradually returned, and the creative energy that had been bottled up in the postwar years was suddenly unleashed. London became the capital of cool in fashion and music in the 'Swinging Sixties'.

The party didn't last long, however, and London returned to the doldrums in the harsh economic climate of the 1970s. Recovery began – for the business community at least – under the iron fist of Margaret Thatcher, elected Britain's first female prime minister in 1979. Her monetarist policy and determination to crush socialism sent unemployment skyrocketing and her term was marked by civil unrest.

In 2000 the modern metropolis got its first Mayor of London (as opposed to the Lord Mayor of the City of London), an elected role covering the City and all 32 urban boroughs. The position was taken in 2008 by Boris Johnson, a Conservative known for his unruly shock of blond hair, appearances on TV game shows and controversial editorials in *Spectator* magazine. One thing the bicycle-riding mayor will have to contend with is the city's traffic snarls. A congestion charge on cars entering the central city had initial success when introduced by his predecessor, but rush-hour congestion has now increased to precharge levels.

July 2005 was a roller-coaster month for London. Snatching victory from the jaws of Paris (the favourites), the city won its bid to host the 2012 Olympics and celebrated with a frenzy of flag waving. The following day, the party abruptly ended as suicide bombers struck on three tube trains and a bus, killing 52 people. Only two weeks later a second terrorist attack was foiled. But Londoners are not easily beaten and they immediately returned to the tube, out of defiance and pragmatism.

Work is continuing in earnest in the East End to transform a 500-acre site into the Olympic Park, complete with new legacy venues and an athletes' village that will be turned into housing post-Olympics. It's expected that the project will rejuvenate this economically depressed area – and with a price tag of £9 billion, you'd certainly hope so. The improved transport connections will certainly help. An expanded East London line will link the East End to Highbury & Islington in the north and Clapham and Crystal Palace in the south.

It won't be ready for the Olympics, but the Crossrail project will add a new east–west route to the colourful spaghetti of the tube map.

ORIENTATION

The M25 ring road encompasses the 609 sq miles that is broadly regarded as Greater London. The city's main geographical feature is the murky Thames, which snakes around but roughly divides the city into north and south.

The old City of London (note the big 'C') is the capital's financial district, covering roughly a square mile bordered by the river and the many gates of the ancient (long-gone) city walls: Newgate, Moorgate etc. The areas to the east of the City are collectively known as the East End. The West End, on the City's other flank, is effectively the centre of London nowadays. It actually falls within the City of Westminster, which is one of London's 32 boroughs and has long been the centre of government and royalty. Surrounding these central areas are dozens of former villages (Camden, Islington, Clapham etc), each with their own High Street, which were long ago swallowed by London's sprawl.

Londoners commonly refer to areas by their postcode. The letters correspond to compass directions from the centre of

London, approximately St Paul's Cathedral. EC means East Central, W means West and so on.

Maps

No Londoner would be without a pocket-sized *London A-Z*, which lists nearly 30,000 streets and still doesn't cover London in its entirety. Lonely Planet also publishes a *London City Map*.

INFORMATION
Bookshops

Daunt Books (Map pp104-5; ☎ 7224 2295; 83 Marylebone High St W1; ❸ Baker St) An exquisitely beautiful store, with guidebooks, travel literature, fiction and reference books all sorted by country.

Forbidden Planet (Map pp108-9; ☎ 7420 3666; 179 Shaftesbury Ave WC2; ❸ Tottenham Court Rd) On a different planet to our lonely one, populated by comic-book heroes, sci-fi figurines, horror and fantasy literature.

Foyle's (Map pp108-9; ☎ 7437 5660; 113-119 Charing Cross Rd WC2; ❸ Tottenham Court Rd) Venerable independent store with an excellent collection of poetry and women's literature.

Grant & Cutler (Map pp108-9; ☎ 7734 2012; 55-57 Great Marlborough St W1; ❸ Oxford Circus) Foreign-language titles.

Judd Books (Map pp98-9; ☎ 7387 5333; 82 Marchmont St WC1; ❸ Russell Sq) Delightfully musty second-hand and bargain bookshop.

Stanfords (Map pp108-9; ☎ 7836 1321; 12-14 Long Acre WC2; ❸ Covent Garden) The granddaddy of travel bookstores.

Travel Bookshop (Map pp100-1; ☎ 7229 5260; 13 Blenheim Cres W11; ❸ Ladbroke Grove) Hugh Grant's haunt in *Notting Hill* and a wealth of guidebooks and travel literature.

Waterstone's Bloomsbury (Map pp98-9; ☎ 7636 1577; 82 Gower St WC1; ❸ Goodge St); Piccadilly (Map pp108-9; ☎ 7851 2400; 203-206 Piccadilly W1; ❸ Piccadilly Circus) Both beautiful branches of the chain. Check out the 5th View bar in the Piccadilly store.

Emergency

Police/Fire/Ambulance (☎ 999)
Rape & Sexual Abuse Support Centre (☎ 8683 3300)
Samaritans (☎ 0845 790 9090)

Internet Access

You'll find free wireless access at many bars, cafes and hotels, and large tracts of London, notably Canary Wharf and the City, are covered by pay-as-you-go wireless services that you can sign up to *in situ* (about £10/5 per

day/hour). You'll usually pay less at an internet cafe (about £1 to £2 per hour). Although it's unlikely you'll be caught, piggybacking off someone's unsecured connection is illegal and people have been prosecuted for it. Reliable internet cafes include:

BTR (Map pp104-5; ☎ 7209 0984; 39 Whitfield St W1; ❸ Goodge St)

easyInternetcafe (www.easy.com) Kensington (Map pp100-1; 160 Kensington High St W8; ❸ High St Kensington); Oxford St (Map pp104-5; 358 Oxford St W1; ❸ Bond St); Trafalgar Sq (Map pp108-9; 456 The Strand WC2; ❸ Charing Cross) Attached to Subway outlets.

Internet Lounge (Map pp102-3; ☎ 7370 1734; 24 Earl's Court Gardens SW5; ❸ Earl's Court)

Internet Resources

The Lonely Planet website (lonelyplanet.com) has lots of London information. You can also try the following:

BBC London (www.bbc.co.uk/london)
Evening Standard (www.thisislondon.co.uk)
Londonist (www.londonist.com)
Time Out (www.timeout.com/london)
Urban Path (www.urbanpath.com)
View London (www.viewlondon.co.uk)
Walk It (www.walkit.com) Enter your destination and get a walking map, time estimate and information on calories burnt and carbon-dioxide saved.

Media

It's hard to avoid London's free press, with vendors pushing freebies in your face outside every central tube stop on weekdays. The best is the reasonably weighty morning *Metro*, while come midafternoon the trashier *London Lite* and *London Paper* are available.

All the national dailies have plenty of London coverage, but the city's only real paper is the tabloid *Evening Standard*, which comes out in early and late editions. Published every Tuesday, *Time Out* (£2.95) is the local listing guide *par excellence*.

Medical Services

To find a local doctor or hospital, consult the local telephone directory or call ☎ 100 (toll free). There is always one local chemist that opens 24 hours (see local newspapers or notices in chemist windows).

Hospitals with 24-hour accident and emergency units include:

Royal Free Hospital (Map pp96-7; ☎ 7794 0500; Pond St NW3; ❸ Belsize Park)

St Thomas' Hospital (Map pp104-5; ☎ 7188 7188; Lambeth Palace Rd SE1; ➌ Waterloo)
University College Hospital (Map pp98-9; ☎ 0845 155 5000; 235 Euston Rd WC1; ➌ Euston Sq)

Money

Banks and ATMs (called cash machines or cash points) are two a penny in central London. You can change cash easily at banks, *bureaux de change*, travel agents and post offices, where rates are usually fair. If you use *bureaux de change*, check commission rates *and* exchange rates; some can be extortionate.

There are decent bureaux in all London's airports, some charging a £3 flat fee. The following are also reliable (both have many branches):
American Express (Amex; Map pp108-9; ☎ 7484 9610; 30-31 Haymarket SW1; ◷ 9am-6pm Mon-Sat, 10am-4pm Sun; ➌ Piccadilly Circus)
Thomas Cook (Map pp108-9; ☎ 0845 308 9570; 30 St James's St SW1; ◷ 9am-5.30pm Mon, Tue, Thu & Fri, 10am-5.30pm Wed; ➌ Green Park)

Post

Most High Streets have a post office, where you'll get to join in the national pastime: queuing. The **Trafalgar Square post office** (Map pp108-9; 24 William IV St WC2; ◷ 8.30am-6.30pm Mon-Fri, 9am-5.30pm Sat; ➌ Charing Cross) has the main *poste restante* service for London. London post offices usually open from around 9am to 5pm, Monday to Friday. Some also open 9am to noon on Saturdays.

Telephone

The only businesses to rival food outlets for sheer number of shopfronts on London's High Streets are mobile-phone stores. It's a good idea to pick up a local SIM card if you're staying for any length of time; not only will you avoid international roaming charges on your home mobile account, some also offer cheap international call-rates (for example, 6p per minute to Australia). Then there's the added advantage of being able to dish out a local number to hotties you meet at bars!
Carphone Warehouse (☎ 0870 087 0870; www.carphone -warehouse.com) has branches all over the city and a bewildering array of prepay plans available. SIMs are often free.

Many internet cafes have booths where you can dial internationally for less than the standard British Telecom (BT) rate. Another handy alternative is to buy a calling card from a corner store which allows you to connect via a local number to an internet-based international service, with charges as low as 2p per minute.

Toilets

If you're caught short around London, public toilets can be hard to find. Only a handful of tube stations have them but the bigger National Rail stations usually do (although they're often coin operated). If you can face five floors on an escalator, department stores are a good bet. In a busy pub, no-one's going to notice you sneaking in to use the loo, but if you're spotted it would be polite to order a drink afterwards.

Tourist Information

For a list of all tourist offices in London and around Britain, see www.visitmap.info/tic.
Britain & London Visitor Centre (Map pp108-9; www.visitbritain.com; 1 Regent St SW1; ◷ 9.30am-6.30pm Mon, 9am-6.30pm Tue-Fri, 10am-4pm Sat & Sun; ➌ Piccadilly Circus) Books accommodation, theatre and transport tickets, and offers a *bureau de change*, international telephones and terminals for accessing tourist information on the web. It's open longer hours in summer.
City of London Information Centre (Map p112; ☎ 7332 1456; www.cityoflondon.gov.uk; ◷ 9.30am-5.30pm Mon-Sat; St Paul's Churchyard EC4; ➌ St Paul's) Tourist information, fast-track tickets to attractions and guided walks (£6, daily in summer). Open Sundays during summer.

Travel Agencies

STA Travel (☎ 0871-230 0040; www.statravel.co.uk) Earl's Court (Map pp102-3; ☎ 7341 3693; 2 Hogarth Rd SW5; ➌ Earl's Court); Soho (Map pp108-9; ☎ 7432 7474; 85 Shaftesbury Ave W1; ➌ Leicester Sq); Tottenham Court Rd (Map pp104-5; ☎ 0871-468 0623; 11 Goodge St W1; ➌ Goodge St); Victoria (Map pp102-3; ☎ 0871-468 0649; 52 Grosvenor Gardens SW1; ➌ Victoria) Long-standing and reliable with several branches in London.
Trailfinders (www.trailfinders.com) One Stop Travel Shop (Map pp100-1; worldwide travel ☎ 7938 3939, visa & passport service 0845 050 5905, immunisation centre 7938 3999; 194 Kensington High St W8; ➌ High St Kensington); Canary Wharf (Map p111; 30A The South Colonnade; ➌ Canary Wharf); City (Map p112; 1 Threadneedle St EC2; ➌ Bank); European Travel (Map pp100-1; 215 Kensington High St W8; ➌ High St Kensington) Also has branches in Waterstones, Piccadilly (opposite), Harrods (p166) and Selfridges (p166).

(Continued on page 114)

GREATER LONDON

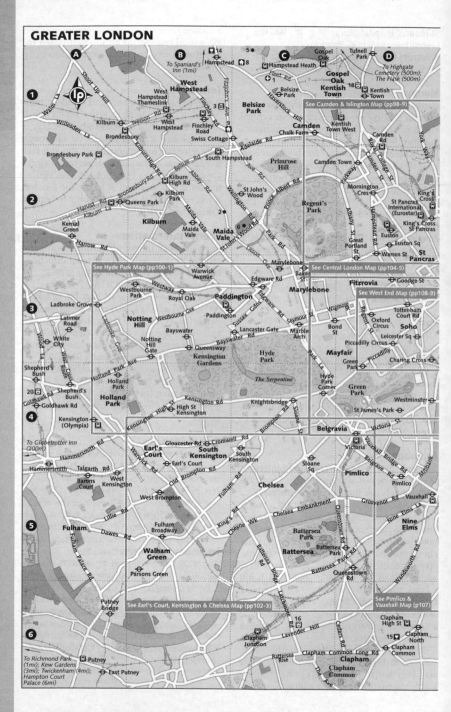

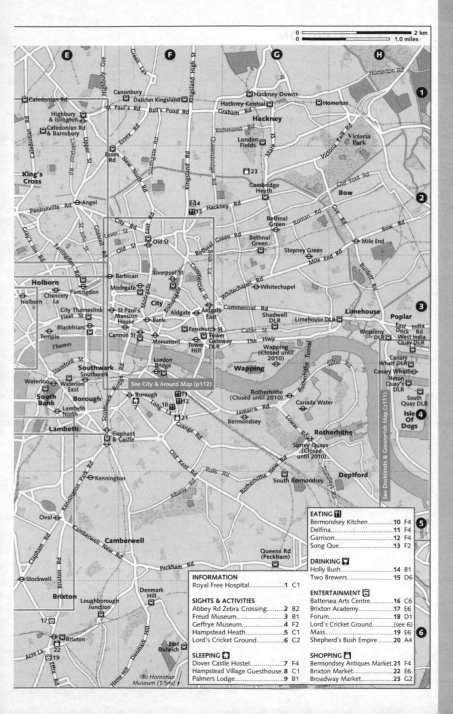

CAMDEN & ISLINGTON

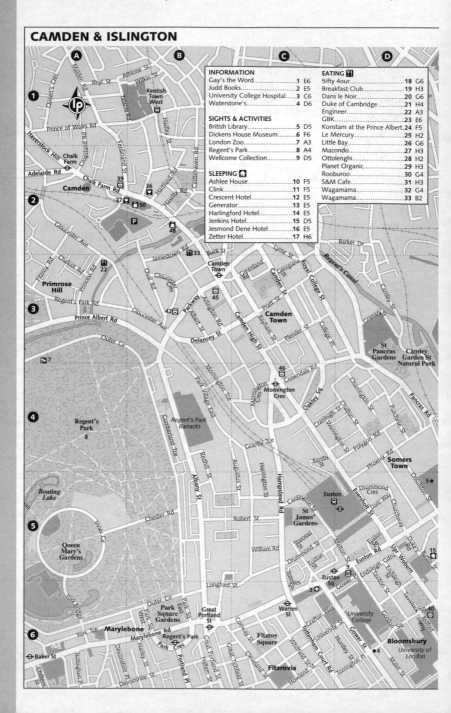

INFORMATION
Gay's the Word.....................1 E6
Judd Books............................2 E5
University College Hospital.....3 C6
Waterstone's.........................4 D6

SIGHTS & ACTIVITIES
British Library........................5 D5
Dickens House Museum.........6 F6
London Zoo..........................7 A3
Regent's Park........................8 A4
Wellcome Collection..............9 D5

SLEEPING 🏠
Ashlee House........................10 F5
Clink.....................................11 F5
Crescent Hotel......................12 E5
Generator..............................13 E5
Harlingford Hotel..................14 E5
Jenkins Hotel........................15 D5
Jesmond Dene Hotel.............16 E5
Zetter Hotel..........................17 H6

EATING 🍴
5ifty 4our.............................18 G6
Breakfast Club......................19 H3
Dans le Noir.........................20 G6
Duke of Cambridge..............21 H4
Engineer...............................22 A3
GBK......................................23 E6
Konstam at the Prince Albert.24 F5
Le Mercury...........................25 H2
Little Bay..............................26 G6
Macondo..............................27 H3
Ottolenghi............................28 H2
Planet Organic......................29 H3
Rooburoo.............................30 G4
S&M Cafe.............................31 H3
Wagamama...........................32 G4
Wagamama...........................33 B2

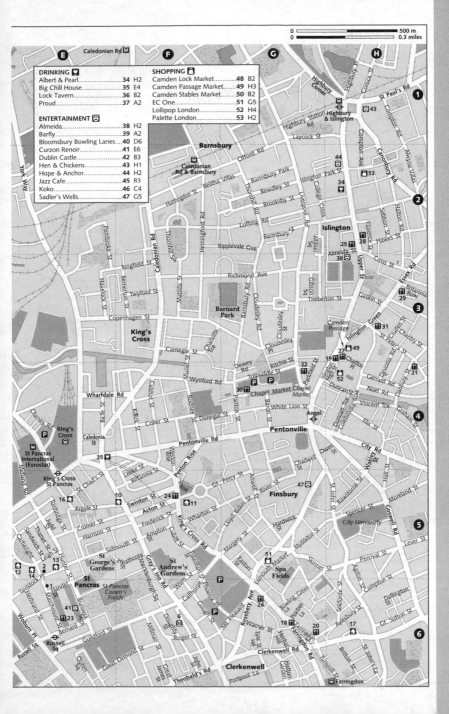

0   500 m
0   0.3 miles

HYDE PARK

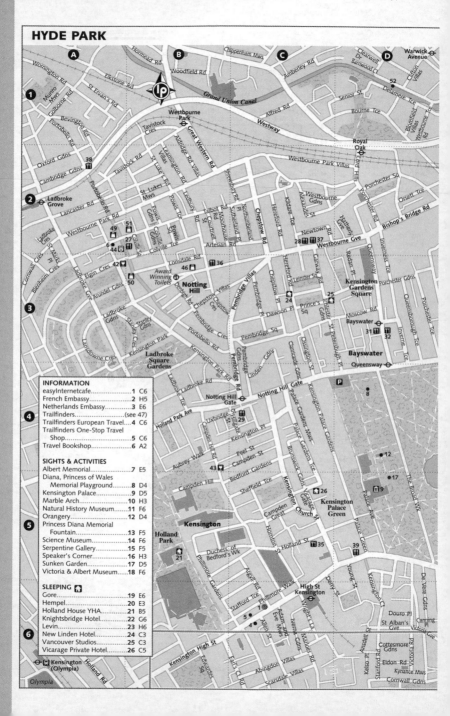

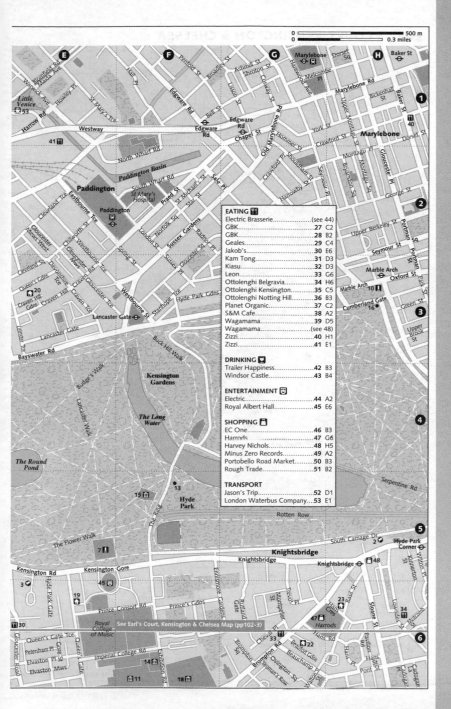

EATING 🍴

Electric Brasserie	(see 44)	
GBK	**27**	C2
GBK	**28**	B2
Geales	**29**	C4
Jakob's	**30**	E6
Kam Tong	**31**	D3
Kiasu	**32**	D3
Leon	**33**	G6
Ottolenghi Belgravia	**34**	H6
Ottolenghi Kensington	**35**	C5
Ottolenghi Notting Hill	**36**	B3
Planet Organic	**37**	C2
S&M Cafe	**38**	A2
Wagamama	**39**	D5
Wagamama	(see 48)	
Zizzi	**40**	H1
Zizzi	**41**	E1

DRINKING 🍷

Trailer Happiness	**42**	B3
Windsor Castle	**43**	B4

ENTERTAINMENT 🎭

Electric	**44**	A2
Royal Albert Hall	**45**	E6

SHOPPING 🛍️

EC One	**46**	B3
Harrods	**47**	G6
Harvey Nichols	**48**	H5
Minus Zero Records	**49**	A2
Portobello Road Market	**50**	B3
Rough Trade	**51**	B2

TRANSPORT

Jason's Trip	**52**	D1
London Waterbus Company	**53**	E1

See Earl's Court, Kensington & Chelsea Map (pp102–3)

EARL'S COURT, KENSINGTON & CHELSEA

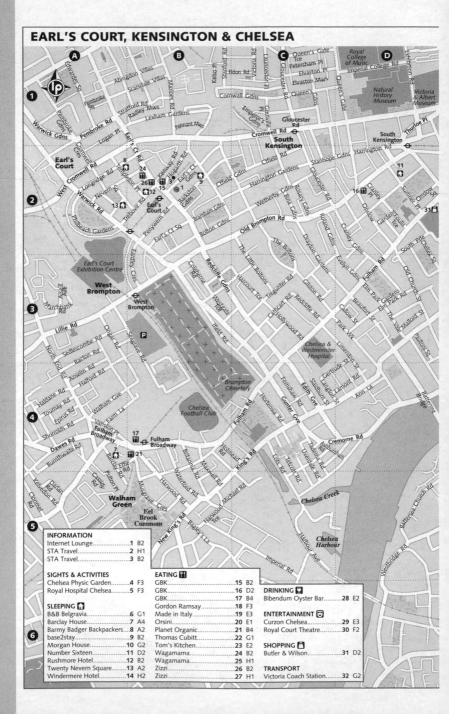

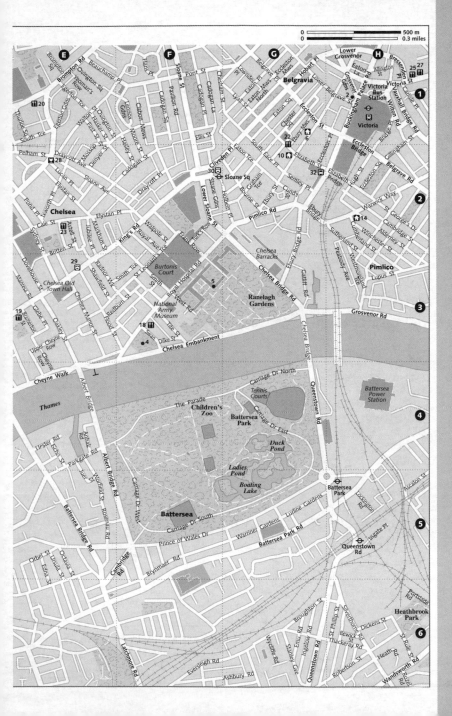

CENTRAL LONDON

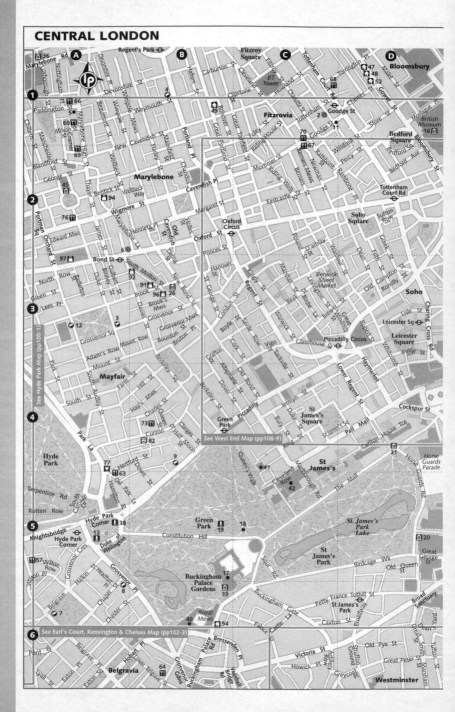

See Hyde Park Map (pp100-1)

See West End Map (pp108-9)

See Earl's Court, Kensington & Chelsea Map (pp102-3)

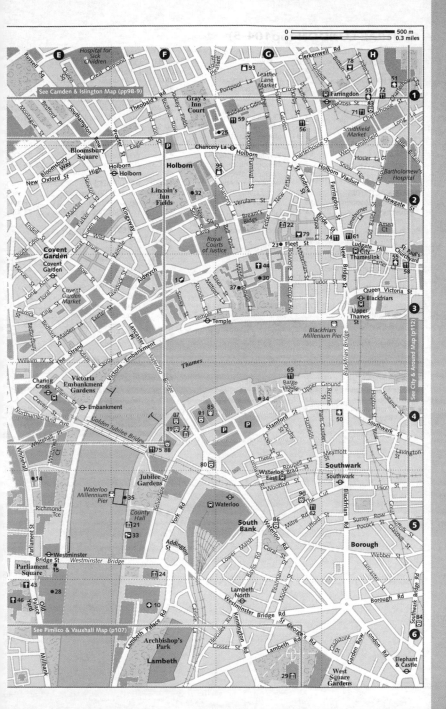

CENTRAL LONDON (pp104-5)

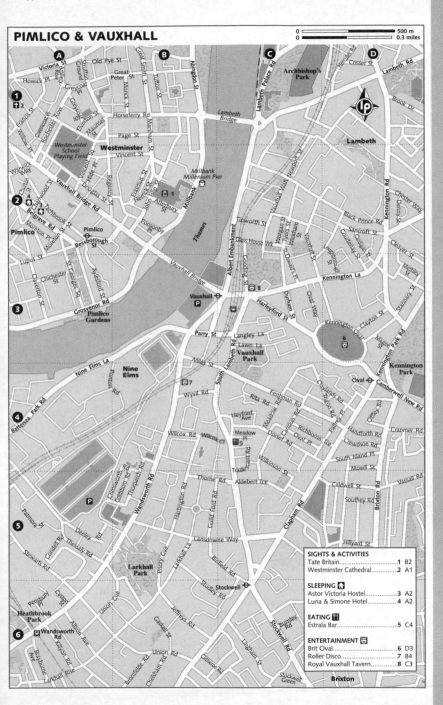

PIMLICO & VAUXHALL

0   500 m
0   0.3 miles

SIGHTS & ACTIVITIES
Tate Britain............................1 B2
Westminster Cathedral............2 A1

SLEEPING
Astor Victoria Hostel................3 A2
Luna & Simone Hotel................4 A2

EATING
Estrala Bar............................5 C4

ENTERTAINMENT
Brit Oval..............................6 D3
Roller Disco..........................7 B4
Royal Vauxhall Tavern.............8 C3

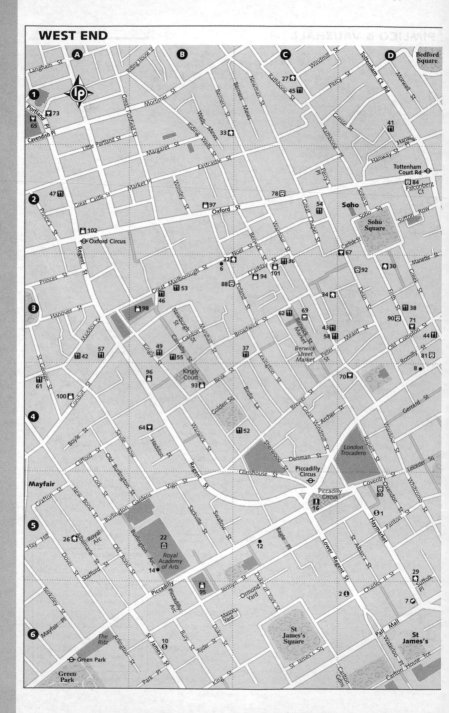

WEST END

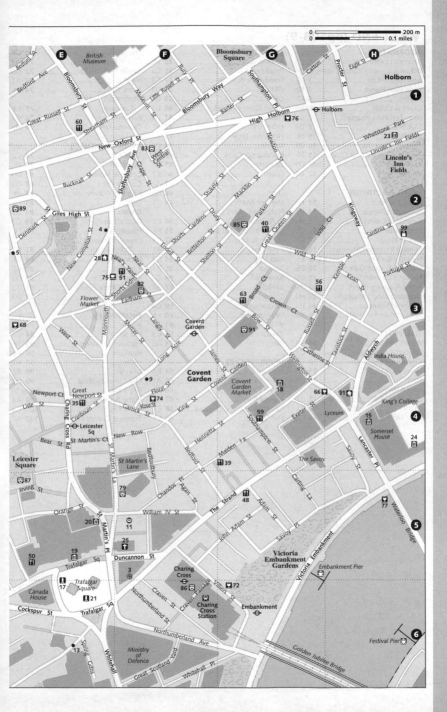

WEST END (pp108-9)

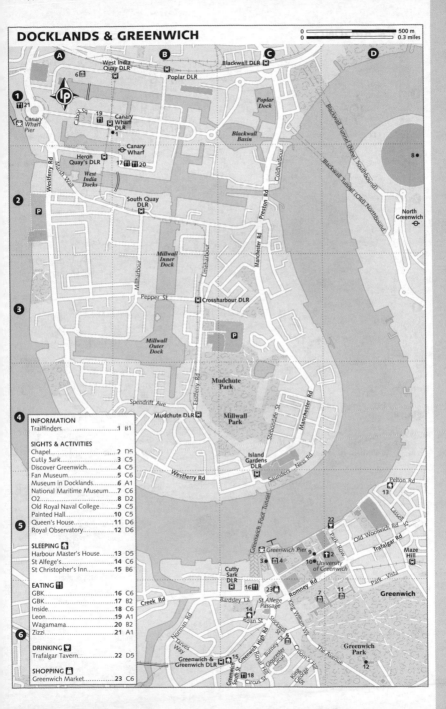

DOCKLANDS & GREENWICH

0 — 500 m
0 — 0.3 miles

CITY & AROUND

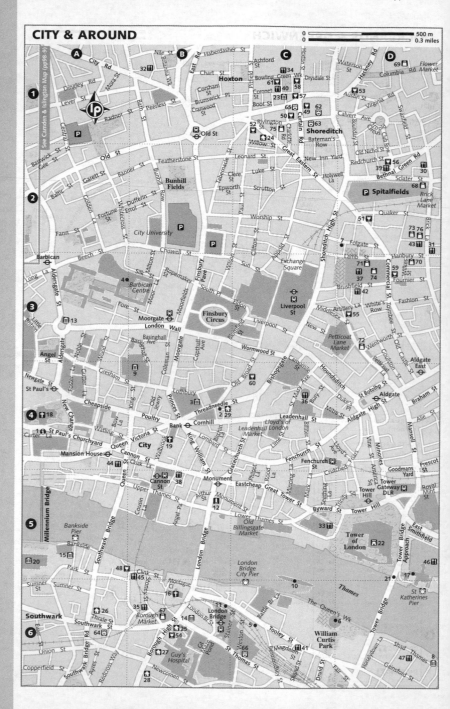

CITY & AROUND (p112)

(Continued from page 95)

DANGERS & ANNOYANCES

Considering its size and disparities in wealth, London is generally safe. That said, keep your wits about you and don't flash your cash unnecessarily. A contagion of youth-on-youth knife crime is cause for concern, so walk away if you sense trouble brewing and take care at night. When travelling by tube, choose a carriage with other people in it and avoid deserted suburban stations. Following reports of robberies and sexual attacks, shun unlicensed minicabs.

Nearly every Londoner has a story about a wallet/phone/bag being nicked from under their noses – or arses, in the case of bags on floors in bars. Watch out for pickpockets on crowded tubes, night buses and streets. That friendly drunk who bumped into you may now be wandering off with your wallet.

Scams

When using ATMs, guard your PIN details carefully. Don't use one that looks like it's been tampered with as there have been incidents of card cloning.

It should come as no surprise that some Soho strip clubs and hostess bars are dodgy, and people should be especially wary of those that tout for business on the street.

SIGHTS

With so much to see and do, it can be hard to know where to start. Weather will be a determining factor: the museums and galleries are great for a rainy day, but when the sun shines make like a Londoner and head to the parks – you never know whether this fine day will be your last. Otherwise, attack the sights by area using the ordering of this section as your guide.

Trafalgar Square

Trafalgar Sq is the public heart of London, hosting rallies, marches and feverish New Year's festivities. Londoners congregate here to celebrate anything from football victories to the ousting of political leaders. Formerly ringed by gnarling traffic, the square's been tidied up and is now one of the world's grandest public places. At the heart of it, Nelson surveys his fleet from the 43.5m-high **Nelson's Column** (Map pp108–9), erected in 1843 to commemorate Nelson's 1805 victory over Napoleon off Cape Trafalgar in Spain. At the edges of the square are four plinths, three of which have permanent statues, while

---

LONDON IN...

Two Days

Only two days? Start in **Trafalgar Square** (above) and see at least the outside of all the big-ticket sights – **London Eye** (p127), **Houses of Parliament** (p116), **Westminster Abbey** (opposite), **St James's Park and Palace** (p118), **Buckingham Palace** (p117), **Green Park** (p118), **Hyde Park** (p129), **Kensington Gardens & Palace** (p129) – and then motor around the **Tate Modern** (p125) until you get booted out. In the evening, explore **Soho** (p119). On day two race around the **British Museum** (p120) then head to the City. Start with our **walking tour** (p133) and finish in the **Tower of London** (p122). Head to the East End for an evening of **ethnic food** (p155) and **hip bars** (p160).

Four Days

Take the two-day itinerary but stretch it to a comfortable pace. Stop at the **National Gallery** (opposite) while you're in Trafalgar Sq, explore inside Westminster Abbey and **St Paul's Cathedral** (p122) and allow half a day for each of the Tate Modern, British Museum and Tower of London. On your extra evenings, check out **Camden** and **Islington** (p161) or splurge on a slap-up dinner in **Chelsea** (p156).

One Week

As above, but add in a day each for **Greenwich** (p131), **Kew Gardens** (p133) and **Hampton Court Palace** (p133).

LONDON FOR FREE

London may be an expensive city to eat, drink and sleep in, but when it comes to sights, most of the very best one are free. Apart from all the breathtaking parks and wonderful buildings, you won't pay a penny to visit any of the following: National Gallery, National Portrait Gallery, Tate Britain, Tate Modern, British Museum, Museum of London, Bank of England Museum, Imperial War Museum, Victoria & Albert Museum, Natural History Museum, Science Museum, Geffrye Museum, British Library, Guildhall, Wellcome Collection and the Wallace Collection.

the **fourth plinth** (Map pp108–9) is given over to temporary modern installations.

The square is flanked by splendid buildings: **Canada House** to the west, the National Gallery and National Portrait Gallery to the north, **South Africa House** and the church of **St Martin-in-the-Fields** (Map pp108–9) to the east. Further south stands **Admiralty Arch** (Map pp108–9), built in honour of Queen Victoria in 1910, beyond which The Mall (rhymes with 'shall', not 'shawl') is the ceremonial route leading to Buckingham Palace.

NATIONAL GALLERY

Gazing grandly over Trafalgar Sq through its Corinthian columns, the **National Gallery** (Map pp108–9; ☎ 7747 2885; www.nationalgallery.org .uk; Trafalgar Sq WC2; admission free; ☼ 10am-6pm Sat-Thu, to 9pm Fri; ⊖ Charing Cross) is the nation's most important repository of art. Four million visitors descend annually to admire its 2300-plus Western European paintings, spanning the years 1250 to 1900.

Highlights include Turner's *The Fighting Temeraire* (voted Britain's greatest painting), Botticelli's *Venus and Mars* and Van Gogh's *Sunflowers*. *Da Vinci Code* fans will make a beeline for Leonardo's *The Virgin of the Rocks*, the sister of the one hanging in the Louvre. The medieval religious paintings in the Sainsbury Wing are fascinating, but for a short, sharp blast of brilliance you can't beat the truckloads of Monets, Manets, Cézannes, Degas and Renoirs in rooms 43 to 46.

It's all a bit overwhelming for one visit, but as admission's free it's possible to dip into it again and again. Free one-hour guided tours leave at 11.30am and 2.30pm daily. If you prefer, you can devise and print off your own tour from the flashy computer screens of Art Start, the gallery's interactive multimedia system. Visit on Friday evenings for live music and free talks.

NATIONAL PORTRAIT GALLERY

The fascinating **National Portrait Gallery** (Map pp108–9; ☎ 7312 2463; www.npg.org.uk; St Martin's Pl WC2; admission free; ☼ 10am-6pm Sat-Wed, to 9pm Thu & Fri; ⊖ Charing Cross) is like stepping into a picture book of English history or, if you're trashy, an *OK* magazine spread on history's celebrities ('what's *she* wearing?').

Founded in 1856, the permanent collection (around 10,000 works) starts with the Tudors on the 2nd floor and descends to contemporary figures. Amongst the modern mob, look out for a full-length painting of Dame Judi Dench, a 3D depiction of JK Rowling and a photographic study of David Bowie, seated in a seedy toilet with a dead-looking Natasha Vojnovic across his lap.

An audio guide (£2) will lead you through the gallery's most famous pictures. Look out for the temporary exhibitions, especially the prestigious National Portrait Award (June to September). There's also an interesting view over the rooftops to Trafalgar Sq and Nelson's backside from the top-floor restaurant.

Westminster & Pimlico

Purposefully positioned outside the old City (London's fiercely independent burghers preferred to keep the monarch and Parliament at arm's length), Westminster has been the centre of the nation's political power for a millennium. The area's many landmarks combine to form an awesome display of power, gravitas and historical import. Neighbouring Pimlico can't compete but it does boast some decent B&Bs and the wonderful Tate Britain gallery.

WESTMINSTER ABBEY

If you're one of those boring sods who boast about spending months in Europe without ever setting foot in a church, get over yourself and make this the exception. Not merely a beautiful place of worship, **Westminster Abbey** (Map pp104–5; ☎ 7222 5152; www.westminster-abbey .org; 20 Dean's Yard SW1; adult/child £12/9, tours/audio guides £5/4; ☼ 9.15am-4.30pm Mon, Tue, Thu & Fri, to 6pm Wed, to 2.30pm Sat; ⊖ Westminster) serves the country's history cold on slabs of stone. For centuries the country's greatest have been interred here, including most of the monarchs from Henry III (died 1272) to George II (1760).

Unlike St Paul's, Westminster Abbey has never been a cathedral (the seat of a bishop). It's what is called a 'royal peculiar' and is administered directly by the Crown. Every monarch since William the Conqueror has been crowned here, with the exception of a couple of unlucky Eds who were murdered (Edward V) or abdicated (Edward VIII) before the magic moment. Look out for the strangely ordinary-looking **Coronation Chair**.

The building itself is an arresting sight. Though a mixture of architectural styles, it is considered the finest example of Early English Gothic in existence. The original church was built in the 11th century by King (later Saint) Edward the Confessor, who is buried in the chapel behind the main altar. Henry III began work on the new building in 1245 but didn't complete it; the French Gothic nave was finished in 1388. Henry VII's magnificent Late Perpendicular–style **Lady Chapel** was consecrated in 1519 after 16 years of construction.

Apart from the royal graves, keep an eye out for the many famous commoners interred here, especially in **Poet's Corner** where you'll find the resting places of Chaucer, Dickens, Hardy, Tennyson, Dr Johnson and Kipling as well as memorials to the other greats (Shakespeare, Jane Austen, Emily Bronte etc). Elsewhere you'll find the graves of Handel and Sir Isaac Newton.

The octagonal **Chapter House** (10.30am-4pm) dates from the 1250s and was where the monks would meet for daily prayer before Henry VIII's suppression of the monasteries. Used as a treasury and 'Royal Wardrobe', the cryptlike **Pyx Chamber** (10.30am-4pm) dates from about 1070. The neighbouring **Abbey Museum** (10.30am-4pm) has as its centrepiece death masks of generations of royalty.

Parts of the Abbey complex are free to visitors. This includes the **Cloister** (8am-6pm), which featured prominently in the *Da Vinci Code*, and the 900-year-old **College Garden** (10am-6pm Tue-Thu Apr-Sep, to 4pm Oct-Mar). Free concerts are held here from 12.30pm to 2pm on Wednesdays from mid-July through August. Adjacent to the abbey is **St Margaret's Church** (Map pp104-5; 9.30am-3.30pm Mon-Fri, to 1.30pm Sat, 2-5pm Sun), the House of Commons'

place of worship since 1614. There are windows commemorating churchgoers Caxton and Milton, and Sir Walter Raleigh is buried by the altar.

Of course, admission to the Abbey is free if you wish to attend a service. On weekdays, Matins is at 7.30am, Holy Communion at 8am and 12.30pm, and Choral Evensong at 5pm. There are services throughout the day on Sundays. You can sit and soak in the atmosphere, even if you're not religious.

HOUSES OF PARLIAMENT

Coming face to face with one of the world's most recognisable landmarks is always a surreal moment, but in the case of the **Houses of Parliament** (Map pp104-5; ☎ 0870 906 3773; www .parliament.uk; Parliament Sq SW1; ⊖ Westminster) it's a revelation. The BBC's standard title shot just doesn't do justice to the ornate stonework and golden filigree of Charles Barry and Augustus Pugin's neo-Gothic masterpiece (1840).

Officially called the Palace of Westminster, the oldest part is **Westminster Hall** (1097), which is one of only a few parts that survived a catastrophic fire in 1834. Its roof, added between 1394 and 1401, is the earliest known example of a hammer-beam roof and has been described as the greatest surviving achievement of medieval English carpentry.

The palace's most famous feature is its clock tower, aka **Big Ben** (Map pp104–5). Ben is actually the 13-ton bell, named after Benjamin Hall, who was commissioner of works when the tower was completed in 1858.

At the business end, Parliament is split into two houses. The green-hued **House of Commons** is the lower house where the 646 elected Members of Parliament sit. Traditionally the home of hereditary bluebloods, the scarlet-decorated **House of Lords** now has peers appointed through various means. Both houses debate and vote on legislation, which must then be approved by the Queen. At the annual State Opening of Parliament (usually in November), the Queen takes her throne in the House of Lords, having processed in the gold-trimmed Irish State Coach from Buckingham Palace. It's well worth lining the route for a gawk at the crown jewels sparkling in the sun.

When Parliament is in session, visitors are admitted to the **House of Commons Visitors' Gallery** (admission free; 2.30-10.30pm Mon & Tue, 11.30am-7.30pm Wed, 10.30am-6.30pm Thu, 9.30am-3pm some Fridays). Expect to queue for at least an hour and possibly longer during Question Time (at the beginning of each day). The **House of Lords Visitors' Gallery** (admission free; ☉ 2.30-10pm Mon & Tue, 3-10pm Wed, 11am-7.30pm Thu, from 10am some Fridays) is also open.

Parliamentary recesses (ie holidays) last for three months over the summer, and a couple of weeks over Easter and Christmas. When parliament is in recess there are guided **tours** (75min tours adult/child £12/5; telephone for times) of both chambers and other historic areas. UK residents can approach their MPs to arrange a free tour and to climb the clock tower.

WESTMINSTER CATHEDRAL
Begun in 1895, the neo-Byzantine **Westminster Cathedral** (Map p107; ☎ 7798 9055; www.westminster cathedral.org.uk; Victoria St SW1; admission free; ☉ 7am-7pm; ⊖ Victoria) is the headquarters of Britain's once suppressed Roman Catholic Church. It's still a work in progress, the vast interior part dazzling marble and mosaic and part bare brick; new sections are completed as funds allow. Look out for Eric Gill's highly regarded stone **Stations of the Cross** (1918).

The **Chapel of St George and the English Martyrs** displays the body of St John Southwark, a priest who was hanged, drawn and quartered in 1654 for refusing to reject the supremacy of the Pope.

The distinctive 83m red brick and white-stone **tower** (adult/child £5/2.50) offers splendid views of London and, unlike St Paul's dome, you can take the lift. Call ahead to book a Cathedral tour (£5).

TATE BRITAIN
Unlike the National Gallery, Britannia rules the walls of **Tate Britain** (Map p107; ☎ 7887 8008; www.tate.org.uk; Millbank SW1; admission free; ☉ 10am-5.50pm; ⊖ Pimlico). Reaching from 1500 to the present, it's crammed with local heavyweights like Blake, Hogarth, Gainsborough, Whistler, Spencer and, especially, Turner, whose work dominates the **Clore Gallery**. His 'interrupted visions' – unfinished canvasses of moody skies – wouldn't look out of place in the contemporary section, alongside the work of David Hockney, Francis Bacon, Tracey Emin and Damien Hirst. The always-controversial annual Turner Prize is exhibited in the gallery from October to January.

There are free hour-long guided tours, taking in different sections of the gallery, held daily at midday and 3pm, as well as additional tours at 11am and 2pm on weekdays. The popular **Rex Whistler Restaurant** (☎ 7887 8825; mains £16), featuring an impressive mural from the artist, is open for breakfast, lunch and snacks.

BANQUETING HOUSE
The beautiful, classical design of the **Banqueting House** (Map pp104-5; ☎ 3166 6154; www.hrp.org.uk /BanquetingHouse; cnr Horse Guards Ave & Whitehall SW1; adult/child £4.50/2.25; ☉ 10am-5pm Mon-Sat; ⊖ Westminster) was conceived by Inigo Jones for James I in 1622. It's the only surviving part of Whitehall Palace after the Tudor bit burnt down in 1698. The key attraction is the ceiling, painted by Rubens in 1635 at the behest of Charles I. Sadly he didn't get to enjoy it for long as in 1649 he was frogmarched out of the 1st-floor balcony to lose his head for treason. A bust outside commemorates the king. An audio guide is included in the price.

CHURCHILL MUSEUM & CABINET WAR ROOMS
The **Cabinet War Rooms** (Map pp104-5; ☎ 7930 6961; www.iwm.org.uk; Clive Steps, King Charles St SW1; adult/child £12/free; ☉ 9.30am-6pm, last entry 5pm; ⊖ Westminster) were Prime Minister Winston Churchill's underground military HQ during WWII. Now a wonderfully evocative and atmospheric museum, the restored and preserved rooms (including Churchill's bedroom) capture the drama of the time. The **Churchill Museum** offers an intriguing exposé of the public and private faces of the man.

St James's & Mayfair
Put on your best rah-rah voice to wander this aristocratic enclave of palaces, famous hotels, exclusive gentlemen's clubs, historic shops and elegant buildings; indeed, there are some 150 historically noteworthy buildings within St James's 36 hectares alone.

BUCKINGHAM PALACE
With so many imposing buildings in the capital, the Queen's well-proportioned but relatively plain city pad is an anticlimax for some. Built in 1803 for the Duke of Buckingham, **Buckingham Palace** (Map pp104-5; ☎ 7766 7302; www.royalcollection.org.uk; The Mall SW1; adult/child £16/8.75; ☉ 9.45am-6pm late Jul-late Sep; ⊖ St James's Park) replaced St James's Palace as the monarch's London home in 1837. When

she's not off giving her one-handed wave in far-flung parts of the Commonwealth, Queen Elizabeth II divides her time between here, Windsor and Balmoral. If you've got the urge to drop in for a cup of tea, a handy way of telling whether she's home is to check whether the yellow, red and blue royal standard is flying.

Nineteen lavishly furnished staterooms are open to visitors when HRH (Her Royal Highness) takes her holidays. The tour includes **Queen Victoria's Picture Gallery** (76.5m long, with works by Rembrandt, Van Dyck, Canaletto, Poussin and Vermeer) and the **Throne Room**, with his-and-hers pink chairs initialled 'ER' and 'P'.

Changing of the Guard

If you're a fan of bright uniforms, bearskin hats, straight lines, marching and shouting, join the throngs outside the palace at 11.30am (daily from May to July and on alternate days for the rest of the year, weather permitting), when the regiment of guards outside the palace changes over in one of the world's most famous displays of pageantry. It does have a certain freak-show value, but gets dull very quickly. If you're here in November, the procession leaving the palace for the State Opening of Parliament is much more impressive (p116).

Queen's Gallery

Originally designed by John Nash as a conservatory, it was smashed up by the Luftwaffe in 1940 before being converted to a **gallery** (Map pp104–5; ☎ 7766 7301; Buckingham Palace Rd SW1; adult/child £8.50/4.25; ⊗ 10am-5.30pm; ⊖ Victoria) in 1962, housing works from the extensive Royal Collection.

Royal Mews

Indulge your Cinderella fantasies while inspecting the exquisite state coaches and immaculately groomed royal horses housed in the **Royal Mews** (Map pp104–5; ☎ 7766 7302; Buckingham Palace Rd SW1; adult/child £7.50/4.80; ⊗ 10am-5pm Aug & Sep, 11am-4pm mid-Mar–Jul & Oct; ⊖ Victoria). Highlights include the stunning gold coach (1762), which has been used for every coronation since George IV, and the 1910 royal weddings' Glass Coach. We're pretty sure these aren't about to change back into pumpkins anytime soon.

ST JAMES'S PARK & ST JAMES'S PALACE

With its manicured flower beds and ornamental lake, **St James's Park** is a wonderful place to stroll and take in the views of Westminster, Buckingham Palace and St James's Palace.

The striking Tudor gatehouse of **St James's Palace** (Map pp104–5; Cleveland Row SW1; ⊖ Green Park), initiated by the palace-mad Henry VIII in 1530, is best approached from St James's St to the north of the park. This was the residence of Prince Charles and his sons before they shifted next door to **Clarence House** (1828), following the death of its previous occupant, the Queen Mother, in 2002. It's a great place to pose for a photograph beside one of the resolutely unsmiling royal guards.

GREEN PARK

Green Park's 47-acre expanse of meadows and mature trees links St James's Park to Hyde Park and Kensington Gardens, creating a green corridor from Westminster all the way to Kensington. It was once a duelling ground and served as a vegetable garden during WWII. Although it doesn't have lakes, fountains or formal gardens, it's blanketed with daffodils in spring and seminaked bodies whenever the sun shines.

The only concession to formality is the **Canada Memorial** (Map pp104–5) near **Canada Gate** (Map pp104–5), which links the park to Buckingham Palace. At its western end is **Hyde Park Corner**, where you'll find the **Australian** and **New Zealand War Memorials** (Map pp104–5).

INSTITUTE OF CONTEMPORARY ARTS

A one-stop contemporary-art bonanza, the exciting program at the **ICA** (Map pp104–5; ☎ 7930 3647; www.ica.org.uk; The Mall SW1; admission Mon-Fri £2, Sat & Sun £3; ⊗ noon-11pm Mon, to 1am Tue-Sat, to 10.30pm Sun; ⊖ Charing Cross), as it's commonly known, includes film, photography, theatre, installations, talks, performance art, DJs, digital art and book readings. Stroll around the galleries, watch a film, browse the bookshop, then head to the bar for a beer.

SPENCER HOUSE

The ancestral home of Princess Diana's family, **Spencer House** (Map pp104–5; ☎ 7499 8620; www.spencerhouse.co.uk; 27 St James's Pl SW1; adult/child £9/7; ⊗ 10.30am-5.45pm Sun Feb-Jul & Sep-Dec; ⊖ Green Park) was built in the Palladian style between 1756 and 1766. It was converted into offices after the Spencers moved out in 1927, but 60 years later an £18 million restoration returned it to its former glory. Visits are by guided tour (last tour 4.45pm). Check the website for the few summer dates when the gardens (£3.50) are opened.

HANDEL HOUSE MUSEUM

George Frideric Handel's pad from 1723 to his death in 1759 is now a moderately interesting **museum** (Map pp104-5; ☎ 7399 1953; www.handelhouse .org; 25 Brook St W1K; adult/child £5/2; ⊙ 10am-6pm Tue, Wed, Fri & Sat, to 8pm Thu, noon-6pm Sun; ⊖ Bond St) dedicated to his life. He wrote some of his greatest works here, including the *Messiah*, and music still fills the house during live recitals (see the website for details).

From songs of praise to *Purple Haze*, Jimi Hendrix lived next door at number 23 many years (and genres) later.

West End

Synonymous with big-budget musicals and frenzied flocks of shoppers, the West End is a strident mix of culture and consumerism. More a concept than a fixed geographical area, it nonetheless takes in Piccadilly Circus and Trafalgar Sq to the south, Regent St to the west, Oxford St to the north and Covent Garden and the Strand to the east.

Elegant **Regent St** and frantic **Oxford St** are the city's main shopping strips. They're beautifully lit at Christmas to coax the masses away from the home fires and into the frying pan sections of the many department stores (see p166).

At the heart of the West End lies **Soho**, a grid of narrow streets and squares hiding gay bars, strip clubs, cafes and advertising agencies. **Carnaby St** was the epicentre of the Swinging London of the 1960s, but is now largely given over to chain fashion stores, although some interesting independent boutiques still lurk in the surrounding streets.

Lisle and Gerrard Sts form the heart of **Chinatown**, which is full of reasonably priced Asian restaurants and unfairly hip youngsters. Its neighbour, pedestrianised **Leicester Sq** (*les*-ter) heaves with tourists – and buskers, inevitably. Dominated by large cinemas, it sometimes hosts star-studded premieres.

PICCADILLY

Named after the elaborate collars (picadils) that were the sartorial staple of a 17th-century tailor who lived nearby, Piccadilly became

---

LONDON CALLING

Download these to your MP3 player before tackling the tube.

- David Bowie – *London Boys*
- The Clash – *Guns of Brixton; London Calling; London's Burning*
- Elvis Costello – *Chelsea*
- Hard-Fi – *Tied Up Too Tight*
- The Jam – *Down In The Tube Station At Midnight*
- The Kinks – *Waterloo Sunset*
- Morrissey – *Piccadilly Palare*
- Pet Shop Boys – *London; West End Girls*
- The Smiths – *London*

---

the fashionable haunt of the well-heeled (and collared), and still boasts establishment icons such as the Ritz hotel and Fortnum & Mason department store (p166). It meets Regent St, Shaftesbury Ave and Haymarket at neon-lit, turbo-charged **Piccadilly Circus**, home to the popular but unremarkable **Eros statue** (Map pp108-9; ⊖ Piccadilly Circus). Ironically the love god looks over an area that's long been linked to prostitution, both male and female, although it's less conspicuous these days.

Royal Academy of Arts

Set back from Piccadilly, the grandiose **Royal Academy of Arts** (Map pp108-9; ☎ /300 8000; www.royal academy.org.uk; Burlington House, Piccadilly W1; admission varies; ⊙ 10am-6pm Sat-Thu, to 10pm Fri; ⊖ Green Park) hosts high-profile exhibitions and a small display from its permanent collection. The crafty Academy has made it a condition of joining its exclusive club of 80 artists that new members donate one of their artworks. Past luminaries have included Constable, Gainsborough and Turner, while Sir Norman Foster, David Hockney and Tracey Emin are among the current crop.

Burlington Arcade

The well-to-do **Burlington Arcade** (Map pp108-9; 51 Piccadilly W1; ⊖ Green Park), built in 1819, is most famous for the Burlington Berties, uniformed guards who patrol the area keeping an eye out for offences such as running, chewing gum or whatever else might lower the arcade's tone.

COVENT GARDEN

A hallowed name for opera fans due to the presence of the esteemed Royal Opera House (p164), Covent Garden is one of London's biggest tourist traps, where chain restaurants, souvenir shops, balconied bars and street entertainers vie for the punters' pound.

In the 7th century the Saxons built Lundenwic here, a satellite town to the City of London. It reverted back into fields until the 1630s, when the Duke of Bedford commissioned Inigo Jones to build London's first planned square. Covent Garden's famous fruit, vegetable and flower market, immortalised in the film *My Fair Lady,* eventually took over the whole piazza, before being shifted in 1974.

In the 18th and 19th centuries, the area immediately north of Covent Garden was the site of one of London's most notorious slums, the 'rookery' of St Giles. Much of it was knocked down in the 1840s to create New Oxford St, but the narrow lanes and yards around Monmouth St still carry an echo of the crammed conditions of the past.

London Transport Museum

Newly refurbished and reopened, this **museum** (Map pp108-9; ☎ 7379 6344; www.ltmuseum.co.uk; Covent Garden Piazza WC2; adult/child £10/free; ☺ 10am-6pm Sat-Thu, 11am-9pm Fri; ⊖ Covent Garden) houses vintage vehicles ranging from sedan chairs to train carriages, along with fascinating posters and photos. You can get your tube map boxer shorts at the museum shop.

THE STRAND

Described by Benjamin Disraeli in the 19th century as Europe's finest street, this 'beach' of the Thames – built to connect Westminster (the seat of political power) and the City (the commercial centre) – still boasts a few classy hotels but has lost much of its lustre. Look for the two Chinese merchants above the door at number 216; Twinings have been selling tea here continuously since 1787, making it London's oldest store.

Somerset House

The first **Somerset House** (Map pp108-9; ☎ 7845 4600; www.somerset-house.org.uk; Strand WC2; ☺ 7.30am-11pm; ⊖ Temple) was built for the Duke of Somerset, brother of Jane Seymour, in 1551. For two centuries it played host to royals (Elizabeth I once lived here), foreign diplomats, wild masked balls, peace treaties, the Parliamentary army

during the Civil War and Oliver Cromwell's wake. Having fallen into disrepair, it was pulled down in 1775 and rebuilt in 1801 to designs by William Chambers. Among other weighty organisations, it went on to house the Royal Academy of the Arts, the Society of Antiquaries, the Navy Board and, that most popular of institutions, the Inland Revenue.

The tax collectors are still here, but that doesn't dissuade Londoners from attending open-air events in the grand central courtyard, such as live performances in summer and ice-skating in winter. The riverside terrace is a popular spot to get caffeinated with views of the Thames.

Near the Strand entrance, the **Courtauld Gallery** (Map pp108-9; ☎ 7848 2733; adult/child £5/free, admission free 10am-2pm Mon; ☺ to 6pm) displays a wealth of 14th- to 20th-century works, including a room of Rubens and works by Van Gogh, Renoir and Cézanne. Downstairs, the **Embankment Galleries** are devoted to temporary exhibitions; prices and hours vary.

Bloomsbury & Fitzrovia

With the University of London and British Museum within its genteel environs, it's little wonder that Bloomsbury has attracted a lot of very clever, bookish people over the years. Between the world wars, these pleasant streets were colonised by a group of artists and intellectuals known collectively as the **Bloomsbury Group**, which included novelists Virginia Woolf and EM Forster and the economist John Maynard Keynes. **Russell Square**, its very heart, was laid out in 1800 and is one of London's largest and loveliest.

Neighbouring Fitzrovia is only marginally less exalted, although media types outnumber intellectuals in the ever-expanding strip of restaurants and bars around Charlotte and Goodge Sts.

BRITISH MUSEUM

The country's largest museum and one of the oldest and finest in the world, this famous **museum** (Map pp104-5; ☎ 7323 8000; www.thebritishmuseum .org; Great Russell St WC1; admission free; ☺ 10am-5.30pm Sat-Wed, to 8.30pm Thu & Fri; ⊖ Tottenham Court Rd or Russell Sq) boasts vast Egyptian, Etruscan, Greek, Oriental and Roman galleries among many others.

Before you get to the galleries, you'll be blown away by the **Great Court**, which was restored and augmented by Norman Foster in 2000. The courtyard now boasts a spectacular

---

BRITAIN & GREECE SQUABBLE OVER MARBLES

Wonderful though it is, the British Museum can sometimes feel like one vast repository for stolen booty. Much of what's on display wasn't just 'picked up' along the way by Victorian travellers and explorers, but taken or purchased under dubious circumstances.

Restive foreign governments occasionally pop their heads over the parapet to demand the return of their property. The British Museum says 'no' and the problem goes away until the next time. Not the Greeks, however. They've been demanding the return of the so-called Elgin Marbles, the ancient marble sculptures that once adorned the Parthenon. The British Museum, and successive British governments, steadfastly refuse to hand over the priceless works that were removed and shipped to England by the British ambassador to the Ottoman Empire, the Lord Elgin, between 1801 and 1805. (When Elgin blew all his dough, he sold the marbles to the government.) The diplomatic spat continues. Only time will tell who blinks first.

---

glass-and-steel roof, making it one of the most impressive architectural spaces in the capital. In the centre is the **Reading Room**, with its stunning blue-and-gold domed ceiling, where Karl Marx wrote the *Manifesto of the Communist Party*. Off to the right is the **Enlightenment Gallery**, the oldest and grandest gallery in the museum, the first section of the redesigned museum to be built (in 1823).

The enthralling exhibits began in 1753 with a 'cabinet of curiosities' bequeathed by Sir Hans Sloane to the nation on his death; this has mushroomed over the years partly through the plundering of the empire.

Among the must-sees are the **Rosetta Stone**, discovered in 1799 and the key to deciphering Egyptian hieroglyphics; the controversial **Parthenon Sculptures**, which once adorned the walls of the Parthenon in Athens (see boxed text, above); the stunning **Oxus Treasure** of 7th to 4th-century BC Persian gold; and the Anglo-Saxon **Sutton Hoo** burial relics.

You'll need multiple visits to savour even the highlights here; happily there are 14 half-hour free 'eye opener' tours between 11am and 3.45pm daily, focussing on different parts of the collection. Other tours include the 90-minute highlights tour at 10.30am, 1pm and 3pm daily (adult/child £8/5), and there is a range of audio guides (£3.50). Given the museum's mind-boggling size and scope, an initial tour is highly recommended.

Holborn & Clerkenwell

In these now fashionable streets, it's hard to find an echo of the notorious 'rookeries' of the 19th century, where families were squeezed into damp, fetid basements, living in possibly the worst conditions in the city's history. This is the London documented so vividly by Dickens. It was also the traditional place for a last drink on the way to the gallows at Tyburn Hill – fitting, as many of the condemned hailed from here, as did many of those who were transported to Australia.

SIR JOHN SOANE'S MUSEUM

Not all of this area's inhabitants were poor, as is aptly demonstrated by the remarkable home of celebrated architect and collector extraordinaire Sir John Soane (1753–1837). Now a fascinating **museum** (Map pp108-9; ☎ 7405 2107; www.soane.org; 13 Lincoln's Inn Fields WC2; admission free, tours 11am Sat £5; ❤ 10am-5pm Tue-Sat, 6-9pm 1st Tue of month; ❸ Holborn), the house has been left largely as it was when Sir John was taken out in a box. Among his eclectic acquisitions are an Egyptian sarcophagus, dozens of Greek and Roman antiquities and the original *Rake's Progress*, William Hogarth's set of caricatures telling the story of a late 18th-century London cad. Soane was clearly a very clever chap – check out the ingenious folding walls in the picture gallery.

DICKENS HOUSE MUSEUM

Mr Dickens' sole surviving **London residence** (Map pp98-9; ☎ 7405 2127; www.dickensmuseum.com; 48 Doughty St WC1; adult/under 16yr/concession £5/3/4; ❤ 10am-5pm Mon-Sat, 11am-5pm Sun; ❸ Russell Sq) is where his work really flourished – *The Pickwick Papers*, *Nicholas Nickleby* and *Oliver Twist* were all written here. The handsome four-storey house opened as a museum in 1925, and visitors can stroll through rooms choc-a-bloc with fascinating memorabilia.

The City

For most of its history, the City of London *was* London. Its boundaries have changed little since the Romans first founded their gated community here two millennia ago. You can always tell when you're within it, as the Corporation of London's coat of arms appears on the street signs.

It's only in the last 250 years that the City has gone from being the very essence of London and it's main population centre to just its central business district. But what a business district it is – you could easily argue that the 'square mile' is the very heart of world capitalism.

Currently fewer than 10,000 people actually live here, although some 300,000 descend on it each weekday where they generate almost three-quarters of Britain's entire GDP before squeezing back onto the tube. On Sundays it becomes a virtual ghost town; it's a good time to poke around, even if you won't be able to smell the fear of the planet's leading bankers coping with the financial crisis.

Apart from the big-ticket sights, visitors tend to avoid the City, which is a shame as it's got enough interesting churches, intriguing architecture, hidden gardens and atmospheric lanes to spend weeks exploring.

ST PAUL'S CATHEDRAL

Dominating the City with a dome second in size only to St Peter's in Rome, **St Paul's Cathedral** (Map p112; ☎ 7236 4128; www.stpauls.co.uk; adult/child £10/3.50; ☆ 8.30am-4pm Mon-Sat; ⊖ St Paul's) was designed by Wren after the Great Fire and built between 1675 and 1710. Four other cathedrals preceded it on this site, the first dating from 604.

The dome is renowned for somehow dodging the bombs during the Blitz, and became an icon of the resilience shown in the capital during WWII. Outside the cathedral, to the north, is a **monument to the people of London**, a simple and elegant memorial to the 32,000 Londoners who weren't so lucky.

Inside, some 30m above the main paved area, is the first of three domes (actually a dome inside a cone inside a dome) supported by eight huge columns. The walkway round its base is called the **Whispering Gallery**, because if you talk close to the wall, your words will carry to the opposite side 32m away. It can be reached by a staircase on the western side of the southern transept (9.30am to 3.30pm only). It is 530 lung-busting steps to the **Golden Gallery** at the very top, and an unforgettable view of London.

The **Crypt** has memorials to up to 300 military demigods including Wellington, Kitchener and Nelson, whose body lies below the dome. But the most poignant memorial is to Wren himself. On a simple slab bearing his name, a Latin inscription translates as: 'If you seek his memorial, look about you'.

Audio tours lasting 45 minutes are available for £4. Guided tours (adult/child £3/1) leave the tour desk at 11am, 11.30am, 1.30pm and 2pm (90 minutes). Evensong takes place at 5pm most weekdays and at 3.15pm on Sunday.

TOWER OF LONDON

If you pay only one admission fee while you're in London, make it the **Tower of London** (Map p112; ☎ 0844-482 7777; www.hrp.org .uk; Tower Hill EC3; adult/child £17/9.50; ☆ 10am-5.30pm Sun & Mon, 9am-5.30pm Tue-Sat Mar-Oct, 10am-4.30pm Sun & Mon, 9am-4.30pm Tue-Sat Nov-Feb; ⊖ Tower Hill). One of the city's three World Heritage Sites (joining Westminster Abbey and Maritime Greenwich), it's a window onto a gruesome and fascinating history.

In the 1070s, William the Conqueror started work on the White Tower to replace the castle he'd previously had built here. By 1285, two walls with towers and a moat were built around it and the defences have barely been altered since. A former royal residence, treasury, mint and arsenal, it became most famous as a prison when Henry VIII moved to Whitehall Palace in 1529 and started dishing out his preferred brand of punishment.

The most striking building is the huge **White Tower**, with its solid Romanesque architecture and four turrets, which today houses a collection from the Royal Armouries. On the 2nd floor is the **Chapel of St John the Evangelist**, dating from 1080 and therefore the oldest church in London.

On the small green in front of the church stood Henry VIII's **scaffold**, where seven people, including Anne Boleyn and her cousin Catherine Howard (Henry's second and fifth wives) were beheaded.

To the north is the **Waterloo Barracks**, which now contains the spectacular **Crown Jewels**. On the far side of the White Tower is the **Bloody Tower**, where the 12-year-old Edward V and his little brother were held 'for their own safety' and later murdered, probably by their uncle, the future Richard III. Sir Walter Raleigh did a 13-year stretch here, when he wrote his *History of the World*, a copy of which is on display.

On the patch of green between the Wakefield and White Towers you'll find the latest in the tower's long line of famous ravens, which legend says could cause the White Tower to collapse should they leave. Their wings are clipped in case they get any ideas.

To help get your bearings, take the hugely entertaining free guided tour with any of the Tudor-garbed Beefeaters. Hour-long tours leave every 30 minutes from the Middle Tower; the last tour's an hour before closing.

TOWER BRIDGE

London was still a thriving port in 1894 when elegant Tower Bridge was built. Designed to be raised to allow ships to pass, electricity has now taken over from the original steam engines. A lift leads up from the modern visitors' facility in the northern tower to the **Tower Bridge Exhibition** (Map p112; ☎ 7403 3761; www.towerbridge.org .uk; adult/child £6/3; ⏰ 10am-6.30pm Apr-Sep, 9.30am-6pm Oct-Mar; ⊖ Tower Hill), where the story of its building is recounted with videos and animatronics. If you're coming from the Tower, you'll pass by Dead Man's Hole, where corpses that had made their way into the Thames (through suicide, murder or accident) were regularly retrieved.

MUSEUM OF LONDON

Visiting the fascinating **Museum of London** (Map p112; ☎ 0870 444 3851; www.museumoflondon.org.uk; 150 London Wall EC2; admission free; ⏰ 10am-5.50pm Mon-Sat, noon-5.50pm Sun; ⊖ Barbican) early in your stay helps to make sense of the layers of history that make up this place. The Roman section, in particular, illustrates how the modern is grafted on to the ancient; several of the city's main thoroughfares were once Roman roads, for instance.

At the time of writing, the section encompassing 1666 (the Great Fire) to the present day was being redesigned. It should reopen in late 2009, featuring the Lord Mayor's ceremonial coach as its centrepiece.

GUILDHALL

Plum in the middle of the 'square mile', the **Guildhall** (Map p112; ☎ 7606 3030; www.cityoflondon.gov .uk; Gresham St EC2; admission free; ⏰ 10am-5pm Mon-Sun May-Sep, reduced hrs Oct-Apr; ⊖ Bank) has been the seat of the City's local government for eight centuries. The present building dates from the early 15th century.

Visitors can see the **Great Hall** where the city's mayor is sworn in and where important fellows like the Tsar of Russia and the Prince Regent celebrated beating Napoleon. It's an impressive space decorated with the shields and banners of London's 12 principal livery companies, carved galleries (the west of which is protected by disturbing statues of giants Gog and Magog) and a beautiful oak-panelled roof. There's also a lovely bronze statue of Churchill sitting in a comfy chair.

Beneath it is London's largest **medieval crypt** (☎ 7606 3030, ext 1463; visit by free guided tour only, bookings essential) with 19 stained-glass windows showing the livery companies' coats of arms.

The **Clockmakers' Museum** (admission free; ⏰ 9.30am-4.45pm Mon-Fri) charts 500 years of timekeeping with more than 700 ticking exhibits, and the **Guildhall Art Gallery** (☎ 7332 3700; adult/child £2.50/1; ⏰ 10am-5pm Mon-Sat, noon-4pm Sun) displays around 250 artworks. Included in admission is entry to the remains of an ancient **Roman amphitheatre**, which lay forgotten beneath this site until 1988.

ST STEPHEN'S WALBROOK

In the 3rd century, a Roman temple stood here, and in the 7th century a Saxon church. Rebuilt after the Great Fire, the current **St Stephen's** (Map p112; ☎ 7626 9000; www.ststephen walbrook.net; 29 Walbrook EC2; ⊖ Bank) is one of Wren's greatest masterpieces, with elegant Corinthian columns supporting a beautifully proportioned dome. Henry Moore sculpted the round central altar from travertine marble in 1972.

INNS OF COURT

All London barristers work from within one of the four atmospheric Inns of Court, positioned between the walls of the old City and Westminster. It would take a lifetime working here to grasp all the intricacies of their arcane protocols – they're similar to the Freemasons, and both are 13th-century creations. It's best just to soak up the dreamy ambience of the alleys and open spaces and thank your lucky stars you're not one of the bewigged barristers scurrying about. A roll call of former members would include the likes of Oliver Cromwell, Charles Dickens, Mahatma Gandhi and Margaret Thatcher.

Lincoln's Inn (Map pp104-5; ☎ 7405 1393; www .lincolnsinn.org.uk; Lincoln's Inn Fields WC2; ⏰ grounds 9am-

6pm Mon-Fri, chapel 12.30-2.30pm Mon-Fri; ⊖ Holborn) is largely intact and has several original 15th-century buildings. It's the oldest and most attractive of the bunch, boasting a 17th-century chapel and pretty landscaped gardens.

Gray's Inn (Map pp104-5; ☎ 7458 7800; www.grays inn.org.uk; Gray's Inn Rd WC1; ☽ grounds 10am-4pm Mon-Fri, chapel to 6pm Mon-Fri; ⊖ Chancery Lane) was largely rebuilt after the Luftwaffe levelled it.

Middle Temple (Map pp104-5; ☎ 7427 4800; www .middletemple.org.uk; Middle Temple Lane EC4; ☽ 10-11.30am & 3-4pm Mon-Fri; ⊖ Temple) and **Inner Temple** (Map pp104-5; ☎ 7797 8247; King's Bench Walk EC4; ☽ 10am-4pm Mon-Fri; ⊖ Temple) both sit between Fleet St and Victoria Embankment – the former is the best preserved while the latter is home to the intriguing **Temple Church** (Map pp104-5; ☎ 7353 8559; www.templechurch.com; ☽ varies, check website or call ahead), another landmark to score a major mention in *The Da Vinci Code.*

BARBICAN

Like Marmite, you either love or hate the concrete **Barbican** (Map p112; ☎ 7638 4141; www .barbican.org.uk; Silk St EC2; ⊖ Barbican). It's true that parts of it are extraordinarily ugly, particularly the forbidding high-rise tower blocks (romantically named Shakespeare, Cromwell and Lauderdale). But at the time of its construction, this vast complex of offices and residences with an arts centre at its heart was revolutionary.

It was designed by Chamberlain, Powell and Bon, disciples of Le Corbusier, to fill a WWII bomb-pummelled space with democratic modern housing. Sadly this dream never really materialised, and today around 80% of the flats are privately owned. It's been fashionable to loath the Barbican in the past, but in 2001 the complex became listed, and more people are finding beauty in its curved roofs, brightly planted window boxes and large central 'lake'.

At its heart is the Barbican Centre (p164). It also houses the **Barbican Art Gallery** (☎ 7638 4141; Level 3; adult/child £8/6; ☽ 11am-8pm Thu-Mon, 11am-6pm Tue & Wed), home to temporary exhibitions of contemporary art, and the smaller **Curve Gallery** (☎ 7638 4141; Level 0; admission free; ☽ 11am-8pm).

BANK OF ENGLAND MUSEUM

Guardian of the country's financial system, the Bank of England was established in 1694 when the government needed to raise cash to support a war with France. It was moved here in 1734 and largely renovated by Sir John Soane. Its **museum** (Map p112; ☎ 7601 5545; www .bankofengland.co.uk; Bartholomew Lane EC2; admission free; ☽ 10am-5pm Mon-Fri; ⊖ Bank) traces the history of the bank and banking system, and is surprisingly interesting.

THE MONUMENT

Designed by Wren to commemorate the Great Fire, the **Monument** (Map p112; ☎ 7626 2717; www.themonument.info; Monument St; ⊖ Monument) is 60.6m high, the exact distance from its base to the bakery on Pudding Lane where the blaze began. Climb the 311 tight spiral steps (not advised for claustrophobics) for an eye-watering view from beneath the symbolic vase of flames. It was closed for repairs at the time of writing but scheduled to reopen in early 2009; check the website for prices and opening hours.

DR JOHNSON'S HOUSE

The Georgian **house** (Map pp104-5; ☎ 7353 3745; www.drjohnsonshouse.org; 17 Gough Sq EC4; adult/child £4.50/1.50; ☽ 11am-5.30pm Mon-Sat May-Sep, to 5pm Mon-Sat Oct-Apr; ⊖ Chancery Lane) where Samuel Johnson and his assistants compiled the first English dictionary (between 1748 and 1759) is full of prints and portraits of friends and intimates, including the good doctor's Jamaican servant to whom he bequeathed this grand residence.

FLEET ST

As 20th-century London's 'Street of Shame', **Fleet St** (Map pp104-5; ⊖ Temple) was synonymous with the UK's scurrilous tabloids until the mid-1980s when the press barons embraced computer technology, ditched a load of staff and largely relocated to the Docklands.

ST KATHARINE DOCKS

A centre of trade and commerce for 1000 years, **St Katharine Docks** (Map p112) is now a buzzing waterside area of pleasure boats and eateries. It was badly damaged during the war but survivors include the popular **Dickins Inn**, with its original 18th-century timber framework, and **Ivory House** (built 1854) which used to store ivory, perfume and other precious goods.

East End

Traditionally the most economically depressed part of the metropolis, a fair bit of cash is being splashed around at present in the lead-up to the 2012 Olympic Games. Dockland's Canary Wharf and Isle of Dogs are now an island of tower blocks, rivalling those of the City itself.

HOXTON, SHOREDITCH & SPITALFIELDS
Fans of the long-running TV soap *Eastenders* may find it hard to recognise its setting in traditionally working class but increasingly trendy enclaves like these. The fact is you're more likely to hear a proper Cockney accent in Essex these days than you are in much of the East End. Over the centuries waves of immigrants have left their mark here and it's a great place to come for diverse ethnic cuisine and vibrant but largely attitude-free nightlife.

Geffrye Museum
If you like nosing around other people's homes, the **Geffrye Museum** (Map pp96-7; ☎ 7739 9893; www.geffrye-museum.org.uk; 136 Kingsland Rd E2; admission free; ☷ 10am-5pm Tue-Sat, noon-5pm Sun; ✪ Old St, then ☐ 243) will be a positively orgasmic experience. Devoted to middle-class domestic interiors, these former almshouses (1714) have been converted into a series of living rooms dating from 1630 to the current Ikea generation. On top of the interiors porn, the back garden has been transformed into period garden 'rooms' and a lovely walled herb garden (April to October only).

Dennis Severs' House
This extraordinary **Georgian House** (Map p112; ☎ 7247 4013; www.dennissevershouse.co.uk; 18 Folgate St E1; ✪ Liverpool St) is set up as if its occupants had just walked out the door. There are half-drunk cups of tea, lit candles and, in a perhaps unnecessary attention to detail, a full chamber pot by the bed. More than a museum, it's an opportunity to meditate on the minutiae of everyday Georgian life through silent exploration.

Bookings are required for the Monday evening candlelit sessions (£12; call for times), but you can just show up on the first and third Sundays of the month (£8; midday to 4pm) or the following Mondays (£5; midday to 2pm).

White Cube
Set in an industrial building with an impressive glazed-roof extension **White Cube** (Map

---

TATE-A-TATE

To get between London's Tate galleries in style, the **Tate Boat** – which sports a Damien Hirst dot painting – will whisk you from one to the other, stopping en route at the London Eye. Services run 10am to 6pm daily at 40-minute intervals. A River Roamer hop-on hop-off ticket (purchased on board) costs £8, single tickets £4.

---

p112; ☎ 7930 5373; www.whitecube.com; 48 Hoxton Sq N1; admission free; ☷ 10am-6pm Tue-Sat; ✪ Old St) has an interesting program of contemporary-art exhibitions from sculptures to video, installations and painting.

DOCKLANDS
The Port of London was once the world's greatest, the hub of the enormous global trade of the British Empire. Since being pummelled by the Luftwaffe in WWII its fortunes have been topsy-turvy, but the massive development of Canary Wharf into a second business district has replaced its crusty seadogs with hordes of dark-suited office workers. It's now an interesting if slightly sterile environment, best viewed while hurtling around on the DLR (p170).

The **Museum in Docklands** (Map p111; ☎ 0870-444 3856; www.museumindocklands.org.uk; Hertsmere Rd, West India Quay E17; annual admission adult/child £5/free; ☷ 10am-6pm Mon-Sat; DLR West India Quay), housed in a heritage-listed warehouse, uses a combination of artefacts and multimedia to chart the history of the Docklands from Roman trading to its renewal in the twilight of the 20th century.

South of the Thames
Londoners once crossed the river to the area controlled by the licentious Bishops of Southwark for all kinds of raunchy diversions frowned upon in the City. It's a much more seemly area now, but the theatre and entertainment tradition remains.

SOUTHWARK
Tate Modern
It's hard to miss this surprisingly elegant former power station on the side of the river, which is fortunate as the tremendous **Tate Modern** (Map p112; ☎ 7887 8888; www.tate.org.uk; Queen's Walk SE1; admission free; ☷ 10am-6pm Sun-Thu,

to 10pm Fri & Sat; (&) ; ⊖ Southwark) really shouldn't be missed. Focussing on modern art in all its wacky and wonderful permutations, it's been extraordinarily successful in bringing challenging work to the masses, becoming one of London's most popular attractions.

Outstanding temporary exhibitions (on the 4th floor; prices vary) continue to spark excitement, as does the periodically changing large-scale installation in the vast Turbine Hall. The permanent collection is organised into four main sections. On floor three you'll find *Material Gestures* (postwar painting and sculpture, including Mark Rothko's affecting *Seagram Murals*) and *Poetry and Dream* (Pablo Picasso, Francis Bacon and surrealism). On the 5th floor, *Idea and Object* showcases minimalism and conceptual art, while in *States of Flux* cubism and futurism rub shoulders with pop art (Roy Lichtenstein, Andy Warhol) and Soviet imagery.

The multimedia guides (£2) are worthwhile for their descriptions of selected works and there are free daily guided tours of the collection's highlights (Level 3 at 11am and midday; Level 5 at 2pm and 3pm). Make sure you cop the view from the top floor's restaurant and bar.

Shakespeare's Globe

Today's Londoners might grab a budget flight to Amsterdam to behave badly. Back in Shakespeare's time they'd cross London Bridge to Southwark. Free from the city's constraints, you could hook up with a prostitute, watch a bear being tortured for your amusement and then head to the theatre, the most famous of which was the **Globe** (Map p112; ☎ 7401 9919; www.shakespeares-globe.org; 21 New Globe Walk SE1; adult/child £9/6.50; ⏰ 10am-6pm May-Sep, last entry 5pm; to 5pm Oct-Apr; ⊖ London Bridge), where a clever fellow was producing box-office smashes like *Macbeth* and *Hamlet*.

Originally built in 1599, the Globe burnt down in 1613 and was immediately rebuilt. The Puritans, who regarded theatres as dreadful dens of iniquity, eventually closed it in 1642. Its present incarnation was the vision of American actor and director Sam Wanamaker, who sadly died before the opening night in 1997.

Admission includes a guided tour of the open-roofed theatre, faithfully reconstructed from oak beams, handmade bricks, lime plaster and thatch. There's also an extensive exhibition about Shakespeare and his times.

Plays are still performed here, and while Shakespeare and his contemporaries dominate, modern plays are also staged (see the website for upcoming performances). As in Elizabethan times, 'groundlings' can watch proceedings for a modest price (£5; seats are £15 to £35), but there's no protection from the elements and you'll have to stand.

Southwark Cathedral

Although the central tower dates from 1520 and the choir from the 13th century, **Southwark Cathedral** (Map p112; ☎ 7367 6700; Montague Close SE1; suggested donation £4-6.50; ⏰ 8am-6pm Mon-Fri, 9am-6pm Sat & Sun; ⊖ London Bridge) is largely Victorian. Inside are monuments galore, including a Shakespeare Memorial; it's worth picking up one of the small guides. Catch Evensong at 5.30pm on Tuesdays, Thursdays and Fridays, 4pm on Saturdays and 3pm on Sundays.

Old Operating Theatre Museum & Herb Garret

One of London's most genuinely gruesome attractions, the **Old Operating Theatre Museum** (Map p112; ☎ 7188 2679; www.thegarret.org.uk; 9A St Thomas St SE1; adult/child £5.45/3; ⏰ 10.30am-4.45pm; ⊖ London Bridge) is Britain's only surviving 19th-century operating theatre, rediscovered in 1956 within the garret of a church. The display of primitive surgical tools is suitably terrifying, while the pickled bits of humans are just unpleasant.

It's a hands-on kind of place, with signs saying 'please touch', although obviously the pointy things are locked away. For a more intense experience, check the website for the regular 20-minute 'special events'.

City Hall

The Norman Foster–designed, wonky-egg-shaped **City Hall** (Map p112; ☎ 7983 4000; www.london .gov.uk; Queen's Walk SE1; admission free; ⏰ 8am-8pm Mon-Fri) is an architectural feast of glass and home to the mayor's office, the London Assembly and the Greater London Assembly (GLA). Visitors can see the mayor's meeting chamber and attend debates. On some weekends the top-floor reception hall, known as **London's Living Room**, is opened for the public to enjoy its panoramic views. It's accessed via a glass winding ramp similar to the one in Berlin's Reichstag (see website for dates).

Design Museum

The whiter-than-white **Design Museum** (Map p112; ☎ 7403 6933; www.designmuseum.org; 28 Shad Thames SE1; adult £8.50; ◷ 10am-5.45pm; ⊖ Tower Hill) is a must for anyone interested in beautiful, practical things. The permanent collection has displays of modern British design and there are also regular temporary exhibitions including the annual *Designs of the Year* competition.

HMS Belfast

Launched in 1938, **HMS Belfast** (Map p112; ☎ 7407 6328; www.iwm.org.uk/hmsbelfast; Morgan's Lane, Tooley St SE1; adult/child £10.30/free; ◷ 10am-6pm Mar-Oct, to 5pm Nov-Feb; ⊖ London Bridge) took part in the D-day landings and saw action in Korea. Explore the nine decks and see the engine room, gun decks, galley, chapel, punishment cells, canteen and dental surgery.

London Dungeon

Older kids tend to love the **London Dungeon** (Map p112; ☎ 0871-423 2240; www.thedungeons.com; 28-34 Tooley St SE1; adult/child £19.95/14.95; ◷ 10.30am-5pm, longer hrs some weeks, check website; ⊖ London Bridge), as the terrifying queues during school holidays and weekends testify. It's all spooky music, ghostly boat rides, macabre hangman's drop-rides, fake blood and actors dressed up as torturers and gory criminals (including Jack the Ripper and Sweeney Todd). Beware the interactive bits.

Britain at War Experience

You can pop down to the London Underground air-raid shelter, look at gas masks and ration books, stroll around Southwark during the Blitz and learn about the battle on the Home Front at the **Britain at War Experience** (Map p112; ☎ 7403 3171; www.britainatwar.co.uk; 64-66 Tooley St SE1; adult/child £11/4.95; ◷ 10am-5.30pm Apr-Sep, to 4.30pm Oct-Mar). It's crammed with fascinating WWII memorabilia.

SOUTH BANK
London Eye

It may seem a bit Mordor-ish to have a giant eye overlooking the city, but the **London Eye** (Map pp104-5; ☎ 0870 5000 600; www.londoneye.com; adult/child £15.50/7.75; ◷ 10am-8pm Jan-May & Oct-Dec, to 9pm Jun & Sep, to 9.30pm Jul & Aug; ⊖ Waterloo) doesn't actually resemble an eye at all, and, in a city where there's a CCTV camera on every other corner, it's probably only fitting. Originally designed as a temporary struc-ture to celebrate the year 2000, the Eye is now a permanent addition to the cityscape, joining Big Ben as one of London's most distinctive landmarks.

This 135m-tall, slow-moving Ferris wheel (although we're not supposed to call it that for all kinds of technical reasons) is the largest of its kind in the world. Passengers ride in an enclosed egg-shaped pod; the wheel takes 30 minutes to rotate completely and offers a 25-mile view on a clear day. It's so popular that it's advisable to book your ticket online to speed up your wait (you also get a 10% discount), or you can pay an additional £10 to jump the queue.

Joint tickets for the London Eye and Madame Tussauds can be purchased (adult/child £35/25), as well as a 40-minute, sight-seeing **River Cruise** (adult/child £12/6) with a multilingual commentary.

London Aquarium

One of the largest in Europe, the **London Aquarium** (Map pp104-5; ☎ 7967 8000; www.london aquarium.co.uk; County Hall SE1; adult/child £14/9.75; ◷ 10am-6pm, last entry 5pm; ⊖ Waterloo) has three levels of fish organised by geographical origin, but you'll be peering over children's excited heads during holidays. Check the website for shark-feeding times.

Dalí Universe

The brochure invites you to 'enter the mind of a genius' – a daunting prospect, as it's a place where clocks melt and telephones morph into lobsters. **Dalí Universe** (Map pp104-5; ☎ 0870 744 7485; www.daliuniverse.com; County Hall SE1; adult/child £12/8; ◷ 9.30am-7pm Sat-Thu, to 8pm Fri; ⊖ Waterloo) is a large collection that focuses on the surrealist master's rare etchings, movies, furniture and sculptures rather than his famous canvasses. Included in the price, **Picasso: Art of a Genius** also concentrates on rare work, such as tapestry and ceramic design. You can download a two-for-one entry voucher from the website; last entry is an hour prior to closing.

Hayward Gallery

Part of the Southbank Centre (p164), the **Hayward** (Map pp104-5; ☎ 0871-663 2587; www.south bankcentre.co.uk/visual-arts; Belvedere Rd SE1; admission prices vary; ◷ 10am-6pm Sat-Thu, to 10pm Fri; ⊖ Waterloo) hosts a changing roster of modern art (video, installations, photography, collage, painting etc).

LAMBETH

Imperial War Museum

You don't have to be a lad to appreciate the **Imperial War Museum** (Map pp104-5; ☎ 7416 5000; www.iwm.org.uk; Lambeth Rd SE1; admission free; ◷ 10am-6pm; ✆ Lambeth North) and its spectacular atrium with spitfires hanging from the ceiling, rockets (including the massive German V2), field-guns, missiles, submarines, tanks, torpedoes and other military hardware. Providing a telling lesson in modern history, highlights include a re-created WWI trench and WWII bomb shelter as well as a **Holocaust Exhibition**.

Florence Nightingale Museum

The thought-provoking **Florence Nightingale Museum** (Map pp104-5; ☎ 7620 0374; www.florence-nightingale.co.uk; 2 Lambeth Palace Rd SE1; adult/child £5.80/4.80; ◷ 10am-5pm Mon-Fri, to 4.30pm Sat & Sun, last admission 1hr before closing; ✆ Waterloo) recounts the story of 'the lady with the lamp' who led a team of nurses during the Crimean War. She established a training school for nurses here at St Thomas' hospital in 1859.

Chelsea, Kensington & Knightsbridge

Known as the royal borough, residents of Kensington and Chelsea are certainly paid royally, earning the highest incomes in the UK (shops and restaurants will presume you do too). Knightsbridge is where you'll find some of London's best-known department stores, including Harrods (p166) and Harvey Nicks (p166), while Kensington High St has a lively mix of chains and boutiques. Thanks to the surplus generated by the 1851 Great Exhibition, which allowed the purchase of a great chunk of land, South Kensington boasts some of London's most beautiful and interesting museums all on one road.

VICTORIA & ALBERT MUSEUM

A vast, rambling and wonderful museum of decorative art and design, the **Victoria & Albert** (V&A; Map pp100-1; ☎ 7942 2000; www.vam.ac.uk; Cromwell Rd SW7; admission free; ◷ 10am-5.45pm Sat-Thu, to 10pm Fri; ✆ South Kensington) is part of Prince Albert's legacy to Londoners in the wake of the Great Exhibition.

It's a bit like the nation's attic, comprising four million objects collected from Britain and around the globe. Spread over nearly 150 galleries, it houses the world's greatest collection of decorative arts, including ancient Chinese ceramics, modernist architectural drawings, Korean bronze, Japanese swords, cartoons by Raphael, spellbinding Asian and Islamic art, Rodin sculptures, actual-size reproductions of famous European architecture and sculpture (including Michelangelo's *David*), Elizabethan gowns, ancient jewellery, an all-wooden Frank Lloyd Wright study and a pair of Doc Martens. Yes, you'll need to plan.

The British Galleries (1500 to 1900) take up the entire western wing, while the eastern wing will hold the revamped Mediterranean and Renaissance Galleries (due to be completed in late 2009).

To top it all off, it's a fabulous building, with an attractive garden cafe as well as the original, lavishly decorated V&A cafe.

NATURAL HISTORY MUSEUM

Let's start with the building itself: stripes of pale blue and honey-coloured stone are broken by Venetian arches decorated with all manner of carved critters. Quite simply, it's one of London's finest.

A sure-fire hit with kids of all ages, the **Natural History Museum** (Map pp100-1; ☎ 7942 5725; www.nhm.ac.uk; Cromwell Rd SW7; admission free; ◷ 10am-5.50pm; ✆ South Kensington) is crammed full of interesting stuff, starting with the giant dinosaur skeleton that greats you in the main hall. In the main dinosaur section, the fleshless fossils are brought to robotic life with a very realistic 4m-high animatronic Tyrannosaurus Rex and his smaller, but no less sinister-looking, cousins.

The Earth Galleries are equally impressive. An escalator slithers up and into a hollowed-out globe where two main exhibits – *The Power Within* and the *Restless Surface* – explain how wind, water, ice, gravity and life itself impact on the earth. For parents not sure on how to broach the facts of life, a quick whiz around the Human Biology section should do the trick – rather graphically.

The **Darwin Centre** (☎ 7942 5011) houses some 22 million zoological exhibits, which can be visited by prearranging a free tour.

SCIENCE MUSEUM

With seven floors of interactive and educational exhibits, the **Science Museum** (Map pp100-1; ☎ 0870 870 4868; www.sciencemuseum.org.uk; Exhibition Rd SW7; admission free; ◷ 10am-6pm; ✆ South Kensington) covers everything from the Industrial Revolution to the exploration of space. There is something for all ages, from vintage cars, trains and aeroplanes to labour-saving devices for the home, a wind tunnel and flight simulator. Kids love the interactive sections. There's also a 450-seat **IMAX cinema**.

KENSINGTON PALACE
Dating from 1605, **Kensington Palace** (Map pp100-1; ☎ 0870 751 5170; www.hrp.org.uk; Kensington Gardens W8; adult/child £13/6.15; ☑ 10am-6pm Mar-Oct, to 5pm Nov-Feb; ⊖ High St Kensington) was the birthplace of Queen Victoria in 1819 but is best known today as the last home of Princess Diana. Hour-long tours take you around the surprisingly small **state-rooms**. A collection of Princess Di's dresses is on permanent display, along with frocks and ceremonial gowns from HRH and her predecessors. There's an audio tour included in the entry fee.

KENSINGTON GARDENS
Blending in with Hyde Park, these **royal gardens** (Map pp100-1; admission free; ☑ dawn-dusk; ⊖ Queensway) are part of Kensington Palace and hence popularly associated with Princess Diana. Diana devotees can visit the **Diana, Princess of Wales Memorial Playground** (Map pp100-1) in its northwest corner, a much more restrained royal remembrance than the over-the-top **Albert Memorial** (Map pp100-1), a lavish marble, mosaic and gold affair opposite the Royal Albert Hall, built to honour Queen Victoria's purportedly humble husband, Albert (1819-61).

The gardens also house the **Serpentine Gallery** (Map pp100-1; ☎ 7402 6075; www.serpentinegallery.org; admission free; ☑ 10am-6pm), one of London's edgiest contemporary art spaces. The **Sunken Garden** (Map pp100-1), near the palace, is at its prettiest in summer, while tea in the **Orangery** (Map pp100-1) is a treat any time of the year.

HYDE PARK
At 145 hectares, **Hyde Park** (Map pp100-1; ☑ 5.30am-midnight; ⊖ Marble Arch, Hyde Park Corner or Queensway) is central London's largest open space. Henry VIII expropriated it from the Church in 1536, when it became a hunting ground and later a venue for duels, executions and horse racing. The 1851 Great Exhibition was held here and during WWII the park became an enormous potato field. These days, it serves as an occasional concert venue and a full-time green space for fun and frolics. There's boating on the Serpentine for the energetic or, near Marble Arch, **Speaker's Corner** (Map

pp100-1) for oratorical acrobats. These days, it's largely possible nutters and religious fanatics who maintain the tradition begun in 1872 as a response to rioting.

A soothing structure, the **Princess Diana Memorial Fountain** (Map pp100-1) is a meandering stream that splits at the top, flows gently downhill and reassembles in a pool at the bottom. It was unveiled here in mid-2004 with inevitable debate over matters of taste and gravitas.

ROYAL HOSPITAL CHELSEA
Designed by Wren, the **Royal Hospital Chelsea** (Map pp102-3; ☎ 7881 5246; Royal Hospital Rd SW3; admission free; ☑ 10am-noon & 2-4pm Mon-Sun; ⊖ Sloane Sq) was built in 1692 to provide shelter for ex-servicemen. Today it houses hundreds of war veterans known as Chelsea Pensioners, charming old chaps who are generally regarded as national treasures. As you wander around the grounds or inspect the elegant chapel and interesting museum, you'll see them pottering about in their winter blue coats or summer reds. The Chelsea Flower Show takes place in the hospital grounds in May.

CHELSEA PHYSIC GARDEN
One for the garden obsessives (the less hardcore should head to the many free parks or Kew), this historic **botanical garden** (Map pp102-3; ☎ 7352 5646; www.chelseaphysicgarden.co.uk; 66 Royal Hospital Rd SW3; adult/child £7/4; ☑ noon-5pm Wed-Fri, to 6pm Sat & Sun; ⊖ Sloane Sq) is one of the oldest in Europe, established in 1673 for apprentice apothecaries to study medicinal plants. An audio guide is included in the price and tours leave at 3pm on Sundays.

MARBLE ARCH
London's grandest bedsit – with a one-room flat inside – **Marble Arch** (Map pp100-1; ⊖ Marble Arch) was designed by John Nash in 1828 as the entrance to Buckingham Palace. It was moved here in 1851.

The infamous Tyburn Tree, a three-legged gallows, once stood nearby. It is estimated that up to 50,000 people were executed here between 1196 and 1783.

Marylebone
With one of London's nicest high streets and Regent's Park on its doorstep, increasingly hip Marylebone is an interesting area to wander.

LONDON

REGENT'S PARK

A former royal hunting ground, **Regent's Park** (Map pp98-9; ⊖ Regent's Park) was designed by John Nash early in the 19th century, although what was actually laid out is only a fraction of the celebrated architect's grand plan. Nevertheless, it's one of London's most lovely open spaces – at once serene and lively, cosmopolitan and local – with football pitches, tennis courts and a boating lake. **Queen Mary's Gardens**, towards the south of the park, are particularly pretty, with spectacular roses in summer. **Open Air Theatre** (☎ 7935 5756; www.openairtheatre.org) hosts performances of Shakespeare here on summer evenings, along with comedy and concerts.

LONDON ZOO

A huge amount of money has been spent to bring **London Zoo** (Map pp98-9; ☎ 7722 3333; www .londonzoo.co.uk; Regent's Park NW1; adult/child £15.40/11.90; ⊗ 10am-5.30pm Mar-Oct, to 4pm Nov-Feb; ⊖ Camden Town), established in 1828, into the modern world. It now has a swanky new £5.3 million gorilla enclosure and is involved in gorilla conservation in Gabon. Feeding times, reptile handling and the petting zoo are guaranteed winners with the kids.

WALLACE COLLECTION

Housed in a beautiful, opulent Italianate mansion, the **Wallace Collection** (Map pp104-5; ☎ 7563 9500; www.wallacecollection.org; Hertford House, Manchester Sq W1; admission free, audio guide £3; ⊗ 10am-5pm; ⊖ Bond St) is a treasure trove of exquisite 18th-century French furniture, Sèvres porcelain, arms, armour and art by masters such as Rubens, Titian, Rembrandt and Gainsborough. Oliver Peyton's Wallace Restaurant occupies a lovely glassed-in courtyard at its centre.

MADAME TUSSAUDS

With so much fabulous free stuff to do in London, it's a wonder that people still join lengthy queues to visit pricey **Madame Tussauds** (Map pp104-5; ☎ 0870 400 3000; www.madame-tussauds .co.uk; Marylebone Rd NW1; adult/child £25/21; ⊗ 9.30am-5.30pm Mon-Fri, 9am-6pm Sat & Sun; ⊖ Baker St), but in a celebrity-obsessed, camera-happy world, the opportunity to pose beside Posh and Becks is not short on appeal.

The life-sized wax figures are remarkably lifelike and are as close to the real thing as most of us will get. It's interesting to see which are the most popular; nobody wants to be photographed with Richard Branson, but Prince Charles and Camilla do a brisk trade.

Honing her craft making effigies of victims of the French revolution, Tussaud brought her wares to England in 1802. Her Chamber of Horrors still survives (complete with the actual blade that took Marie Antoinette's head) but it's now joined by Chamber Live, where actors lunge at terrified punters in the dark. The Spirit of London ride is wonderfully cheesy but the conversion of the old planetarium into the Stardome show is just lame.

Tickets are cheaper when ordered online and for entries after 5pm. Combined tickets with London Eye and London Dungeon are also available (adult/child £50/35).

North London

Once well outside the city limits, the former hamlets of North London have long been gobbled up by the metropolis, and yet still maintain a semblance of a village atmosphere and distinct local identity. Not as resolutely wealthy as the west or as gritty as the east, the Norf is a strange mix of genteel terrace houses and council estates, containing some of London's hippest neighbourhoods.

EUSTON & KING'S CROSS

Most people are content to experience Kings Cross subterraneously, as it's a major interchange on the tube network, but the conversion of spectacular **St Pancras station** (Map pp98–9) into the new Eurostar terminal and a ritzy apartment complex seems to be reviving its fortunes. The streets are still grey and car-choked, but some decent accommodation options and interesting bars have sprung up.

British Library

You need to be a 'reader' (ie member) to use the vast collection of the **library** (Map pp98-9; ☎ 7412 7332; www.bl.uk; 96 Euston Rd NW1; admission free; ⊗ 9.30am-6pm Mon & Wed-Fri, to 8pm Tue, to 5pm Sat, 11am-5pm Sun; ⊖ King's Cross St Pancras), but the Treasures gallery is open to everyone. Here you'll find Shakespeare's first folio, Leonardo da Vinci's notebooks, the lyrics to 'A Hard Day's Night' scribbled on the back of Julian Lennon's birthday card, St Thomas Moore's last letter to Henry VIII, Jane Austen's correspondence, religious texts from around the world and, most importantly, the 8th-century Lindisfarne Gospel and 1215 Magna Carta.

Wellcome Collection

Say what you like about pharmaceutical companies, but when one of their charitable trusts spends £30 million opening a new, free gallery, it's very welcome indeed. The **Wellcome Collection** (Map pp98-9; ☎ 7611 2222; www .wellcomecollection.org; 183 Euston Rd NW1; admission free; ☽ 10am-6pm Tue, Wed, Fri & Sat, to 10pm Thu, 11am-6pm Sun; ⊖ Euston Sq) focuses on the interface of art, science and medicine. There are interactive displays where you can scan your face and watch it stretched into the statistical average; wacky modern sculptures inspired by various medical conditions; and downright creepy things like an actual cross-section of a body.

CAMDEN

Technicolour hairstyles, facial furniture, intricate tattoos and ambitious platform shoes are the look of Bohemian Camden, a lively neighbourhood of pubs, live-music venues, interesting boutiques and, most famously, Camden Market (see p167). There are often a few cartoon punks hanging around earning a few bucks for being photographed by tourists, as well as none-too-discreet dope dealers.

ST JOHN'S WOOD

Posh St John's Wood is famous for two things: cricket and Abbey Road Studios. Local traffic is by now pretty used to groups of tourists lining up on the **zebra crossing** (Map pp96–7) outside 3 Abbey Rd to recreate the cover of The Beatles' 1969 album *Abbey Road*.

Lord's Cricket Ground

The next best thing to watching a test at **Lord's** (Map pp96-7; ☎ 7616 8595; www.lords.org; St John's Wood Rd NW8; tours adult/child £12/6; ☽ tours 10am, noon & 2pm when there's no play; ⊖ St John's Wood) is the absorbingly anecdotal 100-minute tour of the ground and facilities. It takes in the famous (members only) Long Room and the **MCC Museum** featuring evocative memorabilia including the tiny Ashes trophy. For more information on attending test matches, see p165.

HAMPSTEAD & HIGHGATE

These quaint and well-heeled villages, perched on hills above London, are home to an inordinate number of celebrities.

Hampstead Heath

With its 320 hectares of rolling meadows and wild woodlands, **Hampstead Heath** (Map pp96-7; ☒ Gospel Oak or Hampstead Heath) is a million miles away – well, approximately four – from central London. A walk up **Parliament Hill** affords one of the most spectacular views of the city and on summer days it's popular with picnickers. Also bewilderingly popular are the murky brown waters of the separate single-sex or mixed bathing ponds (basically duck ponds with people splashing about in them), although most folk are content just to sun themselves around London's 'beach'.

Kenwood House (☎ 8348 1286; www.english-heritage .org.uk; Hampstead Ln NW3; admission free; ☽ 11.30am-4pm; ⊖ Archway or Golders Green, then ☒ 210) is a magnificent neoclassical mansion on the northern side of the heath, and houses a small collection of paintings by European masters.

Highgate Cemetery

The **cemetery** (☎ 8340 1834; www.highgate-cemetery .org; Swain's Lane N6; ⊖ Archway) weaves a creepy kind of magic, with its Victorian symbols – shrouded urns, obelisks, upturned torches (life extinguished) and broken columns (life cut short) – eerily overgrown graves and the twisting paths on the western side, where admission is by tour only (adult/child £5/1; 2pm weekdays, on the hour 11am to 4pm weekends). On the less atmospheric **eastern side** (admission £3; ☽ 10am-5pm Mon-Fri, 11am-5pm Sat & Sun Apr-Oct, to 4pm Nov-Mar) you can pay your respects to Karl Marx and George Eliot.

From Archway station, walk up Highgate Hill until you reach Waterlow Park on the left. Go through the park; the cemetery gates are opposite the exit.

Freud Museum

After fleeing Nazi-occupied Vienna in 1938, Sigmund Freud lived the last year of his life here. The fascinating **Freud Museum** (Map pp96-7; ☎ 7435 2002; www.freud.org.uk; 20 Maresfield Gardens NW3; adult £5; ☽ noon-5pm Wed-Sun) maintains his study and library much as he left it, with his couch, books and collection of small Egyptian figures and other antiquities. Excerpts of dream analysis are scattered around the house and there's a video presentation upstairs.

Greenwich

Simultaneously the first and last place on earth, Greenwich (*gren*-itch) straddles the hemispheres as well as the ages. More than any of the villages swamped by London, Greenwich has managed to retain its own sense of identity based on splendid architecture and strong connections with the sea and science. All the great architects of the Enlightenment made their mark here, leaving an extraordinary cluster of buildings that have earned 'Maritime Greenwich' its place on Unesco's World Heritage list.

Greenwich is easily reached on the DLR or via train from London Bridge. **Thames River Services** (☎ 7930 4097; www.westminsterpier .co.uk) has boats departing half-hourly from Westminster Pier (single/return £7.50/9.80, one hour), or alternatively take the cheaper Thames Clippers ferry (p171).

OLD ROYAL NAVAL COLLEGE

Also designed by Wren, the **Old Royal Naval College** (Map p111; ☎ 8269 4747; www.oldroyalnaval college.org; 2 Cutty Sark Gardens SE10; admission free; ◷ 10am-5pm Mon-Sat; DLR Cutty Sark) is a magnificent example of monumental classical architecture. Parts are now used by the University of Greenwich and Trinity College of Music, but you can visit the **chapel** and the extraordinary **Painted Hall**, which took artist Sir James Thornhill 19 years of hard graft to complete.

The complex was built on the site of the 15th-century Palace of Placentia, the birthplace of Henry VIII and Elizabeth I. This Tudor connection will be explored in **Discover Greenwich**, a new centre due to open in late 2009. The **tourist office** (☎ 0870 608 2000; www.green wich.gov.uk) will be housed here, but until then look for it in temporary buildings nearby.

NATIONAL MARITIME MUSEUM

Directly behind the old college, the **National Maritime Museum** (Map p111; ☎ 8858 4422; www.nmm .ac.uk; Romney Rd SE10; admission free; ◷ 10am-5pm, last entry 4.30pm; DLR Cutty Sark) completes Greenwich's trump hand of historic buildings. The **museum** itself houses a massive collection of paraphernalia recounting Britain's seafaring history. Exhibits range from interactive displays to humdingers like Nelson's uniform complete with a hole from the bullet that killed him.

At the centre of the site, the elegant Palladian **Queen's House** has been restored to something like Inigo Jones' intention when he designed it in 1616 for the wife of Charles I. It's a stunning setting for a gallery focusing on illustrious seafarers and historic Greenwich.

Behind Queen's House, idyllic **Greenwich Park** climbs up the hill, affording great views of London. It's capped by the **Royal Observatory**, which Charles II had built in 1675 to help solve the riddle of longitude. Success was confirmed in 1884 when Greenwich was designated as the prime meridian of the world, and Greenwich Mean Time (GMT) became the universal measurement of standard time. Here you can stand with your feet straddling the western and eastern hemispheres.

If you arrive just before lunchtime, you will see a bright-red ball climb the observatory's northeast turret at 12.58pm and drop at 1pm – as it has every day since 1833 when it was introduced for ships on the Thames to set their clocks by.

The observatory's newly revamped galleries are split into those devoted to astronomy and those devoted to time. There's also a 120-seat **planetarium** (adult/child £6/4) screening a roster of digital presentations; check the website for details.

CUTTY SARK

A famous Greenwich landmark, this **clipper** (Map p111; ☎ 8858 3445; www.cuttysark.org.uk; King William Walk) was the fastest ship in the world when it was launched in 1869. Despite a fire in 2007, only a fraction of the ship was destroyed as much of its fabric had already been removed for conservation. By early 2010 it should have reopened and be better displayed than ever – you'll even be able to walk under her. Watch the website for details.

FAN MUSEUM

Housed in an 18th-century Georgian house, the engaging **Fan Museum** (Map p111; ☎ 8305 1441; www.fan-museum.org; 12 Croom's Hill SE10; admission £4; ◷ 11am-5pm Tue-Sat, noon-5pm Sun; DLR Cutty Sark) is one of a kind. Only a fraction of its collection of hand-held fans from around the world, dating back to the 17th century, are on display at any one time.

THE O2

The world's largest dome (365m in diameter) opened on 1 January 2000 at a cost of £789m as the Millennium Dome, but closed on 31 December, only hours before the third millennium began. Renamed **The O2** (Map p111; ☎ 8463 2000; www.theo2.co.uk; Peninsula Sq SE10; ✈ North Greenwich), it's now a 20,000-seater sports and entertainment arena surrounded by shops and restaurants. It has hosted some massive concerts, including the one-off Led Zeppelin reunion and a 21-night purple reign by Prince. There are shuttle-boat services from central London on concert nights.

Outside Central London
KEW GARDENS
In 1759 botanists began rummaging around the world for specimens they could plant in the 3-hectare plot known as the **Royal Botanic Gardens, Kew** (Map pp96-7; ☎ 8332 5655; www.kew .org.uk; Kew Rd; adult/child £13/free; ☉ 9.30am-6.30pm Mon-Fri, to 7.30pm Sat & Sun, earlier closing in winter; ⊖ Kew Gardens). They never stopped collecting, and the gardens, which have bloomed to 120 hectares, provide the most comprehensive botanical collection on earth (including the world's largest collection of orchids) as well as a delightful pleasure garden. It's now recognised as a Unesco World Heritage Site.

You can easily spend a whole day wandering around, but if you're pressed for time, the **Kew Explorer** (adult/child £4/1) is a hop-on hop-off road train that leaves from Victoria Gate and takes in the gardens' main sights.

Highlights include the enormous **Palm House**, a hothouse of metal and curved sheets of glass; the stunning **Princess of Wales Conservatory**; the red-brick, 1631 **Kew Palace** (adult/child £5/2.50; ☉ 10am-5pm Easter-30 Sep), formerly King George III's country retreat; the celebrated **Great Pagoda** designed by William Chambers in 1762, due to reopen in 2009 following restoration; and the **Temperate House**, which is the world's largest ornamental glasshouse and home to its biggest indoor plant, the 18m Chilean Wine Palmand.

The gardens are easily reached by tube, but you might prefer to take a cruise on a riverboat from the **Westminster Passenger Services Association** (☎ 7930 2062; www.wpsa.co.uk), which runs several daily boats from April to October, departing from Westminster Pier (return adult/child £16.50/8.25, 90 minutes).

HAMPTON COURT PALACE
Built by Cardinal Thomas Wolsey in 1514 but coaxed out of him by Henry VIII just before the chancellor fell from favour, **Hampton Court Palace** (Map pp96-7; ☎ 0844-482 7777; www.hrp.org .uk/HamptonCourtPalace; adult/child £13.50/6.65; ☉ 10am-6pm Apr-Oct, to 4.30pm Nov-Mar; ⊠ Hampton Court) is England's largest and grandest Tudor structure. It was already one of the most sophis-

ticated palaces in Europe when, in the 17th century, Wren was commissioned to build an extension. The result is a beautiful blend of Tudor and 'restrained baroque' architecture. Take a themed tour led by costumed historians or, if you're in a rush, visit the highlights: **Henry VIII's State Apartments,** including the Great Hall with its spectacular hammer-beamed roof; the **Tudor Kitchens**, staffed by 'servants'; and the **Wolsey Rooms**. You could easily spend a day exploring the palace and its 60 acres of riverside gardens, especially if you get lost in the 300-year-old **maze**.

Hampton Court is 13 miles southwest of central London and is easily reached by train from Waterloo. Alternatively, the riverboats that head from Westminster to Kew (left) continue here (return adult/child £19.50/9.75, 3½ hours).

RICHMOND PARK
London's wildest **park** (Map pp96–7) spans more than 1000 hectares and is home to all sorts of wildlife, most notably herds of red and fallow deer. It's a terrific place for birdwatching, rambling and cycling.

To get there from the Richmond tube station, turn left along George St then left at the fork that leads up Richmond Hill.

HORNIMAN MUSEUM
Set in an Art Nouveau building amid gorgeous gardens, **Horniman Museum** (Map pp96-7; ☎ 8699 1872; www.horniman.ac.uk; 100 London Rd SE23; admission free; ☉ 10.30am-5.30pm; ⊠ Forest Hill) has three main themes: anthropology (Britain's third-most important collection of ethnographical objects), natural history (250,000 specimens) and a fab assortment of musical instruments.

Trains to Forest Hill leave from London Bridge. The museum is a well-signposted five-minute walk from the station, uphill along London Rd.

CITY WALKING TOUR
The City of London has as much history and interesting architecture in its square mile as the rest of London put together. This tour focuses on the City's hidden delights (secluded parks, charming churches) in a journey from the ancient to the ultramodern.

It's fitting to start at **St Bartholomew-the-Great (1)**, as this fascinating 12th-century church was once a site of pilgrimage for travellers to

CITY WALK

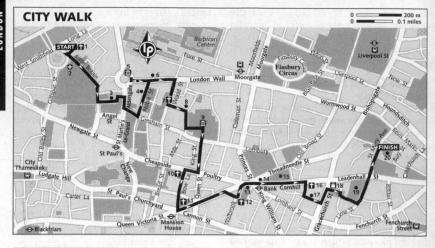

0 ——————— 200 m
0 ——————— 0.1 miles

WALK FACTS

Start: St Bartholomew-the-Great
Finish: 30 St Mary Axe
Distance: 2 miles
Duration: two hours

London. In more recent times, it's been used for scenes in *Four Weddings & A Funeral* and *Shakespeare In Love*.

Head out through the Tudor gatehouse, where in the distance you'll see the Victorian arches of Smithfield's meat market, which has occupied this site just north of the old city walls for 800 years. Executions were held here, most famously the burning of Protestants under Mary I and the grisly killing of Scottish hero William Wallace (Braveheart) in 1305; a plaque on the front of **St Batholemew's Hospital (2)** commemorates him. Also note the shrapnel damage to the wall, the legacy of an attack in 1916 by a German Zeppelin.

Head back towards the gate and turn right into Little Britain. Follow it as it curves to the right and look out for the large oak marking the entrance to **Postman's Park (3)**. This lovely space includes a touching legacy of Victorian socialism: a tiled wall celebrating everyday heroes.

Turn right at the end of the park, then left and left again into Noble St. You're now inside the City's **walls (4)**, remnants of which you'll pass on your left. Take the stairs up to the footbridge and cross towards the **Museum of London (5, p123)**. Its Roman section will give you a feel for the layout of the City.

Turn left when leaving the museum and follow the Highwalk. On your left you'll see **ruins (6)** of the barbicans (defensive towers) that once guarded the northwestern corner of the walls, with the Barbican centre (p124) behind them.

Take the escalator (by Pizza Express) down to Wood St and head towards the remaining tower of **St Alban's (7)**, a Wren-designed church destroyed in WWII. Turn left and you'll find a sweet garden on the site of **St Mary Aldermansbury (8)**, capped by a bust of Shakespeare. The 12th-century church was ruined in the war then shipped to Missouri where it was re-erected.

Turn right onto Aldermansbury and head to the **Guildhall (9, p123)**. Take King St down to Cheapside, cross the road and head right to elegant **St Mary-le-Bow (10)**. The church was rebuilt by Wren after the Great Fire, and then rebuilt again after WWII. The term 'Cockney' traditionally refers to someone born within the sound of this church's bell.

Backtrack to Bow Lane and follow this narrow path to beautiful **St Mary Aldermary (11)**, rebuilt in the Perpendicular Gothic style in 1682 following the fire. Turn left onto Queen Victoria St and then right into Bucklersbury, where you'll see **St Stephen's Walbrook (12, p123)** directly in front of you.

Leaving the church, you'll pass **Mansion House (13)**, built in 1752 as the official residence of the Lord Mayor. As you approach the busy Bank intersection, lined with neo-classical temples to commerce, you might think you've stumbled into the ancient Roman forum (the actual forum was a couple of blocks east). Head for the **equestrian statue of the Iron Duke (14)**, behind which a metal pyramid details the many significant buildings here. Directly behind you is the **Royal Exchange (15)**; walk through it and exit through the door on the right, then turn left onto Cornhill.

If you're not churched out, cross the road to **St Michael's (16)**, a 1672 Wren design which still has its box pews. Hidden in the warren of tiny passages behind the church is its **churchyard (17)**. Head through to Gracechurch St, turn left and cross the road to wonderful **Leadenhall Market (18)**. This is roughly where the ancient forum once stood.

As you wander out the far end, the famous **Lloyd's building (19)** displays its innards for all to see.

Once you turn left onto Lime St, you'll see ahead of you Norman Foster's 180m **30 St Mary Axe building (20)**. Its dramatic curved shape has given birth to many nicknames (the Crystal Phallus, the Towering Innuendo), but it's the Gherkin by which it's fondly referred. Built nearly 900 years after St Bartholomew-the-Great, it's testimony to the City's ability to constantly reinvent itself for the times.

LONDON FOR CHILDREN

London has plenty of sights that parents and kids can enjoy together, and many of them are free, including the Natural History Museum (p128), Science Museum (p128) and all of the city's parks, many of which have excellent playgrounds. Pricier but popular attractions include London Dungeon (p127), London Zoo (p130), Madame Tussauds (p130), Tower of London (p122), London Aquarium (p127) and the London Eye (p127).

On top of that, there are a number of city farms (see www.london-footprints.co.uk/visit farms.htm) and the big galleries have activities for children. However, don't expect a warm welcome in swanky restaurants or pubs.

All top-range hotels offer in-house baby-sitting services. Prices vary enormously from hotel to hotel, so ask the concierge about hourly rates. Alternatively try www.sitters .co.uk: membership costs £12.75 for three months, then sitters cost around £8 per hour plus a £4 booking fee.

TOURS

One of the best ways to get yourself orientated when you first arrive in London is with a 24-hour hop-on/hop-off pass for the double-decker bus tours operated by the **Original London Sightseeing Tour** (☎ 8877 1722; www.theorig inaltour.com; adult/child £22/12) or the **Big Bus Company** (☎ 7233 9533; www.bigbustours.com; adult/child £24/10). The buses loop around interconnecting routes throughout the day, providing a commentary as they go, and the price includes a river cruise and three walking tours. You'll save a couple of pounds by booking online.

There are loads of walking-tour operators, including **Citisights** (☎ 8806 3742; www.chr .org.uk/cswalks.htm), focussing on the academic and the literary; **London Walks** (☎ 7624 3978; www.walks.com), including Harry Potter tours, ghost walks and the ever-popular Jack The Ripper tours; and **Mystery Tours** (☎ 07957 388280; mysterywalks@hotmail.com).

Other unusual tours include:

Black Taxi Tours of London (☎ 7935 9363; www .blacktaxitours.co.uk; 8am-6pm £95, 6pm-midnight £100, plus £5 on weekends) Takes up to five people on a two-hour spin past the major sights with a chatty cabbie as your guide.

City Cruises (☎ 7740 0400; www.citycruises.com; single/return trips from £6.40/7.80, day pass £10.50; ☽ 10am-6pm, later Jun-Aug) Operates a ferry service between Westminster, Waterloo, Tower and Greenwich piers.

London Bicycle Tour Company (Map pp104-5; ☎ 7928 6838; www.londonbicycle.com; 1A Gabriel's Wharf, 56 Upper Ground SE1; tour incl bike £14.95-17.95; ⊖ Waterloo) Offers themed 2½- to 3½-hour tours of the 'East', 'Central' or 'Royal West'.

London Duck Tours (Map pp104-5; ☎ 7928 3132; www.londonducktours.co.uk; County Hall; adult/child £21.50/15.50; ⊖ Waterloo) Cruise the streets in the same sort of amphibious landing craft used on D-Day before making a dramatic plunge into the Thames.

FESTIVALS & EVENTS

Although it's not renowned as a festival city, London has a few events that might sway your plans:

Chinese New Year Late January or early February sees Chinatown (p119) snap, crackle and pop with fireworks, a colourful street parade and eating aplenty.

University Boat Race (www.theboatrace.org) A posh-boy grudge match held annually since 1829 between the rowing crews of Oxford and Cambridge Universities (late March).

Chelsea Flower Show (www.rhs.org.uk/chelsea; Royal Hospital Chelsea; admission £18-41) Held in May, the world's most renowned horticultural show attracts green fingers from near and far.

LONDON

GAY & LESBIAN LONDON

London's had a thriving scene since at least the 18th century, when the West End's 'Mollie houses' were the forerunners of today's gay bars. The West End, particularly Soho, remains the visible centre of gay and lesbian London, with numerous venues clustered around Old Compton St and its surrounds. However, Soho doesn't hold a monopoly on gay life. One of the nice things about the city is that there are local gay bars in many neighbourhoods.

Despite, or perhaps because of, its grimness and griminess, Vauxhall's taken off as a hub for the hirsute, hefty and generally harder-edged sections of the community. The railway arches are now filled with dance clubs, leather bars and a sauna.

Also in southwest London, Clapham's got some of the friendliest gay bars in the city, while Earl's Court (West London), Islington (North London) and Limehouse (East End) have their own miniscenes.

Generally, London's a safe place for lesbians and gays. It's rare to encounter any problem with sharing rooms or holding hands in the inner city, although it would pay to keep your wits about you at night and be conscious of your surroundings.

The easiest way to find out what's going on is to pick up the free press *(Pink Paper, Boyz, QX)* from a venue, but be warned: the mags can be somewhat…confronting. The gay section of *Time Out* is useful, as are www.gaydarnation.com (for men) and www.gingerbeer.co.uk (for women).

Here are some places to get you started:

Candy Bar (Map pp108-9; ☎ 7494 4041; 4 Carlisle St W1; ✆ Tottenham Court Rd) Long-running lesbian hang-out.

Friendly Society (Map pp108-9; ☎ 7434 3805; 79 Wardour St W1; ✆ Piccadilly Circus) Soho's quirkiest gay bar, this Bohemian basement is bedecked in kid's-room wallpaper and Barbie dolls.

G-A-Y Bar (Map pp108-9; ☎ 7494 2756; 30 Old Compton St W1; ✆ Leicester Sq) At the time of research the famous club night of the same name was planning to move. Find out where to from this, its little boozy sister.

Gay's the Word (Map pp98-9; ☎ 7278 7654; 66 Marchmont St WC1; ✆ Russell Sq) Books and mags of all descriptions.

George & Dragon (Map p112; ☎ 7012 1100; 2 Hackney Rd E2; ✆ Old St) Appealing corner pub where the crowd is often as eclectically furnished as the venue.

Ghetto (Map pp108-9; ☎ 7287 3726; 5-6 Falconberg Ct W1; admission £3-7; ✆ Tottenham Court Rd) Home to a roster of crazy nights such as The Cock, with inexpensive drinks and alternative music.

Heaven (Map pp108-9; ☎ 7930 2020; The Arches, Villiers St WC2; ✆ Charing Cross) One of the world's best-known gay clubs, Saturday night's the big one (£15) but Monday's Popcorn is lots of frothy fun (free before midnight, £5 after).

Popstarz (Map pp108-9; www.popstarz.org/popzmini; Sin, Andrew Borde St WC1; admission free-£7; ⏰ 10pm-4am Fri; ✆ Tottenham Court Rd) London's legendary indie club night. The online flyer gets you in cheaper.

Royal Vauxhall Tavern (RVT; Map p107; ☎ 7820 1222; 372 Kennington Ln SE11; admission free-£7; ✆ Vauxhall) A much-loved pub with crazy cabaret and drag acts.

Two Brewers (Map pp96-7; ☎ 7498 4971; 114 Clapham High St SW4; admission free-£5; ✆ Clapham Common) Friendly gay bar with regular acts and a nightclub out the back.

Camden Crawl (www.thecamdencrawl.com; 1/2-day pass £30/50) Your chance to spot the next big thing in the music scene or witness a secret gig by an established act, with 28 of Camden's intimate venues given over to live music for two full days in April.

London Marathon (www.london-marathon.co.uk) Up to half a million spectators watch the whippet-thin champions and often bizarrely clad amateurs take to the streets in late April.

Trooping the Colour Celebrating the Queen's official birthday (in June), this ceremonial procession of troops, marching along the Mall for their monarch's inspection, is a pageantry overload.

Royal Academy Summer Exhibition (www.royal academy.org.uk; Royal Academy of Arts; adult/child £8/3) Running from mid-June to mid-August, this is an annual showcase of works submitted by artists from all over Britain, mercifully distilled to 1200 or so pieces.

Meltdown Festival (www.southbankcentre.co.uk/festivals -series/meltdown) Held late June, where the Southbank Centre hands over the curatorial reigns to a legend of contemporary music (such as David Bowie, Morrissey or Patti Smith) to pull together a full program of concerts, talks and films.

Wimbledon Lawn Tennis Championships (www .wimbledon.org; tickets by public ballot) Held at the end of June, the world's most splendid tennis event is as much about strawberries, cream and tradition as smashing balls.

Pride (www.pridelondon.org) The big event on the gay and lesbian calendar, a technicolour street parade heads through the West End in late June or early July, culminating in a concert in Trafalgar Sq.

Notting Hill Carnival (www.nottinghillcarnival.biz) Held over two days in August, this is Europe's largest and London's most vibrant outdoor carnival, where London's Caribbean community shows the city how to party. Unmissable and truly crazy.

SLEEPING

Take a deep breath and sit down before reading this section because no matter what your budget, London is a horribly pricey city to sleep in – one of the most expensive in the world, in fact. Anything below £80 per night for a double is pretty much 'budget', and at the top end, how does a £3500 penthouse sound? For this book we've defined the price categories for London differently than for the other chapters. Double rooms ranging between £80 and £150 per night are considered midrange; cheaper or more expensive options fall into the budget or the top-end categories respectively.

Ignore the scary money stuff for a minute London has a wonderful selection of interesting hotels, whether they be brimming with history or zany modern decor. Most of the ritzier places offer substantial discounts on the weekends, for advance bookings and at quiet times (if there is such a thing in London).

Public transport is exceptionally good, so you don't need to be sleeping at Buckingham Palace to be at the heart of things. However, if you're planning some late nights and don't fancy enduring the night buses (a consummate London experience, but one you'll want only once) it'll make sense not to wander too far from the action (see p161).

London's a noisy city, so expect a bit of the din to seep into your room. If you're a light sleeper, earplugs are a sensible precaution, as is requesting a room back from the street and higher up.

It's now becoming the norm for budget and midrange places to offer free wireless internet. The expensive places will offer it too, but often charge. Hostels tend to serve up free breakfast (of the toast and cereal variety). If your hotel charges for breakfast, check the prices; anything over £8 just isn't worth it when there are so many eateries to explore.

Budget accommodation is scattered about, with some good options in West London, Southwark, Victoria and King's Cross. For something a little nicer, check out Victoria, Bloomsbury, Fitzrovia, Bayswater and Earl's Court. If you've the cash to splash, consider Mayfair, the West End, Clerkenwell and Kensington.

Westminster & Pimlico

Handy to the big sights but lacking a strong sense of neighbourhood, the streets get prettier the further you stray from Victoria station. Despite being the queen's own hood, there are some surprisingly affordable options.

BUDGET

Astor Victoria Hostel (Map p107; ☎ 7834 3077; www .astorhostels.com; 71 Belgrave Rd SW1; dm £16-19, d & tw £60; 🖳 wi-fi; ❷ Pimlico) This cheap and cheerful hostel has plenty of mixed or women-only dorms but only a scattering of private rooms, so book early. There are two comfortable lounges with PCs, a fully equipped kitchen and weekly dinners for bonding over grub.

Morgan House (Map pp102-3; ☎ 7730 2384; www .morganhouse.co.uk; 120 Ebury St SW1; s/d/tw/tr without bathroom £52/72/72/92, with bathroom £86/92/92/112; ❷ Victoria) More homely than swanky, this pleasant Georgian house offers romantic iron beds (some a little saggy), chandeliers, period fireplaces, sparkling bathrooms and a full English breakfast.

MIDRANGE

Luna & Simone Hotel (Map p107; ☎ 7834 5897; www .lunasimonehotel.com; 47-49 Belgrave Rd SW1; s £45-65, d/tw/ tr/q £95/95/115/140; 🖳 wi-fi; ❷ Pimlico) The ensign of Luna (the moon) and Simone (the owner) is etched into the glass porch and this personal touch continues inside with the friendly service. The blue-and-yellow rooms aren't huge but they're clean and calming; the ones at the back are quieter. A full English breakfast is included.

Windermere Hotel (Map pp102-3; ☎ 7834 5163; www.windermere-hotel.co.uk; 142-144 Warwick Way SW1; s £95-134, d £119-144, tw £126-144, f £159; 🖳 wi-fi; ❷ Victoria) Chintzy but homely, this early-Victorian town house has 22 rooms, all traditionally British in decor. Lively floral curtains correspond with matching bedspreads, tartan headboards complement armchairs, and tables are draped in lace. Most have lacklustre but perfectly adequate en suites.

BOOKING SERVICES

It's possible to make same-day accommodation bookings for free at most tourist offices, and **Visit London** (☎ 08456 443010; www.visitlondonoffers.com) also has good deals.

At Home in London (☎ 8748 1943; www.athomeinlondon.co.uk) Can arrange B&B accommodation and charges percentage booking fees.

British Hotel Reservation Centre (☎ 7592 3055; www.bhrconline.com) Free online booking.

Lastminute (www.lastminute.com) Has kiosks at the Britain & London Visitor Centre (p95) and Victoria station.

London Homestead Services (☎ 7286 5115; www.lhslondon.com) Charges a 5% booking fee.

LondonTown (☎ 7437 4370; www.londontown.com) Hotel, hostel and B&B bookings.

Uptown Reservations (☎ 7937 2001; www.uptownres.co.uk) Books upmarket B&Bs, mainly around Chelsea and the West End.

YHA (☎ 01629-592700; www.yha.org.uk) Operates its own central reservations service, provided you give at least two weeks' notice.

B&B Belgravia (Map pp102-3; ☎ 7259 8570; www.bb-belgravia.com; 64-66 Ebury St SW1; s/d/tw/tr/q £99/115/125/145/155; ☐ wi-fi; ⊖ Victoria) This small hotel's unassuming facade belies a chic, contemporary interior that comprises stylish bathrooms and floor-to-ceiling dark-wood cupboards. The only noticeable design blip is the EasyJet-style orange staff uniform. Outside, the pretty courtyard garden is a suntrap.

Rubens at the Palace (Map pp104-5; ☎ 7834 6600; www.rubenshotel.com; 39 Buckingham Palace Rd SW1; s £129, d £139-279, ste £329-579; 🖭 ☐ wi-fi; ⊖ Victoria) Opposite Buckingham Palace, it's perhaps not surprising to find that Rubens is a firm favourite with Americans looking for that quintessential British experience. With decor and service as traditional as high tea, it doesn't disappoint. The rooms are octogenarian chic, full of heavy patterned fabrics, dark wood, thick drapes and crowns above the beds.

St James's & Mayfair

Home to some of London's most famous 'establishment' hotels (such as the Ritz and Claridges), you'll need to be seriously cashed up to consider staying here.

Brown's Hotel (Map pp108-9; ☎ 7493 6020; www.brownshotel.com; 30 Albemarle St W1; d £325-615, ste £840-3000; ☐ wi-fi; ⊖ Green Park) Stay here and you're in good company – Rudyard Kipling penned many of his works here, Kate Moss has frequented the spa and both Queen Victoria and Winston Churchill dropped in for tea. There's a lovely old-world feel to Browns, but without the snootiness of some others in the neighbourhood. The rooms have every modern comfort.

West End

This is the heart of the action, so naturally accommodation comes at a price, and a hefty one at that. A couple of hostels cater for would-be Soho hipsters of more modest means.

BUDGET

Oxford St YHA (Map pp108-9; ☎ 0845 371 9133; www.yha.org.uk; 14 Noel St W1; dm/tw £25/64; ☐ wi-fi; ⊖ Oxford Circus) In most respects, this is a bog-standard YHA hostel with tidy rooms and all the usual facilities (kitchen, TV room, laundry). What it's got going for it are a terrific (albeit noisy) location and decent views over London's rooftops from some of the rooms.

TOP END

Hazlitt's (Map pp108-9; ☎ 7434 1771; www.hazlittshotel.com; 6 Frith St W1; d/ste from £205/300; ☐ ; ⊖ Tottenham Court Rd) Staying in this charming Georgian house (1718) is a trip back into a time when four-poster beds and claw-footed baths were the norm for gentlefolk. Each of the individually decorated 23 rooms is packed with antiques and named after a personage connected with the house.

Haymarket Hotel (Map pp108-9; ☎ 7470 4000; www.haymarkethotel.com; 1 Suffolk Pl SW1; d £250-325, ste £395-3000; ☐ wi-fi; ⊖ Piccadilly Circus) The building was designed by John Nash (Buckingham Palace's main man) but the rest is Kit Kemp all the way (see boxed text, opposite). We love the gold loungers around the sunset-lit indoor swimming pool.

Soho Hotel (Map pp108-9; ☎ 7559 3000; www.sohohotel.com; 4 Richmond Mews W1; d £280-350, ste £385-2750; ☐ wi-fi; ⊖ Oxford Circus) Hello Kitty! This Kit Kemp–designed hotel (see boxed text, opposite) has a giant cat sculpture in a reception that looks like a psychedelic candy store; try to refrain from licking the walls.

Also recommended:

Covent Garden Hotel (Map pp108-9; ☎ 7806 1000; www.coventgardenhotel.co.uk; 10 Monmouth St WC2; d £235-330, ste £385-1150; 🖳 wi-fi; ⊖ Covent Garden) First-time guests get a complimentary massage in this well-positioned Firmdale hotel.

One Aldwych (Map pp108-9; ☎ 7300 1000; www .onealdwych.com; 1 Aldwych WC2; d £380-460, ste £625-1160; ⊠ 🖳 wi-fi; ⊖ Covent Garden) Granite bathrooms, long swimming pool with underwater music, majestic bar and restaurant, modern art, and a lift that changes colour to literally lift your mood.

Bloomsbury & Fitzrovia

Only one step removed from the West End and crammed with Georgian town-house conversions, these neighbourhoods are much more affordable. You'll find a stretch of lower-priced hotels along Gower St and on the pretty Cartwright Gardens crescent.

BUDGET

London Central YHA (Map pp104-5; ☎ 0845 371 9154; www.yha.org.uk; 104-108 Bolsover St W1; dm £19-32; 🖳 wi-fi; ⊖ Great Portland St) The newest and best of London's YHA hostels, everything's got that just-out-of-the-wrapper look and most of the four- to six-bed rooms have en suites. Communal space is lacking but there's a flash cafe-bar attached to reception.

Generator (Map pp98-9; ☎ 7388 7666; www.generator hostels.com/London; Compton Pl, 37 Tavistock Pl WC1; dm £20-25, s/tw/tr/q £70/70/75/100; 🖳 wi-fi; ⊖ Russell Sq) Lashings of primary colours and shiny metal are the hallmarks of this futuristic but fun hostel. This former police barracks has 850 beds; a bar that stays open until 2am and hosts quizzes, pool competitions, karaoke and DJs; safe-deposit boxes; and a large eating area but no kitchen. Come to party.

Ridgemount Private Hotel (Map pp104-5; ☎ 7636 1141; www.ridgemounthotel.co.uk; 65-67 Gower St WC1; s/d/tr/q without bathroom £42/58/78/92, with bathroom £54/75/93/104; 🖳 wi-fi; ⊖ Goodge St) There's a comfortable, welcoming feel at this old-fashioned, slightly chintzy place that's been in the same family for 40 years.

Arran House Hotel (Map pp104-5; ☎ 7636 2186; www.arranhotel-london.com; 77-79 Gower St WC1; s/d/tr/q without bathroom £50/77/95/101, with bathroom £60/100/118/122; 🖳 wi-fi; ⊖ Goodge St) Period features such as cornicing and fireplaces, a pretty pergola-decked back garden and a

comfy lounge with PCs and TV lift this hotel from the average to the attractive. Squashed en suites or shared bathrooms are the trade-off for these reasonable rates.

MIDRANGE

Jenkins Hotel (Map pp98-9; ☎ 7387 2067; www .jenkinshotel.demon.co.uk; 45 Cartwright Gardens WC1; s/d/tr with bathroom from £72/89/105; ⊖ Russell Sq) This modest hotel has featured in the TV series of Agatha Christie's *Poirot*. Rooms are small but the hotel has charm.

Crescent Hotel (Map pp98-9; ☎ 7387 1515; www .crescenthoteloflondon.com; 49-50 Cartwright Gardens WC1; s £49-81, d/tw/tr/q £97/97/110/120; 🖳 ; ⊖ Russell Sq) One of the cheaper options on the crescent overlooking Cartwright Gardens, there's a homely feel to this humble hotel, despite the odd saggy bed.

Arosfa Hotel (Map pp104-5; ☎ 7636 2115; www .arosfalondon.com; 83 Gower St WC1E; s £60-65, d/tr/q £90/102/110; 🖳 wi-fi; ⊖ Goodge St) While the decor of the immaculately presented rooms is unremarkable, Arosfa's guest lounge has been blinged up with chandeliers, clear plastic chairs and a free internet terminal. Recent refurbishments have added en suites to all 15 bedrooms, but they're tiny (putting the 'closet' back into water closet).

Hotel Cavendish (Map pp104-5; ☎ 7636 9079; www .hotelcavendish.com; 75 Gower St WC1E; s £85, d £105-130, tr/q £120/140; 🖳 wi-fi; ⊖ Goodge St) Following a

---

THE KIT KEMP CLUB

Kit Kemp's interiors purr loudly rather than whisper. She's waved her magically deranged wand over all the hotels of London's boutique Firmdale chain – including Covent Garden (left), Haymarket (opposite), Soho (opposite), Charlotte St (p140), Knightsbridge (p149) and Number Sixteen (p149) – creating bold, playful spaces full of zany fabrics, crazy sculpture and sheer luxury. Yet somehow she manages to create an old-fashioned feel from a thoroughly modern sensibility. While nonconformity is the norm, key values are shared throughout the chain: the staff is welcoming, guest lounges are inviting spaces with honesty bars, each bedroom features a dressmaker's dummy (some in miniature) and each bathroom is crafted from beautiful grey-flecked granite.

complete refurbishment a few years back, bedrooms have a contemporary look, with flat-screen TVs, and all are equipped with compact en suite shower rooms (some have pretty tiles and bumper mirrors). The two gardens at the back are a good place to catch some rays.

Harlingford Hotel (Map pp98-9; ☎ 7387 1551; www .harlingfordhotel.com; 61-63 Cartwright Gardens WC1; s/d/tw/ tr/q £85/110/110/125/135; ☐ wi-fi; ✆ Russel Sq) This family-run hotel sports refreshing, upbeat decor such as bright-green mosaic-tiled bathrooms (with trendy sinks), fuchsia bedspreads and colourful paintings. Lots of stairs and no lift – consider requesting a 1st-floor room.

TOP END

Charlotte Street Hotel (Map pp108-9; ☎ 7806 2000; www.charlottestreethotel.com; 15 Charlotte St W1; d £210-295, ste £350-950; ☐ wi-fi; ✆ Goodge St) Another of the Firmdale clan (see boxed text, p139), this one's a favourite with media types, with a small gym and a screening room.

Sanderson (Map pp108-9; ☎ 7300 1400; www.sand ersonlondon.com; 50 Berners St W1; d £305-875, ste £611-925, apt £2500-3500; ⊠ ☐ wi-fi; ✆ Goodge St) Liberace meets Philippe Starck in an 18th-century French bordello – and that's just the reception. A 3D space scene in the lift shuttles you into darkened corridors leading to blindingly white rooms complete with sleigh beds, oil paintings hung on the ceiling, en suites behind glass walls and pink silk curtains. Très chic.

Holborn & Clerkenwell

The availability of accommodation hasn't kept pace with Clerkenwell's revival, but it's still a great area to stay in. The best pickings aren't exactly cheap.

Rookery (Map pp104-5; ☎ 7336 0931; www.rookery hotel.com; Peter's Lane, Cowcross St EC1; s £175, d £210-495; ☐ wi-fi; ✆ Farringdon) Taking its name from London's notorious slums (Fagin's house in *Oliver Twist* was set a few streets west), this antique-strewn luxury hotel recreates an early 19th-century ambience with none of the attendant grime or crime. For a bird's-eye view of St Paul's, book the Rook's Nest but be warned: Fagin never had a lift.

Zetter Hotel (Map pp98-9; ☎ 7324 4444; www .thezetter.com; 86-88 Clerkenwell Rd EC1M; d £188-400; ☐ wi-fi; ✆ Farringdon) A slick, beautiful 21st-century conversion of a Victorian warehouse. The furnishings are an enticing blend of old and new, and the facilities cutting edge. You can even choose the colour of your room's lighting.

Malmaison (Map pp104-5; ☎ 7012 3700; www .malmaison.com; 18-21 Charterhouse Sq EC1; s from £205, d £225-250, ste £295-475; ☐ wi-fi; ✆ Farringdon) Given Malmaison's grand frontage onto a hidden square, the *Alice in Wonderland* lobby of chessboard carpet, black seats that look like pawns and supersized chairs are a quirky surprise. Once in the rooms, the look is more classical with contemporary fittings in neutral shades.

The City

Bristling with bankers during the week, you can often pick up a considerable bargain in the City on weekends.

St Paul's YHA (Map pp104-5; ☎ 0845 371 9012; www .yha.org.uk; 36 Carter Lane EC4; dm £27; ☐ wi-fi; ✆ St Paul's) The former St Paul's Cathedral Choir Boys School is located just notes away from the cathedral itself. After the lovely facade, the interiors are a bit of a let-down, but the dorms are small and have their own TVs and lockers. There's a licensed cafeteria but no kitchen.

Threadneedles (Map p112; ☎ 7657 8080; www .theetoncollection.com; 5 Threadneedle St EC2; d £370-499, ste £582-617; ⊠ ☐ wi-fi; ✆ Bank) The incredible stained-glass dome in the lobby points to its former status as a bank HQ. Today the bar and restaurant are still popular with suits, but the atmosphere is chic. At weekends this top-end spot is an absolute bargain.

Hoxton, Shoreditch & Spitalfields

It's always had a rough-edged reputation, but London's East End is being gentrified faster than you can say 'awrigh' guv'. Staying here, you'll be handy to some of London's best bars.

ourpick Hoxton (Map p112; ☎ 7550 1000; www.hoxton hotels.com; 81 Great Eastern St; d & tw £59-189; ⊠ ☐ wi-fi; ✆ Old St) A novel approach to pricing means that while all the rooms are identical, the first ones on any given day are offered at £59: an absolute steal for a hotel of this calibre. Rooms are a decent size, scrupulously clean, have comfy beds with quality linen and a well-designed desk space where you can access the internet through the TV.

South of the Thames

Just south of the river is good if you want to immerse yourself in workaday London and still be central.

(Continued on page 149)

Outdoor England

A post box welcomes you to Great Langdale (p722), Lakes District National Park

DAVID TOMLINSON

What's the best way to get off the beaten track as you travel around England? Simple: enjoy some outdoor activities. Fresh air is good for your body and soul, of course, and becoming *actively* involved in the country's way of life is much more rewarding than staring at it through a camera lens or car window.

Walking and cycling are the most popular and accessible of all outdoor activities, because they open up some beautiful corners of the country and can be done virtually on a whim. On foot or two wheels you can enjoy relaxed saunters or work up a sweat on long tours, amble across plains or conquer lofty mountains. There's something for young and old, and these activities are often perfect for families.

England supplies the goods for thrill-seekers too. The coast has excellent spots for surfing and sailing, while rock climbers can test their skills on sheer sea cliffs or inland crags, and that's before we get onto cutting-edge activities like mountain boarding and kitesurfing.

So pack your bags and your sense of adventure. Whatever your budget, a walk or ride through the English countryside – and possibly something involving more adrenaline – could be a highlight of your trip.

WALKING

England is a crowded place, so open areas are highly valued and every weekend millions of people go walking. It might be a short riverside stroll or a major hike over mountain ranges, or anything in between. You could do a lot worse than joining them.

PRACTICAL DETAILS

These pages will hopefully get you in the mood for walking or cycling in England, and possibly for trying some other (more hair-raising) activities. For practical details, and a few more outdoor ideas, see the Directory chapter (p787).

Not a bad view from Exmoor (p361)
MARK DAFFEY

The joy of walking in England comes from the sense of freedom provided by the 'right of way' network – public paths and tracks across private property. If you come from a country where private land is jealously guarded with barbed wire, this can be a major revelation; in England you can follow a right of way through crop fields, paddocks, woods, even farmhouse yards, as long as you keep to the route and do no damage.

Every village and town is surrounded by a web of footpaths, while most open country is crossed by paths and tracks. You can walk from place to place in true backpacker style, or base yourself in one spot for a week or so and go out on day walks to explore the surrounding countryside. The options are limitless.

Where to Walk

The heart and soul of walking in England is the Lake District (p704), a wonderful area of soaring peaks, endless views, deep valleys and, of course, beautiful lakes. For something a little gentler, green valleys and rolling hills make the Yorkshire Dales (p605) one of the most popular walking areas in England.

Further north, keen walkers love the starkly beautiful moors of Northumberland (p774). The high cliffs and vast empty beaches on the nearby coast are less daunting but just as dramatic – perfect for wild seaside strolls.

The gem of central England is the Cotswolds (p240) – classic English countryside, where gentle paths meander through neat fields and mature woodland, past farms and pretty villages spotted with cottages of honey-coloured stone.

The dales of North Yorkshire (p621)   STEPHEN SAKS

Heading southwest, Dartmoor (p387) is high and wild, with rounded hills dotted with granite outcrops called 'tors' and valleys full of Bronze Age sites and other ancient remains. Not far away, Exmoor (p361) has heather-covered hills cut by deep valleys and edged by spectacular cliffs and great beaches.

South of London are two ranges of broad, chalky hills – the North Downs and South Downs (p173) – with the tranquil farmland of the Weald in between. Great for easy walking, and all within easy reach of the capital or the lively resorts on the coast.

In the deep south lies the New Forest (p289). Visitors to England love this name, as the area is more than 1000 years old and there aren't *that* many trees – but the beautiful open areas of gorse and grassland are ideal for easy strolls.

The Seven Sisters Cliffs, one of the sights along the South Downs Way (p173)   DAVID TOMLINSON

Just across the water is the Isle of Wight (p293), a great spot if you're new to walking, or simply not looking for high peaks and wilderness. Many routes are signposted, and you can always get back to your starting point using the island's excellent bus service.

Long-Distance Walks

Many walkers savour the chance of completing one of England's famous longdistance routes, but you don't have to do them end-to-end. Many people walk just a section for a day or two, or use the main route as a basis for loops exploring the surrounding area.

England boasts 12 national trails, with signposting and maintenance ideal for beginners, but there are hundreds more to choose from – some world-famous, others more obscure. Our favourites include the following:

Coast to Coast Walk (190 miles) A top-quality trail across northern England, through spectacular scenery of valleys, plains, mountains, dales and moors.

Cotswold Way (102 miles) A fascinating walk through classic picture-postcard countryside with smatterings of English history.

Cumbria Way (68 miles) A fine hike through Lake District valleys, with breathtaking mountain views.

Hadrian's Wall (84 miles) In the footsteps of the legions, an epic stride across northern England.

Pennine Way (256 miles) The granddaddy of them all, along the mountainous spine of northern England.

South West Coast Path (610 miles) A roller-coaster romp past beaches, bays, shipwrecks, seaside resorts, fishing villages and cliff-top castles.

Thames Path (173 miles) A journey of contrasts beside England's best-known river, from rural Gloucestershire to the heart of London.

CYCLING

A bike is the perfect mode of transport for exploring back-road England. Once you escape the busy main highways, a vast network of quiet country lanes winds through fields and peaceful villages, ideal for cycle-touring. Mountain bikers can go further into the wilds on the tracks and bridleways that cross England's farmlands, forests and high moors.

Whether on- or off-road is your thing, the options are endless. You can cruise through flat or rolling landscapes, taking it easy and stopping for cream teas, or thrash all day through hilly areas, revelling in steep ascents

Resting up in the North York Moors (p642)

Descending to Patterdale (p731)

RICHARD I'ANSON

FIRST STEPS

So you've arrived in a new area, and want to know more about local options for walking or other outdoor activities.

Step 1: Flip to the start of the regional chapter for an overview of the best opportunities in that area.

Step 2: Find the local tourist office to pick up leaflets and maps, find out about bike hire or guided walks, and get info on other activities, such as surf schools and riding stables.

Step 3: Head out, and enjoy!

and swooping downhill sections. You can cycle from place to place, camping or staying in B&Bs (many of which are cyclist-friendly), or you can base yourself in one place for a few days and go out on rides in different directions. With a map and a sense of adventure, the highways and byways of England are yours.

Where to Cycle

While you can cycle anywhere in England, car traffic can be a problem on summer weekends in popular spots, and the hills in some areas can be daunting if you're not a regular cyclist, so the counties of Norfolk (p456) and Suffolk (p446) are a great place to start. The landscape is generally flat, with quiet lanes winding through farmland and picturesque villages, past rivers, lakes and welcoming country pubs.

GRANT DIXON

Join the cyclists of Painswick (p253)
GLENN BEANLAND

The Cotswolds (p240) is another mostly rural area with good cycling options. From the western side of the hills you get fantastic views over the Severn Valley, but you wouldn't want to go up and down the escarpment too often. The Marches (p527), where England borders Wales, is another pastoral delight, with good minor roads relatively free of cars, plus some off-road options in the hills.

Beautiful Cornwall and Devon enjoy the best of the English climate, but the rugged landscape means tough days in the saddle for beginners. West-country neighbours Somerset, Dorset and Wiltshire have less-demanding hills (plus a few steep valleys to keep you on your toes) and a beautiful network of quiet lanes, making the area perfect for leisurely cycle-touring. Off-road fans can head for the tracks on Dartmoor (p387) and the Quantock (p359) or Mendip Hills (p355).

In Hampshire, the New Forest (p289) is especially good for on- and off-road rides, while in Sussex the South Downs (p173) offer numerous mountain-bike options.

And finally, northern England. It's no accident that many of England's top racing cyclists come from this area – the mountain roads make an excellent training ground. Derbyshire's Peak District (p512) is very popular for mountain biking and road cycling, although (or because) the hills are quite steep in places. Leisurely options include cycle routes cutting through the landscape along disused railways – dramatic and effortless at the same time. The North York Moors (p641) and Yorkshire Dales (p605) also offer exhilarating cycle-touring and mountain biking. Once again, these areas are hilly and some routes are strenuous, but the superb scenery of 'God's own country' makes it well worth the effort.

OTHER ACTIVITIES

While walking and cycling can be done at the drop of a hat, many other activities need a bit more organisation – and often a specialist kit, guides or instructors. Coasteering, for example, is not something you can just go off and do on your own. Ask at tourist offices about local operators and adventure centres.

Coasteering

If a simple cliff-top walk doesn't cut the mustard, then coasteering might appeal. It's like mountaineering, but instead of going up a mountain, you go sideways along a rocky coast, with waves breaking around your feet. And if the rock gets too steep, no problem – you jump in and start swimming. The mix of sheer rock, sandy beaches and warm water make Cornwall and Devon prime coasteering spots.

Horse Riding & Pony Trekking

There's a theory that humans are genetically programmed to absorb the world at a horse's walking pace – it's all to do with our nomadic ancestors, apparently. Seeing England from horseback is certainly highly recommended. In rural areas and national parks like Dartmoor (p387) and Northumberland (p774), riding centres cater to all levels of proficiency – with ponies for kids and beginners, and horses for the more experienced.

Kitebuggying

Bring together a wing-shaped parachute, three wheels, a good breeze, and – whoosh – you're picking up serious speed across the beach. Welcome to the world of kitebuggying. Often available wherever you find big stretches of flat sand, a good place to start is Burnham Deepdale (p466) in Norfolk, a great backpacker-friendly base for other activities too.

Mountain boarding, Wiltshire (p314)
RICHARD SMITH /ALAMY

Mountain Boarding & Kiteboarding

Imagine hurtling down a grassy hillside on a gigantic skateboard with four oversize wheels, and you've pretty much got mountain boarding. If that's not enough, add a wing-shaped parachute and it's kiteboarding – so the wind can pull you around whenever gravity gives up. There are mountain boarding centres in Yorkshire, Derbyshire, Shropshire and Cornwall (among other places), but you can do it practically anywhere where there's a grassy slope – as long as you've got the landowner's permission, of course.

Sailing near Devon's Plymouth (p383) is one of many water-based options in England
DAVID TOMLINSON

Rock Climbing & Mountaineering

England's main centre for long multi-pitch routes (as well as some fine short routes) is the Lake District. Other popular climbing areas are the Peak District and Yorkshire Dales. England also offers the exhilaration of sea-cliff climbing, most notably in Cornwall. Nothing makes you concentrate harder on finding the next hold than waves crashing 30m below!

A Peak District climb (p513)

ANDERS BLOMQVIST

Sailing & Windsurfing

England's nautical heritage means sailing is a very popular pastime, in everything from tiny dinghies to ocean-going yachts. In recent years there's been a massive surge in windsurfing, too. Favourite spots include the coasts of Norfolk and Suffolk, southeast England, Devon, Cornwall and the Isle of Wight. There are also many inland lakes and reservoirs, ideal for training, racing or just pottering.

Surfing & Kitesurfing

If you've come from the other side of the world, you'll be delighted to learn that summer water temperatures in England are roughly equivalent to winter temperatures in southern Australia. But wetsuit-protected, you'll have many excellent surf opportunities. Top of the list is the Atlantic-facing west coast of Cornwall and Devon – Newquay (p400) is the surf centre, with all the trappings from Kombi vans to bleached hair – and there are smaller surf scenes (with less posing) in Norfolk and Yorkshire.

If regular surfing doesn't offer enough air time, strap on a wing-shaped parachute and let the wind do the work. It's called kitesurfing and is one of the fastest-growing water sports in the world. Brisk winds, decent waves and great beaches make Cornwall a favourite spot, but it's possible all round the English coastline.

Braving the cold waters to face the surf in Cornwall (p395)

LEE SEARLE /

(Continued from page 140)

BUDGET

Dover Castle Hostel (Map pp96-7; ☎ 7403 7773; www.dovercastlehostel.com; 6a Great Dover St; dm £10-16; 🖳 wi-fi; ✚ Borough) If living in a pub is your fantasy, this is your chance. It's a modest affair (what do you expect for a tenner?), but the dorms are tidy, freshly painted and get loads of natural light. If you fancy a sound sleep, bring earplugs or drink yourself into oblivion downstairs.

St Christopher's Village (Map p112; ☎ 7407 1856; www .st-christophers.co.uk; 163 Borough High St SE1; dm £16-24, d & tw £52; 🖳 ; ✚ London Bridge) With three locations on the same street sharing a main reception, there's quite a range of experiences on offer. The main hub is the Village, a huge, up-for-it party hostel, with a club that opens until 4am on the weekends and a spa pool on the roof terrace. It's either heaven or hell, depending on what side of 30 you're on. The others are much smaller, quieter and, frankly, more pleasant. St Christopher's Inn (121 Borough High St) is situated above a very nice pub, while the Orient (59 Borough High St), above a cafe, has a separate women's floor. For these last two, you still need to book and check in at the Village.

MIDRANGE

Mad Hatter Hotel (Map pp104-5; ☎ 7401 9222; www .fullershotels.com/frames/1044; 3-7 Stamford St SE1; r £145-165; ✚ Southwark) There's nothing particularly mad (or even unusual) about it, but this is a good basic hotel with decent-sized rooms and unassuming decor hiding behind a lovely Victorian frontage. Prices fall well below £100 on weekends.

Southwark Rose Hotel (Map p112; ☎ 7015 1480; www.southwarkrosehotel.co.uk; 47 Southwark Bridge Rd SE1; d weekdays/weekends £180/105, ste £245; 🔀 🖳 wi-fi; ✚ Borough) Though it's somewhat pricey during the week, this business hotel drops its rates considerably to attract the weekender visitors.

Chelsea, Kensington & Knightsbridge

Classy Chelsea and Kensington offer easy access to the museums and fashion retailers. It's all a bit sweetie-darling, along with the prices.

BUDGET

Holland House YHA (Map pp100-1; ☎ 0845 371 9122; www.yha.org.uk; Holland Walk W8; dm £15-25; 🖳 wi-fi;

TOP FIVE SWANKY STAYS

▪ **Browns** (p138)

▪ **One Aldwych** (p139)

▪ **Hempel** (p150)

▪ **Sanderson** (p140)

▪ Any of the **Firmdale hotels** (see boxed text, p139)

✚ High St Kensington) Built out of the bombed-out remains of a 1607 mansion in the heart of Holland Park, there's an unfortunate school-camp vibe to the large dorm rooms. However, it's well looked after and the cheapest option for miles around, and the setting is unforgettable.

MIDRANGE

Vicarage Private Hotel (Map pp100-1; ☎ 7229 4030; www.londonvicaragehotel.com; 10 Vicarage Gate W8; s/d/ tr/q without bathroom £52/88/109/116, with bathroom £88/114/145/160; 🖳 wi-fi; ✚ High St Kensington) If you were staying here 15 years ago, Princess Di would have been your neighbour – you can see Kensington Palace from the doorstep. This grand Victorian town house looks onto a cul-de-sac, so you shouldn't have a problem with noise in the simply furnished rooms. The cheaper ones (without bathrooms) are on floors three and four, so you may get a view as well as a workout.

TOP END

Number Sixteen (Map pp102-3; ☎ 7589 5232; www .numbersixteenhotel.co.uk; 16 Sumner Pl SW7; s £120-165, d £200-270; 🖳 wi-fi; ✚ South Kensington) The least pricey of the Firmdale hotels (see boxed text, p139), with a lovely garden tucked away.

Knightsbridge Hotel (Map pp100-1; ☎ 7584 6300; www.knightsbridgehotel.com; 10 Beaufort Gdn SW3; s £170-185, d £210-295, ste £345-595; 🖳 wi-fi; ✚ Knightsbridge) Another Firmdale (see boxed text, p139), this one's on a quiet, tree-lined cul-de-sac very close to Harrods. It's the most restrained of the chain.

Gore (Map pp100-1; ☎ 7584 6601; www.gorehotel.com; 190 Queen's Gate SW7; r £187-390; 🖳 wi-fi; ✚ Gloucester Rd) A short stroll from the Royal Albert Hall, the Gore serves up British grandiosity (antiques, carved four-posters, a secret bathroom in the Tudor room) with a large slice of camp. How else could you describe the Judy Garland room (complete with ruby slippers) and the Nellie room (Dame Nellie Melba, dahling), named after famous former occupants?

Levin (Map pp100-1; ☎ 7589 6286; www.thelevinhotel .co.uk; 28 Basil St SW3; d £235-445; ⊖ Knightsbridge) As close as you can get to sleeping in Harrods, the Levin knows its market. Despite the baby-blue colour scheme, there's a subtle femininity to the decor, although it's far too elegant to be flouncey.

Notting Hill, Bayswater & Paddington

Don't be fooled by Julia Roberts and Hugh Grant's shenanigans, Notting Hill and the areas immediately north of Hyde Park are as shabby as they are chic. There are some nice gated squares surrounded by Georgian town houses, but the area is better exemplified by the Notting Hill Carnival (p137), where the West Indian community who made the area their home from the 1950s party up big time.

Scruffy Paddington has lots of cheap hotels, with a major strip of unremarkable ones along Sussex Gardens, worth checking if you're short on options.

MIDRANGE

Vancouver Studios (Map pp100-1; ☎ 7243 1270; www .vancouverstudios.co.uk; 30 Prince's Sq W2; apt £85-170; ▣ wi-fi; ⊖ Bayswater) Technically apartments, it's only the addition of kitchenettes and a self-service laundry that differentiate these smart but reasonably priced studios (sleeping from one to three people) from a regular Victorian town-house hotel. In spring, the garden is filled with colour and fragrance.

New Linden Hotel (Map pp100-1; ☎ 7221 4321; www .newlinden.co.uk; 58-60 Leinster Sq W2; s £95, d £129-179, tr/ f/ste £210/150/189; ▣ wi-fi; ⊖ Bayswater) Cramming in a fair amount of style for the price, this terrace-house hotel has interesting modern art in the rooms and carved wooden fixtures from India combined with elegant wallpaper in the guest lounge. The quiet location, helpful staff and monsoon shower heads in the deluxe rooms make this an excellent proposition.

TOP END

Hempel (Map pp100-1; ☎ 7298 9000; www.the-hempel .co.uk; 31-35 Craven Hill Gardens; d £239-315, ste £319-1345; ▣ wi-fi; ⊖ Bayswater) As soon as you enter the expansive all-white lobby with sunken seating areas, supermodern fireplaces and dramatic ceiling-grazing flower arrangement, you know you're in for something special. Created by Anouska Hempel, every detail is a feat of superb design, from the Zen garden to the minimalist but luxurious rooms.

North London
EUSTON & KING'S CROSS
While hardly a salubrious location, King's Cross is handy to absolutely everything and has some excellent budget options.

Ashlee House (Map pp98-9; ☎ 7833 9400; www .ashleehouse.co.uk; 261-265 Grays Inn Rd; dm £21-24, s/tw/tr £57/76/76; ▣ ; ⊖ Kings Cross) This hostel is a cheery surprise in a gritty but central location. There's a large tube map and London scenes on the walls, green dice tables in the small lounge, bright paintwork in the compact rooms and stripy duvets on the blue bunk beds.

Clink (Map pp98-9; ☎ 7183 9400; www.clinkhostel .com; 78 Kings Cross Rd; dm £21-28, tw with/without bathroom £70/60, d/tr £70/78; ▣ wi-fi; ⊖ Kings Cross) If anyone can think of a more right-on London place to stay than the courthouse where The Clash went on trial, please let us know. You can watch TV from the witness box or sleep in the cells, but the majority of the rooms are custom-built and quite comfortable.

Jesmond Dene Hotel (Map pp98-9; ☎ 7837 4654; www.jesmonddenehostel.co.uk; 27 Argyle St; s/d/tw/tr/q from £50/60/60/85/120; ▣ wi-fi; ⊖ Kings Cross) A surprisingly pleasant option for a place so close to busy Kings Cross station, this modest hotel has clean but small rooms, some of which share bathrooms. A full English breakfast is included in the price.

HAMPSTEAD & HIGHGATE
A little further out but still in transport Zone 2, the following are excellent options within walking distance of Hampstead Heath.

Palmers Lodge (Map pp96-7; ☎ 7483 8470; www .palmerslodge.co.uk; 40 College Cres NW3; dm £15-22, tw £46-50, d £52; ▣ wi-fi ℗ ; ⊖ Swiss Cottage) Reminiscent of a period murder mystery (in a good way), this former children's hospital has bags of character. Listed by English Heritage, it's stuffed with cornicing, moulded ceilings, original fireplaces and imposing wooden panelling. Ceilings are high, rooms are spacious, there's a chapel bar with pews, a grand stairway and a roomy lounge. Privacy curtains make the 28-bed men's dorm bearable (imagine you're in the hold of a pirate ship), but they don't shut out the amorous noises in the couples dorm.

Hampstead Village Guesthouse (Map pp96-7; ☎ 7435 8679; www.hampsteadguesthouse.com; 2 Kemplay

Rd NW3; s £55-75, d £80-95, apt £100-175; 🖳 wi-fi; ➔ Hampstead) Eclectic, cluttered and thoroughly charming, this grand Victorian house has an easy-going hostess, comfy beds and a delightful back garden. There's also a studio flat, which can accommodate up to five people.

Greenwich

If you'd rather keep the bustle of central London at arm's length and nightclubbing is your idea of hell, Greenwich offers a villagey ambience and some great old pubs to explore.

BUDGET

St Christopher's Inn (Map p111; ☎ 8858 3591; www .st-christophers.co.uk; 189 Greenwich High Rd SE10; dm £18-22, tw £44-50; 🖳 wi-fi; 🚇 /DLR Greenwich) The nicest of the St Christopher's chain, this lovely old Georgian block is right by the station, with bright six- to eight-bed dorms and bunkstyle twins. The downstairs pub is a nicer place to hang out in than the claustrophobic basement lounge.

MIDRANGE

St Alfege's (Map p111; ☎ 8853 4337; www.st-alfeges.co.uk; 16 St Alfege Passage SE10; s/d £60/90; 🖳 wi-fi; DLR Cutty Sark) Both the house and the host have personality plus, so much so that they were featured on TV's *Hotel Inspector* series. The two double rooms are elegant and comfortable, but the single would suit the vertically challenged and going to the toilet in the wardrobe might take some getting used to.

Harbour Master's House (Map p111; ☎ 8293 9597; http://website.lineone.net/~harbourmaster; 20 Ballast Quay SE10; d £85; 🚇 Maze Hill) The 1855 building is Grade 2-listed and perfectly positioned by the Thames, but don't expect views from this self-contained flat in the vaulted cellar. However, the windows let in natural light and it's great value for its size, with a large lounge and separate kitchen/dining area.

West London

Earl's Court is lively, cosmopolitan and so popular with travelling Antipodeans it's been nicknamed Kangaroo Valley. There are no real sights, but it does have inexpensive digs and an infectious holiday atmosphere.

BUDGET

Barmy Badger Backpackers (Map pp102-3; ☎ 7370 5213; www.barmybadger.com; 17 Longridge Rd SW5; dm £16-18, d & tw £38; 🖳 wi-fi; ➔ Earl's Court) A humble but friendly hostel in a big old house, most of the rooms (including the dorms) have their own toilet. There's a big kitchen and a small garden out the back.

our pick **Globetrotter Inn** (Map pp96-7; ☎ 8746 3112; www.globetrotterinn.com; Ashlar Ct, Ravenscourt Gardens W6; dm £20-24, d & tw £60; 🖳 ; ➔ Stamford Brook) At the far reaches of Zone 2 (so still relatively central), this former nurses' home inhabits an attractive art-deco building in a leafy part of West London. It's certainly not boutique (there are 390 beds), but high ceilings and an attractive central lawn with a fountain give a sense of space, and personal reading lights and curtains in the dorms allow extra privacy.

MIDRANGE

Barclay House (Map pp102-3; ☎ 7384 3390; www.bar clayhouselondon.com; 21 Barclay Rd SW6; s/d £68/88, apt £135-200; 🖳 wi-fi; ➔ Fulham Broadway) A proper homestay B&B, the two comfy bedrooms in this charming Victorian town house share a bathroom and an exceptionally welcoming hostess. You'll be well set up to conquer London with helpful tips, maps, umbrellas and a full stomach. There's also a self-contained, two-bedroom apartment downstairs.

Rushmore Hotel (Map pp102-3; ☎ 7370 3839; www .rushmore-hotel.co.uk; 11 Trebovir Rd SW5; s £69-79, d & tw £89-99, tr/q £115/139; 🖳 wi-fi; ➔ Earl's Court) The soft pastel colours, draped fabrics and simple designs of this modest hotel create a cheery, welcoming atmosphere, heightened by the friendly family that runs the joint. There's no lift, so a complimentary workout is provided for those on the upper floors. The double rooms can be tight but the twins have a bit more space.

Twenty Nevern Square (Map pp102-3; ☎ 7565 9555; www.twentynevernsquare.co.uk; 20 Nevern Sq SW5; s £79-140, d £85-189; 🖳 wi-fi; ➔ Earl's Court) An Ottoman theme runs through this contemporary town house hotel, where a mix of wooden furniture, luxurious fabrics and natural light helps maximise space even though the cheaper bedrooms are not particularly large.

base2stay (Map pp102-3; ☎ 0845 262 8000; www .base2stay.com; 25 Courtfield Gardens SW5; s £93, d £107-127, tw £127; 🖳 wi-fi; ➔ Earl's Court) With smart decor, power showers, flat-screen TVs with internet access and artfully concealed kitchenettes, this boutique establishment feels like a four-star hotel without the hefty price tag.

Airports

Yotel (☎ 7100 1100; www.yotel.com; r per 4/5/6/7-24 hr £38/45/53/59; ☐ wi-fi) Gatwick (**South Terminal**); Heathrow (**Terminal 4**) The best news for early-morning flyers since coffee-vending machines, Yotel's smart 'cabins' offer pint-sized luxury: comfy beds, soft lights, internet-connected TVs, monsoon showers and fluffy towels. Swinging cats isn't recommended, but when is it ever?

EATING

Dining out in London has become so fashionable that you can hardly open a menu without banging into some celebrity chef or restaurateur. Unfortunately, this doesn't automatically guarantee quality – food and service can be hit and miss regardless of price tag. In this section, we steer you towards restaurants and cafes distinguished by their location, value for money, unique features, original settings and, of course, good food. Vegetarians needn't worry; London has a host of dedicated meat-free joints, while most others offer at least a token dish.

Westminster & Pimlico

There's very little action around these parts at night and those restaurants that are worth the detour will set you back a few quid.

our pick **Olivomare** (Map pp104-5; ☎ 7730 9022; 10 Lower Belgrave St SW1; mains £14-19; ⟨Y⟩ lunch & dinner Mon-Sat; ✸ Victoria) The Sardinian seaside comes to Belgravia in a dazzling white dining room with flavoursome seafood dishes and authentic wines. The grilled sea bass with olives and tomato is a treat and the service impeccable.

Thomas Cubitt (Map pp102-3; ☎ 7730 6060; 44 Elizabeth St SW1; mains £16-21; ✸ Victoria) The bar below gets rammed to the impressively high rafters with the swanky Belgravia set, but don't let that put you off this excellent, elegant dining room. The culinary focus is thoroughly British and deftly executed. The downstairs menu is cheaper (£9 to £14).

St James's & Mayfair

Like on the Monopoly board, if you land on Mayfair you may have to sell a house (to afford to eat here).

Sketch (Map pp108-9; ☎ 0870 777 4488; 9 Conduit St W1; Parlour mains £4-14, Gallery mains £11-27, Lecture Room 2-course lunch/8-course dinner £30/90; ✸ Oxford Circus) A design enthusiast's wet dream, with shimmering white rooms, video projections, designer Louis XIV chairs and toilet cubicles

---

TOP FIVE BLOW THE INHERITANCE

- **Gordon Ramsay** (p157)
- Lecture Room at **Sketch** (left)
- **Hibiscus** (below)
- **Hakkasan** (p154)
- **Nobu** (below)

---

shaped like eggs. And that's just the Gallery, which becomes a buzzy restaurant and bar at night. The ground-floor Parlour has decadent cakes and decor, but is surprisingly affordable; perfect for breakfast, or afternoon tea served on fine bone china. The swanky Lecture Room upstairs is the realm of three-Michelin-starred chef Pierre Gagnaire, whose book *Reinventing French Cuisine* gives a hint of what to expect.

Nobu (Map pp104-5; ☎ 7447 4747; Metropolitan Hotel, 19 Old Park Ln W1; dishes £10-26; ✸ Hyde Park Corner) One of London's most famous eateries, Nobu's dining room is surprisingly unremarkable but it does have nice views over Hyde Park. It's nonetheless out of this world when it comes to exquisitely prepared and presented Japanese dishes. Ordering the sublime lunchtime bento box (£28) is a sensible way of limiting the financial pain, especially compared to the £50 to £90 chef's choices.

Wild Honey (Map pp108-9; ☎ 7758 9160; 12 St George St W1; mains £16-22; ✸ Oxford Circus) If you fancy a swanky evening at a top Mayfair restaurant without breaking the bank, Wild Honey offers an excellent value pretheatre menu (£19 for three courses). Of course, the danger is that once you're ensconced in this elegant dining room, you won't be able to resist the delights of the full Modern European menu.

Tamarind (Map pp104-5; ☎ 7629 3561; 20 Queen St W1; mains £16-28; ✸ Green Park) London's only Michelin-starred Indian restaurant serves up mouth-watering spicy classics. The set lunches are a good deal (two-/three-courses £17/19).

Hibiscus (Map pp108-9; ☎ 7629 2999; 29 Maddox St W1; 3-course lunch/dinner £25/60; ✸ Oxford Circus) Claude and Claire Bosi have generated an avalanche of praise from London critics since moving their Michelin-starred restaurant from Shropshire to Mayfair. Expect adventurous French and English cuisine in an elegant dining room.

West End

Soho and Covent Garden are the gastronomic heart of London, with stacks of restaurants and cuisines to choose from at budgets to suit both booze hounds and theatre-goers. If you're craving a decent coffee, this is the place to come.

BUDGET

Nordic Bakery (Map pp108–9; ☎ 3230 1077; 14a Golden Sq W1; snacks £3–5; ☒ 8am-8pm Mon-Fri, 11am-7pm Sat, 11am-6pm Sun; ☻ Piccadilly Circus) As simple and stylish as you'd expect from the Scandinavians, this small cafe has bare wooden walls and uncomplicated Danish snacks such as sticky cinnamon buns and salmon served on dark rye bread.

Neal's Yard Salad Bar (Map pp108–9; ☎ 7836 3233; Neal's Yard WC2; mains £3–12; ☻ Covent Garden) Occupying both sides of the courtyard, this bright-orange salad bar has waiters in black bow ties serving fresh, leafy meals and moist Brazilian cakes.

Yauatcha (Map pp108–9; ☎ 7494 8888; 15 Broadwick St W1; dishes £3–18; ☻ Piccadilly Circus) Dim sum restaurants don't come much cooler than this, and the menu is fantastic and Michelin-starred. Upstairs, the chilled-out teahouse serves pretty cakes.

Fernandez & Wells (Map pp108–9; ☎ 7287 2814; 73 Beak St W1; mains £4–5; ☒ 8am-7pm Mon-Fri, 9am-7pm Sat & Sun; ☻ Piccadilly Circus) With its sister deli around the corner, there's no shortage of delicious charcuterie and cheese to fill the fresh baguettes on the counter of this teensy cafe. The coffee's superb.

Sacred (Map pp108–9; ☎ 7734 1415; 13 Ganton St W1; mains £4–5; ☒ 7.30am-8.30pm Mon-Fri, 9.30am-8pm Sat, 10am-7pm Sun; ☻ Oxford Circus) The spiritual paraphernalia and blatant Kiwiana don't seem to deter the smart Carnaby St set from lounging around this eclectic cafe. It must be something to do with the excellent coffee, appealing counter food and deliciously filling cooked breakfasts (try the scrambled eggs with salmon and goat's cheese).

Hummus Bros (Map pp108–9; ☎ 7734 1311; 88 Wardour St W1; meals £4–7; ☻ Piccadilly Circus) Don't come here if you're chickpea challenged, because this informal place is hummus heaven. It comes in small or regular bowls with a choice of meat or vegie toppings and a side of pitta bread.

Mother Mash (Map pp108–9; ☎ 7494 9644; 26 Ganton St W1; mains £7; ☻ Oxford Circus) If you've survived a London winter, you'll know the importance of good comfort food. This Mother certainly does, offering choices of four types of mashed potato, eight varieties of sausage (including a vegetarian version), six choices of pie and five types of gravy (including the traditional, parsley-based East End 'liquor').

Also recommended:

Breakfast Club (Map pp108–9; ☎ 7434 2571; 33 D'Arblay St W1; ☒ ; ☻ Oxford Circus) See p158.

Konditor & Cook (Map pp108–9; ☎ 7292 1684; Curzon, 99 Shaftesbury Ave W1; ☻ Leicester Sq) See p156.

Red Veg (Map pp108–9; ☎ 7437 3109; 95 Dean St W1; ☻ Tottenham Court Rd) Everyone's favourite communist vegetarian burger bar.

MIDRANGE

Abeno Too (Map pp108–9; ☎ 7379 1160; 17-18 Great Newport St WC2; mains £8–15; ☻ Leicester Sq) Specialists in *okonomi-yaki* (Japanese-style pancakes), which are cooked in front of you on a hotplate. Sit at the bar or by the window and feast. Japanese noodle dishes are also available.

Sarastro (Map pp108–9; ☎ 7836 0101; 126 Drury Ln WC2; mains £8–16; ☻ Covent Garden) This Turkish-influenced restaurant is gaudy, kitsch and loads of fun. The opera theme – with balcony tables, gold everywhere (even the ceiling), crushed velvet and myriad lamps – is totally over the top. Good for pre- and post-theatre meals.

Spiga (Map pp108–9; ☎ 7734 3444; 84-86 Wardour St W1; mains £9–18; ☻ Piccadilly Circus) With Italian movie posters on the walls, warm, colourful decor and a tasty menu of pastas, pizzas, fish and meat dishes, this popular restaurant is a winner.

Kettners (Map pp108–9; ☎ 7734 6112; 29 Romilly St W1; mains £9–20; ☻ Leicester Sq) Founded in 1867 (no, that's not a typo), Kettners has served the likes of Oscar Wilde and Edward VIII. Nowadays it dishes up pizza and burgers, which you can wash down with champagne while soaking in the gently fading grandeur and tinkling piano.

TOP END

National Gallery Dining Rooms (Map pp108–9; ☎ 7747 2525; Sainsbury Wing, National Gallery, Trafalgar Sq WC2; 2 courses £25; ☒ lunch daily, dinner Fri; ☻ Charing Cross) It's fitting that Oliver Peyton's acclaimed restaurant should celebrate British food (such as smoked haddock, traditional Suffolk cob chicken and 'Farmer Shep's aged sirloin'), being in the National Gallery and overlooking Trafalgar Sq. For a much cheaper option with the same views, ambience, quality produce and excellent service, try a salad, pie or tart at the adjoining bakery (mains £4.50 to £9.50).

Bloomsbury & Fitzrovia

Tucked away behind busy Tottenham Court Rd, Fitzrovia's Charlotte and Goodge Sts form one of central London's most vibrant eating precincts.

Salt Yard (Map pp104-5; ☎ 7637 0657; 54 Goodge St W1; tapas £5-8; ⊖ Goodge St) Named after the place where cold meats are cured, this softly lit joint serves delicious Spanish and Italian tapas. Try the roasted chicken leg with gnocchi, wild garlic and sorrel, or flex your palate with courgette flowers stuffed with cheese and drizzled with honey.

Ooze (Map pp104-5; ☎ 7436 9444; 62 Goodge St W1; mains £7-15; ⊖ Goodge St) The humble risotto gets its moment on the catwalk in this breezy Italian restaurant. There are a handful of grills on the menu, but it's the 16 varieties of oozy, but still slightly crunchy, risotto that take centre stage.

La Perla (Map pp108-9; ☎ 7436 1744; 11 Charlotte St W1; mains £9-17; ⓨ closed Sun lunch; ⊖ Goodge St) The service is lovely, but it's the street tacos that have us infatuated: mini tacos loaded up with tomato, coriander, onion, chilli and your choice of pork, prawns or chicken.

Hakkasan (Map pp108-9; ☎ 7907 1888; 8 Hanway Pl W1; mains £10-60; ⊖ Tottenham Court Rd) Hidden down a lane like all fashionable haunts need to be, the first Chinese restaurant to get a Michelin star combines celebrity status, a stunning design, persuasive cocktails and incredibly sophisticated Chinese food.

Holborn & Clerkenwell

Similarly hidden away, Clerkenwell's gems are well worth digging for. Pedestrianised Exmouth Market is a good place to start.

BUDGET

Little Bay (Map pp98-9; ☎ 7278 1234; 171 Farringdon Rd EC1; mains before/after 7pm £6/8; ⊖ Farringdon) The crushed-velvet ceiling, handmade twisted lamps that improve around the room (as the artist got better) and elaborately painted bar and tables showing nymphs frolicking is bonkers but fun. The hearty food is very good value.

It's also worth checking out **Konditor & Cook** (Map pp104-5; ☎ 7404 6300; Gray's Inn Rd, WC1; ⊖ Chancery Ln) – see p156.

MIDRANGE

Bleeding Heart Restaurant & Bistro (Map pp104-5; ☎ 7242 8238; Bleeding Heart Yard EC1; bistro £8-16, restaurant £13-25; ⊖ Farringdon) Locals have taken this place, tucked in the corner of Bleeding Heart Yard, to their hearts. Choose from formal dining in the downstairs restaurant or more relaxed meals in the buzzy bistro – wherever, the French food is divine.

5ifty 4our (Map pp98-9; ☎ 7336 0603; 54 Farringdon Rd; mains £9-13.50; ⊖ Farringdon) Britain and Malaysia go back a long way and this smart-looking restaurant celebrates that fact with tasty fusion dishes like lamb shanks with redang sauce.

Great Queen Street (Map pp108-9; ☎ 7242 0622; 32 Great Queen St WC2; mains £10-14; ⓨ lunch Tue-Sat, dinner Mon-Sat; ⊖ Holborn) There's no tiara on this Great Queen, her claret-coloured walls and mismatched wooden chairs suggesting cosiness and informality. But the food's still the best of British, including brawn, lamb that melts in the mouth and Arbroath smokie (a whole smoked fish with creamy sauce).

Smiths of Smithfield (Map pp104-5; ☎ 7251 7950; 67-77 Charterhouse St EC1; mains 1st fl £11-17, top fl £17-29; ⊖ Farringdon) This converted meat-packing warehouse endeavours to be all things to all people and succeeds. Hit the ground-floor bar for a beer, follow the silver-clad ducts and wooden beams upstairs to a relaxed dining space, or continue up for two more floors of feasting, each slightly smarter and pricier than the last.

St John (Map pp104-5; ☎ 7251 0848; 26 St John St EC1; mains £14-23; ⊖ Farringdon) Bright whitewashed brick walls, high ceilings and simple wooden furniture keep diners free to concentrate on its world-famous nose-to-tail offerings. Expect offal, ox tongue and tripe.

TOP END

Dans le Noir (Map pp98-9; ☎ 7253 1100; 30-31 Clerkenwell Green EC1; 2/3 courses £29/37; ⊖ Farringdon) If you've ever felt in the dark about food, eating in the pitch black might suit you. A visually impaired waiter guides you to your table, plate and cutlery. Then it's up to you to guess what you're eating and enjoy the anonymous conviviality of the dark...

The City

You'll be sorely dismayed if you've got an empty belly on a Sunday morning in the City. Even during the busy weekdays, your best

CHAIN-CHAIN-CHAIN, CHAIN OF FOODS

It's an unnerving, but not uncommon, experience to discover the idiosyncratic cafe or pub you were so proud of finding on your first day in London popping up on every other high street. But amongst the endless Caffe Neros, Pizza Expresses and All-Bar-Ones are some gems, or, at least, great fallback options.

Some of the best include:

GBK (Map pp104-5, pp100-1, pp98-9, pp102-3, p111, p112, pp108-9; www.gbkinfo.com) Producing creative burger constructions in 19 Gourmet Burger Kitchens.

Leon (Map pp104-5, p111, p112, pp108-9; www.leonrestaurants.co.uk) Focussing on fresh, seasonal food (salads, wraps and the like).

Ping Pong (Map pp104-5, pp108-9; www.pingpongdimsum.com) Stylish Chinese dumpling joints.

Wagamama (Map pp104-5, pp100-1, pp98-9, pp102-3, p111, p112, pp108-9; www.wagamama.com) Japanese noodles taking over the world from their London base.

Zizzi (Map pp104-5, pp100-1, pp102-3, p111, p112, pp108-9; www.zizzi.co.uk) Wood-fired pizza.

bets are the chains (above) or the **Konditor & Cook** (Map p112; ☎ 0845 262 3030; 30 St Mary Axe EC3; ⊖ Liverpool St) bakery in the Gherkin.

Hoxton, Shoreditch & Spitalfields

From the hit-and-miss Bangladeshi restaurants of Brick Lane to the Vietnamese strip on Kingsland Rd, and the Jewish, Spanish, French, Italian and Greek eateries in between, the East End's cuisine is as multicultural as its residents.

BUDGET

Brick Lane Beigel Bake (Map p112; ☎ 7729 0616; 159 Brick Lane E2; most bagels less than £2; ⓨ 24hr; ⊖ Liverpool St) A relic of London's Jewish East End, it's more a takeaway than a cafe and sells dirt-cheap bagels. They're a top snack on a bellyful of booze.

Cafe Bangla (Map p112; ☎ 7247 7885; 128 Brick Ln E1; mains £4-13; ⊖ Liverpool St) Dining in the famous curry houses of Brick Lane is inevitably more about the experience than the food. Amongst the hordes of practically interchangeable restaurants, this one stands out for its murals of scantily-clad women riding dragons, alongside a tribute to Princess Di.

Song Que (Map pp96-7; ☎ 7613 3222; 134 Kingsland Rd E2; mains £5-7; ⊖ Old St) If you arrive after 7.30pm, expect to queue as this humble eatery has already had its cover blown as one of the best Vietnamese in London. There's never much time to admire the institutional-green walls, fake lobsters and bizarre horse portrait, as you'll be shunted out shortly after your last bite.

Macondo (Map p112; ☎ 7729 1119; 8-9 Hoxton Sq N1; mains £5-8; ⓨ 9.30am-11pm Sun-Thu, to midnight Fri &

Sat; ⊖ Old St) A welcome respite from the full English breakfast, Macondo brings some Latin loving to eggs on toast, transforming it into eggs on tortilla with spicy *tomatillo* or bitter *anchilo* pepper sauce. Beverages range from excellent coffee to cocktails, best enjoyed on a sunny day on the outdoor tables facing the square.

We also recommend **S&M Cafe** (Map p112; ☎ 7247 2252; 48 Brushfield St E1; ⊖ Liverpool St) – flick to p158.

MIDRANGE

Story Deli (Map p112; ☎ 7247 3137; 3 Dray Walk; pizzas £9-10; ⊖ Liverpool St) This organic cafe with mismatched cutlery poking out of jam jars, vintage mirrors leaning haphazardly against walls, high ceilings and solid wooden furniture (mismatched of course) is justifiably popular. The pizzas are thin and crispy, and you can rest assured that anything fishy has been sustainably caught.

Hoxton Apprentice (Map p112; ☎ 7749 2828; 16 Hoxton Sq N1; mains £9-17; ⊖ Old St) Similar in concept to Fifteen (below), both professionals and apprentices work the kitchen in this restaurant, housed appropriately enough in a former Victorian primary school. The music selection's awful (hotel lobby piano when we visited), but the prices are reasonable and it's under the auspices of the Training For Life charity.

our pick **Fifteen** (Map p112; ☎ 0871-330 1515; www .fifteen.net; 15 Westland Pl N1; breakfast £2-8.50, trattoria £9-18, restaurant £22-24; ⊖ Old St) It can only be a matter of time before Jamie Oliver becomes Sir Jamie. His culinary philanthropy started at Fifteen, set up to give unemployed young people a shot at a career. The Italian food is beyond excellent and, surprisingly, even those on limited budgets can afford a visit. In the trattoria, a croissant and coffee will only set you back £3.50, while a £9 pasta makes for a delicious lunch.

TOP END

Les Trois Garçons (Map p112; ☎ 7613 1924; 1 Club Row E1; mains £18-32; ⊖ Liverpool St) The name may prepare you for the French menu, but nothing on earth could prepare you for the camp decor. A virtual menagerie of stuffed or bronze animals fills every surface, while chandeliers dangle between a set of suspended handbags. The food is good, if overpriced, and the small army of bow-tie-wearing waiters unobtrusively deliver complementary bread and tasty gifts from the kitchen.

South of the Thames

You'll find plenty of touristy eateries on the riverside between Westminster and Tower Bridges, making the most of the constant foot traffic and iconic London views. For a feed with a local feel, head to Borough Market, Bermondsey St or The Cut in Waterloo.

BUDGET

Konditor & Cook (Map p112; ☎ 7407 5100; 10 Stoney St SE1; snacks £2-5; ⊖ London Bridge) The original location of arguably the best bakery in London, it serves excellent muffins, sweets, bread and coffee. There's only one table but everything is yours to take away.

Estrala Bar (Map p107; ☎ 7793 1051; 111-115 South Lambeth Rd SW8; tapas £2-8, mains £8-12; ⓨ breakfast, lunch & dinner; ⊖ Oval) In a Portuguese pocket of South London, Estrala's waistcoated waiters deliver the national dish, *bacalhau* (salt cod), in several different guises, along with excellent tapas.

Mesón Don Felipe (Map pp104-5; ☎ 7928 3237; 53 The Cut SE1; tapas £3-6; ⊖ Waterloo) The Don is tops for tapas and an authentic Spanish atmosphere, helped by bright orange walls and theatrical but friendly staff. Serves are a decent size for the price, which explains why this place is always rammed with satisfied customers.

MIDRANGE

Bermondsey Kitchen (Map pp96-7; ☎ 7407 5719; 194 Bermondsey St SE1; mains £10-15; ⊖ London Bridge) Smart but informal, this place sits somewhere between a restaurant and a gastropub,

serving cocktails and tapas all day. It does an outrageously tasty bouillabaisse, lunch specials under £10 and excellent brunch on the weekends.

Garrison (Map pp96-7; ☎ 7089 9355; 99-101 Bermondsey St SE1; mains £12-15; ⓨ breakfast, lunch & dinner; ⊖ London Bridge) It may be a gastropub but the ambience is more French country kitchen than London boozer, with soft colours and baskets of fresh vegetables proudly displayed. Vegetarians will find they're almost as well served by interesting, beautifully presented options as carnivores.

Delfina (Map pp96-7; ☎ 7357 0244; 50 Bermondsey St SE1; mains £13-16; ⓨ lunch Mon-Fri, dinner Fri; ⊖ London Bridge) This restaurant-cum-art gallery, in a converted Victorian chocolate factory, serves delicious modern cuisine with an Asian twist to a backdrop of contemporary canvases. Studios upstairs house artists, and there's an exhibition space downstairs with more works.

Magdalen (Map p112; ☎ 7403 1342; 152 Tooley St SE1; mains £15-20; ⓨ lunch Mon-Fri, dinner Mon-Sat; ⊖ London Bridge) Roasting up the best of the critters that walk, hop, flap and splash around these fair isles, Magdalen isn't the place to bring a vegetarian or a weight-conscious waif on a date. Carnivorous couplings, however, will appreciate the elegant room and traditional treats presented in interesting ways. Love that pork crackling!

TOP END

Oxo Tower Brasserie (Map pp104-5; ☎ 7803 3888; Barge House St SE1; 2 courses £20; ⊖ Waterloo) The spectacular views are the big drawcard, so skip the restaurant and head for the slightly less extravagantly priced brasserie, or if you're not hungry, the bar. Italian with a twist is the focus of the very proficient kitchen.

Chelsea, Kensington & Knightsbridge

These highbrow neighbourhoods harbour some of London's very best (and priciest) restaurants. Perhaps the Chelsea toffs are secretly titillated by the foul-mouthed telechefs in their midst.

BUDGET

Jakob's (Map pp100-1; ☎ 7581 9292; 20 Gloucester Rd SW7; mains £4-10; ⊖ Gloucester Rd) A charismatic cafe/delicatessen serving a mixture of Armenian, Persian and Mediterranean dishes including salads, falafel and quiches.

Orsini (Map pp102-3; ☎ 7581 5553; 8a Thurloe Pl SW3; snacks £2-6, mains £7-12; ⊖ South Kensington) Marinated in authentic Italian charm, this tiny family-run eatery serves excellent espresso and deliciously fresh baguettes stuffed with Parma ham and mozzarella.

Made in Italy (Map pp102-3; ☎ 7352 1880; 249 King's Rd SW3; pizzas £5-13, mains £15-19; ⊖ Sloane Sq) Pizza is served by the tasty quarter-metre at this traditional trattoria. Sit on the Chelsea roof terrace and dream of Napoli.

Ottolenghi Belgravia (Map pp100-1; ☎ 7823 2707; 13 Motcomb St SW1; ⊖ Knightsbridge); Kensington (Map pp100-1; ☎ 7937 0003; 1 Holland St W8; ⊖ High St Kensington) is another decent option. See p158.

MIDRANGE

Tom's Kitchen (Map pp102-3; ☎ 7349 0202; 27 Cale St SW3; breakfast £2-11; lunch 2 courses £14; mains £17-22; ⊙ breakfast Mon-Fri, lunch & dinner daily; ⊖ South Kensington) Tom Aikens is the notorious kitchen firebrand who's been gradually taking over Chelsea; around the corner you'll find his Michelin-starred, mortgage-your-mother eponymous restaurant as well as his blinged-up fish diner. This excellent, informal British/French restaurant sits between somewhere between the two: dinners can be pricey but a delicious breakfast or lunch needn't break the bank.

TOP END

Boxwood Cafe (Map pp104-5; ☎ 7235 1010; Berkeley Hotel, Wilton Pl SW1; mains £16-31; ⊖ Knightsbridge) A New York–style cafe set up by superchef Gordon Ramsay, in a valiant attempt to kick back with young folk and make fine dining in London 'a little bit more relaxed'.

Gordon Ramsay (Map pp102-3; ☎ 7352 4441; www .gordonramsay.com; 68 Royal Hospital Rd SW3; set lunch/dinner £40/90; ⊖ Sloane Sq) One of Britain's finest restaurants, and the only one in the capital with three Michelin stars. The food is blissful and perfect for a luxurious treat. The only quibble is that you don't get time to linger. Bookings are made in specific eat-it-and-beat-it time slots and, if you've seen the chef on the telly, you won't argue.

Notting Hill, Bayswater & Paddington

Notting Hill teems with good places to eat, from cheap takeaways to atmospheric pubs

and restaurants worthy of the fine-dining tag. Queensway has the best strip of Asian restaurants this side of Soho.

BUDGET

Kam Tong (Map pp100-1; ☎ 7229 6065; 59-63 Queensway W2; yum cha £2-3, mains £7-14; ⊖ Bayswater) When most of the clientele are actually Chinese, you know you're on to a good thing, which can't be said for the trendy dumpling chains that have sprung up around London recently. Kam Tong serves genuine Cantonese dishes and wonderful yum cha, but we can't help wondering where the pushy trolley dollies are (you order from a menu instead).

Kiasu (Map pp100-1; ☎ 7727 8810; 48 Queensway W2; mains £6-8; ⊖ Bayswater) Local Malaysians and Singaporeans rated rate this place highly, as do those who know a tasty cheap thing when they see it. Kiasu serves 'Food from the Straits of Malacca'. You'll also find Thai and Vietnamese food on the menu, but it's hard to go past the delicious and filling *laksa*.

Also recommended:

Ottolenghi (Map pp100-1; ☎ 7727 1121; 63 Ledbury Rd W11; ⊖ Notting Hill Gate) See p158.

S&M Cafe (Map pp100-1; ☎ 8968 8898; 268 Portobello Rd W10; ⊖ Ladbroke Grove) See p158.

MIDRANGE

Geales (Map pp100-1; ☎ 7727 7528; 2 Farmer St W8; mains £8-17; ⊙ closed lunch Mon; ⊖ Notting Hill Gate) It may have opened in 1939 as a humble chippie, but now it's so much more. Fresh fish from sustainable fisheries in Devon and Cornwall star in a variety of guises – either battered and British or with an Italian sensibility. Tables spill out onto the pleasant side street.

Electric Brasserie (Map pp100-1; ☎ 7908 9696; 191 Portobello Rd W11; breakfast £2-8, mains £9-28; ⊖ Ladbroke Grove) The leather-and-cream look is suitably

---

TOP FIVE AFFORDABLE GRUB AT SWISH SPOTS

- Breakfast or a trattoria pasta at **Fifteen** (p155)
- The Parlour at **Sketch** (p152)
- Tapa Room at **Providores** (p158)
- The Bakery at **National Gallery Dining Rooms** (p153)
- Pretheatre menu at **Wild Honey** (p152)

cool for the brasserie that's attached to the Electric Cinema. And the food's very good, too; head to the back area for a darker, more moody dinner.

Marylebone

You won't go too far wrong planting yourself on a table anywhere along Marylebone's charming High Street.

Providores and Tapa Room (Map pp104-5; ☎ 7935 6175; 109 Marylebone High St W1; mains £18-25; ♦ Baker St) New Zealand's greatest culinary export since kiwifruit, chef Peter Gordon works his fusion magic here, matching his creations with exclusively NZ wine. Downstairs, in a cute play on words, the Tapa Room (as in the Polynesian bark-cloth) serves sophisticated tapas, along with excellent brunch on the weekends.

North London

Allow at least an evening to explore Islington's Upper St, along with the lanes leading off it. Camden's great for cheap eats, while neighbouring Chalk Farm and Primrose Hill are salted with gastropubs and upmarket restaurants.

BUDGET

Breakfast Club (Map pp98-9; ☎ 7226 5454; 31 Camden Passage N1; mains £5-9; ⏲ 8am-10pm Mon-Fri, 9.30am-10pm Sat & Sun; ♦ Angel) Eighties survivors will immediately clock this place and, with dishes like *Hungry Like The Wolf* (the big breakfast) and *When Haloumi Met Salad*, they'll feel right at home.

Rooburoo (Map pp98-9; ☎ 7278 8100; 21 Chapel Market N1; mains £5-10; ♦ Angel) 'Waltzing Matilda' isn't in this particular Roo's repertoire, but a hell of a lot of piquant chillies, fresh spices and interesting north and south Indian dishes are. The name means face to face (although you might want to down a breath mint first if you've just finished a meal here).

Ottolenghi (Map pp98-9; ☎ 7226 5454; 287 Upper St N1; mains £5-10; ⏲ 8am-10pm Mon-Sat, 9am-7pm Sun; ♦ Angel) Mountains of meringues tempt you through the door, where a sumptuous array of sweet and savoury bakery treats greets you. The big communal table is great for conversation surfing (aka eavesdropping). Dinners are as light and tasty as the oh-so-white interior design.

S&M Cafe (Map pp98-9; ☎ 7359 5361; 4/6 Essex Rd N1; mains £6-10; ⏲ breakfast, lunch & dinner; ♦ Angel)

The S&M refers to sausages and mash in this cool diner (which featured in the movie *Quadrophenia*) that won't give your wallet a spanking. There's a range of sausages, mashes and gravies.

Le Mercury (Map pp98-9; ☎ 7354 4088; 140A Upper St N1; mains £6-10; ♦ Highbury & Islington) A cosy Gaelic haunt ideal for a romantic dalliance, given that it appears much more expensive than it is. Sunday lunch by the open fire upstairs is a treat, although you'll have to book.

Another place you could try is **Macondo** (Map pp98-9; ☎ 7226 7275; 20 Camden Passage N1; ♦ Angel). See p155.

MIDRANGE

Konstam at the Prince Albert (Map pp98-9; ☎ 7833 5040; 2 Acton St WC1; mains £11-17; ⏲ closed Sundays; ♦ Kings Cross) As London a restaurant as you can get, chef Oliver Rowe sources all but a few of his ingredients from within the tube map. Sit below the bizarrely elegant draped metal beads and watch your often adventurous London-centric dish take shape in the open kitchen.

Duke of Cambridge (Map pp98-9; ☎ 7359 3066; 30 St Peter's St N1; mains £12-17; ♦ Angel) Pioneers in bringing sustainability to the table, this tucked-away gastropub serves only organic food, wine and beer, fish from sustainable sources and locally sourced fruit, vegetables and meat.

our pick Engineer (Map pp98-9; ☎ 7722 0950; 65 Gloucester Ave NW1; mains £13-17; ♦ Chalk Farm) One of London's original gastropubs, Engineer has been serving up consistently good international cuisine to hip north Londoners fo a fair while now. The courtyard garden is a real treat on balmy summer nights.

Greenwich

Inside (Map p111; ☎ 8265 5060; 19 Greenwich South St SE10; mains £13-17; ⏲ /DLR Greenwich) Cap off your genteel Greenwich visit with white linen and smart food (British with a dash of Turkish) in this elegant dining room. The lunch special (two courses for £12) is a steal.

Self-Catering

There are supermarkets absolutely everywhere in central London. Look out for the big names: Waitrose, Tesco, Sainsbury's, Marks & Spencer, Morrisons and Asda.

Planet Organic Bayswater (Map pp100-1; ☎ 7727 2227; 42 Westbourne Grove W2; ♦ Bayswater); Fitzrovia (Map pp104-5; ☎ 7436 1929; 22 Torrington Pl WC1; ⊖ Goodge St); Fulham (Map pp102-3; ☎ 7731 7222; 25 Effie Rd; ⊖ Fulham Broadway); Islington (Map pp98-9; 64 Essex Rd, N1; ⊖ Angel) As the name suggests, everything in this cafe/supermarket is organic. Fresh vegies are sourced (where possible) directly from British farms.

La Fromagerie Cafe (Map pp104-5; ☎ 7935 0341; 2-6 Moxon St W1; mains £8-13; ⊖ Baker St) This providore-cafe has bowls of delectable salads, antipasto, peppers and beans scattered about the long communal table. Huge slabs of bread invite you to tuck in, and all the while the heavenly waft from the cheese room beckons.

DRINKING

As long as there's been a city, Londoners have loved to drink – and, as history shows, often immoderately. The pub is the focus of social life and there's always one near at hand. When the sun shines, drinkers spill out into the streets, parks and squares as well. It was only in 2008 that drinking was banned on the tube!

Soho is undoubtedly the heart of bar culture, with enough variety to cater to all tastes. Camden's great for grungy boozers and rock kids, although it's facing stiff competition on the Bohemian-cool front from the venues around Hoxton and Shoreditch.

Now that Princes William and Harry have hit their stride, the Sloane Ranger scene has been reborn in exclusive venues in South Ken(sington), although the 'Turbo Sloanes' now count megarich commoners among their numbers.

Us mere mortals will find plenty of pub-crawl potential in places like Clerkenwell, Islington, Southwark, Notting Hill, Earl's Court…hell, it's just not that difficult. The reviews below are simply to make sure you don't miss out on some of the most historic, unusual, best-positioned or excellent examples of the genre.

St James's & Mayfair

Absolut Ice Bar (Map pp108-9; ☎ 7478 8910; 31-33 Heddon St W1; admission Thu-Sat £15, Sun-Wed £12; ☽ noon-midnight; ⊖ Piccadilly Circus) At -6°C, this bar made entirely of ice is literally the coolest in London. Entry is limited to 40 minutes and your ticket includes a vodka cocktail served in an ice glass. The compulsory futuristic silver polyester cape is to protect the bar from your body heat, not the other way

around, so wear warm togs. It's a gimmick, sure, but a good one, and there are plenty of places nearby that charge the same for a cocktail alone.

Galvin at Windows (Map pp104-5; ☎ 7208 4021; The Hilton, 22 Park Ln W1; ⊖ Hyde Park Corner) Drinks are well pricey, but the view's astounding from this 28th-floor eyrie.

West End

CAFES

Flat White (Map pp108-9; ☎ 7734 0370; 17 Berwick St W1; ☽ 8am-7pm Mon-Fri, 9am-6pm Sat & Sun; ⊖ Piccadilly Circus) Trailblazers of the unexpected but thoroughly welcome Kiwi invasion of Soho cafes, Flat White is both named after and delivers the holy grail of Antipodean coffee. The beach scenes on the walls are a comfort on a cold day.

Monmouth Coffee Company (Map pp108-9; ☎ 7379 3516; 27 Monmouth St WC2; snacks £1-2; ⊖ Covent Garden) While the array of treats displayed on the counter is alluring, it's the coffee that's the star, nay god, here. Chat to a caffeinated stranger on one of the tight tables at the back, or grab a takeaway and slink off to a nearby lane for your fix.

BARS & PUBS

Be At One (Map pp108-9; ☎ 7240 9889; 23 Wellington St WC2; happy hours 5-8pm Mon & Tue, to 7pm Wed-Sat, 6pm-close Sun; ⊖ Covent Garden) Forgive the silly name and make the most of the generous happy hours (two cocktails for £6.50).

Coach & Horses (Map pp108-9; ☎ 7437 5920; 29 Greek St W1; ⊖ Leicester Sq) This Soho institution has been patronised by Sigmund Freud, Francis Bacon, Dylan Thomas, Peter Cooke and Peter O'Toole. The Wednesday night East End sing-along is tops.

Gordon's Wine Bar (Map pp108-9; ☎ 7930 1408; 47 Villiers St WC2; ⊖ Charing Cross) What's not to love about this cavernous wine cellar lit by candles and practically unchanged over the last 100 years? Choose between wines, sherries, ports and Madeiras accompanied by warming home-cooked grub. In summer, the crowd spills out into Embankment Gardens.

Lamb & Flag (Map pp108-9; ☎ 7497 9504; 33 Rose St WC2; ⊖ Covent Garden) Everyone's Covent Garden 'find', this popular historic pub is often jammed. It was built in 1623, formerly called the 'Bucket of Blood'.

Queen Mary (Map pp108-9; ☎ 7240 9404; Waterloo Pier WC2; ⊖ Embankment) Board this steamer for a welcoming publike atmosphere accompanied by great views of the London Eye and the South Bank.

Holborn & Clerkenwell

Jerusalem Tavern (Map pp104-5; ☎ 7490 4281; 55 Britton St; ✆ Farringdon) Pick a wood-panelled cubbyhole to park yourself in at this gorgeous former 18th-century coffee shop–turned-inn, and choose from a selection of St Peter's beers such as cinnamon and apple, grapefruit or, if you're not feeling fruity, creamy ale or bitter.

Princess Louise (Map pp108-9; ☎ 7405 8816; 208 High Holborn WC1; ✆ Holborn) This late-19th-century Victorian boozer is arguably London's most beautiful pub. Spectacularly decorated with fine tiles, etched mirrors, plasterwork and a gorgeous central horseshoe bar, it gets packed with the after-work crowd.

The City

Vertigo 42 (Map p112; Tower 42, Old Broad St, EC2; ✆ Liverpool St) Book a two-hour slot in this 42nd-floor bar with vertiginous views across London.

Ye Olde Cheshire Cheese (Map pp104-5; Wine Office Ct, 145 Fleet St EC4; ✆ Holborn) Rebuilt six years after the Great Fire, it was popular with Dr Johnson, Thackeray, Dickens and the visiting Mark Twain. Touristy but always atmospheric and enjoyable for a pub meal.

Hoxton, Shoreditch & Spitalfields

Bar Music Hall (Map p112; ☎ 7729 7216; 134 Curtain Rd EC2; ✆ Old St) Keeping the East End music-hall tradition alive but with a modern twist, this roomy space with a central bar amuses the friendly punters with DJs and live bands. Music runs the gamut from punk to jazz to rock and disco.

Commercial Tavern (Map p112; ☎ 7247 1888; 142 Commercial St E1; ✆ Liverpool St) The zany decor's a thing of wonder in this reformed East End boozer. Check out the walls coated in buttons and jigsaw puzzle pieces. The little boy's room has been wallpapered like, well, a little boy's room: Popeye, astronauts and cyclists all make an appearance.

Grapeshots (Map p112; ☎ 7247 8215; 2/3 Artillery Passage E1; ✆ Liverpool St) Half the fun of this wine bar is walking down the Dickensian passage, complete with old street lamps, that leads to it. Once inside, there's a decent wine list and the old-world ambience continues.

Loungelover (Map p112; ☎ 7012 1234; 1 Whitby St E1; ⏱ 6pm-midnight Sun-Thu, to 1am Fri & Sat; ✆ Liverpool St)

Book a table, sip a cocktail and admire the Louis XIV chairs, the huge hippo head, the cage-turned-living room, the jewel-encrusted stag's head and the loopy chandeliers. Utterly fabulous.

Ten Bells (Map p112; ☎ 7366 1721; cnr Commercial & Fournier Sts E1; ✆ Liverpool St) The most famous Jack the Ripper pub, Ten Bells was patronised by his last victim before her grisly end, and possibly by the slayer himself. Admire the wonderful 18th-century tiles and ponder the past over a pint.

The following are all good stops on a Hoxton hop:

Bricklayer's Arms (Map p112; ☎ 7613 0469; 63 Charlotte Rd EC2; ✆ Old St) Back-street pub with an interesting crowd.

Favela Chic (Map p112; ☎ 7613 4228; 91-93 Great Eastern St EC2; entry £5-10 after 9pm; ⏱ 5pm-1am Tue-Thu, to 2am Fri, 6pm-2am Sat; ✆ Old St) Ticks the following boxes: hip young things; crazy theme nights; lumberyard meets jungle decor; fun and funky music.

Mother (Map p112; ☎ 7613 0469; 333 Old St EC1; entry £5 Fri & Sat; ✆ Old St) Red-and-gold flocked wallpaper, chequerboard floors and live alternative music and DJs on weekends. Downstairs, 333 is a part nightclub/part live venue.

Red Lion (Map p112; ☎ 7729 7920; 41 Hoxton St N1; ✆ Old St) Old corner pub with eclectic furniture and cheap drinks.

Zigfrid Von Underbelly (Map p112; ☎ 7613 1988; 11 Hoxton Sq N1; ✆ Old St) Furnished like an oversized lounge room (check out the disturbing family portrait over the fireplace), it's simultaneously the coolest and the most fun of the Hoxton Sq venues.

South of the Thames

Anchor (Map p112; ☎ 7407 1577; 34 Park St SE1; ✆ London Bridge) A 17th-century boozer just east of the Globe Theatre, it has a terrace offering superb views over the Thames. Dr Johnson was once a regular.

George Inn (Map p112; ☎ 7407 2056; Talbot Yard, 77 Borough High St SE1; ✆ London Bridge or Borough) Tucked away in a cobbled courtyard is London's last surviving galleried coaching inn, dating from 1677 and now belonging to the National Trust. Dickens and Shakespeare used to prop up the bar here (not together, obviously). There are outdoor tables for sunny days.

Chelsea, Kensington & Knightsbridge

Bibendum Oyster Bar (Map pp102-3; ☎ 7581 5817; 81 Fulham Rd SW3; ✆ South Kensington) If rubber-clad men happen to be your thing, slurp up a bivalve and knock back a champers in the foyer of the wonderful Art Nouveau Michelin House (1911). The Michelin Man is everywhere: in mosaics, stained glass, crockery and echoed in the architecture itself.

Notting Hill, Bayswater & Paddington

Trailer Happiness (Map pp100-1; ☎ 7727 2700; 177 Portobello Rd W11; ✚ Ladbroke Grove) Think shagpile carpets, 1960s California kitsch and trashy trailer-park glamour. Try the Tiki cocktails and share a flaming volcano bowl of Zombie with a friend to ensure your evening goes off with a bang.

Windsor Castle (Map pp100-1; ☎ 7243 9551; 114 Campden Hill Rd W11; ✚ Notting Hill Gate) A memorable pub with oak partitions separating the original bars. The panels have tiny doors so big drinkers will have trouble getting past the front bar. It also has one of the loveliest walled gardens of any pub in London. Thomas Paine (*The Rights of Man* writer) is rumoured to be buried in the cellar.

Marylebone

Artesian (Map pp108-9; Langham Hotel, 1C Portland Pl W1; ✚ Oxford Circus) For a dose of colonial glamour with a touch of the orient, the sumptuous bar at the Langham hits the mark. Rum is the speciality here – award-winning cocktails (£15) are concocted from the 60 varieties on offer.

Heights (Map pp108-9; 7580 0111; St George's Hotel, 14 Langham Pl W1; ✚ Oxford Circus) Take the lift up to this understated bar with huge windows to showcase the panorama. It's an unusual view, managing to miss most of the big sights, but impressive nonetheless.

North London

EUSTON & KING'S CROSS

Big Chill House (Map pp98-9; 257-259 Pentonville Rd N1; entry £5 after 10pm Fri & Sat; ✚ King's Cross) Come the weekend, the only remotely chilled-out space in this busy bar, split over two levels, is its first-rate and generously proportioned rooftop terrace.

CAMDEN & ISLINGTON

Albert & Pearl (Map pp98-9; ☎ 7354 9993; 181 Upper St; ✚ Highbury & Islington) The chap behind Fabric (p163) also has a finger in this chic, cocktail-filled pie (pie with cocktails – now there's an idea). DJs play until the small hours on Friday and Saturday nights (admission £3 after midnight).

Lock Tavern (Map pp98-9; 35 Chalk Farm Rd NW1; ✚ Camden Town) The archetypal Camden pub, the Lock has both a rooftop terrace and a beer garden and attracts an interesting crowd with its mix of ready conviviality, pleasant surrounds and regular live music.

Proud (Map pp98-9; Stables Market NW1; admission £10 after 7.30pm Mon-Sat; ✚ Camden Town) No, despite the name it's not a gay bar. Proud occupies a former horse hospital within Stables Market, with booths in the stalls, ice-cool rock photography on the walls and deckchairs printed with images of Marilyn Manson and Pete Doherty. Spin around the gallery during the day or enjoy bands at night.

HAMPSTEAD & HIGHGATE

Holly Bush (Map pp96-7; ☎ 7435 2892; 22 Holly Mount NW3; ✚ Hampstead) Dating from the early 19th century, this beautiful pub has a secluded hilltop location, open fires in winter and a knack for making you stay a bit longer than you had intended. It's above Heath St, reached via the Holly Bush Steps.

Flask (Map pp96-7; ☎ 8340 7260; 77 Highgate West Hill N6; ✚ Highgate) Charming candlelit nooks and crannies, an old circular bar complete with pumps (don't knock yourself when you sit down) and a lovely beer garden make this the perfect place for a pint after visiting Highgate Cemetery (p131).

Spaniard's Inn (Map pp96-7; ☎ 8731 6571; Spaniard's Rd NW3; ✚ Hampstead, then bus 21) A marvellous tavern that dates from 1585, complete with dubious claims that Dick Turpin, the dandy highwayman, was born here and used it as a hideout. More savoury sorts like Dickens, Shelley, Keats and Byron also availed themselves of its charms. There's a big, blissful garden and good food.

Greenwich

Trafalgar Tavern (Map p111; ☎ 8858 2909; Park Row SE10; DLR Cutty Sark) An 1837 Regency-style pub that stands above the site of the Placentia Palace where Henry VIII was born. Dickens, Gladstone and Disraeli have all darkened its doors, although they wouldn't have had the wonderful views of the O2 and Canary Wharf highrises to admire.

ENTERTAINMENT

From West End luvvies to End End geezers, Londoners have always loved a spectacle. With bear baiting and public executions no longer an option, they've learnt to make do with having the world's best theatres, night-clubs and live music scene to divert them. Yet the gladiatorial contests that the Romans brought to these shores still survive on the football fields, especially when Chelsea goes head-to-head with Arsenal.

For a comprehensive list of what to do on any given night, check out *Time Out*. The listings in the free tube papers are also handy.

Theatre

London is a world capital for theatre and there's a lot more than mammoth musicals to tempt you into the West End. The term 'West End' – as with Broadway – generally refers to the big-money productions like mu-sicals, but also includes such heavyweights as the **Royal Court Theatre** (Map pp102-3; ☎ 7565 5000; www.royalcourttheatre.com; Sloane Sq SW1; ➋ Sloane Sq), the patron of new British writing; the **National Theatre** (Map pp104-5; ☎ 7452 3000; www .nationaltheatre.org.uk; South Bank SE1; ➋ Waterloo), which has cheaper tickets for both classics and new plays from some of the world's best companies; and the **Royal Shakespeare Company** (RSC; ☎ 0870 609 1110; www.rsc.org.uk), with produc-tions of the Bard's classics and other qual-ity stuff. Kevin Spacey continues his run as artistic director (and occasional performer)

at the **Old Vic** (Map pp104-5; ☎ 0870-060 6628; www .oldvictheatre.com; The Cut SE1; ➋ Waterloo).

On performance days, you can buy half-price tickets for West End productions (cash only) from the official **Leicester Square Half-Price Ticket Booth** (Map pp108-9; ➌ 10am-7pm Mon-Sat, noon-3pm Sun; Leicester Sq; ➋ Leicester Sq), on the south side of Leicester Sq. The booth is the one with the clock tower; beware of touts selling dodgy tickets.

Off West End – where you'll generally find the most original works – includes venues such as the **Almeida** (Map pp98-9; ☎ 7359 4404; www .almeida.co.uk; Almeida St N1; ➋ Highbury & Islington), **Battersea Arts Centre** (Map pp96-7; ☎ 7223 2223; www.bac.org.uk; Lavender Hill SW11; ➋ Clapham Junction) and the **Young Vic** (Map pp104-5; ☎ 7922 2920; www .youngvic.org; 66 The Cut SE1; ➋ Waterloo). The next rung down is known as the Fringe and these shows take place anywhere there's a stage (and can be very good).

Other interesting companies, such as the not-for-profit **Donmar Warehouse** (Map pp108-9; ☎ 0870-060 6624; www.donmarwarehouse.com; 41 Earlham St WC2; ➋ Covent Garden) and the **Menier Chocolate Factory** (Map p112; ☎ 7907 7060; www.menierchocolate factory.com; 55 Southwark St SE1; ➋ London Bridge), have started Off West End and ended up with West End reputations.

As far as the blockbuster musicals go, you can be fairly confident that *Les Miserables* and *Phantom of the Opera* will still be chugging

---

NOVEL NIGHTS OUT

It seems that some of the cool kids are bored with simply going clubbing, listening to a band or propping up a bar with a pint. To plant your finger on the party pulse, check out some of these activity-based haunts.

Bloomsbury Bowling Lanes (Map pp98-9; ☎ 7183 1979; cnr Bedford Way & Tavistock Sq WC1; ➌ noon-2am Mon-Thu, to 3am Fri & Sat, 1-10pm Sun; ➋ Russell Sq) With eight 10-pin bowling lanes, a diner and details down to the carpet all dating from the 1950s and shipped in from America, this place is the real deal. And the fun doesn't stop with dubious footwear and a burger; there are also private karaoke rooms, a cinema screening independent movies, DJs and up-and-coming live bands.

Lucky Voice (Map pp108-9; ☎ 7439 3660; 52 Poland St W1F; 4-person booth per hr £20-40; ➌ 5.30pm-1am Mon-Thu, 3pm-1am Fri & Sat, 3-10.30pm Sun; ➋ Oxford Circus) Moulded on the private karaoke bars of Tokyo, superstylish Lucky Voice is a low-lit maze of dark walls with hidden doors revealing snug leather-clad soundproofed booths for your secret singalong. Select one of 50,000 songs from a touch screen, pick up a microphone and you're away. In the Super Lucky rooms, there are wigs and blow-up guitars to enhance your performance. Drinks and bento boxes are ordered by the touch of a button; expect to spend a fortune in Dutch courage.

Roller Disco (Map p107; ☎ 0844-736 5375; www.rollerdisco.info; Renaissance Rooms, off Wandsworth Rd SW8; admission incl skate hire £10-13; ➌ 8pm-midnight Thu, to 2am Fri & Sat; ➋ Vauxhall) Remember those adolescent roller discos you used to go to? Well, this is your chance to dust off your skating skills and roll to a changing soundtrack of disco, funk, house, garage and R&B. Dressing up like a twat is encouraged.

along, as well as the new revival of *Oliver!* For a comprehensive look at what's being staged where, visit www.officiallondontheatre.co.uk, www.theatremonkey.com or http://london .broadway.com.

Nightclubs

London's had a lot of practice perfecting the art of clubbing – Samuel Pepys used the term in 1660! – and the volume and variety of venues in today's city is staggering. Clubland's no longer confined to the West End, with megaclubs scattered throughout the city wherever there's a venue big enough, cheap enough or quirky enough to hold them. Some run their own regular weekly schedule, while others host promoters on an ad hoc basis. The big nights are Friday and Saturday, although you'll find some of the most cutting-edge sessions midweek. Admission prices vary widely; it's often cheaper to arrive early or prebook tickets.

Cargo (Map p112; ☎ 7739 3440; www.cargo-london .com; 83 Rivington St EC2; admission free-£16; ⊖ Old St) A hugely popular club with local and international DJs and a courtyard where you can simultaneously enjoy big sounds and the great outdoors.

our pick **The End** (Map pp108-9; ☎ 7419 9199; www .endclub.com; 18 West Central St WC1; admission £6-16; ⊙ from around 10.30pm Mon-Sat, 5.30am-midday Sun; ⊖ Tottenham Court Rd) The End offers an eclectic range of cutting-edge nights starting with Durrr on Mondays, devoted to underground music, live acts and kids in skinny jeans. If you've got a Wednesday drum and bass itch, Swerve's where you can scratch it, while the aptly named Jaded kicks off at 5.30am Sundays.

Fabric (Map pp104-5; ☎ 7336 8898; www.fabric london.com; 77A Charterhouse St EC1; admission £13-16; ⊙ 10pm-6am Fri, 11pm-8am Sat; ⊖ Farringdon) In 2008 Fabric was once again voted the world's best club by *DJ* magazine. Fabric's not a meat market but its three dance floors are based in a converted meat cold-store opposite the actual Smithfield meat market. Friday's FabricLive offers an 'urban music soundclash' (drum and bass, breakbeats, hip-hop and live acts), while Saturdays see house, techno and electro.

Guanabara (Map pp108-9; ☎ 7242 8600; www .guanabara.co.uk; cnr Parker St & Drury Lane WC2; admission £5-10; ⊖ Covent Garden) Brazil comes to London with live music seven nights a week. On Wednesdays enjoy an authentic *Roda de*

BURLESQUE IS BACK

Basques, suspenders, cinched waists, circle skirts, tweed, top hats, trilbies, spats, feathers, foxtrot, lindy hop, divas, mime artists and of course cabaret – burlesque's retro sexy sophistication sizzles. Revived by Immodesty Blaize in Blighty and Dita von Teese stateside, there's no hotter trend for night owls. Here are the most decadently divine nights: don't forget to dress up and adopt an air of languid panache.

Agent Lynch (www.agentlynch.com)
Immodesty Blaize (www.immodestyblaize.com)
Jitterbugs (www.jitterbugs.co.uk)
Lady Luck (www.ladyluckclub.co.uk)
Madame Jo Jo's (www.madamejojos.com)
Velvet London (www.myspace.com/velvet london)
Viva Cake (www.myspace.com/vivacakebitches)
Volupté (www.volupte-lounge.com)

Samba, tuck into Brazilian snacks, sip on a *Caipirinha* and shake your booty. Admission is free before 9pm.

Mass (Map pp96-7; ☎ 7738 7875; www.mass-club .com; St Matthew's Church, Brixton Hill SW2; admission £5-10; ⊙ 10pm-6am Fri & Sat; ⊖ Brixton) The congregation's swollen at this Brixton church under its new high priests, with regular services of live music and club nights.

Ministry of Sound (Map pp104-5; ☎ 0870 060 0010; http://club.ministryofsound.com; 103 Gaunt St SE1; admission £12-20; ⊙ 10pm-6am Fri, 11pm-7am Sat; ⊖ Elephant & Castle) Where the global brand started, it's London's most famous club and still packs in a diverse crew with big local and international names.

Plastic People (Map p112; 147-149 Curtain Rd EC2; admission £5-13; ⊖ Old St) Taking the directive 'underground club' literally, Plastic People provides a low-ceilinged subterranean den of dubstep, techno, electro and no-frills fun times.

SeOne (Map p112; ☎ 0870 246 2050; www.seone -london.com; 41-43 Saint Thomas St SE1; ⊖ London Bridge) Under the railway arches of London Bridge, this mammoth venue can (and frequently does) cram in 3000 up-for-it ravers.

Live Music
ROCK & JAZZ

While London may have stopped swinging in the 1960s, every subsequent generation has given birth to a new set of bands in the city's thriving live venues: punk in the 1970s, New Romantics in the 1980s, Brit Pop in the 1990s and the current crop of skinny-jeaned rockers and electro acts thrilling the scenesters today. You'll find interesting young bands gigging around venues all over the city. Big-name gigs sell out quickly, so check www.seetickets.com before you travel.

100 Club (Map pp108–9; ☎ 7636 0933; www.the 100club.co.uk; 100 Oxford St W1; ⊖ Oxford Circus) This legendary London venue once showcased the Stones and was at the centre of the punk revolution. It now divides its time between jazz, rock and even a little swing.

Barfly (Map pp98–9; ☎ 0844-847 2424; www.bar flyclub.com; 49 Chalk Farm Rd NW1; ⊖ Chalk Farm) Pleasantly grungy, and the place to see the best new bands. The same crew run a couple of other joints around town.

Brixton Academy (Map pp96-7; ☎ 0844-477 2000; www.brixton-academy.co.uk; 211 Stockwell Rd SW9; ⊖ Brixton) This Grade 2–listed art-deco venue is always winning awards for 'best live venue' (something to do with the artfully sloped floor, perhaps) and hosts big-name acts in a relatively intimate setting (5000 capacity).

Dublin Castle (Map pp98-9; ☎ 7485 1773; www .thedublincastle.com; 94 Parkway NW1; ⊖ Camden Town) There's live punk or alternative music most nights in this pub's back room.

Forum (Map pp96-7; ☎ 0844-847 2405; www.kentish townforum.com; 9-17 Highgate Rd NW5; ⊖ Kentish Town) A grand old theatre and one of London's best large venues.

Hope And Anchor (Map pp98-9; ☎ 7700 0550; 207 Upper St; admission free-£6; ⊖ Angel) Live music's still the focus of the pub that hosted the first London gigs of Joy Division and U2 (only nine people showed up).

Jazz Cafe (Map pp98-9; ☎ 7485 6834; 5 Parkway NW1; ⊖ Camden Town) Jazz is just one part of the picture at this intimate club that stages a full roster of rock, pop, hip-hop and dance, including famous names.

Koko (Map pp98-9; ☎ 0870 432 5527; www.koko .uk.com; 1A Camden High St NW1; ⊖ Mornington Cres) Occupying the grand Camden Palace theatre, Koko hosts live bands most nights and the regular Club NME (£5) on Friday.

Ronnie Scott's (Map pp108-9; ☎ 7439 0747; www .ronniescotts.co.uk; 47 Frith St W1; ⊖ Leicester Sq) London's legendary jazz club has been pulling in the hep cats since 1959.

Shepherd's Bush Empire (Map pp96-7; ☎ 8354 3300; www.shepherds-bush-empire.co.uk; Shepherd's Bush Green W12; ⊖ Shepherd's Bush) A slightly dishevelled, midsize theatre that hosts some terrific bands.

See also Bar Music Hall (p160), Mother and 333 (p160), and Proud (p161).

CLASSICAL

With four world-class symphony orchestras, two opera companies, various smaller ensembles, brilliant venues, reasonable prices and high standards of performance, London is a classical capital. Keep an eye out for the free (or nearly so) lunchtime concerts held in many of the city's churches.

Barbican Centre (Map p112; ☎ 0845 120 7500; www .barbican.org.uk; Silk St EC2; ⊖ Barbican) This hulking complex has a full program of film, music, theatre, art and dance including loads of concerts from the London Symphony Orchestra, which is based here.

Southbank Centre (Map pp104-5; ☎ 0871-663 2509; www.southbankcentre.co.uk; South Bank; ⊖ Waterloo) Home to the London's Philharmonic Orchestra, Sinfonietta and the Philharmonia Orchestra, amongst others, this centre has three premier venues: the **Royal Festival Hall** (Map pp104–5), the smaller **Queen Elizabeth Hall** (Map pp104–5) and **Purcell Room** (Map pp104–5), which hosts classical, opera, jazz and choral music. The precinct is a riverside people-watching mecca of shops and restaurants. Look out for free recitals in the foyer.

Royal Albert Hall (Map pp100-1; ☎ 7589 8212; www.royalalberthall.com; Kensington Gore SW7; ⊖ South Kensington) A splendid circular Victorian arena that hosts classical concerts and the occasional contemporary act, but is best known as the venue for the Proms.

Opera & Dance

Coliseum (Map pp108-9; ☎ 0871-911 0200; www.eno.org; St Martin's Lane WC2; tickets £10-85; ⊖ Leicester Sq) Home of the progressive English National Opera; all performances are in English.

Royal Opera House (Map pp108-9; ☎ 7304 4000; www.royaloperahouse.org; Bow St WC2; tickets £5-190; ⊖ Covent Garden) The gleaming Royal Opera House has been attracting a younger audience since its £213-million millennium redevelopment, which also seems to have breathed new life into its programming. The Royal Ballet, Britain's premier classical ballet company, is also based here.

Sadler's Wells (Map pp98-9; ☎ 0844-412 4300; www .sadlers-wells.com; Rosebery Ave EC1; tickets £10-49; ⊖ Angel) A glittering modern venue that was in fact first established in the 17th century, Sadler's Wells has been given much credit for bringing modern dance to the mainstream.

Comedy

When London's comics aren't being terribly clever on TV, you might find them doing stand-up somewhere in your neighbourhood. There are numerous venues to choose from, and many pubs getting in on the act.

99 Club (☎ 7739 5706; www.the99club.co.uk; admission £10-25) Not quite the famous 100 Club, this virtual venue takes over various bars around town from Tuesday to Sunday night, with four rival clones on Saturdays.

Comedy Cafe (Map p112; ☎ 7739 5706; www.comedycafe.co.uk; 66-68 Rivington St EC2; admission free-£15; ❺ Old St) Have dinner and watch some comedy; take to the stage on Wednesday if you're brave/foolhardy/drunk.

Comedy Store (Map pp108-9; ☎ 7839 6642; www.thecomedystore.co.uk; 1A Oxendon St SW1; admission £13-18; ❺ Piccadilly Circus) One of London's first comedy clubs, featuring the capital's most famous improvisers, the Comedy Store Players, on Wednesdays and Sundays.

Hen & Chickens (Map pp98-9; ☎ 7704 2001; www.henandchickens.com; 109 St Paul's Rd N1; admission £10-18; ❺ Highbury & Islington) Catch a chuckle in the theatre above this Islington boozer.

Soho Theatre (Map pp108-9; ☎ 7478 0100; www.sohotheatre.com; 21 Dean St W1; ❺ Tottenham Court Rd) Where grownup comedians graduate to once they start pulling the crowds.

Cinemas

Glitzy premieres usually take place in one of the mega multiplexes in Leicester Sq.

For less mainstream movies try **Curzon Cinemas** (☎ 0870 756 4621; www.curzoncinemas.com; tickets £8-12) Chelsea (Map pp102-3; 206 Kings Rd SW3; ❺ Sloane Sq); Mayfair (Map pp104-5; 38 Curzon St W1; ❺ Green Park); Renoir (Map pp98-9; Brunswick Sq WC1; ❺ Russell Sq); Soho (Map pp108-9; 99 Shaftesbury Ave W1; ❺ Leicester Sq). They're some of a clutch of independent cinemas spread throughout the capital.

BFI Southbank (Map pp104-5; ☎ 7928 3232; Belvedere Rd SE1; tickets £9; ❺ Waterloo) A film-lover's fantasy, it screens some 2000 flicks a year, ranging from classics to foreign art house. There's also the Mediatheque viewing stations, where you can explore the British Film Institute's extensive archive of movies and watch whatever you like for free.

BFI IMAX (Map pp104-5; ☎ 0870-787 2525; www.bfi.org.uk/imax; Waterloo Rd SE1; tickets £13; ❺ Waterloo) Watch 3D movies and cinema releases on the UK's biggest screen: 20m high (nearly five double-decker buses) and 26m wide.

Electric (Map pp100-1; ☎ 7908 9696; www.electriccinema.co.uk; 191 Portobello Rd W11; tickets £13-15; ❺ Ladbroke Grove) Grab a glass of wine from the bar, head to your leather sofa (£30) and snuggle down to watch a flick. All cinemas should be like this. Tickets are cheapest on Mondays.

Sport

As the capital of a football-mad nation, you can expect London to be brimming over with sporting spectacles during the cooler months. The Wimbledon Lawn Tennis Championships (p136) is one of the biggest events on the city's summer calendar.

FOOTBALL

Tickets for Premier League football matches are ridiculously hard to come by for casual fans these days, but if you want to try your luck, the contacts for London's Premiership clubs are listed here:

Arsenal (☎ 7704 4040; www.arsenal.com)

Chelsea (☎ 0870 300 2322; www.chelseafc.com)

Fulham (☎ 0870 442 1234; www.fulhamfc.com)

Tottenham Hotspur (☎ 0870 420 5000; www.tottenhamhotspur.com)

West Ham United (☎ 0870 112 2700; www.whufc.com)

RUGBY

Twickenham (☎ 0870 405 2000; www.rfu.com; Rugby Rd, Twickenham; tickets £10-45, more for internationals; ❒ Twickenham) is the home of English rugby union, but as with football, tickets for tests are difficult to get unless you have contacts. The ground also boasts the **World Rugby Museum** (☎ 0870 405 2001; ✆ 10am-5pm Tue-Sat, 11am-5pm Sun), which can be combined with a tour of the stadium (adult/child £10/7; bookings recommended).

CRICKET

Cricket is as popular as ever in the land of its origin. Test matches take place at two venerable grounds: **Lord's Cricket Ground** (Map pp96-7; ☎ 7616 8500; www.lords.org; St John's Wood Rd NW8; ❺ St John's Wood) and the **Brit Oval** (Map pp96-7; ☎ 0871-246 1100; www.surreycricket.com; Kennington SE11; ❺ Oval). Tickets are from £24 to £80, but if you're a fan it's worth it. If not, it's an expensive and protracted form of torture.

SHOPPING

Napoleon famously described Britain as a nation of shopkeepers, which doesn't sound at all bad to us! From world-famous department stores to quirky backstreet retail revelations, London is a mecca for shoppers with an eye for style and a card to exercise. If you're looking for something distinctly British, eschew the Union Jack–emblazoned kitsch of the tourist thoroughfares and fill your bags with Twinings tea, Paul Smith shirts, Royal Doulton china and Marmite. For bookshops, see p94.

Antiques & Crafts

Curios, baubles and period pieces abound along Camden Passage in Islington, Bermondsey Antiques Market and the Saturday market at Portobello (see opposite).

Grays Antiques Market (Map pp104-5; ☎ 7629 7034; 58 Davies St W1; ♦ Bond St) Top-hatted doormen welcome you to this wonderful building full of specialist stallholders. Make sure you head to the basement where the Tyburn River still runs through a channel in the floor.

London Silver Vaults (Map pp104-5; ☎ 7242 3844; 53-63 Chancery Lane WC2; ♦ Chancery Lane) Has 72 subterranean shops forming the world's largest collection of silver under one roof.

Department Stores

London's famous department stores are a tourist attraction in themselves, even if you don't intend to make a personal contribution to the orgy of consumption.

Harrods (Map pp100-1; ☎ 7730 1234; 87 Brompton Rd SW1; ♦ Knightsbridge) An overpriced theme park for fans of Britannia, Harrods is always crowded with slow tourists.

Harvey Nichols (Map pp100-1; ☎ 7235 5000; 109-125 Knightsbridge SW1; ♦ Knightsbridge) This is London's temple of high fashion, jewellery and perfume.

Fortnum & Mason (Map pp108-9; ☎ 7734 8040; 181 Piccadilly W1; ♦ Piccadilly Circus) The byword for quality and service from a bygone era, steeped in 300 years of tradition. It is particularly noted for its old-world, ground-floor food hall, where Britain's elite come for their cornflakes and bananas.

Liberty (Map pp108-9; ☎ 7734 1234; 214-220 Regent St W1; ♦ Oxford Circus) An irresistible blend of contemporary styles and indulgent pampering in a mock-Tudor fantasyland of carved dark wood. Access from Great Marlborough St.

Selfridges (Map pp104-5; ☎ 0870 837 7377; 400 Oxford St W1; ♦ Bond St) The funkiest and most vital of London's one-stop shops, where fashion runs the gamut from street to formal. The food hall is unparalleled and the cosmetics hall the largest in Europe.

Fashion

If there's a label worth having, you'll find it in central London. Oxford St is the place for High St fashion, while Regent St cranks it up a notch. Carnaby St is no longer the hip hub that it was in the 1960s, but the lanes around it still have some interesting boutiques. These days, stylists are more likely to seek out attention-grabbing new looks on Portobello Rd. For something different, head to Camden, Exmouth Market or Islington's Upper and Cross Sts.

Kensington High St has a nice mix of chains and boutiques, Bond St has designers galore, while Knightsbridge draws the hordes with quintessentially English department stores. Savile Row is famous for bespoke tailoring, and Jermyn St is the place for Sir to buy his smart clobber (particularly shirts).

Look out for dress agencies that sell second-hand designer clothes, bags and shoes – there are particularly rich pickings in the wealthier parts of town.

Albam (Map pp108-9; ☎ 3157 7000; 23 Beak St W1; ♦ Oxford Circus) UK-produced classic duds for stylish dudes.

Butler & Wilson Chelsea (Map pp102-3; ☎ 7352 3045; 189 Fulham Rd SW3; ♦ South Kensington); Mayfair (Map pp104-5; ☎ 7409 2955; 20 South Moulton St W1; ♦ Bond St) Camp costume jewellery, antique baubles and vintage clothing.

EC One Clerkenwell (Map pp98-9; ☎ 7713 6185; 41 Exmouth Market EC1; ♦ Farringdon); Notting Hill (Map pp100-1; ☎ 7243 8811; 184 Westbourne Grove W11; ♦ Notting Hill Gate) Husband-and-wife team Jos and Alison Skeates sell beautiful contemporary collections by British and international jewellery designers.

KJ's Laundry (Map pp104-5; ☎ 7486 7855; 74 Marylebone Ln W1; ♦ Bond St) Break out of the High St uniform in this women's boutique, which sources ranges from up-and-coming designers.

Lollipop London (Map pp98-9; ☎ 7226 4005; 114 Islington High St N1; ♦ Angel) A girlie boutique stocking shoes and accessories from independent designers.

Palette London (Map pp98-9; ☎ 7288 7428; 21 Canonbury Ln N1; ♦ Highbury & Islington) Fancy an

ROLL OUT THE BARROW

London has more than 350 markets selling everything from antiques and curios to flowers and fish. Some, such as Camden and Portobello Rd, are full of tourists, while others exist just for the locals and sell everything from lunch to underwear. Here's a sample:

Bermondsey Antiques Market (Map pp96-7; Bermondsey Sq SE1; 4am-1pm Fri; Borough) The place to come for opera glasses, bowling balls, hatpins, costume jewellery, porcelain or other curios.

Borough Market (Map p112; cnr Borough High & Stoney Sts SE1; 11am-5pm Thu, noon-6pm Fri, 9am-4pm Sat; London Bridge) A farmers market sometimes called London's Larder, it has been here in some form since the 13th century. It's wonderfully atmospheric; you'll find everything from organic falafel to boars' heads.

Brick Lane Market (Map p112; Brick Lane E1; early-2pm Sun; Liverpool St) An East End pearler, a sprawling bazaar featuring everything from fruit and vegies to paintings and bric-a-brac.

Brixton Market (Map pp96-7; Electric Ave & Granville Arcade; 10am-dusk Mon-Sat, to 1pm Wed; Brixton) Immortalised in the Eddie Grant song, Electric Ave is a cosmopolitan treat that mixes everything from reggae music to exotic foods and spices.

Broadway Market (Map pp96-7; Broadway Mkt E8; 9am-5pm Sat; Bethnall Green) Graze from the organic food stalls, choose a cooked meal and then sample one of the 200 beers on offer at the neighbouring Dove Freehouse.

Camden Market (10am-5.30pm; Camden Town) London's most famous market is actually a series of markets spread along Camden High St and Chalk Farm Rd. It's been quieter since the major fire in 2008, but the Lock (Map pp98–9) and Stables (Map pp98–9) markets are still the place for punk fashion, cheap food, hippy shit and a whole lotta craziness.

Camden Passage Market (Map pp98-9; Camden Passage N1; 10am-2pm Wed, to 5pm Sat; Angel) Get your fill of antiques and trinkets galore. Not in Camden (despite the name).

Columbia Road Flower Market (Map p112; Columbia Rd; 8am-2pm Sun; Old St) The best place for East End barrow boy banter ('We got flowers cheap enough for ya mother-in-law's grave'). Unmissable.

Greenwich Market (Map p111; College Approach SE10; 11am-7pm Wed, 10am-5pm Thu & Fri, 10am-5.30pm Sat & Sun; DLR Cutty Sark) Rummage through antiques, vintage clothing and collectibles on weekdays, arts and crafts on weekends, or just chow down in the food section.

Petticoat Lane Market (Map p112; Wentworth St & Middlesex St E1; 9am-2pm Sun-Fri; Aldgate) A cherished East End institution overflowing with cheap consumer durables and jumble sale ware.

Portobello Road Market (Map pp100-1; Portobello Rd W10; 8am-6.30pm Mon-Sat, closes 1pm Thu; Ladbroke Grove) One of London's most famous (and crowded) street markets. New and vintage clothes are its main attraction, with antiques at its south end and food at the north.

Spitalfields Market (Map p112; 105a Commercial St E1; 10am-4pm Mon-Fri, 9am-5pm Sun; Liverpool St) Housed in a Victorian warehouse but the market's been here since 1638. Thursdays are devoted to antiques and Fridays to fashion and art, but Sunday's the big day.

Sunday (Up)market (Map p112; The Old Truman Brewery, Brick Lane E1; 10am-5pm Sun; Liverpool St) Handmade handbags, jewellery, new and vintage clothes and shoes, plus food if you need refueling.

original 1970s Halston dress or 1980s Chanel? Vintage meets modern and fashion meets collectables in this interesting store.

Paul Smith Sale Shop (Map pp104-5; ☎ 7493 1287; 23 Avery Row W1; Bond St) Classic Paul Smith shirts and other delights by London's most commercially successful designer, at a discounted price.

Rigby & Peller (Map pp108-9; ☎ 7491 2200; 22A Conduit St W1S 2XT; Oxford Circus) Get into

some right royal knickers with a trip to the Queen's corsetière.

Start (Map p112; ☎ 7729 3334; 42-44 Rivington St EC2; Old St) Spilling over three stores on the same lane (womenswear, menswear and men's formal), your quest for designer jeans starts here.

Topshop Oxford Circus (Map pp108-9; ☎ 7636 7700; 216 Oxford St W1; Oxford Circus) Billed as the 'world's largest fashion store', the Topshop

LONDON

TOP FIVE ECCENTRIC STORES

- **Duke of Uke** (Map p112; ☎ 7247 7924; 22 Hanbury St E1; ✪ Liverpool St) Devoted entirely to ukuleles and banjos.
- **FairyGothMother** (Map p112; ☎ 7247 7924; 15 Lamb St E1; ✪ Liverpool St) Purveyors of custommade corsets and vampy evening wear, not all in black.
- **Hamleys** (Map pp108–9; ☎ 0844-855 2424; 188-196 Regent St W1; ✪ Oxford Circus) A seemingly endless wonderland of toys.
- **International Magic** (Map pp104–5; ☎ 7405 7324; 89 Clerkenwell Rd EC1; ✪ Chancery Ln) If you've ever fancied pulling a rabbit out of hat, here's where you'll find the hat.
- **Old Curiosity Shop** (Map pp108–9; ☎ 7405 9891; 13-14 Portsmouth St WC2; ✪ Holborn) Having been constructed from recycled ship timber in 1567, this is London's oldest shop building. It now sells out-there handmade, high-fashion shoes.

---

branch on Oxford Circus is a constant frenzy of shoppers searching for the latest look at reasonable prices. It's been given a shot of cool by being home to a range by London's favourite local supermodel rock chick, Kate Moss. Topman is next door.

Music

Nick Hornsby's book *High Fidelity* may have done for London music-store workers what *Sweeney Todd* did for barbers, but those obsessive types still lurk in wonderful independent stores all over London. If you'd like to purchase schmaltz without attitude, try the giant Oxford St **HMV** (Map pp108–9; ☎ 7631 3423; 150 Oxford St W1; ☼ 9am-9pm; ✪ Oxford Circus), which has many central branches.

For personality, visit the following:

BM Soho (Map pp108–9; ☎ 7437 0478; 25 D'Arblay St W1; ✪ Oxford Circus) Your best bet for dance – if they haven't got what you're after, they'll know who has.

Minus Zero Records (Map pp100–1; ☎ 7229 5424; 2 Blenheim Cres W11; ✪ Ladbrooke Grove) The place for collectables, like Bowie seven-inch singles.

Ray's Jazz (Map pp108–9; ☎ 7437 5660; Foyle's, 113-119 Charing Cross Rd WC2; ✪ Tottenham Court Rd) Where aficionados find those elusive back catalogues from their favourite jazz and blues artists.

Rough Trade East (Map p112; ☎ 7392 7788; Dray Walk, 91 Brick Ln E1; ✪ Liverpool St); West (Map pp100–1; ☎ 7229 8541; 130 Talbot Rd W11; ✪ Ladbroke Grove) At the forefront of the punk explosion of the 1970s, it's the best place to come for basically anything of an indie or alternative bent.

Sister Ray (Map pp108–9; ☎ 7734 3297; 34-35 Berwick St W1; ✪ Oxford Circus) If you need to be told that this store is named after a 17-minute distorted

Velvet Underground classic about a trannie smack dealer, then this shop's not for you.

GETTING THERE & AWAY

London is the major gateway to England, so further transport information can be found in the main Transport chapter.

Air

For information on flying to/from London see p803.

Bus

Most long-distance coaches leave London from **Victoria Coach Station** (Map pp102–3; ☎ 7824 0000; 164 Buckingham Palace Rd SW1; ✪ Victoria), a lovely art-deco building. The arrivals terminal is in a separate building across Elizabeth St from the main coach station.

Car

See p807 for reservation numbers of the main car-hire firms, all of which have airport and various city locations.

Train

With the reopening of beautiful St Pancras station, London is now only 2¼ hours by train from Paris on the Eurostar (see p805). Its vast vaulted concourse holds all the services you might find in an airport terminal, along with a giant statue of embracing lovers that Londoners love to hate.

London's main-line terminals are all linked by the tube and each serve different destinations. Most stations now have left-luggage facilities (around £4) and lockers, toilets (a 20p coin) with showers (around £3), newsstands and bookshops, and a range of eating and drinking outlets. St Pancras, Victoria and Liverpool St stations have shopping centres attached.

If you can't find your destination below, see the journey planner at www.national rail.co.uk.

Charing Cross (Map pp108-9) Canterbury.

Euston (Map pp98-9) Manchester, Liverpool, Carlisle, Glasgow.

King's Cross (Map pp98-9) Cambridge, Hull, York, Newcastle, Scotland.

Liverpool Street (Map p112) Stansted airport, Cambridge.

London Bridge (Map p112) Gatwick airport, Brighton.

Marylebone (Map pp100-1) Birmingham.

Paddington (Map pp100-1) Heathrow airport, Oxford, Bath, Bristol, Exeter, Plymouth, Cardiff.

St Pancras (Map pp98-9) Gatwick and Luton airports, Brighton, Nottingham, Sheffield, Leicester, Leeds, Paris.

Victoria (Map pp102-3) Gatwick airport, Brighton, Canterbury.

Waterloo (Map pp104-5) Windsor, Winchester, Exeter, Plymouth.

GETTING AROUND
To/From the Airports
HEATHROW

The transport connections to Heathrow are excellent, and the journey to and from the city is painless. The cheapest option is the Underground (p170). The Piccadilly line is accessible from every terminal (£4, one hour to central London, departing from Heathrow every five minutes from around 5am to 11.30pm). If it's your first time in London, it's a good chance to practice using the tube as it's at the beginning of the line and therefore not too crowded when you get on. Although for first timers buying a ticket can still be confusing, with little signage and the sometimes impenetrable accents. If there are vast queues at the airport ticket office, use the automatic machines instead; some accept credit cards as well as cash. Keep your bags near you and expect a scramble to get off if you're hitting the city at rush hour (7am to 9am and 5pm to 7pm weekdays).

The fastest (and easiest) way to central London is the **Heathrow Express** (☎ 0845 600 1515; www.heathrowexpress.co.uk), an ultramodern train to Paddington station (one-way/return £14.50/28, 15 minutes, every 15 minutes 5.10am to 11.25pm). You can purchase tickets on board (£2 extra), from self-service

machines (cash and credit cards accepted) at both stations or online.

There are taxi ranks for black cabs outside every terminal. A black cab to the centre of London will cost you between £40 and £70, a minicab around £35.

GATWICK

There are **National Rail** (www.nationalrail.co.uk) services from Gatwick's South Terminal to Victoria (£9.50, 37 minutes), running every 15 minutes during the day and hourly through the night. Other trains head to St Pancras (£8.90, 63 minutes), stopping at London Bridge, City Thameslink, Blackfriars and Farringdon. If you're racing to make a flight, the **Gatwick Express** (☎ 0845 850 1530; www .gatwickexpress.co.uk) departs Victoria every 15 minutes from 5.50am to 12.35am (one-way/ return £18/31, 30 minutes, first/last train 4.35am/1.35am).

Prices start very low, depending on when you book, for the **EasyBus** (www.easybus.co.uk) mini-bus service between Gatwick and Victoria (return from £11, allow 1½ hours, every 30 minutes from 3am to 1am). You'll be charged extra if you have more than one carry-on and one check-in bag.

Gatwick's taxi partner, **Checker Cars** (www .checkercars), has a counter in each terminal. Fares are quoted and paid for in advance (about £83 for the 65-minute ride to Central London). A black cab costs similar, a minicab around £55.

STANSTED

The **Stansted Express** (☎ 0845 600 7245; www.stanstedexpress.com) connects with Liverpool St station (one way/return £17/26, 46 minutes, departing every 15 minutes 5.10am to 10.55pm, first/last train 4.40am/11.25pm).

EasyBus (above) also has services between Stansted, Baker St and Victoria (return from £13, allow 1¾ hours, every 30 minutes from 3am to 1.05am). The **Airbus A6** (☎ 0870 580 8080; www.nationalexpress.com) links with Victoria coach station (one way/return £10/16, allow 1¾ hours, departing at least every 30 minutes).

A black cab to/from central London costs about £100, a minicab around £55.

LONDON CITY

The Docklands Light Railway connects London City Airport to the tube network, taking 22 minutes to reach Bank station (£4). A black taxi costs around £25 to/from central London.

LONDON'S OYSTER DIET

To get the most out of London, you need to be able to jump on and off public transport like a local, not scramble to buy a ticket at hefty rates each time. The best and cheapest way to do this is with an Oyster card, a reusable smartcard on which you can load either a season ticket (weekly/monthly £24.20/93) or prepaid credit. The card itself is free with a season ticket, otherwise it's £3.

London is divided into six concentric transport zones, although almost all of the places covered in this book are in Zones 1–2. The season tickets quoted above will give you unlimited transport on tubes, buses and most National Rail services within these zones. All you need to do is touch your card to the sensors on the station turnstiles or at the front of the bus.

If you opt for pay as you go, the fare will be deducted from the credit on your card at a much lower rate than if you were buying a one-off paper ticket. An oyster bus trip costs 90p as opposed to £2, while a Zone 1 tube journey is £1.50 as opposed to £4. Even better, in any single day your fares will be capped at the equivalent of the Oyster day-pass rate for the zones you've travelled in (Zones 1-2 peak/off-peak £6.30/4.80).

Assuming you'll avoid the tube during peak hours (before 9.30am), this ready reckoner gives the cheapest options for your length of stay:

- 1–4 days: non-Oyster off-peak daily (£5.30 per day)
- 5–25 days: Oyster weeklies topped up with prepay for any remaining days
- 26–31 days: monthly

LUTON

There are regular **National Rail** (www.nationalrail.co.uk) services from St Pancras (£14, 28 to 48 minutes) to Luton Airport Parkway station, where a shuttle bus (£1) will get you to the airport within 10 minutes. EasyBus (p169) minibuses head from Victoria and Baker St to Luton (return from £12, allow 1¼ hours, departing every 30 minutes). A black taxi costs around £95 to/from central London, minicabs around £55.

Public Transport

Although locals love to complain about it, London's public transport is excellent, with tubes, trains, buses and boats conspiring to get you anywhere you need to go. **Transport for London** (TFL; www.tfl.gov.uk) is the glue that binds the network together. Its website has a handy journey planner and information on all services, including cabs. As a creature of leisure, you'll be able to avoid those bits that Londoners hate (especially the sardine squash of rush-hour tubes), so get yourself an Oyster (above) and make the most of it.

LONDON UNDERGROUND, DLR & OVERGROUND

'The tube', as it's universally known, extends its subterranean tentacles throughout London and into the surrounding counties, with services running every few minutes from 5.30am to roughly 12.30am (from 7am on Sunday).

It's incredibly easy to use. Tickets (or Oyster card top-ups) can be purchased from counters or machines at the entrance to each station using either cash or credit card. They're then inserted into the slot on the turnstiles (or you touch your Oyster card on the yellow reader) and the barrier opens. Once you're through you can jump on and off different lines as often as you need to get to your destination. See the boxed text above for information about fares, zones and Oyster cards.

Also included within the network are the driverless Docklands Light Railway (DLR), and the train lines shown on tube maps as 'Overground'. The DLR links the City to Docklands, Greenwich and London City Airport. It's very Jetsons-like, especially when it hurtles between the skyscrapers of Canary Wharf; try to get the front row seat.

The tube map itself is an acclaimed graphic design work, using coloured lines to show how the 14 different routes intersect. However, it's not remotely to scale. The distances between stations become greater the further from central London you travel, while Leicester Sq and Covent Garden stations are only 250m apart.

BUS

Travelling round London by double-decker bus is an enjoyable way to get a feel for the city, but it's usually more difficult and slower than the tube. A recommended scenic route is number 24, which runs from Victoria to Hampstead Heath through the West End. Heritage 'Routemaster' buses with conductors operate on route 9 (from Aldwych to Royal Albert Hall) and 15 (between Trafalgar Sq and Tower Hill); these are the only buses without wheelchair access.

Buses run regularly during the day, while less-frequent night buses (prefixed with the letter 'N') wheel into action when the tube stops. Single-journey bus tickets (valid for two hours) cost £2 (90p on Oyster, capped at £3 per day); cash day passes are £3.50 and books of six tickets are £6. Children ride for free. At stops with yellow signs, you have to buy your ticket from the automatic machine *before* boarding. Buses stop on request, so clearly signal the driver with an outstretched arm.

TAXI

London's famous black cabs are available for hire when the yellow light above the windscreen is lit. To get an all-London licence, cabbies must do 'The Knowledge', which tests them on up to 25,000 streets within a 6-mile radius of Charing Cross and all the points of interest from hotels to churches. Fares are metered, with flag fall at £2.20 and the additional rate dependent on time of day, distance travelled and taxi speed. A 1-mile trip will cost between £4.40 and £8. To order a black cab by phone, try **Dial-a-Cab** (☎ 7253 5000); you must pay by credit card and will be charged a premium.

Licensed minicabs operate via agencies (most busy areas have a walk-in office with drivers waiting). They're a cheaper alternative to black cabs and quote trip fares in advance. The cars are recognisable by the ⊖ symbol displayed in the window. To find a local minicab firm, visit www.tfl.gov.uk.

There have been many reports of sexual assault and theft by unlicensed minicab drivers. Only use drivers from proper agencies; licensed minicabs aren't allowed to tout for business, so avoid the characters who hang around outside nightclubs or bars.

TRAIN

Particularly south of the river, where tube lines are in short supply, the various rail companies are an important part of the public transport picture. More stations are being fitted with Oyster readers, but you should check before travelling as to whether you need to purchase a separate ticket.

BOAT

The myriad boats that ply the Thames are a great way to travel, avoiding traffic jams while affording great views. Passengers with daily, weekly or monthly travelcards (Oyster or otherwise) get one third off all fares.

Thames Clippers (☎ 0871-781 5049; www.thames clippers.com) runs regular commuter services between Embankment, Waterloo, Bankside, London Bridge, Tower, Canary Wharf, Greenwich and Woolwich piers (adult £2.50 to £6.50, children £1.25 to £3.25) from 7am to 12.30pm (from 9am weekends). Another service runs from Putney to Blackfriars during the morning and evening rush hours.

Leisure services include the Tate-to-Tate boat (see boxed text, p125), Westminster-to-Greenwich services (p131) and a loop route taking in Westminster, Embankment, Festival, Bankside, London Bridge and St Katherine's piers (day pass £7.80/3.70, May to September). For boats to Kew Gardens and Hampton Court Palace, see p133.

London Waterbus Company (Map pp100-1; ☎ 7482 2660; www.londonwaterbus.com, single/return £6.50/9) and **Jason's Trip** (Map pp100-1; ☎ 7286 3428; www.jasons .co.uk; opposite 60 Blomfield Rd W9; single/return £7.50/8.50) both run canal boat journeys between Camden Lock and Little Venice; see websites for times. London has some 40 miles of inner-city canals, mostly built in the 19th century.

Car

Don't even think about it. Driving in London is a nightmare: traffic is heavy, parking is either impossible or expensive and wheel-clampers keep busy. If you drive into central London from 7am to 6pm on a weekday, you'll need to pay an £8 per day congestion charge (visit www.tfl.gov.uk to register) or face a hefty fine. If you're hiring a car to continue your trip, take the tube to Heathrow and pick it up from there.

The Southeast

From the site of the Battle of Hastings to the secret war tunnels at Dover castle and the scattered ruins of Roman palaces, this corner of the country is rich with reminders of its crucial role as the nation's front line of defence against Continental invaders. The formidable cliffs, castles and fortified ports still remain, but these days they're raided by sightseers armed with cameras and picnics rather than belligerent Normans.

The wealthy counties of Kent, East and West Sussex and Surrey are some of the most popular parts of the country to live and visit. It's a middle-class enclave of picturesque villages, narrow country lanes, and faceless commuter-belt towns, wrapped up in manicured farmland and gently sloping downs. A string of resort towns line the shore, with something to please all-comers, from the chi-chi charm of Londoners' favourite Whitstable, to the Bohemian spirit of hedonistic Brighton, to sedate septuagenarian magnet Eastbourne. And all along the coast you can soak up maritime history, dine out on seafood, and charge around battlegrounds and cliff tops.

Here too you'll find England's spiritual heart at Canterbury, with its magnificent cathedral and ancient winding streets. And scattered throughout the countryside, stately homes, royal residences and castles serve as reminders of the region's long-lasting ties with the monarchy.

HIGHLIGHTS

- Shopping, dining and partying in boisterous **Brighton & Hove** (p204)
- Following in the footsteps of pilgrims to ancient **Canterbury Cathedral** (p177)
- Lapping up tales of ghosts and smugglers in the cobbled backstreets of romantic **Rye** (p194)
- Strolling past candy coloured beach huts and feasting on oysters on the beach at **Whitstable** (p182)
- Conjuring up knights and dragons at the romantic moated marvel that is **Leeds Castle** (p193)
- Exploring the atmospheric WWII tunnels under sprawling **Dover Castle** (p188)
- Finding a clear day to amble along the **White Cliffs of Dover** (p190)

■ POPULATION: 8 MILLION	■ AREA: 3,560 SQ MILES	■ NUMBER OF TOWNS WITH THEIR OWN CURRENCY: ONE (LEWES)

Information

Tourism South East (www.visitsoutheastengland.com) is the official website for south and southeast England. Other helpful websites include:
Kent Attractions (www.kentattractions.co.uk)
Visit Kent (www.visitkent.co.uk)
Visit Surrey (www.visitsurrey.com)
Visit Sussex (www.visitsussex.org)

Activities

The southeast of England may be Britain's most densely populated corner, but there are still plenty of off-the-beaten-track walking and cycling routes to enjoy here. We concentrate on the highlights here, but you'll find more information throughout the chapter and in the Outdoor Activities chapter. Regional tourist offices are also well stocked with leaflets, maps and guides to start you off walking, cycling, paragliding, sailing and more.

CYCLING

Finding quiet roads for cycle touring takes a little extra perseverance in the southeast of England, but the effort is richly rewarded. Long-distance routes that form part of the **National Cycle Network** (NCN; www.sustrans.org.uk) include:
Downs & Weald Cycle Route (150 miles; NCN routes 2, 21) London to Brighton and on to Hastings.
Garden of England Cycle Route (165 miles; NCN routes 1, 2) London to Dover and then Hastings.

You'll also find less-demanding routes on the NCN website. Meanwhile there are plenty of uppers and downers to challenge mountain bikers on the South Downs Way National Trail (100 miles), which takes hard nuts two days but mere mortals around four. There are also a number of excellent trails at Devil's Punchbowl in the Surrey Hills.

WALKING

Two long-distance trails meander steadily westward through the region, but there are plenty of shorter ambles to fit your schedule, stamina and scenery wish list.
South Downs Way National Trail (100 miles) At the time of writing the rolling chalk South Downs were hotly tipped to become England's newest national park, and this trail is a beautiful roller-coaster walk along prehistoric drove ways between the ancient capital, Winchester, and the seaside resort Eastbourne.
North Downs Way (153 miles) This popular walk begins near Farnham in Surrey but one of its most beautiful sections runs from near Ashford to Dover in Kent, and there's also a loop that takes in Canterbury near its end.

Both long-distance routes have sections ideal for shorter walks. History buffs will revel in the 1066 Country Walk (p195), which connects with the South Downs Way. Devil's Punchbowl offers breathtaking views, sloping grasslands and romantic wooded areas.

Getting There & Around

The southeast is easily explored by train or bus, and many attractions can be visited in a day trip from London. Contact the **National Traveline** (☎ 0871 200 2233; www.travelinesoutheast.org .uk) for comprehensive information on public transport in the region.

BUS

Explorer tickets (adult/child £6.40/4.50) provide day-long unlimited travel on most buses throughout the region; you can buy them at bus stations or on your first bus.
   Stagecoach Coastline (www.stagecoachbus.com) services run through the coastline, East Kent and East Sussex areas. Travellers can buy an unlimited day (£7) or week (£18) ticket.

TRAIN

If you're based in London but day-tripping around the southeast, the BritRail London Plus Pass allows unlimited regional rail travel for two days in eight (£102), four days in eight (£164), or seven days in fifteen (£197) and must be purchased outside the UK; see p810 for more details.
   You can secure 33% discounts on most rail fares over £10 in the southeast by purchasing a **Network Railcard** (☎ 08457 225 225; www .railcard.co.uk/network/; per yr £20). Children under 15 can save 60%, but a minimum fare of £1 applies.

KENT

Kent isn't described as the garden of England for nothing. Inside its sea-lined borders you'll find a clipped landscape of gentle hills, lush farmland, cultivated country estates and fruitful orchards. It also serves as the booze garden of England, producing the world-renowned Kent hops, some of the country's finest ales and even award-winning wines from its numerous vineyards. At it's heart

THE SOUTHEAST

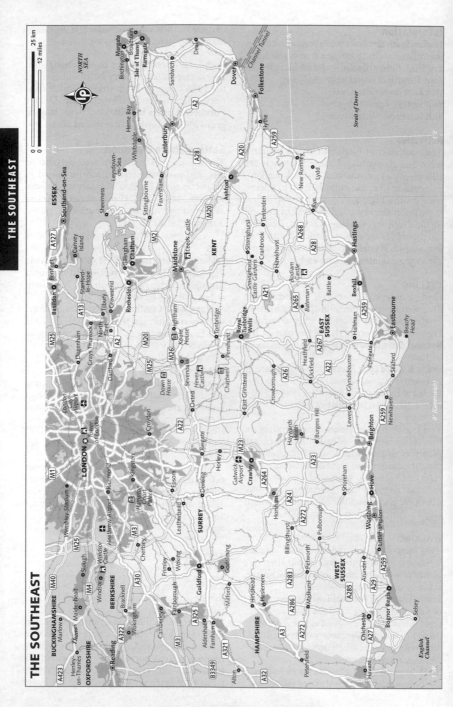

THE SOUTHEAST

KEEP YOUR ENEMIES CLOSE...

Not one to shy away from nepotism, in 1162 King Henry II appointed his good mate Thomas Becket to the highest clerical office in the land, figuring it would be easier to force the increasingly vocal religious lobby to toe the line if he was pally with the archbishop. Unfortunately for Henry, he had underestimated how seriously Thomas would take the job, and the archbishop soon began disagreeing with almost everything the king said or did. By 1170 Henry had become exasperated with his former favourite and, after a few months of sulking, 'suggested' to four of his knights that Thomas was too much to bear. The dirty deed was done on December 29. Becket's martyrdom – and canonisation in double-quick time (1173) – catapulted Canterbury Cathedral to the top of the premier league of northern European pilgrimage sites. Mindful of the growing criticism at his role in Becket's murder, Henry arrived here in 1174 for a dramatic *mea culpa*, and after allowing himself to be whipped and scolded was granted absolution.

---

is spellbinding Canterbury crowned by its fascinating cathedral.

Here too are beautiful coastal stretches dotted with beach towns and villages, from old-fashioned Broadstairs to gentrified Whitstable, to the aesthetically challenged port town of Dover, which is close enough to France to smell the garlic or hop over on a day trip to taste it.

CANTERBURY
pop 43,552

Canterbury tops the charts when it comes to English cathedral cities and is one of southern England's top attractions. The World Heritage–listed cathedral that dominates its centre is considered by many to be one of Europe's finest, and the town's narrow medieval alleyways, riverside gardens and ancient city walls are a joy to explore. But Canterbury isn't just a showpiece to times past; it's a spirited place with an energetic student population and a wide choice of contemporary bars, restaurants and arts. But book ahead for the best hotels and eateries: pilgrims may no longer flock here in their thousands but there's a year-round flood of tourists to replace them.

History

Canterbury's past is as rich as it comes. From AD 200 there was a Roman town here, which later became the capital of the Saxon kingdom of Kent. When St Augustine arrived in England in 597 to carry the Christian message to the pagan hordes, he chose Canterbury as his *cathedra* (primary see) and set about building an abbey on the outskirts of town. Following the martyrdom of Thomas Becket (see boxed text, above), Canterbury became

northern Europe's most important centre of pilgrimage, which in turn led to Geoffrey Chaucer's *The Canterbury Tales*, one of the most outstanding poetic works in English literature (see boxed text, p180).

Blasphemous murders and rampant tourism thrown aside, the city of Canterbury still remains the primary see for the Church of England.

Orientation

The Old Town is enclosed by a bulky medieval city wall that makes a wonderful walk. The Unesco World Heritage Site encompasses the cathedral, St Augustine's Abbey and St Martin's Church. Much of the centre is pedestrianised, but there is parking inside the wall.

Information

BOOKSHOPS

Chaucer Bookshop (☎ 01227-453912; 6-7 Beer Cart Lane) Antiquarian and used books.

Waterstones (☎ 01227-456343; 20-21 St Margaret's St)

INTERNET ACCESS

Dotcafe (☎ 01227-478778; 19-21 St Dunstan's St; per hr £3; 🕙 10am-7pm) Large cyber cafe near the railway station.

Main library (☎ 01227-463608; 18 High St; 🕙 9.30am-6pm Mon-Sat) Free internet access in the same building as the Royal Museum & Art Gallery.

LAUNDRY

Canterbury Laundrette (☎ 01227-452211; Nunnery Fields; 🕙 9am-6pm Mon-Fri, to 4pm Sat, to 3pm Sun)

MEDICAL SERVICES

Canterbury Health Centre (☎ 01227-452444; 26 Old Dover Rd) For general medical consultations.

THE SOUTHEAST

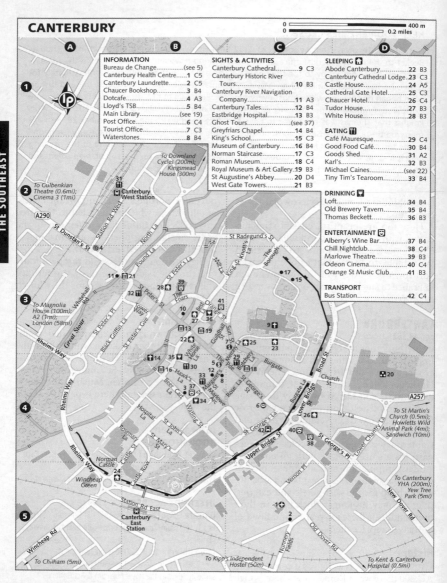

CANTERBURY

0 — 400 m
0 — 0.2 miles

INFORMATION
Bureau de Change..............(see 5)
Canterbury Health Centre......**1** C5
Canterbury Laundrette.........**2** C5
Chaucer Bookshop..............**3** B4
Dotcafe.......................**4** A3
Lloyd's TSB...................**5** B4
Main Library.................(see 19)
Post Office...................**6** C4
Tourist Office................**7** C3
Waterstones...................**8** B4

SIGHTS & ACTIVITIES
Canterbury Cathedral..........**9** C3
Canterbury Historic River
    Tours.....................**10** B3
Canterbury River Navigation
    Company...................**11** A3
Canterbury Tales..............**12** B4
Eastbridge Hospital...........**13** B3
Ghost Tours.................(see 37)
Greyfriars Chapel.............**14** B4
King's School.................**15** C3
Museum of Canterbury..........**16** B4
Norman Staircase..............**17** C3
Roman Museum..................**18** C4
Royal Museum & Art Gallery...**19** B3
St Augustine's Abbey..........**20** D4
West Gate Towers..............**21** B3

SLEEPING 🏠
Abode Canterbury..............**22** B3
Canterbury Cathedral Lodge...**23** C3
Castle House...................**24** A5
Cathedral Gate Hotel..........**25** C3
Chaucer Hotel.................**26** C4
Tudor House...................**27** B3
White House...................**28** B3

EATING 🍽
Café Mauresque................**29** C4
Good Food Café................**30** B4
Goods Shed....................**31** A2
Karl's........................**32** B3
Michael Caines.............(see 22)
Tiny Tim's Tearoom............**33** B4

DRINKING 🍷
Loft..........................**34** B4
Old Brewery Tavern............**35** B4
Thomas Beckett................**36** B3

ENTERTAINMENT 🎭
Alberry's Wine Bar............**37** B4
Chill Nightclub...............**38** C4
Marlowe Theatre...............**39** B3
Odeon Cinema..................**40** C4
Orange St Music Club..........**41** B3

TRANSPORT
Bus Station...................**42** C4

Kent & Canterbury Hospital (☎ 01227-766877;
Etherbert Rd) Has an emergency room and is a mile from
the centre.

MONEY
ATMs and other major banks are on High St,
near the corner of St Margaret's St.
Lloyd's TSB (28 St Margaret's St) Has a bureau de change.

POST
Post office (19 St George's St, inside WH Smiths;
🕑 9am-5.30pm Mon-Sat)

TOURIST OFFICES
Tourist office (☎ 01227-378100; www.canterbury
.co.uk; 12 Sun St; 🕑 9.30am-5pm Mon-Sat, 10am-4pm
Sun Easter-Oct, 10am-4pm Mon-Sat Nov-Easter) Situated

opposite the cathedral gate; the staff can help you book accommodation, excursions and theatre tickets.

Sights
CANTERBURY CATHEDRAL
The Church of England could not have a more imposing mother church than this extraordinary early Gothic **cathedral** (☎ 01227-762862; www.canterbury-cathedral.org; adult/concession £7/5.50; 9am-6.30pm Mon-Sat Easter-Sep, 9am-4.30pm Mon-Sat Oct-Easter, also 12.30-2.30pm & 4.30-5.30pm Sun year-round), the centrepiece of the city's World Heritage Site and repository of more than 1400 years of Christian history.

It's an overwhelming edifice filled with enthralling stories, striking architecture and a very real and enduring sense of spirituality, although visitors can't help but pick up on the ominous undertones of violence and bloodshed that whisper from its walls.

This ancient structure is packed with monuments commemorating the nation's battles. Also here is the grave and heraldic tunic of one of the nation's most famous warmongers, Edward the Black Prince (1330-76). The spot in the northwest transept where Archbishop Thomas Becket met his grisly end has been drawing pilgrims for more than 800 years (see the boxed text, p175). It is marked by a lit candle and striking modern altar.

The doorway to the crypt is beside the altar. This cavernous space is the cathedral's highlight, an entrancing 11th-century survivor from the cathedral's last devastating fire in 1174, which destroyed the rest of the building. Look for original carvings among the forest of pillars.

The wealth of detail in the cathedral is immense and unrelenting, so it's well worth joining a one-hour **tour** (adult/child £5/3; 10.30am, noon & 2.30pm Mon-Fri, 10.30am, noon & 1.30pm Sat Apr-Sep, noon & 2pm Mon-Sat Oct-Mar), or you can take a 30-minute self-guided **audio tour** (adult/child £3.95/1.95). There is an additional charge to take photographs.

When you leave the cathedral, go round the eastern end and turn right into **Green Court**, surrounded on the eastern side by the Deanery and on the northern side (straight ahead) by the early-14th-century Brewhouse and Bakehouse, which now house part of the very exclusive prep school, **King's School**. In the northwestern corner (far left) is the famous **Norman Staircase** (1151).

MUSEUMS
Good for history buffs, the Museum Passport (adult/child £6.20/3.70) grants free admission to all the following. Individual charges are given with each listing.

A fine 14th-century building, once the Poor Priests' Hospital, now houses the absorbing **Museum of Canterbury** (☎ 01227-475202; www.canterbury-museums.co.uk; Stour St; adult/child £3.50/2.25; 10.30am-5pm Mon-Sat year-round, also 1.30-5pm Sun Jun-Sep), which has varied exhibits from pre-Roman times to the assassination of Becket, Joseph Conrad to locally born celebs. The kids' room is excellent, with a memorable glimpse of real medieval poo among other fun activities. There's also a fun Rupert Bear Museum and a gallery celebrating that other children's favourite of old, Bagpuss.

A fascinating subterranean archaeological site forms the basis of the **Roman Museum** (☎ 01227-785575; Butchery Lane; adult/child £3/2; 10am-5pm Mon-Sat year-round, also 1.30-5pm Sun Jun-Oct), which actually lets you handle the artefacts and walk around reconstructed rooms, including a kitchen and a market place. The museum culminates with a display of the original mosaic floors.

The city's only remaining medieval gateway – a brawny 14th-century bulk with murder holes pointing over the passing cars below – is home to the small **West Gate Towers** (☎ 01227-789576; St Peter's St; adult/concession £1.25/75p; 11am-12.30pm & 1.30-3.30pm Mon-Sat), a museum of arms and armour. The rooftop views are worth squeezing up the spiral staircase for.

The mock-Tudor facade of the **Royal Museum & Art Gallery** (☎ 01227-452747; High St; admission free; 10am-5pm Mon-Sat) is a splendid display of Victorian foppery, with intricate carving and big wooden gables. The interior houses mostly ho-hum art and military memorabilia, but has a few surprises from the likes of Pissaro, Henry Moore and Van Dyke.

THE CANTERBURY TALES
A three dimensional interpretation of Chaucer's classic tales through jerky animatronics and audio guides, the ambitious **Canterbury Tales** (☎ 01227-479227; www.canterburytales.org.uk; St Margaret's St; adult/child £7.25/5.25; 10am-5pm Mar-Jun, 9.30am-5pm Jul & Aug, 10am-5pm Sep & Oct, 10am-4.30pm Nov-Feb) is certainly entertaining but could never do full justice to Chaucer's tales. It's a lively and fun introduction for the young or uninitiated, however.

ST AUGUSTINE'S ABBEY

An integral but often overlooked part of the Canterbury World Heritage Site, **St Augustine's Abbey** (EH; ☎ 01227-767345; adult/child £4.20/2.10; ⏰ 10am-6pm Jul & Aug, 11am-5pm Sat & Sun Sep-Mar, 10am-5pm Wed-Sun Apr-Jun) was founded in AD 597, marking the rebirth of Christianity in southern England. Later requisitioned as a royal palace, it was to fall into disrepair and now only stumpy foundations remain. A small museum and a worthwhile audio tour do their best to underline the site's importance and put flesh back on its now humble bones.

ST MARTIN'S CHURCH

This stumpy little **church** (☎ 01227-768072; North Holmes Rd; admission free; ⏰ 11am-4pm Tue, Thu & Sat Apr-Sep, to 3pm Oct-Mar) is thought to be England's oldest parish in continuous use, and where Queen Bertha (the wife of the Saxon King Ethelbert) welcomed Augustine upon his arrival in the 6th century. The original Saxon church has been swallowed by a medieval refurbishment, but it's still worth the 900m walk east of the abbey.

EASTBRIDGE HOSPITAL & GREYFRIARS CHAPEL

A 'place of hospitality' for pilgrims, soldiers and the elderly since 1180, the Hospital of St Thomas the Martyr **Eastbridge** (☎ 01227-471688; www.eastbridgehospital.org.uk; 25 High St; adult/5-16yr/senior/under 5yr £1/50p/75p/free; ⏰ 10am-5pm Mon-Sat) is worth a visit for the Gothic-arched undercroft and historic chapel. Its 16th-century almshouses are still in use today.

In serene riverside gardens behind the hospital you'll find **Greyfriars Chapel** (admission free; ⏰ 2-4pm Mon-Sat Easter-Sep), the first English monastery built by Franciscan monks in 1267.

Tours

Canterbury Historic River Tours (☎ 07790-534744; www.canterburyrivertours.co.uk; adult/child £6.50/5; ⏰ 10am-5pm Apr-Sep) Will take you on a rowing-boat tour including (prebooked) candlelit tours, from behind The Old Weaver's House on St Peter's St.

Canterbury River Navigation Company (☎ 07816-760869; www.crnc.co.uk; Westgate Gardens; adult/child £7/4; ⏰ Apr-Sep) Relaxing punt trips.

Canterbury Walks (☎ 01227-459779; www.canterbury-walks.co.uk; adult/under 12yr/senior & student £4.70/3.20/4.20; ⏰ 2pm daily Apr-Oct, also 11.30am Mon-Sat Jul–mid-Sep) Chaperoned walking tours; leave from the tourist office.

Ghost Tours (☎ 07779-575831; adult/child £7/5.50) Depart from outside Alberry's wine bar in St Margaret's St at 8pm year-round every Friday and Saturday. Only groups need book.

Festivals & Events

Myriad musicians, comedians, theatre groups and other artists from around the world come to the party for two weeks in mid-October, during the **Canterbury Festival** (☎ 01227-452853; www.canterburyfestival.co.uk).

Sleeping
BUDGET

Yew Tree Park (☎ 01227-700306; www.yewtreepark.com; Stone St, Petham; tent & 2 adults £11.80-16.80; ⏰ Mar-Sep; Ⓟ 🖳 wi-fi) Set in gentle rolling countryside 5 miles southeast of the city, this lovely family-run camp site has plenty of soft grass to pitch a tent on and a heated swimming pool. Call for directions and transportation information.

Kipp's Independent Hostel (☎ 01227-786121; www.kipps-hostel.com; 40 Nunnery Fields; dm/s/d £15/20/35; 🖳) This red-brick town house is popular for its laid-back, homely atmosphere with friendly hosts and long-term residents, lots of communal areas, clean though cramped dorms, bike hire and garden. It's just south of the centre.

Canterbury YHA (☎ 0845 371 9010; www.yha.org.uk; 54 New Dover Rd; dm £20.95; Ⓟ 🖳) This grand Victorian Gothic-style villa is a little way out of town, but it's spacious and organised, with a garden and cheaper, prepared-tent accommodation. It's a great deal, and also has single rooms. It's 1¼ miles southeast of the centre, and open year-round by advanced booking. Wheelchair access available.

MIDRANGE

Tudor House (☎ 01227-765650; 6 Best Lane; s £25-35, d £48-55) Three overlapping storeys decorated with whitewashed shingles introduce this historic guest house, which sits beside the river near the High Street. The plain rooms don't make much of its period features, but they're clean and cosy, with sloping floors and the odd exposed beam, and there's a cute little cabin bedroom at the bottom of the garden.

Cathedral Gate Hotel (☎ 01227-464381; www.cathgate.co.uk; 36 Burgate; s/d from £67/100, without bathroom from £42/72) This often-photographed 15th-century hotel adjoins the spectacular cathedral gate, which it predates – a fact that becomes evident upon exploring its labyrinthine passageways, where few rooms lack an angled floor, low door or wonky wall. Rooms are simple but worth it for the fantastic position.

Castle House (☎ 01227-761897; www.castlehouse hotel.co.uk; 28 Castle St; s/d/f from £50/70/90; P 🖳 wi-fi) This historic guest house sits opposite the ruins of Canterbury's Norman castle, and incorporates part of the old city walls. The deep reds of the guest lounge and reception give the hotel a warm feel and many of the tasteful, high-ceilinged rooms have great views.

Magnolia House (☎ 01227-765121; www.magnolia housecanterbury.co.uk; 36 St Dunstan's Tce; s/d from £55/65; P 🖳 wi-fi) A gorgeous Georgian guest house, complete with pretty rooms, lovely gardens and delicious breakfasts.

White House (☎ 01227-761836; www.canterbury breaks.co.uk; 6 St Peter's Lane; s/d £55/70; 🖳) This elegant white Regency town house, supposedly once home to Queen Victoria's head coachman, has a friendly welcome, seven spick-and-span rooms with crisp white linen and country touches, and a grand guest lounge complete with fireplace and beaten leather sofas.

Canterbury Cathedral Lodge (☎ 01227-865350; www.canterburycathedrallodge.org; Canterbury Cathedral precincts; r from £79; 🖳 wi-fi) The position of this modern, circular lodge is unbeatable. It's right opposite the cathedral within the precinct itself. The clean, modern rooms – done out in white and blond wood – have excellent facilities but what really makes this place are the views. Call in good time, as it's often booked up with large groups.

TOP END

Abode Canterbury (☎ 01227-766266; www.abodehotels .co.uk; 30-33 High St; s/d from £89/109) The only boutique hotel in town, rooms here are graded from 'comfortable' to 'fabulous' and for the most part they live up to their names. They come with little features such as handmade beds, cashmere throws, velour bathrobes, beautiful modern bathrooms and little tuck boxes of locally produced snacks. There's a splendid champagne bar, restaurant and tavern here too.

Chaucer Hotel (☎ 01227-464427; www.swallowhotels .com; 63 Ivy Lane; s/d from £105/130; P) Just outside the old city walls, this once elegant red-brick Georgian house now has the aura of a chain hotel: plush but more than a little bland. The position makes up for its lack of personality, however.

Eating

Karl's (☎ 01227-764380; 43 St Peter's St; snacks £3-7; 🕑 9am-6pm Mon-Sat) The walls of this bright little deli are crammed with fine cheeses, artisan breads and pastries, coffee beans and food-friendly wines. You can sample the delicious wares (including fantastic deli sandwiches and cheeseboards) in a comfy dining space at the back of the shop or in the small garden.

Good Food Cafe (☎ 01227-456654; 1 Jewry Lane; soups £3.95, specials £6.95; 🕑 9am-5pm Tue-Sat, noon-4pm Sun) This unfussy little cafe sits above an equally healthy wholefoods store. It's full of delicious locally sourced, organic and biodynamically grown vegies and daily specials such as quiches and lasagne.

Tiny Tim's Tearoom (☎ 01227-450793; 34 St Margaret's St; mains £7-13; 🕑 9.30am-5pm Tue-Sat, 10.30am-4pm Sun) Not a hint of chintz in this English tearoom, it's pure 1930s elegance. Come in to enjoy big breakfasts full of Kentish ingredients or tiers of cakes, crumpets and sandwiches for high tea. There's a sunny courtyard garden outside and there are chutneys, breads and local Kentish wines for sale.

Cafe Mauresque (☎ 01227-464300; www.cafemaur esque.com; 8 Butchery Lane; mains £7-17; 🕑 noon-10pm Sun-Thu, to 10.30pm Fri & Sat) Fun little North African and Spanish spot with a plain cafe upstairs as well as a romantic basement swathed in exotic fabric, serving up rich tagines, couscous and tapas. There are hubbly bubbly hookah pipes to finish off your meal.

our pick Goods Shed (☎ 01227-459153; Station Rd West; lunch £8-12, dinner £10-16; 🕑 market 10am-7pm Tue-Sat, to 4pm Sun, restaurant lunch & dinner Tue-Sun) Farmers market, food hall and fabulous restaurant all rolled into one, this converted station warehouse by the railway is a hit with everyone from self-caterers to sit-down gourmets. The chunky wooden tables sit slightly above the market hubbub but in full view of its appetite-whetting stalls, and country-style daily specials exploit the freshest farm goodies available.

Michael Caines (☎ 01227-826684; Adobe Canterbury Hotel, 30-33 High St; mains £20-28; 🕑 lunch & dinner) Owned by Michelin star–winning chef Michael Caines, this is Canterbury's only 'fine dining' restaurant, with elegant taupe and caramel decor and an elaborate menu of Kentish ingredients, such as shellfish from Whitstable, Romney Marsh lamb or Tamworth pork, twisted into (rather small) culinary delights. It's on the ground floor of the Abode Canterbury Hotel.

THE SOUTHEAST

Drinking

Old Brewery Tavern (☎ 01227-826682; Adobe Canterbury Hotel, 30-33 High St) Trendy boozer in a large open space adorned with black-and-white prints of brewery workers of old and a white brick courtyard with a huge curved wood and soft leather sofa. The choice of beers is plentiful, and there's a good wine list as well as a solid menu of English pub classics like fish pie and gammon, egg and chips – albeit a swanky version. Enter from White Horse Lane.

Thomas Beckett (☎ 01227-464384; 21 Best Lane) A classic English pub with a garden's worth of hops hanging from its timber frame, several quality ales to sample and a traditional decor of copper pots, comfy seating and a fireplace to cosy up to on winter nights. It also serves decent pub grub (mains £6 to £9).

Loft (☎ 01227-456515; 516 St Margaret's St) Miles away from Canterbury's quaint alehouses, this slick bar plays chilled electronic beats in a retro-edged setting with one extremely long couch, a black granite bar and DJs spinning house at the weekend. It draws a youthful crowd and serves a medley of multicoloured cocktails.

Entertainment

NIGHTCLUBS

Alberry's Wine Bar (☎ 01227-452378; St Margaret's St) Every night is different at this after-hours music bar, which puts on everything from smooth live jazz to DJ-led drum and bass to commercial pop. It's a two-level place where you can relax over a French Kiss (cocktail or otherwise) above, before partying in the basement bar below.

Chill Nightclub (☎ 01227-761276; St George's Pl, New Dover Rd; admission £3-6) Canterbury's newest club is a large, fun, cheesy place with a popular student night on Mondays and house anthems and old skool at the weekends.

Orange St Music Club (☎ 01227-760801; www.orangestreetmusic.com; 15 Orange St; ☾ Tue-Sat) This Bohemian music and cultural venue in a 19th-century hall puts on a medley of jazz, salsa, folk, DJ competitions, comedy and even poetry.

CINEMAS

Odeon Cinema (☎ 0871-224 4007; cnr Upper Bridge St & St George's Pl) Catch the latest movies here.

Cinema 3 (☎ 01227-769075; University of Kent) Part of the Gulbenkian Theatre complex. Shows a mix of mainstream and arty films and old classics.

THEATRE

Marlowe Theatre (☎ 01227-787 787; www.marlowetheatre.com; The Friars) Canterbury's central venue for performing arts brings in touring plays, dances, concerts and musicals year-round.

Gulbenkian Theatre (☎ 01227-769075; www.kent.ac.uk/gulbenkian; University of Kent) Out on the university campus, this large long-time venue puts on plenty of contemporary plays, modern dance and great live music.

Getting There & Away

Canterbury is 58 miles from London and 15 miles from Margate and Dover.

BUS

The bus station is just within the city walls on St George's Ln. There are frequent buses to London Victoria (£12.70, two hours, hourly)

THE CANTERBURY TALES

If English literature has a father figure, then it is Geoffrey Chaucer (1342/3–1400). Chaucer was the first English writer to introduce characters – rather than 'types' – into fiction, and he did so to greatest effect in his most popular work, *The Canterbury Tales*.

Written between 1387 and his death, the *Tales* is an unfinished series of 24 vivid stories as told by a party of pilgrims on their journey from London to Canterbury and back. Chaucer successfully created the illusion that the pilgrims, not Chaucer (though he appears in the tales as himself), are telling the stories, which allowed him unprecedented freedom as an author.

Chaucer's achievement remains a high point of European literature, but it was also the first time that English came to match Latin (the language of the Church) and French (spoken by the Norman court) as a language of high literature. *The Canterbury Tales* remains one of the pillars of the literary canon, but more than that it's a collection of rollicking good yarns of adultery, debauchery, crime and edgy romance, and filled with Chaucer's witty observances of human nature. That said, contemporary modern readers tend to make more sense of modern transliterations than the often obscure original Middle English version.

and services to Dover (£5.20, 35 minutes, hourly). There are also buses to Margate (53 minutes, three per hour), Broadstairs (one hour, twice hourly), Ramsgate (80 minutes, twice hourly) and Whitstable (30 minutes, every 15 minutes).

TRAIN
There are two train stations: Canterbury East (for the YHA hostel), accessible from London Victoria; and Canterbury West, accessible from London's Charing Cross and Waterloo East stations.

London-bound trains leave frequently (£20.90, 1½ hours, two to three hourly), as do Canterbury East to Dover Priory trains (£6.70, 16 to 28 minutes, every 30 minutes).

Canterbury will be a stop on the UK's first high-speed rail line, with trains pulling in at London St Pancras from late 2009. It is expected to reduce journey times significantly.

Getting Around
Canterbury's centre is mostly pedestrianised. Car parks are dotted along and just within the walls, otherwise parking is by pay and display. Day trippers may prefer to use one of the city's three park-and-ride sites, which cost £2.50 per day and are connected to the centre by buses every 10 minutes from 7am to 7.30pm Monday to Saturday, or 10am to 6pm Sunday.

Taxi companies include **Cathedral Cars** (☎ 451000) and **Cabwise** (☎ 01227-712929). **Downland Cycles** (☎ 01227-479643; www.downlandcycles.co.uk; ☺ 9.30am-5pm Mon-Sat, 10am-4.30pm Sun) rents bikes from the Malthouse on St Stephen's Rd. Bikes cost £12 per day with helmet.

AROUND CANTERBURY
Howlett's Wild Animal Park
You can trade grins and glowers with the world's largest captive breeding collection of lowland gorillas at this 28-hectare **park** (☎ 01227-721286; www.totallywild.net; Bekesbourne; adult/4-16yr/under 4yr £14.45/11.45/free; ☺ 10am-6pm Apr-Sep, to 5pm Oct-Mar). The animals here live in an environment as close to their natural habitat as possible. Rather than simply keeping the animals in captivity, the park funds projects to reintroduce these rare and endangered animals back to their natural habitat. You'll also see tigers, a black rhino breeding sanctuary, African elephants, monkeys, giant anteaters and more.

A COTTAGE OF YOUR OWN

If you'd prefer a self-catering holiday using a cottage as your base, try these websites as a starting point:

Best of Brighton & Sussex Cottages (www.bestofbrighton.co.uk)

Garden of England Cottages (www .gardenofenglandcottages.co.uk)

Kent Holiday Cottages (www.kentholiday cottages.co.uk)

The park is 4 miles east of Canterbury. By car, take the A257 and turn right at the sign for Bekesbourne, then follow the signs. Several regular buses run from Canterbury bus station to Littlebourne, from where it's about a mile's walk.

Chilham
Five miles southwest of Canterbury on the A252, compact little Chilham is one of the best examples of a medieval village you'll see anywhere in England. Built in typical feudal fashion around a square beside the 12th-century castle, the village consists of a 13th-century church and a cluster of Tudor and Jacobean timber-framed houses.

The town makes a great destination for a lovely day's walk from Canterbury via the North Downs Way (see p173). Alternatively, hourly trains run from Canterbury (nine minutes). The centre is a half-mile walk from the station.

ROCHESTER
pop 27,000
Romans, Saxons and Normans have all occupied this historic riverside town and their architectural remains can be seen to this day, most vividly in a grand Cathedral and a ruined Norman Castle that loom over the town's medieval walls, cobbled streets and half-timbered buildings. Charles Dickens spent a large chunk of his childhood and the last few years of his life here, and many of the town's streets and buildings feature (albeit disguised) in his books.

The **tourist office** (☎ 01634-843666; 95 High St; ☺ 9am-5pm Mon-Fri; 10am-5pm Sat; 10.30am-5pm Sun) has details of local accommodation. Free tours of the town leave here from Easter to September on weekends, bank holidays and Wednesdays at 2.15pm.

OAST HOUSES

While travelling through Kent you're bound to spy the jaunty conical tips of the county's distinctive oast houses peeking out from amid the trees. These giant kilns were used for drying hops, a key ingredient in beer, introduced to the region in the early 15th century. The odd cone-shaped roof was necessary to create a draught for the kiln fire, and the crooked nozzles sticking out from their tops could be moved to regulate the airflow to the fire.

If your curiosity is piqued, you can stick your nose into a few prime examples at the **Hop Farm Country Park** (☎ 01622-872068; www.thehopfarm.co.uk; Paddock Wood, Tonbridge; adult/child £7.50/6.50; ⊙ 10am-5pm), which also re-creates the history of hop picking in Kent. It's signed off the A228 near Paddock Wood, southwest of Maidstone.

Many oast houses have been converted into homes and oast-house B&Bs are becoming more common throughout the county; check with the various tourist offices for information on local possibilities.

Ghost Tours (☎ 07939-241580) leave from Rochester Cathedral at 8pm on the first Wednesday of every month.

For three days in June, the streets of Rochester take on an air of Victorian England during the town's annual **Dickens Festival**, when parades, music and costumed characters make his best-loved novels come to life.

Rochester Castle (☎ 01634-335882; adult/child £5/4; ⊙ 10am-6pm Apr-Sep; to 4pm Oct-Mar) is one of the finest examples of Norman architecture in England and has lived through three sieges and partial demolition. The flooring of the 12th-century, 35m Norman keep is long gone, allowing awesome views of the keep's structure and open roof from the ground. You can also climb to the top of the battlements for panoramas over the town.

Rochester Cathedral (☎ 01634-861232; admission free; guided tours £4; ⊙ 7.30am-6pm; to 5pm Sat), founded in AD 604, is the second-oldest cathedral in England. Although construction on the present building started in 1080 and remodelling has left a mixture of styles, much of the Norman building remains, including an impressive nave and remains of a 13th-century wall painting featuring a wheel of fortune.

Housed in a splendid 17th-century building, **Guildhall Museum** (☎ 01634-848717; High St; admission free; ⊙ 10am-4pm Tue-Sun) contains a range of exhibitions including a Dickens room, where you can find out which parts of the town feature in his books, and a dramatic exhibition of life on hulks – prison ships used to contain convicts in the 18th century.

Eating

Precinct Pantry (☎ 01634-409645; 3 Cottage Yard; ⊙ 10am-5pm Mon-Sat; from 11am Sun) This little cafe has a prime location next to the cathedral and opposite the castle. There's a tiny dining room inside and in summer you can enjoy the great sandwiches, homemade cakes and tea on the pavement tables outside.

Topes (☎ 01634-845270; www.topesrestaurant.com; 60 High St; ⊙ lunch Wed-Sun; dinner Tue-Sat) Deservedly popular, modern-European food served in a cosy restaurant with low-beamed slanted ceilings, wood panelling and a large, inviting fireplace. Some windows look out onto the castle.

Getting There & Away

Trains to London Victoria (£12.30; 40 to 55 minutes) leave four times an hour and there are less frequent services to Charing Cross (£12.30; one hour 10 minutes). Trains to Canterbury leave twice hourly (£9.60; 45 minutes).

WHITSTABLE
pop 30,159

Best known for its succulent oysters, which have been harvested here since Roman times, pretty little Whitstable has transformed into a popular destination for weekending metropolitans, attracted by the clapboard houses, pretty shingle beach and candy-coloured beach huts that line the shore. The town has nevertheless managed to retain the character of a working fishing town, its thriving harbour and fish market coexisting with boutiques, organic delis and swanky restaurants.

The **tourist office** (☎ 01227-275482; www.visitwhit stable.co.uk; 7 Oxford St; ⊙ 10am-5pm Mon-Sat Jul & Aug, to 4pm Mon-Sat Sep-Jun) can help you find and book accommodation, though at the time of writing there were plans to shut the office down, in which case Canterbury would become the nearest tourist office. The nearby **library** (☎ 01227-273309; 31-33 Oxford St; ☿ 9am-6pm Mon-Fri, to 5pm Sat, 10am to 4pm Sun) can make you a temporary member to use its internet terminals.

The modest **Whitstable Museum & Gallery** (☎ 01227-276998; www.whitstable-museum.co.uk; 8 Oxford St; admission free; ☿ 10am-4pm Mon-Sat year-round, 1-4pm Sun Jul & Aug) has good exhibits on Whitstable's oyster and fishing industry as well as a corner dedicated to the actor Peter Cushing, the town's most famous resident, who died in 1994.

For a week at the end of July, the town hosts a seafood, arts and music extravaganza, the **Whitstable Oyster Festival** (www.whitstableoysterfestival .co.uk), offering a packed schedule of events, from history walks, crab-catching and oyster-eating competitions to a beer festival and traditional 'blessing of the waters'.

Sleeping

Pearl Fisher (☎ 01227-771000; www.thepearlfisher.com; 103 Cromwell Rd; s/d £50/75; P) A few minutes' walk from the high street, this B&B has comfortable, themed rooms and plenty of thoughtful touches, such as chocolates on the pillows at night. There's a warm welcome and huge, top-quality breakfasts.

Hotel Continental (☎ 01227-280280; www.hotel continental.co.uk; 29 Beach Walk; s/d/huts from £60/70/100, d with sea view & balcony £100; P) The rooms in this elegant seaside art-deco building are nothing special – come for the quirky converted fishermen's huts right on the beach. Room rates increase by £15 to £100 a night during high season.

Eating & Drinking

Whitstable's famous oysters are harvested between September and April.

Crab & Winkle (☎ 0845 257 1587; South Quay, The Harbour; mains £12-18; ☿ 12pm-9pm) Sitting above the Whitstable Fish Market in a black clapboard house, this bright restaurant has large windows overlooking the harbour, a buzzing vibe and excellent seafood with a few options for meat lovers thrown in.

Wheeler's Oyster Bar (☎ 01227-273311; 8 High St; mains £13-19; ☿ lunch & dinner Thu-Tue) Squeeze onto a stool by the bar or into the Victorian dining room of this teeny pink restaurant, choose from a seasonal menu and enjoy the best seafood in Whitstable. They've been serving oysters since 1856. It's a BYO venue; no credit cards.

Old Neptune (☎ 01227-272262; www.neppy.co.uk; Marine Tce) About as far onto the beach as it's possible to be, with plenty of strategically placed outside tables, wonky wooden floorboards, window seats and even a honky-tonk piano in the corner, Whitstable's most famous pub is ramshackle and fun. It puts on regular live music and there's a friendly vibe, although it can get massively crowded throughout summer.

Getting There & Away

Buses 4 and 6 go to Canterbury (30 minutes) every 15 minutes.

AROUND WHITSTABLE
Herne Bay

The only reason to visit Herne Bay is to join one of its waterborne tours, the best of which is on the **Wildlife** (☎ 01227-366712; www.wildlifesail ing.com; 8 Western Esplanade; ☿ Apr-Oct), a traditionally styled boat with a knowledgeable skipper that sails to an offshore sandbank packed with seals. Trips last five hours and prices depend on group size but start from £19.50 each. Another company to try is **Bayblast Tours** (☎ 01227-373372; www.bayblast.co.uk; 3hr seal trip £32; ☿ Mar-Oct).

There's an enjoyable coastline walk 2 miles east from Herne Bay into **Reculver Country Park** (admission free), where you'll find the remains of a Roman fort built in AD 280 and the 7th-century Saxon Church of St Mary. The church collapsed in 1809 due to coastal erosion, but the distinctive 12th-century twin towers have been rebuilt. It's an atmospheric if melancholic site that dominates the flat scenery around it.

Buses run from Whitstable to Herne Bay (20 minutes, every 15 minutes). Stagecoach bus 7 goes from Herne Bay train station to Reculver Park.

ISLE OF THANET

You won't need a ferry or a wetsuit to reach this island, which was swallowed by the mainland during the first millennium as the Watsun Channel dried up. It now forms a perky peninsula jutting out to sea at the far eastern tip of the country. But in its island days, Thanet was the springboard to several epoch-making episodes of English history. It was here that the Romans kicked off their invasion in the first century AD, and where Augustine landed in AD 597 to begin his conversion of the pagans.

These days, Thanet's pretty coastline is home to a string of Victorian resorts that are only invaded by the summer bathing-suit brigade. Walkers can also look to conquer the **Thanet Coastal Path**, a 20-mile trail that hugs the shore from Margate to Pegwell Bay via Broadstairs and Ramsgate.

Margate
pop 57,000

A popular seaside resort for more than 250 years thanks to its fine-sand beaches, Margate's tatty seafront and amusement arcades seem somewhat removed from the candy-striped beach huts and crowd-pleasing Punch and Judy puppet shows of its Victorian heyday. Major cultural regeneration projects – including the spectacular new Turner Contemporary art gallery – should reverse the town's fortunes.

Visit the **tourist office** (☎ 01843-292019; www.tourism.thanet.gov.uk; 12-13 The Parade; ☉ 9.15am-4.15pm Mon-Fri, 10am-4pm Sat) for maps and information.

SIGHTS

Margate's unique attraction is the mysterious, subterranean **Shell Grotto** (☎ 01843-220008; www.shellgrotto.co.uk; Grotto Hill; adult/child £2.50/1.50; ☉ 10am-5pm daily Easter-Oct, 11am-4pm Sat & Sun Nov-Easter). Discovered in 1835, it's a claustrophobic collection of rooms and passageways embedded with millions of shells arranged in symbol-rich mosaics. It has inspired feverish speculation over the years but presents few answers; some think it a 2000-year-old pagan temple, others an elaborate 19th-century hoax. Either way, it's an exquisite place worth seeing.

A new **Turner Contemporary** (☎ 01843-294208; www.turnercontemporary.org) gallery – to highlight the town's links with the artist JMW Turner – is due to open in 2010.

In the meantime, Turner Contemporary exhibitions take place at the **Turner Contemporary Project Space** (53-57 High Street) and **Droit House** (Stone Pier).

SLEEPING & EATING

Margate YHA (☎ 0870 770 5956; www.yha.org.uk; The Beachcomber, 3-4 Royal Esplanade; dm member/nonmember £15/18; **P** **⬛** wi-fi) Clean and family-friendly hostel in what used to be a hotel, a gentle stroll from a sandy bay and about half a mile west of the tourist office. Book a couple of days in advance.

Walpole Bay Hotel (☎ 01843-221703; www.walpolebayhotel.co.uk; 5th Ave, Cliftonville; s/d from £50/70) For a hefty slice of Victoriana, look no further than this eccentric part-hotel, part-shrine to the 19th century. The pink, flouncy rooms are furnished with antiques, while public spaces are filled by glass-cased displays of memorabilia from the 1800s. The hotel is a mile from central Margate, in Cliftonville.

No 6 Brasserie (☎ 01843-295603; 6 Market Pl; mains £12.95-16.95; ☉ lunch & dinner) One of the best places to eat in Margate – an elegant bar and restaurant full of heavy beams and squishy leather sofas, serving up decent European food and a great selection of cocktails.

GETTING THERE & AWAY

Buses to Margate leave from London Victoria (£12.10, 2½ hours, five daily). From Canterbury, take bus 8 (55 minutes, three hourly).

Trains run twice hourly from London Victoria and less frequently from Charing Cross (£23.90, one hour 50 minutes). Margate is due to be joined to London St Pancras from December 2009 when the UK's first high-speed rail line opens.

Broadstairs
pop 24,370

Unlike its bigger, brasher neighbours, the charming resort village of Broadstairs revels in its quaintness, plays the Victorian nostalgia card at every opportunity, and names every second business after the works of its most famous holidaymaker, Charles Dickens. The town's elegant cliff-top buildings, neatly manicured gardens, wide saffron-sand bay and wistful Punch and Judy shows hide a far grittier history of smuggling and shipbuilding.

The **tourist office** (☎ 01843-861232; 2 Victoria Pde, Dickens House Museum; ☉ 10am-5pm Mon-Sun Jun-Sep, Tue-Sat April-Jun, Wed-Sat Sep-Apr) has details of the annual, week-long **Dickens Festival** in mid-June, which culminates in a banquet-cum-ball in Victorian dress (£18). It's located in the quaint **Dickens House Museum** (☎ 01843-861232; www.dickenshouse.co.uk; 2 Victoria Pde; adult/child £2.50/1.30; ☉ 10am-5pm Apr-Oct), which was actually the home of Mary Pearson Strong, inspiration for the character of Betsey Trotwood in *David Copperfield*. Diverse Dickensiana on display includes letters from the author.

Dickens wrote parts of *Bleak House* and *David Copperfield* in the handsome, if slightly worse for wear, cliff-top house above the pier between 1837 and 1859. Now private property, it suffered severe fire damage in 2006.

SLEEPING & EATING

East Horndon Hotel (☎ 01843-868306; www.easthorn donhotel.com; 4 Eastern Esplanade; s/d £35/66; ☐ wi-fi) This elegant hotel sits on manicured lawns a few yards from the beach. The comfortable rooms are slightly bland but have sea views to make up for it, several with little balconies where you can sit out to enjoy the sunset over the bay.

Copperfields Guest House (☎ 01843-601247; www .copperfieldsbb.co.uk; 11 Queen's Rd; d & tw from £65; ☐ wi-fi) This vegetarian B&B has three homely, if rather chintzy, rooms and a warm welcome from the owners and pet Yorkie. It also caters for vegans and all products in the bathrooms are cruelty free. It's a short hop away from the seafront and there's space to store muddy bikes.

Tartar Frigate (☎ 01843-862013; 42 Harbour St; mains £14-16.50) Dating back to the 18th century, this seafront pub is a great place to be in summer when tourists and locals alike spill out onto the beach. The seafood restaurant upstairs has excellent food and great views of the bay and the pub has regular live folk music.

GETTING THERE & AWAY

The Thanet Loop bus runs every 10 minutes through the day to Ramsgate (£2, 20 minutes) and Margate (£2, 20 minutes).

Bus 8 runs to Canterbury (1½ hours, three per hour) via Margate and bus 9 via Ramsgate (hourly). National Express buses leave High St for London Victoria (£12.10, three hours, five daily).

Trains run to London Victoria (£25.80, two hours, twice hourly) and there are less frequent services to London Bridge and Charing Cross. You may have to change at Ramsgate.

Ramsgate
pop 38,200

The most diverse of Kent's coastal towns, Ramsgate has a friendlier feel than rival Margate and is more vibrant than quaint little neighbour Broadstairs. A forest of sails whistle serenely in the breeze below the town's handsome curved harbour walls, surrounded by laid-back seafront bars and cosmopolitan street cafes that give the town a tang of nearby France. History buffs are kept busy

---

TOP FIVE CASTLES

- Leeds Castle (Kent Weald; p193)
- Dover Castle (Dover; p188)
- Hever Castle (Kent Weald; p192)
- Bodiam Castle (Around Battle; p197)
- Arundel Castle (Arundel; p212)

---

by the town's neo-Gothic architecture and rich maritime heritage, whilst the town's wide Blue Flag beaches appeal to families, surfers and sun worshippers.

On a small alleyway off Leopold St, the **tourist office** (☎ 01843-583333; www.tourism.thanet .gov.uk; 17 Albert Ct; ☺ 9am-5pm Tue-Sat Apr-May, daily Jun-Sep, to 12.15pm Wed-Sat Sep-Mar) has information and a self-guided walking map of the area's smugglers' caves.

SIGHTS & ACTIVITIES

When the sun's out, rollerbladers, surfers and sunbathers all head to the east of the main harbour where Ramsgate's reddish-sand-and-shingle beach and elegant promenade sit under an imposing cliff.

At least 620 ships have been wrecked in the notorious Goodwin Sands off this stretch of coast, and an intriguing assortment of loot from their barnacled carcasses is in the **Ramsgate Maritime Museum** (☎ 01843-290399; www .ekmt.fogonline.co.uk; The Clock House, Royal Harbour; adult/child £1.50/75p; ☺ 10am-5pm Tue-Sun Easter-Sep, 11am-4.30pm Thu-Sun Oct-Easter), inside the town's 19th-century clock tower near the harbour. Here, too, is a line marking Ramsgate's meridian (the town has its own Ramsgate Mean Time).

SLEEPING

Glendevon Guesthouse (☎ 01843-570909; www.glen devonguesthouse.co.uk; 8 Truro Rd; s/d from £35/55) This ecofriendly guest house, run by energetic and outgoing young hosts, is a 10-minute stroll from the action down at the harbour. The hallways of this grand Victorian house are decorated with watercolours by local artists, and there are bookshelves full of games, books and videos to borrow. All the rooms have very comfy beds and small kitchens, and breakfast is a convivial affair taken around one large table.

ourpick Royal Harbour Hotel (☎ 01843-591514; www.royalharbourhotel.co.uk; Nelson Crescent; s/d from £65/85, superior £100-215; (🖳 wi-fi) Occupying two regency town houses on a glorious seafront crescent, this boutique hotel feels enveloped in warmth and quirkiness – an eclectic collection of books, magazines, games and artwork line the hotel, and there's a gramophone with old LPs and an honesty bar in the lounge, complimentary cheese and biscuits in the evening and hot-water bottles when it's chilly. Rooms range from tiny nauticalesque 'cabins' to country-house style, four-poster doubles, most with postcard views over the forest of masts below.

EATING

Pete's Fish Factory (97 Harbour St; fish & chips from £3.50; ☷ 11.30am-11.30pm) Follow the tangy smells of salt and vinegar to this classic fish-and-chip shop (with a roof in the shape of a giant sandcastle), where cheap, sinful and salty treats can be devoured on outside seating.

Surin Restaurant (☎ 01843-592001; www.surin restaurant.co.uk; 30 Harbour St; mains £6-13; ☷ lunch & dinner Tue-Sun) Ramsgate is an unlikely spot to eat some of the best Thai, Cambodian and Laotian food this side of the Hindu Kush, but sure enough, the tasty menu in this restaurant delivers. The restaurant is a dumpling's throw from the seafront and even serves its own label of microbrewed beers.

DRINKING

Miles Cafe Culture (☎ 01843-585008; 54-56 Harbour Pde; ☷ 8am-1.30am) This relaxed and understated bar, cafe and restaurant right next to the harbour attracts an exuberant crowd of all ages. There's a good selection of wine and cocktails to enjoy by candlelight whilst slumped into a deep leather sofa, and the action spills out onto outside tables as well.

Rokka (☎ 01843-599999; 64 Harbour Pde; ☷ 10am-midnight Sun-Thu; till 2am Fri & Sat) This kitsch red-and-white bar looks like the kind of place Austin Powers might frequent: curved, white plastic chairs, red-leather sofas, devilish red chandeliers and beaded curtains. It also does a nice line in cocktails and Mediterranean snacks.

GETTING THERE & AWAY

National Express bus 22 runs to London Victoria (£12.70, three hours, five daily) via Margate and Broadstairs. There are also local buses to Canterbury, Broadstairs and Ramsgate. Trains run to London Victoria and Charing Cross (£25.80, 1¾ to two hours, twice hourly).

There's also a ferry service to Ostend in Belgium run by **Transeuropa Ferries** (☎ 01843-595522; www.transeuropaferries.com) from Ramsgate New Port just west of the centre (five hours, from £36 per passenger with car, four each day).

When the UK's first high-speed rail line opens (due late 2009 at the time of writing), there will be a direct link between Ramsgate and London St Pancras, which should significantly reduce journey times.

SANDWICH
pop 4398

With a top slice of ancient churches, gables and peg-tiled roofs, a juicy filling of medieval streets and timber-framed houses, and a wholesome base slice of riverside strolls and superb golf links, Sandwich makes a very tasty morsel for passing travellers. Today it's a sleepy little inland settlement, but the town retains a certain salty tang from its days as an important Cinque Port before the coastline shifted and its harbour silted up in the 17th century.

Inside the Elizabethan guildhall, the **tourist office** (☎ 01304-613565; www.open-sandwich.co.uk; New St; ☷ 9.30am-4pm Apr-Oct) has information packs on short and long walks in the area. Guided tours of town can be arranged by contacting the **Sandwich Local History Society** (☎ 01304-613 476; tours £2; ☷ evenings only).

Sights & Activities

Sandwich's spiderweb of medieval and Elizabethan streets is perfect for ambling and getting pleasantly lost. **Strand St** in particular has one of the highest concentrations of half-timbered buildings in the country. Steeped gables betray the strong influence of Protestant Flemish refugees who settled in the town in the 16th century.

A cute little flint-chequered **Barbican** tollgate, also dating from this period, controls traffic flow on the waterfront.

Architecture buffs should head for the **Church of St Clement**, which has a handsome Norman tower. The oldest church in Sandwich is **St Peter's** (King St), now out of action. It's a real mixture of styles and years: its tower collapsed in dramatic fashion in 1661 and it was rebuilt with a bulbous cupola. It houses sparse displays on the often scandalous earls of Sandwich, the fourth of which is credited with inventing the sandwich as a quick snack to eat whilst engrossed in gambling.

The historic guildhall hosts a small but thorough **museum** (☎ 01304-617197; adult/child £1/50p; ⊗ 10.30am-12.30pm & 2-4pm Tue, Wed, Fri & Sat, 2-4pm Thu & Sun) on Sandwich's rich past as a Cinque Port.

On fair-weather days, hop aboard the **Sandwich River Bus** (☎ 07958-376183; www.sandwichriverbus.co.uk; adult/child 30min trip £5/4, 1hr £10/7; ⊗ every 30-60min 11am-6pm Thu-Sun Apr-Sep, Sun only Oct-Mar) beside the toll bridge for a quick river jaunt or trip out to Richborough (below).

Sandwich is also home to **Royal St Georges** (☎ 01304-613090; www.royalstgeorges.com), one of the most challenging golf links in England.

Sleeping & Eating

Bell Hotel (☎ 01304-617330; Strand St; s/d from £95/115; P 🖳 wi-fi) The Bell Hotel has been sitting on the town's quays since Tudor times, although much of the remaining building is from the 19th century. A splendid, sweeping staircase leads up to recently redecorated snazzy rooms, some with great views. There's also a smart brasserie serving good food (mains £9.25 to £16.80) below.

King's Arms (☎ 01304-617330; Strand St; mains £7.95-18.75; ⊗ lunch & dinner) This 15th-century inn near the water has a beamed dining room with large fireplace serving quality English food and very popular Sunday lunches. For sunny days there's a walled, vine-covered garden complete with child's playhouse. There are a few B&B rooms upstairs.

Getting There & Away

National Express runs buses from London Victoria to Deal (£12.10, 3¼ hours, two daily), from where a local bus takes you to Sandwich (25 minutes).

Trains run from Dover Priory (23 minutes, half-hourly) or from London's Charing Cross (twice hourly) and from London Victoria (£24.10, two hours, hourly) to Sandwich.

Buses also go to Ramsgate (25 minutes, hourly), Dover (50 minutes, hourly) and Canterbury (40 minutes, hourly).

AROUND SANDWICH
Richborough

Roman Britain began here amid the windswept ruins of **Richborough Roman Fort** (☎ 01304-612013; adult/5-15yr/under 5yr £4.20/2.10/free; ⊗ 10am-6pm Mar-Sep), just 2 miles north of Sandwich. This is the spot from which the successful AD 43 invasion of Britain was launched. To celebrate

their victory, a colossal triumphal arch was planted here, the base of which remains. The fort's clearest features today – high walls and scores of deep defensive ditches that give it the appearance of a vast jelly mould – came later as the Romans were forced to stave off increasingly vicious seaborne attacks.

There's a small onsite museum and an audio tour to steer you through the rise and fall of Roman Richborough. To arrive as the Romans did – by boat – take the Sandwich River Bus (see left) from Sandwich. Return passengers pay an extra £2, but get a 25% discount for fort admission.

Deal

Julius Caesar and his armies set foot on Deal's peaceful shingle beach in 55 BC, for their first exploratory dip into Britain. Today there's a gorgeous little 16th-century **castle** (EH; ☎ 01304-372762; Victoria Rd; adult/5-15yr/under 5yr £4.20/2.10/free; ⊗ 10am-6pm Apr-Sep) with curvaceous bastions that form petals in a Tudor rose shape. Far from delicate, however, it is the largest and most complete of Henry VIII's defence chain along the south coast.

And hardly a mile south is another link in the 16th-century coastal defences, **Walmer Castle** (EH; ☎ 01304-364288; Kingsdown Rd; adult/5-15yr/under 5yr £6.50/3.30/free; ⊗ 10am-6pm Apr-Sep, to 4pm Wed-Sun Mar & Oct) the much-altered and really rather lavish official residence of the warden of the Cinque Ports (see boxed text, p188). English hero, the Duke of Wellington, died here.

DOVER
pop 39,078

As a town itself, depressing Dover's air of decay and run-down, postwar architecture has little to offer to travellers, most of whom pass quickly through on their way to, and from, the Continent. Lucky, then, that the town has a couple of stellar attractions to redeem it. The port's vital strategic position so close to mainland Europe gave rise to a sprawling hilltop castle, with some 2000 years of history to its credit. Also here are the spectacular white cliffs that are as much a symbol of English wartime resilience as Winston Churchill or the Battle of Britain.

Orientation

Dover Castle dominates the town from a high promontory east of town, above the white

CINQUE PORTS

Due to their proximity to Europe, the coastal towns of southeast England were the front line against raids and invasion during Anglo-Saxon times. In the absence of a professional army and navy, these towns were frequently called upon to defend themselves, and the kingdom, at land and sea.

In 1278, King Edward I formalised this already ancient arrangement by legally defining the Confederation of Cinque (pronounced 'sink', meaning five) Ports. The five head ports – Sandwich, Dover, Hythe, Romney and Hastings – were granted numerous perks and privileges in exchange for providing the king with ships and men. At their peak, the ports were deemed England's most powerful institution after Crown and Church.

Even after shifting coastlines silted up several Cinque Port harbours, a professional navy was based at Portsmouth and the ports' real importance evaporated, the pomp and ceremony remains. The Lord Warden of the Cinque Ports is a prestigious post now given to faithful servants of the crown. The Queen Mother was warden until she passed away, succeeded by Admiral Lord Boyce. Previous incumbents include the Duke of Wellington and Sir Winston Churchill.

cliffs. Ferry departures are from the Eastern Docks southeast of the castle. Dover Priory train station is a short walk west of the centre. The bus station is on Pencester Rd.

Information

Banks and ATMs are located on Market Sq.

Mangle laundrette (21 Worthington St; per load £4; 8am-8pm)

Post office (Pencester Rd; 9am-5.30pm Mon-Sat)

Tourist Office (☎ 01304-05108; www.whitecliffs country.org.uk; Biggin St; 9am-5.30pm daily Jun-Aug, 9am-5.30pm Mon-Fri & 10am-4pm Sat & Sun Sep-May) Located in the Old Town Gaol on Biggin St; has accommodation and ferry-booking services (both free).

White Cliffs Medical Centre (☎ 01304-201705; 143 Folkestone Rd)

Sights & Activities

DOVER CASTLE

The almost impenetrable **Dover Castle** (EH; ☎ 01304-211067; adult/5-15yr/under 5yr £10.30/5.20/free; 10am-6pm Apr-Sep, to 5pm Oct, to 4pm Thu-Mon Nov-Mar; P), one of the most impressive in England, was built to bolster the country's weakest point at this, the shortest sea-crossing to mainland Europe. It sprawls across the city's hilltop, commanding a tremendous view of the English Channel as far as the French coastline.

The site has been in use for as many as 2000 years. On the vast grounds are the remains of a **Roman lighthouse**, which date from AD 50 and may be the oldest standing building in Britain. Beside it lies a restored **Saxon church**.

The robust 12th-century **keep**, with walls up to 7m thick, is filled with reconstructed scenes

of Henry VIII's visit, and its base shelters a sound-and-light re-creation of a 13th-century siege. But it's the warren of claustrophobic **secret wartime tunnels** under the castle that are the biggest draw. Excellent 50-minute tours delve into the hillside passageways, which were first excavated during the Napoleonic Wars and then expanded to house a command post and hospital in WWII. They now house reconstructed scenes of their wartime use, complete with sounds, smells and erratic lighting. One of Britain's most famous wartime operations, code-named Dynamo, was directed from here in 1940. It saw the evacuation of hundreds of thousands of troops from the French beaches of Dunkirk.

Buses 90C and 111 run from Dover Priory station to the castle.

ROMAN PAINTED HOUSE

Some of the most extensive, if stunted, Roman wall paintings north of the Alps are on show at the **Roman Painted House** (☎ 01304-203279; New St; adult/child £2/80p; 10am-5pm Tue-Sun Apr-Sep), although they're housed in an amateurish museum. Several scenes depict Bacchus (the god of wine and revelry), which makes perfect sense as this large villa was built around AD 200 as a *mansio* (hotel) for travellers in need of a little lubrication to unwind.

OTHER SIGHTS & ACTIVITIES

By far the most enthralling exhibit in the three-storey **Dover Museum** (☎ 01304-201066; www.dover museum.co.uk; Market Sq; adult/child £2.50/1.50; 10am-5.30pm Mon-Sat year-round, noon-5pm Sun Apr-Aug) is that of an astonishing 3600-year-old Bronze Age

DOVER

0   400 m
0   0.2 miles

INFORMATION			
Mangle Laundrette............1	B3	Grand Shaft............7	B4	Maison Dieu Guest House......15	B2
Post Office............2	B3	Roman Lighthouse............8	D3	Number One Guest House......16	C3
Tourist Office............3	B3	Roman Painted House............9	B3	
White Cliffs Medical Centre......4	A4	Saxon Church............10	D3	**EATING**
		Secret Wartime Tunnels......11	D3	Cullins Yard............17	B4
SIGHTS & ACTIVITIES		White Cliffs Boat Tours......12	B5	La Salle Verte............18	B3
Bronze Age Boat Gallery......(see 6)			
Dover Castle............5	C2	**SLEEPING**		**TRANSPORT**
Dover Museum............6	B3	East Lee Guest House......13	C3	Bus Station............19	B3
		Hubert House............14	C3	Eastern Docks............20	D3

To White Cliffs Tourist
Office (1.2mi);
Deal (7mi);
Sandwich (12mi)

To White
Cliffs (50m)

*Dover
Harbour*

*Western
Docks*

To Ashford
(20mi)

---

boat discovered here in 1992. Vaunted as the world's oldest-known seagoing vessel, it measures a thumping great 9.5m by 2.4m. Kids will love the touchy-feely activities, white coats and microscopes that accompany the exhibit.

The easily dizzied may prefer to avoid the **Grand Shaft** (Snargate St; admission £1; 2-5pm Tue-Sun Jul & Aug), a unique 43m triple staircase cut

into the chalky white cliffs as a short cut for troops during the Napoleonic Wars. Phone the tourist office before arriving as it doesn't open every year.

Sleeping

B&Bs cluster along Castle St, Maison Dieu Rd and Folkestone Rd.

Maison Dieu Guest House (☎ 01304-204033; www
.brguest.co.uk; 108 Maison Dieu Rd; s/d from £25/44; **P** 🖵 wi-
fi) Not the most exciting option in town, guest
house with chintzy decor is good value and
well located.

Hubert House (☎ 01304-202253; www.huberthouse
.co.uk; 9 Castle Hill Rd; s/d incl breakfast from £40/55; **P** 🖵 wi-
fi) The comfortable bedrooms in this Georgian
house may be overly flowery but the welcome
is warm, and it uses ecofriendly and fair-trade
products. It has its own little bistro downstairs
which opens out onto a front terrace.

Number One Guest House (☎ 01304-202007; www
.number1guesthouse.co.uk; 1 Castle Street; d from £45; **P**)
Set in a grand Georgian town house at the
foot of Dover Castle, with rooms decorated
in traditional Victorian style. There's also a
pretty walled garden with lovely views and
breakfast is served in bed.

East Lee Guest House (☎ 01304-210176; www
.eastlee.co.uk; 108 Maison Dieu Rd; d with/without breakfast
from £55/50; **P**) This lovely terracotta-shingled
town house makes quite an impression with
its grand, elegantly decorated communal
areas, energetic hosts, super-comfy beds and
excellent, varied breakfasts.

Eating & Drinking

La Salle Verte (☎ 01304-201547; 14-15 Cannon St; snacks
£2-6; ☽ 9am-4.30pm Mon-Sun) The funkiest little
coffee shop in Dover serves great cakes, coffee
and snacks both inside and in a little suntrap
patio garden. It also lays on regular live music
evenings showcasing local musicians.

Cullins Yard (☎ 01304-211666; 11 Cambridge Rd;
☽ 10am-12pm Mon-Sun) This bar, restaurant and
sometime music venue has a nautical theme
(including a bar in the shape of a boat) and a
great location down by Wellington Docks. A
variety of seafood dishes is on offer as well as
a wide choice of beers from around the world.
Local bands play on Sunday afternoons and
there's jazz on Fridays.

Getting There & Away

Dover is 75 miles from London and 15 miles
from Canterbury.

For information on the Channel Tunnel
services, see p805.

BOAT

Ferries depart for France from the Eastern
Docks (accessible by bus; see right) below the
castle. Fares vary according to season and advance purchase. See the websites for specials.

Norfolk Line (☎ 0870 870 1020; www.norfolkline.com)
Services to Dunkirk (1¾ hours, every two hours).
P&O Ferries (☎ 08716 645645; www.poferries.com)
Runs to Calais (1½ hours, every 40 minutes to an hour).
Seafrance (☎ 0871 423 7119; www.seafrance.com)
Ferries to Calais roughly every hour and a half.
SpeedFerries (☎ 0871 222 7456; www.speedferries
.com) Services to Boulogne (50 minutes, up to five daily).

BUS

Dover's **bus station** (Pencester Rd) is in the heart of
town. Stagecoach East Kent has a Canterbury
to Dover service (35 minutes, hourly).
National Express runs 20 daily coaches from
London Victoria (£12.10, 2¾ hours). Stagecoach buses also go to Deal (40 minutes,
hourly) and Sandwich (55 minutes, hourly).

TRAIN

There are more than 40 trains daily from London Victoria and Charing Cross stations to
Dover Priory via Ashford and Sevenoaks (£26,
two hours). In late 2009, Dover is due to be
linked to London via a high-speed railway.

Getting Around

The ferry companies run regular shuttle buses
between the docks and the train station (five
minutes) as they're a long walk apart.

Heritage (☎ 01304-204420) and **Star Taxis**
(☎ 01304-228822/201010) have 24-hour services.
A one-way trip to Deal costs £15 and £20
to Sandwich.

AROUND DOVER
The White Cliffs

Immortalised in song, film and literature,
these iconic cliffs are embedded in the national consciousness, acting as a big, white
'Welcome Home' sign to generations of travellers and soldiers.

The cliffs rise 100m high and extend for 10
miles on either side of Dover, but it is the 6-
mile stretch east of town – properly known as
the Langdon Cliffs – that particularly captivates
visitors' imaginations. The chalk here is about
250m deep, and the cliffs themselves are about
half a million years old, formed when the melting icecaps of northern Europe were gouging a
channel between France and England.

The Langdon Cliffs are managed by the
National Trust, which has a **tourist office**
(☎ 01304-202756; ☽ 10am-5pm Mar-Oct, 11am-4pm
Nov-Feb) and **car park** (£3 for nonmembers) 2 miles
east of Dover.

KENTISH SAFARI

Spend the day out on a game drive before retiring to your lodge and enjoying a cocktail while watching the wildlife gather round the watering hole...but this isn't the Serengeti, this is rural Kent. The people at Port Lympne safari park, the sister park to Howlett's (p181), have created **Livingstone Safari Lodge** (☎ 01303-234190; www.totallywild.net/portlympne; adult/child £150/80; P ✗), the only place in Europe to run overnight safaris. You're taken on safari drives by a Zimbabwean ranger, you can stay in luxury safari tents, and there's an open-to-the-elements lounge where you eat food cooked on an open fire whilst looking out over the zebra and giraffe filled plains...and over to France. It's different, and great fun.

From the tourist office, you can follow a stony path as it winds its way further east along the cliff tops for a bracing 2-mile walk to the stout Victorian **South Foreland Lighthouse** (NT; ☎ 01304-215484; adult/child £4/2; ⏲ guided tours 11am-5.30pm Fri-Mon mid-Mar–Oct). This was the first lighthouse to be powered by electricity, and is the site of the first international radio transmissions in 1898.

The cliffs are 2 miles east of Dover along Castle Hill Rd and the A258 road to Deal or off the A2 past the Eastern Docks. Buses 113 and 90/1 from Dover stop near the main entrance.

To see them in all their full-frontal glory, **White Cliffs Boat Tours** (☎ 01303-271388; www.white cliffsboattours.co.uk; adult/child £6/3; ⏲ daily Jul & Aug, Sat & Sun Apr-Jun & Sep-Oct) runs 40-minute water tours at 10am, noon, 2pm and 4pm from the Western Docks.

Romney Marsh

This eerie landscape of flat reed beds, sparsely populated and echoing with the whistling wind and lonely squawks of sea birds, was once a favourite haunt of smugglers and wreckers. It's now home to an incredibly cramped tourist attraction: the world's smallest-gauge public railway. Opened in 1927, the pocket-sized **Romney, Hythe & Dymchurch Railway** (☎ 01797-362353; www.rhdr.org .uk; adult/child £12/6; ⏲ daily Apr-Sep, Sat & Sun Nov-Mar) trains trundle and toot their way 13.5 miles from Hythe to Dungeness lighthouse and back (roughly an hour each way). Cute, undoubtedly. But prone to cramped leg space and sore heads? You better believe it.

Dungeness

Sticking out from the western edge of Romney Marsh is a low shingle spit dominated by a brooding nuclear power station. In spite of the apocalyptic desolation, this spot is home

to the largest sea-bird colony in the southeast at the **Royal Society for the Protection of Birds (RSPB) Nature Reserve** (☎ 01797-320588; www.rspb .org.uk; Dungeness Rd; adult/child £3/1; ⏲ 9am-9pm or sunset, visitor centre 10am-5pm Mar-Oct, to 4pm Nov-Feb), which has displays, binocular hire, explorer backpacks for kids, and information on bird-watching hides.

THE KENT WEALD

Taking its name from an old German world *wald,* meaning 'forest', the Weald, as it's known by locals, is all out of woodland these days, but you'll find postcard villages, manicured lawns and ripe fields. The region also has more than its fair share of country estates, castles and gardens.

Sevenoaks
pop 26,699

A bland commuter town off the M25, Sevenoaks is home to one of England's most celebrated country estates. The gates to **Knole House** (NT; ☎ 01732-450608; adult/child £9/4.50; ⏲ noon-4pm Wed-Sun mid-Mar–Oct) sit on the southern High St, and from there it's a beautiful winding walk or drive through a rolling medieval park dotted with bold deer. The estate was built in the 12th century, but in 1456 the Archbishop of Canterbury, Thomas Bouchier, snapped the property up and set about building a vast and lavish house 'fit for the Princes of the Church'. Its curious calendar design encompasses 365 rooms, 52 staircases and seven courtyards. The house was later home to Vita Sackville-West, whose love affair with Virginia Woolf spawned the novel *Orlando,* set at Knole.

The house is 1.5 miles southeast of Sevenoaks **train station** (London Rd). Trains leave from London Charing Cross station (£8.20, 35 minutes, every 15 minutes) and continue to Tunbridge Wells (20 minutes, two per hour) and Hastings (£14.20, one hour).

ENGLISH WINE

Mention English wine not too long ago and you'd likely hear a snort of derision. Not any more. Thanks to warmer temperatures and determined winemakers, English wine, particularly of the sparkling variety, is developing a fan base all of its own.

Legend has it that the Romans first brought over grapevine cuttings 2000 years ago, and that vineyards blossomed in English soil. But by the time the 20th century rolled around, there wasn't a wine producer in sight – until some bright spark started planting vines again in the 1950s.

These days, there are more than 400 English vineyards and interest (and sales) in domestic wine has grown dramatically, with the likes of Nyetimber, Chapel Down and Ridgeview enjoying award-winning success around the world.

The best vineyards are in the south, particularly Sussex, Essex and Kent, whose chalky soil is likened to the Champagne region in France. Many vineyards now offer tours and wine tastings. Two of the most popular are **Chapel Down Vinery** (☎ 01580-763033; www.englishwinesgroup.com; adult/child £6.50/2 ; ☺ tours Jun-Sep), and **Denbies Wine Estate** (☎ 01306-876616; www.denbiesvineyard .co.uk ; adult/child £7.25/3; ☺ tours year-round).

Down House

Charles Darwin's home from 1842 until his death in 1882, **Down House** (EH; ☎ 01689-869119; adult/5-14yr £7.20/3.60; ☺ 11am-5pm Wed-Sun Mar-Jun & Sep-Oct, closed Nov-Feb) witnessed the development of Darwin's theory of evolution by natural selection. The house and gardens have been restored to look much as they would have in Darwin's time, including Darwin's study, where he undertook much of his reading and writing; the drawing room, where he tried out some of his indoor experiments; and the gardens and greenhouse, where some of his outdoor experiments are re-created. There are three self-guided trails in the area, where you can follow in the great man's footsteps. You can pick up trail booklets at the house. At the time of writing, the UK was putting forward Down House, Downe village and the surrounding area as its World Heritage Site Nomination bid for 2009. The same year sees the 200th anniversary of Darwin's birth and the 150th anniversary of the publication of *The Origin of Species*, his seminal work.

Down House is in Luxted Rd, Downe, off the A21. Take bus 146 from Bromley North or Bromley South railway station, or service R8 from Orpington.

Chartwell

The home of Sir Winston Churchill from 1924 until his death in 1965 (see boxed text, p45), **Chartwell** (☎ 01732-868381; Westerham; adult/child £11.20/5.60, garden & studio only £5.60/2.80; ☺ 11am-5pm Wed-Sun Apr-Jun & Sep-Oct, Tue-Sun Jul & Aug), 6 miles east of Sevenoaks, offers a breathtakingly inti-mate insight into the life of England's famous cigar-chomping bombast.

This 19th-century house and its rambling grounds have been preserved much as Winnie left them, full of books, pictures, maps and personal mementos. Churchill was also a prolific painter and his daubings are scattered throughout the house and fill the garden studio.

Transport options are limited without a car. Kent Passenger Services bus 238 runs from Sevenoaks train station (30 minutes, every two hours) on Wednesdays from May to mid-September. Arriva 401 runs on Sundays and Bank Holiday Mondays only.

Hever Castle

This idyllic little **castle** (☎ 01732-865224; www.hever castle.co.uk; adult/5-14yr £11.50/6.30, gardens only £9.30/6; ☺ noon-5pm Mar-Oct, to 4pm Nov) seems to have leapt right out of a film set. It's encircled by a narrow moat and surrounded by family-friendly gardens, complete with cute topiary of woodland creatures and wandering ducks and swans.

The castle is famous for being the childhood home of Anne Boleyn, mistress to Henry VIII and then his doomed queen. It dates from 1270, with a Tudor house added in 1505 by the Bullen (Boleyn) family. The castle later fell into disrepair until 1903, when American multimillionaire William Waldorf Astor bought it, pouring obscene amounts of money into a massive refurbishment. The exterior is unchanged from Tudor times, but the interior is thick with Edwardian panelling.

From London Bridge trains go direct to Hever (£8.50, 40 minutes, hourly), a poorly signposted 1-mile walk from the castle); and to Edenbridge (£8.50, 50 minutes), from where it's a 4-mile taxi or bike ride. If you're driving, Hever Castle is 3 miles off the B2026 near Edenbridge.

Penshurst

The pretty village of Penshurst, on the B2176, just off the A21, is lined with timber-framed Tudor houses and features a fanciful four-spired church, but most people come for grandiose medieval manor house **Penshurst Place** (☎ 01892-870307; www.penshurstplace.com; adult/5-16yr/under 5yr £8.50/5.50/free; ⏰ noon-4pm Apr-Oct). Its pride and joy is the splendid **Baron's Hall**, built in 1341, where a number of royal visitors, including Queen Elizabeth I, were entertained beneath its stunning 18m-high chestnut roof. Just outside the main house is a vintage-toy museum, whose empty-eyed dolls, classic rocking horses and mechanical red-eyed bear are enough to give even adults nightmares.

Outside, Penshurst's famous **walled gardens** (⏰ 10.30am-6pm Apr-Oct) were designed in 1346 and remain virtually unchanged since Elizabethan times. There are also lovely riverside walks in the grounds.

From Edenbridge, buses 231 and 233 leave for Tunbridge Wells via Penshurst every hour (27 minutes).

Leeds Castle

This immense moated pile is for many the world's most romantic **castle** (☎ 01622-765400; www.leeds-castle.com; adult/4-15yr/senior & student £15/9.50/12.50; ⏰ 10.30am-6pm Apr-Oct, to 4pm Nov-Mar), and it's certainly one of the most visited in Britain. While it looks formidable enough from the outside – a hefty structure balancing on two islands amid a large lake and sprawling estate – it's actually known as something of a 'ladies castle'. This stems from the fact that in its more than 1000 years of history, it has been home to a who's who of medieval queens, most famously Henry VIII's first wife, Catherine of Aragon.

The castle was transformed from fortress to lavish palace over the centuries, and its last owner, the high-society hostess Lady Baillie, used it as a princely family home and party pad to entertain the likes of Errol Flynn, Douglas Fairbanks and JFK.

The castle's vast estate offers enough attractions of its own to justify a day trip: peaceful walks, a duckery, aviary and falconry demonstrations. You'll also find a quirky dog-collar museum and a hedge maze, overseen by a grassy bank where fellow travellers can shout encouragement or misdirections.

Since Lady Baillie's death in 1974, a private trust has managed the property. This means that some parts of the castle are periodically closed for private events.

Leeds Castle is just east of Maidstone. National Express runs one direct bus daily from London Victoria coach station, leaving at 9am and returning at 3pm (£12.30, 1½ hours). It must be prebooked. There is a combined entrance and bus fare ticket that costs £22.

You can also get a train from London Bridge, London Victoria or London Cannon St to Bearstead (£15; 50 minutes) from where you can catch a connecting coach to the castle (£5 return).

Sissinghurst Castle Garden

One of England's most famous and romantic gardens is at **Sissinghurst** (NT; ☎ 01580-710700; Sissinghurst; adult/child £9/4.40; ⏰ 11am-6.30pm Fri-Tue mid-Mar–Oct). Though the castle dates to the 12th century, writer Vita Sackville-West crafted the delightful gardens after she bought the estate in 1930. Highlights include the exuberant rose garden and the virginal snowy-bloomed White Garden. Sissinghurst is 2 miles northeast of Cranbrook and 1 mile east of Sissinghurst village off the A262.

EAST SUSSEX

Home to lush countryside, medieval villages and gorgeous coastline, this lovely corner of the country is besieged by weekending Londoners whenever the weather is fine. Here you'll find an air of romance amid the cobbled medieval streets of Rye, historic Battle, where William the Conqueror first engaged the Saxons in 1066, and the breathtaking white cliffs of Beachy Head, near the civilised seaside town of Eastbourne. Brighton, a highlight of a visit here, offers vibrant nightlife, offbeat shopping and shingly shores. But you needn't follow the crowds to enjoy East Sussex. It's just as rewarding to get off the beaten track, linger along its winding country lanes and stretch your legs across the rolling South Downs.

RYE

pop 4195

If you're searching for a perfect example of a medieval village, look no further than Rye. Once a Cinque Port (p188), this exquisitely pretty place looks as if it's been pickled, put on a shelf and promptly forgotten about by old Father Time. Even the most hardened cynic can't fail to be bewitched by Rye's cobbled lanes, mysterious passageways and crooked half-timbered Tudor buildings. Romantics can lap up the townsfolk's tales of resident smugglers, ghosts, writers and artists, and hole up in one of a slew of gorgeous accommodation in its heart.

The town sits prettily atop a rocky outcrop, and sheep graze where the waters once lapped. If you do visit – and you absolutely should – try to avoid summer weekends when hoards of day-trippers dilute the town's time-warp effect.

Information

The **tourist office** (☎ 01797-226696; www.visitrye.co.uk; Strand Quay; ✆ 10am-5pm Apr-Oct, to 4pm Nov, Dec & Mar, to 3pm Jan & Feb) runs a town-model audiovisual

history for £3. More fun is the freaky collection of penny-in-the-slot novelty machines upstairs. It also sells a *Rye Town Walk* map (£1), and rents out multilingual audio tours (adult/child £3/1).

You can jump online at **Rye Internet Cafe** (☎ 01797-224276; 46 Ferry Rd; per min 5p; ✆ 8am-10pm Mon-Sat, 10am-9pm Sun). The **post office** (✆ 8.30am-5.30pm Mon-Fri, to 1pm Sat) is on Cinque Ports St.

Sights

From the tourist office, turn your back to the water, go through Strand Quay and wobble up the cobblestones of famous **Mermaid St**, bristling with 15th-century timber-framed houses with quirky house names such as 'The House with Two Front Doors' and 'The House Opposite'.

Turn right at the T-junction for the striking Georgian **Lamb House** (NT; ☎ 01797-229542; West St; adult/child £3.50/1.80; ✆ 2-6pm Thu & Sat late Mar-Oct), a favourite stomping ground for local apparitions, but not that of its most famous resident, American writer Henry James, who lived here from 1898 to 1916, during which he wrote *The Wings of the Dove*.

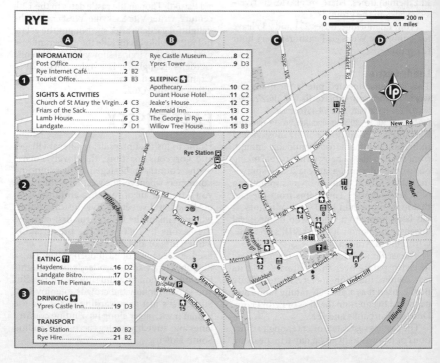

RYE

0 ———————— 200 m
0 ———————— 0.1 miles

INFORMATION
Post Office........................1 C2
Rye Internet Café...............2 B2
Tourist Office....................3 B3

SIGHTS & ACTIVITIES
Church of St Mary the Virgin....4 C3
Friars of the Sack...............5 C3
Lamb House.......................6 C3
Landgate..........................7 D1

Rye Castle Museum.............8 C2
Ypres Tower......................9 D3

SLEEPING
Apothecary......................10 C2
Durant House Hotel...........11 C2
Jeake's House..................12 C3
Mermaid Inn...................13 C3
The George in Rye............14 C2
Willow Tree House............15 B3

EATING
Haydens.........................16 D2
Landgate Bistro...............17 D1
Simon The Pieman............18 C2

DRINKING
Ypres Castle Inn..............19 D3

TRANSPORT
Bus Station.....................20 B2
Rye Hire........................21 B2

Continue around the dogleg into cobbled Church Sq, ringed by historic houses, including the **Friars of the Sack**, which was once part of a 13th-century Augustinian friary but is now a private home. The pretty **Church of St Mary the Virgin** (☺ 9am-6pm Apr-Sep, to 4pm Oct-Mar) is a hotchpotch of medieval and later styles and its turret clock is the oldest in England (1561) still working with its original pendulum mechanism. You can climb the church **tower** (adult/child £2/free) for great views of the town and surrounding countryside.

Turn right at the square's east corner for the sandcastle archetype **Ypres Tower** (tower & museum adult/child £3/1.80; ☺ 10.30am-5pm Thu-Mon Apr-Oct, 10.30am-3.30pm Sat & Sun Nov-Mar), pronounced 'wipers'. This 13th-century building has great views over Romney Marsh and Rye Bay, and houses one part of Rye Castle Museum. It's overseen by a friendly warden, who's full of colourful tales from the tower's long history as fort, prison, mortuary and museum (the last two at overlapping times).

The other branch of the **museum** (☎ 01797-226728; www.ryemuseum.co.uk; 3 East St; adult/child £2.50/1.80; ☺ 10.30am-1pm & 2-5pm Thu-Mon Apr-Oct), a short stroll away on East St, is home to an 18th-century leather fire engine and other intriguing loot.

At the northeastern edge of the village, the thickset pale-stone **Landgate** dates back from 1329, and is the only remaining gate out of four.

Activities

To combine history and a hearty hike, the well-signposted **1066 Country Walk** meanders 31 miles from Rye to Battle and Pevensey where it connects with the South Downs Way.

Festivals & Events

Rye wholeheartedly celebrates its maritime heritage with a two-day festival in August, and in September the town gets arty for the two-week **Rye Arts Festival** (☎ 01797-224442; www.ryefestival.co.uk).

Sleeping

Rye boasts an exceptional choice of unique historic accommodation.

Jeake's House (☎ 01797-222828; www.jeakeshouse.com; Mermaid St; s/d from £55/110; [P]) An inviting, ivy drenched 17th-century town house on cobbled Mermaid St, Jeake's was once home to US poet Conrad Aitken. Today it lives life as a handsomely furnished guest house. You can literally take a pew in the snug book-lined bar and, continuing the theme, breakfast is served in an 18th-century former chapel.

Durant House Hotel (☎ 01797-223182; www.duranthouse.com; 2 Market St; s/d from £70/95) Tucked discreetly away on a cobbled lane, the rooms in this Georgian guest house range from opulent four posters to a little attic nook, some with peaceful views over the river toward Romney Marsh. There's also a snug lounge with an honesty bar.

The George in Rye (☎ 01797-224065; www.thegeorgeinrye.com; 98 High St; d from £125; [] wi-fi) This coaching inn at the heart of Rye has managed to reinvent itself as a contemporary boutique hotel whilst staying true to its roots. Downstairs, an old-fashioned wood-panelled lounge is warmed by roaring log fires, whilst the bedrooms are chic and understated with the odd splash of psychedelic colour. The George's restaurant – dealing in contemporary Sussex-sourced food and good English wine – can compete with the best Rye has to offer.

Mermaid Inn (☎ 01797-223065; www.mermaidinn.com; Mermaid St; d £150-240; [P]) Few inns can claim to be as atmospheric as this ancient hostelry, dating from 1420. Every room is different – but each is thick with dark beams and lit by leaded windows, and some are graced by secret passageways that now act as fire escapes. Small wonder it's such a popular spot – these days you're as likely to spot a celeb or a royal as the resident ghost.

More great choices:

Apothecary (☎ 01797-229157; www.bedandbreakfastrye.com; 1 East St; d from £60) Originally the home of the town's apothecary, this characterful B&B has three rooms and its own coffee shop.

Willow Tree House (☎ 01797-227820; www.willow-tree-house.com; 113 Winchelsea Rd; s/d £70/80; [P]). Lovingly decorated B&B in a listed building, it features a big garden dominated by – you've guessed it – a large weeping willow.

Eating & Drinking

Simon the Pieman (☎ 01797-222207; 3 Lion St; snacks £1.50-5; ☺ 9.30am-5pm Mon-Sat, 1.30-5.30pm Sun) Rye isn't short of quaint little tea shops, and this is one of the more traditional, with calorific cream teas, freshly baked cakes and simple lunches.

Haydens (☎ 01797-224501; 108 High St; snacks/meals from £3/9; ☺ 10am-5pm daily, dinner Fri & Sat) Staunch

THE SOUTHEAST

SOMETHING FOR THE WEEKEND

Start by checking into boutique splendour at the **George in Rye** (p195). Hear tales of the town's ghosts and smugglers over dinner, then out to roam the cobbled medieval streets after dark. After a night untroubled by spirits (unless they come in a glass), set out to explore the town's beauty by daylight. Navigate your way through narrow country lanes to fairytale **Bodiam Castle** (opposite). Explore its ramparts, then picnic in its pretty parkland. In the afternoon, drive on to historic site of the 1066 Battle of Hastings at **Battle** (below), and see the spot where King Harold met his end. Have dinner at the stunning **Pilgrim's Restaurant** (opposite) and then on to Hastings to settle in at the beautiful **Swan House** (p198). After a leisurely breakfast on Sunday, it's time for a bracing stroll around town. Check out the Old Town's galleries and boutiques (p198), before taking the **West Hill Cliff Railway** (p198) up to the ruins of Hastings castle, with awesome views out to sea. When you get back down again, fortify yourself with fish and chips on the beach in time for the long trip home.

---

believers in organic and fair-trade produce, these guys dish up delicious omelettes, ploughman's lunches, salads and pancakes in their light, breezy cafe. There's a wonderful elevated terrace at the back with great views over the town and surrounding countryside.

Ypres Castle Inn (☎ 01797-223248; www.yprescastle inn.co.uk; Gun Gardens; meals £7-15; ☺ lunch noon-3pm, dinner 6-9pm) You can have a match on a boules pitch, enjoy some live bands or chow down on scrumptious seasonal food like Rye bay scallops at this warm, country-style pub. The beer's not bad either.

Landgate Bistro (☎ 01797-222829; www.landgate bistro.co.uk; 5/6 Landgate; mains £13-15.50; ☺ dinner Tue-Sat & Sun before bank holiday, lunch Sat & Sun) There's fine dining to be had in these two old Georgian cottages. Take a seat amongst the beams and exposed brickwork of their graceful dining room for a top-notch feast of local delights such as game, Dover sole and Romney Marsh lamb.

Getting There & Away

Bus 711 runs between Dover (two hours, hourly) and Hastings (30 minutes) via Rye. Trains run to London Charing Cross (£22.60, two hours, three per hour), but you must change either in Hastings or Ashford.

Getting Around

You can rent all-terrain bikes (per day/four hours £12/8) from **Rye Hire** (☎ 01797-223033; 1 Cyprus Pl; ☺ 8am-5pm Mon-Fri, till noon Sat). Call ahead for Sunday hire.

BATTLE
pop 5190

This little, unassuming village has a monumental place in British history. Battle grew up around the point where invading French duke William of Normandy, aka William the Conqueror, scored a decisive victory over local King Harold in 1066, so beginning Norman rule and changing the face of the country forever.

Orientation & Information

The train station is a short walk from High St, and is well signposted. The **tourist office** (☎ 01424-773721; Gatehouse; ☺ 10am-6pm Apr-Sep, to 4pm Oct-Mar) is next to Battle Abbey. The post office, banks and ATMs are also on High St.

Sights

Another day, another photogenic ruin? Hardly. On this spot raged *the* pivotal battle in the last successful invasion of England in 1066: an event with unparalleled impact on the country's subsequent social structure, architecture and well…pretty much everything. Only four years later, the conquering Normans began constructing **Battle Abbey** (EH; ☎ 01424-773792; adult/child £6.50/3.30; ☺ 10am-6pm Apr-Sep, to 4pm Oct-Mar), right in the middle of the battlefield: a penance ordered by the Pope for the loss of life incurred here.

Only the foundations of the original church remain, the altar's position marked by a plaque – also supposedly the spot England's King Harold famously took an arrow in his eye. But other impressive monastic buildings survive and make for atmospheric explorations.

The battlefield's innocently rolling lush hillsides do little to evoke the ferocity of the event, but high-tech interactive presentations and blow-by-blow audio tours do their utmost to bring the battle to life.

Sleeping & Eating

Tollgate Farmhouse (☎ 01424-777436; www.tollgate
farmhouse.co.uk; 59 North Trade Rd; s/d from £35/65; P) A
homely atmosphere can be found 10-minutes'
walk away from the centre of Battle at this
large domestic residence, with a handful of
florid en suite rooms dotted with embroidery
and fake flowers, and several extra surprises
tucked up its sleeve: a Jacuzzi, sauna and outdoor pool among them.

Powdermills (☎ 01424-775511; www.powdermills
hotel.com; Powdermill Lane; s/d £115/125; P) Rebuilt in
the 18th century after a Napoleonic gunpowder works saw off the previous manor with a
bang, this graceful, ivy-covered country-house
hotel has classic four-postered rooms, a wonderful orangery restaurant, a swimming pool
and 200-acre grounds of tranquil lakes and
woodland adjoining Battle Abbey's grounds.

Pilgrim's Restaurant (☎ 01424-772314; www.pil
grims-battle.co.uk; 1 High St; 3-course dinner £19.95; ☽ lunch
& dinner Mon-Sat, lunch Sun) Misshapen beams,
rough-plastered walls and a vaulted ceiling
make this 15th-century pilgrim's lodging
the most spectacular place to eat in Battle.
The food is tasty as well as beautiful to look
at, and the chef is committed to using local
produce.

Getting There & Away

National Express bus 023 from London
(£11.60, 2¼ hours, daily) to Hastings passes
through Battle. Bus 4/5 runs to Hastings (26
minutes, hourly). Trains also run to London
Charing Cross (£18, one hour 20 minutes,
twice hourly).

AROUND BATTLE

Bodiam Castle

Surrounded by a square moat teeming with
oversized goldfish, this four-towered arche-
typal **castle** (NT; ☎ 01580-830436; adult/child £5.20/2.60;
☽ 10am-6pm mid-Feb–Oct, to 4pm Sat & Sun Nov-early Feb)
makes you half expect to see a fire-breathing
dragon appear or a golden-haired princess
lean over its walls. It is the legacy of 14th-
century soldier of fortune (the polite term for
knights who slaughtered and pillaged their
way around France) Sir Edward Dalyngrigge,
who married the local heiress and set about
building a castle to make sure everybody knew
who was boss.

Parliamentarian forces left the castle in
ruins during the English Civil War, but in

TOP FIVE PAMPERED GETAWAYS
■ Mermaid Inn (Rye; p195)
■ Powdermills (Battle; left)
■ Drakes (Brighton; p208)
■ Abode (Canterbury; p179)
■ Swan House (Hastings; p198)

1917 Lord Curzon, former viceroy of India,
bought it and restored the exterior. Much of
the interior remains unrestored, but it's possible to climb to the battlements for some
sweeping views.

You'll most likely hear the tooting of the
nearby **Kent & East Sussex steam railway** (☎ 01580-
765155; www.kesr.org.uk; adult/3-15yr £12/7), which runs
from Tenterden in Kent through 11 miles of
gentle hills and woods to Bodiam village, from
where a bus takes you to the castle. It operates three to five services on most days from
May to September and at the weekend and
school holidays in October, December and
February. It's closed November, January and
most of March.

The castle is 9 miles northeast of Battle
off the B2244. Stagecoach bus 349 stops at
Bodiam from Hastings (38 minutes) once
every two hours during the day Monday
to Saturday.

Bateman's

It was love at first sight when Mr Rudyard
Kipling, author of *The Jungle Book*, set eyes
on **Bateman's** (NT; ☎ 01435-882302; adult/child
£7.20/3.60; ☽ 11am-5pm Sat-Wed mid-Mar–Oct), the
glorious little 1634 Jacobean mansion he
would call home for the last 34 years of
his life, and where he would draw inspiration for *The Just So Stories* and other vivid
tales.

Even today, the house is pervaded by a
sense of Kipling's cosy contentment here.
Everything is pretty much just as the writer
left it after his death in 1936, down to the
blotting paper on his study desk. Furnishings
often reflect his fascination with the East,
with many oriental rugs and Indian artefacts
adding colour.

The house is surrounded by lovely gardens and a small path leads down to a water
mill that grinds corn on Wednesdays and
Saturdays at 2pm.

THE SOUTHEAST

Bateman's is about half a mile south of the town of Burwash along the A259.

HASTINGS
pop 85,000

Forever associated with the Norman invasion of 1066 even though the crucial events took place 6 miles away, Hastings thrived as a Cinque Port, and in its Victorian heyday was one of the country's most fashionable seaside resorts. After a period of steady decline, the town is enjoying a renaissance, and these days, it's an intriguing mix of tacky resort, fishing port and chic Bohemian retreat.

Orientation & Information

The new train station is a five-minute walk up from the seafront on Havelock Rd. National Express buses leave for the bus station on Queen's Rd. The main **tourist office** (☎ 0845 274 1001; Queen's Sq; ☼ 8.30am-6.15pm Mon-Fri, 9am-5pm Sat, 10.30am-4.30pm Sun) is in the Town Hall.

Sights

The best place to hang out is **Old Town**, a hotchpotch of narrow streets and half-timbered buildings filled with antique shops, boutiques, bistros, quaint local pubs and galleries.

Down by the seafront, the **Stade** – the stretch of shingle in front of Rock-a-Nore Rd – is home to distinctive, tall black clapboard **Net Huts**, built as storage for fishing gear back in the 17th century.

There are three nautical attractionson Rock-a-Nore Rd itself: the **Fishermen's Museum** (☎ 01424-461446; www.hastingsfish.co.uk; Rock-a-Nore Rd; admission free; ☼ 10am-5pm Apr-Oct, 11am-4pm Nov-Mar), the **Shipwreck and Coastal Heritage Centre** (☎ 01424-437452; www.shipwreck-heritage.org.uk; Rock-a-Nore Rd; admission free; ☼ 10.30am-5pm Apr-Oct, 11am-4pm Nov-Mar) and the **Blue Reef Aquarium** (☎ 01424-718776; www.bluereefaquarium.co.uk/hastings; Rock-a-Nore Rd; adult/child £7.50/5.50; ☼ 10am-5pm).

To scale up the high cliffs that shelter the town, there are two Victorian funicular railways, the most useful of which is the **West Hill Cliff Railway** (☎ 01424-781030; George St; adult/child £1.80/1.10; ☼ 10am-5.30pm summer, 11am-4pm winter), which takes visitors up to West Hill and the ruins of a Norman fortress built by William the Conqueror in 1069, now known as **Hastings Castle** (☎ 01424-444412; www .discoverhastings.co.uk; Castle Hill Rd; adult/child £3.75/2.70; ☼ 10am-5pm Easter-Sep, 11am-3pm Oct-Easter).

Hokey **Smugglers Adventure** (☎ 01424-444412; www.smugglersadventure.co.uk; St Clement Caves; adult/child £6.75/4.75; ☼ 10am-5.30pm Easter-Sep, 11am-4.30pm Oct-Easter) is also on West Hill. Meander through underground caverns to hear yarns of smuggling along the Sussex coast, told through interactive exhibits and a ghostly narrator.

Sleeping & Eating

Lavender and Lace (☎ 01424-716290; www.lavenderlace1066.co.uk; 106 All Saints St; s/d from £50/70; ☐ wi-fi) Old-world charm comes as standard in this cute little 16th-century house in the old town, along with genial hosts and spotless, comfortable rooms.

our pick **Swan House** (☎ 01424-430014; www.swanhousehastings.co.uk; 1 Hill St; s/d from £70/100; ☐ wi-fi) Inside its ancient, timbered 15th-century shell this place blends contemporary and vintage chic to perfection. Rooms feature organic toiletries, fresh flowers, hand-painted walls and huge beds. The guest lounge, where pale sofas, painted floorboards and striking modern sculpture sit alongside beams and a huge stone fireplace, is a stunner. The hosts are warm but unobtrusive, and their fabulous breakfasts feature kippers, muesli, smoothies and smoked salmon.

Dragon Bar (☎ 01424-423688; 71 George St; ☼ lunch & dinner Mon-Sat, lunch Sun) Atmospheric, laid-back bar full of dark walls, mismatched furniture and beaten leather sofas, attracting the younger end of the alternative old-town crowds. There's an eclectic menu featuring everything from Thai curry to braised goat to pizzas.

Getting There & Away

National Express buses run from London (£12.60, 2½ to 3⅓ hours, twice daily) to Hastings. Trains also run to London Charing Cross (£16.90; one hour 30 minutes, twice hourly) and to London Victoria (two hours, hourly). There are three services an hour to Brighton (£10.60; one hour 10 minutes).

EASTBOURNE
pop 106,562

This classic, old-fashioned seaside resort has long brought to mind images of octogenarians dozing in deck chairs, but whilst many of Eastbourne's seafront hotels still have that retirement-home feel, there's been a con-

THE LAST INVASION OF ENGLAND

The most famous battle in the history of England took place in 1066: a date seared into every English schoolchild's brain. The Battle of Hastings began when Harold's army arrived on the scene on 14 October and created a three-ring defence consisting of archers, then cavalry, with massed infantry at the rear. William marched north from Hastings and took up a position about 400m south of Harold and his troops. He tried repeatedly to break the English cordon, but Harold's men held fast. William's knights then feigned retreat, drawing some of Harold's troops after them. It was a fatal mistake. Seeing the gap in the English wall, William ordered his remaining troops to charge through, and the battle was as good as won. Among the English casualties was King Harold who, as tradition has it, was hit in the eye by an arrow, and struck down by Norman knights as he tried to pull it out. At news of his death the last English resistance collapsed.

In their wonderfully irreverent *1066 And All That* (1930), WC Sellar and RJ Yeatman suggest that 'the Norman conquest was a Good Thing, as from this time onward England stopped being conquered and thus was able to become top nation…' When you consider that England hasn't been successfully invaded since, it's hard to disagree.

certed effort to promote its many charms to sprightlier generations. You certainly can't doubt the appeal of its pebbly beaches, scrupulously snipped seaside gardens and picturesque arcade-free promenade, but if you're looking for cosmopolitan buzz, grab your ice cream and head for Brighton.

The **tourist office** (☎ 0871-663 0031; www.visit eastbourne.com; Cornfield Rd; ⏱ 9.30am-5.30pm Mon-Fri, to 5pm Sat Apr-Sep, to 4.30pm Sat Mar & Oct, to 1pm Sat Nov-Feb) can fix you up with accommodation for £3.

Nearby, email can be found at **Coffee Republic** (☎ 01323-438576; 69 Terminus Rd; per 20min/hr £1/3; ⏱ 7am-6pm).

Sights & Activities

Eastbourne's pretty filigree-trimmed pier, a lovely place to watch the sunset, also has a curious Victorian **Camera Obscura** (adult/child £2/1; ⏱ noon-5pm Apr-Sep) that projects images of the outside world into a dish within a darkened room. In July, daredevils in feathery frocks hurl themselves from the pier in the annual birdman competition.

Eastbourne's two museums are entirely given up to nostalgia. The **Museum of Shops** (☎ 01323-737143; 20 Cornfield Tce; adult/child £4.50/3.50; ⏱ 10am-5pm) is swamped by an obsessive collection of how-we-once-lived memorabilia, while **Eastbourne Heritage Centre** (☎ 01323-411 189; www.eastbourneheritagecentre.co.uk; 2 Carlisle Rd; adult/child £1/free; ⏱ 2-5pm mid-Mar–early Oct) livens up exhibits on the town's history with eccentric asides, such as on Donald McGill, the pioneer of the 'naughty postcard'.

As part of Eastbourne's drive to attract younger visitors, water sports are increasingly popular. **Spray Water Sports Centre** (☎ 01323-417 023; Royal Pde) offers courses in sailing, windsurfing, kayaking and power boating.

At the time of writing, a swanky new **Cultural Centre** (☎ 01323-417961) was due to open in early 2009 at Devonshire Park. It will provide a home for Eastbourne's Towner Art Collection (moved from the town's old Towner Gallery), as well as providing general exhibition space, a cafe and sun terrace.

Tours

City Sightseeing (☎ 0170-8866000; www.city-sightseeing.co.uk; adult/child £7/3.50; ⏱ tours every 30 min 10am-4.30pm May-Sep, every hr till 4pm Oct & mid-Mar–end Apr) runs buses around local sights, including Beachy Head cliffs.

Sleeping

At the time of writing, a new YHA hostel was due to open in Eastbourne in 2009. For further details, contact the **YHA** (☎ 01629-592700; www.yha.org.uk).

Albert & Victoria (☎ 01323-730948; www.albertandvictoria.com; 19 St Aubyns Rd; s/d £45/70) Book ahead to stay at this delightful Victorian terraced house with opulent rooms, canopied beds, crystal chandeliers and wall frescoes in the breakfast room, mere paces from the seafront promenade.

Da Vinci Hotel (☎ 01323-727173; www.davinci.uk .com; 10 Howard Sq; d from £69; 💻) Pegged as an 'art hotel', each room in this boutique B&B is named after a famous artist and prints are hung accordingly, with bold, bright colours to match. There's a space in the reception dedicated to displaying the work of local artists.

Eating

Eastbourne's 'restaurant row' can be found on the seafront end of Terminus Rd.

Beach House (☎ 01323-738228; www.thegreenhouse bar.com; light meals £5-10; ☺ 10am-5pm Mon-Sat) The nicest of Eastbourne's beachfront cafes is a laid-back space with a large wooden deck on the beach outside. It serves great big breakfasts and homemade burgers, as well as wines and beer on tap.

Meze Restaurant (☎ 01323-731893; 15 Pevensey Rd; www.meze-restaurant.com; mains £11-18.50; ☺ lunch & dinner) Great Turkish food is prepared before your eyes over a large open grill at this popular local restaurant. The decor is part bistro, part Turkish bazaar, the large portions are great value and the ebullient proprietor offers a warm welcome.

Getting There & Around

National Express operates buses to London Victoria (£12, 2¾ hours, daily) and to Brighton (£3.20, 55 minutes to 1¼ hours, daily). Bus 12 runs to Brighton (one hour and 15 minutes, three per hour, twice hourly on Sunday).

Trains for London Victoria (£21.60, 1½ hours) leave every half an hour. There's a thrice-hourly service to Brighton (£7.80, 30 to 40 minutes).

Wheely Good Fun (☎ 01323-479077) hires out skates and bikes from Fisherman's Green on Royal Pde.

AROUND EASTBOURNE
Pevensey Castle

The ruins of William the Conqueror's first stronghold, **Pevensey Castle** (EH; ☎ 01323-762604; adult/child £4.20/2.10; ☺ 10am-6pm mid-Apr–Sep, to 4pm Oct, to 4pm Sat & Sun Nov-Mar) sit 5 miles east of Eastbourne, off the A259. Picturesquely dissolving into its own moat, the castle marks the point where William the Conqueror landed in 1066, just two weeks before the Battle of Hastings. And shortly afterwards, Old Bill wasted no time in building upon sturdy Roman walls to create a castle, which was used time and again through the centuries, right up to WWII. You can roam about its decaying husk with an enlightening audio guide, free with entry.

STRANGE SOUTHERNERS

A few oddball regional events include the **World Marbles Championship** on Tinsley Green, near Crawley, in mid-April, when teams compete to knock each other's balls out of action. Another event some may put down to lost marbles is the Isle of Wight's late-August **Newchurch Garlic Festival**, where visitors can achieve new heights of bad breath by trying garlic ice cream, garlic jelly beans, garlic beer and more bulb-inspired products. And what could be more English than October's almighty shouting match – the **National Town Criers Championship** in Hastings? These iconic newspapers-on-legs once roamed the streets with a bell and throaty 'Oyez, Oyez, Oyez…' from as early as 1066 right up to the 19th century.

The 14th-century **Mint House** (☎ 01323-762337; admission £1), just across the road from the castle, is worth visiting for its nutty collection of antiques and curios.

Regular train services between London Victoria and Hastings via Eastbourne (10 minutes) stop at Westham, half a mile from Pevensey.

Beachy Head

The famous cliffs of Beachy Head are the highest point of a string of chalky rock faces that slice across this rugged stretch of coast at the southern end of the South Downs. It's a spot of thrilling beauty, at least until you remember that this is also one of England's top suicide spots.

From Beachy Head, the famous **Seven Sisters Cliffs** roller coaster their way west. Along the way, you'll stumble upon tiny seaside hamlet Birling Gap, where you can stop for a drink, snack or ice cream at the **Birling Gap Hotel** (☎ 01323-423197; **Seven Sisters** Cliffs, Birling Gap, East Dene).

Beachy Head is off the B2103, from the A259 between Eastbourne and Newhaven. Eastbourne's City Sightseeing tour bus (see p207) stops at the cliff top.

The Long Man

If you're travelling along the A27 between Eastbourne and Lewes, be sure to look southwards, just east of the town of Wilmington, to see the spindly stick-figure-like **Long Man of Wilmington**. No one really knows how this leggy 70m-high man – now marked out with white concrete – arrived here or what he represents.

There is a turn-off for the Long Man at the town of Wilmington, 7 miles west of Eastbourne, from where you can get a better view. If you're walking this section of the South Downs you will pass him and get a close-up view.

Charleston Farmhouse

Five miles west of Eastbourne, **Charleston Farmhouse** (☎ 01323-811265; www.charleston.org.uk; Firle, off A27; adult/child £6.50/4.50; ☺ 2-6pm Thu, Fri & Sun, 11.30am-6pm Wed & Sat Apr-Oct) was the Bohemian country getaway of the Bloomsbury Group. Even now that the joyous frescoes and vivid furniture have begun to fade, and the last of its pioneering occupants and visitors have long since passed away, it's still a tangible example of the rich intellectual and aesthetic life that they came to represent (see boxed text, below).

In 1916, Virginia Woolf's sister, painter Vanessa Bell, moved here with her lover Duncan Grant, and they set about redecorating with abandon in a style that owed much to the influence of the post-Impressionists. Hardly a wall, door or piece of furniture was left untouched, and the walls featured paintings by Picasso, Derain, Delacroix and others. There's also a striking garden, interesting outbuildings and medieval dovecote.

Visits are by guided tour only, except on Sunday and bank holiday Mondays. The nearest train station is at Berwick, on the Brighton to Eastbourne line, a 2-mile walk from the farmhouse.

LEWES
pop 15,988

Strung out along a thin High St flanked by elegant Georgian buildings, a part-ruined castle and a traditional brewery just across the River Ouse, Lewes (pronounced 'Lewis') is a charming hillside town with a turbulent past and fiery traditions (see boxed text, p203). Off the main drag, however, there's a more intimate atmosphere as you descend into twisting narrow streets called twittens – the remainder of the town's original medieval street plan. The town occupies a steep ridge between the river and the castle ruins, with High St climbing the spine and the twittens running off it.

The town made headlines in late 2008 when it introduced its own currency to encourage more money to be spent in the local economy. The Lewes Pound has the same value as sterling and can be used in some 70 local businesses and farmers markets.

You'll find the **tourist office** (☎ 01273-483448; lewes.tic@lewes.gov.uk; 187 High St; ☺ 9am-5pm Mon-Fri, 9.30am-5.30pm Sat & 10am-2pm Sun Apr-Sep, 9am-5pm Mon-Fri, 10am-2pm Sat Oct-Mar) at the top of the hill. The **main post office** (High St) is a short walk west.

Lloyds TSB (Cliffe High St) has ATMs at either end of the centre. While you're here it's worth

---

THE BLOOMSBURY GROUP

The Bloomsbury Group was Britain's most influential artistic and intellectual circle to arise from the first half of the 20th century, a set of Cambridge graduates, artists and scholars who all gravitated to London's Bloomsbury area pre-WWI. Its most famous members included Virginia Woolf, Maynard Keynes, Vanessa Bell, Duncan Grant, Lytton Strachey, TS Elliot and EM Forster.

The outspokenly pacifist group gained notoriety for stunts that embarrassed the military forces during WWI, and scandalised London society with their intergroup relationships and, in several cases, bisexuality. Their tastes in post-Impressionist art and avant-garde literature were ahead of their time, and were often savaged by critics only to be later hailed as masterpieces. Woolf of course was winning herself acclaim as a novelist, and with her husband Leonard founded the Hogarth Press. Her artist sister Vanessa and Vanessa's lover Duncan Grant were two of several group members to make a name through the modernist design firm Omega Workshops. Keynes, meanwhile, became one of the foremost economic theorists of the day, and Strachey had several uncompromising biographies under his belt.

Though the group gradually drifted apart after the war and Woolf committed suicide in 1941, their once-controversial views were steadily accepted into the mainstream and their work has continued to influence generations of new writers, poets, artists and musicians.

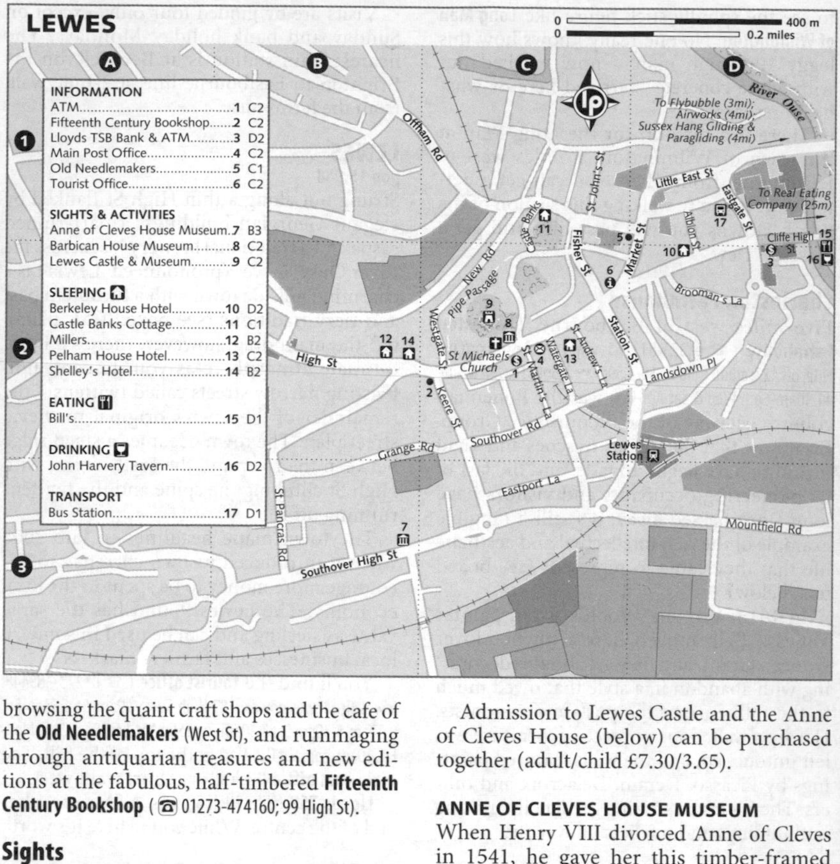
LEWES
0 400 m
0 0.2 miles
A
B
C
D
1
2
3
INFORMATION
ATM.....1 C2
Fifteenth Century Bookshop.....2 C2
Lloyds TSB Bank & ATM.....3 D2
Main Post Office.....4 C2
Old Needlemakers.....5 C1
Tourist Office.....6 C2
SIGHTS & ACTIVITIES
Anne of Cleves House Museum.7 B3
Barbican House Museum.....8 C2
Lewes Castle & Museum.....9 C2
SLEEPING
Berkeley House Hotel.....10 D2
Castle Banks Cottage.....11 C1
Millers.....12 B2
Pelham House Hotel.....13 C2
Shelley's Hotel.....14 B2
EATING
Bill's.....15 D1
DRINKING
John Harvery Tavern.....16 D2
TRANSPORT
Bus Station.....17 D1
River Ouse
To Flybubble (3mi); Airworks (4mi); Sussex Hang Gliding & Paragliding (4mi)
To Real Eating Company (25m)
Offham Rd
St John's St
Little East St
Eastgate St
Castle Banks
Fisher St
Market St
Albion St
Cliffe High St
New Rd
Pipe Passage
Brooman's La
Westgate St
High St
St Michaels Church
St Martin's La
Watergate La
St Andrew's La
Station St
Landsdown Pl
Keere St
Southover Rd
Grange Rd
Lewes Station
Eastport La
St Pancras Rd
Mountfield Rd
Southover High St

browsing the quaint craft shops and the cafe of the **Old Needlemakers** (West St), and rummaging through antiquarian treasures and new editions at the fabulous, half-timbered **Fifteenth Century Bookshop** (☎ 01273-474160; 99 High St).

Sights

LEWES CASTLE & BARBICAN HOUSE MUSEUM

Now little more then a set of ruins, this **castle** (☎ 01273-486290; www.sussexpast.co.uk; 169 High St; adult/child £4.90/2.55; 🕒 10am-5.30pm Tue-Sat, 11am-5.30pm Sun-Mon) was built shortly after the 1066 Norman invasion. It never saw warfare, not counting the riotous celebrations following the Navy's victory over the Spanish Armada in 1588, when happy citizens blew great chunks out of the castle's walls! They left enough standing for it to remain an impressive sight, however, and its windy top affords excellent views over the town. The castle grounds also host summertime plays and concerts.

The attached **Barbican House Museum** has a good collection of prehistoric flint axeheads, Anglo Saxon jewellery and medieval long swords.

Admission to Lewes Castle and the Anne of Cleves House (below) can be purchased together (adult/child £7.30/3.65).

ANNE OF CLEVES HOUSE MUSEUM

When Henry VIII divorced Anne of Cleves in 1541, he gave her this timber-framed **house** (☎ 01273-474610; 52 Southover High St; adult/child £3.65/1.70; 🕒 10am-5pm Tue-Sat year-round, to 5pm Sun & Mon Mar-Oct) as part of her divorce settlement, although she never actually moved in. The creak-and-groan floors and spider's web wooden roof today houses an idiosyncratic folk museum, with everything from a witch's effigy complete with pins to a rack of Tudor costumes to try on.

Activities

Paragliders can get one step closer to heaven in the South Downs near Lewes, an excellent spot for the sport. A half-hour tandem flight costs about £100 to £120. Companies include:

Airworks (☎ 01273-858108; www.airworks.co.uk; Glynde)

Flybubble (☎ 01273-812442; www.flybubble.co.uk; Ringmer)

Sussex Hang Gliding & Paragliding (☎ 01273-858170; www.flysussex.co.uk; Tollgate)

Sleeping

Castle Banks Cottage (☎ 01273-476291; www.castle bankscottage.co.uk; 4 Castle Banks; s/d £32.50/65) Tucked away off the High St in a quiet lane, this tiny, pretty guest house has only two rooms. The easy-going proprietor is a mine of information about the area's local history. Breakfast is served in the pretty garden in summer.

Berkeley House Hotel (☎ 01273-476057; www .berkeleyhouselewes.co.uk; 2 Albion St; s from £55, d £75-105; 🖳 wi-fi) Lovely extras such as a front balcony and a roof terrace looking over the South Downs make this Georgian town house worth a look, as do the tastefully decorated rooms and courteous service.

Shelleys Hotel (☎ 01273-472361; www.the-shelleys .co.uk; High St; s/d from £125/170; 🅿) Full of old-fashioned charm, this 16th-century manor house was once home to the earl of Dorset and was owned by the Shelley family (of Percy Bysshe fame). It has cosy, country rooms and a good restaurant overlooking a lovely walled garden.

Other options:

Millers (☎ 01273-475631; www.millersbedandbreak fast.com; 134 High St; s/d £75/85) Chivalrous service in a 16th-century, timber-framed town house.

Pelham House Hotel (☎ 01273-488600; www.pelham house.com; St Andrews La; s/d from £90/120) Swish contemporary town house hotel with an excellent restaurant.

Eating & Drinking

our pick **Bill's** (☎ 01273 476918; 56 Cliffe High St, snacks £2.50-5, specials £5-10; ❤ lunch) There's something doubly delicious about a forkful of fresh food when its ingredients are piled all around you. Part grocers, part delicatessen, part rustic-styled cafe, Bill's envelopes customers in its colours and smells then dishes up melt-in-the-mouth tartlets, gourmet pizzas, salads, deserts and other artisanal snacks.

Real Eating Company (☎ 01273-402650; 18 Cliffe High St; mains £7-15; ❤ 10.30am-5.30pm Mon, to 11pm Tue-Fri, 8am-11pm Sat, 11.30am-4pm Sun) At the rear of an excellent deli, this large, airy cafe-cum-brasserie stretches back to a lovely outside terrace and serves delicious cheese and charcuterie plates, breakfast, omelettes and top-class main meals such as wood pigeon and braised pork belly.

John Harvey Tavern (☎ 01273-479880; Bear Yard) Warm and friendly place just off the high street serving a great selection of ales from the local Harveys brewery. It also serves pretty decent food and hosts regular live music nights.

Getting There & Away

Lewes is 9 miles northeast of Brighton and 16 miles northwest of Eastbourne, just off the A27.

The bus station is north of the town centre off Eastgate St. Buses 28 and 29 run to Brighton (£2.80, 30 minutes, every 15 minutes) on weekdays and Sundays (hourly). The 29 bus continues north to Tunbridge Wells (one hour).

Lewes is on the main train line between London Victoria and Eastbourne and the coastal link between Eastbourne and Brighton. Trains leave from London Victoria (£19, 1¼ hours, every 10 to 20 minutes) and Brighton (15 minutes) and from Eastbourne (20 minutes, four times an hour).

LEWES' FIERY HISTORY

The English enjoy an evening of frenzied pyromania nationwide on **Guy Fawkes Night** (5th November) in memory of a 1605 plot to blow up the Houses of Parliament. But unassuming little Lewes has double the reason to host one of the craziest fireworks celebrations you're ever likely to see.

In 1555, at the height of Mary Tudor's Catholic revival, 17 protestant martyrs were burned at the stake in the town's High St. Lewes has not forgotten, and every 5 November tens of thousands of people gather for the famous fireworks display, in which effigies of the pope are burnt in memory of the martyrs. These days he's often joined by modern-day figures, prime ministers, presidents and terrorists among them. Locals parade the streets in outlandish medieval garb with flaming crosses, and send barrels filled with bangers to crack and fizzle their way down to the river, chased by local youth.

Though not shy of controversy, there's no sectarian fervour these days and it's one of the most enjoyable nights on the southeastern calendar.

THE SOUTHEAST

AROUND LEWES

In 1934 science teacher John Christie and his opera-singer wife decided to build a 1200-seat opera house in the middle of nowhere. It seemed a magnificent folly at the time. But now, **Glyndebourne** (☎ 01273-812321; www.glynde bourne.com) is one of England's best places to enjoy the lyric arts, with a season that runs from late May to the end of August. Tickets can be like gold dust so book well ahead. And bring your glad rags: dress code is strictly black tie and evening dress. Glyndebourne is 4 miles east of Lewes off the B2192.

BRIGHTON & HOVE

pop 247, 817

Brighton and Hove is the most vibrant seaside resort in England and a high point of any visit to the region. It's a thriving, cosmopolitan city with a Bohemian spirit; home to an exuberant gay community, a dynamic student population and a healthy number of ageing and new-age hippies, as well as traditional candy-floss fun. Brighton rocks all year round, but really comes to life during the summer months, when tourists, language students and revellers from London, keen to explore the city's legendary nightlife, summer festivals and multitude of trendy restaurants, slick boutique hotels and shops, pour into the city.

Brighton has embraced the outlandish ever since the Prince Regent built his party palace here in the 19th century (see boxed text, p206). Celebrities rub shoulders with dreadlocked hippies, drag queens party next to designer-clad urbanites, and kids toddle around the tables of coffee-quaffing media types.

The town's increase in popularity over the past few years isn't all good, however. Chain bars are slowly sneaking into once staunchly alternative areas, and some long-term residents grumble that the city's trendy status and the influx of moneyed Londoners are prompting a sharp rise in prices and pretension, detracting from the very alternative spirit that makes the city unique in the first place.

Orientation

Brighton Town and its western neighbour Hove were jointly made a city in 2000. The train station is half a mile north of the beach, while the tiny bus station is tucked away in Poole Valley close to Brighton Pier. Old Steine (pronounced 'steen') is the major thoroughfare linking pier and centre.

To the west lies the Lanes, a tangle of pedestrian alleyways, packed with pubs, restaurants and shops. A short walk north is the North Laine, full of quirky stores and Bohemian cafes. The city's effervescent gay scene flourishes in Kemptown, east of Old Steine along St James' St.

Brighton's burgeoning marina, east of town, is also a vibrant waterside shopping, dining, drinking and water-sports centre.

Information

BOOKSHOPS

Borders Books (☎ 01273-731122; Churchill Square Shopping Centre; ⊗ 9am-10pm Mon-Sat, 11am-5pm Sun)
Brighton Books (☎ 01273-693845; 18 Kensington Gardens; ⊗ 10am-6pm Mon-Sat) Secondhand bookshop.

INTERNET ACCESS

Internet Junction (☎ 01273-607650; 109 Western Rd; per hr £2.50)
Jubilee Library (☎ 01273-296961; Jubilee St; ⊗ 10am-7pm Mon & Tue, to 5pm Wed, Fri & Sat, to 8pm Thu, 11am-4pm Sun) Bring ID and sign up to use machines for free.
Netpama (☎ 01273-227188; 37 Preston St; per hr £2)

INTERNET RESOURCES

Brighton City Guide (www.brighton.co.uk)
visitbrighton.com (www.visitbrighton.com)

LAUNDRY

Preston Street Laundrette (☎ 01273-738556; 75 Preston St; ⊗ 8am-7.30pm Mon-Sat, 9am-7pm Sun)

MEDICAL SERVICES

Royal Sussex County Hospital (☎ 01273-696955; Eastern Rd) Has an accident and emergency department 2 miles east of the centre.
Wistons Clinic (☎ 01273-506263; 138 Dyke Rd) For general medical consultations, under a mile from the centre.

MONEY

American Express (☎ 01273-712906; 82 North St) Has bureau de change.
NatWest (Castle Sq) Bank with ATM.

POST

Post office (2-3 Churchill Square Shopping Centre; ⊗ 9am-5.30pm Mon-Fri, 9am-3pm Sat)

TOURIST INFORMATION

Tourist office (☎ 0906-7112255; www.visitbrighton .com; Royal Pavilion Shop, Royal Pavilion; ⊗ 9.30am-5.30pm) Overworked staff, along with a 50p-per-minute

BRIGHTON & HOVE

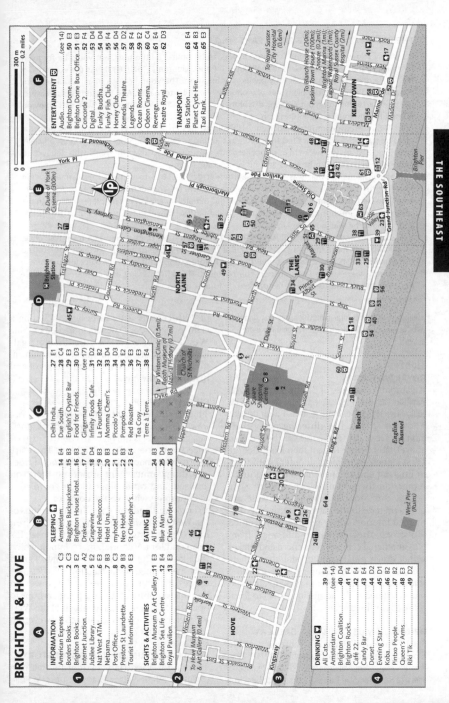

INFORMATION
American Express.....................1	C3
Borders Books.........................2	C3
Brighton Books........................3	E2
Internet Junction......................4	A2
Jubilee Library.........................5	E2
Nat West ATM..........................6	E3
Netpama.................................7	B3
Post Office..............................8	C3
Preston St Laundrette...............9	B3
Tourist Information..................10	E3

SIGHTS & ACTIVITIES
Brighton Museum & Art Gallery..11	E3
Brighton Sea Life Centre...........12	E4
Royal Pavilion.........................13	E3

SLEEPING
Amsterdam............................14	E4
Baggies Backpackers...............15	B3
Brighton House Hotel..............16	B3
Drakes..................................17	F4
Grapevine.............................18	D4
Hotel Pelirocco.......................9	B3
Hotel Una.............................20	B3
myhotel................................21	E2
Neo Hotel.............................22	B3
St Christopher's.....................23	E4

EATING
Al Fresco...............................24	B3
Blue Man..............................25	D4
China Garden.........................26	B3
Delhi India.............................27	E1
Due South.............................28	C4
English's Oyster Bar................29	E3
Food for Friends.....................30	D3
Gingerman...........................(see 7)
Infinity Foods Cafe.................31	D2
La Fourchette........................32	B2
Momma Cherri's.....................33	D4
Piccolo's...............................34	D3
Pompoko..............................35	E2
Red Roaster...........................36	F4
Tea Cosy..............................37	E2
Terre à Terre.........................38	E4

DRINKING
Ali Cats..................................39	E4
Amsterdam.........................(see 14)
Brighton Coalition...................40	D4
Brighton Rocks.......................41	E4
Café 22.................................42	E4
Candy Bar.............................43	E4
Dorset...................................44	D2
Evening Star..........................45	D1
Koba.....................................46	B2
Pintxo People.........................47	B2
Queen's Arms.......................48	E3
Riki Tik..................................49	D2

ENTERTAINMENT
Audio..................................(see 14)
Brighton Dome.......................50	E3
Brighton Dome Box Office........51	E3
Concorde 2............................52	F4
Digital...................................53	D4
Funky Buddha........................54	D4
Funky Fish Club......................55	F4
Honey Club............................56	D4
Komedia Theatre.....................57	D2
Legends.................................58	F4
Ocean Rooms.........................59	E2
Odeon Cinema.......................60	C4
Revenge................................61	E4
Theatre Royal.........................62	D3

TRANSPORT
Bus Station............................63	E4
Planet Cycle Hire....................64	B3
Taxi Rank..............................65	E3

THE SOUTHEAST

THE PRINCE, THE PALACE & THE PARTYING

It's widely known that England's George III was, to be polite, a little nuts. But you'd be forgiven for thinking that 'Mad King George's' eldest son Prince George (1762–1830) was the eccentric in the family upon visiting his princely pavilion at Brighton. The young prince began drinking with abandon and enjoying the pleasures of women while still a teenager. And to daddy's displeasure, he soon started hanging out with his dissolute uncle the Duke of Cumberland, who was enjoying himself royally by the sea in Brighton.

In 1787 George commissioned Henry Holland to design a neoclassical villa as his personal pleasure palace. While he waited to accede to the throne (when his father was declared officially insane in 1810 he was sworn in as Prince Regent), George whiled away the years with debauched parties for himself, his mistresses and his aristocratic mates.

Ever conscious of what was trendy, George decided in 1815 to convert the Marine Pavilion to reflect the current fascination with all things Eastern. He engaged the services of John Nash, who laboured for eight years to create a Mogul Indian–style palace, complete with the most lavish Chinese interior imaginable. George finally had a palace suited to his outlandish tastes and, to boot, he was now the king.

His brother and successor, William IV (1765-1837), also used the pavilion as a royal residence, as did William's niece Victoria (1819-1901). But the conservative queen never really took to the place and in 1850 sold it to the town, but not before stripping it of every piece of furniture – 143 wagons were needed to transport the contents. Thankfully, many original items were later returned and the palace is now restored to its former glory.

telephone line provide local information. You may find the website and on-site 24-hour-accessible computer more helpful.

Sights

ROYAL PAVILION

An absolute must-see of Brighton is the **Royal Pavilion** (☎ 01273-290900; www.royalpavilion.org.uk; adult/under 15yr £8.50/5.10; ☺ 10am-4.30pm Oct-Mar, 9.30am-5pm Apr-Sep), the glittering party-pad-cum-palace of Prince George (see boxed text, above), later Prince Regent then King George IV. It's one of the most decadent buildings in England and an apt symbol of Brighton's reputation for hedonism. The Indian-style domes and Moorish minarets outside are only a prelude to the palace's lavish oriental-themed interior, where no colour is deemed too strong, dragons swoop and snarl from gilt-smothered ceilings, gem-encrusted snakes slither down pillars, and crystal chandeliers seem ordered by the tonne. While gawping is the main activity, you can pick up an audio tour (included in the admission price) to learn more about the palace.

BRIGHTON MUSEUM & ART GALLERY

Set in the Royal Pavilion's renovated stable block, this **museum and art gallery** (☎ 01273-290900; Royal Pavilion Gardens; admission free; ☺ 10am-7pm Tue, to 5pm Wed-Sat, 2-5pm Sun) has a glittering collection of 20th-century art and design, including a crimson Salvador Dali sofa modelled on Mae West's lips. There's also an enthralling gallery of world art, and an 'images of Brighton' multimedia exhibit containing a series of oral histories of the city.

BRIGHTON PIER

This grand old centenarian **pier** (Palace Pier; www.brightonpier.co.uk; admission free), full of glorious gaudiness, is the place to come to experience the tackier side of Brighton. There are plenty of stomach-churning fairground rides and dingy amusement arcades to keep you amused, and candy floss and Brighton rock to chomp on while you're doing so.

Look west and you'll see the sad remains of the **West Pier** (www.westpier.co.uk), a skeletal iron hulk that attracts flocks of birds at sunset. It's a sad end for a Victorian marvel upon which the likes of Charlie Chaplin and Stan Laurel once performed. Construction of a *Jetsons*-esque Brighton i-360 observation tower on this site is imminent, and the planners hope to open to the public in 2010. Much of the West Pier wreckage will be left intact, however, in the hope that it can one day be restored.

BOOTH MUSEUM OF NATURAL HISTORY

This odd Victorian taxidermy **museum** (☎ 01273-292777; 194 Dyke Rd; admission free; ☺ 10am-

5pm Mon-Wed, Fri & Sat, 2-5pm Sun) has several creepy sights such as walls full of mammoth butterflies and cabinets of birds poised to tear apart small mammals. Particularly disturbing if you've seen the Hitchcock movie. The museum is about half a mile north of the train station. Buses 27 and 27A stop nearby on Dyke Rd.

HOVE MUSEUM & ART GALLERY

It may surprise you that Hove can justifiably claim to be the birthplace of British cinema, with the first short film shot here in 1898. You can see it alongside other fascinating films at this attractive Victorian **villa** (☎ 01273-290200; 19 New Church Rd; admission free; ☷ 10am-5pm Tue-Sat, 2-5pm Sun). Another highlight is the kids' room, full of fairy lights and reverberating to the snores of a wizard and the whirr of an underfloor train. Exhibits include old zoetropes, a magic lantern and a small cupboard with a periscope inside. From central Brighton take bus 1, 1A or 6.

BRIGHTON SEA LIFE CENTRE

This grand old Victorian **aquarium** (☎ 01273-604234; www.sealifeeurope.com; Marine Pde; adult/child £12.95/9.50; ☷ 10am-5pm) is the world's oldest operational sea-life centre, and makes for a fun hour or two pressing your nose up against glass and making fishy faces at sea horses, rays, sea turtles and other inhabitants.

Activities

There is a huge range of activities on offer in Brighton, from rollerblading to beach volleyball to skateboarding, to paragliding and of course myriad water sports: ask the tourist office for details. **Lagoon Watersports** (☎ 01273-684260; www.lagoon.co.uk; West Jetty, Brighton Marina) can help you onto the waves, whether in a yacht or dinghy or on water-skis.

Tours

The tourist office can organise a range of guided tours, including:

Brighton Walks (☎ 01273-888596; www.brighton walks.com; adult/child £6/3.50) Offers a huge variety of standard and offbeat themes including a Murder Walk and a Rich & Famous tour. Show up for prescheduled walks or contact to book.

City Sightseeing (www.city-sightseeing.co.uk; adult/child £7/3; ☷ tours every 30min late May-late Sep) Has open-top hop-on hop-off bus tours that leave from Grand Junction Rd near Brighton Pier and take you around the main sights.

Tourist Tracks (www.tourist-tracks.com) Has MP3 audio guides downloadable from its website (£5) or available on a preloaded MP3 player at the tourist office (£6 per half-day).

Festivals & Events

There's always something fun going on in Brighton, from **Gay Pride** (late Jul; www.brighton pride.org) to food and drink festivals, but the showpiece is May's three-week-long **Brighton Festival** (☎ 01273-709 709; www.brighton-festival.org .uk), the biggest arts festival in Britain after Edinburgh, drawing theatre, dance, music and comedy performers from around the globe.

Sleeping

Despite a glut of hotels in Brighton, prices are relatively high and you'd be wise to book well ahead for summer weekends and for the Brighton Festival in May.

BUDGET

Brighton's hostels are a varied bunch. Several cater to raucous stag and hen nights; others are more traditional and homely. Choose wisely!

Baggies Backpackers (☎ 01273-733740; 33 Oriental Pl; dm/d £13/35) A warm familial atmosphere, worn-in charm, motherly onsite owner and clean, snug dorms have made this long-established hostel something of an institution. It's also blessed with a homely kitchen, a cosy basement music room thick with cassettes, and a TV room piled high with videos. Some travellers complain that it can get a little cliquey, though.

Grapevine (☎ 01273-703985; www.grapevinewebsite .co.uk; 75-76 Middle St; per person from £15; ☐ wi-fi) The Spartan rooms in this hostel-cum-budget-hotel have the air of a hospital ward but are generally clean and well kept. It's popular with hen and stag nights so can get noisy but on the plus side it has a great central location and young energetic staff. There's a sister hotel by the seafront on North Rd.

St Christopher's (☎ 01273-202035; www.st-christo phers.co.uk; Palace Hotel, 10/12 Grand Junction Rd; dm £16-19.50, s/d £25/50; ☐) Don't count on getting a peaceful night's sleep at this basic seafront hostel – it's a magnet for party people thanks to its location in the heart of the Brighton action. While quiet is a rare luxury, it boasts sea views, a spot near Brighton Pier and a pub downstairs for cheap meals. There are under-bed cages to stash your stuff (bring a lock) but no kitchen.

MIDRANGE

Brighton is blessed with a wide selection of midrange accommodation.

Snooze (☎ 01273-605797; www.snoozebrighton.com; 25 St George's Tce; s/d incl breakfast from £35/65; ▣ wi-fi) This eccentric Kemptown pad is very fond of retro styling. Rooms feature vintage posters, bright 60s and 70s patterned wallpaper, flying wooden ducks, floral sinks and mad clashes of colour. It's more than just a gimmick though – rooms are comfortable and spotless, and there are great vegie breakfasts.

Brighton House Hotel (☎ 01273-323282; www .brighton-house.co.uk; 52 Regency Sq; s/d from £45/85; ▣ wi-fi) You'll get honest value at this welcoming Regency town-house B&B. Rooms are immaculate and traditionally styled (some with four-posters) and they serve healthy breakfasts with organic ingredients and vegetarian options. Children under 12 not allowed.

Hotel Pelirocco (☎ 01273-327055; www.hotelpeli rocco.co.uk; 10 Regency Sq; s £50-65, d £90-140, ste £300; ▣ wi-fi) One of Brighton's first theme hotels, this is still the nuttiest (and one of the most fun) places to stay in town. There's a range of individually designed rooms, some by artists, some by big-name sponsors, from a basic single done up like a boxing ring, to the Motown room, full of gold satin, LPs and a vintage record player, to the playroom suite with a 3m circular bed, mirrored ceiling and pole-dancing area.

Amsterdam (☎ 01273-688825; www.amsterdam .uk.com; 11-12 Marine Pde; d with bathroom £60-140, without bathroom from £50) Popular gay-run hotel that also welcomes tolerant straights, with tastefully decorated, spacious, bright rooms and wonderful sea views, including a fabulous penthouse suite (£160 to £200). It sits above one of Brighton's best gay bars and saunas, which guests can use for half price. Request a room on higher floors if you're a light sleeper.

Hotel Una (☎ 01273-820464; www.hotel-una.co.uk; 55/56 Regency Sq; s/d from £70/110; ▣ wi-fi) A simple, unpretentious place, Hotel Una is devoid of the themes or kitsch decor that are popular in so many of the city's hotels. Instead you'll find caramel-coloured floorboards and rooms in soothing shades of brown and cream, with the odd miniature sauna or whirlpool bath thrown in.

Paskins Town House (☎ 01273-601203; www .paskins.co.uk; 18/19 Charlotte St; d from £90; ▣ wi-fi) An environmentally friendly B&B spread between two elegant town houses. It prides itself on using ecofriendly products such as recycled toilet paper, low-energy bulbs and biodegradable cleaning materials. The individually designed rooms are beautifully maintained, and excellent organic and vegetarian breakfasts are served in the art deco–inspired breakfast room.

Neo Hotel (☎ 01273-711104; www.neohotel.com; 19 Oriental Pl; d from £105; ▣ wi-fi) You won't be surprised to learn that the owner of this gorgeous hotel is an interior stylist. The eleven rooms could have dropped straight out of the pages of a design magazine, each finished in rich colours and tactile fabrics, with bold floral and Asian motifs and black-tiled bathrooms. Kick back in satin kimono robes and watch a DVD on your flat-screen TV, or indulge in massage and beauty treatments. Wonderful breakfasts include homemade smoothies and fruit pancakes.

TOP END

Drakes (☎ 01273-696934; www.drakesofbrighton.com; 43-44 Marine Pde; r £100-325; ▣ wi-fi) Drakes oozes understated class: a stylish, minimalist boutique hotel that eschews the need to shout its existence from the rooftops. Feature rooms have giant free-standing tubs set in front of full-length bay windows with stunning views out to sea. It also has one of Brighton's best restaurants, Gingerman (see p210).

Blanch House (☎ 01273-603504; www.blanchhouse .co.uk; 17 Atlingworth St; d from £100; ▣ wi-fi) Themed rooms are the name of the game in this boutique hotel, but there's nothing tacky about them – plush fabrics and a Victorian rolltop bath rule in the Decadence suite and the Alice room is an ice-cool vision of silver and white. There's a magnificently stylish fine dining restaurant here – all white leather banquettes and space-age swivel chairs – and a fine cocktail bar.

myhotel (☎ 01273-224300; www.myhotels.co.uk; 17 Jubilee St; r incl breakfast £140-600; ℗ ▣ wi-fi) The rooms in this trendy new hotel look like space-age pods, full of curved white walls, floor-to-ceiling observation windows and suspended flat-screen TVs, with the odd splash of neon orange or pink. You can even hook up your iPod and play music through speakers in the ceiling. There's a cocoon-like cocktail bar downstairs, and if you've money to burn, a suite with a steam room and harpooned vintage carousel horse.

Eating

Brighton easily has the best choice of eateries on the south coast, with cafes, diners and restaurants to fulfil every whim.

BUDGET

Brighton is one of the UK's best destinations for vegetarians, and its innovative meat-free menus are also terrific value for anyone on a tight budget.

Pompoko (☎ 01273-703072; 110 Church St; mains £4-5; ☺ 11am-10pm Tue-Thu, to 11pm Fri & Sat, to 9pm Sun) Simple Japanese food in a small but perfectly formed little cafe. It's quick, cheap and delicious, with an emphasis on home-style curries, soups and noodle dishes.

Deli India (☎ 01273-699985; 81 Trafalgar St; curries £5; ☺ 10am-7pm Tue-Fri, to 6pm Sat, 11am-3pm Sun) Light and healthy Indian food made without artificial flavours, cream or heavy oil is on offer in this delicatessen and teashop. The deli's shelves are packed with lentils, chapatti flours, chutneys, spices and cookbooks to take home.

Infinity Foods Cafe (☎ 01273-670743; 50 Gardner St; mains £5-8; ☺ 9.30am-5pm Mon-Sat) The sister establishment of Infinity Foods wholefoods shop, a Brighton institution, serves a wide variety of vegetarian and organic food, with many vegan and wheat- or gluten-free options including tofu burgers, mezze plates and falafel.

Food for Friends (☎ 01273-202310; www.foodfor friends.com; 17a Prince Albert St; mains £8-13; ☺ lunch & dinner) This airy, glass-sided restaurant attracts the attention of passers-by as much as it does the loyalty of its customers with an ever-inventive choice of vegetarian and vegan food. Children are also catered to.

Other worthy contenders:

Piccolo's (☎ 01273-203701; 56 Ship St; mains £3.60-8.50; ☺ 11.30am-11.30pm) Cheap, tasty pizza served in this fast, friendly and bustling restaurant.

Red Roaster (☎ 01273-686668; 1d St James' St; mains £4-5; ☺ 7am-7pm Mon-Fri, 8am-7pm Sat, 9am-6.30pm Sun) You can smell the aroma of roasting coffee from across the street at this fine independent coffee house, which also serves sandwiches and salads.

Tea Cosy (☎ 01273-677055; 3 George St; Diana Spencer memorial tea £8; ☺ noon-5pm Wed, 11am-6pm Thu-Sat,

noon-6pm Sun) Barmy tearoom full of strict etiquette rules and royal family memorabilia.

MIDRANGE

Al Fresco (☎ 01273-206532; The Milkmaid Pavilion, Kings Rd Arches; mains £9-20; ☺ noon-midnight) The star here is the view. Al Fresco sits a mere 100m from the West Pier, in a curved-glass structure with a huge, staggered outdoor terrace and amazing views up and down the seafront and out to sea. The pizzas, pastas and Italian meat dishes make a tasty accompaniment to the views.

our pick **Terre á Terre** (☎ 01273-729051; 71 East St; mains £10-15; ☺ noon-10.30pm Tue-Fri, to 11pm Sat, to 10pm Sun) Even staunch meat eaters will come out raving about this legendary vegetarian restaurant. Terre á Terre offers a sublime dining experience, from the vibrant, modern space, to the entertaining menus, to the delicious, inventive dishes full of rich robust flavours.

La Fourchette (☎ 01273-722556; www.lafourchette .co.uk; 105 Western Rd; set lunch/dinner from £10/26.50; ☺ lunch & dinner Mon-Thu, 11am-11pm Fri-Sun) Grown up, romantic dining, sleek decor and fine French bistro food are the name of the game at this charming Gallic bistro. There are particularly good, locally caught fish dishes and the service is excellent if a little over-attentive.

English's Oyster Bar (☎ 01273-327980; www.englishs .co.uk; 29-31 East St; mains £10-29; ☺ lunch & dinner) A 60-year institution, this Brightonian seafood paradise dishes up everything from oysters to lobster to Dover sole. It's converted from fishermen's cottages, with echoes of the elegant Edwardian era inside and buzzing alfresco dining on the pedestrian square outside.

Blue Man (☎ 01273-325529; 11 Little East St; mains £11-16; ☺ 3-6pm) Tiny dining room tucked away near the seafront serving excellent, large portions of North African food, in a spicy, cosy atmosphere, full of ambient lighting, mosaic tables and scatter cushions. After you're full, you can sit back and suck on an apple hubble bubble.

Due South (☎ 01273-821218; www.duesouth.co.uk; 139 Kings Rd Arches; mains £14-20; ☺ lunch & dinner Mon-Sat, lunch Sun) Sheltered under a cavernous Victorian arch on the seafront, with a curvaceous front window and small bamboo-screened terrace on the promenade, this refined yet relaxed restaurant specialises in dishes cooked with the best environmentally sustainable and seasonal Sussex produce.

THE SOUTHEAST

Gingerman (☎ 01273-696934; Drake's Hotel, Marine Pde; mains £16-24) Chic and minimalist, this well-loved eatery has a modish menu bolstered by classical French influence. It's set in an exclusive hotel and occupies a curvaceous room with red blinds, cream-leather seating and soft jazz. It also has an equally good but more informal venue on Norfolk Sq.

Also try:

China Garden (☎ 01273-607835; 88-91 Preston St; mains £7-18; ⏲ noon-11.30pm) Well-loved Chinese restaurant, with fantastic dim sum at the weekend.

Momma Cherri's (☎ 01273-325305; 2-3 Little East St; mains £8-14.50; ⏲ lunch & dinner Tue-Sat, noon-7pm Sun) Try ribs, southern-fried chicken or jambalayas at this popular soul-food restaurant.

Drinking

Outside London, Brighton's nightlife is the best in the south, with its unique mix of sea-front clubs and bars. Drunken stag and hen parties and charmless, tacky nightclubs rule on West St, which is best avoided. For more ideas, visit www.drinkinbrighton.co.uk.

Evening Star (☎ 01273-328931; www.eveningstar brighton.co.uk; 55 Surrey St) This cosy, unpretentious pub is a beer-drinker's nirvana, with a wonderful selection of award-winning real ales, Belgian beers, organic lagers and real ciders. It's a short stagger away from the station.

Brighton Coalition (☎ 01273-772842; 171-181 Kings Rd Arches) On a summer's day, there's nowhere better to sit and watch the world go by than at this popular beach bar, diner and club. It's a cavernous place with a funky brick-vaulted interior and a wide terrace spilling onto the promenade. All sorts happen here, from comedy, to live music, to club nights.

Pintxo People (☎ 01273-732323; www.pintxopeople .co.uk; 95 Western Rd; ⏲ to midnight Mon-Fri, to 1am Sat) This place is principally a Spanish restaurant, but go upstairs and you'll find a sultry bar with huge squishy sofas, red-leather stools, a martini station and a staggering cocktail list. Or sit on one of the rustic wooden tables downstairs, sink a few sangrias and nibble on tapas.

Dorset (☎ 01273-605423; www.thedorset.co.uk; 28 North Rd) This laid-back Brighton institution throws open its doors and windows in fine weather and spills tables onto the pavement. You'll be just as welcome for a morning coffee as for an evening pint here, and if you decide not to leave between the two, there's always the decent gastropub menu.

Riki Tik (☎ 01273-683844; 18a Bond St; ⏲ 10am-late) Coffee bar by day, popular preclub venue by night, this place has been pumping out cool cocktails and funky breaks for years. It's stylish, dark and sexy and much bigger than it looks from the outside. DJs play here most nights.

Brighton Rocks (☎ 01273-601139; 6 Rock Pl; ⏲ 4pm-late) This cocktail bar is firmly on the Kemptown gay scene, but welcomes all-comers. The cocktails are tasty, there's a damn fine 'grazing' menu and the bar plays regular host to theme parties and art launches.

Ali Cats (☎ 01273-220902; Brills La; ⏲ 7pm-midnight Wed-Sat) In the early evenings, this super-chilled, windowless, subterranean dive is an informal picture house, playing classic cult movies. Later, it turns into an alternative bar serving cheap beer and playing drum and bass, jungle, electro and old skool.

Entertainment

Brighton offers the best entertainment line-up on the south coast, with clubs to rival London and Manchester for cool. Keep tabs on what's hot and what's not by searching out publications such as the *List*, the *Source* and *What's On*.

NIGHTCLUBS

When Britain's top DJs aren't plying their trade in London, Ibiza or Aya Napia, chances are you'll spy them here. All Brighton's clubs open until 2am, and many as late as 5am.

Funky Buddha (☎ 01273-725541; www.funkybuddha .co.uk; Kings Rd Arches; admission £2-8) Twin giant, brick, subterranean tunnels, with bars at the front and back, playing funky house, 70s, R&B and disco to a stylish and attitude free crowd.

Audio (☎ 01273-606906; www.audiobrighton.com; 10 Marine Pde; admission £3-10) Some of the city's top club nights can be found at this ear-numbing venue, where the music's top priority, attracting a young, up-for-it crowd. Every night is different, with music ranging from breakbeats to electro to indie. Next to the Amsterdam Hotel.

Ocean Rooms (☎ 01273-699069; www.oceanrooms .co.uk; 1 Morley St; admission £3-10) This enduring favourite crams in three floors of dance variety, from an all-white bar to a dance floor where you can lap up the efforts of top DJs, from hip-hop to drum and bass, to breakbeat.

Funky Fish (☎ 01273-699069; www.funkyfishclub.co.uk; 19-23 Marine Pde; admission £3-10) Fun, friendly, and unpretentious little club playing soul, funk, jazz, Motown and old-skool breaks. No big-name DJs or stringent door policies, just cheap drinks and a rocking party atmosphere.

Digital (☎ 01273-227767; www.yourfutureisdigital.com/brighton; 187-193 Kings Rd Arches; admission £3-12) Formerly the famous Zap club, this new place on the Brighton scene hosts indie, house and cheesy student nights.

Honey Club (☎ 01273-202807; www.thehoneyclub.co.uk; 214 Kings Rd Arches; admission £5-12) A cavernous seafront club that jumps from strength to strength, almost as popular with DJs as it is with the weekly queues of clubbers who pile into its glittering depths. Dress up, party hard, then cool off on the balcony chillout area or dip your aching feet in the sea.

Concorde 2 (☎ 01273-673311; www.concorde2.co.uk; Madeira Dr, Kemptown; admission £8-20) Brighton's best-known and best-loved club is a disarm-ingly unpretentious den, where DJ Fatboy Slim pioneered the Big Beat Boutique and still occasionally graces the decks. There's a huge variety of club nights and live bands each month, from world music to rock.

CINEMAS

Odeon Cinema (☎ 0871-224 4007; cnr King's Rd & West St) Check out this seafront cinema for mainstream movies.

Duke of York (☎ 01273-602503; Preston Circus) About a mile north of North Rd, showing art-house films and classics.

THEATRE

Brighton Dome (☎ 01273-709709; www.brighton-dome.org.uk; 29 New Rd) Once the stables and exercise yard of King George IV, this art-deco complex houses three theatre venues within the Royal Pavilion estate. The box office is on New Rd.

THE SOUTHEAST

GAY & LESBIAN BRIGHTON

Perhaps it's Brighton's long-time association with the theatre, but for more than 100 years the city has been a gay haven. Gay icons Noel Coward and Ivor Novello were regular visitors, but in those days the scene was furtive and separate. From the 1960s onwards, the scene really began to open up, especially in the Kemptown area and around Old Steine. Today, with more than 25,000 gay men and 10,000 to 15,000 lesbians living in the city, it is the most vibrant queer community in the country outside London.

Kemptown (aka Camptown), on and off St James' St, is where it's all at. In recent years the old Brunswick Town area of Hove has emerged as a quieter alternative to the traditionally cruisy (and sometimes seedy) Kemptown, but the community here has responded by branching out from the usual pubs that served as nightly pick-up joints. Now you will find a rank of gay-owned businesses, from cafes and hotels to bookshops, as well as the more obvious bars, clubs and saunas.

For up-to-date information on what's going on in gay Brighton, check out the websites www.gay.brighton.co.uk and www.realbrighton.com, or pick up the free monthly magazine **Gscene** (www.gscene.com) from various venues or the tourist office.

For drinking...
Cafe 22 (☎ 01273-626682; 129 St James' St; snacks £2-3; ☽ 8am-6pm Mon-Fri, 10am-6pm Sat & Sun) This cool coffeeshop hangout and internet cafe is *the* place to get word on everything going on in town.
Amsterdam (☎ 01273-688825; www.amsterdam.uk.com; 11-12 Marine Pde; ☽ noon-2am) Hotel, sauna, restaurant and extremely hip bar above the pier; its sun terrace is a particular hit.
Candy Bar (☎ 01273-622424; www.thecandybar.co.uk; 129 St James' St; ☽ 9pm-2am) Slick cafe-bar-club for the girls, with pink-lit arches, curvaceous bar, pool table and dance floor.
Queen's Arms (☎ 01273-696873; www.queensarmsbrighton.com; 7 George St; ☽ 3pm-late) Plenty of camp in the cabaret and karaoke acts at this pub make it a definite stop on the Brighton gay trail.

For dancing...
Bars and pubs may be fun, but the real action takes place on and off the dance floor.
Revenge (☎ 01273-608133; www.revenge.co.uk; 7 Marine Pde; ☽ 10.30pm-3am) Nightly disco with occasional cabaret.
Legends (☎ 01273-624462; 31-34 Marine Pde; ☽ 9am-2am) Club and basement bar underneath the Amsterdam, playing 1990s music and club anthems with the odd touch of drag.

Theatre Royal (☎ 01273-328488; New Rd) Built by decree of the Prince of Wales in 1806, this venue hosts plays, musicals and operas.

Komedia Theatre (☎ 01273-647100; www.komedia .co.uk; Gardner St) This former billiards hall and supermarket is now a stylish comedy, theatre and cabaret venue.

Shopping

A busy maze of narrow lanes and tiny alleyways that was once a fishing village, the **Lanes** is Brighton's most popular shopping district. Its every twist and turn is jam-packed with jewellers and gift shops, coffee shops and boutiques selling everything from antique firearms to hard-to-find vinyls. There's another, less-claustrophobic shopping district in **North Laine**, a series of streets north of the Lanes, including Bond, Gardner, Kensington and Sydney Sts, that are full of retro-cool boutiques and Bohemian cafes. Head west from the Lanes and you'll hit Churchill Square Shopping Centre and Western Rd, where you'll find all the mainstream high street stores.

Getting There & Away

Brighton is 53 miles from London and transport is fast and frequent.

BUS

National Express (☎ 08705 808080; www.national express.com) coaches leave for London Victoria (£10.90, 80 minutes, hourly), and there are regular coach links to all London airports.

Buses 28, 29 and 29A go to Lewes (£2.80, 35 minutes), bus 12 to Eastbourne (£3, 80 minutes), bus 700 to Chichester (£3, 80 minutes) and Arundel (two hours).

TRAIN

There are two hourly services to London Victoria (£19, 50 to 70 minutes) and two to London Bridge (50 minutes to 1¼ hours). For £2 on top of the rail fare, you can get a PlusBus ticket that gives unlimited travel on Brighton & Hove buses for the day. There's one direct service to Portsmouth (£14.50, 1½ hours, hourly), twice-hourly services to Chichester, Eastbourne and Hastings, and links to Canterbury and Dover.

Getting Around

Brighton is a sizable place, but you'll be able to cover most of it on foot. Alternatively, you can buy a day ticket (£3) from the driver to scoot back and forth on Brighton & Hove buses.

Parking can be expensive. Brighton and Hove operates a pay-and-display parking scheme. In the town centre, it's usually £1.50 per half hour with a maximum stay of two hours. Alternatively, there's a park-and-ride on the outskirts of town at Withdean.

Cab companies include **Brighton Streamline Taxis** (☎ 01273-747 474) and **City Cabs** (☎ 01273-205205), and there's a taxi rank on the junction of East St with Market St.

Planet Cycle Hire (☎ 01273-748881; West Pier Promenade; bikes per half day/day £8/12; ⏰ 10am-6pm Thu-Tue May-Sep, to 4pm Fri-Mon Oct-Apr), next to West Pier, rents bikes. Deposit and ID required.

WEST SUSSEX

After the fast-paced adventures of Brighton and East Sussex, West Sussex is welcome respite. The serene hills and valleys of the South Downs ripple across the county, fringed by sheltered coastline. Beautiful Arundel and cultured Chichester make good bases from which to explore the county's winding country lanes and remarkable Roman ruins.

ARUNDEL

pop 3297

Arundel is perhaps West Sussex's prettiest town. Clustered around a vast fairy-tale castle, its hillside streets burst with antique stores, teashops, excellent restaurants and the odd boutique hotel – it makes a great weekend break or stopover. While much of the town appears medieval – the whimsical castle has been home to the dukes of Norfolk for centuries – most of it dates to Victorian times.

Information

The **tourist office** (☎ 01903-882268; www.sussexbythe sea.com; 61 High St; ⏰ 10.30am-4pm Mon-Sat, 2-4pm Sun Easter-Oct, 10am-3pm daily Nov-Easter) has maps, an accommodation-booking service (£1.50) plus a small **museum** (☎ 01903-883890; www.arundelmuseum .org.uk; admission free; ⏰ 10am-3pm Easter-Aug, 11am-1pm Sep-Easter), temporarily located in the Mill Rd car park while it looks for a new home.

Sights & Activities

Originally built in the 11th century, all that's left of the first **Arundel Castle** (☎ 01903-882173; www.arun

---

TOP FIVE BEACH TOWNS

- Brighton & Hove (p204)
- Whitstable (p182)
- Ramsgate (p185)
- Hastings (p198)
- Broadstairs (p184)

---

delcastle.org; adult/under 16yr/student & senior £13/7.50/10.50; 11am-5pm Tue-Sun Easter-Oct) are the modest remains of its keep at its core. Thoroughly ruined during the English Civil War, most of what you see today is the result of passionate reconstruction by the eighth, 11th and 15th dukes of Norfolk between 1718 and 1900. The current duke still lives in part of the castle. Highlights include the atmospheric keep, the massive Great Hall and the library, which has paintings by Gainsborough and Holbein.

The other architectural landmark in town is Arundel's ostentatious 19th-century **cathedral** (☎ 01903-882297; www.arundelcathedral.org; 9am-6pm summer, to dusk winter), built in the French Gothic style by the 15th duke. Inside are the remains of his ancestor, St Philip Howard, now a canonised Catholic martyr who was caught praying for a Spanish victory against the English in 1588.

Kids will most likely opt for the **Arundel Ghost Experience** (☎ 01903-889821; www.arundelghost experience.com; High St; adult/child £4/3; 10am-6pm), where they'll hear hair-raising ghost stories and see old prison cells that are supposedly haunted themselves.

Bird fanciers will be rewarded by a trip to the 4-hectare **Wildfowl & Wetlands Centre** (☎ 01903-883355; www.wwt.org.uk; Mill Rd; adult/child £6.95/3.75; 9.30am-5pm Easter-Oct, to 4.30pm Nov-Easter), a mile east of the centre as the duck flies.

At the foot of High St is the Town Quay, from where you can hire your own boat or hop on a **cruise** (adult/child £6/4) of the River Arun.

Sleeping

Arundel YHA (☎ 0845 371 9002; www.yha.org.uk; Warningcamp; dm £17.95; P) Catering to South Downs walkers and families, this large Georgian hostel has excellent facilities and is set in sprawling grassy grounds on a charming country lane, 20- to 30-minutes' walk from town off the A27 (call for directions).

Norfolk Arms (☎ 01903-882101; www.norfolkarms hotel.com; High St; s/d from £65/90; P wi-fi) You'll be warmly welcomed at this rambling old Georgian coaching inn built by the 10th duke. Although the rooms are spacious, they are looking dated and a little scruffy.

Arundel House (☎ 01903-882136; www.arundel houseonline.com; 11 High St; d from £100; wi-fi) The modern rooms in this lovely 'restaurant with rooms' may be small but they're beautifully styled and very comfortable, with showers big enough for two. The restaurant downstairs serves some of the best food in Arundel (three-course dinner £28), which happily extends to breakfast.

Also worth a look:

April Cottage (☎ 01903-885401; www.april-cottage .co.uk; London Rd; d from £70; P wi-fi) Charming, friendly B&B with countryside views, a 20-minute walk from town.

Town House (☎ 01903-883847; www.thetownhouse .co.uk; 65 High St; d from £85) Stunning Regency-style boutique hotel.

Eating

Pallant of Arundel (☎ 01903-882288; www.pallantof arundel.co.uk; The Square; 9am-6pm Mon-Sat) Set yourself up for an English picnic by the river at this irresistible delicatessen. Choose from local cheese, freshly baked bread, pâté, wine and more sinful treats.

Tudor Rose (☎ 01903-883813; 49 High St; mains £4-10; 9am-6pm) This bustling, kitsch family-run tearoom is cluttered with everything from faux armour to brollies, to ships' wheels, to a portrait of the Queen. As well as tea and cakes, breakfasts, burgers, Sunday roasts and other substantial meals are served here.

Zigs (☎ 01903-884500; www.zigsrestaurant.co.uk; 51 High St; mains £6-18; 9.30am-3.30pm Mon & Tue, to 9.30pm Wed-Sat, to 6pm Sun) The slick, modern furnishings of this Parisian-style bistro fit in perfectly with the low ceilings and oak beams of its old town-house setting. It specialises in *tartines* (*pain Poîlane* – an unusual French bread with a slightly sour flavour – topped with assorted hot and cold toppings) and *piérrades* (hot volcano stones on which you cook your own food at the table).

Town House (☎ 01903-883847; 65 High St; set lunch £14-18, set dinner £22-27.50; Tue-Sat) The only thing that rivals the stunning 16th-century Florentine gilded-walnut ceiling at this elegant eatery is the acclaimed Mediterranean-influenced cuisine and sparkling atmosphere. Book ahead.

Getting There & Away

Trains are the way to go. They run to London Victoria (£20.50, 1½ hours, twice hourly), and to Chichester (20 minutes, twice hourly); change at Ford or Barnham. There are also links to Brighton (£7.80, one hour 20 minutes, twice hourly); change at Ford or Barnham.

AROUND ARUNDEL

Bignor Roman Villa (☎ 01903-869259; www.bignorrom anvilla.co.uk; adult/child £4.35/1.85; ☙ 10am-6pm Jun-Sep, to 5pm May & Oct, Tue-Sun Mar-Apr) is home to an astonishingly fine collection of mosaics preserved within an atmospheric thatched complex that's historic in its own right. Discovered in 1811 by a farmer ploughing his fields, the villa was built around AD 190. The wonderful mosaic floors include vivid scenes of chunky-thighed gladiators, a beautiful Venus whose eyes seem to follow you about the room and an impressive 24m-long gallery design.

While Bignor is well worth the trip, it's a devil of a place to reach without your own wheels. It's located 6 miles north of Arundel off the A29.

CHICHESTER

pop 27,477

Sitting on flat plains between the South Downs and the sea, this prosperous Georgian market town has plenty of country charm. It's home to an array of traditional tea-and-crumpet shops, well-mannered townsfolk, a fine cathedral and streets of handsome 18th-century town houses. It doesn't stint on cosmopolitan culture either. A famous theatre and arts festival takes place every year, and there's a superb modern-art gallery. The administrative capital of West Sussex, the town is within easy reach of some fascinating Roman remains that recall its days as a sprawling port garrison shortly after the invasion of AD 43.

Orientation & Information

Striking crown-shaped Market Cross, built in 1501, marks the centre of town. The streets around it are pedestrianised and everything you'd want to see is within walking distance.

There is a **tourist office** (☎ 01243-775888; www .visitchichester.org; 29a South St; ☙ 9.15am-5.15pm Mon-Sat year-round, also 11am-3.30pm Sun Apr-Sep) and

a **post office** (cnr Chapel & West Sts), and **Internet Junction** (☎ 01243-776644; 2 Southdown Bldg, Southgate; per hr £1; ☙ 9am-8pm Mon-Fri, 11am-8pm Sat & Sun) has double-quick net access.

Sights
CHICHESTER CATHEDRAL

This elegant **cathedral** (☎ 01243-782595; www.chi chestercathedral.org.uk; West St; requested donation £5; ☙ 7.15am-7pm Jun-Aug, to 6pm Sep-May) was begun in 1075 and largely rebuilt in the 13th century. Three storeys of beautiful arches sweep upwards, and Romanesque carvings are dotted around. The freestanding church tower was built in the 15th century and the spire is from the 19th century. There are also a few bold, modern flourishes, including an entrancing stained-glass window by Marc Chagall and the not-so-pretty disembodied likenesses of the Queen and Prince Phillip outside the main entrance.

Guided tours operate at 11.15am and 2.30pm Monday to Saturday, Easter to October, and the excellent cathedral choir is guaranteed to give you goosebumps during the daily **Evensong** (☙ 5.30pm Mon-Sat, 3.30pm Sun).

PALLANT HOUSE GALLERY

One of many handsome Georgian houses in town, **Pallant House** (☎ 01243-774557; www.pallant .org.uk; 9 North Pallant; adult/child/student £6.50/2/3.50; ☙ 10am-5pm Tue-Sat, 12.30-5pm Sun), once owned by a wealthy wine merchant, now houses a superb collection of 20th-century, mostly British, art, with names such as Caulfield, Freud, Sutherland and Moore represented, as well as international artists including Picasso, Cézanne and Rembrandt.

CHURCH OF THE GREYFRIARS

If you fancy a stroll in the park, it's worth a peek at the remains of this **Franciscan church** (☎ 01243-784683; Priory Park; admission free; ☙ noon-4pm Sat Jun–mid-Sep), built in the northeastern corner of the town in 1269. After dissolution in 1536, the structure became the guildhall and, later, a court of law, where William Blake was tried for sedition in 1804.

Festivals & Events

For three weeks in June and July, the annual **Chichester Festivities** (☎ 01243-785718; www.chifest .org.uk) puts on an abundance of terrific theatre, art, guest lectures, fireworks and performances of every musical genre.

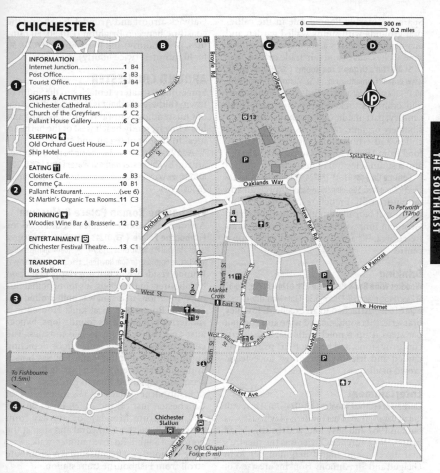

CHICHESTER

INFORMATION		
Internet Junction	1	B4
Post Office	2	B3
Tourist Office	3	B4
SIGHTS & ACTIVITIES		
Chichester Cathedral	4	B3
Church of the Greyfriars	5	C2
Pallant House Gallery	6	C3
SLEEPING		
Old Orchard Guest House	7	D4
Ship Hotel	8	C2
EATING		
Cloisters Cafe	9	B3
Comme Ça	10	B1
Pallant Restaurant	(see 6)	
St Martin's Organic Tea Rooms	11	C3
DRINKING		
Woodies Wine Bar & Brasserie	12	D3
ENTERTAINMENT		
Chichester Festival Theatre	13	C1
TRANSPORT		
Bus Station	14	B4

THE SOUTHEAST

Sleeping

Most accommodation in Chichester is mid-range, with little for budget travellers.

Old Orchard Guest House (☎ 01243-536547; www .oldorchardguesthouse.co.uk; 8 Lyndhurst Rd; s/d from £45/60) Freshly baked bread and jams are served up for breakfast in the garden or conservatory at this disarming central Georgian town house, which has three spacious and gracious old-style rooms.

Old Chapel Forge (☎ 01243-264380; www.oldchapel forge.co.uk; Lagness; d from £60; P wi-fi) For those with their own wheels, this gorgeous, eco-friendly B&B set in a 17th-century house and a stone chapel, is a good bet. The chapel rooms, with high ceilings and open views across the countryside, are particularly special.

Ship Hotel (☎ 01243-778000; North St; s/d £95/120; wi-fi) The grand central staircase in this former Georgian town house leads to 36 polished blonde wood, suede and leather rooms; they're the nicest option in the city centre. The Ship Hotel also boasts an excellent all-day brasserie.

Eating

Pallant Restaurant (☎ 01243-784701; 9 North Pallant; snacks £2-6.50; ☺ 10am-5pm Tue-Sat, 12-5pm Sun) In the Pallant House gallery, this sophisticated cafe has paintings and display cases, and a sunny courtyard that's a good spot for sandwiches, cakes and heartier main meals.

Cloisters Cafe (☎ 01243-783718; Cathedral Cloisters; snacks £2.50-5; ☺ 9am-5pm Mon-Sat, 10am-4pm Sun)

Sparkling marble-floored cafe in the cathedral grounds with sunny walled garden and airy atmosphere. It's a good spot for simple sandwiches, cakes and fair-trade drinks.

St Martin's Organic Tea Rooms (☎ 01243-786715; www.organictearooms.co.uk; 3 St Martins St; mains £4-10; ⏰ 10am-6pm Mon-Sat) A little cocoon of nooks and crannies tucked away in a part-18th-century, part-medieval town house, this passionately organic cafe serves freshly ground coffee and wholesome, mostly vegetarian, food from Welsh rarebits to risottos. There's also a sinful selection of desserts.

Comme Ça (☎ 01243-788724; 67 Broyle Rd; mains £8-13; ⏰ lunch Wed-Sun, dinner Tue-Sat) Family-run and family-friendly French restaurant, offering traditional Normandy cuisine in a converted Georgian inn, with a lovely vine-covered alfresco area. It's a short walk north of the town centre.

Drinking

Woodies Wine Bar & Brasserie (☎ 01243-779895; 10-13 St Pancras St; mains £8-12; ⏰ 5.30-11pm Mon-Thu, to midnight Fri & Sat) Attached to an excellent, low-key brasserie, this sophisticated wine and cocktail bar steps it up a notch with bright colours, corduroy stools and bold pop-art prints. The chilled and friendly vibe draws an eclectic crowd of all ages.

Entertainment

Chichester Festival Theatre (☎ 01243-781312; www.cft.org.uk; Oakland's Park) This modern playhouse was built in 1962 and has a long and distinguished history. Sir Laurence Olivier was the theatre's first director and Ingrid Bergman, Sir John Gielgud and Sir Anthony Hopkins are a few of the other famous names to have played here.

Getting There & Away

Chichester is 60 miles from London and 18 miles from Portsmouth.

BUS

Chichester is served by Coastliner bus 700, which runs between Brighton (2¼ hours, hourly) and Portsmouth (one hour, hourly). National Express has a rather protracted service from London Victoria (£12.60, four hours, twice daily).

TRAIN

Chichester can be reached easily from London Victoria (£20.60, 1¾ hours, half hourly) via Gatwick airport and Arundel. It's also on the coastline between Brighton (£10.50, 50 minutes, twice hourly) and Portsmouth (£6.20, 30 to 40 minutes, twice hourly).

AROUND CHICHESTER

Spreading its watery tentacles to the south of town, **Chichester Harbour** is designated an Area of Outstanding Natural Beauty (AONB) and has a lovely, sandy beach west of the harbour, ideal for a spot of sea air and strolling.

At West Itchenor, 1½-hour harbour cruises are run by **Chichester Harbour Water Tours** (☎ 01243-670504; www.chichesterharbourwatertours.co.uk; adult/child £6.50/3).

Fishbourne Roman Palace & Museum

Anyone mad about mosaics should head for **Fishbourne Palace** (☎ 01243-785859; www.sussexpast.co.uk; Salthill Rd; adult/child £7/3.70; ⏰ 10am-5pm Mar-Jul & Sep-Oct, to 6pm Aug, to 4pm Nov-Feb), the largest known Roman residence in Britain. Happened upon by labourers in the 1960s, it's thought that this once-luxurious mansion was built around AD 75 for a Romanised local king. Housed in a modern pavilion are its foundations, hypocaust and painstakingly re-laid mosaics. The centrepiece is a spectacular floor depicting cupid riding a dolphin flanked by sea horses and panthers. There's a fascinating little museum and replanted Roman gardens.

Fishbourne Palace is 1½ miles west of Chichester, just off the A259. Buses 56 and 700 leave from Monday to Saturday from outside Chichester Cathedral and stop at the bottom of Salthill Rd (five minutes' walk away; roughly hourly). The museum is a 10-minute stroll from Fishbourne train station.

Petworth

On the outskirts of its namesake village, the imposing 17th-century stately home, **Petworth House** (NT; ☎ 01798-342207; adult/child £9.50/4.80; ⏰ 11am-5pm Sat-Wed Apr-Oct), has an extraordinary art collection, the National Trust's finest. JMW Turner was a regular visitor and the house is still home to the largest collection of his paintings outside London's Tate Gallery. There are also many paintings by Van Dyck, Reynolds, Gainsborough, Titian, Bosch and William Blake. Other highlights are the fabulously theatrical grand staircase and the exquisite Carved Room, which ripples with wooden reliefs by master chiseller Grinling Gibbons.

The surrounding **Petworth Park** (adult/child £3.80/1.90; ☿ 8am-sunset) is the highlight – the fulfilment of Lancelot 'Capability' Brown's romantic natural landscape theory. It's home to herds of deer and is the site of open-air concerts in summer.

Petworth is 5 miles from the train station at Pulborough, from where bus 1 runs to Petworth Sq (15 minutes, hourly Monday to Saturday). If driving, it's 12 miles northeast of Chichester off the A285.

SURREY

Surrey is the heart of commuterville, chosen by well-off Londoners when they spawn, move out of the city and buy a country pad. For the most part, though, it's made up of uninspiring towns and dull, sprawling suburbs. Further away from the roaring motorways and packed rush-hour trains, the county reveals some inspiring landscapes made famous by authors Sir Arthur Conan Doyle, Sir Walter Scott and Jane Austen.

FARNHAM
☎ pop 36,298

Farnham is Surrey's nicest market town. Practically empty during the week, it's a relaxing place to visit, and the town's main enticements include exquisite Georgian homes, independent boutiques (some of which are on the pricey side), walking and cycling in the surrounding countryside and popping into one of Surrey's only intact castles.

Orientation & Information

The easiest way to explore Farnham is on foot. The most interesting part of town is its historical centre, where East, West, South and Castle Sts meet.

The Borough (the eastern end of West St) is the town's main shopping street. The train station is at the southern end of South St (Station Hill).

The **tourist office** (☎ 01252-712667; tourism@ farnham.gov.uk; South St; ☿ 9am-noon Mon & Sat, 9.30am-5pm Tue-Fri) has free maps of the town and surrounding countryside, the free *Farnham Heritage Trail* pamphlet and an updated list of accommodation in the area. It also offers free internet access.

You'll find a couple of banks with ATMs on the Borough. The main post office and a bureau de change are on West St, which is the continuation of the Borough.

Guided walks (☎ 01252-718119; adult/child £3/1) of approximately 1½ hours run at 11am on the first Sunday of every month between April and October. Meet at the entrance of the Wagon Yard car park at the southern end of Downing St.

Sights
FARNHAM CASTLE

Constructed in 1138 by Henry de Blois, the grandson of William the Conqueror, there's not much left of the **castle keep** (☎ 01252-713393; admission £3, free audio tour; ☿ noon-5pm Fri-Sun & public holidays 21 Mar-30 Sep) today except the beautiful old ramparts. Even if the keep is closed, it's worth walking around the outside (everyone seems to ignore the 'private' signs) to drink in the lovely view.

A residential palace house, Farnham Castle was built in the 13th century for the bishops of Winchester as a stopover on London journeys. From 1926 to the 1950s, it was taken over by the bishops of Guildford. It's now owned by the Farnham Castle International Briefing & Conference Centre, but you can visit it on a **guided tour** (☎ 01252-721194; adult/child £2.50/1.50; ☿ 2-4pm Wed & 2.30pm Fri Apr-Aug).

Farnham Castle is located up the old steps at the top of Castle St.

MUSEUM OF FARNHAM

This engaging **museum** (☎ 01252-715094; 38 West St; admission free; ☿ 10am-5pm Tue-Sat) is located in the splendid Willmer House, a Georgian town house built for wealthy hop merchant and maltster John Thorne in 1718. Since it opened in 1962, the museum has won many awards, including the European Museum of the Year Award.

The museum traces the history of Farnham through themes such as 'country life', 'art and architecture', 'on the road' and 'town life'. There's also an amazing **1780s dolls' house**, modelled on the house next door, and a morning cap that once belonged to Charles I.

Sleeping

Accommodation in Farnham tends towards the midrange to top end.

Mulberry (☎ 01252-726673; Station Hill; s/d £55/75; P ☐ wi-fi) Right by the station and set over an Indian restaurant and bar, this place has nine spic-and-span en suite rooms.

Hotel de Vie (☎ 01252-823030; 22 Firgrove Hill; s/d from £90) This plush, sexy boutique hotel has a naughty edge – around the lounge, bar and lobby are prints from the *moulin rouge* and pictures of ladies in corsets and killer heels. Rooms (with names like 'Oriental Pleasures' and 'Gothic Nights') come stocked with erotic DVDs and literature; two of them even have a love swing. If you do choose to emerge from your room, there's a pretty good restaurant.

Bush Hotel (☎ 01252-715237; www.mercure-uk.com; The Borough; s/d £120/150; ⊠) This 17th-century inn is right in the heart of the action and benefits from a cosy beamed bar, a pretty garden at the back and recently renovated rooms.

Eating & Entertainment

Farnham contains a good choice of tempting eateries.

Colony Restaurant (☎ 01252-725108; 68 Castle St; mains £5-7.50; lunch & dinner) Big, tasty portions of Peking cuisine on Farnham's attractive Castle St.

Nelson Arms (☎ 01252-716078; 50 Castle St; 2-course lunch £7.95, dinner £9.95-18.95) A rustic, low-ceilinged, cosy bar with a few modern touches, a small terrace at the back and good-value, locally sourced food.

Farnham Maltings (☎ 01252-745444; Bridge Sq; www.farnhammaltings.com) Creative, multipurpose spot with a riverside bar, live music, amateur theatre, exhibitions, workshops and comedy.

Getting There & Away

Train services run from London Waterloo (one hour, half hourly). From Winchester, there are trains to Woking (30 minutes, two per hour). Change there for trains to Farnham (25 minutes, half hourly). The train station is at the end of South St, on the other side of the A31 from the old town centre.

Stagecoach (☎ 0845 121 0190) bus X64 runs from Winchester to Farnham at 10 minutes past the hour (one hour and 10 minutes). The stop is on the Borough.

AROUND FARNHAM
Waverley Abbey

Said to be the inspiration for Sir Walter Scott's eponymous novel, Waverley Abbey sits ruined and forlorn on the banks of the River Wey about 2 miles southeast of Farnham. This was the first Cistercian abbey built in England (construction began in 1128) and was based on a parent abbey at Cîteaux in France.

Across the Wey is the impressive **Waverley Abbey House** (closed to the public), built in 1783 using bricks from the demolished abbey. In the 19th century it was owned by Florence Nightingale's brother-in-law, and the famous nurse was a regular visitor. Fittingly, the house was used as a hospital in WWI. Since 1973 it has been the headquarters of the Crusade for World Revival, a Christian charity.

The abbey and house are off the B3001.

Hindhead

The tiny hamlet of Hindhead, 8 miles south of Farnham off the A287, lies in the middle of the largest area of open heath in Surrey. During the 19th century, a number of prominent Victorians bought up property in the area, including Sir Arthur Conan Doyle (1859-1930), creator of Sherlock Holmes. One of the three founders of the National Trust, Sir Robert Hunter, lived in nearby Haslemere, and today much of the area is administered by the foundation.

The most beautiful part of the area is to the northeast, where you'll find a natural depression known as the **Devil's Punchbowl**. There are a number of excellent trails and bridle paths here. To get the best view, head for **Gibbet Hill** (280m), which was once an execution ground.

The **Hindhead YHA Hostel** (☎ 0845 371 9022; www.yha.org.uk; Devil's Punchbowl, Thursley; dm £12.95) is a completely secluded cottage run by the National Trust on the northern edge of the Punchbowl. It's perfect if you like walking – the nearest bus stop and car park are a half-mile away.

Buses 18 and 19 run hourly to Hindhead from Farnham.

Oxford, the Cotswolds & Around

Dripping with charm and riddled with implausibly pretty villages, this part of the country is as close to the old-world English idyll as you'll get. It's a haven of lush rolling hills, rose-clad cottages, bucolic views and graceful stone churches and is a magnet for tourists and commuters alike.

For some, the glut of thatched roofs, cream teas and antique shops is far too quaint, but get off the tourist trail, find your own romantic bolthole and you'll soon see why it is that A-list celebrities and the merely moneyed rush to buy property here. The honey-coloured villages, fire-lit inns and grandiose manors are very persuasive in their charms.

Beyond this rural Arcady lies the legendary city of Oxford, home to the world-famous university and the academic elite. Renowned for its beautiful colleges, top-notch museums and dreamy atmosphere, it's a great base for exploring the area. To the south, the Queen herself has a weekend pad, the majestic Windsor Castle, and nearby are the sedate and intellectual charms of the scholarly town of Eton.

To the west, you'll find the genteel sophistication of Regency Cheltenham and the elegant cloisters of the magnificent Gloucester Cathedral, and to the east there's the Rothschild pile, Waddesdon Manor, and the unexpected exotica of Woburn Safari Park.

Most of the attractions in this chapter are an easy day trip from London, but Oxford and the Cotswolds deserve at least an overnight stay. Although there is good public transport in the region, a car allows you to get off the beaten track and away from the crowds. Be prepared for busy roads in the summer months, especially around the Cotswolds.

HIGHLIGHTS

- Following in the footsteps of Lyra, Tolkien, CS Lewis and Inspector Morse as you tour the **Oxford colleges** (p226)
- Discovering deserted **Cotswold villages** (p240) straight out of medieval England
- Soaking up the atmosphere in the Queen's very own hideaway, **Windsor Castle** (p269)
- Feeling the hairs on the back of your neck rise as you revel in the reverberations at a concert in **Gloucester Cathedral** (p260)
- Immersing yourself in an African odyssey on a tour through **Woburn Safari Park** (p266)

- POPULATION: 3.8 MILLION
- AREA: 4239 SQ MILES
- UFO HOTSPOT: UFFINGTON

History

The Bronze Age chalk horse at Uffington and the Iron Age hill fort close by are some of the earliest evidence of settlement in this part of England. In Roman times, the region was traversed by a network of roads, some of which still exist today, and as word of the good hunting and fertile valleys spread, the region became heavily populated.

By the 11th century, the wool and grain trade had made the locals rich, William the Conqueror had built his first motte and bailey in Windsor, and the Augustinian abbey in Oxford had begun training clerics. In the 12th century, Henry II fortified the royal residence at Windsor by adding a stone tower and protective walls, and in the 13th century, Oxford's first colleges were established along with its reputation as England's foremost centre of learning.

Meanwhile, local farmers continued to supply London with corn, wool and clothing. The Cotswolds in particular flourished and amassed great wealth. By the 14th century, the wool merchants were rolling in money and happy to show off their good fortune by building the beautiful villages and graceful wool churches that still litter the area today.

The region's proximity to London also meant that it became a popular retreat for wealthy city dwellers. The nobility and aristocracy flocked to Hertfordshire and Buckinghamshire, building country piles as retreats from the city, while the labourers who had once been so important to the wool trade were made redundant by increasing mechanisation and moved back to the towns and cities. Today, the area remains affluent and is home to busy commuters and is a popular choice for wealthy Londoners looking for second homes.

Information

The popularity of the Cotswolds as a holiday destination means that you'll find helpful tourist offices in all towns and a wealth of information on the area. Outside the Cotswolds, the region is far less visited and information points can be rather thin on the ground. St Albans and Windsor are your best bets for assistance, or visit www.visitsoutheastengland.com and www.enjoyengland.com for the local low-down.

Activities

Walking or cycling through the Cotswolds is an ideal way to get away from the crowds and discover some of the lesser-known vistas and villages of the region. You'll also find great walking and cycling opportunities in Buckinghamshire's leafy Chiltern Hills and along the meandering River Thames. For more information, see the Outdoor England chapter (p141) or specific suggestions for walks and rides throughout this chapter.

CYCLING

Gentle gradients and scenic vistas make the Cotswolds ideal for cycling, with only the steep western escarpment offering a challenge to the legs. Plenty of quiet country lanes and gated roads criss-cross the region, or follow the waymarked **Thames Valley Cycle Way** (NCN routes 4, 5).

Mountain bikers can use a variety of bridleways in the **Cotswolds** and **Chilterns**, and in the west of the region the **Forest of Dean** has many dirt-track options, and some dedicated mountain-bike trails.

WALKING

The **Cotswold Hills** offer endless opportunities for day hikes, but if you're looking for something more ambitious, the **Cotswold Way** (www.nationaltrail.co.uk/Cotswold) is an absolute classic. The route covers 102 miles from Bath to Chipping Campden and takes about a week to walk.

Alternatively, the **Thames Path** (www.nationaltrail.co.uk/thamespath) follows the river downstream from its source near Cirencester to London. It takes about two weeks to complete the 184-mile route, but there's a very enjoyable five-day section from near Cirencester to Oxford.

Finally the 87-mile **Ridgeway National Trail** (www.nationaltrail.co.uk/ridgeway) meanders along the chalky grassland of the Wiltshire downs near Avebury, down into the Thames Valley and then along the spine of the Chilterns to Ivinghoe Beacon near Aylesbury in Buckinghamshire offering wonderful views of the surrounding area.

Getting There & Around

Thanks to its proximity to London and the rash of commuters who live in the area, there are frequent trains and buses here from the capital. Getting across the region by public transport can be frustrating and time

OXFORD, THE COTSWOLDS & AROUND

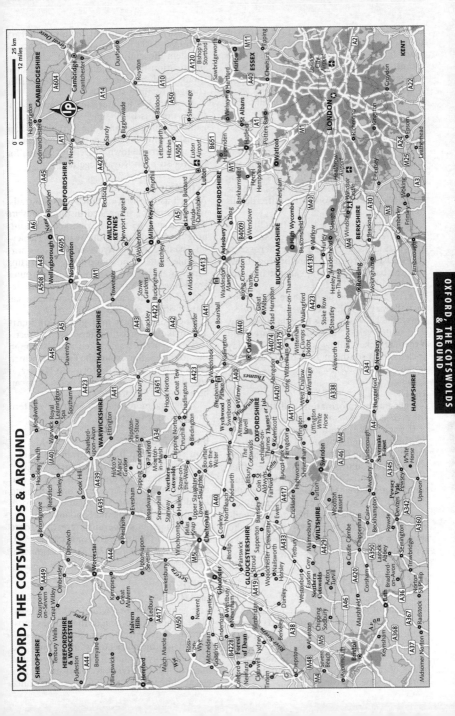

consuming, though. Renting a car gives you the most freedom, but be prepared for busy roads in the Cotswolds during the summer months and daily rush-hour traffic closer to London.

Traveline (☎ 0871-2002233; www.traveline.org.uk) provides timetable information on all public transport.

BUS

Major bus routes are run by **Stagecoach** (www .stagecoachbus.com) and **Arriva** (www.arrivabus.co.uk) with a host of smaller companies offering services to local towns and villages. See the destination information for specific details of routes.

If you plan to do a lot of travelling by bus, there are a variety of bus passes available that allow unlimited travel across the region. Check routes before buying, however, as bad connections can rot up your best-laid plans.

Arriva offers the **Go Anywhere** (£7) ticket that allows you unlimited use of its services across the UK (excluding London) for a day. The better-value Stagecoach **Explorer** and **Megarider** tickets allow one-/seven-/28-day travel across southern England (excluding London) for £8/20/75.

TRAIN

For general rail information, call **National Rail** (☎ 08457-48 49 50; www.nationalrail.co.uk).

If you're planning a lot of rail travel in southern England, it may be worth investing in a **Network Railcard** (www.railcard.co.uk; per yr £20), which allows you and three other adults a 33% discount on rail tickets and up to four children (five to 15 years) a 60% discount. There are some restrictions on travel (such as discounts being only available after 10am on weekdays), but if you're travelling with family or friends it can make for great savings.

OXFORDSHIRE

The whiff of old money, academic achievement and genteel living wafts from Oxfordshire's well-bred, well-preened pores. Rustic charm, good manners and grand attractions are in abundant supply here, with a host of charming villages surrounding the world-renowned university town.

Oxford is a highlight on any itinerary with over 1500 listed buildings, a choice of excellent museums and an air of refined sophistication. Its gorgeous colleges, hushed quads and gowned cyclists seem little changed by time.

Yet there is a lot more to the county. Just to the north is Blenheim Palace, an extravagant baroque pile that's the birthplace of Sir Winston Churchill, while to the south is the elegant riverside town of Henley, famous for its ever-so-posh Royal Regatta.

Activities

As well as the long-distance national trails, walkers may be interested in the **Oxfordshire Way**, a scenic, 65-mile waymarked trail running from Bourton-on-the-Water to Henley-on-Thames, and the **Wychwood Way**, a historic, 37-mile route from Woodstock, which runs through an ancient royal forest. The routes are divided up into manageable sections, described in leaflets available from most local tourist offices and libraries.

The quiet roads and gentle gradients also make Oxfordshire good cycling territory. The main waymarked route through the county is the **Oxfordshire Cycleway**, which takes in Woodstock, Burford and Henley. If you don't have your own wheels, you can hire bikes in Oxford (p235).

You'll find more information at www.oxford shire.gov.uk/countryside.

Getting Around

You can pick up bus and train timetables for most routes at local tourist offices. The main train stations are in Oxford and Banbury and have frequent connections to London Paddington and Euston, Hereford, Birmingham, Bristol and Scotland.

The main bus operators are the **Oxford Bus Company** (☎ 01865-785400; www.oxfordbus.co.uk) and **Stagecoach** (☎ 01865-772250; www.stagecoachbus .com/oxfordshire).

OXFORD
pop 134,248

The genteel city of Oxford is a privileged place, renowned as one of the world's most famous university towns, soaked in history, dripping with august buildings and yet incredibly insular. The 39 colleges that make up the University jealously guard their elegant honey-coloured buildings and, once inside their grounds, a reverent hush and studious calm descends.

Oxford is highly aware of its international standing and yet is remarkably restrained for a city driven by its student population. It's a conservative, bookish kind of place where academic achievement and intellectual ideals are the common currency. The University buildings wrap around narrow cobbled lanes, gowned cyclists blaze along the streets and the vast library collections run along shelves deep below the city streets.

Oxford is a wonderful place to ramble: the oldest colleges date back almost 750 years and little has changed inside the hallowed walls since then. But along with the rich history and tradition, there is a whole other world beyond the college walls. Oxford has a long industrial past and was birthplace of the Morris motor car as well as of Mensa. Today, the new Mini runs off the production lines and the real-world majority still outnumber the academic elite. Along with the all that fine architecture, world-class museums and historic pubs is a working city home to disadvantaged council estates, the usual glut of high-street chain shops and plenty of chi chi restaurants, trendy bars and expensive boutiques.

History

Strategically placed at the confluence of the Rivers Cherwell and Thames (called the Isis here, from the Latin *Tamesis*), Oxford was a key Saxon town heavily fortified by Alfred the Great during the war against the Danes.

By the 11th century, the Augustinian abbey in Oxford had begun training clerics, and when Henry II banned Anglo-Norman students from attending the Sorbonne in 1167, the abbey began to attract students in droves. Whether bored by the lack of distractions or revolted by the ignorance of the country folk we'll never know, but the new students managed to create a lasting enmity with the local townspeople, culminating in the St Scholastica's Day Massacre in 1355 (see boxed text, p226). Thereafter, the king ordered that the university be broken up into colleges, each of which then developed its own traditions.

The first colleges Balliol, Merton and University, were built in the 13th century, with at least three more being added in each of the following three centuries. Newer colleges, such as Keble, were added in the 19th and 20th centuries to cater for an ever-expanding student population. However, old habits die hard at Oxford, and it was 1877 before lecturers were allowed to marry, and another year before female students were admitted. Even then, it still took another 42 years before women would be granted a degree for their four years of hard work. Today, there are 39 colleges that cater for about 20,000 students, and in 2008 the last all-female college, St Hilda's, eventually opened its door to male students.

Meanwhile, the arrival of the canal system in 1790 had a profound effect on the rest of Oxford. By creating a link with the Midlands' industrial centres, work and trade suddenly expanded beyond the academic core. However, the city's real industrial boom came when William Morris began producing cars here in 1913. With the success of his Bullnose Morris and Morris Minor, his Cowley factory went on to become one of the largest motor plants in the world. Although the works have been scaled down since their heyday, new Minis still run off BMW's Cowley production line today.

Orientation

Oxford is fairly compact and can easily be covered on foot. Carfax Tower makes a good central landmark and is a short walk from the bus and train stations, which are conveniently located close to the centre of town.

The university buildings are scattered throughout the city, with the most important and architecturally significant in the centre. Jericho, in the northwest, is the trendy, artsy end of town, with slick bars and restaurants and an art-house cinema, while Cowley Rd, southeast of Carfax, is the edgy student and immigrant area packed with cheap places to eat and drink. Further out, in the salubrious northern suburb of Summertown, you'll find more upmarket restaurants and bars.

Information

BOOKSHOPS

Blackwell (☎ 01865-333000; www.blackwell.co.uk; 48-51 Broad St) 'The Knowledge Retailer' stocks any book you could ever need.

Waterfields (☎ 01865-721809; www.waterfields books.co.uk; 52 High St) Collection of rare, secondhand and antiquarian books.

EMERGENCY

Police (☎ 0845 8 505 505; St Aldate's)

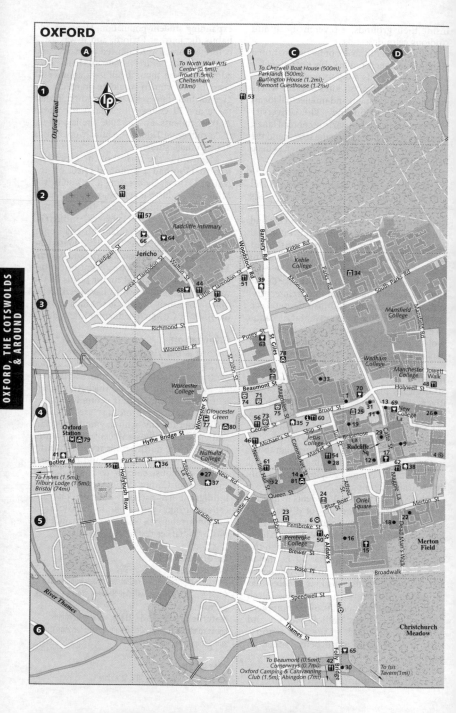

OXFORD

0   300 m
0   0.2 miles

New Marston
Recreation Ground

INFORMATION
Blackwell...........................**1** D4
C-Works...........................**2** C5
Coin Wash........................**3** G6
Links................................**4** D4
Police Station...................**5** C6
Post Office.......................**6** C5
Tourist Office...................**7** C4
Waterfields......................**8** E4

SIGHTS & ACTIVITIES
All Souls College................**9** D4
Ashmolean Museum...........**10** C4
Bodleian Library................**11** D4
Brasenose College.............**12** D4
Bridge of Sighs.................**13** D4
Carfax Tower....................**14** C5
Christ Church Cathedral......**15** D5
Christ Church College.........**16** D5
Church of St Mary the Virgin.**17** D4
Corpus Christi College........**18** D5
Exeter College..................**19** D4
Howard C & Sons...............**20** E5
Magdalen College..............**21** E5
Merton College.................**22** D5
Modern Art Oxford............**23** C5
Museum of Oxford.............**24** C5
Museum of the History of
   Science........................**25** D4
New College......................**26** D4
Oxford Castle....................**27** B5
Oxford Covered Market.......**28** C4
Pitt Rivers Museum.........(see 34)
Radcliffe Camera...............**29** D4
Salter Bros.......................**30** D6
Sheldonian Theatre............**31** D4
St Edmund Hall.................**32** E4
Trinity College..................**33** C4
University Museum.............**34** D3

SLEEPING
Buttery Hotel....................**35** C4
Central Backpackers...........**36** B4
Malmaison........................**37** B5
Old Bank Hotel..................**38** D4
Old Parsonage Hotel...........**39** C3
Orchard House...................**40** F6
YHA Oxford......................**41** A4

EATING
Aziz.................................**42** C6
Aziz.................................**43** H6
Big Bang..........................**44** B3
Café Coco.........................**45** F5
Chutneys..........................**46** C4
Door 74...........................**47** F6
Edamame..........................**48** D4
Fishers.............................**49** F5
G&D's..............................**50** C5
G&D's..............................**51** C3
G&D's..............................**52** G6
Gee's...............................**53** C1
Georgina's........................**54** C4
Jam Factory......................**55** A4
Jamie's Italian...................**56** C4
Jericho Café......................**57** B2
Manos..............................**58** A2
Mortons...........................**59** C4
Mortons.......................(see 28)
Mortons...........................**60** B3
Mortons...........................**61** C5
Quod...............................**62** D4
Vaults..........................(see 17)

DRINKING
Eagle & Child....................**63** C3
Frevd...............................**64** B2
Head of the River..............**65** D6
Jericho Tavern...................**66** B2
Kazbar.............................**67** F5
Raoul's.............................**68** B3
Turf Tavern......................**69** D4
White Horse......................**70** D4

ENTERTAINMENT
Burton Taylor Theatre.........**71** C4
Carling Academy................**72** H6
New Theatre.....................**73** C4
Oxford Playhouse...............**74** C4
Po Na Na.........................**75** C4

TRANSPORT
Cyclo Analysts **76** G6
Gloucester Green Bus/Coach
   Station........................**77** B4
Taxi Rank.........................**78** C3
Taxi Rank.........................**79** A4
Taxi Rank.........................**80** B4
Taxi Rank.........................**81** C5

Cherwell

St
Catherine's
College

Deer
Park

To Brookes (0.8mi);
Victoria Arms (1.8mi);
John Radcliffe
Hospital (2.8mi);
London (57mi)

St Cross Rd

Longwall St

Botanic
Gardens

Rose La

High St

St Clement's St

Iffley Rd

Cowley Rd

Cherwell

To Pegasus
Theatre (0.5mi)

**OXFORD, THE COTSWOLDS
& AROUND**

ST SCHOLASTICA'S DAY MASSACRE

The first real wave of students arrived in Oxford in the 12th century, and right from the start an uneasy relationship grew between the townspeople and the bookish blow-ins. Name calling and drunken brawls escalated into full-scale riots in 1209 and 1330, when browbeaten scholars abandoned Oxford to establish new universities in Cambridge and Stamford respectively. The riots of 10 and 11 February 1355, changed everything, however, and left a bitter scar on relations for hundreds of years.

It all began when celebrations for St Scholastica's Day grew out of hand and a drunken scuffle spilled into the street. Years of simmering discontent and frustrations let loose, and soon students and townspeople took to each other's throats. The chancellor ordered the pealing of the university bells and every student who heard it rushed to join the brawl. By the end of the day, the students had claimed victory and an uneasy truce was called.

The next morning, however, the furious townspeople returned with the help of local villagers armed with pickaxes, shovels and pikes. By sundown, 63 students and 30 townspeople were dead. King Edward III sent troops to quell the rioting and eventually decided to bring the town under the control of the university.

To prove its authority, the university ordered the mayor and burgesses (citizens) to attend a service and pay a penny for every student killed on the anniversary of the riot each year. For 470 years, the vengeful practice continued, until one mayor flatly refused to pay the fine. His successors all followed suit, but it took another 130 years for the university to extend the olive branch and award a Doctorate of Civil Law to Mayor William Richard Gowers, MA, Oriel in 1955.

INTERNET ACCESS

C-Works (☎ 01865-722044; 1st fl, New Bailey Hse, New Inn Hall St; per 50min £1; ☼ 9am-9pm Mon-Sat, to 7pm Sun)
Links (☎ 01865-204207; 33 High St; per 45min £1; ☼ 10am-9pm Mon-Sat, 10am-8pm Sun)

INTERNET RESOURCES

Try these sites if you want to get the low-down on local happenings.
Daily Info (www.dailyinfo.co.uk) Daily listings for events, gigs, performances, accommodation and jobs.
Oxford City (www.oxfordcity.co.uk) Accommodation and restaurant listings as well as entertainment, activities and shopping.
Oxford Online (www.visitoxford.org) Oxford's official tourism website.

LAUNDRY

Coin Wash (127 Cowley Rd; per load £3.50; ☼ 8am-10pm)

MEDICAL SERVICES

John Radcliffe Hospital (☎ 01865-741166; Headley Way, Headington) Three miles east of the city centre.

MONEY

You'll find that every major bank and ATM is handily represented on or close to Cornmarket St.

POST

Post office (☎ 0845-7223344; 102 St Aldate's; ☼ 8.30am-5.30pm Mon, 9.30am-5.30pm Tue, 9am-5.30pm Wed-Sat)

TOURIST INFORMATION

Tourist office (☎ 01865-252200; www.visitoxford.org; 15-16 Broad St; ☼ 9.30am-5pm Mon-Sat, to 6pm Thu-Sat Jul & Aug, 10am-4pm Sun) Stocks a *Welcome to Oxford* brochure (£1), which features a walking tour and college opening times, as well as the *University of Oxford* leaflet and *Oxford Accessible Guide* for travellers with disabilities. It can book accommodation for a £4 fee plus a 10% deposit.

UNIVERSITIES

Oxford Brookes (☎ 01865-484848; www.brookes .ac.uk; Gipsy Lane) Oxford's lesser-known university.
Oxford University (☎ 01865-270000; www.ox.ac.uk)

Sights
UNIVERSITY BUILDINGS & COLLEGES
Christ Church College

The largest and grandest of all of Oxford's colleges, **Christ Church** (☎ 01865-276492; www.chch .ox.ac.uk; St Aldate's; adult/under 16yr £4.90/3.90; ☼ 9am-5pm Mon-Sat, 1-5pm Sun) is also its most popular. The magnificent buildings, illustrious history and latter-day fame as a location for the Harry Potter films have tourists coming in droves.

The college was founded in 1525 by Cardinal Thomas Wolsey, who suppressed 22 monasteries to acquire the funds for his lavish building project. Over the years numerous luminaries have been educated here including Albert Einstein, philosopher John Locke, poet WH Auden, Charles Dodgson (Lewis Carroll) and 13 British prime ministers.

The main entrance is below imposing **Tom Tower**, the upper part of which was designed by former student Sir Christopher Wren. Great Tom, the 7-ton tower bell, still chimes 101 times each evening at 9.05pm (Oxford is five minutes west of Greenwich), to sound the curfew imposed on the original 101 students.

Mere visitors, however, are not allowed to enter the college this way and must go further down St Aldate's to the side entrance. Immediately on entering is the 15th-century cloister, a relic of the ancient Priory of St Frideswide, whose shrine was once a focus of pilgrimage. From here, you go up to the **Great Hall**, the college's magnificent dining room, with its hammer-beam roof and imposing portraits of past scholars.

Coming down the grand staircase, you'll enter **Tom Quad**, Oxford's largest quadrangle, and from here, **Christ Church Cathedral**, the smallest cathedral in the country. Inside, brawny Norman columns are topped by elegant vaulting, and beautiful, stained-glass windows adorn the walls. Look out for a rare depiction of the murder of Thomas Becket.

You can also explore another two quads and the **Picture Gallery**, with its modest collection of Renaissance art. To the south of the college is **Christ Church Meadow**, a leafy expanse bordered by the Isis and Cherwell rivers and ideal for leisurely walking.

Magdalen College

Set amid 40 hectares of lawns, woodlands, river walks and deer park, **Magdalen** (mawd-len; ☎ 01865-276000; www.magd.ox.ac.uk; High St; adult/under 16yr £4/3; ☺ noon-6pm Jul-Sep, 1pm-6pm/dusk Oct-Jun) is one of the wealthiest and most beautiful of Oxford's colleges.

An elegant Victorian gateway leads into a medieval chapel, with its glorious 15th-century tower, and on to the remarkable cloisters, some of the finest in Oxford. The strange gargoyles and carved figures here are said to have inspired CS Lewis' stone statues in *The Chronicles of Narnia*. Behind the cloisters, the lovely Addison's Walk leads through the grounds and along the banks of the River Cherwell for just under a mile.

Magdalen has a reputation as an artistic college, and some of its most famous students and fellows have included Oscar Wilde, Poet Laureate Sir John Betjeman and Nobel Laureate Seamus Heaney.

The college also boasts a fine choir that sings *Hymnus Eucharisticus* at 6am on May Day (1 May) from the top of the 42m bell tower. The event now marks the culmination of a solid night of drinking for most students as they gather in their glad rags on Magdalen Bridge to listen to the dawn chorus.

Opposite the college and sweeping along the banks of the River Cherwell are the beautiful **Botanic Gardens** (☎ 01865-286690; www.botanic-garden.ox.ac.uk; adult/under 16yr £3/free; ☺ 9am-6pm May-Aug, to 4.30pm Oct-Apr). The gardens are the oldest in Britain and were founded in 1621 for the study of medicinal plants.

Sheldonian Theatre

The monumental **Sheldonian Theatre** (☎ 01865-277299; www.sheldon.ox.ac.uk; Broad St; adult/under 16yr £2/1; ☺ 10am-12.30pm & 2-4.30pm Mon-Sat Mar-Oct, 10am-12.30pm & 2-3.30pm Mon-Sat Nov-Feb) was the first major work of Christopher Wren, at that time a university Professor of Astronomy. Inspired by the classical Theatre of Marcellus in Rome, it has a rectangular front end and a semicircular back, while inside, the ceiling of the main hall is blanketed by a fine 17th-century painting of the triumph of truth over ignorance. The Sheldonian is now used for college ceremonies and public concerts, but you can climb to the cupola for good views of the surrounding buildings.

Bodleian Library

Oxford's **Bodleian Library** (☎ 01865-277224; www.bodley.ox.ac.uk; Broad St) is one of the oldest public libraries in the world, and one of England's three copyright libraries. It holds more than seven million items on 118 miles of shelving and has seating space for up to 2500 readers.

The oldest part of the library surrounds the stunning Jacobean-Gothic **Old Schools Quadrangle** (☺ 9am-5.15pm Mon-Fri, to 4.45pm Sat), which dates from the early 17th century. On the eastern side of the quad is the **Tower of Five Orders**, an ornate building depicting the five classical orders of architecture. On the west side is the **Divinity School** (adult/under 14yr £2/free; ☺ 9am-5pm Mon-Fri, to 4.30pm Sat), the university's first teaching room. It is renowned as a masterpiece of 15th-century English Gothic architecture and has a superb fan-vaulted ceiling. A self-guided **audio tour** (£2.50, 40 minutes) to these areas is available.

Most of the rest of the library is closed to visitors, but **library tours** (admission £6; tours 10.30am, 11.30am, 2pm & 3pm) allow access to the medieval Duke Humfrey's library, where, the library proudly boasts, no less than five kings, 40 Nobel Prize winners, 25 British prime ministers and writers such as Oscar Wilde, CS Lewis and JRR Tolkien studied. You'll also get to see 17th-century **Convocation House and Court**, where parliament was held during the Civil War. The tour takes about an hour and is not suitable for children under 11 years old.

Radcliffe Camera

Just south of the library is the **Radcliffe Camera** (Radcliffe Sq; no public access), the quintessential Oxford landmark and one of the city's most photographed buildings. The spectacular circular library was built between 1737 and 1749 in grand Palladian style, and boasts Britain's third-largest dome. The only way to see the library is to join an **extended tour** (£12), which also explores the warren of underground tunnels and passages leading to the library's vast book stacks. Tours take place once a month (more often in July and August) on Saturdays at 10.30am and last about an hour and a half. Advanced booking is recommended.

For excellent views of the Radcliffe Camera and surrounding buildings, climb the 14th-century tower in the beautiful **Church of Saint Mary the Virgin** (01865-279111; www.university -church.ox.ac.uk; High St; tower admission adult/under 16yr £2.50/1.50; 9am-6pm Jul & Aug, 9am-5pm Sep-Jun). On Sunday the tower does not open until about noon, after the morning service.

New College

From the Bodleian, stroll under the **Bridge of Sighs**, a 1914 copy of the famous bridge in Venice, to **New College** (01865-279555; www.new.ox.ac .uk; Holywell St; admission Easter-Sep £2, Oct-Easter free; 11am-5pm Easter-Sep, 2-4pm Oct-Easter). This 14th-century college was the first in Oxford to accept undergraduates and is a fine example of the glorious Perpendicular style. The chapel here is full of treasures including superb stained glass, much of it original, and Sir Jacob Epstein's disturbing statue of Lazarus.

During term time, visitors may attend the beautiful Evensong, a choral church service held nightly at 6pm. Access for visitors is through the New College Lane gate from Easter to early October, and through the Holywell St entrance the rest of the year.

William Spooner was once a college warden here, and his habit of transposing the first consonants of words gave rise to the term 'spoonerism'. Local lore suggests that he once reprimanded a student by saying, 'You have deliberately tasted two worms and can leave Oxford by the town drain'.

Merton College

From the High St, follow the wonderfully named Logic Lane to **Merton College** (01865-276310; www.merton.ox.ac.uk; Merton St; admission free; 2-4pm Mon-Fri, 10am-4pm Sat & Sun), one of Oxford's original three colleges. Founded in 1264, Merton was the first to adopt collegiate planning, bringing scholars and tutors together into a formal community and providing a planned residence for them. The charming 14th-century **Mob Quad** was the first of the college quads.

Just off the quad is a 13th-century **chapel** and the **Old Library** (admission on guided tour only), the oldest medieval library in use. It is said that Tolkien spent many hours here writing *The Lord of the Rings*. Other literary giants associated with the college include TS Eliot and Louis MacNeice.

During the summer months it may be possible to join a guided **tour** (£2, 45 minutes) of the college grounds. These usually take place in the afternoon, but are dependent on the availability of the graduate students who run them. If you're visiting in summer, look out for posters advertising candlelit concerts in the chapel.

All Souls College

One of the wealthiest of Oxford's colleges and unique in not accepting undergraduate students, **All Souls** (01865-279379; www.all-souls .ox.ac.uk; High St; admission free; 2-4pm Mon-Fri) is primarily an academic research institution. It was founded in 1438 as a centre of prayer and learning, and today fellowship of the college is one of the highest academic honours in the country. Each year, the university's top finalists are invited to sit a fellowship exam, with an average of only two making the grade annually.

Much of the college facade dates from the 1440s, and, unlike other older colleges, the front quad is largely unchanged in five centuries. It also contains a beautiful 17th-century sundial designed by Christopher Wren. Most obvious, though, are the twin mock-Gothic towers on the north quad. Designed by Nicholas Hawksmoor in 1710, they were lambasted for ruining the Oxford skyline when first erected.

Other Colleges

Much of the centre of Oxford is taken up by graceful university buildings and elegant colleges, each one individual in its appearance and academic specialities. However, not all are open to the public. You'll find details of visiting hours and admission at www.ox.ac.uk/colleges.

Set back off Broad St, **Trinity College** (☎ 01865-279900; www.trinity.ox.ac.uk; Broad St; adult/under 16yr £1.50/75p; 10am-noon & 2-4pm Mon-Fri, 2-4pm Sat & Sun term time) is worth a visit for the exquisite carvings in its chapel and for Wren's beautiful Garden Quad.

Nearby **Exeter College** (☎ 01865-279600; www.exeter.ox.ac.uk; Turl St; admission free; 2-5pm) is known for its elaborate 17th-century dining hall and ornate Victorian Gothic chapel housing *The Adoration of the Magi*, a William Morris tapestry.

Small and select **Brasenose College** (☎ 01865-277830; www.bnc.ox.ac.uk; Radcliffe Sq; admission £1; 2-5pm) is an elegant 16th-century place with more charm than many of the larger colleges. Look out for the doorknocker hanging above the high table in the dining hall – and ask about its fascinating history.

The sole survivor of the original halls, the teaching institutions that preceded colleges in Oxford, medieval **St Edmund Hall** (☎ 01865-279000; www.seh.ox.ac.uk; Queen's Lane; admission free; noon-4pm Mon-Fri term time only) is worth a visit to see its small chapel decorated by William Morris and Edward Burne-Jones.

Sandwiched between Christ Church and Merton, you'll find the small and beautiful **Corpus Christi College** (☎ 01865-276700; www.ccc.ox.ac.uk; Merton St; admission free; 1.30-4.30pm). Look out for the pelican sundial in the middle of the front quad.

ASHMOLEAN MUSEUM

A vast, rambling collection of art and antiquities is on display at the mammoth **Ashmolean** (☎ 01865-278000; www.ashmolean.org; Beaumont St; admission free; 10am-5pm Tue-Sat, noon-5pm Sun), Britain's oldest public museum. Established in 1683, it is based on the extensive collection of the remarkably well-travelled John Tradescant, gardener to Charles I, and it is housed in one of Britain's best examples of neo-Grecian architecture.

Bursting with Egyptian, Islamic and Chinese art; rare porcelain, tapestries and silverware; priceless musical instruments; and extensive displays of European art (including works by Raphael and Michelangelo), it's impossible to take it all in at once. At the time of writing, the Ashmolean was undergoing a £61 million redevelopment with 39 new galleries due to open in a state-of-the-art building in late 2009. The 'Treasures of the Ashmolean Museum' exhibition offers a cross-section of highlights from the vast collection. At the time of writing, the entire museum was due to close temporarily from January 2009, so check the website for up-to-date details.

UNIVERSITY & PITT RIVERS MUSEUMS

Housed in a glorious Victorian Gothic building with slender, cast-iron columns, ornate capitals and a soaring glass roof, the **University Museum** (☎ 01865-272950; www.oum.ox.ac.uk; Parks Rd; admission free; 10am-5pm) is worth a visit for its architecture alone. However, the real draw is the mammoth natural-history collection of more than five million exhibits ranging from exotic insects and fossils to a towering T-Rex skeleton.

Pitt Rivers Museum (☎ 01865-270927; www.prm.ox.ac.uk; admission free; 10am-4.30pm Tue-Sun, noon-4.30pm Mon), hidden away through a door at the back of the main exhibition hall, is a treasure trove of weird and wonderful displays to satisfy every armchair adventurer's wildest dreams. In the half-light inside are glass cases and mysterious drawers stuffed with Victorian explorers' prized booty. Feathered cloaks, necklaces of teeth, blowpipes, magic charms, Noh masks, totem poles, fur parkas, musical instruments and shrunken heads lurk here, making it a fascinating place for adults and children. At the time of writing the museum was closed for renovations, due to reopen in spring 2009.

Both museums run workshops for children almost every weekend and are known for their child-friendly attitude.

OXFORD CASTLE

Oxford Castle Unlocked (☎ 01865-260666; www.oxford castleunlocked.co.uk; 44-46 Oxford Castle; adult/under 15yr £7.50/5.35; 10am-5pm, last tour 4pm) explores the

THE BRAINS BEHIND THE OED

In 1879, the Oxford University Press began an ambitious project: a complete re-examination of the English language. The four-volume work was expected to take 10 years to complete. Recognising the mammoth task ahead, editor James Murray issued a circular appealing for volunteers to pore over their books and make precise notes on word usage. Their contributions were invaluable but after five years, Murray and his team had still only reached the word 'ant'.

Of the thousands of volunteers who helped out, the most prolific of all was Dr WC Minor, a US Civil War surgeon. Over the next 20 years, he became Murray's most valued contributor, providing tens of thousands of illustrative quotations and notes on word origins and usage. Murray received all of the doctor's contributions by post from Broadmoor, a hospital for the criminally insane. When he decided to visit the doctor in 1891 however, he discovered that Minor was not an employee but the asylum's longest-serving inmate, a schizophrenic committed in 1872 for a motiveless murder. Despite this, Murray was deeply taken by Minor's devotion to his project and continued to work with him, a story told in full in Simon Winchester's book *The Surgeon of Crowthorne*.

Neither Murray nor Minor lived to see the eventual publication of *A New English Dictionary on Historical Principles* in 1928. Almost 40 years behind schedule and 10 volumes long, it was the most comprehensive lexicographical project ever undertaken, and a full second edition did not appear until 1989.

Today, the updating of such a major work is no easier and the public were again asked for help in 2006. This time, the BBC ran a TV program, *Balderdash and Piffle*, encouraging viewers to get in contact with early printed evidence of word use, new definitions and brand-new entries for the dictionary. A second edition of the program was broadcast a year later.

For a full history of the famousdictionary and the development of printing, pay a visit to the **Oxford University Press Museum** (☎ 01865-353527; Great Clarendon St; admission free; ☺ by appointment only).

1000-year history of Oxford's castle and prison. Tours begin in the 11th-century Crypt of St George's Chapel, possibly the first formal teaching venue in Oxford, and continue on into the Victorian prison cells and the 18th-century Debtors' Tower where you can learn about the inmates' grisly lives, daring escapes and cruel punishments. You can also climb the Saxon St George's Tower, which has excellent views of the city, and clamber up the original medieval motte.

OTHER ATTRACTIONS

Far removed from Oxford's musty hallways of history, **Modern Art Oxford** (☎ 01865-722733; www.modernartoxford.org.uk; 30 Pembroke St; admission free; ☺ 10am-5pm Tue-Sat, noon-5pm Sun) is one of the best contemporary-art museums outside London, with a wonderful gallery space and plenty of activities for children.

Nearby, the **Museum of Oxford** (☎ 01865-252761; www.museumofoxford.org.uk; St Aldate's; admission free; ☺ 10am-5pm Tue-Fri, noon-5pm Sat & Sun) is dedicated to the history of the city and its university, and explores everything from Oxford's prehistoric mammoths to its history of car manufacturing.

Science, art, celebrity and nostalgia come together at the **Museum of the History of Science** (☎ 01865-277280; www.mhs.ox.ac.uk; Broad St; admission free; ☺ noon-5pm Tue-Fri, 10am-5pm Sat, 2-5pm Sun), where the exhibits include everything from a blackboard used by Einstein to the world's finest collection of historic scientific instruments, all housed in a beautiful 17th-century building.

Oxford's central landmark, **Carfax Tower** (☎ 01865-792653; adult/under 16yr £2.10/1; ☺ 10am-5.15pm Apr-Sep, to 4.15pm Mar & Oct, to 3pm Nov-Feb), is the sole reminder of medieval St Martin's Church and offers good views over the city centre.

A haven of traditional butchers, fishmongers, cobblers and barbers, the **Oxford Covered Market** (www.oxford-covered-market.co.uk; ☺ 8.30am-5.30pm Mon-Sat) is the place to go for Sicilian sausage, handmade chocolates, traditional pies, funky T-shirts and expensive brogues. It's a fascinating place to explore and, if you're in Oxford at Christmas, a must for its traditional displays of freshly hung deer, wild boar, ostrich and turkey.

Activities

A quintessential Oxford experience, **punting** is all about sitting back and quaffing Pimms as you watch the dreaming spires float by. Which, of course, requires someone else to do the hard work – punting is far more difficult than it appears. Be prepared to spend much of your time struggling to get out of a tangle of low branches or avoiding the path of an oncoming eight. For tips on how to punt, see p434.

Punts are available from mid-March to mid-October, 10am to dusk, and hold five people including the punter (£12/14 per hour weekdays/weekends).

The most central location to rent punts is at Magdalen Bridge, from **Howard C & Sons** (☎ 01865-202643; High St; deposit £30). From here, you can punt downstream around the Botanic Gardens and Christ Church Meadow or upstream around Magdalen Deer Park. Alternatively, head for the **Cherwell Boat House** (☎ 01865-515978; www.cherwellboathouse.co.uk; Bardwell Rd; deposit £60) for a countryside amble, where the destination of choice is the busy boozer, the **Victoria Arms** (☎ 01865-241382; Mill Lane). To get to the boathouse, take bus 2 or 7 from Magdalen St to Bardwell Rd and follow the signposts.

Tours

Blackwell (☎ 01865-333606; oxford@blackwell.co.uk; 48-51 Broad St; adult/child £6.50/4; ☉ late May-Oct) Oxfords most famous bookshop runs 1½ -hour tours including a literary tour (2pm Tuesday, 11.30am Thursday), an 'Inklings' – an informal literary group whose membership included CS Lewis and JRR Tolkien – tour (11.45am Wednesday) and a town-and-gown tour (2pm Friday).

City Sightseeing (☎ 01865-790522; www.citysight seeingoxford.com; adult/under 16yr £11.50/6; ☉ every 10-15min 9.30am-6pm Apr-Oct) Runs hop-on hop-off bus tours from the bus and train stations or any of the 20 dedicated stops around town.

Tourist office (☎ 01865-252200; www.visitoxford .org; 15-16 Broad St; ☉ 9.30am-5pm Mon-Sat, 10am-4pm Sun) Runs two-hour tours of Oxford city and colleges (adult/under 16yr £7/3.50; ☉ 11am & 2pm year-round, also 10.30am & 1pm July and August), Inspector Morse tours (£7.50/4; ☉ 1.30pm Sat), family walking tours (£5.50/3.50; ☉ 1.30pm school holidays) and a selection of themed tours (adult/child £7.50/4) that run on various dates throughout the year.

Oxford River Cruises (☎ 08452-269396; www.oxford rivercruises.com) Choose from a range of Thames tours including river sightseeing trips (adult/child £15/7.50; 50 minutes) and lunchtime picnics trips (adult/under 12 years £42/29) Thursday and Sunday March to October, plus sunset dinner cruises (£42) Wednesday and Saturday May to September.

Oxon Carts (☎ 07747-024600; www.oxoncarts.com; 15min taster tour £10, 1hr tour £30) Runs a fleet of five pedicabs around Oxford's narrow lanes where the buses simply can't go. Passengers receive a copy of a 1904 map of the city and a personal guide to its buildings and history.

Salter Bros (☎ 01865-243421; www.salterssteamers.co .uk; Folly Bridge; boat trips adult/child £8.50/4.80; ☉ mid-May–mid-Sep) Boat trips along the Isis to Abingdon.

Sleeping

Oxford accommodation is generally overpriced and underwhelming, with suffocating floral patterns the B&B norm. The following places stand out for their value for money and good taste. Book ahead between May and September, and if you're stuck you'll find a string of B&Bs along the Iffley, Abingdon, Banbury and Headington roads.

BUDGET

Oxford Camping & Caravanning Club (☎ 01865-244088; www.campingandcaravanningclub.co.uk; 426 Abingdon Rd; sites per person £9) This well-run campsite is conveniently close to the city centre but consequently lacks character and can be noisy. It's a popular spot however, especially on weekends, so book well in advance.

Central Backpackers (☎ 01865-242288; www.central backpackers.co.uk; 13 Park End St; dm £16-19; ☐) A good budget option right in the centre of town, this small hostel has basic, bright and simple rooms that sleep four to 12 people. There's a small but decent lounge with satellite TV, a rooftop terrace and free internet and luggage storage.

Oxford YHA (☎ 0845 371 9131; www.yha.org.uk; 2A Botley Rd; dm/d £22/56; ☐) Bright, well-kept, clean and tidy, this is Oxford's best budget option with simple but comfortable dorm accommodation, private rooms and loads of facilities including a restaurant, library, garden, laundry and a choice of lounges. All rooms are en suite and are bright and cheery, a far better option than some of the city's cheapest B&Bs.

MIDRANGE

Oxford Rooms (www.oxfordrooms.co.uk; r £40-120) Didn't quite make the cut for a place at Oxford? Well at least you can experience life inside the hallowed college grounds and breakfast in a grand college hall by staying overnight in one of their student rooms. Most rooms

OXFORD, THE COTSWOLDS & AROUND

are singles and pretty functional with basic furnishings, shared bathrooms and internet access, though there are some en suite, twin and family rooms available. Some rooms have old-world character and views over the college quad, while others are more modern but in a nearby annexe.

There's limited availability during term time, but a good choice of rooms during university holidays, and you'll get a full description before you book.

Beaumont (☎ 01865-241767; www.oxfordcity.co.uk /accom/beaumont; 234 Abingdon Rd; s £45-55, d £60-78) A class above most B&Bs at this price, this place is all crisp, white linen, pale and trendy flock wallpaper, mosaic bathrooms and beautiful, hand-picked furniture. The simple but elegant decor gives it a really tranquil atmosphere, despite being close to the city centre.

Cornerways (☎ 01865-240135; jeakings@btopenworld .com; 282 Abingdon Rd; s £48, d £76-98; **P**) Bright, modern rooms with simple but attractive decor make this a good bet within walking distance of town. The genial hosts can help with planning your stay, and breakfast is served in a lovely conservatory overlooking the small patio garden.

Tilbury Lodge (☎ 01865-862138; www.tilburylodge .com; 5 Tilbury Lane; s £70, d £80-90; **P** 💻) Spacious, top-of-the-line rooms with plush, modern decor and excellent bathrooms make this stylish B&B worth the trip outside the centre of town. Giant pillows in funky fabrics adorn the big beds, light streams through the large windows and, downstairs, there's a conservatory for guest use.

our pick **Orchard House** (☎ 01865-249200; www .theorchardhouseoxford.co.uk; 225 Iffley Rd; s £75-85, d £85-95; **P**) Set in beautiful secluded gardens just a short walk from the city centre, this lovely arts-and-crafts-style house is a wonderful retreat from the city. The two bedrooms are sleek and stylish and very spacious, each with its own sofa and breakfast table, and the limestone bathrooms are luxuriously modern.

Burlington House (☎ 01865-513513; www.burling ton-house.co.uk; 374 Banbury Rd; s £65, d £85-95; **P** 💻) Simple, elegant rooms decked out in restrained, classical style are available at this Victorian merchant house. The rooms are big, bright and uncluttered, with plenty of period character and immaculately kept bathrooms. Burlington isn't central, but it has good public transport to town and is well worth the trip.

Buttery Hotel (☎ 01865-811950; www.thebuttery hotel.co.uk; 11-12 Broad St; s/d from £60/95; 💻) Right in the heart of the city with views over the college grounds, the Buttery is Oxford's newest hotel. Considering its location, it's a great deal, with spacious, modern rooms, decent bathrooms and the pick of the city's attractions on your doorstep.

Remont Guesthouse (☎ 01865-311020; www.remont -guesthouse.co.uk; 367 Banbury Rd; s £82, d £107-135, tr £135; **P** 💻) All modern style, subtle lighting and plush furnishings, this 25-room guest house is a bit of a hike from the city centre but has regular buses just outside the door. The rooms here are decked out in cool neutrals with silky bedspreads and abstract art on the walls, and the flat-screen TVs, soundproofing, free wi-fi and modern garden just add to the appeal.

TOP END

Malmaison (☎ 01865-268400; www.malmaison-oxford .com; 3 Oxford Castle; d/ste from £160/245; 💻) Lock yourself up for the night in one of Oxford's most spectacular settings. This former Victorian prison has been converted into a sleek and slinky hotel with plush interiors, sultry lighting, dark woods and giant beds. If you're planning a real bender, go for the Governor's Suite, complete with four-poster bed and mini cinema. Look out for online promotions when you can bag a room for as little as £99.

our pick **Old Parsonage Hotel** (☎ 01865-310210; www.oldparsonage-hotel.co.uk; 1 Banbury Rd; r £170-250; **P** 💻) Wonderfully quirky and instantly memorable, the Old Parsonage is a small boutique hotel with just the right blend of old-world character, period charm and modern luxury. The 17th-century building oozes style with a contemporary-art collection, artfully mismatched furniture and chic bedrooms with handmade beds and marble bathrooms.

Old Bank Hotel (☎ 01865-799599; www.oldbank-hotel .co.uk; 92 High St; r £185-325; **P** 💻) Slap bang in the centre of Oxford, rooms here look over the college walls and dreaming spires into the very heart of the university. The rooms are sleek and spacious, all neutral colours and silky throws but lack a little soul. Downstairs the buzzing restaurant, Quod (see opposite), makes up for it with brash modern artworks and a tumult of eager diners.

Eating

Oxford has plenty of choice when it comes to eating out, but unfortunately ubiquitous chain restaurants dominate the scene, especially along George St and around the pedestrianised square at the castle. Head to Walton St in Jericho, to St Clements, Summertown or up the Cowley Rd for a more quirky selection of restaurants.

BUDGET

our pick Edamame (☎ 01865-246916; 15 Holywell St; sushi £2.50-3.50, mains £6-7; ☽ lunch Wed-Sun, dinner Thu-Sat) You'll find this tiny Japanese place by looking for the queue out the door as you head down Holywell St, but it's well worth the wait. The food here is simply divine with the best rice and noodle dishes in town and sushi (Thursday night only) to die for.

Manos (☎ 01865-311782, 105 Walton St; mains £6-9; ☽ closed Sun dinner) For delicious home-cooked tastes of the Med, head for this Greek deli and restaurant where you'll find a great selection of dishes bursting with flavour. The ground floor has a cafe and deli, while downstairs has more style and comfort, with giant cushions surrounding low tables.

Jericho Cafe (☎ 01865-310840; 112 Walton St; mains £7-9) Chill out and relax with the paper over a coffee and a doorstep of cake, or go for some of the wholesome lunch and dinner specials, which encompass everything from sausages and mash to Lebanese lamb *kibbeh*. There are plenty of hearty salads, lots of choice for vegies and bulging platters of meze.

Cafe Coco (☎ 01865-200232; 23 Cowley Rd; mains £7-14) Chilled out but always buzzing, this Cowley Rd institution is a sort of hip hang-out, with classic posters on the walls and a bald clown in an ice bath. The food is vaguely Mediterranean, with everything from pizzas to *merguez* thrown in, and can be a bit hit and miss but most people come for the atmosphere.

Quick Eats

Vaults (☎ 01865-279112; Church of St Mary the Virgin; mains £3.25-4.95; ☽ 10am-5pm) Does a great selection of wholesome soups, salads, pastas and paellas with plenty of choice for vegetarians. Set in a vaulted 14th-century Congregation House with lovely gardens, overlooking Radcliffe Sq, it's one of the most beautiful lunch venues in Oxford.

Georgina's (☎ 01865-249527; Ave 3, Oxford Covered Market; mains £5-8; ☽ 8.30am-5pm Mon-Sat) Hidden up a scruffy staircase in the covered market and plastered with old cinema posters, this is a funky little cafe serving a bumper crop of

bulging salads, hearty soups and such goodies as goat's cheese quesadillas and scrumptious cakes.

A couple of chains worth keeping your eye out for:

G&D's (☽ 8am-midnight) Cowley Rd (104 Cowley Rd); Little Clarendon St (☎ 01865-516652; 55 Little Clarendon St); St Aldate's (94 St Aldate's) The best ice cream, brownies and desserts in town. You'll also get copies of the *Beano and Dandy* and regular silly-hat, cow-dunking and mooing competitions.

Mortons (baguettes £2.40-2.80) Broad St (22 Broad St); Little Clarendon St (36 Little Clarendon St); New Inn Hall St (22 New Inn Hall St); Oxford Covered Market (☎ 01865-200867; 103 Covered Market) For a quick bite en route between colleges, the ever-popular Mortons has a fine selection of baguettes.

MIDRANGE

Aziz (☎ 01865-794945; 228 Cowley Rd; mains £8-10) Thought by many to be Oxford's best curry house, this award-winning restaurant attracts vegans, vegetarians and curry lovers in hoards. There's an extensive menu, chilled surroundings and portions generous enough to ensure you'll be rolling out the door. There's a second branch on Folly Bridge (☎ 01865-247775).

Jam Factory (☎ 01865-244613; www.thejamfactory oxford.com; 27 Park End St; mains £8-12) Arts centre, bar and restaurant rolled into one, the Jam Factory is a laid-back, boho kind of place, with changing exhibitions and hearty breakfasts, an excellent-value, £10 two-course lunch and an understated menu of modern British dishes.

Door 74 (☎ 01865-203374; 74 Cowley Rd; mains £8-13; ☽ closed Mon & Sun dinner) This cosy little place woos its fans with a rich mix of largely Mediterranean flavours, friendly service and a quirky interior. The menu is limited, but each dish is cooked to perfection and combines classic ingredients with a modern twist.

Jamie's Italian (☎ 01865-838383; 24-26 George St; mains £8-18) Celebrity chef Jamie Oliver's new 'neighbourhood' restaurant is all rustic Italian, with wooden crates of freshly made pasta tempting you from the windows and a menu of authentic but affordable Italian dishes. Packed since opening, the crowds come as much for the name as the heaped plates of bruschetta and the steaming bowls of pasta.

Quod (☎ 01865-202505; www.quod.co.uk; 92 High St; mains £10.50-15.50) Bright, buzzing and decked out with modern art and beautiful people, this designer joint dishes up Mediterranean brasserie-style food to the masses. It doesn't take reservations, is always heaving and, at worst, will tempt you to chill by the bar with a cocktail while you wait.

Other options:

Big Bang (☎ 01865-511441; 124 Walton St; mains £8-12) Dated decor, but packed to the gills, thanks to its simple menu of divine sausages and mash.

Chutneys (☎ 01865-724241; 36 St Michael's St; mains £8-11) Top-notch Indian with consistently great food and chilled atmosphere.

Fishers (☎ 01865-243003; 36-37 St Clements; mains £9-15) Oxford's finest seafood restaurant with simple but heavenly plates of Shetland mussels, yellow-fin tuna and New England lobster.

TOP END

Gee's (☎ 01865-553540; www.gees-restaurant.co.uk; 61 Banbury Rd; mains £15-21.50) Set in a Victorian conservatory, this top-notch restaurant is a sibling of Quod's but much more conservative. Popular with the visiting parents of university students, the food is modern British and European and the setting stunning, but it's all a little stiff.

Drinking
PUBS

Turf Tavern (☎ 01865-243235; 4 Bath Pl) Hidden away down narrow alleyways, this tiny medieval pub is one of the town's best-loved and bills itself as 'an education in intoxication'. It's always heaving with a mix of students, professionals and the lucky tourists who manage to find it, and has plenty for outdoor seating for sunny days.

Eagle & Child (☎ 01865-302925; 49 St Giles) Affectionately known as the 'Bird & Baby', this atmospheric place has been a pub since 1650 and is still a hotchpotch of nooks and crannies. It was once the favourite haunt of Tolkien, CS Lewis and their literary friends and still attracts a mellow crowd.

White Horse (☎ 01865-728318; 52 Broad St) This tiny olde-worlde place was a favourite retreat for TV detective Inspector Morse, and it can get pretty crowded in the evening. It's got buckets of character and makes a great place for a quiet afternoon pint and intellectual conversation.

Oxford has some wonderful riverside pubs worth checking out, most of which can be reached by a stroll along the towpaths.

Head of the River (☎ 01865-721600; Folly Bridge) Right in the centre of town and a great place to watch struggling punters go by.

Fishes (☎ 01865-249796; North Hinksey; mains £10-17.50) Old and quaint on the outside but sleek and modern inside, this popular summer haunt also does good food.

Trout (☎ 01865-302071; 195 Godstow Rd; mains £10-15.50) Charming old-world pub with a modern interior, lovely garden and roaming peacocks. Book ahead if you plan to eat.

BARS

Raoul's (☎ 01865-553732; 32 Walton St) This trendy retro-look bar is one of Jericho's finest and is always busy. Famous for its perfectly mixed cocktails and funky music, it's populated by effortlessly cool punters trying hard not to spill their drinks as people squeeze by.

Kazbar (☎ 01865-202920; 25-27 Cowley Rd) This funky Moroccan-themed bar has giant windows, low lighting, warm colours and a cool vibe. It's buzzing most nights with hip young things sipping cocktails and filling up on the Spanish and North African tapas (£3 to £5).

Jericho Tavern (☎ 01865-311775; 56 Walton St) Chilled out and super cool with big leather sofas, tasselled lamps and boldly patterned wallpaper, this hip bar also has a live-music venue upstairs. Adorned with giant portraits of John Peel, Supergrass and Radiohead, it's supposedly where Radiohead (who hail from nearby Abingdon) played their first gig.

Frevd (☎ 01865-311171; 119 Walton St) Once a neoclassical church, now a happening bar, Frevd is a cavernous place with soaring ceilings, distressed walls, quirky artwork and a mixed bag of punters. It's popular with a young style-conscious clientele and cocktail-sipping luvvies by night.

Entertainment
NIGHTCLUBS

Despite its large student population, Oxford's club scene is fairly limited, with several cattle-mart clubs in the centre of town and a lot of crowd-pleasing music. Try the following for something a little more adventurous.

Carling Academy (☎ 01865-813500; www.carling-academy.co.uk; 190 Cowley Rd; club admission up to £6; ⏱ box office noon-5.30pm Mon-Fri, to 4pm Sat) Oxford's best club and live-music venue had a recent makeover and now hosts everything from big-name DJs to indie sounds, hard rock, funk nights and chart-busting bands.

Po Na Na (☎ 01865-249171; 13-15 Magdalen St; admission up to £6; ⏱ Thu-Sat) Looking a little rough around the edges now, this small cave-like place is hung with Moroccan lanterns and drapes and, in between the regular club nights, attracts some big-name DJs and live events. Expect funk, soul, electro, drum 'n' bass, house and indie rock.

THEATRE

The city's main stage for quality drama is the **Oxford Playhouse** (☎ 01865-305305; www.oxfordplay house.com; Beaumont St), which also hosts an impressive selection of touring theatre, music and dance productions. Just around the corner, the **Burton Taylor Theatre** (☎ 01865-305305; www .burtontaylor.co.uk; Gloucester St) puts on quirky student shows, while the **Pegasus Theatre** (☎ 01865-722851; www.pegasustheatre.org.uk; Magdalen Rd) holds alternative independent productions.

For ageing pop stars, comedians and plenty of fanfare, try the **New Theatre** (☎ 0870 606 3500; www.newtheatreoxford.org.uk; George St), and for drama, dance, live music and art, there's the **North Wall Arts Centre** (☎ 01865-319452; www .thenorthwall.com; South Parade).

Performing in a variety of non-traditional venues including city parks, the BMW plant and Oxford Castle, **Creation Theatre** (☎ 01865-761393; www.creationtheatre.co.uk) produces highly original, mostly Shakespearean shows featuring plenty of magic and special effects. If you're in town when a performance is running, don't miss it.

CLASSICAL MUSIC

With a host of spectacular buildings with great acoustics and two orchestras, Oxford is an excellent place to attend a classical concert. You'll find the widest range of events at www .musicatoxford.com. Alternatively, watch out for posters around town or contact one of these groups:

City of Oxford Orchestra (☎ 01865-744457; www .cityofoxfordorchestra.co.uk)

Oxford Contemporary Music (☎ 01865-488369; www.ocmevents.org)

Oxford Philomusica (☎ 01865-736202; www.oxford phil.com)

Getting There & Away

BUS

Oxford's main bus/coach station is at **Gloucester Green**, in the heart of the city. Competition on the Oxford–London route is fierce, with two companies running buses (£15 return, four per hour) at peak times. Services run all through the night and take about 90 minutes to reach central London:

Oxford Espress (☎ 01865-785400; www.oxfordbus .co.uk)

Oxford Tube (☎ 01865-772250; www.oxfordtube.com)

The Heathrow Express (£18, 70 minutes) runs half-hourly 4am to 10pm and at midnight and 2am, while the Gatwick Express (£22, two hours) runs hourly 5.15am to 8.15pm and every two hours 10pm to 4am.

National Express has five direct buses to Birmingham (£11, two hours), and one service to Bath (£9.50, two hours) and Bristol (£13.80, 2¾ hours). All these destinations are easier to reach by train.

Stagecoach serves most of the small towns in Oxfordshire and runs the X5 service to Cambridge (£9, 3½ hours) roughly every half-hour. If you're planning a lot of bus journeys it's worth buying a Goldrider pass (£20), which allows unlimited bus travel in Oxfordshire for seven days.

CAR & MOTORCYCLE

Thanks to a complicated one-way system and a shortage of parking spaces, driving and parking in Oxford is a nightmare. Drivers are strongly advised to use the five park-and-ride car parks on major routes leading into town. Three car parks are free to use, the others cost £1. The return bus journey to town (10 to 15 minutes, every 10 minutes) costs £2.50.

TRAIN

There are half hourly services to London Paddington (£22.50, one hour) and roughly hourly trains to Birmingham (£22, 1¼ hours), Worcester (£29, 1½ hours) and Hereford (£17.40, two hours). Hourly services also run to Bath (£19.60, 1¼ hours) and Bristol (£21.40, 1½ hours), but require a change at Didcot Parkway.

Getting Around

BICYCLE

The *Cycle into Oxford* map available from the tourist office shows all local cycle routes. You can hire bikes from **Cyclo Analysts** (☎ 01865-424444; 150 Cowley Rd; per day/week £14/40).

BUS

If sightseeing has worn you out, buses 1 and 5 go to Cowley Rd from Carfax, 2 and

7 go along Banbury Rd from Magdalen St, and 16 and 35 run along Abingdon Rd from St Aldate's.

A multi-operator Plus Pass (per day/week/month £5/17/46) allows unlimited travel on Oxford's bus system.

TAXI

There are taxi ranks at the train station and bus station, as well as on St Giles and at Carfax. Be prepared to join a long queue after closing time. For a green alternative, call **Oxon Carts** (☎ 07747 024600; info@oxoncarts.com), a pedicab service.

WOODSTOCK

pop 2389

The charming village of Woodstock is full of picturesque creeper-clad cottages, elegant town houses, buckled roofs, art galleries and antique shops. It's an understandably popular spot, conveniently close to Oxford, yet a quintessential rural retreat. The big draw here is Blenheim Palace, the opulent country pile of the Churchill family, but the village itself is a gracious and tranquil spot even on busy summer days.

The hub of the village is the imposing **town hall**, built at the Duke of Marlborough's expense in 1766. Nearby, the **Church of St Mary Magdalene** had a 19th-century makeover but retains its Norman doorway, early English windows and a musical clock.

Opposite the church, the **Oxfordshire Museum** (☎ 01993-811456; Park St; admission free; ☺ 10am-5pm Tue-Sat, 2-5pm Sun) has displays on local history, art, archaeology and wildlife. It also houses the **tourist office** (☎ 01993-813276).

Blenheim Palace

One of the country's greatest stately homes, **Blenheim Palace** (☎ 08700 602080; www.blenheim palace.com; adult/under 16yr £16.50/10, park & garden only £9.50/4.80; ☺ 10.30am-5.30pm daily mid-Feb–Oct, Wed-Sun Nov–mid-Dec, park open year-round) is a monumental baroque fantasy designed by Sir John Vanbrugh and Nicholas Hawksmoor between 1705 and 1722. The land and funds to build the house were granted to John Churchill, Duke of Marlborough, by a grateful Queen Anne after his decisive victory at the 1704 Battle of Blenheim. Now a Unesco World Heritage Site, Blenheim (pronounced *blen*-num) is home to the 11th duke and duchess.

Inside, the house is stuffed with statues, tapestries, ostentatious furniture and giant oil paintings in elaborate gilt frames. Highlights include the **Great Hall**, a vast space topped by 20m-high ceilings adorned with images of the first duke in battle; the opulent **Saloon**, the grandest and most important public room; the three **state rooms** with their plush decor and priceless **china cabinets**; and the magnificent 55m **Long Library**.

From the library, you can access the **Churchill Exhibition**, which is dedicated to the life, work and writings of Sir Winston, who was born at Blenheim in 1874 (see boxed text, p45). For an insight into life below stairs, the **Untold Story** exhibition explores the family's history through the eyes of the household staff.

If the crowds in the house become too oppressive, retire to the lavish gardens and vast parklands, parts of which were landscaped by Lancelot 'Capability' Brown. To the front, an artificial lake sports a beautiful bridge by Vanbrugh, and a mini train is needed to take visitors to a maze, adventure playground and butterfly house. For a quieter and longer stroll, glorious walks lead to an arboretum, cascade and temple.

Sleeping & Eating

Woodstock has a good choice of accommodation, but it's not cheap. Luxurious, old-world hotels are the thing here so plan a day trip from Oxford if you're travelling on a budget.

Laurel's Guesthouse (☎ 01993-812583; www.laurels guesthouse.co.uk; 40 Hensington Rd; s/d £75/80; closed Dec & Jan; P) Packed with Victorian charm and character, this comfortable B&B has rooms featuring cast-iron or ornate wood beds, antique furniture and open fireplaces. The rooms are small and the bathrooms are tiny, but it's the period charm you'll remember.

Kings Arms Hotel (☎ 01993-813636; www.kings -hotel-woodstock.co.uk; 19 Market St; s/d £75/140; ☐) Set in a lovely Georgian town house, the rooms are sleek and stylish with warm woods, soft, neutral tones and black-and-white images on the walls. Downstairs, there's a bright bistro serving modern British fare (mains £10 to £15) and a good bar with leather sofas and cheaper snacks.

Bear Hotel (☎ 01993-811124; www.macdonald hotels.co.uk/bear; Park St; d from £92; P ☐) One of England's oldest hotels, the lavish Bear has long been a hideaway for romantic couples. The 13th-century coaching inn has recently

OXFORD, THE COTSWOLDS & AROUND

been refurbished and, along with the open fireplaces, stone walls and exposed beams, you'll get the height of modern luxury. Book in advance and you could be in for a great deal.

Hampers (☎ 01993-811535; 31-33 Oxford St; snacks £1.50-5; ☽ lunch) On a fine day you couldn't do better than a picnic in the grounds of the palace, and this deli provides all the essential ingredients: fine cheeses, olives, cold meats, Cotswold smoked salmon and delicious cakes. If it's raining, pop in to the cafe and feast on the delicious soups, sambos and cakes instead.

Brotherton's Brasserie (☎ 01993-811114; 1 High St; mains £9-14; ☽ closed Tue in winter) Set in an atmospheric 17th-century house clad in Virginia creeper and lit with the warm glow of gaslight, this popular brasserie is one of the best spots in town. Deep-red walls, scrubbed wooden floors and bare tables give it a rustic but homely feel, and the menu features everything from light pastas to hearty wild boar casserole.

Getting There & Away
Stagecoach bus 20 runs every half-hour (hourly on Sunday) from Oxford bus station (20 minutes). **Cotswold Roaming** (☎ 01865-308300; www.cotswold-roaming.co.uk) offers a Cotswolds/ Blenheim combination tour (adult/under 15 years £40/27.50), with a morning at Blenheim and a half-day Cotswolds tour in the afternoon. The price includes admission to the palace.

DORCHESTER & THE WITTENHAMS
A winding street flanked on either side by old coaching inns, quaint cottages and timber-framed buildings flows through sleepy **Dorchester-on-Thames**. The town's main draw is the magnificent medieval church, **SS Peter & Paul** (www.dorchester-abbey.org.uk; admission free; ☽ 8am-6pm), or Dorchester Abbey, as it is more commonly known. It is a beautiful space, built on the site of a Saxon cathedral and home to a wonderful Jesse window, a rare Norman font and, in the Cloister Gallery, a collection of medieval decorated stones. There's also a small **museum** (admission free; ☽ 2-5pm Apr-Sep) in the Old School Room in the grounds.

From the village you can take a pleasant 3-mile walk to **Wittenham Clumps**, two ancient tree-topped hills offering wonderful views of the surrounding area. At the bottom of the hills lies the village of **Little Wittenham**, a rustic idyll. Known for its beautiful cottages and the

imposing **St Peter's Church**, it has made its mark on the international sporting calendar by hosting the **Pooh Sticks World Championships** in March each year. Teams from all over the world compete by dropping sticks into the river and watching them 'race' to the finish line.

In nearby **Clifton Hampden**, you'll find a row of stunning thatched cottages and the atmospheric 15th-century **Barley Mow Inn** (☎ 01865-407847; Clifton Hampden), where Jerome K Jerome wrote most of his timeless classic *Three Men in a Boat*.

Buses 105 and 106 connect Dorchester with Oxford (45 minutes, hourly Monday to Saturday). To get to Clifton Hampden, take bus X39 to Berinsfield and change to bus 107 (25 minutes in total, five daily Monday to Saturday). Dorchester-on-Thames is on the A4074, 7 miles south of Oxford. Clifton Hampden is on the A415.

HENLEY-ON-THAMES
pop 10,513

A conservative but well-heeled kind of place, Henley is an attractive town set on the banks of the river, studded with elegant stone houses, a few Tudor relics and a host of chichi shops. The town bursts into action in July when it becomes the location for the Henley Royal Regatta, a world-famous boat race and weeklong posh picnic hosted by high-end corporate entertainers.

The **tourist office** (☎ 01491-578034; www.visit henley-on-thames.com; The Barn; King's Rd; ☽ 10am-5pm Mon-Sat Jun-Sep, to 4pm Mar-May & Oct, to 3pm Nov-Feb) is next to the handsome town hall.

Sights
Life in Henley has always focused on the river, and the impressive **River & Rowing Museum** (☎ 01491-415600; www.rrm.co.uk; Mill Meadows; museum only adult/child £3.50/2.50, museum & Wind in the Willows adult/under 18yr £7/5; ☽ 10am-5.30pm May-Aug, 10am-5pm Sep-Apr) takes a look at the town's relationship with the Thames, the history of rowing and the wildlife and commerce the river supports. Hands-on activities and interactive displays mak e it a good spot for children, and the *Wind in the Willows* exhibition brings Kenneth Grahame's stories of Ratty, Mole, Badger and Toad to life.

Walking around Henley, you'll come across a wealth of historic buildings, with many Georgian gems lining Hart St, the main drag. You'll also find the imposing **town hall** here, and the 13th-century **St Mary's Church** with its 16th-century tower topped by four octagonal turrets.

Festivals & Events

HENLEY ROYAL REGATTA

The first ever Oxford and Cambridge boat race was held in Henley in 1839, and ever since the cream of English society has descended on this small town each year for a celebration of boating, back slapping and the beau monde.

The five-day **Henley Royal Regatta** (☎ 01491-572153; www.hrr.co.uk) has grown into a major fixture in the social calendar of the upwardly mobile, and is a massive corporate entertainment opportunity. These days, hanging out on the lawn swilling champagne and looking rich and beautiful is the main event, and although rowers of the highest calibre compete, most spectators appear to take little interest in what's happening on the water.

The regatta is held in the first week of July, but you'll need contacts in the rowing or corporate worlds to get tickets in the stewards' enclosure. Mere mortals should head for the public enclosure (tickets £11 to £14), where you can lay out your gourmet picnic and hobnob with the best of them.

HENLEY FESTIVAL

In the week following the regatta, the town continues its celebrations with the **Henley Festival** (☎ 01491-843404; www.henley-festival.co.uk), a vibrant black-tie affair that features everything from big-name international stars to quirky, alternative acts – anything from opera to rock, jazz, comedy and swing. The main events take place on a floating stage on the Thames, and tickets vary in price from £59 for a seat in the grandstand to £35 for a space on the promenade.

Sleeping & Eating

Henley has a good choice of accommodation, especially at the top end, but if you're planning to visit during either festival, book well in advance.

Apple Ash (☎ 01491-574198; www.appleash.com; Woodlands Rd, Harpsden Woods; s/d £50/70 **P**) Lovingly maintained and beautifully decorated, it's well worth the 2-mile trip from town to stay at this charming Edwardian country house. The rooms are spacious and dripping in period character, but the styling is modern and

comfortable, with pale fabrics and plenty of scatter cushions.

Old School House (☎ 01491-573929; www.oldschoolhousehenley.co.uk; 42 Hart St; d £75-85; **P**) This small, quiet guesthouse in the town centre is a 19th-century school house in a walled garden, with a choice of two pretty guest rooms decked out in simple but comfortable style. Exposed timber beams and rustic furniture give it plenty of character, and the central location can't be beaten at this price.

Milsoms (☎ 01491-845789; www.milsomshotel.co.uk; 20 Market Pl; r £95) Set in an 18th-century former bakery, Milsoms offers sleek and stylish rooms, with bespoke artwork, subtle lighting and a muted colour scheme. They can be pretty compact, though, so ask for light and airy room 1 for more space. Downstairs, Loch Fyne (☎ 01491-845780; mains £10 to £18) serves its usual impeccably prepared fish dishes in bright surroundings.

our pick **Hotel du Vin** (☎ 01491-848400; www.hotelduvin.com; New St; d £145-295; **P** **⌨**) Set in the former Brakspears Brewery, this upmarket hotel chain scores highly for its blend of industrial chic and top-of-the-line designer sophistication. The spacious rooms and opulent suites are slick and stylish and are matched by a walk-in humidor, incredible billiards rooms, huge wine cellar and a popular bistro (mains £15 to £21).

Green Olive (☎ 01491-412220; 28 Market Pl; meze £4-10) A popular Henley haunt, Green Olive dishes up piled plates of traditional Greek meze in a bright and airy building with a lovely garden to the rear. Choose from over 50 dishes including spanakopitta, souvlaki, mussels with feta, stifado and moussaka.

Chez Gerard Brasserie (☎ 01491-411099; 40 Hart Street; mains £9-15) A welcome addition to the Henley restaurant scene, this stalwart chain of French brasseries has a chilled atmosphere, wooden floors, modern art on the walls and a selection of mismatched furniture. The menu features French classics as well as Moroccan *tagines*, pastas and grills.

Getting There & Around

There are no direct train or bus services between Henley and Oxford. Trains to London Paddington take about one hour (£12.50, hourly).

If you fancy seeing the local area from the river, **Hobbs & Son** (☎ 01491-572035; www.hobbs-of-henley.com) runs hour-long afternoon river trips from April to September (adult/under 16 years £7/5) and hires five-seater rowing boats (£13 per hour) and four-seater motorboats (£25 per hour).

WANTAGE
pop 10,613

Sleepy but handsome Wantage is a medieval market town of sturdy timber-framed buildings, old coaching inns and crooked cottages. The market square is dominated by a statue of Alfred the Great (see p37), who was born here in AD 849, and traders still flog their wares beneath his feet every Wednesday and Saturday. To the west of the square is the beautiful 13th-century church of St Peter & St Paul, with its hammer-beam roof and beautiful corbels. Wantage also provides easy access to the ancient Ridgeway trail (see p220), less than 3 miles to the south.

There's a **visitor information point** (☎ 01235-760176; www.wantage.com; ⊗ 10am-4pm Mon-Sat) in the **Vale & Downland Museum** (☎ 01235-771447; www.wantage.com/museum; Church St; adult/student under 25yr £2.50/1; ⊗ 10am-4pm Mon-Sat). Set in a converted 16th-century cloth merchant's house, the museum covers local geology and archaeology, as well as everything from King Alfred and Victorian kitchens to the local Williams Formula 1 team.

Sleeping & Eating

Courthill Centre (☎ 01235-760253; www.courthill.org.uk; Court Hill; dm per adult/under 18yr £16.50/12.50, tepee £70) Set in a series of converted barns just 500m from the Ridgeway, this hostel is an ideal base for walkers. It has basic but spacious dorms, an oak-beamed dining room and excellent views over the Vale. There's also a choice of family rooms and tepees (sleeping six) to rent. The hostel is about 2 miles south of Wantage off the A338.

Manor Farm (☎ 01235-763188; www.manorfarm-wantage.co.uk; Silver Lane, West Challow; s/d £45/75; P) By far the most atmospheric place to stay in the area, this early-15th-century Queen Anne manor house makes a wonderful base and is incredible value for money. The charming rooms have high ceilings, cast-iron fireplaces, antique furniture and buckets of period style.

King Alfred's Head (☎ 01235-765531; 31 Market Pl; mains £9.50-11.50; ⊗ closed Mon) The best bet in town for food, this rustic pub serves everything from bangers and mash to tagliatelle with butternut squash, walnut and sage. The rustic interior is full of old church pews and scrubbed tables, while the courtyard garden is a good bet on sunny days.

Getting There & Away

Bus X30 runs directly from Monday to Saturday to Oxford (35 minutes, hourly).

AROUND WANTAGE
Uffington White Horse

One of England's oldest chalk carvings, the **Uffington White Horse** is a stylised image cut into a hillside almost 3000 years ago. No-one is sure why the people of the time went to so much trouble to create the image or what exactly it is supposed to represent, but the mystery only adds to the sense of awe. This huge figure measures 114m long and 49m wide but is best seen from a distance, or, if you're lucky enough, from the air, because of the stylised lines of perspective.

Just below the figure is **Dragon Hill** so called because it is believed that St George slew the dragon here – and above it the grass-covered earthworks of **Uffington Castle**. From the Courthill Centre, near Wantage, a wonderful 5-mile walk leads along the Ridgeway to the White Horse.

DETOUR: OLDE BELL

With country pubs all getting a makeover and everyone jumping on the gastropub band wagon, it can sometimes be hard to choose where to go. Just outside Henley, however, is a gastropub extraordinaire complete with designer interior and perfectly mismatched furniture, sheepskin throws and open fires. **Olde Bell** (☎ 01628-825881; www.theoldebell.co.uk; Hurley) is within easy striking distance of London, and popular with well-heeled patrons keen to dine on the superb modern British food (mains £10 to £14) dished up in chic surroundings. It's not all new-world sophistication here, though: you'll still get the exposed beams, tasteful knick-knacks and even tea cosies knitted by the local WI (Women's Institute).

Hurley is on the A4130, 8 miles east of Henley.

HIGHWAYMAN'S HIDEOUT

Crooked Billet (☎ 01491-681048; www.the
crookedbillet.co.uk; Stoke Row; mains £12-20)
Hidden down a back lane and surrounded
by trees, the 17th-century Crooked Billet
is an inn famous as the one-time hideout
of highwayman Dick Turpin. Today it is little changed – beer is drawn directly from
casks in the cellar and the low beams, flagstone floor and inglenook fireplace are all
original.

However, it's the food that really draws
the crowds here, with local produce being
whipped into modern, mouth-watering fare
such as warm pigeon salad with wild mushrooms and roast garlic, or venison fillet with
McSweens haggis, baby spinach and roast
figs. Book well in advance.

In the nearby village of Uffington, you can
visit the lovely 13th-century **St Mary's Church**,
known locally as the 'Cathedral of the Vale',
and the **Uffington Museum** (☎ 01367-820259; Broad
St; admission free; ☽ 2-5pm Sat & Sun Easter-Oct). The
museum is set in the old school room featured
in Thomas Hughes' *Tom Brown's Schooldays*
and features displays on the author, local history and archaeology.

THE COTSWOLDS

Glorious honey-coloured villages riddled with
beautiful, old mansions, thatched cottages,
atmospheric churches and rickety almshouses
draw crowds of tourists to the Cotswolds, but,
despite its popularity, it's easy to get off the
beaten track.

The booming medieval wool trade brought
the area its wealth and left it with such a glut
of beautiful buildings that its place in history
is secured for ever more. If you've ever craved
exposed beams, dreamed of falling asleep
under English-rose wallpaper or lusted after
a cream tea in the mid-afternoon, there's no
finer place to fulfil your fantasies.

This is prime tourist territory, however, and
the most popular villages can be besieged by
tourists and traffic in summer. Plan to visit the
main centres early in the morning or late in
the evening, focus your attention on the south
or take to the hills on foot or by bike to avoid
the worst of the crowds. Better still, just leave

the crowds behind and meander down deserted country lanes and bridleways until you
discover your very own bucolic village seemingly undisturbed since medieval times.

Orientation & Information

The limestone hills of the Cotswolds extend
across a narrow band of land east of the M5,
stretching almost as far as Oxford at their
widest point, north to Chipping Campden
and almost as far south as Bath. Most of
the region lies within Gloucestershire, but
parts leak out into Oxfordshire, Wiltshire,
Somerset, Warwickshire and Worcestershire.
The Cotswolds are protected as an Area of
Outstanding Natural Beauty (AONB).

For information on attractions, accommodation and events:

Cotswolds (www.the-cotswolds.org)
Cotswolds Tourism (www.cotswolds.com)
Oxfordshire Cotswolds (www.oxfordshirecotswolds.org)

Activities

The gentle hills of the Cotswolds are perfect
for walking, cycling and riding.

The long-distance **Cotswold Way** (102 miles)
gives walkers a wonderful overview of the
area. The route meanders from Chipping
Campden to Bath, with no major climbs or
difficult stretches, and is easily accessible from
many points en route if you fancy tackling a
shorter section. Ask at local tourist offices for
details of day hikes or pick up a copy of one of
the many walking guides to the region.

Away from the main roads, the winding
lanes of the Cotswolds make fantastic cycling
territory, with little traffic, glorious views and
gentle gradients. Again, the local tourist offices
are invaluable in helping to plot a route.

A COTTAGE OF YOUR OWN

If you'd like to rent your own Cotswold cottage, try these websites:

Campden Cottages (www.campdencottages
.co.uk)
Cotswold Cottage Company (www
.cotswoldcottage.co.uk)
Cotswold Cottages (www.cotswold-cottages
.org.uk)
Cotswold Retreats (www.cotswoldretreats
.co.uk)
Manor Cottages & Cotswold Retreats
(www.manorcottages.co.uk)

THE COTSWOLDS

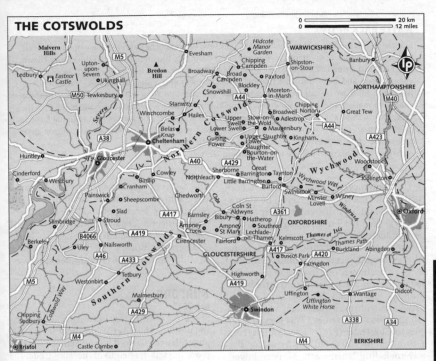

For more information on companies operating self-guided and guided tours of the region, see the boxed text, p248.

Getting Around

Public transport through the Cotswolds is fairly limited, with bus services running to and from major hubs only, and train services just skimming the northern and southern borders. However, with a little careful planning and patience, you can see all the highlights. Tourist offices stock useful *Explore the Cotswolds* brochures with bus and rail summaries.

For the most flexibility, and the option of getting off the beaten track, your own car is unbeatable; car hire can be arranged in most major centres (see p807).

Alternatively, **Cotswold Roaming** (☎ 01865-308300; www.cotswold-roaming.co.uk) runs guided bus tours from Oxford between April and October. Half-day tours of the Cotswolds (adult/under 15 £20/12) include Minster Lovell, Burford and Bibury, while full-day tours of the North Cotswolds (adult/under 15 £30/20) feature Bourton-on-the-Water, Lower Slaughter, Chipping Campden and Stow-on-the-Wold.

WITNEY
pop 22,765

The sleepy town of Witney is firmly on Oxford's commuter belt, but make your way through the traffic and new housing developments to the centre of town and you'll find a charming village green flanked by pretty, stone houses. At one end is a glorious wool church and 18th-century almshouses, at the other a 17th-century covered market. Witney built its wealth through blanket production and the mills, wealthy merchants' homes and blanket factories can still be seen today. The baroque, 18th-century Blanket Hall dominates genteel High St, while at Wood Green you'll find a second village green and a cluster of stunning old stone cottages.

Pick up a copy of the *Witney Wool & Blanket Trail* from the **tourist office** (☎ 01993-775802; witney.tic@westoxon.gov.uk; 3 Welch Way; ✆ 9am-5.30pm Mon-Thu, to 5pm Fri, 9.30am-5pm Sat) to guide you around the town's old buildings and give you some insight into its history.

If you'd like to stay overnight, your best bet for a meal and a bed is the **Fleece** (☎ 01993-892270; www.fleecewitney.co.uk; 11 Church Green; s/d £80/90;

A STEP BACK IN TIME

Squirreled away in the gorgeous village of Great Tew, is a pub little changed since medieval times, its flagstone floors, open fireplaces, low beams and outside loo all part of its 16th-century charm. The **Falkland Arms** (☎ 01608-683653; www.falklandarms.org.uk; Great Tew; r £80-110) sits right on the village green and plays host to a fine collection of local ales, ciders and wines. Traditional clay pipes and snuff are on sale behind the bar, and the clientele are a mix of lucky locals and those willing to make a special trip to enjoy its mellow atmosphere and beautiful surroundings. The food (mains £5 to £9) ranges from homemade soups and crusty baguettes to traditional Sunday roasts with all the trimmings; upstairs, the six guest rooms offer four-poster or cast-iron beds and period style. It doesn't get much more authentic than this.

Great Tew is about 4 miles east of Chipping Norton.

P), a contemporary pub, restaurant and B&B on the main village green. The rooms are sleek and stylish, while the spacious brasserie (mains £9 to £15) offers an ambitious modern menu.

Stagecoach bus 100 runs from Oxford to Witney roughly every 20 minutes Monday to Saturday, hourly on Sunday (30 minutes). **Swanbrook** (www.swanbrook.co.uk) runs three buses Monday to Saturday (one on Sunday) between Cheltenham (£7, one hour) and Oxford (30 minutes) via Witney. This service also goes to Gloucester (£7, 1½ hours) and serves a number of Cotswold towns along the way including Northleach, Minster Lovell and Burford.

MINSTER LOVELL
pop 1200

Set on a gentle slope leading down to the meandering River Windrush, Minster Lovell is a gorgeous village with a cluster of stone cottages nestled beside an ancient pub and riverside mill. One of William Morris' favourite spots, the village has changed little since medieval times and is a glorious place for an afternoon pit stop, quiet overnight retreat or start to a valley walk.

The main sight here is the ruins of **Minster Lovell Hall**, the 15th-century manor-house home to Viscount Francis Lovell. Lovell fought with Richard III at the Battle of Bosworth in 1485, and joined Lambert Simnel's failed rebellion after the king's defeat and death. Lovell's mysterious disappearance was never explained, and when a skeleton was discovered inside a secret vault in the house in 1708, it was assumed he had died while in hiding.

The **Mill & Old Swan** (☎ 0844 980 2313; www .deverevenues.co.uk; d £70-170; **P** **⌨**) offers charming period-style rooms in the 17th-century

Old Swan or sleek, contemporary design in the 19th-century converted mill. The Old Swan serves decent pub food (£9 to £14).

Swanbrook coaches stop here on the Oxford to Cheltenham run. Stagecoach bus 233 between Witney and Burford stops here Monday to Saturday (10 minutes each way, 10 daily).

BURFORD
pop 1877

Slithering down a steep hill to a medieval crossing point on the River Windrush, the remarkable village of Burford is little changed since its glory days at the height of the wool trade. It's a stunningly picturesque place with higgledy-piggledy stone cottages, fine Cotswold town houses and the odd Elizabethan or Georgian gem. A glut of antique shops, tearooms and specialist boutiques peddle nostalgia to the hoards of visitors who make it here in summer, but despite the crowds it's easy to get off the main drag and wander along quiet side streets seemingly lost in time.

The helpful **tourist office** (☎ 01993-823558; Sheep St; ⏰ 9.30am-5.30pm Mon-Sat Mar-Oct, to 4pm Mon-Sat Nov-Feb) provides the Burford Trail leaflet (10p) with information on walking in the local area.

Sights & Activities

Burford's main attraction lies in its incredible collection of buildings, including the 16th-century **Tolsey House** (Toll House; High St; admission free; ⏰ 2-5pm Tue-Fri & Sun, 11am-5pm Sat Mar-Oct), where the wealthy wool merchants held their meetings. This quaint building perches on sturdy pillars and now houses a small museum on Burford's history.

Just off the High St, you'll find the town's 14th-century **almshouses** and the gorgeous

Church of St John the Baptist. The Norman tower here is topped by a 15th-century steeple, and inside you'll find a fine fan-vaulted ceiling and medieval screens dividing the chapels.

Younger visitors will enjoy a visit to the excellent **Cotswold Wildlife Park** (☎ 01993-823006; www.cotswoldwildlifepark.co.uk; adult/under 16yr £10/7.50; ◷ 10am-4.30pm Mar-Sep, to 3.30pm Oct-Feb), set around a Victorian manor house. The park is home to everything from penguins to white rhinos and giant cats.

If you have the time and fancy getting away from the crowds, it's worth the effort to walk east along the picturesque river path to the untouched and rarely visited village of **Swinbrook** (3 miles), where the beautiful church has some remarkable tombs.

Sleeping & Eating

Burford has a wonderful choice of atmospheric, upmarket hotels but far fewer options at more affordable prices.

Cotland House (☎ 01993-822382; www.cotland house.com; Fulbrook Hill; s/d £40/70) A five-minute walk from town, this delightful B&B effortlessly mixes contemporary style with period charm. Although the rooms aren't spacious, they are gloriously comfortable with cast-iron beds, crinkly white linen and soft throws.

Westview House (☎ 01993-824723; www.westview -house.co.uk; 151 The Hill; d £65-85) This lovely old stone cottage has two bright and spacious guest rooms with plenty of period character. The Heritage Room has exposed beams, stone walls and a cast-iron bed, while the Windrush Room has its own private balcony overlooking the garden.

our pick **Lamb Inn** (☎ 01993-823155; www.cotswold -inns-hotels.co.uk/lamb; Sheep St; r £145-255; P ◻ wi-fi) Step back in time with a stay at the Lamb, a 15th-century inn just dripping with character. Expect flagstone floors, beamed ceilings, creaking stairs and a charming, laid-back atmosphere downstairs, and luxurious period-style rooms with antique furniture and cosy comfort upstairs. You'll get top-notch modern British food in the restaurant (three-course dinner £27 to 33) or less formal dining (mains £9 to £13) in the bar.

Angel (☎ 01993-822714; www.theangelatburford .co.uk; 14 Witney St; mains £15-16) Set in a lovely 16th-century coaching inn, this atmospheric brasserie serves up an innovative menu of modern British and European food. Dine-in by roaring fires in winter, or eat al fresco in the lovely walled garden in warmer weather.

Getting There & Away

From Oxford, Swanbrook runs three buses a day (one on Sunday) to Burford (45 minutes) via Witney. Stagecoach bus 233 runs between Witney and Burford 10 times a day, Monday to Saturday (20 minutes). Bus 853 goes to Cheltenham three times daily Monday to Saturday and once on Sunday.

CHIPPING NORTON
pop 5688

The sleepy but attractive town of Chipping Norton – or 'Chippy' as it is locally known – is somewhat spoiled by the traffic running along the main street but has plenty of quiet side streets to wander and none of the Cotswold crowds. Handsome Georgian buildings, stone cottages and old coaching inns cluster around the market square, and on Church St you'll find a row of beautiful honey-coloured **alms-houses** built in the 17th century. Further on is the secluded **Church of St Mary**, a classic example of the Cotswold wool churches, with a magnificent 15th-century Perpendicular nave and clerestory.

Chippy's most enduring landmark, however, is the arresting **Bliss Mill** (now converted to apartments) on the outskirts of town. This monument to the industrial architecture of the 19th century is more like a stately home

---

TOP FIVE PUBS FOR SUNDAY LUNCH

- **Crooked Billet** (p240; Stoke Row) Top-notch food, old-world charm and tales of dashing highwaymen.

- **Falkland Arms** (opposite; Great Tew) Real ales, clay pipes and snuff behind the bar; it doesn't get more authentic than this.

- **Plough** (p244; Kingham) Quaint village pub with sublime food and chilled atmosphere.

- **Swan** (p250; Southrop) Sophisticated fare from ex-London foodies at a traditional village inn.

- **Olde Bell** (p239; Hurley) Sophisticated country pub with designer interior and excellent nosh.

than a factory, topped by a domed tower and chimney stack of the Tuscan order.

For overnight accommodation, **Norten's B&B** (☎ 01608-645060; www.nortens.co.uk; 10 New St; s £35-50, d £50-65) offers a range of modern rooms with simple, stylish design. The downstairs cafe (10am to 10pm) serves a good range of Mediterranean food (mains £4 to £7).

Alternatively, make your way 4 miles southwest of town to the pretty village of Kingham, where two fine gastropubs offer stylish rooms and sublime food. Set on the village green, **Plough** (☎ 01608-658327; www.kinghamplough.co.uk; The Green, Kingham; s £65-75 d £75-95; P wi-fi) has simple, elegant rooms and a short but exquisite menu (mains £12 to £14). Just around the corner is **Tollgate Inn** (☎ 01608-658389; www.thetollgate .com; Church St, Kingham; s/d £60/90), with contemporary but rustic rooms and sophisticated fare.

Stagecoach bus 20 runs between Chippy and Oxford roughly every half-hour.

MORETON-IN-MARSH

pop 3198

Home to some beautiful buildings but utterly ruined by through traffic, Moreton-in-Marsh is a major road hub and useful for its transport links. On Tuesday, the town bursts into life for its weekly market.

Just east of Moreton, **Chastleton House** (NT; ☎ 01608-674355; adult/under 18yr £7/3.50; 1-5pm Wed-Sat mid-Mar–late-Sep, 1-4pm Wed-Sat Oct) is one of England's finest and most complete Jacobean houses, full of rare tapestries, family portraits and antique furniture. Outside, there's a classic Elizabethan topiary garden and a lovely 12th-century church nearby.

Pulhams Coaches (☎ 01451-820369; www.pulhams coaches.com) runs seven services between Moreton and Cheltenham (one hour, Monday to Saturday) via Stow-on-the-Wold (15 minutes) and Bourton-on-the-Water (20 minutes). Two Sunday services run from May to September only.

There are trains roughly every 90 minutes to Moreton from London Paddington (£29, 1½ hours) via Oxford (£9.70, 35 minutes) and on to Worcester (£10.60, 45 minutes) and Hereford (£14.30, 1½ hours).

CHIPPING CAMPDEN

pop 1943

An unspoiled gem in an area full of achingly pretty villages, Chipping Campden is a glorious reminder of life in the Cotswolds in medieval times. The graceful curving main street is flanked by a wonderful array of wayward stone cottages, fine terraced houses, ancient inns and historic homes, liberally sprinkled with chichi boutiques and upmarket shops. Despite its obvious allure, the town remains relatively unspoiled by tourist crowds and is a wonderful place to visit.

Pop into the helpful **tourist office** (☎ 01386-841206; www.visitchippingcampden.com; High St; 10am-5pm Mon-Fri) to pick up a town trail guide for information on the most historic buildings and to get you off the main drag and down some of the gorgeous back streets. If you're visiting on a Wednesday between July and September, it's well worth joining a guided tour (2.30pm, suggested donation £2.50) run by the Cotswold Wardens.

The most obvious sight is the wonderful 17th-century **Market Hall**, with multiple gables and elaborate timber roof. Further on, at the western end of the High St, is the 15th-century **St James's**, one of the Cotswolds' great wool churches. Built in the Perpendicular style, it has a magnificent tower and some graceful 17th-century monuments. Nearby on Church St is a remarkable row of **almshouses** dating from the 17th century, and the Jacobean lodges and gateways of the now-ruined Campden House.

The surviving **Court Barn** (☎ 01386-841951; www.courtbarn.org.uk; Church St; adult/under 16yr £3.75/ free; 10.30am-5.30pm Tue-Sat, 11.30am-5.30pm Sun Apr-Sep, 11am-4pm Tue-Sat, 11.30am-4pm Sun Oct-Mar) is now a museum of craft and design featuring work from the Arts and Crafts Movement (see p534). CR Ashbee and the Guild of Handicrafts moved to Chipping Campden in 1902 and a collection of their work is showcased here.

About 4 miles northeast of Chipping Campden, **Hidcote Manor Garden** (NT; ☎ 01386-438333; Hidcote Bartrim; adult/under 18yr £8.50/4.25; 10am-5pm Sat-Wed mid-Mar–Oct, Fri Jul & Aug) is one of the finest examples of Arts and Crafts landscaping in Britain.

Sleeping & Eating

Manor Farm (☎ 01386-840390; www.manorfarmnb .demon.co.uk; s/d £55/65) Set in a beautiful 17th-century farmhouse, this lovely B&B has all the period charm of a Cotswold home but with contemporary style and modern facilities. Along with the exposed oak beams and creaking stairs, you'll find king-size beds, power showers and neutral colour schemes.

THE COTSWOLDS OLIMPICKS

The medieval sport of shin-kicking lives on in Chipping Campden, where each year the townspeople gather to compete at the Cotswolds Olimpicks, a traditional country sports day first celebrated in 1612. It is one of the most entertaining and bizarre sporting competitions in England, and many of the original events such as welly wanging (throwing), the sack race and climbing a slippery pole are still held. The competition was mentioned in Shakespeare's *Merry Wives of Windsor* and has even been officially sanctioned by the British Olympic Association. It is held annually at the beginning of June.

Eight Bells (☎ 01386-840371; www.eightbellsinn .co.uk; Church St; s £55-85, d £85-125) Dripping with old-world character and charm, but also decidedly modern, this 14th-century inn has a range of sleek, comfortable rooms and a well-respected restaurant serving a British and Continental menu (mains £11 to £12) in rustic settings.

our pick Cotswold House Hotel (☎ 01386-840330; www.cotswoldhouse.com; The Square; r £150-650; P 💻) If you're after a spot of luxury, look no further than this chic Regency town house turned boutique hotel. Bespoke furniture, massive beds, Frette linens, cashmere throws, private gardens and hot tubs are the norm here. You can dine in style at Juliana's (two/three course set dinner £39.50/49.50) or take a more informal approach at Hick's Brasserie (mains £9 to £18), a slick operation with an ambitious menu.

If you're wiling to stay a little out of town, there are two fine options well worth going the extra mile:

Churchill Arms (☎ 01386-594000; www.thechurchill arms.com; Paxford; s/d £40/70) A gastropub with pretty rooms and a menu (mains £10 to £16) that draws crowds from miles around.

Malt House (☎ 01386-840295; www.malt-house.co .uk; Blockley, Broad Campden; s/d £85/135) A charming country guest house set in a stunningly picturesque village.

Getting There & Around

Between them, buses 21 and 22 run almost hourly to Stratford-upon-Avon or Moreton-in-Marsh. Bus 21 also stops in Broadway. There are no Sunday services.

To catch a real glimpse of the countryside, try hiring a bike from **Cotswold Country Cycles** (☎ 01386-438706; www.cotswoldcountrycycles .com; Longlands Farm Cottage; per day £15) and discovering the quiet lanes and gorgeous villages around town.

BROADWAY
pop 2496

This absurdly pretty village has inspired writers, artists and composers in times past with its graceful, golden-hued cottages set at the foot of a steep escarpment. It's a quintessentially English place pitted with antiques shops, tearooms and art galleries, and is justifiably popular in the summer months, but take the time to wander away from the main street and you'll be rewarded with quiet back roads lined with stunning cottages, flower-filled gardens and picturesque churches.

The **tourist office** (☎ 01386-852937; www.beautiful broadway.com; Russell Sq; ⏰ 10am-5pm Mon-Sat, 2-5pm Sun) is just off the High St.

Beyond the charm of the village itself, there are few specific attractions. If you're feeling energetic, the lovely, 12th-century **Church of St Eadburgha** is a signposted 1-mile walk from town. Near here, a more challenging path leads uphill for 2 miles to **Broadway Tower** (☎ 01386-852390; www.broadwaytower.co.uk; adult/under 14yr £3.80/2.30; ⏰ 10.30am-5pm Apr-Oct, 11am-3pm Sat & Sun Nov-Mar), a crenulated, 18th-century Gothic folly on the crest of the escarpment. It has a small William Morris exhibition on one floor and stunning views from the top.

Broadway is littered with chintzy B&Bs, but for something more modern, try **Hadley House** (☎ 01386-853486; www.cotswolds.info/webpage/hadley -house.htms; Leamington Rd; s/d £60/70; P 💻 wi-fi), a cosy B&B with beautiful rooms in soothing pale colours with a splash of deep red.

Alternatively, **Windrush** (☎ 01386 853577; www .broadway-windrush.co.uk; Station Rd; d £80-100; P) is a friendly B&B with newly refurbished rooms decked out in simple neutral colours, with flat-screen TVs, bathrobes and complimentary toiletries.

For food, the **Swan** (☎ 01386-852278; www .theswanbroadway.co.uk; 2 The Green; mains £8-15) is an informal place with stylish, contemporary decor, wooden floors, leather seats and a mouth-watering, modern menu.

Sleek and stylish **Russells** (☎ 01386-853555; www.russellsofbroadway.com; 20 High St; mains £10-21) has upmarket modern British fare. It also has a selection of slick, modern rooms (£120 to £325) with simple design, flat-screen TVs and lots of little luxuries.

Getting There & Away
Bus 22 goes to Moreton-in-Marsh, Chipping Campden and Stratford (20 minutes, four daily Monday to Saturday) and bus 606 goes to Cheltenham (50 minutes, four Monday to Saturday).

AROUND BROADWAY
About 3 miles south of Broadway is **Snowshill Manor** (NT; ☎ 01386-852410; Snowshill; adult/under 18yr £8.10/4.10, garden only £4.40/2.20; 🕑 noon-5pm Wed-Sun mid-Mar–Oct), a wonderful Cotswold mansion once home to the marvellously eccentric Charles Paget Wade. The house contains Wade's extraordinary collection of craftsmanship and design including everything from musical instruments to Victorian perambulators and Japanese armour. Outside, the lovely gardens were designed as an extension of the house, with pools, terraces and wonderful views.

Also worth visiting, nearby, is the stunning Jacobean mansion **Stanway House** (☎ 01386-58469; www.stanwayfountain.co.uk; Stanway; adult/under 14yr £6/4.50, garden only £4/1; 🕑 2-5pm Tue & Thu Jun-Aug, garden only Sat Jun-Aug). Little has changed since it was a family home: it contains much of its original furniture and is surrounded by wonderful, baroque water gardens including the world's highest gravity fountain.

WINCHCOMBE
pop 3682
Winchcombe is a sleepy Cotswold town, very much a working, living place with butchers, bakers and small independent shops giving it a very lived-in, authentic feel. It was capital of the Saxon kingdom of Mercia and one of the most important towns in the Cotswolds until the Middle Ages, and today the remnants of its illustrious past can be seen in the beautiful houses lining the streets, and the picturesque cottages on Vineyard St and Dents Tce and in majestic Sudeley Castle. Winchcombe is also blessed with good accommodation and fine-dining choices, making it a great base for exploring the area.

The helpful **tourist office** (☎ 01242-602925; www.winchcombe.co.uk; High St; 🕑 10am-1pm & 2-5pm Mon-Sat, 10am-4pm Sun Apr-Oct, to 4pm Sat & Sun Nov-Mar) can help plan an itinerary.

When wandering around town, look out for the fine gargoyles that adorn the lovely St Peter's Church. Just outside the town are the evocative ruins of Cistercian **Hailes Abbey** (EH; ☎ 01242-602398; adult/under 15yr £3.50/1.80; 🕑 10am-5pm Easter-Oct), once one of the country's main pilgrimage centres.

The town's main attraction is magnificent **Sudeley Castle** (☎ 01242-602308; www.sudeleycastle.co.uk; adult/under 15yr £7.20/4.20; 🕑 10.30am-5pm Sun-Thu mid-March–Oct), once a favoured retreat of Tudor and Stuart monarchs. The house is still used as a family home, and much of the interior is off limits to visitors, but you can get a glimpse of its grand proportions while visiting the exhibitions of costumes, memorabilia and paintings and the surrounding gardens. If you want an insight into real life in the castle, join one of the 'Connoisseur Tours' (£15, Tuesday, Wednesday and Thursday 11am, 1pm and 3pm, mid-March to October).

If you're feeling energetic, there's easy access to the Cotswold Way from Winchcombe, and the 2½-mile hike to Belas Knap is one of the most scenic short walks in the region. Five-thousand-year-old Belas Knap is the best-preserved neolithic burial chamber in the country and, although visitors are not allowed inside, the views down to Sudeley Castle and across the surrounding countryside are breathtaking.

Sleeping & Eating
White Hart Inn (☎ 01242-602359; www.the-white-hart-inn.com; r £40-115) An excellent option in the centre of town. Choose the cheaper 'rambler' rooms with shared bathrooms or go for more luxury in a superior room. You'll also get a good choice of food in the bar (mains £7 to £8) and modern British fare in the main restaurant (mains £10.50 to £19.50).

Parks Farm (☎ 01242-603874; www.parksfarm.co.uk; Sudeley; d £50-60; P) Stay on a 17th-century Cotswold hill farm just outside the town for an insight into local life. This friendly B&B has two cosy rooms with views over the rolling hills, and guests are served breakfast in a beamed kitchen with one large table and a roaring Aga.

our pick **5 North St** (☎ 01242-604566; 5 North St; 2/3-course lunch £20.50/24.50, 3-course dinner £33-43; 🕑 lunch Wed-Sat, dinner Tue-Sun) The top spot to eat for miles around, this Michelin-starred restaurant has no airs and graces, just beautifully prepared food in down-to-earth surroundings. Deep-red walls, wooden tables and friendly service make it a very unpretentious place, but the food is thoroughly ambitious with a keen mix of British ingredients and French flair.

Getting There & Away

Bus 606 runs from Broadway (65 minutes, four daily Monday to Saturday) to Cheltenham via Winchcombe.

STOW-ON-THE-WOLD
pop 2074

A popular stop on a tour of the Cotswolds, Stow is anchored by a large market square surrounded by handsome buildings and steep-walled alleyways, originally used to funnel the sheep into the fair. The town has long held a strategic place in Cotswold history, standing as it does on the Roman Fosse Way and at the junction of six roads. Today, it's littered with antique shops, boutiques, tearooms and delis, thronging with people from passing coach tours. On a quiet day, it's a wonderful place, but all a little artificial if you're looking for true Cotswold charm.

The **tourist office** (☎ 01451-831081; Hollis House; 9.30am-5.30pm Mon-Sat) on Market Sq sells discounted tickets to local attractions.

Sleeping & Eating

Stow-on-the-Wold YHA (☎ 0845 371 9540; www.yha .org.uk; The Square; dm £15.95; P 🖳) Slap bang on the market square, this hostel is in a wonderful 16th-century town house and has small dorms, a children's play area and a warm welcome for families.

Number 9 (☎ 01451-870333; www.number-nine .info; 9 Park St; s £45-50, d £65-75) Centrally located and wonderfully atmospheric, this beautiful B&B has three simple, chic rooms with plenty of space, brand-new bathrooms and subtle decor.

Grapevine Hotel (☎ 01451-830344; www.vines .co.uk; Sheep St; s £85-95, d £140-160) Set in a charming 17th-century building, the grapevine has a range of elegant, classically furnished rooms with exposed stone walls and beams. It also has a choice of three restaurants offering everything from bar food, pizza and pasta to fine dining.

Eagle & Child (☎ 01451-830670; Digbeth St; mains £10-16) Although the atmosphere is decidedly medieval with exposed beams and old-world charm, the menu is modern

with traditional English favourites given a contemporary twist.

Old Butchers (☎ 01451-831700; www.theoldbutchers .com; 7 Park St; mains £12-17) Simple, smart and sophisticated, this is Stow's top spot for dining, serving robust, local ingredients whipped up into sublime dishes. For all its fanfare, there's little pretension here, just fine modern British cuisine with more than a hint of Continental European influence thrown in.

Getting There & Away

Bus 55 links Stow with Moreton, Bourton, Northleach and Cirencester (eight daily Monday to Saturday). Bus 801 runs to Cheltenham, Moreton and Bourton (four daily Monday to Friday, nine on Saturday).

The nearest train stations are 4 miles away at Kingham and Moreton-in-Marsh.

BOURTON-ON-THE-WATER
pop 3093

An undeniably picturesque town, Bourton has sold its soul to tourism, becoming a Cotswolds theme park with its handsome houses and pretty bridges overshadowed by a series of crass, commercial attractions. Take your pick from the model railway and village, bird-conservation project, perfume factory, maze and motor museum, or visit in the winter when the village's understated charm is free to reveal itself.

One occasion worth battling the crowds for is the annual **water football match**, held in the river on the August Bank Holiday Monday. This traditional frolic dates back to the 1800s.

If you'd like to stay chic and stylish, **Dial House** (☎ 01451-822244; www.dialhousehotel.com; The Chestnuts; r £110-230) is unpretentious but seriously luxurious, with hand-painted wallpaper, giant beds, silky throws and a wonderful mix of period charm and designer style. The restaurant (mains £10 to £23) serves up excellent modern British cuisine.

Bus 801 operates to Cheltenham, Moreton and Stow (up to four daily Monday to Friday, nine Saturday).

THE SLAUGHTERS
pop 400

An antidote to the commercialism of Bourton, the picture-postcard villages of Upper and Lower Slaughter still attract the crowds of tourists, yet manage to maintain

---

THROW AWAY YOUR GUIDEBOOK!

As wonderful as the Cotswolds villages may be, in the summer months they can be a nightmare of camera-wielding crowds, slow-moving pensioners and chaotic coach parking. However, most tourists stick to a well-trodden path, so it's easy to get away from the crowds and discover the rarely visited villages lurking in the hills. Stick to the B-roads and visit places like **Guiting Power** near Bourton, **Broadwell**, **Maugersbury**, **Adlestrop** and the **Swells** near Stow, **Sheepscombe** and **Slad** near Painswick, **Blockley** near Chipping Campden, **Great Tew** near Chipping Norton, **Taynton**, **Sherborne** and the **Barringtons** near Burford, **Ampney St Mary** and **Ampney Crucis** near Cirencester, or **Coln St Aldwyns** and **Hatherop** near Bibury. Or better still, see the region on foot or by bike and just meander at your own pace, or join a walking tour with **Cotswold Walking Holidays** (☎ 01242-518888; www.cotswoldwalks.com) or a bike tour with **Cotswold Country Cycles** (☎ 01386-438706; www.cotswoldcountrycycles.com).

---

their unhurried medieval charm. The village names are derived from the Old English 'sloughtre', meaning slough or muddy place, but today the River Eye is contained within limestone banks and meanders peacefully through the village past the 17th-century Lower Slaughter Manor (now a top-notch hotel) to the **old mill** (☎ 01451-820052; www.oldmill-lowerslaughter.com; admission £2; ⏰ 10am-6pm Mar-Oct) which houses a small museum and teashop.

To see the Slaughters at their best, arrive on foot from Bourton (a 1-mile walk) across the fields. From here you can continue for another mile across the fields to Upper Slaughter, with its own fine manor house and glorious cottages.

NORTHLEACH
pop 1923

Little visited and under appreciated, Northleach is a lovely little market town of half-timbered Tudor houses, imposing merchants' stores and late-medieval cottages. There's a wonderful mix of architectural styles clustered around the market square and the narrow laneways leading off it, but the highlight is the **Church of St Peter and St Paul**, a masterpiece of Cotswold Perpendicular style. The large traceried stained-glass windows and collection of memorial brasses are unrivalled in the region.

Near the square is Oak House, a 17th-century wool house that contains **Keith Harding's World of Mechanical Music** (☎ 01451-860181; www.mechanicalmusic.co.uk; adult/child £7.50/3; ⏰ 10am-6pm), a fascinating museum of self-playing musical instruments, where you can hear Rachmaninoff's works played on a reproducing piano.

Just outside town is **Chedworth Roman Villa** (NT; ☎ 01242-890256; Yanworth; adult/under 18yr £5.70/3.35; ⏰ 10am-5pm Tue-Sun Mar-Nov), one of the largest Roman villas in England. Built as a stately home in about AD 120, it contains some wonderful mosaics illustrating the seasons, bathhouses, and, a short walk away, a temple by the River Coln. It's 3 miles northwest of Fossebridge off the A429.

For overnight stays, try the **Wheatsheaf** (☎ 01451-860244; www.wheatsheaf.cotswoldinns.com; West End; d £85-145; ▯ wi-fi). It has eight en suite rooms that have recently been refurbished. The restaurant serves a good selection of light lunches (£6 to £8) and a modern British dinner menu (mains £11 to £18).

Getting There & Away
Swanbrook runs six buses Monday to Saturday between Cheltenham (30 minutes) and Northleach, and three to Oxford (one hour).

CIRENCESTER
pop 15,861

Refreshingly unpretentious, with narrow, winding streets and graceful town houses, charming Cirencester is an affluent, elegant kind of place. The lovely market square is surrounded by wonderful 18th-century and Victorian architecture, and the nearby streets showcase a harmonious medley of buildings from various eras.

Under the Romans, Cirencester was second only to London in terms of size and importance and, although little of this period remains, you can still see the grassed-over ruins of one of the largest amphitheatres in the country. The medieval wool trade was also good to the town, with wealthy merchants funding the building of a superb church.

Today, Cirencester is the most important town in the southern Cotswolds and retains an authentic, unaffected air, with the lively Monday and Friday markets as important as the expensive boutiques and trendy delis that line its narrow streets.

The **tourist office** (☎ 01285-654180; Park St; ☷ 10am-5pm Mon-Sat, 2-5pm Sun) is located in the museum and has a leaflet detailing a guided walk around the town and its historic buildings.

Church of St John the Baptist

Standing elegantly on the Market Sq, the cathedral-like **St John's** (suggested donation £3; ☷ 10am-5pm) is one of England's largest parish churches. An outstanding Perpendicular-style tower with wild flying buttresses dominates the exterior, but it is the majestic three-storey south porch that is the real highlight. Built as an office by late-15th-century abbots, it subsequently became the medieval town hall.

Soaring arches, magnificent fan vaulting and a Tudor nave adorn the light-filled interior, where you'll also find a 15th-century, painted stone pulpit and memorial brasses recording the matrimonial histories of important wool merchants. The east window contains fine medieval stained glass, and a wall safe displays the **Boleyn Cup**, made for Anne Boleyn, second wife of Henry VIII, in 1535.

Corinium Museum

Modern design, innovative displays and computer reconstructions bring one of Britain's largest collections of Roman artefacts to life at the **Corinium Museum** (☎ 01285-655611; www.cotswolds.gov.uk/museum; Park St; adult/under 16yr £3.95/2; ☷ 10am-5pm Mon-Sat, 2-5pm Sun). You can dress as a Roman soldier, meet an Anglo-Saxon princess and discover what Cirencester was like during its heyday as a wealthy medieval wool town. Highlights of the Roman collection include the beautiful Hunting Dogs and Four Seasons floor mosaics, and a reconstructed Roman kitchen and butcher's shop.

Other Sights

Set in a beautifully converted Victorian brewery, the **Brewery Arts Centre** (☎ 01285-657181; www.breweryarts.org.uk; Brewery Ct; admission free; ☷ 9.30am-5.30pm Mon-Sat, 10am-4pm Sun) is home to 12 resident craft workers and hosts regular exhibitions, workshops and classes.

Also worth visiting is **Cirencester Park** (Cecily Hill; ☷ 8am-5pm), the baroque landscaped grounds of the Bathurst Estate. The park features magnificent geometrical landscaping and has a lovely short walk along Broad Ride.

The remains of the **Roman amphitheatre** are on Cotswold Ave.

Sleeping & Eating

Old Brewhouse (☎ 01285-656099; www.theoldbrew house.com; 7 London Rd; s £50-55, d £65-70; **P**) Set in a charming 17th-century town house, this lovely B&B has bright, pretty rooms with cast-iron beds and subtle, country-style florals or patchwork quilts. The beautiful garden room even has its own patio.

Corinium Hotel (☎ 01285-659711; www.corinium hotel.com; 21 Gloucester St; s £55-70, d £74-109; **P**) This Elizabethan wool merchant's house is now a family-run hotel with 15 rooms ranging from simple doubles to four-posters with exposed beams and corner baths. The understated decor, subtle colour schemes and mix of period features make it a good bet.

No 12 (☎ 01285-640232; ww.no12cirencester.co.uk; 12 Park St; d £85) This Georgian town house right in the centre of town has gloriously unfussy rooms kitted out with a tasteful mix of antiques and modern furnishings. Think feather pillows, merino blankets, extra-long beds, slick modern bathrooms and a host of little extras to make you smile.

Piazza Fontana (☎ 01285-643133; 30A Castle St; mains £9-17; closed Sun) An authentic family-run Italian joint hidden away in a courtyard, serving up a great selection of traditional pastas, meat and fish dishes just done to perfection. It's well worth seeking out for its informal atmosphere and top-notch service.

Jesse's Bistro (☎ 01285-641497; Blackjack St; mains £12.50-21.50; ☷ lunch Mon-Sat & dinner Tue-Sat) Hidden away in a cobbled stable yard with its own fishmonger and cheese shop, Jesse's is a great little place with flagstone floors, wrought-iron chairs and mosaic tables. The modern menu features a selection of great dishes, but the real treat is the fresh fish and meat cooked in the wood-burning oven.

Getting There & Away

National Express buses run roughly hourly from Cirencester to London (£17, 2½ hours) and to Cheltenham Spa (30 minutes) and Gloucester (one hour). Stagecoach bus 51 also runs to Cheltenham Monday to Saturday (40

OXFORD, THE COTSWOLDS & AROUND

THE GOOD LIFE

The Cotswolds' mellow charms attract moneyed city folk, A-list celebrities and wealthy downsizers in equal measure, but mere mortals can get a slice of the good life at one of the numerous luxury hotels in the area. Here are just a few to whet your fancy.

Lygon Arms (☎ 01386-852255; www.barcelo-hotels.co.uk/lygonarms; High St, Broadway; d £99-209; P ☐) Choose medieval splendour or modern chic at this 16th-century inn in the heart of Broadway.

Cotswolds 88 (☎ 01452-813688; www.cotswolds88hotel.com; Painswick; d £170-450) Quirky, ostentatious and opulently designed, this latest arrival to the Cotswolds uber-hotel club aims to be rock 'n' roll cool and has the tragically hip attitude to go with it.

Lords of the Manor (☎ 01451-820243; www.lordsofthemanor.com; Upper Slaughter; d £195-370; P ☐) A former rectory just dripping in character, this place has a genteel air with lavishly elegant rooms and the foresight to leave a pristine pair of wellies at your door just in case you'd like to explore the gardens.

Cowley Manor (☎ 01242-87900; www.cowleymanor.com; Cowley; d £245-470; P ☐) Handmade furniture and fabrics by young British designers adorn the simple, but elegant, rooms at this super-slinky hotel.

Barnsley House (☎ 01285-740000, www.barnsleyhouse.com; Barnsley; d £295-525; P ☐) For funky chic and indulgent sophistication, this hideout for the rich and famous is just the spot for a romantic weekend.

---

minutes, hourly). Bus 852 goes to Gloucester (four daily Monday to Saturday).

BIBURY
pop 623

Once described by William Morris as 'the most beautiful village in England', Bibury is another Cotswold gem with a cluster of gorgeous riverside cottages and tangle of narrow streets flanked by wayward stone buildings. It's an impossibly quaint place whose main attraction is **Arlington Row**, a stunning sweep of cottages now thought to be the most photographed street in Britain. Originally built as a sheep house in the 14th century, the building was converted into weavers' cottages in the 17th century. Also worth a look is the 17th-century **Arlington Mill**, just a short stroll away across Rack Isle, a wildlife refuge once used to dry cloth.

Few visitors make it past these two sights, but for a glimpse of the real Bibury, venture into the village proper behind Arlington Row, where you'll find a cluster of stunning cottages and the Saxon **Church of St Mary**. Although much altered since its original construction, many 8th-century features are still visible among the 12th- and 13th-century additions.

Despite its popularity Bibury, is seriously lacking in decent accommodation. The best place to stay is in the nearby village of Coln, where the jasmine-clad **New Inn** (☎ 01285-750651; www.new-inn.co.uk; Coln-St-Aldwyns; d £120-180) offers

contemporary rooms in 16th-century surroundings. It's also the best bet in the area for food with its modern British menu (mains £9 to £15) served in the main restaurant, bar and gorgeous garden.

Buses 860, 863, 865, 866 and 869 pass through Bibury en route to Cirencester at least once daily from Monday to Saturday (20 minutes).

LECHLADE-ON-THAMES
pop 2415

A quiet backwater dominated by the graceful spire of St Lawrence's Church, the attractive market town of Lechlade is temptingly close to two wonderful period houses.

Just 3 miles east, signposted off the A417, is the gorgeous Tudor pile **Kelmscott Manor** (☎ 01367-252486; www.kelmscottmanor.co.uk; adult/under 16yr £8.50/4.25, garden only £2; ☼ house & garden 11am-5pm Wed Apr-Sep & selected Sat in summer, garden only 2-5pm Thu Jun-Sep), once the summer home of William Morris, the poet, artist and founder of the Arts and Crafts Movement (p534). The house contains many of Morris' personal effects, as well as fabrics and furniture designed by him and his associates.

Another worthwhile trip from Lechlade is **Buscot Park** (NT; ☎ 01367-240786; www.buscot-park.com; adult/child £7.50/3.75, grounds only £5/2.50; ☼ 2-6pm Wed-Fri, grounds only Mon & Tue Apr-Sep & selected weekends), an ornate, Italianate country house set in gardens designed by Harold Peto. The house is now

---

SOMETHING FOR THE WEEKEND

Kick-start your weekend by checking into the seductively stylish **Cotswold House Hotel** (p245) in Chipping Campden, and take a sunset stroll around the village before dining at Juliana's or Hick's Brasserie. First thing the following morning, blow away the cobwebs with a short stroll and magnificent views at **Broadway Tower** (p245) and then head south to **Winchcombe** (p246), where you can loll about the lovely village or take in some history at the Tudor pile **Sudeley Castle** (p246).

Stop for lunch at the seriously unpretentious but exceptionally good **5 North St** (p246), before taking the cross-country route to stunning **Lower Slaughter** (p247). If you're feeling sprightly, follow the trail over the rolling hills to Upper Slaughter, or just sit and feed the ducks before swinging back to Bourton to check into the sumptuous **Dial House** (p247) for an evening of luxury and fine food.

On Sunday, head east to **Woodstock** to ramble the grounds or the stately rooms of **Blenheim Palace** (p236), and work up an appetite for a hearty traditional lunch at the glorious thatched **Falkland Arms** (see boxed text, p242) in Great Tew.

---

home to the Faringdon art collection, which includes paintings by Rembrandt, Reynolds, Rubens, Van Dyck and Murillo. The house is 2¾ miles southeast of Lechlade on the Faringdon road (A417).

If you're visiting either attraction, it's well worth making a detour to the pretty village of Southrop, 4 miles northwest of Lechlade, to dine at the atmospheric pub **Swan** (☎ 01367-850205; www.theswanatsouthrop.co.uk; mains £11-15; ✆ closed Sun dinner). This 17th-century inn has the stone floors and exposed beams you'd expect, but is refreshingly bright and uncluttered and serves extremely sophisticated food at reasonable prices.

Bus 877 runs from Lechlade to Cirencester (40 minutes, three times daily from Monday to Saturday).

TETBURY
pop 5250

Once a prosperous wool-trading centre, Tetbury has managed to preserve most of its architectural heritage – its busy streets are lined with medieval cottages, sturdy old town houses and Georgian Gothic gems. It's an unspoilt place with a rather regal character: even HRH Prince Charles has a shop here – Highgrove – though it's unlikely you'll find him serving behind the counter.

Along with goodies from the Highgrove Estate, Tetbury is a great place for antique fans with a shop of old curios on almost every corner. You'll also find plenty of chichi boutiques and interior-design shops, but they're tempered by the bakers, butchers and delis that ground the town and give it a sense of real identity.

As you wander round, look out for the row of gorgeous medieval weavers' cottages that line the steep hill at **Chipping Steps**, leading up to the **Chipping** (market), which is surrounded by graceful 17th- and 18th-century town houses. From here, it's a short stroll to Market Sq, where the 17th-century **Market House** stands as if on stilts. Close by, the Georgian Gothic **Church of St Mary the Virgin** has a towering spire and wonderful interior.

Just south of Tetbury is the **National Arboretum** (☎ 01666-880220; www.forestry.gov.uk /westonbirt; adult £5-8, under 18yr £2; ✆ 9am-dusk) at Westonbirt. The park boasts a magnificent selection of temperate trees, with some wonderful walks and great colour throughout the year, especially in autumn.

The friendly **tourist office** (☎ 01666-503552; www.visittetbury.co.uk; 33 Church St; ✆ 9.30am-4.30pm Mon-Sat Mar-Oct, to 2.30pm Nov-Feb) has plenty of information on the town and its history and stocks a trail guide to the arboretum.

Sleeping & Eating

Ormond's Head (☎ 01666-505690; www.theormond.co.uk; 23 Long St; s £59-99, d £69-140; **P**) This modern hotel has a range of individually styled rooms with subtle, but striking, fabrics and funky wallpapers. It's an unassuming place that offers excellent value for money. Expect duck-down duvets, flat-screen TVs, a DVD library and warm welcome for families. The modern bar and grill downstairs serve excellent-value food (mains £9 to £15).

Talboys House (☎ 01666-503597; www.talboyshouse .com; 17 Church Street; s £45, d £95-120) Grab a slice of India in this quirky joint with exotic rooms decked out in Bollywood style. This 19th-century wool merchant's house is now a haven of sultry colour schemes, embroidered fabrics, carved woods and Indian toiletries.

Chef's Table (☎ 01666-504466; 49 Long St; bistro mains £8-13; 9.30am-3.30pm) This fantastic deli and bistro is the place to go to stock up for a picnic in the Arboretum or a mouth-watering lunch of local organic ingredients rustled up into stunning rustic dishes – go for rabbit and tarragon pie or shellfish and saffron chowder. If you're feeling inspired, you can learn how to cook the dishes under the guidance of Michelin-starred chef Michael Bedford – his cookery school runs on selected days during the summer months (day course £120).

Blue Zucchini (☎ 01666-505852; 7-9 Church St; dinner mains £10-14; lunch & dinner Tue-Sat, lunch Sun & Mon) This popular cafe and bistro is a bright, cheery place that's usually buzzing. It's great for a coffee and a look at the papers and serves a good selection of contemporary classics for lunch and dinner.

Getting There & Away

Bus 29 runs between Tetbury and Stroud (30 minutes, six daily Monday to Saturday). Bus 620 goes to Bath (1¼ hours, six daily Monday to Friday, four on Saturday), stopping at Westonbirt Arboretum en route.

ULEY

pop 1100

This lovely little hamlet, with its quaint village green and jumble of pretty houses, sits below the overgrown remains of the largest Iron Age hill fort in England, **Uley Bury**. Dating from about 300 BC, the fort and its 2-mile perimeter walk provide spectacular views over the Severn Vale. To walk there, follow the steep path that runs from the village church. If you're driving, access to the car park is off the B4066, north of the village.

Just east of Uley you'll find the wonderfully romantic **Owlpen Manor** (☎ 01453-860261; www.owlpen.com; adult/under 14yr £5.50/2.50; 2-5pm Tue, Thu & Sun May-Oct), a Tudor mansion nestled in a wooded valley and surrounded by formal terraced gardens. The house was built between 1450 and 1616 and has a magnificent Tudor **Great Hall**, which contains unique painted wall hangings. Owlpen suffered 100 years of neglect in the 19th century and was rescued and partially refurbished in 1926 by architect Norman Jewson, a follower of William Morris. The house now contains a rich collection of Arts and Crafts (see p534) furniture and fittings.

Virtually untouched since the mid-1870s, **Woodchester Mansion** (☎ 01453-861541; www.woodchestermansion.org.uk; adult/under 14yr £5.50/free; 11am-4pm Sun Easter-Oct plus Sat Jul & Aug) is an incredible place, abandoned before it was finished, yet amazingly grand and graceful. Doors lead nowhere, fireplaces are stuck halfway up walls, and corridors end at ledges with views of the ground below. The house also features an impressive set of gruesome gargoyles and is home to a large colony of bats and several resident ghosts. It's a mile north of Uley on the B4066; bus 20 runs between Uley and Stroud (55 minutes, hourly Monday to Saturday).

BERKELEY

pop 1865

An astounding relic from medieval times, **Berkeley Castle** (☎ 01453-810332; www.berkeley-castle.com; adult/under 16yr £7.50/4.50, grounds only £4/2; 11am-5.30pm Sun late Mar-late Oct, daily Jul & Aug) has remained virtually untouched since it was built as a sturdy fortress in Norman times. Edward II was imprisoned and then murdered here on the order of his wife, Queen Isabella, and her lover in 1327, and you can still see the King's Gallery with its cell and dungeon. You can also visit the castle's **state rooms**, as well as the medieval **Great Hall**, **Picture Gallery** and **kitchen**. Regular jousting events and medieval banquets are held here in summer.

Berkeley is also home to the **Jenner Museum** (☎ 01453-810631; www.jennermuseum.com; Church Lane; adult/under 18yr £4.25/2.50; 12.30-5.30pm Tue-Sat, 1-5.30pm Sun Apr-Oct), which honours the life and works of Edward Jenner, country doctor and pioneer of vaccination. The museum is in the beautiful Queen Anne house, where the doctor performed the first smallpox vaccination in 1796. To get to the museum on foot, follow the path from the castle through **St Mary's churchyard**.

Bus 207 does the route between Berkeley and Gloucester (40 minutes, daily Monday to Saturday).

STROUD

pop 32,052

Stroud once hummed with the sound of industry, with over 150 cloth mills operating around the town, but when the bottom fell out of the market it fell heavily into decline, and is only today recovering from the downturn in its fortunes. Although only a handful of the handsome old mills are still operating, many others have been converted into apartments or offices and the pleasant town has become a Bohemian enclave littered with fair-trade and wholefood shops, delis and organic cafes. The picturesque Shambles still holds a market three times weekly and the Tudor town hall is also worth a look.

In the centre of town, the imposing Subscription Rooms are home to the **tourist office** (☎ 01453-760960; George St; ☟ 10am-5pm Mon-Sat), which can help with information for visiting mills in the area.

The main attraction is the diverting **Museum in the Park** (☎ 01453-763394; www.stroud.gov.uk /museum; Stratford Pk; admission free; ☟ 10am-5pm Tue-Fri, 11am-5pm Sat & Sun Apr-Oct, 10am-4pm Tue-Fri, 11am-4pm Sat & Sun Oct-Mar), set in an 18th-century mansion surrounded by parkland. The museum tells the history of the town and its cloth-making, and there are displays of everything from dinosaurs to Victorian toys and the world's first lawnmower.

For food, head for **Star Anise** (☎ 01453-761938; Gloucester St; mains £6-8; ☟ 8am-6pm Mon-Sat, 10am-2.30pm Sun), a vegetarian arts cafe serving good, fresh local produce, and a popular spot for Sunday brunch. It's also open for dinner (mains £9 to £11) on Saturday nights and often features live music.

Another good bet is **Woodruffs Organic Cafe** (☎ 01453-759195; 24 High St; mains £5-8; ☟ 9am-5.30pm Mon-Sat), a small, cheerful place with a wholesome selection of salads, soups and stews.

The nicest place to stay is in nearby Nailsworth at the 16th-century **Egypt Mill** (☎ 01453-833449; www.egyptmill.com; s £80-95, d £90-110; ℗), where you can fall asleep to the sound of the gurgling weir. The rooms vary quite a bit and it's definitely worth paying the extra tenner for a superior option.

Bus 46 runs hourly to Painswick (10 minutes) and Cheltenham (30 minutes), while bud 93 runs roughly hourly to Gloucester (25 minutes), both from Monday to Saturday. Trains run roughly hourly to London (£38, 1½ hours), Gloucester (£4.50, 20 minutes) and Cheltenham (£6.40, 40 minutes).

PAINSWICK

pop 1666

One of the most beautiful and unspoilt towns in the Cotswolds, hilltop Painswick is an absolute gem. Largely untouched since medieval times, totally unassuming and gloriously uncommercial, it's like gaining access to an outdoor museum that is strangely lost in time. Despite its obvious charms, Painswick sees only a trickle of visitors, so you can wander the narrow winding streets and admire the picture-perfect cottages, handsome stone town houses and medieval inns in your own good time.

The village centres on **St Mary's Church**, a fine, Perpendicular wool church surrounded by table-top tombs and 99 clipped yew trees. Legend has it that, should the hundredth yew tree be allowed to grow, the devil would appear and shrivel it. They planted it anyway – to celebrate the millennium – but there's been no sign of the Wicked One.

Sliding downhill beside and behind the church is a series of gorgeous streetscapes. Look out for **Bisley St**, the original main drag, which was superseded by the now ancient-looking New St in medieval times. Just south of the church, rare **iron stocks** stand in the street.

If you're visiting in late May, enquire about the **Coopers Hill cheese-rolling competition** (www .cheese-rolling.co.uk), held in the nearby village of Cranham. A 200-year-old tradition sees locals running, tumbling and sliding down a local hill in pursuit of a seven-pound block of Double Gloucester cheese. For the truly committed, there is also an uphill competition.

Painswick Rococo Garden

Just a mile north of town, the ostentatious **Painswick Rococo Garden** (☎ 01452-813204; www .rococogarden.co.uk; adult/under 16yr £5.50/2.75; ☟ 11am-5pm Jan-Oct) is the area's biggest attraction. These flamboyant pleasure gardens were designed by Benjamin Hyett in the 1740s and have now been restored to their former glory. Winding paths soften the otherwise strict geometrical precision, bringing visitors around the central vegetable garden to the many Gothic follies dotted in the grounds. There's also a children's nature trail and maze.

Sleeping & Eating

St Michaels (☎ 01452-814555; www.stmichaelsrestaurant .co.uk; Victoria St; d £80, 2/3-course dinner £28/32.50; ☟ lunch & dinner Wed-Sat, dinner Sun; ☐) The three rooms at St Michaels are a handsome mix of luxurious fabrics, exposed stone work, rustic furniture and carved woods. Each is individual in style and features flat-screen TVs, fresh-cut flowers and a sense of tranquil calm. The restaurant downstairs serves modern British and European cuisine with a touch of Asian and Czech influence.

Cardynham House (☎ 01452-814006; www.cardyn ham.co.uk; The Cross; s £65-85 d £80-185) The rooms at 15th-century Cardynham House offer four-poster beds, heavy-patterned fabrics and buckets of character. Choose the Shaker-style New England room, the opulent Arabian Nights room, the chintzy Old Tuscany room or for a private pool and garden, the Pool Room. Downstairs, the Bistro (mains £11.50-16.50; lunch Tuesday to Sunday, dinner Tuesday to Saturday) serves modern British cuisine.

For a light lunch or evening meal, the **Royal Oak Inn** (☎ 01452-813129; St Mary's St; mains £8-12) and the **Falcon Inn** (☎ 01452-814222; New St; mains £9-13) both do decent, if fairly standard, grub.

Getting There & Around
Bus 46 connects Cheltenham (30 minutes) and Stroud (10 minutes) with Painswick hourly Monday to Saturday. Bus 256 connects Painswick to Gloucester twice daily on Wednesday and Saturday.

GLOUCESTERSHIRE

After the crowds and coaches of the Cotswolds, Gloucestershire's languid charms are hard to beat, with its host of mellow stone villages and rustic allure. The county's greatest asset, however, is the elegant Regency town of Cheltenham, with its graceful, tree-lined terraces of pristine period houses, its upmarket boutiques and its tempting collection of accommodation and dining options.

The county capital, Gloucester, seems a dowdy cousin by comparison, but is well worth a visit for a glimpse of its magnificent Gothic cathedral. To the north, Tudor Tewkesbury follows the ecclesiastical splendour with a gracious Norman abbey surrounded by a town full of crooked, half-timbered houses. To the west, the picturesque Forest of Dean is a leafy backwater perfect for cycling and walking.

Information
Much of Gloucestershire falls into the Cotswold district. Information on sights, activities, accommodation and transport can be found on www.glos-cotswolds.com.

Activities
Gloucestershire's quiet roads, gentle gradients and numerous footpaths are ideal for walking and cycling. Tourist offices can help with route planning and they stock numerous guides to the trails.

Compass Holidays (☎ 01242-250642; www.compass -holidays.com; bikes per day/week from £12/52) hires bikes and also offers a bag-drop service along the Cotswold Way (£8 per bag per day, minimum two bags) as well as guided cycling tours of the area.

Getting Around
A host of companies operate bus services in Gloucestershire. Most tourist offices stock local bus timetables or can help with finding connecting services. As always, **Traveline** (☎ 0871 200 22 33; www.traveline.org.uk) has details of all routes.

CHELTENHAM
pop 98,875
The shining star of the region, Cheltenham is a historic but cosmopolitan hub at the western edge of the rustic Cotswolds. The city oozes an air of gracious refinement, its streetscapes largely left intact since its heyday as a spa resort in the 18th century. At the time, it rivalled Bath as *the* place for the sick, hypochondriac and merely moneyed to go, and today it is still riddled with historic buildings, beautifully proportioned terraces and manicured squares.

Cheltenham is an affluent kind of place, its well-heeled residents attracted by the genteel architecture, leafy crescents, wrought-iron balconies and expansive parks – all of which are kept in pristine condition. Bolt on a slew of festivals of all persuasions and a host of fine hotels, restaurants and shops, and it's easy to come to the conclusion that it's the perfect base to explore the region.

History
Cheltenham languished in relative obscurity, until pigeons were seen eating and thriving on salt crystals from a local spring in the early 18th century. It wasn't long before a pump was bored and Cheltenham began to establish itself as a spa town. Along with the sick, property speculators arrived in droves and the town started to grow dramatically. Graceful terraced housing was thrown up, parks were laid out and the rich and famous followed.

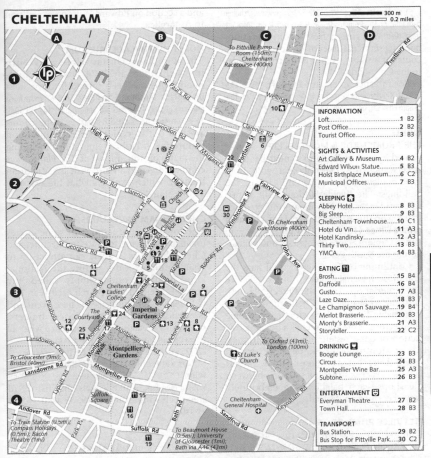

CHELTENHAM

INFORMATION	
Loft	1 B2
Post Office	2 B2
Tourist Office	3 B3

SIGHTS & ACTIVITIES	
Art Gallery & Museum	4 B2
Edward Wilson Statue	5 B3
Holst Birthplace Museum	6 C2
Municipal Offices	7 B3

SLEEPING	
Abbey Hotel	8 B3
Big Sleep	9 B3
Cheltenham Townhouse	10 C1
Hotel du Vin	11 A3
Hotel Kandinsky	12 A3
Thirty Two	13 B3
YMCA	14 B3

EATING	
Brosh	15 B4
Daffodil	16 B4
Gusto	17 A3
Laze Daze	18 B3
Le Champignon Sauvage	19 B3
Merlot Brasserie	20 B3
Monty's Brasserie	21 A3
Storyteller	22 C2

DRINKING	
Boogie Lounge	23 B3
Circus	24 B3
Montpellier Wine Bar	25 A3
Subtone	26 B3

ENTERTAINMENT	
Everyman Theatre	27 B2
Town Hall	28 B3

TRANSPORT	
Bus Station	29 B2
Bus Stop for Pittville Park	30 C2

OXFORD, THE COTSWOLDS & AROUND

By the time George III visited in 1788, the town's fate had been sealed and Cheltenham became the most fashionable holiday destination for England's upper crust. Handel, Samuel Johnson and Jane Austen all came here, and by the mid-19th century, the Victorian neo-Gothic Cheltenham College had sprung up, and, soon after, the genteel Cheltenham Ladies' College.

The town retained its period glamour and allure, and in the 20th century became known as the 'Anglo-Indian's Paradise' as so many Empire-serving, ex-military men retired here. Today, Cheltenham is the most complete Regency town in England, with millions being spent propping up the quick-buck buildings that the Regency entrepreneurs rushed to erect.

Orientation

Central Cheltenham is fairly compact and easy to get around on foot. High St runs roughly east–west; to its south is the Promenade, a more elegant shopping area, which extends into Montpellier, the town's most exclusive area. Pittville Park and the old Pump Room are a mile or so north of High St.

The bus station is behind the Promenade in the town centre, but the train station is out on a limb to the west; bus D runs to the town centre every 10 minutes.

Information

You'll find all the major banks and the main **post office** (☎ 0845 722 3344; 225-227 High St) on High St.

The **tourist office** (☎ 01242-522878; www.visitchelten
ham.info; 77 The Promenade; ⏱ 9.30am-5.15pm Mon-Sat,
from 10am Wed) runs a free accommodation-
booking service, sells event tickets and stocks
copies of walking, cycling and driving guides
to the Cotswolds.

For internet access, try the **Loft** (☎ 01242-
539573; 8-9 Henrietta St; per hr £4; ⏱ 10am-7pm Mon-Thu,
to 6pm Fri & Sat, noon-5pm Sun).

Sights

THE PROMENADE & MONTPELLIER
Famed as one of England's most beautiful
streetscapes, the **Promenade** is a wide, tree-
lined boulevard flanked by imposing period
buildings. The **Municipal Offices**, built as private residences in 1825, are among the most
striking on this street and they face a **statue of
Edward Wilson** (1872–1912), a local man who
joined Captain Scott's ill-fated second expedition to the South Pole.

Continuing on from here, you'll pass the
grandiose **Imperial Gardens**, built to service
the Imperial Spa (now the Queens Hotel),
en route to **Montpellier**, Cheltenham's most
fashionable district. Along with the handsome
architecture of the area, there's a buzzing collection of bars, restaurants and boutiques.
Along Montpellier Walk, **caryatids** (draped
female figures based on those on the Acropolis
in Athens) act as structural supports between
the shops, each balancing an elaborately
carved cornice on its head.

PITTVILLE PUMP ROOM
Built in 1830 as a centrepiece to a vast estate,
the **Pittville Pump Room** (☎ 01242-227979; www
.pittvillepumproom.org.uk; Pittville Park; admission free;
⏱ 10am-4pm Wed-Mon) is Cheltenham's finest
Regency building. Originally used as a spa
and social centre, it is now used as a concert
hall. You can wander into the main auditorium and sample the pungent spa waters, or
just explore the vast parklands and lake it
overlooks.

ART GALLERY & MUSEUM
Cheltenham's excellent **Art Gallery & Museum**
(☎ 01242-237431; www.cheltenham.artgallery.museum;
Clarence St; admission free; ⏱ 10am-5.20pm Mon-Sat) is well
worth a visit for its depiction of Cheltenham
life through the ages. It also has wonderful
displays on William Morris and the Arts and
Crafts Movement (p534), as well as Dutch and
British art, rare Chinese and English ceramics

and a section on Edward Wilson's expedition
to Antarctica.

HOLST BIRTHPLACE MUSEUM
The composer Gustav Holst was born
in Cheltenham in 1874, and his childhood home has been turned into the **Holst
Birthplace Museum** (☎ 01242-524846; www.holst
museum.org.uk; 4 Clarence Rd; adult/under 16yr £3.50/3;
⏱ 10am-4pm Tue-Sat mid-Feb–mid-Dec). The rooms
are laid out in typical period fashion and
feature much Holst memorabilia, including
the piano on which most of *The Planets* was
composed. You can also visit the Victorian
kitchen, which explains what life was like
'below stairs'.

CHELTENHAM RACECOURSE
The town is more famous in some circles
for its horse racing than its architecture, and
Cheltenham's racecourse can attract up to
40,000 punters a day during the National
Hunt Festival, often simply called 'the
Festival'. Held in mid-March each year, this
is England's premier steeplechase event and
is attended by droves of breeders, trainers,
riders and spectators. To experience what all
the fuss is about, buy your **tickets** (☎ 01242-
226226; www.cheltenham.co.uk) well in advance.

For race enthusiasts the **Hall of Fame museum** (☎ 01242-513014; admission free; ⏱ 8.30am-
5.30pm Mon-Fri), which charts the history of
steeplechasing since 1819, is well worth
a visit.

Tours
Guided 1¼-hour **walking tours** (£4; ⏱ 11am Mon-Fri,
11.30am Sat late Jun–mid-Sep) of Regency Cheltenham
depart from the tourist office. You can also
book tickets for a rolling program of day-long
coach tours (adult/under 12yr £29/14) to various locations in the Cotswolds here.

Festivals & Events
Cheltenham is renowned as a city of festivals,
and throughout the year you'll find major
events going on in the city. For more information or to book tickets, visit www.cheltenham
festivals.com.
Folk Festival A showcase of traditional and new-age folk
talent in February.
National Hunt Festival The hottest week in the racing
calendar on both sides of the Irish Sea; in March.
Jazz Festival An imaginative program hailed as the UK's
finest jazz fest, held in April.

Science Festival Exploring the delights and intrigues of the world of science in June.

Music Festival A celebration of traditional and contemporary sounds with a geographical theme, in July.

Literature Festival A 10-day celebration of writers and the written word in October.

Sleeping

Cheltenham has an excellent choice of hotels and B&Bs, but few options in the budget range. Book as far in advance as possible during the festivals – especially for race week.

YMCA (☎ 01242-524024; www.cheltenhamymca.com; 6 Victoria Walk; dm/s £18.50/27.50) This elegant building right in the city centre now houses the cheapest beds in town. The four-bed dorms are fairly basic and well worn, but it's a great location and you'll find nothing else at this rate.

Big Sleep (☎ 01242-696999; www.thebigsleephotel .com; Wellington St; r £65-90; P 🖳) A luxury budget hotel, the Big Sleep chain offers stylish minimalism with thoroughly modern rooms featuring flat-screen TVs. At this price, it's an absolute steal, and if you're travelling with friends or family, the large family or group rooms make it an even better deal. You can also bring your own food and eat it in the bar.

Cheltenham Townhouse (☎ 01242-221922; www .cheltenhamtownhouse.co.uk; 12 Pittville Lawn; s £55-95, d £70-120; P 🖳) Modern decor with pale, neutral colours, stylish accessories, DVD players and broadband make this central option a good bet for a midrange budget. The Townhouse is set on a quiet street just out of the centre, but the spacious rooms and sparkling bathrooms make it worth the trip.

Beaumont House (☎ 01242-223311; www.bhhotel .co.uk; 56 Shurdington Rd; s £63-184, d £86-201; P 🖳) Set in a large garden just a short way from the centre of town, this boutique guesthouse is a memorable place with a range of carefully designed rooms with opulent decor. Go for the full-on safari look in Out of Africa, sultry boudoir in Out of Asia or more subtle design in the Prestbury Suite.

Hotel Kandinsky (☎ 01242-527788; www.aliashotels .com; Bayshill Rd; s £95, d £125-155; P) Gloriously quirky, keenly priced and extravagantly decked out, this is a 'funkier than average' hotel, with lots of eclectic modern art, exotic furniture, designer style and an extremely efficient but laid-back attitude. The slick, modern Cafe Paradiso (mains £14 to £19) serves an ambitious modern British menu.

our pick Thirty Two (☎ 01242-771110; www.thirty twoltd.com; 32 Imperial Square; s/d from £139/154; P 🖳 wifi) In a league of its own, this slick, boutique B&B is a rare find. It may charge hotel prices, but it's well worth it. You get the personal service of a B&B but the luxury, style and comfort of a top-notch hotel. Expect views over the Imperial gardens, muted colours, contemporary artwork, luxurious fabrics and rooms that could easily feature in a glossy style magazine.

Other options:

Abbey Hotel (☎ 01242-516053; www.abbeyhotel -cheltenham.com; 14-16 Bath Pde; s/d from £35/75; P) Convenient location and affordable prices but lacklustre rooms.

Hotel du Vin (☎ 01242-588450; www.hotelduvin.com; Parabola Rd; r from £145; P 🖳) Sleek, stylish and very hip – another winning offer from this luxury hotel chain.

Eating

Cheltenham has a great choice of top-end places to eat, but apart from the usual chains there's little choice for those on a meagre budget. For the best range of options, head to Montpellier or the area around Suffolk Square.

Gusto (☎ 01242-239111; 12 Montpellier Walk; mains £6-8; 🕒 9.30am-6pm Mon-Thu, to 6.30pm Fri, to 5.30pm Sat) This Italian-style deli and cafe is a great place for lunchtime treats made with authentic Italian ingredients. Choose from pizzas, salads, meats and gorgeous pastas (try the gorgonzola and walnut for a real taste sensation).

Storyteller (☎ 01242-250343; 11 North Pl; mains £8-15) Feel-good comfort food draws the crowds to this enduringly popular restaurant that dishes up generous portions of barbecue ribs, seafood platters and vegetarian burritos on a menu fusing tastes from as far afield as Mexico and Asia.

Laze Daze (☎ 01242-257878; 81 The Promenade; mains £9-17) Overlooking the Promenade and just a stone's throw from the tourist office, this relaxed place serves a good range of contemporary brasserie-style food ranging from Barbary duck and venison steak to stuffed peppers and steamed mussels. The lunch and early evening set menus are a great deal (two/three courses £10/13).

Merlot Brasserie (☎ 01242-574008; 2a Ormond Terrace, Regent St; mains £11-16) A popular option right in the centre of town, the Merlot offers a menu of modern Mediterranean flavours.

It's a stylish place with contemporary design, subtle lighting and leather seats, and is a good option for lunch (mains £8 to £9).

Brosh (☎ 01242-227277; 8 Suffolk Pde; mains £14-18; ⊙ dinner Wed-Sat) This lovely little place serves excellent eastern Mediterranean food with a great selection of meze and vegetarian dishes, as well as such delicacies as roast quail, lamb kefta and chargrilled chicken with sumac.

Daffodil (☎ 01242-700055; 18-20 Suffolk Pde; mains £14-19) A perennial favourite, the Daffodil is as loved for its top-notch modern British brasserie-style food as for its flamboyant surroundings. Set in a converted art-deco cinema, it harks back to the Roaring Twenties and features live jazz and blues every Monday night.

Other good options:

Le Champignon Sauvage (☎ 01242-573449; 24-26 Suffolk Rd; set menu 2-/3-course £39/48; ⊙ Tue-Sat) An unpretentious but oh-so-delectable restaurant that has earned two Michelin stars for its inspired French cuisine.

Monty's Brasserie (☎ 01242-227678; 41 St George's Rd; mains £12-19; ⊙ lunch & dinner) Bright, buzzing brasserie and seafood restaurant with a great lunch menu (£8 to £10).

Drinking

Thanks to its rather genteel nature, Cheltenham isn't the spot for a raucous night out. The following are the best in town.

Boogie Lounge (☎ 01242-238001; 1A Imperial Lane; admission £2-5; ⊙ 10pm-2am Wed-Sat) Late-night club and music venue featuring everything from 1970s funk to '80s cheese and '90s pop. It's real floor-filling stuff and can get packed despite having two bars.

Subtone (☎ 01242-575925; 117 The Promenade; admission £2-6; ⊙ 8pm-late Thu-Sat) One of the city's most popular venues, Subtone has three floors of DJs and live music at its basement club and piano bar. Expect everything from jazz and house to funk and rock.

Montpellier Wine Bar (☎ 01242-527774; Bayshill Lodge, Montpellier St; ⊙ 10am-11pm) Slick, sophisticated and self-consciously cool, this is where Cheltenham's beautiful people come to hang out, sip wine and dine on modern British food (mains £12 to £17). There's an extensive wine list, cask ales and plenty of people-watching.

Circus (☎ 01242-578393; 5 Queen's Circus; ⊙ 11am-11pm Mon-Sat, noon-10.30pm Sun) Giant windows look out over the busy street at this chic but relaxed Montpellier bar. It's the kind of place where you chill out in a big leather chair and sup a drink, rather than downing a few pints before a night out.

Entertainment

The **Everyman Theatre** (☎ 01242-572573; www .everymantheatre.org.uk; Regent St) is Cheltenham's main stage and hosts everything from Elvis impersonators to comedy and panto, while the modern **Bacon Theatre** (☎ 01242-258002; www .bacontheatre.co.uk; Hatherly Rd) showcases touring shows, jazz and ballet. Classical-music lovers should look out for concerts at the **Pittville Pump Room** (☎ 01242-227979; www.pittvillepumproom .org.uk; Pittville Park). The **town hall** (☎ 01242-227979; www.cheltenhamtownhall.org.uk; Imperial Sq) offers more mainstream talent as well as hosting many festival events.

Getting There & Away

For information on public transport to and from Cheltenham, pick up a free copy of the handy *Getting There by Public Transport* guide from the tourist office.

BUS

National Express runs buses to London roughly hourly (£18, 3½ hours), and Swanbrook bus 853 goes to Oxford three times daily Monday to Saturday and once on Sunday (£7, 1½ hours).

Bus 94 (30 minutes) runs to Gloucester every 10 minutes Monday to Saturday and every 20 minutes on Sunday. Bus 51 goes to Cirencester (40 minutes, hourly).

Pulhams bus 801 runs to Moreton (one hour) via Bourton (35 minutes) and Stow (50 minutes) seven times daily Monday to Saturday. Castleways Coaches 606 runs four times daily Monday to Saturday to Broadway (50 minutes) via Winchcombe (20 minutes).

TRAIN

Cheltenham has trains to London (£50, 2¼ hours), Bristol (£9.20, 50 minutes), Gloucester (£3.10, nine minutes) and Bath (£14.30, 1¼ hours) roughly every half-hour.

Getting Around

Compass Holidays (☎ 01242-250642; www.compass -holidays.com; bikes per day/week from £12/52) has bicycles for hire at the train station. Bus D runs to Pittville Park from Portland St every 10 minutes.

TEWKESBURY

pop 9978

Tudor-heavy Tewkesbury hit the headlines in July 2007 when the Rivers Avon and Severn, which meet here, burst their banks and the town suffered some of the worst flooding in British history. Today there's little evidence to suggest anything untoward happened at all, the crooked half-timbered houses, buckled roof lines and narrow alleyways remain stuck in medieval glory, and the town's higgledy-piggledy charm is as apparent as ever. Take time to wander the ancient passageways that lead up to the town from the rivers, and then wander along Church St to the town's most glorious building, the magnificent medieval abbey church.

The **tourist office** (☎ 01684-855040; www.visitcots woldsandsevernvale.gov.uk; 100 Church St; ☿ 9.30am-5pm Mon-Sat year-round, 10am-4pm Sun Easter-Oct) is housed in a 17th-century hat shop that's also home to the **Out of the Hat** (www.outofthehat.org.uk; adult/child £4.70/2.50) heritage centre. It explores the history of the town and the restoration of the building and has plenty of interactive games for young visitors.

The town also has a second small **museum** (☎ 01684-292901; www.tewkesburymuseum.org; 64 Barton St; adult/child £1.50/75p; ☿ 1-4.30pm Tue-Fri, 11am-4pm Sat Mar-Aug, noon-3pm Tue-Fri, 11am-3pm Sat Sep-Oct, Sat only Nov-Mar) housed in a timber-framed building, which displays finds from Roman and medieval times as well as hosting an exhibition on Antarctic exploration.

Tewkesbury Abbey

This magnificent **abbey** (☎ 01684-850959; www .tewkesburyabbey.org.uk; guided tours £3; ☿ 7.30am-6pm, to 5pm Oct-Apr) is one of Britain's largest churches, far bigger than many of the country's cathedrals. The Norman abbey, built for the Benedictine monks, was consecrated in 1121 and was one of the last monasteries to be dissolved by Henry VIII. Although many of the monastery buildings were destroyed, the abbey church survived after being bought by the townspeople for the princely sum of £453 in 1542.

The church has a massive 40m-high tower and some spectacular Norman piers and arches in the nave. The Decorated-style chancel dates from the 14th century, however, and still retains much of its original stained glass. The church also features an organ dating from 1631, originally made for Magdalen College, Oxford, and an extensive collection of medieval tombs. The most interesting is that of John Wakeman, the last abbot, who is shown as a vermin-ridden skeleton.

The church makes a wonderfully atmospheric venue for a range of summer concerts. You can find information on the website or at the **visitor centre** (☿ 10am-5.30pm Mon-Sat Apr-Sep) by the gate, which also houses an exhibition on the abbey's history.

Sleeping & Eating

Ivydene House (☎ 01684-592453; www.ivydenehouse .net; Uckinghall; s/d £45/70; **P**) This gorgeous B&B is well out of town but such a gem you'll be delighted you made the effort to get here. The rooms are luxuriously styled with a mix of contemporary fashion, classic furniture, soft colour schemes and gorgeous fabrics. Uckinghall is 7 miles north of Tewkesbury off the A38.

Aubergine (☎ 01684-292703; 73 Church St; mains £10-17; ☿ Tue-Sat) Set in a 15th-century building that's decidedly modern inside, this place is a welcome change from Tewkesbury's tearooms. The menu ranges from standard fare to more adventurous dishes such as venison casserole with honey and roast cardamom vegetables.

My Great Grandfathers (☎ 01684-292687; www .mygreatgrandfathers.com; 84-85 Church St; mains £9-15; ☿ Wed-Sun) Exposed oak beams and half-timbered walls set the tone in this otherwise modern place serving excellent afternoon teas and an interesting menu of classic and modern British cuisine.

Getting There & Away

Bus 41 (25 minutes) runs to Cheltenham every 15 minutes and hourly on Sunday, and bus 71 (30 minutes, hourly) goes to Gloucester. The nearest train station is 1½ miles away at Ashchurch.

GLOUCESTER

pop 123,205

Gloucester (*glos*-ter) began life as a settlement for retired Roman soldiers, but really came into its own in medieval times when the pious public brought wealth and prosperity to what was then a prime pilgrimage city. The faithful flocked to see the grave of Edward the II and soon financed the building of what remains one of England's most beautiful cathedrals with an exquisite cloister.

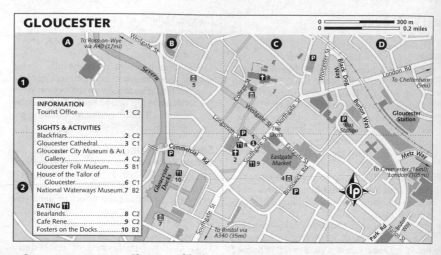

In more recent years, Gloucester felt the brunt of hard times and the city fell into serious decline. The centre remains a rather dowdy, workaday place with brutalist architecture and a glut of greasy spoon cafes. But scratch under the surface and you'll find a glimmer of medieval character and the beginnings of a city trying hard to transform its fortunes. The historic docks are now home to trendy apartments, lively restaurants and interesting museums and are well worth a wander. Despite this, Gloucester makes a better day trip than a destination in itself.

Orientation & Information

The city centre is based on a medieval cruciform pattern, with Northgate, Southgate, Eastgate and Westgate Sts converging on the Cross.

The **tourist office** (☎ 01452-396572; www.visit gloucester.info; 28 Southgate St; ⏱ 10am-5pm Mon-Sat Sep-Jun, 11am-3pm Sun Jul & Aug) is conveniently located in the centre of town.

Sights

GLOUCESTER CATHEDRAL

The main reason to visit Gloucester is to see its magnificent **Gothic cathedral** (☎ 01452-528095; www.gloucestercathedral.org.uk; College Green; suggested donation £3; ⏱ 8am-6pm), a stunning example of English Perpendicular style. Originally the site of a Saxon abbey, a Norman church was built here by a group of Benedictine monks in the 12th century, and when Edward II was murdered in 1327, the church was chosen as

his burial place. Edward's tomb proved so popular, however, that Gloucester became a centre of pilgrimage and the income generated from the pious pilgrims financed the church's conversion into the magnificent building seen today.

Inside, the cathedral skilfully combines the best of Norman and Gothic design with sturdy columns, creating a sense of gracious solidity and wonderful Norman arcading draped with beautiful mouldings. From the elaborate 14th-century wooden choir stalls, you'll get a good view of the imposing **Great East Window**, one of the largest in England.

To see the window in more detail, head for the **Tribune Gallery**, where you can also see an **exhibition** (admission £2; ⏱ 10.30am-4pm Mon-Fri, to 3pm Sat) on its creation. As you walk around the **Whispering Gallery**, you'll notice that even the quietest of murmurs reverberates across the wonderfully elaborate lierne vaulting. Beneath the window in the northern ambulatory is Edward II's magnificent tomb, and nearby is the late-15th-century **Lady Chapel**, a glorious patchwork of stained glass.

One of the cathedral's greatest treasures, however, is the exquisite **Great Cloister**. Completed in 1367, it is the first example of fan vaulting in England and is only matched in beauty by Henry VIII's Chapel at Westminster Abbey. You (or your children) might recognise the cloister from the first two Harry Potter films: it was used in the corridor scenes at Hogwart's School.

A wonderful way to take in the glory of the cathedral is to attend one of the many musical recitals and concerts held here. The stunning acoustics and breathtaking surroundings are pretty much guaranteed to make your hair stand on end.

For more cathedral insights and a fantastic view of the town, climb the 69m **tower** on an hour-long guided **tour** (adult/under 16yr £3/1; ☺ tours 2.30pm Wed-Fri, 1.30pm & 2.30pm Sat & bank holidays). Because of the steep steps it's not recommended for children under 10. Civic Trust volunteers also provide guided tours of the **cathedral** (☺ 10.45am-3.15pm Mon-Sat, noon-2.30pm Sun).

OTHER SIGHTS & ACTIVITIES

A major part of the city's regeneration is taking place at **Gloucester Docks**, once Britain's largest inland port. Fifteen beautiful Victorian warehouses, many now restored, surround the canal basins and house a series of museums, shops and cafes, plus a large antiques centre.

The largest warehouse, Llanthony, is home to the newly revamped **National Waterways Museum** (☎ 01452-318200; www.nwm.org.uk; adult/under 16yr £4/3; ☺ 10am-5pm), a hands-on kind of place where you can discover the history of inland waterways. Exhibitions explain what life was like living, working and moving on the water, featuring plenty of historic boats and interactive exhibits that are great for children. Included in the admission price is a 45-minute **boat trip** (non-museum visitors adult/under 16yr £4.75/3.50; ☺ noon, 1.30 & 2.30pm Apr-Oct) along the canal.

For more local history, the **Gloucester Folk Museum** (☎ 01452-396868; 99-103 Westgate St; admission free, ☺ 10am-5pm Tue-Sat) examines domestic life, crafts and industries from 1500 to the present. The museum is housed in a wonderful series of Tudor and Jacobean timber-framed buildings dating from the 16th and 17th centuries.

Also worth visiting are 13th-century **Blackfriars** (Ladybellgate St; admission free), one of Britain's best-preserved Dominican friaries, and the **Gloucester City Museum & Art Gallery** (☎ 01452-396131; www.gloucester.gov.uk/citymuseum; Brunswick Rd; admission free; ☺ 10am-5pm Tue-Sat), which houses everything from dinosaur fossils and Roman artefacts to paintings by the artists Turner and Gainsborough.

Tours

The Civic Trust operates one-hour guided **walking tours** (☎ 01452-396572; adult £3-4; ☺ Jun-Sep) of the city leaving from the tourist office on Southgate St at 2pm. Tours include a Historic

Gloucester Walk, Beatrix Potter tours, cathedral tours, ghost walks, historic dock tours and Blackfriars tours. You can also pick up a free *Via Sacra* self-guided walk brochure from the tourist office, which will guide you on an hour-long walking trail around the city's most historic buildings.

Sleeping & Eating

Gloucester's accommodation options are pretty grim. You'd be far better off staying in Cheltenham (10 minutes by train) instead.

Fosters on the Docks (☎ 01452-300990; Kimberley Warehouse; mains £7-10; ☺ 10am-11.30pm Mon-Sat, 11am-10.30pm Sun) The most lively option down at the historic docks is this cheerful place serving tapas, traditional grills and Mediterranean dishes including pizza and pasta. There's a nice conservatory overlooking the water, as well as more cosy dining in the industrial chic interior.

Cafe Rene (☎ 01452-309340; www.caferene.co.uk; 31 Southgate St; mains £7-10; ☺ noon-11.30pm) For a decent but predictable choice of pub grub head to this cheery joint through the archway on Southgate. There's live music on Wednesday nights and a pleasant beer garden outside. Food is served until 9.30pm and includes everything from wraps and sandwiches (£4.50) at lunch to burgers, chilli, pasta and curry by night.

Bearlands (☎ 01452-419966; Longsmith St; 2/3-course dinner £23/25; ☺ closed Mon & Sun) Crisp white linen, a large airy conservatory and an atmospheric vaulted wine cellar make Bearlands an interesting and popular venue. It's a stylish place serving a competent modern British menu in relaxing surroundings.

Getting There & Away

National Express has buses roughly every two hours to London (£18, 3½ hours). Bus 94 runs to Cheltenham (30 minutes, six hourly), with an express bus X94 cutting the journey to 15 minutes during rush hour. The quickest journey between the two cities is by train (10 minutes, every 20 minutes).

FOREST OF DEAN
pop 79,982

An ancient woodland with a unique, almost magical character, the Forest of Dean is the oldest oak forest in England and a wonderfully scenic place to walk, cycle or paddle. Its steep, wooded hills, winding, tree-lined

THE TAILOR OF GLOUCESTER

Beatrix Potter's magical tale of good-hearted mice saving a feverish Gloucester tailor from ruin was inspired by a local legend about real-life tailor John Prichard. Like the tailor in Potter's tale, Prichard had been commissioned to make a coat for the mayor, but left the garment at cutting stage on a Friday night. He returned on Monday to find it finished, save for a single button hole. A note pinned to it read 'No more twist'.

Commercially minded Mr Prichard was soon encouraging people to come in and see his workshop where 'waistcoats are made at night by the fairies'. In reality, his two assistants had slept off a Saturday night bender at the workshop and woke to see the faithful heading to the cathedral for mass. Consumed by guilt and hoping to make amends, they had tried to finish the coat but ran out of thread.

The **House of the Tailor of Gloucester** (☎ 01452-422856; 9 College Ct; ☸ 10am-4pm Mon-Sat, to 4pm Sun), the house that Potter used in her illustrations, is now a museum and souvenir shop dedicated to the author.

roads and glimmering lakes make it a remarkably tranquil place, and an excellent spot for outdoor pursuits.

The forest was formerly a royal hunting ground and a centre of iron and coal mining, and its mysterious depths were supposedly the inspiration for Tolkien's setting in *The Lord of the Rings* and for JK Rowling's Harry Potter adventures. Numerous other writers, poets, artists and craftspeople have been inspired by the stunning scenery, designated England's first National Forest Park in 1938.

Covering 42 sq miles between Gloucester, Ross-on-Wye and Chepstow, the forest is in an isolated position, but Coleford, the main population centre, has good transport connections.

The **tourist office** (☎ 01594-812388; www.visit forestofdean.co.uk; High St, Coleford; ☸ 10am-5pm Mon-Sat Apr-Sep, to 2pm Sun Jul & Aug, to 4pm Mon-Fri Oct-Mar, to 2pm Sat Oct, Feb & Mar) stocks walking and cycling guides and also offers a free accommodation booking service. If you've got your own transport, pick up the *Royal Forest Route* and *Heritage Trail* leaflets, which describe tours through the forest and its most significant sights.

Sights & Activities

Your first stop should be the **Dean Heritage Centre** (☎ 01594-822170; www.deanheritagemuseum .com; Camp Mill, Soudley; adult/under 16yr £5/3; ☸ 10am-5pm Mar-Oct, to 4pm Sat & Sun Nov-Feb), which explains the history of the forest and its free miners from medieval times to the industrial age. There's also a reconstructed forest home, adventure playground and art gallery on site.

If you're travelling with children, **Puzzle Wood** (☎ 01594-833187; www.puzzlewood.net; adult/ under 12yr £4/3; ☸ 10am-5.30pm Apr-Sep, 11am-4pm Oct) is a must. This overgrown pre-Roman, open-cast ore mine has a maze of paths, weird rock formations, tangled vines and eerie passageways and offers a real sense of discovery. Puzzle Wood is 1 mile south of Coleford on the B4228.

Mined for iron ore for more than 4000 years, the **Clearwell Caves** (☎ 01594-832535; www .clearwellcaves.com; adult/under 16yr £5.50/3; ☸ 10am-5pm Feb-Oct) are a warren of passageways, caverns and pools that help explain the forest's history of mining. The caves are signposted off the B4228 a mile south of Coleford.

In contrast to the caves, **Hopewell Colliery** (☎ 01594-810706; www.hopewellcoalmine.co.uk; adult/ under 14yr £4/3; ☸ 10am-4pm Easter-Oct) offers underground tours of the mine workings, with miners as guides. The colliery is on the B4226 between Coleford and Cinderford.

In Newland, you can visit the 'Cathedral of the Forest', the 13th-century **All Saints**. The church was restored and partially rebuilt in the 19th century and houses some fine stained-glass windows, as well as a unique brass depicting a miner with a *nelly* (tallow candle) in his mouth, a pick in his hand and a *billy* (backpack) on his back.

Sleeping & Eating

our pick **St Briavels Castle YHA** (☎ 0845 371 9042; www .yha.org.uk; Lydney; dm from £15.95; **P**) Live like a king for a night at this unique hostel set in an imposing moated castle once used as King John's hunting lodge. Loaded with character and a snip at this price, the hostel also hosts lively medieval banquets on Mondays, Wednesdays and Saturdays in August.

Old Nibley Farmhouse (☎ 01594-516770; www .oldnibleyfarmhouse.co.uk; Nibley Hill, Blakeney; s/d £36/72) Set in a 300-year-old farmhouse, this warm and friendly B&B has a range of bright and pretty rooms with pale fabrics and furnishings livened up with a dash of colour in the cushions and throws. The sitting room has a large fireplace and exposed beams; a cosy enclave on a wet weekend.

Tudor Farmhouse Hotel (☎ 01594-833046; www .tudorfarmhousehotel.co.uk; High St, Clearwell; s £60, d £90-140) You'll find oak beams, exposed stonework and old-world charm at this rustic 13th-century hotel and former farmhouse. There's a wide variety of rooms, from comfortable singles to luxurious four-posters and a popular restaurant (dinner mains £15 to £20) serving modern British fare.

Three Choirs Vineyard (☎ 01531-890223; www .threechoirs.com; Newent; s £85-125, d £95-135; P) This working vineyard has a range of extremely comfortable, classically styled rooms overlooking the sweeping fields of vines. You can also take a guided tour of the vineyard (£8), try the award-winning wines and then relax over lunch (mains £11 to £15) or dinner (mains £17 to £20) in the bright and airy restaurant. There's also a gift shop and microbrewery on site.

Garden Cafe (☎ 01594-860075; www.gardencafe .co.uk; Lwr Lydbrook; mains £8-13; ☾ lunch Fri, Sat & Sun, dinner Fri, Sat & Mon) An award-winning organic cafe on the banks of the River Wye, this place is set in a converted malt house and surrounded by a beautiful walled garden. The food ranges from classic dishes such as pork schnitzel to the more exotic Imam Byaldi: stuffed aubergine with pine nuts, tomato and raisins.

Getting There & Around

From Gloucester, bus 31 (one hour, half-hourly) runs to Coleford and there are trains to Lydney (20 minutes, hourly). The **Dean Forest Railway** (☎ 01594-845840; www.deanforestrailway.co.uk) runs steam trains from Lydney to Parkend (day tickets adult/under 16 years £9/5) on selected days from March to December.

You can hire road/mountain/premium bikes (£14/18/22 per day), buy maps and get advice on cycling routes at **Pedalabikeaway** (☎ 01594-860065; www.pedalabikeaway.com; Cannop Valley; ☾ Tue-Sun) near Coleford.

HERTFORDSHIRE

Firmly on the commuter belt and within easy reach of the capital, Hertfordshire is a small, sleepy county liberally scattered with satellite towns that threaten to overtake the fast-disappearing countryside. However, it is also home to the historic town of St Albans, with its elegant Georgian streetscapes and Roman remains, and to Hatfield House, a spectacular stately home well worth the effort to visit.

ST ALBANS
pop 114,710

A bustling market town with a host of crooked Tudor buildings and elegant Georgian town houses, St Albans makes a pleasant day trip from London. The town was founded as Verulamium after the Roman invasion of AD 43, but was renamed St Albans in the 3rd century after a Roman soldier, Alban, lost his head in punishment for sheltering a Christian priest. He became England's first Christian martyr and the small city soon became a site of pilgrimage.

The pilgrims brought business and, subsequently, wealth to the town, and eventually the object of their affection was enshrined in what is now a magnificent cathedral. The town is also home to an excellent Roman museum, an array of chichi shops and upmarket restaurants and some wonderful pubs.

Orientation & Information

St Peter's St, 10 minutes' walk west of the train station on Victoria St, is the focus of the town but is scarred by an ugly array of plastic shop fronts. Get off the main drag to discover the quiet back streets lined with elegant buildings or follow George St into Fishpool St, a charming lane that winds its way past old-world pubs to leafy Verulamium Park.

The **tourist office** (☎ 01727-864511; www.stalbans .gov.uk; Market Pl; ☾ 10am-5pm Mon-Sat, to 4pm every 2nd Sun & mid-Jul–mid-Sep) is in the grand town hall in the marketplace. It stocks the *St Albans City Trail*, a free guide to the town's most historic buildings. It's also the best place for information on a dizzying array of themed guided walks (adult/child £3/1.50) that take place throughout the year.

Sights
ST ALBANS CATHEDRAL

Set in tranquil grounds away from the din of the main streets, St Albans' magnificent

cathedral (☎ 01727-890200; www.stalbanscathedral.org.uk; admission by donation; ☯ 8am-5.45pm) is a lesson in architectural history. The church began life as a Benedictine monastery in 793, built by King Offa of Mercia around the tomb of St Alban. In Norman times, it was completely rebuilt using material from the old Roman town of Verulamium, and then, in the 12th and 13th centuries, Gothic extensions and decorations were added.

The deceptively simple nave gives way to stunningly ornate ceilings, semi-lost wall paintings, an elaborate nave screen and, of course, the shrine of St Alban. There's also a luminescent rose window from the 20th century. The best way to appreciate the wealth of history contained in the building is to join a **free guided tour** (☯ 11.30am & 2.30pm Mon-Fri, 11.30am & 2pm Sat, 2.30pm Sun). If you miss the tour you can pick up a very helpful free plan and guide at the entrance.

VERULAMIUM MUSEUM & ROMAN RUINS

A fantastic exposé of everyday life under the Romans, the **Verulamium Museum** (☎ 01727-751810; www.stalbansmuseums.org.uk; St Michael's St; adult/child £3.30/2; ☯ 10am-5.30pm Mon-Sat, 2-5.30pm Sun) is home to a large collection of arrowheads, glassware and grave goods. Its centrepiece, however, is the **Mosaic Room**, where five superb mosaic floors, uncovered between 1930 and 1955, are laid out. You can also see recreations of Roman rooms, and learn about life in the settlement through interactive and audiovisual displays. Every second weekend, the museum is invaded by Roman soldiers who demonstrate the tactics and tools of the Roman army.

Adjacent **Verulamium Park** has remains of a basilica, bathhouse and parts of the city wall. You can pick up a map of the area with information on the site from the museum or tourist office.

Across the busy A4147 are the grassy foundations of a **Roman theatre** (☎ 01727-835035; www.romantheatre.co.uk; adult/child £2/1; ☯ 10am-5pm Mar-Oct, to 4pm Nov-Feb), which once seated 2000 spectators.

OTHER SIGHTS

For a potted history of St Albans, take a look at the local **museum** (☎ 01727-819340; www.stalbansmuseums.org.uk; Hatfield Rd; admission free; ☯ 10am-5pm Mon-Sat, 2-5pm Sun), which houses displays from Roman times to the present.

ST ALBANS BEER FESTIVAL

Beer is big business in England, and to pint-swilling connoisseurs, real ale is the only brew that matters. To celebrate its key role in national culture, Camra (the Campaign for Real Ale) hosts a four-day beer festival in St Albans at the end of September. Close to 5000 people converge on the Alban Arena off St Peter's St to sample and talk about the 300-odd real ales on tap. (For more information on real ales, see p79). With food, music and ale on offer, and tickets a mere £2.50 to £4, it's a great excuse for a party. For more information, see www.stalbansbeerfestival.info.

On High St, you'll find England's only medieval **clock tower** (High St; adult/child 80/40p; ☯ 10.30am-5pm Sat, Sun & bank holidays Apr-Oct), a fine flint tower built around 1410. 'Gabriel' (the original bell) is still there.

Sleeping & Eating

Park House (☎ 01727-811910; www.parkhouseonline.co.uk; 30 The Park; s/d £35/55; P 🖳 wi-fi) Bright rooms with crisp, white linens, white wicker chairs and subtle floral patterns give this small B&B a fresh and airy feel. It's set in a quiet residential area within walking distance of town, and is a good deal for the price.

St Michael's Manor (☎ 01727-864444; www.stmichaelsmanor.com; Fishpool St; r from £145; P 🖳) Set in beautiful grounds complete with a glistening lake, this elegant, classically styled hotel has a range of comfortable rooms with views over the gracious gardens. An air of restrained luxury permeates the place, with tip-top service in the modern British restaurant (mains £14 to £20).

Lussmanns Eatery (☎ 01727-851941; Waxhouse Gate; mains £7-16; ☯ 11.30am-10pm Mon-Thu, to 10.30pm Fri & Sat, to 9pm Sun) This bright, modern restaurant just off the High St is enduringly popular with locals despite ample competition around town. It serves a menu of mainly Mediterranean dishes in a bright, modern space with oak, leather and metal decor.

Mantra (☎ 01727-811115; 6 The Collonade; mains £9-12; ☯ closed dinner Sun) Excellent modern Japanese food is on the menu at this slick joint where sushi, sashimi and maki compete with wonderful curries, noodles and grills. You'll probably have to make a return visit to fit it all in.

OXFORD, THE COTSWOLDS & AROUND

Darcy's (☎ 01727-730777; 2 Hatfield Rd; mains £11-18)
This stylish, contemporary restaurant has a
menu of modern European dishes with the
odd Aussie influence thrown in. Go for barbecue kangaroo with aubergine relish or play it
safe with sea bass on a bed of Catalan stew.

Drinking

our pick **Ye Olde Fighting Cocks** (☎ 01727-869152;
16 Abbey Mill Lane) Reputedly the oldest pub in
England, this unusual, octagonal-shaped inn
has oodles of charm. Oliver Cromwell spent
a night here, stabling his horses in what's now
the bar, and underground tunnels lead to the
cathedral. Drink in this historic atmosphere
while you nurse your pint.

Rose & Crown (☎ 01727-851903; 10 St Michael's St)
Another St Albans favourite, this 16th-century
pub with a beautiful beer garden features live
music during the week.

Getting There & Away

Trains depart London St Pancreas station to
St Albans station (£8.90, 23 minutes, every 10
minutes), which is on Victoria St, a 10-minute
walk east of St Peter's St.

AROUND ST ALBANS
Hatfield House

For over 400 years, **Hatfield House** (☎ 01707-
287010; house & garden adult/child £10/4.50, garden only
£2.50/1.50; ☼ noon-4pm Wed-Sun & public holidays,
gardens 11am-5.30pm Easter-Sep) has been home to
the Cecils, one of England's most influential
political families. This magnificent Jacobean
mansion was built between 1607 and 1611
for Robert Cecil, first earl of Salisbury and
secretary of state to both Elizabeth I and
James I, and is awash with grandiose portraits, tapestries, furnishings and armour.
Look out for the grand marble hall, the stunning carved-oak staircase and the stained
glass in the chapel.

Outside, the vast grounds were landscaped
by 17th-century botanist John Tradescant,
and you can see an old oak tree that marks
the spot where Elizabeth I, who spent much
of her childhood here, first heard of her
accession to the throne.

If you'd really like to get into the character of the house, you can attend a four-
course Elizabethan banquet, complete with
minstrels and court jesters, in the atmospheric Great Hall on Friday nights (£47.50).
Book on ☎ 01707-262055.

The house is opposite Hatfield train station, and there are trains from London
King's Cross station (£7.40, 20 minutes,
half-hourly). Between them, buses 300, 301
and 724 run every 10 minutes between St
Albans and Hatfield (32 minutes).

Shaw's Corner

Preserved in time and much as he left it,
Shaw's Corner (NT; ☎ 01438-820307; www.nationaltrust
.org.uk/shawscorner; Ayot St Lawrence; adult/child £4.95/2.50;
☼ 1-5pm Wed-Sun mid-Mar–Nov) is a tranquil Arts
and Crafts building that was home to George
Bernard Shaw (1856–1950) for the last 44
years of his life. His study contains his type-
writer, pens, inkwell and dictionaries, and
in the garden you can see his writing hut
(which revolves to catch the sun) where he
penned several works including *Pygmalion,*
the play on which the film *My Fair Lady* was
based. The Oscar he received for the screen-
play is also on display.

Ayot St Lawrence is 6 miles north of
St Albans, off the B651. Bus 304 from St
Albans will drop you off at Gustardwood,
1.5 miles from Ayot St Lawrence.

BEDFORDSHIRE

Sleepy and understated Bedfordshire is a
rural hideaway home to the majestic stately
pile, Woburn Abbey, and to the attractive
market town of Bedford. The River Great
Ouse weaves across the pastoral fields of the
north of the county, creating several pristine
nature reserves and some good woodland
walks. To the south, the last gasps of the
Chiltern hills protect the county from the
worst of the industrialisation of the capital.

BEDFORD
pop 82,488

The historic county town of Bedford enjoys
a lovely riverside setting on the banks of the
Great Ouse. Although the centre of town is
overrun with high-street chain shops, if you
wander a little further you'll find a host of
interesting sites connected to the town's most
famous export, John Bunyan (1628–88), the
17th-century Nonconformist preacher and
author of *The Pilgrim's Progress.*

Located in the town hall, the **tourist office**
(☎ 01234-221712; www.bedford.gov.uk/tourism; Town
Hall, St Paul's Sq; ☼ 9am-4.30pm Mon-Sat & 10am-2pm

Sun May-Aug, 9.30am-5pm Mon-Sat Sep-Apr) stocks a free guide to places with a Bunyan connection, and runs free guided walks on Sunday mornings and Wednesday evenings between May and August.

If you're visiting in July 2010, you can join the festivities at the **Bedford River Festival**, a bi-annual event featuring theatre, dance, music, historic re-enactments, rowing and Dragon Boat racing.

Sights

Want to know just how Glenn Miller, Ronnie Barker and Nelson Mandela are connected to the area? Start your sightseeing with a trip to the **Bedford Room** at the tourist office for a potted history of the town.

The **Bunyan Meeting Free Church** (☎ 01234-213722; www.bunyanmeeting.co.uk; Mill St; 🕙 10am-4pm Tue-Sat Mar-Oct) was built in 1849 on the site of the barn where Bunyan preached from 1671 to 1688. The church's bronze doors, inspired by Ghiberti's doors for the Baptistry in Florence, show 10 scenes from *The Pilgrim's Progress*, and inside the stained-glass windows also show scenes from the tome.

Next door, the **John Bunyan Museum** (☎ 01234-213722; admission free; 🕙 10am-3.45pm Tue-Sat Mar-Oct) has displays on the author's life including his time in prison, as well as 169 editions of *The Pilgrim's Progress* from around the world. There are recreated scenes from the period including a kitchen, and various artefacts such as his writing desk, a violin he made and his prison door from the county jail, which was demolished in 1801.

Although closed for renovation works until late 2009, the excellent **Cecil Higgins Art Gallery** (☎ 01234-211222; Castle Lane; admission free; 🕙 11am-5pm Tue-Sat, 2-5pm Sun) houses work by Blake, Turner, Rossetti, Picasso and Edvard Munch.

Next door, the **Bedford Museum** (☎ 01234-353323; www.bedfordmuseum.org; admission free; 🕙 11am-5pm Tue-Sat, 2-5pm Sun) has archaeological and historical exhibits telling Bedford's story.

Eating

Santaniello (☎ 01234-353742; 9 Newnham St; pizzas £5-9; 🕙 lunch & dinner Sat, lunch Tue-Sun) Bedford has quite a large Italian community, and this cheery, bustling place with red-and-white tablecloths and lively waiters serves up Italian favourites with a smile.

Tokyo (☎ 01234-266100; 21 Greyfriars; dinner buffet adult/child £12.90/6.50; 🕙 lunch Sat & Sun, dinner Tue-Sun) This bright, cheery Japanese restaurant has a sushi conveyor the length of the room, and serves a wide range of à la carte dishes. The evening buffet is excellent value and includes sushi, tempura, dumplings and noodle dishes.

Getting There & Away

Stagecoach X5 runs from Bedford to Cambridge (£4.50, 1½ hours) and Oxford (£8, two hours) every half-hour.

There are frequent trains from London St Pancreas (£15.90, 45 minsutes, every 10 minutes) to Bedford's Midland station, a well-signposted 500m walk west of the High St.

WOBURN ABBEY & SAFARI PARK

The pretty Georgian village of Woburn is home to Bedfordshire's biggest attractions: a palatial stately home and Europe's largest conservation park.

Once a Cistercian abbey but dissolved by Henry VIII and awarded to the earl of Bedford, **Woburn Abbey** (☎ 01525-290333; www .woburnabbey.com; adult/child £10.50/6; 🕙 11am-5.30pm Apr-Oct, last entry 4pm) is a wonderful country pile set within a 1200-hectare deer park. The house is stuffed with 18th-century furniture, porcelain and silver, and displays paintings by Gainsborough, Van Dyck and Canaletto. Highlights include Queen Victoria's bedroom, where she slept with Prince Albert; the beautiful wall hangings and cabinets of the Chinese Room; the mysterious story of the Flying Duchess; and the gilt-adorned dining room. An audio tour brings the history of the house and the people who lived here to life. Outside, the gardens are well worth a wander and host theatre and music events during the summer months.

On an equally grand scale is **Woburn Safari Park** (☎ 01525-290407; www.woburnsafari.co.uk; adult/child £17.50/13.50; 🕙 10am-6pm Apr-Oct, 11am-4pm Sat & Sun Nov-Feb, last entry 1hr before closing), the country's largest drive-through animal reserve. Rhinos, tigers, lions, zebras, bison, monkeys, elephants and giraffes roam the grounds, while in the 'foot safari' area, you can see sea lions, penguins and lemurs. Pick up a timetable on arrival for information on feeding times, keeper talks and animal demonstrations.

For both attractions, buy a passport ticket (adult/child £20.50/16) that can be used on two separate days within any 12-month period.

The abbey and safari park are easily accessible by car off the M1 motorway. First Capital Connect run trains from King's Cross to Flitwick, the nearest station. From here it's a 15-minute taxi journey (£15 to £20) to Woburn.

BUCKINGHAMSHIRE

The chalky, forested Chiltern Hills and sweeping valleys of Buckinghamshire are pitted with the stately homes and country estates of the rich and famous. The gentle, rolling countryside won the hearts of the Rothschild dynasty in the 19th century, and they duly invested in some plum real estate around the historic town of Aylesbury. The pièce de résistance is the magnificent Renaissance-style chateau Waddesdon Manor.

Buckinghamshire was also a favourite with the more poetic types: John Milton lived in Chalfont St Giles; Robert Frost spent time in Beaconsfield; and TS Eliot and Percy Bysshe Shelley both lived in Marlow, 100 years apart.

The south of the county is dominated by the beech woods of the scenic Chilterns, and the forest walks and mountain-bike trails that criss-cross the region are popular throughout the year.

AYLESBURY
pop 69,021

Make your way past the confusing road system and modern eyesores to Aylesbury's old town and you'll be rewarded with narrow winding streets flanked by pretty 17th-century houses, a thriving local market and the lovely, medieval St Mary's Church.

Henry VIII courted Anne Boleyn in the local inn, the King's Head, now home to the **tourist office** (☎ 01296-330559; King's Head Passage; ⏱ 9.30am-5pm Mon-Sat Apr-Oct, 10am-4.30pm Mon-Sat Nov-Mar). You can pick up an informative heritage-walk leaflet (50p) here for information on the town's sights.

The main sight is the **Buckinghamshire County Museum** (☎ 01296-331441; www.buckscc.gov.uk/museum; Church St; admission free; ⏱ 10am-5pm Mon-Sat Mar-late Jun & late-Aug to Oct, from 1pm late Jun-late Aug, 10am-4pm Nov-Feb), which takes visitors through life in the county from Roman times to the present.

In the award-winning **Roald Dahl Children's Gallery** (⏱ 3-5pm Apr-Oct, 10am-5pm school holidays;

adult/child £4.50/4), kids of all ages can investigate the beasts inside James' Giant Peach, explore Fantastic Mr Fox's tunnel and see the Twit's upside-down bedroom.

Trains run to and from London Marylebone (£11.80, one hour, every 15 minutes).

AROUND AYLESBURY
Waddesdon Manor

Dripping with gilt, crystal chandeliers, tapestries, fine porcelain and elaborate furniture, **Waddesdon Manor** (☎ 01296-653226; www.waddesdon .org.uk; adult/child house & gardens £15/11; ⏱ noon-4pm Wed-Fri, 11am-4pm Sat & Sun mid-Mar–late Oct) is a stunning Renaissance-style chateau built by Baron Ferdinand de Rothschild to showcase his collection of French decorative arts. The baron liked to do things on a grand scale, and the ostentatious magnificence of the house, designed by French architect Destailleur and completed in 1889, is almost overwhelming.

Very little space is left unadorned – only the Bachelor's Wing stands out as being noticeably more restrained. The baron used the house for his glamorous parties, and it's not hard to imagine the great and good of the 19th century living it up in the palatial rooms. Visitors can view his outstanding collection of art, Sèvres porcelain, expensive furniture and the extensive wine cellar. The houses hosts a variety of events throughout the year, from Christmas fairs to wine-tasting days, Valentine's dinners and opera and theatre events. Weekends get busy, so book tickets in advance.

The beautiful **gardens** (gardens only adult/child £7/3.50; ⏱ 10am-5pm Wed-Sun mid-Mar–late Oct, Sat & Sun Jan–mid-Mar) boast rare flowers, divine views and a Rococo-revival aviary filled with exotic birds.

If the idea of grand living whets your appetite, spend the night at the **Five Arrows** (☎ 01296-651727; www.waddesdon.org.uk/five_arrows; High St, Waddesdon; s £65, d £85-175; ℗ 🖳), a stunning, half-timbered lodge at the gates to the estate. Built in 1887 by Baron Rothschild to house the architects and craftsmen who were working on his house, the five arrows refer to the Rothschild coat of arms and represent the five sons of the dynasty's founder, Mayer Amschel Rothschild. Rooms are furnished with antiques and original pieces from the manor, and the restaurant (mains £12 to £18) serves a seasonal modern British menu.

Waddesdon is 6 miles northwest of Aylesbury off the A41. From the Aylesbury bus station, take bus 16 (15 minutes, hourly Monday to Friday, every two hours Saturday).

Bletchley Park

Once England's best-kept secret, **Bletchley Park** (☎ 01908-640404; www.bletchleypark.org.uk; The Manor, Bletchley; adult/12-16 yr/under 12 yr £10/8/free; 9.30am-5pm Mon-Fri, 10.30am-5pm Sat & Sun) was the scene of a huge code-breaking operation during WWII, dramatised in the film *Enigma*. Almost 8,500 people worked here in total secrecy intercepting, decrypting, translating and interpreting enemy correspondence. Exhibitions explain the complex process and the hard work, frustration and successes that shaped this secret war effort. You can also see a collection of Churchill memorabilia, a computer museum tracing the development of computers from the early Bletchley model 'Colossus' to the modern day, and get an idea of what life was like for civilians during the war.

Bletchley is just south of Milton Keynes off the B4034. There are regular trains running from London Euston to Bletchley (40 minutes).

STOWE

Stowe, the sort of private school so exclusive that its driveway is half a mile long, is housed in the neoclassical splendour of **Stowe House** (☎ 01280-818166; www.shpt.org; adult/child £4/2.50; tours 2pm Wed-Sun Apr & Jul-Oct, Sat & Sun Nov-Mar & Jun, noon-5pm selected days Jul & Aug). Mere mortals are permitted to visit the eight state rooms which connect in a 137m enfilade and offer stunning views of the wonderful grounds. Although the rooms are left bare (the house's contents were sold off to rescue the original owners from financial disaster), the sheer scale and ornamentation of the building is highly impressive. An interpretive centre explains the rise and fall of the family who lived here and offers a glimpse into the elaborate world of Britain's landed gentry in the 18th century. The opening hours for the house are complex, so check the website before travelling.

For many, the real draw at Stowe is not the house but the extraordinary **Georgian gardens** (NT; ☎ 01280-822850; www.nationaltrust.org.uk; adult/child £6.90/3.50; 10.30am-5.30pm Wed-Sun Mar-Oct, to 4pm Sat & Sun Nov-Feb, last admission 1½ hr before closing), which cover 400 hectares and were worked on by the greatest British landscape gardeners,

including Charles Bridgeman, William Kent and Capability Brown.

The gardens are best known for their 32 temples, created in the 18th century by the wealthy owner Sir Richard Temple (no kidding), whose family motto was *Templa Quam Delecta* (How Delightful Are Your Temples). There are also arches, lakes and a Palladian bridge among other buildings.

Stowe is 3 miles northwest of Buckingham off the A422. There are buses from Aylesbury to Buckingham (45 minutes, hourly) from where it's an £8 taxi ride.

BERKSHIRE

Long known as the 'Royal County of Berkshire', this rather posh and prosperous part of the world acts as a country getaway for some of England's most influential figures. Within easy reach of London and yet entirely different in character, the pastoral landscape is littered with handsome villages and historic houses as well as some of the top attractions in the country. Few visitors make it past the historic towns of Windsor and Eton, home to the Queen's favourite castle and the world-renowned public school, but wander further afield and you'll be rewarded with tranquil rural countryside and exquisitely maintained villages.

WINDSOR & ETON
pop 30,568

Dominated by the massive bulk and heavy influence of Windsor Castle, these twin towns have a rather surreal atmosphere, with the morning pomp and ceremony of the changing of the guards in Windsor and the sight of school boys dressed in formal tail coats wandering the streets of Eton.

Windsor Castle, with its romantic architecture and superb state rooms, is an absolute must-see, while across the bridge over the Thames, England's most famous public school has an altogether different flavour. To cater for the droves of tourists that visit these star attractions, Windsor town centre is full of expensive boutiques, grand cafes and trendy restaurants. Eton, by comparison, is far quieter, its pedestrianised centre lined with antique shops and art galleries. Both towns exude an air of affluence, and if you're travelling on a tight budget, a day trip from London is probably your best bet.

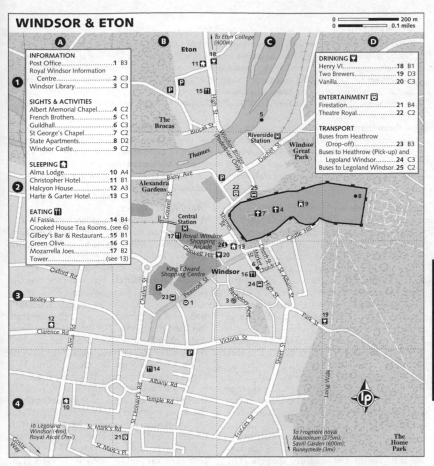

Orientation

Windsor and Eton are separated by the River Thames, with a pedestrianised bridge linking the two towns. The massive castle marks the centre of Windsor, with the town's main drag, Peascod St, leading away from its soaring stone walls. Castle Hill and Thames St skirt the edge of the castle, the latter leading down to the bridge to Eton.

Information

The **Royal Windsor Information Centre** (☎ 01753-743900; www.windsor.gov.uk; Old Booking Hall, Windsor Royal Shopping Arcade; ☺ 10am-5pm Mon-Sat, to 4pm Sun) sells bus and local attraction tickets, and has an **accommodation booking service** (☎ 01753-743907; £5).

There are plenty of banks with ATMs along the High and Thames Sts. The **post office** is in Peascod St and you'll get free internet access at the **Windsor library** (☎ 01753-743940; Bachelors Acre).

Sights
WINDSOR CASTLE

The largest and oldest occupied fortress in the world, **Windsor Castle** (☎ 020-7766 7304; www.royalcollection.org.uk; adult/child £15/8.50; ☺ 9.45am-4pm Mar-Oct, to 3pm Nov-Feb) is a majestic vision of battlements and towers used for state occasions and as the Queen's weekend retreat.

William the Conqueror first established a royal residence in Windsor in 1070 when he built a motte and bailey here, the only naturally defendable spot in the Thames valley.

DIY WEEKEND

Buckinghamshire is littered with pretty villages with half-timbered houses, rose-clad cottages, old coaching inns and ancient parish churches. Grab a map, forget the guidebook and just take to the back roads to explore some of the lesser-known treasures lurking in London's backyard. Visit **Amersham** for half-timbered buildings and charming cottages; **Chenies** for old manor houses and an ancient parish church; **West Wycombe** for cottages and inns so quaint they're protected by the National Trust; or **Chalfont St Giles** and **Chalfont St Peter** for historic connections and picturesque settings.

Further north between Aylesbury and Buckingham, you'll find **Winslow**, home to an 8th-century hall designed by Sir Christopher Wren, and just south of Aylesbury, the quaint thatched cottages of **Wendover** and the half-timbered and Georgian shops in **Great Missenden**. To the north and west of Aylesbury, you'll find the extraordinary architecture of **Claydon House** in Middle Claydon, the duck decoy and tower at **Boarstall** and the 15th-century courthouse in **Long Crendon**.

Since then successive monarchs have rebuilt, remodelled and refurbished the castle complex to create the massive and sumptuous palace that stands here today. Henry II replaced the wooden stockade in 1165 with a stone round tower and built the outer walls to the north, east and south; Charles II gave the state apartments a baroque makeover; George IV swept in with his preference for Gothic style; and Queen Victoria refurbished a beautiful chapel in memory of her beloved Albert.

The castle largely escaped the bombings of WWII, but in 1992 a devastating fire tore through the building destroying or damaging more than 100 rooms. By chance, the most important treasures were in storage at the time, and with skilled craftsmanship and painstaking restoration, the rooms were returned to their former glory.

Join a free guided tour (every half hour) or take a multilingual audio tour of the lavish state rooms and beautiful chapels. The State Apartments and St George's Chapel are closed at times during the year; check the website for details. If the Queen is in residence, you'll see the Royal Standard flying from the Round Tower.

Windsor Castle is one of England's most popular attractions. Come early and be prepared to queue.

Queen Mary's Dolls' House

Your first sight will be an incredible dolls' house, designed by Sir Edwin Lutyens for Queen Mary in 1924. The attention to detail is spellbinding – there's running water, electricity and lighting and vintage wine in the cellar! The house was intended to accurately depict households of the day, albeit on a scale of 1:12.

State Apartments

After the dolls' house, a **gallery** with drawings by Leonardo da Vinci and a **China Museum**, visitors enter the stunning State Apartments, home to some exquisite paintings and architecture and still used by the Queen.

The **Grand Staircase** sets the tone for the rooms, all of which are elaborate, opulent and suitably regal. Highlights include **St George's Hall**, which incurred the most damage during the fire of 1992. The dining chairs here, dwarfed by the scale of the room, are standard size. On the ceiling, the shields of the Knights of the Garter (originally from George IV's time here) were recreated after the fire.

For intimate gatherings (just 60 people), the Queen entertains in the **Waterloo Chamber** – the super shiny table is French-polished and then dusted by someone walking over it with dusters on their feet. During large parties, this room is used for dancing and the table is tripled in size and set up in St George's Hall.

The **King's Dressing Room** has some of the most important Renaissance paintings in the royal collection. Alongside Sir Anthony Van Dyck's magnificent *Triple Portrait* of Charles I, you will see works by Hans Holbein, Rembrandt, Peter Paul Rubens and Albrecht Dürer. Charles II kipped in here instead of in the **King's Bedchamber** – maybe George IV's magnificent bed (now on display) would have tempted him.

St George's Chapel

This elegant chapel, commissioned for the Order of the Garter by Edward IV in 1475, is one of Britain's finest examples of Perpendicular Gothic architecture. The nave and fan-vaulted roof were completed under

Henry VII but the final nail was struck under Henry VIII in 1528.

The chapel – along with Westminster Abbey – serves as a **royal mausoleum**, and its tombs read like a history of the British monarchy. The most recent royal burial occurred in April 2002, when the body of George VI's widow, Queen Elizabeth, the Queen Mother (1900–2002), was transported here in a splendid and sombre procession and buried alongside her husband. And in April 2005, Prince Charles and Camilla Parker-Bowles were blessed here following their civil marriage in the town's Guildhall.

St George's Chapel closes on Sunday, but time your visit well and you can attend Evensong at 5.15pm daily except Wednesday, or services at 10.45am, 11.45am and 5.15pm.

Albert Memorial Chapel

Originally built in 1240 and dedicated to Edward the Confessor, this small chapel was the place of worship for the Order of the Garter until St George's Chapel snatched that honour. After the death of Prince Albert at Windsor Castle in 1861, Queen Victoria ordered its elaborate redecoration as a tribute to her husband. A major feature of the restoration is the magnificent vaulted roof, whose gold mosaic pieces were crafted in Venice. There's a monument to the prince, although he's actually buried with Queen Victoria in the Frogmore Royal Mausoleum in the castle grounds.

Windsor Great Park

Stretching behind Windsor Castle almost all the way to Ascot, Windsor Great Park covers about 40 sq miles and features a lake, walking tracks, a bridleway and gardens. The **Savill Garden** (☎ 01753-860222; www.theroyallandscape.co.uk; adult/child £7/3.50; ◷ 10am-6pm Mar-Oct, to 4pm Nov-Feb) is particularly lovely and has a stunning visitor centre.

The **Long Walk** is a 3-mile jaunt along a tree-lined path from King George IV Gate to the Copper Horse statue (of George III) on Snow Hill, the highest point of the park. The Queen can occasionally be spotted driving down the Long Walk, accompanied only by a bodyguard. The walk is signposted from the town centre.

Changing of the guard

A fabulous spectacle of pomp, with loud commands, whispered conversations, triumphant

tunes from a military band and plenty of shuffling and stamping of feet, the **changing of the guard** (11am Mon-Sat Apr-Jun, alternate days Jul-Mar) draws the crowds to the castle gates each day. It's a must for any visitor, but you'll get a better view if you stay to the right of the crowd.

ETON COLLEGE

Cross the bridge over the Thames to Eton and you'll enter another world, one where old-school values and traditions seem to ooze from the very walls. The streets here are surprisingly hushed as you make your way down to the most enduring and most illustrious symbol of England's class system, **Eton College** (☎ 01753-671177; www.etoncollege.com; adult/child £4.20/3.45, tours £5.50/4.50; ◷ 10.30am-4.30pm Mar-Apr, Jul-Sep [school holidays], 2-4.30pm term time, guided tours 2.15pm & 3.15pm).

Those who have studied here include nineteen prime ministers, countless princes, kings and maharajahs, famous explorers, authors and economists, among them the Duke of Wellington, Princes William and Harry, George Orwell, Ian Fleming, Aldous Huxley, Sir Ranulph Fiennes and John Maynard Keynes.

Eton is the largest and most famous public (meaning very private) school in England. It was founded by Henry VI in 1440 with a view towards educating 70 highly qualified boys awarded a scholarship from a fund endowed by the king. Every year since then, 70 King's Scholars (aged 12 to 14) have been chosen based on the results of a highly competitive exam; these pupils are housed in separate quarters from the rest of the 1300 or so other students who are known as Oppidans.

While the King's Scholars are chosen exclusively on the basis of exam results, Oppidans must be able to foot the bill for £26,000 per-annum fees as well as passing entrance exams. All the boys are boarders and must comply with the strong traditions at Eton. The boys still wear formal tail coats, waistcoats and white collars to lessons, the school language is full of in-house jargon and fencing, and shooting, polo and beagling are on the list of school sporting activities.

Luckily for the rest of us, the college is open to visitors and a guided tour can go a long way to giving you an insight into how this most elite of schools functions. Tours take in the **chapel** (which you can see from Windsor Castle), the **cloisters**, the **Museum of Eton Life**,

A WORLD FIRST

In June 1215, King John met his barons and bishops in a large field 3 miles southeast of Windsor, and over the next few days they hammered out an agreement on a basic charter of rights guaranteeing the liberties of the king's subjects and restricting the monarch's absolute power. The document they signed was the Magna Carta, the world's first constitution. It formed the basis for statutes and charters throughout the world's democracies. (Both the national and state constitutions of the United States, drawn up more than 500 years later, paraphrase directly from this document.)

Runnymede – from the Anglo-Saxon words *ruinige* (take council) and *moed* (meadow) – was chosen because it was the largest piece of open land between the king's residence at Windsor and the bishop's palace at Staines. Today, the field remains pretty much as it was, except now it features two **lodges** (1930) designed by Sir Edward Lutyens. In the woods behind the field are two **memorials**, the first to the Magna Carta designed by Sir Edward Maufe (1957). The second is to John F Kennedy, and was built by Geoffrey Jellicoe in 1965 on an acre of land granted in perpetuity to the US government following Kennedy's assassination.

Runnymede is on the A308, 3 miles south east of Windsor. Bus 41 stops near here on the Windsor to Egham route.

the **lower school** and the **school yard**. As you wander round, you may recognise some of the buildings, as the college is often used as a film set. *Chariots of Fire, The Madness of King George, Mrs Brown* and *Shakespeare in Love* are just some of the classics that have been filmed here.

LEGOLAND WINDSOR

A fun-filled theme park of white-knuckle rides, **Legoland** (☎ 08705 040404; www.legoland.co.uk; adult/3-15yr £34/26; ☼ hours vary) is more about the thrills of scaring yourself silly than the joys of building your own make-believe castle from the eponymous bricks. The professionals have already done this for you, with almost 40 million Lego bricks transformed into some of the world's greatest landmarks. You'll also get live shows, 3-D cinema and slightly tamer activities for the less adventurous. If you prebook online, you save about £3 off the whopping ticket prices.

The Legoland shuttle bus departs from High St and Thames St from 10am, with the last bus returning 30 minutes after the park has closed. If you're planning to take the first bus of the morning, use the High St stop as it often fills up here and consequently does not stop in Thames St.

Tours

Open-top double-decker bus tours of the town are run by **City Sightseeing Tours** (☎ 0871-666 0000; www.city-sightseeing.com; adult/child £7/4; ☼ every ½hr daily mid-Mar–mid-Nov, Sat & Sun mid-Nov–Dec) and

leave from Castle Hill opposite the Harte & Garter Hotel. From Easter to October, **French Brothers** (☎ 01753-851900; www.frenchbrothers.co.uk; Clewer Court Rd; ☼ 11am-5pm) runs a variety of boat trips to Runnymede, Maidenhead and around Windsor and Eton. The 45-minute round trip to Runnymede costs £4.90 for adults and £2.45 for children. Boats leave from just next to Windsor Bridge. If you fancy doing the hop-on-hop-off bus plus a 35-minute boat trip, a combined boat and bus ticket costs £11.50/6.25 per adult/child.

Sleeping

Windsor has a good selection of quality hotels and B&Bs, but few budget options.

Alma Lodge (☎ 01753-855620; www.almalodge .co.uk; 58 Alma Rd; s £45-60, d £60-75; P wi-fi) This elegant Victorian house, within walking distance of the centre of town, has large en suite rooms with plenty of period features. A sweeping staircase greets you on arrival and ferries you up to rooms with ornate ceilings, original fireplaces and period style.

Halcyon House (☎ 01753-863262; www.halcyon-house .co.uk; 21 Clarence Rd; s/d £70/80; P wi-fi) Another fine Victorian house, this place offers an entirely different experience with simple stylish rooms that feature muted colour schemes and sparkling new bathrooms. The period features, such as the old fireplaces, remain but the overall effect is far more modern.

Christopher Hotel (☎ 01753-852359; www.thechris topher.co.uk; High St, Eton; r £99-200; P wi-fi) Set in a former coaching inn, this modern hotel offers clean-cut, uncluttered rooms with contemporary, if a little corporate, styling. The grill downstairs has big windows overlooking the street, and it serves up a modern European menu (mains £8 to £13) in slick surroundings.

Harte & Garter (☎ 01753-863426; www.harteandgarter.com; High St; r £105-145; 🖳) Right opposite the castle and newly renovated, this Victorian hotel blends period style with modern furnishings. High ceilings, giant fireplaces, decorative cornices and dark woods seamlessly combine with contemporary fabrics, plasma-screen TVs and roll-top baths. Some rooms enjoy wonderful views over the castle and all guests can enjoy the luxurious spa in the converted stable block.

Eating

Green Olive (☎ 01753-866655; 10 High St; meze £4-10) A great spot for a light lunch or tantalising evening meal, this place dishes up generous portions of traditional Greek meze in bright, simple surroundings. You can choose from over 50 different dishes and combine a riot of flavours before rolling out the door.

Mozzarella Joes (01753-751121; www.mozzarellajoes.com; 31 Windsor Royal Station; mains £5.90-8.90) For quick eats, this bright and airy pizza joint in the station is a good bet with simple wooden tables, a good choice of tasty pizzas, pastas and salads and a friendly attitude to children.

Tower (☎ 01753-863426; High St; mains £9.50-17.50; ⏰ 7-10pm) Giant windows with views over the castle give this place an immediate allure, as do the grand chandeliers and high ceilings. The menu is brasserie style with a choice of classic British cuisine featuring grills, fish and steaks simply and perfectly done. It's also a good spot to sample the finest of English institutions, afternoon tea.

Gilbey's Bar & Restaurant (☎ 01753-854921; 82-83 High St, Eton; mains £12.50-21.50, set menu 2-course/3-course £13.75/18.75) This small restaurant in Eton has the feel of a Continental cafe, with terracotta tiling and a sunny courtyard garden and conservatory. The superb modern British menu is almost surpassed by the wide and interesting choice of wines, making it one of the top spots to eat in town.

Other options include:

Al Fassia (☎ 01753-855370; 27 St Leonard's Rd; mains £9.50-13.50) An atmospheric Moroccan restaurant with traditional decor and menu.

Crooked House Tea Rooms (☎ 01753-857534; 51 High St; afternoon tea £7-12; ⏰ 10.30am-6pm Mon-Fri,

> ### DETOUR: ROYAL ASCOT
>
> Get out your glad rags and join the glitterati at **Royal Ascot** (☎ 0870-727 1234; www.ascot.co.uk) for the biggest racing meet of the year. The royal family, A-list celebs and the rich and famous gather here to show off their Jimmy Choos and place the odd bet. The four-day festival takes place in mid-June and it's essential to book tickets well in advance. You can soak up the atmosphere from the Silver Ring for a mere £15 per day, or head for the Grandstand and Paddock where you can rub shoulders with the great and the good for £54 per day. Just make sure you dress to impress.

10am-7pm Sat & Sun) A traditional tearoom complete with sloping floors, wooden beams and royal cream teas.

Drinking

Windsor and Eton are packed with pubs, with a cluster under the railway arches of the central station.

our pick **Two Brewers** (☎ 01753-855426; 34 Park St) This 17th-century inn perched on the edge of Windsor Great Park is close to the castle's tradesmen's entrance and supposedly frequented by staff from the castle. It's a quaint and cosy place with dim lighting, obituaries to castle footmen and royal photographs with irreverent captions on the wall.

Henry VI (☎ 01753-866051; 37 High St, Eton) Another old pub, but this time the low ceilings and subtle lighting are mixed with leather sofas and modern design. It's the kind of place where you can sit back with an afternoon pint and read the paper. There's a nice garden for alfresco dining and live music at weekends.

Vanilla (☎ 01753-831122; 15A Goswell Hill; admission £2-10) This uber-trendy boutique bar and club plays everything from funk and rock to indie and house beats, and it has a champagne-and-cocktail bar and a snappy dress code.

Entertainment

Firestation (☎ 01753-866865; www.windsorartscentre.org; cnr St Leonard's & St Mark's Rds) hosts a range of comedy, film, theatre, music and dance events with plenty for interest for kids.

The **Theatre Royal** (☎ 01753-853888; www.theatreroyalwindsor.co.uk; 32-34 Thames St) features a wide repertoire of theatre productions from pantomime to first runs.

OXFORD, THE COTSWOLDS & AROUND

READING FESTIVAL

Each August Bank Holiday weekend about 240,000 revellers descend on the rather industrial town of Reading for one of the country's biggest music events. The **Reading Festival** (www.readingfestival.com) is a three-day extravaganza that features top acts in pop, rock and dance music. Tickets will set you back about £65 per day or £155 for a three-day pass.

Getting There & Away

Windsor is 21 miles west of central London and only about 15 minutes by car from Heathrow airport.

BUS

Green Line bus 702 departs for Windsor and Legoland from London Victoria coach station (£2 to £8 depending on time of travel, 1½ hours, hourly, about every two hours Sunday). Bus 77 connects Windsor with Heathrow airport (one hour). Buses depart from the High St, Windsor, opposite the Parish Church.

TRAIN

There are two Windsor and Eton train stations – trains from Central station on Thames St go to London Paddington (27 to 43 minutes) and trains from Riverside station, near the bridge to Eton, go to London Waterloo (56 minutes). Services run half-hourly from both stations and tickets cost £7.70.

Wessex

The land stretching west from Hampshire and encompassing Dorset, Wiltshire, Bristol, Bath and Somerset was once the core of the now nonexistent Anglo-Saxon realm of Wessex. However, the area still rings to tales of its ruler, Alfred the Great, who made Winchester his power base. Legends linger everywhere, often accompanied by contemporary delights. Somerset's rolling green hills give way to the hippie haven of Glastonbury with its Arthurian tales, grail quests and fabled faery kings. The shaded lanes of Wiltshire wind towards awe-inspiring megalithic monuments at Stonehenge and Avebury. In Dorset, myth-rich Iron Age hill forts shelter behind a coast peppered with shimmering blue bays, sparkling sandy coves and fossils waiting to be found. In genteel Bath the legend is one of conquest, while the legacy is Britain's most impressive cluster of Roman buildings – a stunning Regency cityscape adds to the appeal.

Evidence of more-modern myth-makers abounds. The Wessex wordsmith Thomas Hardy wove Dorset's market towns into his writings, while Hampshire and Bath celebrate their links with the novelist Jane Austen. Portsmouth has 18th-century naval hero Admiral Nelson and a rejuvenated waterfront; in Bristol, reminders of engineering genius Isambard Kingdom Brunel now nestle amid innovative restaurants, clubs and bars. Add the great escape of remote Exmoor's cliffs and moors, the activities of the New Forest, and the funky holiday hot spot that is the Isle of Wight, and Wessex emerges as not just a lost kingdom laced with legends, but also as a region ripe with adventure, alive to the present and demanding to be explored.

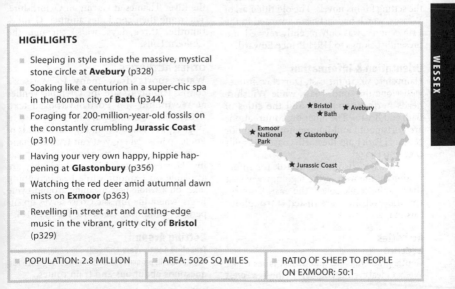

HIGHLIGHTS

- Sleeping in style inside the massive, mystical stone circle at **Avebury** (p328)
- Soaking like a centurion in a super-chic spa in the Roman city of **Bath** (p344)
- Foraging for 200-million-year-old fossils on the constantly crumbling **Jurassic Coast** (p310)
- Having your very own happy, hippie happening at **Glastonbury** (p356)
- Watching the red deer amid autumnal dawn mists on **Exmoor** (p363)
- Revelling in street art and cutting-edge music in the vibrant, gritty city of **Bristol** (p329)

- ★ Bristol ★ Avebury
- ★ Bath
- ★ Exmoor National Park ★ Glastonbury
- ★ Jurassic Coast

| ▪ POPULATION: 2.8 MILLION | ▪ AREA: 5026 SQ MILES | ▪ RATIO OF SHEEP TO PEOPLE ON EXMOOR: 50:1 |

History

Wessex can trace its human history back as far as the Stone Age – a 9000-year-old skeleton was found at Cheddar Gorge (p354). By 3000 BC a complex tribal society with clearly defined social hierarchies and shared religious beliefs had developed. This so-called Wessex culture constructed the magnificent stone circles of Avebury (p326) and Stonehenge (p320), as well as the many barrows and processional avenues scattered across the region. Centuries later, Iron Age peoples engineered massive forts at Maiden Castle (p307) and Old Sarum (p319), before being subjugated by the Romans – it is their city of Aquae Sulis that we now known as Bath (p341).

The Anglo-Saxon kingdom of Wessex was founded by King Cerdic in the 6th-century after the Romans withdrew. At the kingdom's heart was land now covered by Hampshire, Dorset, Wiltshire and Somerset, but borders shifted over the centuries, and at its height the kingdom stretched from Kent in the east to Cornwall in the west. The most famous ruler was King Alfred (r 871–99), who made Winchester his capital and ensured Wessex was the only sizeable part of the Anglo-Saxon lands not overrun by the Danes. Wessex was officially incorporated into the kingdom of England in the mid-9th century.

Dorset novelist Thomas Hardy revived the name of Wessex 1000 years later and used it as the setting for his novels. The old title Earl of Wessex, which had last been awarded in the 11th century, was only recently revived and presently belongs to HRH Prince Edward.

Orientation & Information

Hampshire sits to the east, Dorset continues west along the south coast, while Wiltshire heads north to Somerset and the cities of Bath and Bristol. The other big conurbations are Portsmouth and Bournemouth. Exmoor National Park hugs the north coast and spills over into Devon.

See www.visitsouthwest.co.uk for information on the west of the region; www.visit-hampshire.co.uk covers the east. County-specific websites are listed throughout this chapter.

Activities

CYCLING

Gentle gradients and quiet rural lanes make Wessex ideal cycling country. In the **New Forest** (see boxed text, p290) hundreds of miles of cycle-paths snake through a historic, wildlife-rich environment. Wiltshire is another highlight – the 160-mile circular **Wiltshire Cycleway** (p315) is a good basis for long or short rides. The **Isle of Wight** (p293) has 62 miles of bike-friendly routes and its own cycling festival.

The **West Country Way** (p362) is a fabulously varied 250-mile jaunt from Bristol to Padstow in Cornwall. **Exmoor** (p362) provides some superb, and testing, off-road cycling, as do the fields, woods and heathland of the 19km long **Quantock Hills** (p359), an Ares of Outstanding Natural Beauty (AONB) which peaks at 300m. The **North Wessex Downs** provide gentler terrain and take in the World Heritage Site of Avebury, the market towns of Marlborough and Hungerford and the western part of the Ridgeway National Trail.

WALKING

This is a fantastic region for hitting the trail. Top spots include **Exmoor** (p363), the **Mendips** (p355), the **Quantock Hills** (p359) and the **Isle of Wight** (p293). The rugged **South West Coast Path** (www.southwestcoastpath.com) runs along the region's northern and southern shores, cutting through some of the main coastal towns en route.

In northeastern Wiltshire, the **Ridgeway National Trail** (p328) starts near Avebury and winds 44 miles through chalk hills to meet the River Thames at Goring in Oxfordshire. The route then continues another 41 miles (another three days' walk) through the Chiltern Hills.

OTHER ACTIVITIES

Water sports draw many to Wessex's coasts. Highlights are the Olympic venues at Weymouth and Portland (boxed text, p309), the yachting havens of the Isle of Wight (p294), and the watery playgrounds of Poole (p301), where you can try your hand at everything from kitesurfing to powerboating. Horse riding, fishing and falconry are available on Exmoor while beachcombing takes on a whole new meaning around Lyme Regis, where the Jurassic Coast serves up superb fossil hunting (see boxed text, p310).

Getting Around

Traveline South West (☎ 0871 200 22 33; www.travelinesw.com; calls per min 10p) can answer regionwide questions about bus and train routes.

WESSEX

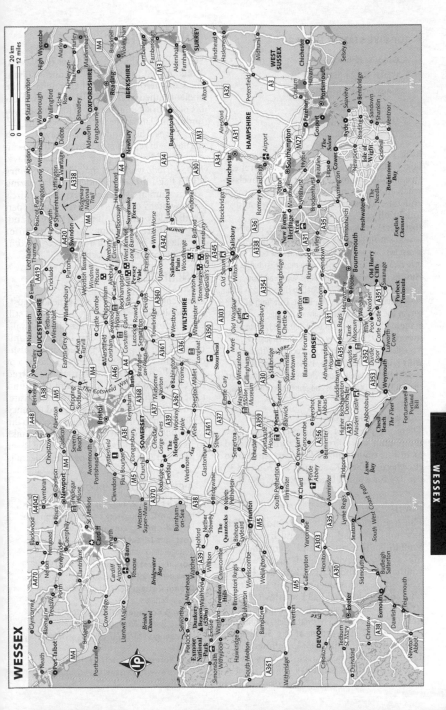

TOP FIVE STATELY HOMES

■ Osborne House (p295)

■ Wilton House (p319)

■ Kingston Lacy (p302)

■ Longleat (p322)

■ Montacute House (p360)

BUS

Local bus services are fairly comprehensive, but it pays to have your own wheels to reach the more-remote spots. Route maps and timetables are available online and at tourist offices.

First Travel (☎ timetables 0871 200 22 33, customer service 0870 010 6022; www.firstgroup.com) The region's largest bus company. The FirstDay Southwest ticket (adult/child £7/5.20) is valid for one day on most First buses.

PlusBus (www.plusbus.info) Allows you to add local bus travel to your train ticket. Participating cities include Bath, Bristol, Taunton and Weymouth. Tickets cost from £2 to £3 per day and can be bought at railway stations.

Stagecoach (☎ timetables 0871 200 22 33, customer service 0845 121 0190) A key provider in Hampshire. A one-day Explorer Ticket costs £7/4 per adult/child.

Wilts & Dorset (☎ 01202-673555; www.wdbus.co.uk) One-day Explorer tickets (adult/child £7/4) cover transport on most Wilts & Dorset buses and some other companies.

CAR & MOTORCYCLE

There are plenty of car-hire companies in the region, often around the airports and main-line train stations. Rates are similar to elsewhere in the UK, starting at around £35 per day for a small hatchback (see p807).

TRAIN

The main railway hub is Bristol, which has links to London, the southwest, the Midlands, the north and Scotland. In the south, Weymouth, Bournemouth, Southampton and Portsmouth are linked to London and Bath. For more information contact **National Rail Enquiries** (☎ 0845 748 4950; www.nationalrail.co.uk) or **Traveline South West** (☎ 0871 200 22 33; www.travelinesw.com; calls per min 10p). The **Freedom of the SouthWest Rover pass** (adult/child £95/45) allows eight days' unlimited travel over 15 days in an area that includes Salisbury, Bath, Bristol and Weymouth.

HAMPSHIRE

Hampshire is the historic heart of Wessex. Kings Alfred the Great, Knut and William the Conqueror all based their reigns in the ancient cathedral city of Winchester. Its jumble of historic buildings sits in the centre of an undulating landscape of chalk downs and fertile valleys. The county's coast is awash with heritage – in rejuvenated Portsmouth you can clamber aboard the pride of Nelson's navy, *HMS Victory*, wonder at the *Mary Rose* (Henry VIII's flagship), and wander wharfs buzzing with restaurants, shops and bars. Hampshire's southwestern corner claims the lovely open heath and woodlands of the New Forest and, just off shore, the happy holiday haven of the Isle of Wight – both areas are covered in separate sections in this chapter.

WINCHESTER
pop 41,420

Calm, collegiate Winchester is a mellow must-see for all visitors to the region. The past still echoes strongly around the flint-flecked walls of this ancient cathedral city. It was the capital of Saxon kings and a power base of bishops, and its statues and sights evoke two of England's mightiest myth-makers: Alfred the Great and King Arthur (he of the round table). Winchester's architecture is exquisite, from the handsome Elizabethan and Regency buildings in the narrow winding streets to the wondrous cathedral at the town's core. Thanks to its location, nestled in a valley of the River Itchen, there are also charming waterside trails

A COTTAGE OF YOUR OWN

After a rural bolt-hole far from the maddening crowd? Then check out these companies for self-catering cottages.

Cottages Direct (☎ 0870 197 6964; www .cottagesdirect.com)

Dorset Coastal Cottages (☎ 0800 980 4070; www.dorsetcoastalcottages.com)

Dream Cottages (☎ 01305-789000; www .dream-cottages.co.uk)

Farm & Cottage Holidays (☎ 01237-479146; www.holidaycottages.co.uk)

Hideaways (☎ 01747-828170; www.hideaways .co.uk)

New Forest Self Catering (☎ 01425-653908; www.newforestcottages.com)

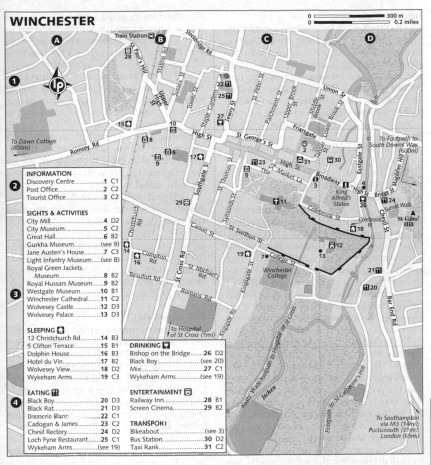

WINCHESTER

0   300 m
0   0.2 miles

INFORMATION
Discovery Centre...............**1** C1
Post Office........................**2** C2
Tourist Office...................**3** C2

SIGHTS & ACTIVITIES
City Mill...........................**4** D2
City Museum....................**5** C2
Great Hall........................**6** B2
Gurkha Museum.............(see 9)
Jane Austen's House.........**7** C3
Light Infantry Museum....(see 8)
Royal Green Jackets
   Museum.........................**8** B2
Royal Hussars Museum.....**9** B2
Westgate Museum.........**10** B1
Winchester Cathedral....**11** C2
Wolvesey Castle.............**12** D3
Wolvesey Palace............**13** D3

SLEEPING
12 Christchurch Rd.........**14** B3
5 Clifton Terrace............**15** B1
Dolphin House................**16** B3
Hotel du Vin...................**17** B2
Wolvesey View...............**18** D2
Wykeham Arms...............**19** C3

EATING
Black Boy........................**20** D3
Black Rat........................**21** D3
Brasserie Blanc...............**22** C1
Cadogan & James...........**23** C2
Chesil Rectory................**24** D2
Loch Fyne Restaurant.....**25** C1
Wykeham Arms.............(see 19)

DRINKING
Bishop on the Bridge......**26** D2
Black Boy......................(see 20)
Mix.................................**27** C1
Wykeham Arms............(see 19)

ENTERTAINMENT
Railway Inn.....................**28** B1
Screen Cinema................**29** B2

TRANSPORT
Bikeabout.......................(see 3)
Bus Station.....................**30** D2
Taxi Rank........................**31** C2

To Dawn Cottage (800m)

To Footpath to South Downs Way (600m)

To Hospital of St Cross (1mi)

To Southampton via M3 (14mi); Portsmouth (31mi); London (65mi)

St Giles' Hill

WESSEX

---

to explore, and the city marks the beginning of the beautiful South Downs Way (see p173).

History

The Romans first put their feet under the table here, but Winchester really took off when the powerful West Saxon bishops moved their episcopal see here in AD 670. Thereafter, Winchester was the most important town in the powerful kingdom of Wessex. King Alfred the Great (r 871–99) made it his capital, and it remained so under Knut (r 1016–35) and the Danish kings. After the Norman invasion of 1066, William the Conqueror arrived here to claim the throne of England. In 1086 he commissioned local monks to write the all-important *Domesday Book*, an adminis-trative survey of the entire country and the most significant clerical accomplishment of the Middle Ages. Winchester thrived up until the 12th century, when a fire gutted most of the city – after this, London took its crown. A long slump lasted until the 18th century, when the town revived as a trading centre.

Orientation

The city centre is compact and easily managed on foot. The partly pedestrianised High St runs from west to east, where you'll find a towering statue of a wild-looking King Alfred the Great. The bus station is in the middle of town opposite the Guildhall and tourist office; the train station is five minutes' walk northwest.

Information

The **tourist office** (☎ 01962-840500; www.visitwinchester.co.uk; High St; ☼ 9.30am-5.30pm Mon-Sat, 11am-4pm Sun May-Sep, 10am-5pm Mon-Sat Oct-Apr), in the Gothic Revival Guildhall, has information and an accommodation booking service. The new **Discovery Centre** (☎ 0845 603 5631; Jewry St; admission free; ☼ 9am-7pm Mon-Fri, 9am-5pm Sat, 10am-4pm Sun), a library-cum-entertainment space, has free internet access. There's a **post office** (☼ 9.30am-6pm Mon-Sat) on Middle Brook St, and there are plenty of banks and ATMs on High St.

Sights

WINCHESTER CATHEDRAL

Almost 1000 years of history are crammed into Winchester's superb **cathedral** (☎ 01962-857200; www.winchester-cathedral.org.uk; adult/child £5/free, combined admission & tower tour £8; ☼ 8.30am-6pm Mon-Sat, to 5.30pm Sun), which is not only the city's star attraction but one of southern England's most awe-inspiring buildings. The exterior, with a squat tower and a slightly sunken rear, isn't at first glance appealing, despite a fine Gothic facade. But the interior contains one of the longest medieval naves (164m) in Europe, and a fascinating jumble of features from all eras.

The cathedral sits beside foundations that mark the town's original 7th-century minster church. The cathedral was begun in 1070 and completed in 1093, and subsequently entrusted with the bones of its patron saint, St Swithin (bishop of Winchester from 852 to 862). He is best known for the proverb that states that if it rains on St Swithin's Day (15 July), it will rain for a further 40 days and 40 nights.

Soggy ground and poor workmanship spelled disaster for the early church; the original tower collapsed in 1107 and major restructuring continued until the mid-15th century. Look out for the monument at the rear to diver William Walker, who saved the cathedral from collapse by delving repeatedly into its waterlogged underbelly from 1906 to 1912 to bolster rotting wooden foundations with vast quantities of concrete and brick.

On the south side of the nave, the **Cathedral Library & Triforium Gallery** (adult/child £1/50p; ☼ 11am-4pm Tue-Sat, 1.30-4pm Mon Apr-Oct) provide a fine elevated view of the cathedral body, and contains the dazzlingly illuminated pages of the 12th-century *Winchester Bible* – its colours as bright as if they were painted yesterday.

You can also see the grave of one of England's best-loved authors, Jane Austen. It's near the entrance in the northern aisle. Austen died a stone's throw from the cathedral in 1817 at **Jane Austen's House** (8 College St), where she spent her last six weeks. It's now a private residence and is marked by a slate plaque.

The transepts are the most original parts of the cathedral, and the intricately carved medieval choir stalls are another must-see, sporting everything from mythical beasts to a mischievous green man.

Flooding often prevents tours of the **crypt** (tours free; ☼ 10.30am, 12.30pm & 2.30pm Mon-Sat) from going ahead; if it is open, look out for the poignant solitary sculpture by Anthony Gormley called *Sound 2*.

Cathedral body **tours** (free; ☼ hourly 10am-3pm Mon-Sat) last one hour. There are also **tower and roof tours** (£5; ☼ 2.15pm Mon-Fri, 11.30am & 2.15pm Sat Jun-Sep, 2.15pm Wed, 11.30am & 2.15pm Sat Oct-May) up narrow stairwells and with views as far as the Isle of Wight. Sunday services take place at 8am, 10am and 11.15am, with evensong at 3.30pm. Evensong is also held at 5.30pm Monday to Saturday.

THE GREAT HALL

Winchester's other showpiece is the cavernous **Great Hall** (☎ 01962-846476; Castle Ave; suggested donation adult/child £1/50p; ☼ 10am-5pm), the only part of 11th-century Winchester Castle that Oliver Cromwell spared from destruction. Crowning the wall like a giant-sized dartboard of green and cream spokes is what centuries of mythology have called **King Arthur's Round Table**. It's actually a 700-year-old fake, but a fascinating one nonetheless. It's thought to have been constructed in the late 13th century and later painted in the reign of Henry VIII (King Arthur's image is unsurprisingly reminiscent of Henry's youthful face).

This hall was also the stage for several dramatic English courtroom dramas, including the trial of adventurer Sir Walter Raleigh in 1603, who was sentenced to death but received a reprieve at the last minute.

Outside, near the hall's entrance, there's also a section of an old Roman wall, built around AD 200, and more remains of Winchester Castle, built around 1000 years later.

MUSEUMS

City Museum (☎ 01962-863064; The Square; admission free; ☼ 10am-5pm Mon-Sat, noon-5pm Sun Apr-Oct,

10am-4pm Tue-Sat, noon-4pm Sun Nov-Mar) whizzes through Winchester's fascinating Roman and Saxon history, lingers on its Anglo-Norman golden age, pays homage to Jane Austen, and reconstructs several early-20th-century Winchester shops.

Fitting snugly into one of Winchester's two surviving medieval gateways, **Westgate Museum** (☎ 01962-869864; High St; admission free; 10am-5pm Mon-Sat, noon-5pm Sun Apr-Oct, 10am-4pm Tue-Sat, noon-4pm Sun Feb & Mar) was once a debtors' prison with a macabre set of gibbeting irons last used to display an executed criminal's body in 1777. Scrawled crudely all over the interior walls is the 17th-century graffiti of prisoners.

There's a clutch of army museums dotted around the Peninsula Barracks on Romsey Rd. The highlight is the **Royal Green Jackets Museum** (☎ 01962-828549; www.winchestermilitarymuseums.co.uk; adult/child £2/1; 10am-5pm Mon-Sat, noon-4pm Sun Mar–mid-Nov), which has a mini rifle-shooting range, a room of 6000 medals and an impressive blow-by-blow diorama of Napoleon's downfall, the Battle of Waterloo.

The militarily minded may also enjoy the jungle tableau of the **Gurkha Museum** (☎ 01962-842832; www.thegurkhamuseum.co.uk; adult/senior/child £2/1/free; 10am-5pm Mon-Sat, noon-4pm Sun), the **Light Infantry Museum** (☎ 01962-828550; admission free; 10am-4pm Tue-Sat, noon-4pm Sun), complete with a chunk of the Berlin Wall, and the **Royal Hussars Museum** (☎ 01962-828541; admission free; 10am-4pm Tue-Fri, noon-4pm Sat & Sun), which gallops through combat history from the Charge of the Light Brigade to armour-clad vehicles.

WOLVESEY CASTLE & PALACE

The fantastic, crumbling remains of early-12th-century **Wolvesey Castle** (EH; ☎ 023-9237 8291; admission free; 10am-5pm Apr-Sep) huddle in the protective embrace of the city's walls, despite the building having been largely demolished in the 1680s. According to legend, its odd name comes from a Saxon king's demand for an annual payment of 300 wolves' heads. It was completed by Henry de Blois, and it served as the Bishop of Winchester's residence throughout the medieval era. Queen Mary I and Philip II of Spain celebrated their wedding feast here in 1554. Access via College St. Today the bishop lives in the adjacent **Wolvesey Palace**.

CITY MILL

The city's 18th-century water-powered **mill** (NT; ☎ 01962-87005/; Bridge St; adult/child £3.40/1.70;

11am-5pm Mar-Dec) is now working again – you can see the process in action and buy stone-ground flour in the shop.

HOSPITAL OF ST CROSS

Monk, bishop, knight, politician and grandson of William the Conqueror, Henry de Blois was a busy man. But he found time to establish this still-impressive **hospital** (☎ 01962-851375; www.st crosshospital.co.uk; St Cross Rd; adult/child/senior £2.50/50p/£2; 9.30am-5pm Apr-Oct, 10.30am-3.30pm Mon-Sat Nov-Mar) in 1132. As well as healing the sick and housing the needy, the hospital was built to feed and bed pilgrims and crusaders en route to the Holy Land. It's the oldest charitable institution in the country, and is still roamed by 25 elderly black- or red-gowned brothers in pie-shaped trencher hats, who continue to hand out alms. Take a peek into the stumpy church, the brethren hall, the kitchen and the peaceful gardens. The best way to arrive is via the 1-mile Keats' Walk (below). Upon entering, claim the centuries-old traditional Wayfarer's Dole – a crust of bread and horn of ale (now a small swig of beer) from the Porter's Gate.

Activities
WALKS

Winchester has a tempting range of rambles. The 1-mile **Keats' Walk** meanders through the water meadows to Hospital of St Cross (above). Its beauty is said to have prompted the poet to pen the ode *To Autumn* – pick up the trail near Wolvesey Castle. Alternatively, head down Wharf Hill, through the water meadows to **St Catherine's Hill** (1 mile). The tranquil **Riverside Walk**, meanwhile, trails a short distance from the castle along the bank of the River Itchen to High St. The stiffer **Sunset Walk** up St Giles' Hill rewards with fine city views, especially at dusk – to get here head up East or Magdalen Hills. St Giles' Hill is also the beginning (or end) of the **South Downs Way** (p173).

Tours

The tourist office runs a wide variety of 1½-hour **guided walks** (adult/child £4/free; 11am Mon-Fri year-round, 2.30pm Sat Apr-Oct, 11am Sat Nov-Mar); look out for the evening strolls, which sometimes feature Jane Austen's Winchester and a 'Bring Out Your Dead' plague tour.

Sleeping

Wolvesey View (☎ 01962-852082; www.wintonian.com; 10 Colebrook Pl; s/d £40/68; P) Book the Yellow

WESSEX

Room here and you'll open the curtains to grandstand views of Wolvesey Castle's fairytale tumblings. It's a simply furnished, family-run affair, with shared bathrooms – all hidden away in a quiet cul-de-sac.

Dolphin House (☎ 01962-853284; www.dolphinhouse studios.co.uk; 3 Compton Rd; s/d £55/70; P) A kind of B&B-plus, the two rooms (with attached bathroom) in this charming town house share a compact kitchen to which your Continental breakfast is delivered – allowing for lazy lie-ins. The terrace, complete with cast-iron tables and chairs, overlooks a gently sloping lawn.

5 Clifton Terrace (☎ 01962-890053; chrissiejohnston@ hotmail.com; 5 Clifton Tce; s/d/f £55/65/89; P ▢) Blending old and new, this tall Georgian town house sees plush furnishings rub shoulders with antiques, and modern comforts coexist alongside claw-foot baths. The owners are utterly charming.

ourpick Wykeham Arms (☎ 01962-853834; www .accommodating-inns.co.uk; 75 Kingsgate St; s £90-100, d £105-150) At 250-odd years old, the Wykeham is bursting with history – it used to be a brothel and also put up Nelson for a night (some say the two events coincided). Creaking, winding stairs lead to the cosy, traditionally styled bedrooms above the pub, while the posher rooms (over the converted post office, opposite) look out onto a pocked-sized courtyard garden.

Hotel du Vin (☎ 01962-841414; www.hotelduvin.com; Southgate St; r £135-205; P ▢ wi-fi) Tucked in behind a red-brick facade and gleaming white porticoes, this oh-so-chic hotel boasts ultracool minimalist furniture, ornate chaise longues and opulent stand-alone baths. The bistro delivers Georgian elegance and modern versions of English and French classics (mains £16).

Also recommended:

12 Christchurch Rd (☎ 01962-854272; 12 Christchurch Rd; s/d £35/50) A reassuringly traditional B&B, with lace doilies, feather beds and a flower-filled conservatory.

Dawn Cottage (☎ 01962-869956; dawncottage@ hotmail.com; 99 Romsey Rd; s/d £55/68; P) A tranquil, vine-covered house a mile from the middle of town. Has lovely views, a sun deck and pretty gardens.

Eating

Cadogan & James (☎ 01962-840805; 31A The Square; 9.30am-5.30pm Mon-Sat) Self-caterers will need to be dragged out of this delightful delicatessen, full of the smells of freshly baked breads, herbs and spices, and gourmet goodies.

Wykeham Arms (☎ 01962-853834; 75 Kingsgate St; mains £9-14; lunch & dinner Mon-Sat, lunch Sun)

Somehow reminiscent of an endearingly eccentric old uncle, this charming pub-restaurant has 1400 tankards hanging from the ceilings, as well as an impressive array of school canes. The food is legendary – try the pan-fried salmon, or sausages flavoured with local bitter, then finish off with some seriously addictive sticky toffee pudding.

Brasserie Blanc (☎ 01962-810870; 19 Jewry St; mains £13; lunch & dinner) Get a taste of French home cooking, Raymond (Blanc) style, at this super-sleek chain. The celebrity chef may not necessarily sauté your starter himself, but the chicken stuffed with morel mushrooms and the Toulouse sausage with onion gravy are full of Gallic charm.

Black Rat (☎ 01962-844465; 88 Chesil St; mains £17; dinner Mon-Fri, lunch & dinner Sat & Sun) Worn wooden floorboards and warm red-brick walls give this relaxed restaurant a cosy feel. Duck with brioche, mushrooms with truffle-oil and woodpigeon with pine nuts all find their way onto the sanded-down tables.

Chesil Rectory (☎ 01962-851555; 1 Chesil St; 1-/2-/3-course lunch £15/19/23, 2-/3-/6-course dinner £39/49/65; dinner Tue, lunch & dinner Wed-Sat) Duck through the hobbit-sized door, settle down amid the 15th-century beams and prepare to enjoy some fine modern Continental cuisine. Confit of duck, Solent sea bass with oyster sauce, and ravioli of lobster with diver-caught scallops all feature on the assured menu.

Also recommended:

Loch Fyne Restaurant (☎ 01962-872930; 18 Jewry St; mains £9-15; breakfast, lunch & dinner) Quality seafood served surrounded by a stunning array of twisted Tudor beams and wooden galleries.

Black Boy (☎ 01962-861754; 1 Wharf Hill; mains £8-10; dinner Tue, lunch & dinner Wed-Sat, lunch Sun) Dishes up decent pub grub in a completely quirky environment.

Drinking

Winchester isn't big on late-night revelry, though the students head for cheap pubs along Jewry St.

Black Boy (☎ 01962-861754; 1 Wharf Hill; noon-11pm) This adorable old pub is filled with obsessive and sometimes freaky collections, from pocket watches to wax facial features, bear traps and sawn paperbacks.

Bishop on the Bridge (☎ 01962-855111; 1 High St; noon-11pm) The riverside beer garden of this contemporary pub makes a great spot to down a drink; you'll be overlooking the rushing water below.

Mix (☎ 01962-860900; 10 Jewry St; ☺ 4pm-1am Mon-Sat, 4pm-1am Sun) A poseur's paradise: perch elegantly on a velvet dressing-table chair in this black, pink and aquamarine champagne and cocktail bar.

The **Wykeham Arms** (see Eating, opposite) is a wonderfully characterful place for a pint.

Entertainment

For listings, pick up the free *What's On in Winchester* from the tourist office.

Railway Inn (☎ 01962-867795; www.liveattherailway .co.uk; 3 St Paul's Hill; ☺ 5pm-midnight Sun-Thu, to 2am Fri, to 1am Sat) Catch live bands from 8pm at this grungy place behind the station.

Screen Cinema (☎ 01962-877007; www.screencinemas .co.uk; Southgate St) Watch movies in a converted 19th-century military chapel.

Getting There & Away

Winchester is 65 miles west of London and 14 miles north of Southampton.

BUS

National Express has several direct buses to London Victoria bus station (£13, 2¼ hours). Buses also run to Southampton (40 minutes). Wilts & Dorset Explorer tickets (adult/child £7.50/4.50) let you roam the region to the west, including the New Forest.

TRAIN

Trains leave every 20 minutes from London Waterloo (£24, one hour) and Southampton (15 to 23 minutes) and hourly from Portsmouth (£8.60, one hour). There are also fast links to the Midlands.

Getting Around

There's plenty of day parking within five minutes' walk of the centre or you can use the park-and-ride for £2.70 per day. The **Bikeabout** (☎ 01962-840500; www.winchester.gov.uk/ bikeabout; membership £20) scheme lets members borrow bikes free for 24 hours at a time. Bikes can be picked up and dropped off at the tourist office.

For a taxi try the rank outside Sainsbury's on Middle Brook St or phone **Wintax Taxis** (☎ 01962-878727).

PORTSMOUTH

pop 187,056

Prepare to splice the main brace, hoist the halyard and potter around the poop deck.

Portsmouth is the principal port of Britain's Royal Navy, and its historic dockyard ranks alongside Greenwich as one of England's most fascinating centres of maritime history. Here you can jump aboard Lord Nelson's glorious warship *HMS Victory*, which led the charge at Trafalgar, and glimpse the atmospheric remains of Henry VIII's 16th-century flagship, the *Mary Rose*.

Regeneration at the nearby Gunwharf Quays has added new glitz to the city's waterfront. A spectacular millennium-inspired structure, the Spinnaker Tower – keelhauled by the British media for delays and spiralling costs – finally opened here in 2005, with views to knock the wind from the critics' sails.

However, Portsmouth is by no means a city noted for its beauty; it was heavily bombed during WWII and a combination of sometimes soulless postwar architecture and surprisingly deserted waterfront promenades can leave a melancholy impression. But the city's fine array of naval museums justifies an overnight stay, while the suburb of Southsea boasts some fair beaches, bars and good restaurants.

Orientation

It's easy to find Portsmouth's key sights – the futuristic Spinnaker Tower (p285) soars into the sky to point the way. The central quay area alongside, known as The Hard, also has the Historic Dockyard, tourist office, train station and the passenger-ferry terminal for the Isle of Wight. Just southeast lies Old Portsmouth, where more ancient buildings feature amid the postwar rebuild. Next door sits the Point, a cluster of seaworn, atmospheric buildings around the old harbour. Southsea is about 2 miles south.

Information

Laundry Care (☎ 023-9282 6245; 59 Osborne Rd; ☺ 8am-6pm)

Online Cafe (☎ 023-9283 1106; 163 Elm Grove, Southsea; internet access per 10min/1hr 50p/£2.60; ☺ 9am-9pm Mon-Fri, 10am-9pm Sat & Sun)

Post office (Palmerston Rd, Southsea)

Tourist office (☎ 023-9282 6722; www.visitports mouth.co.uk; The Hard; ☺ 9.30am-5.45pm Apr-Sep, to 5.15pm Oct-Mar) Can arrange walking tours (£2), and has an accommodation service.

Tourist office branch (☎ 023-9282 6722; Clarence Esplanade, Southsea; ☺ 9.30am-5.45pm Jul & Aug, to

WESSEX

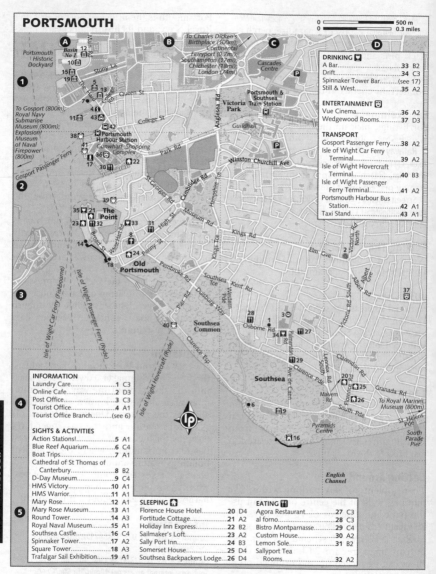

PORTSMOUTH

0 ___ 500 m
0 ___ 0.3 miles

DRINKING 🍸
A Bar.................................**33** B2
Drift...................................**34** C3
Spinnaker Tower Bar.........(see 17)
Still & West......................**35** A2

ENTERTAINMENT 🎭
Vue Cinema......................**36** A2
Wedgewood Rooms...........**37** D3

TRANSPORT
Gosport Passenger Ferry......**38** A2
Isle of Wight Car Ferry
  Terminal........................**39** A2
Isle of Wight Hovercraft
  Terminal........................**40** B3
Isle of Wight Passenger
  Ferry Terminal...............**41** A2
Portsmouth Harbour Bus
  Station..........................**42** A1
Taxi Stand.......................**43** A1

INFORMATION
Laundry Care......................**1** C3
Online Cafe........................**2** D3
Post Office.........................**3** C3
Tourist Office.....................**4** A1
Tourist Office Branch........(see 6)

SIGHTS & ACTIVITIES
Action Stations!..................**5** A1
Blue Reef Aquarium............**6** C4
Boat Trips...........................**7** A1
Cathedral of St Thomas of
  Canterbury......................**8** B2
D-Day Museum...................**9** C4
HMS Victory.....................**10** A1
HMS Warrior....................**11** A1
Mary Rose........................**12** A1
Mary Rose Museum...........**13** A1
Round Tower.....................**14** A3
Royal Naval Museum.........**15** A1
Southsea Castle.................**16** C4
Spinnaker Tower...............**17** A2
Square Tower.....................**18** A3
Trafalgar Sail Exhibition......**19** A1

SLEEPING 🛏
Florence House Hotel..........**20** D4
Fortitude Cottage................**21** A2
Holiday Inn Express............**22** B2
Sailmaker's Loft................**23** A2
Sally Port Inn.....................**24** B3
Somerset House.................**25** D4
Southsea Backpackers Lodge....**26** D4

EATING 🍴
Agora Restaurant...............**27** C3
al forno.............................**28** C3
Bistro Montparnasse...........**29** C4
Custom House...................**30** A2
Lemon Sole.......................**31** B2
Sallyport Tea
  Rooms............................**32** A2

WESSEX

5.15pm Mar-Jun, to 4pm Sep-Feb) Next to the Blue Reef Aquarium, this branch gives discounts to several attractions (if you buy tickets in advance).

Sights & Activities
PORTSMOUTH HISTORIC DOCKYARD
Portsmouth's blockbuster attraction is the **Historic Dockyard** (☎ 023-9283 9766; www.historic dockyard.co.uk; adult/child single-attraction ticket £10/8, all-inclusive ticket £18.50/14; ⏰ 10am-6pm Apr-Oct, 10am-5.30pm Nov-Mar, last admission 1½hr before closing). Set in the heart of the country's most important naval port, it comprises three stunning ships and a clutch of museums that pay homage to the historical might of the Royal Navy. Together they make for a full day's outing,

though you may spend much of your time swimming through a tide of schoolchildren. The all-inclusive ticket provides access for one year to all the ships and museums, and it includes a harbour tour (see Tours, p286) – the single ticket limits you to just one of the attractions.

The Ships

As resplendent as she is venerable, the dockyard's star sight is **HMS Victory** (www.hms-victory .com), Lord Nelson's flagship at the 1805 Battle of Trafalgar and the site of his infamous 'Kiss me, Hardy…' dying words when victory over the French had been secured. This remarkable ship is topped by a forest of ropes and masts, and weighted by a swollen belly filled with cannon and paraphernalia for an 850-strong crew. Clambering through the low-beamed decks is a stirring experience and there's huge demand for the excellent 40-minute tours – arrive early to bag a place (you can't book in advance).

Equally thrilling are the remains of 16th-century warship and darling of Henry VIII, the **Mary Rose** (www.maryrose.org), the only such ship on display in the world. This 700-tonne floating fortress sank off Portsmouth after a mysterious incident of 'human folly and bad luck' in 1545. In an astoundingly ambitious piece of marine archaeology, the ship was raised from its watery grave in 1982. It now presents a ghostly image that could teach Hollywood a few tricks, its vast flank preserved in dim lighting, dripping and glistening in a constant mist of sea water.

Anywhere else, the magnificent warship **HMS Warrior**, built in 1860, would grab centre stage. This stately dame was at the cutting edge of technology in her day, riding the transition from wood to iron and sail to steam. Visitors can wander freely around the four decks to imagine life in the Victorian navy.

Mary Rose Museum

At this museum, which is set away from the ship herself, you can bear witness to the Herculean salvage operation to raise the *Mary Rose* from the seabed. Crammed full of recovered treasures and fascinating facts, displays also feature a 15-minute film showing just how they managed to extract her from Portsmouth Harbour. A single-attraction ticket to this museum also includes admission to the ship (see above).

Royal Naval Museum

This huge museum has five galleries of naval history, model ships, battle dioramas, medals, paintings and much more. Audiovisual displays recreate the Battle of Trafalgar and one even lets you take command of a battleship – see if you can cure the scurvy and avoid mutiny. One gallery is entirely devoted to Lord Nelson.

Trafalgar Sail Exhibition

This small **exhibition** (🕙 10am-5pm Apr-Oct, to 4pm Nov-Mar) showcases HMS *Victory*'s only remaining sail from the Battle of Trafalgar. Clearly bearing the scars of conflict, it's riddled with the holes made by Napoleonic cannon – a telling illustration of the battle's ferocity.

Action Stations!

Stumble into this warehouse-based **interactive experience** (www.actionstations.org) and you'll soon be controlling a replica Merlin helicopter, commanding a warship, upping periscope or jumping aboard a jerky simulator. The whole set-up is a thinly disguised recruitment drive for the modern navy, but it's a fun one, nonetheless.

SPINNAKER TOWER

Soaring to 170m above Gunwharf Quays, **Spinnaker Tower** (☎ 023-92857520; www.spinnakertower .co.uk; Gunwharf Quays; adult/child £7/5 50; 🕙 10am-10pm Aug, 10am-6pm Sun-Fri, 10am-10pm Sat Sep & Oct, 10am-6pm Nov Jul) is Portsmouth's unmistakable new landmark, a symbol of the city's new-found razzle-dazzle. Its two sweeping white arcs resemble a billowing sail from some angles, and a sharp skeletal ribcage from others.

As the UK's tallest publicly accessible structure, it offers truly extraordinary views over Portsmouth, the Isle of Wight, the South Downs and even Chichester, 23 miles to the east. Observation Deck 1 has a hair-raising view through the glass floor, while the roofless Crow's Nest on Deck 3 allows you to feel the wind in your hair. Below, the glitzy mall and promenades dotted with palm trees complete the designers' vision of 21st-century Portsmouth.

GOSPORT

Gosport sits on the other side of Portsmouth Harbour, and is easily reached by ferry from The Hard.

Less than a mile from the ferry port, **Royal Navy Submarine Museum** (☎ 023-9252 9217; www .rnsubmus.co.uk; adult/child £7/5.50; ⏲ 10am-5.30pm Apr-Oct, to 4.30pm Nov-Mar) includes a bona-fide ex-service submarine – clambering aboard provides a revealing insight into the claustrophobic conditions.

Or, if it's things that go bang that float your boat, head for **Explosion! Museum of Naval Firepower** (☎ 023-9250 5600; www.explosion.org.uk; Priddy's Hard; adult/child £4/2; ⏲ 10am-4pm Sat & Sun), less than a mile from the Gosport ferry terminal, in the opposite direction from the Royal Navy Submarine Museum. An old gunpowder magazine, built in 1771, houses this museum of munitions and ordinance.

OTHER SIGHTS & ACTIVITIES

A short waterside walk from Gunwharf Quays, but a world apart in atmosphere, the **Point** is home to characterful cobbled streets dotted with salty sea-dog pubs. It's a top spot from which to gaze at the Spinnaker Tower and the passing parade of ferries and navy ships.

Just off the Point you can mount the **Round Tower** (originally built by Henry V), the **Square Tower** of 1494, and take a stroll along the old fort walls. A short walk from the water, the airy **Cathedral of St Thomas of Canterbury** (☎ 023-9282 3300; www.portsmouthcathedral.org.uk; High St; ⏲ 9am-5pm) retains fragments of its 12th- and 17th-century incarnations, but a striking modern makeover has introduced some quirky little statuettes by Peter Eugene Ball; look for Thomas Becket with a sword through his mitred head.

There's a cluster of attractions on Clarence Esplanade at the Southsea end of the waterfront. **Blue Reef Aquarium** (☎ 023-9287 5222; www .bluereefaquarium.co.uk; adult/child £9/7; ⏲ 10am-5pm Mar-Oct, to 4pm Nov-Feb) has open-topped tanks, huge underwater walkways and a captivating 'seahorse ranch' – a sure hit with kids. A short stroll away is bunkerlike **D-Day Museum** (☎ 023-9282 7261; www.ddaymuseum.co.uk; Clarence Esplanade; adult/child £6/4.20; ⏲ 10am-5.30pm Apr-Sep, to 5pm Oct-Mar), which recounts Portsmouth's important role as departure point for the Allied D-Day forces in 1944.

Alongside, squat **Southsea Castle** (☎ 023-9282 7261; www.southseacastle.co.uk; adult/child £3.50/2.50; ⏲ 10am-5.30pm Apr-Sep) was built by Henry VIII and is said to be where he watched his beloved *Mary Rose* sink. The castle was much altered in the early 19th century and there's now a lighthouse plonked on top.

Further south, **Royal Marines Museum** (☎ 023-9281 9385; www.royalmarinesmuseum.co.uk; Barracks Rd; adult/child £5.25/3.25; ⏲ 10am-5pm) tells the story of the navy's elite force, and has a jungle-warfare display complete with live snakes and scorpions.

East of the Historic Dockyard you can also poke your nose into **Charles Dickens' Birthplace** (☎ 023-9282 7261; www.charlesdickensbirthplace.co.uk; 393 Old Commercial Rd; adult/child £3.50/2.50; ⏲ 10am-5.30pm mid-Apr–Oct); the hard-hitting author was born here in 1812. He also died here in 1870 – you can see the couch upon which he breathed his last breath.

Tours

Boat trips (☎ 023-9272 8060; Historic Dockyard; ⏲ 11am-3pm Easter-Oct) Weather permitting, 40-minute harbour tours leave on the hour from just inside the entrance to the Historic Dockyard. They're free with the all-inclusive Dockyard ticket or can be bought separately (adult/child £5/3).

Walking tours (adult/child £3/free; ⏲ 2.30pm Sun) The tourist office runs a program of guided tours; check with the office for details and departure points.

Sleeping

Most B&Bs are in Southsea. Centrally located spots fill up quickly, so book ahead.

Southsea Backpackers Lodge (☎ 023-9283 2495; www.portsmouthbackpackers.co.uk; 4 Florence Rd, Southsea; dm £15, d £33-38; P ▢) This old-fashioned backpackers hostel is a warren of four- to eight-bed dorms. The shower-to-people ratio isn't that high, but there are other extras like a pool table, patio and BBQ.

Fortitude Cottage (☎ 023-9282 3748; www.fort itudecottage.co.uk; 51 Broad St, The Point; s from £45, d £70-80) The ferry-port views from this fresh and airy B&B are interesting, if industrial. The lovely bay-windowed breakfast area is ideal for munching a sausage as the ships come in.

Sally Port Inn (☎ 023-9282 1860; High St, Old Portsmouth; s/d/f £45/70/80) The slightly worn bedrooms in this 16th-century inn are showing their age; they also share bathrooms. But history buffs might enjoy the slanting floors, beams scavenged from shipwrecks and a Georgian cantilever staircase built with a ship's mast.

Florence House Hotel (☎ 023-9275 1666; www.flor encehousehotel.co.uk; 2 Malvern Rd, Southsea; d £70-140; P ▢ wi-fi) Edwardian elegance combines beautifully with modern flourishes at this

WESSEX

superstylish oasis of boutique bliss. It's a winning combination of plush furnishings, sleek bathrooms, open fireplaces and the odd chaise longue – the suite, complete with spa bath, is top-notch.

our pick **Somerset House** (☎ 023-9275 3555; www .somersethousehotel.co.uk; 10 Florence Rd, Southsea; d £110-190) At this late-Victorian sister to Florence House (opposite), opposite, the same team has created another achingly tasteful haven of designer calm. Here, stained glass, dark woods and polished floors cosy up to Balinese figurines and the very latest word in luxury bathrooms.

Also recommended:

Sailmaker's Loft (☎ 023-9282 3045; sailmakersloft@ aol.com; 5 Bath Sq, The Point; s/d £28/55) Unbeatable views across the water towards Gosport.

Holiday Inn Express (☎ 0870 417 6161; www.hi express.com; The Plaza; r £105; P ⌨) Spotlessly bland, but set right amid Gunwharf Quays' restaurants and bars.

Eating

Sallyport Tea Rooms (☎ 023-9281 6265; 35 Broad St, The Point; breakfast £3.75-5.25, lunch £3-5; ✆ 10am-5pm Tue-Sun) Just as a traditional teashop should be: civilised, filled with fussy collectibles and serving up loose-leaf speciality teas and other old-fashioned delights to the strains of 1940s jazz.

Custom House (☎ 023-9283 2333; Gunwharf Quays; mains £8; ✆ lunch & dinner) The best of Gunwharf Quays' numerous swanky eateries. Custom House is in the 1790 Vernon Building, now a traditional-style pub with better-than-average bar food.

al forno (☎ 023-9282 0515; 39 Osborne Rd; mains £8; ✆ noon-10pm) This cool little Italian brings a touch of la dolce vita to not-terribly Continental Southsea. The decor may not be traditional (think burgundy candy stripes and elegant chairs), but the chef still rustles up all the old pasta and pizza favourites.

Agora Restaurant (☎ 023-9282 2617; 9 Clarendon Rd, Southsea; mains £8.50-10.50; ✆ dinner) Festooned with fake beams, this familial little Turkish hookah bar serves up tasty Mediterranean food, washed down with ouzo and raki. Watch out for its occasional belly-dancing nights.

our pick **Lemon Sole** (☎ 023-9281 1303; 123 High St, Old Portsmouth; mains £9.50-18; ✆ lunch & dinner) A colourful little pick-your-own seafood restaurant, Lemon Sole lets you size up freshly netted critters at a counter, then choose how you want them cooked. Try the seafood and shellfish chowder, the devilled mackerel or the stunning fish platters (£39 for two). The menu includes vegie and meat options, too. It's all tucked away in a lemon-yellow, gold and blue interior with a whole wall full of wine bottles at the end.

Bistro Montparnasse (☎ 023-9281 6754; 103 Palmerston Rd, Southsea; lunch mains £11-22, 2-/3-course dinner £27/32; ✆ lunch & dinner Tue-Sat) Along with polished wooden floors and chic decor, this classy, cosy bistro serves up French classics with an English twist. Wild mushroom and spinach Wellington, and local sea bass with crab ravioli are among the treats.

Drinking

For a taste of modern Portsmouth, pick your way through the rows of bars and trendy terraced and balconied eateries that line Gunwharf Quays.

A Bar (☎ 023-9281 15585; 58 White Hart Rd, Old Portsmouth; ✆ 11am-11pm) There's actually been a pub here since 1784 – these days it's home to worn floorboards, squishy leather sofas, a soundtrack of groovy tunes and a chilled, gently trendy vibe.

Still & West (☎ 023-9282 1567; 2 Bath Sq, The Point) This relaxed salty-sea-dog pub has served many a sailor and smuggler in the last 300 years. The waterside terrace is a great spot to down a beer to a backdrop of passing yachts and ferries.

Drift (☎ 023-9277 9839; www.driftbar.com; 78 Palmerston Rd, Southsea; ✆ 10pm-3am) All slick chrome and smooth wood, this hip London-style bar languishes behind a frosted glass and pebble-dashed front. The lounge showcases DJs at the weekends and acoustic sets on Sundays.

Spinnaker Tower Bar (☎ 023-9285 7520; Gunwharf Quays; ✆ 10am-11pm) OK, it's the most touristy cafe-bar in Portsmouth, but it provides a prime coffee-sipping, wine-supping, boat-watching vantage point.

Entertainment

Southsea is thick with nightclubs and live-music venues.

Wedgewood Rooms (☎ 023-9286 3911; www.wedge woodrooms.co.uk; Albert Rd, Southsea) One of Portsmouth's best live-music venues; also hosting DJs and comedians.

For cinema, head to **Vue** (www.myvue.com; Gunwharf Quays).

WESSEX

Getting There & Away

Portsmouth is 100 miles southwest of London.

BOAT

P&O Ferries (☎ 08716 645 645; www.poferries.com) sails twice a week to Bilbao in Spain (10 hours). **Brittany Ferries** (☎ 0870 366 5333; www.brittanyferries .co.uk) has overnight services to St Malo (10¾ hours), Caen (5½ hours) and Cherbourg (three hours) in France. **LD Lines** (☎ 0844 576 8836; www.ldlines.co.uk) has overnight ferries to Le Havre (8½ hours) in France. **Condor Ferries** (☎ 0845 609 1024; www.condorferries.co.uk) runs a weekly car-and-passenger service to Cherbourg (5½ hours).

Prices for all routes vary wildly depending on times and dates of travel – an example fare is £152 return for a car and two adults on the Portsmouth–Cherbourg route. Book in advance, be prepared to travel off-peak and look out for special deals.

The Continental Ferryport is north of the Historic Dockyard.

For details on how to reach the Isle of Wight from Portsmouth, see p294.

BUS

There are 15 National Express buses from London (£14.30, 2½ hours) daily; some go via Heathrow airport (£14.30, 2¾ hours) and continue to Southampton (50 minutes). Bus 700 runs to Chichester (one hour) and Brighton (3½ hours) half-hourly Monday to Saturday, and hourly on Sunday.

TRAIN

Trains run every 15 minutes from London Victoria (£24.40, two hours 20 minutes) and Waterloo Stations (£24.40, one hour and 40 minutes). Trains also go to Southampton (£7.80, 40 to 55 minutes, four hourly), Brighton (£12.80, one hour and 40 minutes, hourly), Winchester (£7.90, one hour, hourly) and Chichester (£5.60, 30 to 46 minutes, twice an hour).

For the Historic Dockyard get off at the final stop, Portsmouth Harbour.

Getting Around

Bus 6 operates between the Portsmouth Harbour bus station and South Parade Pier in Southsea, via Old Portsmouth.

The **Gosport Passenger Ferry** (☎ 023-9252 4551; www.gosportferry.co.uk; adult/child return £2.10/1.40, bicycle 70p) shuttles between The Hard and Gosport every 10 to 15 minutes.

For a taxi try **Aquacars** (☎ 023-9266 6666, 9265 4321) in Southsea, or the rank near the bus station.

SOUTHAMPTON

pop 234,224

A no-nonsense port city and gateway to the Isle of Wight, Southampton lies deep in the folds of the Solent, an 8-mile inlet fed by the rivers Itchen and Test. The city was once a flourishing medieval port but its centre was gutted by merciless bombing in WWII and consequently there's little left of its early heritage. Southampton today is more a transport hub than an appealing place to stay. Its gritty waterfront waved the *Titanic* off on its ill-fated voyage in 1912, while larger-than-life ocean liners such as the *QEII* still dock here.

The **tourist office** (☎ 023-8083 3333; www.visit -southampton.co.uk; 9 Civic Centre Rd; ⏲ 9.30am-5pm Mon-Sat, 10.30am-3.30pm Sun) has details of free 90-minute **guided walks** (⏲ 10.30am Jul & Sep, 10.30am & 2.30pm Aug, 10.30am Sun Oct-Jun), which meet at the Bargate on High St.

Sights & Activities

Set in a 14th-century waterfront warehouse, the **Maritime Museum** (☎ 023-8063 5904; The Wool House, Town Quay; adult/child £2/1; ⏲ 10am-4pm Tue-Sat, 1-4pm Sun) tells the tragic story of the *Titanic* and outlines Southampton's history. The building was once a prison – look out for the inmates' names carved in the impressive timber roof.

For a glimpse of Southampton's medieval heyday, visit the nearby **Medieval Merchant's House** (EH; ☎ 023-8022 1503; French St; adult/child £3.70/2; ⏲ noon-5pm Sun late Mar-Sep), which dates back to 1290.

The **Southampton Art Gallery** (☎ 023-8083 2277; www.southampton.gov.uk/art; Commercial Rd; admission free; ⏲ 10am-5pm Tue-Sat, 1-4pm Sun) features work by some of the best names in 20th-century British art, including Spencer, Turner and Gainsborough.

Getting There & Away

AIR

Southampton International Airport (☎ 0870 040 0009; www.southamptonairport.com) has links to 40 UK and European destinations, including Amsterdam, Paris and Dublin. There are five trains an hour between the airport and the main train station (seven minutes).

BOAT
Red Funnel (☎ 0844 844 9988; www.redfunnel.co.uk)
runs regular passenger and car ferries to the
Isle of Wight (see p294). There's a half-hourly
ferry service (☎ 023-8084 0722; one-way adult/child
£3.20/2.40) from the Town Quay to Hythe in the
New Forest.

BUS
National Express runs to London and Heathrow
16 times a day (£13.80, 2½ hours). It also runs
a 7.20pm bus to Lymington (40 minutes) via
Lyndhurst (20 minutes) in the New Forest.

Bus M27 runs to Portsmouth six times
daily (40 minutes). Buses 31 and 32 run to
Winchester (one hour) every two hours
Monday to Saturday, and half-hourly on
Sunday. Buses 56 and 56A go to all the main
towns in the New Forest hourly (every two
hours on Sunday). Ask about the good-value
Explorer tickets that are valid on these routes.

TRAIN
Trains to Portsmouth run every 15 minutes
(£7.80, 40 to 55 minutes) and to Winchester
(20 minutes) every 20 minutes.

NEW FOREST

With typical accidental English irony, the New
Forest is anything but new. It's also not much
of a forest, being mostly moorland ('forest' is
from the Old French for 'hunting ground').
This ancient swathe of land has a unique
history and archaic traditions that date back
almost 1000 years (see boxed text, p291). Its
incarnation as a national park is much more
modern, having been awarded that status in
2005. The forest's combined charms make it
a joy to explore. Wild ponies mooch around
pretty scrubland, deer flicker in the distance
and rare birds flit among the foliage. Genteel
villages lightly dot the landscape, connected
by a web of walking and cycling routes.

The park is also a hugely popular destination
for campers; Lyndhurst's tourist office has a free
brochure detailing designated areas. For more
information, go to www.thenewforest.co.uk.

Activities
CYCLING
With all that picturesque scenery, the New
Forest makes for superb cycling country, and

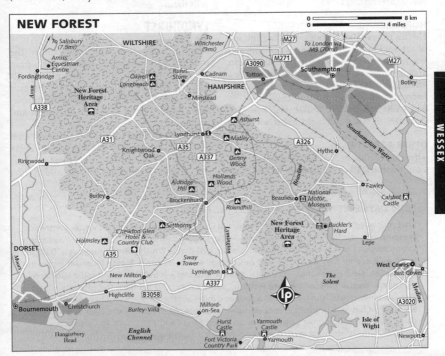

hundreds of miles of trails link the main villages and the key railway station at Brockenhurst

New Forest Cycle Map (£2) shows the approved off-road and quieter 'on-road' routes. *New Forest Cycle Experience Route Pack* (£4) features seven trips, ranging from a 4-mile jaunt through the forest to a 24-mile leg test round the cliffs of the Isle of Wight. David Hancock's *Mountain Bike Guide to Hampshire and the New Forest* (£5) outlines routes of 13 to 20 miles. Maps and guides can be bought from Lyndhurst tourist office (right) or via its website.

There are several rental shops. You'll need to pay a deposit (usually £20) and provide identification.

AA Bike Hire (☎ 023-8028 3349; www.aabikehirenew forest.co.uk; Fern Glen, Gosport Lane, Lyndhurst; adult/child per day £10/5)

Country Lanes (☎ 01590-622627; www.countrylanes .co.uk; Railway Station, Brockenhurst; bike/tandem per day £14/25; ☙ Easter-Oct)

Cyclexperience (☎ 01590-624204; www.newforest cyclehire.co.uk; Brookley Rd, Brockenhurst; adult/child per day £11/6)

Forest Leisure Cycling (☎ 01425-403584; www .forestleisurecycling.co.uk; The Cross, Village Centre, Burley; adult/child per day from £11/6)

HORSE RIDING

No, we're *not* talking about saddling up one of the wild ponies. But riding *is* a wonderful way to roam the New Forest. These stables can arrange rides, and they welcome beginners:

Arniss Equestrian Centre (☎ 01425-654114; Godshill, Fordingbridge; per hr £20)

Burley-Villa (Western Riding; ☎ 01425-610278; per 1-/ 2hr hack £28/48) It's off the B3058, just south of New Milton.

OTHER ACTIVITIES

There are regular guided walks with Forestry Commission staff called **Rambles with a Ranger**

(☎ 023-8028 3141; walks per person £4). **New Forest Activities** (☎ 01590-612377; www.newforestactivities .co.uk), near Beaulieu, offers canoeing (adult/ child per hour £15/12, per two hours £25/20), kayaking (per two hours £25) and archery (per 1½ hours adult/child £20/15).

Getting There & Around

There are regular bus services from Southampton and Bournemouth. Trains run every hour to Brockenhurst from London Waterloo (£29.50, two hours) via Winchester (£8, 31 minutes) and on to Bournemouth (£5, 25 minutes). Local trains also link Brockenhurst with Lymington (see p293).

The **New Forest Tour Bus** (☎ 023-8061 8233; www.thenewforesttour.info; adult/child £9/4.50; ☙ tours hourly 10am-4pm late May-Aug) is a two-hour hop-on hop-off bus service that passes through Lyndhurst's main car park, Brockenhurst Station, Lymington and Beaulieu; buses also have cycle trailers.

A **Wilts & Dorset** (www.wdbus.co.uk) Network Ticket offers unlimited travel on main bus lines in the region (one/seven days costs £7.50/20); the tourist office in Lyndhurst also sells them.

LYNDHURST
pop 2281

A good base from which to explore the national park or simply stop off for a pint, a cuppa or a map, the quaint country village of Lyndhurst is one of the New Forest's larger settlements. It has an excellent information centre, as well as several cosy pubs and restaurants.

The **tourist office** (☎ 023-8028 2269; www.thenew forest.co.uk; High St; ☙ 10am-5pm) sells a wide variety of information on the New Forest, including camping guides and walking and cycling

---

FOUR DAYS FREEWHEELING THROUGH THE FOREST

Start your woodland two-wheeled adventure with some research at Lyndhurst's **visitor centre and museum** (above). Then limber up with an 8-mile, largely off-road jaunt via Denny Wood south to Brockenhurst before checking into the pamper pad that is **Whitley Ridge** (opposite). Day two is a 9-mile peddle east via copses and quiet roads to the **National Motor Museum** (opposite) at **Beaulieu**. Next comes the 2-mile dash south to **Buckler's Hard** (p292) and some supercomfy digs at the **Master Builder's House Hotel** (p292). The next day it's back to Brockenhurst, via a more southerly route, and from there a further 8 miles southwest leads to **Chewton Glen Hotel & Country Club** (p293), where an unbelievably luxurious spa should soothe away any aches and pains. Day four is a 15-mile power north via lanes, forest and pubs back to Lyndhurst, having explored some of the best cycle trails the New Forest has to offer.

VERDERERS, AGISTERS & PONIES

The woods of the New Forest are some of the few areas of England to remain largely untouched since Norman times, partly thanks to their unsuitability as agricultural land. But more significantly, the New Forest has also been protected by an 11th-century law: William the Conqueror officially declared the whole area a royal hunting preserve in 1079, thereby protecting it from development. The crown still owns 260 sq km of the New Forest, though the Forestry Commission has maintained it since 1924.

The remaining 130 sq km are owned by commoners, and by verderers, who, in the pre-automobile age, reared ponies as work horses. Today the animals are either schooled as riding ponies or left to graze the land at will. The verderers' status is protected by the Commoners' Charter, first laid down in 1077, which guaranteed them six basic rights, the most important of which is the right to pasture. Every year, the 300-odd verderers gather to elect five agisters, who are responsible for the daily management of the forest's 3000 ponies, 1800 cattle and smaller numbers of donkeys, pigs and sheep.

You can wander freely throughout the forest, but don't feed or touch the wild ponies. To protect ponies, cyclists and walkers, there is a 40mph speed limit. If you find an injured pony phone Lyndhurst Police on ☎ 0845 045 45 45.

maps. It also sells the more detailed Ordnance Survey (OS) map (No 22, £8). The displays of the **New Forest Museum** (☎ 023-8028 3444; www .newforestmuseum.org.uk; adult/child £3/free), alongside, run through the unique ecology and social history of the region.

Just across the car park, the **library** (☎ 023-8028 2675; ☺ 10am-1pm Fri & Sat, 10am-1pm & 4-7pm Tue, 3-5pm Wed) has free internet access.

Sleeping & Eating

Acorns (☎ 023-8028 4559; www.acornsoflyndhurst.co.uk; 31 Romsey Rd; d £50-70; **P**) One of many B&Bs along the A337 into the village from the south, Acorns gains from being set back from the road. Simple rooms, decked out in cream and pine, sit behind a flower-filled front garden.

Crown Hotel (☎ 023-8028 2922; www.crownhotel -lyndhurst.co.uk; 9 High St; s/d £88/145; **P** 🖵) There's such a deeply established feel to this oak-panelled, old-English coaching inn that you half expect to see a well-trained butler gliding up the grand stairs. The mullioned windows and ancient beams frame bedroom furnishings that are sometimes a little staid, and sometimes surprisingly snazzy.

Waterloo Arms (☎ 023-8028 2113; Pikes Hill; mains £7-15; ☺ lunch & dinner) This cosy 17th-century thatched pub serves good-value meals in a snug wood-beamed interior. On the town's northern edge, it's signposted off the A337 to Cadnam.

our pick **Whitley Ridge** (☎ 01590-622354; www.whit leyridge.com; Beaulieu Rd; Brockenhurst; r £95) If you hanker after a country-house atmosphere, head here. Set in 6 hectares of dappled grounds, this ivy-clad Georgian pile pampers guests amid elegant period-style rooms finished with contemporary twists (think flat-screen TVs and gilt mirrors). The classy restaurant conjures up organic, seasonal, locally sourced creations finished with dashes of Anglo-French flair, and it's all tucked away 4 miles south of Lyndhurst at Brockenhurst.

Getting There & Away

Buses 56 and 56A run twice hourly to Southampton (30 minutes) Monday to Saturday, with five buses on Sunday. Lyndhurst has no train station, and the nearest stop is at Brockenhurst, 8 miles south (see opposite).

White Horse Ferries (☎ 023-8084 0722; www.hythe ferry.co.uk) operates a service from Southampton to Hythe, 13 miles east of Lyndhurst, every half-hour (£4 off-peak return, 12 minutes).

AROUND LYNDHURST

Petrol-heads, historians and ghost-hunters all gravitate to **Beaulieu** (☎ 01590-612345; www .beaulieu.co.uk; adult/child/family £16/8/44; ☺ 10am-6pm Jun-Sep, to 5pm Oct-May) – pronounced *bew*-lee – a tourist complex based on the site of what was once England's most important 13th-century Cistercian monastery. Following Henry VIII's monastic land-grab of 1536, the abbey fell to the ancestors of current proprietors, the Montague family.

Motor-maniacs will be in raptures at Lord Montague's **National Motor Museum**, a splendid

WESSEX

collection of vehicles that will sometimes leave you wondering if they are really are cars, or strange hybrid planes, boats or metal bubbles with wheels. It's hard to resist the romance of the early classics, or the oomph of winning F1 cars. Here, too, are several jet-powered land-speed record-breakers including *Bluebird*, which famously broke the record (403mph, or 649km/h) in 1964. There are even celebrity bangers – look out for Mr Bean's Austin Mini and James Bond's whizz-bang speed machines.

Beaulieu's grand but indefinably homely **palace** began life as a 14th-century Gothic abbey gatehouse, but received a 19th-century Scottish Baronial makeover from Baron Montague in the 1860s. Don't be surprised if you hear eerie Gregorian chanting or feel the hairs on the back of your neck quiver – the abbey is supposedly one of England's most haunted buildings.

The New Forest Tour Bus stops directly outside the complex on its circular route via Lyndhurst, Brockenhurst and Lymington. You can also get here from Lymington (35 minutes) by catching bus 112, which continues to Hythe and the ferry to Southampton.

BUCKLER'S HARD

For such a tiny place, this picturesque huddle of 18th-century cottages, near the mouth of the River Beaulieu, has a big history. It started life in 1722, when one of the dukes of Montague decided to build a port to finance an expedition to the Caribbean. His dream was never realised, but when the war with France came, this embryonic village with a sheltered gravel waterfront became a secret boatyard where several of Nelson's triumphant Battle of Trafalgar warships were built. In the 20th century it played its part in more clandestine wartime manoeuvrings – the preparations for the D-Day landings.

The hamlet is now a fascinating heritage centre – **Buckler's Hard Story** (☎ 01590-616203; www.bucklershard.co.uk; adult/child £5.70/4.10; ☻ 10am-5pm Mar-Oct, to 4.30pm Nov-Feb) – which features immaculately preserved 18th-century labourers' cottages. The maritime museum charts the inlet's shipbuilding history and its role in WWII – for a little light relief, seek out Nelson's dinky baby clothes.

The luxurious **Master Builder's House Hotel** (☎ 01590-616253; www.themasterbuilders.co.uk; d £94-127; P) is also part of the complex. This

beautifully restored 18th-century hotel has 25 chintz and candy-striped rooms, topped off with suitably nautical pictures. The acclaimed restaurant (mains £10 to £18) overlooks the river, while the Yachtsman's Bar serves pub grub from £4.

Swiftsure boats operate 30-minute **river cruises** (adult/child £4/2.50) from the waterfront between Easter and October.

Buckler's Hard is 2 miles downstream from Beaulieu; a lovely riverside walking trail links the two.

LYMINGTON

pop 14,227

Yachting haven, New Forest base and jumping-off point to the Isle of Wight – the bustling harbour town of Lymington has several strings to its tourism bow. This pleasing Georgian town also boasts a range of inns, nautical stores and quirky bookshops, as well as a few stretches of utterly quaint cobbled streets.

Information

Lymington's main **library** (☎ 01590-673050; North Close; ☻ 9.30am-7pm Mon, Tue, Thu & Fri, 9.30am-1pm Wed, 9.30am-5pm Sat) has free internet access.

Lymington Laundrette (☎ 01590-672898; 11 New St; ☻ 8am-6pm Mon-Fri, to 1pm Sat) can make hiking gear smell sweet again; it's next door to the tourist office.

ATMs, banks and shops line the High St. There's a post office at the end of the High St near St Thomas Church.

The **tourist office** (☎ 01590-689000; www.thenewforest.co.uk; New St; ☻ 10am-5pm Mon-Sat Jul-Sep, to 4pm Mon-Sat Oct-Jun), a block off the High St next to the museum, sells walking tours of town and can help with accommodation.

Sights

Lymington was once known as a contrabandist port, and tales of local smugglers, saltmakers and yachties pack the **St Barbe Museum** (☎ 01590-676969; www.stbarbe-museum.org.uk; New St; adult/child £3/2; ☻ 10am-4pm Mon-Sat).

Sleeping & Eating

Durlston House (☎ 01590-677364; www.durlstonhouse.co.uk; 61 Gosport St; s £45, d £60-70; P) For good value, head to this B&B of pine cabinets, subdued furnishings and neat-as-a-pin rooms, a few minutes' walk from town.

Angel Inn (☎ 01590-672050; www.roomattheinn.co.uk; 108 High St; s £50, d £80-100; P) There's a snug feel to this swish hotel, which is set in a renovated Georgian coaching inn. The rooms are warmly decorated and full of wood, while the cosy pub-bistro dishes up seared tuna, blue-cheese and chive tart, and Aberdeen Angus burgers (mains £7 to £18).

our pick **Stanwell House** (☎ 01590-677123; www.stanwellhouse.com; 14 High St; s £99-135, d £135-165, ste £195; 🖳) The epitome of discreet luxury, this beautiful boutique hotel is the place to wait for your ship to come in. Cane chairs dot the elegant conservatory, flowers frame a long, walled garden, and the rooms are an eclectic mix of stand-alone baths, rococo mirrors, gently distressed furniture and plush throws. The seafood restaurant (open noon to 10pm daily; tapas £6, mains £13 to £35) rustles up bouillabaisse and seafood platters, and the chic bistro tempts you with fine dining (two/three courses from £20/24). There's even a vaguely decadent satin-cushion-strewn bar.

Getting There & Away

The bus station is just off High St. Lymington has two train stations: Lymington Town and Lymington Pier. The latter is where the Isle of Wight ferry drops off and picks up. Trains to Southampton (£7.80, 45 minutes) via Brockenhurst leave every half-hour.

Wightlink Ferries (☎ 0870 582 7744; www.wightlink.co.uk) cross to Yarmouth on the Isle of Wight (see p294).

ISLE OF WIGHT

This lovely island, just a few miles off the Hampshire coast, does its utmost to bottle and sell traditional childhood-holiday nostalgia. A popular escape for yachties, cyclists, walkers and the bucket-and-spade brigade since Victorian times, it alternates between chocolate-box quaint and crazy-golf kitsch, and between rosy-cheeked activity and rural respite. But the 21st century has also seen a youthful buzz inject life into the island's southern resort towns, attracting a new generation of urbanites and romantic weekenders with gastropubs, slick hotels and big music festivals. Still, the island's principal appeal remains: a surprisingly mild climate, myriad outdoorsy activities and lush green hills that roll down to 25 miles of clean, unspoilt beaches.

For good online information, check out www.islandbreaks.co.uk.

Activities

CYCLING

The Isle of Wight will make pedal-pushers smile – there is a 62-mile cycleway, and the island has its very own **Cycling Festival** (☎ 01983-203891; www.sunseaandcycling.com) every September. The tourist office has exhaustive information and sells trail guides.

Bike rentals are available all over the island for around £14 per day or £45 per week. Recommended companies:

Tavcycles (☎ 01983-812989; www.tavcycles.co.uk; 140 High St, Ryde)

Wight Cycle Hire (☎ 01983-731800; www.wightcyclehire.co.uk) Brading (Station Rd, Brading); Yarmouth (Station Rd, Yarmouth) Offers delivery and collection across the island.

Wight Off Road (☎ 01983-408587; 105 High St, Sandown)

WALKING

This is one of the best spots in southern England for gentle rambling; the island has a network of 500 miles of well-marked walking paths, including 67 miles of coastal routes. The island's **Walking Festival** (☎ 01983-813813; www.isleofwightwalkingfestival.co.uk), held over

WESSEX

two weeks in May, is feted as the largest in the UK. Tourist offices sell trail pamphlets (from £3).

OTHER ACTIVITIES

Water sports are a serious business on Wight's northern shores – especially sailing but also windsurfing, sea-kayaking and surfing. Powerboat trips also run out to the Needles (p297). Wight also offers **gliding** lessons, **paragliding**, and even **llama-trekking**. Tourist offices can help fix you up with all of these.

Getting There & Away

The cost of car fares to the Isle of Wight can vary enormously – make savings by booking ahead, asking about special offers and travelling in off-peak periods.

Wightlink (☎ 08705 82 77 44; www.wightlink.co.uk) operates a passenger ferry from The Hard in Portsmouth to Ryde pier (day-return adult/child £13.50/6.50, 20 minutes) and a car-and-passenger ferry to Fishbourne (day-return adult/child £11/5.40, 40 minutes). Both run every half-hour. Car fares start at £47 for a short-break return.

The Wightlink car ferry between Lymington and Yarmouth costs £10.80/5.40 per adult/child (day return), and from £40 for cars (30 minutes, every half-hour).

Hovertravel (☎ 01983-811000; www.hovertravel .co.uk) hovercrafts shuttle foot passengers between Southsea (near Portsmouth) and Ryde (day-return adult/child £12.50/6.25, 10 minutes, every half-hour).

Red Funnel (☎ 08448 44 99 88; www.redfunnel.co.uk) operates car ferries between Southampton and East Cowes (day-return adult/child £12/6, from £40 with car, 55 minutes) and high-speed passenger ferries between Southampton and West Cowes (day-return adult/child £16.60/8.30, 25 minutes). Check for deals that include admission to island attractions.

Getting Around

1st Call (☎ 01983-400055; 15 College Close, Sandown) provides car hire (from £23 per day), collecting and delivering vehicles islandwide.

Southern Vectis (☎ 01983-827000; www.islandbuses .info) operates buses between the eastern towns about every 30 minutes; regular services are less frequent to the remoter southwest side be-

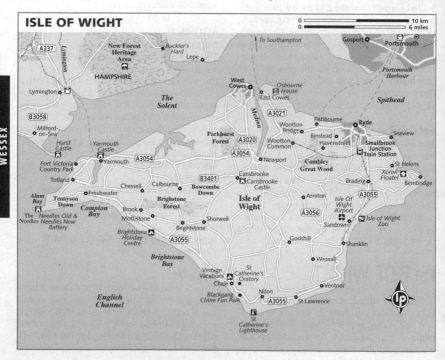

ISLE OF WIGHT

WIGHT'S OWN WOODSTOCK

The tranquil Isle of Wight is commonly described as 'England, only a few decades ago', referring to its genteel traditions and often unspoilt charm. But the last few years have seen an altogether different revival of past decades. For this island was once the setting for a series of infamous rock festivals that burned short but bright from 1968 to 1970.

The final 1970 festival is the stuff of rock legend: an incredible 600,000 hippies gathered here to see the likes of the Doors, the Who, Joni Mitchell and – most famously – the last performance of rock icon Jimi Hendrix, who was to die less than three weeks later, aged just 27. The festival itself bit the dust after a bunch of revellers ran amok; the incident led to an Isle of Wight Act being passed in parliament, and all gatherings of over 10,000 people were henceforth banned.

But the noughties have seen a rekindling of the island's revolutionary festivals, which are fast growing into some of England's top music events. The new generation of **Isle of Wight Festivals** (www.isleofwightfestival.org), held in mid-June, has already been headlined by the likes of REM, Coldplay, The Feeling, the Kaiser Chiefs and Keane, while dance-oriented **Bestival** (www.bestival .net), in early to mid-September, has seen the Pet Shop Boys, Scissor Sisters and more.

tween Blackgang Chine Fun Park and Brook. Twice daily between Easter and September the Island Coaster compensates by shuttling (each way) from Ryde, in the northeast, all the way around the southern shore to Alum Bay in the far southwest.

Stagecoach Island Line (www.island-line.com) runs trains twice-hourly from Ryde to Shanklin (25 minutes). The **Isle of Wight Steam Railway** (☎ 01983-885923; www.iwsteamrailway.co.uk; ☯ May-Sep) branches off Smallbrook Junction and goes to Wootton Common (adult/child £9/4.50, 1st class £13/8.50).

Rover Tickets provide unlimited use of buses and trains for a day (adult/child £10/5), two days (£15/7.50) or a week (adult/child/family £20/10/40).

COWES

Pack your yachting cap – this hilly Georgian harbour town on the island's northern tip is famous for **Cowes Week** (www.skandiacowesweek .co.uk), one of the longest-running and biggest annual sailing regattas in the world. Started in 1826, the regatta still sails with as much gusto as ever in late July or early August. Fibreglass toys and vintage sailboats line Cowes' waterfronts, which are lopped into East and West Cowes by the River Medina; a chain ferry shuttles regularly between the two (foot passengers free, cars £1.50).

The **tourist office** (☎ 01983-813813; ☯ 9.30am-5pm Mon-Sat Easter-Oct, 10am-3.30pm Tue-Sat Nov-Easter) is at Fountain Quay.

Cowes' must-see sight is Queen Victoria's right-royal hideaway, **Osborne House** (EH; ☎ 01983-200022, 281784; East Cowes; adult/child £10/5; ☯ 10am-6pm Apr-Sep, 10am-4pm Oct, pre-booked tours only Nov-Mar), which is the kind of lemon-frosted confection of pomp that only the Victorian era knew how to execute. Built between 1845 and 1851, Queen Victoria grieved here for many years after the death of her husband, and died here herself in 1901. The obscenely extravagant rooms include the stunning Durbar Room, while the gardens have a delightful Swiss Cottage where the royal ankle-biters would play.

Sleeping & Eating

Anchorage (☎ 01983-247975; www.anchoragecowes .co.uk; 23 Mill Hill Rd, West Cowes; s £40, d £60-80; P) A five-minute walk from town leads to this B&B of unfussy cream and blue rooms. There's also a green theme, with ecofriendly water and heating systems, and breakfasts full of fair-trade and island foods.

Fountain (☎ 01983-292397; www.fountaininn-cowes .com; High St, West Cowes; s £75, d £95-120) It may be a classic old pub, but the bedrooms are all airy drapes, white linen and leather headboards – the best have views across the Solent. The cool cafe is the venue for espressos and pastries; the bar's the place for hearty pub grub (mains £7 to £12); and the seafront patio is the spot to watch the world drift by.

NEWPORT & AROUND

The capital of the Isle of Wight, rambling Newport has little for holidaymakers except nearby **Carisbrooke Castle** (EH; ☎ 01983-522107; adult/child £6.50/3.20; ☯ 10am-5pm Apr-Sep, to 4pm Oct-Mar). An oft-repeated local saying states that whoever controlled this medieval castle

WESSEX

also controlled the island. While scrambling around the sturdy ramparts, spare a thought for the unfortunate Charles I, who was imprisoned here before his execution in 1649.

RYDE

The nippiest foot-passenger ferries to Wight alight in this unglamorous Victorian town that's lined with kiss-me-quick seafront arcades. The **tourist office** (☎ 01983-813813; 81-83 Union St; 9.30-5pm Mon-Sat, 10am-3.30pm Sun Apr-Oct) can help with accommodation and transport.

More North Africa than East Wight, the funky B&B-cum-bar that is **Kasbah** (☎ 01983-810088; www.kas-bah.co.uk; 76 Union St; s/d £50/80, mains £7; lunch & dinner; wi-fi) brings a hot blast of the Mediterranean to Ryde. Intricate lanterns, stripy throws and furniture fresh from Marrakesh dot the smoothly comfy rooms. Falafel, tapas and paella are on offer in the chilled bar downstairs.

BRADING

The cutesy little village of Brading, 4 miles south of Ryde, is home to the island's oldest standing house. A higgledy-piggledy timber-framed building dating from the 13th century, it now endures the indignity of housing a kitsch waxworks museum, the **Brading Experience** (☎ 01983-407286; www.brading theexperience.co.uk; 46 High St; adult/child £7.25/5.25; 10am-5.30pm Easter-Oct, to 5pm Nov-Easter).

Just south of the village, the fascinating remains at nearby **Brading Roman Villa** (☎ 01983-406223; www.bradingromanvilla.co.uk; adult/child £4.25/2.20; 9.30am-5pm Mar-Oct, to 4pm Nov-Feb) feature some exquisitely preserved mosaics (including a famous cockerel-headed man) that illustrate the original owner's notoriously bacchanal pursuit of pleasure.

About 4 miles east of Brading you can go to sleep in a gunboat – the **Xoron Floatel** (☎ 01983-874596; www.xoronfloatel.co.uk; Bembridge Harbour; s/d £35/56) was a warship in WWII, but is now a cheery, bunting-draped houseboat B&B, with cosy cabins (and attached bathrooms).

Trains (11 minutes) and buses 2 and 3 (16 minutes) run regularly from Ryde to Brading.

SANDOWN & SHANKLIN

The island's southeast coast is traditional family-holiday heaven. Hordes of sunburned vacationers wielding buckets and spades descend in droves to the beaches framing the twin resort towns of Sandown and Shanklin. After indulging in candy floss and funfair rides, many go and growl at Britain's largest collection of tigers in the sprawling **Isle of Wight Zoo** (☎ 01983-403883; Sandown; adult/child £6/5; 10am-6pm Apr-Sep, 10am-4pm Oct).

VENTNOR

The Victorian town of Ventnor slaloms so steeply down the island's southern coast that you'd be forgiven for mistaking it for the south of France. The winding streets are also home to a scattering of quirky boutiques, musicians and artists.

The staid, self-contained flats at **Spy Glass Inn** (☎ 01983-855338; www.thespyglass.com; The Esplanade; apt £70) have swirling carpets and creaky cane furniture, but also rudimentary balconies overlooking the sea. The busy bar below is festooned with nautical knick-knacks and serves up crowd-pleasing grub (mains £8).

Up the hill at the chintz-free **Hambrough** (☎ 01983-856333; www.thehambrough.com; Hambrough Rd; d £150-187, ste £210;), it's hard to say which are the better views: the 180-degree vistas out to sea, or the rooms themselves, full of subtle colours, clean lines and satiny furnishings. Espresso machines, dressing gowns and heated floors keep the luxury gauge set to high; one room overlooks the hills behind.

SOUTH WIGHT

The southernmost point of the island is marked by the stocky mid-19th-century **St Catherine's Lighthouse**. Far more exciting, however, is the nearby stone rocket-ship lookalike, **St Catherine's Oratory**. This odd construction is a lighthouse dating from 1314 and marks the highest point on the island.

The kids will love **Blackgang Chine Fun Park** (☎ 01983-730052; www.blackgangchine.com; admission £9.50; 10am-10pm mid-Jul–Aug, 10am-5pm Apr-early Jul, Sep & Oct), a couple of miles northwest of St Catherine's Lighthouse. This Victorian landscaped garden–turned–theme park has water gardens, animated shows and a hedge maze.

Slightly further west, you'll find a dose of pure hippie-chic: **Vintage Vacations** (☎ 07802-758113; www.vintagevacations.co.uk; Chale; 4-person caravans per weekend £150-220, per week £360-495; Apr-Oct;) is a dairy farm that rents out 10 1960s aluminium Airstream trailers from California. All are lovingly refitted with retro furnishings – camping has never been so cool.

WEST WIGHT

Rural and remote, the Isle of Wight's westerly corner is where the island really comes into its own. Sheer white cliffs rear from a surging sea and the stunning coastline peels away to Alum Bay in the far west and the most famous chunks of chalk in the region: the **Needles**. These jagged rocks rise shardlike out of the sea, forming a line like the backbone of a prehistoric sea monster.

Established in 1862, the **Needles Old Battery** (NT; ☎ 01983-754772; adult/child £4.65/2.35; ☻ 10.30am–5pm Jul & Aug, 10.30am–5pm Tue–Sun mid-Mar–Jun, Sep & Oct, 11am–3pm Sat & Sun Feb–mid-March) was used as an observation post during WWII – trek down the 60m tunnel through the cliff to a searchlight lookout. The same site also houses the **New Battery** (☎ 01983-754772; admission free; ☻ 11am–4pm Tue & Sat mid-Mar–Oct), with its exhibitions on the clandestine space-rocket testing carried out here in the 1950s.

You can hike to the battery along the cliffs from Alum Bay (1 mile) or hop on the tourist bus that runs between the bay and battery hourly (twice hourly in July and August).

Alum Bay is also home to the happy hullabaloo of kiddies' rides, boat trips and souvenir shops at **Needles Park** (☎ 0870 458 0022; www.theneedles.co.uk; admission free; ☻ 10am–5pm Easter–Nov), which also has a chairlift down to the beach. Look out for the fireworks nightly in August.

Twenty-minute **boat trips** (☎ 01983-761587; www.needlespleasurecruises.co.uk; adult/child £4/3; ☻ 10.30am–4.30pm Apr–Oct) head out from Alum Bay to the Needles, providing close-up views of those jagged white cliffs.

Four miles east along the north coast is the port of Yarmouth, an appealing tangle of cafes, pubs and restaurants. It's also home to Henry VIII's last great fortress, **Yarmouth Castle** (EH; ☎ 01983-760678; Quay St; adult/child £3.50/1.80; ☻ 11am–4pm Sun–Thu Apr–Oct). The facade, which is all that's left of it now, dates from 1547.

Sleeping

Totland Bay YHA (☎ 0845 371 9348; www.yha.org.uk; Hirst Hill, Totland; dm £15.95; P) This large, marvellous Victorian house overlooking the water has mostly family-oriented dorms and a maximum of eight beds per room.

Brighstone Holiday Centre (☎ 01983-740244; www.brighstone-holidays.co.uk; 1-/2-person tents £7/9, caravans from £16, B&B per adult/child £28/14, 2-person cabins per week from £300; P) What a view to wake up to – this B&B, campsite and cabin park perches atop cliffs looking towards the spectacular bluffs at Alum Bay. It's located on the A3055, 6 miles east of Freshwater.

DORSET

For many, Dorset conjures up the kind of halcyon holiday memories you find in flickering 1970s home movies. But this county's image deserves a dramatic revamp. In partytown Bournemouth the snapshots are as likely to be of stag and hen party frenzies as buckets and spades on the sand; Poole provides images of the super-rich; and Dorset's Jurassic Coast would catch the eye of even the most jaded cinematographer. This stunning shoreline is studded with exquisite seacarved bays and creamy-white rock arches around Lulworth Cove, while beaches at Lyme Regis are littered with fossils ripe for the picking. Dorchester provides a biopic of Thomas Hardy; the massive Iron Age hill fort at Maiden Castle is a battle-ground epic; and the really rather rude chalk figure at Cerne Abbas will linger long in the memory. Then comes the regenerated resort of Weymouth, preparing to be catapulted onto TV screens worldwide as the sailing venue for England's 2012 Olympics.

Orientation & Information

Dorset stretches along the south coast from Lyme Regis on the western (Devon) border, to Christchurch, which abuts Hampshire on the east. Dorchester, the county town, sits in between providing a central base for exploring, but Lyme Regis or Weymouth will suit those who prefer the coast.

Dorset has several useful websites:
Dorset County Council (www.dorset-cc.gov.uk)
Rural Dorset (www.ruraldorset.com)
West Dorset (www.westdorset.com)

Getting Around

Dorset has two slow railway lines – one running from Bristol and Bath through Dorchester West to Weymouth, the other chugging from London and Southampton to Bournemouth and Poole.

WESSEX

The main bus company in east and central Dorset is **Wilts & Dorset** (☎ 01202-673555; www .wdbus.co.uk). For western Dorset and on to Devon and southern Somerset, **First** (☎ 0870 010 6022; www.firstgroup.com) is the main operator.

Regional timetables are available free from tourist offices or bus stations, or by downloading from the companies' websites. Otherwise call **Traveline South West** (☎ 0871 200 22 33; www.travelinesw.com).

BOURNEMOUTH

pop 163,600

In Bournemouth, four worlds collide: old folks, families and corporate delegates meet club-loads of boozers out on a bender. Sometimes the edges rub – painfully. On weekend evenings parts of town transform into a massive frenzy of stag and hen parties, full of angels with L plates and blokes in frocks, blond wigs and slingbacks. But there's also a much sunnier side to the town. In 2007 a survey revealed Bournemouth had the happiest residents in the UK – thanks partly to its glorious 7-mile sandy beach. The town sprang to life as a resort in the Victorian era but these days it's busy adding a much more modern attraction: Europe's first artificial surf reef (see boxed text, below) is set to bring even bigger barrels and more amped-up board riders to the town.

Orientation & Information

Bournemouth sprawls along the coast towards Poole to the west and Christchurch to the east. The main pier marks the central seafront area; the town centre and train station are northeast from here.

Bournemouth Library (☎ 01202-454848; 22 The Triangle; ☼ 10am-7pm Mon, 9.30am-7pm Tue, Thu & Fri, 9.30am-5pm Wed) Internet access.

Cyber Place (☎ 01202-290099; 25 St Peter's Rd; per hr £2; ☼ 9.30am-midnight)

Tourist office (☎ 0845 051 1700; www.bournemouth .co.uk; Westover Rd; ☼ 10am-5.30pm Mon-Fri Sep-Jun, to 6pm Jul & Aug, 10.30am-5pm Sun)

Sights & Activities

Backed by 3000 deckchairs, Bournemouth's expansive, sandy **beach** regularly clocks up seaside awards. It stretches from Southborne in the far east to Alum Chine in the west – an immense promenade backed by ornamental gardens, cafes and toilets. The resort also prides itself on two piers (Bournemouth and Boscombe). Around Bournemouth Pier you can hire beach **chalets** (☎ 01202-451781; per day/ week from £11/52; ☼ 9am-6pm Apr-Oct), deckchairs (£2 per day), windbreaks (£2) and parasols (£4), as well as sit-on-board **kayaks** (☎ 07970 971867; per 30min £5). For surfing, see boxed text, below.

Bournemouth's **Pleasure Gardens** are one part of the Victorian town that has survived – they're even Grade II listed. This colourful belt of greenery, shrubs and herbaceous perennials stretches 1.5 miles northwest from the seafront. Sadly, much of Bournemouth's Victorian architecture has been smothered by modern development, but the area is still noted for its chines (sharp-sided valleys), many of which are lined with holiday villas. **Alum Chine**, a mile west of the centre, is a good example.

An ostentatious mix of Italianate holiday home and Scottish baronial pile, the **Russell-Cotes Art Gallery & Museum** (☎ 01202-451858; www .russell-cotes.bournemouth.gov.uk; Russell-Cotes Rd; admission free; ☼ 10am-5pm Tue-Sun) is set in landscaped grounds that include a formal Japanese garden, with views across Poole Bay. It's renowned for Victorian art and sculpture, and for a fine Japanese collection gathered by the museum's benefactors, Sir Merton and

---

SURF'S UP?

In a bid to turn itself into south-coast surf-central, Bournemouth's been busy building the **Boscombe Artificial Reef** just east of Boscombe Pier. Construction has been delayed by bad weather several times but when the reef is completed, 60m-long, submerged sand-filled bags are set to produce heavy breaking, barrelling 2.5m waves – doubling the current size and creating a challenging ride. The £8 million redevelopment at Boscombe Spa Village will add a new wave of beach huts, showers, surf shops and restaurants to the mix.

Contact the tourist office for the latest about the reef and surf hire and tuition. You could also try **Surf Steps Bournemouth Surf School** (☎ 0800 043 7873; www.bournemouthsurfschool.co.uk; ☼ Feb-Nov), based 300m west of Boscombe Pier. It offers surf lessons (adult/child £35/30 per three hours) and half-day body-boarding sessions (£25).

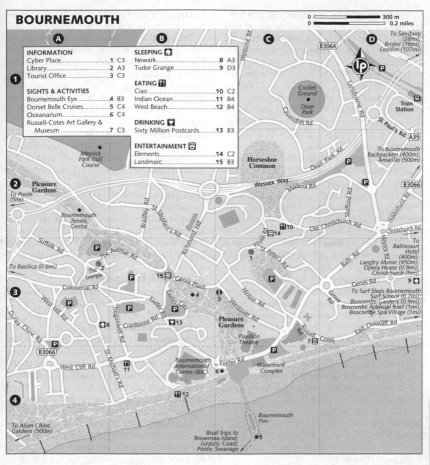

BOURNEMOUTH

INFORMATION	
Cyber Place	1 C3
Library	2 A3
Tourist Office	3 C3
SIGHTS & ACTIVITIES	
Bournemouth Eye	4 B3
Dorset Belle Cruises	5 C4
Oceanarium	6 C4
Russell-Cotes Art Gallery & Museum	7 C3
SLEEPING	
Newark	8 A3
Tudor Grange	9 D3
EATING	
Ciao	10 C2
Indian Ocean	11 B4
West Beach	12 B4
DRINKING	
Sixty Million Postcards	13 B3
ENTERTAINMENT	
Elements	14 C2
Landmarc	15 B3

Lady Russell-Cotes, during a visit to Japan in 1885.

Right next to Bournemouth Pier, the **Oceanarium** (☎ 01202-311933; www.oceanarium.co.uk; adult/child £8.50/6; ⏰ 10am-5pm) recreates various marine habitats from around the world, including the Great Barrier Reef, the Amazon River and the inky realms of the deep sea. Highlights are the guitarfish, flesh-eating piranhas and giant sea turtles.

Some say a trip in the **Bournemouth Eye** (☎ 01202-314539; www.bournemouthballoon.com; Lower Gardens; adult/child £10/6; ⏰ 7am-11pm Apr-Sep) hot-air balloon cures vertigo. Ascents to 150m last about 15 minutes, so at least you'll find out fast whether or not they're right. The views from the top extend 25 miles and are amazing.

Leaving from Bournemouth Pier, **Dorset Belle Cruises** (☎ 01202-558550; www.dorsetbelles.co.uk) runs trips (adult/child £13/6, 2½ hours, 10.30am Thursday to Tuesday) to the sheer chalk cliffs at Old Harry – the start of the Jurassic Coast (see boxed text, p303) – as well as ferries to Swanage, Poole and Brownsea Island (p301).

Sleeping

Bournemouth has huge concentrations of budget B&Bs, especially around the central St Michael's Rd and to the east of the train station.

Bournemouth Backpackers (☎ 01202-299491; www.bournemouthbackpackers.co.uk; 3 Frances Rd; dm £13-15) Containing aluminium bunk beds and set in a suburban house, the dorms in this hostel may be plain but the place is cheap and friendly. Reservations can only be made by email or by phoning between 5pm and 7pm on Sundays.

Tudor Grange (☎ 01202-291472; www.tudorgrange hotel.co.uk; 31 Gervis Rd; s £60-90, d £80-120, f £100-140) Five hundred years of history positively waft from the panelled walls and grand staircase of this pint-sized baronial pile. Rooms are either antique and flowery or historic with a twist – old oak meets buff throws.

Balincourt Hotel (☎ 01202-552962; www.balincourt .co.uk; 58 Christchurch Rd; s/d from £50/80) This Victorian B&B is a labour of love – even the china on the tea tray is hand painted to match each room's colour scheme. The decor is bright and deeply tasteful – respecting both the house's heritage and modern anti-frill sensibilities.

our pick **Langtry Manor** (☎ 0800 988 5720; www .langtrymanor.com; Derby Rd; s £79-148, d £98-236) Prepare for a delicious whiff of royal indiscretion – this minimansion was built by Edward VII for his mistress Lillie Langtry. It instantly immerses you in a world of opulent grandeur – from the red carpet rolled out in the entrance to the immense chandeliers and intricately carved wood inside. The rooms combine Edwardian elegance with modern touches – recessed lights and Jacuzzis. The King's Suite is a real jaw-dropper: a monumental, climb-up-to-get-in four-poster bed, and a tile fireplace big enough to have two seats inside.

Also recommended:

Amarillo (☎ 01202-553884; www.amarillohotel.co.uk; 52 Frances Rd; s £25-45, d £50-90, f £80) Minimalist decor, beige throws and clumps of twisted willow – a budget Bournemouth B&B with style.

Newark (☎ 01202-294989; www.thenewarkhotel.co.uk; 65 St Michael's Rd; s from £28, d £40-50) A Victoriana-meets-modern B&B of gold flocked wallpaper, glinting chandeliers and 21st-century curtains.

Eating

Indian Ocean (☎ 01202-311222; 4 West Cliff Rd; mains £8-11; ✆ lunch & dinner) Don't be fooled by this place's unimpressive glass frontage – the interior is modern and funkily lit and the menu includes unusual karai and Bangladeshi specials as well as tried and tested Indian favourites.

Ciao (☎ 01202-555657; 144 Old Christchurch Rd; mains £8-14; ✆ lunch & dinner) A cool hang-out with slabs of red paint on the walls, a huge glass-backed bottle-filled bar, and tables that spill out onto the street. The food is firmly focused on pizza, pasta and gourmet panini.

Basilica (☎ 01202-757722; 73 Seamoor Rd; tapas from £3, mains £6-10; ✆ Mon-Sat) The menu at this groovy bistro visits more Mediterranean countries than your average InterRailer – expect mezze, Parma ham parcels, grilled halloumi and pasta with chorizo. The brick-lined interior is dotted with tables hacked out of single chunks of wood, and with jars of olives.

our pick **West Beach** (☎ 01202-587785; West Promenade; mains £21; ✆ lunch & dinner) The venue of choice for Bournemouth's foodie crowd, this buzzy restaurant delivers both the best views and the best meals in town. The seafood is exemplary: rock oysters with shallot vinegar, monkfish medallions with Parma ham and a seafood platter crammed with crab claws, lobster, razor clams and crevettes (£30 per person). The view is of the seafront – it's so close to the beach that sand drifts right up to the door.

Drinking & Entertainment

Most of the main entertainment venues are clustered around Firvale Rd, St Peter's Rd and Old Christchurch Rd.

Sixty Million Postcards (☎ 01202-292697; 19 Exeter Rd; ✆ noon-midnight Sun-Wed, to 1am Thu, to 2am Fri & Sat) A hip crowd inhabits this quirky drinking den. The worn wooden floors, battered sofas and fringed lampshades are home to everything from DJ sets (including indie, synth-pop and space disco), to board games and impromptu Sunday jumble sales.

Landmarc (☎ 01202-589868; www.thelandmarc .com; Exeter Rd; mains £9; ✆ show nights 7pm-1am) The preacher wouldn't recognise this vibrant bistro-cum-music venue, set in a former church – the old stained glass now merges with bright red neon. Acoustic acts, tribute bands and comedians entertain crowds tucking into Swiss burgers, grilled tuna steak and Thai chicken curry.

Also recommended:

Elements (☎ 01202-311178; www.elements-nightclub .co.uk; Firvale Rd) Massive queues and club anthems.

Opera House (☎ 01202-399922; www.operahouse .co.uk; Boscombe Arcade; 570 Christchurch Rd) Restored Victorian theatre lining up gigs (from jazz to rude-boy punk), DJ sets (from Northern soul to drum and bass), gay nights and comedy.

Getting There & Away

National Express shuttles to London (£18, 2½ hours, hourly), Bristol (£15.40, four hours, one daily) and Oxford (£19, three hours, three daily).

Bus X3 runs from Salisbury (1¼ hours, half-hourly Monday to Saturday, nine on Sunday), while the X35 comes from Southampton (1¾ hours, two daily Monday to Saturday). There's a multitude of M1 and M21 buses between Bournemouth and Poole (15 minutes).

Trains run from London Waterloo (£26.10, two hours, half-hourly Monday to Saturday, hourly Sunday). There are regular connections to Poole (10 minutes, half-hourly), Dorchester South (£9, 45 minutes, hourly) and Weymouth (£11.40, one hour, hourly).

POOLE
pop 144,800

Just a few miles west of Bournemouth, Poole was once the preserve of hard-drinking sailors and sunburned day-trippers. But these days you're as likely to encounter super-yachts and Porsches, because the town borders Sandbanks, one of the most expensive chunks of real estate in the world. However, you don't have to be knee-deep in cash to enjoy Poole's agreeable ancient port, thanks to a quaint old harbour dotted with restaurants and nautical pubs, some irresistible boat trips and a wide variety of tempting water sports.

The **tourist office** (☎ 01202-253253; www.poole tourism.com; Poole Quay; ☼ 9.15am-6pm Jul & Aug, 10am-5pm Apr-Jun, Sep & Oct, 10am-4pm Mon-Sat Nov-Mar) is on the quay.

Sights & Activities
BROWNSEA ISLAND

This small wooded **island** (NT; ☎ 01202-707744; adult/child £4.90/2.40; ☼ 10am-6pm mid-Jul–Aug, 10am-5pm mid-Mar–Jul & Sep, 10am-4pm Oct) in Poole Bay is now a nature reserve and wildlife haven run by the National Trust (NT). There are several tranquil walks around the island, which is home to a population of deer, peacocks and rare red squirrels, as well as terns, gulls and wading birds.

To get to the island, catch a ferry from Poole Quay. Try **Brownsea Island Ferries** (☎ 01929-462383; www.brownseaislandferries.com; adult/child £8/5.50), which also offers **cruises** to Sandbanks (adult/child £8/5.50) and the other bay islands, as well as a daily trip to Wareham (£5). It also runs occasional cruises along the Jurassic Coast (see boxed text, p303; adult/child £13/5) to the Old Harry rocks – a set of limestone stacks

that have been separated from each other by sea erosion.

POOLE OLD TOWN & HARBOUR

Poole Old Town has rows of attractive 18th-century buildings, including a wonderful Customs House and Guildhall. The town's rightly proud of the new-look **Poole Museum** (☎ 01202-262600; 4 High St; admission free; ☼ 10am-5pm Mon-Sat, noon-5pm Sun Apr-Oct). Housed in a sensitively restored 18th-century harbour warehouse, it cracks through Poole's history both ashore and afloat – the star attraction is the 30ft-long Iron Age log boat, carved from a single tree 2300 years ago, which was recovered from the depths of Poole Harbour.

WATER SPORTS

Poole's beaches sit 3 miles southeast of the old town at **Sandbanks**, a 2-mile, wafer-thin peninsula of land that curls around the expanse of Poole Harbour. The houses in this super-rich suburb are some of the most exclusive in the world, but the beaches that border them are free, and have some of the best water-quality standards in the country.

A clutch of water-sport operators base themselves at Sandbanks – **H2O Sports** (☎ 01202-733744; www.h2o-sports.co.uk; 91 Salterns Rd) offers courses in windsurfing and power-kiting (£49 per three hours). **FC Watersports Academy** (☎ 01202-708283; www.fcwatersports.co.uk) hires out kayaks (£10 per hour) and sailing dinghies (£20 per hour) and runs windsurfing tuition (from £25 per hour), kitesurfing classes (£100 per day) and a two-day start-sailing course (£165). Or try to wakeboard with **Surface2Air** (☎ 01202-738448; www.s2as.com; 14 Station Rd), at £60 per hour.

Towards Hamworthy, west of Poole, you can learn to sail at **Moonfleet** (☎ 0800 019 1369; www.moonfleet.net; Cobbs Quay Marina), with two/five days costing £185/425, or cling to a jet ski with **Absolute Aqua** (☎ 01202-666118; www.absoluteaqua .co.uk; Parkstone Marina) from £135 a day.

POOLE LIGHTHOUSE

This cutting-edge **arts centre** (☎ 0844 406 8666; www.lighthousepoole.co.uk; 21 Kingland Rd) hosts a vibrant events calendar, including live music, theatre, film and exhibitions.

Sleeping & Eating

our pick **Saltings** (☎ 01202-707349; www.the-saltings .com; 5 Salterns Way; d £70-85) You can almost hear

WESSEX

the languid drawl of Noël Coward in this utterly delightful 1930s B&B, where charming art-deco flourishes include curved windows, arched doorways and decorative up-lighters. Immaculate rooms feature dazzling white, spearmint and pastel blue as well as mini-fridges, digital radios and Lush toiletries. One room is more like a little suite, with its own seating area and pocket-sized balcony. Saltings is halfway between Poole and Sandbanks.

Milsoms Hotel (☎ 01202-609000; www.milsomshotel .co.uk; 47 Haven Rd; d £75; P) Supersleek and semi-boutique, this minihotel sits above Poole's branch of the Loch Fyne seafood restaurant chain. Bedrooms are decked out in achingly tasteful tones of mauve and cream, and finished with thoughtful extras such as cafetières and Molton Brown bath products.

our pick **Guildhall Tavern** (☎ 01202-671717; 15 Market St; mains £15-20; lunch & dinner Tue-Sun) More Provence than Poole, the grub at this French-run brasserie is Gallic gourmet charm at its best: unpretentious and top-notch. Expect chargrilled sea bass flambéed with Pernod, or beef with Roquefort sauce. Exquisite aromas fill the dining room, along with the quiet murmur of people enjoying very good food.

Other options:

Quayside (☎ 01202-683733; www.poolequayside.co.uk; 9 High St; s £35-50, d £55-75, f £60-80) Snug rooms, pine, and jazzy prints in the heart of the old harbour.

Custom House (☎ 01202-676767; Poole Quay; mains from £12; lunch & dinner) Harbourside terrace, funky bar-bistro and fine-dining venue all rolled into one.

Storm (☎ 01202-674970; 16 High St; mains £13-18; dinner) Superb fish restaurant – the robust, eclectic menu depends on what the owner's caught.

Getting There & Away

Countless buses cover the 20-minute trip to Bournemouth. National Express runs hourly to London (£18, three hours). Train connections are as for Bournemouth (p300); just add 13 minutes to times to London Waterloo (£26).

Sandbanks Ferry (☎ 01929-450203; www.sandbanks ferry.co.uk; pedestrian/car 90p/£3) shuttles to Studland every 20 minutes. This is a short-cut from Poole to Swanage, Wareham and the west Dorset coast, but summer queues can be horrendous.

Brittany Ferries (☎ 0870 907 6103; www.brittany-ferries .com) sails between Poole and Cherbourg in France (2¼ to 6½ hours, one to three daily); expect to pay around £90 per foot passenger, or £335 for a car and two passengers.

To hire a bike, call ☎ 01202-855383 and it'll be dropped off at your hotel or B&B (per day £8).

Bus 152 goes from Poole to Sandbanks (15 minutes, three hourly Easter to September, hourly October to Easter). For a taxi try **Dial-a-Cab** (☎ 01202-666822).

WIMBORNE
pop 14,844

Just 10 miles from Bournemouth, but half a world away, Wimborne sits in the middle of a peaceful, pastoral landscape. Its imposing minster, complete with an intriguing chained library, oversees a central array of Georgian houses, sedate tearooms and creaky old pubs. With the impressive ancestral pile of Kingston Lacy nearby, it is a soothing antidote to a sometimes cocksure coast.

The **tourist office** (☎ 01202-886116; wimbornetic@ eastdorset.gov.uk; 29 High St; 9.30am-5.30pm Mon-Sat Apr-Sep, to 4.30pm Oct-Mar), based near the minster, sells a good town trail leaflet (£1). Wimborne's annual **folk festival** is in June.

Sights
WIMBORNE MINSTER

St Cuthburga founded a monastery in Wimborne in around 705, but most of the present-day **Wimborne Minster** (☎ 01202-884753; 9.30am-5.30pm Mon-Sat, 2-5pm Sun) was built by the Normans between 1120 and 1180. As well as the impressive Perpendicular tower and its unusual 'Quarterjack', which strikes the quarter-hour, the minster also houses a remarkable 14th-century astronomical clock. In **Holy Trinity Chapel** is the tomb of Ettricke, the 'man in the wall', a local eccentric who refused to be buried in the church or village and was instead interred in the church wall.

Above the choir vestry is the famous **chained library** (10.30am-12.30pm & 2-4pm Mon-Fri Easter-Oct). Established in 1686, it's filled with some of the country's oldest medieval books, 12th-century manuscripts written on lambskin, and ancient recipes, including ones for making ink out of oak apples.

KINGSTON LACY

Looking every inch the setting for a period drama, **Kingston Lacy** (NT; ☎ 01202-883402; house & grounds adult/child £10/5, grounds only £5/2.50; house 11am-4pm Wed-Sun Mar-Oct) became home to the aristocratic Bankes family when they were evicted from Corfe Castle (p304) by the

Roundheads. This grand, 17th-century country mansion was later clad in stone by Charles Barry, architect of the Houses of Parliament (p116), but it's best known for its resplendent Spanish Room, which is hung with gilded leather. The property's wonderfully preserved interior is dotted with paintings by Titian, Brueghel and Van Dyck. Outside, the extensive landscaped gardens encompass the Iron Age hill fort of Badbury Rings. Kingston Lacy is 2.5 miles northwest of Wimborne off the B3082.

Sleeping & Eating

Old George (☎ 01202-888510; chrissie_oldgeorge@yahoo .co.uk; 2 Corn Market; d £60-80) Hidden away in a tiny square beside the minster, this charming 18th-century house has chic bedrooms decked out in light greens and russets as well as scatterings of dinky cushions and elegant armchairs.

our pick **Percy House** (☎ 01202-881040; www.per-cyhouse.jazzland.co.uk; 4 East Borough; s/d/f £60/80/100) A sauna, hot tub in the garden, and a river in which to fish make this gorgeously Georgian house a slice of B&B heaven. An impressive staircase sweeps up to rooms where the style is rustic-meets-elegant: raspberry red walls, antique furniture and stripped woods.

Getting There & Away

Bus 3, the 'Wimborne Flyer', goes to Poole (30 minutes, two to four per hour). Bus 13 connects with Bournemouth (50 minutes, half-hourly Monday to Saturday, seven on Sunday).

SOUTHEAST DORSET

With its string of glittering bays and towering rock formations, the southeast Dorset shoreline is the most beautiful in the county. Also known as the 'Isle' of Purbeck (although its actually a peninsula), it's also the start of the Jurassic Coast (see boxed text, below) and the scenery and geology, especially around Lulworth Cove, make swimming irresistible and hiking memorable. The hinterland harbours the immense, fairy-tale ruins of Corfe Castle and some intriguing sights linked to Lawrence of Arabia.

Wareham & Around

pop 2568

Saxons established the sturdy settlement of Wareham on the banks of the River Frome in the 10th century, and their legacy lingers in the remains of their defensive walls and one of Dorset's last remaining Saxon churches. Wareham is also famous for its connections to the enigmatic TE Lawrence, the British

---

A BOX-OFFICE COAST

The kind of massive, hands-on geology lesson you wish you had at school, the Jurassic Coast is England's first natural World Heritage Site (England's other World Heritage Sites are cultural). This puts it on a par with the Great Barrier Reef and the Grand Canyon. This exquisite shoreline, stretching from Exmouth in East Devon to just beyond Swanage in Dorset, encompasses 185 million years of the Earth's history in just 95 miles – so in a few hours' walk you can cover millions of years of geology.

The area was formed when massive earth movements tilted the rocks from west to east. Gradually, erosion exposed the different strata – leaving the oldest formations in the west and the youngest in the east. It's a tangible timeline: Devon's rusty-red Triassic rocks are some 200 to 250 million years old; the dark clay Jurassic cliffs around Lyme Regis (see boxed text, p310) ensure superb fossil hunting; and the bulk of the coast from Lyme Regis to the Isle of Purbeck is around 140 to 200 million years old. Pockets of much younger creamy coloured Cretaceous rocks (a mere 65 to 140 million years old) also pop up, notably around Lulworth Cove (p305), where erosion has sculpted a stunning display of cliffs, coves and arches – particularly at Durdle Door (p305).

The website www.jurassiccoast.com has more information, and local tourist offices sell the *Official Guide to the Jurassic Coast* (£4.95). Responsible fossil hunting is encouraged – these nuggets of prehistory would otherwise be destroyed by the sea. Be aware, though, that the coast is highly unstable in places – official advice is to keep well away from the cliffs, stay on public paths, check tides times, only pick up from the beach (never dig out from cliffs), always leave some behind for others, and tell the experts if you find a stunner.

soldier immortalised in the 1962 David Lean epic *Lawrence of Arabia*.

The **Purbeck tourist office** (☎ 01929-552740; www .purbeck.gov.uk; Holy Trinity Church, South St; 9.30am-5pm Mon-Sat, 10am-4pm Sun Easter-Oct, 9.30am-5pm Mon-Sat Nov-Easter) is opposite the library.

SIGHTS

TE Lawrence was the British scholar, military strategist and writer made legendary for his role in helping unite Arab tribes against Turkish forces in WWI. The tiny cottage of **Clouds Hill** (NT; ☎ 01929-405616; adult/child £4/2; noon-5pm Thu-Sun Apr-Oct) was Lawrence's rural retreat and remains largely unchanged since his death in 1935. There's a small exhibition exploring his incredible life and wartime achievements, and a few relics that hint at his enduring fascination with the art and culture of the Middle East. Clouds Hill is 8 miles northeast of Wareham on an unclassified road.

The bijou **Wareham Museum** (☎ 01929-553448; East St, Wareham; admission free; 10am-4pm Mon-Sat Easter-Oct) provides a good potted history of Lawrence's life, along with press cuttings on the speculation surrounding his death.

Wareham's delightful Saxon **St Martin's Church** in North Street dates from about 1020. Inside there's a 12th-century fresco on the northern wall, and a marble effigy of Lawrence of Arabia.

Lawrence was stationed at Bovington Camp, now a **Tank Museum** (☎ 01929-405096; www.tankmuseum.org; adult/child £11/7; 10am-5pm), 6 miles east of Wareham. He died at Bovington Military Hospital six days after a motorcycle accident nearby. The museum has a collection of more than 300 armoured vehicles, from the earliest WWI prototypes to remnants from the first Gulf War.

Nearby is **Monkey World** (☎ 01929-462537; www .monkeyworld.co.uk; Longthorns; adult/child £10.50/7.25; 10am-5pm Sep-Jun, to 6pm Jul & Aug), a sanctuary for rescued chimpanzees, orang-utans, gibbons, marmosets and some ridiculously cute ring-tailed lemurs.

SLEEPING & EATING

our pick Trinity (☎ 01929-556689; www.trinitybnb.co.uk; 32 South St; d £60, f £80) You wouldn't be surprised to meet a bloke in doublet and hose here – this 15th-century B&B oozes so much character. Bedrooms are framed by fantastic brickwork and inglenook fireplaces; the staircase is a swirl of ancient timber; floors creak under stately rugs; and rooms are alive with nooks and crannies.

Anglebury (☎ 01929-552988; www.angleburyhouse .co.uk; 15 North St; mains £9-13, s/d £35/70; lunch daily, dinner Tue-Sat) Lawrence of Arabia and Thomas Hardy have, apparently, both had cuppas in the coffee shop attached to this 16th-century inn. Simple rooms are done out in creams, floral fabrics and pine while the restaurant dishes up hearty fare such as trout wrapped in bacon, and lamb in Pernod.

GETTING THERE & AWAY

Wareham is on the main railway line from London Waterloo to Weymouth (2½ hours); trains run hourly.

Buses 142 and 143 run hourly between Poole (35 minutes) and Swanage via Wareham (every two hours on Sunday).

Corfe Castle

The massive, shattered ruins of Corfe Castle loom so dramatically from the landscape it's like blundering into a film set. The defensive fragments tower over an equally photogenic village, which bears the castle's name, and makes for a romantic spot for a meal or an overnight stay.

Corfe Castle (NT; ☎ 01929-481294; adult/child £5.10/2.50; 10am-6pm Apr-Sep, 10am-5pm Feb, Mar & Oct, 10am-4pm Nov-Jan) was the ancestral home of Sir John Bankes, right-hand man and attorney general to Charles I, and was besieged by Cromwellian forces during the Civil War. Following a six-week defence directed by the plucky Lady Bankes, the castle was eventually betrayed from within and gunpowdered to pieces by the Roundheads. The Bankes family established its new family seat at Kingston Lacy (p302).

The 450-year-old **Bankes Hotel** (☎ 01929-481288; www.dorset-hotel.co.uk; East St; mains £8-14, s £50-75, d £60-90; lunch & dinner) is an atmospheric place for a pint and quality pub grub. The bedrooms are a mass of mullioned windows, creaking floors and slightly worn bathrooms.

Buses 142 and 143 run to Corfe Castle hourly from Poole (50 minutes) via Wareham (15 minutes), before going on to Swanage (20 minutes).

The **Swanage Steam Railway** (☎ 01929-425800; www.swanagerailway.co.uk; Day Rover adult/child £12/10; hourly Apr-Oct plus many weekends Nov, Dec, Feb & Mar) runs between Swanage and Norden (20 minutes) and stops at Corfe Castle.

ELIZABETHAN EXTRAVAGANCE

Morton's House Hotel (☎ 01929-480988; www.mortonshouse.co.uk; East St, Corfe Castle; r £149-249; P) This heart-meltingly beautiful 16th-century manor was built in the shape of an 'E' in honour of Queen Elizabeth, and it certainly makes an impressive tribute. Built from solid grey Purbeck stone, the house is crammed with Elizabethan and Jacobean character. Stone fireplaces and wood-panelled friezes adorn the downstairs drawing room, and the luxuriant heritage feel runs into the upstairs bedrooms – bag the Elizabethan-themed suite, if you can. It's a place to languish in front of a crackling fire or stuff yourself silly with a rich Sunday roast – traditional, classic and very, very English. Some rooms are in a more modern annexe.

Blue Pool

Sometimes green, sometimes turquoise, the **Blue Pool** (☎ 01929-551408; www.bluepooluk.com; Furzebrook; adult/child £5/2.50; 9.30am-5pm Mar-Nov) is a former clay pit that has an extraordinary knack of changing colour in different conditions – it's all down to tiny particles refracting light through the water. The surrounding woods are home to green sand lizards and shy Dartford warblers. The pool is 4 miles northwest of Corfe Castle, signposted from the A351; buses 142 and 143 from Wareham (10 minutes) stop nearby.

Lulworth Cove & the Coast

South of Corfe Castle the coast steals the show. For millions of years the elements have been creating an intricate shoreline of curved bays, caves, stacks and weirdly wonderful rock formations – most notably the massive natural arch at Durdle Door.

At **Lulworth Cove**, a pleasing jumble of thatched cottages and fishing gear leads down to a perfect circle of white cliffs. It's a charismatic place to stay; inevitably, it draws coach party crowds in the height of summer.

The coast's iconic feature is **Durdle Door**, an immense, 150-million-year-old Portland stone arch that plunges into the sea 3 miles west of Lulworth Cove. Part of the Jurassic Coast (see boxed text, p303), it was created by a combination of massive earth movements and then erosion. Today it's framed by shimmering bays – bring a swimsuit and head down the hundreds of steps for an unforgettable dip. There's a car park at the top of the cliffs, but its best to hike along the coast from Lulworth Cove (1 mile); this route takes you past the delightfully named **Lulworth Crumple**, where layers of rock have been forced into dramatically zigzagging folds

Creamy, dreamy-white, **Lulworth Castle** (EH; ☎ 01929-400352; www.lulworth.com; East Lulworth; admis-

sion £7; 10.30am-6pm Sun-Fri Apr-Oct, to 4pm Sun-Fri Nov-Mar) looks more like a French chateau than a traditional English castle. Built in 1608 as a hunting lodge, it's survived extravagant owners, extensive remodelling and a disastrous fire in 1929. It has now been sumptuously restored. Check out the massive four-poster bed, and the suits of armour in the basement.

Jurassic Kayak Tours (☎ 01305-835301; www.jurassic-kayaking.com; Lulworth Cove Visitor Centre, Main St) offers a seal's-eye view of the cliffs on a paddle from Lulworth Cove to Durdle Door, on sit-aboard kayaks (£40, three hours). Weather dependent, they run most weekends in summer.

The bedrooms at the cool **Bishops Bistro** (☎ 01929-400880; www.bishopscottage.co.uk; Main St, Lulworth Cove; s £35-45, d £60-100, f £160, mains £3-8; 9am-5pm May-Sep) throw together antique furniture and slinky modern fabrics – and make it work. The funky cafe serves up spicy seafood or ploughman's with cider.

Rose Cottage (☎ 01929-400150; www.rosecottage.fsworld.co.uk; Main St, Lulworth Cove; s £35-50, d £70-80) is an archetypal thatched cottage with flowers winding around the door, thick walls, low lintels and rooms full of rustic charm.

Lulworth Beach (☎ 01929-400404; www.lulworthbeachhotel.com; Lulworth Cove; d £80-95) is an oh-so-stylish hotel 180m from the beach with rooms finished in blondwood, coconut matting and flashes of leather and lime – the best room has its own private sea-view deck.

There's a basic single-storey **YHA** (☎ 0870 770 5940; www.yha.org.uk; School Lane; dm £14; Mar-Oct), in West Lulworth, and a great clifftop campsite at **Durdle Door Holiday Park** (☎ 01929-400200; www.lulworth.com; sites per tent £10-20; Mar-Oct).

DORCHESTER

pop 16,171

With Dorchester, you get two towns in one: a real-life, bustling county town, and Thomas Hardy's fictional Casterbridge. The writer

WESSEX

was born just outside Dorchester and clearly used it to add authenticity to his writing – so much so that his literary locations can still be found amid the town's white Georgian terraces and red-brick buildings. You can also visit his former homes here and see his original manuscripts. Incredibly varied museums (teddy bears, terracotta warriors and Tutankhamen) and some attractive places at which to sleep and eat combine to make an appealing base for a night or two.

Orientation & Information

Most of Dorchester's action takes place along South St, which runs north into pedestrianised Cornhill and then emerges at High St.

The **tourist office** (☎ 01305-267992; www.westdorset.com; Antelope Walk; ☺ 9am-5pm Mon-Sat Apr-Oct, to 4pm Mon-Sat Nov-Mar) brims over with Hardy information, and sells 'location' guides to the places in his novels.

Sights

THOMAS HARDY SITES

The Hardy collection in the **Dorset County Museum** (☎ 01305-262735; www.dorsetcountymuseum.org; High West St; adult/child £6/5; ☺ 10am-5pm Jul-Sep, 10am-5pm Mon-Sat Oct-Jun) is the biggest in the world. It offers extraordinary insight into his creative process – reading his cramped handwriting, it's often possible to spot where he's crossed out one word and substituted another. There's also a wonderful reconstruction of his study at Max Gate (see below), and a letter from Siegfried Sassoon, asking Hardy if Sassoon can dedicate his first book of poems to him.

A trained architect, Hardy designed **Max Gate** (NT; ☎ 01305-262538; Alington Ave; adult/child £3/1.50; ☺ 2-5pm Mon, Wed & Sun Apr-Sep), where he lived from 1885 until his death in 1928. *Tess of the D'Urbervilles* and *Jude the Obscure* were both written here, and the house contains several pieces of original furniture, but otherwise it's a little slim on sights. The house is a mile east of Dorchester on the A352.

The small cob-and-thatch **Hardy's Cottage** (NT; ☎ 01305-262366; admission £3.50; ☺ 11am-5pm Sun-Thu Apr-Oct), where the author was born, is again short on attractions, but it makes an evocative stop for Hardy completists. It's in Higher Bockhampton, 3 miles northeast of Dorchester.

Track down Hardy's statue at the top of High West St in Dorchester and what's thought to be the red and grey brick inspi-

ration for the house of the mayor (of the book *The Mayor of Casterbridge*). The house is now a Barclays Bank in South Street. The Maumbury Rings (below) are the location of Henchard's secret meetings in the same novel.

OTHER SIGHTS

Dorchester was once a thriving Roman settlement: you can see evidence of this in the remains of a 1st-century **Roman villa** – look out for the foundations and remarkable mosaic floors behind the town hall. The steep-sided ridges of the **Maumbury Rings** (admission free, ☺ 24hr), just south of town, were a neolithic henge before the Romans turned them into an amphitheatre.

As well as its superb Hardy exhibits, the **Dorset County Museum** (left) has some impressive fossils from the Jurassic Coast, including a huge ichthyosaur on one wall, and a 1m dinosaur skull hanging over the stairs. Reflecting the area's rich Bronze and Iron Age past, there are also archaeological finds from Maiden Castle (opposite) and a treasure trove of gold neck rings and bronze coins.

At the **Tutankhamen Exhibition** (☎ 01305-269571; www.tutankhamun-exhibition.co.uk; High West St; adult/child £7/5.50; ☺ 9.30am-5.30pm) you get to experience the sights, sounds and smells of ancient Egypt in a fake-gold mock-up of the pharaoh's tomb. The **Terracotta Warriors Museum** (☎ 01305-266040; www.terracottawarriors.co.uk; East Gate, East High St; adult/child £5.75/4; ☺ 10am-5pm Apr-Oct, to 4.30pm Nov-Mar) whisks you off to 8th century China for a reconstruction of the famous figures. The **Teddy Bear Museum** (☎ 01305-266040; East Gate, East High St; adult/child £5.75/4; ☺ 10am-5pm Apr-Oct, to 4.30pm Nov-Mar) rounds off this surreal exhibition combo – it's populated by historical and famous bears, as well as a rather disturbing family of human-sized teddies.

On the northern side of town is **Poundbury**, a cod-Georgian town dreamt up by Prince Charles as a model housing development for the 21st century.

Sleeping

our pick **Beggar's Knap** (☎ 01305-268191; beggarsknap@hotmail.co.uk; 2 Weymouth Ave; s £45, d £65-75) Fabulous and far from impoverished, this vaguely decadent guest house spins the clock back to the Victorian era. Opulent, raspberry-red rooms drip with chandeliers and gold brocade, while beds (ranging from four-poster to French sleigh) are draped in fine cottons. The breakfast room, with its towering plants and a huge harp, is gorgeous.

Slades Farm (☎ 01305-264032; www.bandbdorset.org.uk; Charminster; s £45 d£70-90) Barn conversions don't come much more stylish than this – oatmeal and cream walls meeting ceilings in gentle curves. The riverside paddock is perfect to laze in after a breakfast full of local delicacies. You'll find this place 2 miles north of Dorchester on the Cerne Abbas road (it's on the latter bus route).

Casterbridge Hotel (☎ 01305-264043; www.casterbridgehotel.co.uk; 49 High East St; s £60-65, d £70-125, f £110-155) In the 1780s this hotel was the town jail. Now marble fireplaces, ruched furnishings and Thomas Hardy books in the rooms make it worth spending a night in an old prison. Six bedrooms are in a 1980s annexe.

Also recommended:

Aquila Heights B&B (☎ 01305-267145; www.aquilaheights.co.uk; 44 Maiden Castle Rd; s £34, d £66-75, f £90-110) Pine and photo-placemat-style B&B with fabulous breakfast choices.

Westwood House (☎ 01305-268018; www.westwoodhouse.co.uk; 29 High West St; s £45-50, d £60-85, f £120) Elegant Georgian B&B with prettily painted wicker chairs.

Eating

Prezzo (☎ 01305-259678; 6 High West St; mains £8-11; ☽ lunch & dinner) A reliable outpost of this Italian chain. The baroque interior is filled with black-leather sofas and twisted willow – top-notch pizzas and pastas are on the menu.

Sienna (☎ 01305-250022; 36 High West St; 2-course set lunch/dinner £19.50/30.50; ☽ lunch & dinner Tue-Sat) This smart little bistro is home to some fine pan-European flavour combos. Roast pollack with crab gnocchi, asparagus risotto with parmesan ice cream and Dorset lamb with shepherd's pie, all sit cosily on the same menu.

Getting There & Around

There's a direct daily National Express coach to London (£19.80, four hours).

Bus 31 travels from Dorchester to Weymouth (30 minutes, hourly), and to Lyme Regis (1¾ hours). Bus 10 travels to Weymouth (35 minutes, three per hour Monday to Saturday, six on Sunday), and bus 387 goes to Poole (1¼ hours, three daily Monday to Saturday).

There are two train stations – Dorchester South and Dorchester West. Trains run at least hourly from Weymouth (11 minutes)

to London Waterloo (£41.30, 2½ hours) via Dorchester South, Bournemouth (£9, 45 minutes) and Southampton (£18.60, 1¼ hours).

Dorchester West has connections to Bath (£13, 1¾ hours) and Bristol (£13, two hours); trains run every two hours.

Dorchester Cycles (☎ 01305-268787; 31 Great Western Rd) hires out bikes for £15 per day.

AROUND DORCHESTER
Maiden Castle

Occupying a massive slab of horizon on the southern fringes of Dorchester, **Maiden Castle** (EH; admission free; ☽ 24hr) is the largest and most complex Iron Age hill fort in Britain. The huge, steep-sided chalk ramparts flow along the contour lines of the hill and surround 48 hectares – the equivalent of 50 football pitches. The first hill fort was built on the site around 500 BC and in its heyday was densely populated with clusters of roundhouses and a network of roads. The Romans besieged and captured it in AD 43 – an ancient Briton skeleton with a Roman crossbow bolt in the spine was found at the site. The sheer scale of the ramparts is awe-inspiring, especially from the ditches immediately below, and the winding complexity of the west entrance reveals just how hard it would be to storm. Finds from the site are displayed at Dorset County Museum (opposite). Maiden Castle is 1½ miles southwest of Dorchester.

Cerne Abbas & the Cerne Giant

If you had to describe an archetypal sleepy Dorset village, you'd come up with something a lot like Cerne Abbas: its houses run the gamut of England's historical architectural styles, roses climb countless doorways, and half-timbered houses frame a honey-coloured, 12th-century church.

But this village also packs one heck of a surprise – a real nudge-nudge, wink-wink tourist attraction in the form of the **Cerne Giant**. Nude, full frontal and notoriously well endowed, this chalk figure is revealed in all his glory on a hill on the edge of town. And he's in the kind of stage of excitement that wouldn't be allowed in most magazines. The giant is around 60m high and 51m wide and his age remains a mystery; some claim he's Roman but the first historical reference comes in 1694, when three shillings were set aside for his repair. The Victorians found it all deeply embarrassing and allowed grass to grow over his most outstanding feature. Today the hill is grazed on by sheep and cattle – though only the sheep are allowed to do their nibbling over the giant – the cows would do too much damage to his lines.

The village has the not-so-new **New Inn** (☎ 01300-341274; www.newinncerneabbas.co.uk; 14 Long St; d from £90; P), a 13th-century pub with rustic, comfy rooms (avoid the newer extension), and an excellent menu of bar food. For top-notch dining head for the ivy-smothered, thatched **Royal Oak** (☎ 01300-341797; Long St; mains from £7; lunch & dinner) and its menu of whole crab or lobster salad, Dartmouth smokehouse eels and Lyme Bay scallops in lemon butter.

Dorchester, 8 miles to the south, is reached on bus D12 (20 minutes, three daily Monday to Saturday).

WEYMOUTH & AROUND

As the venues for the sailing events in Britain's 2012 Olympics, Weymouth and neighbouring Portland are in the middle of a multimillion-pound building spree. But despite the bustle and the waterfront spruce-up, evidence of their core characters remains. Weymouth's billowing deckchairs, candy-striped beach kiosks and Punch and Judy stands are the epitome of a faded Georgian kiss-me-quick resort, while Portland's pock-marked central plateau and remote cliffs still proudly proclaim a rugged, quarrying past.

Weymouth
pop 48,279
Weymouth has been a popular seaside spot since King George III (the one who suffered from a nervous disorder) took an impromptu dip here in 1789. Some 2½ centuries later, it's still popular with beachgoers.

ORIENTATION & INFORMATION
Weymouth is strung out along its seafront. To the west the rejuvenated old harbour is a vibrant jumble of brightly painted Georgian town houses, restaurants and pubs. The Isle of Portland, really a 4-mile-long peninsula, lies a few miles south.

The **tourist office** (☎ 01305-785747; www.visit weymouth.co.uk; The Esplanade; 9.30am-5pm Apr-Oct, 10am-4pm Nov-Mar) sells discounted tickets to many local attractions and can, for a fee, help arrange local accommodation.

SIGHTS & ACTIVITIES
The fine sandy **beach** is a place to surrender to your inner kitsch and rent a deckchair,

sun-lounger or pedalo (each £5 per hour). Alternatively, go all Californian and join a volleyball game. For sailing, kitesurfing, diving and windsurfing lessons, see the boxed text, opposite.

The 19th-century **Nothe Fort** (☎ 01305-766626; www.fortressweymouth.co.uk; Barrack Rd; adult/child £4.50/1; 10.30am-5.30pm May-Sep, 2.30-4.30pm Sun Oct-Apr) is full of cannons, rifles, searchlights and 12-inch coastal guns. It also details the Roman invasion of Dorset, a Victorian soldier's drill, and Weymouth in WWII. Commanding an armoured car and clambering around the magazine prove popular with regiments of children.

Beside the old harbour, Brewer's Quay has a shopping centre and plentiful attractions, including **Timewalk** (☎ 01305-777622; Hope Sq; adult/child £4.50/3.25; 10am-5.30pm Mar-Oct), which explores various key events in Weymouth's history. These include the Black Death, the Spanish Armada and the town's transition from fishing harbour to tourist resort. **Weymouth Museum** (☎ 01305-777622; admission free; 10am-4.30pm), alongside, has displays on smuggling, paddle steamers and shipwrecks. Nearby, **Tudor House** (☎ 01305-779711; 3 Trinity St; adult/child £4/1; 1-3.45pm Tue-Fri Jun-Sep, 2-4pm 1st Sun of month Oct-May) is one of the few 17th-century buildings left in Weymouth and is furnished in period style.

Seals, otters and seahorses entertain you at the 3-hectare aquatic park at **Sea Life** (☎ 01305-761070; www.sealife.co.uk; Lodmoor Country Park; adult/child £15/10.50; 10am-4pm).

White Motor Boats (☎ 01305-785000; www.white motorboat.freeuk.com; return adult/child £7/5; Apr-Oct) runs a cracking 35-minute jaunt across to Portland Castle (p310) from Cove Row on the harbour (three to four daily).

SLEEPING
There are also plenty of campsites near Chesil Beach and Weymouth Bay.

Chatsworth (☎ 01305-785012; www.thechatsworth .co.uk; 14 The Esplanade; s £35-45, d £80-108) Watery views are everywhere at this supertrendy B&B – the terrace is just a yardarm from yacht berths, while bedrooms overlook the seafront or the harbour. Inside, the views are of purple satins, vanilla candles and worn wood.

our pick **Harbourside** (☎ 01305-777150; www .harbourside2let.co.uk; 5 Trinity Rd; 2-/4-person apt £80/125) This stylish two-bedroom Regency apartment is elegance personified. Antique chairs, brass

WATER SPORTS IN WEYMOUTH & PORTLAND

Stunning to look at, the seas round Weymouth and Portland are also a massive watery playground. So good, they're to host the sailing events for the 2012 Olympics. In part it's due to Portland Harbour – 890 hectares of sheltered water created by breakwaters begun by convict labour in the mid-1800s.

You can beat the Olympians to it by learning to sail at the new **Weymouth & Portland National Sailing Academy** (☎ 0845 337 3214; www.sail-laser.com; Portland Harbour; per 2/4 days £175/315). **Windtek** (☎ 01305-787900; www.windtek.co.uk; 109 Portland Rd, Wyke Regis) offers windsurfing lessons (£90/150 per one/two days), and hires out gear (£15 per hour) if you have a Royal Yachting Association card. Staff can teach you to kitesurf, too (£95 per day).

There's a huge variety of depths, seascapes and wrecks for divers – sunken ships range from paddle steamers and East Indiamen to WWII vessels. For experienced divers **Scimitar Diving** (☎ 07765 326728; www.scimitardiving.co.uk) sets off from Weymouth Harbour for off-shore dives (from £40 per diver, per day). It also rents out a range of gear, from £25. **Fathom and Blues** (☎ 01305-826789; www.fathomandblues.co.uk; Boscawen Centre, Castletown, Portland) runs training courses for divers, from £95 per day.

bedsteads and fine Egyptian cotton fill a bedroom and lounge that look out directly onto the bustling harbour. It's often rented out as a weekly let (£300 to £700), but the nightly rates are a bargain.

Old Harbour View (☎ 01305-774633; fax 750828; 12 Trinity Rd; d £75-85) A few doors down from Harbourside, fresh, suitably nautical bedrooms are tucked away in a pretty Georgian terrace.

EATING

King Edward's (☎ 01305-786924; 100 The Esplanade; mains £6; ☒ lunch & dinner) It has to be done: sitting on Weymouth seafront and scoffing fish 'n' chips. King Edward's is a classic chippy – all burgundy tiles and wrought iron. You can eat inside or out, and then chase it down with an ice cream from the kiosks dotting the prom. For a waterside drink, head off to the pubs and bars lining the old harbour.

La Baroque (☎ 01305-750666; 19 Trinity Rd; tapas £4, mains £13; ☒ lunch & dinner) Baroque by name, baroque by nature: munch tapas surrounded by raspberry walls and heavy gilt pictures in the wine bar, or pop upstairs to Toulouse Lautrec prints and classy dining.

our pick Perry's (☎ 01305-785799; 4 Trinity Rd; mains £12-18; ☒ lunch Tue-Fri, dinner Tue-Sat) Effortlessly stylish, but also relaxed, this Georgian town house is a study of snowy white tablecloths and flashes of pink. You won't be able to resist the Lyme Bay scallops, twice baked Dorset Blue Vinny cheese soufflé or crab soup. Weymouth's cognoscenti book the window table on the 1st floor (it has a fabulous harbour view) for a two-course lunch – a bargain at £15.

GETTING THERE & AWAY
Bus

There's one direct National Express coach to London (£19.80, 4¼ hours) each day.

Bus 10 is the quickest to Dorchester (30 minutes, three per hour Monday to Saturday, six buses on Sunday). The hourly bus 31 also stops in Dorchester en route to Lyme Regis (two hours) and Axminster. The X53 travels from Weymouth to Wareham (50 minutes, six daily) and Poole (1¼ hours), and to Abbotsbury (35 minutes), Lyme Regis (1½ hours) and Exeter (three hours) in the opposite direction. Bus 1 travels regularly over to Portland (30 minutes).

Train

Trains run hourly to London (£43, 2¾ hours) via Dorchester South (11 minutes) and Bournemouth (£11.40, one hour), and every two hours to Dorchester West, Bath (£13.20, two hours) and Bristol (£13.80, 2¼ hours).

Portland

The multimillion-pound pre-Olympic building boom is hugely apparent on the Isle of Portland. Waterside waste ground is being transformed into restaurants, a shiny new sailing centre, glitzy apartment blocks and a hotel. But inland on Portland's 500ft central plateau, the peninsula's quarrying past still holds sway – evidenced by the huge craters and large slabs of limestone still littering the landscape. Proud, and at times bleak and rough around the edges, it's decidedly different from the rest of Dorset, but it's also curiously compelling. The water sports on offer, the rich birdlife and the stark beauty of its wind-whipped coasts make it worthy of at least a day trip.

Portland is a comma-shaped rock peninsula, fused to the mainland by the ridge of Chesil Beach (see below). Its unique white limestone has been quarried here for centuries, and has been used in some of the world's finest buildings – including the British Museum, St Paul's Cathedral and the UN headquarters in New York. One abandoned quarry, **Tout Quarry**, has been transformed into a sculpture park where snaking footpaths lead past 50 works of art that have been carved into the rock in situ. The *Philosopher's Stone*, *Fallen Fossil* and *Green Man* are particularly worth hunting out. Tout Quarry is signed off the main road, just south of Fortuneswell.

The sea views from Portland's rugged cliff tops are breathtaking, especially around the red-and-white-striped **lighthouse** (☎ 01305-820495; ☿ 11am-5pm Apr-Sep) on Portland Bill – climb to the top of its 12m tower (adult/child £2.50/1.50) and look down at The Race, a surging vortex of conflicting tides. A summer-only **tourist office** (☎ 01305-861233; ☿ 11am-5pm Apr-Sep) sits alongside.

Sturdy **Portland Castle** (EH; ☎ 01305-820539; adult/child £4/2; ☿ 10am-6pm Jul & Aug, to 5pm Apr-Jun & Sep, to 4pm Oct) is one of the finest examples of the defensive forts constructed during Henry VIII's castle-building spree. You can try on period armour while enjoying great views over Portland harbour.

Housed in two thatched cottages, **Portland Museum** (☎ 01305-821804; 217 Wakeham St; adult/child £2.50/free; ☿ 10.30am-5pm Fri-Tue Easter-Oct) explores Portland's history of smuggling and shipwrecks, and also has some huge fossils and ammonites collected from the Jurassic Coast.

Bus 1 runs to Portland from Weymouth every half-hour, and it goes onto Portland Bill between June and September. For the ferry from Weymouth, see White Motor Boats, p308.

Chesil Beach

One of the most breathtaking beaches in Britain, Chesil is 17 miles long, 15m high and moving inland at the rate of 5m a year. This mind-boggling, 100-million-tonne pebble ridge is the baby of the Jurassic Coast (see boxed text, p303); a mere 6000 years old, its stones range from pea-sized in the west to hand-sized in the east. More recently it became famous as the setting for Ian McEwan's acclaimed novel about sexual awakening, *On Chesil Beach*.

Chesil Beach Centre (☎ 01305-760579; Ferrybridge; ☿ 10am-5pm Apr-Sep, 11am-4pm Oct-Mar), just over the bridge to Portland, is a good place to get onto the ridge. It also provides information, and organises talks and guided walks.

LYME REGIS
pop 4406

Fantastically fossiliferous, Lyme Regis packs a heavyweight historical punch. Rock-hard relics of the past pop out repeatedly from the surrounding cliffs – exposed by the landslides of a retreating shoreline. Now a pivot point of the World Heritage Site Jurassic Coast (see boxed text, p303), fossil fever is definitely in the air and everyone, from proper palaeontologists to those out for a bit of fun, can engage in a spot of coastal rummaging.

Lyme was also famously the setting for *The French Lieutenant's Woman* – starring Meryl Streep, the film version immortalised the iconic Cobb harbour defences in movie history. Add sandy beaches and some delightful places at which to stay and dine, and you get a charming base for explorations.

Information

Lyme Regis' **tourist office** (☎ 01297-442138; lyme.tic@westdorset-dc.gov.uk; Guildhall Cottage, Church St; ☿ 10am-5pm Mon-Sat, to 4pm Sun Apr-Oct, to 3pm Mon-Sat Nov-Mar) is on the corner of Church and Bridge Sts.

FOSSIL FEVER

In Lyme, fossil fever is catching. The town sits in one of the most unstable sections of Britain's coast and regular landslips mean nuggets of prehistory are constantly popping out of the cliffs. If you are bitten by the bug, the best cure is one of the regular **fossil walks** run by Dinosaurland Fossil Museum (see opposite). Alternatively, meet **Dr Colin Dawes** (☎ 01297-443758; ☿ tours 1pm Sun year-round, plus Wed & Fri May-Sep) at the Old Forge Fossil Shop in Broad St. Walks cost from £8 for adults, £5 for children. For the best chances of a find, time your trip to Lyme to within two hours of low tide.

Sights & Activities

Mary Anning found the first full ichthyosaurus skeleton near Lyme in 1814, and the site of her former home is now the excellent **Lyme Regis Philpot Museum** (☎ 01297-443370; www.lymeregismuseum.co.uk; Bridge St; adult/child £3/free; ☼ 10am-5pm Mon-Sat, from 11am Sun Easter-Oct, 11am-4pm Wed-Sun Nov-Easter). An incredibly famous fossilist in her day, Miss Anning did much to pioneer the science of modern-day palaeontology; the museum exhibits her story along with spectacular fossils and other prehistoric finds.

The **Dinosaurland Fossil Museum** (☎ 01297-443541; www.dinosaurland.co.uk; Coombe St; adult/child £4.50/3.50; ☼ 10am-5pm, closed some weekdays Nov-Feb) is a mini, indoor Jurassic Park – packed with the remains of belemnites and the graceful plesiosaurus. Lifelike dinosaur models will thrill youngsters – the fossilised tyrannosaurus eggs and 73kg dinosaur dung will have them in raptures.

The **Cobb**, a curling harbour wall–cum–sea defence, was first built in the 13th century. It's been strengthened and extended over the years so it doesn't present the elegant line it once did, but it's still hard to resist wandering its length for a wistful, sea-gazing Meryl moment at the tip.

Sleeping

Old Lyme Guest House (☎ 01297-442929; www.oldlymeguesthouse.co.uk; 29 Coombe St; s from £40, d £70; **P**) Once home to Lyme's old post office, this stone-fronted house is now an award-winning B&B. It has several frilly rooms finished in pale creams and soft hues, topped off by patterned curtains and china trinkets.

our pick **Coombe House** (☎ 01297-443849; www.coombe-house.co.uk; 41 Coombe St; d £52-58) Easygoing and stylish, this is a fabulous-value B&B of airy rooms, bay windows, wicker and white

wood. There's also a self-contained, ground-floor studio flat, complete with minikitchen. Breakfast is delivered to your door on a trolley, complete with toaster – perfect for a lazy lie-in in Lyme.

Alexandra (☎ 01297-442010; www.hotelalexandra.co.uk; Pound St; s £65, d £105-165; ☼ lunch & dinner) This grand 18th-century hotel was once home to a countess; today, it's all dignified calm and murmured chatter. Rooms are scattered with antique chairs and fine drapes and most have captivating views of the Cobb and the sea. The glorious terrace prompts urges to peruse the *Telegraph* in a panama hat.

Eating

Jurassic Seafood (☎ 01297-444345; 47 Silver St; mains £10-15; ☼ dinner) Bright and buzzy in blue and orange, this bistro revels in its prehistoric theme: fossil maps, hunting tips and replica dinosaur remains abound. A tasty, eclectic menu includes crab sushi, mussels and chips and local mackerel, as well as salads and steaks.

our pick **Broad Street** (☎ 01297-445792; 57 Broad St; 3 courses £27; ☼ dinner Thu-Sat, plus Tue, Wed & Sun in high season). Whitewashed walls, crisp white linen and old chapel chairs dot the interior of this innovative restaurant. The food has flair, too: confit of duck, roast tomato and beetroot purée sit alongside pot roast pollack with spinach and leeks. The ingredients' local credentials are outlined on the menu, and include wild garlic gathered from the woods. Bookings are essential.

The pubs clustered at the foot of the Cobb are great for harbourside bustle. The **Harbour Inn** (☎ 01297-442299; Marine Pde; mains £5-10; ☼ lunch & dinner), with stone walls and wooden settles, pips the others for atmosphere and

WESSEX

DETOUR: ABBOTSBURY SWANNERY

Every May some 600 free-flying swans choose to nest at the **Abbotsbury Swannery** (☎ 01305-871858; New Barn Rd, Abbotsbury; adult/child £8.50/5.50; ☼ 10am-5pm mid-Mar–Oct), which is protected by the pebble banks of Chesil Beach. The swannery was founded by the monks of Abbotsbury's monastery about 600 years ago, and feathers from the Abbotsbury swans are still used in the helmets of the Gentlemen At Arms (the Queen's official bodyguard). Wandering the network of trails that wind between their nests is an awe-inspiring experience that is often punctuated by occasional territorial displays (think snuffling cough and stand-up flapping), ensuring even the liveliest children are stilled. A few isolated cases of bird flu were reported here in early 2008, but they didn't affect opening.

sheer range of pub grub. Alongside, the **Cobb Arms** (☎ 01297-443242; Marine Pde) pulls a good pint.

Getting There & Away

Bus 31 runs to Dorchester (1¼ hours, hourly) and Weymouth (1¾ hours). Bus X53 goes west to Exeter (1¾ hours, six daily) and east to Weymouth (1½ hours).

AROUND LYME REGIS
Forde Abbey

A former Cistercian monastery, **Forde Abbey** (☎ 01460-221290; www.fordeabbey.co.uk; abbey & gardens adult/child £9/free, gardens only £7.20/free; ☼ abbey noon-4pm Tue-Fri & Sun Apr-Oct, gardens 10am-4.30pm) was built in the 12th century, updated in the 17th century, and has been a private home since 1649. The building boasts magnificent plasterwork ceilings and fine tapestries but it's the gardens that are the main attraction: 12 hectares of lawns, ponds, shrubberies and flower beds with many rare and beautiful species. It's 10 miles north of Lyme Regis; public transport is a nonstarter.

SHERBORNE
pop 9350

Sherborne gleams with a mellow, orangey-yellow stone – it's been used to build a central cluster of 15th-century buildings and the impressive abbey church at their core. This serene town exudes wealth. The five local fee-paying schools include the famous Sherborne School, and its pupils are a frequent sight as they head off to lessons from boarding houses scattered around the town. The number of boutique shops and convertibles in the car parks reinforces the well-heeled feel. Evidence of splashing the cash 16th- and 18th-century style lies on the edge of town: two castles, one a crumbling ruin, the other a marvellous manor house, complete with a Capability Brown lake.

Sherborne's **tourist office** (☎ 01935-815341; sherborne.tic@westdorset-dc.gov.uk; Digby Rd; ☼ 9am-5pm Mon-Sat Apr-Oct) stocks the free *All About Sherborne* leaflet, which has a map and town trail. There are **walking tours** (£3; ☼ 11am Fri May-Sep) that depart from the tourist office and last 1½ hours.

Sherborne Museum (☎ 01935-812252; www.sherbornemuseum.co.uk; Church Lane; adult/child £2/free; ☼ 10.30am-4.30pm Tue-Sat, 2.30-4.30pm Sun Apr-Oct) has a digital version of the *Sherborne Missal*,

the most exquisite illuminated manuscript to survive from the Middle Ages. With this high-tech copy you can turn the virtual pages and zoom in on sections of text.

Sights
SHERBORNE ABBEY

At the height of its influence, the magnificent **Abbey Church of St Mary the Virgin** (☎ 01935-812452; suggested donation £2; ☼ 8.30am-6pm late Mar-late Oct, to 4pm Nov–mid-Mar) was the central cathedral of the 26 Saxon bishops of Wessex. Established early in the 8th century, it became a Benedictine abbey in 998 and functioned as a cathedral until 1075. The church boasts the oldest fan vaulting in the country, and there are several intriguing tombs – it's worth tracking down the elaborate marble effigy marking the one belonging to John Lord Digby, Earl of Bristol, flanked by his two wives. Ethelred and Ethelbert are buried in the corner of the abbey.

On the edge of the abbey lie the beautiful 15th-century **St Johns' Almshouses** (admission £1.50; ☼ 2-4pm Tue & Thu-Sat May-Sep); look out, too, for the six-sided **conduit** now at the foot of Cheap St. This arched structure used to be the monks lavatorium (washhouse), but was moved to provide the townsfolk with water when the abbey was disbanded.

OLD CASTLE

These days the epitome of a picturesque ruin, Sherborne's **Old Castle** (EH; ☎ 01935-812730; adult/child £2.50/1.30; ☼ 10am-6pm Jul & Aug, to 5pm Apr-Jun & Sep, to 4pm Oct) was built by Roger, Bishop of Salisbury in around 1120. Queen Elizabeth gave it to her one-time favourite Sir Walter Raleigh in the late 16th century. He spent large sums of money modernising it before opting for a new-build instead – moving across the River Yeo to start work on the next Sherborne Castle. The old one became a Royalist stronghold during the English Civil War, but Cromwell reduced the 'malicious and mischievous castle' to rubble after a 16-day siege in 1645.

SHERBORNE CASTLE

Having had enough of the then 400-year-old Old Castle, Sir Walter Raleigh began building **New Castle** (☎ 01935-813182; www.sherbornecastle.com; castle & gardens adult/child £9/free, gardens only £4.50/free; ☼ 11am-4.30pm Tue-Thu & Sun, 2-4.30pm Sat Apr-Oct), really a splendid manor house, in

1594. Raleigh got as far as the central block before falling out of favour with the royals and ending up back in prison – this time at the hands of James I. In 1617 James sold the castle to Sir John Digby, Earl of Bristol, who added the wings we see today. In 1753, the grounds received a mega-makeover at the hands of landscape-gardener extraordinaire Capability Brown – visit today and marvel at the massive lake he added, along with a remarkable 12 hectares of waterside gardens.

Sleeping & Eating

Cumberland House (☎ 01935-817554; sandie@bandb dorset.co.uk; Green Hill; s £45, d £64-74) There are few straight lines in this 17th-century B&B; instead, walls undulate towards each other then in charming rooms finished in white, beige and tiny bursts of vivid pink. Breakfast is either Continental (complete with chocolate croissants) or full English – either way, there's freshly squeezed orange juice.

Eastbury Hotel (☎ 01935-813131; www.theeastbury hotel.co.uk; Long St; s £68, d £120-160) The best rooms here have real 'wow' factor – black and gold lacquer screens frame minimalist free-standing baths, and shimmering fabrics swathe French sleigh beds. The standard rooms are much more standard, but are still elegant with stripy furnishings and pared-down wicker chairs.

Also recommended:

Antelope (☎ 01935-812077; www.theantelopehotel .co.uk; Green Hill; s £54-60, d £60-85) A creaking old coaching inn with simple rooms at the top of town.

Stoneleigh Barn (☎ 01935-815964; www.stoneleigh barn.com; North Wootton; s/d/f £56/80/95) A flower-smothered, tastefully converted 18th-century barn, 2 miles southeast of town.

Eating

Pear Tree Deli (☎ 01935-812828; Half Moon St; mains £4-8; ☑ 9am-5pm Mon-Sat, 10am-4pm Sun) Full of mouth-watering aromas, this delectable deli is packed with gourmet picnic supplies. Spinach and feta pie, homemade soups and a wealth of local cheeses are coupled with irresistible cakes and puds.

Paprika (☎ 01935-816429; Half Moon St; mains £7-12; ☑ lunch & dinner) Expect excellent, well-spiced food in this Indian restaurant. The menu is a mix of the usual fare and some surprises: honey and cashew chicken, garlic masala and Thai prawn risotto.

Green (☎ 01935-813821; 3 The Green; 2/3 courses £25/30; ☑ lunch & dinner Tue-Sat) Local food features

strongly at this intimate, cream and green restaurant at the top of Cheap St. Tempting flavour combos include Dorset venison with butternut squash, or local crab with tarragon and avocado.

Getting There & Away

Bus 57 runs from Yeovil (30 minutes, half-hourly Monday to Saturday), as does bus 58 (15 minutes, every two hours Monday to Saturday, six buses on Sunday), which sometimes continues to Shaftesbury (1½ hours, four daily Monday to Saturday). Buses D12 and D13 run to Dorchester (one hour, three to six daily Monday to Saturday).

Hourly trains go to Exeter (£14.50, 1¼ hours), London (£38.40, 2½ hours) and Salisbury (£10.10, 45 minutes).

SHAFTESBURY & AROUND
pop 6665

Perched on an idyllic hilltop overlooking a panorama of pastoral meadows and hog-backed hills, the village of Shaftesbury was home to the largest community of nuns in England until 1539, when Henry VIII came knocking during the Dissolution. These days its attractions are rather more prosaic; the town's best-known landmark is Gold Hill. This cobbled slope, lined by chocolate-box cottages, graces many a local postcard and also starred in a famous TV advert for Hovis bread.

The **tourist office** (☎ 01747-853514; www.shaftes burydorset.com; 8 Bell St; ☑ 10am-5pm Apr-Sep, 10am-3pm Mon-Sat Oct-Mar) is by the Bleke St car park.

Sights

Sitting on a terrace with sweeping views across the hills, **Shaftesbury Abbey** (☎ 01747-852910; www .shaftesburyabbey.org.uk; Park Walk; adult/child £4/1; ☑ 10am-5pm Apr-Oct) was at one time England's largest and richest nunnery. It was founded in 888 by King Alfred the Great, and was the first religious house in Britain built solely for women; Alfred's daughter, Aethelgifu, was its first abbess. St Edward is thought to have been buried here, and King Knut died at the abbey in 1035. Most of the buildings were dismantled by Henry VIII and his cronies, but you can still wander around its foundations with a well-devised audio guide, and you can visit the intriguing museum.

The small **Gold Hill Museum** (☎ 01747-852157; Sun & Moon Cottage, Gold Hill; adult/child £4/1;

WESSEX

(☪ 10.30am-4.30pm Thu-Tue) is worth visiting for its 18th-century fire engine, a collection of Dorset decorative buttons, and the ornamental Byzant, used during the town's ancient water ceremony.

Old Wardour Castle

The six-sided **Old Wardour Castle** (EH; ☎ 01747-870487; adult/child £3.50/1.80; ☪ 10am-6pm Jul & Aug, to 5pm Apr-Jun & Sep, to 4pm Oct, to 4pm Sat & Sun Nov-Mar) was built around 1393 and suffered severe damage during the English Civil War, leaving the magnificent remains you see today. It's an ideal spot for a picnic and there are fantastic views from the upper levels. Bus 26 runs from Shaftesbury (four daily Monday to Friday), 4 miles west.

Sleeping & Eating

Retreat (☎ 01747-850372; www.the-retreat.org.uk; 47 Bell St; s/d/f £45/84/78; **P**) The rooms in this Georgian town house are large and stately, if a little staid – all moulded ceilings, antique chairs and pieces of 19th-century china. Two minutes' walk from town.

Cobwebbs (☎ 01747-853505; www.cobwebbs.me.uk; 14 Gold Hill; d £70-75) If it's a picturesque setting you're after, head for this miniature whitewashed cottage halfway up Gold Hill. Unsurprisingly, it's on the snug side but you get a sitting room as well as double bedroom, and the patio doors lead onto the lovely rear terrace.

Fleur de Lys (☎ 01747-853717; www.lafleurdelys.co.uk; Bleke St; s £80, d £110-145, f £175, 2/3 courses £24/29, mains £24; ☪ lunch Wed-Sun, dinner Mon-Sat) For a lovely dollop of luxury, immerse yourself in the world of Fleur de Lys. Fluffy bathrobes, minifridges and laptops ensure you click into pamper mode; the elegant restaurant rustles up quail with raspberry and smoked salmon with samphire.

our pick **Bell Street Cafe** (☎ 01747-850022; 17 Bell St; mains £10-15; ☪ lunch Tue-Sat, dinner Wed-Sat) The flavours in this chilled bistro are from Lombardy, Gascony and Burgundy but the ingredients are often local, seasonal and organic. Ancient wooden stairs and whitewashed walls give it a funky feel – helped by regular live bands that play flamenco and swing.

Mitre Inn (☎ 01747-852549; 23 The High St; mains £6-10; ☪ lunch & dinner Mon-Sat, lunch Sun) For a good pint, imaginative pub grub and a deck with stunning hill views, pop into this atmospheric pub.

Getting There & Away

Bus 58 goes to Sherborne (1½ hours) and on to Yeovil (two hours, four daily Monday to Saturday). Buses 26 and 27 go to Salisbury (1¼ hours, five to seven Monday to Saturday).

One National Express bus (£17.20, 3¾ hours) a day runs from Shaftesbury to London Victoria, via Heathrow.

WILTSHIRE

With Wiltshire you get the very best of ancient England. This verdant landscape is rich with the reminders of ritual and is littered with more ancient barrows, processional avenues and mysterious stone rings than anywhere else in Britain. It's a place that teases and tantalises the imagination – here you'll find the prehistoric majesty of Stonehenge, atmospheric Avebury and, in soaring Silbury Hill, the largest constructed earth mound in Europe. Then there's the serene 800-year-old cathedral at Salisbury – a relatively modern religious monument. Add the supremely stately homes at Stourhead and Longleat and the impossibly pretty villages of Castle Combe and Lacock, and you have a county crammed full of English charm waiting to be explored.

Information

The **Visit Wiltshire** (www.visitwiltshire.co.uk) website is a good source of info.

Activities

WALKING

Wiltshire is great walking country, much of it flat or rolling farmland, cut by steep-sided valleys, edged with grassy hills and downs providing stunning views, and dotted with a wealth of ancient monuments.

The 87-mile **Ridgeway National Trail** starts near Avebury (p328), but there are plenty of shorter walks, including hikes around Stonehenge (p320), Old Sarum (p319) and the Stourhead Estate (p322).

The *Walking in Wiltshire* booklet (£3) details 10 easy strolls, while the *White Horse Trail* leaflet (£6) covers a 90-mile route, taking in all of Wiltshire's eight chalk horses. Both are available from tourist offices. The Visit Wiltshire website also has some useful downloadable walking routes, ranging from 2 to 10 miles.

Foot Trails (☎ 01747-861851; www.foottrails.co.uk) leads guided walks and can help you plan your own self-guided route.

CYCLING

Cyclists should pick up the *Wiltshire Cycleway* leaflet (£3) in tourist offices, which includes a detailed route guide and lists handy cycle shops. The waterproof *Off-Road Cycling in Wiltshire* (£6) includes trail maps for mountain-bikers. The Visit Wiltshire website has five downloadable cycling routes, ranging from 16 to 33 miles.

Dedicated cycling tours are offered by several operators, including **History on Your Handlebars** (☎ 01249-730013; www.historyonyourhandlebars.co.uk; Lacock).

CANAL TRIPS

The 87-mile-long **Kennet & Avon Canal** runs all the way from Bristol to Reading. If you fancy getting out on the water, contact **Sally Boats** (☎ 01225-864923; www.sallyboats.ltd.uk; Bradford-on-Avon) or **Foxhangers** (☎ 01380-828795; www.foxhangers.co.uk; Devizes), which both have narrowboats for hire. Weekly rates start at around £630 for four people in winter, rising to about £1500 for a 10-berth boat in high summer.

Getting Around

BUS

The bus coverage in Wiltshire can be patchy, especially in the northwest of the county. The two main operators:

First (☎ 0871 200 22 33; www.firstgroup.com) Serves the far west of the county.

Wilts & Dorset Buses (☎ 01722-336855; www.wdbus .co.uk) Covers most destinations; its Explorer ticket is valid for a day (adult/child £7.50/4.50).

TRAIN

Rail lines run from London to Salisbury and beyond to Exeter and Plymouth, branching off north to Bradford-on-Avon, Bath and Bristol, but most of the smaller towns and villages aren't served by trains.

SALISBURY

pop 43,335

Centred on a majestic cathedral that's topped by the tallest spire in England, the gracious city of Salisbury makes a charming base from which to explore the rest of Wiltshire. It's been an important provincial city for more than 1000 years, and its

---

TOP FIVE ANCIENT SITES

- Avebury (p326) Bigger than Stonehenge in atmosphere and acreage, this huge stone ring encases an entire village.

- Stonehenge (p320) The world's most famous collection of megaliths – shame no one has a clue what it was for.

- Maiden Castle (p307) Massive and rampart-ringed, this is the biggest Iron Age hill fort in Britain.

- Glastonbury Tor (p356) Myth-rich and mighty hard to climb, this iconic mound looks down onto the Vale of Avalon.

- Old Sarum (p319) A stunning Iron Age stronghold on Salisbury Plain.

---

streets form an architectural timeline ranging from medieval walls and half-timbered Tudor town houses to Georgian mansions and Victorian villas. Salisbury is also a lively, modern place, boasting plenty of bars, restaurants and terraced cafes, as well as a concentrated cluster of excellent museums.

Orientation

From miles around, Salisbury Cathedral's soaring spire points you towards the centre of town, which stretches north to Market Sq, an expanse dominated by its impressive Guildhall. The train station is a 10-minute walk to the west of the market, while the bus station is 90m north up Endless St.

Information

Library (☎ 01722-324145; Market Pl; 🕙 10am-7pm Mon, 9am-7pm Tue, Wed & Fri, 9am-5pm Thu & Sat) Provides 30 minutes of internet access for free.

Post office (cnr Castle St & Chipper Lane)

Tourist office (☎ 01722-334956; www.visitwiltshire .co.uk/salisbury; Fish Row, Market Sq; 🕙 9.30am-6pm Mon-Sat, 10.30am-4.30pm Sun Jun-Sep, 9.30am-5pm Mon-Sat, 10.30am-4pm Sun May, 9.30am-5pm Mon-Sat Oct-Apr)

Washing Well Laundrette (☎ 01722-421874; 28 Chipper Lane; 🕙 8am-9pm)

Sights

SALISBURY CATHEDRAL

England is endowed with countless stunning churches, but few can hold a candle to the grandeur and sheer spectacle of **Salisbury Cathedral** (☎ 01722-555120; www.salisburycathedral.org.uk;

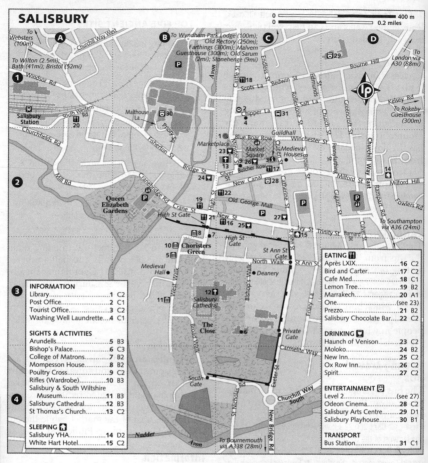

requested donation adult/child £5/3; 7.15am-6.15pm Sep-May, to 7.15pm Jun-Aug). Built between 1220 and 1258, the cathedral bears all the hallmarks of the early English Gothic style, with an elaborate exterior decorated with pointed arches and flying buttresses, and a sombre, austere interior designed to keep its congregation suitably pious.

Beyond the highly decorative **West Front**, a small passageway leads into the 70m-long nave, lined with handsome pillars of Purbeck stone. In the north aisle look out for a fascinating **clock** dating from 1386, probably the oldest working timepiece in the world. At the eastern end of the ambulatory the glorious **Prisoners of Conscience** stained-glass window (1980) hovers above the ornate tomb

of Edward Seymour (1539–1621) and Lady Catherine Grey. Other monuments and tombs line the sides of the nave, including that of **William Longespée**, son of Henry II and half-brother of King John. When the tomb was excavated a well-preserved rat was found inside Longespée's skull.

The splendid **spire** was added in the mid-14th century. At 123m, it's the highest in Britain, and represented an enormous technical challenge for its medieval builders; it weighs around 6500 tons and required an elaborate system of cross-bracing, scissor arches and supporting buttresses to keep it upright. Look closely and you'll see that the additional weight has buckled the four central piers of the nave.

Sir Christopher Wren surveyed the cathedral in 1668 and calculated that the spire was leaning by 75cm. A **brass plate** in the floor of the nave is used to measure any shift, but no further lean was recorded in 1951 or 1970. Despite this, reinforcement of the notoriously 'wonky spire' continues to this day.

There are 1½-hour tower **tours** (adult/child £5.50/4.50; ☉ 2.15pm year-round, plus 11.15am Mar-Oct & Dec, plus 3.15pm Apr-Sep, plus 5pm mid-Jun–mid-Aug), which climb up 332 vertigo-inducing steps to the base of the spire. From here there are jaw-dropping views across the city and the surrounding countryside.

One of the four surviving copies of the **Magna Carta**, the historic agreement made between King John and his barons in 1215, is kept in the cathedral's **Chapter House** (☉ 9.30am-5.30pm Mar–mid-Jun & mid-Aug–Oct, to 6.45pm mid-Jun–mid-Aug, 10am-4.30pm Nov-Feb).

CATHEDRAL CLOSE

The medieval cathedral close, a tranquil enclave surrounded by beautiful houses, has an other-worldly feel. Many of the buildings date from the same period as the cathedral, although the area was heavily restored during an 18th-century clean-up by James Wyatt. The close is encircled by a sturdy outer wall, constructed in 1333; the stout gates leading into the complex are still locked every night.

The highlight of the **Salisbury & South Wiltshire Museum** (☎ 01722-332151; www.salisburymuseum.org.uk; 65 The Close; adult/child £5/2; ☉ 10am-5pm Mon-Sat Sep-Jun, 10am-5pm Mon-Sat, 2-5pm Sun Jul & Aug) is the interactive Stonehenge gallery. There are also archaeological finds recovered from Old Sarum (p319) and lots of ceramics, historical artefacts and paintings, including a dreamy watercolour of Stonehenge by JMW Turner.

You can have a nose around **Arundells** (☎ 01722-326546; www.arundells.org.uk; 59 The Close; admission £8; ☉ tours 1-4pm Sat-Tue late Mar-Sep), the fine, grey-stone home of late British prime minister Edward Heath (1916–2005). Look out for the paintings by Winston Churchill that nestle amid sailing memorabilia and political cartoons. The house is open for guided tours only, which have to be prebooked.

Built in 1701, **Mompesson House** (NT; ☎ 01722-335659; The Close; adult/child £4.50/2.20; ☉ 11am-5pm Sat-Wed Mar-Oct) is a fine Queen Anne building with magnificent plasterwork ceilings, exceptional period furnishings and a wonderful carved

staircase. All that made it the perfect location for the 1995 film *Sense and Sensibility*.

Military buffs will revel in the **Rifles** (☎ 01722-419419; www.thewardrobe.org.uk; 58 The Close; adult/child £3.25/1; ☉ 10am-5pm Apr-Oct, 10am-5pm Tue-Sun Nov-Mar). Also referred to as the Wardrobe, this museum is home to detailed displays about the Royal Berkshire, Wiltshire and Duke of Edinburgh regiments.

Just inside narrow High St Gate is the **College of Matrons**, founded in 1682 for widows and unmarried daughters of clergymen. South of the cathedral is the **Bishop's Palace**, now the private Cathedral School, parts of which date back to 1220.

ST THOMAS'S CHURCH

This elegant **church** (Minster St) was built for cathedral workmen in 1219 and named after St Thomas Becket. Modified in the 15th century, its most famous feature is the amazing **doom painting** above the chancel arch, painted in 1475. This depicts Christ on the day of judgment, sitting astride a rainbow flanked by visions of Heaven and Hell; on the Hell side, look out for two naked kings and a nude bishop, a miser with his moneybags, and a female alehouse owner, the only person allowed to hang on to her clothes.

MARKET SQUARE

Markets were first held here in 1219, and the square still bustles with traders every Tuesday and Saturday. On these days you can pick up anything from fresh fish to discount digital watches. The narrow lanes surrounding the square reveal their medieval specialities: Oatmeal Row, Fish Row and Silver St. The 15th-century **Poultry Cross** is the last of four market crosses that once stood on the square.

Tours

Salisbury City Guides (☎ 01722-320349; www.salisbury cityguides.co.uk; adult/child £4/2; ☉ 11am Apr-Oct, 11am Sat & Sun Nov-Mar) leads 1½-hour tours from the tourist office. There is also an 8pm ghost walk on Fridays from May to September.

Festivals & Events

The **Salisbury Festival** (☎ 01722-332977; www.salisbury festival.co.uk) is a prestigious, wide-ranging arts event that encompasses classical, world and pop music, plus theatre, literature and art. It runs over three weeks from late May to early June.

Sleeping

BUDGET

Salisbury YHA (☎ 0845 371 9537; www.yha.org.uk; Milford Hill; dm £17.50; **P**) A real gem: a rambling, welcoming hostel in a listed 19th-century building. Rooms range from doubles to dorms, while a cafe-bar, laundry and dappled gardens add to the appeal.

MIDRANGE

Old Rectory (☎ 01722-502702; www.theoldrectory-bb.co.uk; 75 Belle Vue Rd; s £35-50, d £55-80; **P**) This serene, airy B&B is full of spick-and-span rooms decked out in cream and shades of blue. The delightful enclosed garden has views of St Edmund's Church – you can even cook up a storm on the B&B's BBQ.

Websters (☎ 01722-339779; www.websters-bed-breakfast.com; 11 Hartington Rd; s £40-45, d £55-58; **P** **▯**) Websters' exterior charms include quaint blue shutters and dinky arched windows. Inside it's all flowery wallpaper, patterned duvets, extra tea-tray treats and a genuinely warm welcome.

Wyndham Park Lodge (☎ 01722-416517; www.wyndhamparklodge.co.uk; 51 Wyndham Rd; s £40-45, d £55-60; **P** **▯** wi-fi) The best rooms in this tall, red-brick B&B are the huge 1st-floor family suite and the stylish garden double (which leads onto a private patio). Extras include kippers or pancakes for breakfast.

Rokeby Guesthouse (☎ 01722-329800; www.rokebyguesthouse.co.uk; 3 Wain-a-long Rd; s/d from £45/55; **P** **▯** wi-fi) Fancy furnishings, free-standing baths and lovely bay windows make this cheerful B&B stand out from the crowd. The decking overlooking the lawn and the mini-gym help, too.

Also recommended:

Farthings (☎ 01722-330749; www.farthingsbandb.co.uk; 9 Swaynes Close; s/d £35/60; **P**) Victorian-era B&B with quilted beds and a pleasant garden; the cheaper rooms share facilities.

Malvern Guesthouse (☎ 01722-327995; www.malvernguesthouse.com; 31 Hulse Rd; d from £55; **P**) Family-run guest house with floral-themed rooms and homemade marmalade.

TOP END

White Hart Hotel (☎ 01722-327476; St John St; www.mercure-uk.com; s from £90, d £120; **P** **▯**) For a bit of pomp and pampering, duck under the porticos of this 17th-century hotel. Standing right opposite the cathedral close, the service is appropriately attentive and rooms are suitably swish – the wood-rich four-poster bedrooms are positively opulent.

Eating

BUDGET

Salisbury Chocolate Bar (☎ 01722-327422; 33 High St; ☽ 9.30am-5pm Tue-Sat, 10.15am-5pm Mon) With a scattering of tables that hug counters brim-full of handmade chocs and sweet pastries, there is no better place to blow a diet.

our pick **Bird and Carter** (☎ 01722-417908; 3 Fish Row, Market Sq; snacks from £4; ☽ 8.30am-6pm Mon-Sat, 10am-4pm Sun) Nestling amid 15th-century beams, this deli-cum-cafe blends old-world charm with a tempting array of antipasti, charcuterie and local goodies. Grab a goats' cheese and aubergine panini to go, or duck upstairs to eat alongside weathered wood, stained glass and old church pews.

MIDRANGE

Prezzo (☎ 01722-341333; 52-54 High St; mains £8-10; ☽ lunch & dinner) Housed in a decidedly wonky half-timbered house, this sleek Italian does all the standard pizza and pasta dishes fantastically well, plus Sicilian chicken and a delicious red-pesto burger.

Lemon Tree (☎ 01722-333471; 92 Crane St; mains £8-13; ☽ lunch & dinner Mon-Sat) The menu at this tiny bistro is packed with character – how about crispy duck with cherry sauce, pear and brie toast or roasted mozzarella wrapped in Parma ham? The patio-garden makes warm weather dining a delight.

One (☎ 01722-411313; 1-5 Minster St; mains £8-15; ☽ lunch & dinner) Sloping floors, slanting beams and fake pony-hide chairs surround you in this quirky restaurant, located above the Haunch of Venison pub (opposite). The menu is equally eclectic, featuring hot smoked mackerel salad, grilled bratwurst and good old English cottage pie.

Cafe Med (☎ 01722-328402; 68 Castle St; mains £9-20; ☽ lunch & dinner Mon-Fri, dinner Sat) Bringing some Mediterranean vim to Salisbury's streets, this breezy bistro blends British classics with sun-kissed flavours – think sirloin steak with grilled vine tomatoes, or roast cod with pancetta.

Marrakech (☎ 01722-411112; 129-133 South Western Rd; mains £9; ☽ lunch Tue-Sat, dinner daily) For a taste of Casablanca without leaving Wiltshire, dive into this funky little restaurant's terracotta-coloured dining room, where five-vegetable couscous, marinated chicken *tagine*, falafel and meze all end up on tiled Moroccan tables.

Après LXIX (☎ 01722-340000; 69 New St; mains £10-18; ✍ lunch & dinner Mon-Sat) With artfully soft lighting and whitewashed walls, this Soho-style bistro is ideal for a romantic meal. Dishes reflect Italian, French and British influences – try the wild-boar sausages with red-wine jus or the seared tuna salad.

Drinking

Haunch of Venison (☎ 01722-322024; 1-5 Minster St) Featuring wood-panelled snugs, spiral staircases and wonky ceilings, this 14th-century pub is packed with atmosphere – and ghosts. One is a cheating whist player whose hand was severed in a game (track down his mummified bones inside).

Spirit (☎ 01722-330053; 46 Catherine St; ✍ 4pm-midnight Tue-Sat) This hip hang-out is packed with the young and beautiful, who enjoy the banging tunes on the decks and a choice of multicoloured cocktails.

Moloko (☎ 01722-507050; 5 Bridge St) Red radiators, red banquets and red Soviet stars lend this Russian-themed bar a Cold War feel. The flavoured vodkas are definitely post-1984.

Try the **Ox Row Inn** (☎ 01722-424921; 11 Ox Row, Market Sq) for local ales; the walled beer garden at the 14th-century **New Inn** (☎ 01722-326662; 41 New St) overlooks the Cathedral.

Entertainment

Salisbury Arts Centre (☎ 01722-321744; www.salisburyartscentre.co.uk; Bedwin St) Housed in the converted St Edmund's church, this innovative arts centre showcases cutting-edge theatre, dance and live gigs; photography and arts exhibitions are held in the foyer.

Salisbury Playhouse (☎ 01722-320333; www.salisburyplayhouse.com; Malthouse Lane) The town's big arts venue, hosting top touring shows, musicals and new plays.

Odeon Cinema (☎ 0871 22 44 007; New Canal) Quite possibly the only cinema in the world with a heavily beamed medieval foyer.

Level 2 (☎ 01722-330053; 48 Catherine St; ✍ 10.30pm-2am Thu-Sat) The club above Spirit (see above), Level 2 pumps out dance-floor fillers and drum and bass, and has guest DJs on Friday.

Getting There & Away

BUS

Three National Express coaches run direct to London via Heathrow each day (£14.40, 3½

hours). There's a daily coach to Bath (£8.80, 1½ hours) and Bristol (£8.80, two hours).

Buses X4 and X5 travel to Bath (two hours, hourly Monday to Saturday) via Bradford-on-Avon (1½ hours). Regular buses run to Shaftesbury, Devizes and Avebury.

Tour buses leave Salisbury for Stonehenge regularly; see p322.

TRAIN

Trains run half-hourly from London Waterloo (£27.60, 1½ hours) and hourly on to Exeter (£25.70, two hours) and the southwest. Another line runs from Portsmouth (£14.40, 1½ hours, hourly) via Southampton (£7.20, 30 minutes), with connections to Bradford-on-Avon (£9.40, 40 minutes, hourly), Bath (£8, one hour, hourly) and Bristol (£9.50, 1¼ hours, hourly).

AROUND SALISBURY
Old Sarum

The huge ramparts of **Old Sarum** (EH; ☎ 01722-335398; adult/child £3/1.50; ✍ 9am-6pm Jul & Aug, 10am-5pm Apr-Jun & Sep, 10am-4pm Oct & Mar, 11am-3pm Nov-Feb) sit on a grassy rise about 2 miles from Salisbury. It began life as a huge hill fort during the Iron Age, and was later occupied by both the Romans and the Saxons. By the mid-11th century it was a town – one of the most important in the west of England; William the Conqueror convened one of his earliest councils here, with the first cathedral being built in 1092, snatching the bishopric from nearby Sherborne Abbey. But Old Sarum always had problems: it was short on water and exposed to the elements, and in 1219 the bishop was given permission to move the cathedral to a new location beside the River Avon, founding the modern-day city of Salisbury. By 1331 the cathedral had been demolished for building material and Old Sarum was practically abandoned; a scale model in Salisbury Cathedral (p315) illustrates how the site once looked.

There are free guided tours at 3pm in June, July and August, and medieval tournaments, open-air plays and mock battles are held on selected days.

Between them, buses 5, 6 and 9 run four times an hour from Salisbury to Old Sarum (hourly on Sundays).

Wilton House

For an insight into the exquisite, rarefied world of the British aristocracy, head to

Wilton House (☎ 01722-746714; www.wiltonhouse
.com; house & gardens adult/child £12/6.50, gardens only
£5/3.50; ⏱ house noon-5pm Sun-Thu Apr-Aug, noon-5pm
Tue-Thu Sep, gardens 11am-5.30pm Apr-Sep), one of the
finest stately homes in England. The Earls of
Pembroke have lived here since 1542, and it's
been expanded, improved and embellished
by successive generations since a devastating
fire in 1647. The result is quite staggering and
provides a whistle-stop tour of the history of
English art and architecture: magnificent period furniture, frescoed ceilings and elaborate
plasterwork frame paintings by Van Dyck,
Rembrandt and Joshua Reynolds. Highlights
are the Single and Double Cube Rooms, designed by the pioneering 17th-century architect Inigo Jones. The fine landscaped grounds
were largely laid out by Capability Brown.

All that architectural eye candy makes the
house a favoured film location: *The Madness
of King George*, *Sense and Sensibility* and a
recent version of *Pride and Prejudice* were
all shot here. But Wilton was serving as an
artistic haven long before the movies – famous guests include Ben Jonson, Edmund
Spenser, Christopher Marlowe and John
Donne, and Shakespeare's *As You Like It* was
performed here in 1603, shortly after the bard
had written it.

Wilton House is 2½ miles west of Salisbury;
buses 60, 60A and 61 run from Salisbury (10
minutes, four hourly Monday to Saturday,
hourly on Sunday).

STONEHENGE

Stonehenge (EH/NT; ☎ 01980-624715; adult/child
£6.50/3.30; ⏱ 9am-7pm Jun & Aug, 9.30am-6pm mid-
Mar–May & Sep–mid-Oct, 9.30am-4pm mid-Oct–mid-Mar) is
Britain's most iconic archaeological site. This
compelling ring of monolithic stones has been
attracting a steady stream of pilgrims, poets
and philosophers for the last 5000 years.

Despite the constant flow of traffic from
the main road beside the monument, and the
huge numbers of visitors who traipse around
the perimeter on a daily basis, Stonehenge
still manages to be a mystical, ethereal place –
a haunting echo from Britain's forgotten
past, and a reminder of the people who once
walked the many ceremonial avenues across
Salisbury Plain. Even more intriguingly, it's
still one of Britain's great archaeological mysteries: despite countless theories about what
the site was used for, ranging from a sacrifi-
cial centre to a celestial timepiece, in truth,
no one really knows what drove prehistoric
Britons to expend so much time and effort
on its construction.

You can't stroll around the centre of the site
during normal opening hours, but unforgettable evening and early-morning **Stone Circle
Access Visits** (☎ 01722-343834; adult/child £13/6) can be
arranged. Each visit only takes up to 26 people,
so you'll need to book well in advance.

The Site

The first phase of construction at Stonehenge
started around 3000 BC, when the outer circular bank and ditch were erected. A thousand
years later, an inner circle of granite stones,
known as bluestones, was added. It's thought
that these mammoth 4-ton blocks were hauled
from the Preseli Mountains in South Wales,
some 250 miles away – an almost inexplicable
feat for Stone Age builders equipped with
only the simplest of tools. Although no one
is entirely sure how the builders transported
the stones so far, it's thought they probably

MYSTERIOUS PAST, MYSTERIOUS FUTURE

For such a celebrated site, Stonehenge has seen a surprising amount of upheaval. While the
reasons behind its creation have provoked debate, how the site is used today has proved equally
controversial. The tense stand-offs between solstice-goers and police that marked the 1980s and
'90s have been replaced by fresh controversy about the impact the modern world has on the jewel
in Britain's archaeological crown. This World Heritage Site is hemmed in by busy roads and wire
barricades; jammed with visitors throughout the summer; and underscored by a cacophony of
traffic. It's a long way from the haven of peace and spiritual tranquillity many expect to find.

Ambitious plans to tunnel the A303 under the monument, to turn the surrounding arable
fields back into chalk downland and to bus people in from 2 miles away have now been rejected.
English Heritage has to come up with other, smaller scale, changes – set to be in place by 2012,
these will still feature a new visitor centre and may include closing the quieter A344, but the
wider future of this supremely mystical site looks as mysterious as its past.

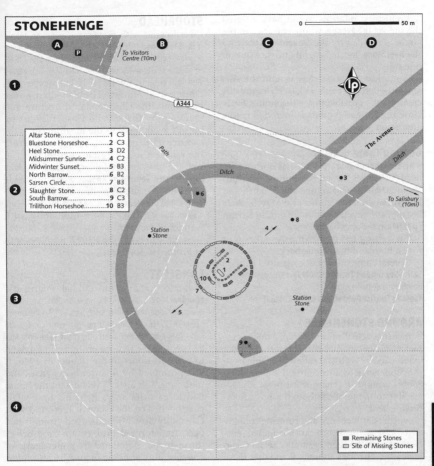

STONEHENGE

0 ———— 50 m

Altar Stone	1	C3
Bluestone Horseshoe	2	C3
Heel Stone	3	D2
Midsummer Sunrise	4	C2
Midwinter Sunset	5	B3
North Barrow	6	B2
Sarsen Circle	7	B3
Slaughter Stone	8	C2
South Barrow	9	C3
Trilithon Horseshoe	10	B3

To Visitors Centre (10m)

A344

The Avenue

Ditch

Path

Ditch

To Salisbury (10mi)

Station Stone

Station Stone

■ Remaining Stones
□ Site of Missing Stones

WESSEX

used a system of ropes, sledges and rollers fashioned from tree trunks – Salisbury Plain was still covered by forest during Stonehenge's construction.

Around 1500 BC, Stonehenge's main stones were dragged to the site, erected in a circle and crowned by massive lintels to make the trilithons (two vertical stones topped by a horizontal one). The sarsen (sandstone) stones were cut from an extremely hard rock found on the Marlborough Downs 20 miles from the site. It's estimated dragging one of these 50-ton stones across the countryside would require about 600 people.

Also around this time, the bluestones from 500 years earlier were rearranged as an inner **bluestone horseshoe** with an **altar stone** at the

centre. Outside this the **trilithon horseshoe** of five massive sets of stones was erected. Three of these are intact; the other two have just a single upright. Then came the major **sarsen circle** of 30 massive vertical stones, of which 17 uprights and six lintels remain.

Much further out, another circle was delineated by the 58 **Aubrey Holes**, named after John Aubrey, who discovered them in the 1600s. Just inside this circle are the **South and North Barrows**, each originally topped by a stone. Like many stone circles in Britain (including Avebury, p327), the inner horseshoes are aligned to coincide with sunrise at the midsummer solstice, which some claim supports the theory that the site was some kind of astronomical calendar.

Prehistoric pilgrims would have entered the site via the **Avenue**, whose entrance to the circle is marked by the **Slaughter Stone** and the **Heel Stone**, located slightly further out on one side.

A marked pathway leads around the site, and although you can't walk freely in the circle itself, it's possible to see the stones fairly close up. An audio guide is included in the admission price.

Getting There & Away

The **Stonehenge Tour** (☎ 01722-336855; return adult/child £11/5) leaves Salisbury's railway and bus stations half-hourly in June and August, and hourly between September and May. Tickets last all day, so you can hop off at Old Sarum (p319) on the way back.

Taxis charge £35 to go to the site – they wait for an hour and then come back.

Several companies offer organised tours:
Salisbury Guided Tours (☎ 01722-337960; www .salisburyguidedtours.com)
Wessex Tourist Guides (☎ 01980-623463)

AROUND STONEHENGE

Stonehenge actually forms part of a huge complex of ancient monuments, a fact that's often overlooked by visitors. Leaflets available from the Stonehenge visitor centre detail walking routes around the main sites; most are accessible to the public although a few are on private land.

North of Stonehenge and running roughly east–west is the **Cursus**, an elongated embanked oval; the slightly smaller **Lesser Cursus** is nearby. Theories abound as to what these sites were used for, ranging from ancient sporting arenas to processional avenues for the dead.

Other prehistoric sites around Stonehenge include a number of burial mounds, such as the **New King Barrows**, and **Vespasian's Camp**, an Iron Age hill fort.

Just north of Amesbury and 1½ miles east of Stonehenge is **Woodhenge**, a series of concentric rings that would once have been marked by wooden posts. It's thought there might be some correlation between the use of of wood and stone in both structures, but it's unclear what the materials would have meant to ancient Britons. Excavations in the 1970s at Woodhenge revealed the skeleton of a child with a cloven skull, buried near the centre.

STOURHEAD

Overflowing with vistas, temples and follies, **Stourhead** (NT; ☎ 01747-841152; Stourton; house or garden adult/child £6.30/3.80, house & garden £10.50/5.80; ◷ house 11.30am-4.30pm Fri-Tue mid-Mar–Oct, garden 9am-7pm or sunset year-round) is landscape gardening at its finest. The Palladian house has some fine Chippendale furniture and paintings by Claude and Gaspard Poussin, but it's a sideshow to the magnificent 18th-century gardens, which spread out across the valley. A lovely 2-mile circuit takes you past the most ornate follies, around the lake and to the **Temple of Apollo**; a 3½-mile side trip can be made from near the **Pantheon** to **King Alfred's Tower** (adult/child £2.20/1.20; ◷ 11.30am-4.30pm mid-Mar–Oct), a 50m-high folly with wonderful views.

Stourhead is off the B3092, 8 miles south of Frome (in Somerset).

LONGLEAT

Half ancestral mansion and half safari park, **Longleat** (☎ 01985-844400; www.longleat.co.uk; house & grounds adult/child £10/6, safari park £11/8, all-inclusive passport £22/16; ◷ house 10am-5pm year-round, safari park 10am-4pm Apr-Nov, other attractions 11am-5pm Apr-Nov) became the first stately home in England to open its doors to the public, in 1946. It was prompted by finance: heavy taxes and mounting bills after WWII meant the house had to earn its keep. Britain's first safari park opened on the estate in 1966, and soon Capability Brown's landscaped grounds had been transformed into an amazing drive-through zoo, populated by a menagerie of animals more at home in an African wilderness than the fields of Wiltshire. These days the zoo is backed up by a throng of touristy attractions, including a narrow-gauge railway, Dr Who exhibit, Postman Pat village, pets' corner and butterfly garden. Under all these tourist trimmings it's easy to forget the house itself, which contains fine tapestries, furniture and decorated ceilings, as well as seven libraries containing around 40,000 tomes. The highlight, though, is an extraordinary series of paintings and psychedelic murals by the present-day marquess, who trained as an art student in the '60s and upholds the long-standing tradition of eccentricity among the English aristocracy – check out his website at www.lordbath.co.uk.

Longleat is just off the A362, 3 miles from both Frome and Warminster.

BRADFORD-ON-AVON
pop 8800

Tumbling down the slopes of a wooded hillside towards the banks of the River Avon, the beautiful amber-coloured town of Bradford is one of Wiltshire's prettiest – a handsome jumble of Georgian town houses and riverside buildings that makes a pleasant day trip from Bath, just 8 miles away.

The **tourist office** (☎ 01225-865797; www.bradford onavon.co.uk; 50 St Margaret's St; ☼ 10am-5pm Apr-Oct, 10am-4pm Mon-Sat, 11am-3pm Sun Nov-Mar) stocks leaflets on rambles around the town and can help with accommodation.

Sights & Activities

Bradford grew rich in the 17th and 18th centuries as a thriving centre for the weaving industry, and the town's elegant architecture is a reminder of its former wealth – some of the best examples are along **Middle Rank** and **Tory**, northwest of the town centre. But the town's most important building dates back to the early 11th century: the tiny **Church of St Laurence** (Church St) is one of the last surviving Saxon churches in Britain, and is particularly noted for the twin angels carved above the chancel arch.

Near the river is **Westbury House** (St Margaret's St), where a riot against the introduction of factory machinery in 1791 led to three deaths. The machinery in question was subsequently burned on **Town Bridge**. The unusual room jutting out from the bridge was originally a chapel but was later used as a jail.

Across the river, a waterside path leads to the 14th-century **Tithe Barn** (EH; admission free; ☼ 10.30am-4pm) on the bank of the Kennet & Avon Canal. The barn originally belonged to monks from nearby Shaftesbury Abbey, and was used to store tithes (a 10% tax made on local landowners) during the Middle Ages. It's worth visiting for its wood-vaulted interior and stone-tiled roof.

The tiny **Bradford-on-Avon Museum** (☎ 01225-863280; Bridge St; admission free; ☼ 10.30am-12.30pm & 2-4pm Wed-Sat, 2-4pm Sun Easter-Oct) is above the library.

Sleeping & Eating

Georgian Lodge Hotel (☎ 01225-862268; www.geor gianlodgehotel.com; 25 Bridge St; s/d £40/80) Shutters, ornate fireplaces and Georgian architectural plans dot the rooms of this old town-centre coaching inn. The supersmooth restaurant

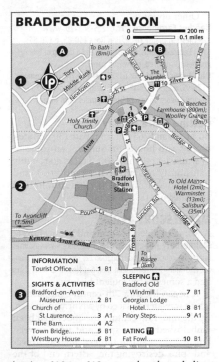

BRADFORD-ON-AVON

INFORMATION	
Tourist Office	1 B1

SIGHTS & ACTIVITIES	
Bradford-on-Avon Museum	2 B1
Church of St Laurence	3 A1
Tithe Barn	4 A2
Town Bridge	5 B1
Westbury House	6 B1

SLEEPING ⌂	
Bradford Old Windmill	7 B1
Georgian Lodge Hotel	8 B1
Priory Steps	9 A1

EATING 🍴	
Fat Fowl	10 B1

(mains £10 to £18; open lunch and dinner) rustles up generous portions of classic British fare.

Priory Steps (☎ 01225-862230; www.priorysteps.co.uk; Newtown; s £68, d £84-92) This cosy little hillside hideaway has been created by knocking six weavers' cottages together. Now the charming rooms house antique wooden furniture and sparkling new bathrooms – the views down onto the River Avon are lovely.

Bradford Old Windmill (☎ 01225-866842; www .bradfordoldwindmill.co.uk; 4 Masons Lane; s £59-99, d £89-109; P) One for the 'places-I-have-stayed' photo album: a circular, three-storey former windmill boasting eyebrow-raising features. Queen-sized waterbeds and satin sheets cosy up to conical ceilings and spiral staircases. The whole slightly saucy affair clings to a hill overlooking town.

Fat Fowl (☎ 01225-863111; Silver St; dinner mains £15; ☼ breakfast, lunch & dinner, closed dinner Sun) Catering to all your needs, this French-inspired bistro tempts you with crumbly breakfast pastries, leisurely lunches (mains from £6), tasty tapas (£4) and classy dinners. Sometimes live jazz and blues are laid on, too.

WESSEX

Other options:

Beeches Farmhouse (☎ 01225-865170; www
.beeches-farmhouse.co.uk; Holt Rd; s £50-85, d £70-85;
Ⓟ) Exposed beams, rustic charm and a dollop of luxury
in a honey-coloured, converted barn.

Old Manor Hotel (☎ 01225-777393; Trowle Common;
s £75-95, d £95-140; Ⓟ) Rambling, regal rooms in a
beautiful Georgian manor house 2 miles from town.

Getting There & Away

Buses 264 and 265 run from Bath (30 minutes, hourly, two hourly on Sunday) en route to Warminster (40 minutes). Trains go roughly half-hourly to Bath (£3, 15 minutes), and hourly to Warminster (£4.30, 20 minutes) and Salisbury (£9.40, 45 minutes).

MALMESBURY ABBEY

A wonderful blend of ruin and living church, **Malmesbury Abbey** (☎ 01666-826666; www.malmes
buryabbey.com; suggestion donation £2; ☼ 10am-5pm Mon-Sat mid-Mar–Oct, 10am-4pm Mon-Sat Nov–mid-Mar) has had a somewhat turbulent history.

It began life as a 7th-century monastery, which was later replaced by a Norman church. By the mid-15th century the abbey had been embellished with a spire and twin towers, but in 1479 a storm toppled the east tower and spire, destroying the eastern end of the church. The west tower followed suit in 1662, destroying much of the nave. The present-day church is about a third of its original size, and is flanked by ruins at either end. Notable features include the Norman doorway decorated with biblical carvings, the Romanesque **Apostle** carvings and a four-volume illuminated bible dating from 1407. A window at the western end of the church depicts Elmer the Flying Monk, who in 1010 strapped on wings and jumped from the tower. Although he broke both legs during this leap of faith, he survived and became a local hero.

Just below the abbey are the **Abbey House Gardens** (☎ 01666-822212; www.abbeyhousegardens
.co.uk; adult/child £6.50/2.50; ☼ 11am-5.30pm mid-Mar–Oct), which include a herb garden, river, waterfall and 2 hectares of colourful blooms.

Bus 31 runs to Swindon (45 minutes, hourly Monday to Saturday), while £10 92 heads to Chippenham (35 minutes, hourly Monday to Saturday).

CASTLE COMBE

Proudly trumpeting itself as the 'prettiest village in England', the little hamlet of Castle Combe presents a picture-perfect image of English countryside – its quiet streets and stone-walled cottages doubled as the fictional village of Puddleby-on-the-Marsh in the 1967 film of *Doctor Dolittle*. The village grew up around a medieval castle and later became an important centre for the local wool trade: old weavers' cottages are huddled around the medieval packhorse bridge, and the riverbanks were once lined with more than 20 clattering mills. In the centre of the village is a 13th-century **market cross**, and nearby, the medieval **church of St Andrew** contains the carved tomb of Sir Walter de Dunstanville, the 13th-century lord of the manor who fought in the Crusades and was killed in battle in 1270.

The best place to stay in the village is the 12th-century **Castle Inn** (☎ 01249-783030; www
.castle-inn.info; s £85-95, d £110-175), where rich fabrics cover wooden-framed beds, and soft lights illuminate worn beams and whirlpool baths. The restaurant (mains £11 to £18), which is open for lunch and dinner, serves up classic British fare including tenderloin of pork, rack of lamb and a smashing Sunday lunch.

Head to the **White Hart** (☎ 01249-782295; mains £6-12; ☼ lunch & dinner) for real ales, cheap eats and country atmosphere.

Bus 35 runs to Chippenham bus station (30 minutes) six times daily Monday to Friday, and four times on Saturday. There's also a direct bus to Bath on Wednesday (one hour).

LACOCK

With its geranium-covered cottages, higgledy-piggledy rooftops and idyllic location next to a rushing brook, pockets of the medieval village of Lacock seem to have been preserved in aspic since the mid-19th century. The village has been in the hands of the National Trust since 1944, and in many places is remarkably free of modern development – there are no telephone poles or electric street lights, and although villagers drive around the streets, the main car park on the outskirts keeps it largely traffic-free. Unsurprisingly, it's also a popular location for costume dramas and feature films – the village and its abbey pop up in the Harry Potter films, *The Other Boleyn Girl* and BBC adaptations of *Moll Flanders* and *Pride and Prejudice*.

Sights

LACOCK ABBEY

Lacock Abbey (NT; ☎ 01249-730459; abbey, museum, cloisters & grounds adult/child £9/4.50, abbey, cloisters & grounds

---

DETOUR: WOOLLEY GRANGE

Mixing boutique style with a refreshing family-friendly attitude, **Woolley Grange** (☎ 01225-864705; www.woolleygrangehotel.co.uk; Woolley Green; B&B & dinner per 2 people £240-440; **P**) is one of the most welcoming country-house hotels in Wiltshire. With its designer bedrooms, laid-back attitude and quietly impressive service, it's a place whose raison d'être seems to be keeping everyone in a state of mild euphoria throughout their stay. While the little 'uns are kept lavishly entertained with everything from giant trampolines to PlayStation 2s at the Woolley Bear Den, mum and dad can relax with a truly indulgent range of spa treatments, aromatherapy massages, gourmet meals, and sparkling-wine cocktails by the heated outdoor pool. Rooms are all individually styled, with a smattering of patchwork quilts, shiny antiques and funky fixtures. Children can share their parents' room for free; you pay only for their meals. This little oasis of family fun is on the edge of Bradford-on-Avon, and is 8 miles from Bath.

£7.20/3.60; ☑ abbey 1-5.30pm Wed-Mon mid-Mar–Oct, cloisters & grounds 11am-5.30pm Mar-Oct, museum 11am-5.30pm late Feb-Oct plus Sat & Sun Nov-Jan) was founded as an Augustinian nunnery in 1232 by Ela, Countess of Salisbury. After the Dissolution the abbey was sold to Sir William Sharington in 1539, who converted the nunnery into a home, demolished the church, tacked a tower onto the corner of the abbey and added a brewery. The wonderful Gothic entrance hall is lined with bizarre terracotta figures; spot the scapegoat with a lump of sugar on its nose. Some of the original 13th-century structure is evident in the cloisters and there are traces of medieval wall paintings. The recently restored botanic garden is also worth a visit.

In the early 19th century, William Henry Fox Talbot (1800–77), a prolific inventor, developed the photographic negative while working at the abbey: the **Fox Talbot Museum of Photography** (NT; ☎ 01249-730459; museum, cloisters & grounds adult/child £5.50/2.70; ☑ 11am-5.30pm Mar-Oct, 11am-4pm Sat & Sun Nov-Feb) details his ground-breaking work and displays a fine collection of his snapshots.

Sleeping & Eating

King John's Hunting Lodge (☎ 01249-730313; king johns@amserve.com; 21 Church St; s/d £60/90, f £115-140; ☑ tearooms 11am-5.30pm) Housed in Lacock's oldest building, this tearoom-cum-B&B is run by an ex-shepherdess, who's now a celebrity chef. Tearoom (snacks £3 to £8) specialities include 'priddy oggies' (a pastry with pork and Stilton), cheese muffins and homemade elderflower cordial. Upstairs, snug, resolutely old-fashioned rooms are crammed with creaky furniture and Tudor touches.

our pick **Sign of the Angel** (☎ 01249-730230; www .lacock.co.uk; 6 Church St; s £82, d £120-145, mains from £14; **P**) If you want to slumber amid a slice of

history, check into this 15th-century beamed bolt-hole. Crammed with antique beds, tapestries and burnished chests, comfort levels are brought up to date with free-standing sinks and slipper baths. The restaurant revels in English classics – try the 'angel plate' of cold meats and bubble and squeak, then squeeze in treacle tart with clotted cream.

Other options:

George Inn (☎ 01249-730263; 4 West St; mains from £8; ☑ lunch & dinner) A horse brass–hung pub dispensing grub and local ales.

Lacock Pottery B&B (☎ 01249-730266; www.lacock bedandbreakfast.com; s £49-59, d £76-96; **P**) An oatmeal colour scheme and antiques grace this airy former workhouse, which is overlooked by the church.

Getting There & Away

Bus 234 runs hourly, Monday to Saturday, from Chippenham (15 minutes).

AROUND LACOCK
Corsham Court

Two miles northwest of Lacock, the Elizabethan mansion of **Corsham Court** (☎ 01249-712214; www .corsham-court.co.uk; adult/child £6.50/3; ☑ 2-5.30pm Tue-Thu, Sat & Sun late Mar-Sep, 2-4.30pm Sat & Sun Oct, Nov & Jan-late Mar) dates from 1582, although the house and grounds were later improved by John Nash and Capability Brown. The house is renowned for its superb art collection, which features works by Reynolds, Caravaggio, Rubens and Van Dyck. It's also known for its formal gardens, which contain some stunning ornamental box hedges and a Gothic bathhouse.

DEVIZES
pop 14,379

The busy market town of Devizes is famous for its grand semicircular marketplace – the largest anywhere in England – but apart from some intriguing Georgian architecture and two fine churches, there's not a huge amount to keep you entertained. Nevertheless, the town makes a handy base for exploring southern Wiltshire and nearby Avebury.

The **tourist office** (☎ 01380-729408; ATIC@ kennet.gov.uk; Cromwell House, Market Pl; ☺ 9.30am-5pm Mon-Sat) has a couple of useful leaflets for walks around town, and can help with local accommodation.

Sights

Between St John's St and High St, **St John's Alley** has a wonderful collection of Elizabethan houses, their upper storeys cantilevered over the street. **St John's Church**, on Market Pl, displays elements of its original Norman construction, particularly in the solid crossing tower. Other interesting buildings include the **Corn Exchange** (topped by a figure of Ceres, goddess of agriculture), and the **Old Town Hall**, built 1750 to 1752.

The **Wiltshire Heritage Museum & Gallery** (☎ 01380-727369; www.wiltshireheritage.org.uk; 41 Long St; adult/child £4/1, Sun free; ☺ 10am-5pm Mon-Sat, noon-4pm Sun) has artefacts from Avebury, Stonehenge and other burial barrows across Wiltshire.

The **Kennet & Avon Canal Museum** (☎ 01380-729489; The Wharf; adult/child £2/75p; ☺ 10am-4pm Easter-Dec) brings to life the heritage of this historic canal. On the western outskirts of Devizes are the 29 successive locks at **Caen Hill**, which raise the water level 72m in just 2½ miles.

Sleeping & Eating

ourpick **Rosemundy Cottage** (☎ 01380-727122; www .rosemundycottage.co.uk; London Rd; s/d £37/60; P ☐ wi-fi) There can't be many B&Bs that, like this one, can boast a canalside terrace and heated pool. The cheerful owners delight in going the extra mile, providing plunger coffee and DVD players in the airy bedrooms, and local honey, sausages and free-range duck eggs for breakfast.

Bear Hotel (☎ 01380-722444; www.thebearhotel .net; Market Pl; s £80, d £105-130; P) They've been putting up weary travellers at this rambling coaching inn since 1559. Smart rooms are decked out in cream and lime candy stripes; the best one has bay windows, oil paintings and a whopping four-poster bed.

ourpick **Bistro** (☎ 01380-720043; 7 Little Brittox; mains £12; ☺ lunch & dinner Tue-Sat) Delivering a burst of fragrant, Mediterranean flavours to

market town Devizes, this lovely, two-floor eatery champions the cause of connecting local producers and communities – the owner even holds tasting sessions at nearby schools. Good intentions infuse the menu, too: try the grilled Somerset goats' cheese with pesto and chilli jam, or the risotto with Wiltshire wine and parmesan cheese.

Eastleigh House (☎ 01380-726918; www.eastleigh house.co.uk; 3 Eastleigh Rd; s/d £36/65; P) A relaxed, welcoming B&B of simple colours and plain fabrics.

Blounts Court Farm (☎ 01380-727180; www .blountscourtfarm.co.uk; s £36-42, d £60-70; P) Bordering a village cricket ground, this is a farmhouse B&B full of rustic charm.

Getting There & Away

Bus 49 serves Avebury (25 minutes, hourly Monday to Saturday, five on Sunday), while bus 2 runs from Salisbury (1¼ hours, hourly Monday to Saturday).

AROUND DEVIZES
Bowood House

Stately **Bowood House** (☎ 01249-812102; www.bo wood.org; adult/child £8/6.50; ☺ 11am-5.30pm mid-Mar-Oct) was first built around 1725 and has been home to the successive earls of Shelburne (now the marquess of Lansdowne) since 1754. The house has an impressive picture gallery and a fine sculpture gallery, as well as the laboratory where Dr Joseph Priestly discovered oxygen in 1774. The grounds, designed by Capability Brown, are an attraction in themselves and include a terraced rose garden.

Bowood is 3 miles southeast of Chippenham and 6 miles northwest of Devizes.

AVEBURY

While the tour buses usually head straight for Stonehenge, prehistoric purists make for the massive ring of stones located at **Avebury**. Though it lacks the huge slabs of rock and dramatic trilithons of its sister site across the plain, Avebury is arguably a much more rewarding place to visit. A large section of the village is actually inside the stone circle; you get much closer to the action than you do at Stonehenge; and it's bigger, older and a great deal quieter. It may also have been a more important ceremonial site, judging by its massive scale and its location at the centre of a complex of barrows, burial chambers and processional avenues.

Orientation & Information

Two main roads bisect the village, but it's much easier to use the National Trust car park on the A4361, just a short walk from the village. The **tourist office** (☎ 01380-734669; www.visitwiltshire.co.uk; Chapel Centre, Green St; ☒ 9.30am-5pm Wed-Sun Apr-Oct, 9.30am-4.30pm Thu-Sun Nov-Mar) is housed in a converted chapel near the centre of the village.

Sights

STONE CIRCLE

With a diameter of about 348m, Avebury is the largest stone circle in the world. It's also one of the oldest, dating from around 2500 to 2200 BC, between the first and second phase of construction at Stonehenge. The site originally consisted of an outer circle of 98 standing stones from 3m to 6m in length, many weighing up to 20 tons, carefully selected for their size and shape. The stones were surrounded by another circle delineated by a 5.5m-high earth bank and a 6m- to 9m-deep ditch. Inside were smaller stone circles to the north (27 stones) and south (29 stones).

The present-day site represents just a fraction of the circle's original size; tragically, many of the stones were buried, removed or broken up during the Middle Ages, when Britain's pagan past became something of an embarrassment to the church. In 1934, wealthy businessman and archaeologist Alexander Keiller supervised the re-erection

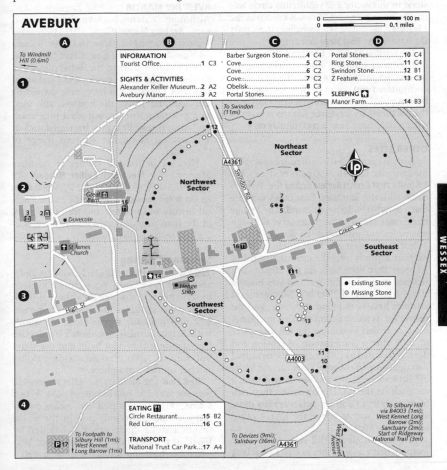

AVEBURY

0 — 100 m
0 — 0.1 miles

INFORMATION
Tourist Office.................1 C3

SIGHTS & ACTIVITIES
Alexander Keiller Museum...2 A2
Avebury Manor.................3 A2

Barber Surgeon Stone.........4 C4
Cove..........................5 C2
Cove..........................6 C2
Cove..........................7 C2
Obelisk.......................8 C3
Portal Stones.................9 C4

Portal Stones................10 C4
Ring Stone...................11 C4
Swindon Stone................12 B1
Z Feature....................13 C3

SLEEPING
Manor Farm...................14 B3

To Windmill Hill (0.6mi)

To Swindon (11mi)

Northeast Sector

A4361 Swindon Rd

Northwest Sector

Great Barn

Dovecote

St James Church

14

Henge Shop

Southwest Sector

High St

Southeast Sector

Green St

● Existing Stone
○ Missing Stone

16

EATING
Circle Restaurant............15 B2
Red Lion.....................16 C3

TRANSPORT
National Trust Car Park......17 A4

To Footpath to Silbury Hill (1mi); West Kennet Long Barrow (1mi)

To Devizes (9mi); Salisbury (36mi)

A4361

West Kennet Avenue

To Silbury Hill via B4003 (1mi); West Kennet Long Barrow (2mi); Sanctuary (2mi); Start of Ridgeway National Trail (3mi)

A4003

WESSEX

of the buried stones, and planted markers to indicate those that had disappeared; he later bought the site for posterity using funds from his family's marmalade fortune.

Modern roads into Avebury neatly dissect the circle into four sectors. Start at High St, near the Henge Shop, and walk round the circle in an anticlockwise direction. There are 11 standing stones in the southwest sector, including the **Barber Surgeon Stone**, named after the skeleton of a man found under it. The equipment buried with him suggested he was a medieval travelling barber-surgeon, possibly killed when a stone accidentally fell on him.

The southeast sector starts with the huge **portal stones** marking the entry to the circle from West Kennet Ave. The **southern inner circle** stood in this sector and within this circle was the **Obelisk** and a group of stones known as the **Z Feature**. Just outside this smaller circle, only the base of the **Ring Stone** remains.

The northwest sector has the most complete collection of standing stones, including the massive 65-ton **Swindon Stone**, the first stone encountered and one of the few never to have been toppled. In the northern inner circle in the northeast sector, three sarsens remain of what would have been a rectangular **cove**.

OTHER SITES

Avebury is surrounded by a network of ancient monuments. Lined by 100 pairs of stones, the 1.5-mile **West Kennet Avenue** linked the Avebury circle with the **Sanctuary**. Post holes indicate that a wooden building surrounded by a stone circle once stood at the Sanctuary, although no one knows quite what the site was for.

Just to the west, the huge dome of **Silbury Hill** rises abruptly from the surrounding fields. At more than 40m high, it's the largest constructed mound in Europe, and was built in stages from around 2500 BC. No significant artefacts have been found at the site, and the reason for its construction remains unclear. A massive project to stabilise the hill took place in 2008 after a combination of erosion and damaged caused by earlier excavations caused part of the top to collapse. Direct access to the hill isn't allowed, but you can view it from a car park on the A4. Hiking across the fields from Avebury (1.5 miles each way) is a more atmospheric way to arrive; the tourist office sells guides (50p).

Just east of Silbury Hill you can take the footpath half a mile further to **West Kennet Long**

Barrow. Set in the fields south of Silbury Hill, this is England's finest burial mound and dates from around 3500 BC. Its entrance is guarded by huge sarsens and its roof is made out of gigantic overlapping capstones. About 50 skeletons were found when it was excavated, and finds are on display at the Wiltshire Heritage Museum & Gallery in Devizes (p326).

Northwest of the Avebury circle you'll find **Windmill Hill**, a neolithic enclosure or 'camp' dating from about 3700 BC (the earliest site in the area).

The **Ridgeway National Trail** starts near Avebury and runs eastwards across Fyfield Down, where many of the sarsen stones at Avebury (and Stonehenge) were collected.

AVEBURY MANOR

Although it dates back to the 16th century, **Avebury Manor** (NT; ☎ 01672-539250; manor & garden adult/child £4/2, garden only £3/1.50; ☺ manor 2-4.40pm Mon, Tue & Sun, gardens 11am-5pm Fri-Tue) was modified during the Edwardian era. Keiller bought the manor in 1939 and spent much of his later life here; now owned by the National Trust, the house is still used as a private residence, but it's a little scant on attractions. Entry is by timed ticket. The manor is on the western fringe of the village.

Housed in the old stables of Avebury Manor, the **Alexander Keiller Museum** (NT; ☎ 01672-539250; adult/child £4.20/2.10; ☺ 10am-6pm Apr-Oct, to 4pm Nov-Mar) explores the archaeological history of the circle and traces the story of the man who dedicated his life to unlocking the secret of the stones.

Sleeping & Eating

our pick **Manor Farm** (☎ 01672-539294; fax 01672-539294; High St; s/d £60/80) Your chance to sleep in style inside a stone circle – this red-brick farmhouse snuggles just inside the henge. The quietly comfy rooms blend old woods with bright furnishings; there's a splendid free-standing claw-foot bath; and the views out onto the 4000-year-old standing stones ratchet up the atmosphere.

Red Lion (☎ 01672-539266; redlion.avebury@whitbread.com; Swindon Rd; mains from £10, s/d £50/80; ☺ lunch & dinner; ℗) Having a pint here means downing a drink at the only pub in the world inside a stone circle. It's also haunted by Flori, who was killed during the Civil War when her husband threw her down a well –

WESSEX

it now forms the centrepiece of the dining room, where you can tuck into hearty pub grub of the pie 'n' mash school. The rustic rooms upstairs are peeling in places, but they do look out onto those famous stones.

Circle Restaurant (☎ 01672-539514; mains from £7; ⊗ lunch) This vegie and wholefood cafe beside the Great Barn serves delicious sandwiches, cakes and afternoon teas.

Getting There & Away

Bus 5 runs to Avebury from Salisbury (1¾ hours, five or six Monday to Saturday). Bus 49 serves Swindon (30 minutes) and Devizes (25 minutes, hourly Monday to Saturday, five on Sunday).

BRISTOL

pop 393,300

Boom-town Bristol may not be as pretty as her older sister Bath (and really, she isn't) but she's just as interesting. After being in the doldrums for decades, this former hub of shipbuilding, manufacturing and the railways has undergone a transformative regeneration. Crumbling docks have been prettified, cutting-edge restaurants have sprung up, and hotels and designer bars occupy sites that were, until recently, derelict. But despite her new-found swagger, Bristol is also a city with a complex past; here you can explore the legacies of engineering genius Isambard Kingdom Brunel as well as those of the transatlantic slave trade. Mix in the work of guerrilla graffiti artist Banksy and a cutting-edge club scene and you get something real, and just a little rough around the edges. But there's also a sense that this little sister's time has come.

HISTORY

A small Saxon village at the confluence of the Rivers Frome and Avon became the thriving medieval Brigstow (later Bristol) as the city began to develop a European trade in cloth and wine. Religious houses were established on high ground (now the suburb of Temple) above the marshes, and it was from here that celebrated 'local hero' John Cabot (actually a Genoese sailor called Giovanni Caboto) sailed to discover Newfoundland in 1497. Over the following centuries, Bristol became one of Britain's major ports, and grew fat on the proceeds of the transatlantic slave trade (see boxed text, p334), as well as from dealing in cocoa, sugar and tobacco.

By the 18th century the city was suffering from competition, from Liverpool in particular. With large ships having difficulty reaching the city-centre docks, some trade moved to new ports at Avonmouth and Portishead instead.

Bristol repositioned itself as an industrial centre, becoming an important hub for shipbuilding, as well as the terminus for the pioneering Great Western Railway line from London to the southwest. World War II saw Bristol become a key target for German bombing, and much of the city centre was reduce to rubble. The postwar rush for reconstruction left Bristol with plenty of concrete carbuncles, but over the last decade or so the city has undergone extensive redevelopment, especially around the dockside.

ORIENTATION

The city centre, north of the river, is easy to get around on foot, but it's hilly. The central area centres on the narrow streets by the markets and Corn Exchange and the newly developed docklands. Park St is lined with trendy shops

WESSEX

BRISTOL IN TWO DAYS

Start off with a tour around Bristol's historic dockside, taking a few hours to explore the cutting-edge **Arnolfini** (p332) and the hands-on science displays of **Explore @ Bristol** (p332). Have a sumptuous lunch at **Bordeaux Quay** (p338) before cruising down the river aboard the **Bristol Ferry Boat** (p340). Check into the **Mercure Brigstow** (p336), dine out in style at the **Glassboat** (p338) and catch an evening film at the **Watershed** (p339), if there's time.

On day two catch a bus over to Clifton, stopping at the **Georgian House** (p332) and the **City Museum & Art Gallery** (p332) en route, before taking a wander around Clifton's many shops, boutiques and cafes. Enjoy an afternoon stroll across the marvellous **suspension bridge** (p333) and around the **Clifton Downs** (p334) nearby, and finish up with a slap-up supper at **Quartier Vert** (p338) on Whiteladies Rd.

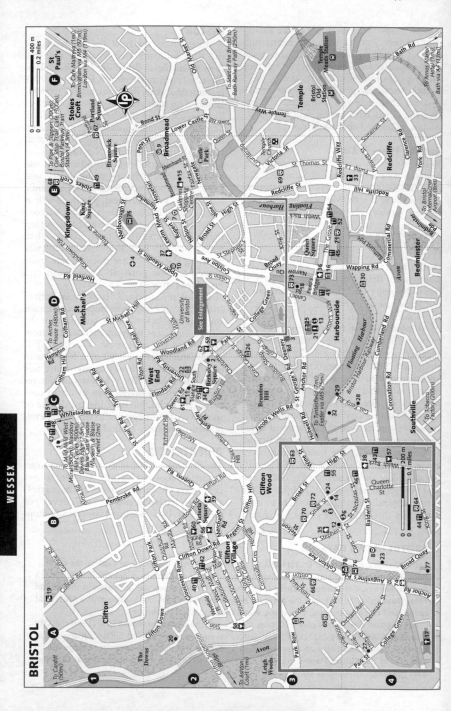

and cafes, while a strip of Whiteladies Rd (northwest of Park St), is the hub of bar and restaurant life. The genteel suburb of Clifton, with its Georgian terraces and boutique shops, is on the hilltop west of the centre.

As in any big city, it pays to keep your wits about you after dark, especially around the suburb of St Paul's, just northeast of the centre. It's a run-down area with a heavy drug scene, and is best not visited alone at night.

The main train station is Temple Meads, a mile southeast of the centre. Some trains use Bristol Parkway, 5 miles to the north. The bus station is on Marlborough St, northeast of the city centre.

INFORMATION
Bookshops
Blackwell's/George's (☎ 0117-927 6602; 89 Park St) This vast bookshop sells both second-hand and new titles.
Stanfords (☎ 0117-929 9966; 29 Corn St) You'll find a superb collection of maps and books at this travel specialist.
Waterstones (☎ 0117-925 2274; The Galleries, Broadmead) General bookshop in the Galleries shopping centre.

Emergency
Police station (☎ 0845 456 7000; Nelson St)

Internet Access
Bristol Central Library (☎ 0117-903 7200; College Green; access free; ⌚ 9.30am-7.30pm Mon, Tue & Thu, 10am-5pm Wed, 9am-5pm Fri & Sat, 1-5pm Sun)

Internet Resources
This is Bristol (www.thisisbristol.com) Web edition of the *Bristol Evening Post*.
Venue (www.venue.co.uk) Online version of Bristol's listings guide, with reviews of clubs, bars and restaurants.
Visit Bristol (www.visitbristol.co.uk) Official tourism website with info on events, accommodation, transport and exploring the city.
What's on Bristol (www.whatsonbristol.co.uk) Useful online city guide with comprehensive listings.

Laundry
Alma Laundrette (☎ 0117-973 4121; 78 Alma Rd; ⌚ 7am-9pm)

Medical Services
Bristol Royal Infirmary (☎ 0117-923 0000; 2 Marlborough St)

Money
You'll find all the main banks along Corn St, including Barclays at number 40, Lloyds at 55, and NatWest at 32.

WESSEX

Post

Post office (☎ 0845 722 3344) Baldwin St **(Baldwin St)**;
The Galleries **(The Galleries, Broadmead)**; Upper Maudlin St
(Upper Maudlin St)

Tourist Information

Free touch-screen kiosks known as i-plus
points are located around the city, providing
tourist information.
Tourist office (☎ enquiries 0906 711 2191 per min
50p, accommodation 0845 408 0474; www.visitbristol
.co.uk; Explore @ Bristol, Anchor Rd; 🕙 10am-6pm
Mar-Oct, 10am-5pm Mon-Sat, 11am-4pm Sun Nov-Feb)
Well stocked with leaflets, transport maps and local info;
books accommodation for £3.

Travel Agencies

STA Travel (☎ 0871 230 8569; 43 Queen's Rd)
Trailfinders (☎ 0117-929 9000; 48 Corn St;
🕙 9am-6pm)

SIGHTS

Explore @ Bristol (☎ 0117-9155000; www.at-bristol.org
.uk; Anchor Rd; adult/child £9/7; 🕙 10am-5pm Mon-Fri, to
6pm Sat, Sun & school holidays) is Bristol's impressive
science museum, with several zones spanning
space, technology and the human brain. In
the Curiosity Zone you get to walk through
a tornado, spin on a human gyroscope and
strum the strings of a virtual harp. It's fun,
imaginative and highly interactive, and should
keep kids of all ages enthralled for a few hours.
A £4-million aquarium is due to open at the
same site in 2009.

One of Bristol's most famous sons was Cary
Grant (aka Archibald Leach), who was born
here in 1904; look out for his **statue** in neighbouring Millennium Sq.

Museums & Galleries

Housed in a stunning Edwardian baroque
building, the **City Museum & Art Gallery** (☎ 0117-
922 3571; Queen's Rd; admission free; 🕙 10am-5pm) has an
excellent collection of British and French art;
galleries dedicated to ceramics and decorative arts; and archaeological, geological and
natural-history wings. Look out for it's best-
known resident, Alfred the Gorilla.

The 18th-century **Georgian House** (☎ 0117-921
1362; 7 Great George St; admission free; 🕙 10am-5pm Wed-
Sat) provides an atmospheric illustration of
aristocratic life in Bristol during the Georgian
era – and the city's links to the slave trade (see
boxed text, p334). The six-storeyed house was
home to West India merchant John Pinney,

along with his slave Pero – after whom Pero's
Bridge across the harbour is named. It's still
decorated throughout in period style, typified
by the huge kitchen (complete with cast-iron
roasting spit) and the grand drawing rooms.

The Elizabethan **Red Lodge** (☎ 0117-921 1360;
Park Row; admission free; 🕙 10am-5pm Wed-Sat) was built
in 1590 but was much remodelled in 1730,
and its architecture reflects both periods. The
highlight is the Elizabethan Oak Room, which
still features its original oak panelling, plasterwork ceiling and carved chimneypiece.

In the northern suburb of Henbury lies
Blaise Castle House Museum (☎ 0117-903 9818; Henbury
Rd; admission free; 🕙 10am-5pm Wed-Sat), a late-18th-
century house and social-history museum.
Displays include vintage toys, costumes and
other Victorian ephemera. Across the road is
Blaise Hamlet, a cluster of picturesque thatched
cottages designed for estate servants by John
Nash in 1811. Bus 43 (45 minutes, every 15
minutes) passes the castle from Colston Ave;
bus 1 (20 minutes, every 10 minutes) from St
Augustine's Pde doesn't stop quite as close,
but is quicker and more frequent.

The massive avant-garde **Arnolfini Arts Centre**
(☎ 0117-917 2300; www.arnolfini.org.uk; 16 Narrow Quay;
admission free; 🕙 10am-6pm Tue-Sun) has had an impressive facelift, and remains the top venue in
town for exhibitions of dance, photography
and art.

A £25-million scheme to turn the city's old
Industrial Museum into a flagship **Museum of
Bristol** is due to be completed by 2011. Sited
on the Harbourside inside huge 1950s transit
sheds, displays will include historic working cranes, boats and trains. A steam railway
runs from the site along to Brunel's SS *Great
Britain*, below.

The British Empire & Commonwealth
Museum closed in autumn 2008 ahead of a
planned relocation to London.

SS Great Britain

In 1843 Brunel designed the mighty **SS Great
Britain** (☎ 0117-926 0680; www.ssgreatbritain.org; Great
Western Dockyard; adult/child £11/5.65; 🕙 10am-5.30pm
Apr-Oct, to 4.30pm Nov-Mar), the first transatlantic
steamship to be driven by a screw propeller. For 43 years the ship served as a luxury
ocean-going liner and cargo vessel, before
being damaged in 1886 near the Falkland
Islands. The cost of repairs proved uneco-
nomical and the ship's owners sold her off
as a coal hulk, an ignominious fate for such a

BRISTOL & BRUNEL

Bristol is packed with reminders of one of its towering figures: the extravagantly named **Isambard Kingdom Brunel** (1806–59) – industrial genius, visionary engineer, and general all-round Renaissance man.

The precocious young Isambard was educated at the Lycée Henri-IV in Paris and the University of Caen in Normandy, and was barely 20 years old when he was appointed chief engineer of the pioneering Thames Tunnel between Rotherhithe and Wapping in London. The project was fraught with technical difficulties and considerable danger, including explosive gases and floods; in one such flood Brunel was almost drowned while trying to rescue trapped workers. While recovering, he entered a competition to design a bridge over the Avon at Clifton, eventually winning first prize with his vision for a suspension bridge (below).

During his 30-year career Brunel was responsible for many of the landmark projects of Victorian engineering, including the construction of the first rail bridge over the River Tamar; the foundation of the Great Western Railway line from London to the southwest; and the design of the ground-breaking transatlantic vessels *Great Western* and *Great Eastern*, as well as the first iron-hulled, screw-propeller steamship, SS *Great Britain* (opposite), now in Bristol. He also modernised the docks at Bristol, Plymouth and Cardiff; designed the first prefabricated field hospital for use during the Crimean War; and worked on railway projects everywhere from India to Italy.

Despite surviving on a diet of four hours' sleep and 40 cigars a day, Brunel's closest shave came when he nearly choked to death having accidentally swallowed a coin while performing a conjuring trick for his children. His eventual end was rather more prosaic; he suffered a stroke in 1859, just before the *Great Eastern* made its first voyage to New York, and he died 10 days later at the age of 53.

grand vessel. By 1937 she was no longer watertight and was abandoned near Port Stanley in the Falklands. There she remained, forgotten and rusted, before finally being towed back to Bristol in 1970.

Since then a massive 30-year program of restoration costing £11.3 million has allowed the ship to rediscover her former splendour. The ship's rooms have been refurbished in impeccable detail, including the ship's galley, surgeon's quarters, mess hall, and the great engine room; but the highlight is the amazing 'glass sea' on which the ship sits, enclosing an airtight dry dock that preserves the delicate hull and allows visitors to see the ground-breaking screw propeller up close. Moored nearby is a replica of John Cabot's ship **Matthew**, which sailed from Bristol to Newfoundland in 1497.

Tickets to the SS *Great Britain* also allow access to the neighbouring **Maritime Heritage Centre** (☎ 0117-927 9856; Great Western Dockyard, Gas Ferry Rd; ☼ 10am-5.30pm Apr-Oct, to 4.30pm Nov-Mar), which has various exhibits relating to the ship's illustrious past, and the city's boat-building heritage.

The steam-powered **Bristol Harbour Railway** (single/return £2/3; ☼ Sat & Sun late-May-early-Sep) runs along the dock from the site of the new Museum of Bristol to the SS *Great Britain* and the maritime centre.

Clifton & the Suspension Bridge

During the 18th and 19th centuries, wealthy Bristol merchants transformed the former spa resort of Clifton into an elegant hilltop suburb packed with town houses and porticoed mansions – especially around **Cornwallis Cres** and **Royal York Cres**. These days, Clifton is still the poshest postcode in Bristol, with a wealth of streetside cafes and designer shops, and a villagey atmosphere that's far removed from the rest of the city.

Clifton's most famous (and photographed) landmark is another Brunel masterpiece, the 76m-high **Clifton Suspension Bridge** (www.clifton-suspension-bridge.org.uk), which spans the Avon Gorge from Clifton over to Leigh Woods in northern Somerset. Undoubtedly one of Britain's most elegant bridges, initial construction began in 1836, but, sadly, Brunel died before the bridge's completion in 1864. It was mainly designed to carry light horse-drawn traffic and foot passengers, but these days around 12,000 cars cross it every day – testament to the quality of the construction and the vision of Brunel's design. It's also become a magnet for stunt artists and suicides; in 1885 Sarah Ann Hedley

HUMAN CARGO

It's a sobering thought that some of Bristol's 18th-century wealth and splendour was fuelled by brutality and human exploitation. In the late 1600s, the first slave ship set sail from Bristol harbour, kick-starting the city's connections with the so-called 'triangular trade'. Africans were kidnapped from their homes, shipped across the Atlantic to America and the Caribbean and sold into a life of slavery. Conditions on the boats were unimaginably horrific; it was expected that one in 10 of those captured would die en route – in reality, many more did. The enslaved people who survived endured a lifetime of brutal, inhuman conditions, often being forced to work on sugar plantations. Meanwhile, the merchants stocked their vessels with luxury goods such as sugar, rum, indigo, tobacco and cotton, and sailed back to Britain.

Bristol, London and Liverpool (see International Slavery Museum, p681) were the three main British ports engaged in the practice. By the time the slave trade (not slavery itself) was finally abolished in the British Empire in 1807, it's thought that 500,000 Africans were enslaved by Bristol merchants – one-fifth of all people sold into slavery by British vessels.

The financial profits for Bristol's traders were immense, and that legacy lingers. Many of the grand houses in Clifton were built on the proceeds of the 'trade', and several of the city's most elegant edifices – such as the Bristol Old Vic theatre – were partly financed by slave-trading investors.

There are many more connections – for further insights, download the MP3 audio tour from the **Visit Bristol** (www.visitbristol.co.uk) website, or pick up the *Slave Trade Trail* leaflet (£3) from the tourist office.

jumped from the bridge after a lovers' tiff, but her voluminous petticoats parachuted her safely to earth and she lived to be 85.

It's free to walk or cycle across the bridge; car drivers pay a 30p toll. There's a **visitor information point** (☎ 0117-974 4665; visitinfo@clifton-suspension-bridge.org; ⏰ 10am-5pm) near the tower on the Leigh Woods side. Free guided tours of the bridge take place at 3pm on Sundays between Easter and mid-September.

The grassy parks of Clifton Down and Durdham Down (often referred to as just the **Downs**) beside the bridge make a fine spot for a picnic. Nearby, a well-worn observatory houses Britain's only **camera obscura** (☎ 0117-974 1242; adult/child £2/1; ⏰ from 10.30am Easter-Oct, from 10.30am Sat & Sun Nov-Easter), which offers incredible views of the suspension bridge. Hours are weather dependent – it closes when there's reduced visibility.

Bristol Zoo Gardens (☎ 0117-974 7399; www.bristolzoo.org.uk; College Rd, Clifton; adult/child £12/7.40; ⏰ 9am-5.30pm high season, to 5pm low season) is renowned as much for its conservation work as for its exotic residents. Attractions include a group of West African gorillas, underwater walkways for viewing seals and penguins, and a Brazilian rainforest where you can get up close and personal with agouti, capybara and golden lion tamarins.

See p340 for details of buses to Clifton and the zoo.

Bristol Cathedral

Originally founded as the church of an Augustinian monastery in 1140, **Bristol Cathedral** (☎ 0117-926 4879; www.bristol-cathedral.co.uk; College Green; donations requested; ⏰ 8am-6pm) has a remarkably fine Norman chapter house and gate, while the attractive chapels have eccentric carvings and beautiful heraldic glass. Although much of the nave and the west towers date from the 19th century, the 14th-century choir has fascinating misericords depicting apes in hell, quarrelling couples and dancing bears. The south transept shelters a rare Saxon carving of the *Harrowing of Hell*, discovered under the chapter-house floor after a 19th-century fire.

St Mary Redcliffe

St Mary Redcliffe (☎ 0117-929 1487; www.stmaryredcliffe.co.uk; Redcliffe Way; ⏰ 9am-5pm Mon-Sat, 8am-7.30pm Sun) boasts a soaring 89m-high spire, a grand hexagonal porch and a vaulted ceiling decorated with gilt bosses. At the entrance to the America Chapel is a whale rib presented to the church by John Cabot as a souvenir of his trip to Newfoundland in 1497.

BRISTOL FOR CHILDREN

There's no shortage of things to keep kids happy in Bristol, with loads of hands-on activities and interesting events. Most hotels and some B&Bs can rustle up a baby cot or heat up a bottle; confirm that when you book.

Baby-changing facilities are available in most supermarkets, department stores, shopping centres and major attractions.

The brilliant **Bristol Zoo Gardens** (opposite) has enough hairy apes and even hairier spiders to keep whippersnappers entertained for hours, and there are plenty of hands-on exhibits at the **Explore @ Bristol** (p332) science museum on the old Harbourside. Chug along the dockside on the steam **Bristol Harbour Railway** (p333) to the **SS Great Britain** (p332), where kids can join a detective trail in search of the missing ship's cat, Sinbad.

At the **City Museum & Art Gallery** (p332), Alfred the Gorilla guides youngsters through a world of dinosaurs, Egyptology and archaeology; there are also self-led trails, an activity program and a touch-the-artefact zone for children aged zero to five. Seadogs, meanwhile, can trawl for treasure on a **Pirate Walk** (right). In August, look to the skies for Bristol's **balloon and kite festivals** (right).

Bristol Babysitting Agency (☎ 07791-478028; www .bristolbabysitting.co.uk) can recommend accredited local childminders.

TOURS

The **Bristol Highlights Walk** (☎ 0870 444 0654; www .bristolvisitor.co.uk; adult/under 12yr £3.50/free; 🕑 11am Sat Apr-Sep) tours the old town, city centre and Harbourside. It's run every Saturday; just turn up outside the tourist office. Themed tours exploring Clifton, Brunel and the history of Bristol traders are run on request.

MP3 Tours (www.visitbristol.co.uk/site/sightseeing-and-tours; free), which can be downloaded from the Visit Bristol website, cover Brunel, the slave trade, pirates, churches and general heritage.

City Sightseeing (☎ 0870 444 0654; www.city-sight seeing.com; 24hr ticket adult/child £10/5, single trips £1/50p; 🕑 10am-4pm Easter-Sep) has an open-topped hop-on, hop-off bus visiting all the major attractions. Buses leave Broad Quay hourly (every 30 minutes from July to September).

Bristol Packet Boat Trips (☎ 0117-927 3416; www .bristolpacket.co.uk; 24hr ticket adult/child £4.75/2.75; 🕑 Mar-Oct) offers cruises around the harbour area, as well as weekend day trips to Avon Gorge (return adult/child £12/8.75, May to October) and Bath (single adult/child £22.50/15, Sunday late May to September).

Pirate Walk (☎ 07950 566483; adult/child/family £5/3.50/12.50; 🕑 tours 6.15pm Apr-Sep, 2pm Sat & Sun Oct-Mar) is a child-friendly, swashbuckling two-hour trail of pirates, smugglers and other ne'ers-do-well, which leaves from the tourist office.

FESTIVALS & EVENTS

Bristol has an ever-expanding program of annual events; the tourist office can advise on dates and details.

Bristol Shakespeare Festival (www.bristolshake speare.org.uk) Between May and September, venues across the city host this festival, the largest open-air event of its type in Britain.

St Paul's Carnival (☎ 0117-944 1478) This giant street party takes place on the first Saturday of July.

Bristol Harbour Festival (☎ 0117-922 3719) The city's biggest waterside event is held in early August – expect bands, theatre and circus entertainment to a backdrop of tall ships and maritime displays.

AEROSOL ANTIHERO

Bristol brings you closer to a man who specialises in stencils, subverted art and stunts: the guerilla graffiti artist **Banksy** (www.banksy.co.uk). Banksy's true identity is a closely guarded secret, but it's rumoured he was born in 1974 in Yate (near Chipping Sodbury), 12 miles from Bristol, and cut his teeth in a city graffiti outfit. Headline-grabbing works include issuing spoof British £10 notes (with Princess Diana's head on them instead of the Queen's); replacing 500 copies of Paris Hilton's debut album in record shops with remixes (featuring tracks titled *Why Am I Famous?* and *What Have I Done?*); painting an image of a ladder going up and over the Israeli West Bank Barrier; and covertly inserting his own version of a primitive cave painting (with a human hunter-gatherer pushing a shopping trolley) into the British Museum in London.

His works feature in the streets of Bristol, too. Look out for his notorious **love triangle** stencil (featuring an angry husband, a two-timing wife, and a naked man dangling from a window) at the bottom of Park St. Banksy's ghostly take on Charion, the River Styx boatman, graces the side of the **Thekla Social** (p339), and there's a large mural called **Mild Mild West** featuring a Molotov cocktail–wielding teddy bear on Cheltenham Rd, opposite the junction with Jamaica St.

For more, check out www.banksy.co.uk; the tourist office has produced a free miniguide.

WESSEX

International Balloon Fiesta (☎ 0117-953 5884; www.bristolfiesta.co.uk) Held in August at Ashton Court, over the Clifton Suspension Bridge.

International Kite Festival (☎ 0117-977 2002; www.kite-festival.org.uk) Held in September, also at Ashton Court.

Encounters (☎ 0117-929 9188; www.encounters -festival.org.uk) This film festival is held at the Watershed every November.

Christmas market Held in evenings in late November and December, at St Nicholas Market.

SLEEPING
Budget

Bristol Backpackers (☎ 0117-925 7900; www.bristol backpackers.co.uk; 17 St Stephen's St; dm/tw £15/36; 🖳) This long-standing travellers' friend is a decent budget option, although the dorms and doubles are cramped, and crowded in summer. There's no curfew, so prepare to join in the noise at weekends.

Bristol YHA (☎ 0870 770 5726; www.yha.org.uk; 14 Narrow Quay; dm £18-20, s £25-35, d £40-45; 🖳) You can pay through the nose for a location like this, in the heart of the Harbourside action, just steps away from the water. Facilities are superb: modern four-bed dorms and doubles, a cycle store, games room and the excellent Grainshed coffee lounge.

Midrange

Arches House (☎ 0117-924 7398; www.arches-hotel.co.uk; 132 Cotham Brow; s £29-45, d £52-63) Vegetarians will love this Victorian guest house – breakfasts are meat-free and packed with organic, fairtrade treats. The rooms are traditional but the thinking is very modern: electricity comes from renewable sources; cleaning products are ecofriendly; and the owners could run classes in recycling and composting.

Downs Edge (☎ 0117-968 3264; www.downsedge.com; Saville Rd; s £55-59, d £75-80; 🅿 🖳 wi-fi) A few miles from the centre of town and surrounded by botanical gardens, this double-gabled B&B provides a soothing slice of rural life. Elegant, antique-filled rooms create a country house atmosphere, reinforced by breakfasts full of compotes, overnight porridge and softly poached eggs.

Victoria Square Hotel (☎ 0117-973 9058; www .vicsquare.com; Victoria Sq; s £59-95, d £75-115, f £85-125; 🅿 🖳 wi-fi) Split across two Victorian town houses overlooking a tree-shrouded Clifton square, this hotel is owned by Best Western, so function takes precedence over flair, but most rooms have traces of Victorian character and soft beds.

Top End

Berkeley Square Hotel (☎ 0117-925 4000; www .cliftonhotels.com; 15 Berkeley Sq; s £79-137, d £115-180; 🅿 🖳 wi-fi) In the middle of the kind of leafy square in which a nightingale would sing, this hip hotel brings baroque imagination to a Georgian town house. Painted gazelle heads, Day-Glo settees and rococo mirrors dot the lobby, while the bedrooms mix DVD players and gratis sherry with classic finishes.

Arnos Manor Hotel (☎ 0117-971 1461; www.arnos manorhotel.co.uk; 470 Bath Rd; s/d from £105/125; 🅿 🖳 wi-fi) Built for the Bristol magnate William Reeve in 1760, this smart hotel has an original crenellated chateau plus an extension tacked on the side. The poshest rooms are in the old building, and boast half-tester beds, spa baths and bags of space; the annexe rooms are more corporate, but still have rubber ducks in the bath.

Mercure Brigstow Hotel (☎ 0117-929 1030; www .mercure.com; Welsh Back; r midweek £149-250, weekend £99-250; 🖳 wi-fi) Despite an ugly concrete-and-glass facade, this is one of Bristol's funkiest, freshest places to stay. Bedrooms boast trendy floating beds, curved wood-panel walls and tiny TVs set into bathroom tiles. Make sure you bag a room with a river view.

ourpick Hotel du Vin (☎ 0117-925 5577; www .hotelduvin.com; Narrow Lewins Mead; d £145-160, ste £195-215; 🅿 🖳 wi-fi) This enclave of stylish, sexy luxury is housed in converted sugar warehouses, neatly signalling the sweet indulgence found within. Fabulous futon beds, claw-foot baths, frying-pan showerheads and a mix of chic furniture, industrial beams and iron pillars grace sumptuous rooms. The stunning double-height loft suites may make you weep when you have to leave.

EATING

Eating out in Bristol is a real highlight – the city is jammed with restaurants of every description, ranging from classic British 'caffs' to designer dining emporiums.

Budget
CAFES & QUICK EATS

Bar Chocolat (☎ 0117-974 7000; 19 The Mall; ⏰ 9am-6pm Mon-Sat, 11am-5pm Sun) Don't even try to resist this holy temple to the cocoa bean – it'll get you anyway, so succumb with a smile. Hot chocolates, chocolate-flavoured coffees and chocolate with a fair-trade conscience are all on offer at this cosy cafe – just remember to leave room for some handmade chocolates before you leave.

Pieminister (☎ 0117-942 9500; 24 Stokes Croft; pies £3; ☺ 10am-7pm Sat, 11am-4pm Sun) Offering so much more than just steak 'n' kidney, Pieminister drags the good old British pie into the 21st century. Try the wittily named Poussin Boots (red wine, chicken and pancetta) or the vegie Bush pie (cheddar cheese, cabbage, mushroom and onion).

Rocotillo's (☎ 0117-929 7207; 1 Queens Row; mains from £4; ☺ breakfast & lunch) Bristol's version of a traditional American diner, complete with bar stools, leather booths and an open grill kitchen, serves gourmet burgers and the best milkshakes in town (including dubious concoctions such as Crunchie and mint choc-chip).

RESTAURANTS

Obento (☎ 0117-929 7392; 69 Baldwin St; mains £4-9; ☺ lunch & dinner Tue-Sun) Somewhere to satisfy those wasabi cravings, this minimalist Japanese restaurant finds diners tucking into teriyaki chicken, fresh sushi and hot noodles at sleek bench tables. Its neatly packaged, three-course bento lunch boxes are practically works of art.

One Stop Thali Cafe (☎ 0117-942 6687; 12A York Rd; set meal £6.95; ☺ lunch) The bustle and buzz of an Indian street market comes to this cute Montpelier diner, which serves traditional thalis (multicourse Indian dishes) that change depending on what the chef's picked up. It's fresh, spicy and authentic, and the six-course £6.95 menu is ridiculously cheap.

SELF-CATERING

Papadeli (☎ 0117-973 6569; 84 Alma Rd) This Italian deli is stocked with the kind of zesty flavours and sweet treats you'd normally only find in a Tuscan street market. Fresh pasta salads, salami sandwiches and goats' cheese tarts are served in the main cafe, or you can load up with picnic supplies and Italian cakes at the counter.

St Nicholas Market (Corn St; ☺ 9.30am-5pm Mon-Sat) The city's lively street market has a bevy of food stalls selling everything from artisan bread to cheese toasties. Look out for local farmers markets on Wednesdays, and a slow-food market on the first Sunday of each month.

Midrange

riverstation (☎ 0117-914 4434; The Grove; mains £8-19; ☺ lunch & dinner) Yet another riverside restaurant that satisfies Bristol's style-conscious gourmands – this one is a split-level eatery with a fabulous barrelled roof. The downstairs cafe rustles up light lunches, coffee and featherlight pastries, while up on the 1st floor it's all effortless elegance and European cuisine.

Planet Pizza (☎ 0117-907 7112; 83 Whiteladies Rd; pizzas from £10; ☺ 11am-11pm; 🖳 wi-fi) A top option for huge, freshly made pizzas, this brightly coloured eatery serves a huge choice of 12-inch specials, all named after astronomical bodies and big enough to share.

Clifton Sausage (☎ 0117-973 1192; 7-9 Portland St; mains £10-18; ☺ lunch & dinner) Hog heaven for sausage lovers, this groovy Clifton gastropub serves up no fewer than eight types of bangers 'n' mash, including Gloucester Old Spot and a vegie-friendly cheddar, leak and mustard. Worn wooden floorboards and tables complement the comfort eating – while the rhubarb crumble and sorbet round things off nicely.

WESSEX

DETOUR: WHATLEY MANOR

If you happen to be a holidaying film star or celebrity supermodel, then it's time to whip out a platinum card and book a suite at the jaw-dropping **Whatley Manor** (☎ 01666-822888; www .whatleymanor.com; Easton Grey; d £285-485, ste £650-850; Ⓟ), which takes luxury and designer pampering to a whole new level. Housed in a stunningly restored Cotswold manor house in the village of Easton Grey, 25 miles northeast of Bristol (3 miles west of Malmesbury), it's quite simply one of the poshest, plushest hotels in Britain, blending period architecture and a glorious country setting with a razor-sharp eye for interior design. Underfloor heating, Bang & Olufsen stereos, presidential beds and massive bathroom suites feature in the rooms; there are also two award-winning restaurants, nearly 5 hectares of landscaped gardens, and a futuristic spa that's been voted the best in Europe. Oh, and there's a private cinema, too, just in case you need somewhere to screen your latest directorial creations.

Picture House (☎ 0117-973 9302; 44 Whiteladies Rd; mains £11-18; ☒ lunch & dinner) The whir of a projector has been replaced by dining room chatter at this former cinema, now one of the best midrange options on the Whiteladies strip. The menu mixes Albion classics (slow-cooked mutton, pig-in-a-blanket, Eton Mess) with fancier fare (smoked eel, wild boar, squirrel).

Quartier Vert (☎ 0117-973 4482; 84 Whiteladies Rd; mains £11.50-18.50; ☒ lunch & dinner) The QV has been a Whiteladies staple for two decades, and after several revamps has settled on Spanish and southern Med flavours, supplemented with designer cheeses, sausages, tapas and home-baked bread. Wine-tasting and slow-food courses will knock that philistinic palate into shape.

Severnshed (☎ 0117-925 1212; The Grove; mains from £12; ☒ lunch & dinner) Typifying 'new-Bristol', this former boathouse was built by Brunel – now it's home to a designer bar, bistro and waterside cafe. The renovation is a beautiful blend of industrial trappings and contemporary chrome, while the food is a winning fusion of flavours – try the beef with oyster mushrooms, spicy Thai monkfish or the bouillabaisse. The 977 menu (served before 7pm) features two courses for £9.77.

Other recommendations:

Mud Dock (☎ 0117-934 9734; 40 The Grove; mains £9-16; ☒ lunch & dinner Mon-Sat, 10am-4.30pm Sun) Ultratrendy combo of bar, bistro and bike shop, in a brick warehouse by the harbour.

La Taverna Dell'Artista (☎ 0117-929 7712; 33 King St; mains £13-25; ☒ dinner Tue-Sat) This chaotic, cramped Italian is an old fave with the post-theatre crowd.

Top End

Cafe Maitreya (☎ 0117-951 0100; 89 St Marks Rd; 3 courses £20.95; ☒ dinner Tue-Sat) Regularly notching up awards and rave reviews, the Maitreya has firmly established itself as one of the city's most inventive eateries. The seasonal menu is renowned for its culinary creativity, and dabbles in everything from red onion *tartelette* to cashew-nut roulade.

Glassboat (☎ 0117-929 0704; Welsh Back; lunch mains £7-8, dinner mains £16; ☒ closed Sun) With its floor-to-ceiling glass windows, this double-decked barge has some of the most romantic tables in the city. The fine wood-panelled interior is lit by soft globe lanterns, the menu is a happy marriage of British and French country dishes, and the views across the water are dreamy.

our pick Bordeaux Quay (☎ 0117-943 1200; Canons Way; brasserie mains £10, restaurant mains £17-21; ☒ lunch & dinner) Funky, friendly, Bordeaux Quay neatly fulfils all your food needs in one: it's a restaurant, brasserie, bar, deli, bakery and cookery school. Its efforts to shrink the food-miles map have produced a menu bursting with organic, seasonal, regionally sourced ingredients, and proves 'sustainable' can equal 'delectable'. Settle down at a sanded wooden table in the cool, calm interior and tuck into the squash and rocket linguini or the roast sea bass with *beurre rouge* (a butter and red-wine sauce). Great, green, guilt-free food.

DRINKING

The fortnightly listings magazine *Venue* (www.venue.co.uk, £1.50) contains the latest info on what's hot and what's not. The freebie mag *Folio* is published monthly.

Elbow Room (☎ 0117-930 0242; 64 Park St; ☒ noon-2am Sun-Thu, to 4am Fri & Sat) Part dimly lit bar, part hustler's pool hall, this is a favourite hang-out for Bristol's style-conscious crowd. Rack up the balls and knock back the bourbons to a soundtrack of jazz and funk – for budding Fast Eddies, there's a pool competition every Monday.

Woods (☎ 0117-925 0890; 1 Park St Ave; ☒ 4pm-2am Sun-Thu, to 4am Fri, to 6am Sat) Cultured and cool, this is another haunt for Bristol's beautiful people, crammed with glitter balls, refectory benches and Victoriana sofas, plus 50 whiskies behind the bar.

Apple (☎ 0117-925 3500; Welsh Back; ☒ noon-midnight Mon-Sat, to 10.30pm Sun) Bristol's legendary cider boat stocks an impressive 40 varieties of the golden elixir and specialises in organic and craft-produced varieties – staff even offer taster samples (try a tipple of the raspberry and strawberry varieties). You can sip your scrumpy on the covered deck, or at tables that spill over onto the quayside.

Park (☎ 0117-940 6101; Triangle St West; ☒ 4.30pm-1am Sun-Wed, to 2am Thu, to 4am Fri & Sat) This place has got the metropolitan bar aesthetic nailed – stripped wood, banquette seats and moody lighting abound. Funk and hip hop on Wednesday and Thursday give way to classic beats at weekends.

Avon Gorge Hotel (☎ 0117-973 8955; Sion Hill; www.avongorge-hotel-bristol.com; ☒ 11am-11pm Mon-Sat, 11.30am-10.30pm Sun) The golden age of this huge Victorian hotel has long since passed, but its panoramic drinks terrace is still the top place to watch the sun set over the Avon Gorge.

MBargo (☎ 0117-925 3256; 30 Triangle St West; 🕙 noon-2am) Marble and leather set the scene for a swanky bar with a huge cocktail list – the soundtrack ranges from 1970s and '80s crowd-pleasers to uberhip hip hop.

Hophouse (☎ 0117-923 7390; 16 King's Rd) Lime and chocolate candy stripes, (presumably) ironic flock wallpaper and oh-so-polished wood make this Clifton bar a trendy spot to sip a designer beer and watch the neighbourhood's media types stroll on by.

Pipe & Slippers (☎ 0117-942 7711; 118 Cheltenham Rd) Bath Ales on tap and a menu of Pieminister pies make this unpretentious pub a reliable bet for late-night drinking, as well as for Sunday lunch.

Albion (☎ 0117-975 3522; Boyce's Ave) Another venerable pub packed with evening drinkers from Clifton's well-heeled streets.

ENTERTAINMENT
Cinemas
Watershed (☎ 0117-927 5100; www.watershed.co.uk; 1 Canon's Rd) This is the city's leading art-house cinema and digital media centre, specialising in new indie releases and the occasional silver-screen classic.

Nightclubs
The Bristol club scene moves fast, so check the latest listings to see where the big nights are happening.

Timbuk2 (☎ 0117-945 8459; 22 Small St; admission £5-10; 🕙 9am-2pm) A scruffy-chic club-venue, crammed underneath the arches off Corn St. It hosts a mixed bag of breaks, house, drum and bass and jungle.

Native (☎ 0117-930 4217; www.nativebristol.co.uk; 15 Small St; admission £5-8; 🕙 10pm-4am) Bristol's top ticket, this tiny 200-cover club is right on the cutting edge, with drum and bass, Latin, jungle, dubstep, hip hop and jazz all making the playlist, along with a revolving line-up of guest DJs.

Thekla Social (☎ 0117-929 3301; www.thekla.co.uk; The Grove; admission £5-7; 🕙 9pm-2am) After a hefty refit, Bristol's venerable club-boat is back with nights to cater for all tastes: electro-punk, indie, disco and new wave, plus live gigs and, once a month, legendary leftfield night Blowpop.

Carling Academy (☎ 0117-927 9227; Frogmore St; admission £6-10; 🕙 10pm-3am Fri & Mon, 7-11pm gig nights) Bristol's original superclub can hold a 2000-strong crowd on its biggest nights, but it's practically never that busy. There's indie and

R&B during the week, and big house nights on weekends.

Cosies (☎ 0117-942 4110; www.cosies.co.uk; 34 Portland Sq; admission after 9pm £2; 🕙 10am-2am Thu & Fri, 8pm-2am Sat & Sun, 10am-10pm Mon-Wed) This diminutive club is a real gem, especially if you're sick of the big beats and designer attitude of some of Bristol's larger venues. Upstairs there's a bistro and wine bar, but it's the weekend reggae nights that draw in the crowds.

Theatre
Tobacco Factory (☎ 0117-902 0344; www.tobaccofactory .com; Raleigh Rd) This small-scale theatre venue stages cutting-edge drama and dance. Catch bus 24 or 25 from Broadmead to the Raleigh Rd stop.

The **Bristol Old Vic** (King St) pulled down the curtain and launched a £9 million refurbishment appeal in 2007, to save it from permanent closure. For the latest see www .bristol-old-vic.co.uk.

Live Music
Big names play at the **Carling Academy** (see left), while a host of smaller venues feature emerging acts.

Fleece & Firkin (☎ 0117-945 0996; www.fleecegigs .co.uk; St Thomas St) A small, intimate venue, much favoured by indie artists and breaking names on the local scene.

Colston Hall (☎ 0117-922 3686; www.colstonhall.org; Colston St) Bristol's biggest concert hall hosts everything from big-name comedy to touring bands. A £20-million refit will see a swanky glass and recycled-copper foyer tacked onto the old red-brick building.

Croft (☎ 0117-987 4144; www.the-croft.com; 117-119 Stokes Croft) Chilled venue with a policy of supporting new names and Bristol-based artists. There's usually no cover charge if you arrive by 10pm Sunday to Thursday.

Bierkeller (☎ 0117-926 8514; www.bristolbierkeller .co.uk; All Saints St) A legendary place that has played host to plenty of rock stars down the years, and still gets packed out on weekends.

GETTING THERE & AWAY
Air
Bristol International Airport (☎ 0871 334 4344; www.bristolairport.co.uk) is 8 miles southwest of the city. Many flights are holiday charters but there are also scheduled flights to European destinations.

WESSEX

Air Southwest (☎ 0870 043 4553; www.airsouthwest
.com) Several UK destinations including Jersey, Leeds,
Manchester, Newquay and Plymouth.

easyJet (☎ 0871 244 2366, per min 10p; www.easyjet
.com) Budget flights to UK destinations including Belfast,
Edinburgh, Glasgow, Newcastle and Inverness, as well as
numerous European cities.

Ryanair (☎ 0871 246 0000, per min 10p; www.ryanair
.com) Flights to Irish airports including Derry, Dublin and
Shannon, as well as European destinations.

Bus

National Express coaches go to Birmingham
(£17, two hours, nine daily), London (£18, 2½
hours, at least hourly), Cardiff (£7, 1¼ hours,
nine daily) and Exeter (£12.40, two hours,
four daily). There's also a direct daily bus to
Nottingham (£26, five hours) and Oxford
(£13.80, three hours).

Bus X39 (one hour, several per hour) runs
to Bath. Buses 375 and 376 go to Wells (one
hour) and Glastonbury (1¼ hours) every half-
hour (hourly on Sunday). There are buses
to most destinations around Somerset and
Wiltshire from Bath and Wells.

Train

Bristol is an important rail hub, with regular
connections to London (£62, 1¾ hours) and the
southwest, including Exeter (£19, 1¼ hours),
Plymouth (£44, 2½ hours) and Penzance (£60,
four hours). **Cross Country** (www.crosscountrytrains
.co.uk) trains travel north to Glasgow (£101, 5¾
hours, five direct daily) via Birmingham (£31,
1½ hours, eight direct daily). Most main-line
trains arrive at Temple Meads.

Bath makes for an easy day trip (single
£5.50, 11 minutes, four per hour).

GETTING AROUND
To/From the Airport

Bristol International Flyer runs bus services
to the airport (single/return adult £7/8, child

£6/7, 30 minutes, half-hourly 5am to 11pm)
from Marlborough St bus station and Temple
Meads train station. A taxi to the airport costs
around £25.

Bicycle

To hire a bike, try the **Ferry Station** (☎ 0117-
376 3942; Narrow Quay; half-/full day £7/12; ☺ 8am-6pm
Mon-Fri, 10am-6pm Sat & Sun) on the waterfront or
Blackboy Hill Cycles (☎ 0117-973 1420; 180 Whiteladies
Rd; per day £10; ☺ 9am-5.30pm Mon-Sat). The 13-mile
off-road **Bristol to Bath Railway Path** (www.bristol
bathrailwaypath.org.uk) follows the course of an old
train track between the two cities. In Bristol
pick it up around half a mile northeast of
Temple Meads Train Station.

Boat

The most scenic way to travel around the city
is with the **Bristol Ferry Boat Co** (☎ 0117-927 3416;
www.bristolferry.com), which runs two routes. One
is from the city centre to Temple Meads (40
minutes, six to 10 daily April to September,
weekends only October to March), stopping
at Welsh Back, Bristol Bridge and Castle Park
(for Broadmead shopping centre). The other
route goes from the city centre to Hotwells
(40 minutes, 12 to 16 daily year-round), stopping at the SS *Great Britain* and Mardyke.
An adult single fare is £1.60 (child £1.30), or
you can pay £7 for a day's unlimited travel
(child/family £5/20).

Bus

Every 15 minutes, bus 73 runs from Parkway
Station to the centre (30 minutes). Buses 8 and
9 run every 15 minutes from St Augustine's
Pde to Clifton (10 minutes), the foot of
Whiteladies Rd and Bristol Zoo Gardens; add
another 10 minutes from Temple Meads.

FirstDay tickets (adult/child £4/2.80) are valid on
all buses for one day in zones one and two,
which contain all the key sites. The **FirstFamily**

DETOUR: TYNTESFIELD

Formerly the aristocratic home of the Gibbs family, gorgeously Gothic **Tyntesfield** (NT; ☎ 01275-
461900; Wraxall; adult/child £9.45/4.75; ☺ 11am-5pm Sat-Wed mid-Mar–Oct) is an ornate Victorian pile
that prickles with spiky turrets and towers. The house was built in grand Gothic Revival style
by the architect John Norton, and is crammed with Victorian decorative arts, a working kitchen
garden and a magnificent private chapel. The house is undergoing extensive renovation (due
to finish in 2012); until then, some facilities are a little basic, but you do get an insight into the
conservation process. Call the info line (☎ 0844 800 4986) for updates. Tyntesfield is 7 miles
southwest of Bristol, off the B3128.

ticket (£7.30) buys one days' travel for two adults and three children, but is only valid after 9am Monday to Friday.

Car & Motorcycle

Bristol has a seriously confusing one-way system and very heavy traffic – it's best to avoid driving altogether and instead use public transport or the **park-and-ride** (☎ 0117-922 2910; before 10am return Mon-Fri £3, after 10am Mon-Fri £2.50, Sat £2), which runs every 10 minutes (Monday to Saturday) from Portway, Bath Rd and Long Ashton. Park-and-ride car parks are well signed on routes into the city.

Taxi

The taxi rank on St Augustine's Pde is a central but rowdy place on weekend nights. There are plenty of companies; try **Streamline Taxis** (☎ 0117-926 4001).

BATH

pop 90,144

If you only explore one English city outside London, make it Bath. Tucked into the folds of seven grassy hills and blessed by healing thermal springs, this romantic city of honey-coloured stone blends past and present with imagination and ease. Here you'll find one of the finest Roman bathhouses in the world, extensive, exquisite Regency architecture and a chic new spa that lets you swim alfresco in a heated rooftop pool after a mud wrap and full body massage. With its grand Georgian terraces, Palladian parades and lofty town houses, Bath boasts so many listed buildings that the whole city has been named a World Heritage Site by Unesco. Yes, it can be expensive and too busy for its own good, but add hip hotels, excellent eateries and an absorbing collection of museums and you have one of Britain's most appealing cities. The Romans never had it so good.

HISTORY

Prehistoric peoples probably knew about the hot springs; legend has it King Bladud, a Trojan refugee and father of King Lear, founded Bath some 2800 years ago and was cured of leprosy by a dip in the muddy swamps. The Romans established the town of Aquae Sulis in AD 44 and built the extensive baths complex and a temple to the goddess Sulis-Minerva.

Long after the Romans decamped, the Anglo-Saxons arrived, and in 944 a monastery was founded on the site of the present abbey. Throughout the Middle Ages, Bath was an ecclesiastical centre and a wool-trading town, and it wasn't until the early 18th century that Ralph Allen and Richard 'Beau' Nash (see boxed text, p345) made Bath the centre of fashionable society. Allen developed the quarries at Coombe Down, constructed Prior Park (p350) and employed the two John Woods (father and son) to create the glorious buildings you see today.

As the 18th century wore on, Beau Nash lost his influence, and sea bathing started to draw visitors away from Bath. By the mid-19th century the city was thoroughly out of fashion and in 1970 what was then the last spa closed. But fast forward to the 21st century and Bath is experiencing a rebirth: you can once again soak in style in those soothing waters, thanks to Thermae Bath Spa (see boxed text, p344); the refurbished Milsom Place is set to be home to a celebrity chef; and the £360-million mock-Georgian SouthGate development will add 60 new shops and 100 apartments to the mix.

ORIENTATION

Like Rome, Bath is famed for its seven hills, and although the city centre is compact it will test your legs. Most street signs are carved into the golden stone of the buildings.

The most obvious landmark is the abbey, across from the Roman Baths and Pump Room. Just under £20 million is being spent on jazzing up Bath's public transport stations – after two years in a temporary home on Avon St, by mid-2009 the bus station will be alongside the train station.

INFORMATION

Scattered around the city you'll find i-plus points, which are free touch-screen kiosks providing tourist information.

Bath Quarterly (www.bathquarterly.com) Guide to sights, accommodation, restaurants and events.

Laundrette (4 Margarets Bldgs; per load £2; ⏱ 6am-9pm)

Main post office (☎ 0845 722 3344; 27 Northgate St)

Police station (☎ 0845-456700; Manvers St; ⏱ 7am-midnight)

WESSEX

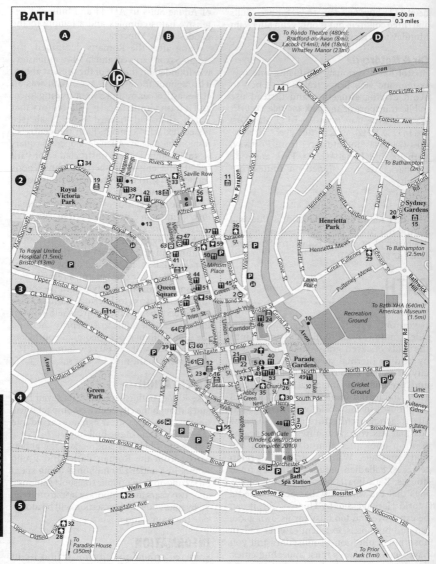

BATH

Retailer Internet (☎ 01225-443181; 13 Manvers St;
per 20min £1; ⏱ 9am-9pm Mon-Sat, 3-9pm Sun)
Royal United Hospital (☎ 01225-428331; Combe Park)
Tourist office (☎ 0906 711 2000, per min 50p; www
.visitbath.co.uk; Abbey Churchyard; ⏱ 9.30am-5pm Mon-
Sat, 10am-4pm Sun)
What's On (www.whatsonbath.co.uk) Up-to-date listing
of the city's events and nightlife.

SIGHTS
Baths

Ever since the Romans arrived in Bath, life in
the city has revolved around the three natural springs that bubble up near the abbey.
In typically ostentatious style, the Romans
constructed a glorious complex of bathhouses
above these thermal waters, to take advan-

tage of their natural temperature – a constant 46°C. The buildings were left to decay after the Romans departed and, apart from a few leprous souls who came looking for a cure in the Middle Ages, it wasn't until the end of the 17th century that Bath's restorative waters again became fashionable. It's no longer possible to take a dip in the Roman Baths themselves; for modern-day dunks head for the sparkling new Thermae Bath Spa (see boxed text, p344).

The 2000-year-old baths now form one of the best-preserved ancient Roman spas in the world. The **Roman Baths Museum** (☎ 01225-477785; www.romanbaths.co.uk; Abbey Churchyard; adult/child £11/6.80, incl Fashion Museum £14/8.30; ⏰ 9am-6pm Mar-Jun, Sep & Oct, 9am-10pm Jul & Aug, 9.30am-5.30pm Nov-Feb) gets very, very busy in summer; you can usually dodge the worst crowds by visiting early on a midweek morning, or by avoiding July and August. An audio guide (read by the bestselling author Bill Bryson) is included in the admission price.

The first sight inside the complex is the **Great Bath**. Head down to water level and along the raised walkway to see the Roman paving and lead base. A series of excavated passages and chambers beneath street level leads off in several directions and lets you inspect the remains of other smaller baths and hypocaust (heating) systems.

One of the most picturesque corners of the complex is the 12th-century **King's Bath**, built around the original sacred spring; 1.5 million litres of hot water still pour into the pool every day. You can see the ruins of the vast **Temple of Sulis-Minerva** under the **Pump Room**, and recent excavations of the **East Baths** give an insight into its 4th-century form.

Bath Abbey

King Edgar was crowned in a church in Abbey Courtyard in 973 – though he had ruled since 959 – but the present **Bath Abbey** (☎ 01225-422462; www.bathabbey.org; requested donation £2.50; ⏰ 9am-6pm Mon-Sat Easter-Oct, to 4.30pm Nov-Easter, 1-2.30pm & 4.30-5.30pm Sun year-round) was built between 1499 and 1616, making it the last great medieval church raised in England. The nave's wonderful fan vaulting was erected in the 19th century.

Outside, the most striking feature is the west facade, where angels climb up and down stone ladders, commemorating a dream of the founder, Bishop Oliver King. The abbey boasts the second-largest collection of wall monuments after Westminster Abbey. Among those buried here are Sir Isaac Pitman, who devised the Pitman method of shorthand, and Beau Nash.

On the abbey's southern side, the steps lead down to the small **Heritage Vaults Museum**

WESSEX

(admission free; ⏰ 10am-3.30pm Mon-Sat), which explores the abbey's history and its links with the nearby baths. It also contains fine stone bosses, archaeological artefacts and a weird model of the 10th-century monk Aelfric, dressed in his traditional black Benedictine habit.

Royal Crescent & The Circus

The crowning glory of Georgian Bath and the city's most prestigious address is Royal Crescent, a semicircular terrace of majestic houses overlooking a private lawn and the green sweep of Royal Victoria Park. Designed by John Wood the Younger (1728–82) and built between 1767 and 1775, the houses would have originally been rented for the season by wealthy socialites. These days flats on the crescent are still keenly sought after, and entire houses almost never come up for sale.

For a glimpse into the splendour and razzle-dazzle of Georgian life, head for **No 1 Royal Crescent** (☎ 01225-428126; www.bath-preservation-trust .org.uk; adult/child £5/2.50; ⏰ 10.30am-5pm Tue-Sun Feb-Oct, to 4pm Tue-Sun Nov), which contains an astonishing amount of period furniture. Only materials available during the 18th century were used in its refurbishment, so it's about as authentically Georgian as you can get; the same can't be said for the endearingly hammy staff dressed in period costume.

A walk east along Brock St from the Royal Crescent leads to the **Circus**, a magnificent ring of 30 houses. Plaques on the houses commemorate famous residents such as Thomas Gainsborough, Clive of India and David Livingstone. To the south is the restored 18th-century **Georgian Garden**, where gravel replaces grass (to protect women's long dresses from unsightly stains).

Assembly Rooms & Fashion Museum

Opened in 1771, the city's glorious **Assembly Rooms** (☎ 01225-477789; Bennett St; admission free; ⏰ 11am-6pm Mar-Oct, to 5pm Nov-Feb) were where fashionable Bath socialites once gathered to waltz, play cards and listen to the latest chamber music. You're free to wander around the rooms, as long as they haven't been reserved for a special function. Highlights include the card room, tearoom and the truly splendid ballroom, all of which are lit by their original 18th-century chandeliers.

In the basement, the **Fashion Museum** (☎ 01225-477173; www.fashionmuseum.co.uk; adult/child £7/5, incl Roman Baths Museum £14/8.30; ⏰ 10.30am-5pm Mar-Oct, to 4pm Nov-Feb) displays costumes worn from the 16th to late-20th centuries, including some alarming crinolines that would have forced women to approach doorways side on.

Jane Austen Centre

Bath is known to many as a location in Jane Austen's novels. *Persuasion* and *Northanger Abbey* were both largely set in the city; the writer visited it many times and lived here from 1801 to 1806 (a plaque marks one of her former houses at **No 4 Sydney Pl**, opposite the Holburne Museum). The author's connections with the city are explored at the **Jane Austen Centre** (☎ 01225-443000; www.janeausten .co.uk; 40 Gay St; adult/child £6.50/3.50; ⏰ hours vary), where displays also include period costume and contemporary prints of Bath.

Other Museums

Housed in an 18th-century Gothic chapel, the **Building of Bath Museum** (☎ 01225-333895; www.bath-preservation-trust.org.uk; The Vineyards, The

---

BATH'S REBIRTH

Larking about in the Roman Baths might be off the agenda, but thankfully you can still sample the city's curative waters at **Thermae Bath Spa** (☎ 0844 888 0844; www.thermaebathspa.com; Hot Bath St; New Royal Bath spa session per 2hr/4hr/day £22/32/52, spa packages from £65; ⏰ New Royal Bath 9am-10pm). Here the old **Cross Bath**, incorporated into an ultramodern shell of local stone and plate glass, is now the setting for a variety of spa packages. The New Royal Bath ticket includes steam rooms, waterfall shower and a choice of bathing venues – including the jaw-dropping open-air rooftop pool, where you can swim in the thermal waters in front of a backdrop of Bath's stunning cityscape. Other exotic treatments include peat baths, body cocoons, Vichy showers and the ominous-sounding 'Kraxen stove' (an Alpine hay chamber, apparently).

Across the street are treatment rooms above the old **Hot Bath**, while the Hetling Pump Room, opposite, houses a **visitor centre** (⏰ 10am-5pm Mon-Sat, to 4pm Sun) that explores the history of bathing in Bath.

> **QUITE A BEAU**
>
> If Ralph Allen, John Wood the Elder and John Wood the Younger were responsible for the physical construction of Georgian Bath, Richard 'Beau' Nash was the force that shaped its high-society heyday. Dandy, gambler and womaniser, Nash was purportedly charming, friendly, witty, influential and (at least to some degree) philanthropic.
>
> Born in Wales in 1674, Richard Nash was an Oxford scholar and ex-soldier and in 1705 was appointed Master of Ceremonies in Bath. By revitalising spa culture and providing entertainment for the rich, Nash effectively created a prestigious social milieu over which he would rule, imposing strict regulations on behaviour and dress, for almost 50 years. But by the 1750s Nash's influence was waning and he died in poverty in 1761. Yet Bath had been changed irrevocably by his presence – it simply wouldn't be what it is without his legacy.

Paragon; admission £4; 10.30am-5pm Tue-Sun mid-Feb–Nov) details how Bath's Georgian splendour came into being, tracing the city's evolution from a sleepy spa town to one of the centres of Georgian society. There are some intriguing displays on contemporary construction methods, and the museum also explores the way in which social class and interior decor were intimately linked during the Georgian era; heaven forbid should you use a wallpaper that outstripped your station...

The 18th-century **Holburne Museum** (01225-466669; Great Pulteney St; adult/child £4.50/3.50; 10am-5pm Tue-Sat, 11am-5pm Sun) houses the booty of Sir William Holburne, a 19th-century Bath resident who brought together an outstanding collection of porcelain, antiques, and paintings by great 18th-century artists such as Gainsborough, Turner and Guardi.

In 1781 astronomer William Herschel discovered Uranus from the garden of his home, which now houses the **Herschel Museum of Astronomy** (01225-446865; 19 New King St; adult/child £4/2.50; 1-5pm Mon, Tue, Thu & Fri, 11am-5pm Sat & Sun Feb-Dec). The house is decorated as it would have been in the 18th century; an astrolabe in the garden marks where Herschel would probably have placed his telescope.

The **Victoria Art Gallery** (01225-477233; www.victoriagal.org.uk; Pulteney Bridge; admission free; 10am-5pm Tue-Sat, 1.30-5pm Sun) houses the city's main arts collection, with most items dating from the 15th to 20th centuries. There are some particularly fine canvases by Gainsborough, Turner and Sickert, as well as a wonderful series of Georgian caricatures from the wicked pens of artists such as James Gillray and Thomas Rowlandson.

The **American Museum** (01225-460503; www.americanmuseum.org; Claverton Manor; adult/child £7.50/4; noon-5pm Tue-Sun mid-Mar–Oct) houses a collection of stateside artefacts, memorabilia and furniture dating from the 17th century. There are 15 individually decorated rooms scattered around the manor house, including a suitably sparse Shaker Room and a New Orleans room, decked out in the lavish style of a plantation villa. Even the trees and plants in the surrounding grounds have a Yankee provenance. The museum is 2 miles southeast of the city centre; bus 18 and several other buses to the university stop nearby.

The **Museum of East Asian Art** (01225-464640; www.meaa.org.uk; 12 Bennett St; adult/child £4/1.50; 10am-5pm Tue-Sat, noon-5pm Sun) contains more than 500 jade, bamboo, porcelain and bronze objects from Cambodia, Korea and Thailand, and substantial Chinese and Japanese carvings, ceramics and lacquerware.

TOURS
Guided Tours

The most popular, and daftest, guided stroll around the city is the **Bizarre Bath Comedy Walk** (01225-335124; www.bizarrebath.co.uk; adult/student £8/5; 8pm Mar-Sep), a chaotic and frequently hilarious blend of street theatre, live performance and guided tour. Wallflowers be warned – you'll probably find yourself being roped into the act whether you like it or not. Tours leave from outside the Huntsman Inn on North Parade Passage (south of York St) and last about 1½ hours.

Jane Austen's Bath (01225-443000; adult/child £5/4) focuses on the Georgian city and sites associated with the author. Tours leave from the Abbey Churchyard at 11am on Saturday, Sunday and bank holidays.

The free, two-hour **Mayor's Guide walking tour** (01225-477411; www.thecityofbath.co.uk), a good all-round introduction to Bath, sets off from outside the Pump Room at 10.30am and 2pm Sunday to Friday, and at 10.30am Saturday. From May to September there are additional tours at 7pm on Tuesday, Friday and Saturday.

Bath City Sightseeing (☎ 01225-330444; www.city -sightseeing.com) provides a hop-on hop-off **city tour** (adult/child £10/6; 🕑 9.30am-5pm Mar-May, Oct & Nov, to 6.30pm Jun-Sep) on an open-topped bus. Commentary is in seven languages. Buses stop every 20 minutes or so at various points around town. There's also a second route, the **Skyline tour** that runs year-round and travels out to Prior Park (p350); the same tickets are valid on both routes.

There are also minibus tours to some of the attractions around Bath:

Mad Max Tours (☎ 07990 505970; www.madmax tours.co.uk) One-day tours to Stonehenge, Avebury, Lacock and Castle Combe (£27.50), and half-day tours to Stonehenge and Lacock (£15).

Scarper Tours (☎ 07739 644155; www.scarpertours .com) Twice-daily tour to Stonehenge (adult/child £14/8).

Boat Trips

Various cruise operators offer boat trips up and down the River Avon; try **Bath City Boat Trips** (☎ 07974 560197; www.bathcityboattrips.com; adult/ child £7/5; 🕑 11am-5pm) or the **Pulteney Princess** (☎ 07791 910650; www.pulteneyprincess.co.uk; adult/child £7/3; 🕑 11.30am-5pm). Trips for both companies leave from the landing stage just to the east of Pulteney Bridge.

For cruises to Bristol, see Tours, p335.

FESTIVALS & EVENTS

The annual events calendar in Bath would keep even the most demanding Georgian socialite busy, with a varied program of music, arts and theatre throughout the year. **Bath Festivals** (☎ 01225-463362; www.bathfestivals.org.uk; 2 Church St; 🕑 9.30am-5.30pm Mon-Sat) has an overview and handles all bookings.

Bath Literature Festival (www.bathlitfest.org.uk) This annual festival takes place in late February or early March, and attracts bookworms and big-name authors alike.

Bath International Music Festival (www.bathmusic fest.org.uk) From mid-May to early June this festival takes over the city, with a main program of classical music and opera, as well as jazz, world and folk gigs in the city's smaller venues.

Bath Fringe Festival (www.bathfringe.co.uk) Hits town around mid-May to early June; it's the biggest fringe festival in Britain after Edinburgh, with all kinds of theatre shows and street acts dotted around town.

Jane Austen Festival (www.janeausten.co.uk/festival) Held in September, the highlight of this festival is a grand Georgian costumed parade through the city's streets, all the way to the Royal Crescent.

Mozartfest (www.bathmozartfest.org.uk) Takes place annually in mid-October.

Bath Film Festival (www.bathfilmfestival.org.uk) Held in early November.

SLEEPING

Bath gets incredibly busy; the tourist office books rooms for a £3 fee, and sells the brochure *Bath & Beyond* (£1; free through the website). If you can, avoid weekends, when room prices can rise dramatically.

Budget

Bath Backpackers' Hostel (☎ 01225-446787; bath@ hostels.co.uk; 13 Pierrepont St; dm £12-13; 🖳) It may be grungy (expect peeling paint, worn carpets and saggy beds), but Bath's indie hostel is a friendly affair and slap-bang in the middle of town. There's a party 'dungeon' in the cellar, no curfew and a fair bit of noise at night.

Bath YHA (☎ 0845 371 9303; www.yha.org.uk; dm £14, d from £35; 🅿 🖳) Hostels don't come much grander than this Italianate mansion, a steep climb (or a short hop on bus 18) from the city centre. The refurbished rooms are surprisingly modern and many look out across the private tree-lined gardens; book early if you're after a double.

YMCA (☎ 01225-325900; www.bathymca.co.uk; International House, Broad St Pl; dm £14-16, s £26-30, d & tw £40-48; 🖳) Despite bright fabrics in the dorms and funky sofas in the lounge, this huge hostel has an institutional feel. But with its excellent facilities (a health suite and on-site cafe), a super-central location and knock-down prices, do you care?

Midrange

There's a wide range of midrange options; generally you'll get better value for money the further you head from the city centre.

Henry Guest House (☎ 01225-424052; www.the henry.com; 6 Henry St; s £35-65, d £70-130, f from £105) Some of the best-value rooms in town are just five minutes' walk from the centre of Bath, at this stylish Georgian terrace. Crisp linens and a judicious scattering of cushions give the rooms a light, airy feel; the odd ornate fireplace and mock-Georgian chair help with the heritage mood.

SOMETHING FOR THE WEEKEND

To kick off your trip in glorious, Georgian Bath, check into one of the city's excellent hotels – try the **Queensberry** (below) for boutique chic. Then explore the city's key sights: the **Roman Baths** (p343), **Bath Abbey** (p343), the **Royal Crescent** and the **Circus** (p344). Lunch at the smart **Circus** (p348) restaurant, soak up more Georgian splendour at the **Building of Bath Museum** (p344) and the **Assembly Rooms** and **Fashion Museum** (p344), before indulging in a spot of pampering and an open-air rooftop swim at **Thermae Bath Spa** (see boxed text, p344). Laugh your socks off on the **Bizarre Bath Comedy Walk** (p345), tuck into a slap-up meal at **Onefishtwofish** (p349) – vegetarians should head to Demuth's (p349) – then round off the night with a late-night gig at **Moles** (p349), the city's top music venue.

On Sunday head east from Bath to **Bradford-on-Avon** (p323), famous for its 14th-century tithe barn, and **Lacock** (p324), with its beautiful medieval abbey. Grab a delicious country lunch at the **Sign of the Angel** (p325) before heading on to **Avebury** (p326), Britain's largest and arguably most spectacular stone circle, best seen in the light of late afternoon. And for the ultimate weekend getaway, head for **Whatley Manor** (see boxed text, p337) – one of the most luxurious night's sleep anywhere in Britain.

Oldfields (☎ 01225-317984; www.oldfields.co.uk; 102 Wells Rd; s £49-99, d £65-135, f from £85; **P**) This has to be one of the best deals in Bath: spacious rooms and soft beds for comfort; brass bedsteads and antique chairs for character; and Laura Ashley fabrics and Molton Brown bathstuffs for luxury. It's all wrapped up in a lemon-coloured stone house with views over Bath's rooftops.

Three Abbey Green (☎ 01225-428558; www.three abbeygreen.com; 3 Abbey Green; d £85-125, f £125-175) Built when 'Beau' Nash was a teenager, this great-value B&B sits near the abbey in the kind of secluded square around which he would have strolled. It's not quite as stylish as the dandy inside, where simplicity and smartness see plain whites offset by tartan checks or colour tints.

Paradise House (☎ 01225-317723; www.paradise -house.co.uk; 88 Holloway; s £60-115, d £65-170; **P**) If the tourist crowds become too much for you, beat a retreat to this chimney-crowned villa and its charming walled garden. It's an old-world treat, with half-tester beds, gilded mirrors and oil paintings in the drawing room, and a lighter palette in the bedrooms (plus Jacuzzis and four-posters for the high-rollers).

Dorian House (☎ 01225-426336; www.dorianhouse .co.uk; 1 Upper Oldfield Park; s £65-78, d £80-155; **P** 💻 wi-fi) Owned by a cellist with the London Symphony Orchestra, this chic B&B is a symphony of sumptuous style. The marble bathrooms, scattered antiques, elaborate floor tiles and plush throws all chime together perfectly, with never a duff note.

Brocks (☎ 01225-338374; www.brocksguesthouse.com; 32 Brock St; d £87-125) Part of the Georgian terrace linking the Circus and the Royal Crescent, Brocks nestles in the heart of elegant Bath. Teddy bears sit in lemon, cream and blue rooms – the ones to the rear have views of yet more classy architecture and the leafy hills beyond.

Also recommended:

Abbey Rise (☎ 01225-316177; www.abbeyrise.co.uk; 97 Wells Rd; s £48-58, d £68-78, f £75-90; **P**) Attractively refurbished, contemporary B&B whose owner trained as a housekeeper at Buckingham Palace.

Milsoms (☎ 01225-750128; www.milsomshotel.co.uk; 24 Milsom St; d from £85) Smooth city-chic and cocoa-bean colours above Loch Fyne Restaurant.

Top End

ᴏᴜʀ ᴘɪᴄᴋ Queensberry Hotel (☎ 01225-447928; www .thequeensberry.co.uk; 4 Russell St; s £95-300, d £105-425; **P**) One to save your pennies for – this boutique barnstormer is sexy, swanky and super. Hidden away in four town houses, modern fabrics, muted colour schemes and funky throws meet polished wardrobes, feature fireplaces and Zen-tinged furniture. Gleaming bathrooms house his 'n' hers sinks and posh smellies, while designer-print cushions pepper sofas and oversized beds. The walled garden is a chilled refuge from the city fizz. Prepare to be pampered.

Dukes (☎ 01225-787960; www.dukesbath.co.uk; Great Pulteney St; s £115, d £135-175, ste £170-215; **P**) The rooms at this Grade I–listed Palladian pile are some of the most regal you'll find in Bath. Themes include Asian finery, Italianate splendour, English botanica or French baroque – either way, you get original cornicing and carved plasterwork.

Royal Crescent Hotel (☎ 01225-823333; www.royal crescent.co.uk; 16 Royal Cres; d £290-850; P 🖵 wi-fi) Set right in the middle of the poshest postcode in town, this opulent hotel's ornaments and antiques would have welcomed guests in the 18th century. Expect paintings by Gainsborough, a sweeping secret garden and more chaise longues, chandeliers and sash windows than your average royal palace.

EATING

As befits a historic watering hole, Bath has some top-notch restaurants. Look out for TV chef Jamie Oliver's new Milsom Pl eatery, **Jamie's Italian** (www.jamieoliver.com/Italian) – it wasn't yet open at the time of writing, but we expect that its quality will match that of Jamie's other restaurants.

Budget
CAFES & QUICK EATS
Parisienne (☎ 01225-447147; Milsom Pl; mains £7-13; ☾ breakfast & lunch) This delightful cafe has an air of Paris' Left Bank, thanks to its lovely courtyard terrace and an authentic menu of baguettes, croissants, *croques-monsieurs* (toasted cheese-and-ham sandwiches) and *moules marinières* (mussels cooked in white wine).

Adventure Cafe (☎ 01225-462038; 5 Princes Bldgs, George St; mains £4-8; ☾ breakfast, lunch & dinner) Californian bohemia mixes with urban chic at this groovy cafe-cum-hang-out, all picture windows, distressed wood and deep sofas. Cappuccinos by morning, ciabattas at noon and cocktails after dark.

Cafe Retro (☎ 01225-339347; 18 York St; mains £5-11; ☾ breakfast, lunch & dinner Tue-Sat, breakfast & lunch Mon) A place to make a stand (well, actually a laid-back 'sit') against bland, insidious global coffee-shop chains, Cafe Retro is a quirky gem. Settle down alongside Bath's boho trendies and munch a burger, linger over brunch or sink a salad – smashing.

Boston Tea Party (☎ 01225-313901; 19 Kingsmead Sq; mains from £4; ☾ 7.30am-7pm Mon-Sat, from 8.30am Sun) With a lovely outside terrace spilling onto Kingsmead Sq, the Bath outpost of this small southwest franchise is always full to bursting at lunchtime – thanks to its prodigious selection of sandwiches, homemade soups and sweet treats.

RESTAURANTS
Number 8 Manvers St (☎ 01225-331888; 8 Manvers St; lunch mains £4-8, dinner mains £7-12; ☾ breakfast, lunch & dinner Fri & Sat, 8am-7pm Mon-Thu) There's a fresh feel to the food and furnishings at this airy brasserie. Slender chairs, stripped wood and local artwork set the scene for pan-global offerings such as king prawn and coriander linguini, wild mushroom risotto and gourmet burgers.

Sally Lunn's (☎ 01225-461634; 4 North Parade Passage; lunch mains £5-6, dinner mains from £8; ☾ lunch & dinner) People have been taking afternoon tea here since the 1680s, and it's still high on many a tourist to-do list. The atmosphere – quintessential English chintz – makes it a genteel spot to devour the trademark Sally Lunn's bun.

Walrus & the Carpenter (☎ 01225-314864; 28 Barton St; mains £7-15; ☾ lunch & dinner) Another Bath classic, this bistro eschews snootiness in favour of a homelier mix of mismatched furniture, chummy service and down-home food. The menu's divided into 'befores' and 'afters' – the kebabs, moussakas and huge burgers are old faves.

SELF-CATERING
Deli Shush (☎ 01225-443563; 8A Guildhall Market; ☾ 8am-5.30pm Mon-Sat) Serrano ham, antipasti, samosas and 20 types of olives fill the shelves of this designer deli that's set inside the Guildhall Market. You'll also find delicious crêpes, tangy cheeses and a wealth of other takeaway goodies at the nearby stalls.

our pick Paxton & Whitfield (☎ 01225 466403; 1 John St; ☾ Mon-Sat) Cheese lovers be warned – you will simply never want to leave. This upmarket fromagerie overflows with utterly oozing brie, whiffy Stilton and the kind of extra-mature cheddar that makes your tongue stick to the roof of your mouth. If they could bottle the smell they could sell that, too.

Chandos Deli (☎ 01225-314418; George St; ☾ Mon-Sat) Gourmet sarnies, fresh pasta and Italian cakes are the mainstays of this excellent deli – perfect for stocking up on picnic supplies.

Midrange
Circus (☎ 01225-318918; 34 Brock St; lunch mains £7, dinner mains £11; ☾ lunch & dinner Mon-Sat) As elegant as the architectural edifices that surround it, this bistro near the Royal Crescent plays on its superchic surrounds. The ladies who lunch like the fresh, fashionable food, too.

FishWorks (☎ 01225-448707; 6 Green St; mains from £13; ☾ lunch & dinner) The embodiment of the old seafood gag ('I'm on a seafood diet: I see food and I eat it'), FishWorks is a fishmonger, cookery school and seafood restaurant in one. Select something from the ice-packed trays, pick a treatment then enjoy the flavours of the sea.

Firehouse Rotisserie (☎ 01225-482070; 2 John St; mains £11-15; ⊗ lunch & dinner Mon-Sat) Stateside flavours and a Californian vibe characterise this excellent American restaurant, run by a couple of ex-LA chefs. The menu evokes Mexico and the deep South, with signature dishes including rotisserie chicken, Louisiana catfish and Texan steak.

Onefishtwofish (☎ 01225-330236; 10A North Pde; mains £13-18; ⊗ dinner Tue-Sun) Tables are crammed in under a barrel-brick roof, full of twinkly light in this cosy cellar restaurant. Seafood is shipped in from Devon ports, and chefs cook up everything from wonton salmon to Marseillaise bouillabaisse.

our pick **Pinch** (☎ 01225-421251; 11 Margarets Bldgs; 2-course lunch £10, dinner mains £14-20; ⊗ lunch & dinner Wed-Sat) Bringing the flavours of Bordeaux, Burgundy and the Left Bank to Bath, many Brits will dearly wish there were more snug eateries like this over here. The menu is packed with duck, rabbit, langoustine and beef and is suffused with classic French flavours: garlic and thyme; cinnamon and saffron; Champagne and brandy.

Demuth's (☎ 01225-446059; 2 North Parade Passage; mains £11.50-16; ⊗ lunch & dinner) Having made Bath's vegetarians smile for more than 20 years, Demuth's still delights. Imaginative, superbly flavoured seasonal fare includes asparagus tart, spinach and chickpea curry, and a 'vitality salad'. If that sounds too healthy, finish off with the devilish apricot and calvados tart.

Bistro Papillon (☎ 01225-310064; 2 Margarets Bldgs; 2-course lunch £8.50, mains £11-15; ⊗ lunch & dinner Tue-Sat) Rustic Mediterranean dishes dominate at this Gallic bistro, with a thoroughly French ambience of checked tablecloths, sunbaked colours and clattering pans.

Top End

Olive Tree Restaurant (☎ 01225-447928; 4 Russell St; lunch/dinner mains £14/18; ⊗ lunch Tue-Sun, dinner Mon-Sun) Break out the glad-rags – the Queensberry Hotel's (p347) restaurant is a posh, pricey extravaganza of boutique British cuisine. You'll need a gastronomic glossary – expect galantine of woodpigeon and dark chocolate *panna cotta* with griottine cherries.

Hole in the Wall (☎ 01225-425242; 16 George St; mains £15-20; ⊗ lunch & dinner Mon-Sat) This long-standing favourite with Bath's gourmands takes you on a cook's tour through Anglo-French flavours – braised pork with Puy lentils, or Chew Magna lamb with potato fondant. The cellar dining room is half country restaurant, half urbane elegance.

DRINKING

Common Room (☎ 01225-425550; 2 Saville Row; ⊗ 6pm-2am Mon-Sat) Next door to an anarchic antiques shop, this tiny bar is a favourite with Bath's beautiful people. It's got all the designer credentials – exposed brickwork, blondwood floors, black leather sofas – and a more chilled atmosphere than the drinking dens on George St.

Revolution (☎ 01225-336168; George St; ⊗ 11am-midnight Mon-Sat, noon-10.30pm Sun) This is a swish Manhattan-style bar with the standard-issue blend of retro lamps and chrome fixtures, and a selection of cocktails served by the jug.

Raven (☎ 01225-425045; Queen St) Highly respected by real ale aficionados, this fine city drinking den commands a devoted following for its well-kept beer, traditional atmosphere and blues and jazz nights.

Porter (☎ 01225-424104; George St) It's somehow typical of Bath that it has a vegetarian pub; this spit-and-sawdust affair is run by the folk behind Moles nightclub and it's usually jammed to the rafters on Friday and Saturday nights.

Bath Tap (☎ 01225-404344; 19-20 St James Pde; ⊗ to 2am Thu-Sat) The classic pub hang-out for Bath's gay community, with a late weekend licence and a fun range of theme nights ranging from drag to cabaret.

Crystal Palace (☎ 01225-482666; Abbey Green) You couldn't ask for a nicer location for this popular pub, tucked away in the shadow of the abbey on a tree-shaded green. Local beers and a gorgeous patio garden make this a top spot for a quiet pint.

ENTERTAINMENT

Venue magazine (www.venue.co.uk; £1.50) has comprehensive listings of Bath's theatre, music and gig scenes. Pick up a copy at -any newsagency.

Nightclubs

Moles (☎ 01225-404445; www.moles.co.uk; 14 George St; admission £5-7; ⊗ 9pm-2am Mon-Thu, to 4am Fri & Sat,

WESSEX

8pm-12.30am Sun) The best venue in town goes from strength to strength, hosting a regular line-up of cutting-edge new acts and breaking bands, as well as occasional club nights.

Porter Cellar Bar (☎ 01225-424104; George St; ☼ 11.30am-midnight Mon-Thu, to 1am Fri & Sat, noon-11.30pm Sun) Just across the street and also run by the folk at Moles, this crowded, rustic venue hosts the bands who aren't yet big enough to play at the larger venue.

Delfter Krug ☎ 01225-443352; Sawclose; ☼ noon-late Mon-Sat) A massive, rambling pub opposite the theatre, equipped for all eventualities – upstairs club for housey tunes and DJs, downstairs bar for dedicated drinkers, and a street terrace for when the weather's fine.

Theatre & Cinemas

Theatre Royal (☎ 01225-448844; www.theatreroyal .org.uk; Sawclose) This high-class theatre features drama, opera and ballet in the main auditorium, experimental productions in the Ustinov Studio, and young people's theatre at 'the egg'.

Rondo Theatre (☎ 01225-463362; www.rondotheatre .co.uk; St Saviours Rd, Larkhall) This small rep theatre mixes up a varied program of comedy, music, dance and drama.

Little Theatre (☎ 0871 704 2061; St Michael's Pl) Bath's art-house cinema, screening fringe and foreign-language flicks.

GETTING THERE & AWAY

Bath's bus and train stations are having a multimillion-pound revamp. By mid-2009 the bus station should have left its temporary home of Avon St and be back alongside the train station on Dorchester St.

Bus

National Express coaches run to London (£21.25, 3½ hours, 10 daily) via Heathrow (£17.50, 2¾ hours), and to Bristol (45 minutes, every 30 minutes) for buses to the north. Services to most other cities require a change at Bristol or Heathrow.

Buses X39 and 339 (55 minutes, several per hour) and 332 (50 minutes, hourly, seven on Sunday) run to Bristol. Other useful services include buses 264 and 265 to Bradford-on-Avon (30 minutes, half-hourly), X71 and X72 to Devizes (one hour, hourly Monday to Saturday, six on Sunday) and 173 and 773 to Wells (1¼ hours, hourly Monday to Saturday, seven on Sunday).

Train

There are trains to London Paddington (£60.50, 1½ hours, half-hourly) and Cardiff (£14.90, 1¼ hours, four hourly), and several each hour to Bristol (£5.50, 11 minutes), from where you can connect with the main-line trains to northern England and the southwest.

Trains travel to Oxford approximately hourly (£17.20, 1½ hours, change at Didcot Parkway); Weymouth (£12.60, two hours) every two hours via Bradford-on-Avon (15 minutes) and Dorchester West (£12.30, 1¾ hours); and Portsmouth (£29, 2½ hours) hourly via Salisbury (£13, one hour).

GETTING AROUND

Bicycle

The 13-mile **Bristol & Bath Railway Path** (www .bristolbathrailwaypath.org.uk) runs along the disused track of the old Midland Railway, which was decommissioned in the late 1960s. At the time of going to press there weren't any bike-hire companies operating in Bath, so you could bring your own bike, or hire a bike in Bristol and start the ride there (for bike hire in Bristol, see p340).

Bus

Bus 18 runs from the bus station, High St and Great Pulteney St up Bathwick Hill past the YHA to the university every 10 minutes. Bus 4 runs every 20 minutes to Bathampton from the same places. A FirstDay pass for unlimited bus travel in the city costs £4/2.70 per adult/child.

Car & Motorcycle

Bath has serious traffic problems (especially at rush hour). **Park-and-ride** (☎ 01225-394041; ☼ 6.15am-7.30pm) services operate at Lansdown to the north, Newbridge to the west and Odd Down to the south (tickets return £2.50, 10 minutes to the centre, every 10 to 15 minutes).

AROUND BATH

Prior Park

Celebrated landscape gardener Capability Brown and satirical poet Alexander Pope both had a hand in the creation of **Prior Park** (NT; ☎ 01225-833422; adult/child £4.50/2.50; Ralph Allen Dr, Bath; ☼ 11am-5.30pm Wed-Mon Mar-Oct, 11am-dusk Sat & Sun Nov-Jan), an 18th-century ornamental garden dreamt up by local entrepreneur Ralph Allen. Cascading lakes, a Gothic temple and a famous Palladian bridge can be found around the garden's winding walks, and the sweeping views of the Bath skyline are something to behold.

Prior Park is 1 mile south of Bath's centre; it can be reached on foot or by bus 2 (every 10 minutes), as well as by the City Skyline tour (p346).

SOMERSET

Sleepy Somerset provides the type of pleasing pastoral wanderings that are reminiscent of a simpler, calmer, kinder world. Its landscape of knotted hedgerows, hummocks and russet-coloured fields is steeped in ancient rites and scattered with ancient sites. The cloistered calm of the cathedral city of Wells acts as a springboard for the spectacular limestone caves and gorges around Cheddar; hippie haven Glastonbury brings an ancient abbey, mud-drenched festival and masses of Arthurian myth; while the lyrical landscape of the Quantocks is one that inspired Romantic poet Samuel Taylor Coleridge. Whether you're into 'Olde Worlde' or New Age, this is a place to wander, ponder and drink in the sights at your own laid-back pace.

Orientation & Information

Somerset hugs the coast of the Bristol Channel. The Mendip Hills (the Mendips) follow a line below Bristol, just north of Wells and Cheddar, while the Quantock Hills (the Quantocks) sit just east of Exmoor National Park (p361). Most places of interest are in northern Somerset. Bath makes a good base in the east; Glastonbury and Wells are more-central options.

Individual towns have tourist offices; the **Somerset Visitor Centre** (☎ 01934-750833; www.visit somerset.co.uk; Sedgemoor Services M5 South, Axbridge; ☒ 9.15am-5pm daily Easter-Oct, Mon-Fri Nov-Easter) provides general information.

Getting Around

Most buses in Somerset are operated by **First** (☎ 0845 606 4446; www.firstgroup.com), supplemented by a few smaller operators. For timetables and general travel information contact **Traveline South West** (☎ 0871 200 22 33; www.travelinesw.com).

Area timetables are available at bus stations and tourist offices.

Key train services link Bath, Bristol, Bridgwater, Taunton and Weston-Super-Mare. The M5 heads south past Bristol, to Bridgwater and Taunton, with the A39 leading west across the Quantocks to Exmoor.

WELLS
pop 10,406

With Wells, small is beautiful. This tiny, picturesque metropolis is England's smallest city, and only qualifies for the 'city' title thanks to a magnificent medieval cathedral, which sits in the centre beside the grand Bishop's Palace. Wells has been the main seat of ecclesiastical power in this part of Britain since the 12th century, and is still the official residence of the Bishop of Bath and Wells. Medieval buildings and cobbled streets radiate out from the cathedral green to a marketplace that has been the bustling heart of Wells for some nine centuries (Wednesday and Saturday are market days). A quiet provincial city, Wells' excellent restaurants and busy shops help make it a good launching pad for exploring the Mendips and northern Somerset.

Information

Tourist office (☎ 01749-672552; www.wellstourism .com; Market Pl; ☒ 9.30am-5.30pm Mon-Sat, 10am-4pm Sun Easter-Oct, 10am-4pm Mon-Sat Nov-Easter) Stocks the *Wells City Trail* leaflet (30p) and sells discount tickets to the nearby attractions of Wookey Hole and Cheddar Gorge.
Wells Laundrette (☎ 01458-830409; 39 St Cuthbert St; ☒ 8am-8pm) Opposite St Cuthbert's Church.

Sights
WELLS CATHEDRAL

Set in a marvellous medieval close, the **Cathedral Church of St Andrew** (☎ 01749-674483; www .wellscathedral.org.uk; Chain Gate, Cathedral Green; requested donation adult/child £5.50/2.50; ☒ 7am-7pm Apr-Sep, 7am-dusk Oct-Mar) was built in stages between 1180 and 1508. The building incorporates several Gothic styles, but its most famous asset is the wonderful **west front**, an immense sculpture gallery decorated with more than 300 figures, built in the 13th century and restored to its original splendour in 1986. The facade would once have been painted in vivid colours, but has long since reverted to its original sandy hue. Apart from the figure of Christ, installed in 1985 in the uppermost niche, all the figures are original.

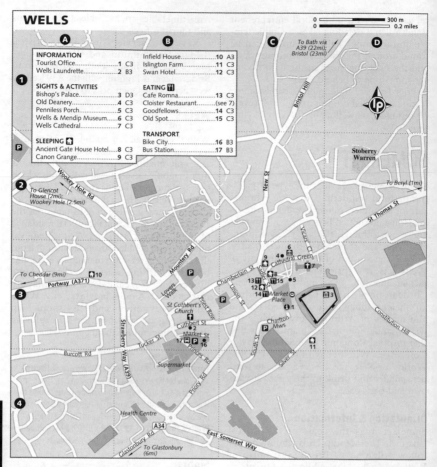

WELLS

| 0 | 300 m |
| 0 | 0.2 miles |

INFORMATION
| Tourist Office | 1 | C3 |
| Wells Laundrette | 2 | B3 |

SIGHTS & ACTIVITIES
Bishop's Palace	3	D3
Old Deanery	4	C3
Penniless Porch	5	C3
Wells & Mendip Museum	6	C3
Wells Cathedral	7	C3

SLEEPING
Ancient Gate House Hotel	8	C3
Canon Grange	9	C3
Infield House	10	A3
Islington Farm	11	C3
Swan Hotel	12	C3

EATING
Cafe Romna	13	C3
Cloister Restaurant	(see 7)
Goodfellows	14	C3
Old Spot	15	C3

TRANSPORT
| Bike City | 16 | B3 |
| Bus Station | 17 | B3 |

To Bath via A39 (22mi); Bristol (23mi)

Stoberry Warren

To Beryl (1mi)

To Glencot House (2mi); Wookey Hole (2.5mi)

To Cheddar (9mi)

Portway (A371)

St Cuthbert's Church

Market Place

To Glastonbury (6mi)

East Somerset Way

Health Centre

Supermarket

WESSEX

Inside, the most striking feature is the pair of **scissor arches** that separate the nave from the choir, designed to counter the subsidence of the central tower. High up in the north transept you'll come across a wonderful **mechanical clock** dating from 1392 – the second-oldest surviving in England after the one at Salisbury Cathedral (p316). The clock shows the position of the planets and the phases of the moon.

Other highlights are the elegant **Lady chapel** (1326) at the eastern end and the seven **effigies** of Anglo-Saxon bishops ringing the choir. The 15th-century **chained library** houses books and manuscripts dating back to 1472. It's only open at certain times during the year or by prior arrangement.

From the north transept follow the worn steps to the glorious **Chapter House** (1306), with its delicate ceiling ribs sprouting like a palm from a central column. Externally, look out for the **Chain Bridge** built from the northern side of the cathedral to Vicars' Close to enable clerics to reach the cathedral without getting their robes wet. The **cloisters** on the southern side surround a pretty courtyard.

Guided tours (Mon-Sat) of the cathedral are free, and usually take place every hour. Regular **concerts** (01749-672773) and cathedral choir **recitals** (01749-674483) are held here throughout the year. You need to buy a permit (£3) from the cathedral shop to take pictures. As you wander, keep an eye out for the cathedral cat, a ginger tabby called Louis.

CATHEDRAL CLOSE

Wells Cathedral forms the centrepiece of a cluster of ecclesiastical buildings dating back to (and even earlier than) the Middle Ages. Facing the west front, on the left are the 15th-century **Old Deanery** and the **Wells & Mendip Museum** (☎ 01749-673477; 8 Cathedral Green; www.wellsmuseum.org.uk; adult/child £3/1; ☾ 10am-5.30pm Easter-Oct, 11am-4pm Wed-Mon Nov-Easter), with exhibits on local life, cathedral architecture and the infamous Witch of Wookey Hole.

Further along, **Vicars' Close** is a stunning cobbled street of uniform houses dating back to the 14th century, with a chapel at the end; members of the cathedral choir still live here. It is thought to be the oldest complete medieval street in Europe. Passing under the Chain Bridge, inspect the outside of the Lady chapel and a lovely medieval house called the Rib, before emerging at a main road called the Liberty.

Penniless Porch, a corner gate leading onto Market Sq and built by Bishop Bekynton around 1450, is so-called because beggars asked for alms here.

BISHOP'S PALACE

Beyond the cathedral, the moated 13th-century **Bishop's Palace** (☎ 01749-678691; www.bishopspalacewells.co.uk; adult/child £1.10; ☾ 10.30am-6pm Sun-Fri, to 2pm Sat Jan-Oct, 10.30am-3.30pm Wed-Sun Nov & Dec) is a real delight. Purportedly the oldest inhabited building in England, ringed by water and surrounded by a huge fortified wall, the palace complex contains several fine Italian Gothic state rooms, an imposing Great Hall and beautiful tree-shaded gardens. The natural wells that gave the city its name bubble up in the palace's grounds, feeding the moat and the fountain in the market square. The swans in the moat have been trained to ring a bell outside one of the windows when they want to be fed.

Sleeping

Islington Farm (☎ 01749-673445; www.islingtonfarmatwells.co.uk; Silver St; s/d £50/65; P) Set beside a rushing stream, this ivy-clad farmhouse is two minutes' walk south of the city centre and yet still has idyllic rural views. Snug rooms have all the beams, fireplaces and old-world charm you could want. A self-catering cottage in the old stables sleeps four (£650 per week).

our pick Beryl (☎ 01749-678738; www.beryl-wells.co.uk; Hawkers Lane; s £65-75, d £85-120; P) A mile from the city centre, this tree-shaded, gabled Victorian mansion is set in 5 hectares of private parkland and boasts the kind of luxurious accommodation you'd normally find at double (or triple) the price. The richly furnished rooms have bags of country character, with swags, frills and elegant drapes and a smattering of veneered antiques. Wake up to views of rolling countryside, elegant lawns or Wells Cathedral, then take a dip in the heated outdoor swimming pool.

Ancient Gate House Hotel (☎ 01749-672029; www.ancientgatehouse.co.uk; Sadler St; s £76, d £91-105; P) Wildly wonky walls, a stone spiral staircase and plenty of beams make this 15th-century inn a characterful place to rest your head. Firmly traditional furnishings add to the atmosphere, while a handful of rooms look out directly onto the Cathedral.

Swan Hotel (☎ 01749-836300; www.swanhotelwells.co.uk; Sadler St; s £82-112, d £104-180; P) Antique furnishings and quilted fabrics help you sink into the history of this 600-year-old hotel, as do the quirky antiques and the padded armchairs in the bedrooms. Winter sees log fires blazing in the studylike lounges; in summer the red-brick walled garden is perfect for lazy, sunny afternoons.

Also recommended:

Infield House (☎ 01749-670989; www.infieldhouse.co.uk; 36 Portway; s/d £40/60; P) Simple, spacious rooms in a Victorian B&B.

Canon Grange (☎ 01749-671800; www.canongrange.co.uk; Cathedral Green; d £70; P) Old-fashioned B&B in a 15th-century house overlooking Cathedral Green.

Eating

Cloister Restaurant (☎ 01749-676543; Wells Cathedral, Cathedral Green; mains £6; ☾ 10am-5pm Mon-Sat, 1-5pm Sun Mar-Oct, 10am-5pm Mon-Sat Nov-Feb) Tucked away under ancient stone arches inside the cathedral's west cloister, this atmospheric bistro dishes up hearty, homemade soul food: rich risottos, exquisite quiches and wicked cakes.

Cafe Romna (☎ 01749-670240; 13 Sadler St; mains £10-15; ☾ lunch & dinner Mon-Sat) A stylish Bangladeshi fusion restaurant featuring futuristic chairs, low lighting and an unusual mix of menu options. Try the *zingha bhajee* (Bangladeshi vegetable curry) or the *chingri palack* (tiger prawns cooked with garlic and spinach).

Goodfellows (☎ 01749-673866; 5 Sadler St; cafe mains £7, restaurant mains £13-17; ☾ cafe lunch Mon & Tue, lunch & dinner Wed-Sat, restaurant lunch Mon, lunch & dinner Tue-Sat) This sophisticated eatery can satisfy

WESSEX

pretty much any hunger pang you have: the cafe rustles up treats like warm goats' cheese bruschetta; the in-store bakery proves there is an art to piling fresh fruit and custard onto pastry cases; and the formal dining room serves up a classy blend of Somerset produce and French-inspired cuisine.

Old Spot (☎ 01749-689099; 12 Sadler St; 2/3 courses £18.50/21.50; ☺ lunch Wed-Sun, dinner Tue-Sat) Worn floorboards, a tiled and mirrored bar and very comfy chairs set the scene at this superstylish restaurant. The menu is imaginative, too: flavour favourites include black-pudding salad, cod with garlic purée, and warm apple and almond pud.

Getting There & Around

The bus station is south of Cuthbert St, on Princes Rd. National Express runs direct to London once a day (£19, 4½ hours), although it's usually more convenient to travel to Bristol by local bus, and from there catch a more frequent coach to London.

Bus 173 runs from Bath to Wells (1¼ hours, hourly, seven on Sunday). Bus 376 travels to Wells from Bristol (one hour, hourly) before continuing on to Glastonbury (15 minutes) and Street (25 minutes). Bus 29 travels to Taunton (1¼ hours, seven daily Monday to Friday, five or six on weekends) via Glastonbury. Bus 126 runs to Cheddar (25 minutes) hourly Monday to Saturday and every two hours on Sunday. There's no train station in Wells.

Bike City (☎ 01749-671711; 31 Market St; ☺ 9am-5.30pm Mon-Thu, to 5pm Fri & Sat) charges £15 per day for bike hire.

WOOKEY HOLE

On the southern edge of the Mendips, the River Axe has carved out a series of deep caverns collectively known as **Wookey Hole**

(☎ 01749-672243; www.wookey.co.uk; adult/child/family £15/10/45; ☺ 10am-5pm Apr-Oct, 10.30am-4pm Nov-Mar). The caves are littered with dramatic natural features, including a subterranean lake and some fascinating stalagmites and stalactites (one of which is supposedly the legendary Witch of Wookey Hole, who was turned to stone by a local priest). The caves were inhabited by prehistoric people for some 50,000 years, but these days the deep pools and underground rivers are more often frequented by cave divers – the deepest subterranean dive ever recorded in Britain was made here in September 2004, when divers reached a depth of more than 45m.

Admission to the caves is by guided tour. The rest of the complex is taken up by an assortment of child-friendly attractions including mirror mazes, an Edwardian penny arcade and a valley stuffed with 20 giant plastic dinosaurs. You can also have a go at making your own sheet of paper in the Victorian paper-mill. Some prehistoric finds are on show at the on-site museum, but many are on display at the Wells & Mendip Museum (p353).

Bus 670 runs from Wells (10 minutes, nine daily, four on Sunday).

CHEDDAR GORGE

If Wookey Hole is a little too touristy for your tastes, then you'd better brace yourself for **Cheddar Gorge Caves** (☎ 01934-742343; www.cheddarcaves.co.uk; Explorer Ticket adult/child £15/9.50; ☺ 10am-5.30pm Jul & Aug, 10.30am-5pm Sep-Jun), a spectacular series of limestone caverns that's always jammed with visitors throughout the summer months.

Despite the tourist throng, the natural wonders on display are still genuinely impressive. Although the network of caves extends deep into the surrounding rock, only a few

---

DETOUR: GLENCOT HOUSE

A breathtaking 19th-century mansion built in opulent Jacobean style, **Glencot House** (☎ 01749-677160; www.glencothouse.co.uk; Wookey Hole; d £165-230, r with 4-poster-bed £245-260; **P**)) is a place to indulge your senses and live out your lord-of-the-manor fantasies. It's surrounded by 7 hectares of private woods and riverside grounds, and even has its own cricket pitch. Walnut panelling, carved ceilings and dazzling chandeliers decorate the public rooms, while the bedrooms drip with flowing furnishings, swags and drapes and are peppered with chaise longues, country prints and antique dressers. Downstairs there's a billiard room, fire-lit drawing room, minicinema, sauna and plunge pool, as well as a wood-beamed dining hall that could have fallen straight from the pages of *The Remains of the Day*.

A CHEESY STORY

As well as its spectacular cave system, Cheddar is also famous as the spiritual home of the nation's favourite cheese. Cheddar's strong, crumbly, tangy cheese is the essential ingredient in any self-respecting ploughman's sandwich, and has been produced in the area since at least the 12th century; Henry II boldly proclaimed cheddar to be 'the best cheese in Britain', and the king's accounts from 1170 record that he purchased 10,240lbs (around 4644kg) of the stuff. In the days before refrigeration, the Cheddar caves made the ideal cool store for the cheese, with a constant temperature of around 7°C. However, the powerful smell attracted rats and the practice was eventually abandoned.

These days most cheddar cheese is made far from the village, but if you're interested in seeing how the genuine article is made, head for the **Cheddar Gorge Cheese Company** (☎ 01934-742810; www.cheddargorgecheeseco.co.uk; adult £1.95, 2 accompanying children free; ☷ 10am-4pm). You can take a guided tour of the factory from Easter to October, and pick up some tangy, whiffy souvenirs at the on-site shop.

are open to the public. The most impressive are Cox's Cave and Gough's Cave, both decorated by an amazing gallery of stalactites and stalagmites, and subtly lit to bring out the spectrum of colours in the limestone rock. After the end of the last ice age, the caves were inhabited by prehistoric people; a 9000-year-old skeleton (imaginatively named 'Cheddar Man') was discovered here in 1903, and genetic tests have revealed that some of his descendants are still living in the surrounding area.

Outside the caves, the 274 steps of **Jacob's Ladder** lead up to an impressive panorama of the surrounding countryside; on a clear day you can see all the way to Glastonbury Tor and Exmoor.

Nearby, a signposted 3-mile-round walk follows the cliffs along the most spectacular parts of **Cheddar Gorge**, which cuts a mile-long swathe through the southern side of the Mendip Hills. At some points the cliff walls tower 138m above the winding narrow road that lies at its base. Most visitors only explore the first section of the path, and you can usually escape the crowds by venturing further up the valley.

The **tourist office** (☎ 01934-744071; cheddar.tic@ sedgemoor.gov.uk; ☷ 10am-5pm Easter-Sep, 10.30am-4.30pm Oct, 11am-4pm Sun only Nov-Easter) is at the southern end of the gorge, and has some useful information on local walks and caving trips.

Look out for the **Big Green Gathering** (☎ 01458-834699; www.big-green-gathering.com) in late July and early August, when some 20,000 eco-aware campers descend on the fields near Cheddar for a festival of music, performance, therapies and good causes.

A mile southwest of the caves on the western side of Cheddar village is the **Cheddar YHA** (☎ 0845 371 9730; www.yha.org.uk; Hillfield; dm £14), set in an old stone house.

Bus 126 runs to Wells (25 minutes) hourly Monday to Saturday and every two hours on Sunday.

MENDIP HILLS

The Mendip Hills are a picturesque sequence of limestone ridges stretching from the coast near Weston-Super-Mare to Frome in eastern Somerset. Their highest point is Black Down (326m) to the northwest – but because they rise sharply, there are panoramic views towards Exmoor and across northwest Wiltshire.

Historically, the area has seen its share of action, and neolithic earthworks, Bronze Age barrows and Iron Age forts can be found scattered over the hills. More recently, lead and coal mining have left their mark, with remains of mines dotting the area around Radstock and Midsomer Norton. Quarrying for stone is an important (and controversial) industry to this day.

Until the Middle Ages, large tracts of land lay beneath swampy meadows, and the remaining wetlands provide an important habitat for wildlife and flora. The marshland hid relics, too, including a lake village that was excavated at the turn of the 20th century (see Lake Village Museum, p357).

The landscape is peppered with pretty hamlets and isolated pubs that once served the thirsty miners. Mendip villages are also home to some delightful timbered houses, and several have fine Perpendicular church towers.

GOING UNDERGROUND

If a visit to the Cheddar caves piques an interest in the strange subterranean world beneath the gorge, then you might like to take a **caving trip** to explore further. **Rocksport** (☎ 01934-742343; caves@visitc heddar.co.uk) offers 1½-hour abseiling and climbing trips around the gorge (£16), as well as adventurous subterranean trips into the more-remote caverns (from £20). Needless to say, you'll get cold, wet and muddy, and you'll need to be up to the physical challenges of underground caving. If you're even vaguely claustrophobic, don't even think about it.

The one at **Chewton Mendip** (off the A37 between Bristol and Wells) is especially striking and has an impressive medieval churchyard cross. Further west, the village of **Priddy**, the highest village in the Mendips, has a massive sheep fair on the green in mid-August, while the village of **Compton Martin** has a Norman church with a 15th-century tower. A mile to the east, **West Harptree** is prettier, with two 17th-century former manor houses. Near **East Harptree** are the remains of the Norman castle of Richmond. Local tourist offices stock leaflets with information on walking and cycling in the area.

The A371 skirts the southern side of the Mendip Hills, and any of the towns along it make good touring bases, though Wells has the best range of facilities.

GLASTONBURY

pop 8429

Realign those chakras and open that third eye – you've just touched down in England's hippie central. A bohemian haven and centre for New Age culture since the days of the Summer of Love, Glastonbury is still a favourite hang-out for festival-goers, mystics and counter-cultural types of all descriptions. Crammed with goddess temples, trance workshops and Beltane ceremonies, this is the place to answer the call of the shaman, hear the healing drum and possibly even take part in a mystical singing-bowl experience. But look past the tie-dye and through the crystals, and you'll find Glastonbury is also much more. The town claims to be the birthplace of Christianity in England, and boasts some

absorbing museums as well as fabulous places to stay and eat (including a lovely old pub where there isn't a joss stick in sight).

Information

The **tourist office** (☎ 01458-832954; www.glastonburytic .co.uk; The Tribunal, 9 High St; ☺ 10am-5pm Apr-Sep, to 4pm Oct-Mar) stocks maps and accommodation lists, and sells leaflets describing local walks and the *Glastonbury Millennium Trail* (60p).

Sights

GLASTONBURY ABBEY

Legend has it that Joseph of Arimathea, greatuncle of Jesus, owned mines in this area and returned here with the Holy Grail (the chalice from the Last Supper) after the death of Christ. Joseph supposedly founded England's first church on the site, now occupied by the ruined **abbey** (☎ 01458-832267; www.glastonbury abbey.com; Magdalene St; adult/child £5/3; ☺ 9.30am-6pm or dusk Sep-May, from 9am Jun-Aug), but the earliest proven Christian connection dates from the 7th century, when King Ine gave a charter to a monastery in Glastonbury. In 1184 the church was destroyed by fire and reconstruction began in the reign of Henry II.

In 1191, monks claimed to have had visions confirming hints in old manuscripts that the 6th-century warrior-king Arthur and his wife Guinevere were buried in the abbey grounds. Excavations uncovered a tomb containing a skeletal couple, who were reinterred in front of the high altar of the new church in 1278. The tomb survived until 1539, when Henry VIII dissolved the monasteries and had the last abbot hung, drawn and quartered on the tor.

The remaining ruins at Glastonbury mainly date from the church that was built after the 1184 fire. It's still possible to make out some of the nave walls, the ruins of the St Mary's chapel, and the remains of the crossing arches, which may have been scissor-shaped, like those in Wells Cathedral (p351). The site of the supposed tomb of Arthur and Guinevere is marked in the grass. The grounds also contain a small museum, cider orchard and herb garden, as well as the **Holy Thorn** tree, which supposedly sprung from Joseph's staff and mysteriously blooms twice a year, at Christmas and Easter.

GLASTONBURY TOR

The iconic hump of Glastonbury Tor is crowned by a ruined tower and rears steeply

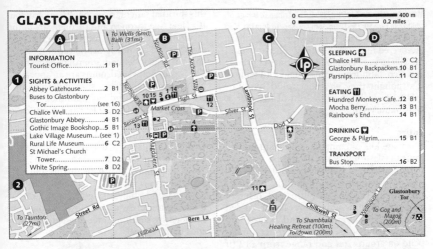

from the Somerset flatlands. This 160m-high grassy mound on the edge of town provides both glorious views over the surrounding countryside, and a focal point for a bewildering array of myths. According to some it's the home of a faery king, while an old Celtic legend identifies it as the stronghold of Gwyn ap Nudd (ruler of Annwyn, the Underworld) – but the most famous legend identifies the tor as the mythic Isle of Avalon, where King Arthur was taken after being mortally wounded in battle by his nephew Mordred, and where Britain's 'once and future king' sleeps until his country calls again.

Whatever the truth of the legends, the tor has been a site of pilgrimage for many years, and was once topped by the medieval church of **St Michael**, although today only the tower remains. On the way up to the tor look out for **Gog** and **Magog**, two gnarled oak trees believed to be the last remains of an ancient processional avenue.

It takes 45 minutes to walk up and down the tor. Parking is not permitted nearby, but the **Tor Bus** (adult/child £2.50/1.50) leaves from Dunstan's car park near the abbey. The bus runs every 30 minutes from 10am to 7.30pm from April to September, and from 10am to 3.30pm from October to March. It also stops at Chalice Well and the Rural Life Museum.

CHALICE WELL & GARDENS
Shaded by knotted yew trees and surrounded by peaceful paths, the **Chalice Well & Gardens** (☎ 01458 831154; www.chalicewell.org.uk; Chilkwell St; adult/child £3.25/2.70; ☺ 10am-5.30pm Apr-Oct, to 4pm Nov-Mar) have been sites of pilgrimage since the days of the Celts. The iron-red waters from the 800-year-old well are rumoured to have healing properties, good for everything from eczema to smelly feet; some legends also identify the well as the hiding place of the Holy Grail. You can drink the water from a lion's-head spout, or rest your feet in basins surrounded by flowers.

The Chalice Well is also known as the 'Red Spring' or 'Blood Spring'; its sister, **White Spring**, surfaces across Wellhouse Lane. Spigots from both springs empty into the street, where there's often a queue to fill containers.

RURAL LIFE MUSEUM
Somerset's agricultural heritage is explored at the **Rural Life Museum** (☎ 01458-831197; Abbey Farm, Chilkwell St; admission free; ☺ 10am-5pm Tue-Fri, 2-6pm Sat & Sun Apr-Oct, 10am-5pm Tue-Sat Nov-Mar), which contains a varied collection of artefacts relating to traditional trades such as willow growing, peat digging, cider making and cheese making. There are often live displays of local skills, so if you fancy trying your hand at beekeeping, lace making and spinning, this is the place to do it. The late-14th-century tithe barn has fine carvings on the gables and porch, and an impressive timber roof; it now houses a collection of vintage agricultural machinery.

LAKE VILLAGE MUSEUM
Upstairs from Glastonbury's tourist office, in the medieval courthouse, the **Lake Village**

WESSEX

Museum (EH; ☎ 01458-832954; The Tribunal, 9 High St; adult/child £2/1.50; ☺ 10am-5pm Apr-Sep, to 4pm Oct-Mar) displays finds from a prehistoric bog village discovered in nearby Godney. The houses in the village were clustered in about six groups and were built from reeds, hazel and willow. It's thought they were occupied by summer traders who lived the rest of the year at Glastonbury Tor.

Tours

There are lots of companies offering guided tours of Glastonbury's main sights.

Mystical Tours of Glastonbury (☎ 01458-831453; www.gothicimagetours.co.uk; 7 High St) is based at the Gothic Image bookshop and offers a range of tours including three-hour guided trips to Wearyall Hill, Gog and Magog and Glastonbury Tor itself. Prices per person depend on group sizes and range from £12 (if there are more than four people) to £70. It also runs day tours to Stonehenge and Avebury (£140 per person).

Sleeping

If you're a fan of wind chimes, organic brekkies and homemade muesli, then Glastonbury's B&Bs won't disappoint.

Glastonbury Backpackers (☎ 01458-833353; www.glastonburybackpackers.com; 4 Market Pl; dm/tw/d £14/35/40; P 🖳) A happy, hippie hang-out, Glastonbury's hostel is a friendly, welcoming affair, with doubles and dorms decked out jazzy colours. There's a TV lounge, kitchen and cafe-bar downstairs.

Tordown (☎ 01458-832287; www.tordown.com; 5 Ashwell Lane; s £36-40, d £60-64; P) As well as a peaceful sleep and a massive vegie breakfast, this B&B also offers a range of treatments, including higher-self sessions and rainbow massage. The downstairs rooms are a tad fuddy-duddy; the two upstairs are smarter and have grandstand views over the Vale of Avalon.

Parsnips (☎ 01458-835599; www.parsnips-glastonbury .co.uk; 99 Bere Lane; s/d £50/65; P 🖳) Swimming against the tie-dye and crystal tide, this stylish B&B has opted instead for a fresh design topped with gingham flourishes and plumpedup quilts. There's a comfy guest lounge, a bright conservatory and a refreshing lack of spiritual guidance.

Shambhala Healing Retreat (☎ 01458-831797; www.shambhala.co.uk; Coursing Batch; s £48-66, d £76-112) If you're not in touch with your inner goddess,

this spiritual sanctuary probably isn't for you. It's New Age through and through, from the meditation tent on the top floor to the reiki massage and colonic hydrotherapy on offer – you can even meet your guardian angel here. The 'clear energy' bedrooms are an appealing blend of airy fabric and snazzy designs in a choice of Tibetan and Egyptian themes,

our pick Chalice Hill (☎ 01458-830828; www.chalice hill.co.uk; Dod Lane; s/d £70/90; P) This luxurious, utterly delightful B&B is aet in a rambling Georgian house. It's dripping with quirky charm – stripped wooden floors combine with a sweeping staircase, ornate mirrors and stylish modern art. The effect is deeply elegant, but also wonderfully easy-going. The fact that it's a five-minute walk into town, and is surrounded by soothing, tree-shaded grounds, adds to the appeal.

Eating & Drinking

Rainbow's End (☎ 01458-833896; 17A High St; mains £4-7; ☺ 10am-4pm) The classic Glastonbury wholefood cafe, with ranks of potted plants and wooden tables and a rotating menu of organic offerings such as vegie moussaka, sweet-potato flan and fiery chilli. The carrot cake is divine.

Mocha Berry (☎ 01458-832149; 14 Market Pl; mains £5-8; ☺ Sun-Wed) This ever-popular cafe is the top spot in Glastonbury for a frothy latte, a fresh milkshake or a stack of breakfast pancakes.

Hundred Monkeys Cafe (☎ 01458-833386; 52 High St; mains £5-10; ☺ 10am-6pm Mon-Wed, to 9pm Thu-Sat, to 3.30pm Sun) A refreshingly nonalternative option with leather sofas, pine tables and a huge blackboard listing fresh pastas, salads and mains. If you've a spare half-hour ask about the origin of the name – the original 100th monkey.

George & Pilgrim (☎ 01458-831146; 1 High St; mains £7-10; ☺ lunch daily, dinner Mon-Sat) The creaking timbers and stone arches in this 15th-century inn are evidence that Glastonbury's New Age incarnation is a mere blip on a very ancient timeline. The snug interior is home to a warm welcome, an excellent pint and some above-average pub grub – try the homemade beef and onion burger.

Getting There & Away

There's one early-morning National Express service to Bath (£6.10, 1¼ hours), which goes on to London (£19, 4¼ hours).

THE OTHER GLASTONBURY

To many people, the village of Glastonbury is synonymous with the **Glastonbury Festival of Contemporary Performing Arts** (www.glastonburyfestivals.co.uk), an often mud-soaked extravaganza of music, street theatre, dance, cabaret, carnival, ecology, spirituality and general all-round weirdness that's been held on and off on farmland near Glastonbury for well over 30 years. The first event was held in 1970, when young dairy farmer Michael Eavis invited some bands to play on makeshift stages in his field; 30 years later, the festival has become the longest-running performing-arts festival in the world, attracting some of the world's biggest acts and crowds of more than 120,000 festival-goers. Glastonbury is more a way of life than a music festival, and it's a rite of passage for every self-respecting British teenager – ask about the toilets to anyone who's been to the festival, and prepare to hear some horror stories.

Bus 29 travels to Glastonbury from Taunton (50 minutes, five to seven daily). Bus 376 travels to Wells (30 minutes, hourly) and Bristol (1¼ hours), and also to Street (15 minutes). Bus 377 goes to Yeovil, while bus 375 heads to Bridgwater (both one hour, hourly Monday to Saturday, every two hours Sunday).

There is no train station in Glastonbury.

QUANTOCK HILLS

The curving, 12-mile ridge of the Quantocks forms a romantic, lyrical landscape of rolling red sandstone hills. Unsurprisingly, poet Samuel Taylor Coleridge was partial to roaming around the hills during his six-year sojourn in the village of Nether Stowey. The hills are still popular with walkers today – linking the Vale of Taunton Deane with the Somerset coast, they're only 384m at their highest point. The area is designated an AONB (Area of Outstanding Natural Beauty), and some of the most attractive country is owned by the National Trust – including the Beacon and Bicknoller Hills, which offer views of the Bristol Channel and Exmoor to the northwest.

The **AONB Service** (☎ 01823-451884; www.quantockhills.com; ⏰ 9am-5pm Mon-Fri) runs an excellent program of guided walks and is based at **Fyne Court** (NT; ☎ 01823-652400; admission free; ⏰ 9am-6pm or dusk), a National Trust nature reserve at Broomfield, in the south Quantocks. The **tourist office** (☎ 01278-436438; King Sq; ⏰ 9am-5pm Mon-Fri) in Bridgwater can also advise about the area. Mountain-biking is very popular in the Quantocks.

Nether Stowey & Holford

The pretty village of Nether Stowey is best known for its association with Coleridge, who moved to the village in 1796 with his wife Sara

and son Hartley. They lived at **Coleridge Cottage** (NT; ☎ 01278-732662; adult/child £3.90/1.90; ⏰ 2-5pm Thu-Sun Apr-Sep), where the poet composed some of his great early work, including *The Rime of the Ancient Mariner*. Wordsworth and his sister Dorothy spent 1797 at nearby Alfoxden House in **Holford**; during that year they all worked on the poems for *Lyrical Ballads* (1798), a short booklet that heralded the beginning of the British Romantic movement.

The area has a great variety of places to sleep. All wobbly walls and low lintels, **Stowey Brooke House** (☎ 01278-733356; www.stoweybrookehouse.co.uk; 18 Castle St, Nether Stowey; s £40, d £55-65) manages to combine old-world character with new-fangled comfort. An array of ancient beams sits above plump furnishings, brass bedsteads and free-standing baths, while the guest lounge has a huge inglenook fireplace to relax beside.

For even more luxury, head half a mile out of Nether Stowey to **Castle of Comfort** (☎ 01278-741264; www.castle-of-comfort.co.uk; s £42-92, d £104-142; ℗), a Grade II-listed manor set in rolling fields on the northern slopes of the Quantock Hills.

Tucked away in a wooded valley, **Combe House** (☎ 01278-741382; www.combehouse.co.uk; Holford Combe; s £65-95, d £95-135; ℗) is one of the most famous pamper pads in the Quantocks. The best rooms boast huge four-poster beds and views over the private wooded gardens; there's also a gorgeous indoor pool, a private sauna and a fine country restaurant (mains £15.50 to £24.50) finished in gleaming Cornish oak. You can even play croquet on the lawn.

Crowcombe

One of the prettiest Quantock villages, Crowcombe is graced with a cluster of cottages made of stone and cob (a mixture of mud and

WESSEX

straw), many with thatched roofs. The ancient **Church of the Holy Ghost** has wonderful carved 16th-century bench ends with surprisingly pagan themes (the Green Man is common). Part of its spire still stands in the churchyard where it fell when lightning struck in 1725.

Crowcombe is a little short on places to stay and eat – the best option is the village inn, the **Carew Arms** (☎ 01984-618631; www.thecarewarms. co.uk; s £44-54, d £64-84; **P**)), where the six upstairs bedrooms sport snazzy, polka-dot throws. The bar is all ancient atmosphere (expect huge fireplaces, high-backed wooden benches and antlers on the walls), while the chefs rustle up great pub grub (mains £11 to £16) including a tasty steak with whisky and Stilton sauce.

There's also a good campsite, the **Quantock Orchard Caravan Park** (☎ 01984-618618; www.quantock orchard.co.uk; Flaxpool; sites per tent or caravan £11-20).

Getting There & Away

Bus services around the Quantocks can be very limited. Bus 14 travels from Bridgwater to Nether Stowey (45 minutes, four daily Monday to Saturday, six on Sunday). Buses 23A and 23B travel from Taunton to Nether Stowey (30 minutes, two to three daily Monday to Friday) en route to Bridgwater.

Half-hourly bus 28 runs from Taunton to Minehead but only stops at Crowcombe (30 minutes) once daily, Monday to Saturday.

TAUNTON
pop 58,241

There's not much to draw visitors to Somerset's main county town and administrative capital, but it's a handy transport hub and is the main gateway to the Quantocks.

The **tourist office** (☎ 01823-336344; www.heartof somerset.com; Paul St; ⏰ 9.30am-5pm Mon-Sat) is in the library and has some useful leaflets on exploring the Quantocks and northern Somerset.

One of Taunton's most famous landmarks is the **Church of St Mary Magdalene** (⏰ 10am-4pm Mon-Fri, to 1pm Sat), with its 50m-high tower carved from red Quantock rock. The striking 12th-century **Taunton Castle**, on Taunton Green, is home to the **Somerset County Museum**, which is due to reopen in 2010, after a two year refit.

Sleeping

Blorenge House (☎ 01823-283005; www.blorengehouse .co.uk; 57 Staple Grove Rd; s £44-55, d £68-80; **P**)) An unusual B&B – this enormous Victorian villa

has 24 bedrooms and a heated outdoor pool. The decor is a blast from the past, featuring pine furniture, quilted bedspreads and a scattering of antiques. The cheaper rooms share bathrooms.

Salisbury House Hotel (☎ 01823-272083; 14 Billetfield; s/d from £58/66; **P**)) Probably the most comfortable place to stay in town, this large detached town house near Vivary Park has traces of country-club atmosphere: large heritage-style bedrooms, pocket-sprung beds and snug sitting areas.

Getting There & Away

National Express coaches run to London (£16.70, four hours, six daily), Bristol (£6.60, 1½ hours, four daily) and Exeter (£6.10, one hour, six daily).

Bus 28 (hourly Monday to Saturday, nine on Sunday) crosses the Quantocks to Minehead (1¼ hours). Bus 29 travels to Wells (1¼ hours, seven daily Monday to Friday, five or six on weekends) via Glastonbury (one hour).

Trains run to London (£39.50, two hours, every one to two hours), to Exeter (£9, 30 minutes, half-hourly) and to Plymouth (£23, 1½ hours, half-hourly).

AROUND TAUNTON
Montacute House

Elizabethan **Montacute House** (NT; ☎ 01935-823289; house & garden adult/child £8.50/4, garden only £5.10/2.50; ⏰ house 11am-5pm Wed-Mon mid-Mar–Oct, garden 11am-6pm Wed-Mon mid-Mar–Oct, 11am-4pm Wed-Sun Nov–mid-Mar) was built in the 1590s for Sir Edward Phelips, a Speaker of the House of Commons, and contains some of the finest 16th- and 17th-century interiors in the country. The house is particularly renowned for its remarkable plasterwork, fine chimneypieces and magnificent tapestries, but the highlight is the Long Gallery, decorated with Elizabethan-era portraits borrowed from the National Portrait Gallery (p115) in London.

Bus 81 from Yeovil (40 minutes, hourly Monday to Saturday) to South Petherton passes close by.

Haynes Motor Museum

The 300-strong car collection at **Haynes Motor Museum** (☎ 01963-440804; www.haynesmotormuseum .com; Sparkford; adult/child £7.50/4; ⏰ 9.30am-5.30pm Apr-Oct, 10am-4.30pm Nov-Mar) includes an array of the outstanding, the old, and, frankly, the odd. Aston Martins and Ferraris rub shoulders

---

BEER & BREAKFAST?

You'll want to raise a toast this one – Old Cider House (☎ 01278-732228; www.oldciderhouse.co.uk; 25 Castle St, Nether Stowey; d £60-80; P) is quite possibly the only B&B in Britain where guests design and brew their own beer. The process involves as much formulation, mashing, boiling and fermenting as ale addicts could possibly want. Once your top tipple is ready, it's bottled up, labelled and shipped to your door. All-inclusive, two-night beer-brewing breaks start at £225 per person; nonparticipants pay £99. Bedrooms are unfussy in plain colours and pine. But then, take part in enough 'tutored tasting sessions' and you probably won't notice the bedspread. If you're not staying, ask for a pint of the B&B's Stowey Brewery Ale in the local Rose and Crown.

---

with Bentleys and, well, the Sinclair C5. And yes, it is *that* Haynes, of the ubiquitous car-repair manuals that you'll find in charity shops throughout the country. The museum is on the A359 off the A303, northwest of Yeovil.

West Somerset Steam Railway

Railway buffs will love the **West Somerset Steam Railway** (☎ 01643-704996; www.west-somerset-railway .co.uk), which chugs through the Somerset countryside from Bishops Lydeard to Minehead, 20 miles away (return adult/child £13.40/6.70, 1¼ hours). There are stops at Dunster and other stations, depending on the time of year. Trains run pretty much daily from mid-March to October, otherwise occasional days only.

Bus 28 runs to Bishops Lydeard from Taunton (15 minutes, 11 daily Monday to Saturday, nine on Sunday).

EXMOOR NATIONAL PARK

Exmoor is an adventure. From dawn deer-spotting safaris to test-your-mettle hikes, from moorland gallops to cracking cycle rides, from clambering the coast path to a summertime dip in a cold, cold sea. This compact national park is a bit like England's version of the Wild West, except here cliffs replace cowboys, red deer replace cattle, and gumboots replace gunslingers. Part wilderness expanse, part rolling fields, these days Exmoor isn't all rustic B&Bs and hugger-mugger pubs. Instead, it's scattered with pockets of boutique bliss, from refined restaurants to sumptuous country-house hotels where the service is sublime, the beds are soft and a fire crackles in the grate.

The amiable market town of Dulverton shelters south of the swathes of bracken-smothered higher moorland that encircle the picturesque village of Exford. This unfenced wilderness plunges down to a coast dotted with charming stop-off points, from the twin villages of Lynton and Lynmouth in the west, via the pretty harbour at Porlock to the medieval town of Dunster, complete with a brooding red-brick castle. Expansive and exciting – Exmoor awaits.

Orientation

The park is only about 21 miles wide from west to east and stretches just 12 miles from north to south. Waymarked paths criss-cross the moor, and a dramatic section of the South West Coast Path runs from Minehead (a family-fun resort just outside the park) to Padstow in Cornwall.

Information

There are several tourist offices within the park:

Dulverton (☎ 01398-323841; NPCDulverton@exmoor -nationalpark.gov.uk; 7-9 Fore St; ☽ 10am-5pm Apr-Oct, 10.30am-3pm Nov-Mar)

Dunster (☎ 01643-821835; NPCDunster@exmoor -nationalpark.gov.uk; Dunster Steep; ☽ 10am-5pm Easter-Oct, limited hr Nov-Easter)

Lynmouth (☎ 01598-752509; Lyndale Car Park; ☽ 10.30am-3pm Easter-Oct)

Lynton (☎ 01598-752225; info@lyntourism.co.uk; Lynton Town Hall, Lee Rd; ☽ 10am-4pm Mon-Sat, to 2pm Sun)

Porlock (☎ 01643-863150; www.porlock.co.uk; West End, High St; ☽ 10am-5pm Mon-Sat, to 1pm Sun Mar-Oct, 10.30am-1pm Tue-Fri, 10am-2pm Sat Nov-Mar)

All information outlets stock the free *Exmoor Visitor* newspaper, an excellent source of information about accommodation, guided walks, activities, attractions, transport and the moor's fragile environment.

There are four comprehensive websites covering Exmoor:

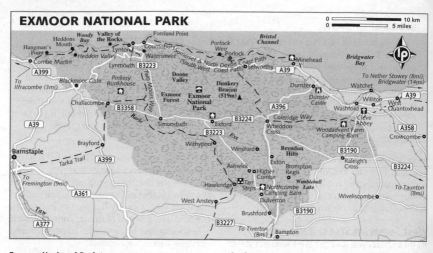

EXMOOR NATIONAL PARK

Exmoor National Park (www.exmoor-nationalpark.gov
.uk) The official National Park Authority site.

Exmoor Tourist Association (www.exmoor.com) Lists
details on accommodation and activities.

Visit Exmoor (www.visit-exmoor.info) Excellent information site with advice on activities, events, accommodation
and eating out.

What's On Exmoor (www.whatsonexmoor.com) Local
listings and information.

Activities

Active Exmoor (☎ 01398-324599; www.activeexmoor
.com) is a central contact point for all the park's
outdoor activity providers, ranging from riding to rowing and sailing to surfing. It also
has information for more-experienced white-
water kayakers and rock climbers.

Wimbleball Lake Watersports Centre (☎ 01398-
371460) runs a range of courses from sailing,
windsurfing and kayaking taster sessions
(£18 for one hour), to two-day windsurfing
(£145 per person) and sailing courses (£145
per person).

CYCLING

A network of bridleways and quiet lanes
makes Exmoor great cycling country, but
you're not going to get away without tackling
a few hills. Popular trails travel through the
Brendon Hills, the Crown Estate woodland
and along the old Barnstaple railway line.
National Park Authority (NPA) centres sell
the map *Exmoor for Off-Road Cyclists* (£10),
and the *Bike It Dunster* and *Bike It Wimbleball*
leaflets (75p) – both of which feature a fam-

ily, beginner and explorer route. All are also
available at the NPA's online shop.

Several sections of the **National Cycle Network**
(NCN; www.sustrans.org.uk) cross the park, includ-
ing the **West Country Way** (NCN route 3) from
Bristol to Padstow, and the **Devon Coast to Coast
Cycle Route** (NCN route 27) between Exmoor
and Dartmoor.

Located near Minehead, **Exmoor Mtb Experiences** (☎ 01643-705079; www.exmoormtbexperiences
.co.uk), runs guided off-road days from £25 and
all-inclusive weekends from £150. For bike
hire, see Getting Around, opposite.

MOORLAND SAFARIS

Several companies offer 4WD 'safari' trips
across the moor, which stop at the main beauty
spots and provide lots of background info.
If you're a nature-lover or a keen photographer, bird- and deer-watching safaris can be
arranged. Half-day trips start at around £20.

Barle Valley Safaris (☎ 01643-851386; www.exmoor
-barlevalley-safaris.co.uk) Located at Dulverton, Dunster and
Minehead.

Discovery Safaris (☎ 01643-863444; Porlock)

Exmoor Safari (☎ 01643-831229; www.exmoorsafari
.co.uk; Exford)

PONY TREKKING & HORSE RIDING

Exmoor is popular riding country and lots
of stables offer pony and horse treks from
around £25 per hour – see the *Exmoor Visitor*
for full details.

Brendon Manor Riding Stables (☎ 01598-741246)
Near Lynton.

Burrowhayes Farm (☎ 01643-862463; www.burrow hayes.co.uk; Porlock)

Outovercott Stables (☎ 01598-753341; www .outovercott.co.uk; Lynton)

WALKING

The open moors and profusion of marked bridleways make Exmoor an excellent area for hiking. The best-known routes are the **Somerset & North Devon Coast Path**, which is part of the **South West Coast Path** (www.southwestcoastpath .com), and the Exmoor section of the **Two Moors Way**, which starts in Lynmouth and travels south to Dartmoor and beyond.

The **Coleridge Way** (www.coleridgeway.co.uk) winds for 36 miles through Exmoor, the Brendon Hills and the Quantocks, taking in Coleridge's home at Nether Stowey and the village of Porlock, where he's said to have written *Kubla Khan*.

Part of the 180-mile **Tarka Trail** falls within the park. A combination of cycling and walking paths, road routes and even a train journey, it is based on the countryside that inspired Henry Williamson's Tarka the Otter. Join it at Combe Martin, hike along the cliffs to Lynton/Lynmouth, then head across the moor towards Barnstaple.

Organised **walks** run by the NPA are held throughout the year – visit www.exmoor -nationalpark.gov.uk or see the listings in *Exmoor Visitor* for details. Its autumn dawn safaris to see rutting stags are superb, as are its summertime evening deer-watching hikes. Short walks cost £3; longer walks are £5.

For hard-core hikers, **Mountains I Moor** (☎ 01643-841610; www.mountainsandmoor.co.uk; Mine-head), offers navigation lessons (from £80 per two days) and summer mountain-craft courses (£110/270 per two/five days), which include camp-craft, rope work and river crossings, and take the form of mini-expeditions.

Dulverton (p364), Exford (p364) and Lynton (p365) make good bases.

Sleeping & Eating

There are **YHA hostels** (☎ 01629-592700; www.yha.org .uk) in Minehead and Ilfracombe (outside the park), and Exford (p364) within the park.

The YHA also runs camping barns (from £7.50 per person) at Woodadvent Farm near Roadwater and at Northcombe Farm near Dulverton (p364). There are a number of official campsites along the coast.

For more-comfy sleeping options, Exmoor's accommodation ranges from rustic rooms

above pubs to cosy B&Bs to spoil-yourself-silly country-house hotels. We outline many; however, for an overview, see www.exmoor .com. If you'd like to hire a cottage, contact **Exmoor Holiday Group** (www.exmoor-holidays.co.uk).

Getting There & Around

Once outside the key towns, getting around Exmoor by bus can be tricky, as regular services are very limited. Bus 300 shuttles regularly along the coast between Minehead and Lynmouth, while bus 400, the **Exmoor Explorer** (round trip adult/child £6/3) offers a handy circular route that takes in Minehead, Dunster, Wheddon Cross, Exford and Porlock. It operates only on Saturday and Sunday between June and September (two daily); from late July to the end of August it also runs on Tuesday and Thursday.

BICYCLE

Several places hire out bikes:

Fremington Quay (☎ 01271-372586; www.bike trail.co.uk; Fremington; per day adult/child £10/7.50; ⏰ 10am-5pm Wed-Sun) Delivers bikes to your door.

Pompys (☎ 01643-704077; www.pompyscycles.co.uk; Minehead; per day £12.50; ⏰ 9am-5pm Mon-Sat) Offers full-suspension mountain bikes from £25.

Tarka Trail (☎ 01271-324202; Train Station, Barnsta-ple; per day adult/child £10/7; ⏰ 9.15am-5pm Apr-Oct) Can be picked up 15 miles west of the park boundary.

BUS

National Express runs buses to Tiverton from London (£16.50, 4¾ hours, three daily) and Bristol (£14.80, two to three hours, one daily), and to Taunton from London (£16.70, four hours, seven daily) and Bristol (£6.60, 1½ hours, four daily).

Regular main-line trains also serve Tiverton and Taunton. Once there, local buses link to Dulverton (p364), Dunster (p368) and beyond.

The *Taunton & West Somerset Public Transport Guide,* free from tourist offices, con-tains timetables for all the main bus routes.

DULVERTON

Dulverton is the southern gateway to Exmoor National Park., and sits at the base of the Barle Valley near the confluence of two key rivers, the Exe and Barle. It's a no-nonsense sort of country town, home to a collection of gun-sellers, fishing-tackle stores and gift shops, as well as the **NPA Visitor Centre** (☎ 01398-323841;

WESSEX

www.exmoor-nationalpark.gov.uk; 7-9 Fore St; ⏲ 10am-5pm Apr-Oct, 10.30am-3pm Nov-Mar).

Activities

WALKING

There's a lovely 12-mile (including hills) circular walk along the river from Dulverton to **Tarr Steps** – an ancient stone clapper bridge haphazardly placed across the River Barle and shaded by gnarled old trees. The bridge was supposedly built by the devil for sunbathing. It's a four- to five-hour trek for the average walker. You can add another three or four hours to the walk by continuing from Tarr Steps up Winsford Hill for distant views over Devon.

Sleeping & Eating

Town Mills (☎ 01398-323124; www.townmillsdulverton .co.uk; High St; s/d £50/75; **P**) The glossy rooms in this converted mill are resolutely 'un-country' – all crisp fabrics, sparkling bathrooms and bright artwork, topped off by original fireplaces and snazzy mirrors. It's all best surveyed while sipping a glass of complimentary sherry.

Three Acres (☎ 01398-323730; www.threeacrescoun tryhouse.co.uk; Brushford; s £55-70, d £80-110; **P**) Full of genteel elegance, this fine country retreat makes a wonderful base from which to explore the southern moor. A sweeping drive leads to a hideaway that bristles with huge beds, Egyptian linen, snug armchairs and deep free-standing baths with delightfully old-fashioned taps.

our pick **Tarr Farm** (☎ 01643-851507; www.tarrfarm .co.uk; s/d £90/150, mains £13-18; ⏲ lunch & dinner; **P**) One of Exmoor's best bolt-holes. Snuggled in a beguiling wooded valley next to the tourist honey-pot of Tarr Steps (above), this old Somerset farmhouse has been transformed into a superstylish retreat. The beds are draped in fine cottons and sprinkled with satin cushions; luxury touches include fluffy bathrobes, power-showers and organic bath products. The restaurant plates up new-country treats – expect Exmoor beef with wild mushrooms, and local lamb with red onion confit.

Lewis' Tea Rooms (☎ 01398-323850; 13 High St; mains £5-18; ⏲ breakfast & lunch Mon-Sat, dinner Thu-Sat Jul & Aug) The sumptuous array of homemade goodies in this cosy cafe will blow that diet – the chefs love 'experimenting with cakes'. Dinner's a belt-buster, too: try the monkfish with cream and saffron sauce (at least you can walk it off on a hefty moorland hike).

Woods (☎ 01398-324007; 4 Bank Sq; mains £11-18; ⏲ lunch & dinner) This deservedly popular gastropub has built up a devoted following by giving excellent local ingredients imaginative treatments, all helped along by a rustic atmosphere and excellent service. Tummy treats include local lobster, pork belly with samphire, and Ruby Red sirloin steak.

Other recommendations:

Northcombe Camping Barn (☎ 0870 770 8868; www.yha.org.uk; per person £7.50) A converted watermill about 1 mile from town.

Ashwick House (☎ 01398-323868; www.ashwick house.com; s £84-94, d £138-158) A grand, gorgeous minibaronial pile crammed full of Edwardian features. Near Ashwick, 4 miles from Dulverton.

Tongdam (☎ 01398-323397; 26 High St; mains £8-13; ⏲ lunch & dinner) A thrill for choice-starved vegetarians, this excellent Thai restaurant has a whole page of vegie dishes to choose from.

Getting There & Away

Bus 398 (six daily Monday to Saturday) stops at Dulverton on its way from Minehead (50 minutes) and Dunster (40 minutes) to Tiverton (55 minutes). Bus 25B shuttles to Taunton (1½ hours, seven daily Monday to Saturday).

EXFORD

Nestled on the banks of the River Exe at the heart of the moor, Exford is a delightful muddle of cottages and slate-roofed houses clustered around a village green. The village is the base of Devon and Somerset Staghounds, and meets are still an important part of life here, despite the hunting ban. Exford is also a centre for shooting, fishing, horse riding and hiking – Exmoor's highest point is 4 miles northeast of the village at Dunkery Beacon (519m), and the village is surrounded by secluded hills and quiet bridleways.

Sleeping & Eating

Exford YHA (☎ 0845 371 9634; www.yha.org.uk; Exe Mead; dm £13.95; **P**) Probably one of Exmoor's best budget bases, this brick Victorian house is just a short walk from the village centre – and the pub. The dorms are small and a smidgen institutional, but the hordes of hikers and cyclists aren't too bothered.

Exmoor House (☎ 01643-841432; www.exmoorhouse .com; Wheddon Cross; B&B only per person £39, 3-course dinner & B&B per person from £60; **P**) Rich, dark woods and unfussy pastel fabrics fill this homely restaurant-cum-B&B in nearby Wheddon Cross. Grab a local beer from the bar, read up on the moor in the cosy library, then feast on Exmoor produce: smoked trout pâté, local rabbit in Somerset cider and pungent Exmoor Jersey Blue cheese.

Edgcott House (☎ 01643-831495; info@edgcotthouse .co.uk; s £40, d £70-90; **P**) A 10-minute walk from the village, this beautiful 17th-century house is set in private riverside gardens. It's packed with period features, including a terracotta-tiled hallway and an amazing 15m 'Long Room' decorated with hand-painted murals. The bedrooms revel in their venerable character, so don't expect too many flat-screen TVs or designer flourishes.

Crown Hotel (☎ 01643-831554; www.crownhotelexmoor .co.uk; Chapel St; mains £13-25, s £70, d £110-140; ☽ lunch & dinner; **P**) For a taste of traditional Exmoor try the Crown, where hunting prints and stags' heads preside over leather armchairs and a colour scheme of racing-green and cream. The restaurant packs a few surprises: rabbit is paired with langoustine, while the free-range chicken comes with a Madeira and truffle sauce.

Getting There & Away

Exford is a 7-mile walk over the moors from Porlock; from Minehead it's a 10-mile hike, from Dunster it's 12 miles and from Lynton it's 15 miles.

Bus 398 from Tiverton to Minehead stops at Exford twice daily Monday to Saturday. The circular bus 400 (Exmoor Explorer) links Exford to Minehead, Dunster and Porlock twice on Saturday and Sunday between June and September, plus Tuesday and Thursday from late July to the end of August.

LYNTON & LYNMOUTH

The attractive harbour of Lynmouth is rooted at the base of a steep, tree-lined valley, where the West Lyn River empties into the sea along Exmoor's northern coastline. Its similarity to the harbour at Boscastle (p398) is striking, and, in fact, the two harbours share more than just a common geography: like Boscastle, Lynmouth is famous for a devastating flash flood. A huge wave of water swept through Lynmouth in 1952 and the town paid a much heavier price than its Cornish cousin; 34 people lost their lives, and memory of the disaster remains strong in the village today.

Today Lynmouth is a busy tourist harbour town lined with pubs, souvenir sellers and fudge shops. At the top of the rocky cliffs is the more genteel Victorian resort of Lynton, which can be reached via an amazing water-operated railway, or a stiff climb up the cliff path.

The **tourist office** (☎ 01598-752225; info@lyntour ism.co.uk; Lynton Town Hall, Lee Rd; ☽ 10am-4pm Mon-Sat, to 2pm Sun) provides a free newspaper called *Lynton & Lynmouth Scene* (www.lyntonand lynmouthscene.co.uk), which has accommodation, eating and activities listings.

There's a small **NPA visitor centre** (☎ 01598-752509; Lyndale Car Park; ☽ 10am-3pm Easter-Oct) near Lynmouth harbour.

Sights & Activities

The history of Lynmouth's flood is explored at the **Lyn & Exmoor Museum** (☎ 01598-752317; St Vincent's Cottage, Market St, Lynton; adult/child £1/20p; ☽ 10am-12.30pm & 2-5pm Mon-Fri, 2-5pm Sun Apr-Oct), which also houses some interesting archaeological finds and a collection of tools, paintings and period photos.

The **Cliff Railway** (☎ 01598-753486; www.cliff railwaylynton.co.uk; single/return adult £1.95/2.85, child £1.10/1.85; ☽ 10am-6pm Easter-Oct, later at peak times) is an extraordinary piece of Victorian engineering that was designed by George Marks, believed to be a pupil of Brunel. Two cars linked by a steel cable descend or ascend the slope according to the amount of water in the cars' tanks. It's been running like clockwork since 1890, and it's still the best way to commute between the two villages. The views aren't bad, either.

From the Lynmouth crossroads follow the signs 200m to **Glen Lyn Gorge** (☎ 01598-753207; adult/child £4/3; ☽ Easter-Oct), the steepest of the two valleys into Lynmouth. There are several lovely gorge walks and a small **exhibition centre** devoted to hydroelectric power.

WALKING

There are some beautiful short walks in and around the two villages, as well as access to some longer routes: the South West Coast Path, the Coleridge Way and the Tarka Trail all pass through Lynmouth, and it is the official starting point of the Two Moors Way.

The most popular hike is to the stunning **Valley of the Rocks**, described by poet laureate Robert Southey as 'rock reeling upon rock, stone piled upon stone, a huge terrifying reeling mass'. It's just over a mile west of Lynton, and is believed to mark the original course

WESSEX

of the River Lyn. Many of the tortuous rock formations have been named over the years – look out for the Devil's Cheesewring and Ragged Jack – the valley is also home to a population of feral goats.

Other popular trails wind to the lighthouse at **Foreland Point**, east of Lynmouth, and **Watersmeet**, 2 miles upriver from Lynmouth, where a handily placed National Trust teashop is housed in a Victorian fishing lodge.

Sleeping

There are plenty of mid-price B&Bs dotted along Lee Rd in Lynton.

Sea View Villa (☎ 01598-753460; www.seaviewvilla .co.uk; 6 Summer House Path, Lynmouth; s £40, d £90-120) Adding a dash of Georgian grandeur to seaside Lynmouth, this 1721 villa makes for a supremely elegant night's kip. Egyptian cotton, Indian silk and suede fabrics grace rooms done out in 'Champagne', 'ginger' and 'vanilla'. Eggs Benedict, smoked salmon and cafetière coffee ensure the breakfast is classy, too.

Hunters' Inn (☎ 01598-763230; www.thehuntersinn .net; s £55-80, d £80-130) Tucked away in the heart of the heavily wooded Heddon Valley, west of Lynton, this 19th-century coaching inn is an Exmoor institution. Cosy, creaky rooms add to the atmosphere, as do views over tumbling hills and the sense of sleeping snugly somewhere in the middle of nowhere. Local ales and excellent pub grub are on offer in the welcoming, well-worn bar.

Victoria Lodge (☎ 01598-753203; www.victorialodge .co.uk; Lee Rd, Lynton; s £60-120, d £70-140) The rooms here positively drip with swags, pelmets and padded cushions, often in hard-to-ignore patterns – that they're named after princesses provides a clue to opulence levels. You'll also tuck into a right royal breakfast of homemade kedgeree, Victoria omelette or the enormous Exmoor Works.

our pick **St Vincent House** (☎ 01598-752244; www .st-vincent-hotel.co.uk; Castle Hill, Lynton; d £74; P) Run by an Anglo-Belgian couple and named Hotel of the Year by Les Routiers, no less, this elegant establishment brings a dollop of class to the quiet streets of Lynton. The house once belonged to a comrade of Nelson's, and all the delightful, pared-back rooms are named after battleships from Horatio's fleet. There's a relaxed, old-world atmosphere and a spiral staircase so sweeping that you'll feel like a film star.

Eating

Greenhouse (☎ 01598-753358; 6 Lee Rd; mains £9; 9am-9.30pm) Cole Porter tunes, a log-burning stove and conservatory-style dining create a cafe-cum-restaurant with gently eccentric charm. Evenings see a smooth segue from gourmet baguettes, cinnamon-scented toast and superb cream teas to suppertime comfort food like pan-fried salmon with hollandaise, and crab with new potatoes.

St Vincent Restaurant (☎ 01598-752244; Castle Hill, Lynton; 2/3 courses £24/27; dinner Wed-Sun Easter-Oct) Part of the St Vincent House hotel (left), this cracking little eatery is the top table in town. Subdued lighting, polished wooden floors and intimate tables set the scene for dishes that fuse Mediterranean flavours with Exmoor fish and game. The Westcountry lamb with olives, tomatoes, capers and garlic is hard to resist, but leave room for the crème Catalane brûlée.

Entertainment

Lynton Cinema (☎ 01598-753397; www.lyntoncinema .co.uk; Lee Rd; adult/child £4.25/2.75), This 68-seater cinema, set in a converted Methodist church, is a superbly atmospheric spot to catch the latest movies.

Getting There & Away

Bus 300 runs from Lynmouth to Minehead (55 minutes), via Porlock (30 minutes), three to four times daily.

If you're driving, the most scenic route to Porlock is the steep, twisting road that hugs the coast all the way from Lynmouth. The scenery is worth the £2 toll, and you get to avoid the notoriously steep descent via Porlock Hill.

PORLOCK & AROUND

The small village of Porlock is one of the prettiest on the north Exmoor coast; the huddle of thatched cottages lining its main street is framed on one side by the sea, and on the other by a jumble of houses that cling to the steeply sloping hills behind. Winding lanes lead to the picturesque breakwater of Porlock Weir, a compact collection of pubs, shops and hotels, 2 miles to the west. Coleridge's famous poem *Kubla Khan* was written during a brief sojourn in Porlock (helped along by a healthy slug of laudanum and a vicious head cold), and the villages are popular with summertime tourists, as well as walkers on the Coleridge Way and the South West Coast Path.

The village of **Selworthy**, 2½ miles southeast of Porlock, forms part of the 5060-hectare Holnicote Estate, the largest NT-owned area of land on Exmoor. Though its cob-and-thatch cottages look ancient, the village was almost entirely rebuilt in the 19th century by local philanthropist and landowner Thomas Acland, to provide accommodation for elderly workers on his estate.

Porlock's **tourist office** (☎ 01643-863150; www .porlock.co.uk; West End, High St; ☷ 10am-5pm Mon-Sat, 10am-1pm Sun Mar-Oct, 10.30am-1pm Tue-Fri, 10am-2pm Sat Nov-Mar) is a mine of local knowledge, and is also the point of contact for information on the Coleridge Way.

For interesting artefacts and photos of the village, check to see if the tiny **Dovery Manor Museum**, housed in a pretty, 15th-century building in High St, has reopened after refurbishments.

Sleeping & Eating

Reines House (☎ 01643-862913; www.reineshouse.co.uk; Parson St; s £25, d £50-54) Simplicity and bargain prices define this snug, central B&B. Expect shades of subtle cream and buttercup-yellow, tasteful scatter cushions and views of the church from the front rooms. Two rooms share bathrooms.

Ship Inn (☎ 01643-862507; www.shipinnporlock.co.uk; High St, Porlock; mains £7-14, s/d £40/60; ☷ lunch & dinner; **P**) Once a favoured haunt of smugglers and the poet Coleridge, this 13th-century thatched inn is still a snug spot for a pint and some great grub. Try the 'Chef's Pie of the Day' – the beef and horseradish is a triumph. The pine and faintly floral bedrooms feature all the home comforts you need after a day on the moors.

ourpick **SeaView** (☎ 01643-863456; www.seaview porlock.co.uk; High Bank; s £27, d £50-55) You can lie in bed and gaze across Porlock Bay to the cliffs of Wales (they're only 12 miles away) in this delightful, village-centre B&B. It's crammed full of quirky charm, from art-deco bedroom furniture and distressed cabinets to a dining room dripping with oil paintings and antiques. The compact single is more like a minisuite, while the attic room looks out onto the tree-covered Porlock Hill behind. Smoked haddock, local organic eggs and dry-cured bacon make breakfast a treat.

Getting There & Away

Bus 300 runs from Lynmouth to Porlock (30 minutes, three to four times daily) and on to Minehead (20 minutes). Bus 39 (six daily Monday to Saturday) links Porlock to Porlock Weir (seven minutes) and Minehead (20 minutes).

DUNSTER

Dominated by a striking russet-red castle and centred on a chaotically cobbled market square, the pretty village of Dunster can not only claim to be easy on the eye, but also architecturally interesting. It's unusual features include a medieval packhorse bridge, a 16th-century stone dovecote and a curious octagonal yarn market. In high summer it's a favourite on the coach-tour trail, but make a visit outside that time and the village is still a joy to explore.

The beautiful **St George's Church** dates mostly from the 15th century and boasts a wonderfully carved fan-vaulted rood screen. Further down the road is the **watermill** (☎ 01643-821759; Mill Lane; adult/child £3.20/1.95; ☷ 11am-4.45pm Jun-Sep, 11am-4.45pm Sat-Thu Apr, May & Oct), a working 18th-century mill.

The **NPA visitor centre** (☎ 01643-821835; Dunster Steep; ☷ 10am-5pm Easter-Oct, limited hr Nov-Easter) is in the main car park.

Dunster Castle

Although it served as a fortress for around 1000 years, present-day **Dunster Castle** (NT; ☎ 01643-821314; castle & garden adult/child £8.60/4.20, garden only £4.80/2.20; ☷ castle 11am-4.30pm mid-Mar–late Jul, Sep & Oct, to 5pm late Jul-Aug, gardens 11am-4pm Feb–mid-Mar & Nov-Jan, 10am-5pm mid-Mar–Oct) bears little resemblance to the original Norman stronghold. The 13th-century gateway is probably the only original part of the castle; the turrets, battlements and towers were all added later during a romantic remodelling at the hands of Victorian architects. Despite its 19th-century makeover, the castle is still an impressive sight, and is decorated with Tudor furnishings, gorgeous 17th-century plaster-work and ancestral portraits of the Luttrell family. The terraced gardens are also worth exploring, with fine views across Exmoor and the coastline, and an important national collection of strawberry trees.

Sleeping & Eating

ourpick **Spears Cross** (☎ 01643-821439; www.spears cross.co.uk; 1 West St; s £48, d £75-85) Beam enthusiasts will be in hog-heaven in this 15th-century gem of a B&B – the bedrooms are a mass of

MOOR ELEGANCE

Andrews on the Weir (☎ 01643-863300; www.andrewsontheweir.co.uk; Porlock Weir; mains £14-20, 2-course lunch £10, d £100-180; ☒ lunch & dinner Wed-Sun) Every meal becomes an 'experience' at this outlandishly fine restaurant-with-rooms, hovering beside the lapping waves on Porlock Weir. Local contacts (including Porlock fishermen and Exmoor farmers) help the chefs source the very best produce, from farm-reared meat to seafresh fish. The cuisine is classic British with a dash of Gallic panache, the atmosphere is all effortless elegance, and the tablecloths are sharp enough to enough to cut your finger on. Classy with a capital 'C'.

burnished old-English planking and latticeworks of ancient wood and painted plaster. Posh new bathrooms and fluffy bathrobes ensure you're steeped in luxury as well as history, and breakfast is a smorgasbord of locally sourced delights – don't miss out on the sausages made from local free-range, rare-breed pork.

Yarn Market Hotel (☎ 01643-821425; www.yarn markethotel.co.uk; High St; s £60-65, d £90-100, f £120-160; Ⓟ) Despite a historic exterior, the rooms in this small hotel are all modern identikit furniture and floral fabrics. But the suites may suit families, and wet walkers and unlucky cyclists will find the drying rooms and emergency puncture-repair kits very handy.

Luttrell Arms (☎ 01643-821555; www.luttrellarms .co.uk; High St; B&B d £116-150; Ⓟ) In medieval times this glorious old coaching inn was the guest house of the Abbots of Cleeve – lucky abbots. Huge flagstones, heavy armchairs and faded tapestries dot the lounge and bar, and the lavish four-poster-bed bedrooms put some royal retreats to shame. Weekends require a two-night dinner, bed and breakfast booking (doubles £160 to £190).

Cobblestones Cafe (☎ 01643-821595; High St; £7-14; ☒ lunch Sun, Mon & Wed-Fri, dinner Sat) One for a lunchtime treat: choose to fuel your sightseeing with ham terrine, spiced potted shrimps or braised shallot and goats' cheese tart. Saturday evenings see candlelit dinners and more seriously good fare; try the sea bass or Moroccan lamb tagine.

Reeve's Restaurant (☎ 01643-821414; High St; mains £15-25; ☒ lunch & dinner Tue-Sat) Reeve's is all rusticchic – slim leather chairs and boxy wooden tables accompany some extremely stylish food. The menu's full of the flavours of the local moors and shores; escallop of venison sits alongside pan-seared red mullet and slowcooked honey-glazed belly pork.

Getting There & Away

Bus 28 runs from Minehead to Taunton via Dunster hourly Monday to Saturday, and nine times on Sunday. Bus 398 travels from Dunster to Exford (30 minutes, once daily except Sunday) and Dulverton (40 minutes, six daily except Sunday), and to Minehead (10 minutes, six daily except Sunday) in the opposite direction. Bus 398 goes to Tiverton (1½ hours, six daily).

The West Somerset Steam Railway (p361) stops at Dunster during the summer.

WESSEX

Devon & Cornwall

England's two most westerly counties tend to saunter into your soul, wander around and leave a trail of sandy footprints. These are places for barefoot beachcombing and sunset strolls, storm watching and star gazing, island hopping and moorland mooching. Devon and Cornwall are a blend of quiet hamlets, jewel-green meadows and breathtaking coast, and their charms range from ancient to modern, with all the best bits in between. From mystical stone circles on Dartmoor to the myth-rich castles at Tintagel and St Michael's Mount; from a creaking maritime history at Falmouth and Plymouth to cobbled fishing villages at Colvelly, Looe, Polperro and Fowey.

Devon and Cornwall are also alive with regeneration. Gastropubs, designer bars and boutique hotels are opening up practically everywhere you look. Old fishing harbours, derelict mining towns and faded seaside resorts are reinventing themselves as cultural centres, artistic havens and celebrity chef–run gastronomic hubs. In both counties you can check into supremely hip hotels, learn to ride the surf and then stuff yourself silly at elegant eateries – before hiking it off the next day on the moors. Party through the night in Newquay and Plymouth or get environmental inspiration at the Eden Project, ecofriendly Totnes or west Cornwall's exotic gardens. And then there's Exeter's stately cathedral, art-rich St Ives and the enticing Isles of Scilly – a Cornish archipelago with a touch of the Med. In fact, Devon and Cornwall have such a surfeit of charms it hardly seems fair on the rest of England. Make some space in your soul and prepare for sandy feet.

HIGHLIGHTS

- Becoming a barefoot castaway in the blissfully beguiling **Isles of Scilly** (p419)
- Hiking the myth-rich, mist-shrouded wilderness that is **Dartmoor** (p387)
- Hanging 10, or just hanging on, in the exhilarating surf off **Newquay** (p402)
- Discovering your inner gardener at subtropical **Trebah** (p411), Agatha Christie's **Greenway** (p380) and the huge biomes of the **Eden Project** (p406)
- Gazing up at the supremely serene, gloriously Gothic cathedral in **Exeter** (p375)
- Treating your tummy at great-for-gourmands **Padstow** (p400) and **Dartmouth** (p381)

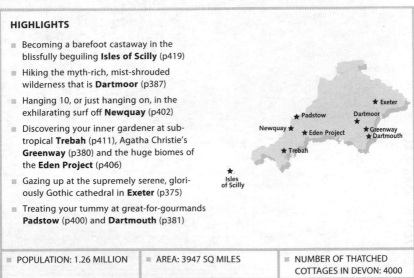

- **POPULATION: 1.26 MILLION**
- **AREA: 3947 SQ MILES**
- **NUMBER OF THATCHED COTTAGES IN DEVON: 4000**

DEVON & CORNWALL

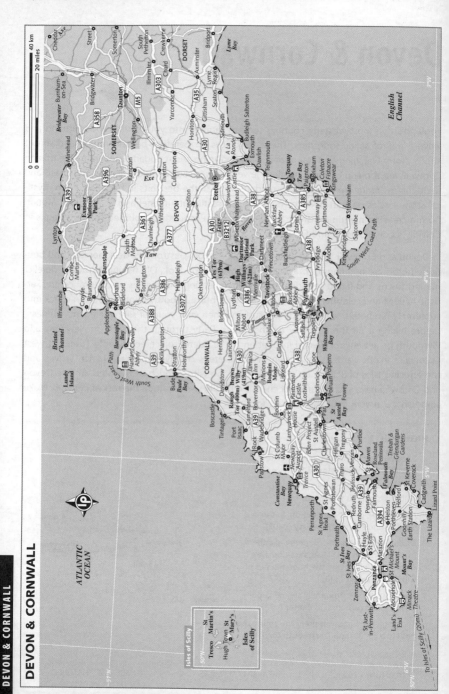

DEVON & CORNWALL

History

Devon and Cornwall positively ripple with the past. The counties are doted with stone circles, tombs and Bronze Age houses, especially on Dartmoor (p390), Bodmin Moor and in west Cornwall (p404 and p416). The Roman's invaded in AD 55 and their crumbling city wall still winds through Exeter's streets. When the legionnaires decamped (around 400) legend has it King Arthur ruled the roost – many claim that spray-dashed Tintagel Castle (p398) was his stronghold. Certainly the counties were part of King Alfred the Great's 9th-century kingdom of Wessex. From Tudor times onwards Devon and Cornwall helped England build an empire – plaques on Plymouth's Barbican (p383) note the departures of Sir Francis Drake, America's first settlers and emigrant ships to Australia and New Zealand.

The late 1800s saw a sharp decline in Cornwall's mining industry and mass migration – some communities were cut by a third; today ruined engine houses still dot the county's cliffs, most dramatically at Geevor and Botallack (p415). The Victorian era brought the railways, mass tourism and resorts – notably at Torquay (p379) and Penzance (p412). WWII brought devastating bombing and hundreds of thousands of American servicemen. The following decades saw the death of the mining industry, and fishing and farming slip into decline; despite the holiday image the region still has among the lowest wages in the country.

Orientation & Information

Devon's historic capital, Exeter, sits in the east, Dartmoor straddles the middle of the county while south-coast Plymouth signals Devon's western edge. From there, Cornwall's dramatic coast heads west, tapering sharply and sandwiching the capital, Truro, en route to Land's End. The Isles of Scilly are 28 miles offshore.

The moors of Dartmoor and Bodmin aside, many of the region's attractions line the coast. Although parts of Exmoor National Park (p361) fall within north Devon, we cover the whole park in our Wessex chapter.

The **South West Tourist Board** (www.visitsouthwest .com) covers Devon and Cornwall; its themed subsites cover nature, adventure, family and heritage holidays.

The free monthly listings magazine *twenty4-seven* (www.twenty4-seven.co.uk) covers all the latest bars, gigs and clubs, and is available from tourist offices, bars and restaurants.

Activities

There's a distinct whiff of adrenalin in Devon and Cornwall. Their landscapes lend themselves to activities ranging from amped-up adventure to chilled-out wanderings. The tourist board's subsite (www.itsadventuresouthwest .co.uk) offers an overview; local tourist offices can also advise.

CYCLING

Encompassing canal paths, country lanes and precipitous moorland slopes, Devon and Cornwall have a huge variety of cycle-routes. Several sections of the National Cycle Network (NCN) cross the region, including the **West Country Way** (NCN route 3), a 250-mile jaunt from Bristol to Padstow on the north Cornwall coast. The 102-mile **Devon Coast to Coast** (NCN route 27) has 71 car-free miles, and skirts Dartmoor to link Ilfracombe with Plymouth.

Many cycle trails trace the routes of old railway lines, including the largely traffic-free, 11-mile **Granite Way**, which winds between Okehampton and Lydford. The 17-mile **Camel Trail** (p399) is completely car free and sweeps from Bodmin Moor to Padstow. Bikes can be hired in most large towns; we specify options throughout.

SURFING

Cornwall is a magnet for Britain's surfers, with excellent breaks running all the way from Porthleven (near Helston) in Cornwall, west around Land's End and along the north coast. Popular spots include Newquay (p402), Perranporth, St Agnes and Bude (p397) in Cornwall, and Croyde (p394) in north Devon. The latest surf updates can be found at www.a1surf.com.

WALKING

Britain's longest national trail is the 630-mile **South West Coast Path**, which takes in dazzling bays, pretty fishing villages and cliffs crowned by tin mines. The whole trail takes about eight weeks, but most people opt for shorter hikes. The trail's official website (www.southwest coastpath.com) has a detailed overview; the South West Coast Path Association (www .swcp.org.uk) publishes an annual guide.

DEVON & CORNWALL

CAMPER CAPERS

Want to tour the southwest in style? Then you'll need your own vintage VW campervan, complete with grill, fridge, crockery, cutlery, four bunk beds and the kitchen sink. Contact **O'Connor's Campers** (☎ 01837-659599; www.oconnorscampers.co.uk) in Okehampton or **Kernow Kampers** (☎ 01637-830027; www.kernowkampers.co.uk) near Newquay. Prices start from around £425 per week; surfboards and sunglasses not included.

Walkers also delight in tramping the region's wildernesses: Dartmoor (p389) and the smaller Bodmin Moor (p404). Both provide history, testing terrain and a great escape.

OTHER ACTIVITIES

Devon and Cornwall also offer horse riding on Dartmoor, climbing on Cornwall's cliffs, wreck diving, windsurfing, wakesurfing, kitesurfing, caving, coasteering and mountainboarding. Check out www.itsadventure southwest.co.uk for details.

Getting There & Around

To reach some remote spots you will need your own wheels. However, if you're determined, many rural areas are accessible by public transport, and if you're sticking to the main towns and sights, it's perfectly possible to get around by bus and train. Timetables and transport maps are available from stations and tourist offices, and the handy *Car-Free Days Out* (www.carfreedaysout.com) booklet has comprehensive public-transport listings.

For all bus and train timetables, call **Traveline South West** (☎ 0871 200 2233; www.travelinesw.com).

BUS

The region's main towns and cities are served by regular National Express coaches. For local buses, the more remote the area, the less regular the service; parts of Dartmoor and west Cornwall can be particularly tricky to navigate.

First Group (☎ 0845 600 1420, timetables 0871 200 2233; www.firstgroup.com) provides many of region's bus services. The Firstday Southwest pass (adult/child £7/5.20) is valid on most First buses in Devon and Cornwall, plus Bristol, Somerset, Gloucestershire and Dorset. The one-day Ride Cornwall pass (adult/child £12/7.50) allows off-peak travel on trains and buses in Cornwall and Plymouth. Other local bus operators do cheap day tickets, so it's worth asking the driver.

TRAIN

Devon and Cornwall's main railway line follows the coast as far as Penzance, with spurs to Barnstaple, Paignton, Gunnislake, Looe, Falmouth, St Ives and Newquay. The line from Exeter to Penzance is one of England's most scenic routes.

Some key operators and lines:

First Great Western (☎ 08457 000125; www .firstgreatwestern.co.uk) Links London Paddington with Exeter, Penzance, Plymouth and Truro; plus branch lines to Exmouth, Falmouth, Newquay, St Ives and Torquay.

CrossCountry (☎ 0844 811 0124 www.crosscountry trains.co.uk) Shuttles between the southwest and Scotland, the north and the midlands.

South West Trains (☎ 0845 6000 650; www.south westtrains.co.uk) Runs services between London Waterloo and Axminster and Exeter.

Several regional rail passes are available from train stations, including the **Freedom of the South West Rover** (adult £95), which allows eight days' unlimited travel over 15 days in an area west of (and including) Salisbury, Bath, Bristol and Weymouth.

The **Devon and Cornwall Rover** allows unlimited train travel throughout Devon and Cornwall. It's available for three days' travel in one week (£40), or eight days' travel in 15 (£60).

DEVON

If counties were capable of emotions, those in the rest of England would envy Devon. It's all to do with a rippling landscape studded with prehistoric sites, historic homes, vibrant cities, ancient villages, intimate coves and wild, wild moors. If exhilaration is your thing, you'll be right at home: here you can get churned around by crashing surf, ride whitewater rapids or hike hundreds of miles along precipitous cliffs. Landscape and lifestyle ensure food is fresh from furrow or sea – eat a Michelin-starred meal at a swanky restaurant or a fresh crab sandwich sitting on the beach – it's up to you. In Devon a day's drive can take you from Exeter's serene cathedral, via Torbay's kiss-me-quick coast to the yachting haven of Dartmouth, where Agatha Christie's mysterious gardens wait in the wings. Totnes provides the eco-awareness, Plymouth provides the party and wilderness, Dartmoor provides the great escape, while the north coast – rugged, remote and surf-dashed – tempts you into the waves. Whether you see them as envy-inducing, green-tinged or green-fringed, the delights of Devon are tempting indeed.

Orientation & Information

To the east Devon is bordered by Somerset and Dorset – the county boundary stretches from north-coast Exmoor to south-coast Lyme Regis. To the west the border with Cornwall follows the River Tamar from its source in north Devon to the estuary at Plymouth. Dartmoor occupies much of the centre of the county.

Discover Devon (☎ 0870 608 5531; www.discover devon.com) has plenty of useful information.

Getting Around

Traveline South West (☎ 0871 200 2233; www.travel inesw.com) can answer timetable questions. Tourist offices stock timetables, the *Devon Bus Map* and the *Discovery Guide to Dartmoor*.

First (see opposite) is the key bus operator in north, south and east Devon, and Dartmoor; **Stagecoach Devon** (☎ 01392-427711; www.stagecoach bus.com) operates mostly local buses, especially in Exeter and Torbay.

The Day Explorer (£2.20 to £4.50) allows one day's travel on Stagecoach Devon buses (prices vary depending on the area), while the Goldrider pass (£6 to £12) is valid for one week.

Devon's rail network skirts the south coast through Exeter and Plymouth to Cornwall.

Key lines branching off include the 39-mile Tarka Line from Exeter to Barnstaple, the 15-mile Tamar Valley Line from Plymouth to Gunnislake and the scenic Exeter to Paignton line, which runs via Torquay. The Devon Day Ranger (£10) allows a day's unlimited travel on the county's trains.

EXETER
pop 116,393

Well-heeled and comfortable, Exeter exudes evidence of its centuries-old role as the spiritual and administrative heart of Devon. The city's gloriously Gothic cathedral presides over stretches of cobbled streets, fragments of the terracotta Roman city wall and a tumbling of medieval and Georgian buildings. A snazzy new shopping centre brings bursts of the modern, thousands of university students ensure a buzzing nightlife and the vibrant quayside acts as a launch pad for cycling or kayaking trips. Throw in some super-stylish places to stay and eat and you have a relaxed but lively base for further explorations.

History

Exeter's past can be read in its buildings. The Romans marched in around AD 55 – their 17-hectare fortress included a 2-mile defensive wall, crumbling sections of which remain, especially in Rougemont and Northernhay Gardens. Saxon and Norman times saw growth: a castle went up in 1068, the cathedral 40 years later. The Tudor wool boom brought Exeter an export trade, riches and half-timbered houses; prosperity continued into the Georgian era when hundreds of merchants built genteel homes. The Blitz of WWII brought devastation. In just one night in 1942, 156 people died and 12 hectares of the city were flattened. Fast forward to 2007 and the

---

SOMETHING FOR THE WEEKEND

Start off in style by checking into the super-chic **Hotel Barcelona** (p376) and supping a cocktail at its movie-themed bar: **Kino** (p377). Then it's time for a slap-up meal at **Michael Caines** (p377) before checking out Exeter's nightspots, including the **Cavern Club** (p377) and the **Phoenix Arts Centre** (p377). Day one is set aside for exploring the villages and tors of wild **Dartmoor** (p387), with a hearty pub lunch in **Chagford** (p393) or **Widecombe** (p392) and a luxurious night's sleep at the lavish **Holne Chase Hotel** (p392). On Sunday take a leisurely drive down to designer **Dartmouth** (p380), allowing time for a visit to Agatha Christie's home at **Greenway** (p380), a swanky lunch at the **New Angel** (p381) or a quay-side crab roll from the **Crab Shell** (p381) kiosk. Finish off your weekend with a cruise along the River Dart to chill out at hippie haven **Totnes** (p382).

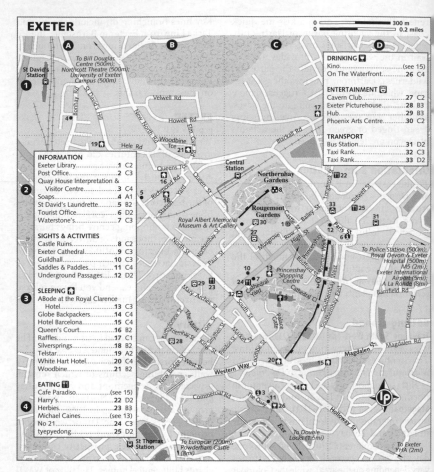

EXETER

£220 million Princesshay shopping centre has
added shimmering glass and steel lines to the
architectural mix.

Orientation

South of the ruined castle, the city centre radi-
ates out from the grassy square around the ca-
thedral; the redeveloped quay is 500m south.
There are two main train stations, Central and
St David's; most long-distance trains use St
David's, a mile northwest of the centre.

Information
BOOKSHOPS

Waterstone's (☎ 01392-218392; 48-49 High St;
🕑 9am-5.30pm Mon-Fri, 9am-6pm Sat, 10.30am-
4.30pm Sun)

EMERGENCY

Police station (☎ 08452 777444; Heavitree Rd;
🕑 24hr)
Royal Devon & Exeter Hospital (☎ 01392-411611;
Barrack Rd)

INTERNET ACCESS

Exeter Library (☎ 01392-384200; Castle St;
🕑 9.30am-7pm Mon, Tue, Thu & Fri, 10am-5pm Wed,
9.30am-4pm Sat, 11am-2.30pm Sun) First 30 minutes free,
then £3 per hour.

LAUNDRY

St David's Laundrette (St David's Hill; per load £2.20;
🕑 8am-9pm)
Soaps (☎ 01392-491930; Isambard Pde; 🕑 8.15am-
7.45pm Mon-Sat, 9.15am-5.45pm Sun; per load £1.70)

MEDIA
The List magazine (50p) details events, listings, bars and restaurants in the Exeter area.

POST
Main branch (☎ 01392-223344; Bedford St; ⏰ 9am-5.30pm Mon-Sat)

TOURIST INFORMATION
Quay House Interpretation & Visitor Centre (☎ 01392-271611; The Quay; ⏰ 10am-5pm Easter-Oct, 11am-4pm weekends only Nov-Easter)
Tourist office (☎ 01392-265700; www.exeter.gov .uk/visiting; Paris St; ⏰ 9am-5pm Mon-Sat year-round, 10am-4pm Sun Jul & Aug)

Sights
EXETER CATHEDRAL
Magnificent in warm, honey-coloured stone, Exeter's **Cathedral Church of St Peter** (☎ 01392-255573; www.exeter-cathedral.org.uk; Cathedral Cl; suggested donation £4; ⏰ 9.30am-6.30pm Mon-Fri, 9am-5pm Sat, 7.30am-6.30pm Sun), is framed by lawns and wonky half-timbered buildings – a quintessentially English scene often peopled by picnickers snacking to the sound of the bells.

The site has been a religious one since at least the 5th-century but the Normans started the current building in 1114; the towers of today's cathedral date from that period. In 1270 Bishop Bronescombe remodelled the whole building, a process that took 90 years and introduced a mix of Early English and Decorated Gothic styles.

Above the **Great West Front** scores of weather-worn figures line a screen that was once brightly painted. It now forms the largest collection of 14th-century sculpture in England. Inside, the ceiling is mesmerising – the longest unbroken Gothic vaulting in the world, it sweeps up to meet ornate ceiling bosses in gilt and vibrant colours. Look out for the 15th-century **Exeter Clock** in the north transept: in keeping with medieval astronomy it shows the earth as a golden ball at the centre of the universe with the sun, a fleur-de-lys, travelling round. Still ticking and whirring, it chimes on the hour.

The huge oak canopy over the **Bishop's Throne** was carved in 1312, while the 1350 **minstrels' gallery** is decorated with 12 angels playing musical instruments. Cathedral staff will point out the famous sculpture of the **lady with two left feet** and the tiny **St James Chapel**, built to repair the one destroyed in the Blitz in 1942. Look out for its unusual carvings: a cat, a mouse and, oddly, a rugby player.

In the **Refectory** (☎ 01392-285988; ⏰ 10am-4.45pm Mon-Sat) you can tuck into cakes, quiches and soups at trestle tables surrounded by vaulted ceilings, stained glass and busts of the great, the good and the dead.

Free 45-minute guided tours run at 11am and 2.30pm Monday to Friday, 11am on Saturday and 4pm on Sunday, April to October. Evensong is at 5.30pm Monday to Friday and 3pm on Saturday and Sunday.

UNDERGROUND PASSAGES
Prepare to crouch down, don a hard hat and possibly get spooked in what is the only system of its kind open to the public in England. These medieval, vaulted **passages** (☎ 01392-665887; Paris St; adult/child £5/3.50; ⏰ 9.30am-5.30pm Mon-Sat, 10.30am-4pm Sun Jun-Sep, 11.30am-5.30pm Tue-Fri, 9.30am-5.30pm Sat, 11.30am-4pm Sun Oct-May) were built to house pipes bringing fresh water to the city. Unlike modern utility companies, the authorities opted to have permanent access for repairs, rather than dig up the streets each time – genius. Guides lead you on a scramble through the network regaling you with tales of ghosts, escape routes and cholera. The last tour is an hour before closing.

BILL DOUGLAS CENTRE
A delightful homage to film and fun, the **Bill Douglas Centre** (☎ 01392-264321; www.billdouglas.org; University of Exeter, Old Library, Prince of Wales Rd; admission free; ⏰ 10am-4pm Mon-Fri) is a compact collection of all things celluloid, from magic lanterns to Mickey Mouse. Inside discover just what the butler did see and why the flicks are called the flicks. In a mass of movie memorabilia Charlie Chaplin bottle stoppers mingle with Ginger Rogers playing cards, James Bond board games and Star Wars toys.

GUILDHALL
The earliest parts of the medieval **Guildhall** (☎ 01392-665500; High St; admission free) date from 1330, making it the oldest municipal building still in use in the country. A gloriously ornate barrel roof arches above wooden benches and crests of dignitaries – the mayor still sits in the huge throne-like chair at the end. Opening hours depend on civic functions.

Activities
Saddles & Paddles (☎ 01392-424241; www.sadpad.com; 4 Kings Wharf, The Quay; ⏰ 9.30am-5.30pm) on Exeter quayside rents out bikes (adult/child per hour

£5/4, per day £14/10) and Canadian canoes (per one/six hours £10/35) allowing you to explore Exeter's canal and the footpaths that wind toward the sea.

Tours

Redcoat Guided Tours (☎ 01392-265203; www.exeter .gov.uk/visiting; 2-5 daily Apr-Oct, 2-3 daily Nov-Mar) are free and hugely varied. Themes range from ghosts and murder to Romans and religion – there's even a torch-lit prowl through the catacombs. Tours leave from Cathedral Yard or the quay, pick up a program from the tourist office.

Sleeping
BUDGET

Globe Backpackers (☎ 01392-215521; www.exeterback packers.co.uk; 71 Holloway St; dm £15, 7th night free, d £40; ☐) This relaxed hostel is housed inside a rambling house near the quay. It's spotlessly clean and run by a friendly husband-and-wife team. There's only one double room so plan ahead.

Exeter YHA (☎ 0845 371 9516; www.yha.org.uk; 47 Countess Wear Rd; dm £15.95; P ☐) Exeter's official hostel is in a spacious 17th-century house overlooking the River Exe. The facilities are good and the dorms are reasonably sized, but being 2 miles out of town is a drawback. Catch bus K or T from High St, or 57 or 85 from the bus station to School Lane and follow the signs.

MIDRANGE

Woodbine (☎ 01392-203302; www.woodbineguesthouse .co.uk; 1 Woodbine Tce; s/d £38/65) A bit of a surprise sits behind this archetypal flower-framed B&B facade: fresh, contemporary rooms with low beds and flashes of burgundy – there's even underfloor heating in the showers.

our pick **Raffles** (☎ 01392-270200; www.raffles-exeter .co.uk; 11 Blackall Rd; s/d/f £38/68/78; P) Creaking with antiques and oozing atmosphere, this late-Victorian B&B is a lovely blend of old woods and tasteful modern fabrics. Plant stands and dado rails add to the turn-of-the-century feel, while the largely organic breakfasts, walled garden and much coveted parking make it a great value choice.

White Hart Hotel (☎ 01392-279897; www.room attheinn.info; 66 South St; s £60, d £70-75; P) They've been putting people up here since the Plantagenets were on the throne. The court-yard is a wisteria-fringed bobble of cobbles

and the bar is book-lined and beamed. Rooms are either traditional (dark woods and rich drapes) or contemporary (laminate floors and light fabrics).

Silversprings (☎ 01392-494040; www.silversprings .co.uk; 12 Richmond Rd; s £55, d £80-90, f £95, ste £100) This oh-so-chi-chi Georgian town house will either leave you longing to recline and varnish your nails or slightly overwhelmed. Rooms are all gilt mirrors and silky, vibrant fabrics – the best have real coffee, a free half-bottle of wine and fluffy bathrobes.

Other recommendations:

Telstar (☎ 01392-272466; www.telstar-hotel.co.uk; 75-77 St David's Hill; s £30-40, d £55-70) Friendly, traditional B&B with plain rooms and a tiny courtyard garden.

Queen's Court (☎ 01392-272709; www.queenscourt -hotel.co.uk; 6-8 Bystock Tce; s £87, d £97-105) Leather sofas and zebra prints spice up this Victorian town house.

TOP END

our pick **Hotel Barcelona** (☎ 01392-281000; www.alias hotels.com; Magdalen St; s £105, d £125-145; P ☐) The fabulous revamp of this former eye hospital has more wit than a festival full of come-dians. The building's medical past features alongside ultra-arty twists: plush deep-green carpets slice across the original hospital floor-ing, while the hospital lift still ferries guests up and down. But with rich woods, vivid furnishings and deeply luxurious bathrooms, it's unlike any institution you've ever seen. You can even sleep in the old operating thea-tre (room 220) without a trolley bed (or a surgeon) in sight.

ABode at the Royal Clarence Hotel (☎ 01392-319955; www.abodehotels.co.uk/exeter; Cathedral Yard; r £125-250) Georgian grandeur meets minimal-ist chic in these, the poshest rooms in town, where wonky floors and stained glass blend with pared-down furniture and neutral tones. The top-end suite is bigger than most people's apartments; its slanted ceilings and beams frame a grandstand Cathedral view.

Eating

Herbies (☎ 01392-258473; 15 North St; mains £5-9; ✆ lunch Mon-Sat, dinner Tue-Sat) Cosy and gently groovy, Herbies has been cheerfully feeding Exeter's vegetarians for 20 years. It's *the* place in town to tuck into delicious butterbean and vegetable pie, Moroccan *tagine* or cashew nut loaf. They're strong on vegan dishes too.

tyepyedong (☎ 01392-251888; 175 Sidwell St; mains £7-9; ✆ lunch & dinner Mon-Sat) Tucked away in an unlikely terrace of modern shops, this fusion food and noodle bar has a pristine, modern feel and rustles up great value *ramen* and *udon* noodles – their lunchtime dish-and-a-drink deal costs £5.

Harry's (☎ 01392-202234; 86 Longbrook St; mains £7-19; 🕑 lunch & dinner) Harry's is the kind of welcoming neighbourhood bistro you wish was on your own doorstep, but rarely is. The decor is all wooden chairs, blackboards and gilt mirrors; the food includes goat's cheese and walnut burgers, chargrilled chicken and classic pizzas.

Cafe Paradiso (☎ 01392-281000; Magdalen St; mains lunch £4-9, dinner £11-28; 🕑 lunch & dinner) Set in a futuristic glass-sided circus top, Hotel Barcelona's funky restaurant is dotted with Rothko-esque artwork and (intriguingly) painted white bicycles. Lunch is chic: silver mullet with herb gnocchi, while there's stylish dining at night – try the wood-fired trout.

No 21 (☎ 01392-210303; 21 Cathedral Yard; lunch £4-9, dinner £14-18; 🕑 breakfast, lunch & dinner Tue-Sat, 9am-5pm Sun & Mon) This mellow little eatery features subtle art, subtle lighting and imaginative fish, meat and vegie options – try their sea bass and chorizo or open mushroom ravioli.

Michael Caines (☎ 01392-223638; www.michaelcaines.com; Cathedral Yard; mains £24; 🕑 breakfast, lunch & dinner) Housed in the Royal Clarence and run by a locally famous Michelin-starred chef, the food here is a complex fusion of Westcountry ingredients and full-bodied French flavours. Top tips are the monkfish with red-wine butter or the Devon lamb with ratatouille. There's a bargain two-course lunch (£14.50) and a seven-course tasting menu (£58).

Drinking

On The Waterfront (☎ 01392-210590; The Quay; 🕑 lunch & dinner) In 1835 this was a warehouse, now its red-brick, barrel-vaulted ceilings stretch back from a minimalist bar. The tables that stretch along the quayside are perfect for a riverside pint.

Kino (☎ 01392-281000; Hotel Barcelona; Magdalen St; 🕑 6pm-1.30am Mon-Sat) More like a film set than a cocktail lounge, Kino's centrepiece is a stunning 1930s-style bar. Original film posters line the walls, while all around wannabe movie stars sip the seriously good cocktails and ponder their profiles.

Double Locks (☎ 01392-256947; Canal Banks) A bit of a local legend, this atmospheric former lockhouse sits 2 miles south of the quay beside the Exeter Ship Canal. Scarred floorboards, battered board games and excellent ale lend it a chilled vibe – helped by the real fires, waterside terrace and better than average bar food (mains £8).

Entertainment

GALLERIES, THEATRES & CINEMAS

Phoenix Arts Centre (☎ 01392-667080; www.exeterphoenix.org.uk; Gandy St) The city's art and soul; Phoenix is a vibrant hub of exhibitions, performance, music, dance, film, classes and workshops. There's a buzzing cafe-bar too.

Exeter Picturehouse (☎ 01392-435522; www.picturehouses.co.uk; 51 Bartholomew St West) This intimate, independent cinema screens mainstream and art-house movies.

Northcott Theatre (☎ 01392-493493; www.northcott-theatre.co.uk; University of Exeter Campus, Stocker Rd) The recently revamped Northcott stages a mix of home-grown and touring productions – look out for their open-air summer Shakespeare in Rougemont Gardens.

NIGHTCLUBS

Hub (☎ 01392-424628; 1 Mary Arches St; 🕑 8pm-midnight, 9pm-2am when bands play) A showcase for everything from thrash metal to alternative rock and DJs.

Cavern Club (☎ 01392-495370; www.cavernclub.co.uk; 83-84 Queen St; 🕑 11am-5pm Mon-Sat & 8pm-1am Sun-Thurs, to 2am Fri & Sat) A long-standing venue for big-name DJs and breaking acts from the indie scene.

Getting There & Away

AIR

Scheduled services connect **Exeter International Airport** (☎ 01392-367433; www.exeter-airport.co.uk) with cities in Europe and the UK, including Glasgow, Manchester and Newcastle, as well as the Channel Islands and the Isles of Scilly. A key operator is **FlyBe** (☎ 0871 700 2000; www.flybe.com).

BUS

Bus X38 goes to Plymouth (£6, 1¼ hours, hourly). Bus X9 runs to Bude (£5.50, three hours, five daily, two on Sunday) via Okehampton.

On Sundays throughout the year, bus 82 runs two to five times daily across Dartmoor from Exeter to Plymouth (£6, 2¼ hours), taking in Moretonhampstead (45 minutes) Postbridge (1¼ hours) and Princetown (one hour 20 minutes). It also runs twice on Saturdays between May and September. Between late July and late August it also runs twice a day Monday to Friday, but only between Moretonhampstead and Plymouth – bus 359 from Exeter to Moretonhampstead connects with the service. Bus X64 runs to Totnes (one hour, six daily Monday to Saturday, two on Sunday).

TRAIN
Trains run from Exeter St David's station to London Paddington (£58, 2¾ hours, hourly), Bristol (£20, 1¼ hours, half-hourly) and Penzance (£15, three hours, hourly) stations. Main-line trains run to Plymouth (£6.90, one hour, two or three per hour), and a branch line also shuttles to Torquay (£6, 45 minutes, hourly) and Paignton (£6.30, 50 minutes). Frequent trains also go to Totnes (£8.50, 45 minutes).

The picturesque Tarka Line connects Exeter Central with Barnstaple (£7, 1¼ hours, every two hours Monday to Saturday, four to six on Sunday).

Getting Around
TO/FROM THE AIRPORT
Buses 56 and 379 run from the bus station and Exeter St David's train station to Exeter International Airport (20 to 30 minutes, hourly), 5 miles east of the city. The service stops at 6pm.

BICYCLE
For bike hire see Saddle & Paddles (p375).

DETOUR: COMBE HOUSE

The sumptuous **Combe House** (☎ 01404-540400; www.thishotel.com; Gittisham; s £150, d £170-280, ste £320-240) is more like a National Trust property than a hotel. The great hall of this Elizabethan country manor is floor-to-ceiling wood panels, while ancient oak furniture and original Tudor paintings pop up everywhere. The historic splendour is matched by modern luxuries – guests are pampered with crisp cottons, monogrammed towels, rain showers and sumptuous throws – one room even has a vast copper washtub for a bath. It's all set on a massive estate near Gittisham, 14 miles east of Exeter.

BUS
The one-day Explorer pass (adult/child £6/4) gives unlimited travel on Stagecoach's Exeter buses. Bus H links St David's and Central train stations, passing near the bus station.

CAR
The tourist office has a list of car-hire offices; try **Europcar** (☎ 01392-275398; Water Lane; ☑ 8.30am-5.30pm Mon-Fri, to 1pm Sat). Park-and-ride buses run from Matford (Bus PR5) and Honiton Rd (PR2), every 10 minutes.

TAXI
There are taxi ranks at St David's train station and on High St, or call **Capital Taxis** (☎ 01392-433433), **Club Cars** (☎ 01392-213030) or **Gemini** (☎ 01392-666666).

AROUND EXETER
Powderham Castle
Powderham (☎ 01626-890243; www.powderham.co.uk; adult/child £8.50/6.50; ☑ 10am-5.30pm Easter-Oct, closed Sat) is the historic home of the earl of Devon. A stately but still friendly place, it was built in 1391, damaged in the Civil War and remodelled in the Victorian era. A visit takes in a fine wood-panelled Great Hall, parkland with 650 deer and a glimpse of life 'below stairs' in the kitchen. The earl and family are still resident and, despite its grandeur, for charming, fleeting moments it feels like you're actually wandering through someone's sitting room.

Powderham is on the River Exe near Kenton, 8 miles south of Exeter. Bus 2 runs from Exeter (20 minutes, every 15 minutes Monday to Saturday, every 30 minutes Sunday).

A La Ronde
A La Ronde (NT; ☎ 01395-265514; Summer Lane, Exmouth; adult/child £5.40/2.70; ☑ 11am-5pm Sat-Wed late Mar-Oct) is a DIY job with a difference. This delightfully quirky 16-sided cottage was built in 1796 for two spinster cousins to display a mass of curiosities acquired on a 10-year European grand tour. Its glass alcoves, low lintels and tiny doorways mean it's like clambering through a doll's house – highlights are a delicate feather frieze in the drawing room and a gallery smothered with a thousand seashells. In a fabulous collision of old and new, this can only be seen via remote control CCTV from the butler's pantry. The house is 10 miles south of Exeter, near Exmouth; bus 57 runs close by.

SOUTH DEVON COAST
Torquay & Paignton
pop 110,370

For decades the bright 'n' breezy seaside resort of Torquay pitched itself as an exotic 'English Riviera' – playing on a mild microclimate, palm trees and promenades. But these days Torquay's nightclubs and bars attract a much younger crowd and the result is a sometimes bizarre clash of cultures: coach parties meet stag parties on streets lined by fudge shops and slightly saucy postcards. Chuck in some truly top-notch restaurants, a batch of good beaches and an Agatha Christie connection, and it all makes for some grand days out beside the sea. Just to the south of Torquay is Paignton with its seafront prom, multicoloured beach huts and faded 19th-century pier.

The **tourist office** (☎ 0870 707 0010; www.theenglish riviera.co.uk; Vaughan Pde; 🕑 9.30am-5pm Mon-Sat, 10am-4.30pm Sun May-Sep, 9.30am-5pm Mon-Sat Oct-Apr) sells discounted tickets to local attractions.

SIGHTS & ACTIVITIES

Torquay has two famous former residents: Agatha Christie, who was born in Torquay in 1890 and lived at the manor house of Greenway (p380), near Dartmouth; and Basil Fawlty, the deranged Torquay hotelier played memorably by John Cleese in the classic British comedy *Fawlty Towers*.

Torquay Museum (☎ 01803-293975; 529 Babbacombe Rd; adult/child £4/2.50; 🕑 10am-5pm Mon-Sat, 1.30-5pm Sun Jul-Sep) has an intriguing selection of Agatha Christie memorabilia including family photos, 1st-edition novels and a couple of display cases devoted to her famous detectives Hercule Poirot and Miss Marple.

Torbay Belle (☎ 01803-528555) runs boat trips to Brixham (p380; adult/child return £6/3) from North Quay in the Harbour, and to Dartmouth (p380; adult/child return £14/7) from Haldon Pier. The trips to Agatha Christie's garden at Greenway leave from Princess Pier.

Torquay is surrounded by 20 beaches, the best of which is family-friendly **Babbacombe**, about 2 miles north of the centre, which still has a working 1920s **funicular** (☎ 01803-328750; adult/child return £1.75/1.20; 🕑 9.30am-5.25pm Easter-Sep) connecting the beach to the clifftop.

SLEEPING

Torquay is practically wall-to-wall B&Bs and hotels, with a concentrated cluster around Avenue and Bridge Rds.

Torquay International Backpackers (☎ 01803-299924; www.torquaybackpackers.co.uk; 119 Abbey Rd; dm/d £14/30) Relics of happy travels (world maps, board games and homemade wind chimes) are everywhere in this funky, friendly, laid-back hostel. The owners hand out guitars and organise barbecues, beach trips and local pub tours.

Headland View (☎ 01803-312612; www.headland view.com; Babbacombe Downs; s/d £45/64) Set high on the cliffs at Babbacombe, this B&B is awash with nauticalia: from boat motifs on the curtains to 'welcome' lifebelts on the walls. Four rooms have tiny flower-filled balconies overlooking a cracking stretch of sea.

our pick Lanscombe House (☎ 01803-606938; www.lanscombehouse.co.uk; Cockington Lane; s £50-60, d £75-110) Laura Ashley herself would love the lashings of tasteful fabrics, four-poster beds, and free-standing slipper baths on show here. Set amid the calm of Cockington Country Park between Torquay and Paignton, it has a lovely English cottage garden where you can hear owls hoot at night.

Hillcroft (☎ 01803-297247; www.thehillcroft.co.uk; 9 St Lukes Rd; d £75-85, ste £130-180) Full of boutique flourishes, the themed rooms in this mini hotel veer from French antique to Asian chic. The sumptuous bathrooms range from grotto-esque to sleekly styled, and the top-floor suite is gorgeous.

Other recommendations:

Norwood Hotel (☎ 01803-294236; www.norwood hoteltorquay.co.uk; 60 Belgrave Rd; s/d/f £38/54/70) Four-storey B&B draped with lemon and gold satin.

Haven Hotel (☎ 01803-293390; www.havenhotel.biz; 11 Scarborough Rd; s/d £40/60) Cream, pristine B&B with clean modern lines and beige throws.

EATING & DRINKING

Torbay sizzles with some seriously good restaurants, including one with a Michelin star, as well the full complement of chippies.

Number 7 (☎ 01803-295055; Beacon Tce; mains £15; 🕑 dinner & lunch Wed-Sat) Fabulous smells fill the air at this buzzing harbourside fish bistro, where the menu is packed with super-fresh crab, lobster and monkfish, often with unexpected twists. Try the king scallops with vermouth or fish and prawn tempura.

Orange Tree (☎ 01803-213936; 14 Park Hill Rd; mains £18; 🕑 dinner) This award-winning brasserie adds a dash of Continental flair to local fish, meat and game. Prepare to enjoy lemon sole with Armagnac and prawns, or Devon scrumpy pork (it's stuffed with apples). Then loosen your belt for Vesuvius – a dark chocolate fondant cooked to order.

Elephant (☎ 01803-200044; www.elephantrestaurant .co.uk; 3 Beacon Tce; 2-/3-courses £33/40, brasserie mains £14; ☯ dinner Tue-Sat, brasserie lunch & dinner Tue-Sat, lunch Sun) One to remember. Torbay's Michelin-starred restaurant is full of imaginative flavour fusions: try venison with vanilla and beetroot or sea bass with hog's pudding gnocchi. If that's a bit much, they'll do you a steak. There's fine dining in The Room or brasserie fare downstairs.

Other recommendations:

Pier Point (☎ 01803-299935; Torbay Pier; mains £5-20; ☯ lunch & dinner) Tasty salads, pizzas and burgers at the foot of Torquay Pier.

Hole In The Wall (☎ 01803-200755; 6 Park Lane) Heavily beamed, Tardis-like boozer – an atmospheric spot for a pint.

GETTING THERE & AWAY

Bus 12 runs to Paignton from Torquay (20 minutes, every 10 minutes) and onto Brixham (40 minutes). Bus X80 goes to Totnes (one hour, every two hours) and onto Plymouth (£5.20, 1¾ hours). Bus 111 goes to Dartmouth (1¾ hours, hourly Monday to Saturday, three on Sunday).

A branch train line runs from Exeter via Torquay (£6, 45 minutes, hourly) to Paignton (£6.30, 50 minutes). The **Paignton & Dartmouth Steam Railway** (☎ 01803-555872; www.paignton-steam railway.co.uk; adult/child return £8/5.50) puffs from Paignton on the charming 7-mile trip (30 minutes) to Kingswear on the River Dart, linked by ferry to Dartmouth (car/pedestrian £3.30/1, six minutes). Generally four to nine trains run daily between April and October, but there are exceptions – check with the operator.

Brixham
pop 17,460

An appealing, pastel-painted tumbling of fishermen's cottages leads down to Brixham's horseshoe harbour, signalling a very different place from Torquay. Here gently tacky arcades coexist with winding streets, brightly coloured boats and one of England's busiest working fishing ports. Although picturesque, Brixham is far from a neatly packaged resort, and its brand of gritty charm offers a more accurate glimpse of life along Devon's coast.

The **tourist office** (☎ 0870 707 0010; www.theenglish riviera.co.uk; Old Market House, The Quay; ☯ 9.30am-

5pm Mon-Sat, 10am-4pm Sun Apr-Oct) is right beside the harbour.

A full-sized replica of Devon seafarer Sir Francis Drake's ship, the **Golden Hind** (☎ 01803-856223; adult/child £3/2; ☯ 10am-4pm Mar-Sep), is tied up in Brixham harbour. Remarkably small, the Elizabethan original had a crew of 60. Today you get to cross the gangplank, peer in the tiny captain's cabin and prowl around the poop deck.

The displays at **Brixham Heritage Museum** (☎ 01803-856267; www.brixhamheritage.org.uk; Bolton Cross; adult/child £2/1.50; ☯ 10am-5pm Mon-Fri, 10am-1pm Sat, closed Nov-Jan) explore the town's salty history with exhibits on smuggling and the curious items dragged up by local trawlers.

There are plenty of chippies scattered around the quay but for a real taste of the British seaside, try a pot of prawns or fresh crab from **Browse Seafoods** (☎ 01803-882484), next to the tourist office.

Bus 22 runs along the coast to Kingswear (30 minutes, half-hourly Monday to Saturday, hourly Sunday) from where you can catch the river ferry over to Dartmouth. Bus 12 connects Torquay and Bixham via Paignton (see left).

Dartmouth
pop 5693

A bewitching blend of primary-coloured boats and delicately shaded houses, Dartmouth is hard to resist. Buildings cascade down steep, wooded slopes towards the River Dart while 17th-century shops with splendidly carved and gilded fronts line narrow lanes. Its popularity with a trendy sailing set risks imposing too many boutiques and upmarket restaurants, but Dartmouth is also a busy port and the constant traffic of working boats ensures an authentic tang of the sea. Agatha Christie's summer home and a captivating art-deco house are both nearby, adding to the town's appeal.

Dartmouth hugs the quay on the west side of Dart estuary, the village of Kingswear on the east bank provides a key transport link to Torbay and is connected by an array of car and foot ferries. Dartmouth's **tourist office** (☎ 01803-834224; www.discoverdartmouth.com; Mayor's Ave; ☯ 9.30am-5.30pm Mon-Sat year-round, plus 10am-2pm Sun Apr-Oct) houses the Newcomen Engine, an early (1712) steam engine.

Greenway (NT; ☎ 01803-842382; Greenway Rd, Galmpton; adult/child £6/3; ☯ 10.30am-5pm Wed-Sun Mar-

Sep), the enchanting summer home of crime writer Agatha Christie, sits beside the River Dart near Dartmouth. Woods speckled with splashes of magnolias, daffodils and hydrangeas, hug the water, while the planting creates intimate, secret spaces – the boathouse and views over the river are delightful. After extensive renovation the house was due to open in 2009. Driving to Greenway is discouraged; you can hike along the Dart Valley Trail from Kingswear (4 miles) or sail up river from Dartmouth on the **Greenway Ferry** (☎ 01803-844010; adult/child £6/4). Boats run only when the property is open; times vary and it's best to book.

Coleton Fishacre (NT; ☎ 01803-752466; Brownstone Rd, Kingswear; adult/child £6.40/3.20; ☽ garden 10.30am-5pm, house 11am-4.30pm Wed-Sun mid-Mar–Oct) was built in the 1920s for the D'Oyly Carte family of theatre impresarios – they also owned London's Savoy Hotel. Its gorgeous art-deco embellishments include original Lalique tulip uplighters, comic bathroom tiles and a stunning saloon – complete with tinkling piano. The croquet terrace leads to deeply shelved subtropical gardens and suddenly revealed vistas of the sea. Hike the 4 miles along the cliffs from Kingswear, or drive.

Dartmouth Castle (EH; ☎ 01803-833588; adult/child £4/2; ☽ 10am-6pm Jul & Aug, 10am-5pm Apr-Jun & Sep, 10am-4pm Oct, 10am-4pm Sat & Sun only Nov-Mar), at the mouth of the estuary, is great for some battlement scrambling. In the centre of town the row of wonky timber-framed houses that looks near to collapse is the **Butterwalk** – it's actually managed to remain standing since the late 17th century.

SLEEPING

Hill View House (☎ 01803-839372; www.hillviewdart mouth.co.uk; 76 Victoria Rd; s £39-47, d £57-70) This eco-conscious place to kip features environmentally-friendly toiletries, natural cotton, long-life light bulbs and organic breakfasts. Rooms are tastefully decked out in cream and brown and there's a 5% discount for travellers not using cars.

Brown's Hotel (☎ 01803-832572; www.brownshotel dartmouth.co.uk; 29 Victoria Rd; s £65, d £85-170) How do you combine leather curtains, pheasant feather-covered lampshades, animal-print chairs and still make it look classy? The owners of this smoothly sumptuous hotel have worked it out. Look out for the lobster and frites evenings in their tapas bar too.

Orleans (☎ 01803-835450; www.orleans-guesthouse -dartmouth.co.uk; 24 South Town; d £85-95, ste £165) Purple and gold fabrics, marble fireplaces and bare floorboards grace this oh-so-chic guest house. There's a bay window in which to enjoy a game of chess – if you can tear your eyes away from the boats on the water below.

EATING & DRINKING

our pick Crab Shell (☎ 01803-839036; 1 Raleigh St; sandwiches £4; ☽ lunch, closed Jan-Mar) The shellfish gracing the sarnies here has been landed on the quay a few steps away, and much of the fish has been smoked locally. Opt to fill your bread with mackerel with horseradish mayo, kiln-roast salmon with dill, or classic, delicious Dartmouth crab.

Alf Resco (☎ 01803-835880; Lower St; mains from £6; ☽ breakfast, lunch & dinner Wed-Sun) Tucked under a huge canvas awning, this cool cafe brings a dash of cosmopolitan charm to town. Rickety wooden chairs and old street signs fill the front terrace; frothy lattes and ciabatta sandwiches fill the menu.

Taylor's (☎ 01803-832748; 8 The Quay; mains £15; ☽ lunch Tue-Sat, dinner Fri & Sat Sep-Jun, nightly Jul & Aug) The huge bay windows here mean you can watch boats bobbing about, while the menu ensures a tastebud treat too. There's everything from grilled lobster or Devon lamb to asparagus and goat's-cheese tart.

New Angel (☎ 01803-839425; 2 South Embankment; mains £18-23; ☽ breakfast, lunch & dinner Tue-Sat, breakfast & lunch Sun & Mon) The fanciest, most famous joint in town. Awarded a Michelin star and run by celebrity chef John Burton Race (of *French Leave* fame) it serves up pheasant, Devon duck and local fish with more than a soupçon of continental flair.

GETTING THERE & AWAY

Bus 93 runs to Plymouth (£5.30, two hours, hourly, four on Sunday) via Kingsbridge (one hour). Bus 111 goes to Torquay (1¾ hours, hourly Monday to Saturday, three on Sunday) via Totnes. Ferries shuttle across the river to Kingswear (car/pedestrian £3.30/1) every six minutes; they run from 6.30am to 10.45pm.

River Link (☎ 01803-834488; www.riverlink.co.uk; adult/child return £9/6; ☽ Apr-Oct) runs cruises along the River Dart to Totnes (1¼ hours, two to four daily).

For details of the Paignton & Dartmouth Steam Railway, see opposite.

Totnes

pop 8194

Totnes has such a reputation for being alternative that local jokers wrote 'twinned with Narnia' under the town sign. For decades famous as Devon's hippie haven, eco-conscious Totnes also became Britain's first 'transition town' in 2005, when it began trying to wean itself off a dependence on oil. Sustainability aside, Totnes boasts a gracious Norman castle, a mass of fine Tudor buildings, an unusual Jazz Age house and a tempting vineyard.

The **tourist office** (☎ 01803-863168; www.totnes information.co.uk; Coronation Rd; ☼ 9.30am-5pm Mon-Sat) is in the town's old mill.

SIGHTS & ACTIVITIES

The white and vivid blue Modern Movement **High Cross House** (☎ 01803-864114; Dartington Hall Estate; adult/child £3.50/2.50; ☼ 10.30am-12.30pm & 2-4.30pm Tue-Fri late Jul-Aug, 2-4.30pm May–mid-Jul, Sep & Oct) was built in 1932, making its rectilinear and curved design one of the first examples of its kind in the country. The interior is gorgeous: all pared-down shapes, smooth woods and understated elegance. High Cross sits alongside the main road inside the Dartington Hall Estate, 1.5 miles west of Totnes.

Sharpham Vineyard (☎ 01803-732203; www.sharpham .com; Ashprington; tours £5-10, Sharpham Experience £50; ☼ 10am-5pm Mon-Sat Mar-Dec plus Sun Jun-Aug) shelters in a tranquil riverside setting. It provides the chance to wander among the vines, learn about vinification and indulge in tutored tastings – they also make cheese on the estate so you can nibble that too. The vineyard is 3 miles south of Totnes, signed off the A381 – or walk from town along the Dart Valley Trail.

Totnes Castle (EH; ☎ 01803-864406; adult/child £2.50/1.30; ☼ 10am-6pm Jul & Aug, to 5pm Easter-Sep, to 4pm Oct) occupies a commanding position on a grassy hilltop above town. Little remains of the original Norman motte-and-bailey fortress but the outer keep is still standing, and the views of the town and surrounding fields are fantastic.

The bijou but lovely **Devonshire Collection of Period Costume** (☎ 01803-863168; High St; adult/child £2/80p; ☼ 11am-5pm Tue-Fri May-Sep) features beautifully displayed garments.

Canoe Adventures (☎ 01803-865301; www.canoe adventures.co.uk; per 5hr £17) organises trips on the Dart in 12-seater Canadian canoes. They often work in a campfire or a pub visit, and their monthly moonlit paddles are a treat.

SLEEPING

Old Forge (☎ 01803-862174; www.oldforgetotnes.com; Seymour Pl; s £52, d £62-82, f £107) This 600-year-old B&B used to be a smithy and the town jail – thankfully comfort has replaced incarceration: deep red and sky blue furnishings cosy up to bright throws and spa baths. The delightful family room even has its own decked sun terrace.

Maltsters Arms (☎ 01803-732350; www.tuckenhay .com; d from £75-110) The rooms in this old creekside pub are anything but ordinary, ranging from silky and eastern to authentically nautical – one even sports painted oil drums and real anchors. It's hidden away in the hamlet of Tuckenhay, 4 miles south of Totnes.

Steam Packet Inn (☎ 01803-863880; www.steampacket inn.co.uk; St Peters Quay; d/f £80/110) Plucked from the pages of a design magazine, the minimalist bedrooms of this wharfside former warehouse are full of painted wood panels, willow arrangements and neutral tones. Ask for a riverview room then watch the world float by.

EATING

Willow Vegetarian Restaurant (☎ 01803-862605; 87 High St; mains £5.50; ☼ lunch Mon-Sat, dinner Wed, Fri & Sat) The hang-out of choice for Totnes' New Agers, this rustic wholefood cafe does a nice line in couscous, quiches, hotpots and homemade cakes. Look out for their curry nights.

Rumour (☎ 01803-864682; 30 Fore St; mains £10.50-14; ☼ 10am-11pm Mon-Sat, 6-10.30pm Sun) It's so friendly here it's almost like dining in a friend's front room. The menu is packed with pizzas, panfried sea trout and Salcombe ice cream; their pioneering eco-policy includes using heat from the kitchen to warm the water.

our pick **Riverford Field Kitchen** (☎ 01803-762074; www.riverford.co.uk; Wash Barn, nr Buckfastleigh; 2 courses adult/child £14/7; ☼ lunch, plus some Fri & Sat dinner) For a taste of ecofriendly Totnes head to this futuristic farm bistro. Vegetables are plucked to order from the fields in front of you, the meats are organic and locally sourced, and the dining area is a huge, hip hangar-like canteen. The food treatments are imaginative too – try the marinated grilled Moroccan lamb and cumin and saffron veg. Planning laws require you to book and take a tour of the fields. The farm is 3 miles west of Totnes.

GETTING THERE & AWAY

Bus X64 runs to Exeter (one hour, six daily Monday to Saturday, two on Sunday). Bus

X80 comes from Plymouth (1¼ hours, hourly) and goes onto Paignton (20 minutes) and Torquay (30 minutes).

Frequent trains go to Exeter (£8.50, 45 minutes) and Plymouth (£5, 30 minutes, hourly). The privately run **South Devon Railway** (☎ 0845 345 1420; www.southdevonrailway.org) is beside the main-line station. Its steam trains chuff to Buckfastleigh (adult/child return £9.30/5.60, four or five daily Easter to October) on the edge of Dartmoor.

You can also cruise down the river to Dartmouth (p381).

PLYMOUTH
pop 256,633

If parts of Devon are costume dramas or nature programs, Plymouth is a healthy dose of reality TV. Gritty, and certainly not always pretty, its centre has been subjected to buildings even the architects' mothers might question. But despite often being dismissed for its partying, poverty and urban problems, this is a city that's huge in spirit and it comes with great assets. Its setting on the fringes of an impressive natural harbour and just a few miles from the wilderness expanse of Dartmoor makes it an ideal base for activities. Add a rich maritime history, a Barbican area creaking with half-timbered houses, some unusual attractions and a decidedly lively nightlife, and you have a place to reconnect with the real before another foray into the delights of Devon's chocolate-box-pretty moors and shores.

History

Plymouth's history is dominated by the sea. The first recorded cargo left the city in 1211 and by the late 16th century it was the port of choice for explorers and adventurers. It's waved off Sir Francis Drake, Sir Walter Raleigh, the fleet that defeated the Spanish Armada, the pilgrims who founded America, Charles Darwin, Captain Cook and countless boats carrying emigrants to Australia and New Zealand.

During WWII Plymouth suffered horrendously at the hands of the Luftwaffe – more than 1000 civilians died in the Blitz, which reduced the city centre to rubble. The 21st-century has brought large-scale regeneration of the city's waterfront areas and the architectural mishmash of the £200 million pound Drake Circus shopping centre.

Orientation

Plymouth's pedestrianised centre is south of the train station. Further south again the headland Hoe area is packed with guest houses and B&Bs; to the east of the Hoe the regenerated Barbican is packed with good places to eat and drink.

Information

Hoegate Laundrette (☎ 01752-223031; 55 Notte St; ⊙ 8am-6pm Mon-Fri, 9am-1pm Sat)
Plymouth Library (☎ 01752-305923; Drake Circus; ⊙ 9am-7pm Mon-Fri, 9am-5pm Sat) Free internet access.
Police station (Charles Cross; ⊙ 24hr)
Post office (5 St Andrew's Cross; ⊙ 9am-5.30pm Mon-Sat)
Tourist office (☎ 01752-306330; www.visitplymouth .co.uk; 3-5 The Barbican; ⊙ 9am-5pm Mon-Sat, 10am-4pm Sun Apr-Oct, 9am-5pm Mon-Fri, 10am-4pm Sat Nov-Mar) Housed inside the Plymouth Mayflower building.
University Bookseller (☎ 01752-660428; 42 Drake Circus; ⊙ 10am-4pm Mon-Sat)

Sights & Activities
PLYMOUTH HOE

Francis Drake supposedly spied the Spanish fleet from this grassy headland overlooking Plymouth Sound; the fabled bowling green on which he finished his game was probably where his **statue** now stands. Later the Hoe became a favoured holiday spot for the Victorian aristocracy, and the headland is backed by an impressive array of multistoreyed villas and once-grand hotels.

The red-and-white-striped former lighthouse, **Smeaton's Tower** (☎ 01752-603300; The Hoe; adult/child £2/1; ⊙ 10am-4pm Tue-Sat Apr-Oct, to 3pm Nov-Mar), was built 14 miles off shore on the Eddystone Rocks in 1759, then moved to the Hoe in 1882. Climbing its 93 steps provides an illuminating insight into lighthouse keepers' lives and a stunning view of the city, Dartmoor and the sea.

BARBICAN

To get an idea of what old Plymouth was like before the Blitz, head for the Barbican, with its many Tudor and Jacobean buildings (now converted into galleries, craft shops and restaurants).

The Pilgrim Fathers' *Mayflower* set sail for America from the Barbican on 16 September 1620. The **Mayflower Steps** mark the point of departure (track down the passenger list displayed on the side of a shop

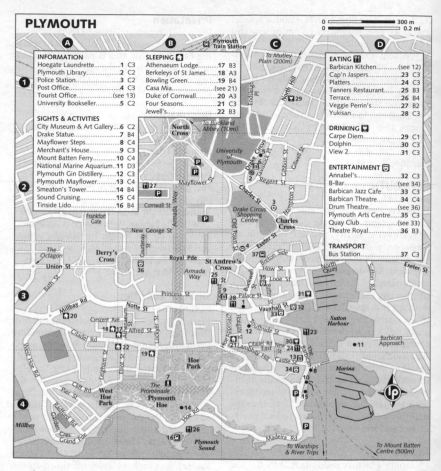

PLYMOUTH

0   300 m
0   0.2 mi

INFORMATION
Hoegate Laundrette................1 C3
Plymouth Library.................2 C2
Police Station.....................3 C2
Post Office........................4 C3
Tourist Office.................(see 13)
University Bookseller........5 C2

SIGHTS & ACTIVITIES
City Museum & Art Gallery...6 C2
Drake Statue.......................7 B4
Mayflower Steps.................8 C4
Merchant's House...............9 C3
Mount Batten Ferry..........10 C4
National Marine Aquarium..11 D3
Plymouth Gin Distillery.....12 C4
Plymouth Mayflower..........13 C4
Smeaton's Tower...............14 B4
Sound Cruising..................15 C3
Tinside Lido......................16 B4

SLEEPING
Atheneaum Lodge...........17 B3
Berkeleys of St James......18 A3
Bowling Green.................19 B4
Casa Mia......................(see 21)
Duke of Cornwall.............20 A3
Four Seasons..................21 C3
Jewell's........................22 B3

EATING
Barbican Kitchen............(see 12)
Cap'n Jaspers.................23 C3
Platters.........................24 C3
Tanners Restaurant...........25 B3
Terrace..........................26 B4
Veggie Perrin's................27 B2
Yukisan.........................28 C3

DRINKING
Carpe Diem.....................29 C1
Dolphin..........................30 C3
View 2...........................31 C3

ENTERTAINMENT
Annabel's.......................32 C3
B-Bar..........................(see 34)
Barbican Jazz Cafe...........33 C3
Barbican Theatre..............34 C4
Drum Theatre................(see 36)
Plymouth Arts Centre........35 C3
Quay Club...................(see 33)
Theatre Royal..................36 B3

TRANSPORT
Bus Station.....................37 C3

nearby); scores of other famous voyages are also marked by plaques at the steps, including one led by Captain James Cook, who set out from the Barbican in 1768 in search of a southern continent.

Plymouth Mayflower (☎ 01752-306330; 3-5 The Barbican; ⊙ 9am-5pm Mon-Sat, 10am-4pm Sun Apr-Oct, 9am-5pm Mon-Fri, 10am-4pm Sat Nov-Mar) is a hi-tech rundown through Plymouth's nautical heritage, providing the background to the Pilgrim Fathers' trip with plenty of interactive gizmos and multisensory displays.

The **Plymouth Gin Distillery** (☎ 01752-665292; www.plymouthgin.com; 60 Southside St; tours £6; ⊙ 10.30am-4.30pm Mon-Sat, 11.30am-3.30pm Sun) is the oldest producer of this kind of spirit in the world – they've been making gin here

since 1793. The Royal Navy ferried it round the world in countless officers' messes and the brand was specified in the first recorded recipe for a dry martini in the 1930s. Tours wind past the stills and take in a tutored tasting before depositing you in the heavily beamed medieval bar for a free tipple.

A footbridge leads from the Barbican across the harbour to the **National Marine Aquarium** (☎ 01752-220084; The Barbican; www .national-aquarium.co.uk; adult/child £9.50/5.75; ⊙ 10am-6pm Apr-Oct, 10am-5pm Nov-Mar). Here sharks swim in coral seas teaming with moray eels, turtles and vividly coloured fish, while other displays highlight successful breeding programs of cardinal fish, coral and incredibly cute seahorses.

AN ART DECO DIP

Tucked between the Hoe and the shore **Tinside Lido** (☎ 01752-261915; Hoe Rd; adult/child £3.65/2.40; ☉ noon-6pm Mon-Fri, 10am-6pm Sat & Sun late May–late Jul, from 10am daily late Jul–early Sep) is an outdoor, saltwater art-deco pool first opened to the public in 1935. During its heyday in the '40s and '50s, thousands of Plymouthians flocked to the pool on summer days (backed by the soothing strains of a string orchestra). In the '70s and '80s the pool fell into disrepair before closing in 1992. It's since been restored to its former glory thanks to a hefty £3.4 million refurbishment and now it's packed throughout summer with school kids and sun worshippers; sadly, though, there's no sign of the string orchestra returning just yet.

MERCHANT'S HOUSE

The 17th-century **Merchant's House** (☎ 01752-304774; 33 St Andrews St; adult/child £1.50/1; ☉ 10am-5pm Tue-Sat Apr-Sep) is packed with curiosities; from manacles, truncheons and a ducking stool, to a replica 19th-century school room and an entire Victorian pharmacy where you get to try old-fashioned pill rolling.

CITY MUSEUM & ART GALLERY

At the time of writing, the **City Museum & Art Gallery** (☎ 01752-304774; Drake Circus; admission free; ☉ 10am-5.30pm Tue-Fri, 10am-5pm Sat) was remaining partially open during a £750,000 revamp, due for completion in 2009. New galleries highlight its world-cultures, archaeological and maritime collections.

BOAT TRIPS & WATER SPORTS

Sound Cruising (☎ 01752-671166; www.soundcruising.com; Phoenix Warf) offers regular boat trips from Phoenix Warf out to the warships at Plymouth's naval base (1½ hour trips adult/child £6/2.75) and up the River Tamar to the Cornish village of Calstock (4½ hour trips adult/child £9.50/6.50)

The little yellow **Mount Batten Ferry** (adult/child return £3/2, 10 minutes, half hourly) shuttles from beside the Mayflower Steps across to the Mount Batten Peninsula, where the **Mount Batten Centre** (☎ 01752-404567; www.mount-batten-centre.com; 70 Lawrence Rd, Mount Batten) does lessons in kayaking (£75 for two days) and sailing (£145 for two days).

Sleeping

Fertile B&B hunting grounds are just back from Hoe, especially around Citadel Rd.

BUDGET & MIDRANGE

Jewell's (☎ 01752-254760; 220 Citadel Rd; s £25, d £45-55, f £60-65) Traces of the Victorian era linger in the high ceilings and ornate plasterwork

of this friendly B&B. Rooms are bright and modern with lilac armchairs and filmy blue curtains; top-quality bathrooms add another layer of class.

Casa Mia (☎ 01752-265742; www.casa-mia-onthehoe.com; 201 Citadel Rd East; s/d/f from £30/55/65; ☐ wi-fi) A flower-filled patio and a highly polished brass step hint at what to expect here: a cheerful, traditional and spotlessly clean B&B. Tucked away from main roads, it's still only a few minutes' walk from the Barbican.

Four Seasons ☎ 01752-223591; www.fourseasonsguesthouse.co.uk; 207 Citadel Rd East; s £31-46, d £50-62, f £60) This place is crammed full of treats, from the big bowls of free sweets to the mounds of Devon bacon for breakfast. They've got the basics right too: tasteful rooms decorated in gold and cream.

Bowling Green (☎ 01752-209090; www.bowlinggreenhotel.co.uk; 10 Osborne Pl; s £46-56, d £66, f £76) Some of the airy cream-and-white rooms in this family-run hotel look out onto the modern incarnation of Drake's famous bowling green. If you tire of watching people throw woods after jacks you can play chess in the conservatory.

Other recommendations:

Athenaeum Lodge (☎ 01752-665005; www.athenaeumlodge.com; 4 Athenaeum St; s £32, d £46-60; ☐) Grade II Georgian B&B with a few frills and flounces.

Berkeleys of St James (☎ 01752-221654; www.onthehoe.co.uk; 4 St James Pl East; s/d/f £40/57/75) Cosy B&B dishing up breakfasts full of local, organic goodies.

TOP END

Duke of Cornwall (☎ 01752-275850; www.thedukeofcornwallhotel.com; Millbay Rd; s £94, d £87-160) With one of the most striking edifices in Plymouth, this grand turret-topped, gable-studded pile is the most luxurious place to stay in town. The rooms are massive, if a touch old fashioned; the four-poster suite, complete with champagne and complimentary fruit basket, is the pick of the bunch.

Eating

CAFES

our pick **Cap'n Jaspers** (☎ 01752-262444; www.capn
-jaspers.co.uk; Whitehouse Pier, Quay Rd; snacks £3-5;
◷ 7.45am-11.45pm) Unique, quirky and slightly
insane, this outdoor cafe has been delighting
bikers, tourists and locals for decades with its
motorised gadgets and teaspoons attached by
chains. The menu is of the burger and bacon
butty school – trying to eat their 'half a yard of
hot dog' is a Plymouth rite of passage. Try the
local crab rolls – the filling could have been
caught by the bloke sitting next to you.

Terrace (☎ 01752-603533; Madeira Rd; mains £3-6;
◷ breakfast & lunch) Tucked away beside the
Tinside Lido, this bright and breezy cafe has
the best location of any eatery in town, with
sweeping views across Plymouth Sound and a
selection of sandwiches, coffees and generous
jacket potatoes.

RESTAURANTS

our pick **Barbican Kitchen** (☎ 01752-604448; 60 Southside St; snacks £5, mains £11-16; ◷ lunch & dinner, closed
dinner Sun) In this bistro-style baby sister of
Tanners Restaurant (below), the wood and
stone interior fizzes with bursts of shocking
pink and lime. The food is attention grabbing
too – try the calves' liver with horseradish
mash or the honey, goat's cheese and apple
crostini. Their Devon beefburger, with a slab
of stilton, is divine.

Platters (☎ 01752-227262; 12 The Barbican; mains £13;
◷ lunch & dinner) The fish in this down-to-earth
eatery is so fresh it's just stopped flapping – try
their skate in butter or the locally caught sea
bass. You could pay twice as much nearby and
end up with something half as good.

Tanners Restaurant (☎ 01752-252001; www.tan
nersrestaurant.com; Finewell St; 2-/3-course dinner £26/32;
◷ lunch & dinner Tue-Sat) Plymouth's top table is
run by the (locally famous) Tanner brothers. Renowned for reinventing British and
French classics, they dish up lamb with
gnocchi, chargrilled asparagus with soft-
poached egg, and roasted quail with pancetta.
Gourmands should try to book the five-course
meal (£37).

Also recommended:

Yukisan (☎ 01752-250240; 51 Notte St; mains £14;
◷ lunch & dinner) Super-fresh sushi, light tempura and
noodles worth mastering chopsticks for.

Veggie Perrin's (☎ 01752-252888; 97 Mayflower St;
mains £8; ◷ lunch & dinner Mon-Sat) Excellent, authentic, vegetarian Indian food.

Drinking

Like any Navy city, Plymouth has a more than
lively nightlife. Union St is clubland; Mutley
Plain and North Hill have a studenty vibe,
while the Barbican has more restaurants amid
the bars. All three areas get rowdy, especially
at weekends.

Carpe Diem (☎ 01752-252942; 50 North Hill; ◷ 11am-
midnight) A beautifully lit, funky bar done out
in a kaleidoscope of colours – there's a heated,
open-air chill-out room too.

View 2 (☎ 01752-252564; Vauxhall Quay; ◷ to 2am,
later at weekends) Just round from the heart of the
Barbican, this cool venue's waterside terrace is
perfect for a lunchtime pizza or drink. In the
evening enjoy comedy, salsa, easy listening,
soul, funk and R&B.

Dolphin (☎ 01752-660876; 14 The Barbican) This
wonderfully unreconstructed Barbican boozer
is all scuffed tables, padded bench seats and
an authentic, no-nonsense atmosphere.

Entertainment

BARS & NIGHTCLUBS

Barbican Jazz Cafe (☎ 01752-672127; 11 The Parade; admission Fri & Sat £2; ◷ noon-2am Mon-Sat, noon-midnight
Sun) Nightly jazz and guest DJs keep the
crowd happy at this barrel-vaulted venue.

Quay Club (☎ 01752-224144; 11 The Parade;
◷ 10am-2am, to 3am Fri, to 4am Sat) Next to the
Jazz Cafe, this cavernous club is a favourite
with Plymouth's night owls, with rock and
indie on Thursdays; funk, soul and Latin on
Fridays; and chart and dance on Saturday.

Annabel's (☎ 01752-260555; 88 Vauxhall St; ◷ to
2am Fri & Sat) The stage spots in this quirky
cabaret-cum-dance venue are filled by an
eclectic collection of acts; crowd-pleasing
tunes fill the dance floor while classy cocktails fill your glass.

THEATRES & CINEMAS

Theatre Royal (☎ 01752-267222; www.theatreroyal
.com; Royal Pde) Plymouth's main theatre stages
large-scale touring and home-grown productions; its studio Drum Theatre is renowned
for featuring new writing.

Barbican Theatre (☎ 01752-267131; www.barbican
theatre.co.uk; Castle St) A tiny theatre with regular dance and drama, and a buzzing bar –
the B-Bar.

Plymouth Arts Centre (☎ 01752-206114; www
.plymouthac.org.uk; 38 Looe Street; ◷ 10am-8.30pm Mon-
Sat, 5.30-8.30pm Sun) A place to feed body and

mind – this centre combines an independent cinema, modern-art exhibitions, and a licensed vegie-friendly cafe (lunch Monday to Saturday, dinner Tuesday to Saturday).

Getting There & Away

BUS

National Express runs regular coaches to Birmingham (£43.50, 5½ hours, four daily), Bristol (£26, three hours, four daily), London (£29, five to six hours, eight daily) and Penzance (£6.90, 3¼ hours, seven daily).

Bus X38 runs to Exeter (£6, 1¼ hours, hourly); Bus X80 runs every half-hour to Torquay (1¾ hours) via Totnes (one hour 10 minutes) from Monday to Saturday, and hourly on Sunday.

Bus 82 (the Transmoor link) runs across Dartmoor between Plymouth and Exeter via Princetown, Postbridge and Moretonhampstead. On Sundays year-round there are two to five buses; between May and September it also runs twice on Saturdays; and between late July and late August it also runs twice on weekdays, with one bus connection onto Exeter.

TRAIN

Services run to London (£63, 3½ hours, half-hourly), Bristol (£40, two hours, two or three per hour), Exeter (£6.90, one hour, two or three per hour) and Penzance (£9, two hours, half-hourly).

AROUND PLYMOUTH
Buckland Abbey

Stately **Buckland Abbey** (NT; ☎ 01822-853607; Yelverton; adult/child £7/3.50; 🕙 10.30am-5.30pm Fri-Wed mid-Mar–Oct, 2-5pm Sat & Sun Nov–mid-Mar) was originally a Cistercian monastery and 13th-century abbey church, but was transformed into a family residence by Sir Richard Grenville before being purchased in 1581 by his cousin and nautical rival Sir Francis Drake. Its displays include Drake's Drum, said to beat by itself when Britain is in danger of being invaded. There's also a very fine Elizabethan garden.

Buckland Abbey is 11 miles north of Plymouth. You'll need your own transport to get here.

DARTMOOR NATIONAL PARK

Dartmoor is an ancient, compelling landscape, so different from the rest of Devon that a visit can feel like falling straight into *The Return of the King*. Exposed granite hills (called tors) crest on the horizon, linked by swathes of honey-tinged moors. On the fringes, streams tumble over moss-smothered boulders in woods of twisted trees. The centre of this 368-sq-mile wilderness is the higher moor; a vast, treeless expanse. Moody and utterly empty you'll find its desolate beauty exhilarating or chilling, or quite possibly a bit of both.

Dartmoor can be picture-postcard pretty; ponies wander at will here and sheep graze beside the road, but peel back the picturesque and there's a core of hard reality – stock prices mean many farming this harsh environment struggle to make a profit. It's also a mercurial place where the urban illusion of control over our surroundings is stripped away and the elements are in charge. Dartmoor inspired Sir Arthur Conan Doyle to write *The Hound of the Baskervilles* and in sleeting rain and swirling mists you suddenly see why; the moor morphs into a bleak, wilderness where tales of a phantom hound can seem very real indeed.

But Dartmoor is also a natural breakout zone with a checklist of charms: superb walking, cycling, riding, climbing and white-water kayaking; rustic pubs and fancy restaurants; wild camping nooks and posh country-house hotels – the perfect bolt holes when the mists roll in.

WARNING

The military uses three separate areas of Dartmoor as training ranges where live ammunition is used. The national park information centres can explain their locations; they're also marked on OS maps. In general you're advised to check if the route you're planning falls within a range; if it does, find out if firing is taking place when you want to walk via the **Firing Information Service** (☎ 0800 458 4868; www.dartmoor-ranges.co.uk). In the day red flags fly at the edges of the range if it's being used, and red flares burn at night. Even when there's no firing, beware of unidentified metal objects lying in the grass. Don't touch anything you find: note its position and report it to the police or the Commandant (☎ 01837-650010).

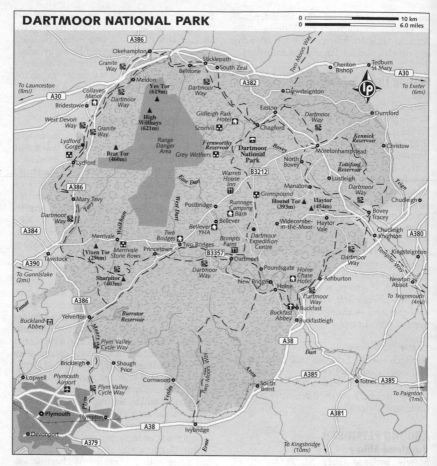

DARTMOOR NATIONAL PARK

Orientation

Dartmoor occupies a massive chunk of central Devon, stretching within 7 miles of Plymouth and 6 miles of Exeter. The A38 dual carriageway borders its southeast edge and the A30 skirts the north en route from Exeter to Cornwall via Okehampton. The B3212 carves a path across the centre, linking Moretonhampstead, Postbridge and Princetown. From there the B3357 leads into Tavistock.

The northwest moor is the highest and most remote, peaking at 621m at High Willhays. The lower, southwest moor is particularly rich in prehistoric sites. About 40% of Dartmoor is common land but 15% is leased to the Ministry of Defence for live firing practice and access can be restricted – see p387.

Information

The main **High Moorland Visitors Centre** (☎ 01822-890414; www.dartmoor-npa.gov.uk; ⏰ 10am-5pm Apr-Oct, 10am-4pm Nov-Mar) is located in Princetown (p390); there are smaller centres at **Haytor** (☎ 01364-661520; 10am-5pm Easter-Oct, 10am-4pm Sat & Sun Nov & Dec) and **Postbridge** (☎ 01822-880272; 10am-5pm Easter-Oct, 10am-4pm Sat & Sun Nov & Dec), p391.

The free *Dartmoor Visitor* newspaper is packed with useful info, including details of guided walks. The larger centres also stock walking guides, Ordnance Survey (OS) maps and books; all have leaflets on hiking, horse riding, cycling and other activities.

The **Dartmoor Tourist Association** (www.discover dartmoor.co.uk) is another useful information source.

Don't feed the Dartmoor ponies as this encourages them to move dangerously near to the roads.

Activities
WALKING
Every year thousands of people explore Dartmoor's open heaths and rocky tors. There are some 730 miles of public footpaths and bridleways to discover, and following changes in the law much of the rest of the moor is now open to enthusiastic ramblers.

Jarrold's *Dartmoor, Short Walks* (£5.99) is a good introduction for family day strolls, and the **national park information centres** can advise on all types of self-guided trails.

It also runs a range of **guided walks** (£3-8, free if you show your bus ticket). Themes include Sherlock Holmes, myths, geology, industry and archaeology. Look out for their magical, moonlit rambles amid stone rows.

CYCLING
There are a couple of marked cycling routes around the moor including the 7-mile, traffic-free **Plym Valley Cycle Way** along the disused Great Western Railway between Plymouth and Yelverton, and the **Dartmoor Way**, a 90-mile circular cycling and walking route through Okehampton, Chagford, Buckfastleigh, Princetown and Tavistock.

A good option for bike hire is **Devon Cycle Hire** (☎ 01837-861141; www.devoncyclehire.co.uk; Sourton Down, nr Okehampton; bikes per day £12), which is handily situated along the 11-mile Okehampton to Lydford **Granite Way**. Alternatively try **Okehampton Cycles** (☎ 01837-53248; North Rd, Okehampton).

HORSE RIDING
There are lots of places to saddle up on Dartmoor. *Dartmoor Visitor* has full details. A half-day ride costs around £30.

Babeny Farm Riding Stables (☎ 01364-631296; Poundsgate)
Skaigh Stables (☎ 01837-840917; www.skaighstables.co.uk; Belstone)
Shilstone Rocks (☎ 01364-621281; Widecombe-in-the-Moor).

WHITE WATER
The raging River Dart makes Dartmoor a top spot for thrill seekers. Experienced kayakers can get permits from www.dartaccess.co.uk or the **British Canoe Union** (BCU; ☎ 0845 370 9500; www.bcu.org.uk). **CRS Adventures** (☎ 07891 635964; www.crsadventures.co.uk) in Ashburton runs a range of white-water activities (from £70 for a half day). Rivers are only open in the winter.

CLIMBING
Experienced climbers will have to book at some popular sites – the park information centres can provide a free leaflet and further advice. For lessons, try the **Rock Centre** (☎ 01626-852717; www.rockcentre.co.uk; Rock House, Chudleigh; per half-/full day £15/25).

Sleeping
From spoil-yourself-silly luxury (try Gidleigh Park, p393, or Holne Chase, p392) to snoozing under the stars, with some lovely thatched cottages in between, Dartmoor has the widest range of sleeping options around. We detail them throughout the chapter.

There are YHA hostels at Postbridge (p391) and Okehampton (p393); the association also has bare-bones camping barns, such as the one near Postbridge (p391). For YHA bookings call ☎ 01629-592700. There are independent hostels and camping barns at Moretonhampstead (p392), Widecombe-in-the-Moor (p392) and Princetown (p391).

Dartmoor is also a top venue for a spot of 'wild camping' – so called by devotees to

---

DARTMOOR HIKES
The **West Devon Way** (part of the Dartmoor Way, below) is a 14-mile hike between Tavistock and Okehampton, while the 18-mile **Templer Way** is a two- to three-day leg stretch from Haytor to Teignmouth. The 90-mile **Dartmoor Way** circles from Buckfastleigh in the south, through Moretonhampstead, northwest to Okehampton and south through Lydford to Tavistock. But the blockbuster route is the 103-mile **Two Moors Way**, which runs from Ivybridge on the southern fringes of Dartmoor across Dartmoor and Exmoor to Lynmouth on the north Devon coast.

Be prepared for Dartmoor's notoriously fickle weather and carry a map and compass as many trails are not way-marked. OS Explorer Map No 28 (1:50,000) is the most comprehensive and shows park boundaries and MOD firing-range areas, see p387.

PREHISTORIC DARTMOOR

The first settlers arrived on Dartmoor somewhere around 12,000 years ago, after the end of the last ice age. The moor looked very different then; it was almost entirely covered by trees, which provided a rich source of food, fuel and natural shelter. Evidence of prehistoric people is dotted all over Dartmoor; over 1500 cairns and burial chambers have been discovered, and the area has more ceremonial rows and stone circles than anywhere else in Britain. The **Grey Wethers** stone circles stand side by side on a stretch of open moor halfway between Chagford and Postbridge, about a third of a mile from another stone circle near **Fernworthy**. **Scorhill** stone circle, near Gidleigh, is sometimes called the Stonehenge of Dartmoor, although only half of the original stones remain. Another intriguing site is at **Merrivale**, on the main road from Princetown to Tavistock, where you'll find several stone rows and standing stones, as well as a small ceremonial circle and the remains of several stone huts. But the most impressive site is the Bronze Age village of **Grimspound**, just off the B3212, where you can wander around the circular stone wall that once surrounded the village, and the ruins of several granite round houses.

---

ensure it is properly distinguished from the 'mild camping' of official sites. Pitching a tent on some sections of the open moor is allowed provided you stick to some simple but strict rules – pick up a free leaflet from the park information centres then pack your pack.

The **Dartmoor Tourist Association** (☎ 01822-890567; www.discoverdartmoor.com; High Moor Visitors Centre, Princetown) produces an annual *Dartmoor Guide* with full accommodation listings.

Eating & Drinking

Dartmoor can cater for all tastes – and budgets. There's the double-Michelin-starred Gidleigh Park (p393) near Chagford and classy Holne Chase (p392) near Widecombe-in-the-Moor. Or try the stylish bar food at the Rugglestone Inn at Widecombe (p392), the hiker-friendly grub and authentic pub atmosphere at the Warren House Inn in Postbridge (opposite), or some of the best cream teas in Devon at Brimpts Farm (opposite).

Getting There & Around

The park authorities advocate using public transport for environmental reasons and, with a bit of planning, it is a real option. The *Discovery Guide to Dartmoor*, free from most tourist offices, details bus and train services in the park. Buses travel into the moor from various points including Totnes, Exeter, Plymouth and Okehampton.

First's bus 82 (the Transmoor link) runs across Dartmoor between Plymouth and Exeter via Princetown, Two Bridges, Postbridge, the Warren House Inn and Moretonhampstead. Frequencies vary wildly: on Sundays year-round there are two to five

buses, between May and September it also runs twice on Saturdays, and between late July and late August it also runs twice on weekdays – these services stop at Moretonhampstead, with only one bus connection onto Exeter.

The Dartmoor Sunday Rover ticket (adult/child £6/4, June to September) buys unlimited travel on most bus routes, and train travel on the Tamar Valley line from Plymouth to Gunnislake. Buy tickets from bus drivers or at Plymouth train station.

The only main-line train station within easy reach of the park is Okehampton (p393)

Princetown

Set in the heart of the remote, higher moor, Princetown is dominated by the grey, foreboding bulk of **Dartmoor Prison**. The jail has dictated the town's fortunes for hundreds of years. When it stopped housing French and American prisoners of war in the early 1800s, Princetown fell into decline and parts of the town still have a bleak, neglected feel. But the settlement is also a useful insight into the harsh realities of moorland life and makes an atmospheric base for some excellent walks.

The prison reopened as a convict jail in 1850 and just up from its looming gates the **Dartmoor Prison Heritage Centre** (☎ 01822-892130; adult/child £2/1; ☺ 9.30am-12.30pm & 1.30-4.30pm, to 4pm Fri & Sun) provides a chilling glimpse of life (past and present) inside – look out for the straight jackets, manacles and mock-up cells, and the escape tale of Frankie 'the mad axeman' Mitchell, supposedly sprung by 1960s gangster twins the Krays. The centre also sells the bizarrely cheery garden ornaments made by the inmates.

The **High Moorland Visitors Centre** (☎ 01822-890414; www.dartmoor-npa.gov.uk; �}10am-5pm Apr-Oct, 10am-4pm Nov-Mar) stocks maps, guides and books. The building started life as Princetown's main hotel, where Arthur Conan Doyle began his classic Dartmoor tale *The Hound of the Baskervilles*. Ask staff to point you towards Foxtor Mires (2 to 3 miles away), the inspiration for the book's Grimpen Mire, then detect the story's other locations.

The **Plume of Feathers** (☎ 01822-890240; www.theplumeoffeathers.co.uk; Plymouth Hill; dm/s/d £13/35/70, sites £13; �} 11.30am-8.30pm) in the heart of town serves up typical bar food. It also offers no-nonsense rooms with shared bathrooms, as well as camping and bunk-bed dorms. The similar **Railway Inn** (☎ 01822-890240; s/d £35/70) is next door.

GETTING THERE & AWAY
Between late July and late August bus 82 (the Transmoor Link) runs twice each weekday from Princetown to Postbridge (10 minutes) and Moretonhampstead (30 minutes). It also runs to Plymouth (50 minutes) in the opposite direction. The service also runs twice on Saturdays between May and September, when it goes onto Exeter (40 minutes). There are between two and five services on Sundays year-round.

Postbridge
There's not much to the quaint village of Postbridge apart from a couple of shops, pubs and whitewashed houses. It's best known for its 13th-century **clapper bridge** across the East Dart, made of large granite slabs supported by stone pillars.

There's a **park information centre** (☎ 01822-880272; �} 10am-4pm Apr-Oct) in the car park, and a **post office** and **shop** in the village.

SLEEPING & EATING
Runnage Camping Barn (☎ 01822-880222; www.runnagecampingbarns.co.uk; sites per adult/child £4.50/3.50, dm £7.50) Set in a working farm, this converted hayloft allows you to bed down to the soundtrack of bleating sheep. It's 1½ miles from Postbridge: take the 'Widecombe' turning off the Moretonhampstead road.

Bellever YHA (☎ 0845 371 9622; www.yha.org.uk; dm £14; �} Mar-Oct) This former farm on the edge of a conifer plantation has bags of character: expect a huge kitchen, lots of rustic stone walls and cosy dorms. It's a mile south of the village.

our pick **Two Bridges** (☎ 01822-890581; www.twobridges.co.uk; Two Bridges; s £95-120, d £140-190) There's a real feel of a classy country house to this classic moorland hotel. That's no doubt down to the gently elegant rooms, huge inglenook fireplaces and squishy leather sofas; former guests Wallace Simpson, Winston Churchill and Vivien Leigh probably liked it too. It's 3 miles southwest of Postbridge.

our pick **Warren House Inn** (☎ 01822-880208; mains £4-9; �} 11am-11pm, food served noon-8.30pm, to 4pm Mon & Tue Nov-Mar) Plonked amid miles of open moor, this former tin miners' haunt exudes the kind of hospitality you only get in a pub in the middle of nowhere. A Dartmoor institution, its stone floors, trestle tables and hearty food are warmed by a fire that's reputedly been crackling since 1845. It's on the B3212, 2 miles northeast of Postbridge.

Brimpts Farm (☎ 01364-631450; Dartmeet; cream teas £3; �} 11.30am-5.30pm weekends & school holidays, 2-5.30pm weekdays) They've been serving cream teas here since 1913, and its still one of the best places to tuck in on the moor. Expect freshly baked scones, homemade jams and utterly, utterly gooey clotted cream. It's signed off the B3357, Two Bridges to Dartmeet road.

GETTING THERE & AWAY
Bus 82 (the Transmoor Link) runs from Plymouth via Princetown, Two Bridges, Postbridge and Warren House Inn to Moretonhampstead. Between late July and late August it runs twice each weekday. It also goes twice on Saturdays between May and September – there are between two and five services on Sundays year-round.

Widecombe-in-the-Moor
pop 652
This is archetypal Dartmoor, down to the ponies grazing on the village green. Widecombe's honey-grey, 15th-century buildings circle a church whose 40m tower has seen it dubbed the Cathedral of the Moor. Inside search out the boards telling the fire-and-brimstone tale of the violent storm of 1638 – it knocked a pinnacle from the roof, killing several parishioners. As ever on Dartmoor the devil was blamed, said to be in search of souls.

The village is commemorated in the traditional English folksong of Widecombe Fair; the event of the same name takes place on the second Tuesday of September.

DETOUR: HOLNE CHASE HOTEL

Holne Chase Hotel (☎ 01364-631471; www.holne-chase.co.uk; Tavistock Rd; s £120, d £160-180, ste £200-210; dinner £35; **P**) Hidden away in a beautiful wooded valley beside the River Dart, this is one of the finest country-house hotels on Dartmoor. Built as a hunting lodge for nearby Buckfast Abbey, it commands sweeping views across private parkland, and is decorated with style and sophistication. Antique furniture, wide fireplaces and effortlessly chic furnishings are dotted throughout the bedrooms, while several detached 'stable suites' cluster beside the main hotel. The in-house restaurant is renowned for its inventive country-inspired cuisine, and the hotel even provides a luxury weekend getaway for visitors of the canine kind. One to remember.

SLEEPING & EATING

Dartmoor Expedition Centre (☎ 01364-621249; www.dartmoorbase.co.uk; dm £12, loft room £14; **P**) The real fires, hot showers and dorm beds at this 300-year-old converted barn are all best enjoyed after the climbing, orienteering and caving the centre organises. It's 2 miles west of Widecombe.

Higher Venton Farm (☎ 01364-621235; www.ventonfarm.com; Widecombe; d £50-60; **P**) This 16th-century farmhouse could be used to define the architectural style 'picture-postcard thatch'. With low lintels and winding stone stairs, there's not a straight line in the place.

Rugglestone Inn (☎ 01364-621327; mains £5-10; Widecombe; ☽ lunch & dinner) You'll find plenty of locals in front of this intimate old pub's wood-burning stove. Its stone floor and low beams also set the scene for hearty helpings of hand-made sausages and mash or fisherman's pie.

Old Inn (☎ 01364-621207; The Green; mains £9; ☽ lunch & dinner) Right beside the village green, this 14th-century hostelry has been carefully, if incongruously, renovated in blond beams, light panelling and quirky quotes. Somewhere to sip a cappuccino and dine on steak-and-ale pie or smoked-fish crumble.

GETTING THERE & AWAY

Bus 272 goes to Tavistock (1¼ hours, three buses, late May to early September) via Two Bridges (50 minutes) and Princetown (55 minutes), but only on Sundays in the summer.

Bus 274 runs to Okehampton (1¾ hours, three on summer Sundays only) via Moretonhampstead. Several other buses also stop at Widecombe on Sunday as part of the Sunday Rover scheme: check with the park information centres.

Moretonhampstead
pop 1721

The small market town of Moretonhampstead stands at an old crossroads where two of the main routes across Dartmoor meet. It makes a handy base for exploring the eastern moor.

SLEEPING & EATING

Sparrowhawk Backpackers (☎ 01647-440318; www.sparrowhawkbackpackers.co.uk; 45 Ford St; dm/d £15/35) The bright, light dorms in this ecofriendly hostel are set in converted stables. The central courtyard, ringed by rickety outbuildings, is a great spot to swap traveller's tales.

Cookshayes (☎ 01647-440374; www.cookshayes.co.uk; Court St; s £25, d £50-70; **P**) Ask for a room with a view of the fields edging the moor at this Victorian B&B. Rooms are fairly plain and traditional, except the four-poster one, which is a vivid pink.

White Hart Hotel (☎ 01647-441340; www.whitehartdartmoor.co.uk; The Square; s £70-85, d £120-140; ☽ lunch & dinner) The mail coaches used to change horses here in Georgian days; today it's a smoothly comfy hotel with tartan carpets, deep terra-cotta walls and CD players in the rooms. The food (mains £14) is tasty and substantial; try the steak with local blue cheese or sea bass with a pine-nut crust.

GETTING THERE & AWAY

Bus 82 runs across the moor from Moretonhampstead to Plymouth (1½ hours) via Postbridge and Princetown (40 minutes). Between late July and late August it runs twice each weekday. It also goes twice on Saturdays between May and September – there are between two and five services on Sundays year-round.

Bus 359 goes to Exeter (seven daily Monday to Saturday).

Chagford
pop 1470

With its wonky thatches and cream-and-white-fronted buildings, Chagford gathers round a busy square – at first glance every inch a timeless moorland town. But the purveyors of waxed jackets and hip flasks have also been joined by health-food shops and contemporary pottery galleries. A former Stannary town (where local tin was weighed and checked), Chagford was also the first town west of London to get electric street lights.

SLEEPING & EATING

Sandy Park (☎ 01647-433267; www.sandyparkinn.co.uk; Sandy Park; s/d £50/90; ☯ lunch & dinner Mon-Sat, lunch Sun) Part pub (mains £8 to £12), part chic place to stay, at this 17th-century thatch you can sip a pint of real ale in a cosy, exposed-beam bar, sample classy Dartmoor fare in the restaurant, then totter upstairs to sleep amid plump pillows and classic furnishings.

Easton Court (☎ 01647-433469; www.easton.co.uk; Easton Cross, Easton; s/d £60/75) It's worth staying here just for breakfast – choices include fresh fish or soufflé omelette. The rooms are lovely too with their cast-iron beds, soft sofas and views of wooded hills.

Three Crowns Hotel (☎ 01647-433444; www.chagford-accom.co.uk; High St; mains £8; d £90; ☯ lunch & dinner) Crowd in among ghosts, massive beams and Civil War–style armour at this 700-year-old pub, where the grub is solid and the creaking bedrooms are full of dark woods.

GETTING THERE & AWAY

Bus 179 runs to Okehampton (one hour, two to three daily). Bus 173 travels from Moretonhampstead to Exeter via Chagford twice daily.

Okehampton

pop 7029

Okehampton has a staging post feel, huddling as it does on the edge of the mind-expanding sweep of the higher moor; an uninhabited tract of bracken-covered slopes and granite tors. With its clusters of traditional shops and pubs, it's an agreeable place to stock up before a foray into the wilderness. The **tourist office** (☎ 01837-53020; oketic@visit.org.uk; Museum Courtyard, 3 West St; ☯ 10am-5pm Mon-Sat Easter-Oct) can help with local accommodation and walks.

SIGHTS & ACTIVITIES

A Norman motte and ruined keep are all that remain of Devon's largest **castle** (EH; ☎ 01837-52844; adult/child £3/1; ☯ 10am-5pm Apr-Jun & Sep, 10am-

> ### DETOUR: GIDLEIGH PARK HOTEL
>
> **Gidleigh Park Hotel** (☎ 01647-432367; www.gidleigh.com; s £360 d £480-1325; ☯ lunch & dinner) Brace yourself (and your bank balance) – staying somewhere this prestigious doesn't come cheap. This sumptuous oasis of supreme luxury teams crests, crenellations and roaring fires with shimmering sanctuaries of blue marble, waterproof TVs and private saunas. Rates include dinner at the double-Michelin-starred restaurant, where three courses would normally set you back a hefty £85 – crafty local gourmands opt for the £33 two-course lunch instead. This dollop of utter extravagance is 2 miles west of Chagford.

6pm Jul & Aug). This towering, crumbling ruin teeters on top of a wooded spur and provides picturesque rampart clambering; a free audio guide fills in the missing parts.

The **Finch Foundry** (NT; ☎ 01837-840046; adult/child £4/2; ☯ 11am-5.30pm Wed-Mon Apr-Oct), with its three working water wheels, is a charming 3½-hour walk along the Tarka Trail in Sticklepath.

SLEEPING & EATING

Okehampton YHA (☎ 0845 371 9651; www.yha.org.uk; Klondyke Rd; dm £14; **P**) This former railway shed has had a bright revamp and is now a hugely popular hostel. No doubt something to do with the sailing, rock-climbing and kayaking courses it runs.

Collaven Manor (☎ 01837-861522; www.collavenmanor.co.uk; Sourton; s £65, d £106-146) The bedrooms in this delightful, clematis-clad mini manor house are framed by tapestries and window seats; dinner includes venison stroganoff and guinea fowl in Madeira sauce (three-courses £25.50) – non-residents need to book.

Tors (☎ 01837-840689; Belstone; mains £8-15; ☯ lunch & dinner) Tucked away in the picturesque village of Belstone, this welcoming country pub offers simple, traditional rooms (singles/doubles £30/60, hearty food and views onto the moor. It's 2 miles east of Okehampton.

GETTING THERE & AWAY

Bus X9 runs from Exeter (50 minutes, hourly Monday to Saturday, two on Sunday) via Okehampton to Bude (one hour). Bus 179 goes two or three times daily to Chagford (30 minutes) and Moretonhampstead (50 minutes).

DETOUR: LYDFORD GORGE

The 1½-mile rugged riverside walk at **Lydford Gorge** (NT; ☎ 01822-820320; adult/child £4.80/2.40; ⏱ 10am-4pm late Mar-Oct, 11am-3.30pm Sat & Sun Nov-late Mar) snakes past a series of bubbling whirlpools (including the fearsome 'Devil's Cauldron') to the thundering, 30m-high White Lady waterfall. You can also drive to the car park at the other end of the track, near the waterfall itself. Lydford is 9 miles southwest of Okehampton.

NORTH DEVON

Intensely rugged and, in places, utterly remote, the north Devon coast is a coast to inspire. It's also hugely varied: drastically concertinaed cliffs, excellent surf breaks and ancient fishing villages rub shoulders with classic, slightly faded British seaside resorts.

Braunton & Croyde
pop 8319

The cheerful, chilled village of Croyde is Devon's surf central. Here olde-worlde meets new wave: thatched roofs peep out over racks of wetsuits; crowds of cool guys in board shorts sip beer outside 17th-century inns. Inland, Braunton also has surf shops and board hire. The **tourist office** (☎ 01271-816400; www.brauntontic.co.uk; The Bakehouse Centre, Braunton; ⏱ 10am-4pm Mon-Sat Easter-Oct, plus Sun Jul & Aug) provides information and also houses a small local museum.

The water's hard to resist. **Le Sport** (☎ 01271-890147; Hobbs Hill, Croyde; ⏱ 9am-5.30pm, to 9pm at peak times) is among those hiring wetsuits and boards (half-/full day £12/18). The British Surfing Association (BSA)–approved **Surf South West** (☎ 01271-890400; www.surfsouthwest .com; Croyde Burrows Beach; ⏱ late Mar-Oct) and **Surfing Croyde Bay** (☎ 01271-891200; www.surfing croydebay.co.uk; 8 Hobbs Hill, Croyde) provide lessons from around £33 per half-day.

SLEEPING & EATING

Croyde gets very busy in the summer – book ahead, even for campsites.

Bay View Farm (☎ 01271-890501; www.bayviewfarm .co.uk; sites from £20) On the road from Braunton, this is one of the area's best campsites, with laundry and showers.

Mitchum's Campsites (☎ 07875 406473; www .croydebay.co.uk; sites £24-30) There are two locations, one in Croyde village and one by the beach, but they're only open on certain weekends in summer, so phone ahead.

Chapel Farm (☎ 01271-890429; www.chapelfarm croyde.co.uk; Hobbs Hill, Croyde; s/d £44/68; **P**) This lovely old thatched farmhouse has beamed rooms, rustic furniture and an inglenook fireplace; there's also self-catering in the old smithy behind the house.

Thatch (☎ 01271-890349; www.thethatch-croyde .co.uk; 14 Hobbs Hill, Croyde; d £60-80) Set above a legendary surfer's hang out, the bedrooms in this cavernous ancient pub are smart and modern, featuring delicate creams, browns and subtle checks. Some share bathrooms.

Billy Budd's (☎ 01271-890606; Hobbs Hill, Croyde; mains £4-10) Another board-rider's favourite, Billy Budd's serves jacket potatoes, chilli, nachos and huge sandwiches, as well as more substantial main meals and local ales.

GETTING THERE & AWAY

Bus 308 runs from Barnstaple (40 minutes, hourly Monday to Saturday, five on Sunday).

Ilfracombe
pop 12,430

Like a matinée idol past his prime, for years Ilfracombe had a sagging, crumpled feel. The steeply sloping streets of this Victorian watering hole are lined by town houses with cast-iron balconies; formal gardens, crazy golf and ropes of twinkling lights line the promenade. But these days there's more to Ilfracombe, as evidenced by a string of smart eateries and places to sleep, a Damien Hirst connection and the chance to go surfing or take a 'dip' in the past.

The best local beach is 5 miles west at Woolacombe – try the **Nick Thorn Hunter Surf Academy** (☎ 01271-871337; www.nickthornhuntersurf academy.com; wetsuit & board hire half/full day £14/18; ⏱ 9am-5pm Apr-Sep) where lessons cost from £30 for 2½ hours. Ilfracombe's **tourist office** (☎ 01271-863001; www.visitilfracombe.co.uk; ⏱ 10am-5pm Mon-Sat, plus Sun Apr-Oct) is inside the Landmark Theatre.

Tunnelsbeaches (☎ 01271-879882; www.tunnels beaches.co.uk; Granville Rd; adult/child £1.95/1.50; ⏱ 10am-5pm Easter-Oct, 9am-9pm Jul & Aug) is a beautifully evocative series of Victorian tidal swimming pools. Passageways hacked out of solid rock in the 1800s lead to a pocket-sized beach where you can still plunge into the sea water. Displays show the same spot in the 19th-century, conveying a world of woollen bathing suits, segregated swimming and boating etiquette ('Gentlemen who cannot swim should never take ladies upon the water').

SLEEPING & EATING

Ocean Backpackers (☎ 01271-867835; www.oceanbackpackers.co.uk; 29 St James Pl; dm £10-14, d £35) The dorms aren't that big but this indie hostel favourite is well run and the owners can help organise surfing, kayaking and archery.

Norbury House Hotel (☎ 01271-863888; www.norburyhouse.co.uk; Torrs Park; d £70-80, f & ste £100; P) This former gentleman's residence is now dotted with low-level beds, cool lamps and artfully placed cushions. Set on the hill overlooking Ilfracombe, there are impressive views from its terraced gardens.

Westwood (☎ 01271-867443; www.west-wood.co.uk; Torrs Park Rd; d £90-105; P) Modern, minimal and marvellous; this ultra-chic B&B is a study of neutral tones and dashes of vivid colour. It's graced by pony-skin chaises longues and stand-alone baths; some rooms have sea glimpses.

our pick **11, The Quay** (☎ 01271-868090; www.11thequay.com; 11 The Quay; cafe mains from £5, restaurant £10-20; ☒ lunch & dinner) Full of Chelsea chic, this supremely distinctive eatery is owned by the artist Damien Hirst (famous for preserving dead cows and sharks). Chose from tasty cafe fare in the Bakery or chi chi dining with superb views upstairs. Seared skate or Lundy lobster and chips feature on the menu; Mr Hirst's artwork features on the walls – including chunks of his *Pharmacy* installation and, with delicious irony, fish in formaldehyde.

GETTING THERE & AWAY

Bus 3 (40 minutes, every half-hour Monday to Saturday, hourly Sunday) runs to Barnstaple. Bus 300 heads to Lynton (one hour) and Minehead (two hours) three times daily.

Clovelly
pop 452

Clovelly is picture-postcard pretty. Its white cottages cascade down cliffs to meet a curving crab claw of a harbour, which is lined with lobster pots and set against a deep blue sea. Clovelly's cobbled streets are so steep cars can't negotiate them so supplies are still brought in by sledge – you'll see these big

bread baskets on runners leaning outside lots of homes. Clovelly's tenants enjoy enviably low rents (around £400 a year) and although the village is often branded artificial, 98 percent of the houses are occupied – in some westcountry villages half the properties are second homes.

Entry to the privately owned village is via the **visitor centre** (☎ 01237-431781; adult/child £5.50/3.50). Land Rovers ferry visitors up and down the slope for £2 from Easter to October.

Charles Kingsley, author of the children's classic *The Water Babies*, spent much of his early life in Clovelly. You can visit his former house, as well as an old fisherman's cottage and the village's twin chapels.

Bus 319 runs five times daily to Bideford (40 minutes) and Barnstaple (one hour).

Hartland Abbey

This 12th-century **monastery-turned-stately-home** (☎ 01237-441264; www.hartlandabbey.com; adult/child £8/2; ☒ house 2-5pm Sun-Thu, grounds noon-5pm Sun-Fri late May-Sep) was another post-Dissolution handout, given to the sergeant of Henry VIII's wine cellar in 1539. It boasts some fascinating murals, ancient documents, paintings by English masters, Victorian photos, as well as marvellous gardens.

Hartland Abbey is 15 miles west of Bideford, off the A39 between Hartland and Hartland Quay.

CORNWALL

If you were creating a perfect holiday haven from scratch, you'd probably come up with Cornwall. This rugged wedge of rock offers impossibly pretty beaches, improbably quaint villages and impressively craggy cliffs. Beloved by the bucket and spade brigade for generations, these days the entire county is in the midst of a renaissance that ranges from cooking to culture. Sample Rick Stein's foodie empire at Padstow or Jamie Oliver's cooking-cum–community program just along the coast. Indulge in an adrenalin sports frenzy at party-town Newquay or explore global habitats at the Eden Project – the planet's biggest greenhouses. Bed down amid styles that range from backpacker basic, via brushed-up B&B, to full-blown boutique chic. Hang out at funky festivals or chill out

---

WHEN DID CORNISH DIE?

A Celtic language akin to Welsh, Kernewek (Cornish) was spoken west of the River Tamar until the 19th century. Written evidence indicates it was still widely spoken at the time of the Reformation, but suppressed after a Cornish uprising in 1548. By the 17th century only a few people in the far west of Cornwall still claimed it as their mother tongue.

Towards the end of the 18th century linguistic scholars foresaw the death of Cornish and scoured the peninsula for people who still spoke it. One such expert, Daines Barrington, visited Mousehole in 1768 and recorded an elderly woman called Dolly Pentreath abusing him in Cornish for presuming she couldn't speak her own language. The decline continued and an 1891 tombstone in Zennor commemorates John Davey as 'the last man to possess any considerable knowledge of the Cornish language'.

It's now estimated there are around 300 Cornish speakers. For years the language's development was hindered because there were a number of different versions, but in 2008 a single written form was agreed, opening the way for it to be taught more widely with EU support, and for it to be used more on signs and in leaflets. Brush up on your own language skills before your trip to Kernow (Cornwall) at www.cornish-language.org.

---

in the exotic gardens at Heligan, Tresco and Trebah. Go all mystical at Arthurian Tintagel or sit in a stone circle as the sun sets in the far west. Pack an easel, pick up a paintbrush and immerse yourself in art at St Ives, or kick off your shoes, grab a knapsack and go island-hoping around the enchanting Isles of Scilly. Better still, do it all – and in one trip. In Cornwall you can. It really is rather wonderful way out west.

Orientation & Information

Cornwall is shaped like a giant door wedge. Around 88 miles from end to end, it's 50 miles wide in the east but tapers down to only eight miles wide in the west. At the time of writing, a new unitary authority is due to take over from Cornwall's district councils in April 2009. **Visit Cornwall** (☎ 01872-322900; www.visitcornwall.co.uk) has information on everything from Cornish cuisine to events, accommodation and adventure sports.

Getting Around

Most of Cornwall's main bus, train and ferry timetables are collected into one handy brochure (available free from bus stations and tourist offices). **Traveline South West** (☎ 0871 200 2233; www.travelinesw.com) can also answer timetable queries.

BUS

The main bus operator in Cornwall is **First** (☎ timetables 0871 200 2233, customer services 0845 600 1420; www.firstgroup.com). A FirstDay ticket (adult/

child £7/5.20) offers unlimited travel on their network for 24 hours.

Smaller, county-wide operator **Western Greyhound** (☎ 01637-871871; www.westerngreyhound.com) also does Day Rover tickets (adult/child £7/4.50). Many tourist attractions (including the Eden Project) offer discounts if you arrive by bus.

TRAIN

Key routes from London, Bristol and the north pass through Exeter, Plymouth, Liskeard, Truro and Camborne en route to Penzance; there are also branch lines to St Ives, Falmouth, Newquay and Looe.

The **Devon and Cornwall Rover** allows unlimited travel across the counties. Three days' travel in one week costs £40; eight days' travel in 15 days costs £60. You can buy it at most main train stations.

The **Freedom of the South West Rover pass** (adult £95) allows eight days' travel in 15 days in an area west of (and including) Salisbury, Bath, Bristol and Weymouth.

NORTH CORNWALL

The north Cornish coast is where Atlantic rollers smack hard into the county's granite cliffs and, for many, it's the quintessential Cornish landscape – a wild mix of grassy headlands, craggy bluffs and pounding surf. It's also where you'll find the county's best beaches and biggest waves, so in summer the winding clifftop roads can be jammed with tourists. But visit in the low-season when the weather's cooler and the holidaymakers have left for home, and you might have some of Cornwall's finest sand all to yourself.

Bude
pop 9242

Tucked in at the end of the River Neet and a 19th-century canal, Bude is both a popular family getaway and surfing hang-out, thanks to its fantastic nearby beaches. Closest to town is Summerleaze, a classic bucket-and-spade affair with bags of space at low tide; just to the north is Crooklets, which often has decent surf, as does Widemouth Bay (pronounced widmouth) 3 miles south of town.

Bude Visitor Centre (☎ 01288-354240; www.visitbude.info; The Crescent; 🕑 10am-5pm Mon-Sat, plus 10am-4pm Sun summer) is in a car park at the end of town. The **Castle Heritage Centre** (☎ 01288-357301; The Castle; adult/child £3.50/2.50; 🕑 10am-6pm Easter-Oct, 10am-4pm Nov-Easter) evokes Bude's maritime, geological and social history with great imagination – look out for exhibits on local inventor Sir Goldsworth Gurney whose pioneering creations included theatrical limelight and steam carriages. **Outdoor Adventure** (☎ 01288-362900; www.oasurfschool.co.uk) runs surf lessons at Widemouth Bay from £25 for a half day.

The nine fresh, uncluttered rooms at **Dylan's Guesthouse** (☎ 01288-354705; www.dylansguesthouseinbude.co.uk; Downs View; s/d £45/60) are decked out in white linen, chocolate throws and pleasant pine.

Life's a Beach (☎ 01288-355222; Summerleaze Beach; mains £11-16; 🕑 Mon-Sat) transforms from a lunchtime bistro to a snazzy candlelit restaurant by night and specialises in seafood. Or check out **Scrummies** (☎ 01288- 359522; Lansdown Rd; mains from £7; 🕑 8am-10pm), a fab fish cafe where the skate and monkfish are caught by the owner – try their crab pasta or lobster (half/whole £12/24) and chips.

Bus 595 runs between Bude and Boscastle (30 minutes, six daily Monday to Saturday, four on summer Sundays), where you can pick up connections to Tintagel, Wadebridge, St Columb Major and onto Truro. Bus 581 links Bude with Widemouth Bay (10 minutes, hourly Monday to Saturday, four on summer Sundays).

FESTIVAL FEVER

Cornwall has much more going on than just sand, sea and spectacular views. The county's calendar is packed with festivals and events.

- **Padstow Obby Oss** (1 May) Cornwall's oldest, and quite possibly weirdest, pagan festival – expect people-packed streets, two profoundly disturbing man-made 'osses and enough booze to make your liver quiver (see My Kingdom for an Oss, p400).
- **Helston Flora Day** (8 May) This centuries-old spring festival fizzes with street dancing, traditional music and a lively community atmosphere (see Cornwall's Furry Fling, p412).
- **Golowan Arts Festival** (Jun; www.golowan.org) Lively arts and music festival held around Penzance.
- **Eden Sessions** (Jun & Jul; http://sessions.edenproject.com) The Eden Project's biomes are transformed into the county's most spectacular live venue over four nights in June and July.
- **Port Eliot Litfest** (Jul; www.porteliotlitfest.com) Dubbed 'Glastonbury for books', this cult east Cornwall literary festival took a year off in 2008; check the website for July 2009 and beyond.
- **Fowey Regatta Week** (Aug; www.fowey.co.uk) Yachts and yachties converge on Fowey for this annual sailing festival.
- **St Ives September Festival** (Sep; www.stivesseptemberfestival.co.uk) A creative arts shindig crammed with exhibitions, gigs, readings and workshops.
- **Falmouth Oyster Festival** (Oct; www.falmouthoysterfestival.co.uk) Three days of mollusc-themed feasting on the Falmouth quayside.
- **Cornwall Film Festival** (mid-Nov; www.cornwallfilmfestival.com) A fiesta of short films, documentaries, animations and student work, held in Falmouth.
- **City of Lights** (late Nov) Withy lanterns and giant paper puppets take to Truro's streets for this Christmassy spectacle in late November.

DEVON & CORNWALL

SOMETHING FOR THE WEEKEND

Start your great Cornish escape by checking into the boutique bliss of the **Primrose Valley Hotel** (p418) in St Ives, then take a leisurely drive down to Porthcurno for an alfresco evening performance at the cliffside **Minack Theatre** (p415). Saturday brings an exploration of the extraordinary art in the **Tate St Ives** (p416) and **Barbara Hepworth Museum** (p416). After a chic bistro lunch at the sea-view **Porthminster Beach Cafe** (p419) potter around Penwith's myth-rich **prehistoric sights** (p404) before motoring east, via a swim at **Perranporth** (p403), to Newquay to check into **The Hotel** (p402) at Watergate Bay. Jamie Oliver's budding chefs rustle up a slap-up dinner for you at **Fifteen Cornwall** (p402), before you head into town for a late-night boogie at **Koola** (p403).

Sunday brings learning to **surf** at Fistral Beach and the thrills (and spills) of **kitesurfing** (see Surf's Up, p402), with a gourmet lunch at the **Beach Hut** (p402) squeezed in, in between. After strolling barefoot along the beach at sunset, you then leave a message on your bosses' answer phone, saying you won't be coming back.

Boscastle

On 16 August 2004 the pretty, sleepy harbourside village of Boscastle was catapulted onto TV screens worldwide. The most devastating flash flood to hit Britain for 50 years forced 440 million gallons of water through the heart of the village in just a few hours. It swept away a hundred cars and caused devastating damage to many of village's oldest buildings; 58 properties were flooded and much of the village was evacuated by helicopter. Miraculously not a single person lost their life.

Residents have spent years piecing Boscastle back together, with many properties now completely refurbished. The new **visitor centre** (☎ 01840-250010; www.visitboscastle andtintagel.com; ☉ 10am-5pm Mar-Oct) sits by the harbour.

The quirky **Museum of Witchcraft** (☎ 01840-250111; The Harbour; adult/child £3/2.50; ☉ 10.30am-6pm Mon-Sat, 11.30am-6pm Sun) has the world's largest collection (apparently) of witch-related memorabilia. Among its artefacts are spooky poppets (a kind of voodoo doll), wooden witch mirrors, enchanted skulls and a hideous cast-iron 'witch's bridle' designed to extract confessions from suspected hags.

SLEEPING & EATING

Riverside Hotel (☎ 01840-250216; www.hotelriverside .co.uk; s/d £35/65) Housed in one of the village's oldest buildings, this lovely B&B has fresh, modern rooms (think pink, peach or raspberry red) and a delightful riverside terrace for sandwiches and cream teas.

Old Rectory (☎ 01840-250225; www.stjuliot.com; St Juliot; s/d £58/86; ☉ Mar-Nov; ℗) Formerly the home of the vicar of St Juliot, the Old Rectory

is famous as the house where Thomas Hardy fell in love with his future wife, Emma Lavinia Gifford (the rector's sister-in-law). Period antiques, Victorian knick-knacks and heavy drapes recreate the Hardy-era atmosphere; bookworms can stroll through the woods to St Juliot Church, which features in the pages of Hardy's novel *A Pair Of Blue Eyes*.

Wellington Hotel (☎ 01840-250202; www.boscastle -wellington.com; The Harbour; d £80-184; ℗) Closer to a fortified castle than a hotel, this traditional coaching inn has welcomed weary travellers for more than 500 years (previous guests include Edward VII and Thomas Hardy). Bag a turret room for an antique atmosphere, chunky rugs, gentlemen's armchairs and unbeatable views.

Other recommendations:

St Christopher's (☎ 01840-250412; www.st-christo phers-boscastle.co.uk; High St; d £60-70) Flouncy rooms in tints of lemon and rose inside a former merchant's house.

Bottreaux Hotel (☎ 01840-250231; www.bos castlecornwall.co.uk; d £70-94; ℗) Elegant guest house sporting king-size beds and seagrass floors.

GETTING THERE & AWAY

For buses see the Getting There & Away section for Tintagel, opposite.

Tintagel

pop 1822

The spectre of King Arthur looms large over the village of Tintagel and its spectacular clifftop **castle** (EH; ☎ 01840-770328; adult/child £4.70/2.40; ☉ 10am-6pm Apr-Sep, 10am-5pm Oct, 10am-4pm Nov-Mar). Though the present-day ruins mostly date from the 13th century, archaeological digs have revealed the foundations of a much earlier fortress, fuelling speculation that the legendary king may indeed have been born at the castle as local fable claims. Part of the crumbling stronghold stands on a rock tower cut off from the mainland, accessed via a bridge and steep steps, and it's still possible to make out several sturdy walls and much of the castle's interior layout.

The village is awash with touristy shops and tearooms making the most of the King Arthur connection, but there's not much to keep you for long. The **Old Post Office** (NT; ☎ 01840-770024; Fore St; adult/child £2.80/1.40; ☑ 11am-5.30pm mid-Mar–Sep, 11am-4pm Oct) is a beautiful example of a traditional Cornish longhouse and mostly dates from the 1500s; it was still used as the village's post office during the 19th-century.

The **tourist office** (☎ 01840-779084; www.visit boscastleandtintagel.com; Bossiney Rd; ☑ 10am-5pm Mar-Oct, 10.30am-4pm Nov-Feb) has a few exhibits exploring local history and the Arthur legend.

GETTING THERE & AWAY

Bus 597 runs from Truro to St Columb Major where the connecting 594 goes via Wadebridge to Tintagel (two hours, seven daily Monday to Saturday) and onto Boscastle (10 minutes).

Padstow
pop 3162

If anywhere symbolises Cornwall's culinary renaissance it's Padstow. Decades ago this was an industrious fishing village where the day's catch was battered and served up in newspaper. Today it's seared, braised or chargrilled, garnished with wasabi and dished up in some of the poshest restaurants this side of the Tamar. The transformation is largely due to one man, celebrity chef Rick Stein (see p480), whose property portfolio now includes three eateries, three shops, six places to stay and even (with glorious irony) a fish and chip outlet. Some locals wryly refer to the town as 'Pad-stein' while others warmly welcome the jobs. Either way it's hard not to be charmed by Padstow's seaside setting, with a cluster of cafes and fishermen's cottages nestled around its old harbour.

The **tourist office** (☎ 01841-533449; www .padstowlive.com; North Quay; ☑ 10am-5pm Mon-Sat) charges £3 to book accommodation.

Much favoured by directors of costume dramas, the stately manor house of **Prideaux Place** (☎ 01841-532411; admission £7, grounds only £2; ☑ 12.30-4pm Sun-Thu Easter–mid-Apr & mid-May–Sep) above the village was built by the Prideaux-Brune family (who still reside here), purportedly descendants of William the Conqueror.

The disused Padstow-to-Bodmin railway now forms the **Camel Trail**, one of Cornwall's most popular cycling tracks. Starting in Padstow, it runs east through Wadebridge (5¾ miles), Bodmin (11 miles) and beyond. Bikes can be hired from **Padstow Cycle Hire** (☎ 01841-533533; www.padstowcyclehire.com; South Quay; ☑ 9am-5pm) and **Brinhams** (☎ 01841-532594; South Quay; ☑ 9am-5pm) for £9 to £12 per day.

The **Jubilee Queen** (☎ 07836-798457) offers one-hour boat trips (adult/child £8/4) around the bay and offshore islands, leaving from the harbourside.

Padstow is surrounded by some excellent beaches, including the ones at **Treyarnon Bay** and **Polzeath**, where the beachside **Animal Surf Academy** (☎ 01208-880617; www.animalsurfacademy .co.uk; Polzeath) does tuition (from £20 per 2½ hours) and **Ann's Cottage** (☎ 01208-863317; www .annscottagesurf.co.uk; Polzeath) rents boards and wetsuits (£3 per hour each).

SLEEPING

Treyarnon Bay YHA (☎ 0845 371 9664; www.yha.org .uk; Tregonnan; dm £14; P ⌨) This 1930s beach house is arguably Cornwall's best hostel. Its unbeatable setting above Treyarnon Bay is topped off by a home-cooking cafe, designer lounge and comfy dorms with top-drawer sea views. Bus 556 from Padstow stops at nearby Constantine several times daily.

Ballaminers House (☎ 01841-540933; www .ballaminershouse.co.uk; Little Petherick; tw/d £70/85; P) Two miles south of Padstow, this smart stone

TOP FIVE BEACHES

- For superb swimming: Perran Sands, Perranporth (p403)

- For scenic views: Bedruthan Steps, near Newquay (p400)

- For peaceful strolling: Gwithian and Godrevy Towans, near St Ives (p417)

- For family fun: Holywell Bay, near Newquay (p400)

- For learning to surf: Fistral or Watergate Bay, both near Newquay (p402)

DEVON & CORNWALL

MY KINGDOM FOR AN OSS

Padstow's raucous May Day fertility rite, featuring the fabled Obby Oss (hobby horse) is believed to be the oldest such event in the country. The ritual begins just before midnight on 30 April, as villagers sing to the innkeeper at the Golden Lion with the news that summer is 'a-come'. Then, at 10am the next morning the Blue Ribbon Oss – a man garbed in a huge hooped sailcloth dress and wild-looking horse headdress – dances around the town, grabbing any woman close enough and daubing her with coal (or, often, pinching her – it's believed to aid child-bearing!). He's followed at 11am by the Old Original (or Red) Oss and the madness continues until late.

---

farmhouse blends old-world atmosphere and modern elegance. Rooms feature Balinese furniture and antique chests, and boast sweeping views of the surrounding fields.

Althea Library (☎ 01841-532717; www.althealibrary .co.uk; 27 High St; d £76-120; P) One of central Padstow's nicest B&Bs, Althea has a couple of cosy, tasteful rooms tucked away on the 1st floor of this listed cottage, as well as a more expensive 'nook suite'. The pretty lounge has a CD player and board games, and the range-cooked breakfasts will keep you going for hours.

Treverbyn House (☎ 01841-532855; www.trever bynhouse.com; Station Rd; d from £75) Harry Potter would feel at home at this charming villa of five colour-coded rooms – it's even got a turret hideaway. Pine beds, pocket-sprung mattresses, stunning views and a choice of three breakfasts make this a top Padstow choice.

EATING

Rojano's (☎ 01841-532796; 9 Mill Sq; pizzas £7, pasta £8; ☒ lunch & dinner Tue-Sun) This bright, buzzy Italian joint turns out excellent pizza and pasta, served either in the snug, sunlit dining room or the tiny front terrace.

Rick Stein's Cafe (☎ 01841-532700; Middle St; mains £8.50-15; ☒ closed Sun) Stripped-down versions of Stein's Seafood Restaurant fare are on offer at this Continental backstreet cafe-bistro. It's buzzy and busy, with a faint seaside feel; everything from homemade carrot cake to grilled mackerel fillets occupy the specials blackboard.

Pescadou (☎ 01841-532359; South Quay; mains £14-18; ☒ lunch & dinner) Mr Stein isn't the only person around town who manages to turn out top-notch seafood, and this brightly toned brasserie next to the Old Custom House pub is the proof. Our tip? Go for the rosemary-roasted turbot.

our pick **Seafood Restaurant** (☎ 01841-532700; www.rickstein.com; Riverside; mains £18-45; ☒ lunch & dinner) The place that kick-started the Stein empire, and still the best of the bunch. Unsurprisingly, superb seafood is the menu's cornerstone, and huge swathes of the ingredients are certified Cornish. You'll need friends in high places to get a table, but this is one eatery that lives up to the hype.

GETTING THERE & AWAY

Bus 555 goes to Bodmin Parkway (50 minutes, hourly, six on summer Sundays) via Wadebridge. Bus 554 travels to St Columb Major, with connecting buses to Truro (1¼ hours, five daily Monday to Saturday), while bus 556 serves Newquay (1¼ hours, seven daily Monday to Saturday, five on summer Sundays).

Newquay
pop 19,423

Hoards of hard-core surfers, party-animals and wannabe board riders all make a beeline for bright, breezy, brash Newquay. Perched on the cliffs above a cluster of white-sand beaches and packed with enough pubs, bars and dodgy clubs to give Ibiza a run for its money, it's the capital of Cornish surfing, and if you're looking to learn how to brave the waves, this is the place to do it.

INFORMATION

Laundrette (☎ 01637-874487; 90 Tower Rd; ☒ 8am-8pm)

Tad & Nick's Talk'n'Surf (☎ 01637-874868; 72 Fore St; per min/hr 5p/£3; ☒ 10am-6pm)

Tourist office (☎ 01637-854020; www.newquay.co .uk; Marcus Hill; ☒ 9.30am-5.30pm Mon-Sat, 9.30am-12.30pm Sun)

SIGHTS & ACTIVITIES

Newquay is set amid some of the finest beaches on the north coast. **Fistral**, west of Towan Head, is England's best-known surfing beach and the venue for the annual Boardmasters surfing festival. Below town are **Great Western** and **Towan**; a little further up the coast you'll find Tolcarne, Lusty Glaze and Porth. All the beaches are good for swimming and supervised by lifeguards in summer.

Just east of Newquay is **Watergate Bay**, home to the latest branch of Jamie Oliver's Fifteen Cornwall restaurant, a swish new hotel and some superb adventure sports (see Surf's Up, p402). The stately rock towers of **Bedruthan Steps**, are a few miles further east towards Padstow; **Crantock** beach lies 3 miles to the southwest; a little further west again is family-friendly **Holywell Bay**.

Back in Newquay, the **Blue Reef Aquarium** (☎ 01637-878134; www.bluereefaquarium.co.uk; Towan Promenade; adult/child £8.50/6; ☁ 10am-5pm) displays a selection of weird and wonderful aquatic characters, including jellyfish, seahorses, octopi and rays.

Most of Newquay is relentlessly modern, but on the cliff above Towan Beach stands the 14th-century **Huer's House**, a lookout for approaching pilchard shoals. Until they were fished out early in the 20th century, these shoals were enormous: one catch of 1868 netted a record 16.5 million fish.

SLEEPING

Although Newquay has stacks of sleeping options, in high season prices rocket, the best get booked up, and some require a week's booking.

Budget

There are plenty of surf lodges in Newquay – the best ones have secure board storage and links with local surf schools.

Base Surf Lodge (☎ 01637-874852; www.basesurf lodge.com; 20 Tower Rd; dm £15-20) A superior surf lodge; slatted blinds, tiled floors and big sunset murals brighten up the lounge-bar, while pine bunk-beds and off-white walls characterise the upstairs dorms.

Goofys (☎ 01637-872684; www.goofys.co.uk; 5 Headland Rd; dm £15-25, d £30-60; P □) Friendly, funky Goofys bridges the gap between surf lodge and B&B. Rooms range from simple, airy doubles to quads with bunk beds; all are en suite and the price includes bedding, towels and a hearty buffet breakfast.

Reef Surf Lodge (☎ 01637-879058; www.reefsurf lodge.info; 10-12 Berry Rd; dm £15-30, d £35-70; □) An oh-so-fancy foyer and bar (think stripped

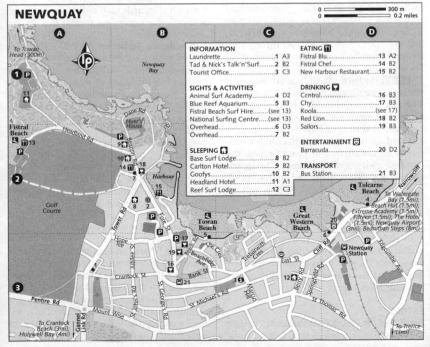

NEWQUAY

0	300 m
0	0.2 miles

INFORMATION
Laundrette...................1 A3
Tad & Nick's Talk'n'Surf...2 B2
Tourist Office................3 C3

SIGHTS & ACTIVITIES
Animal Surf Academy...........4 D2
Blue Reef Aquarium............5 B3
Fistral Beach Surf Hire........(see 13)
National Surfing Centre........(see 13)
Overhead......................6 D3
Overhead......................7 B2

SLEEPING 🏠
Base Surf Lodge...............8 B2
Carlton Hotel.................9 B2
Goofys.......................10 B2
Headland Hotel...............11 A1
Reef Surf Lodge..............12 C3

EATING 🍴
Fistral Blu...................13 A2
Fistral Chef..................14 B2
New Harbour Restaurant.....15 B2

DRINKING 🍷
Central......................16 B3
Chy..........................17 B3
Koola......................(see 17)
Red Lion.....................18 B3
Sailors......................19 B3

ENTERTAINMENT 🎭
Barracuda....................20 D2

TRANSPORT
Bus Station..................21 B3

DEVON & CORNWALL

SURF'S UP

Dig out the board shorts, slip on the shades and prepare to dangle your toes off the nose – Newquay is one of the country's top places for learning to **surf**. In high summer every other person is carrying a board and the town is awash with surf schools offering everything from half-day taster lessons (£25 to £30) to full-blown multiday 'surfaris' (from £130). Reputable operators include the BSA's **National Surfing Centre** (☎ Fistral Beach 01637-850737, Lusty Glaze 01637-851487; www.nationalsurfingcentre.com), **Animal Surf Academy** (☎ Newquay 01637-850808, Polzeath 01208-880617; www.animalsurfacademy.co.uk) and the **Extreme Academy** (☎ 01637-860840; Watergate Bay; www.extreme academy.co.uk). If you choose another school, make sure it's BSA approved.

Lots of surf shops around Newquay hire out equipment, including boards (£10/25/45 for one/ three/seven days) and wetsuits (£5/12/25 for one/three/seven days). Try a branch of **Overhead** (☎ 01637-850808; Beacon Rd & 19 Cliff Rd) or **Fistral Beach Surf Hire** (☎ 01637-850584; Fistral Beach).

For those after even more thrills and spills, Extreme Academy (above) also offers lessons in kitebuggying, waveskiing and the new craze: stand-up paddle-surf. They also do kitesurfing, as do **Mobius Kite School** (☎ 08456 430630; Cubert; www.mobiusonline.co.uk). Lessons happen at whichever beach has the best conditions on the day.

---

pine, brushed aluminium and a sign-cum–water feature) give this place a super-slick feel. And it is cleaner, smarter and better organised than many – but it *is* still a surf lodge, so expect dorms, shared facilities and chronic overcrowding in the summer.

Midrange & Top End

Carlton Hotel (☎ 01637-872658; www.carltonhotel newquay.co.uk; 6 Dane Rd; s £45, d £68-94; **P**) Swanky rooms, frilly edged beds, DVD players and country-cream furnishings run throughout this upmarket B&B on a quiet terrace just off Headland Rd.

ourpick The Hotel (☎ 01637-860543; www.water gatebay.co.uk; Watergate Bay; d £95-295, ste £205-400; **P**) This chic surf-side hotel is a kind of upmarket beachcombers paradise. Set plumb on the headland at Watergate Bay, its bedrooms are all pared-down simplicity, with crinkly linen, creaky wicker chairs and gauzy drapes; the best have mini sea-view balconies. The decked terrace, complete with bar and outdoor pool, overlooks the bay, and the whole little holiday haven is just steps from the beach.

Headland Hotel (☎ 01637-872211; www.headland hotel.co.uk; Fistral Beach; d £95-350; **P** **⌨**) Clinging to cliffs above Fistral beach, this red-brick pile is all about old-style pampering. Ritzy rooms range from budget singles to ornate sea-view suites, and there are even pools, tennis courts and nine holes of golf.

EATING

Fistral Chef (☎ 01637-850718; 2 Beacon Rd; breakfasts £2-6, mains £6-10; ☾ breakfast & lunch) Fantastic all-day breakfasts and chunky sandwiches are the mainstays of this popular all-day cafe, which also opens for Thai meals several nights a week.

Fistral Blu (☎ 01637-879444; Fistral Beach; mains £7-19; ☾ lunch & dinner) Right on Fistral Beach, this modern glass-fronted eatery experiments with Thai and Mediterranean flavours, as well as Cornish standards such as fish pie and local scallops. Tuck into less formal fare in the downstairs cafe.

New Harbour Restaurant (☎ 01637-874062; South Quay Hill; mains £10-15; ☾ lunch & dinner) In a lovely spot beside the old harbour, this relaxed restaurant is a fine place to escape the crowds along Newquay's main drag. Fish and seafood are the menu's staple – think crab claws, homemade fishcakes and skate wing.

ourpick Beach Hut (☎ 01637-860877; Watergate Bay; mains £13-17; ☾ breakfast, lunch & dinner) Surf boards on the walls, panoramic views of the waves and floorboards patterned by sandy footprints help make this beachside bistro the perfect hang-out. The menu redefines 'surf 'n' turf': miso-blackened mackerel, Fowey mussels with Cornish cider and homemade burgers with smoked Tintagel cheese. In the winter they tend to close at dusk.

ourpick Fifteen Cornwall (☎ 01637-861000; www .fifteencornwall.com; Watergate Bay; lunch mains £18, 6-course dinner menu £50; ☾ breakfast, lunch & dinner) Celebrity chef Jamie Oliver opened the second UK branch of his Fifteen restaurant in 2006 in a stunning location on Watergate Bay. Designed to give underprivileged Cornish youngsters an opportunity to train and work in a professional restaurant environment, Fifteen is one of the hottest tickets in the county. If you manage to bag a table, the beach views, electric atmosphere and contemporary cooking won't disappoint.

DRINKING & ENTERTAINMENT

Chy (☎ 01637-873415; www.the-chy.co.uk; 12 Beach Rd; ☾ 10am-3am Fri, Sat & Mon, to 6pm Tue-Thu & Sun) Chrome, wood and leather dominate this stylish cafe-bar overlooking Towan Beach. The patio is perfect for a gourmet breakfast or lunchtime salad, or pitch up late when the DJs take to the decks, the beers flow and the beautiful people arrive en masse.

Koola (☎ 01637-873415; www.thekoola.com; 12 Beach Rd; ☾ 10pm-3am daily summer, Mon & Sat winter) Underneath the Chy, the Koola is the venue of choice for connoisseur clubbers, with house, latin, and drum and bass nights, and a regular slot for local DJs Jelly Jazz.

Central (☎ 01637-878310; 11 Central Sq) As its name suggests, this rowdy pre-club pub is right in the heart of town, and the outside patio is always overflowing on warm summer nights.

Red Lion (☎ 01637-871195; North Quay Hill) Established surfer's pub with regular live music and plenty of ales on tap.

Barracuda (☎ 01637-875800; 27-29 Cliff Rd; ☾ 9pm-3am) One of the largest clubs in town with big-name DJs on weekends.

Sailors (☎ 01637-872838; Fore St) Pub-club playing cheesy house and chunky choons.

GETTING THERE & AWAY

Newquay Airport (☎ 01637-860600, www.newquaycorn wallairport.com) has regular flights to UK airports, including London, Belfast, Birmingham, Cardiff, Edinburgh and the Isles of Scilly. Bus 556 travels hourly to the airport from town.

National Express has direct buses to London (£38.50, seven hours, four to five daily), Plymouth (£6.40, 1½ hours, five daily) and Penzance (£7.20, 1¾ hours, two to seven daily).

There are trains every couple of hours between Newquay and Par (£5.20, 45 minutes) on the main London–Penzance line.

Trerice

Built in 1751, the charming Elizabethan manor of **Trerice** (NT; ☎ 01637-875404; adult/child £6/3; ☾ 11am-5pm Sun-Fri Mar-Oct) is famous for the elaborate barrel-roofed ceiling of the Great Chamber, but has plenty of other intriguing features, including ornate fireplaces, original

plasterwork and a fine collection of period furniture. There's also an amusing lawn-mower museum in the barn, with over 100 grass-cutters going back over a century.

Trerice is 3 miles southeast of Newquay. Bus 527 runs from Newquay to Kestle Mill, about a mile from the manor house.

Perranporth

Perranporth's best asset is an immense, 3-mile long sandy beach, which is backed by wind-whipped dunes and pounded by surf. The workman-like town is thronged with holiday-makers in summer and all but deserted in the winter months.

There are some decent campsites nearby including **Tollgate Farm Touring Park** (☎ 01872-572130; Budnick; sites £11-14; ☾ Easter-Oct), about a mile from the beach, and **Perranporth Camping and Touring Park** (☎ 01872-572174; Budnick; sites £8-18; ☾ Easter-Oct).

Set amid the dunes, the **Watering Hole** (☎ 01872-572888; Perranporth Beach) is one of the liveliest beach bars on the north coast, with outside tables on the sand, regular bands and a buzzy surf-shack vibe.

GETTING THERE & AWAY

For buses see Getting There & Away for Porthtowan & St Agnes, p404.

Porthtowan & St Agnes

The secluded beaches and reliable swells around the coastal towns of St Agnes and Porthtowan are popular with surfers and holi-daymakers alike. The tiny National Trust cove of **Chapel Porth**, tucked away at the bottom of a beautiful river valley, is a particularly fine spot; a dramatic coast path snakes along the clifftops to the abandoned mine at **Wheal Coates** and breathtaking views at **Tubby's Head**.

The **Rose-in-Vale Hotel** (☎ 01872-552202; www .rose-in-vale-hotel.co.uk; Mithian; B&B £164; P) is a lovely country-house hotel with flower-filled grounds 2 miles from St Agnes. It has 18 taste-ful rooms and an ubersmart restaurant.

Alternatively, the **Driftwood Spars** (☎ 01872-552428; www.driftwoodspars.com; d £86-102; P), a lively beachside pub at Trevaunance Cove near St Agnes, has 15 delightful rooms upstairs, many of which have sea views and attractive nautical touches.

Over at Porthtowan, the buzzing **Blue Bar** (☎ 01209-890329; www.blue-bar.co.uk; Porthtowan; ☾ lunch & dinner) is a popular surfers' hang-out with beachside tables tailor-made for sinking a cold one at sundown.

GETTING THERE & AWAY

Bus 501 travels along the north coast from Newquay to St Ives, Sunday to Friday, between late May and October (three to four buses daily), stopping at St Agnes and Perranporth en route. Bus T1 travels from Truro to St Agnes (40 minutes, hourly), but only a few daily buses travel on to Perranporth (15 minutes, five daily Monday to Saturday).

Bodmin Moor

Cornwall's 'roof' is a high heath pock-marked with bogs and granite hills, including Rough Tor (pronounced *row-tor*, 400m) and Brown Willy (419m), Cornwall's highest points. It's a desolate place that works on the imagination; for years there have been reported sightings of the Beast of Bodmin, a large, black cat-like creature, although no one's ever managed to snap a decent picture.

Bodmin tourist office (☎ 01208-76616; www.bodmin live.com; Mount Folly; ☺ 10am-5pm Mon-Sat) is in the Shire Hall. It also houses the **Charlotte Dymond Courtroom Experience** (adult/child £3.75/2.25; ☺ 11am-4pm Mon-Sat Easter-Oct, Mon-Fri Nov-Easter), which re-creates one of Cornwall's most notorious Victorian court cases – you get to cast your own verdict at the end.

The A30 cuts across the centre of the moor from **Launceston**, which has a medieval **castle** (EH; ☎ 01566-772365; adult/child £2.50/1.30; ☺ 10am-6pm Jul & Aug, 10am-5pm Apr-Jun & Sep, 10am-4pm Oct) and an interesting granite **church**.

Jamaica Inn (☎ 01566-86250; www.jamaicainn.co.uk; s £65, d £80-110; ℗), out on the desolate moor near Bolventor, was made famous by Daphne du Maurier's novel of the same name. Modernised and inevitably touristy, on a misty winter's night the inn can still feel hugely atmospheric; it also has a small smuggling museum and a room devoted to du Maurier.

About a mile south is **Dozmary Pool**, said to have been where Arthur's sword, Excalibur, was thrown after his death. It's a 4-mile walk northwest of Jamaica Inn to Brown Willy.

The **Bodmin & Wenford Railway** (☎ 0845 125 9678; www.bodminandwenfordrailway.co.uk; adult/child return £7.50/4; ☺ Mar-Oct) is the last standard-gauge railway in Cornwall plied by steam locomotives. Trains are still decked out in original 1950s livery and chug from Bodmin Parkway and Bodmin General station to

---

STONES & STORIES

Bodmin Moor is strewn with reminders of its ancient past. Perhaps the most impressive prehistoric monument is the **Hurlers**, a series of three stone circles near the village of Minions. Legend has it the stones were once local men who were petrified for playing the local game of hurling on the Sabbath. Around a mile across the moor is the **Cheesewring**, a 20-foot stack of stones balanced on top of each other. Although it looks man-made, in fact it's an entirely natural formation that's been sculpted by the elements over several million years. The far west of Cornwall is also rich in ancient sites, see Searching for Stones, p416.

Boscarne Junction, where you can join up with the Camel Trail cycle route (p399). There are two to four return trips daily depending on the season.

GETTING THERE & AWAY

Bodmin has bus connections with St Austell (bus 529; one hour, hourly Monday to Saturday, five on Sunday) as well as Bodmin Parkway (bus 555; 15 minutes, hourly Monday to Saturday, six on summer Sundays) on the London–Penzance train line.

SOUTHEAST CORNWALL

Dotted with picturesque fishing villages and traced by a patchwork of fields, southeast Cornwall offers a much gentler side to the county than the stark, sea-pounded granite cliffs of the north. Carpeted with wildflowers and criss-crossed by hedgerows, this is still working dairy country, where much of Cornwall's famously rich milk and clotted cream is produced.

Looe
pop 5280

Looe is a pleasing mixture of breezy bucket-and-spade destination and historic fishing port. Although the industry has declined, Looe has the second-biggest fish market in Cornwall (after Newlyn), and high tide still brings the bustle of landing and ice-packing the catch. The port has been a holiday hotspot since Victorian times when bathing machines rolled up to the water's edge off **Banjo Pier**. Split into East and West Looe and divided by a broad estuary, inter-village rivalry is intense, with locals referring to living on the 'sunny' or the 'money' side of town.

The **tourist office** (☎ 01503-262072; www.visit -southeastcornwall.co.uk; Fore St; ☒ 10am-5pm Easter-Oct, plus occasional days Nov-Easter) is in the Guildhall.

Half a mile west, the **Monkey Sanctuary** (☎ 01503-262532; www.monkeysanctuary.org; St Martins; adult/child £6/3.50; ☒ 11am-4.30pm Sun-Thu Easter-Sep) is guaranteed to raise a few 'aaahhhhs' over its unfeasibly cute (and disturbingly human) woolly and capuchin monkeys. The sanctuary is also strong on rehabilitation, conservation and anti-cruelty campaigns.

Hannafore Point is the headland just round from West Looe; half a mile off-shore is tiny St George's Island (known locally as Looe Island), a 9-hectare nature reserve run by the Cornwall Wildlife Trust. The boat **Islander** (☎ 07814 139223; adult/child return £7.50/4) will drop you off and collect you; trips run three hours either side of high tide. Other boat trips set out from **Buller Quay** for destinations including Polperro (£19) and Fowey (£12). Check the signs on the quay for sailings, then leave your contact details in one of the books alongside.

SLEEPING
Beach House (☎ 01503-262598; www.thebeachhouse looe.com; Hannafore Point; d £80-120; ℗) The guest house goes grandiose at this double-gabled pile overlooking Hannafore Point. The compact rooms are named after Cornish beaches and the balconies, puffy beds and breakfast pancakes make for a luxurious night's stay.

Barclay House (☎ 01503-262929; www.barclayhouse .co.uk; St Martins Rd, East Looe; d from £110; ℗ ▯) A swimming pool, sauna and gym may well tempt you to this grand mini hotel in East Looe. That, or the classy modern fixtures, bold colours (think aquamarine, gold and pistachio) and river views.

Schooner Point (☎ 01503-262670; www.schoonerpoint .co.uk; 1 Trelawney Tce; d £50-60; ℗) Pastel-shaded, chintz-free B&B with great vegie breakfasts and great views.

Trehaven Manor (☎ 01503-262028; www.trehaven hotel.co.uk; Station Rd; d £68-122; ℗) Antique wardrobes, original fireplaces and deep armchairs fill this old-world B&B.

GETTING THERE & AWAY
Trains travel the scenic Looe Valley Line from Liskeard (£2.90, 30 minutes, 11 daily

Monday to Saturday, eight on Sunday) on the London–Penzance line.

Bus 572 travels to Plymouth (1¼ hours, six daily Monday to Saturday); bus 573 goes to Polperro (30 minutes, hourly Monday to Saturday, five on Sunday).

Polperro
The ancient fishing village of Polperro is a picturesque muddle of narrow lanes and cottages set around a tiny harbour, best approached along the coastal path from Looe or Talland. It's always jammed with day trippers and coach tours in summer, so arrive in the evening or out of season if possible.

Polperro was once heavily involved in pilchard fishing by day and smuggling by night; the displays at the small **Heritage Museum** (☎ 01503-272423; The Warren; adult/child £1.60/50p; ☒ 10.50am-5pm Easter-Oct) include sepia photos, pilchard barrels and fascinating smuggling memorabilia, including a mean-looking cutlass.

For buses to Polperro see Getting There & Away under Looe, left.

Fowey
pop 2273
Nestled on the steep tree-covered hillside overlooking the River Fowey, opposite the old fishing harbour of Polruan (pronounced Foy) is a pretty tangle of pale-shaded houses and snaking lanes. Its long maritime history includes being the base for 14th-century raids on France and Spain; to guard against reprisals Henry VIII constructed **St Catherine's Castle** (EH; admission free) above Readymoney Cove, south of town. The town later prospered by shipping china clay extracted from pits at St Austell, but the industrial trade has now long declined and Fowey has now reinvented itself for summer-time tourists and second-home owners.

The **tourist office** (☎ 01726-833616; www.fowey .co.uk; 5 South St; ☒ 9am-5.30pm Mon-Sat, 10am-5pm Sun) is also home to the compact **Daphne du Maurier Literary Centre** (same details as the tourist office), which is devoted to the author of *Rebecca*, *Frenchman's Creek* and the short story that inspired Hitchcock's film *The Birds*. Du Maurier (1907–89) lived at houses in nearby Polridmouth Cove, Readymoney Cove and Ferryside, overlooking the Bodinnick ferry (none of these are open to the public). Every

May Fowey hosts the **Daphne du Maurier Literary Festival** (www.dumaurier.org) in her honour.

Fowey is at the southern end of the Saints' Way, a 26-mile waymarked trail running to Padstow on the north coast. **Ferries** (☎ 01726-870232; car/pedestrian £2.30/90p; ☺ schedule varies) cross the river to Bodinnick. A **passenger ferry** (foot passengers & bikes only; £1) shuttles over the estuary to the village of **Polruan**, which provides a quaint starting point for some cracking coastal walks.

SLEEPING & EATING

Golant YHA (☎ 0845 371 9019; www.yha.org.uk; Penquite House; dm £15.50; ℗ ▣) Sheltering amid 16 hectares of tree-shaded grounds, this whitewashed Georgian manor house makes a fantastic base. It has a cafe-bar, games room and views of the estuary. You can even rent a tepee.

Globe Posting House Hotel (☎ 01726-833322; www.globepostinghouse.co.uk; 19 Fore St; s/d £50/70) This tiny cob-walled cottage in the middle of Fore St has a clutch of snug, low-ceilinged rooms arranged around its rabbit-warren corridors.

Old Quay House (☎ 01726-833302; 28 Fore St; www.theoldquayhouse.com; d £160-300) Set in a blissful waterside location, this boutique beauty proves that the British seaside can be sexy. Rooms are all natural fabrics, rattan chairs and achingly tasteful tones – the best have stunning estuary-view balconies.

Marina Villa Hotel (☎ 01726-833315; www.the marinahotel.co.uk; The Esplanade; d £172-264) Accolades aplenty ensure the beautiful crowd flocks to this collection of nautical-chic rooms (think deluge showers, ornate mirrors and sleigh beds). The pricier rooms have riverside balconies too.

Sam's (☎ 01726-832273; 20 Fore St; mains £4-10) Forget razor-sharp napkins and snooty service – this great little local's favourite is a cross between *Cheers* and a backstreet French bistro. Squeeze into one of the booths, sink a beer and tuck into mussels, calamari rings or stacked-up Samburgers.

Food For Thought (☎ 01726-832221; 4 Town Quay; menu £19.95; ☺ lunch & dinner) There's a touch of the French Riviera to this smart restaurant on the corner of Town Quay, which has an excellent fixed-price menu and a pleasant awning-shaded terrace.

GETTING THERE & AWAY

Bus 25 from St Austell (55 minutes, hourly) runs to Fowey via Par, the closest train station.

Lanhydrock House

Lanhydrock (NT; ☎ 01208-265950; adult/child £9/4.50, gardens only £5/2.50; ☺ house 11am-5.30pm Tue-Sun mid-Mar–Sep, to 5pm Oct, gardens 10am-6pm year-round) is reminiscent of the classic 'upstairs-downstairs' film *Gosford Park*. Set in 365 hectares of sweeping grounds above the River Fowey, parts date from the 17th century but the property was extensively rebuilt after a fire in 1881, creating the quintessential Victorian county house. Highlights include the gentlemen's smoking room (complete with old Etonian photos, moose heads and tigerskin rugs), the children's toy-strewn nursery, and the huge original kitchens.

Lanhydrock is 2½ miles southeast of Bodmin; you'll need your own transport to get here.

Restormel Castle

A glorious, fairy-tale crumbling ruin, the 13th-century **Restormel Castle** (☎ 01208-872687; adult/child £2.50/1; ☺ 10am-6pm Jul & Aug, 10am-5pm mid-Mar–Jun & Sep, 10am-4pm Oct) has one of the best-preserved circular keeps in England. A series of wooden steps snakes past the remains of the 1st-floor rooms and onto the 2nd-floor crenellated battlements. One of the past owners, Edward, the Black Prince, is thought to have stayed here at least twice – perhaps drawn to hunt the 300 deer in his surrounding land. The castle is 1½ miles north of Lostwithiel, on the main London–Penzance rail line.

The Eden Project

If any one thing is emblematic of Cornwall's regeneration, it is the **Eden Project** (☎ 01726-811911; www.edenproject.com; Bodelva; adult/child £15/5; ☺ 10am-6pm Apr-Oct, 10am-4.30pm Nov-Mar). Ten years ago the site was a dusty, exhausted clay pit, a symbol of the county's industrial decline. Now it's home to the largest plant-filled greenhouses in the world and is effectively a superb, monumental education project about how much man depends on the natural world. Tropical, temperate and desert environments have been recreated inside the massive biomes, so a single visit carries you from the steaming rainforests of South America to the dry deserts of North Africa.

The Core, a newly built education centre (constructed according to the Fibonacci sequence, one of nature's most fundamental building blocks) was opened in 2006. In summer the biomes become a spectacular backdrop to a series of gigs known as the **Eden Sessions** (recent artists include The Verve, Goldfrapp and The Kaiser Chiefs), and from November to February Eden transforms itself into a winter wonderland for the **Time of Gifts** festival, complete with a full-size ice rink.

It's impressive and immensely popular: crowds (and queues) can be large, so avoid peak times. Eden is about 3 miles northeast of St Austell. Shuttle buses run from St Austell, Newquay and Truro: check times with **Traveline South West** (☎ 0871 200 22 33; www.travelinesw.com). Combined bus and admission tickets are available on board. Alternatively, if you arrive by bike or on foot, you'll get £3 off the admission price. Last entry is 90 minutes before the site closes.

The Lost Gardens of Heligan

Before he dreamt up the Eden Project, ex-record producer Tim Smit was best known for rediscovering the lost gardens of **Heligan** (☎ 01726-845100; www.heligan.com; Pentewan; adult/child £8.50/5; ⏱ 10am-6pm Mar-Oct, 10am-5pm Nov-Feb). Heligan was the former home of the Tremayne family, and during the 19th century was renowned as one of Britain's finest landscaped gardens. The grounds fell into disrepair following WWI (when many staff were killed) and are only now being restored to their former glory. Formal terraces, flower gardens, a working kitchen garden and a spectacular jungle walk through the 'Lost Valley' are just some of Heligan's secrets.

The Lost Gardens of Heligan are 1½ miles from Mevagissey and 7 miles from St Austell. Bus 526 (30 minutes, six daily, three on Sunday) links Heligan with Mevagissey and St Austell train station.

Roseland Peninsula

Stretching into the sea south of Truro, this beautiful rural peninsula gets its name not from flowers but from the Cornish word *ros*, meaning promontory. Highlights include the coastal villages of **Portloe**, a wreckers' hang out on the South West Coast Path, and **Veryan**, awash with daffodils in spring and framed by two thatched roundhouses. Nearby are the beaches of **Carne** and **Pendower**, which join at low tide to form one of the best stretches of sand on Cornwall's south coast.

St Mawes has a rare, beautifully preserved clover-leaf **castle** (EH; ☎ 01326-270526; admission £3.60; ⏱ 10am-6pm Jul & Aug, 10am-5pm Sun-Fri Apr-Jun

---

TOP FIVE GARDENS

■ Glendurgan – The Helford (p411)

■ Heligan – near Mevagissey (left)

■ Trebah – The Helford (p411)

■ Trelissick – near Falmouth (p410)

■ Tresco Abbey – Isles of Scilly (p421)

Check out www.gardensofcornwall.com for further tips.

& Sep, 10am-4pm Oct, 10am-4pm Fri-Mon Nov-Mar), commissioned by Henry VIII and designed as the sister fortress to Pendennis (p409) across the estuary.

St Just-in-Roseland boasts one of the most beautiful churchyards in the country, full of flowers it tumbles down to a creek filled with boats and wading birds.

TRURO
pop 17,431

Cornwall's capital city has been at the centre of the county's fortunes for over eight centuries. Truro first grew up around a now vanished hilltop castle, built by Richard Lucy, a minister of Henry II's. Throughout the Middle Ages it was one of Cornwall's five stannary towns, where tin and copper was assayed and stamped. The 18th and 19th centuries saw it become a key industrial centre, and its wealthy merchants built swathes of elegant town houses, best seen along Lemon St and Falmouth Rd. Truro was granted its own bishop in 1877, with the city's three-spired cathedral following soon after. Today the city makes an appealing base, with a good selection of shops, galleries and restaurants and Cornwall's main museum.

Information

Library (☎ 01872-279205; Union Pl; ⏱ 9am-6pm Mon-Fri, 9am-4pm Sat) Net access costs £3 per hour.
Post office (High Cross; ⏱ 9am-5.30pm Mon-Sat)
Tourist office (☎ 01872-274555; www.acornishriver.co.uk; Boscawen St; ⏱ 9am-5pm Mon-Fri, plus Sat Apr-Oct).

Sights

The **Royal Cornwall Museum** (☎ 01872-272205; www.royalcornwallmuseum.org.uk; River St; admission free; ⏱ 10am-4.45pm Mon-Sat) has excellent displays exploring the county's industrial and archaeo-logical past. There are also temporary exhibitions of art, photography and local craft.

Built on the site of a 16th-century parish church in soaring Gothic Revival style, **Truro Cathedral** (☎ 01872-276782; www.trurocathedral.org.uk; High Cross; suggested donation £4; ☼ 7.30am-6pm Mon-Sat, 9am-7pm Sun) was finally completed in 1910, making it the first new cathedral in England since London's St Paul's. It contains a soaring high-vaulted nave, some fine Victorian stained glass and the impressive Father Willis Organ.

The **Lemon St Market** (Lemon St) houses craft shops, cafes, delicatessens and an upstairs art gallery. There are also several excellent galleries around town, including the upmarket **Lemon St Gallery** (☎ 01872-275757; 13 Lemon St; ☼ 10.30am-5.30pm Mon-Sat).

Sleeping

Carlton Hotel (☎ 01872-272450; www.carltonhotel.co.uk; 49 Falmouth Rd; s £47-57, d £67-77; P) The furnishings may be standard B&B (pastel colours, easy-clean carpets, ancient kettles) but extras such as Sky TV and a guest sauna and Jacuzzi seal the deal.

Bissick Old Mill (☎ 01726-882557; www.bissickoldmill .co.uk; Ladock; d £75-95; P 🖳) There's not a corn sack in sight at this beautifully converted 17th-century mill. Instead it's all Egyptian-cotton sheets, handmade soap and in-room fridges, topped off by plenty of beams and old mill wheels. Ladock is 7 miles northeast of Truro.

DETOUR: LUGGER HOTEL

Lugger Hotel (☎ 01872-501322; www.lugger hotel.co.uk; Portloe; r £160-350) Teetering over the harbour's edge in the beautiful old fishing town of Portloe, this supremely indulgent boutique hotel is the ultimate romantic getaway. A range of higgledy-piggledy rooms are dotted around the old smugglers' inn and a couple of adjoining fishermen's cottages, creating a charming mix of rough oak beams, clean, contemporary furnishings and huge, decadent beds. Downstairs the elegant restaurant serves fish fresh from the boats, and the panoramic portside terrace makes the ideal place for watching the sun go down. You may find it very hard to leave.

Royal Hotel (☎ 01872-270345; www.royalhotelcorn wall.co.uk; Lemon St; s £80, d £100-110; P 🖳) The bedrooms at this Georgian-fronted hotel are zingy affairs thanks to bold, bright designs and citrus tints. There are super-sleek 'aparthotels' just behind the main building too (£140 a night).

Other recommendations:

Fieldings (☎ 01872-262783; www.fieldingsintruro.com; 35 Treyew Rd; s/d £23/46) Homely Edwardian house with great city views.

Alverton Manor (☎ 01872-276633; www.alverton manor.co.uk; Tregolls Rd; s £80, d £95-180; P) A convent-turned-hotel crammed with antiques, sleigh beds and flowery drapes.

Eating

Xen Noodle Bar (☎ 01872-222998; 47-49 Calenick St; mains £4-8; ☼ lunch & dinner, closed Sun) Minimalistic and moreish, this inventive noodle bar keeps the crowds happy with Szechuan, Hong Kong and Canton flavours as well as Chinese classics.

Fodder's (☎ 01872-271384; Pannier Market, Lemon Quay; mains £6-9; ☼ 9am-5.30pm Mon-Sat) Hidden away above Truro's Pannier Market, this reliable wholefood cafe is still rustling up great chunky butties, thick bean soup and tasty carrot cake.

Saffron (☎ 01872-263771; Quay St; mains £8-16; ☼ lunch & dinner Mon-Sat) Asparagus, Cornish meats, seafood and strawberries: Saffron is all about local, seasonal food dished up with flair. Daily changing mains include Cornish lamb, spider-crab chowder, Cajun monkfish, and falafel with crème fraiche.

Tabbs (☎ 01872-262110; 85 Kenwyn St; mains £12.50-19; ☼ lunch & dinner) A stylish interior – dark slate floors, pale tones and futuristic fireplaces – is matched by a sophisticated menu at this renowned (if slightly stuffy) eatery – try the Provençale fish soup or the wild pigeon with brandy cream.

Indaba Fish (☎ 01872-274700; Tabernacle St; mains £14-18; ☼ dinner) The chef here used to work for Rick Stein, and this swish fish emporium has a similar emphasis on classic, straightforward seafood, ranging from Falmouth oysters and Newlyn lobster to sea bream with garlic mash. Vegetarians and fish-phobes are catered for too.

Drinking

Old Ale House (☎ 01872-271122; Quay St) What a relief – a city-centre pub that eschews chrome 'n' cocktails and sticks with burnished wood 'n' beer mats. The daily ales are chalked up behind the bar and there's often live jazz at weekends.

Heron (☎ 01872-272773; Malpas; ◷ 11am-3pm & 6-11pm Mon-Sat, 7-10.30pm Sun) Two miles along the river estuary from Truro, this creekside pub in the tiny village of Malpas, serves good beer and excellent pub grub.

MI Bar (☎ 01872-277214; Lemon Quay; ◷ 10am-1am Fri & Sat, 10am-midnight Sun-Thu) A sleek city-slicker style bar whose guest DJs have a fondness for hip hop, jazz, funk and soul.

Entertainment

Hall for Cornwall (☎ 01872-262466; www.hallforcornwall .co.uk; Lemon Quay) The county's main venue for touring theatre and music, housed in Truro's former town hall on Lemon Quay.

Plaza Cinema (☎ 01872-272894; www.wtwcinemas .co.uk; Lemon St) A four-screen cinema showing mainly mainstream releases.

L2 (☎ 01872-261199; Calenick St; cover charge £3-5; ◷ 9pm-1.30am Mon, 9.30pm-1am Wed-Thu, 9.30pm-3am Fri & Sat) Truro's biggest nightclub features a wide variety of themed nights – it can get rowdy at kicking-out time.

Getting There & Away
BUS

There are direct National Express coaches to London Victoria (£38.50, eight hours, four daily). Bus X18 travels to Penzance (one hour, hourly Monday to Saturday, six on Sunday) via Redruth and Camborne, and bus 14B travels to St Ives (1½ hours, hourly Monday to Saturday); lots of services travel to Falmouth and Newquay. The bus station is beside Lemon Quay.

TRAIN

Truro is on the main line between London Paddington (£70, 4½ to five hours, hourly) and Penzance (£7, 45 minutes, hourly). There's a branch line to Falmouth (£3.50, 20 minutes, every two hours).

WEST CORNWALL

For exhilarating swathes of wind-blasted, spray-dashed coast, it's hard to top west Cornwall, especially around St Just-in-Penwith and Zennor. Sleepy fishing villages, such as Mousehole, provide the picturesque; the Tate St Ives adds art history; the Lizard Peninsula supplies stunning gardens; while

Penzance provides an authentic maritime atmosphere and bursts of seaside chic.

Falmouth
pop 20775

Falmouth is a pleasing blend of bustling port, holiday resort and mildly alternative student town. Flanked by the third deepest natural harbour in the world, its fortunes were made in the 18th and 19th centuries when clippers, trading vessels and mail packets from across the world stopped off to unload their cargoes. Today Falmouth still has an important shipyard as well as an absorbing National Maritime Museum. Thousands of students from the nearby Combined Universities in Cornwall campus lend the town a laid-back vibe, as does the batch of sandy beaches just around the headland to the south of town.

The **tourist office** (☎ 01326-312300; www.acornish river.co.uk; 11 Market Strand; ◷ 9.30am-5.15pm Mon-Sat Mar-Oct, Mon-Fri Nov-Feb, plus 10.15am-1.45pm Sun Jul & Aug) is beside the Prince of Wales Pier.

SIGHTS & ACTIVITIES
National Maritime Museum

This **museum** (☎ 01326-313388; www.nmmc.co.uk; Discovery Quay; adult/child £7.95/5.25; ◷ 10am-5pm) is home to one of the largest maritime collections in the UK, second only to its sister museum in Greenwich in London. At the heart of the complex is the huge Flotilla Gallery, where boats dangle from the ceiling on slender steel wires, while suspended walkways wind their way around the collection of yachts, schooners, punts and canoes. Other highlights include the Set Sail exhibit, which tells the story of nine ground-breaking boats, and the Lookout, with a 360-degree panorama of Falmouth Bay.

Pendennis Castle

Perched on a promontory overlooking Falmouth harbour, **Pendennis Castle** (EH; ☎ 01326-316594; adult/child £5.50/2.80; ◷ 10am-6pm Jul & Aug, 10am-5pm Apr-Jun & Sep, 10am-4pm Oct-Mar, closes 4pm Sat year-round) provides an evocative taste of its 460-year-old history. Henry VIII first constructed Cornwall's largest fortress here to defend the entrance to the Fal estuary in tandem with its sister fortress at St Mawes (p407), on the opposite side. Highlights include a superbly atmospheric Tudor gun deck (complete with cannon flashes, smoke and shouted commands), a WWI guard house and remarkable re-creation of a WWII observation post.

Boat Trips
Boat trips set out from the Prince of Wales Pier to the River Helford (opposite) and Frenchman's Creek (£8 return), the 500-year-old Smuggler's Cottage pub (£6.50 return) and Truro (£8 return, one hour). The pier is lined with boat companies' booths; try **Enterprise Boats** (☎ 01326-374241) or **Newman's Cruises** (☎ 01872-580309).

Passenger ferries make the harbour-mouth dash across to St Mawes and Flushing from the pier every hour in summer.

Beaches
The nearest beach to town is busy **Gyllyngvase**, a short walk from the town centre, where you'll find plenty of flat sand and a decent beach cafe. Further around the headland, **Swanpool** and **Maenporth** are usually quieter.

SLEEPING
Falmouth is crammed with B&Bs and hotels, especially along Melvill Rd and Avenue Rd.

Hawthorne Dene Hotel (☎ 01326-311427; www .hawthornedenehotel.co.uk; 12 Pennance Rd; s/d £40/80; P) Edwardian elegance rules the roost at this family-run hotel, with its ranks of old photos and booklined gentleman's lounge. The antique-themed bedrooms feature springy beds, polished woods and teddy bears – most also have a sea view.

Dolvean Hotel (☎ 01326-313658; www.dolvean .co.uk; 50 Melvill Rd; s £41, d £70-92; P wi-fi) There's hardly a piece of fabric in this plush five-star B&B that isn't ruched, swagged and draped. The bigger rooms sport brass bedsteads and antique mirrors, while the lounge is a shrine to Victoriana.

Chelsea House (☎ 01326-212230; www.chelseahouse hotel.com; 2 Emslie Rd; d £61-86) Displaying as many

styles as it has rooms, Chelsea takes you on a whirlwind decor tour. There's everything from plain cream and beige to wood-themed dens, flouncy twins and a sloped-ceiling attic snug.

St Michael's Hotel (☎ 01326-312707; www.st michaelshotel.co.uk; s £90-150, d £120-200; P) Bedrooms with gingham checks, light candy stripes and painted, slatted wood make this luxurious hotel reminiscent of a Long Island beach retreat. The cracking sea views, spa, swimming pool and sauna also help the holiday mood.

Other recommendations:
Trelawney (☎ 01326-316607; 6 Melvill Rd; s £30-40, d £48-90) Modern cream-and-pine rooms and brekkies full of organic goodies.
Greenbank (☎ 01326-312440; www.greenbank-hotel .co.uk; Harbourside; d £120-215, ste £260; P) Upmarket hotel where fabrics veer from traditional quilted to bursts of animal print.

EATING & DRINKING
Boathouse (☎ 01326-315425; Trevethan Hill; mains £6-10; lunch & dinner) This fantastic gastropub is so laid-back it's almost horizontal. It's especially popular with Falmouth's creative crowd, who come for the generous plates of food, cold beer and chilled-out vibe.

Harbour View (☎ 01326-315315; 24 Arwenack St; mains £7-15; lunch & dinner Wed-Mon, lunch only Sun-Tue winter) On a fine summer evening settle into a candy-coloured chair on this bistro's funky deck and enjoy a captivating view of the water. Then choose between Cornish sardines, Fal estuary scallops or the delicate, delicious seafood linguini.

our pick Hunky Dory (☎ 01326-212997; 46 Arwenack St; mains £12-25; dinner) Fishermen often ferry their just-caught catch past diners at this stylish restaurant – the seafood is that fresh. The design blends pale wood and rough whitewashed walls; while the menu

---

DETOUR: TRELISSICK

At the head of the Fal estuary, 4 miles south of Truro, **Trelissick** (NT; ☎ 01872-862090; Feock; adult/ child £6.60/3.30; 10.30am-5.30pm Feb-Oct, 11am-4pm Nov-Jan) is one of Cornwall's most beautiful landscaped gardens, with several tiered terraces covered in magnolias, rhododendrons and hydrangeas. A lovely walk runs all the way from the main garden along the river to the estate's private beach.

Enterprise Boats (☎ 01326-374241; www.enterprise-boats.co.uk; adult/child one way £4.50/3) operates boats from Falmouth and Truro that call in at Trelissick Gardens, otherwise you'll need your own transport.

mixes European and Asian flavours with classic Cornish produce – try the crispy-skinned sea bass or the Newlyn cod wrapped in prosciutto.

Top spots for a pint include the **Quayside** (☎ 01326-312113; Arwenack St), with outside seating on the harbour, and the nearby **Chain Locker** (☎ 01326-311685; Quay St), which is nautical but nice.

ENTERTAINMENT

Poly (☎ 01326-212300; www.thepoly.org; 24 Church St) The former Falmouth Arts Centre has been reinvented an excellent art-house cinema.

GETTING THERE & AWAY

Falmouth is at the end of the branch train line from Truro (£3.50, 20 minutes, every two hours).

Buses 89 and 90 run to Truro (1¼ hours, half-hourly Monday to Saturday) and onto Newquay.

The Lizard

For a taste of Cornwall's stormier side, head for the ink-black cliffs, rugged coves and open heaths of the mercurial Lizard Peninsula. Wind-lashed in winter, in summer it bristles with wildflowers, butterflies and coves that are perfect for a secluded swim. The Lizard used to be at the centre of Cornwall's smuggling industry and is still alive with tales of Cornish 'free-traders', contraband liquor and the government's preventive boats. The most notorious excise dodger was John Carter, the so-called King of Prussia – Prussia Cove near Marazion is named after him.

For more information visit www.lizard-peninsula.co.uk.

GOONHILLY EARTH STATION

The last thing you'd expect to find in the middle of the Lizard are the vast dishes of the **Goonhilly Earth Station** (☎ 0800 679593; www.goonhilly.bt.com; adult/child £7.95/5.50; ⏰ 10am-6pm Jul & Aug, 10am-5pm mid-Mar–Jun, Sep & Oct, 11am-4pm Nov–mid-Mar), which make up the largest satellite station on earth. The multimedia visitor centre has lots of interactive exhibits and romps through the last 200 years of telecommunications.

RIVER HELFORD

The **River Helford** flows across the north of the Lizard. Lined with overhanging oaks and hidden inlets it is the perfect smugglers'

DETOUR: FERRYBOAT INN

Ferryboat Inn (☎ 01326-250625; Helford Passage; mains £5-15; ⏰ lunch & dinner) Tucked away along the beautiful Helford estuary, this riverfront pub is an old favourite with locals and visiting yachties alike. On summer nights the creekside patio is packed with a lively crowd tucking into huge plates of beer-battered fish or triple-decker club sandwiches, and in winter it becomes the quintessential smugglers' pub, perfect for Sunday lunch in front of a roaring log fire.

---

hideaway. **Frenchman's Creek**, the inspiration for Daphne du Maurier's novel of the same name, can be reached on foot from the car park in **Helford** village.

On the northern bank of the river is **Trebah** (☎ 01326-252200; www.trebahgarden.co.uk; adult/child Mar-Oct £7/2, Nov-Feb £3/1; ⏰ 10.30am-6.30pm, last entry 5pm), billed as Cornwall's 'Garden of Dreams'. First planted in 1840, it's one of Cornwall's finest subtropical gardens, dramatically situated in a steep ravine filled with giant rhododendrons, huge Brazilian rhubarb plants and jungle ferns.

Glendurgan Gardens (NT; ☎ 01326-250906; adult/child £6/3; ⏰ 10.30am-5.30pm Tue-Sat Feb-Oct, plus Mon Aug) are just east of Trebah. They were established in the 18th century by the wealthy Fox family, who imported exotic plants from the New World. Look out for the stunning views of the River Helford, the 19th-century maze and the secluded beach near Durgan village.

Six miles from Helston at the western end of the river, the **National Seal Sanctuary** (☎ 01326-221361; www.sealsanctuary.co.uk; Gweek; adult/child £11.50/8.50; ⏰ 10am-5pm May-Sep, 9am-4pm Oct-Apr) cares for sick and orphaned seals washed up along the Cornish coastline before returning them to the wild.

LIZARD POINT & AROUND

Three miles west of Helston is **Porthleven**, another quaint fishing port with excellent beaches nearby. **Cadgwith** is the quintessential Cornish fishing village, with thatched, white-washed cottages and a small harbour.

Lizard Point is a 3½-mile walk along the South West Coast Path. At the peninsula's tip is the **Lizard Lighthouse** (☎ 01326-290065; adult/child £3.50/2.50; ⏰ 11am-6pm Jul & Aug, 11am-5pm Sun-Thu May & Jun, noon-5pm Sun-Wed Mar & Apr), built in 1751

DEVON & CORNWALL

and now entirely automated. Lizard Point is one of the most dangerous bits of coast in Cornwall: hundreds of ships have foundered on its rocky shores. The views from the surrounding cliff tops are some of the most dramatic in all of Cornwall.

A mile west is beautiful **Kynance Cove**, overlooked by towering cliffs and flower-covered headland; much of the red-green serpentine rock fashionable during the Victorian era was mined here.

SLEEPING

Coverack YHA (☎ 0845 371 9014; www.yha.org.uk; Coverack; dm from £10; ☿ Mar-Oct) Set above the pretty harbour of Coverack, this is a good option with spacious dorms arranged over several floors in an old gentleman's town house.

Lizard YHA (☎ 0845 371 9550; www.yha.org.uk; dm £16; ☿ Apr-Oct) Few top-end hotels can boast the kind of spectacular sea view enjoyed by this gloriously situated hostel, in a renovated Victorian hotel right below the lighthouse on Lizard Point.

Housel Bay Hotel (☎ 01326-290417; www.housel bay.com; The Lizard; d £90-140; **P**) By far the most impressive hotel on Lizard Point, this grand gabled manor was built by a group of luxury-loving Victorian entrepreneurs. It's still a gorgeous place to stay, with plenty of antiques, period rugs and a charming old-world atmosphere.

GETTING THERE & AWAY

Bus T2 runs from Truro to Helston (50 minutes, eight daily Monday to Saturday, five on Sunday) and onto Goonhilly (20 minutes), Coverack (30 minutes) and St Keverne (40 minutes).

To reach Lizard village, near Lizard Point, catch bus T34 from Helston (45 minutes, hourly Monday to Saturday, five on Sunday).

St Michael's Mount

Looming up from the waters of Mount's Bay, the island abbey of **St Michael's Mount** (NT; ☎ 01736-710507; adult/child £6.60/3; ☿ 10.30am-5pm Sun-Fri Mar-Oct) is one of Cornwall's iconic landmarks. Set on a collection of craggy cliffs and connected to the mainland by a cobbled causeway that's submerged by the rising tide, there's been a monastery here since at least the 5th century. After the Norman conquest the island was given to the Benedictine monks of Mont St Michel in Normandy, who raised a new chapel on the site in 1135. The mount later served as a fortified stronghold and is now the family home of the St Aubyns, and under the stewardship of the National Trust.

Highlights include the rococo Gothic drawing room, the original armoury, the 14th-century priory church and its subtropical **gardens** (adult/child £3/1), which teeter dramatically above the sea. You can walk across the causeway at low tide, or catch a ferry at high tide in the summer.

Bus 2 passes Marazion as it travels from Penzance to Falmouth (half hourly Monday to Saturday, six on Sunday).

Penzance
pop 21,168

Stretching along the glittering sweep of Mount's Bay, Penzance has been the last stop on the main railway line from London back since the days of the Great Western Railway. With its hotchpotch of winding streets, old shopping arcades and its grand seafront promenade, Penzance is much more authentic than the polished-up, prettified towns of Padstow and St Ives, and makes an excellent base for exploring the rest of west Cornwall and Land's End.

CORNWALL'S FURRY FLING

Helston, the only real town on the Lizard, is famous for its annual **Flora Day**, held every year on 8 May. Believed to be rooted in old pagan celebrations marking the coming of spring, this ancient festival is a peculiar mixture of street dance, musical parade and floral pageant. Locals dress up in traditional finery and cover the town in blossoms from the surrounding countryside. The day itself is marked by several stately dances – the first is at 7am, followed by the lively Hal-An-Tow pageant and a children's dance. The highlight of the day is the Furry Dance, which kicks off at noon and processes around the town's streets; participants take part by invitation only, and the dance is always led by a local couple. After the final dance the entire town piles into the pubs for a hard-earned pint, or six. Unsurprisingly, the Victorians took a dim view of the proceedings and the festival was banned in the 19th century for promoting 'drunken revelry'.

INFORMATION
Library (☎ 01736-363954;Morrab Rd; internet access per hr £3; ⏱ 9.30am-6pm Mon-Fri, to 4pm Sat)
Polyclean Laundrette (☎ 01736-364815; 4 East Tce; ⏱ 9am-7.30pm) Opposite the railway station.
Tourist office (☎ 01736-362207; www.visit-west cornwall.com; Station Approach; ⏱ 9am-5pm Mon-Fri, plus 10am-4pm Sat Easter-Sep & 10am-2pm Sun Jul & Aug) Next to the bus station.
Penzance OnLine (www.penzance.co.uk) Useful local guide to Penzance and the surrounding area.

SIGHTS & ACTIVITIES
Despite what you may have heard from Messrs Gilbert and Sullivan, Penzance was never renowned for its pirates – instead it was famous for trading in tin, grain and pilchards (a local delicacy was 'stargazey pie', so called because the fishes' heads gazed up through the pie's crust). The export trade brought riches and the old town is littered with elegant Georgian and Regency houses, especially around Chapel St; hunt down the 19th-century **Egyptian House**, which is a bizarre blend of Georgian town house and Egyptian sarcophagus.

At the eastern end of Penzance's 19th-century promenade, the glorious 1930s **Jubilee Pool** (☎ 01736-334832; www.jubileepool.co.uk; adult/child/family £3.85/2.75/12.20; ⏱ 10.30am-6pm May-Sep) offers you the chance to take a dip in a classic art-deco lido. Since falling into disrepair in the 1980s, it's been thoroughly spruced-up and is now open to alfresco bathers throughout the summer – just don't expect the water to be warm.

The busy fishing harbour of **Newlyn**, on the western edge of Penzance, was the centre of the Newlyn School of artists in the late 19th century; the **Newlyn Art Gallery** (☎ 01736-363715; www.newlynartgallery.co.uk; ⏱ 10am-5pm Mon-Sat Easter-Sep, Wed-Sat Oct-Easter) showcases their modern counterparts.

SLEEPING
Budget
Penzance has lots of low-price B&Bs, especially along Alexandra Rd and Morrab Rd.

Penzance Backpackers (☎ 01736-363836; www .pzbackpack.com; Alexandra Rd; dm/d £15/32; 🖳) The rooms and dorms of this laid-back indie hostel are small and a touch worn, but it's clean, fun and friendly, so globe-trotting backpackers will feel right at home.

Penzance YHA (☎ 0845 371 9653; www.yha.org.uk; Castle Horneck, Alverton; dm £15.50; P 🖳) Housed inside an 18th-century Georgian manor on the outskirts of town, this official hostel has an on-site cafe, laundry and four- to 10-bed dorms. Buses 5 and 6 run from the bus station to Alverton; it's a 500m walk from the bus stop.

Glencree House (☎ 01736-362026; www.glencree house.co.uk; 2 Mennaye Rd; d £40-62; P) Modest sea views, a budget bill and a slap-up breakfast make this old fashioned B&B worth booking; the smoked kippers, proper coffee and croissants will leave you crying off lunch.

Midrange & Top End
Chy-an-Mor (☎ 01736-363441; Regent Tce; s £35, d £72-84; P) This reliable guest house is decked out in standard-issue shades and off-the-shelf furnishings, but worth considering for the seafront location.

Camilla House (☎ 01736-363771; www.camillahouse .co.uk; 12 Regent Tce; s £35, d £74-85; P 🖳) Set in a Georgian Master Mariner's house, this five-star B&B stands out for its classy rooms, period features and environmentally conscious stance. Fluffy bathrobes, pillow treats and views over the prom will tempt you too.

Summer House (☎ 01736-363744; www.summer house-cornwall.com; Cornwall Tce; s £85, d £95-125; ⏱ closed Nov-Mar; P) For a touch of Chelsea-on-Sea chic, check into this elegant Regency house. Checks, pinstripes and cheery colours characterise the five bedrooms, and downstairs there's a Mediterranean restaurant with alfresco terrace.

Abbey Hotel (☎ 01736-366906; www.theabbeyonline .co.uk; Abbey St; d £130-200) Bucking the pared-down trend, this flower-filled, period town house offers a taste of Penzance's 17th-century heyday. All the cosy rooms have their own offbeat style and higgledy-piggledy layout, topped off with floral fabrics and canopied beds.

EATING
Bar Coco's (☎ 01736-350222; 13 Chapel St; tapas £2-6; ⏱ lunch & dinner Mon-Sat) More Cádiz than Cornwall, this funky little tapas bar is an ideal spot to sample miniplatters of *patatas*

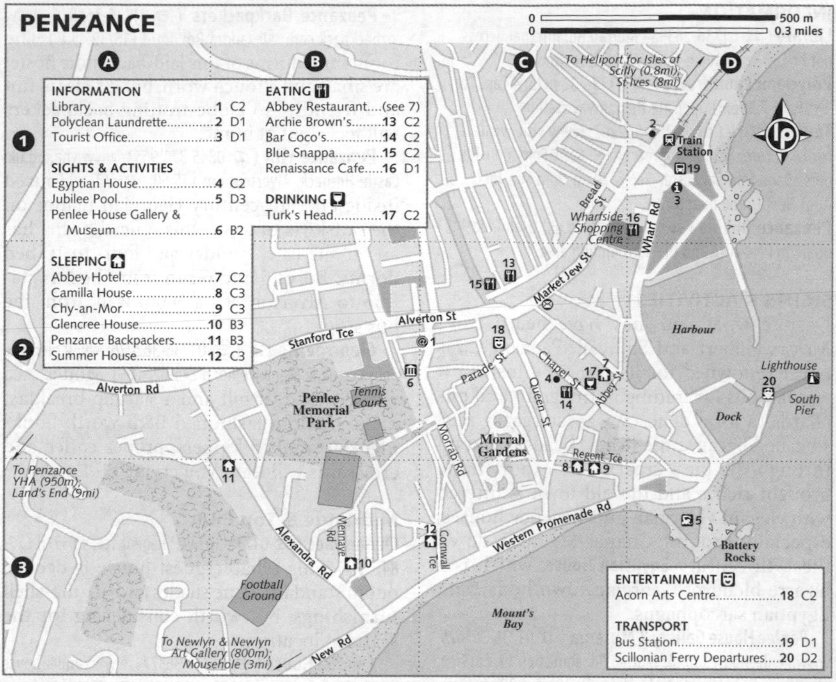
PENZANCE
0 500 m
0 0.3 miles
A
B
C
D
1
2
3
INFORMATION
Library....................1 C2
Polyclean Laundrette....................2 D1
Tourist Office....................3 D1
SIGHTS & ACTIVITIES
Egyptian House....................4 C2
Jubilee Pool....................5 D3
Penlee House Gallery & Museum....................6 B2
SLEEPING
Abbey Hotel....................7 C2
Camilla House....................8 C3
Chy-an-Mor....................9 C3
Glencree House....................10 B3
Penzance Backpackers....................11 B3
Summer House....................12 C3
EATING
Abbey Restaurant....(see 7)
Archie Brown's........13 C2
Bar Coco's........14 C2
Blue Snappa........15 C2
Renaissance Cafe.....16 D1
DRINKING
Turk's Head........17 C2
ENTERTAINMENT
Acorn Arts Centre....................18 C2
TRANSPORT
Bus Station....................19 D1
Scillonian Ferry Departures....20 D2
To Heliport for Isles of Scilly (0.8mi); St Ives (8mi)
Train Station
Bread St
Wharfside Shopping Centre
Wharf Rd
Market Jew St
Harbour
Alverton St
Stanford Tce
Parade St
Chapel St
Queen St
Abbey St
Lighthouse
South Pier
Dock
Alverton Rd
Penlee Memorial Park
Tennis Courts
Morrab Gardens
Morrab Rd
Regent Tce
To Penzance YHA (950m); Land's End (9mi)
Western Promenade Rd
Battery Rocks
Alexandra Rd
Mennaye Rd
Cornwall Tce
Football Ground
Mount's Bay
To Newlyn & Newlyn Art Gallery (800m); Mousehole (3mi)
New Rd

and chorizo. You can also say '*buenas tardes*' to Mediterranean-style sardines, tuna and monkfish.

Archie Brown's (☎ 01736-362828; Bread St; mains £4-6; 9.30am-5pm Mon-Sat) This much-loved vegie/vegan cafe serves up hearty portions of old faves including homity pie, hot chilli and crumbly carrot cake.

Renaissance Cafe (☎ 01736-366277; 6 Wharfside Shopping Centre; mains £5-12; 10am-10pm) Despite being hidden away in the Wharfside Shopping Centre, this Continental-style cafe-bar has floor-to-ceiling vistas of Mount's Bay. A great bistro menu (think gourmet burgers and seafood specials) does its best to distract you from the view.

Blue Snappa (☎ 01736-363352; 35 Market Pl; mains £6-15; breakfast, lunch & dinner Mon-Sat, breakfast & lunch Sun) They do a good line in hip surfer chic at this buzzing bar-brasserie; the menu meanwhile will leave you torn between slow-roast belly pork, smoked pollack with garlic or a flavoursome vegie risotto.

Abbey Restaurant (☎ 01736-330680; Abbey St; mains £16-20, 2/3 courses £19/23; lunch & dinner Tue-Sat) Underpinned by top-quality produce, the Abbey turns out consistently fabulous food in a light-filled dining room. It's not cheap, but tucking into your roast monkfish or hot chocolate soufflé, you'll feel it's money well spent.

DRINKING & ENTERTAINMENT

Turk's Head (☎ 01736-363093; Chapel St) They pull a fine pint of real ale at this, the oldest boozer in Penzance. It's said a smugglers' tunnel used to link the pub with the harbour – handy for sneaking in that liquid contraband.

Acorn Arts Centre (☎ 01736-363545; www.acornartscentre.co.uk; Parade St) An excellent independent arts centre, with regular programs of film, theatre and live music.

GETTING THERE & AWAY

The *Scillonian* ferry regularly sails from Penzance to the Isles of Scilly, see p423; helicopters to the Isles of Scilly leave from just outside town, see p422.

Bus

National Express coaches travel to London (£38.50, nine hours, five daily), Exeter (£24, five hours, two daily) and Plymouth (£7.20,

3½ hours, seven daily). For buses to Land's End see right.

Train
Regular services journey to London Paddington (£90, six hours, eight daily) via Truro. There are frequent trains to St Ives (£4.80, 20 minutes, hourly) via St Erth.

Mousehole
The compact harbour town Mousehole (pronounced mow-zel) was once at the heart of Cornwall's thriving pilchard industry, but these days it's better known for its colourful Christmas lights. Despite hideously high numbers of second homes, it's still one of Cornwall's most appealing villages, with a tight-packed knot of slate-roofed cottages gathered around the harbour

The designer decor at the **Old Coastguard Hotel** (☎ 01736-731222; www.oldcoastguardhotel .co.uk; d £140-210) would have bemused ancient mariners, but guests love the arty lighting, smooth leather chairs and balconies with jaw-dropping sea views. The sunlit restaurant also looks out over the glittering bay and specialises, unsurprisingly, in fantastic seafood.

Bus 6 makes the 20-minute journey to Penzance half-hourly.

Minack Theatre
At the **Minack** (☎ 01736-810181; www.minack.com; tickets from £8.50) the actors are constantly upstaged by the setting. Carved directly into the steep cliffs overlooking Porthcurno Bay, this alfresco amphitheatre is the legacy of Rowena Cade, an indomitable local woman who came up with the idea in the 1930s, helped with the construction for 20 years and oversaw the theatre until her death in 1983. From the original production of *The Tempest* in 1932, the Minack has grown into a full-blown theatrical venue, with 750 seats and a 17-week season running from mid-May to mid-September. The cliffs provide the scenery, the sea provides the back drop, while basking sharks and the moon rising over the waves provide charming distractions. Regulars bring a bottle of wine, umbrellas and lots of blankets.

The **visitor centre** (adult/child £3.50/1.40; ☯ 9.30am-5.30pm Apr-Sep, 10am-4pm Oct-Mar) recounts the story of the making of the theatre; it's closed when there's a matinée.

The Minack is above beautiful Porthcurno beach, 3 miles from Land's End and 9 miles from Penzance. Bus 1A from Penzance to Land's End stops at Porthcurno, Monday to Saturday.

Land's End
The most westerly point of mainland England, Land's End's coal-black cliffs, heather-covered headlands and booming Atlantic surf should steal the show. Unfortunately the tawdry **Legendary Land's End** (☎ 0870 458 0099; www.lands end-landmark.co.uk; adult/child £11/7; ☯ 10am-5pm summer, 10am-3pm winter) theme park does rather get in the way. But you can bypass the kitsch models and multimedia shows and opt for an exhilarating clifftop stroll instead. On a clear day the Isles of Scilly are visible, 28 miles out to sea.

Land's End is 9 miles from Penzance (and 886 miles from John O'Groats). Buses 1 and 1A travel from Penzance (one hour, seven to 10 daily Monday to Saturday). Bus 300 heads to St Ives (one hour 20 minutes, four daily May to October).

St Just-in-Penwith
pop 1890
It's hard to imagine today, but a century ago the grey-granite settlement of St Just was at the heart of a vibrant tin and copper mining industry. The old **Geevor Tin Mine** (☎ 01736-788662; www.geevor.com; adult/child £7.50/4.50; ☯ 9am-5pm Sun-Fri Easter-Oct, to 3pm Nov-Mar) at Pendeen, north of St Just, finally closed in 1990, and now offers hourly tours of the underground shafts (three daily in winter), providing an amazing insight into the dark and dangerous conditions in which Cornwall's miners worked.

Clinging to the cliffs nearby is **Botallack Mine** (not open to the public), one of Cornwall's most dramatic engine houses, which have abandoned mine shafts extending right out beneath the raging Atlantic waves.

Land's End YHA (☎ 0845 371 9643; www.yha.org .uk; Letcha Vean; dm £10; ☯ Easter-Oct; Ⓟ) is in an isolated spot half a mile south of the village. This no-frills affair has smallish dorms and a basic kitchen, but is ideal if you're hiking the coast path.

St Just is 6 miles north of Land's End. Buses 17/17A/17B travel from St Ives (1¼ hours) via Penzance (half-hourly Monday to Saturday, five on Sunday).

Zennor
pop 217
A stunning 6-mile stretch of the South West Coast Path runs from St Ives to the windswept

village of Zennor, where DH Lawrence wrote much of *Women in Love*. **St Senara's Church** dates from at least 1150. Look for the carved Mermaid Chair; legend tells of a beautiful, mysterious woman who lured a chorister into the sea at nearby Mermaid's Cove, where you can still hear them singing.

The **Wayside Folk Museum** (☎ 01736-796945; admission £3; ⏰ 10.30am-5pm Sun-Fri May-Sep, 11am-5pm Sun-Fri Apr & Oct) houses a treasure trove of artefacts gathered by inveterate collector Colonel 'Freddie' Hirst in the 1930s. The displays range from blacksmiths' hammers and cobblers' tools to an 18th-century kitchen and two reclaimed watermills.

Even if you normally don't 'do' dorms, the **Old Chapel Backpackers Hostel** (☎ 01736-98307; dm/f £15/50; ℗) is a top sleeping spot. Set in a sensitively renovated former church, the smart rooms sleep four to six – ask for one with a sea view. There's a comfy, high-ceilinged cafe-lounge too.

DH Lawrence's local while he lived at Zennor was the **Tinner's Arms** (☎ 01736-792697; lunch £7-10), a classic Cornish inn with a rambling main bar sheltering under a slate roof. Pub lunches and local ales are served either inside or on the sea-view patio.

Bus 300 (30 minutes, five daily) heads to St Ives.

St Ives
pop 9870

Sitting on the fringes of a glittering arc-shaped bay, St Ives was once one of Cornwall's busiest pilchard-fishing harbours, but it's better known now as the centre of the county's arts scene. From the old harbour, cobbled alleyways and switchback lanes lead up into the jumble of buzzy galleries, cafes and brasseries that cater for thousands of summer visitors. It makes for an intriguing mix of boutique chic and traditional seaside, and while the high-season traffic can take the shine off things, St Ives is still an essential stop on any Cornish grand tour.

INFORMATION

Library (☎ 01736-795377; 1 Gabriel St; internet access per hr £3; ⏰ 9.30am-9.30pm Tue, to 6pm Wed-Fri, to 12.30pm Sat)

Post office (☎ 01736-795004; Tregenna Pl; ⏰ 9am-5.30pm Mon-Fri, 9am-12.30pm Sat)

St Ives Info (www.stives-cornwall.co.uk) Official town website with accommodation and activity guides.

Tourist office (☎ 01736-796297; ivtic@penwith.gov .uk; Street-an-Pol; ⏰ 9am-5.30pm Mon-Fri, 9am-5pm Sat, 10am-4pm Sun) Inside the Guildhall.

SIGHTS & ACTIVITIES
Tate St Ives

The artwork almost takes second place to the surroundings at the stunning **Tate St Ives** (☎ 01736-796226; www.tate.org.uk/stives; Porthmeor Beach; adult/under 19yr £5.75/free, joint ticket with Barbara Hepworth museum £8.75/free; ⏰ 10am-5pm Mar-Oct, 10am-4pm Tue-Sun Nov-Feb), which hovers like a white concrete curl above Porthmeor Beach. Built in 1993, the gallery contains work by celebrated local artists, including Terry Frost, Patrick Heron and Barbara Hepworth, and hosts regular special exhibitions. On the top floor there's a stylish cafe-bar with imaginative bistro food and some of the best sea views in St Ives.

There are plenty more galleries around town; at the **Sloop Craft Centre** you'll find a treasure trove of tiny artists' studios selling everything from handmade jewellery to driftwood furniture.

Barbara Hepworth Museum & Sculpture Garden

Barbara Hepworth (1903–75) was one of the leading abstract sculptors of the 20th century, and a key figure in the St Ives art scene; fittingly her former studio has been transformed into a moving archive and **museum** (☎ 01736-796226; www.tate.org.uk/stives; Barnoon Hill; adult/under 19yr £4.75/free, joint ticket with Tate St Ives £8.75/free; ⏰ 10am-5pm Mar-Oct, 10am-4pm Tue-Sun Nov-Feb). The studio itself has remained almost untouched since her death in

---

SEARCHING FOR STONES

The area between St Just and St Ives is remarkably rich in ancient sites and dotted with dolmens, menhirs and mysterious stone circles. Track down **Lanyon Quoit** (a table-shaped dolmen between Madron and Morvah), the **Mên-an-Tol stone** (a ring-shaped stone near Madron), the **Merry Maidens** (Cornwall's most complete stone circle, near Trewoofe) and **Chysauster Iron Age Village** (☎ 07831 757934; adult/child £2.50/1.30; ⏰ 10am-6pm Jul & Aug, 10am-5pm Apr-Jun & Sep, 10am-4pm Oct), the most complete prehistoric settlement in Cornwall. Bodmin Moor also has plenty of ancient monuments (see Stone & Stories p404).

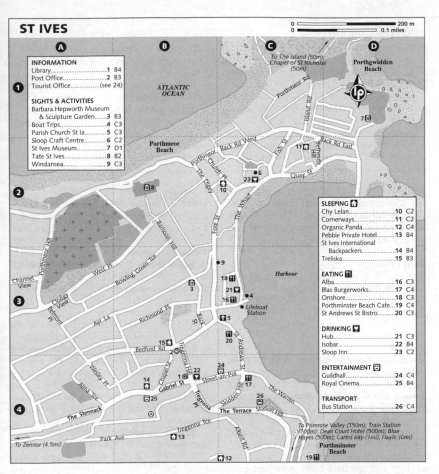

ST IVES

INFORMATION
Library..............................1 B4
Post Office.......................2 B3
Tourist Office..............(see 24)

SIGHTS & ACTIVITIES
Barbara Hepworth Museum
& Sculpture Garden.....3 B3
Boat Trips.........................4 C3
Parish Church St Ia.........5 C3
Sloop Craft Centre..........6 C2
St Ives Museum................7 D1
Tate St Ives.......................8 B2
Windansea.........................9 C3

SLEEPING
Chy Lelan.........................10 C2
Cornerways......................11 C2
Organic Panda.................12 C4
Pebble Private Hotel........13 B4
St Ives International
Backpackers..................14 B4
Treliska............................15 B3

EATING
Alba..................................16 C3
Blas Burgerworks............17 C4
Onshore...........................18 C3
Porthminster Beach Cafe..19 C4
St Andrews St Bistro........20 C3

DRINKING
Hub...................................21 C3
Isobar...............................22 B4
Sloop Inn..........................23 C2

ENTERTAINMENT
Guildhall..........................24 C4
Royal Cinema...................25 B4

TRANSPORT
Bus Station......................26 C4

a fire, and the adjoining garden contains some of her most famous sculptures. Hepworth's work is scattered throughout St Ives; look for her sculptures outside the Guildhall and inside the 15th-century parish church of St Ia.

St Ives Museum
Housed in a pier-side building variously used as a pilchard-packing factory, sailors' mission and copper mine, **St Ives Museum** (☎ 01736-796005; Wheal Dream; adult/child £1.50/50p; ☺ 10am-5pm Mon-Fri, to 4pm Sat, mid-Mar–Oct) contains local artefacts relating to blacksmithery, fishing and shipwrecks.

Beaches
The largest town beaches are **Porthmeor** and **Porthminster**, but the tiny cove of **Porthgwidden**

is also popular. Nearby, on a tiny peninsula of land known locally as The Island, the pre-14th-century **Chapel of St Nicholas**, patron saint of children and sailors, is the oldest (and smallest) church in St Ives. **Carbis Bay**, to the southeast, is popular with families and sun seekers.

On the opposite side of the bay from St Ives, the receding tide reveals over 3 miles of golden beach at **Gwithian** and **Godrevy Towans**, both popular spots for kiteboarders and surfers. The lighthouse just offshore at Godrevy was the inspiration for Virginia Woolf's classic stream-of-consciousness novel *To The Lighthouse*.

Several places on Porthmeor Beach and Fore St rent wetsuits and surfboards; try

DEVON & CORNWALL

ST IVES & THE ARTS

Ever since Turner sketched the town in 1811, St Ives has been a focal point for British art. During the 19th century St Ives was linked with the Newlyn School, a group of figurative painters headed by Stanhope Forbes, who found ideal subjects among rustic local characters and landscapes. Whistler and Sickert made regular visits and, by the beginning of the 20th century, there were scores of artists working in and around St Ives. The 1930s and '40s saw the scene flourish and the work of abstract painters like Peter Lanyon, Henry Moore and Ben Nicholson, and his wife, the sculptor Barbara Hepworth, led to the formation of the Penwith Society of Artists in 1949. Their avant-garde techniques inspired a third wave of St Ives artists in the 1960s and '70s, including Terry Frost, Patrick Heron and Roger Hilton. Today St Ives continues to hold an enduring fascination – the Penwith area supports more working artists than almost anywhere else in Britain.

Windansea (☎ 01736-794830; 25 Fore St; per 24hr £5). The BSA-approved **Shore Surf School** (☎ 01736-755556; per half-day £25) is based at Hayle, 6 miles away; lessons are held where the conditions are best on the day however.

Boat Trips

Boats heading out on sea-fishing trips and cruises to the grey seal colony on Seal Island (adult/child £9/6), include those of the **St Ives Pleasure Boat Association** (☎ 07821 774178).

SLEEPING
Budget

St Ives International Backpackers (☎ 01736-799444; www.backpackers.co.uk/st-ives; The Stennack; dm £12-18; 🖳) Not one of the smartest backpackers around, this shabby indie hostel is pretty battered with cramped dorms and threadbare carpets, but it is handy for town.

Chy Lelan (☎ 01736-797560; www.chylelan.co.uk; Bunkers Hill; d £50-60) Set in the heart of St Ives' winding cobbled streets, these two 17th-century cottages have been converted into vaguely floral rooms. They're on the small side, but some provide glimpses of the sea.

Cornerways (☎ 01736-796706; www.cornerwaysstives .com; 1 Bethesda Pl; d £50-80) The bedroom size at this former fisherman's cottage suggests past seafarers weren't big blokes. But the pastel decor is fresh, you get free tickets to the Tate and you're just steps away from the harbour and the beach.

Midrange

Pebble Private Hotel (☎ 01736-794168; www.pebble -hotel.co.uk; 4 Park Ave; s £35-45, d £84-110) Swirly retro fabrics, gorgeous glossy satins and mock-flock wallpaper set this groovy B&B a world away from its chintz and pine cousins. It also makes it a favourite sleep for hip young things.

Treliska (☎ 01736-797678; www.treliska.com; 3 Bedford Rd; s £40-60, d £64-80) Another beautifully finished B&B that's far beyond lace doilies and photo placemats – here it's all clean lines, chrome bath taps and elegantly understated wooden furniture.

Organic Panda (☎ 01736-793890; www.organicpanda .co.uk; 1 Pednolver Tce; d £80-120; P 🖳 wi-fi) Sleep with a clear conscience (and in style) at this super-sleek B&B, which is run along all-organic lines. Spotty cushions, technicolour artwork and timber-salvage beds keep the funk factor high; the sea views steal the show outside.

Dean Court Hotel (☎ 01736-796023; www.dean courthotel.com; Trelyon Ave; d £90-132; P) There's an upmarket feel to this 12-room Victorian town house where restrained rooms feature rich carpets, brass bedsteads and the occasional quilted duvet cover. Some look onto a glittering St Ives Bay.

our pick **Primrose Valley** (☎ 01736-794939; www .primroseonline.co.uk; Porthminster Beach; d £105-155, ste £175-225; P) One of St Ives' secret gems, this swish guest house–cum–boutique hotel has ecofriendly credentials and a real eye for interior design. All the rooms have characteristic quirks – some boast blonde wood, leather armchairs and exposed brick, while others delight with sea blues, Philippe Starck lights and mosaic-lined bathrooms. Throw in a locally sourced breakfast, Manhattan-style lounge-bar and fab location near Porthminster Beach, and you have one of the best little boltholes in Cornwall.

Top End

Blue Hayes (☎ 01736-797129; www.blue-hayes.co.uk; Trelyon Ave; r £160-190; P) Another boutique beauty, Blue Hayes boasts five luxurious cream-coloured suites (including one with its own private roof patio), body-jet showers and a balustraded breakfast terrace overlooking the bay.

EATING

St Ives' harbourside is awash with brasseries, but the backlanes house top options too.

Blas Burgerworks (☎ 01736-797272; The Warren; burgers £5-9; ☺ dinner Tue-Sun) The humble burger becomes a work of art at this fab diner where creations range from beetburgers in sunflower baps to black-bean burgers laced with lashings of chilli sauce.

Onshore (☎ 01736-796000; The Wharf; pizzas £8-16; ☺ lunch & dinner) Sometimes you just want a pizza – and this bright and breezy outlet delivers gourmet versions baked to perfection in a wood-fired oven.

St Andrews St Bistro (☎ 01736-797074; 16 Andrews St; mains £9-15; ☺ dinner) A hectic heap of North African rugs and oddball furniture covers this eatery where modern-British fare meets African and Middle Eastern cuisine. Artisan bread, lentil curries, grilled fish and spicy casseroles all feature on the menu.

Porthminster Beach Cafe (☎ 01736-795352; Porthminster Beach; lunch £9-17, dinner £17-22) More bistro than beach cafe, this buzzy eatery directly overlooks Porthminster Beach. Balconies and picture windows make the most of an azure view, while the monkfish curry and Cornish scallops make the most of the fruits of the sea.

our pick **Alba** (☎ 01736-797222; Old Lifeboat House; mains £15-20; ☺ lunch & dinner) The award-winning Alba is a byword for sophisticated seafood in a stylish, open-plan setting. Try the Provençale fish soup, whisky-cured salmon or lobster pasta – but do leave room for the chocolate and rum mousse. In-the-know locals bag tables five, six or seven for their gorgeous harbour views.

DRINKING

Hub (☎ 01736-799099; The Wharf; ☺ 10am-late) This funky open-plan cafe-bar cranks up DJs and live music by night, and serves up lattes and hot chocolate by day.

Isobar (☎ 01736-796042; Tregenna Pl; ☺ to 2am) St Ives' main nightspot boasts a pared-back bar on the ground floor and a hot-and-sweaty club upstairs, with regular funk, house and techno nights, and the odd crowd-pleasing burst of cheese.

Sloop Inn (☎ 01736-796584; The Wharf) A classic old fishermen's boozer, complete with low ceilings, tankards behind the bar and a comprehensive selection of Cornish ales.

ENTERTAINMENT

Royal Cinema (☎ 01736-796843; www.merlincinemas.co.uk; Royal Sq) Shows new films and often has cheap matinées.

Guildhall (☎ 01736-796888; 1 Street-An-Pol) Plays host to regular programs of music and theatre, especially during the St Ives September Festival.

GETTING THERE & AWAY

National Express coaches go to London (£38.50, 8½ hours, two daily) and Plymouth (£7.20, three hours, four daily).

Buses 17, 17A and 17B travel to Penzance (30 minutes) regularly; the circular bus 300 stops at Land's End en route.

St Ives is on a scenic branch train line from St Erth (£2.50, 20 minutes, hourly), which is on the main London–Penzance line.

ISLES OF SCILLY

Flung far into the sea off the end of England, the captivating Isles of Scilly have something of the Mediterranean about them. The archipelago is scattered 28 miles west of Land's End where, washed by the Gulf Stream, they enjoy a comparatively balmy climate. Only five of the 140 islands are inhabited; St Mary's is the largest and busiest, closely followed by Tresco, while only a few hardy souls live on Bryher, St Martin's and St Agnes. Traditionally farming, fishing and flower growing were the key industries, but these days tourism is by far the biggest money spinner. Whether enjoying the laid-back lifestyle, island hopping or some of the best beaches in England, many visitors find themselves Scilly addicts – drawn back again and again by the subtropical gardens, barefoot beachcombing and castaway vibe.

Information

The **Isles of Scilly Tourist Board** (☎ 01720-422536; tic@scilly.gov.uk; Hugh Town, St Mary's; ☺ 8.30am-6pm Mon-Fri, 9am-5pm Sat, 9am-2pm Sun May-Sep, shorter hr in winter) is on St Mary's.

Useful websites include www.scillyonline.co.uk and the tourist office's site (www.simplyscilly.co.uk), which has full accommodation listings.

The islands get extremely busy in summer, while many businesses shut down completely in winter. All of the islands, except Tresco,

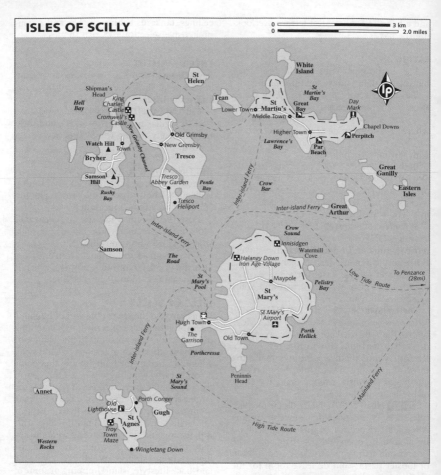

ISLES OF SCILLY

have a simple campsite, but many visitors choose to stay in self-catering accommodation – check out **Island Properties** (☎ 01720-422082; www.scillyhols.com; St Mary's).

St Mary's

The largest and busiest island in the Scillys is St Mary's, which contains many of the islands' big hotels, B&Bs, restaurants and shops. The Scillonian ferry and most flights from the mainland arrive on St Mary's, but the other main islands (known as the 'off-islands') are easily reached via the inter-island launches that leave regularly from the harbour.

About a mile west of the airport is the main settlement of **Hugh Town**, where you'll find the bulk of the island's hotels and guest houses.

The islands have an absorbing, unique history, which is explored to the full in the **Isles of Scilly Museum** (☎ 01720-422337; Church St; adult/child £2/50p; ◷ 10am-4.30pm summer, 10am-noon Mon-Sat winter, or by arrangement) where exhibits include artefacts recovered from shipwrecks (including muskets, a cannon and a ship's bell), Romano-British finds and a fully rigged 1877 pilot gig.

A little way east of Hugh Town is **Old Town**, once the island's main harbour but now home to a few small cafes, a village pub and a curve of beach. Look out for the minuscule Old Town Church where evocative services are still conducted by candlelight – the graveyard contains a memorial to Augustus Smith, founder of the Abbey Garden, as well as the grave of former British prime minister Harold Wilson.

The small inlets scattered around the island's coastline are best reached on foot or by bike (p423): Porth Hellick, Watermill Cove and the remote Pelistry Bay are worth seeking out. The pick of St Mary's prehistoric sites are the Iron Age village at Halangy Down, a mile north of Hugh Town, and the barrows at Bant's Carn and Innisidgen.

Scilly Walks (☎ 01720-423326; www.scillywalks .co.uk) leads excellent three-hour archaeological and historical tours, costing £5/2.50 per adult/child, as well as visits to the off-islands. **Will Wagstaff** (☎ 01720-422212) runs regular bird-watching tours.

For diving on St Mary's contact **Island Sea Safaris** (☎ 01720-422732); it also offers white-knuckle speedboat rides around the islands (£20 to £30) and snorkelling trips to the local seal colonies (£40).

The traditional sport of pilot-gig racing is still hugely popular in the Scillys. These six-oared wooden boats were originally used to race out to secure valuable pilotage of sailing ships. The modern season runs between May and September – look out for the races on Wednesday and Friday evenings, when boats from the different islands battle it out amid heaving seas. Island Sea Safaris (above) will take you alongside (£10). Every May St Mary's hosts the World Pilot Gig Championships, which attracts teams from as far away as Holland and the USA.

SLEEPING

Evergreen Cottage (☎ 01720-422711; www.evergreen cottageguesthouse.co.uk; The Parade, Hugh Town; d £60) The pint-sized rooms in this 300-year-old cottage are decked out in patterned fabrics and topped off by vases of flowers. There's a lovely garden patio out front.

Crebinick Guest House (☎ 01720-422968; www .crebinick.co.uk; Church St, Hugh Town; d £70-84) They've been putting up guests in this sturdy granite house since before WWII. The traditional rooms are a little small but are homely affairs, and the owners are full of helpful holiday tips.

Blue Carn Cottage (☎ 01720-422214; Old Town; d £74) Removed from the relative bustle of Hugh Town, this whitewashed B&B near Old Town is a truly welcoming affair, run by a family of Scilly flower farmers. DVD players and cosy surroundings distinguish the rooms, while there's a game-stocked guest lounge and huge breakfasts with fair-trade ingredients.

Star Castle Hotel (☎ 01720-422317; www.star-castle .co.uk; The Garrison; d £160-288, ste £220-328) Shaped like an eight-pointed star, this former fort on Garrison Point is one of the fanciest places to stay on Scilly, with higgledy-piggledy, heritage-themed rooms filled with plush sofas and vast beds.

St Mary's Hall Hotel (☎ 01720-422316; www.st maryshallhotel.co.uk; Church St, Hugh Town; d £180-250, ste £260-280) Say *ciao* to this Italianate mansion which is full of grand wooden staircases, bits of art and panelled walls. Rooms are either flowery and chintzy or candy-striped, while the superplush designer suites have LCD TVs and a galley kitchen.

A 4-hectare **campsite** (☎ 01720-422670; tedmoul son@aol.com; Tower Cottage, Garrison; sites per person £6-8) sits on the garrison above Hugh Town. Fairly basic facilities, but a cut above many other sites on Scilly.

Tresco

Once owned by Tavistock Abbey, Tresco is the second-largest island, and the second most visited after St Mary's. The main attraction is the magical **Tresco Abbey Garden** (☎ 01720-424105; www.tresco.co.uk; adult/child £9/free; ☺ 9.30am-4pm), first laid out in 1834 on the site of a 10th-century Benedictine abbey. The terraced gardens feature more than 5000 subtropical plants, including species from Brazil, New Zealand and South Africa, and the intriguing Valhalla collection made up of figureheads and nameplates salvaged from the many ships that have foundered off Tresco's shores.

There are only two places to stay on the island, apart from self-catering cottages.

At **New Inn** (☎ 01720-422844; www.tresco.co.uk; d £140-230) they've been whetting Scillonian whistles for several centuries. Smart bedrooms are done out in subtle colours, with some boasting views over the channel to Bryher. The dining (mains £5 to £18) has made Michelin's *Eating Out in Pubs*.

The bedrooms at **Island Hotel** (☎ 01720-422883; www.tresco.co.uk; d £260-550, ste £360-720; ⛆) will make you smile, even if the bill makes you wince. Sleep amid gingham checks or in luxurious gold and navy blue suites, then plump for a private garden patio or sea-view balcony. Thankfully, the price includes dinner.

Bryher & Samson

Only around 70 people live on Bryher, Scilly's smallest and wildest inhabited island. Covered by rough bracken and heather, this chunk of rock takes the full force of Atlantic storms; Hell Bay in a winter gale is a powerful sight. Watch Hill provides cracking view over the islands, and Rushy Bay is one of the finest beaches in the Scillys. From the quay, occasional boats visit local seal and bird colonies and deserted Samson Island, where abandoned settlers' cottages tell a story of hard subsistence living.

The bare-bones **campsite** (☎ 01720-422886; www.bryhercampsite.co.uk; sites from £8.50) is near the quay.

Hell Bay Hotel (☎ 01720-422947; www.tresco.co.uk; d £260-600) is a real pamper pad. This oasis of luxury consists entirely of upmarket, impeccably finished suites, most of which boast sleek, contemporary decor, sitting rooms and private balconies. Prices include dinner.

St Martin's

The most northerly of the main islands, St Martin's is renowned for its beautiful beaches. The largest settlement is **Higher Town** where you'll find a small village shop and **Scilly Diving** (☎ 01720-422848; www.scillydiving.com; Higher Town), which offers two-hour snorkelling safaris (£22), subaqua trips for experienced divers (from £35) and lessons and taster sessions (from £33). A short way to the west is **Lower Town**, home to a cluster of tightly huddled cottages and the island's only hotel.

There are several small art galleries scattered across the island, as well as a tiny vineyard and a flower farm.

Worth hunting out are Lawrence's Bay on the south coast, which becomes a broad sweep of sand at low tide; Great Bay on the north, arguably Scilly's finest beach; White Island in the northwest, which you can cross to (with care) at low tide; the red-and-white candy-striped Day Mark in the east, a navigational aid built back in 1687; and the secluded cove of Perpitch in the southeast.

The **campsite** (☎ 01720-422888; chris@stmartins campsite.freeserve.co.uk; Middle Town; sites £6.50-8.50) is towards the western end of Lawrence's Bay.

Polreath (☎ 01720-422046; Higher Town; d £80-100) is a traditional cottage and one of the few B&Bs on the island. Rooms are snug and cosy, and it's handy for the island bakery and post office.

St Martin's on the Isle (☎ 01720-422090; www.st martinshotel.co.uk; d £300-560) is the only hotel on St Martin's, and arguably one of the best in the Scillys, with landscaped grounds, an indoor swimming pool and a private quay. The 30 lavish, elegant bedrooms have sea or garden views, and rates include a supremely classy dinner.

St Agnes

England's most southerly community somehow transcends even the tranquillity of the other islands in the Isles of Scilly; with its cloistered coves, coastal walks and a scattering of prehistoric sites, it's an ideal spot to stroll, unwind and reflect. Visitors disembark at **Porth Conger**, near the decommissioned **Old Lighthouse** – one of the oldest lighthouses in the country. Other points of interest include the 200-year-old stone **Troy Town Maze**, and the inlets of Periglis Cove and St Warna's Cove (dedicated to the patron saint of shipwrecks). At low tide you can cross over to the island of **Gugh**, where you'll find intriguing standing stones and Bronze Age remains.

The **campsite** (☎ 01720-422360; www.troytownscilly .co.uk; Troy Town Farm; sites £6.50-10.50) is at the southwestern corner of the island.

The little stone-walled **Covean Cottage** (☎ 01720-422620; d £58-70) is the perfect location for getting away from the crowds; it offers four pleasant, good-value rooms and serves excellent cream teas, light meals and sticky treats during the day.

The most southwesterly pub in all of England, the **Turk's Head** (☎ 01720-422434; mains £6.50-10) is a real treat, with fine views, excellent beers, good pub grub and a hearty island atmosphere.

Getting There & Away

There's no transport to or from the islands on Sundays.

AIR

The **Isles of Scilly Skybus** (☎ 0845 710 5555; www.ios -travel.co.uk) flies between St Mary's and Land's End (adult/child £125/76, 15 minutes) and Newquay (£145/88, 30 minutes) several times daily year-round. Cheaper saver fares are available for flights leaving Land's End after 2pm, or leaving St Mary's before noon. There's also at least one daily flight to Exeter (£232/138, 50 minutes) and Bristol (£278/162, 70 minutes). All prices are return fares.

British International (☎ 01736-363871; www .Isles of Scillyhelicopter.com) helicopters fly to St Mary's (20 minutes, 11 daily Monday to Friday, 17 on Saturday late June to late

September, seven to 10 daily late September to late June) and Tresco (20 minutes, four to six daily Monday to Saturday April to October, four daily November to March) from Penzance heliport.

Standard return fares are £152/90 for an adult/child; a cheap day return cost £102/65. Parking at the heliport costs £6 per day.

BOAT

The *Scillonian* ferry (☎ 0845 710 5555; www .ios-travel.co.uk) sails between Penzance and St Mary's (adult/child £92/46 return, two hours 40 minutes, daily Monday to Saturday). The crossing can be notoriously rough – landlubbers might be better off taking the chopper.

Getting Around

Inter-island launches sail regularly from St Mary's harbour in summer to the other main islands. The boats usually leave in the morning and return late afternoon, although there are several boats daily to Tresco. A return trip to most off-islands costs £7 – ask around at the harbour to see what's on offer.

If you're travelling between the islands, make sure you label luggage clearly with your name and the island you're going to.

The airport bus service (one way £3) leaves from the Strand in Hugh Town around 40 minutes before each flight. A circular bus shuttles around St Mary's several times daily in summer (£1 to all destinations).

There's a twice-daily trip around St Mary's on **Island Rover** (☎ 01720-422131; www.islandrover .co.uk, £6), a vintage open-top bus. It leaves at 10.15am and 1.30pm from the park. Ferry passengers can buy bus tickets on board the boat.

Bikes are available from **Buccaboo Hire** (☎ 01720-422289; Porthcressa, Hugh Town) from around £8 per day.

For taxis, try **Island Taxis** (☎ 01720-422126) or **Scilly Cabs** (☎ 01720-422901).

East Anglia

Unfurling gently eastwards to the sea, the vast flatlands of Cambridgeshire, Essex, Suffolk, and Norfolk are a rich web of lush farmland, melancholy fens and sparkling rivers. Between them they offer miles of sweeping sandy beaches and a host of picture-postcard villages, magnificent cathedral cities and Edwardian resorts. The region's most renowned attraction, however, is the world-famous university town of Cambridge, an ancient seat of learning with a hushed and earnest attitude and a backdrop of some of England's most stunning classical architecture.

While the country's upper crust and brilliant minds were busy establishing the university as one of England's most exclusive institutions, the rest of East Anglia was growing rich on the backs of the medieval wool trade. Right across the region soaring churches and cathedrals, implausibly picturesque villages and pretty market towns remain testament to the enormous wealth amassed during medieval times when the wool and weaving industries flourished. No expense was spared on the delicate stonework of the superb cathedrals in Ely, Peterborough, Norwich and Bury St Edmunds. And in rural areas, half-timbered houses still exist, and elaborate decorative pargeting (plasterwork) and ornate thatch still adorn the former homes and halls of rich wool merchants.

In between, gentle hills and placid valleys shelter slow-flowing rivers and the same bucolic scenes that once inspired Constable and Gainsborough. The big skies and dramatic sunsets are still a magnet for artists and tourists alike. The coast too remains largely untouched with broad, sandy beaches, pretty seaside villages, traditional resorts and a whole host of new gastropubs and boutique hotels to cater for trendy city visitors.

HIGHLIGHTS

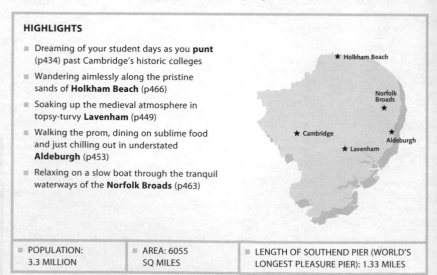

- Dreaming of your student days as you **punt** (p434) past Cambridge's historic colleges

- Wandering aimlessly along the pristine sands of **Holkham Beach** (p466)

- Soaking up the medieval atmosphere in topsy-turvy **Lavenham** (p449)

- Walking the prom, dining on sublime food and just chilling out in understated **Aldeburgh** (p453)

- Relaxing on a slow boat through the tranquil waterways of the **Norfolk Broads** (p463)

★ Holkham Beach

Norfolk Broads ★

★ Cambridge

★ Aldeburgh

★ Lavenham

▪ POPULATION: 3.3 MILLION	▪ AREA: 6055 SQ MILES	▪ LENGTH OF SOUTHEND PIER (WORLD'S LONGEST PLEASURE PIER): 1.33 MILES

History

East Anglia was a major Saxon kingdom and the treasures unearthed in the Sutton Hoo burial ship (see p447) proved that they enjoyed something of the good life here.

The region's heyday, however, was in the Middle Ages, during the wool and weaving boom, when Flemish weavers settled in the area and the grand churches and the world-famous university began to be established.

By the 17th century much of the region's marshland and bog had been drained and converted into arable land and the good times rolled. The emergence of a work-happy urban bourgeoisie coupled with a strong sense of religious duty resulted in the parliamentarianism and Puritanism that would climax in the Civil War. Oliver Cromwell, the uncrowned king of the parliamentarians, was a small-time merchant residing in Ely when he answered God's call to take up arms against the fattened and corrupt monarchy of Charles I.

East Anglia's fortunes waned in the 18th century, however, when the Industrial Revolution got under way up north. The cottage industries of East Anglia dwindled and today crops have replaced sheep as the rural mainstay. During WWII East Anglia became central to the fight against Nazi Germany. With plenty of flat open land and its proximity to mainland Europe, it was an ideal base for the RAF and the United States Air Force. The remains of these bases can still be seen today.

Information

You can get tourist information for the region from the **East of England Tourist Board** (☎ 01284-727470; www.visiteastofengland.com).

Activities

East Anglia is a great destination for walking and cycling enthusiasts with miles of coastline to discover, vast expanses of flat land for leisurely touring and plenty of inland waterways for quiet boating. We concentrate on the highlights here, but you'll find more information throughout the chapter and on p790. Regional tourist websites are packed with walking, cycling and sailing information, and tourist offices are stacked high with leaflets, maps and guides covering outdoor activities.

CYCLING

East Anglia is famously flat and riddled with quiet roads; even the unfit can find vast swaths

for a gentle potter on two wheels. All four counties boast networks of quiet country lanes, where the biggest natural hazard is the wind sweeping in unimpeded from the coast. When it's behind you though, you can freewheel for miles. There's gorgeous riding to be had along the Suffolk and Norfolk coastlines and in the Fens. Finding quiet roads in Essex is a little more of a challenge but not impossible. Mountain bikers should head for Thetford Forest, near Thetford, while much of the popular on- and off-road Peddars Way (below) walking route is also open to cyclists.

WALKING

East Anglia is not everybody's idea of classic walking country; you won't find any challenging peaks here, but gentle rambles through farmland, beside rivers and lakes and along the wildlife-rich coastline are in ample supply.

The **Peddars Way and Norfolk Coast Path** (www .nationaltrail.co.uk/peddarsway) is a six-day, 88-mile national trail from Knettishall Heath near Thetford to Cromer on the coast. The first half trails along an ancient Roman road, then finishes by meandering along the beaches, sea walls, salt marshes and fishing villages of the coast. Day trippers and weekend walkers tend to dip into its coastal stretches, which also cover some of the best bird-watching country in England.

Curving round further south, the 50-mile **Suffolk Coast Path** (www.suffolkcoastandheaths.org) wanders between Felixstowe and Lowestoft, via Snape Maltings, Aldeburgh, Dunwich and Southwold, but is also good for shorter rambles.

OTHER ACTIVITIES

With wind and water so abundant here, it's a popular destination for **sailing**, both along the coast and in the Norfolk Broads, where you can easily hire boats and arrange lessons. It's also possible to just put-put your way around the Broads in **motorboats**. Alternatively, the wide and frequently empty beaches of the Norfolk coast make great spots for **land yachting** and **kitesurfing**.

Getting There & Around

Getting about East Anglia on public transport, both rail and coach, is straightforward. Consult **Traveline** (☎ 0871 200 2233; www.travelineeastanglia.org.uk) for all public transport information.

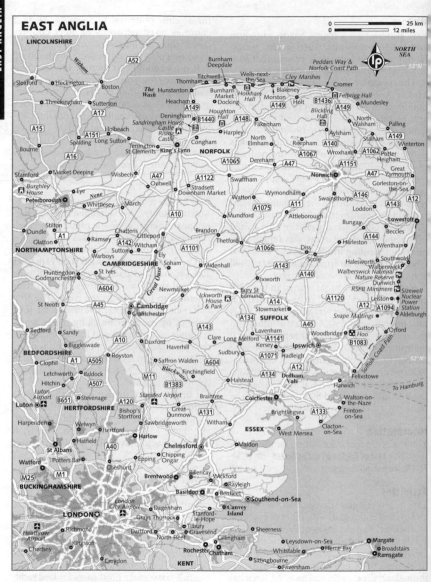

BUS

First Group (www.firstgroup.com) offer a FirstDay pass for a day's unlimited bus travel on its regional services. It costs £10/6.50 per adult/child. There's also a FirstWeek pass costing £25 or £17 respectively.

    Stagecoach (www.stagecoachbus.com) Explorer and Megarider tickets allow one-/seven-/28-day

travel across Southern England (excluding London) for £8/20/75.

TRAIN

National Express East Anglia (☎ 0845 600 7245; www.nationalexpresseastanglia.com) offers some handy regional rail passes to explore Norfolk, Suffolk and parts of Cambridgeshire. The Anglia

Plus Pass is a great option for families and gives unlimited regional travel after 8.45am on weekdays and any time at weekends. It costs £13 for one day (plus £2 each for up to four accompanied children) or £26 for any three separate days over a period of seven days (plus £2 each for up to four children).

You can also get discounts of up to 33% on most rail fares over £10 in the southeast by purchasing a **Network Railcard** (☎ 08457 225 225; www.railcard.co.uk/network; per yr £20). Children under 15 can save 60%, but a minimum £1 fare applies.

CAMBRIDGESHIRE

Many visitors to Cambridgeshire never make it past the beautiful university town of Cambridge, where august old buildings, gowned cyclists, wobbly punters and glorious chapels await. But beyond the breathtaking city and its brilliant minds lies a county of vast open landscapes, epic sunsets and unsullied horizons. The flat reclaimed fen, lush farmland and myriad waterways make perfect walking and cycling territory while the extraordinary cathedrals at Peterborough and Ely, and the rip-roaring Imperial War Museum at Duxford, would be headline attractions anywhere else.

Getting Around

The region's public transport radiates from Cambridge, which is a mere 55-minute train ride from London. This line continues north through Ely to King's Lynn in Norfolk. From Ely, branch lines run east through Norwich, southeast into Suffolk and northwest to Peterborough. The useful *Cambridgeshire and Peterborough Passenger Transport Map* is available in tourist offices.

CAMBRIDGE
pop 108,863

Drowning in exquisite architecture, steeped in history and tradition and renowned for it quirky rituals, Cambridge is a university town extraordinaire. The tightly packed core of ancient colleges, the picturesque 'Backs' leading onto the river and the leafy green meadows that seem to surround the city give it a far more tranquil appeal than its historic rival Oxford.

Like 'the other place', as Oxford is known, the buildings here seem unchanged in cen-

turies and it's possible to wander the college buildings and experience them as countless prime ministers, poets, writers and scientists have done. The sheer weight of academic achievement seems to seep from the very walls with cyclists loaded down with books negotiating narrow cobbled passageways, earnest students relaxing on manicured lawns and great minds debating life-changing research in historic pubs. Meanwhile distracted punters drift into the river banks as they soak up the breathtaking views, tills whir with brisk trade in the city's designer boutiques, and those long past their student days wonder what it would have been like to study in such auspicious surroundings.

History

First a Roman fort and then a Saxon settlement, Cambridge was little more than a rural backwater until 1209, when the university town of Oxford exploded in a riot between town and gown (see boxed text, p226). Fed up with the constant brawling between locals and students, a group of scholars upped and left to found a new university in Cambridge.

Initially students lived in halls and religious houses but gradually a collegiate system, where tutors and students lived together in a formal community, developed. The first Cambridge college, Peterhouse, was founded in 1284. The collegiate system is still intact today and unique to Oxford and Cambridge.

By the 14th century the royalty, nobility, church, trade guilds and anyone rich enough to court the prestige that their own institution offered began to found their own colleges. It was 500 years before female students were allowed into the hallowed grounds though, and even then in women-only colleges Girton and Newnham, founded in 1869 and 1871 respectively. By 1948 Cambridge minds had broadened sufficiently to allow the women to actually graduate.

The honour roll of famous Cambridge graduates reads like an international who's who of high achievers: 81 Nobel Prize winners (more than any other institution in the world), 13 British prime ministers, nine archbishops of Canterbury, an immense number of scientists, and a healthy host of poets and authors. Crick and Watson discovered DNA here, Isaac Newton used Cambridge to work on his theory of gravity, Stephen Hawking is a professor of

EAST ANGLIA

CAMBRIDGE

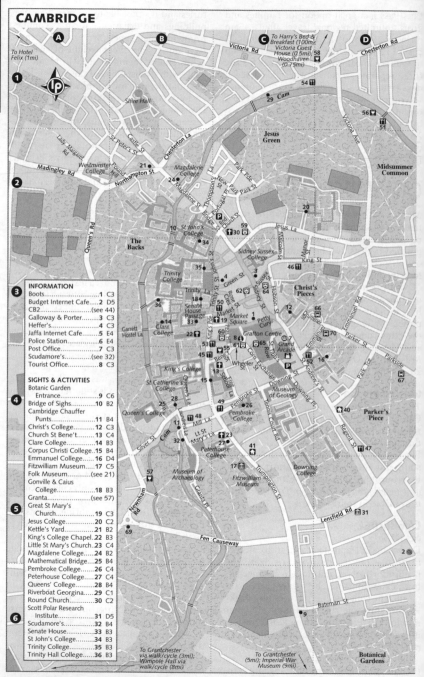

INFORMATION
Boots.........................1	C3
Budget Internet Cafe.....2	D5
CB2.........................(see 44)	
Galloway & Porter.........3	C3
Heffer's.....................4	C3
Jaffa Internet Cafe.......5	E4
Police Station.............6	E4
Post Office.................7	C3
Scudamore's...........(see 32)	
Tourist Office.............8	C3

SIGHTS & ACTIVITIES
Botanic Garden	
Entrance...................9	C6
Bridge of Sighs...........10	B2
Cambridge Chauffer	
Punts.....................11	B4
Christ's College.........12	C3
Church St Bene't.......13	C4
Clare College.............14	B3
Corpus Christi College..15	B4
Emmanuel College......16	D4
Fitzwilliam Museum.....17	C5
Folk Museum............(see 21)	
Gonville & Caius	
College....................18	B3
Granta.....................(see 57)	
Great St Mary's	
Church...................19	C3
Jesus College.............20	C2
Kettle's Yard.............21	B2
King's College Chapel..22	B3
Little St Mary's Church..23	C4
Magdalene College.....24	B2
Mathematical Bridge....25	B4
Pembroke College......26	C4
Peterhouse College.....27	C4
Queens' College.........28	B4
Riverboat Georgina.....29	C1
Round Church............30	C2
Scott Polar Research	
Institute.................31	D5
Scudamore's..............32	B4
Senate House............33	B3
St John's College.......34	B3
Trinity College...........35	B3
Trinity Hall College.....36	B3

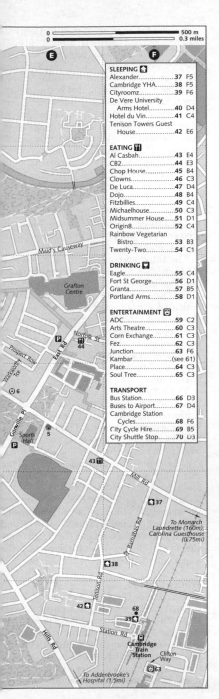

mathematics here, and Charles Darwin, William Wordsworth, Vladimir Nabokov, David Attenborough and John Cleese all studied here.

Today the university remains one of the top three for research worldwide, and international academics have polled it as the top university in the world for science. Thanks to some of the earth-shaking discoveries made here, Cambridge is inextricably linked to the history of mankind. The university celebrates its 800th birthday in 2009; look out for special events, lectures and concerts to mark its intriguing eight centuries.

Orientation

The colleges and university buildings comprise the centre of the city. The central area, lying in a wide bend of the River Cam, is easy to get around on foot or by bike. The best-known section of the Cam is the Backs, which combines lush river scenery with superb views of six colleges, and King's College Chapel. The other 25 colleges are scattered throughout the city. The bus station is on Drummer St, but the train station is a 20-minute walk to the south. For cheap and cheerful restaurants, internet cafes, launderettes and late night shops try Mill Rd.

Information
BOOKSHOPS
Galloway & Porter (☎ 01223-367876; 30 Sidney St) Remaindered and damaged stock.
Heffers (☎ 01223 568568; 20 Trinity St) Vast temple of academic tomes and lighter reads.

EMERGENCY
Police station (☎ 01223-358966; Parkside)

INTERNET ACCESS
The going rate for internet access is about £1 per hour.
Budget Internet Cafe (☎ 01223-313875; 30 Hills Rd; 🕙 9am-11pm)
CB2 (☎ 01223-508503; 5-7 Norfolk St; 🕙 noon-midnight)
Jaffa Internet Cafe (☎ 01223-308380; 22 Mill Rd; 🕙 10am-10pm)

INTERNET RESOURCES
Visit Cambridge (www.visitcambridge.org) The official tourism site for the city.
What's On (www.cam.ac.uk/whatson) Listing of all public events at the University.

LAUNDRY

Monarch Laundrette (☎ 01223-247599; 161 Mill Rd; per wash £3.50; ☯ 8.30am-8pm) Near the train station.

LEFT LUGGAGE

Scudamore's (☎ 01223-359750; www.scudamores .com; Granta Pl; per piece £5)

MEDICAL SERVICES

Addenbrooke's Hospital (☎ 01223-245151; Hills Rd) Southeast of the centre.
Boots (☎ 01223-350213; 28 Petty Cury)

MONEY

You'll find all the major banks and a host of ATMs around St Andrew's St and Sidney St.

POST

Post office (☎ 01223-323325; 9-11 St Andrew's St)

TOURIST INFORMATION

Tourist office (☎ 0871 266 8006; www.visitcambridge .org; Wheeler St; ☯ 10am-5.30pm Mon-Fri, 10am-5pm Sat, 11am-3pm Sun Apr-Sep, 10am-5.30pm Mon-Fri, 10am-5pm Sat Oct-Mar) This large, busy office helps with maps, accommodation, tours and tickets. You can pick up a guide to the Cambridge colleges (£3.99) here or a leaflet (£1.20) outlining a city walk.

Sights

CAMBRIDGE UNIVERSITY

Cambridge University comprises 31 colleges; five of these – King's, Queen's, Clare, Trinity and St John's – charge tourists admission. Some other colleges deem visitors too disruptive and simply deny them entry. Most colleges close to visitors for the Easter term and all are closed for exams from mid-May to mid-June. Opening hours vary year to year, so contact the colleges or the tourist office for up to date information.

King's College Chapel

In a city crammed with show-stopping architecture, this is the show-stealer. Chances are you will already have seen it on a thousand postcards, tea towels and choral CDs before you catch your first glimpse of the grandiose **King's College Chapel** (☎ 01223-331212; www .kings.cam.ac.uk/chapel; King's Pde; adult/concession £5/3.50; ☯ during term 9.30am-3.30pm Mon-Fri, 9.30am-3.15pm Sat, 1.15pm-2.30pm Sun, outside academic terms 9.30am-4.30pm Mon-Sat, 10am-5pm Sun), but still it inspires awe. It's one of the most extraordinary examples of Gothic architecture in England, and was

begun in 1446 as an act of piety by Henry VI and finished by Henry VIII around 1516.

While you can enjoy stunning front and back views of the chapel from King's Pde and the river, the real drama is within. Mouths drop open upon first glimpse of the inspirational **fan-vaulted ceiling**, its intricate tracery soaring upwards before exploding into a series of stone fireworks. This vast 80m-long canopy is the work of John Wastell and is the largest expanse of fan vaulting in the world.

The chapel's length is also remarkably light, its sides flanked by lofty **stained-glass windows** that retain their original glass, rare survivors of the excesses of the Civil War in this region. It's said that these windows were ordered to be spared by Cromwell himself, who knew of their beauty from his own studies in Cambridge.

The antechapel and the choir are divided by a superbly carved **wooden screen**, designed and executed by Peter Stockton for Henry VIII. The screen bears his master's initials entwined with those of Anne Boleyn. Look closely and you may find an angry human face – possibly Stockton's – amid the elaborate jungle of mythical beasts and symbolic flowers. Above is the magnificent bat-wing organ originally constructed in 1686 though much altered since.

The thickly carved wooden stalls just beyond the screen are a stage for the chapel's world-famous **choir**. You can hear them in full voice during the magnificent **Evensong** (admission free; ☯ 5.30pm Mon-Sat, 10.30am & 3.30pm Sun term time only). If you happen to be visiting at Christmas it is also worth queuing for admission to the incredibly popular Festival of Nine Lessons and Carols on Christmas Eve.

Beyond the dark-wood choir, light suffuses the **high altar**, which is framed by Rubens masterpiece *Adoration of the Magi* (1634) and the magnificent east window. To the left of the altar in the side chapels, an **exhibition** charts the stages and methods of building the chapel.

Trinity College

The largest of Cambridge's colleges, **Trinity** (☎ 01223-338400; www.trin.cam.ac.uk; Trinity St; adult/child £2.50/1 Mar-Oct; ☯ library noon-2pm Mon-Fri, hall 3-5pm chapel 10am-5pm), is entered through an impressive Tudor gateway first created in 1546. As you walk through have a look at the statue of the college's founder Henry VIII that adorns it. His left hand holds a golden orb, while his right grips not the original sceptre but a table leg, put there by student pranksters and never replaced. It's a wonderful introduction to one of Cambridge's most venerable colleges, and a reminder of who really rules the roost.

As you enter the **Great Court**, scholastic humour gives way to wonderment, for it is the largest of its kind in the world. To the right of the entrance is a small tree, planted in the 1950s and reputed to be a descendant of the apple tree made famous by Trinity alumnus Sir Isaac Newton. Other alumni include Tennyson, Francis Bacon, Lord Byron, HRH Prince Charles and at least nine prime ministers, British and international, and a jaw-dropping 31 Nobel Prize winners.

The square is also the scene of the run made famous by the film *Chariots of Fire* – 350m in 43 seconds (the time it takes the clock to strike 12). Although many students attempt it, Harold Abrahams (the hero of the film) never actually did, and the run wasn't even filmed here. If you fancy your chances remember that you'll need Olympian speed to even come close.

The college's vast hall has a dramatic hammer-beam roof and lantern, and beyond this are the dignified cloisters of Nevile's Court and the renowned **Wren Library** (☼ noon-2pm Mon-Fri, plus during term 10.30am-12.30pm Sat). It contains 55,000 books dated before 1820 and more than 2500 manuscripts, including AA Milne's original *Winnie the Pooh*. Both Milne and his son, Christopher Robin, were graduates.

Henry VIII would have been proud to note, too, that his college would eventually come to throw the best party in town, the lavish May Ball in June.

Gonville & Caius College

Known locally as Caius (pronounced keys), **Gonville and Caius** (☎ 01223-332400; www.cai.cam.ac.uk; Trinity St) was founded twice, first by a priest called Gonville, in 1348, and then again in 1557 by Dr Caius (Keys – it was common for academics to use the Latin form of their names), a brilliant physician who supposedly spoilt his legacy by insisting the college admit no 'deaf, dumb, deformed, lame, chronic invalids, or Welshmen'! Fortunately for the college his policy didn't last long, and the wheelchair-using megastar of astrophysics, Stephen Hawking, is now a fellow here.

The college is of particular interest thanks to its three fascinating gates: Virtue, Humility and Honour. They symbolise the progress of the good student, since the third gate (the *Porta Honoris,* a fabulous domed and sundial-sided confection) leads to the Senate House and thus graduation.

Trinity Hall College

Henry James once wrote of the delightfully diminutive **Trinity Hall** (☎ 01223-332500; www.trinhall.cam.ac.uk; Trinity Lane), 'If I were called upon to mention the prettiest corner of the world, I should draw a thoughtful sigh and point the way to the gardens of Trinity Hall.' Wedged cosily among the great and the famous, but unconnected to better-known Trinity, it was founded in 1350 as a refuge for lawyers and clerics escaping the ravages of the Black Death, thus earning it the nickname of the 'Lawyers' College'. The college's 16th-century library has original Jacobean reading desks and chained books (an early antitheft device) on the shelves. Writer JB Priestley, astrophysicist Stephen Hawking and actress Rachel Weisz are among Trinity Hall's graduates.

St John's College

After King's College, **St John's** (☎ 01223-338600; www.joh.cam.ac.uk; St John's St; adult/child £2.80/1.70; ☼ 10am-5pm Mon-Fri, 9.30am-5pm Sat & Sun Mar-Oct, Sat & Sun only Nov-Feb) is one of the city's most photogenic colleges, and is also the second-biggest after Trinity. Founded in 1511, it sprawls along both banks of the river, joined by the Bridge of Sighs, a masterpiece of stone tracery. Over the bridge is the 19th-century New Court, an extravagant neo-Gothic creation, and out to the left stunning views of the Backs.

Christ's College

Over 500 years old and a grand old institution, **Christ's** (☎ 01223-334900; www.christs.cam.ac.uk; St Andrew's St; ☼ 9am-dusk) is worth visiting if only for its gleaming Great Gate emblazoned with heraldic carving of spotted Beaufort yale (antelope-like creatures), Tudor roses and portcullis. Its founder, Lady Margaret Beaufort, hovers above like a guiding spirit. A stout oak door leads into First Court, which has an unusual circular lawn, magnolias and wisteria creepers. Pressing on through the Second Court there is a gate to the Fellows' Garden, which contains a mulberry tree under which 17th-century poet John Milton reputedly wrote *Lycidas*. In 2009 the college celebrates the 200th anniversary of the birth of Charles Darwin, who studied here, with a special exhibition in his college rooms.

Corpus Christi College

Entry to this illustrious **college** (☎ 01223-338000; www.corpus.cam.ac.uk; Trumpington St) is via the so-called New Court that dates back a mere 200 years. To your right is the door to the Parker Library, which holds the finest collection of Anglo-Saxon manuscripts in the world. As you enter take a look at the statue on the right, that of the eponymous Matthew Parker, who was college master in 1544 and Archbishop of Canterbury to Elizabeth I. Mr Parker was known for his curiosity, and his endless questioning gave rise to the term 'nosy parker'. Meanwhile monastic atmosphere still oozes from the inner Old Court, which retains its medieval form. Look out for the fascinating sundial and plaque to playwright and past student Christopher Marlowe (1564–93), author of *Dr Faustus* and *Tamburlaine*.

Other Colleges

Tranquil 15th-century **Jesus College** (☎ 01223-339339; www.jesus.cam.ac.uk; Jesus Lane), was once a nunnery before its founder, Bishop Alcock, expelled the nuns for misbehaving. Highlights include a Norman arched gallery, a 13th-century chancel and art-nouveau features by Pugin, William Morris (ceilings), Burne-Jones (stained glass) and Madox Brown.

Originally a Benedictine hostel, riverside **Magdalene College** (☎ 01223-332100; www.magd.cam.ac.uk; Magdalene St) has the dubious honour of being the last college to allow women students; when they were finally admitted in 1988, male students wore black armbands and flew the college flag at half-mast. Its greatest asset is the Pepys Library, housing the magnificent collection of books the famous mid-17th-century diarist bequeathed to his old college.

The oldest and smallest college, **Peterhouse** (☎ 01223-338200; www.pet.cam.ac.uk; Trumpington St), is a charming place founded in 1284. Much of the college was rebuilt or added over the years, including the exceptional little chapel built in 1632, but the main hall is bona fide 13th century and beautifully restored. Just to the north is **Little St Mary's Church**, inside which is a memorial to Peterhouse student Godfrey Washington, great-uncle of George. His family coat of arms was the stars and stripes, the inspiration for the US flag.

The gorgeous 15th-century **Queen's College** (☎ 01223-335511; www.queens.cam.ac.uk; Silver St; adult £2) sits elegantly astride the river and has two enchanting medieval courtyards: Old Court and Cloister Court. Here too is the beautiful half-timbered President's Lodge and the tower in which famous Dutch scholar and reformer Desiderius Erasmus lodged from 1510 to 1514. He had plenty to say about Cambridge: the wine tasted like vinegar, the beer was slop and the place was too expensive, but he did note that the local women were good kissers.

The 16th-centry **Emmanuel College** (☎ 01223-334200; www.emma.cam.ac.uk; St Andrew's St) is famous for its exquisite chapel designed by Sir Christopher Wren. Here too is a plaque commemorating John Harvard (BA 1632) a scholar here who later settled in New England and left his money to found his namesake university in the Massachusetts town of Cambridge.

THE BACKS

Behind the grandiose facades, stately courts and manicured lawns of the city's central colleges lies a series of gardens and parklands butting up against the river. Collectively known as the Backs, these tranquil green spaces and shimmering waters offer unparalleled views of the colleges and are often the most enduring image of Cambridge for visitors. The picture-postcard views of college life, graceful bridges and weeping willows can be seen from the pathways that cross the Backs, from the comfort of a chauffeur-driven punt or from the lovely pedestrian bridges that meander across the river.

The fanciful **Bridge of Sighs** (built in 1831) at St Johns is best observed from the stylish bridge designed by Wren just to the south. The oldest crossing is at **Clare College**, built in 1639 and ornamented with decorative balls. Its architect was paid a grand total of 15p for his design and, feeling aggrieved at such a measly fee, it's said he cut a chunk out of one of the balls adorning the balustrade so the bridge would never be complete. Most curious of all is the flimsy-looking wooden construction joining the two halves of Queen's College known as the **Mathematical Bridge**, first built in 1749. Despite what unscrupulous guides may tell you, it wasn't the handiwork of Sir Isaac Newton (he died in 1727), originally built without nails, or taken apart by students who then couldn't figure how to put it back together.

GREAT ST MARY'S CHURCH

Cambridge's staunch university **church** (☎ 01223-741716; www.gsm.cam.ac.uk; Senate House Hill; tower adult/child £2.50/1.25; ☺ 9am-5pm Mon-Sat, 12.30-5pm Sun, to 4pm Sep-Apr) was built between 1478 and 1519 in the late-Gothic Perpendicular style. If you're fit and fond of a view, climb the 123 steps of the tower for superb vistas of the dreamy spires, albeit marred by wire fencing.

The beautiful classical building directly across King's Pde is the **Senate House**, designed in 1730 by James Gibbs; graduations are held here in summer, when gowned and mortarboarded students parade the streets to pick up those all-important scraps of paper.

ROUND CHURCH

The beautiful **Round Church** (☎ 01223-311602; www.christianheritageuk.org.uk; Bridge St; adult/child £2/free; ☺ 10am-5pm Tue-Sat, 1-5pm Sun) is another of Cambridge's gems and one of only four such structures in England. It was built by the mysterious Knights Templar in 1130 and shelters an unusual circular nave ringed by chunky Norman pillars. It now houses an exhibition on Cambridge's Christian heritage.

CHURCH OF ST BENE'T

The oldest structure in the county, the **Saxon tower** of this Franciscan **church** (www.stbenets.org.uk; Bene't St) was built around 1025. The round holes above the belfry windows were designed to offer owls nesting privileges; they were valued as mouse killers.

FITZWILLIAM MUSEUM

Fondly dubbed 'the Fitz' by locals, this colossal neoclassical pile was one of the first public **art museums** (☎ 01223-332900; www.fitzmuseum.cam.ac.uk; Trumpington St; admission free; ☺ 10am-5pm Tue-Sat, noon-5pm Sun) in Britain, built to house the fabulous treasures that the seventh Viscount Fitzwilliam had bequeathed to his old university. An unabashedly over-the-top building, it sets out to mirror its contents in an ostentatious jumble of styles that mixes mosaic with marble, Greek with Egyptian and more. It was begun by George Basevi in 1837, but he did not live to see its completion: while working on Ely Cathedral he stepped back to admire his handiwork, slipped and fell to his death.

The lower galleries are filled with priceless treasures from ancient Egyptian sarcophagi to Greek and Roman art, Chinese ceramics to English glass, and some dazzling illuminated manuscripts. The upper galleries showcase works by Leonardo da Vinci, Titian, Rubens, the Impressionists, Gainsborough and Constable, right through to Rembrandt and Picasso.

SCOTT POLAR RESEARCH INSTITUTE

For anyone interested in polar exploration or history the **Scott Polar Research Institute** (☎ 01223-336540; www.spri.cam.ac.uk/museum; Lensfield Rd; admission free; ☺ 11am-1pm & 2-4pm Tue-Fri, noon-4pm Sat) has a fantastic collection of artefacts, journals, paintings, photographs, clothing, equipment and maps in its museum. You can learn about the great polar explorers and their harrowing expeditions and read the last messages left to wives, mothers and friends by Scott and his polar crew. You can also examine Inuit carvings and scrimshaw (etched bones), sledges and snow scooters and see the scientific and domestic equipment used by various expeditions.

CAMBRIDGE UNIVERSITY BOTANIC GARDEN

Founded by Charles Darwin's mentor, Prof John Henslow, the beautiful **Botanic Garden** (☎ 01223-336265; www.botanic.cam.ac.uk; entrance on Bateman St; adult/under 16yr £4/free; ☺ 10am-6pm Apr-Sep, to 5pm Feb-Mar & Oct, to 4pm Nov-Jan) is home to 8000 plant species, a wonderful arboretum, tropical houses, a winter garden and flamboyant herbaceous borders.

KETTLE'S YARD

Neither gallery nor museum, this **house** (☎ 01223-352124; www.kettlesyard.co.uk; cnr Northampton & Castle Sts; admission free; ☺ house 2-4pm Tue-Sun, gallery 11.30am-5pm Tue-Sun) nonetheless oozes artistic excellence, with a collection of 20th-century art, furniture, ceramics and glass that would be the envy of many an institution. It is the former home of HS 'Jim' Ede, a former assistant keeper at the Tate Gallery in London, who opened his home to young artists, resulting in a beautiful collection by the likes of Miro, Henry Moore and others. There are also exhibits of contemporary art in the modern **gallery** next door.

While here, take a peek in the neighbouring **Folk Museum** (☎ 01223-355159; www.folkmuseum.org.uk; 2/3 Castle St; adult/child £3.50/1; ☺ 10.30am-5pm Mon-Sat, 2-5pm Sun), a 300-year-old former inn now cluttered with the detritus of centuries of local domesticity.

HOW TO PUNT

Punting looks pretty straightforward but, believe us, it's not. As soon as we dried off and hung our clothes on the line, we thought it was a good idea to offer a couple of tips on how to move the boat and stay dry.

1. Standing at the end of the punt, lift the pole out of the water at the side of the punt.

2. Let the pole slide through your hands to touch the bottom of the river.

3. Tilt the pole forward (that is, in the direction of travel of the punt) and push down to propel the punt forward.

4. Twist the pole to free the end from the mud at the bottom of the river, and let it float up and trail behind the punt. You can then use it as a rudder to steer with.

5. If you haven't fallen in yet, raise the pole out of the water and into the vertical position to begin the cycle again.

Activities

PUNTING

Gliding a self-propelled punt along the Backs is a blissful experience once you've got the knack, though it can also be a manic challenge to begin. If you wimp out you can always opt for a relaxing chauffeured punt.

Cambridge Chauffer Punts (☎ 01223-354164; www .punting-in-cambridge.co.uk; Silver St; per hr £16, chauffeured per punt £60 or per person £11)

Granta (☎ 01223-301845; www.puntingincambridge .com; Newnham Rd; per hr £14, chauffeured per person £10)

Scudamore's (☎ 01223-359750; www.scudamores .com; Silver St; per hr £18, chauffeured per person £12-14)

WALKING & CYCLING

For an easy stroll into the countryside, you won't find a prettier route than the 3-mile walk to Grantchester (see p439) following the meandering River Cam and its punters southwest through flower-flecked meadows.

Scooting around town on a bike is easy thanks to the pancake-flat landscape, although the surrounding countryside can get a bit monotonous. The Cambridge tourist office stocks several useful guides including the free *Cambridge Cycle Route Map*.

Tours

City Sightseeing (☎ 01223-423578; www.city-sight seeing.com; adult/child £10/5; ☷ 10am-4pm) Hop-on hop-off tour buses with 21 stops around town.

Green Wheels Pedicabs (☎ 01223-858485) Trishaw tours around the city on 20-minute (£6 per person) or 45-minute (£10 per person) loops. Minimum two people.

Riverboat Georgina (☎ 01223-307694; www.geor gina.co.uk; per person £16-24) Two-hour cruises from the river at Jesus Lock including a cream tea or boatman's lunch.

Walking tours (☎ 01223-457574; tours@cambridge .gov.uk; tickets incl entry to King's/St John's Colleges adult/

under 12yr £10/5; ☷ tours 11.30pm & 1.30pm, with extra tours at 10.30am & 2.30pm Jul & Aug;) The tourist office also arranges colourful 'Ghost Tours' (adult/under 12 years £5/3; 6pm Friday) and 'Punt and Ghost Tours' (adult/under 12 years £15/7.50; 7pm Saturday). The tourist office has more details; book in advance.

Festivals & Events

Cambridge has a jam-packed schedule of almost continual events from beer festivals to hippie fairs, of which the tourist office has exhaustive listings. One of the biggies is late July's **Folk Festival** (☎ 01223-357851; www .cambridgefolkfestival.co.uk), which has hosted the likes of Elvis Costello, Paul Simon, kd Lang and Joan Armatrading. Although you'll need to be a student to join in, the biggest event in the college year are the **May Balls** (held in June) when students glam up and get down after exams. Also popular are the traditional rowing races, the **Bumps** (☎ 01223-467304; www .cucbc.org), held in March and May, in which college boat clubs compete to collide with the crew in front.

Cambridge University mark's its **800th birthday** in 2009. A series of special events is planned to celebrate throughout the year. Ask at the tourist office for details.

Sleeping

BUDGET

Cambridge YHA (☎ 0845 371 9728; www.yha.org.uk; 97 Tenison Rd; dm incl breakfast £19.95; ☐) Within walking distance of the city centre and cheap and cheerful; it's hard to knock this well-worn hostel close to the train station. The dorms are small and pretty basic and with lots of groups using the hostel it can be noisy, but it's got a great atmosphere and a surprisingly good breakfast.

Cambridge Rooms (www.cambridgerooms.co.uk; r £40-120) If you fancy experiencing a night inside the hallowed college grounds you can rent one of the student rooms and see how life is on the inside. Accommodation varies from functional singles (with shared bathroom) overlooking the college quad to more modern, en suite rooms in a nearby annexe. Although some twin and family rooms do exist, most rooms are singles, but the website will give a clear indication of what you can expect before you make a booking. If you do decide to stay you can wander the grounds, see the chapel and have breakfast in the ancient college hall. There's limited availability during term time but a good choice of rooms during university holidays.

MIDRANGE

Some of Cambridge's most central B&Bs use their convenient location as an excuse not to upgrade. Some of the better places are a bit of a hike from town but well worth the effort.

Carolina (☎ 01223-247015; www.carolinaguesthouse.co.uk; 138 Perne Rd; s/d from £30/55; P 🖳 wi-fi) This lovely, bright B&B is a homely place with cosy rooms decked out in pale blue colour schemes, crisp linens and rustic wooden furniture. Almost all rooms are en suite and there's a spacious garden as well as free wi-fi. It's a 30-minute walk from the city centre but right on a regular bus route.

Woodhaven (☎ 01223-226108; www.stayatwoodhaven.co.uk; 245 Milton Rd; s £30-45, d £60-75; P 🖳 wi-fi) Although a 10-minute bus trip from town, this place is worth the effort for its warm welcome and bright, simple rooms with pine furniture and uncluttered style. Cheaper rooms share bathrooms but all have free wi-fi.

Victoria Guest House (☎ 01223-350086; www.cambridge-accommodation.com; 55-57 Arbury Rd; s £35-60, d £50-75, all incl breakfast; P 🖳 wi-fi) A fairly central option worth seeking out, the Victoria has a range of tasteful rooms with contemporary decor and a hint of period character. Rooms vary in size and not all have en suite facilities but the friendly owners and incredible breakfasts are a real bonus.

Tenison Towers Guest House (☎ 01223-363924; www.cambridgecitytenisontowers.com; 148 Tenison Rd; s/d £35/60) This exceptionally friendly and homely B&B is really handy if you're arriving by train, but well worth seeking out whatever way you arrive in town. The rooms are bright and simple with pale colours and

fresh flowers and the aroma of freshly baked muffins greets you on arrival.

Alexander (☎ 01223-525725; www.beesley-schuster.co.uk; 56 St Barnabas Rd; d & tw incl breakfast £60-75) Set in a Victorian house in quiet residential area, the Alexander has two homely rooms with period fireplaces, big windows and lots of light. There's a two-night minimum stay but with a convenient location and friendly atmosphere it's worth booking in advance. Continental breakfast only.

Other possibilities:

Cityroomz (☎ 01223-304050; www.sleeperz.com; Station Rd; s/d £45/65; P) Modern minimalist rooms, a good location and great rates make this place a popular option but it can be pretty noisy and the single rooms are simply tiny.

Harry's Bed & Breakfast (☎ 01223-503866; www.welcometoharrys.co.uk; 39 Milton Rd; s £60-65, d £70-75; P 🖳 wi-fi) An incredibly warm welcome and plenty of little extras such as free calls to UK landlines make this place stand out from the crowd. It's just north of the centre.

TOP END

our pick **Hotel du Vin** (☎ 01223-227330; www.hotelduvin.com; Trumpington St; d from £140; 🖳 wi-fi) This boutique hotel chain really knows how to do things right. Its Cambridge offering has all the usual trademarks from quirky but incredibly stylish rooms with monsoon showers and luxurious Egyptian cotton sheets to the atmospheric vaulted cellar bar and the French-style bistro (mains £12.75 to £22.75). The central location, character-laden building and top-notch service make it a great deal at this price.

Hotel Felix (☎ 01223-277977; www.hotelfelix.co.uk; Whitehouse Lane, Huntingdon Rd; s/d incl breakfast from £145/180; P 🖳) This luxurious boutique hotel occupies a lovely grey-brick Victorian villa in landscaped grounds a mile from the city centre. Its 52 rooms embody designer chic with minimalist style but lots of comfort. The slick restaurant serves Mediterranean cuisine with a modern twist (mains £14.50 to £19).

De Vere University Arms Hotel (☎ 0845 375 2808; www.devere-hotels.com; Regent St; d from £155; P 🞮 🖳) The grande dame of Cambridge hotels, this Victorian pile dominates Parker's Piece and exudes an air of old-school refinement. Inside the public spaces ooze gentleman's-club atmosphere, while the bedrooms are very traditional in style.

Eating

You won't go hungry in Cambridge, it's packed with chain restaurants, particularly around the city centre and on Bridge St. If you're looking for something more authentic though you'll have to search a little harder.

QUICK EATS

Bright and airy **Origin8** (☎ 01223-354434; 62 St Andrew's St; mains £3-6.50; ☻ 8am-6pm Mon-Sat, 11am-5pm Sun) is a cafe-cum-deli and butchers shop and prides itself on its local organic ingredients. It's a great place to stop for lunch or pick up some goodies for a picnic. Alternatively try **Fitzbillies** (☎ 01223-352500; www.fitzbillies.co.uk; 52 Trumpington St; ☻ shop 9am-5.30pm, restaurant 9am-9.30pm), Cambridge's oldest bakery, beloved by generations of students for its ultrasticky buns and quaint wood shopfront. For a heartier meal, **Dojo** (☎ 01223-363471; 1-2 Miller's Yard, Mill Lane; mains £6-7; ☻ lunch & dinner) is a popular student haunt offering a great range of Chinese, Thai, Japanese, Vietnamese and Malaysian noodle and rice dishes served up in generous portions.

BUDGET

our pick **Michaelhouse** (☎ 01223-309167; Trinity St; mains £3.55-6.35; ☻ 9.30am-5pm Mon-Sat) You can sup fair-trade coffee and nibble focaccia among soaring medieval arches or else take a pew within reach of the altar at this stylishly converted church, which still has a working chancel. The simple lunch menu is mostly vegetarian, and wine and beer is offer to sweeten the deal.

CB2 (☎ 01223-508503; 5-7 Norfolk St; mains £4-13; ☻ noon-midnight) Internet cafe, bistro, music venue and cinema all rolled into one, this lively place dishes up a great range of rustic global cuisine in a relaxed and friendly atmosphere. The menu features everything from salads, pastas and wraps to heartier bistro specials. There's live music on the top floor on Wednesday nights and every other Thursday.

Clowns (☎ 01223-355711; 54 King St; mains £5-9; ☻ 8am-midnight) A cheap and cheerful Cambridge institution frequented by students and dons, town and gown, this thoroughly laid-back place dishes up some of the best Italian dishes in town. It also does a range of great sandwiches and gelato, best consumed on the roof terrace.

MIDRANGE

Al Casbah (☎ 01223-579500; www.al-casbah.co.uk; 62 Mill Rd; mains £7.50-9) Decked out like a Bedouin tent, this Algerian restaurant dishes up steaming plates of classic North African favourites. Expect tabouleh, felafel, brochettes, *merguez* (spicy lamb sausage) and wonderful grills from the indoor charcoal barbecue.

De Luca (☎ 01223-356666; www.delucacucina.co.uk; 83 Regent St; mains £8-19.50; ☻ 11am-late) Contemporary style and classic Italian food collide in this light-filled restaurant in the centre of town. The open kitchen, glass ceiling and exposed brickwork make it a bright and lively place to dine and with a great wine list and plenty of cocktails it's as popular for long lunches as it is for boozy nights out.

our pick **Rainbow Vegetarian Bistro** (☎ 01223-321551; www.rainbowcafe.co.uk; 9a King's Pde; mains £8.50-9.50; ☻ 10am-10pm Tue-Sat) First-rate vegetarian food and a pious glow emanate from this snug subterranean gem, accessed down a narrow passageway off King's Pde. It's decorated in funky colours and serves up organic dishes with a hint of the exotic, such as scrumptious Indonesian gado gado and Moroccan *tagine*.

Chop House (☎ 01223-359506; 1 Kings Pde; mains £9-15; ☻ 11am-10.30pm Mon-Fri, to 11pm Sat, 10am-10.30pm Sun) Set on the busy corner of Kings Pde and Bene't St, this place has giant windows overlooking the street, wooden floors and a menu of classic English cuisine. If you're craving for sausage and mash, a sizzling steak, suet pudding, fish pie or potted ham, look no further.

TOP END

Twenty-Two (☎ 01223-351880; www.restaurant22.co.uk; 22 Chesterton Rd; set dinner £27.50; ☻ 7-9.45pm Tue-Sat) Discretely disguised amid a row of Victorian terraced housing is this outstanding restaurant, blessed by both its romantic candlelit ambiance and its wonderful gourmet English and European menu with a commitment to local produce.

Midsummer House (☎ 01223-369299; www.midsummerhouse.co.uk; Midsommer Common; set lunch £30, 3-course dinner £60; ☻ lunch Wed-Sun, dinner Tue-Sat) For sheer gastronomic delight this sophisticated place serves up what is possibly the best food in East Anglia. With two Michelin stars and a host of rave reviews from famous foodies it's *the* place to go for a special occasion. The menu is French Mediterranean and the setting a wonderful Victorian villa backing onto the river.

SOMETHING FOR THE WEEKEND

Start your weekend in style by ensconcing yourself for a night of romance and fine dining at Cambridge's **Hotel du Vin** (p435) and venture out for a nightcap at the celebrated pub the **Eagle** (below). Next morning check out the university colleges, dip into the sublime **King's College Chapel** (p430) and then reward yourself with lunch at swanky **Midsummer House** (opposite). In the afternoon, work off your excesses by **punting** (p434) along the Backs before bidding farewell to the dreamy spires and breezing east to the **Stour Valley** (p448) and the time-transcending streets of gorgeous **Lavenham** (p449). Install yourself in the spectacular and none-too-frugal **Lavenham Priory** (p449), and explore the town's higgledy-piggledy lanes to work up an appetite for slick French cuisine at the **Great House** (p450). On Sunday morning roll west to check out the twin stately homes of **Long Melford** (p448) then east for the picture-postcard hamlet of **Kersey** (p450), where you can toast the weekend with a pint and pub lunch at the medieval **Bell Inn** (p456).

Drinking

Cambridge is awash with historic pubs that echo with the same equal mix of intellectual banter and rowdy merrymaking that they have done for centuries past.

Eagle (☎ 01223-505020; Bene't St) Cambridge's most famous pub has loosened the tongues and pickled the grey cells of many an illustrious academic in its day; among them Nobel Prize–winning scientists Crick and Watson, who discussed their research into DNA here. It's a traditional 16th-century pub with five cluttered cosy rooms, the back one popular with WWII airmen, who left their signatures on the ceiling.

Fort St George (☎ 01223-354327; Midsummer Common) The ideal English summertime pub sandwiched between the grassy expanse of Midsummer Common and the punt-littered River Cam, this place has lots of outdoor seating and great views of the river. The 16th-century interior with its crooked beams and sloping floors makes a fine alternative when the sun goes in.

Portland Arms (☎ 01223-357268; 129 Chesterton Rd) The best spot in town to catch a gig and see the pick of up-and-coming bands, the Portland is a popular student haunt and music venue. Its wood-panelled interior, unpretentious attitude and spacious terrace make a good bet any day of the week.

Granta (☎ 01223-505016; Newnham Rd) If the exterior of this picturesque waterside pub, overhanging a pretty mill pond, looks strangely familiar it could be because it's the darling of many a TV director. Its terrace sits directly beside the water and when your Dutch courage has been sufficiently fuelled, there are punts for hire alongside.

Entertainment

Thanks to a steady stream of students and tourists there's always something on in Cambridge. Look out for the noticeboards around town laden down with posters advertising classical concerts, theatre shows, academic lectures and live music. It's also worth picking up a *What's On* events guide from the tourist office or logging on to www.cam.ac.uk/whatson for details of university events.

NIGHTCLUBS

Despite the huge student population, Cambridge isn't blessed with the best clubs in the country. Many students stick to the colleges bars late at night and swear that they are the best venues in town. Pity they're not open to the rest of us.

Fez (☎ 01223-519224; www.cambridgefez.com; 15 Market Passage; admission £5-10; ⏰ 8pm-3am) Hip-hop, dance, R&B, techno, funk – whatever you're into you'll find it at Cambridge's most popular club, the Moroccan-themed Fez. Famous for booking top-name DJs, hosting great club nights and its sought-after VIP lounges, it's well worth arriving early to avoid the massive queues.

The Place (☎ 01223-324600; www.placenightclub.co.uk; 22 Sidney St; admission £5; ⏰ 10pm-2am) This sleek club aims to be *the* place to see and be seen in the city, with designer decor and VIP booths with moody blue lighting and white leather sofas. In reality it's pretty mainstream with club classics, crowd-pleasing tunes and the usual suspects on the dance floor.

Other options:

Kambar (☎ 01223-842725; www.kambar.co.uk; Wheeler St; admission £3-5; ⏰ 9pm-3.30am Tue-Sat) Cambridge's alternative venue is a dark and dingy place

---

CAMBRIDGE FOR CHILDREN

Consider taking your little bears to meet the original Winnie the Pooh in a manuscript by ex-alumnus AA Milne at Trinity College's **Wren Library** (p431). Or take advantage of myriad events laid on partly or wholly for kids, including the **Midsummer Fair** (mid-June), the **Big Weekend** (mid-July) and the **Children's Marquee** (early August); details for all these events can be found at www.cambridge-summer.co.uk. Another possibility is to book them in for a 90-minute guided walk with **Cambridge Junior Explorers** (☎ 01223-246990; www.geocities.com/cambridgejuniorexplorers; adult/child £4/3).

Alternatively, if you're hoping a little of the university's vast reserves of knowledge will rub off, there are a host of museums on **Downing St**, covering subjects such as geology, archaeology and anthropology, zoology and the history of science.

---

playing Gothic, industrial, '80s, punk, metal, indie, electro and rock.

Soul Tree (☎ 01223-462277; www.soultree.co.uk; 1-6 Guildhall Chambers, Corn Exchange St; admission £1-4; ☿ 10pm-3am Mon & Thu-Sat) Funk, disco, '80s classics, and not-so-big name DJs at this popular club.

THEATRE

Corn Exchange (☎ 01223-357851; www.cornex.co.uk; Wheeler St) This colossal ex-market building near the tourist office is the city's main centre for arts and entertainment, attracting the top names in pop and rock to ballet.

Arts Theatre (☎ 01223-503333; www.cambridgearts theatre.com; 6 St Edward's Passage) Cambridge's biggest bona-fide theatre puts on everything from pantomime to drama fresh from London's West End.

ADC (☎ 01223-300085; www.adctheatre.com; Park St) Students' theatre and current home to the university's Footlights comedy troupe, which jump-started the careers of scores of England's comedy legends, including John Cleese and Peter Cook.

Junction (☎ 01223-511511; www.junction.co.uk; Cambridge Leisure Park, Clifton Way) Theatre, dance, comedy, live music and club nights at Cambridge's newest venue near the railway station. Tickets can be bought at the Corn Exchange box office.

Getting There & Away

Cambridge is quite well served by trains, though not so well by bus. Trains run at least every 30 minutes from London's King's Cross and Liverpool St stations (£17.90, 45 minutes to 1¼ hours). There are also three trains per hour to Ely (£3.30, 15 minutes) and hourly connections to Bury St Edmunds (£7.60, 44 minutes) and King's Lynn (£8.30, 48 minutes).

From Parkside, Parker's Piece there are regular buses to Stansted airport (£10.50, 55 minutes), Heathrow (£26, 2½ to three hours) and Gatwick (£30.50, 3¾ hours) airports while a Luton (£13, 1½ hours) service runs every two hours.

Buses to Oxford (£9, 3¼ hours) are regular but take a very convoluted route.

Getting Around

BICYCLE

There aren't many cities that are more bike-friendly than Cambridge, and joining the ranks of students on their mad dashes to lectures or leisurely rides around town is an experience in itself.

Cambridge Station Cycles (☎ 01223-307125; www .stationcycles.co.uk; Station Bldg, Station Rd; per half-day/ day/week £8/10/20)

City Cycle Hire (☎ 01223-365629; www.citycyclehire .com; 61 Newnham Rd; per half-day/day/week from £5/10/15)

BUS

A free gas-powered City Shuttle runs around the centre stopping at Emmanuel St every 15 minutes from 9am to 5pm. City bus lines run around town from Drummer St bus station; C1, C3 and C7 stop at the train station. Dayrider passes (£3) offer unlimited travel on all buses within Cambridge for one day; Megarider passes (£10) are valid for one week. Buy them on board.

CAR

Cambridge's centre is largely pedestrianised. It's best to use one of the five free Park & Ride car parks on the outskirts of town. Shuttle buses (£2.20) run to the centre every 10 minutes between 7am and 7pm daily, then every 20 minutes until 10pm.

TAXI
For a taxi, phone **Camtax** (☎ 01223-242424) or **Panther** (☎ 01223-715715).

AROUND CAMBRIDGE
Grantchester
Old thatched cottages with gardens dripping in flowers, breezy meadows and some classic cream teas aren't the only reason to make the pilgrimage along the river to the picture-postcard village of Grantchester. You'll also be following in the footsteps of some of the world's greatest minds on a 3-mile walk, cycle or punt that has changed little since Edwardian times.

The journey here is idyllic on a sunny day and once you arrive you can flop into a deckchair under a leafy apple tree and wolf down calorific cakes at the quintessentially English **Orchard tea garden** (☎ 01223-845788; www .orchard-grantchester.com; Mill Way; ☺ approx 9.30am-5.30pm). This was the favourite haunt of the Bloomsbury Group (see p120) and other cultural icons who came to camp, picnic, swim and discuss their work. If you're after something stronger to whet your thirst the riverside **Red Lion** (☎ 01223-840121; 33 High St, Grantchester) makes a good stop.

Imperial War Museum
The romance of the winged war machine is alive and well at Europe's biggest **aviation museum** (☎ 01223-835000; www.iwm.org.uk; adult/under 16yr £16/free; ☺ 10am-6pm mid-Mar–Sep, to 4pm Oct–mid-Mar) in Duxford, 9 miles south of Cambridge at Junction 10 of the M11. Almost 200 lovingly waxed aircraft from dive bombers to biplanes, Spitfire to Concorde are housed on this vast airfield, which was a frontline fighter station in WWII. Once home to the Dambuster squadron of Lancasters, it is now home to the Red Arrows.

Also included is the stunning **American Air Museum** hangar, designed by Norman Foster, which has the largest collection of American civil and military aircraft outside the USA, and the slick **AirSpace hangar** which houses an exhibition on British and Commonwealth aviation. WWII tanks and artillery can be seen in the **land-warfare hall** and the regular **airshows** of modern and vintage planes are legendary.

Monday to Saturday, Stagecoach bus Citi7 runs to Duxford (45 minutes, every half-hour) from Emmanuel St in Cambridge. The last bus back from the museum is at 5.30pm. The service runs hourly on Sundays.

ELY
pop 15,102
A small but charming city steeped in history and dominated by a jaw-dropping cathedral, Ely (*ee-lee*) makes an excellent day trip from Cambridge. Beyond the dizzying heights of the cathedral towers lie medieval streets, pretty Georgian houses and riverside walks reaching out into the eerie fens that surround the town. The abundance of eels that once inhabited the undrained fens gave the town its unusual name and you can still sample eel stew or eel pie in local restaurants. Ely is a sleepy kind of place where traditional tearooms and antiques shops vie for attention, but it also ranks as one of the fastest-growing cities in Europe, so change is surely on the way.

Information
The helpful **tourist office** (☎ 01353-662062; http://visit ely.eastcambs.gov.uk; 29 St Mary's St; ☺ 10am-5pm Apr-Oct, 11am-4pm Mon-Fri & Sun, 10am-5pm Sat Nov-Mar) makes accommodation bookings and dishes out leaflets on the town's 'Eel Trail' walk. The tourist office also organises a guided walking tour of the city at 2.30pm on Sundays (£3.50).

Sights
ELY CATHEDRAL
Dominating the town and visible across the flat fenland for vast distances, the stunning silhouette of **Ely Cathedral** (☎ 01353-667735; www .cathedral.ely.anglican.org; adult/under 16yr/concession £5.50/ free/4.70; ☺ 7am-7pm Easter-Aug, 7.30am-6pm Mon-Sat, to 5pm Sun Sep-Easter) is locally dubbed the 'Ship of the Fens'.

Walking into the early-12th-century Romanesque nave, you're immediately struck by its clean, uncluttered lines and lofty sense of space. The cathedral is renowned for its entrancing ceilings and the masterly 14th-century octagon and lantern towers, which soar upwards in shimmering colours.

The vast 14th-century Lady Chapel is the biggest in England; it's filled with eerily empty niches that once held statues of saints and martyrs. They were hacked out unceremoniously by iconoclasts during the English Civil War. However, the astonishingly delicate tracery and carving remain.

The cathedral is a breathtaking place, its incredible architecture and light making

EAST ANGLIA

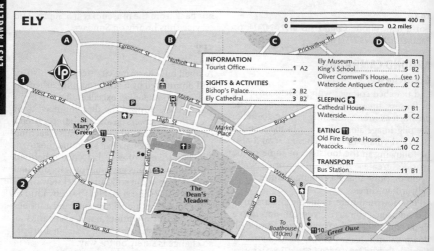

ELY

INFORMATION
Tourist Office.......................1 A2

SIGHTS & ACTIVITIES
Bishop's Palace......................2 B2
Ely Cathedral........................3 B2

Ely Museum.........................4 B1
King's School.......................5 B2
Oliver Cromwell's House.......(see 1)
Waterside Antiques Centre......6 C2

SLEEPING
Cathedral House....................7 B1
Waterside...........................8 C2

EATING
Old Fire Engine House.............9 A2
Peacocks...........................10 C2

TRANSPORT
Bus Station........................11 B1

it a popular film location. You may recognise some of its fine details from scenes in *Elizabeth: The Golden Age* or *The Other Boleyn Girl* but wandering back to the streets it can be difficult to imagine how such a small and tranquil city ended up with such a fine monument.

Although a sleepy place today, Ely has been a place of worship and pilgrimage since at least 673 when Etheldreda, daughter of the king of East Anglia, founded a nunnery here. A colourful character, Ethel shrugged off the fact that she had been twice married in her determination to become a nun and was canonised shortly after her death. The nunnery was later sacked by the Danes, rebuilt as a monastery, demolished and then resurrected as a church after the Norman Conquest. In 1109 Ely became a cathedral, built to impress mere mortals and leave them in no doubt about the power of the church.

For more insight into the fascinating history of the cathedral join a free **guided tour** (10.45am, 1pm, 2pm & 3pm May-Sep, 10.45am, 2pm & 3pm Oct-Apr). You can also explore the **Octagon Tower** (£3.50; 10.45am, 1pm, 2.15pm, 3pm May-Sep) on a tour or attend the spine-tingling **Evensong** (5.30pm Mon-Sat, 4pm Sun) or Sunday **choral service** (10.30am).

Near the entrance a **stained-glass museum** (01353-660347; www.stainedglassmuseum.com; adult/ child £3.50/2.50; 10.30am-5pm Mon-Fri, to 5.30pm Sat, to 6pm Sun Easter-Oct, to 5pm Nov-Easter) tells the history of decorated glasswork from the 14th century onwards. Joint admission to the ca-

thedral and museum is £8 for adults and £6.50 for children.

OTHER SIGHTS & ACTIVITIES
Historic sites cluster about the cathedral's toes. Within spitting distance of the tower are both the former **Bishop's Palace**, now used as a nursing home, and **King's School**, which keeps the cathedral supplied with fresh-faced choristers.

A short hop across St Mary's Green is the attractive half-timbered **Oliver Cromwell's House** (01353-662062; adult/under 16yr £4.85/3; 10am-4pm Apr-Oct, 11am-4pm Nov-Mar), where England's warty warmonger lived with his family from 1636 to 1646, when he was the local tithe collector. The house now has Civil War exhibits, portraits, waxworks and echoes with canned commentaries of – among other things – the great man's grisly death, exhumation and posthumous decapitation. You can take a guided tour of the house (included in the admission price) on Saturdays at 2.30pm.

If you're interested in the history of the town and the surrounding fens, **Ely Museum** (01353-666655; www.elymuseum.org.uk; Market St; adult/ child £3/free; 10.30am-5pm Mon-Sat, 1-5pm Sun May-Oct, 10.30am-4pm Wed-Mon Nov-Apr) has everything from Roman remains to archive footage of eel catching. The museum is housed in the Old Gaol House complete with prisoners' cells and their scrawled graffiti.

Ely is also a great place for rummaging through antiques, and signs lead down to the river and bargain-hunting heaven **Waterside**

ANGLIAN ANTICS

Ah, the English; stiflingly proper, embarrassingly prudish and impeccably reserved. And just a little bit eccentric. Where else could you see laser technology employed to shoot peas, watch Elvis roll a wooden blue cheese down a village high street or find grown adults painting snails with racing stripes? Well, East Anglia of course.

Here you can enter your own pet invertebrate in the **World Snail Racing Championships** (www.snailracing.net) in Congham, about 7 miles east of King's Lynn. Each year over 300 racing snails gather here in mid-July to battle it out for a tankard full of juicy lettuce leaves.

In Witcham, about 8 miles west of Ely, it's the **World Pea Shooting Championships** that draws contestants from far and wide. The school-room prank of blasting dried peas through a tube at a target (not the school master this time round) is alive and well with shooters gathering in early July on the Village Green.

And in the village of Stilton, a few miles south of Peterborough, every May Day bank holiday sees teams in fancy dress scramble along the High St to become **Stilton cheese rolling champions**.

Antiques Centre (☎ 01353-667066; The Wharf; 9.30am-5.30pm Mon-Sat, 11.30am-5.30pm Sun). From here, charming riverside ambles flank the **Great Ouse**; turn left for a quiet walk, or right for the pub and tea garden. If you continue along this path you'll see the Fens stretching to the horizon.

Sleeping & Eating

Accommodation is mostly one- or two-room B&Bs so book ahead for your first choice.

Cathedral House (☎ 01353-662124; www.cathedral house.co.uk; 17 St Mary's St; s £50, d £75-90; P) Set in a lovely Georgian house bursting with antiques and curios, this elegant B&B offers three individually decorated rooms all with period features and cast-iron baths. Outside there's a beautiful walled garden and views of the cathedral.

Waterside (☎ 01353-614329; www.29waterside.org.uk; 29 Waterside; d £60) This pocket-sized B&B is in a wonderfully character-rich 18th-century oak-beamed and wooden-floored building near the waterfront. It's furnished with reclaimed pine and has a pretty walled garden.

Peacocks (☎ 01353-661100; www.peacockstearoom .co.uk; 65 Waterside; cream tea £5.50; 10.30am-5pm Wed-Sun) Voted one of Britain's top teashops by the ladies who know at the Tea Guild, this wisteria-clad place serves a vast selection of leaf teas, as well as luscious homemade cakes, and soups, salads and sambos.

Boathouse (☎ 01353-664388; www.cambscuisine .com; 5 Annesdale; 2-/3-course set lunch £11/15, dinner mains £10-17; noon-2.30pm daily, 6.30-9.30pm Mon-Sat, 6.30-8.30pm Sun) This sleek riverside restaurant dishes up excellent modern English food at very reasonable prices. It has wonderful patio dining overlooking the water, while the stylish interior is lined with oars.

Old Fire Engine House (☎ 01353-662582; www.the oldfireenginehouse.co.uk; 25 St Mary's St; mains £14-17; closed dinner Sun) Backed by beautiful gardens and showcasing a variety of artwork, this delightfully homely place serves classic English food and top-notch afternoon teas. Expect the likes of steak-and-kidney pie or roast pheasant with bread sauce and redcurrant jelly, washed down with a carefully chosen wine.

Getting There & Away

Ely is on the A10, 15 miles northeast of Cambridge. Following the Fen Rivers Way (map available from tourist offices), it's a lovely 17-mile towpath walk.

The easiest way to get to Ely from Cambridge is by train (15 minutes, every 20 minutes); don't even consider the bus, it takes a round-about route and five times as long. There are also twice hourly trains to Peterborough (£8.10, 35 minutes) and Norwich (£13.50, one hour), and hourly services to King's Lynn (£5.40, 30 minutes).

PETERBOROUGH
pop 156,061

A lively city that's shopping mad, Peterborough is riddled with shopping malls but the real reason to visit is the glorious cathedral, which alone makes it worthy of a day trip from Cambridge or London. There's a scattering of other mildly interesting attractions to beef up the town's credentials, but really, see the cathedral and you can leave happy.

Peterborough's bus and train stations are an easy walk west of the city centre. The **tourist office** (☎ 01733-452336; www.visitpeterborough.com; 3-5 Minster Precincts; 🕑 9am-5pm Mon & Wed-Fri, 10am-5pm Tue, 10am-4pm Sat) is in front of the cathedral's west front.

Peterborough Cathedral

England may be filled with fine cathedrals boasting ostentatious facades, but few can rival the instant 'wow' factor of Peterborough's unique early-13th-century western front, with its three cavernous Gothic arches.

Visitors enter the **cathedral** (☎ 01733-355300; www.peterborough-cathedral.org.uk; requested donation £3; 🕑 9am-5.15pm Mon-Fri, to 5pm Sat, noon-5pm Sun), which was founded in 1118, through an odd 14th-century porch that peeks out between the arches. Inside, you'll be immediately struck by the height of the magnificent three-storeyed Norman nave and by its lightness, created by the mellow local stone and fine clerestory windows. The nave is topped by a breathtaking early-13th-century painted-timber ceiling that is one of the earliest and most important of its kind in Europe, and still sports much of its original diamond-patterned paintwork.

Press on below the Gothic tower, which was painstakingly reconstructed in the 19th century, to the northern choir aisle and you'll find the rather plain tombstone of Henry VIII's first wife, the tragic Catherine of Aragon, buried here in 1536. Her divorce, engineered by the king because she could not produce a male heir, led to the Reformation in England. Her only child (a daughter) was not even allowed to attend her funeral. Just beyond this is the cathedral's wonderful 15th-century eastern tip, which has superb fan vaulting thought to be the work of master mason John Wastell, who worked on King's College Chapel in Cambridge.

Loop around into the southern aisle, and you'll find gold lettering marking the spot where the ill-fated Mary, Queen of Scots was once buried. On the accession of her son, James, to the throne, her body was moved to Westminster Abbey.

Getting There & Away

There are regular trains to London (£24.50, 55 minutes to 1½ hours), Cambridge (£13, 50 minutes) and Ely (£8.90, 35 minutes).

ESSEX

Ah, Essex; home to chavs, bottle blondes, boy racers and brash seaside resorts – or so the stereotype goes. The county's inhabitants have been the butt of some of England's cruellest jokes and greatest snobbery for years, but beyond the fake Burberry bags and slots 'n' dodgems resorts there's a rural idyll of sleepy medieval villages and rolling countryside. One of England's best-loved painters, Constable, found inspiration here, and the rural Essex of his time remains hidden down winding lanes little changed for centuries. Here too is the historic town of Colchester, Britain's oldest, with a sturdy castle and vibrant arts scene, and even Southend-on-Sea, the area's most popular resort, has a softer side in the traditional cockle-sellers and cobbled lanes of sleepy suburb Leigh.

COLCHESTER

pop 104,390

Dominated by its sturdy castle and ancient walls, Colchester claims the title as Britain's oldest recorded city, with settlement noted here as early as the 5th century BC. Centuries later in AD 43, the Romans came, saw, conquered and constructed their northern capital Camulodunum here. So too the invading Normans, who saw Colchester's potential and built the monstrous war machine that is the castle.

Today the city is a maze of narrow streets but despite its historic setting and the odd half-timbered gem, the city has a rather dowdy atmosphere. But at the time of writing this was set to change, with a series of major redevelopments planned for the city, including a spectacular new cultural centre, Firstsite.

Orientation & Information

There are two train stations, but most services stop at North station, about half a mile north of the centre. The current bus station is off Queen St near the tourist office, but by 2010 will move to a new location on Vineyard St.

The **tourist office** (☎ 01206-282920; www.visitcolchester.com; 1 Queen St; 🕑 9.30am-6pm Mon-Sat, 11am-4pm Sun Apr-Sep, 10am-5pm Mon-Sat Oct-Mar) is opposite the castle. **Compuccino** (☎ 01206-519090; 7-19 Priory Walk; Centurion House, St John's St; per hr £2.50; 🕑 9am-6.30pm Mon-Sat, 11am-5pm Sun) has internet access. There are a couple of **post offices** (North

Hill & Longe Wyre St) while banks with ATMs can be found on the High St.

Sights & Activities

England's largest surviving Norman keep, bigger even than that of the Tower of London and once a hair-raising symbol of foreign invasion, now slumbers innocently amid a lush park. **Colchester Castle** (☎ 01206-282939; www.colchester museums.org.uk; adult/child £5.20/3.40; ☯ 10am-5pm Mon-Sat, 11am-5pm Sun) was begun in 1076, building upon the foundations of a Roman fort. The interactive castle museum is exceptional, with plenty of try-on togas and sound effects to keep young curiosity alive. There are also illuminating guided tours (adult/child £2.10/1.10) of the Roman vaults, Norman rooftop chapel and castle walls.

Beside the castle, a solid Georgian town house hosts the **Hollytrees Museum** (☎ 01206-282940; admission free; High St; ☯ 10am-5pm Mon-Sat, 11am-5pm Sun), which trawls through 300 years of domestic life with quirky surprises that include a shipwright's boat-cum-pram and a make-your-own Victorian silhouette feature.

Tymperleys, a magnificent timber-framed 15th-century building 100m east of the castle just off the High St, also houses the hypnotic **Clock Museum** (☎ 01206-282939; admission free; ☯ 10am-1pm & 2-5pm Tue-Sat Apr-Oct), which echoes to the steady tick-tocking of one of the largest clock collections in Britain.

A short stroll north of High St will bring you to the Tudor **Dutch Quarter**, where the half-timbered houses and rickety roof lines remain as a testament to the 16th-century Protestant weavers who fled here from Holland.

Sidestep the town's lacklustre natural-history museum in favour of the world-class naturalistic enclosures of **Colchester Zoo** (☎ 01206-331292; www.colchester-zoo.com; Maldon Rd, Stanway; adult/child £14.99/7.99; ☯ 9.30am-6pm Apr-Jun & Sep, to 6.30pm Jul & Aug, to dusk Oct-Mar), 5 miles northeast of the castle. Bus 75 stops at the zoo.

Already being promoted as a future star attraction at the time of writing, **firstsite: newsite** (☎ 01206-577067; www.firstsite.uk.net) will be a massive purpose-built arts and education centre in St Botolph's. The stunning curved glass and copper building will contain gallery space, a library, auditorium and conference facilities and will play host to exhibitions, events and performances. Although construction has been much delayed, it is hoped the centre will open in late 2009. Check the website or tourist office for the latest information.

Tours

The tourist office has a variety of themed, guided **walking tours** (adult/child £3/2; ☯ 11.30am Mon-Sat, 2pm Sun Jul & Aug, 11.30am Sat Mar-Jun, Sep & Oct) of the town and sells tickets for **City Sightseeing** (www.city-sightseeing.com; adult/child £7.50/3; ☯ Apr-Sep) open-top bus tours.

Sleeping & Eating

Colchester has some excellent, lovingly cared for and reasonably priced B&Bs that give the town's ancient hotels a real run for their money. Independent restaurants are in short supply but you'll find all the usual chains along North Hill.

our pick Charlie Browns (☎ 01206-517451; www .charliebrownsbedandbreakfast.co.uk; 60 East St; s £30-45, d £45-60; P ☐ wi-fi) A former hardware shop turned boutique B&B, this place offers incredible value with a couple of stunning rooms blending 14th-century character with 21st-century style. Antique and modern furniture mix seamlessly with the half-timbered walls, limestone bathrooms and rich fabrics to create an intimate, luxurious feel. It's an absolute steal at these rates and should be your first port of call.

Rutland House (☎ 01206-573437; www.rutlandhouse bandb.co.uk; 121 Lexden Rd; s £40-55, d£60-75; P) This is another great B&B with three gorgeous individually furnished rooms in a 1920s house. Choose from Victorian character, 1930s style or contemporary design. Each room has TV and DVD, soft colour schemes and plenty of little extras.

Red Lion (☎ 01206-577986; www.red-lion-hotel.co.uk; High St; s £65-95, d £70-105; ☐ wi-fi) This oak-timbered hotel built in 1465 overhangs the High St and is an atmospheric old place complete with exposed oak beams, wattle-and-daub walls, sloping floors and a resident ghost. The rooms are decked out in Tudor style and are cosy but a bit rickety while the high-beamed banqueting hall serves classic English fayre.

Life Cafe (☎ 01206-574777; 3 Culver St; mains £5-5.50; ☯ 8am-7pm Mon-Fri, to 5pm Sat) This cafe-cum-gallery is bathed in light from the giant floor-to-ceiling windows that look out over the busy street. The menu features a good selection of interesting panini, pastas and salads, as well as plenty of cakes and speciality brews.

Lemon Tree (☎ 01206-767337; www.the-lemon-tree .com; 48 St John's St; mains £11-15; ☒ 10.30am-9.30pm Mon-Sat) This zesty little eatery is graced by a knobbly Roman wall and serves creative English and Continental cuisine. Decor strikes a nice chic-to-rustic balance and there are tasty blackboard specials, frequent gourmet nights and occasional live jazz.

Getting There & Around

Colchester is 62 miles from London. There are three daily National Express buses from London Victoria (£10.30, 2¼ hours) and rail services every 15 to 20 minutes from London Liverpool St (£18.70, 55 minutes). For a cab, call **A1 Taxis** (☎ 01206-544744).

AROUND COLCHESTER
Dedham Vale

'I love every stile and stump and lane… these scenes made me a painter'
John Constable (1776–1837)

Born and bred in East Bergholt, John Constable's romantic visions of country lanes, springtime fields and babbling creeks were inspired by and painted in this serene vale. The area has hung onto its rural charm despite the intervening centuries, and although you may not see the rickety old cart pictured in his renowned painting *The Hay Wain*, the background of picturesque cottages, beautiful countryside and languid charm remains.

Now known as Constable country, Dedham Vale centres on the villages of Dedham, East Bergholt and Flatford. There's a **tourist office** (☎ 01206-299460; flatford@babergh.gov.uk; Flatford Lane; ☒ 10am-4.45pm Easter-Oct, 11am-2.45pm Sat & Sun Nov–mid-Mar) beside the vale's top attraction, a riverside mill once owned by the artist's family. **Flatford Mill** is now used as an education centre and there is no public access.

Near the mill is thatched **Bridge Cottage** (NT; ☎ 01206-298260; Flatford Lane, East Bergholt; admission free; ☒ 10.30am-5.30pm May-Sep, 11am-4pm Oct, 11am-5pm Wed-Sun Mar & Apr, 11am-3.30pm Wed-Sun Nov & Dec, 11am-3.30pm Sat & Sun Jan-Feb), which has an exhibition on the artist, a tea garden and boat hire.

If you'd like to base yourself here try **Dedham Hall** (☎ 01206-323027; www.dedhamhal .demon.co.uk; Dedham; s/d £55/95), an atmospheric 15th-century manor house where you can also take three-/seven-day painting courses (£190/230) if you fancy following in Constable's footsteps.

The area is best explored by bike or in your own car, though there are bus and train services. Buses 93 and 93A from Colchester run to East Bergholt, from where it's less than a mile to the mill. Or come by train to Manningtree (eight minutes), and you get a lovely 1¾-mile walk along pretty footpaths.

SAFFRON WALDEN
pop 14,313

The sleepy, higgledy-piggledy town of Saffron Walden is a delightful knot of half-timbered houses, narrow lanes, crooked roofs and ancient buildings. It's a really lovely place to wander with some real architectural gems and a host of antique shops, galleries and second-hand bookshops to catch your eye.

The town gets its curious title from the saffron crocus, which was cultivated in the surrounding fields from the 15th century right through to the first half of the 20th century.

The **tourist office** (☎ 01799-524002; www.saffron walden.gov.uk; 1 Market Pl; ☒ 9.30am-5.30pm Mon-Sat Apr-Oct, 10.30am-1pm Sun Apr-Aug, 10am-5pm Mon-Sat Nov-Mar) provides a useful town trail leaflet with information on the town's historic buildings.

Sights

The town's most famous building is probably the 14th-century **Sun Inn** (Church St), an ornate wooden structure once used as Cromwell's HQ. The inn is famous for its stunning 17th-century pargeting (decorative plaster work).

Nearby is the jumbo-sized 15th-century **Church of St Mary the Virgin** (Church St). A symbol of the town's saffron-inspired golden age, it is one of the largest in the county and sports some impressive Gothic arches and decorative wooden ceilings.

In the little **museum** (☎ 01799-510333; www .saffronwaldenmuseum.org; Museum St; adult/under 18yr £1/free; ☒ 10am-5pm Mon-Sat, 2-5pm Sun Mar-Oct, closes 4.30pm Nov-Feb), itself dating from 1835, you'll find an eclectic collection of artefacts covering everything from local history to costume and needlecraft, Victorian toys and ancient Egypt. The bramble-covered ruins of **Walden Castle Keep**, built about 1125, lie in the grounds.

Tucked down at the end of quiet lanes off Bridge St and Castle St is **Bridge End Garden** (www.bridgeendgarden.org; admission free; ☒ daylight hr), a restored Victorian garden, and on the eastern side of the town, a tiny turf **labyrinth** thought to be 800 years old.

Sleeping & Eating

Saffron Walden YHA (☎ 0845 371 9137; www.yha.org
.uk; 1 Myddylton Pl; dm member/nonmember £13.95/17.95;
☼ mid-Apr–mid-Sep) This stunning medieval
timber-framed hostel is the town's oldest inhabited building. It was once a malt house,
and although facilities are relatively basic the
place just drips with character. The hostel
often gets booked up with groups so make a
reservation in advance.

Archway Guesthouse (☎ 01799-501500; www
.archways.co.uk; 13 Church St; s/d from £40/60; **P** 💻)
Contemporary style and unfussy decor de-
sign make this bright, airy place well worth an
overnight stay. The rooms feature big, comfortable beds, modern art on the walls and
flat-screen TVs. There's a warm welcome for
children and a family suite available.

Eight Bells (☎ 01799-522790; 18 Bridge St; mains £11-
16; ☼ lunch & dinner Mon-Sat, lunch only Sun) A warm
mix of medieval character and contemporary
style, this 16th-century gastropub is the top
spot in town. Scrubbed wooden floors, half-
timbered walls, abstract art, deep leather sofas
and roaring fires make it a great place to sip
on a pint or enjoy a top-notch meal from the
modern European menu.

Getting There & Away

On weekdays, trains leave London Liverpool
St twice hourly (£15.40, one hour) for
Audley End station, 2.5 miles west of town.
Services run hourly on Sunday. Trains from
Cambridge (18 minutes) run approximately
every 20 minutes.

Buses 301 and 59 run from the station into
Saffron Walden (six minutes) regularly on
weekdays, less often on weekends.

The Citi7 bus runs into Cambridge hourly
(70 minutes).

AROUND SAFFRON WALDEN

Positively palatial in its scale, style and the all-
too-apparent ambition of its creator, the first
earl of Suffolk, the fabulous early-Jacobean
Audley End House (EH; ☎ 01799-522399; adult/child
house & garden £10.50/5.30, garden only £5.50/2.80;
☼ 11am-5pm Wed-Fri & Sun, 11am-3.30pm Sat late Mar-
Sep, 11am-4pm Wed-Sun Oct) eventually did become
a royal palace when it was bought by Charles
II in 1668.

Although hard to believe, the enormous
building today is only one-third of its original size, but it's still magnificent. Its lavishly
decorated rooms glitter with silverware, priceless furniture and paintings, making it one
of England's grandest country homes. The
sumptuous interior was remodelled in Gothic
style by the third Baron Braybrooke in the
19th century and much of his creations are
what remain today. You can also visit the
service wing where a new exhibition explores
the lives of those who worked in the house in
Victorian times.

Outside, the house is surrounded by
dreamy landscaped **park** (☼ 10am-6pm Wed-Sun,
to 5pm Mar & Oct, to 4pm Nov, Dec & Feb) designed by
Lancelot 'Capability' Brown. The grounds
play host to a series of concerts throughout
the summer months.

Audley End House is 1 mile west of Saffron
Walden on the B1383. Audley End train station is 1¼ miles from the house. Taxis will
ferry you here from the town marketplace
for around £4.

SOUTHEND-ON-SEA

pop 160,257

Crass, commercialised and full of flashing
lights, Southend is London's lurid weekend
playground, full of gaudy amusements and
seedy nightclubs. But beyond the tourist tat,
roller coasters and slot machines there's a glorious stretch of sandy beach, an absurdly long
pier and in the suburb of Old Leigh, a traditional fishing village of cobbled streets, cockle
sheds and thriving art galleries. Southend is
also becoming increasingly well known for
its live music scene and is a good place to
catch a gig.

Information

The **tourist office** (☎ 01702-215120; www.visitsouthend
.co.uk; Southend Pier, Western Esplanade; ☼ 8.15am-6pm
Mon-Fri, 8.15am-8pm Sat & Sun Apr-May & Oct, 8.15am-8pm
Jun-Sep, 8.15am-4pm Mon-Fri, 8.15am-6pm Sat & Sun Nov-
Mar) is at the entrance to the pier. Banks and
shops crowd along the High St.

Sights & Activities

Other than miles upon miles of tawny
imported-sand and shingle **beaches**, Southend's
main attraction is its **pier** (☎ 01702-215620; pier train
adult/child £3/1.50; pier walk & ride £2.50/1.50; ☼ 8.15am-
8pm Easter-Oct, 8.15am-4pm Mon-Fri, 8.15am-6pm Sat &
Sun Nov-Easter), built in 1830. At a staggering
1.34 miles long – the world's longest – it's
an impressive edifice and a magnet for boat
crashes, storms and fires, the last of which ravaged its tip in 2005. It's a surprisingly peaceful

stroll to the lifeboat station at its head and you can hop on the Pier Railway to save the long slog back.

Afterwards, dip beneath the pier's entrance to see the antique slot machines at the **museum** (☎ 01702-611214; www.southendpiermuseum.co.uk; adult/under 12yr £1/free; ☑ 11am-5pm Tue-Wed, Sat & Sun May-Oct) and embrace Southend's tacky seaside soul on the head-spinning rides at **Adventure Island** (☎ 01702-443400; www.adventureisland.co.uk; Western Esplanade; ☑ roughly 11am-8pm daily Apr-Aug, Sat & Sun Sep-Mar).

If the seaside tat is not your thing, swap the candyfloss for steaming cockles wrapped in newspaper in the traditional fishing village of **Old Leigh**, just west along the seafront. Wander the cobbled streets, cockle sheds, art galleries and craft shops for a taste of life before the amusement arcades took over. The **Leigh Heritage Centre** (☎ 01702-470834; High St, Old Town, Leigh-on-Sea; ☑ 10.30am-3pm) offers an insight into the history and heritage of the village and its buildings.

Sleeping & Eating

Beaches (☎ 01702-586124; www.beachesguesthouse.co.uk; 192 Eastern Esplanade; s £40, d £65-85; ☐ wi-fi) A welcome respite from violent florals and heavy swag curtains, rooms at Beaches are bright, simple and tasteful with white Egyptian-cotton bed linen, feather duvets and subtle colour schemes. The uncluttered rooms, Continental breakfast and quiet location make it one of the best deals around.

Pebbles (☎ 01702-582329; www.mypebbles.co.uk; 190 Eastern Esplanade; s from £45, d £60-85; ☐) Almost next door is Pebbles, with its subtle, contemporary style. The rooms here still retain their Victorian features but the decor is modern with funky wallpapers, plenty of cushions and big, comfy beds.

Pipe of Port (☎ 01702-614606; www.pipeofport.com; 84 High St; mains £9-16) A Southend institution, this subterranean wine bar–cum–bistro is an atmospheric place with old-world character, candlelit tables, sawdust-covered floor and its own unique charm. It's famous for its pies, casseroles and fish dishes as well as the lengthy wine list.

Fleur de Provence (☎ 01702-352987; www.fleurde provence.co.uk; 52 Alexandra St; mains £16-18, 3-course set meal £15; ☑ lunch & dinner Mon-Fri, dinner Sat) Chic, sleek and sophisticated, this is probably Southend's top dining establishment, serving modern French cuisine with a flourish.

It's away from the centre of town but well worth the trip for its romantic ambience and fine food.

Entertainment

Southend has a lively music scene with a powerful new wave of bands collectively known as the 'Southend sound' putting the town on the map and forcing the national music press to sit up and take notice. Along with local hopefuls you'll also get regular gigs by big-name bands at **Chinnerys** (☎ 01702-467305; www.chinnerys.co.uk; 21 Marine Pde) and the **Riga Music Bar** (☎ 01702-348020; www.rigamusicbar .co.uk; 228 London Rd).

Getting There & Around

The easiest way to arrive is by train. There are trains roughly every 15 minutes from London Liverpool St to Southend Victoria and from London Fenchurch St to Southend Central (£8.90, 55 minutes). The seafront is a 10- to 15-minute walk from either train station. Trains leave Southend Central for Leigh-on-Sea (10 minutes) every 10 to 15 minutes.

SUFFOLK

Littered with picturesque villages seemingly lost in time, and quaint seaside resorts that have doggedly refused to sell their souls to tourism, this charming county makes a delightfully tranquil destination. Suffolk built its wealth and reputation on the back of the medieval wool trade and although the once-busy coastal ports little resemble their time in the limelight, the inland villages remain largely untouched, with magnificent wool churches and lavish medieval homes attesting to the once-great might of the area. To the west are the picture-postcard villages of Lavenham and Long Melford; further north the languid charm and historic buildings attract visitors to Bury St Edmunds; and along the coast the genteel seaside resorts of Aldeburgh and Southwold seem miles away from their more brash neighbours to the north and south.

Information

You can whet your appetite for the region further by visiting these two websites:

www.visitsuffolkattractions.co.uk and www
.visit-suffolk.org.uk.

Getting Around

Consult **Suffolk County Tourism** (www.suffolkonboard
.com) or **Traveline** (☎ 0871 200 2233; www.traveline
eastanglia.co.uk) for local transport information.
The two main bus operators in rural areas
are **Beestons** (www.beestons.co.uk) and **Chambers**
(www.chamberscoaches.co.uk).

IPSWICH
pop 117,069

Suffolk's county capital was one of the very
first Saxon towns in England and a thriving medieval centre, but today its handful
of medieval churches and beautiful timber-framed buildings are lost in the sea of
plastic shopfronts. Change is nigh though
with waterfront warehouses filling up with
trendy bars and restaurants. Ipswich doesn't
merit a detour or an overnight stay, but it's
the main transport hub of the region and
has a few gems worth seeking out if you're
passing through.

The **tourist office** (☎ 01473-258070; www.visit-ips
wich.com; ☺ 9am-5pm Mon-Sat) is in 15th-century St
Stephen's Church, off St Stephen's Lane. The
tourist office is a 15-minute walk northeast of
the train station, across the roundabout and
along Princes St.

Just north of the tourist office is the glorious wedding-cake facade of decorative pargeting on the 17th-century **Ancient House** (40
Buttermarket; ☺ 9am-5.30pm Mon-Sat), its four panels each representing the known continents
at the time. It's one of the finest examples
of the craft you'll see anywhere and crawls
with mythological creatures and characters.
The building now houses a kitchen outfitters,
but you can take a peek at the hammer-beam
roof inside.

Set in a lovely rolling park 300m north
of town, the multigabled 16th-century
Christchurch Mansion (☎ 01473-433554; Soane St;
admission free; ☺ mansion & gallery 10am-5pm Mon-Sat,
noon-4.30pm Sun Apr-Oct, 10am-dusk Tue-Sat, 2.30pm-dusk
Sun Nov-Mar) is filled with period furniture, and
displays works by the likes of Constable and
Gainsborough.

our pick **Samford Restaurant** (☎ 01473-786616;
Suffolk Food Hall, Orwell Bridge; mains £8-12; ☺ 10am-
6pm Mon-Sat, 10.30am-4.30pm Sun) in the Suffolk
Food Hall looks down over the river and the
busy deli, butcher, cheesemonger, baker and

vegetable stalls below. The menu features a
bumper crop of seasonal dishes using local
ingredients. Everything is made to order and
even the butcher is on hand to explain the
cuts of meat to you.

Alternatively try **Seventy Seven** (☎ 01473-
231177; 77 Fore Hamlet; mains £10-15; ☺ 11am-11pm Tue-
Sat, noon-6pm Sun) with its giant windows and an
open-plan layout. Despite the stylish look,
it's down to earth with friendly service and a
tempting modern English menu.

There are trains every 20 minutes to
London's Liverpool St station (£34.50, 1¼
hours), twice hourly to Norwich (£11.50,
40 minutes) and Bury St Edmunds (£6.40,
30 to 40 minutes). There are bus services
roughly every half-hour to Sudbury (one
hour) Monday to Saturday and less frequently
on Sunday.

AROUND IPSWICH
Sutton Hoo

Somehow missed by plundering grave robbers
and left undisturbed for 1300 years, the hull
of an enormous Anglo-Saxon ship was discovered here in 1939, buried under a mound
of earth. The ship was the final resting place
of Raedwald, King of East Anglia until AD
625, and was stuffed with a fabulous wealth
of Saxon riches. The massive effort that went
into his burial gives some idea of just how
important an individual he must have been.

Many of the original finds and a full-scale
reconstruction of his ship and burial chamber
can be seen in the **visitors centre** (NT; ☎ 01394-
389700; www.nationaltrust.org.uk/suttonhoo; Woodbridge;
adult/child £6.20/3.20; ☺ 10.30am-5pm daily Jul & Aug, Wed-
Sun mid-Mar–Jun, Sep & Oct, Sat & Sun 11am-4pm Nov–mid-
Mar). The finest treasures, including the king's
exquisitely crafted helmet, shields, gold ornaments and Byzantine silver, are displayed in
London's British Museum (p120) but replicas
are on show here.

Access to the original burial mounds is
restricted but you can join a one-hour **guided
tour** (adult/child £2.50/1.25) which explores the area
and does much to bring this fascinating site
back to life.

Sutton Hoo is 2 miles east of Woodbridge
and 6 miles northeast of Ipswich off the
B1083. Buses 71 and 73 visit Sutton Hoo 10
times per day Monday to Saturday, passing
through Woodbridge (10 minutes) en route
to Ipswich (40 minutes).

STOUR VALLEY

The soft, pastoral landscape and impossibly pretty villages of the Stour Valley have provided inspiration for some of England's best-loved painters. Constable and Gainsborough grew up or worked here, and the topsy-turvy timber-framed houses and elegant churches that date to the region's 15th-century weaving boom are still very much as they were. This now-quiet backwater once produced more cloth than anywhere else in England, but in the 16th century, production gradually shifted elsewhere and the valley reverted to a tranquil, pastoral landscape.

Long Melford
pop 3675

Strung out along a winding road, the village of Long Melford is home to a clutch of historic buildings and two impressive country piles. The 2-mile High St is supposedly the longest in England and is flanked by some stunning timber-framed houses, Georgian gems and Victorian terraces, and at one end has a sprawling village green lorded over by the magnificently pompous **Great Church of the Holy Trinity** (☎ 01787-310845; ☻ 10am-5pm Apr-Sep, to 4pm Mar & Oct, to 3pm Nov-Feb). A spectacular example of a 15th-century wool church, it has wonderful stained-glass windows and a tower dating from 1903.

From outside, the romantic Elizabethan mansion of **Melford Hall** (NT; ☎ 01787-376395; www .nationaltrust.org.uk/melfordhall; adult/child £5.80/2.90; ☻ 1.30-5pm Wed-Sun May-Sep, 1.30-5pm Sat & Sun Apr & Oct) seems little changed since it entertained the queen in 1578. Inside, there's a panelled banqueting hall, much Regency and Victorian finery and a display on Beatrix Potter, who was related to Parker family who owned the house from 1786 to 1960.

There's a noticeably different atmosphere at Long Melford's other red-brick Elizabethan mansion, **Kentwell Hall** (☎ 01787-310207; www .kentwell.co.uk; adult/child £8.50/5.50; ☻ 11am-5pm Apr-Sep). Despite being full of Tudor pomp and centuries-old ghost stories, it is still used as a private home and has a wonderfully lived-in feel. It's surrounded by a rectangular moat and there's a Tudor-rose maze and a rare-breeds farm that'll keep the kids happy. Kentwell hosts special events throughout the year, including several full Tudor re-creations when the whole estate bristles with bodices and hose. Check the website for details.

Long Melford is also famed for its **antique shops**, thanks in part to a hit '80s TV series called *Lovejoy* that was shot here. Viewing appointments are required in some.

SLEEPING & EATING
High Street Farmhouse (☎ 01787-375765; www.high streetfarmhouse.co.uk; High St; s/d incl breakfast £35/60; Ⓟ) This 16th-century farmhouse offers a choice of big, bright rooms full of rustic charm. Expect patchwork quilts, pretty florals, knotty pine and cast-iron or four-poster beds. There's a lovely mature garden outside and hearty breakfasts on offer.

Black Lion Hotel & Restaurant (☎ 01787-312356; www.blacklionhotel.net; the Green; s £97.50-110, d £150-195; Ⓟ) Flamboyant rooms with serious swag curtains, four-poster and half-tester beds, rich fabrics and a creative combination of contemporary style and traditional elegance are on offer at this small hotel on the village green. Go for the deep red Yquem for pure, sultry passion or try the Sancerre for something a little more restful. The hotel has two restaurants (mains £12 to £17) and a lovely walled Victorian garden.

Scutcher's Bistro (☎ 01787-310200; www.scutchers .com; Westgate St; mains £12-19; ☻ lunch & dinner Tue-Sat) Despite the rather mismatched decor this unpretentious place is renowned throughout the Stour Valley for its exquisite food. The menu features classic and modern English dishes that leave locals coming back regularly for more.

GETTING THERE & AWAY
Buses leave from the High St outside the post office. There are hourly services Monday to Saturday to Bury St Edmunds (52 minutes) and twice-hourly to Sudbury (10 minutes).

Sudbury
pop 11,933

Birthplace of celebrated portrait and landscape painter Thomas Gainsborough (1727–88) and the model for Charles Dickens' fictional town Eatanswill in *The Pickwick Papers* (1836–37), Sudbury is a bustling market town that makes for a pleasant hour or two of wandering.

The **tourist office** (☎ 01787-881320; sudburytic@ babergh.gov.uk; Market Hill; ☻ 9am-5pm Mon-Fri year-round, plus 10am-4.45pm Sat Apr-Oct, 10am-2.45pm Sat Oct-Mar) dispenses advice from alongside the town hall.

Most visitors come to see the birthplace of painter Thomas Gainsborough, **Gainsborough's House** (☎ 01787-372958; 46 Gainsborough St; www.gainsborough.org; adult/child £4/1.50; ⏰ 10am-5pm Mon-Sat), which showcases the largest collection of his work in the world. The 16th-century house and gardens feature a Georgian facade built by Gainsborough's own father in the 18th century, and a mulberry tree that features in some of his son's paintings. Inside, look for his earliest known work, *A Boy and a Girl in a Landscape*, and the exquisite *Lady Tracy*, celebrated for its delicate portrayal of drapery.

Sudbury has a train station with an hourly service to London (£20.40, 1¼ hours). **Beestons** (www.beestons.co.uk) runs about eight buses daily Monday to Saturday to Ipswich (one hour), while **Chambers** (www.chamberscoaches.co.uk) runs regular services to Long Melford, Lavenham, Bury St Edmunds and Colchester.

Lavenham
pop 1738

One of East Anglia's most beautiful and rewarding towns, topsy-turvy Lavenham is home to a wonderful collection of exquisitely preserved medieval buildings that lean and lurch to dramatic effect. Lavenham's 300 half-timbered and pargeted houses and thatched cottages have been left virtually untouched since its heyday in the 15th century when it made its fortunes on the backs of the wool trade. Curiosity shops, art galleries, quaint tearooms and ancient inns line the streets, where the predominant colour is 'Suffolk pink', a traditional finish of whitewash mixed with red ochre. On top of the medieval atmosphere and beautiful streetscapes, Lavenham has an excellent choice of accommodation making it one of the most popular spots in the area with visitors.

If you're visiting at a weekend it's well worth joining a guided village walk (£3, 2.30pm Saturday, 11am Sunday) run by the **tourist office** (☎ 01787-248207; lavenhamtic@babergh.gov.uk; Lady St; ⏰ 10am-4.45pm mid-Mar–Oct, 11am-3pm Sat & Sun Nov–mid-Mar).

SIGHTS

Many of Lavenham's most enchanting buildings cluster along High St, Water St and around Market Pl, which is dominated by the early-16th-century **guildhall** (NT; ☎ 01787-247646; www.nationaltrust.org.uk/lavenham; adult/child £4/1.65; ⏰ 11am-5pm Apr-Oct, 11am-4pm Sat & Sun Nov,

---

A COTTAGE OF YOUR OWN

For self-catering country cottages in the area, have a browse through these sites:
Farm Stay Anglia (www.farmstayanglia.co.uk)
Holiday Cottages Cambridge (www.holidaycottagescambridge.co.uk)
Just Suffolk (www.justsuffolk.com)
Norfolk Cottages (www.norfolkcottages.co.uk)
Suffolk Secrets (www.suffolk-secrets.co.uk)

11am-4pm Wed-Sun Mar), a superb example of a close-studded, timber-framed building. It is now a local-history museum with displays on the wool trade, and in its tranquil garden you can see dye plants that produced the typical medieval colours.

Also on the Market Pl, the atmospheric 14th-century **Little Hall** (☎ 01787-247019; www.littlehall.org.uk; adult/child £2.50/free; ⏰ 2-5.30pm Wed, Thu, Sat & Sun Easter-Oct) is another gem, with soft ochre plastering, timber frame and crown-post roof. Once home to a successful wool merchant, it's now a private residence open to the public.

At the village's high southern end rises the stunning **Church of St Peter & St Paul** (⏰ 8.30am-5.30pm Apr-Sep, to 3.30pm Oct-Mar), a late Perpendicular church that seems to lift into the sky with its beautifully proportioned windows and soaring steeple. Built between 1485 and 1530, it was one of Suffolk's last great wool churches, completed on the eve of the Reformation, and now a lofty testament to Lavenham's past prosperity.

SLEEPING & EATING

De Vere House (☎ 01787-249505; www.deverehouse.co.uk; Water St; s £75, d £80-95; P) This stunning medieval house is just dripping with character and the two guest rooms are decked out in classical style. One features a carved four-poster bed, chaise longue and roll-top bath while the other is all exposed beams and Edwardian style. There's a private reading room for guests and a courtyard garden for breakfast.

our pick **Lavenham Priory** (☎ 01787-247404; www.lavenhampriory.co.uk; Water St; s/d from £75/100; P) A rare treat, this sumptuously restored 15th-century B&B steals your heart as soon as you walk in the door. Every room oozes Elizabethan charm with cavernous fireplaces, leaded windows and exquisite period features. Now an upmarket six-room B&B, it must be booked well in advance.

Swan Hotel (☎ 01787-247477; www.theswanatlaven ham.co.uk; High St; s £75-85, d £115-280; **P**) A warren of stunning timber-framed 15th-century buildings now shelters one of the region's best-known hotels. Rooms are suitably spectacular, some with immense fireplaces, colossal beams and magnificent four-posters. Elsewhere the hotel cultures a gentlefolk's country-club feel. The stunning beamed Great Hall is an atmospheric place to try the modern English cuisine (three-course set dinner £31.95).

Great House (☎ 01787-247431; www.greathouse.co.uk; Market Pl; s £85-120, d £85-180; 💻 wi-fi) Chic design blends effortlessly with 15th-century character at this much-loved restaurant with rooms in the centre of town. The guest accommodation is decidedly contemporary with funky wallpaper, sleek furniture and plasma-screen TVs but there are plenty of period features and a decanter of sherry on the side. The acclaimed French restaurant (thee-course lunch/dinner £16.95/26.95) serves classic French dishes with a modern flourish.

GETTING THERE & AWAY

Chambers Buses connects Lavenham with Bury St Edmunds (30 minutes) and Sudbury (20 minutes) hourly until 6pm Monday to Saturday (no service on Sunday). The nearest train station is Sudbury.

Kersey

Slithering down either side of a steep slope to a shallow ford, picture-perfect Kersey is a pocket-sized hamlet lined with handsome timber-framed houses. Strolling the length of the street takes all of five minutes, after which there is little to do here save snap photos, visit the wonderful church of **St Mary** at the top of the hill, pop into the **Kersey Pottery** (☎ 01473-822092; www.kerseypottery .com; The Street; 🕑 10am-5.30pm Tue-Sat, 11am-5pm Sun) by the ford, or grab some lunch and a pint at the 14th-century, oak-timbered **Bell Inn** (☎ 01473-823229).

Kersey is 8 miles southeast of Lavenham off the A1141, though there are no direct buses connecting the two. Bus No 772 runs from Kersey to Hadleigh from where you can pick up hourly services to Ipswich or Sudbury.

Hadleigh
pop 7239

Though it's hard to envisage now, the quiet country town of Hadleigh was once one of the biggest and busiest wool towns in East Anglia, and hidden just off the High St is a lovely cluster of buildings to prove it.

The town's principal jewel is its handsome three-storeyed 15th-century **guildhall** (☎ 01473-827752; Church St; www.fohg.co.uk; admission free; 🕑 2-5pm Sun-Fri late Jun-late Sep), timber framed and topped by a splendid crown-post roof. Next door, there are some fabulous original features (including a very stiff oaken door) to appreciate in 12th-century **St Mary's Church**, with its lanky spire and lofty ceiling.

Also beside the church is the high-and-mighty **Deanery Tower**, built in 1495 as a gatehouse to an archbishop's mansion that never actually got built. It's a very fanciful affair embellished with decorous battlements and oriel windows.

Hadleigh is 2 miles southeast of Kersey. There are hourly buses from Ipswich (28 minutes) and Sudbury (28 minutes).

BURY ST EDMUNDS
pop 36,218

Once home to one of the most powerful monasteries of medieval Europe, Bury has long attracted travellers for its powerful history, atmospheric ruins, handsome Georgian architecture and bustling agricultural markets. It's a genteel kind of place with tranquil gardens, a newly completed cathedral and a lively buzz. Bury is also home to Greene King, the famous Suffolk brewer.

History

Bury's slogan 'Shrine of a King, Cradle of the Law' recalls two defining events in the town's history. St Edmund, last Saxon king of East Anglia, was decapitated by the Danes in 869 and in 903 the martyr's body was reburied here. Soon a series of ghostly miracles emanated from his grave and the shrine became a centre of pilgrimage and the core of a new Benedictine monastery. In the 11th century, King Canute built a new abbey which soon became one of the most famous and wealthy in the country. Meanwhile the town thrived on the flocks of visiting pilgrims and with the creation of a planned town surrounding the abbey, came an influx of craftspeople.

In 1214 the English barons chose the abbey to draw up a petition that would form the basis of the Magna Carta, making it a 'Cradle of the Law' and setting the country on the road to a constitutional government. In me-

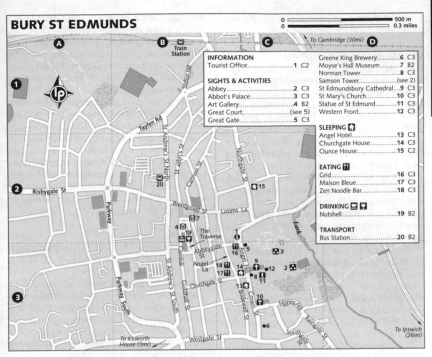

BURY ST EDMUNDS

0 ————— 500 m
0 ————— 0.3 miles

To Cambridge (30mi)

INFORMATION	
Tourist Office	1 C2

SIGHTS & ACTIVITIES	
Abbey	2 C3
Abbot's Palace	3 C3
Art Gallery	4 B2
Great Court	(see 5)
Great Gate	5 C3
Greene King Brewery	6 C3
Moyse's Hall Museum	7 B2
Norman Tower	8 C3
Samson Tower	(see 2)
St Edmundsbury Cathedral	9 C3
St Mary's Church	10 C3
Statue of St Edmund	11 C3
Western Front	12 C3

SLEEPING	
Angel Hotel	13 C3
Churchgate House	14 C3
Ounce House	15 C2

EATING	
Grid	16 C3
Maison Bleue	17 C3
Zen Noodle Bar	18 C3

DRINKING	
Nutshell	19 B2

TRANSPORT	
Bus Station	20 B2

To Ipswich (26mi)

To Ickworth House (3mi)

dieval times the town grew rich on the wool trade and prospered until Henry VIII got his grubby hands on the abbey in 1539 and closed it down as part of the Dissolution.

Orientation & Information

Bury is easily navigated thanks to the original 11th-century grid layout. The train station is 900m north of the tourist office, with frequent buses to the centre. The bus station is in the town's heart.

Bury's **tourist office** (☎ 01284-764667; tic@stedsbc .gov.uk; 6 Angel Hill; ⏰ 9.30am-5pm Mon-Sat Easter-Oct, 10am-3pm Sun May-Sep, 10am-4pm Mon-Fri, 10am-1pm Sat Nov-Easter) has maps and advice and is also the starting point for guided walking tours (£3, 2.30pm Easter to September). Audio tours (adult/child £2.50/1.50) of the abbey ruins are also available.

Sights

ABBEY & PARK

Now a picturesque ruin residing in beautiful gardens behind the cathedral, the once all-powerful **abbey** (admission free; ⏰ dawn-dusk) still impresses despite the townspeople hav-

ing made off with much of the stone after the Dissolution. The Reformation also meant an end to the veneration of relics, and St Edmund's grave and bones have long since disappeared.

You enter the park via one of two well-preserved old gates: opposite the tourist office, the staunch mid-14th-century **Great Gate** is intricately decorated and ominously defensive, complete with battlements, portcullis and arrow slits. The other entrance sits further up Angel Hill, where a gargoyle-studded early-12th-century **Norman Tower** looms.

Just beyond the Great Gate is a peaceful garden where the **Great Court** was once a hive of activity, and further on a dovecote marks the only remains of the **Abbot's Palace**. Most impressive, however, are the remains of the **western front**, where the original abbey walls were burrowed into in the 18th century to make way for houses. The houses are still in use and look as if they have been carved out of the stone like caves. Nearby is **Samson Tower** and in front of it a beautiful **statue of St Edmund** by Dame Elisabeth Frink (1976). The rest of the abbey spreads eastward like a ragged skeleton, with various lumps and pillars hinting at its immense size.

ST EDMUNDSBURY CATHEDRAL

Completed in 2005, the 45m-high Millennium Tower of **St Edmundsbury Cathedral** (St James; ☎ 01284-748720; www.stedscathedral.co.uk; Angel Hill; requested donation £3; ✆ 8am-6pm) is a vision in Lincolnshire limestone, and its traditional Gothic-style construction gives a good idea of how the towers of many other English cathedrals must once have looked fresh from the stonemason's chisel.

Most of the rest of the building dates from the early 16th century, though the eastern end is postwar 20th century, and the northern side was completed in 1990. The overall effect is light and lofty, with a gorgeous hammer-beam roof and a striking sculpture of the crucified Christ by Dame Elisabeth Frink in the north transept. The impressive entrance porch has a tangible Spanish influence, a tribute to Abbot Anselm (1121–48), who opted against pilgrimage to Santiago de Compostela in favour of building a church dedicated to St James (Santiago in Spanish) right here.

For a proper insight into the church's history and heritage join one of the guided tours of the cathedral at 11.30am from May to September.

ST MARY'S CHURCH

One of the biggest parish churches in England, **St Mary's** (☎ 01284-754680; www.stmarystpeter .net/stmaryschurch; Honey Hill; ✆ 10am-4pm Mar-Oct, to 3pm Nov-Feb) contains the tomb of Mary Tudor (Henry VIII's sister and a one-time queen of France). Built around 1430, it also has a host of somewhat vampirish angels swooping from its roof, and a bell is still rung to mark curfew, as it was in the Middle Ages.

GREENE KING BREWERY

Churning out some of England's favourite booze since Victorian times, this famous **brewery** (☎ 01284-714297; www.greeneking.co.uk; Crown St; day/evening tours £8/10; ✆ museum 10.30am-4.30pm Mon-Sat, tours 11am Mon, 2pm Tue, 11am & 2pm Wed-Fri, 10.30am, 12.30pm & 2.30pm Sat, 11.30am Sun, evening tour 7pm Mon-Fri) has a museum (admission free) and runs tours, after which you can appreciate what all the fuss is about in its brewery bar. Tours are popular so book ahead.

ART GALLERY & MOYSE'S HALL MUSEUM

Bury's grand **art gallery** (☎ 01284-762081; www .burystedmundsartgallery.org; Cornhill; adult/child £1/50p; ✆ 10.30am-5pm Tue-Sat) is housed in a beautiful 18th-century former theatre and hosts a top-notch selection of temporary exhibitions of contemporary art.

Just across the square, **Moyse's Hall Museum** (☎ 01284-706183; Cornhill; adult/child £3/2; ✆ 10am-5pm) wows with its impressive 12th-century undercroft and tells some particularly gruesome stories in a room dedicated to death, burial and witchcraft. Among other curiosities, you'll discover a mummified cat that was purposefully buried alive in a building's walls, and a book bound in the tanned skin of an infamous murderer.

Sleeping

Churchgate House (☎ 01284-750233; www.churchgate house.co.uk; 35 Churchgate St; s/d from £55/90; P ☐ wi-fi) This beautiful Georgian house in the centre of town has spacious rooms decked out in glorious period style. From the antique beds and dressers to the gilt-framed prints and cosy armchairs this place just oozes tradition.

Ounce House (☎ 01284-761779; www.ouncehouse .co.uk; Northgate St; s/d from £75/110; P) Heavy swag curtains, plenty of gilt, antique furniture and tasteful florals abound at this dignified Victorian merchant's house in the centre of town. There are only a few rooms up for grabs here so if classical elegance is your thing, book in advance.

Angel Hotel (☎ 01284-714000; www.theangel.co.uk; 3 Angel Hill; s/d from £75/137; P ☐) Peeking from behind a shaggy mane of vines, this famous old coaching inn has hosted many a dignitary in its long history, including fictional celebrity Mr Pickwick who, Dickens wrote, enjoyed an 'excellent roast dinner' here. Rooms are split between a slick contemporary wing and a traditional Georgian building.

Eating

Zen Noodle Bar (☎ 01284-723559; 6 Angel Lane; mains £7-9; ✆ closed Sun) Floor-to-ceiling windows bathe this sleek and contemporary Japanese restaurant in light. The menu also features Thai and Chinese rice dishes and a tempting array of starters for sharing.

Grid (☎ 01284-706004; www.thegridrestaurant.co.uk; 34 Abbeygate St; mains £9-15, set 2-course lunch/dinner £10.50/14.95) Set in a 16th-century building but all slick, modern style, this relaxed restaurant

THE ECCENTRIC EARL

The Hervey family had such a reputation for eccentricity that it was said of them that when 'God created the human race he made men, women and Herveys'. Perhaps the biggest weirdo of them all was the creator of Ickworth House, Frederick. As Bishop of Derry (Ireland) he was renowned not for his piety but for his agnosticism, vanity and oddity: he would force his clergymen to race each other through peat bogs in the middle of the night, sprinkle flour on the floor of his house to catch night-time adulterers, champion the cause of Catholic emancipation (he was, after all, a Protestant bishop) and earn himself the sobriquet of 'wicked prelate' from George III.

Not content with his life in Ireland, in later years Frederick took to travelling around Europe, where he indulged each and every one of his passions: women, wine, art and intrigue. He tried to pass himself off as a spy in France, horrified visiting English aristocrats with his dress sense and manners in Italy, and once chucked a bowl of pasta onto a religious procession because he hated the sound of tinkling bells.

serves a good selection of sandwiches (£6) and light bites (£5) as well as full meals during the day and a menu of modern English dishes by night.

Maison Bleue (☎ 01284-760623; www.maisonbleue .co.uk; 31 Churchgate St; mains £13.50-19.95; 🕙 lunch & dinner Tue-Sat) Muted colours, pale leather banquettes, white linens and contemporary style merge with a menu of imaginative dishes in this seafood restaurant. Although the menu is heavy on fish and seafood there are some vegetarian and meat dishes available.

Drinking

Nutshell (☎ 01284-764867; The Traverse) Recognised by the *Guinness Book of Records* as Britain's smallest, this midget-sized timber-framed pub is an absolute gem and a tourist attraction in its own right. Mind how you knock back a pint here as in the crush you never know who you're going to elbow.

Getting There & Away

Centrally placed, Bury is a convenient point from which to explore western Suffolk. There are three daily National Express buses to London (£12.80, 2½ hours). From Cambridge, Stagecoach runs bus 11 to Bury (65 minutes) hourly from Monday to Saturday; the last bus back to Cambridge leaves at 7.45pm.

Trains go to Ipswich (£6.40, 30 to 40 minutes, two per hour), Ely (£7.60, 30 minutes, six daily) and hourly to Cambridge (£7.60, 44 minutes), all of which have links to London.

AROUND BURY ST EDMUNDS
Ickworth House & Park

The puffed-up pomposity of stately home **Ickworth House** (NT; ☎ 01284-735270; www.national trust.org/ickworth; adult/child house & park £8.30/3.30, park only £4.20/1.10; 🕙 house 1-5pm Fri-Tue mid-Mar–Sep, to 4.30pm Oct, park 8am-8pm year-round) is palpable from the minute you catch sight of its immense oval rotunda and wide outspread wings. The building is the whimsical creation of fourth earl of Bristol and Bishop of Derry, Frederick Hervey (1730–1803; see above), and contains fine paintings by Titian, Gainsborough and Velasquez. There's also a lovely Italian garden, parkland bearing the landscaping eye of Capability Brown, a deer enclosure and a hide to explore.

The east wing of the house now functions as the slick **Ickworth Hotel** (☎ 01284-735350; www .ickworthhotel.com; d from £290; 🅿 🖵), where the traditional surroundings mix with designer furniture and contemporary style to create a luxurious country hideout. Despite its glam design families are very welcome with a play group and games room laid on.

Ickworth is 3 miles southwest of Bury on the A143. Burtons buses 344 and 345 from Bury train station (15 minutes) to Haverhill can drop you nearby.

ALDEBURGH
pop 2790

One of the region's most charming coastal towns, the small fishing and boat-building village of Aldeburgh has an understated charm that attracts visitors back year after year. Ramshackle fishing huts sell fresh-from-the-nets catch, handsome pastel-coloured houses, independent shops and art galleries line the High St and a sweeping shingle beach stretches along the shore offering tranquil big-sky views. Although it's a popular place, the town remains defiantly unchanged with a low-key atmosphere and a great choice of food and accommodation.

Aldeburgh also has a lively cultural scene. Composer Benjamin Britten and lesser-known poet George Crabbe both lived and worked here; Britten founded East Anglia's primary arts and music festival, the **Aldeburgh Festival** (☎ 01728-687110; www.aldeburgh.co.uk), which takes place in June and has been going for over 60 years. Britten's legacy is commemorated by Maggi Hambling's wonderful *Scallop* sculpture, a short stroll left along the seashore.

Aldeburgh's other photogenic gem is the intricately carved and timber-framed **Moot Hall** (☎ 01728-454666; www.aldeburghmuseum.ork.uk; adult/child £1/free; 2.30-5pm Sat & Sun Apr, 2.30-5pm May, Sep & Oct, noon-5pm Jun-Aug), which now houses a local history museum.

If you fancy a day in the kitchen, the popular **Aldeburgh Cookery School** (☎ 01728-454039; www .aldeburghcookeryschool.com; 84 High St) offers hands-on day courses (£150) ranging from fish or Italian food classes to Thai, vegetarian, and shellfish, and cookery courses aimed specifically at men.

Information can be found at the **tourist office** (☎ 01728-453637; atic@suffolkcoastal.gov.uk; 152 High St; 9am-5.30pm Apr-Oct, 9am-5.30pm Mon-Sat, 9am-5pm Sun Nov-Mar).

Activities

A fun way to enjoy the bracing salt air is by following the Suffolk Coast and Heaths Path, which passes around half a mile north of Aldeburgh, along the coast for a few miles. Alternatively, from Aldeburgh follow the path inland for a 3-mile walk towards the village of Snape, through some pleasant wooded areas and fields.

Sleeping

Blaxhall YHA (☎ 0845 371 9305; www.yha.org.uk; Heath Walk; dm £15.95; P) Housed in an old school building that gives it an extra-institutional aura, this hostel nonetheless has small great-value dorms. It's situated in good walking, cycling and birding country 6 miles from Aldeburgh, and west of Snape Maltings. Book ahead as it's popular with groups.

Toll House (☎ 01728-453239; www.tollhouse.travel bugged.com; 50 Victoria Rd; s/d £60/75; P) You'll find small but immaculate rooms at this lovely Victorian-era B&B on the way in to town. The rooms have cast-iron beds, pretty floral bedspreads and simple but tasteful style.

our pick **Ocean House** (☎ 01728-452094; www.ocean housealdeburgh.co.uk; 25 Crag Path; s/d £70/90) Right on seafront and with only the sound of the waves to lull you to sleep at night, this beautiful Victorian guest house has wonderfully cosy, period-styled rooms. Expect pale pastels, subtle florals and tasteful furniture and the sound of classical music wafting from the rooms occupied by visiting music students. There's a grand piano on the top floor, a gaily painted rocking horse, bikes to borrow and table tennis in the cellar.

Dunan House (☎ 01728-452486; www.dunanhouse .co.uk; 41 Park Rd; r incl breakfast £75-85) Set well back off the street in lovely gardens, this charming B&B has a range of individually styled rooms mixing contemporary and traditional elements to surprisingly good effect. With friendly hosts and breakfast assembled from local, wild and home-grown produce it's a real treat.

Eating

Fish and Chip Shop (☎ 01728-452250; 226 High Street; fish & chips £4-5; noon-2pm & 5-8pm Mon-Sat, noon-7pm Sun) Aldeburgh has a reputation for the finest fish and chips in the area, and this place generally has a queue coming right out onto the street thanks to its succulent battered fish, and crisp and airy chips.

Regatta Restaurant (☎ 01728-452011; www .regattaaldeburgh.com; 171 High St; mains £8.50-13.50; noon-2pm & 6-10pm) Good ol' English seaside food is given star treatment at this sleek, contemporary restaurant where local fish is the main attraction. The celebrated owner-chef supplements his wonderful seafood with meat and vegetarian options and regular gourmet nights.

Lighthouse (☎ 01728-453377; www.lighthouserest aurant.co.uk; 77 High St; mains £9-17; 10am-2pm & 6.30-late) This unassuming bistro-style restaurant is a fantastic place to dine, with wooden tables and floors, a menu of simple but sensational international dishes, and a relaxed and friendly atmosphere. Despite the top-notch food and accolades piled upon it children are very welcome.

Cafe 152 (☎ 01728-454594; www.152aldeburgh.co .uk; 152 High St; mains £10-15; 10am-3pm & 6-10pm) Freshly netted seafood is always the dish of the day in this stylishly minimalist bistro, which serves a creative seasonal menu of modern English dishes ranging from fantastic fish to local beef and pork.

Getting There & Away

Aldeburgh is not well connected in terms of transport and your best bet is to take one of the frequent bus services to Ipswich (1½ hours) and to continue on from there.

AROUND ALDEBURGH

Strung along the coastline north of Aldeburgh is a poignant trail of serene and little-visited coastal heritage towns that are gradually succumbing to the sea. Most dramatically, the once-thriving port town of Dunwich is now a quiet village, with 12 churches and chapels and hundreds of houses washed away by the sea.

The region is a favourite haunt of the binocular-wielding bird-watcher brigade, and **RSPB Minsmere** (☎ 01728-648281; Westleton; adult/child £5/1.50; ☼ 9am-dusk) flickers with airborne activity year-round. Another step south towards Aldeburgh is the odd early-20th-century 'Tudorbethan' holiday village of **Thorpeness**, which sports idiosyncratic follies, a windmill and a boating lake. Looming just north of Thorpeness is **Sizewell**, a notorious nuclear-power plant topped by a golf-ball-shaped tumour.

With public transport lacking you'll need your own wheels, or the will to walk or bike this stretch of peaceful and varied coastline.

Orford

This diminutive village, 6 miles south of Snape Maltings, is worth visiting for the odd polygonal keep of the English Heritage **Orford Castle** (☎ 01394-450472; adult/child £4.90/2.50; ☼ 10am-6pm Apr-Sep, 10am-4pm Thu-Mon Oct-Mar), an innovative 12th-century, 18-sided drum design with three square turrets.

From here you can catch a ferry to **Orford Ness** (NT; ☎ 01728-648024; admission incl ferry crossing adult/child £6.50/3.25; ☼ 10am-5pm Tue-Sat Jul-Sep, Sat only May-Jun & Oct), the largest vegetated shingle spit in Europe. Once used as a secret military testing ground, it is now home to a nature reserve and many rare wading birds, animals and plants. There's a 3-mile path lined with information boards and military installations. Ferries run from Orford Quay: the last ferry departs at 2pm and returns from the reserve at 5pm.

On your return make a beeline for the **Butley Orford Oysterage** (☎ 01394-450277; www.butley orfordoysterage.co.uk; mains £7-10), where you'll find fresh seafood, smoked fish and local oysters just waiting to be gobbled up. For overnight stays try the **Old Butcher's Shop B&B** (☎ 01394-450517; www.oldbutchers-orford.co.uk; 111 Church St; s/d from £45/65), a handsome 19th-century house with simple, traditional rooms.

SOUTHWOLD
pop 3858

Southwold is the kind of genteel seaside resort where beach huts cost an arm and a leg (one reputedly changed hands recently for a whopping £48,000) and the visitors are ever so posh. Its reputation as a well-heeled holiday getaway has earned it the nickname 'Kensington-on-Sea' after the upmarket London borough, and its lovely sandy beach, pebble-walled cottages, cannon-dotted clifftop and rows of beachfront bathing huts are all undeniably picturesque. Over the years the town has attracted many artists, including Turner, Charles Rennie Mackintosh, Lucian Freud and Damien Hirst.

However, this down-to-earth town also has a traditional pier, boat rides, fish and chips and its very own brewery **Adnams** (☎ 01502-727200; www.adnams.co.uk; Adnams Pl, Sole Bay Brewery). The **tourist office** (☎ 01502-724729; www.visit-southwold.co.uk; 69 High St; ☼ 10am-5pm Mon-Sat, 11am-4pm Sun Easter-Oct, 10.30am-3.30pm Mon-Fri, to 4.30pm Sat Oct-Mar) can help with accommodation and information.

Starting inland, the **Church of St Edmund** (Church St; admission free; ☼ 9am-6pm Jun-Aug, to 4pm rest of year) is worth a quick peek for its fabulous medieval screen and 15th-century bloodshot-eyed Jack-o-the-clock, which grumpily overlooks the church's rear. A mere stone's throw away is an old weavers' cottage that now houses the **Southwold Museum** (☎ 01502-726097; www.south woldmuseum.org; 9-11 Victoria St; admission free; ☼ 10.30am-noon & 2-4pm Aug, 2-4pm Apr-Oct), where you can gen up on the explosive 132-ship and 50,000-men Battle of Solebay (1672), fought just off the coast.

But Southwold's shorefront is really the place to be. Take time to amble along its promenade and admire the squat 19th-century **lighthouse** before ending up at the cute little **pier** (☎ 01502-722105; www.southwoldpier.co.uk), first built in 1899 but recently reconstructed. In the 'under the pier' show you'll find a quirky collection of handmade slot machines, a mobility masterclass for zimmerframe-users and a dog's-eye view of Southwold.

If you fancy a bit of a water jaunt, the **Coastal Voyager** (☎ 07887 525082; www.coastalvoyager.co.uk)

offers a range of boat trips, including a 30-minute high-speed Sea Blast (adult/child £18/9), a leisurely river cruise (£22/11) to nearby Blythburgh and a three-hour trip to Scroby Sands (£27/13) to see a seal colony and wind farm.

Southwold's hippest event is the **Latitude Festival** (www.latitudefestival.co.uk) held in Henham Park in mid-July. An eclectic mix of music, literature, dance, drama and comedy, its stunning location and manageable size make it popular with festival-goers fed up with fields of mud and never-ending queues.

Sleeping & Eating

Despite Southwold's charm and popularity, decent accommodation is thin on the ground.

Gorse House (☎ 01502-725468; www.gorsehouse .com; 19B Halesworth Rd; Reydon; d from £55; P) A 10-minute walk from the seafront but well worth the effort, this lovely B&B is one of the best in the area. The two rooms here are newly decorated in simple, contemporary style with subtle-patterned wallpapers, silky throws and flat-screen TVs.

Home @ 21 (☎ 01502-722573; www.northparade .southwold.info; 21 North Pde; r £65-85) This friendly place has rooms with four-poster or half-tester beds that are slightly out of keeping with their surroundings but comfortable none the less.

Sutherland House (☎ 01502-724544; www.suther landhouse.co.uk; 56 High St; d £140-200; P 💻 wi-fi) Set in a beautiful 15th-century house dripping with character and period features, this small hotel has just three rooms featuring pargeted ceilings, exposed beams and elm floorboards but decked out in sleek, modern style. The top-notch restaurant (mains £10 to £20) specialises in local food with the menu showing how many miles the principal ingredient in each dish has travelled.

Crown (☎ 01502-722275; www.adnams.co.uk; 90 High St; mains £12-17; 🕙 lunch & dinner) This special old posting inn has a superb restaurant that changes its meaty seasonal menu daily. It also has a wine bar, wood-panelled snugs and serves real ales. It also has a few plush rooms (doubles from £132).

Getting There & Away

Bus connections are surprisingly limited: your best bet is to catch one of the hourly services to Lowestoft (45 minutes) or Hales-worth train station (30 minutes) and continue from there.

AROUND SOUTHWOLD
Walberswick

These days it requires an interstellar leap of the imagination to picture the sleepy seaside village of Walberswick as the thriving medieval port it once was. Nestled behind sandy dunes, it's a tranquil little backwater popular with well-heeled holidaymakers and home to a huddle of fresh-fish stalls.

If you've got your timing right, don't miss the chance to participate in the bizarre **British Open Crabbing Championships** (☎ 01502-722359; www.walberswick.ws/crabbing), held here in July or August, in which contestants compete to capture the heaviest crustacean. Anyone can take part, and competition is fierce with baits a closely guarded secret.

Just south of the village is the largest block of freshwater reedbed in Britain, incorporated into the **Walberswick National Nature Reserve** (☎ 01502-676171; www.naturalengland.org.uk) and home to otters, deer and rare butterflies. It's accessed by a web of public footpaths.

Oak beams, open fires and flagstone floors make the 600-year-old **Bell Inn** (☎ 01502-723109; www.bellinn-walberswick.co.uk; mains £8-10) your best bet by far for food and bedding (singles/doubles from £70/90). The bar downstairs serves award-winning seafood but also invites hiding behind high wooden settles with a pint and newspaper. The spacious en suite rooms have pretty decor and muted colour schemes.

Walberswick is a mile south of Southwold separated by the River Blyth. Pick up the path from Southwold's High St to reach a pedestrian bridge, or catch the summer **ferry** (70p; 🕙 10am-12.30pm & 2-5pm Jun-Sep, 10am-5pm weekends only Easter-May & Oct), which crosses at half-hourly intervals.

NORFOLK

Big skies, sweeping beaches, windswept marshes, meandering inland waterways and pretty flint houses make up the county of Norfolk, a handsome rural getaway with a thriving regional capital. You're never far from water here, whether it's the tranquil setting of rivers and windmills in the Norfolk Broads or the wide sandy beaches, fishing boats and nature reserves along the coast. They say the locals have 'one foot on the land, and one in the sea' and beach and boating holidays are certainly a highlight of the area, but twitchers flock here too for some of the country's best bird-watching, and in Norwich, the county's bustling capital, you'll find a stunning cathedral and castle, medieval churches, a lively market and an excellent choice of pubs, clubs and restaurants.

Information

Some handy websites:

Independent Traveller's Norfolk (www.itnorfolk .co.uk)

Norfolk Coast (www.norfolkcoast.co.uk)

Norfolk Tourist Attractions (www.norfolktourist attractions.co.uk)

Visit Norfolk (www.visitnorfolk.co.uk)

Visit West Norfolk (www.visitwestnorfolk.com)

Activities

Waymarked walking trails include the well-known Peddars Way and Norfolk Coast Path (p425). Other long-distance paths include the **Weavers Way**, a 57-mile trail from Cromer to Great Yarmouth, and the **Angles Way** (www.east suffolklinewalks.co.uk/anglesway), which negotiates the valleys of the Rivers Waveney and Little Ouse for 70 miles. Meanwhile the **Wherryman's Way** (www.wherrymansway.net) is a 35-mile walking and cycling route through the Broads, following the River Yare from Norwich to Great Yarmouth.

For a real challenge, the **Around Norfolk Walk** is a 220-mile circuit that combines most of the above.

If you're planning to do the Norfolk Coast Path and don't fancy carrying your bags, **Walk Free** (☎ 01328-711902; www.walk-free.co.uk; per bag £5) provides a bag courier service.

Getting Around

For comprehensive travel advice and timetable information contact **Traveline East Anglia** (☎ 0871 200 22 33; www.travelineeastanglia.co.uk).

NORWICH

pop 121,550

The affluent and easy-going city of Norwich (pronounced norritch) is a rich tapestry of meandering laneways liberally sprinkled with the spoils of the city's heyday at the height of the medieval wool boom. A magnificent cathedral lords it over the city centre from one end and a sturdy Norman castle from the other. Around these two landmarks a series of leafy greens, grand squares, quiet lanes, crooked half-timbered buildings and a host of medieval churches pan out across this compact and artsy city. Meanwhile thriving markets, modern shopping centres, contemporary-art galleries and a young student population give the city a genial, debonair attitude that makes it one of the most appealing cities in East Anglia. Add easy access to the Broads and sweeping beaches along the coast and you have an excellent base to use for touring the area.

History

Though Norwich's history stretches back well over a thousand years, the city's golden age was during the Middle Ages, when it was England's most important city after London. Its relative isolation meant that it traditionally had stronger ties to the Low Countries than to London and when Edward III encouraged Flemish weavers to settle here in the 14th century this connection was sealed. The arrival of the immigrants helped establish the wool industry that fattened the city and sustained it right through to the 18th century.

Mass immigration from the Low Countries peaked in the troubled 16th century. In 1579 more than a third of the town's citizens were foreigners of a staunch Protestant stock, which proved beneficial during the Civil War when the Protestant parliamentarians caused Norwich little strife.

Today the spoils of this rich period in the city's history are still evident, with 36 medieval churches (see www.norwichchurches .co.uk) adorning the streets whose layout is largely unchanged since this time.

Orientation

The castle crowns central Norwich, surrounded by a compact medieval street plan. Within the circle of river and city walls, there are scattered medieval churches and the Anglican cathedral. At the city's heart is its candy-stripe canopied market (Market Square; open approximately 8am to 4.30pm), one of the biggest and oldest markets in England, running since 1025. The enormous modern Forum building houses Norfolk's main library and the tourist office.

NORWICH

0 — 400 m
0 — 0.2 miles

INFORMATION		
Battlenet	1	B4
Boots	2	C4
Library	(see 4)	
Post Office	3	C4
Tourist Office	4	B4

SIGHTS & ACTIVITIES		
Art Gallery	(see 10)	
Bridewell Museum	5	C4
Broads Boatrains	6	C2
Discover Norwich pick up point	7	B4
Dragon Hall	8	D4
Museum	(see 10)	
Mustard Shop	9	B3
Norwich Castle	10	C3
Norwich Cathedral	11	C3
Royal Norfolk Regimental Museum	12	C3
Strangers' Hall	13	B3

SLEEPING		
By Appointment	14	B2
Georgian House Hotel	15	A4
No3 Princes St	16	C3

EATING		
Britons Arms Coffee House & Restaurant	17	C3
Caley's Cocoa Cafe	18	B3
Elm Hill Brasserie	19	C3
Greenhouse	20	B3
Library	21	B3
Pinocchio's	22	B3
Pulse Cafe	23	B3
Shiki	24	C3
Tatlers	25	C3
Waffle House	26	B3

DRINKING		
Adam & Eve's	27	D2
Erpingham House	28	C3
Ten Bells	29	A3

ENTERTAINMENT		
Mercy	30	D3
Norwich Arts Centre	31	A3

Norwich Puppet Theatre	32	C2
Optic	33	C3
St Andrew's & Blackfriars' Hall	34	C3
Theatre Royal	35	B4

TRANSPORT		
Bus Station	36	B4
Bus to Sainsbury Centre	37	C3

Information

Banks and ATMs can be found around the Market Square.

Battlenet (☎ 01603-765595; 2a Queens Rd; per hr £2; ☽ 11am-6pm Mon-Tue, 11am-9pm Wed, 11am-10pm Thu & Fri, 10am-7pm Sat, 10am-6pm Sun) Internet cafe popular with gamers.

Boots (☎ 01603-767970; 19 Castle Mall) Well-stocked pharmacy.

Library (☎ 01603-774774; The Forum; ☽ 9am-9.30pm Mon-Fri, 9am-8.30pm Sat, 10.30am-4.30pm Sun) Free internet for those with ID and the patience to fill out a few forms.

Norfolk & Norwich University Hospital (☎ 01603-286286; Colney Lane) Four miles west of the centre.

Post office (☎ 01603-761635; 84-85 Castle Mall)

Tourist office (☎ 01603-727927; www.visitnorwich .co.uk; The Forum; ☽ 9.30am-6pm Mon-Sat, 10.30am-

4.30pm Sun Apr-Oct, 9.30am-5.30pm Mon-Sat Nov-Mar) Just inside the Forum on Millennium Plain.

Sights

NORWICH CASTLE, MUSEUM & ART GALLERY

Perched on a hilltop overlooking central Norwich, this massive Norman **castle keep** (☎ 01603-493636; www.museums.norfolk.gov.uk; castle & exhibitions adult/child £5.80/4.25, exhibitions £3/2.20; ☽ 10am-4.30pm Mon-Fri, 10am-5pm Sat, 1-5pm Sun, 10am-5.30pm Mon-Sat school hols) is a sturdy example of 12th-century aristocratic living. The castle is one of the best-preserved examples of Anglo-Norman military architecture in the country, despite a 19th-century facelift and a gigantic shopping centre grafted to one side.

It's now home to an art gallery and superb interactive museum. The **museum** crams in a wealth of history, including lively exhibits on Boudicca and the Iceni, the Anglo-Saxons and Vikings, natural-history displays and even an Egyptian gallery complete with mummies. Every room is enlivened with plenty of fun for kids, but best of all is the atmospheric keep itself, which sends shivers down the spine with graphic displays on grisly punishments meted out in its days as a medieval prison. Guided tours (£2) also run around the battlements (minimum age eight) and dungeons (mini mum age five).

Meanwhile the **art gallery** houses paintings of the acclaimed 19th-century Norwich School of landscape painting founded by John Crome and – trust the English – the world's largest collection of ceramic teapots.

A claustrophobic tunnel from the castle also emerges into a reconstructed WWI trench at the **Royal Norfolk Regimental Museum** (☎ 01603-493649; www.rnrm.org.uk; Shirehall, Market Ave; adult/child £2/1.20; ⊗ 10am-4.30pm Tue-Fri, 10am-5pm Sat), which details the history of the local regiment since 1830. It has another less dramatic entrance from the road.

NORWICH CATHEDRAL

Norwich's most stunning landmark is the magnificent Anglican **cathedral** (☎ 01603-218300; www.cathedral.org.uk; suggested donation £5; ⊗ 7am-7pm mid May–mid-Sep, to 6pm mid-Sep–mid-May), its barbed spire soaring higher than any in England except Salisbury, while the size of its cloisters is second to none.

Begun in 1096, the cathedral is one of the finest Anglo-Norman abbey churches in the country, rivalled only perhaps by Durham. The sheer size of its nave is impressive but its most renowned feature is the superb Gothic rib-vaulting added in 1463. Among the spidery stonework are 1200 sculpted roof bosses depicting bible stories. Together they represent one of the finest achievements of English medieval masonry.

Similar bosses can be seen in closer detail in the cathedral's remarkable cloisters. Built between 1297 and 1430, the two-storey cloisters are unique in England today and were originally built to house a community of about 100 monks.

Outside the cathedral's eastern end is the grave of the WWI heroine Edith Cavell, a Norfolk-born nurse who was executed for helping hundreds of Allied soldiers escape from German-occupied Belgium. The cathedral close also contains handsome houses and the old chapel of King Edward VI School (where English hero Admiral Nelson was educated). Its current students make up the choir, which performs in at least one of the three services held daily.

Fascinating guided tours of the cathedral (minimum donation £1.50) take place daily at 10.45am, 12.30pm and 2.15pm.

ELM HILL

Head west from the cathedral up Wensum St to reach Elm Hill, an utterly charming medieval cobbled street of crooked timber beams and doors, intriguing shops and snug cafes. It's one of the oldest intact streets in the city and now centre of the local antique business. At the far end of Wensum St is Tombland, where the market was originally located. Despite its ominous overtones, 'tomb' is an old Norse word for empty, hence space for a market.

OTHER MUSEUMS

Though it's more shop than museum, the **Mustard Shop** (☎ 01603-627889; www.colmansmustard shop.com; 15 Royal Arcade; admission free; ⊗ 9.30am-5pm Mon-Sat) tells the 200-year story of Colman's Mustard, a famous local product. It's in the lavish art-nouveau Royal Arcade.

Nearby is **Bridewell Museum** (☎ 01603-629127; Bridewell Alley; adult/child £3.20/1.75; ⊗ 10am-4.30pm Tue-Fri, 10am-5pm Sat Easter-Oct), housed in a former merchant's house and 14th-century bridewell or 'prison for women, beggars and tramps', and filled with fascinating paraphernalia and reconstructions of Norwich's principal shops and industries.

Two-hundred and fifty metres west, along St Andrew's St and Charing Cross, is the mazelike **Strangers' Hall** (☎ 01603-667229; adult/child £3.20/1.75; ⊗ 10.30am-4.30pm Wed & Sat), an early-14th-century town house with atmospheric rooms furnished in period styles from Tudor to Victorian. Another remarkable medieval building, originally used as a trading hall, is **Dragon Hall** (☎ 01603-663922; www.dragonhall.org; 115-123 King St; adult/child £5/3; ⊗ 10am-5pm Mon-Fri, 11am-4pm Sun), with a stunning crown-post roof and a timber-framed great hall dating from 1430.

SAINSBURY CENTRE FOR VISUAL ARTS

Housed in the first major building by Norman Foster, now the darling of Britain's architectural set, the **Sainsbury Centre** (☎ 01603-593199; www.scva.org.uk; admission free; ☼ 10am-5pm Tue & Thu-Sun, to 8pm Wed) is the most important centre for the arts in East Anglia. Filled with an eclectic collection of works by Picasso, Moore, Degas and Bacon displayed beside art from Africa, the Pacific and the Americas, it also houses changing exhibitions that cover everything from local heritage to international art movements. Even if you're not an art buff you're almost guaranteed to find something of interest going on here.

To get here take bus 25, 26 or 27 from Castle Meadow (20 minutes).

Tours

The tourist office organises a dizzying array of guided **city walks** (adult/child £4/1.50) between March and October, with daily walks from June to September. Walks depart at 11.30am or 2pm from the office. Check for up-to-date details online at www.visitnorwich.co.uk. **City Sightseeing** (☎ 0871 666000; www.city-sightseeing.com; adult/child £8/4; ☼ hourly 10.15am-4.15pm Apr-Oct) runs a hop-on hop-off bus service stopping at nine destinations around the city centre including city hall. You can take a similar tour by road train with **Discover Norwich** (☎ 01603-440015; www.discovernorwich.com; adult/child £4/2) from Easter to October. Trains depart from opposite Theatre Royal five times a day from 10am to 3pm, with an evening tour at 7pm Thursday to Saturday from June to August (must be prebooked). Or if you prefer to potter about on the river, **Broads Boatrains** (☎ 01603-701701; www.cityboats.co.uk; 1hr city cruise adult/child £8.50/6.50) runs a variety of cruises from Griffin Lane, Station Quay, and Elm Hill Quay.

Sleeping

BUDGET

Norwich has a bit of a dearth of budget-range accommodation, and floral-patterned B&Bs that have seen better days are your only choice in this price category. You'll find most of them around the train station or outside the ring road.

Edmar Lodge (☎ 01603-615599; www.edmarlodge.co.uk; 64 Earlham Rd; s/d from £38/43; P □ wi-fi) Although the rooms here are somewhat dated, the facilities are modern with en suite bathrooms, flat-screen TVs, DVD players and free

wi-fi. It's a 10-minute walk from town but worth the trip.

Eaton Bower (☎ 01603-462204; www.eatonbower.co.uk; 20 Mile End Rd; s/d from £40/50; P □ wi-fi) A little out of town but worth the effort, this small B&B has a choice of cosy rooms with subtle patterns and traditional styling. En suite bathrooms, free wi-fi, private parking and a touch of period character make it one of the best bets in this price range.

Abbey Hotel (☎ 01603-612915; 16 Stracey Rd; s/d with bathroom £50/65, without bathroom £29/58) This Victorian terraced house behind the station has a range of simple floral rooms, most of which share bathrooms. It's a good deal close to the city centre and has friendly service but there's little character.

MIDRANGE & TOP END

Beaufort Lodge (☎ 01603-667402; www.beaufortlodge.com; 60-62 Earlham Rd; s/d £45/60; P □) Giant windows wash the rooms in this Victorian house with light, and the spacious bedrooms feature pretty fabrics and wallpapers in period style. The effect is bright and airy, with tasteful traditional touches, en suite bathrooms and plenty of space. It's a great deal and just a 10-minute walk from town.

Gothic House (☎ 01603-631879; www.gothic-house-norwich.com; King's Head Yard, Magdalen St; s/d £55/90; P □ wi-fi) Set in a quiet courtyard in the heart of the city, this Grade II Regency house has two immaculate rooms with faithful period decor. Each has a private bathroom, great character and buckets of charm.

No3 Princes St (☎ 01603-662692; www.3princes-norwich.co.uk; 3 Princes St; s/d incl breakfast £60/85; □ wi-fi) There are four simple, tasteful rooms in this handsome red-brick Georgian home in the city's heart. Each is individually styled and has its own unique character. Three overlook St Andrew's; the other has a view of a pretty gravel-filled back courtyard. The Continental breakfasts are eaten in your room.

our pick **By Appointment** (☎ 01603-630730; www.byappointmentnorwich.co.uk; 25-29 St George's St; s/d incl breakfast from £70/110; □) This fabulously theatrical and delightfully eccentric B&B occupies three heavy-beamed 15th-century merchant's houses, also home to a labyrinthine restaurant well known for its classic English fare. Its antique furniture, creaky charm and superb breakfasts make this well worth booking in advance.

Georgian House Hotel (☎ 01603-615655; www
.georgian-hotel.co.uk; 32-34 Unthank Rd; s/d from £90/115;
P 🗐 wi-fi) A rambling, elegant Victorian
house turned hotel, this place has a choice
of spacious, modern rooms decked out in
contemporary style. There's a large tree-filled
garden and a popular restaurant (mains £12
to £18).

Eating

Norwich has a great choice of places to eat
with plenty of options for vegetarians.

BUDGET

Greenhouse (☎ 01603-631007; www.greenhousetrust
.co.uk; 42-48 Bethel St; snacks & mains £3.50-6; 🕑 10am-
5pm Tue-Sat) This organic, free-trade, vegetar-
ian/vegan cafe is bound to leave you feeling
wholesome with a menu of simple dishes,
noticeboards crammed with posters for community events, and a lovely vine-covered,
herb-planted terrace.

our pick Pulse Cafe (☎ 01603-765562; Labour in Vain
Yard, Guildhall Hill; mains £4.50-7.50; 🕑 10am-6.30pm Mon,
10am-10pm Tue & Wed, 10am-11pm Thu-Sat, 11.30am-4pm
Sun) This funky lounge bar in the old fire station stables serves a bumper crop of hearty
vegetarian dishes from Thai curries to smoked
tofu and mushroom stroganoff, and leek and
potato pie. There's also a great choice of sambos, organic ciders and beers and scrummy
deserts. Eat in the tranquil courtyard or in
the stylish upstairs lounge.

Waffle House (☎ 01603-612790; www.wafflehouse
.co.uk; 39 St Giles St; waffles £5-9; 🕑 10am-10pm Mon-
Sat, 11am-10pm Sun) Pop in for a crisp and light
Belgian waffle with sweet or savoury toppings at this down-to-earth and friendly cafe
beloved by Norwich families, students and
professionals. Organic and free-range ingredients are used to concoct such delicacies as
vegetable and cashew stir-fry and a stunning
chocolate mousse.

The Library (☎ 01603-616606; 4a Guildhall Hill; 1/2/3
courses £6/8/10.50; 🕑 closed dinner Sun) Set in a 19th-
century library complete with original shelving, this chilled brasserie is a great spot for
a good-value lunch. The menu is heavy on
meats and fish with dishes cooked in a nifty
wood-fired grill, while the interior is sleek and
stylish with exhibitions of work by contemporary local artists.

Other options:
Caley's Cocoa Cafe (☎ 01603-629364; Guildhall,
Market Square; snacks £2-6; 🕑 9am-5pm Mon-Sat) Local

chocolate-maker's cafe serving light meals and luscious
sweets in the confection-like Guildhall's old Court of Record.
Britons Arms Coffee House & Restaurant
(☎ 01603-623367; 9 Elm Hill; mains £7; 🕑 9.30am-5pm
Mon-Sat) Fifteenth-century thatched restaurant serving
classic English dishes in a historic setting.

MIDRANGE

Pinocchio's (☎ 01603-613318; 11 St Benedict's St; mains
£7-8; 🕑 noon-2pm Tue-Sat, 5-11pm Mon-Sat) This bubbly Italian brasserie has a cheerful modern interior with plenty of quirky features including
a giant modern mural. The menu features the
usual array of pizzas and pastas as well as some
top-notch specials including slow-cooked wild
boar with juniper, orange and thyme. There's
live music on Monday and Thursday evenings
when it's best to book ahead.

Shiki (☎ 01603-619262; 6 Tombland; sushi £3-5, mains
£9-11; 🕑 closed Sun) This minimalist Japanese
restaurant has a stylish, contemporary interior
and a reputation for some of the best Asian
food in town. From delicate sushi to superb
teppanyaki, it's a firm local favourite with a
particularly friendly vibe.

Elm Hill Brasserie (☎ 01603-624847; www.elmhill
brasserie.co.uk; 2 Elm Hill; mains £11-16; 🕑 closed Sun) On
the corner of the city's most famous street,
this simple and elegant restaurant is bathed
with light from its giant windows. Scrubbed
wooden floors, contemporary style, a relaxed atmosphere and a menu of unfussy,
classic French dishes made from seasonal,
local ingredients has the punters coming
in droves.

Tatlers (☎ 01603-766670; www.tatlers.com; 21 Tombland; set lunch £14-18, dinner mains £12-17; 🕑 closed Sun)
This converted Victorian town house is home
to one of the city's best eateries, where local
suppliers and ingredients are as important
as the final menu. The truly divine dishes
are modern English with a strong French
influence and are served in a series of unpretentious dining rooms. The set lunch is an
excellent-value choice but book in advance.

Drinking

It was once said that Norwich had a pub
for every day of the year and although that
may not be completely true, there's certainly plenty of choice. You'll find hip and
trendy or quaint and traditional pubs all
across the city centre, but start your quest
in Tombland or St Benedict's St for a taste
of what's on offer.

Adam & Eve's (☎ 01603-667423; www.adamandevenor wich.co.uk; Bishopsgate) A 13th-century brew-house built to quench the thirst of cathedral builders, this is now Norwich's oldest-surviving pub, and an adorable little sunken-floored gem. It's a tiny place just loaded with character and has a pleasant outdoor courtyard.

Ten Bells (☎ 01603-667833; 76 St Benedict's St) This is this kind of faded 18th-century pub where people feel instantly at ease, calmed by the real ales, mellow red velvet and quirky memorabilia, and amused by the red phone booth in the corner. It also fancies itself as an intellectuals' hang-out, with poetry readings and arts-school regulars.

Erpingham House (☎ 01603-630090; www.kitchen andbar.co.uk; 22 Tombland; ☺ noon-midnight Mon-Thu, noon-2am Fri & Sat) If you're looking for something more modern, this stylish bar and brasserie is set in a grand old house by the cathedral. There's a sleek interior and plenty of wine and cocktail-drinking luvvies to mingle with.

Entertainment

Norwich has a flourishing arts scene and pulsating weekend nightlife. For what's on information from ballet to boozing try www.norwichtonight.com or for live music www.norfolkgigs.co.uk.

NIGHTCLUBS

Nightclubs seem to cluster around the Prince of Wales Rd and run from 9pm or 10pm to at least 2am.

Mercy (☎ 01603-627666; www.mercynightclub.com; 86 Prince of Wales Rd; admission free-£8; ☺ Thu-Sat) A former cinema complete with mock-marble entrance and Renaissance-inspired decor, Mercy is a massive club with three dance floors, huge projection screens and DJs that favour R&B and club classics.

Optic (☎ 01603-617977; www.optic-club.co.uk; 50 Prince of Wales Rd; admission free-£8.50; ☺ Mon & Wed-Sat) This place markets itself as Norwich's upmarket club, with a strict dress code and a dislike for Burberry, facial piercings and excessive tattoos. Club nights feature everything from '70s funk to chart-topping anthems.

THEATRE

St Andrew's and Blackfriars' Halls (☎ 01603-628477; www.standrewshall.co.uk; St Andrew's Plain) Once home to Dominican Blackfriars, this spookily Gothic-looking place now serves as an impressive civic centre where concerts, markets and festivals are held.

Theatre Royal (☎ 01603-630000; www.theatreroyal norwich.co.uk; Theatre St) Features programs by touring drama, opera and ballet companies.

Norwich Arts Centre (☎ 01603-660352; www.norwich artscentre.co.uk; St Benedict's St) Also in a medieval church; has a wide-ranging program of alternative drama, concerts, dance and jazz.

Norwich Puppet Theatre (☎ 01603-629921; www .puppettheatre.co.uk; St James, Whitefriars) Set in a cute little repurposed church; goes down a treat with small and big kids.

Getting There & Away

Norwich International Airport (☎ 0844 748 0112; www .norwichinternational.com) is just 4 miles north of town, and has cheap flights to Europe and several British destinations. Bus 11 runs from the airport to the bus and rail stations hourly.

National Express runs buses to London (£14.90, three hours, five daily). First Eastern Counties runs hourly buses to King's Lynn (1½ hours) and Cromer (one hour). There are twice-hourly services to Great Yarmouth (40 minutes).

There are twice hourly train services to Ely (£13.50, one hour), hourly services to Cambridge (£12.40, 1¼ hours), as well as regular links to Peterborough (£15, 1½ hours). Twice hourly trains also go to London Liverpool Street (£40, two hours). For city cabs, call **Loyal Taxis** (☎ 01603-619619).

If you're driving, the city has six Park & Ride locations (£3.30 per vehicle).

AROUND NORWICH

Largely remodelled in the 17th century for Sir Henry Hobart, James I's chief justice, **Blickling Hall** (NT; ☎ 01263-738030; www.nationaltrust .org.uk/blickling; Blickling; adult/child £9.10/4.50, garden only £6/3; ☺ house 11am-5pm Wed-Sun mid-Mar–Jul, Sep & Oct, 11am-5pm Wed-Mon Jul & Aug, gardens 10.15am-5.15pm Wed-Sun mid-Mar–Oct, 11am-4pm Thu-Sun rest of year) began life in the 11th century as a manor house and bishop's palace. Today it is a grand Jacobean mansion set in vast parklands and as famous for its ghostly sightings as its spectacular Long Gallery.

In 1437 the isolated house was claimed by the Boleyn family and passed through the generations to Thomas, father of Anne Boleyn. Poor old Anne was executed by her husband Henry VIII in 1533 and it's said that on the anniversary of her death a coach drives up to the house, drawn by headless horses, driven by headless coachmen and containing the queen with her head on her lap.

If you're not around to witness the spectacle that day there's still quite a lot to see. The grand state rooms are stuffed with fine Georgian furniture, pictures and tapestries and the Long Gallery has an impressive Jacobean plaster ceiling. There's also an exhibition describing life below stairs with stories from those who lived and worked at Blickling over the centuries.

Blickling Hall is 15 miles north of Norwich off the A140. Sanders runs hourly buses here from Norwich bus station from June to August (20 minutes). Aylsham is the nearest train station, 1.5 miles away.

NORFOLK BROADS

A mesh of navigable slow-moving rivers, freshwater lakes, wild water meadows, fens, bogs and saltwater marshes make up the Norfolk Broads, a 125-mile stretch of lock-free waterways and the county's most beautiful attraction. The official name of the national park is the 'Norfolk and Suffolk Broads', but as most of the lakes and waterways are in Norfolk, the area is generally called simply the Norfolk Broads. The Broads are home to some of the UK's rarest plants and animals and are protected as a national park, with flourishing nature reserves and bird sanctuaries attracting gangs of bird-watchers. But the area's appeal reaches far further, with boaters, families and those in search of scenic tranquillity arriving in droves.

Despite the area's popularity, it's easy to lose yourself in the hypnotic peace of the waterways. A boat is by far the best vantage point from which to spy on its myriad wildlife, and anyone fond of splashing about will undoubtedly want to linger here. Apart from the waterways and the wildlife there are restored windmills, medieval churches and glorious gardens to explore. Walkers and cyclists will also find a web of trails crossing the region, and with the Broads' highest point, How Hill, just 12m above sea level, they're accessible for all.

The low-lying nature of the land here was the key to its modern appearance. In the 12th century the land was dug for peat, the only local source of fuel. But dig gaping holes in low-lying land and they're bound to spring a leak. Water gradually seeped through, causing marshes and eventually lakes to develop. As water levels rose, the peat-cutting industry died out and the broads became a landscape of interconnected lakes and rivers. In no other area of England has human effort changed the natural landscape so dramatically. Around How Hill you'll find many of the picturesque wind pumps first built to drain the marshland and to return water to the rivers.

Orientation
The Broads form a triangle, with the Norwich–Cromer road, the Norwich–Lowestoft road and the coastline as the three sides.

Wroxham, on the A1151 from Norwich, and Potter Heigham, on the A1062 from Wroxham, are the main centres. Along the way there are plenty of waterside pubs, villages and market towns where you can stock up on provisions, and stretches of river where you can feel you are the only person around.

Information
Details on scores of conservation centres and bird-watching hides can be found through the **Broads Authority** (☎ 01603-610734; www.broads-authority.gov.uk), including those at Berney Marshes and Breydon Water, Cockshoot Broad, Hickling Broad, Horsey Mere, How Hill, Ranworth, Strumpshaw Fen, Surlingham Church Marsh and Whitlingham. There's more information on Norfolk Broads at www.norfolkbroads.com and the RSPB at www.rspb.org.uk.

Getting Around
You can hire a variety of launches from large cabin cruisers to little craft with outboards for a couple of hours' gentle messing about on the water.

Boating holidays are operated by **Blakes** (☎ 0870 220 2498; www.blakes.co.uk) and **Hoseasons** (☎ 01502-502588; www.hoseasons.co.uk) among others. Depending on boat size, facilities and season, a boat for two to four people costs around £450 to £850 for a week including fuel and insurance.

Meanwhile boat yards around Wroxham and Potter Heigham hire out boats for shorter cruises, from an hour to several days. Look out for the traditional flat-bottomed boats known as wherries. In the height of summer, prices start from £30 for two hours, £55 for four hours and £80 for one day. Prices drop outside summer.

No previous experience is necessary, but remember to stay on the right-hand side of the river, that the rivers are tidal and to stick to the speed limit – you can be prosecuted for speeding.

If you don't feel like piloting your own boat, try **Broads Tours** (☎ Potter Heigham 01692-670711, Wroxham 01603-782207; www.broads.co.uk), which runs 1½-hour pleasure trips (adult/child £6.50/5) from April to October.

Bike and canoe hire are available from the **Broads Authority** (☎ 01603-782281; www.broads-author ity.gov.uk) from Easter to October. Bikes cost £11 per day (you can also hire child seats and tandems) while Canadian canoes cost £25 per day or £15 per half day. Bikes and canoes are available at Whitlingham, Bungay and Burgh St Peter, canoes only at Wayford Bridge, Geldeston and Wroxham, and bikes only at Clippesby, Ludham Bridge and Stokesby.

GREAT YARMOUTH
pop 90,810

On first glance Great Yarmouth is little more than a tatty traditional seaside resort complete with neon-lit esplanade, jingling amusement arcades, grim greasy spoons, crazy golf and cheek-by-jowl hotels. But scratch under the surface and you'll find the old town rich in history and heritage.

The **tourist office** (☎ 01493-846345; www.great -yarmouth.co.uk; 25 Marine Pde; ⏰ 9.30am-5.30pm daily Easter-Oct, 9.30am-4.30pm Sat & Sun Nov-Easter) is on the seafront and can point you towards the lovely Weavers Way (p457) walking trail, which cuts into the Broads from here.

Most absorbing of Yarmouth's museums is **Time & Tide** (☎ 01493-743930; www.museums.norfolk .gov.uk; Blackfriars Rd; adult/child £5/4.15; ⏰ 10am-5pm Easter-Oct, 10am-4pm Mon-Fri, noon-4pm Sat & Sun Nov-Mar), in a Victorian herring-curing works. It tackles everything from prehistory to penny arcades and naughty postcards, but dwells on maritime heritage and reconstructs typical 17th-century row houses. There's plenty for kids, from touch screens to taking the wheel of a coastal drifter.

You can see how life was in Great Yar-mouth's **Row Houses** (EH; ☎ 01493-857900; South Quay; adult/child £3.70/1.90; ⏰ noon-5pm Apr-Sep) in these preserved houses reconstructed as they would have been in 1870 and 1942. Displays show how the 'herring girls' lived and how life was for tenants over the centuries, from wealthy merchants to tenement families.

A cluster of other museums surround his-toric South Quay. The 16th-century **Elizabethan House Museum** (NT; ☎ 01493-855746; 4 South Quay; adult/child £3.20/1.75; ⏰ 10am-5pm Mon-Fri, 1.15-5pm Sat & Sun Easter-Oct) is a fine merchant's house faithfully reconstructed to showcase Tudor and Victorian domestic life, and home to the 'Conspiracy Room' where Cromwell and his cronies decided Charles I must be executed.

Around the corner, the **Tolhouse Museum** (☎ 01493-745526; Tolhouse St; adult/child £3.20/1.75; ⏰ 10am-5pm Mon-Fri, 1.15-5pm Sat & Sun Easter-Oct) is a medieval jail dating back 700 years; it dwells on macabre inmates, witchcraft, grisly mur-ders and nasty punishments, and you can peek inside the spooky cells, all of which make it an instant hit with kids.

The **Norfolk Nelson Museum** (☎ 01493-850698; www.nelson-museum.co.uk; 26 South Quay; adult/child £3.20/1.90; ⏰ 10am-5pm Mon-Fri, 1-4pm Sun Apr-Oct, to 4pm Nov & Jan-Mar) celebrates the life, times, romances and death of the one-eyed hero of Trafalgar, who was a regular visitor to Great Yarmouth.

B&Bs are everywhere, especially chock-a-block Trafalgar St, and cost from £20 to £40 per person. One of the best is **No. 78** (☎ 01493-850001; www.no78.co.uk; 78 Marine Pde; s £35, d £45-80; 🖵) a chic, modern place that bucks the chintzy local trends and offers really beautiful, bright, contemporary rooms with an eco-conscience. The toilets have water-saving devices, tea and coffee come in resealable containers, the house uses 'green' electricity and you're asked to separate recyclables rather than binning them in your room.

There are hourly buses (40 minutes) and trains (£5.20, 33 minutes) to Norwich.

NORTH COAST NORFOLK

The north coast of Norfolk has something of a split personality, with a string of busy sea-side towns with brash attractions and hoards of people clustering along the eastern end and a collection of small villages with trendy gastropubs and boutique hotels littering the western end. In between sit stunning beaches, and the marshy coast that attracts hoards of visiting seabirds.

Cromer
pop 3800

Once a fashionable Victorian coastal resort, Cromer is now firmly part of the bucket-and-spade brigade, with a wonderful stretch of safe, sandy beachfront, family entertainment on the pier, a glut of fish and chip shops and plenty of trashy amusement arcades. The town has recently seen some major investment and may yet return to its former glory.

Stay long enough to wander off the beach and you'll find the quaint **Cromer Museum** (☎ 01263-513543; www.museums.norfolk.gov.uk; East Cottages, Tucker St; adult/under 16yr £2.90/1.75; ☽ 10am-5pm Mon-Sat, 2-5pm Sun Mar-Oct, 10am-4pm Mon-Sat Nov-Feb), set in a Victorian fisherman's cottage. The museum depicts life in the town in the 19th century and displays a series of historic photos of the area.

Just 2 miles southwest of town off the B1436 is **Felbrigg Hall** (NT; ☎ 01263-837444; adult/child £7.90/3.70; ☽ 11am-5pm Sat-Wed Mar-Oct) an elegant stately home with a fine Georgian interior. The walled gardens and orangery are particularly lovely, with access to the **Weavers Way** running through the estate.

If you wish to overnight the superb **Captain's House** (☎ 01263-515434; www.captains-house .co.uk; 5 The Crescent; d £70-140; P ⌨) is a bright and airy Georgian house with lovingly decorated rooms. There's plenty of white linen with pale pastel accents, giant, comfy beds, designer bathrooms and modern but not minimalist style.

Cromer has direct trains to Norwich hourly Monday to Saturday and services every two hours on Sunday (£5.20, 44 minutes).

Cley Marshes

One of England's premier bird-watching sites, Cley (pronounced cly) Marshes, is a mecca for twitchers with over 300 species recorded here. There's a **visitors centre** (☎ 01263-740008; www.norfolkwildlifetrust.org.uk; adult/child £3.75/free; ☽ 10am-5pm Apr-Oct, to 4pm Nov-Mar) built on high ground and a series of hides hidden amid the golden reedbeds.

If you wish to stay in the area, the stunning 17th-century **Cley Windmill** (☎ 01263-740209; www .cleymill.co.uk; d £78-145) has nine bedrooms with the one at the top reached by ladder alone. It's a wonderfully quirky place to stay, with a circular living room, great views across the marshes and rooms with four-poster, half-tester or cast-iron beds.

Blakeney Point

The pretty village of **Blakeney** was once a busy fishing and trading port before its harbour silted up. These days it's a good place to jump aboard boat trips out to a 500-strong colony of common and grey seals that live, bask and breed on nearby Blakeney Point. The hour-long trips (adult/child £8/4) run daily April to October but the best time to come is between June and August when the common seals pup. Trips run either from Blakeney Harbour or nearby Morston.

Beans Boat Trips (☎ 01263-740505; www.beansboat trips.co.uk; Morston)

Bishop's Boats (☎ 01263-740753; www.norfolkseal trips.co.uk; Blakeney Harbour)

Temples Seal Trips (☎ 01263-740791; www.sealtrips .co.uk; Morston)

Wells-next-the-Sea
pop 2451

Thronged with crowds on holiday weekends, this harbour town has plenty of seaside tat on the waterfront but a surprisingly tranquil old town set back from the sea. Attractive Georgian houses and flint cottages surround a large green, while kids bounce between toy shops and ice-cream parlours, and pensioners check out the curios.

The small **tourist office** (☎ 0871 200 3071; www .visitnorthnorfolk.com; Staithe St; ☽ 10am-5pm Mon-Sat, 10am-4pm Sun Mar–mid-Jul, Sep & Oct) can help with all inquiries and information on the **narrow-gauge steam train** (☎ 01328-711630; www.wells walsinghamrailway.co.uk; adult/child return £7.50/6) that chuffs 5 miles to **Little Walsingham**, where there are shrines and a ruined abbey that have drawn pilgrims since medieval times. The train trip takes 30 minutes and there are three to five departures daily April to October.

If you fancy staying overnight, the **Wells YHA** (☎ 0845 371 9544; www.yha.org.uk; Church Plains; dm £15.95; P) has simple rooms in an ornately gabled early-20th-century church hall. Alternatively try the tranquil **Fern Cottage** (☎ 01328-710306; www.ferncottage.co.uk; Standard Rd; s/d £60/80; P). Set in a beautiful Georgian house, the rooms here retain some period character with open fireplaces and cast-iron beds.

For food the **Globe Inn** (☎ 01328-710206; www .globeatwells.co.uk; mains 8-14; ☽ noon-2.30pm & 6-9pm) is a good bet. It's on the green and also has a selection of bright, spacious rooms with contemporary style (£65 to £110).

The Coast Hopper bus goes through Wells roughly hourly in summer on its way between Hunstanton (50 minutes) and Sheringham (45 minutes).

Wells-next-the-Sea To King's Lynn

Once past Wells the atmosphere changes: gone are the tacky seaside resorts and the crowds of weekenders and back come the beautiful Norfolk villages, their flint cottages and narrow streets awash with coloured render and beautiful flowering gardens. Along this stretch of the Norfolk coast are a string of small, quiet villages that seem largely untouched by the tourist crowds save for the wonderful choice of gastropubs, trendy B&Bs and boutique hotels.

HOLKHAM

The pretty village of Holkham is well worth a stop for its imposing stately home, incredible stretch of beach and for the pleasure of walking its picturesque streets lined with elegant buildings.

The main draw here is **Holkham Hall** (☎ 01328-710227; www.holkham.co.uk; hall & museum adult/child £10/5; ⊙ noon-5pm Sun-Thu Easter & Jun-Sep), a grand Palladian mansion set in a vast deer park designed by Capability Brown. The slightly industrial-looking brick mansion is the ancestral seat of the Earls of Leicester and has a sumptuous interior, dripping with gilt, tapestries, fine furniture and family history. The Marble Hall (it's actually alabaster), magnificent state rooms and giant kitchen shouldn't be missed. The public entrance brings you to the rear of the building; for the best views continue along the road around the house and past the ice house to see the building as originally intended. You can also visit the **Bygones Museum** (museum only adult/child £5/2.50) in the stable block. It showcases everything from mechanical toys to agricultural equipment and vintage cars.

For many, Holkham's true delight is not the stately home but the pristine 3-mile **beach** that meanders along the shore. Regularly voted one of England's best, it's a popular spot with walkers but the vast expanse of sand swallows people up and gives a real sense of isolation with giant skies stretching overhead. The only place to park for access to the beach is Lady Anne's Drive (parking £3.50).

Recover after a jaunt on the beach with tea or a snack at the **Marsh Larder** (☎ 01328-711285; Main Rd; ⊙ 10am-5pm) in the stunning Ancient House or a more substantial meal at the much-lauded **Victoria Arms** (☎ 01328-711008; www.victoriaatholkham.co.uk; Park Rd; mains £12-17; ⊙ noon-2.30pm daily, 7-9pm Mon-Fri, 7-9.30pm Sat & Sun). The menu here is modern English with an em-

RURAL ROMANTICS

Valentine's Day forces most people into one of two camps: misty-eyed romantic or born cynic. In Norfolk, however, it seems everyone turns Cupid. Here a mysterious character called Jack Valentine, a kind of loved-up February Father Christmas deposits a doorstep gift, rattles on the door and then promptly disappears into thin air. In Victorian times lovers went to great lengths to swap parcels on Valentine's Eve, and children rose before dawn the next day to sing valentine rhymes and beg for sweets. The tradition continues today with whole streets waking up and finding valentine's treats stuck to their doors.

phasis on local ingredients. The Victoria also has a choice of individually decorated rooms (£120 to £170) with a relaxed, colonial feel. You'd be well advised to book ahead.

The Coast Hopper bus goes through Holkham roughly hourly in summer on its way between Hunstanton (40 minutes) and Sheringham (55 minutes).

BURNHAM DEEPDALE

In-the-know backpackers and walkers flock to this lovely coastal spot, with its tiny twin villages of Burnham Deepdale and **Brancaster Staithe** (www.brancasterstaithe.co.uk) strung along a rural road. Stroked by the beautiful Norfolk Coastal Path, surrounded by beaches and reedy marshes alive with birdlife, criss-crossed by cycling routes, and a base for a whole host of water sports, Burnham Deepdale is also home to one of the country's best backpacker hostels.

The hostel operates a **tourist office** (☎ 01485-210256; ⊙ 10am-4pm Apr-Sep, closed Tue & Wed Oct-Mar), which is flush with information on the surrounding area, and can help arrange accommodation and activities. It's the best place to go to organise kitesurfing or windsurfing on nearby beaches.

Anywhere else it might seem odd to have campers poking their heads out of Native American–style tepees, but at ecofriendly backpackers haven and hostel **Deepdale Farm** (☎ 01485-210256; www.deepdalefarm.co.uk; camping per adult/child £8/4, dm £9.50-12.50, tw £28-42, tepees for 2 /6£60/£90; ℗ ☐) it's just part of a wonderful experience. The set-up includes small and stylish en suite dorms in converted 17th-century stables, camping space, a coffee shop, laundry, barbecue, lounges and picnic tables. Bike hire is also available.

Just west of the hostel is the award-winning **White Horse** (☎ 01485-210262; www.whitehorsebran caster.co.uk; mains £10-14; 🕑 lunch & dinner; 🅿 🖳), a gastropub with a menu strong on fish and seafood. It also has some light and fresh guest rooms (doubles £100 to £148) but it lacks soul and has terraces overlooking the car park.

The Coast Hopper bus stops outside Deepdale Farm roughly hourly in summer on its run between Sheringham (65 minutes) and Hunstanton (25 minutes); it also goes less frequently to King's Lynn (one hour). Ask at the tourist office for timetables.

AROUND BURNHAM DEEPDALE

Littered with pretty little villages and a host of ancient watering holes, trendy gastropubs and boutique hotels, this part of the Norfolk coast is one of the most appealing.

At the lovely Georgian town of Burnham Market you'll find plenty of elegant old buildings, flint cottages, delis and independent retailers. It's another excellent base with a trio of accommodation options to suit any taste. The **Hoste Arms** (☎ 01328-738777; www.hostearms.co.uk; The Green; d £95-305; 🅿) and its sister properties the **Vine House** (d £125-280) and the **Railway Inn** (d £74-140) offer everything from over-the-top classical rooms with swags and florals to trendy, contemporary suites with bold wallpaper, luscious fabrics and mountains of towels.

Just past Burnham Deepdale you come to Titchwell, home to **Titchwell Manor** (☎ 01485-210221; www.titchwellmanor.com; Titchwell; d £130-250; 🅿 🖳), a slick contemporary hotel set in a grand Victorian house. The conservatory restaurant serves modern English cuisine (mains £11 to £19) and there's a large garden loved by visiting children.

Continue west along the coast road to the village of Thornham for a choice of two more great places to eat. Right by the road is the **Orange Tree** (☎ 01485-512213; www.theorangetree thornham.co.uk; High St; mains £10-15; 🕑 bar 11am-11pm Mon-Sat, to 10.30pm Sun) an old-world pub with a modern interior. The food here is excellent and reasonably priced, and there's a garden with playground for children. Hidden from passing traffic on the village back road is the **Lifeboat Inn** (☎ 01485-512236; www.lifeboatinn.co.uk; Ship Lane; 3-course dinner £29) a 16th-century inn

laden with character and famous for its food. The menu features anything that has been 'caught, shot, picked or dug locally'.

KING'S LYNN
pop 34,565

Once one of England's most important ports, the area around King's Lynn's medieval harbour is awash with cobbled lanes and narrow streets flanked by old merchants' houses. Unfortunately, the rest of the town is not so pretty, with modern architectural blunders and high-street chain stores blighting the landscape. Stick to the waterfront though and you'll get some sense of just how important the town once was.

Long labelled 'the Warehouse on the Wash', the port was once so busy that it was said you could cross from one side of the River Great Ouse to the other by simply stepping from boat to boat. Something of the salty port-town tang can still be felt in old King's Lynn, though the petite modern-day port barely passes as a shadow of its former self.

Orientation

Old King's Lynn huddles along the eastern bank of the river. The train station is on its eastern side, while unexciting modern King's Lynn and the bus station are between them. Three markets still take place weekly on Tuesday, Friday and Saturday. The biggest is the Tuesday market, held in er, Tuesday Marketplace, while the others are conducted in front of St Margaret's Church.

Information

Banks and ATMs can be found around Tuesday Marketplace.

Post office (☎ 01553-692185; Baxter's Plain)

Tourist office (☎ 01553-763044; www.visitwestnorfolk .com; 🕑 10am-5pm Mon-Sat, noon-5pm Sun Apr-Sep, 10.30am-4pm Mon-Sat, noon-4pm Sun Oct-Mar) In the Custom House (Purfleet Quay). Guided walks of historic Lynn start from here between May and Oct (☎ 01553-774297; adult/child £3/1). The walks take 1½ to two hours.

Sights

Start your tour of Old Lynn at grand **St Margaret's Church** (Margaret Plain), which bears flood-level marks by the west door. Inside, two extraordinarily elaborate Flemish brasses are etched with vivid details of a peacock feast, strange dragonlike beasts and a mythical wild man. You can also see a remarkable

EAST ANGLIA

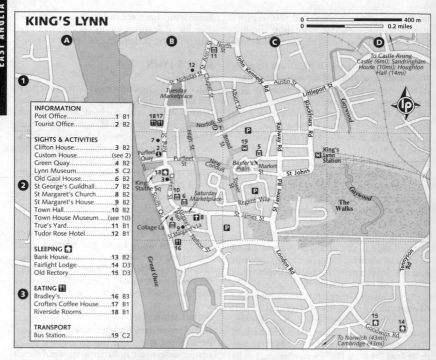

KING'S LYNN

0   400 m
0   0.2 miles

To Castle Rising
Castle (6mi); Sandringham
House (10mi); Houghton
Hall (14mi)

INFORMATION
Post Office...................**1** B1
Tourist Office................**2** B2

SIGHTS & ACTIVITIES
Clifton House..................**3** B2
Custom House.............(see 2)
Green Quay....................**4** B2
Lynn Museum.................**5** C2
Old Gaol House..............**6** B2
St George's Guildhall.......**7** B2
St Margaret's Church........**8** B2
St Margaret's House.........**9** B2
Town Hall....................**10** B2
Town House Museum......(see 10)
True's Yard..................**11** B1
Tudor Rose Hotel............**12** B1

SLEEPING
Bank House..................**13** B2
Fairlight Lodge..............**14** D3
Old Rectory..................**15** D3

EATING
Bradley's....................**16** B3
Crofters Coffee House.......**17** B1
Riverside Rooms.............**18** B1

TRANSPORT
Bus Station..................**19** C2

To Norwich (43mi);
Cambridge (43mi)

17th-century moon dial, which tells the tide, not the time.

Wander across Margaret Plain to take a look at 15th-century **St Margaret's House**, once the warehouse or 'steelyard' of the Hanseatic League (the Northern European merchants' group), then loop around the corner to **Green Quay** (☎ 01553-818500; www.thegreenquay.co.uk; South Quay; admission free; ⏰ 9am-5pm), a museum charting life in the Wash, and housed in an old Tudor warehouse. Exhibitions look at the wildlife, flora and fauna of the area and the effects of climate change.

Turn right on College Lane to explore the old cells and gawp at the town's priceless civic treasures in the **Old Gaol House** (☎ 01553-774297; adult/child £2.90/2.10; ⏰ 10am-5pm Mon-Sat Easter-Oct, 10am-4pm Tue-Sat Nov-Easter); its pride and joy is the breathtaking 650-year-old King John Cup, exquisitely decorated with scenes of hunting and hawking.

Next door is the flint-and-brick **town hall**, dating back to 1421, and the petite **Town House Museum** (☎ 01553-773450; 46 Queen St; adult/under 10yr £3/1.65; ⏰ 10am-5pm Mon-Sat May-Sep), which deals with the history of the town from the Middle

Ages up to the 1950s. Quirkier exhibits include an outdoor privy and basket made from an unfortunate armadillo.

Continue along Queen St past **Clifton House**, with its barley-sugar columns and strange merchant's watchtower, to **Purfleet Quay**, in its heyday the principal harbour. The odd boxy building with the lantern tower is the 17th-century **Custom House**, which houses the tourist office. Inside are displays on the merchants and smugglers of the Lynn in times past.

A short hop north again is the biggest 15th-century guildhall in England. **St George's Guildhall** has been variously incarnated as a warehouse, courthouse and armoury and now contains art galleries, a theatre and eateries. Then topping King St is the roomy **Tuesday Marketplace**, flanked by handsome old buildings.

Turn right into St Nicholas St to see the **Tudor Rose Hotel**, a late-15th-century house with its original main door. North of here, on the corner of St Ann's St, is **True's Yard** (☎ 01553-770479; www.truesyard.co.uk; North St; adult/child £3/1.50; ⏰ 10am-4pm Tue-Sat), a museum exploring the Lynn's maritime past. Housed in two restored fishermen's cottages, the museum looks at the difficult life fishermen endured and the traditions and lifestyle of the close-knit community that once lived in this part of the city.

From here head back towards the centre of town to visit the newly revamped **Lynn Museum** (☎ 01553-775001; www.museums.norfolk.gov.uk; Market St; adult/child Apr-Sep £3/1.65, Oct-Mar free), which features displays on maritime life in Lynn, Norfolk history, and Victorian fairgrounds, but its highlight is the new Seahenge gallery which displays a 4000-year-old timber circle and explores the lives of the people who created it.

Festivals

The July **King's Lynn Festival** (☎ 01553-767557; www .kingslynnfestival.org.uk) is East Anglia's most important cultural gathering. It offers a diverse program of concerts and recitals of all kinds from medieval ballads to opera. The main festival is preceded by a free rock-and-pop bash **Festival Too** (www.festivaltoo.co.uk), now one of Europe's biggest free festivals.

Sleeping

Fairlight Lodge (☎ 01553-762234; www.fairlightlodge .co.uk; 79 Goodwins Rd; s/d incl breakfast £35/52; P) Simple, fresh rooms with subtle florals and plenty of little extras such as homemade biscuits make this B&B excellent value. Not all rooms are en suite but there's a pretty garden, great breakfasts and friendly hosts.

Old Rectory (☎ 01553-768544; www.theoldrectory -kinslynn.com; 33 Goodwins Rd; s/d incl breakfast £38/52; P) Set in an elegant former rectory, this B&B offers tastefully decorated rooms with en suite bathrooms. Just a short walk from town via parkland, this place also offers free pick up from the bus and rail stations.

Bank House (☎ 01553-660492; www.thebankhouse .co.uk; Kings Staithe Sq; s £80-90, d £100-120, all incl breakfast; P 🖳) This outstanding B&B has ticks in all the right boxes: history, location, atmosphere, comfort and welcome. On the waterfront near the tourist office, this 18th-century former bank is now an elegantly furnished town house with five hotel-standard rooms, mixing original features and modern furnishings.

Eating

Crofters Coffee House (☎ 01553-773134; 27 King St; meals £4.50-7; 🕙 9.30am-5pm Mon-Sat) This long brick-vaulted undercroft, once used as a Civil War gunpowder store and now a low-lit cafe, scores top marks for atmosphere and serves

light lunches, hot drinks and cakes. It's in the guildhall arts centre.

Riverside Rooms (☎ 01553-773134; 27 King St; mains £12-19; 🕙 lunch & dinner Mon-Sat) Overlooking the water from a converted 15th-century warehouse, with criss-crossing beams overhead and elegant white-linen tables below, this place serves a confident but uninspired menu of classic dishes.

Bradley's (☎ 01553-819888; www.bradleysbytheriver .co.uk; 10 South Quay; mains £13-19; 🕙 lunch & dinner Mon-Sat, lunch Sun) Eat in the elegant Georgian dining room at this riverside restaurant, or relax at the bar with some lighter snacks (£8); either way you're bound to be pleased as this is probably the finest food the city has to offer.

Getting There & Away

King's Lynn is 43 miles north of Cambridge on the A10. There are hourly trains from Cambridge (£8.30, 48 minutes) and London Kings Cross (£25.90, two hours). First Eastern Counties runs hourly buses to Norwich. Bus 29 goes to Hunstanton from where you can catch the Coasthopper service along the north Norfolk coast.

AROUND KING'S LYNN
Castle Rising Castle

There's something bordering on ecclesiastical about the beautifully embellished keep of this **castle** (EH; ☎ 01553-631330; www.castlerising.co.uk; adult/child £4/2.50; 🕙 10am-6pm Apr-Oct, 10am-4pm Wed-Sun Nov-Mar), built in 1138 and set in the middle of a massive earthwork upon which pheasants scurry about like guards. So extravagant is the stonework that it's no surprise to learn that it shares stonemasons with some of East Anglia's finest cathedrals. It was once the home of Queen Isabella, who (allegedly) arranged the gruesome murder of her husband, Edward II.

It's well worth the trip 4 miles northeast of King's Lynn off the A149. Bus 41 runs here (13 minutes) hourly from King's Lynn bus station.

Sandringham House

Royalists and those bemused by the English sovereigns will have plenty to mull over at this, the Queen's country **estate** (☎ 01553-612908; www .sandringhamestate.co.uk; adult/5-15yr £9/5, gardens & museum only £6/3.50; 🕙 11am-4.45pm late Mar-Oct unless royal family is in residence), set in 25 hectares of landscaped gardens and lakes, and open to the hoi polloi when the court is not at home.

Queen Victoria bought the estate in 1862 for her son, the Prince of Wales (later Edward VII), but he promptly had it overhauled in the style later named Edwardian. Half of the surrounding 8000 hectares is leased to farm tenants, while the rest is managed by the Crown Estate as forestry.

Visitors can shuffle around the ground-floor rooms, regularly used by the royal family, then head out to the old stables, which house a flag-waving **museum** filled with diverse royal memorabilia. The superb royal vintage-car collection includes the very first royal motor from 1900, darling electrical toy cars driven by various princes and the buggy in which the recently deceased Queen Mother would bounce around race tracks. For another oddity, look for the pet cemetery just outside the museum.

There are guided tours of the gardens on offer Friday and Saturday at 11am and 2pm. The **shop** is also worthy of a visit if only to browse the organic goodies produced on the sprawling estate.

Sandringham is 6 miles northeast of King's Lynn off the B1440. First Eastern Counties bus 411 or Coastliner run here from the bus station (24 minutes, every 15 minutes).

Houghton Hall

Built for Britain's first de facto Prime Minister Sir Robert Walpole in 1730, the pompous Palladian-style **Houghton Hall** (☎ 01485-528569; www.houghtonhall.com; adult/child £8/3; ☉ 1.30-5pm Wed, Thu & Sun Easter-Sep) is worth seeing for the ornate staterooms alone; you could build another half-dozen houses with the amount of swirling decorative plasterwork here. The interiors are sumptuous and dripping with gilt, tapestries, squeaky velvets and ostentatious furniture. Six hundred deer roam the surrounding parkland and there's an obsessive model-soldiers exhibit with over 20,000 of the little guys.

Houghton is 14 miles northeast of King's Lynn off the A148 but beyond the reach of buses; a taxi ride from King's Lynn will set you back about £13.

The East Midlands

The East Midlands doesn't have the best of reputations: much of the region is ignored by visitors, under the impression that it's dull, grey and industrial. But while the region does have its fair share of grim settlements, it's for the most part very rural – home to fertile agricultural land, quintessential English villages, waterways, forests and the iconic calling card of the Peak District.

The gentle landscape of Northamptonshire and Rutland is flecked with handsome old towns, infused with warmth by the local honey-coloured limestone with which they're built. Charming villages and stately homes pocket nearby Nottinghamshire and Leicestershire, testament to the area's rich past. And for city slickers there's vibrant Leicester, a multicultural success story, and Nottingham, now as well known for its shopping and clubbing as for its association with a certain man in tights. Further east, the hilltop city of Lincoln has one of the most striking medieval cathedrals in the land. Around it, a carpet of rich farmland, fens and rivers unfolds gently towards a long sandy stretch of coastline, ringed with marshes and nature reserves dense with birdsong.

The region's big name draw, the Peak District, may be a tourist honey pot but it still feels isolated and wild, and its hills and moorland are graced with pretty little stone cottages and handsome settlements including the graceful spa town of Buxton.

HIGHLIGHTS

- Walking or cycling the many footpaths and trails in the **Peak District National Park** (p513)
- Strolling past grand Georgian architecture and through leafy parks in the former spa town of **Buxton** (p516)
- Visiting exquisite **Hardwick Hall**, one of the country's finest Elizabethan mansions (p512)
- Marvelling at the vast facade of Lincoln's **cathedral** in this historic hilltop town (p492)
- Sampling an authentic curry on multicultural Leicester's **Golden Mile** (p486)
- Picturing yourself in a Jane Austen novel as you stroll the historic streets of **Stamford** (p496)
- Exploring **Chatsworth House** (p525), the resplendent country home of the Duke and Duchess of Devonshire

★ Buxton ★ Hardwick Hall
★ ★ Chatsworth ★ Lincoln
Peak District
National Park

Stamford
★
★
Leicester

| POPULATION: 4.2 MILLION | AREA: 6,400 SQ MILES | NUMBER OF BAKEWELL PUDDINGS SOLD IN BAKEWELL DURING HIGH SEASON: 12,000 A WEEK |

Information

East Midlands Tourism (www.enjoyenglandseast midlands.com) is the official website for the East Midlands. Other helpful websites:

Go Leicestershire (www.goleicestershire.com)
Peak District & Derbyshire (www.visitpeakdistrict.com)
Visit Nottinghamshire (www.visitnottingham.com)
Visit Lincolnshire (www.visitlincolnshire.com)

Activities

Regional tourist websites are packed with walking, cycling and sailing information, and tourist offices are stacked high with leaflets, maps and guides covering activities offered in the area.

CYCLING

Derbyshire and the Peak District are full of country lanes for touring cyclists, and tracks and bridleways for mountain bikers – with something for every level of ability. Bikes can be hired at various points around the Peak District, especially in the areas where old railway lines have been converted into delightful walking and cycling tracks. The Pennine Bridleway starts south of the Pennine Way national trail and is designed for off-road cycling and horse riding as well as walking. Just over one third of a planned 350-mile route is now open.

There are quiet country roads and purpose-built cycle ways in the National Forest in Leicestershire and you can hire bikes at Rutland Water in Oakham.

WALKING

The Peak District National Park is one of the finest areas in England for walking; more details are given in the introduction to the Peak District section (p512). It's also home to the start of the Pennine Way national trail, which leads keen walkers for 268 miles through Yorkshire and Northumberland into Scotland. Mammoth walking trails aside, the Peak District is criss-crossed with a vast network of paths for walkers. Ideal bases include the villages and towns of Buxton, Matlock Bath, Edale and Castleton, or the national park centre at Fairholmes on the Derwent Reservoirs.

To follow in the footsteps of history, the 140-mile **Viking Way** (p490) trails from the Humber Bridge through the Lincolnshire Wolds to Oakham in Leicestershire.

There are also pleasant walking trails in the National Forest and at Rutland Water.

OTHER ACTIVITIES

Sailors, windsurfers and water-lovers of all levels also flock to Rutland Water, a giant reservoir. You could also try steering a boat through the waterways of the Lincolnshire fens.

Getting There & Around

There is good public transport throughout most of the region although in Northamptonshire and Lincolnshire you're better off with a car. For public transport information, consult **Traveline East Midlands** (☎ 0871 200 2233; www.travelineeastmidlands.org.uk).

NORTHAMPTONSHIRE

While it lacks a major 'must-see' attraction, Northamptonshire is a great place to explore. Winding country lanes punctuate the gentle countryside, which is studded with fetching, honey-coloured limestone towns, storybook thatched cottages, historic Saxon Churches and grand country estates including Althorp House, the final resting place of Princess Diana. What's more, Northamptonshire is refreshingly free from the tourist hordes, so you won't have to fight to take in its charms.

Orientation & Information

Northamptonshire is roughly 50 miles long and 20 miles wide, running southwest to northeast. The M1 cuts diagonally across the county just below Northampton, which lies in the middle. Attractions are scattered.

For general information about the county, check the website www.explorenorthampton shire.co.uk. Otherwise, visit Northampton's tourist office (p474).

Getting Around

A car can be a convenient way of getting around Northamptonshire. Turning a corner on a winding country lane to discover a sleepy village is one of the joys of a visit here. All the major car-hire companies have branches in Northampton.

Buses services run to most places of interest from Northampton and other nearby towns, but can be sporadic; some run only a few times daily, so check times with the operator.
Stagecoach (www.stagecoachbus.com/northants)
Traveline (☎ 0871 200 2233; www.travelineeastmidlands .org.uk)

THE EAST MIDLANDS

NORTHAMPTON
pop 194,458

Hugging the banks of the River Nene, this unassuming market town played a surprisingly significant role in English history. In the Middle Ages, it was one of the largest towns in the country, a thriving commercial centre with strong links to royalty. Today the city's rich past is blighted by some nasty examples of postwar town planning, although there are a few remaining buildings of architectural note. The town is also famous for footwear and was once the heart of the boot and shoe industry.

Orientation

The town is centred on Market Sq, with the main pedestrianised shopping route, Abington St, running east from it, where it becomes Kettering Rd, with its hotels and bars. To the south of Market Sq are the guildhall and the tourist office. The town's infamously ugly bus station is to the north.

Information

The helpful **tourist office** (☎ 01604-838800; www .explorenorthamptonshire.co.uk; The Guildhall, St Giles Sq; ☺ 10am-5pm Mon-Sat) was in a temporary home next to the Derngate Royal Theatre at the time of writing but will move to Sessions House on George Row during 2009.

Sights & Activities

Even those without a shoe fetish can get a kick out of the impressive displays at **Northampton Museum & Art Gallery** (☎ 01604-838111; Guildhall Rd; admission free; ☺ 10am-5pm Mon-Sat, 2-5pm Sun), where you can learn about the history of shoemaking through interactive exhibits and follow the height of footwear fashion throughout the ages. There are also some fine paintings and an exhibition on Northampton's history from the Stone Age onwards.

St Peter's Church (Marefair) is a marvellous Norman edifice built in 1150 and restored in the 19th century by Gilbert Scott. Beautiful Norman-era carvings still adorn the pillars.

The **Church of the Holy Sepulchre** (☎ 01604-754782; ☺ noon-4pm Wed, 2-4pm Sat May-Sep) is Northampton's oldest building at nine centuries and counting. It is also one of the few surviving round churches in the country. Founded after the first earl of Northampton returned from the Crusades in 1100, it is modelled on its Jerusalem namesake.

Eating & Drinking

Church Bar & Restaurant (☎ 01604-603800; 67-83 Bridge St; mains £12-19; ☺ noon-2.30pm & 6-11pm Tue-Sat, noon-4pm Sun) This dramatic, airy dining room has been a hospice, a railway station and a church in previous lives. It now serves good-quality, beautifully presented European dishes. There's a chapel bar attached.

Malt Shovel Tavern (☎ 01604-234212; 121 Bridge St) Despite its slightly desolate position on the outskirts of town opposite the Carlsberg brewery, this favourite has a great selection

of real ales, a cosy atmosphere and regular live music. It also hosts its own beer festival twice yearly.

Getting There & Away

Northampton has good rail links with Birmingham (£10.70, one hour, hourly) and London Euston (£21.20, one hour, three hourly). The train station is about half a mile west of town along Gold St.

National Express coaches run services to London (£11.50, 2¼ hours, five daily), to Nottingham (£11.60, 2½ hours, daily) and to Birmingham (£6.40, one hour 40 minutes, twice daily). Greyfriars bus station is on Lady's Lane, just north of the Grosvenor shopping centre.

AROUND NORTHAMPTON

Althorp

Althorp House (bookings ☎ 01604-770107; www.althorp .com; adult/child £12.50/6, plus access to upstairs of house £2.50; ☺ 11am-5pm Jul & Aug, last entry 4pm) is most famous as the resting place of Diana, Princess of Wales, who is commemorated in a memorial and museum in the grounds of her ancestral home.

The stern looking 16th-century mansion was already well known for its outstanding collection of art and books, and you'll see works by Rubens, Gainsborough and Van Dyck. Profits from ticket sales go to the Princess Diana Memorial Fund. The limited number of tickets available must be booked by phone or on the web. Althorp should be pronounced *altrup*.

Althorp is off the A428, 5.5 miles northwest of Northampton. Bus number 207 (five daily, not Sundays) links Northampton with Althorp, leaving from Greyfriars bus station.

Stoke Bruerne

This charming little village nestles against the Grand Union Canal, the main drag of England's canal network, 8 miles south of Northampton.

On its banks in a converted corn mill, the engaging **National Waterways Museum** (☎ 01604-862229; www.nwm.org.uk/stoke; adult/child £4.75/3.25; ☺ 10am-5pm daily Mar-Oct, to 4pm Tue-Sun Nov-Mar) charts the history of the waterways system and the sometimes difficult lives of those working on it.

Nowadays, the canals are all about leisure time: you can mess about on boats in summer on the **Indian Chief** (☎ 01604-862428, ☺ Sun

& Bank Holiday weekends only), run by the Boat Inn (see following). Trips range from 25 minutes to six hours (£3 to £16).

For longer stays, try **Waterways Cottage** (☎ 01604-863865; www.waterwayscottage.co.uk; Bridge Rd; s/d incl breakfast £40/55), a sweet little B&B in a thatched cottage right in the middle of the action.

The **Boat Inn** (☎ 01604-862428; www.boatinn.co.uk; mains £5-12) is an old-fashioned canalside pub, one of several in the village.

Buses 86 and 87 each call in at Stoke Bruerne from Northampton (30 minutes, five daily Monday to Saturday).

Sulgrave Manor

Built by Lawrence Washington after Henry VIII sold him the property in 1539, **Sulgrave Manor** (☎ 01295-760205; www.sulgravemanor.org.uk; adult/child £6.25/3; ☽ 2-5.30pm Tue-Thu, noon-5.30pm Sat & Sun Apr-Oct, last entry 4pm) is a well-preserved Tudor mansion. The draw for many overseas visitors is a certain family descendant named George Washington, who became the first president of the USA 250 years later. The family lived here for almost 120 years before Colonel John Washington sailed to Virginia in 1656.

Sulgrave Manor is located just off the B4525, 7 miles northeast of Banbury where the nearest train station is. Public transport links are poor; you'll probably need to get a taxi from there.

Brixworth

The village itself is nothing special; it's the ancient **All Saints Church** (☎ 01604-880286; ☽ usually 10am-5pm Apr-Sep, to 4pm Oct-Mar) that lures in visitors. One of the country's oldest churches, it was built back in Saxon times, around AD 680, and although it's been through plenty of changes since then, the nave remains the same. It is thought to be based on a Roman basilica plan, and was an early example of effective recycling: disused Roman brickwork was used in its construction. The tower and stair turret were added after 9th-century Viking raids, and the spire was built around 1350.

Brixworth is 6 miles north of Northampton off the A508. Bus X7 runs from Northampton (10 minutes, hourly Monday to Saturday, five on Sunday).

Earls Barton

Earls Barton's wonderful place of worship, **All Saints** (☎ 01604-810045; ☽ 10.30am-12.30pm & 2-4pm Mon-Sat Apr-Sep), is notable for its solid Saxon tower with patterns that seem to imitate earlier wooden models. Probably built during the reign of Edgar the Peaceful (r 959–75), it has a 1st-floor door that may have offered access to the tower during Viking raids. Around 1100 the Norman nave was added to the original tower, with other features added in subsequent centuries.

Earls Barton is 8 miles east of Northampton off the A4500. Bus 45 runs from Northampton (20 minutes, every 20 minutes Monday to Saturday, seven on Sunday).

Rushton Triangular Lodge

This mysterious **lodge** (EH; ☎ 01536-710761; adult/child £2.60/1.30; ☽ 11am-4pm Thu-Mon Apr-Oct), with its esoteric inscriptions, shows the power of Sir Thomas Tresham's Catholic faith; he designed a number of buildings in the area and was imprisoned more than once for expressing his beliefs. With three of everything, from sides to floors to gables, the lodge is in a magical setting among rapeseed fields and is Tresham's enduring symbol of the trinity. It was built at the end of the 16th century.

The lodge is 4 miles northwest of Kettering. Stagecoach bus 19 from Kettering stops in Desborough, 2 miles away (20 minutes, every 20 to 30 minutes Monday to Saturday, every two hours on Sunday). Kettering is 15 miles northeast of Northampton along the A43.

Kirby Hall

Known as the 'Jewel of the English Renaissance', **Kirby Hall** (EH; ☎ 01536-203230; adult/child £4.90/2.50; ☽ 10am-5pm Thu-Mon Apr-Jun, Sep & Oct, to 6pm daily Jul & Aug, to 4pm Thu-Mon Nov-Mar), one of the country's finest Elizabethan mansions, began life in 1570 and went through several modifications over the next few hundred years. By the mid-19th century, however, the house had fallen into disrepair. Today, it may be an uninhabited shell but it's a wonderfully atmospheric one, with fine filigree stonework, ravens cawing in the empty halls and peacocks strutting around its restored formal parterre gardens.

Kirby Hall is 4 miles northeast of Corby, which is 9 miles north of Kettering along the A43.

THE EAST MIDLANDS

Oundle & Fotheringhay

The village of **Oundle** is the photogenic face of Northamptonshire, with streets and squares graced with the honey-coloured Jurassic limestone and the Colleyweston slate roofs of 16th- and 17th-century buildings. It's a good base for visiting nearby **Fotheringhay**, birthplace of Richard III (demonised by the Tudors and Shakespeare) and execution place of Mary, Queen of Scots, in 1587. The castle in which these events took place is now merely a hillock, but Fotheringhay is an appealing village with thatched cottages and a pub, the **Falcon** (☎ 01832-226254; www .thefalcon-inn.co.uk; mains £7-15), known for its excellent, locally sourced food.

Oundle's **tourist office** (☎ 01832-274333; www .explorenorthamptonshire.co.uk; 14 West St; 9am-5pm Mon-Sat, 1-4pm Sun Easter-Aug) has several leaflets that help visitors explore its picture-postcard streets.

Built in 1626, the **Talbot Hotel** (☎ 01832-273621; www.thetalbot-oundle.com; New St; s/d £79/99), has comfortable rooms, wooden beams and open fires, making for a lovely olde-worlde atmosphere. The hotel's oak staircase was apparently rescued from the ruins of nearby Fotheringhay Castle. Spook-lovers will be pleased to know that Mary descended these very steps on the way to her execution – her ghost is rumoured to wander the building.

Bus X4 runs to Oundle from Northampton (two hours, hourly) and from Peterborough (30 minutes, hourly) in the other direction.

LEICESTERSHIRE & RUTLAND

Leicestershire isn't at the forefront of most people's minds when it comes to the country's tourist destinations, but this compact county shouldn't be overlooked. At its heart, Leicester is a vital mix of different cultures and faiths, and the surrounding countryside is home to rolling hills and woodland as well as some major historical sites including magnificent Belvoir Castle.

Tiny Rutland was merged with Leicestershire in 1974, but in April 1997 regained its 'independence' as a county. With magnificent Rutland Water and charming settlements, it's a hit with lovers of water sports and picturesque villages.

Orientation & Information

Leicestershire and Rutland together look like an upside-down map of Australia. Leicester is virtually bang in the centre of its county, with the M1 motorway running north–south just to the west, dividing the largely industrial towns and National Forest of the west from the more rural east including Belvoir Castle. To the east of Leicester, Rutland, wedged between four counties, revolves around central Rutland Water.

For general countywide information, contact **Leicestershire Tourism** (☎ 0844 8885181; www .goleicestershire.com).

Getting There & Around

Arriva Midlands (www.arrivabus.co.uk) Operates Leicestershire bus services.

Traveline (☎ 0871 200 2233; www.travelineeastmid lands.org.uk) Latest timetables, bus routes & numbers.

LEICESTER

pop 279,923

Filled with the sense of excitement that comes from a mix of cultures and ethnicities, Leicester (*les*-ter) may not be beautiful but it has a lot going on. Around since the Roman times, it had an unwelcome refurbishment at the hands of the Luftwaffe, while industrial decline hollowed it out and poor urban planning capped off the aesthetic crimes against the city.

But Leicester, home to a large, dynamic Asian community, has reinvented itself as a socially and environmentally progressive melting pot, and many of the city's most interesting events are staged around festivals such as Diwali and Eid-ul-Fitr. Current regeneration projects including a new 'cultural quarter' topped with a bold, curved-glass performing-arts centre, are set to broaden its appeal further.

Orientation

For drivers, Leicester is plagued by a maze of one-way streets and forbidden turns. Although there isn't a ring road as such, the A594 does almost a whole circuit and most attractions flank it or are contained within it.

The centre of the Asian community, Belgrave Rd (the 'Golden Mile'), is about a mile northeast of the centre. Castle Park, with many historic attractions, lies immediately west of the centre.

(Continued on page 485)

Meet the
Locals

Experts on the Street

NAME	Eric Green
OCCUPATION	*Big Issue* vendor
RESIDENCE	London

Few people know the streets of London better than its *Big Issue* vendors. With its motto of 'Working, Not Begging', the magazine provides an income for many of the city's homeless.

'Without a doubt, the best source of local directions is the *Big Issue* man', says 43-year-old Eric Green, who's been selling the mag for about a year. 'We know our patch'.

Eric's patch is the King's Rd in upmarket Chelsea.

'Chelsea's beautiful', he says. 'I've got a lot of friends there…well, acquaintances, who stop and chat.'

Unsurprisingly his favourite places in London are the parks: they're free, and following a marriage breakup he's been sleeping rough a lot. 'I like Regent's Park (p130), St James's Park (p118), Green Park (p118), but my favourite is Kensington Gardens (p129). It's beautiful and open, with nice fountains.'

Any other tips for travellers? 'The best places for cheap food are Kilburn, Ladbroke Grove near Portobello Rd, and Camden, especially the Chinese places by the stables just before closing.'

The day dawns over a frosty Regent's Park (p130)

JANE SWEENEY

Life as an Oxford Student

NAME	Ben Wong
OCCUPATION	Mathematics student
RESIDENCE	Brasenose College (p229)

'Oxford University works on a collegiate system. You eat, sleep and socialise in your college but your lectures are with another faculty, so you make a really diverse set of friends. Another difference from other unis is the importance of tradition. We have to wear a suit, white collar and tie, and a gown to exams and to the regular candle-lit dinners in the ancient college hall.

'All the traditions are bemusing at first, but you soon appreciate that they're part of the Oxford experience. Even when you stay in college rooms it's at the back of your mind that someone really famous could have slept there before you.

'Academic achievement is really important and everything is done to help you concentrate on your studies. It's easy to take life here and the beautiful surroundings for granted, but I'll really miss it when I finish.'

'the traditions are bemusing at first, but you soon appreciate that they're part of the Oxford experience'

Spires and domes – pretty standard for Oxford (p222)

DOUG MCKINLAY

Culinary Cornwall

NAME	Rick Stein
OCCUPATION	Celebrity chef, restaurant owner
RESIDENCE	Cornwall

'there is some-
where in this
overcrowded
island where you
can feel a little bit
on your own'

What makes Cornwall great for gourmands, in Rick's opinion, is that 'there's a natural enthusiasm in the British for Cornwall, and restaurants and hotels have started to live up to their expectations'. He doesn't believe that regeneration could overwhelm the county: 'Cornwall hasn't been overrun with tourism. It still has the appeal it used to. But of course it's changed. Padstow (p399) now is more prosperous and doesn't look like it did when I first opened a restaurant there more than 30 years ago.'

Asked why he loves living and cooking in Cornwall, Rick says: 'The feeling that there is somewhere in this overcrowded island where you can feel a little bit on your own. And I love the local fish – red gurnards, John Dory, Dover sole, I just look at fish like that and think bloody hell – this is fantastic.'

Any eating recommendations? 'Well apart from my own restaurants, of course! Fifteen Cornwall (p402), Jamie Oliver's place in Newquay, is good, as are the Beach Hut (p402), right underneath it on the beach, and Alba (p419) in St Ives.'

Freshly caught
mackerel lands at
St Ives (p416),
Cornwall

Leicester's Lord Mayor

NAME	Manjula Sood
OCCUPATION	Lord Mayor of Leicester 2008–09
RESIDENCE	Leicester

When Manjula Sood arrived in Leicester from the Punjab in 1970, it was snowing, dark and cold, and a very different place to the city it has become today. 'Leicester was not ready to accept different communities', she says. The word multiculturalism didn't even exist, in Leicester or elsewhere, so she never dreamed that she'd end up serving as the country's first Asian female Lord Mayor.

Today things are very different. Over 38 languages are spoken in Leicester, and it will soon become the UK's first ethnic-majority city.

'Leicester is a more successful multicultural city than London or Birmingham because it truly celebrates its diversity', says Manjula. The Caribbean Carnival (p485) is the biggest in the country after Notting Hill, the Diwali lights (p485) are the biggest in Europe, and there are major Hanukkah and Christian celebrations.

It's because of this harmonious spirit that Manjula loves living in this city. 'Leicester is the jewel of the Midlands; you can feel the warmth wherever you go.'

'Over 38 languages are spoken in Leicester, and it will soon become the UK's first ethnic-majority city'

The Caribbean Carnival (p485) is one colourful way Leicester celebrates its cultural diversity
FLAB / ALAMY

Ghost Tours

NAME	Andy Dextious
OCCUPATION	Ghost tour guide
RESIDENCE	York

'In the streets around the Minster you're always within a breath of a ghost tale'

There's a lot that Andy enjoys about living in York: 'Its outstanding architecture, the maze of snickleways (narrow alleys), the street entertainment and festivals, and haunted pubs like the Old White Swan and the Golden Fleece (p628). In the streets around the Minster you're always within a breath of a ghost tale.' His list of places where a ghost-hunter would retire for a drink in the evenings includes the Punch Bowl, Stonegate, and the Blue Bell (p631).

And where would Andy take a friend to show them the best of Yorkshire? 'The Forbidden Corner (p614) near Leyburn. Or drive to Levisham and take the North Yorkshire Moors Railway (p645) to Goathland, then walk to Mallyan Spout waterfall. Include a drink at the Birch Hall Inn at Beck Hole. Or take a walk along Sutton Bank (p644) followed by a meal at the Star (p643) at Harome. For a good meal in York, I'd take them to El Piano (p630) for vegie and vegan food in a place that welcomes children. For somewhere special out of town there's the Stone Trough (p632) at Kirkham.'

The trains continue to run along the restored North Yorkshire Moors Railway (p645)

DAVID ELSE

Manchester Music Tour

NAME	Craig Gill
OCCUPATION	DJ, ex-drummer of Inspiral Carpets, tour guide
RESIDENCE	Manchester

As drummer for Inspiral Carpets, Craig Gill was there when Madchester (p667) was born, even though the name came later: 'By the time the word 'Madchester' was being used it was pretty much over, even if the likes of the Haçienda were still full until it closed in 1997.'

Craig's not too happy that great clubs like the Haçienda have now been converted into office blocks, but it'd take far more than that to kill the city's musical spirit. 'Manchester's always had a brilliant musical heritage. It's what happens when creative people are stifled by boredom and unemployment. They just start doing stuff for themselves and their mates.' Asked where the best 'stuff' is going on in the city these days, he reels off a few names. 'I love bars like the Temple of Convenience (p665) and Bluu (p665), while you'll hear great music in new venues like the Ruby Lounge (p668) and Moho Live (p667).' Craig still DJs regularly in South (p666), while his new tour business, Manchester Music Tours (www .manchesterm-usictours.com), takes visitors on a journey through the city's great musical history.

'Craig's not too happy that great clubs like the Haçienda have now been converted into office blocks, but it'd take far more than that to kill the city's musical spirit'

The distinctive sign for South (p666), one of the many clubs of Manchester

DOMINIC HARRISON / ALAMY

Geordie by Choice

NAME	Jonathan Edwards, CBE
OCCUPATION	Broadcaster, former Olympic athlete
RESIDENCE	Gosforth, Newcastle

'where I live in Gosforth, the people have lived there all their lives, as did their parents and their parents before for them'

'There is an amazing warmth and depth to northerners that you don't get to the same extent in the south; I think it's because northern communities are more settled – where I live in Gosforth, the people have lived there all their lives, as did their parents and their parents before them.

'If friends come to visit me here, I always take them to the Quayside (p747); the bridges are beautiful, but the Sage (p755) and the Baltic (p751) are the real highlights. But you've got to get out of the city and up the Northumberland coast. My favourite place is Warkworth (p779); with the castle as a backdrop to the sand dunes, it's the most beautiful part of the whole region.

'I'm not much for nightlife, but in Newcastle it's not intimidating – I always feel safe here, and even the drunken scuffles are usually pretty good-natured. Still, there's never a scuffle in my favourite, which conveniently is my local, the County on Gosforth High St.'

Newcastle's futuristic Millennium Bridge (p748) and Sage Gateshead (p755)

CHRIS MELLOR

(Continued from page 476)

Information

Ice Mango (☎ 0116-262 6255; www.icemango.co.uk; 4 Market Pl; per hr £2; 🕑 9.30am-6.30pm Mon-Fri, to 7pm Sat, noon-5.30pm Sun) Relaxed coffee house with computers for Internet access.

Tourist office (☎ 0844 888 5181; www.goleicester shire.com; 7-9 Every St; 🕑 10am-5.30pm Mon-Fri, 10am-5pm Sat)

Sights

JEWRY WALL & MUSEUMS

All Leicester's **museums** (www.leicester.gov.uk /museums) are free.

Despite its name, **Jewry Wall** is one of the country's largest surviving Roman civil structures and has nothing to do with Judaism. You can wander the excavated remains of the Roman public baths, which date back almost two millennia.

Notwithstanding its grim external appearance, the **Jewry Wall Museum** (☎ 0116-225 4971; St Nicholas Circle; 🕑 11am-4.30pm Feb-Oct & some school holidays) contains wonderful Roman mosaics and frescoes, as well as an interactive exhibition, 'the Making of Leicester', which explains the history of the city from the Iron Age to the year 2000 with archaeological reconstructions and paintings.

Leicester's oldest museum, the **New Walk Museum & Art Gallery** (☎ 0116-225 4900; New Walk; 🕑 10am-5pm Mon-Sat, from 11am Sun) has a huge range of exhibits on offer, from child-friendly interactive explorations of the natural world, to a quirky mummy-filled gallery set up like an Egyptian tomb, to a collection of 20th-century German art.

Newarke Houses Museum (☎ 0116-225 4980; The Newarke; 🕑 10am-5pm Mon-Sat, from 11am Sun) is made up of two 16th-century buildings. Revolving around the theme 'ordinary people, extraordinary lives', it shows how Leicester residents would have lived during different time periods. Features include reconstructed living rooms, a toy gallery and a gallery telling the story of the Royal Leicestershire Regiment.

One of the best-preserved timber-framed halls in England, the late-14th-century **guildhall** (☎ 0116-253 2569; Guildhall Lane; 🕑 11am-4.30pm Mon-Wed & Sat, 1-4.30pm Sun) is reputed to be the most haunted building in Leicester. Here you can peer into old police cells and inspect the town gibbet, which was used to publicly display the body of an executed murderer.

NATIONAL SPACE CENTRE

This **centre** (☎ 0116-261 0261; www.spacecentre.co.uk; adult/child £12/10; 🕑 10am-5pm Tue-Sun, plus Mon during Leicester school holidays, last entry 3.30pm) does an excellent job of helping us ordinary mortals understand space science. Interactive displays cover cosmic myths, the history of astronomy and the development of space travel, while in the Space Now! area you can check on the status of all current space missions. Films in the domed Space Theatre (included in the admission price) launch you to the far reaches of the galaxy, and in the Human Spaceflight exhibition you can test out your astronaut capabilities and take a space-shuttle flight simulator to an ice moon.

The centre is off the A6 about 1.5 miles north of the city centre. Take bus No 54 from Charles St in the centre.

TEMPLES

Materials were shipped in all the way from India to convert a disused church into a **Jain Centre** (☎ 0116-254 1150; www.jaincentre.com; 32 Oxford St; 🕑 8.30am-8.30pm Mon-Fri, to 6.30pm Sun), the first Jain temple outside the subcontinent and the only one in Europe. The building is faced with marble, and the temple boasts a forest of beautifully carved pillars inside.

Close to the Jewry Wall is the Sikh **Guru Nanak Gurdwara** (☎ 0116-262 8606; 9 Holy Bones; 🕑 1-4pm Thu, 7-8.30pm Sat). There is a small museum, which contains an impressive model of the Golden Temple in Amritsar, India, and a Sikh/Panjabi heritage exhibition.

Festivals & Events

Leicester hosts numerous cultural and religious festivals throughout the year. Contact the tourist office for details.

Leicester Comedy Festival (☎ 0116-261 6812; www .comedy-festival.co.uk) Held in February, this is the country's longest-running comedy festival, drawing big names as well as fresh comic talent.

Leicester Caribbean Carnival (www.lccarnival.org.uk) In August the city hosts the biggest UK Caribbean carnival outside London's Notting Hill Carnival.

Diwali The Hindu community celebrates this during autumn, and the celebration, the largest of its kind outside India, draws visitors from around the world.

Sleeping

Spindle Lodge (☎ 0116-233 8801; www.spindlelodge .com; 2 West Walk; s/d from £49/67; **P** 🖳) Housed

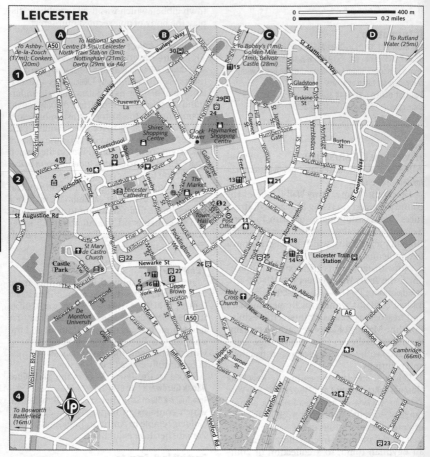

in an elegant Victorian building, the inside is looking pretty shabby, and it's not the most welcoming of places, but the location is good.

Belmont House Hotel (☎ 0116-254 4773; www .belmonthotel.co.uk; De Montfort St; s/d £115/120; P ❑) In an elongated Georgian building, this hotel has spotless rooms, although it looks a little old-fashioned. There are normally great deals to be had if you book ahead.

Ramada Hotel (☎ 0116-255 5599; www.ramadajarvis .co.uk; Granby St; s/d Sun-Thu from £115/145, Fri-Sun from £41/82; P ❑) In a listed Victorian building, the city's top hotel is clinically comfortable. Rates vary according to availability. Get a room set back from the street, away from the blare of pubgoers below on weekend nights – unless you're doing the blaring.

ourpick Hotel Maiyango (☎ 0116-251 8898; www .maiyango.com; 13-21 St Nicholas Pl; d from £135; ❑) The nicest place to stay in Leicester has spacious, sexy rooms, decorated with handmade Asian furniture, bright contemporary art and massive plasma TVs. There are complimentary snacks and magazines in all rooms and the hotel lobby doubles up as a large, airy bar complete with wraparound terrace and views over the city. There's another bar and a restaurant downstairs.

Eating

The **Golden Mile** on Belgrave Rd is located a mile to the north of the centre (take bus 22 or 26 from Haymarket bus station). It's well known for its excellent Indian restaurants and has some of the best Indian vegetarian food in the country. It's also a good place to buy saris and jewellery and is the epicentre of Leicester's Diwali festival.

Halli (☎ 0116-255 4667; www.hallirestaurant.com; 5 Guildhall Lane; dishes £3-6; ☽ noon-3pm Mon-Fri, to 11pm Sat, to 8pm Sun) Great-value, tasty South Indian vegetarian cooking including excellent *dosas*, served in simple surroundings.

Good Earth (☎ 0116-262 6260; 19 Free Lane; mains £3.25-6.25; ☽ noon-3pm, 10am-4pm Sat) Tucked away on a side street, this wholesome vegetarian restaurant is justifiably popular for its vegie bakes, huge, fresh salads and homemade cakes.

Bobby's (☎ 0116-251 0555; 154 Belgrave Rd; mains £5-12; ☽ noon-10pm Tue-Sun) A Belgrave Rd institution, this Indian restaurant serves up tongue-tingling vegetarian curries cooked

without onions or garlic. There's a counter downstairs selling Indian sweets, and samosas and the like.

Haveli (☎ 0116-251 0555; 61 Belgrave Gate; mains £5-12; ☽ 6pm-midnight Tue-Sun) Delicious and varied Indian menu served up by extremely friendly staff in a large, lively dining room with some interesting decor including life-size fake humans.

Watsons (☎ 0116-222 7770; www.watsons-restaurant .com; 5-9 Upper Brown St; mains £12-17; ☽ lunch & dinner Mon-Sat) Set in a converted cotton mill opposite the Phoenix Theatre, this is one of Leicester's finest places to eat out. Mediterranean-inspired food is served in a bright dining room to a soundtrack of mellow jazz. There's also a courtyard bar.

Tinseltown Diner (☎ 0116-2544 696; 5-9 Upper Brown St; mains £13-22; ☽ noon-midnight Mon-Thu, 24hr Fri & Sat) Fancy a triple-decker chilli burger or an Oreo cookie and peanut butter milkshake at three in the morning? This brightly decorated US-style diner is the place to come.

Drinking

Amid the rash of chain pubs in the centre, there are a few places for more discerning drinkers.

Bossa (☎ 0116-255 9551; 110 Granby St; ☽ 11am-10.30pm Mon-Thu, to 1am Fri & Sat) Latin rhythms, cheap, tasty snacks and a relaxed, Bohemian crowd populate this pint-sized, gay-friendly bar-cafe.

Globe (☎ 0116-262 9819; 43 Silver St; ☽ Sun-Thu 11am 11pm, to 1am Fri & Sat) At last, that rare beast: a traditional old pub (built in 1720) in a city centre overrun with chains and style bars – just fine draught ales, a warm atmosphere and little alcoves to lose yourself in.

Long Bar (☎ 0116-254 6115; 29 Market St; ☽ noon-11pm Mon-Thu, to 1am Fri & Sat) This upbeat, corridor-shaped bar, decked out in lime green and purple, attracts a laid-back crowd to sample its eclectic cocktail menu and graze on tasty Mediterranean snacks.

Maiyango (☎ 0116-251 8898; www.maiyango.com; 13-21 St Nicholas Pl) Moroccan lamps, scatter cushions and low seating create a chilled-out atmosphere in this teeny bar attached to the Maiyango hotel and restaurant. A small DJ booth plays mellow jazz, hip hop and house.

Orange Tree (☎ 0116-223 5256; 99 High St) This unpretentious, relaxed bar is a relief among the neighbouring chain pubs. It's kitted out with colourful modern art and there's a beer

THE EAST MIDLANDS

garden that packs out in the summer. Meals are £4.50 to £7.45.

Quarter (☎ 0116-251 1889; 41 Halford St; ☼ noon-midnight) Leading the way in the city's new cultural quarter, this place has an airy, high-ceilinged bar and restaurant that spills outside in summer. The funky basement lounge is all blue mood lighting and plush sofas set to a soundtrack of soul, world music and jazz.

Entertainment

NIGHTCLUBS

Charlotte (☎ 0116-255 3956; www.thecharlotte.co.uk; 8 Oxford St; ☼ doors open 8pm) Leicester's legendary venue has staged Oasis and the Stone Roses, among others, before they became megastars. It's a small, grungy, lively place with a late licence and club nights catering for all sorts of musical tastes.

De Montfort Hall (☎ 0116-233 3111; www.demontfort hall.co.uk; Granville Rd) Bigger bands sometimes play at this hall, southeast of the centre, which also stages everything from cheesy crooners to gospel choirs.

Original Four (☎ 0116-254 1638; 2 King St; Sat £12) Behind a mock-Tudor facade, this place cooks up four floors of diverse beats: a bar, cocktail lounge, dance floor and dedicated space for live music. It has seen more popular days but is still one of the best clubbing options in town.

THEATRE & COMEDY

Phoenix Arts Centre (☎ 0116-255 4854; www.phoenix .org.uk; Newarke St) This is Leicester's main venue for art-house films, fringe plays, comedy and dance events.

Other venues for plays include the **Little Theatre** (☎ 255 1302; www.thelittletheatre.net; Dover St); **Haymarket Theatre** (☎ 0116-253 0021; 1 Belgrave Gate), which has some innovative theatre; and the **Y** (☎ 255 7066; www.leicesterymca.co.uk; 7 East St), a theatre and bar attached to the YMCA, hosting concerts, cabaret, poetry and plays.

Getting There & Away

National Express operates from St Margaret's bus station on Gravel St, north of the centre. Buses run to Nottingham (£3.50, one hour, twenty daily), and Coventry (£5.70, 45 minutes, four daily). Other options for Coventry include the X67 (one hour, hourly).

Trains run to London's St Pancras Station (£21, one hour 20 minutes, four hourly) and Birmingham (£8.40, one hour, twice hourly).

A tourist jaunt rather than a serious transport option, the classic **Great Central Railway** (☎ 01509-230726; www.gcrailway.co.uk; return adult/child £12/8) operates steam locomotives between Leicester North station on Redhill Circle and Loughborough Central. This dual-track railway runs the 8-mile route along which Thomas Cook ran his original package tour in 1841. The trains run regularly from June to August and some weekends the rest of the year. Take bus 70 from Haymarket bus station.

Getting Around

Central Leicester is easy to get around on foot. As an alternative to local buses, the open-top bus run by **Discover Leicester** (☎ 0844 888 5151; adult/under 15yr £7/5; ☼ around 10 past the hour 10am-4pm Jul-Sep) runs a jump-on jump-off bus around the city and up to Belgrave Rd, the Great Central Railway and the National Space Centre, with on-board commentary from a local expert. It starts by the Thomas Cook statue outside Leicester train station.

AROUND LEICESTER

Bosworth Battlefield

The **Battlefield Heritage Centre** (☎ 01455-290429; bosworthbattlefield.com; admission £3.25; ☼ 11am-5pm Apr-Oct) features an interactive exhibition about the Wars of the Roses and the battle that ended it – the Battle of Bosworth. This is one of the most important battle sites in England, where Richard III was defeated by the future Henry VII in 1485. 'A horse, a horse, my kingdom for a horse' was Richard's famous death cry (at least according to William Shakespeare). He may be known as a villain for his supposed role in the murder of the 'princes in the tower', but Leicester has adopted him as something of a folk hero, not the hunchback of Shakespearean spin. The battle is re-enacted annually in August.

The battlefield is 16 miles southwest of Leicester at Sutton Cheny, off the A447. Bus 153 runs hourly from Leicester to Market Bosworth, 3 miles to the north. The **Bosworth Gold Cars** (☎ 01455-291999) taxi firm can also take you there.

Ashby-de-la-Zouch
pop 12,758

The real draw of Ashby-de-la-Zouch is its **castle** (EH; ☎ 01530-413343; adult/child £3.70/1.90; ⏰ 10am-6pm daily Jul-Aug, to 5pm Thu-Mon Apr-Jun, Sep & Oct, noon-4pm Thu-Mon Nov-Mar). Built in Norman times and owned by the Zouch family until 1399, it was extended in the 14th and 15th centuries and then reduced to its present picturesquely ruined state in 1648 after the English Civil War. A lively audio guide introduces the characters and details the history. Bring a torch to explore the underground passageway connecting the tower with the kitchen.

For accommodation, contact the **tourist office** (☎ 01530-411767; North St; ⏰ 9.30am-5pm Mon-Fri, to 4pm Sat). Ashby is on the A511 about 15 miles northwest of Leicester. Bus X2 runs hourly from St Margaret's bus station in Leicester. An open-top bus run by **Discover Leicester** (☎ 0844 888 5181; adult/under 15yr £7/5; ⏰ 9.30am, 11am, 1.30pm & 3pm mid-Jul–end Aug) runs a jump-on jump-off **Heart of the Forest** tour. It leaves from Lloyds TSB and takes in a circular route, passing through Conkers and other local attractions before coming back into town.

Conkers & the National Forest

The National Forest is an ambitious project to generate sustainable woodland by planting 30 million trees from Leicester through Derbyshire into Staffordshire. The purpose-built attraction, **Conkers** (☎ 01283-216633; www.visitconkers.com; Rawdon Rd, Moira; adult/child £6.95/4.50; ⏰ 10am-6pm Apr-Sep, to 4.30pm Oct-Mar), is central to the scheme, containing interactive displays on woodland life, biology and the environment. There's lots of touching, smelling and hearing: it's a multisensory experience to captivate children, but it's engaging for all ages.

There's also an excellent new **YHA hostel** (☎ 0845 371 9672; www.yha.org.uk; beds from £11.95 P ⏰) in the National Forest. It's packed with ecofriendly features and has a great restaurant serving local produce and organic wines. It's 300m west of Conkers' entrance along Bath Lane.

Conkers is 20 miles northwest of Leicester off the A444.

Belvoir Castle

Deep in the countryside, **Belvoir** (*bee*-ver) **Castle** (☎ 01476-871000; www.belvoircastle.com; adult/child £12/6; ⏰ 11am-5pm Sat-Thu May-Aug, Sat & Sun Sep, sporadically in Oct, Mar & Apr) is a magnificent baroque and Gothic fantasy rebuilt in the 19th century after suffering serious damage during the English Civil War. It is also home to the duke and duchess of Rutland. Much of the sumptuous interior is open to the public, and collections of weaponry, medals and art (including pieces by Reynolds, Gainsborough and Holbein) are highlights. There are marvellous views across the countryside, and peacocks roam the gardens.

Belvoir is 6 miles west of Grantham, off the A1; Grantham is about 25 miles east of Nottingham along the A52.

RUTLAND

Rutland's motto 'Multum in Parvo' (So much in so little) refers to its status as England's smallest county. Rutland Water, one of the largest reservoirs in Europe, makes it a haven for water-sport lovers, as well as climbers and bird-watchers. The **Oakham tourist office** (☎ 01572-758441; Catmose St, Oakham ⏰ 10.30am-5pm Mon-Sat, 2-4pm Sun) is housed in the Rutland County Museum, and there's also a **Rutland Water tourist office** (☎ 01572-653026; Sykes Lane, Empingham; ⏰ 10am-5pm Easter-Sep, to 4pm Tue-Sat Oct-Mar, shorter hr in winter).

In Rutland Water, the **Rutland Belle** (☎ 01572-787630; www.rutlandwatercruises.com; the Harbour, Whitwell Park; adult/child £7/4.50) offers pleasure cruises every afternoon from April to September. The **Watersports Centre** (☎ 01780-460154; Whitwell) organises windsurfing, canoeing and sailing and offers tuition, and the **Rutland Sailing School** (☎ 01780-721999; www.rutlandsailingschool.co.uk; Edith Weston) offers tuition to sailors of all abilities, from catamarans to dinghies.

For bike hire, contact **Rutland Water Cycling** (☎ 01780-460705; www.rutlandcycling.co.uk; Whitwell Car Park).

The sleepy county town of **Oakham** has a famous school and **Oakham Castle** (admission free; ⏰ 10.30am-1pm & 1.30-5pm Mon-Sat, 2-4pm Sun, shorter hr Nov-Feb), where an impressive Great Hall from a 12th-century Norman structure still stands.

South of Oakham is the village of Lyddington, home to the **Bede House** (EH; ☎ 01572-822438; adult/child £3.70/1.90; ⏰ 10am-5pm Thu-Mon Apr-Sep). Originally a wing of the medieval rural palace of the bishops of Lincoln, it was converted into almshouses in 1600. Look out for the beautifully carved cornice in the Great Chamber.

our pick **Hambleton Hall** (☎ 01572-756991; Hambleton, Oakham; mains £32-36; ⏰ lunch & dinner) surveys the countryside from a regal peninsula in Rutland Water. The elegant Victorian is one of England's finest country retreats. Its Michelin-starred restaurant attracts food and wine lovers from miles around, who come to dine on passionate cooking featuring wonderfully fresh ingredients such as herbs and vegetables from its own garden and wild mushrooms picked in local woods. After the main event, relax in one of the countrified luxury rooms, stroll the glorious grounds, or work it off in the pool or on the tennis courts.

Bus 19 runs from Nottingham's Broadmarsh bus station to Oakham (1¼ hours, hourly). Trains run hourly from Leicester, Peterborough and Birmingham.

LINCOLNSHIRE

This sparsely populated corner of Eastern England has a reputation for being flat, plain and proper, although on closer look it's uncommonly friendly and remarkably varied: the stunning stately homes and time-capsule towns of rural Lincolnshire are ready fodder for a steady stream of moviemakers searching for ready-made period sets.

The county capital, Lincoln, is the perfect place to start, with a stunning Gothic cathedral and Tudor streetscapes in a dramatic hilltop location. The gently rippling hills

---

DETOUR: OLIVE BRANCH

Picturesque county pub **Olive Branch** (☎ 01780-410355; Main St, Clipsham; mains £12-19; ⏱ lunch & dinner Tue-Sat), sitting pretty in the little village of Clipsham, may have a reputation for the finest food in the area but you wouldn't know it from its chilled-out, unpretentious air. The interior is warm and rustic – full of books, magazines, old wine and champagne bottles, wooden tables, mismatched chairs and log fires – and there's a daily, changing menu of fantastic, fresh, seasonal and flavoursome food. For overnighters, there are sumptuous rooms to sink into at their little B&B across the road – a delightful butterscotch-coloured period house.

The Olive Branch is 9 miles northeast of Oakham, off the A1.

---

of the Lincolnshire Wolds smooth down to eastern marshlands and sandy coast, and the dyke-scored Lincolnshire Fens flat-iron the southeast. While flamboyant medieval churches, red-roofed stone houses and windmills grace many towns, here too you'll find brash beach resort Skegness and rich wildlife reserves where the loudest din is birdsong.

Information

South West Lincs (www.southwestlincs.com)
Visit Lincolnshire (www.visitlincolnshire.com)
Visit the Fens (www.visitthefens.co.uk)

Activities

The 140-mile **Viking Way** trails from the Humber Bridge through the Lincolnshire Wolds to Oakham in Leicestershire. It can be more rewarding to explore the area by bike; leaflets on county cycle trails are available at tourist offices.

To mess around on boats, the **Lincolnshire Fens** offer a rich and varied choice of navigable waterways.

Getting There & Away

Other than a speedy rail link between Grantham and London, Lincolnshire isn't the easiest county to get to and around. You're better off on the buses to reach Stamford and Lincoln, and don't be surprised if you have to change services en route.

Getting Around

For regional travel information, contact **Traveline** (☎ 0871 200 2233; www.travelineeastmidlands .org.uk) or consult the travel pages of the **Lincolnshire County Council** (www.lincolnshire.gov .uk) website. Useful bus operators include **Lincs Interconnect** (☎ 0845 234 3344; www.lincs interconnect.com) and **Stagecoach** (www.stage coachbus.com/lincolnshire).

LINCOLN
pop 85,595

An undervisited delight, Lincoln's tightly knotted core of cobbled streets and majestic medieval architecture is enough to leave visitors breathless, albeit as much for its punishing slopes as for the superb stonework and timber-framed treasures to be found there. An extraordinary cathedral, an unusual Norman castle and compact Tudor streets crown Lincoln's hilltop; the town then tumbles down

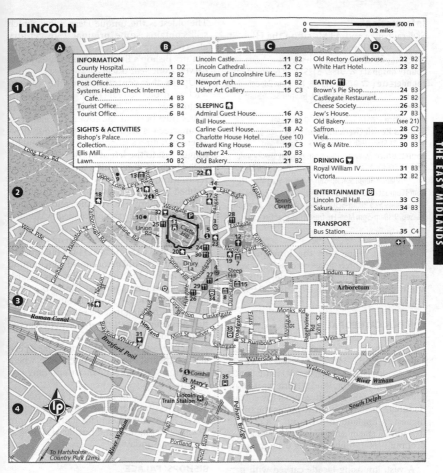

LINCOLN

INFORMATION		
County Hospital............................1	D2	
Launderette....................................2	B2	
Post Office.....................................3	B2	
Systems Health Check Internet		
Cafe..4	B3	
Tourist Office.................................5	B2	
Tourist Office.................................6	B4	
SIGHTS & ACTIVITIES		
Bishop's Palace.............................7	C3	
Collection......................................8	C3	
Ellis Mill...9	B2	
Lawn..10	B2	

Lincoln Castle..............................11	B2	
Lincoln Cathedral.........................12	C2	
Museum of Lincolnshire Life........13	B2	
Newport Arch..............................14	B2	
Usher Art Gallery.........................15	C3	
SLEEPING		
Admiral Guest House...................16	A3	
Bail House....................................17	B2	
Carline Guest House....................18	A2	
Charlotte House Hotel..........(see 10)		
Edward King House......................19	C3	
Number 24...................................20	B3	
Old Bakery...................................21	B2	

Old Rectory Guesthouse..............22	B2	
White Hart Hotel..........................23	B2	
EATING		
Brown's Pie Shop........................24	B3	
Castlegate Restaurant..................25	B2	
Cheese Society.............................26	B3	
Jew's House.................................27	B3	
Old Bakery...........................(see 21)		
Saffron..28	B3	
Viela...29	B3	
Wig & Mitre..................................30	B3	
DRINKING		
Royal William IV..........................31	B3	
Victoria...32	B2	
ENTERTAINMENT		
Lincoln Drill Hall..........................33	C3	
Sakura..34	B3	
TRANSPORT		
Bus Station...................................35	C4	

THE EAST MIDLANDS

---

the hillside losing charm and picking up modern pace as it goes.

At the hill's base, the university breathes life into a waterfront quarter where bars are positioned to watch boats come and go. While there's little to keep you for a longer stay, Lincoln has a welcoming aura and enough cultural clout in its centre to keep you very happy for a day or two at a stretch.

History
With a hill that affords views for miles around and a river for swift sea access, it's hardly surprising that Lincoln's defensive location has been exploited by invading forces for the last 2000 years. The Romans set up camp soon after arriving in Britain and in the 11th century the Normans speedily constructed a castle after their invasion. The city yo-yoed between Royalist and Parliamentarian forces during the Civil War, and the warfare theme continued into the 20th century, when Lincoln's heavy-engineering industry spawned the world's first tank, which saw action in WWI.

Orientation
The cathedral stands imperiously on top of the hill in the old city, with the castle and other attractions clustered nearby. Three-quarters of a mile downhill is the new town, and the bus and train stations. Joining the two is the appositely named Steep Hill, and believe us, they're not kidding – even locals stop to catch their breath.

Information

Several banks and ATMs sit on the High St. Check www.lincolntoday.co.uk and www .lincoln.gov.uk for events listings.

County hospital (☎ 01522-512512; off Greetwell Rd)
Launderette (☎ 01522-543498; 8 Burton Rd; per load £3; 🕙 8.30am-8pm Mon-Fri, to 5pm Sat & Sun) Self-service laundrette.
Post office (☎ 01522-526031; 90 Bailgate)
Systems Health Check Internet Cafe (☎ 01522-522635; 61 Steep Hill; per hr £2; 🕙 10am-7pm)
Tourist office (www.visitlincolnshire.com) Main branch (☎ 01522-873213; 9 Castle Hill; 🕙 9.30am-6pm Mon-Sat, 10.30am-4.30pm Sun Jul-Sep, 9.30am-5pm Mon-Fri, from 10am Sat & Sun Oct-Jun); Cornhill (☎ 01522-873256; 21 Cornhill; 🕙 9.30am-5.30pm Mon-Sat, 11am-3pm Sun Jul-Sep, 9.30am-5pm Mon-Fri, from 10am Sat Oct-Jun)

Sights

The tourist office sells the Lincoln Time Travel Pass, which gives access to several heritage sites including the castle, cathedral and Bishop's Palace (single/family £9.99/20) and lasts three days.

LINCOLN CATHEDRAL

All kinds of marvels and mischief can be found in the county's top attraction, **Lincoln Cathedral** (☎ 01522-544544; www.lincolncathedral.com; adult/under 16yr £4/1; 🕙 7.15am-8pm Mon-Fri, to 6pm Sat & Sun Jun-Aug, 7.15am-6pm Mon-Sat, to 5pm Sun Sep-May). This soaring edifice has three great towers that dominate the city, one of which is the third-highest in England at 81m, but it's claimed that until a storm in 1547 its spire was a jaw-dropping 160m high, topping even the great pyramids of Giza.

A vast, imposing facade carved with gargoyles, kings, dragons and hunters leers over the Great West Door. On closer inspection, you'll spot that the facade is divided into two eras, the lower of which is from the Norman cathedral toppled in an earthquake in 1185; the rest dates to the building's 12th- and 13th-century reconstruction by Bishop Hugh of Avalon (St Hugh). The saint himself tops a pinnacle on one side of the West Front, and his counterpart on the other side is a swineherd who devoted his meagre lifesavings to the cathedral's reconstruction.

Inside the lofty nave, there's a chunky black-marble font from the 11th century, ringed with fearsome mythological beasts. Two magnificent stained-glass rose windows face each other, lighting the great transept.

The oldest is the unique Dean's Eye, which still contains some original 13th-century glass picturing the Last Judgement. The 14th-century Bishop's Eye has some truly exquisite carved stone-leaf tracery.

Up in the central tower, the veteran Victorian bell, Great Tom, still swings its ponderous 2m, 270kg bulk to sound the hours. Just beyond the tower, the elaborate choir screen is studded with grotesque characters including a stonemason sticking out his tongue just to the left of the door.

St Hugh's Choir, which is currently under restoration, is topped by an unusual vault, dubbed the 'crazy vault' for its odd angles, while the superbly carved and canopied stalls below are a classic example of medieval craftsmanship. Just beyond this, the Angel Choir is graced by 28 angels carved high up the walls. It was built as a shrine to St Hugh but modern pilgrims are mostly preoccupied with hunting for the famous Lincoln Imp, a lovably roguish little horned character that is now the city's emblem. Various legends surround the imp, the most fun being that the mischievous creature was caught chatting up one of the carved angels and was promptly turned to stone.

For one last stop before leaving, take a peek at the cathedral's round Chapterhouse, where the climax of *The Da Vinci Code* film was shot in 2005.

There are one-hour tours at least twice a day plus less-frequent tours of the roof and the tower. Evensong takes place daily at 5.30pm (3.45pm on Sunday) and Eucharist is sung at 9.30am on Sunday.

BISHOPS' PALACE

Beside the cathedral are the ravaged but still imposing ruins of the 12th-century **Bishops' Palace** (EH; ☎ 01522-527468; adult/child £4/2; 🕙 10am-6pm daily Jul & Aug, to 5pm Apr-Jun, Sep & Oct, to 4pm Thu-Mon Nov-Mar), which was gutted by parliamentary forces during the Civil War. In its day, it was the power base of medieval England's largest diocese, and, scrambling around its remaining walls, highlights include a barrel-vaulted undercroft and walled terrace garden with views over the town below. The free audio tour is particularly entertaining.

LINCOLN CASTLE

After installing himself as king in 1066, William the Conqueror speedily set about building castles to keep his new kingdom

in line, and **Lincoln Castle** (☎ 01522-511068; www
.lincolnshire.gov.uk/lincolncastle; adult/child £4/2.65;
🕓 10am-6pm daily May-Aug, to 5pm Apr & Sep, to 4pm
Oct-Mar) was one of his first. Highlights include
a castle-wall walkway, from which you can
survey the town, and one of the four surviving
copies of the democratic milestone **Magna Carta**
(dated 1215; see p38).

Lincoln Castle also has its gruesome side.
It was home to the city's court and prison for
centuries, and public executions here used to
draw thousands of bloodthirsty spectators.
The castle has a chilling Victorian prison
chapel with coffin-style pews that inmates
were locked into.

There are free tours of the castle at 11am
and 2pm daily from April to September and
on weekends in winter.

THE COLLECTION
Opened to acclaim in 2005, this **archaeology
museum** (☎ 01522-550990; www.thecollection.lincoln
.museum; Danes Tce; admission free; 🕓 10am-4pm) details
the archaeological history of Lincolnshire and
is full of child-friendly exhibits to inspire budding Indiana Joneses. Kids can measure their
height against a woolly mammoth, design
their own beast on a touch screen or deck
themselves out like a knight or a Roman soldier. Other interesting artefacts include an
impressive 7m log dugout and a 4000-year-old
local skull.

Just east is the historic **Usher Art Gallery**
(☎ 01522-527980; Lindum Rd; admission free; 🕓 10am-
4pm), which now belongs to the same complex but sits separately in a grand mansion
amid parkland. It holds an impressive selection of portraits, and the largest collection of
paintings and drawings by leading English
watercolour practitioner, Peter de Wint
(1784–1849) as well as works by JMW Turner,
LS Lowry and others.

OTHER SIGHTS
The whole length of **Steep Hill** is a delight to
explore (at least until the climb back up),
crowded with black-and-white Tudor beauties and curious antiquarian bookshops. Of
particular note, however, is the Romanesque
stone **Jew's House**, which is easily one of the
best and earliest examples of 12th-century
domestic architecture in Britain. It's now an
upmarket restaurant (see p494).

Back up and through town, rough-edged
Newport Arch (Bailgate) dates back even further

as it was built by the Romans, and is the oldest arch in Britain that still has traffic passing
through it.

If you're barmy about botany, don't miss a
trip to the **Lawn** (☎ 01522-568080; www.thelawninlincoln
.co.uk; admission free; Union Rd; 🕓 10am-5pm, shorter
hrs Nov-Feb), a former lunatic asylum – but
also where you'll find the steamy Sir Joseph
Banks Conservatory, containing descendants
of some of the plants brought back by this
Lincoln explorer who accompanied Captain
Cook to Australia.

History buffs may also make the short
trek north to the **Museum of Lincolnshire Life**
(☎ 01522-528448; adult/child £2.25/1.50; 🕓 10am-5pm
daily May-Oct, Mon-Sat Nov-Apr), displaying everything from a reconstructed Edwardian nursery to an early tank named 'flirt' that was
famous for all the wrong reasons during
WWI. Round the corner from the museum
is the cute little **Ellis Mill** (☎ 528448; Mill Rd; adult/
child £1/0.65) windmill.

Tours
Guided 1½-hour **walking tours** (adult/child £3/1.50)
run from outside the tourist office in Castle
Hill at 11am and 2pm daily in July and August,
and at weekends only from June to October.
Also from the tourist office, a 1¼-hour **ghost
walk** (☎ 01522-874056; www.lincolnhistorywalks.co.uk;
adult/under 12yr £4/2) departs at 7pm Wednesday
to Saturday.

Horse-drawn tours (£25) also run around the
city from Castle Hill in summer. Down below
the centre on Brayford Wharf, several boats
offer one-hour summer **boat trips** (adult/child £6/3;
🕓 10.30am-4pm) along Fossdyke Canal and the
River Witham.

Sleeping
BUDGET
Hartsholme Country Park (☎ 01522-873578; hartsholme
cp@lincoln.gov.uk; Skellingthorpe Rd; tent sites £7-15; 🕓 Mar-
Oct) Decent camping ground with OK facilities.
The main draw is that it's next to a sprawling
nature reserve filled with lovely lakes, woods
and meadows. It's 3 miles southwest of the
train station. Take the regular daytime SB6 or
evening 66A bus towards Birchwood Estate
from Lincoln bus station; alight at Swanpool
(15 minutes).

Old Rectory Guesthouse (☎ 01522-514774;
19 Newport; s/d/f from £28/50/65; Ⓟ) Lovely old
Edwardian building, well kept and charmingly
run but with seriously old-fashioned rooms.

Admiral Guest House (☎ 01522-544467; nicola.major1@ntlworld.com; 16-18 Nelson St; s/d/f £30/50/55; **P**) This place suffers from a mismatched, chintzy interior, but is good value, well located and run by friendly, knowledgeable hosts.

MIDRANGE

Edward King House (☎ 01522-528778; www.ekhs.org.uk; The Old Palace, Minster Yard; **P**) This one's different. It's a Christian-run pilgrim's house in the former home to Bishops of Lincoln, alongside the historic palace ruins. The accommodation was being given a thorough overhaul at the time of writing and will be ready to take visitors in 2009. Call ahead.

Carline Guest House (☎ 01522-530422; www.carlineguesthouse.co.uk; 1-3 Carline Rd; s/d from £35/55; **P**) Occupying a refined Edwardian house, this 12-room place has rather plushly decorated en suite rooms for such a modestly priced guest house, and each is quite different in character.

Old Bakery (☎ 01522-576057; www.theold-bakery.co.uk; 26-28 Burton Rd; r from £53; 🖵 wi-fi) This wonderful guest house, set above an excellent restaurant (right), has four sweet, characterful rooms. The welcome is warm but unobtrusive and the delicious breakfasts feature goodies such as homemade muffins.

our pick **Number 24** (☎ 01522-514650; www.number24.biz; 24 Drury Lane; s/d from £50/90; **P**) Make sure you get in here early – there's only one room and it's a corker. A short stroll away from the cathedral, it's decked out in unfussy country style with marvellous views of castle and cathedral, a private sitting room and roof terrace, and lots of thoughtful touches like a selection of books and magazines, fresh fruit, flowers and chocolates.

Bail House (☎ 01522-520883; www.bailhouse.co.uk; 34 Bailgate; s/d from £65/79, d superior £139-165; **P** 🖵 wi-fi) Stone walls, worn flagstones, Mediterranean-style gardens and one room with an extraordinary medieval, timber-vaulted ceiling are only a few of the charms of this lovingly restored town house in central Lincoln. There's even a heated outdoor swimming pool for fair-weather days.

White Hart Hotel (☎ 01522-526222; www.whitehart-lincoln.co.uk; Bailgate; s/d £75/100; **P** 🖵 wi-fi) You can't get more central or venerable than Lincoln's grand dame of hotels, neatly sandwiched between castle and cathedral, and with a history of hostelry dating back 600 years. It has four dozen luxurious country-

casual rooms, a few with partial views of the cathedral facade.

TOP END

Charlotte House Hotel (☎ 01522-541000; www.charlottehouselincoln.com; The Lawns; d £145-195; **P** 🖵 wi-fi) This refurbished 1930s art-deco building has 14 extremely slick rooms featuring such delights as plasma-screen TVs, huge walk-in showers, ultra-modern free-standing baths and underfloor heating. There's also a nice little bar with resident parrot and large outdoor terrace.

Eating

our pick **Brown's Pie Shop** (☎ 01522-527330; 33 Steep Hill; pies £7-11; 🕑 lunch & dinner) Not strictly a pie shop, this restaurant dishes up large servings of speciality pies, steaks and other hearty fare. Eat in the bustling, bright, white dining room, or in a lovely brick-vaulted basement area for candlelit evenings. The local wild-rabbit and beef-and-stout pies are particularly tasty and there are regularly changing guest-star pies.

Castlegate Restaurant (☎ 01522-541000; Union Rd; mains £10-20 🕑 lunch & dinner) Owned by the Charlotte House Hotel, this former coach house has a prime position right outside Lincoln Castle gate. There's elegant, fine dining on offer and lighter snacks throughout the day, and there's a bar.

Wig & Mitre (☎ 01522-535190; www.wigandmitre.com; 30 Steep Hill; mains £11-20; 🕑 8am-midnight) Civilised pub-restaurant the Wig & Mitre has an excellent, upscale menu but manages to retain the mellow cosiness of a local pub. No music will disturb your meal here, and the candlelit evening meals are good for romantic liaisons.

Jew's House (☎ 01522-524851; Steep Hill; set lunch/dinner £12/27; 🕑 lunch & dinner Tue-Sun) Pass through the ancient round-arched doorway of this 12th-century stone house and you'll immediately know you're in for a treat. This ancient house, an attraction in its own right, is flush with antiques and oil paintings, and its award-winning Anglo-French cuisine will not disappoint. Dress smart and book ahead.

Old Bakery (☎ 01522-576057; www.theold-bakery.co.uk; 26-28 Burton Rd; mains £15-21; 🕑 lunch & dinner Tue-Sun) This old bakery conversion in the shadow of Lincoln Castle's walls is one of the town's most popular restaurants. The pretty dining room, which opens up into an airy, slate-floored conservatory, serves award-winning, impeccably presented local produce, including very addictive bread, baked fresh on the premises of course.

Some more options:

Cheese Society (☎ 01522-511003; 1 St Martins Lane; ☺ 10am-4.30pm Mon-Sat) Cafe-deli that sends aficionados of fermented foodstuffs straight to the moon.

Saffron (☎ 01522-548377; 7 Eastgate; mains £7-12; ☺ noon-2.30pm & 5-11pm Sun-Thu, 5pm-midnight Fri & Sat) Fresh, vibrant Indian food in an elegant town house setting opposite the cathedral.

Viela (☎ 01522-576765; 8-9 The Strait, Steep Hill; meals £20-22; ☺ lunch & dinner Mon-Sat, lunch only Sun) The place to come for huge portions of Brazilian BBQ.

Drinking

Victoria (☎ 01522-536048; 6 Union Rd) A serious beer-drinker's pub with a pleasant patio looking up at the castle's western walls, Victoria has a huge selection of guest brews, cask ales, thick stouts and superb ciders, and preserves a mellow historic ambience undisturbed by sports or flashy lights. The pub runs two beer festivals a year.

Royal William IV (☎ 01522-528159; Brayford Wharf; ☺ 10am-11pm Sun-Thu, to midnight Fri & Sat) This friendly pub provides some respite from the brash chain bars, pubs and restaurants that line the regenerated Brayford Wharf beside the university. There's plenty of outdoor seating, though, if you want to watch the action.

Entertainment

Lincoln Drill Hall (☎ 01522-873894; www.lincolndrillhall .com; Free School Lane) The city's premier venue for music, theatre and comedy.

Sakura (☎ 01522-525828; 280-281 High St; ☺ 10pm-3am Mon-Sat) Every night is different at this Japanese-themed chain club, which alternately rocks to old-school funk, garage, R&B, '80s and '90s nights and house music, with some high-profile guest DJs to get the party started. It has some kaleidoscopic cocktails, and sake-based drinks.

Getting There & Away

Lincoln is 142 miles from London, 94 miles from Cambridge and 81 miles from York.

National Express runs a direct service between Lincoln and London (£21, 4¾ hours, daily). Buses also run from Lincoln to Birmingham (£14.50, three hours, daily).

Getting to and from Lincoln usually involves changing trains. There are links to Boston (£9.20, 1¼ hours, hourly) and Skegness

(£12.60, two hours, hourly); change at Sleaford. There are also trains to Cambridge (£21.90, 2½ hours, hourly), change at Peterborough or Ely; and links to Grantham (£8.20, 1½ hours, twice hourly).

Getting Around

BUS

Regular buses link the lower town bus and train stations with the uptown cathedral area. To avoid the climb up Steep Hill, a 'Walk and Ride' electric bus also runs every 20 minutes during the day from outside the House of Fraser store on High St to Castle Sq (adult/child £1/50p, five minutes).

GRANTHAM

pop 34,592

This sedate red-brick town is notable for its famous former inhabitants. Sir Isaac Newton was born and brought up in the area and is celebrated with a proud statue in front of the town's guildhall. More famously, Britain's first female prime minister, Margaret Thatcher, started life above her father's grocery shop at 2 North Pde, now a chiropractor's clinic; there's a small plaque on the house to honour its former resident, although the Iron Lady is yet to be granted her own plinth.

The **tourist office** (☎ 01476-406166; granthamtic @southkesteven.gov.uk; St Peter's Hill; ☺ 9.30am-4.30pm Mon-Fri, 9.30am-1pm Sat) is in the guildhall complex.

Until a commemorative statue is erected, Maggie must content herself with her latex puppet from the hit 1980s political satire *Spitting Image*, in the town's **museum** (☎ 01476-568783; St Peter's Hill; admission free; ☺ 10am-4pm Mon-Sat). Here too is one of her sparkly evening gowns and famous handbags, as well as displays on Sir Isaac Newton.

You can easily spot the part 13th-, part 16th-century parish church of **St Wulfram's** (☺ 9am-4pm Mon-Sat Apr-Sep, to 12.30pm Mon-Fri, 10am-1pm Sat Oct-Mar) thanks to its pin-sharp 85m spire. It has an interesting crypt chapel, and hidden up a steep stairwell is a 16th-century chained library where a young Newton once pored over his studies.

A dream location for English period dramas (several have been filmed here), serene Restoration country mansion, **Belton House** (NT; ☎ 01476-566116; A607; adult/under fiver £9.50/5.50, grounds only £7.50/4.50; ☺ 12.30-5pm Wed-Sun Apr-Oct), stands in a 400-hectare park 3 miles northeast of Grantham. Built in 1688 for Sir John

Brownlow, it shelters some astonishingly ornate woodcarvings attributed to the master Dutch carver Grinling Gibbons. In the beautiful gardens is a sundial made famous in Helen Cresswell's children's classic *Moondial*. Bus 609 (15 minutes) runs here from near Grantham's train station.

Sleeping & Eating

Red House (☎ 01476-579869; www.red-house.com; 74 North Pde; s/d from £30/48; P 🖳 wi-fi) This handsome Georgian town house near Maggie's birthplace has large, spick-and-span rooms. The welcome is very friendly, beauty treatments are available and rooms have mini fridges and microwaves.

Angel & Royal Hotel (☎ 01476-565816; www.angel androyal.co.uk; High St; s/d from £68/100; P 🖳 wi-fi) This veteran coaching inn claims to be England's oldest, with no less than seven kings of England purportedly having stayed here since 1200. Its 29 rooms are each individually decorated, with beds occupied by a teddy bear, quaint floral patterns and copious olde-English charm. There's a grand restaurant in a baronial hall for fine dining and Sunday lunches.

Blue Pig (☎ 01476-563704; 9 Vine St) Cosy oldworlde pub in a half-timbered Tudor building serving a fine selection of real ales and substantial English meals.

Getting There & Away

Grantham is 25 miles south of Lincoln, and Stagecoach bus 1 runs between the two (one hour 20 minutes, twice hourly Monday to Saturday, five times on Sunday). Bus 4 run by Kimes Coaches runs to Stamford (1½ hours, four daily Monday to Saturday), as does National Express (£6.40, 30 minutes).

You'll need to change at Newark to get to Lincoln by train (£8.20, 1½ hours, two hourly). Direct trains run from London King's Cross to Grantham (£28.20, 1¼ hours, twice hourly).

STAMFORD

pop 19,525

This handsome town has a sunny disposition all year round thanks to the warm honeycoloured Lincolnshire limestone of its buildings. Nestling against the River Welland and a lush waterside park, handsome Stamford's tangle of streets are bursting with fine medieval and Georgian constructions. And if you feel as though you're walking through a period

---

A TALE OF LITTLE & LARGE

Stamford guides are fond of telling the story of the unfortunate Daniel Lambert, who was born a healthy baby in 1770, but who soon began to tip the scales at ever more alarming totals. Despite just eating one meal per day, he ballooned to an astounding 336kg and was hailed by contemporaries as 'the most corpulent man of whom authentic record exists'. When the reluctant celebrity died here in 1809, a wall of his house had to be dismantled to remove the coffin, and 20 pallbearers were needed to heave it to the graveyard. Then, adding insult to injury, after Lambert's death his suits were displayed in a local pub where the mischievous dwarf Charles Stratton (1838–83), otherwise known as 'General Tom Thumb', would cause hilarity by disappearing up the armholes.

---

drama, there's a reason: Stamford has been used as a set for more drama productions than you can shake a clapperboard at.

The **tourist office** (☎ 01780-755611; stamfordtic@ southkesteven.gov.uk; 27 St Mary's St; 🕙 9.30am-5pm Mon-Sat, 10am-3.30pm Sun Apr-Oct) is in the Stamford Arts Centre, and helps with accommodation. They can also arrange guided town walks and chauffeured punt trips.

The **Stamford Museum** (☎ 01780-766317; Broad St; admission free; 🕙 10am-4pm Mon-Sat) has a muddle of displays on the town's history including models of circus-performing midget Charles Stratton (aka Tom Thumb) and local heavyweight Daniel Lambert (see boxed text, above).

Sleeping & Eating

Rock Lodge (☎ 01780-481758; www.rock-lodge.co.uk; 1 Epingham Rd; s/d £70/90; P) This imposing Edwardian town house sits haughtily above clipped green lawns, but the welcome is all smiles. The country casual rooms are well looked after and breakfasts (complete with homemade jams) are excellent.

our pick **George** (☎ 01780-750750; www.george hotelofstamford.com; 71 St Martin's St; s/d from £90/130, 4-poster d £205; P 🖳 wi-fi) Recognised by a gallows sign across the road, welcoming travellers but warning off highwaymen, this wonderful riverside hotel likes to call itself 'England's greatest coaching inn', and with some justification.

Parts of it date back a thousand years and its long history is reflected in its 47 luxurious rooms, each of which has its own unique character and flair, decor and price tag. The oak-panelled restaurant serves classy British and international cuisine

Finnans (☎ 01780-752505; www.finnansbrasserie .co.uk; 8-9 Paul's St; mains £8-14; 🕑 lunch & dinner Tue-Thu, from 9am Fri & Sat) Seasonal, local food from a delicious, unpretentious and regularly changing menu is served up at this friendly brasserie.

Other recommendations:

Dolphin Guest House (☎ 01780-757515; mik@mik dolphin.demon.co.uk; 12 East St; r £25-60; 🅿) Bland modern-ish rooms but central.

Stamford Lodge (☎ 01780-482932; www.stamford lodge.co.uk; 66 Scotgate; s/d £50/70) A former bakehouse with modern rooms, a friendly hostess and excellent breakfasts.

Getting There & Away

Stamford is 46 miles from Lincoln and 21 miles south of Grantham.

National Express serves Stamford from London (£13.10, 2¾ hours, daily). Kimes operates between Stamford and Grantham (1½ hours, four daily Monday to Saturday), as does National Express (£6.40, 30 minutes, two daily). Delaine Buses run to Peterborough (one hour, hourly).

There are trains to Cambridge (£16, 1¼ hours, hourly) and Ely (£10.80, 55 minutes, hourly). Trains to Norwich (£22, 2¼ hours) usually involve changing at Ely or Peterborough.

AROUND STAMFORD
Burghley House

Built to impress back in the 16th century, this dizzyingly flamboyant **Elizabethan palace** (☎ 01780-752451; www.burghley.co.uk; adult/child incl sculpture garden £10.90/5.40; 🕑 11am-5pm Sat-Thu Easter-Oct) still does a damn fine job of it today. Lying just a mile south of Stamford, Burghley (bur-lee) is the home of the Cecil family and was built by Queen Elizabeth's adviser William Cecil. These days it's a regular star of the silver screen, with hit films like *The Da Vinci Code* and *Elizabeth: The Golden Age* just some of the productions utilising its flashy interior as a dramatic stage.

Its roof bristles with cupolas, pavilions, belvederes and chimneys, and every inch of its 18 magnificent staterooms seems drenched with lavish finery. Hundreds of masterpieces from Gainsborough to Brueghel hang from the walls, while other rooms skip the frames and are splashed with wonderful 17th-century Italian murals overflowing with muscles, mammaries and mythology. Most impressive is the Heaven Room, which writhes with floor-to-ceiling gods and goddesses; on the flip side, there's the nearby stairway to Hell, which depicts Satan as a giant cat-eyed uterus devouring the world. Other highlights include cavernous Tudor kitchens decorated with turtle skulls left over from the master's soup and an exhibit detailing the career of David Cecil, the Lord Burghley who was an Olympic athlete and part inspiration for the film *Chariots of Fire*.

Meanwhile, the landscaped deer park outside is now home to a splendid **sculpture garden** with organic-looking contemporary works sprinkled sympathetically and often humorously throughout the grounds.

The house is a pleasant 15-minute walk through the park from Stamford train station. The internationally famous **Burghley Horse Trials** take place here in early September.

BOSTON
pop 35,124

During the Middle Ages, Boston was a major port and wool-trading centre, but the town's true claim to fame came in the 1607, when pilgrims from Nottinghamshire tried to get from Boston to the Netherlands. These religious separatists suffered persecution and imprisonment but were able to make it to the Netherlands the year after and later to the New World. When word of their success made it back here, a crowd of locals followed them across the Atlantic to found a namesake town in the new colony of Massachusetts.

Lying near the mouth of the River Witham, in the bay known as the Wash, the town has been well and truly eclipsed by its US namesake and is a shadow of its former self. Although there isn't much to keep you here for long, the labyrinthine streets are pleasant enough to wander around and much of the Tudor heritage is still in evidence .

The **tourist office** (☎ 01205-356656; South St; ticboston@boston.gov.uk; Market Pl; 🕑 9.30am-5pm Mon-Sat) is in the Haven Gallery, just down from the guildhall.

Sights & Activities

Appropriate to the town's big-shot status in medieval times, the early 14th-century **St Botolph's Church** (☎ 01205-362864; church free, tower adult/under 18yr £2.50/1; ☺ 9am-4.30pm Mon-Sat, btwn services Sun) has a showy 88m-high tower, fondly dubbed the Boston Stump for its square tip, as its fenland base was not firm enough to support a thin spire. Puff your way up the 365 steps on a clear day and you'll see to Lincoln, 32 miles away.

Downstairs, there's a 17th-century **pulpit** from which John Cotton, the fiery vicar of St Botolph, delivered lengthy sermons in the 1630s, apparently convincing his parishioners to follow in the footsteps of the Pilgrim Fathers.

You can see the very cells in which the Pilgrim Fathers were imprisoned in the 14th-century **guildhall** (☎ 01205-365954; South St; adult/child £3/2; ☺ 10am-4.30pm Mon-Sat, 1.30-4.30pm Sun May-Sep), one of Lincolnshire's oldest brick buildings and testament to Boston's great wealth at the time. The guildhall has recently emerged from renovations and there are fun, interactive exhibits (for example, you can sit in the famous cells and close the bars behind you), as well as a restored 16th-century courtroom, and a mock up of a Georgian kitchen.

About 800m northeast of Market Pl is the fully functional, five-sailed **Maud Foster Windmill** (☎ 01205-352188; www.maudfoster.co.uk; adult/child £2.50/1.50; ☺ 10am-5pm Wed, 11am-5pm Thu-Sat, noon-5pm Sun Jul & Aug, Wed, Sat & Sun only Sep-Jun), built in 1819 and the tallest working windmill in the country with no fewer than seven floors that creak and tremble with its flour-grinding exertions. It's well worth the walk, just don't wear black or you'll come out grey.

Sleeping & Eating

Palethorpe House (☎ 3 01205-59000; 138 Spilsby Rd; s/d £50/70; **P** 🖳) This delightful vine-covered Victorian villa has just two beautifully refurbished en suite rooms complete with living room, and it's situated a 10-minute walk from Boston's centre. It only serves Continental breakfasts during the week.

Maud's Tea Rooms (☎ 01205-352188; Maud Foster Windmill, Willoughby Rd; mains £5-8; ☺ 10am-5pm Wed, from 11am Thu-Sat, from noon Sun Jul & Aug, Wed, Sat & Sun only Sep-Jun) Quirky teashop Maud's is set in its namesake tower windmill, and uses organic flour straight from the millstone to whip up a delicious array of cakes. More substantial meals are also on offer incorporating local produce such as Boston sausage and Lincolnshire Poacher cheese.

Getting There & Away

Brylaine Travel bus 5 runs between Lincoln and Boston (1½ hours, hourly), or you can take the train from Lincoln, changing at Sleaford (£9.20, 1¼ hours).

SKEGNESS
pop 16,806

If candyfloss, gaudy funfairs and a seafront parade drowning in amusement arcades and greasy fish-and-chip shops are your bag, then 'Skeggy' is the place to come. Thousands of classic seaside-fun seekers head here every year to do brave impressions of sunbathing on vast bucket-and-spade beaches, and live it up at cabaret shows, bingo halls and cheesy discos. But the resort also works to keep fresh generations of punters rolling in, and its more recent attractions include an orphaned seal-pup sanctuary, facilities for windsurfing and kitesurfing and a fancy skate park.

Cheap and cheerful B&Bs are just about everywhere and start at just £18 per person, but the **tourist office** (☎ 01754-899887; www .funcoast.co.uk; Grand Pde; ☺ 9.30am-5pm daily Easter-Oct, to 4.30pm Mon-Fri Nov-Easter) will also help you find digs. It sits opposite the **Embassy Centre** (☎ 0845 6740505; www.embassytheatre.co.uk), the mothership of Skeggy's cabaret scene, which puts on anything from comedy to Elvis tributes. From July to September, this stretch of beach saturates the night sky with light pollution as 25,000 glowing light bulbs ignite the town's famous light display, the **Skegness Illuminations**.

Skegness is simple to reach by public transport, with Stagecoach 7 buses departing from Boston (1¼ hours, hourly Monday to Saturday), and Stagecoach 6 buses from Lincoln (1¾ hours, hourly Monday to Saturday, five on Sunday).

There are trains between Skegness and Boston (40 minutes, at least hourly Monday to Saturday, nine on Sunday).

LOUTH
pop 15,930

Louth sits on the River Lud, sandwiched between the Wolds and the marches of the

Lincolnshire coast. This largely Georgian market town is cleaved into two hemispheres, – east and west – as the zero longitude line splits the town; it is marked by a plaque in Eastgate and sculptures dot the line as part of the Louth Art Trail. Louth was also once the scene of a dramatic, if short-lived, revolt against Henry VIII in 1536.

The **tourist office** (☎ 01507-609289; louthinfo@ e-lindsey.gov.uk; New Market Hall, off Cornmarket; ☯ 9am-5pm Mon-Sat, to 4.30pm Oct-Easter) has maps and can help find accommodation.

While mustering the strength to climb Louth's main attraction – the tallest parish church spire in England – pop into **Louth Museum** (☎ 01507-601211; www.louthmuseum.co.uk; 4 Broadbank; adult/child £2/1.20; ☯ 10am-4pm Tue-Sat Apr-Oct) to see its reproduction of an enormous panorama of Louth, which was painted from the top of the church's tower in the 19th century.

To make the comparison with today's views, head for the spire itself. The part medieval, part Tudor **St James' Church** (☯ 10.30am-4pm Easter-Christmas) was described by Sir John Betjeman as 'one of the last great medieval Gothic masterpieces' and is propped up by dramatic buttresses and fortified by battlements.

Inside, take a good look down the nave and you'll see that the left row of pillars – which are older than their opposite twins – are lurching off balance. Strange to think that the famous New World adventurer Captain John Smith, of Pocahontas fame, once worshipped here. A long elbow-scraping climb up to the tower (£1.50) is rewarded by views better still than you'd hoped.

Louth's most elegant street is Georgian Westgate, which runs from beside the church. Opposite the mid-17th-century **church precincts** at No 47 is Westgate Pl. Sneak through its archway and you'll find an impossibly cute row of terraced houses, one of which bears a plaque commemorating Tennyson's four-year residence here.

Stay at the **Priory** (☎ 01507-602930; www.the prioryhotel.com; 149 Eastgate; s/d/f from £45/60/110; Ⓟ), which was half-castle, half-house but never a priory. It's a glorious, whitewashed Gothic-style building from 1818, set in sprawling gardens complete with folly and lake. Rooms have beautiful period-style furnishings, dinner is available most nights and children are very welcome.

The **Mad Hatter's Tearooms** (☎ 01507-609986; 117 Eastgate; 10am-5pm Tue-Wed, Fri & Sat, to 3pm Thu) is an eccentric place sitting at the back of an old-fashioned ladies-clothing store. Its menu features a decent selection of cakes, sandwiches and soups.

Louth is 23 miles northeast of Lincoln, from where bus 10 runs (one hour, two hourly).

AROUND LOUTH
Saltfleetby-Theddlethorpe Dunes National Nature Reserve

One of the Fens' most attractive **nature reserves** (☎ 01507-338611; www.english-nature.org.uk; admission free; ☯ dawn-dusk), Saltfleetby-Theddlethorpe is perhaps at its most beautiful in early summer when the marshes are dusted with yellow and mauve orchids. Spring and autumn can be equally lovely, though, as migratory wildfowl flock to the reserve and birdsong rings out across the grassy dunes. Criss-crossing the whole area are dozens of short and long trails to keep your feet dry as you negotiate the myriad lagoons.

You'll need your own transport to get here. The reserve is 10 miles east of Louth at the end of the B1200. Turn right onto the A1031 and follow the signs.

NOTTINGHAMSHIRE

Nottinghamshire is awash with myth and storytelling. Home to outlaw Robin Hood and his band of thieves, it's is also the birthplace of provocative writer DH Lawrence and played host to hedonist poet Lord Byron. The city of Nottingham is the vibrant hub, drawing business people, shoppers and clubbers from around the region. Delve into the surrounding countryside and you'll come across the occasional gem of a stately home.

Orientation & Information

Nottinghamshire is tall and thin, spreading a surprising distance north of Nottingham to finish level with Sheffield. Most of the county's attractions are in the southern half including Nottingham, with Newstead and Eastwood just north, Sherwood Forest in the centre and Newark-on-Trent and Southwell to the east.

Find countywide information at www .visitnottingham.co.uk.

THE EAST MIDLANDS

THE FENS

One of England's most melancholy landscapes, the man-made Fens were once strange and deso-late marshlands that stretched north from Cambridge to The Wash and beyond into Lincolnshire. Amid the wilderness, lived isolated pockets of people who survived by fishing and farming scraps of land among a maze of waterways. Though Romans and land-hungry medieval monasteries dabbled with building flood banks to exploit the fertile land, it took the 17th-century arrival of Dutch engineer Sir Cornelius Vermuyden to begin the wholesale draining of the Fens. Not that the scheme proved easy or unopposed – unhappy Fen folk were known to diligently dig the dykes during the day, then sneak back at night when their landlords weren't looking and fill in their hard work! However, with the aid of wind and, later, steam pumps, the flat, open plains with their rich, black soil were created. Now an eerie windswept but strangely mesmerising landscape, the region has inspired a wealth of literature including Graham Swift's excellent novel *Waterland*.

As the world's weather pattern changes and the sea level rises, however, the Fens are begin-ning to disappear underwater again. It's estimated that by the year 2030 up to 400,000 hectares could be lost. To find out more on the past and future of the Fens, visit **Fenscape Discovery Centre** (☎ 761161; www.fenscape.org; A151 at A16; admission free) near Spalding, Lincolnshire, or ap-preciate its wildlife at **Wicken Fen National Nature Reserve** (☎ 01353-720274; www.wicken.org.uk; Lode Lane, Wicken; adult/child £5.25/2.65; ☾ dawn-dusk), 8 miles south of Ely.

Getting Around

A journey planner and comprehensive bus, rail, tram and plane information can be found at www.itsnottingham.info. **Sherwood Forester buses** (☎ 0845 9 808080; Ranger ticket adult/child £6/3; ☾ Sun & Bank Holidays Jun-Aug) go to tourist attrac-tions all over Nottinghamshire; some offer admission discounts if you show the ticket.

NOTTINGHAM
pop 266,988

Forever associated with merry men in tights and a cranky sheriff, Nottingham today is a dynamic mix of medieval and modern. Multistorey car parks and postwar architectural eyesores live alongside centuries-old landmarks and an old town formed from a warren of former lace shops and factories, on which the city's wealth was built in the 19th century. The city's industrial heyday is long gone, but its nightlife, culture and shopping are booming. Fashion designer Paul Smith is a local lad, while the clubs and bars are some of the liveliest in the country.

Orientation

Like other Midlands cities, Nottingham is en-closed by an inner ring road within which lie most of the attractions, bars and restaurants. The train station is on the southern edge of the centre. There are two bus stations: Victoria bus station is hidden away behind the Victoria shopping centre, just north of the centre, while Broadmarsh bus station is beneath Broadmarsh shopping centre to the south.

Information

HSBC Bank (☎ 08457 404404; 12 Victoria St; 9am-5pm Mon-Fri)

Post office (☎ 0845 722 3344; Queen St; 9am-5.30pm Mon-Fri, 9am-4.30pm Sat)

Tourist office (☎ 0115-915 5330; www.visitnottingham .com; 1-4 Smithy Row; ☾ 9am-5.30pm Mon-Fri, to 5pm Sat, 10am-4pm Sun) The staff here are very helpful. Ask them about discount combination tickets for major attrac-tions. There are a few terminals to access the internet here.

Sights & Activities

NOTTINGHAM CASTLE MUSEUM & ART GALLERY

William the Conqueror erected Nottingham's original castle, but the stately building that stands there now – more of a mansion than a castle – has been around since the 1670s; the last Nottingham Castle was demolished after the English Civil War.

The **castle museum** (☎ 0115-915 3700; adult/child £3.50/2 joint ticket with the Brewhouse Yard Museum; ☾ 10am-5pm Mar-Oct, to 4pm Nov-Feb) opened in 1878. It vividly sets out Nottingham's his-tory and displays some of the medieval ala-baster carvings for which Nottingham was noted. Textiles and costumes peculiar to the city are also on show. Upstairs, there's an **art gallery** with changing exhibitions and some fine permanent pieces including works by Dante Gabriel Rossetti. There's also a stylish cafe and an excellent shop.

An underground passageway, **Mortimer's Hole** (45min tours £2; ☾ tours 11am, 2pm & 3pm Mon-Sat,

THE EAST MIDLANDS

noon, 1pm, 2pm, 3pm Sun May-Aug), leads from the castle to Brewhouse Yard. Roger Mortimer, who arranged Edward II's murder, is said to have been captured by supporters of Edward III who entered via this passage. Ask to see the Sheriff Room (there is still a Sheriff of Nottingham today, a purely symbolic role).

CAVES OF NOTTINGHAM

Nottingham stands on Sherwood sandstone that's riddled with artificial caves dating back to medieval times. Bizarrely, the entrance to the most fascinating, readily accessible **caves** (☎ 0115-988 1955; www.cityofcaves.com; adult/child £5.50/4.25; ☺ 10.30am-4pm Mon-Sun) is inside Broadmarsh shopping centre, on the upper level. These contain an air-raid shelter, a medieval underground tannery, several pub cellars and a mock-up of a Victorian slum dwelling.

TALES OF ROBIN HOOD

The **tales** (☎ 0115-948 3284; www.robinhood.uk.com; 30-38 Maid Marian Way; adult/child £8.95/6.95; ☺ 10am-5.30pm summer, to 5pm winter) is a tacky journey through mock-ups of Nottingham Castle and Sherwood Forest back in the days when Robin and the Sheriff were doing battle. At the weekend, those so inclined can join Robin and Maid Marian for a four-course **medieval banquet** complete with jesters and serving wenches (£40, with disco and unlimited booze with your meal).

WOLLATON HALL

Built in 1588 by land and coal-mine owner, Sir Francis Willoughby, **Wollaton Hall** (☎ 0115-15 3900; Wollaton Park, Derby Rd; admission free, tours £2.50/1.50; ☺ 11am-5pm Apr-Oct, to 4pm Nov-Mar) is a magnificent example of Elizabethan architecture at its most extravagant. Architect Robert Smythson was also responsible for the equally avant-garde Longleat in Wessex (p322). The Hall reopened in 2008 after a major restoration project.

The **Industrial Museum**, in the 18th-century stable block, displays lace-making equipment, Raleigh bicycles, a gigantic 1858 beam engine and oddities such as a locally invented, 1963 video recorder that never got off the ground.

Wollaton Hall is on the western edge of the city, 2.5 miles from the centre; get there on the number 30 bus, which stops right in front (15 minutes). Wollaton Park, surrounding the hall, is a popular picnic spot.

BREWHOUSE YARD MUSEUM

Housed in five 17th-century cottages carved into the cliff below the castle, this engaging **museum** (☎ 0115-915 3600; Castle Blvd; adult/child £3.50/2 joint admission with Nottingham Castle; ☺ 10am-4.30pm) re-creates everyday life in Nottingham over the past 300 years with particularly fine reconstructions of traditional shops.

GALLERIES OF JUSTICE

In the impressive Shire Hall building, the well-presented **Galleries of Justice** (☎ 0115-952 0555; www.galleriesofjustice.org.uk; High Pavement; adult/child £8.95/6.95; ☺ 10am-4pm Tue-Sun Apr-Sep, 10am-3pm Tue-Fri, 11am-4pm Sat & Sun Nov-Mar) takes you through an interactive history of the judicial system. From medieval ordeals by water or hot iron to modern crime detection, 'gaolers' and 'prisoners' guide you through – you could even end up being 'sent down' yourself.

Tours

Nottingham Tours (☎ 0115-925 9388; www.nottinghamtours.com) Offers a well-respected walking tour of the city, as well as tours of Sherwood Forest and boat trips. **Original Nottingham Ghost Walk** (☎ 01773-769300; www.ghost-walks.co.uk; adult/child £4/3; 7pm Sat Jan-Nov) Departs from Ye Olde Salutation Inn, Maid Marian Way, to delve into the city's supernatural past – descend into the medieval caves if you dare…

Festivals & Events

A **Shakespeare Festival** has been held in July each summer for almost a decade at the Nottingham Playhouse (p505). Meanwhile, the Nottingham Castle Museum & Art Gallery (opposite) plays host to a **Robin Hood Pageant** in October each year, reliving the times of the local outlaw legend.

The city's famed **Goose Fair** dates back to the Middle Ages. These days, it's an outsized funfair that takes place around the beginning of October in the Forest Recreation Ground, a mile north of the city centre.

Sleeping

Igloo Backpackers Hostel (☎ 0115-947 5250; www.igloohostel.co.uk; 110 Mansfield Rd; dm £13.50) A favourite of backpackers, this basic 36-bed independent hostel is a short walk north of Victoria bus station (entrance on Fulforth St). It's always full at weekends so book ahead. Breakfast is extra.

Greenwood Lodge City Guest House (☎ 0115-962 1206; www.greenwoodlodgecityguesthouse.co.uk; Third

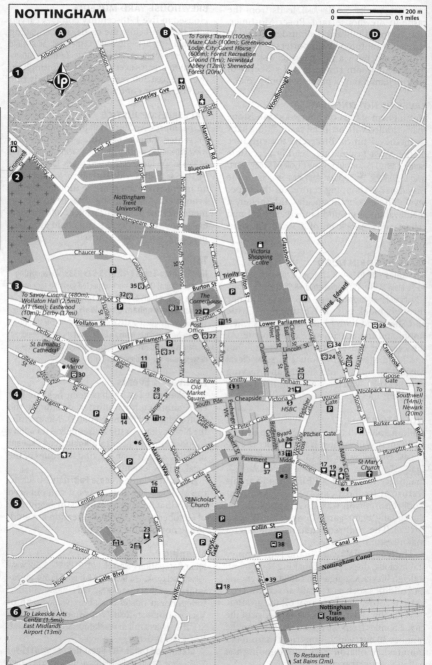

NOTTINGHAM

0   200 m
0   0.1 miles

THE EAST MIDLANDS

THE EAST MIDLANDS

Avenue, Sherwood Rise; s/d £45/75; P) This fantastic B&B is set in a large Victorian house. Pretty rooms are decorated with antiques and old paintings, and great big breakfasts are served with panache in a bright conservatory overlooking the pretty courtyard garden.

Park Hotel (☎ 0115-978 6299; www.parkhotel nottingham.co.uk; 5-7 Waverley St; s/d from £60/85; 🖳 wifi) This rather sinister-looking, turn-of-the-century mansion has recently been transformed into a slick, modern hotel with comfortable rooms decked out in warms reds and browns. Breakfast is extra.

Lace Market Hotel (☎ 0115-852 3232; www.lace markethotel.co.uk; 29-31 High Pavement; s/d £90/115; P) This is a lovely boutique hotel in a beautifully historic, well-heeled pocket of the city centre. It's in an old town house with a slick and contemporary interior and young, attentive staff. Check the website for weekend discounts.

Harts (☎ 0115-988 1900; www.hartsnottingham.co.uk; Standard Hill, Park Row; s/d from 120; P 🖳 wi-fi) A swish boutique hotel in a striking modern building, it's a short walk away from the castle. Rooms are the pinnacle of understated chic and there's an outstanding, buzzy restaurant as well as a lovely garden with sweeping views out over the countryside. Regular discounts are available through the website.

Eating

Delilah (☎ 0115-948 4461; delilahfinefoods.co.uk; 15 Middle Pavement; dishes £4-10; 🕑 9am-6pm Mon-Sat) This fine food and wine shop is brimming with fantastic cheese, meats, olives, breads and other gourmet favourites. At their food bar, you can take a seat to enjoy a tapas-style grazing menu, or grab an outstanding sandwich or deli platter to take away.

our pick Alley Cafe (☎ 0115-955 1013; www.alleycafe .co.uk; Cannon Court; mains £5-6; 🕑 11am-6pm Mon & Tue, till late Wed-Sat) This pint-sized cafe bar has created quite a buzz with its excellent, globally inspired vegetarian and vegan dishes, not to mention its funky DJs and tunes. It's hidden down an ancient back alley – seek it out.

World Service Restaurant (☎ 0115-847 5587; www .worldservicerestaurant.com; Newdigate House, Castlegate; dinner mains £13-21; 🕑 lunch & dinner) Set in a 17th-century house with vaguely oriental styling, in-crowd favourite World Service has the air of a colonial mansion. The food is modern British with plenty of local produce used in the exquisitely presented, tantalising menu. It's expensive, but there are great-value lunchtime menus

Petit Paris (☎ 0115-947 3767; petitparisrestaurant .co.uk; 2 King's Walk; 2/3-course menu from £15/18; 🕑 lunch & dinner Mon-Sat) Great value two- and three-course menus are to be had at this informal and lively French bistro hidden up a little alleyway in the town centre. There are plenty of traditional favourites like coq au vin and frogs' legs, and there's a daily changing specials board.

Restaurant Sat Bains (☎ 0115-986 6566; Lenton Lane; www.restaurantsatbains.com; set dinner £49; 🕑 lunch & dinner) Tucked away on the outskirts town, Nottingham's only Michelin-starred restaurant delivers outstanding, inventive modern European cooking. There are also a few beautiful rooms on offer for that full-on luxury experience. Book well in advance.

Other recommended places:

Brown Betty's (☎ 0115-941 3464; 17B St James St; sandwiches & salads £3-7; 🕑 9am-6pm Mon-Sat) Cheap and delicious sandwiches, pastas and salads. The huge 'hungry man' breakfast ciabattas are particularly mouth-watering.

Memsaab (☎ 0115-957 0009; www.mem-saab.co.uk; 12-14 Maid Marian Way; mains £10-18; ☯ 5.30-10.30pm Mon-Thu, to 11pm Fri & Sat, 5-10pm Sun) Glam, spacious Indian restaurant serving fabulous regional specialties.

Drinking

Brass Monkey (☎ 0115-840 4101; www.brassmonkeybar .co.uk; High Pavement) A chilled and happy clientele sip on cocktails in the corridor-like bar or on the two heated roof terraces of this funky little place. There's an eclectic soundtrack and it's less manic than some of the nearby options.

Pit & Pendulum (☎ 0115-950 6383; 17 Victoria St) Cavernous gothic-style pub with rough stone walls and plenty of nooks and crannies to lose yourself in. The dull orange lighting and horror-themed decorations, including flaming-torch brackets at the entrance, thrones, chains, stocks and toilets accessed through a fake bookcase, make it look like Dracula's local.

Saltwater (☎ 0115-954 2664; www.saltwater-restaurant .com; The Cornerhouse, Forman St; ☯ noon-midnight Sun-Wed, to 1am Thu, to 2am Fri & Sat) The entrance – through the chain restaurants of the Cornerhouse shopping centre – is less than salubrious, but inside you'll find a stylish, buzzing bar with a well-turned out clientele and great cocktails. Best is the expansive plant-filled rooftop terrace with awesome views over the city's rooftops. There's also a restaurant serving top-notch modern British and European food.

our pick **Ye Olde Trip to Jerusalem** (☎ 0115-947 3171; Brewhouse Yard, Castle Rd) Tucked into the cliff below the castle, this fantastically atmospheric alehouse claims to be England's oldest pub – it supposedly slaked the thirst of departing crusaders. The phrase 'nooks and crannies' could have been invented for here. Just when you think there are no more, you'll find another – and there are usually more than enough to accommodate the many tourists who come to sample the brews.

Other good places to drink:

Canal House (☎ 0115-955 5011; 48-52 Canal St; ☯ 11am-midnight Sun-Wed, to 1am Thu, to 2am Fri & Sat) Large, convivial pub with outside tables overlooking the canal. The surprise is the interior – there's a footbridge and two small canal boats that can be sailed in and out.

Cock & Hoop (☎ 0115-852 3231; 25 High Pavement) Atmospheric town-house pub with an almost genteel atmosphere far removed from some of the gaudy, loud nightspots that surround it. There are real ales, great Sunday lunches and it's dog-friendly.

Lincolnshire Poacher (☎ 0115-941 1584; 161-163 Mansfield Rd) This great pub for the beer-drinking connoisseur has ales from Suffolk to Belgium, and boasts eight different types of sausage on its menu. Live bands rock the joint on Sunday nights.

Entertainment

NIGHTCLUBS

Nightclub fads come and go at breakneck speed in Nottingham. Check the local guides for info.

our pick **Bodega Social Club** (☎ 0115-950 5078; www .thebodegasocialclub.co.uk; 23 Pelham St) The sister club of the Social in London plays everything from house to electro to classic rock to hip hop. DJs rock the upstairs dance floor and they put on hugely popular live shows from up-and-coming indie bands to burlesque.

Gatecrasher (☎ 0115-910 1101; Elite Bldg, Queen St; ☯ 10pm-4am Fri & Sat, to 3am Thu) This four-level behemoth is the Nottingham branch of the original Sheffield superclub. It has two clubs and four bars that play house, dance, R&B, hip hop and disco, and hosts regular international guest DJs.

NG1 (☎ 0115-958 8440; www.ng1club.co.uk; 76-80 Lower Parliament St; admission £3-10) Nottingham's very own gay superclub, NG1 is pure, unpretentious, hedonistic fun, with two dance floors belting out classic funky house, pop, cheese or indie depending on the night.

Plan B (15-16 Hurts Yard; admission free) Stashed away up an alley, this sexy little club plays house, electro and indie and has regular acoustic jams. It also does a nice line in cheap cocktails.

Stealth (☎ 0115-958 0672; www.stealthattack.co.uk; Masonic Pl, Goldsmith St; admission £2-10) One of the city's best clubs, Stealth has an eclectic music mix, from electro to drum and bass, to highly charged all-nighters that lure an up-for-it crowd from miles around. Next door, a venue called the Rescue Rooms hosts regular live bands.

LIVE MUSIC

Malt Cross (☎ 0115-941 1048; www.maltcross.com; 16 St James's St; ☯ 11am-11pm Mon-Thu, to 12.30am Fri & Sat) In an old Victorian music hall with a colourful history (it was a brothel in a previous incarnation), this place has a friendly, laid-back vibe. Good live music and decent food are all dished up under the glass arched roof, an architectural treasure in itself.

Maze Club (☎ 0115-947 5650; 257 Mansfield Rd; ⏰ 6pm-midnight Mon, 4pm-midnight Tue-Thu, 4pm-2am Fri & Sat, noon-4pm & 7pm-midnight Sun) Behind the Forest Tavern traditional alehouse, this popular revamped venue puts on live music – mostly of an indie persuasion – almost every night. It also runs regular comedy evenings.

Rock City (☎ 0115-941 2544; www.rock-city.co.uk; 8 Talbot St) The dance floor packs out here on the popular 'Tuned' student night on Thursdays, and on '90s night every Friday. Big-name pop acts usually head here.

THEATRE, CINEMAS & CLASSICAL MUSIC

Broadway Cinema (☎ 0115-952 6611; www.broadway.org.uk; 14-18 Broad St; adult/concession £6/4) The Broadway is the city's art-house film centre.

Lakeside Arts Centre (☎ 0115-846 7777; www.lakesidearts.org.uk; DH Lawrence Pavilion, University Park) A multipurpose venue southwest of the city, this centre hosts films, classical music, comedy and dance.

Savoy Cinema (☎ 0115-947 5812; 233 Derby Rd) This child-friendly independent cinema west of the city has double seats and an ice-cream interval during kids' films.

Screen Room (☎ 0115-924 1133; 25B Broad St) This place claims to be the world's smallest cinema with only 21 seats. It shows mostly art-house films

The city's dedicated theatres include the lower-profile **Arts Theatre** (☎ 0115-947 6096; www.artstheatre.org.uk; George St), which also stages amateur productions, and the **Nottingham Playhouse** (☎ 0115-941 9419; www.nottinghamplayhouse.co.uk; Wellington Circus), a respected venue outside of which sits *Sky Mirror*, a superb Anish Kapoor sculpture.

For musicals or established music acts, try the **Royal Concert Hall** or the **Theatre Royal**, which share a **booking office** (☎ 0115-989 5555; www.royalcentre-nottingham.co.uk; Theatre Sq) and an imposing building close to the centre.

Shopping

Paul Smith is the local boy who conquered London's heady fashion scene. He's done so well, he has not one, but two upmarket exclusive shops in the city centre: one on Byard Lane (☎ 0115-9506 712; 10 Byard Lane) and one in Willoughby House (☎ 0115-968 5990; Willoughby House, 20 Low Pavement).

Getting There & Away

Nottingham is well situated for both trains and buses. The train station just to the south of the town centre has frequent – but not fast – services that go to Birmingham (£13, 1½ hours), Manchester (£17, two hours) and London (£21, two hours).

Coaches are the cheaper option, mostly operating from the dingy confines of Broadmarsh bus station. There are five direct services to Birmingham and around 10 to London. Bus services to outlying villages are regular and reliable too. Services to Southwell, Eastwood and Newark mostly depart from Broadmarsh bus station. If you're going further, the nearby airport might be your best bet.

There are several train companies serving Nottingham. Useful services:

Cross Country Trains (☎ 0870 010 0084; www.crosscountrytrains.co.uk) Goes to Birmingham and as far as Cardiff.

East Midlands Airport (☎ 0871 919 9000; www.nottinghamema.com)

East Midlands Trains (☎ 08457 125678; www.eastmidlandstrains.co.uk) Serves East Midlands, London and up north.

London Midland (☎ 0844 811 0133; www.londonmidland.com) Links up to Liverpool to the northwest, and as far south as London St Pancras.

Trent Barton (☎ 01773-712265; www.trentbuses.co.uk) Buses depart from Broadmarsh and Victoria bus stations.

Getting Around

For information on buses within Nottingham, call **Nottingham City Transport** (☎ 0115-950 6070; www.nctx.co.uk). The Kangaroo ticket gives you unlimited travel on buses and trams within the city for £3.40.

The city tram system (www.thetram.net; single/day ticket from £1.50/£2.70) runs to the centre from Hucknall, 7 miles to the north of central Nottingham, through to the town centre and the train station.

Full details on Nottingham transport can be found at the **Nottingham Travelwise Service** (www.itsnottingham.info). You can also pick up a free transport planner and map from the tourist office.

Bunneys Bikes (☎ 0115-947 2713; 97 Carrington St; bike hire per day £8.99; ⏰ 9am-5.30pm Mon-Fri, to 5pm Sat, 11am-3pm Sun) is near the train station.

AROUND NOTTINGHAM

Newstead Abbey

With its attractive gardens, evocative lakeside ruins and notable connections with Romantic poet Lord Byron (1788–1824), whose country pile it was, **Newstead Abbey** (☎ 01623-455900; www .newsteadabbey.org.uk; adult/child £7/4, gardens only £3/2; ☻ house noon-5pm Apr-Sep, garden 9am-dusk) is a popular weekend destination for tourists and local families alike. Founded as an Augustinian priory around 1170, it was converted into a home after the Dissolution of the Monasteries in 1539. Beside the still-imposing facade of the priory church are the remains of the manor. It now houses some interesting Byron memorabilia, from pistols to manuscripts, and you can have a peek at his old living quarters. Many of the rooms are re-created in convincing period styles.

The house is 12 miles north of Nottingham, off the A60. Pronto buses run from Victoria Bus Station, stopping at Newstead Abbey gates (30 minutes, three hourly Monday to Saturday, hourly on Sunday), from where you will have to walk a mile to the house and gardens. The Sherwood Forester bus runs right there on summer Sunday and Bank Holiday Mondays.

DH Lawrence Sites

The **DH Lawrence Birthplace Museum** (☎ 01773-717353; 8A Victoria St, Eastwood; admission Mon-Fri free, Sat & Sun £2; ☻ 10am-5pm Apr-Oct, to 4pm Nov-Mar), former home of the controversial Nottingham author (1885–1930), has been reconstructed as it would have been in his childhood, with period furnishings.

Down the road, the **Durban House Heritage Centre** (☎ 01773-717353; Mansfield Rd; admission Mon-Fri free, Sat & Sun £2; ☻ 10am-5pm Apr-Oct, to 4pm Nov-Mar) sheds light on the background of Lawrence's books by re-creating the life of the mining community at the turn of the 20th century. A combined weekend ticket for Durben House and the DH Lawrence Birthplace Museum costs £3.50.

Eastwood is about 10 miles northwest of the city. Take Trent Barton service 1 or follow the A610.

Sherwood Forest Country Park

You'll have to put in some effort to lose yourself like an outlaw: today's Sherwood Forest can be incredibly crowded, especially in summer. Stray off the main circuit, though, and you can still find peaceful (and beautiful) spots. The **Sherwood Forest Visitor Centre** (☎ 01623-824490; www.sherwoodforest.org .uk; admission free, parking £3; ☻ 10am-5.30pm Apr-Oct, to 4.30pm Nov-Mar) houses 'Robyn Hode's Sherwode', a deeply naff exhibition of wooden cut-outs, murals and life-size figures describing the lifestyles of bandits, kings, peasants and friars. One of the most popular attractions is the **Major Oak**, a 1-mile walk from the visitors centre and supposedly once a hiding place for Mr Hood; these days it seems to be on its last legs. The **Robin Hood Festival** is a massive medieval re-enactment that takes place here every August.

Sherwood Forest YHA (☎ 0845 371 9139; www.yha .org.uk; Forest Corner, Edwinstowe; dm member/nonmember £17.95/20.95) is a modern hostel with comfortable dorms just a bugle-horn cry away from the visitor centre.

Sherwood Forester buses run the 20 miles to the park from Nottingham on Sunday and Bank Holiday Mondays (May to September). Catch bus 33 from Nottingham Monday to Saturday.

SOUTHWELL

pop 6285

Southwell is a sleepy market town straight out of a Jane Austen novel. **Southwell Minster** (☎ 01636-812649; suggested donation £3; ☻ 8am-7pm May-Sep, to dusk Oct-Apr) is a grand Gothic cathedral, its two heavy, square front towers belying the treats within. The nave dates from the 12th century, although there is evidence of an earlier Saxon church floor, itself made with mosaics from a Roman villa. A highlight of the building is the chapterhouse, filled with 13th-century carvings of leaves, pigs, dogs and rabbits. The library is fascinating, with illuminated manuscripts and heavy tomes from the 16th century and earlier.

A visit to **Southwell Workhouse** (NT; ☎ 01636-817250; Upton Rd; adult/child £5.80/3; ☻ noon-5pm Wed-Sun Apr-Sep, 11am-4pm Sat & Sun Oct-Mar) is a sobering but fascinating experience. An audio guide, narrated by 'inmates' and 'officials', describes the life of paupers in the mid-19th century to good (if grim) effect.

Bus 100 runs from Nottingham (50 minutes, every 20 minutes, hourly on Sunday), and Stagecoach bus 29 runs to Newark-on-Trent (25 minutes, every 30 minutes, every two hours on Sunday).

NEWARK-ON-TRENT
pop 25,376

Another market town with a colourful history, Newark-on-Trent was once a place of strategic importance and a royalist stronghold during the Civil War. Evidence lies in the ruins of **Newark Castle** (free; 🕙 until dusk), which held out against Cromwell's men, only to be condemned to destruction when Charles I ordered surrender. An impressive Norman gate remains, part of the structure in which King John died in 1216. Entry to the gate itself is by guided tour only; contact the **tourist office** (☎ 01636-655765; gilstrap@nsdc.info; Gilstrap Centre, Castlegate; 🕙 9am-5pm Apr-Sep, to 4pm Oct-Mar) for details. The office also houses a small display on the town's history. Pick up the *Walkabout Tour* leaflet and explore.

The town has a large, cobbled square overlooked by the fine, timber-framed, 14th-century **Olde White Hart Inn** (now a building society) and the **Clinton Arms Hotel** (now a shopping precinct), from where former prime minister Gladstone made his first political speech and where Lord Byron stayed while his first book of poems was published.

Gannets Daycafe (☎ 01636-702066; 35 Castlegate; snacks £2-5) scoops the lunchtime trade with fresh, tasty, local food. There are excellent puddings and a decent selection of vegie options.

The riverside setting of **Cafe Bleu** (☎ 01636-610141; 14 Castlegate; mains £11-14; 🕙 lunch daily, dinner Mon-Sat) is part of this sophisticated (and pricey) restaurant's charm. Live jazz accompanies the modern European cooking. In winter, the log fire roars, while in summer the courtyard garden is open.

Bus 90 runs to Nottingham (55 minutes, hourly, every two hours Sunday). An East Midlands train service also leaves from here.

DERBYSHIRE

Derbyshire is one of the most beguiling parts of the country, home to romantic bronze and purple moors, remote windswept farms, stark villages and rolling green hills lined with stone fences and speckled with sheep.

Part of the county lies within the Peak District National Park, and for many visitors the two areas are synonymous – although the park overlaps several other counties, and Derbyshire has a great deal to offer outside the confines of the park. There's the incongruous seaside jollity of Matlock Bath, the twisted spire of Chesterfield cathedral, and some wonderful stately homes including magical, ramshackle Calke Abbey and majestic Chatsworth.

Derbyshire is one of the most visited counties in England, and justifiably so.

Orientation

Derbyshire's main city, Derby, lies toward the south of this very pretty county, which stretches much taller than it does wide. The north contains some of the prettiest stretches of the Peak District, but south is also blessed with some fine scenery, perhaps most instantly accessible from the pretty market town of Ashbourne. Matlock Bath is almost plumb in the county's centre.

Activities

Outdoor activities in Derbyshire include walking, cycling, rock climbing, caving and paragliding, to name but a few. Many take place inside the Peak District National Park, and are covered under the Activities heading in that section (p513).

Getting There & Around

Derbyshire Wayfarer (☎ 0871 200 2233, Traveline; day pass adult/child/family £8/£4/13) Covers buses and trains throughout the county and beyond (eg to Manchester and Sheffield).

Trent Barton Buses (☎ 01773-712265; www.trentbarton.co.uk; day ticket £4) Operates the TransPeak bus service.

DERBY
pop 229,407

Once a relaxed market town, the Industrial Revolution created a major manufacturing centre out of Derby, which made its fortune churning out silk, china, railways and Rolls-Royce aircraft engines. It's not the most attractive of towns but it is a useful stepping stone to some lovely Derbyshire countryside. History buffs can learn about the development of English engineering, and bone-china fans can take a tour of the Royal Crown Derby Factory.

Orientation & Information

Derby has a pedestrianised shopping centre and a small but attractive old-town district. A partly cobbled central thoroughfare called Irongate, with a few good pubs and cafes, leads up to the cathedral.

The helpful **tourist office** (☎ 01332-255802; www .visitderby.co.uk; Market Pl; ☽ 9.30am-5.30pm Mon-Fri, to 5pm Sat, 10.30am-2.30pm Sun) is in the main square.

Sights

Derby's grand 18th-century **cathedral** (Queen St; ☽ 9.30am-4.30pm Mon-Sat) boasts a 64m-high tower and impressive wrought-iron screens. Large windows enhance the magnificent light interior. Tours run at 10.30am on the second Monday in the month. Don't miss the huge tomb of Bess of Hardwick, one of Derbyshire's most formidable residents in days gone by. For more about her, see Hardwick Hall (p512). Bird-lovers should watch out for peregrines, regularly spotted around the tower.

Next to the River Derwent in a former silk mill (Britain's first 'modern' factory), the **Derby Museum of Industry & History** (☎ 01332-255308; Silk Mill Lane; admission free; ☽ 11am-5pm Mon, 10am-5pm Tue-Sat, 1-4pm Sun & Bank Holidays) tells the city's manufacturing history; trainspotters will have a field day, while plane buffs should get a buzz out of displays on the development of the Rolls-Royce aero-engine.

The factory of **Royal Crown Derby** (☎ 01332-712841; www.royalcrownderby.co.uk; Osmaston Rd; tours £4.95, demonstration studio only £2.95/2.75; ☽ 9am-5pm Mon-Sat, 10am-4pm Sun, tours 4 daily Mon-Fri) turns out some of the finest bone china in England. In the demonstration studio, you'll see workers skilfully making delicate china flowers, using little more than a hat pin, a spoon handle and even a head-lice comb.

Sleeping

Crompton Coach House (☎ 01332-365735; www.coach housederby.co.uk; 45 Crompton St; s/d incl breakfast £30/60) Bright, sunny rooms along with cheery hosts make this colourful B&B the best option in a city short on choices for the cash-conscious traveller. It lies just south of the central shopping area.

Cathedral Quarter Hotel (☎ 01332-8523207; www .cathedralquarterhotel.com; 16 St Mary's Gate; s/d from £100/120; ☐ wi-fi) A taste of boutique comes to Derby in this new luxury hotel in a character-ful late-19th-century building, complete with grand, sweeping staircase. Rooms are suitably plush and there's an on-site spa as well as a wood-panelled, fine-dining restaurant.

Eating & Drinking

our pick **Soul Restaurant and Deli** (☎ 01332-346989; 26-28 Green Lane; sandwiches £5-8; ☽ 11.30am-4pm & 5.30-11.30pm Tue-Sat) This outstanding, bright, bustling deli and restaurant is dedicated to using local ingredients in its sandwiches, mezze platters, cheeses, cakes and salads. It also serves heavier, but no less delicious, two- and three-course lunch and dinner menus and has regular live jazz.

Darleys (☎ 01332-362987; Waterfront, Darley Abbey; mains £15-21; ☽ lunch & dinner Mon-Sat, lunch only Sun) Just outside of town in Darley Abbey Village, this restaurant has a gorgeous setting in a bright converted mill overlooking the river. The modern British food's not bad either. Book ahead at weekends.

Brunswick Inn (☎ 01332-290677; www.brunswickinn .co.uk; 1 Railway Tce) This award-winning inn has a warm ambience and a warren of rooms done out in maroon leather upholstery and wood panels, but the real reason to come here is the beers (some made on-site), which are a dream for real-ale lovers.

Victoria Inn (☎ 01332-740091; www.thevicinn.co.uk; 12 Midland Pl) Directly across from the station, and has live-music gigs – from punk to indie – several nights a week.

Getting There & Away

At the time of writing, a brand-new bus station is scheduled to open in 2009. In the meantime, buses are running from temporary stands on Full St, Derwent St, Corporation St, Morledge St and Albert St. TransPeak buses run between Nottingham and Manchester via Derby, Matlock, Bakewell and Buxton (Derby to Nottingham 30 minutes, Derby to Bakewell one hour, hourly). Outgoing services currently leave from Derwent St just north of the tourist office. From London, there are trains to Derby (two hours, hourly), continuing to Chesterfield, Sheffield and Leeds. There is also a direct service from Birmingham (45 minutes, three per hour).

AROUND DERBY

Kedleston Hall

Sitting proudly in vast landscaped parkland, the superb neoclassical mansion of **Kedleston Hall** (NT; ☎ 01332-842191; adult/child £7/3; ☽ noon-4pm Sat-Wed Easter-Oct) is a must for fans of stately homes. The Curzon family has lived here since the 12th century; Sir Nathaniel Curzon tore down an earlier house in 1758 so this stunning masterpiece could be built. Meanwhile, the poor old peasants in Kedleston village had their humble dwellings moved a mile down the road, as they interfered with the view. Ah, the good old days…

Entering the house through a grand portico, you reach the breathtaking **Marble Hall** with its massive alabaster columns and statues of Greek deities. Curved corridors on either side offer splendid views of the park – don't miss the arc of floorboards, specially cut from bending oak boughs. Other highlights include richly decorated bedrooms and a circular saloon with a domed roof, modelled on the Pantheon in Rome.

Another great building, Government House in Calcutta (now Raj Bhavan), was modelled on Kedleston Hall, as a later Lord Curzon was viceroy of India around 1900. His collection of oriental artefacts is on show, as is his wife's 'peacock' dress – made of gold and silver thread and weighing 5kg.

If the sun is out, take a walk around the lovingly restored 18th-century-style **pleasure gardens**.

Kedleston Hall is 5 miles northwest of Derby, off the A52. By bus, service 109 between Derby and Ashbourne goes within about 1½ miles of Kedleston Hall (25 minutes, every two hours Saturday only).

Calke Abbey

Like an enormous, long-neglected cabinet of wonders, **Calke Abbey** (NT; ☎ 01332-863822; adult/child £9/4; ☼ 12.30-5pm Sat-Wed Apr-Oct) is not your usual opulent stately home. Built around 1703, it's passed through a dynasty of eccentric and reclusive baronets and has been left much as it was in the late 1800s – a mesmerising example of a country house in decline. The result is a ramshackle maze of secret corridors, underground tunnels and rooms crammed with ancient furniture, mounted animal heads, dusty books, stuffed birds and endless piles of bric-a-brac from the last three centuries. Some rooms are in fabulous condition, while others are deliberately untouched, complete with crumbling plaster and mouldy wallpaper. (You exit the house via a long, dark tunnel – a bit more thrilling than one might like, given the state of the buildings.) A stroll round the gardens is a similar time-warp experience – in

the potting sheds nothing has changed since about 1930, but it looks like the gardener left only yesterday.

Admission to Calke Abbey house is by timed ticket at busy times. On summer weekends it's wise to phone ahead and check there'll be space. You can enter the gardens and grounds at any time. Calke is 10 miles south of Derby off the A514. Visitors coming by car must enter via the village of Ticknall. The Arriva bus 68A from Derby to Swadlincote stops at Ticknall (40 minutes, hourly) and from there it's a 2-mile walk through the park.

Ashbourne
pop 7600

Standing at the very southern edge of the Peak District National Park, pretty little Ashbourne throngs during the holidays and weekends with hikers and other visitors, who come to this stone town to recharge in the flurry of cafes, pubs and antique shops on the precariously slanted main street. (Things get even busier once a year when the game of Shrovetide Football is rigorously pursued; see the boxed text, p510).

The **tourist office** (☎ 01335-343666; Market Pl; ☼ 9.30am-5pm Apr-Oct, 10am-4pm Mon-Sat Nov-Feb) can provide leaflets or advice on B&Bs in the area.

Ashbourne is of particular interest to walkers and cyclists because it's the southern terminus of the **Tissington Trail**, a former railway line and now a wonderful easy-gradient path cutting through fine west-Derbyshire countryside. The Tissington Trail takes you north towards Buxton and connects with the High Peak Trail running south towards Matlock Bath.

About a mile outside town along Mapleton Lane, **Ashbourne Cycle Hire** (☎ 01335-343156; day hire £14) is on the Tissington Trail, with a huge stock of bikes and trailers for all ages, and free leaflets showing the route with pubs and teashops along the way.

Ivy-covered **Bramhall's** (☎ 01335-346158; www .bramhalls.co.uk; 6 Buxton Rd; s/d £40/70) lies just up the road from the main market square. Its has a fine restaurant and some lovely B&B rooms.

Patrick & Brooksbank (☎ 01335-346753; 22 Market Pl) is a great little deli and cafe with excellent homemade cookies, handmade chocolates, cheeses, breads and meats – just right for a takeaway to eat out on the hills.

SHROVE TUESDAY FOOTBALL

Shrove Tuesday comes before Ash Wednesday, the first day of Lent – the Christian time of fasting – so Shrove Tuesday is the day to use up all your rich and fattening food. This led to the quaint tradition of Pancake Day in England and the flamboyant Mardi Gras festival in other parts of the world.

On Shrove Tuesday, various English towns celebrate with pancake races, but in Ashbourne they go for something much more energetic. Here they play Shrovetide Football, but it's nothing like the football most people are used to. For a start, the goals are 3 miles apart, the 'pitch' is a huge patch of countryside, and the game lasts all afternoon and evening (then starts again the day after). There are two teams, but hundreds of participants, and very few rules indeed. A large leather ball is fought over voraciously as players maul their way through fields and gardens, along the river, and up the main street – where shop windows are specially boarded over for the occasion. Visitors come from far and wide to watch, but only the brave should take part!

Down-to-earth **Smith's Tavern** (☎ 01335-342264; 36 St John's St) is a cosy, cluttered and popular pub with great cask ales and a regularly changing menu of tasty grub.

Without your own transport, bus is the only way to get to Ashbourne and the trip takes from 40 minutes to just under an hour. Direct buses include the Arriva 109 (five services daily Monday to Saturday), and the One, operated by Trent Barton (hourly Monday to Saturday). On Sundays, TM Travel's 108 has four services to Ashbourne.

Dovedale

About 3 miles northwest of Ashbourne, the River Dove winds through the steep-sided valley of Dovedale. It's one of the most accessible ways to sample the beauty of Derbyshire, so it can get crowded on summer weekends – especially near the famous Stepping Stones that cross the river – but the crowds thin out as you go further up, and midweek it's a lovely place for a walk.

The quaint *Dovedale Guide* (£1.50), available from Ashbourne's tourist office, has more background and a map showing footpaths. Romantic Victorian travellers went on outings to Dovedale, bestowing fanciful names on the natural features, so today we can admire the hills and rocky buttresses called Thorpe Cloud, Dovedale Castle, Lovers' Leap, the Twelve Apostles, Tissington Spires, Reynard's Kitchen and Lion Head Rock.

Another early visitor was Izaak Walton, the 17th-century fisherman and author of *The Compleat Angler*. The ivy-covered **Izaak Walton Hotel** (☎ 01335-350555) at the southern end of Dovedale is named in his honour, and the public bar, lush lawns and tasty cream teas make it well worth a stop for after-walk refreshment.

MATLOCK BATH
pop 2202

Unashamedly tacky, Matlock Bath is like a seaside resort that lost its way and ended up at the foot of the Peak District National Park. Wander down the gaudy promenade and you'll find amusement arcades, Victorian cafes, pubs and souvenir shops, while the rest of the town stretches up the hillside behind. Bisected by the smooth, twisty A6, the town's buzz becomes a roar of engines at the weekend, as hundreds of motorcyclists flock here and the crowds of leather-clad bike enthusiasts only adds to the town's fun atmosphere.

It sits next to the pleasant town of Matlock, which has little in the way of sights but is a handy gateway to the scenic dales.

Orientation & Information

Matlock Bath is 2 miles south of Matlock. Everything revolves around North Pde and South Pde, a line of seaside-style shops, attractions, pubs and places to eat along one side of the main road (the A6) through town, with the murmuring River Derwent and a plush gorge on the other side.

Matlock Bath's **tourist office** (☎ 01629-55082; www.derbyshire.gov.uk; the Pavilion; ☑ 9.30am-5pm daily Mar-Oct, 10.30am-4pm Nov-Feb) is run by helpful staff armed with reams of leaflets and guidebooks.

Sights & Activities

You can amuse yourself quite nicely simply strolling along the promenade, chomping on chips or candyfloss. For a scenic detour, you can walk across the river to the park on the other side where steep paths lead to some great cliff-top viewpoints.

At the enthusiast-run **Mining Museum** (☎ 01629-583834; www.peakmines.co.uk; the Pavilion; adult/child £3/2; ☒ 10am-5pm May-Sep, 11am-3pm Nov-Apr) you can clamber through the shafts and tunnels where Derbyshire lead miners once eked out a risky living. Bizarrely, part of the museum was once a dancehall. For £2/1 extra per adult/child, you can go down **Temple Mine** and pan for 'gold'.

For a different view, go to the **Heights of Abraham** (☎ 01629-582365; adult/child £11/8; ☒ 10am-5pm daily Mar-Oct, to 4.30pm Nov-Feb), which claims to be the Peak District's 'oldest attraction'. It's a great family day out, with cavern tours, woodland walks and an adventure playground. The price includes a spectacular cable-car ride up from the valley floor.

Near the cable-car base, **Whistlestop Countryside Centre** (admission free; ☒ 10am-5pm Tue-Sun Apr-Oct, Sat & Sun Nov-Mar), at the old train station, has wildlife and natural garden exhibits, and runs children's activities in the summer.

From the cable-car base, walking trails lead up to viewpoints on top of **High Tor**. You can see down to Matlock Bath and over to **Riber Castle**, a Victorian folly.

Gulliver's Kingdom (☎ 01925-444888; admission £9.95; ☒ usually 10.30am-5pm late May-early Sep, weekends & holidays Oct-Apr) is a theme park for younger kids with the usual favourites: log flume, pirate ship, dodgems and roller coaster. Under 12s will love it, and it includes a non-violent Punch and Judy show (presumably just with Judy).

A mile south of Matlock Bath is **Masson Mills Working Textile Museum** (☎ 01629-581001; adult/child £2.50/1.50; ☒ 10am-4pm Mon-Fri, 11am-5pm Sat, 11am-4pm Sun), built in 1783 for pioneering industrialist Sir Richard Arkwright it was seen as a masterpiece in its time. Today it's a working museum, and one of the **Derwent Valley Mills** (www.derwentvalleymills.org) that make up this Unesco World Heritage Site, with renovated looms and weaving machines, and the world's largest collection of bobbins bringing over 200 years of textile history to life. It has the added attraction of a 'shopping village' including three floors of High St textile and clothing names.

From the beginning of September to October, don't miss the **Matlock Illuminations** (Derwent Gardens; adult/under 16yr £4/free; ☒ from dusk Fri-Sun), with streams of pretty lights, outrageously decorated Venetian boats on the river and fireworks.

Sleeping

Matlock Bath has several B&Bs in the heart of things on North Pde and South Pde, and a few places just out of the centre. There are also more choices in nearby Matlock.

Hodgkinson's Hotel & Restaurant (☎ 01629-582170; www.hodgkinsons-hotel.co.uk; 150 South Pde; s/d from £38/76; ℗) This eccentric hotel is seemingly stuck in the 19th century. Oddly shaped rooms with carved wooden bedposts, antique chairs and beams are soaked in Victorian atmosphere and charm.

Sunnybank Guesthouse (☎ 01629-584621; sunnybankmatlock@aol.com; Clifton Rd; s/d £40/64) This lovely, well-kept guest house is blessed with bright bedrooms, most with fine views over the surrounding countryside. The comfortable, wooden-floored breakfast room has a reassuring and lingering scent of marmalade and toast.

Temple Hotel (☎ 01629-583911; www.templehotel.co.uk; Temple Wk; s/d £65/92; ℗) The views from this hillside hotel are fantastic – so lovely that Lord Byron once felt inspired to etch a poem on the restaurant window. The hotel itself feels slightly old-fashioned and the rooms don't seem to have been updated for years. Bar meals are available.

Eating & Drinking

North Pde and South Pde are lined end to end with cafes, teashops and takeaways serving artery-clogging fish and chips, fried chicken, pies and burgers.

Temple Hotel (☎ 01629-583911; Temple Wk) On the hillside, the bar at this hotel has reasonable pub food and a fine restaurant.

Fishpond (☎ 01629-581000; 204 South Pde) This pub gets a lively, spirited crowd and is surprisingly boisterous for a pub in rural Derbyshire. It has a mixed bag of live music.

Victorian Tea Shop (☎ 01629-583325; 118 North Pde; ☒ 10am-5.30pm Mon-Fri) For the pick of the teahouses, this place is all lace curtains, cream cakes and delicate crockery.

Getting There & Away

The Peak District is extremely well served by public transport, and Matlock is a hub. Buses 213 and 214 go to and from Sheffield (one hour 10 minutes) several times a day.

There are buses to and from Derby (1¼ hours, hourly) and Chesterfield (35 minutes, hourly). Several trains a day serve Derby (30 minutes).

AROUND MATLOCK BATH

From just outside Matlock town centre, about 2½ miles from Matlock Bath, steam trains and scenic railcars trundle along **Peak Rail** (☎ 01629-580381; www.peakrail.co.uk; adult/child return £7/4) via stops at Darley Dale to the northern terminus near the village of Rowsley. For train buffs and families, it's a great ride. There are nine services daily Saturday and Sunday, Sunday only November to March and extra weekday services June to September.

From Rowsley train station a riverside path leads to **Caudwell's Mill** (☎ 01629-734374; admission free; ☽ 10am-6pm Apr-Oct, to 5pm Nov-Mar), a huge, fascinating flour mill full of working belts, shafts and other machinery – some almost a century old. There's a tearoom, several craft workers and a shop selling gifts including plenty of flour. You can get to Rowsley direct from Matlock by bus; it's on the road to Bakewell.

CHESTERFIELD
pop 100,879

This town has nothing much to recommend it except for one famous landmark: the startling crooked spire of **St Mary & All Saints Church** (☎ 01246-206506; admission free; tours adult/child £4/2; ☽ 9am-5pm). Dating from 1360, the giant spire corkscrews 68m high and leans almost 3m southwest. There are various theories why: it probably was due to green-timber warping, although some still prefer to believe that when a virgin got married in the church the spire was so shocked that it twisted to see the sight for itself. Tour times vary; call to arrange.

The **tourist office** (☎ 01246-345777; Rykneld Sq; ☽ 9am-5.30pm Mon-Sat Apr-Oct, to 5pm Nov-Mar) is right opposite the crooked spire in a sleek black building. It's very useful for planning a trip to the Peak District.

The easiest way to get here is by train. Chesterfield is between Nottingham/Derby (20 minutes) and Sheffield (10 minutes), with services about hourly. The station is just east of the centre.

HARDWICK

Elizabethan **Hardwick Hall** (NT; ☎ 01246-850430; adult/child £9.50/4.75; ☽ noon-4.30pm Wed, Thu, Sat & Sun Mar-Oct, 11am-3pm Sat & Sun Dec) should rank high on your list of must-see stately homes. It was home to the 16th century's second-most powerful woman, Elizabeth, countess of Shrewsbury – known to all as Bess of Hardwick. Bess gained power and wealth by marrying upwards four times and she unashamedly modelled herself on the era's most famous woman – Queen Elizabeth I.

Bess's fourth husband died in 1590, leaving her with a huge pile of cash to play with, and she had Hardwick Hall built using the designs of eminent architect Robert Smythson. Glass was a status symbol, so she went all out on the windows; as a contemporary ditty quipped, 'Hardwick Hall – more glass than wall.' Also magnificent are the High Great Chamber and Long Gallery. These and many other rooms and broad stairways are decorated with tremendous tapestries.

Next door is Bess's first house, **Hardwick Old Hall** (EH; adult/child £4/2, joint ticket £11/5; ☽ 11am-6pm Mon & Wed-Sun Apr-Sep, to 5pm Oct), now a romantic ruin.

Also fascinating are the formal gardens, and the hall sits in the great expanse of **Hardwick Park** with short and long walking trails leading across fields and through woods. Ask at the ticket office for details. Just near the south gate is the sandstone **Hardwick Inn** (☎ 01246-850245; Hardwick Park, Doe Lea), a historic pub with a sunny little patio and a surprisingly sophisticated menu.

Hardwick Hall is 10 miles southeast of Chesterfield, just off the M1. The pronto bus from Chesterfield to Nottingham stops at Glapwell, from where it's a 2-mile walk to Hardwick Hall.

PEAK DISTRICT

One of the most beautiful parts of the country, the Peak District National Park crams in pretty villages, wild moorland, grand houses, deep, dark limestone caves and the southernmost hills of the Pennines. No one knows for certain how the Peak District got its name – certainly not from the landscape, which has hills, moors and valleys, but no peaks. It's rumoured to be named after an Anglo-Saxon tribe, the Peacsaetna, who once lived here.

This is one of England's best-loved national parks (it's the busiest in Europe, and the world's second-busiest after Mt Fuji), but don't be put off by its popularity. Escaping the crowds is no problem if you avoid summer weekends, and even then, with a bit of imagination, it's easy to find your own peaceful spot to take it all in.

Orientation & Information

The Peak District is principally in Derbyshire but spills into five adjoining counties including Yorkshire, Staffordshire and Cheshire; it's one of the largest national parks in England. This 555-sq-mile protected area is divided into two distinct zones: the harsher, higher, untamed Dark Peak to the north, characterised by peaty moors and dramatic gritstone cliffs called 'edges'; and the lower, prettier, more pastoral White Peak to the south, with green fields marked by dry-stone walls, divided by deep dales.

There are tourist offices (those run by the national park are called visitor centres) in Buxton, Bakewell, Castleton, Edale and other locations, all overflowing with maps, guidebooks and leaflets detailing walks, cycle rides and other activities. For general information, the free *Peak District* newspaper and the official park website at www.peakdistrict.org cover transport, activities, local events, guided walks and so on.

Activities

CAVING & CLIMBING

The Peak District limestone is riddled with caves and caverns including 'showcaves' open to the public in Castleton, Buxton and Matlock Bath (described in each of those sections). For serious caving (or potholing) trips, tourist offices can provide a list of accredited outdoor centres, and if you know what you're doing, Castleton makes a great base.

For guidebooks, gear (to buy or hire) and a mine of local information, contact **Hitch n Hike** (☎ 01433-651013; www.hitchnhike.co.uk; Mytham Bridge, Bamford, Hope Valley, Derbyshire), a specialist caving and outdoor-activity shop in Bamford, near Castleton. The website also has more info about caving in the area.

If you're keen on climbing, the Peak District is a great place to indulge and has long been a training ground for England's top mountaineers. There are multipitch routes on limestone faces such as High Tor, overlooking Matlock Bath, and there's a great range of short climbing routes on the famous gritstone 'edges' of Froggatt, Curbar and Stanage.

CYCLING

The Peak District is a very popular cycling area, especially the White Peak and the parts of Derbyshire south of here around Matlock and Ashbourne, which have a network of quiet lanes and tracks for mountain bikers. In the Dark Peak there are fewer roads, and they are quite busy with traffic, although there are some good off-road routes. A good place to start any ride is a tourist office, which can supply maps, books and leaflets for cyclists and mountain bikers.

In the Dark Peak, Edale is a popular starting point for mountain bikers, and near the Derwent Reservoirs is also good. In the White Peak, all the villages mentioned in this section make good bases for cycle tours.

For easy traffic-free riding, head for the 17.5-mile **High Peak Trail**, a route for cyclists and walkers on the mostly flat track of an old railway. You can join the trail at Cromford, near Matlock Bath, but it starts with a very steep incline, so if you seek easy gradients, a better start is Middleton Top, a mile or so north. The trail winds through beautiful hills and farmland to a village called Parsley Hay, and continues on for a few more miles towards Buxton.

At Parsley Hay another former railway turned walking-and-cycling route, the **Tissington Trail**, heads south for 13 miles to Ashbourne. You can go out and back as far as you like, or make it a triangular circuit, following the busy B5053 or (a better choice) the quiet lanes through Bradbourne and Brassington.

The **Pennine Bridleway** is another good option, suitable for horse riders, cyclists and walkers.

There are several cycle-hire centres in the Peak District including **Derwent Cycle Hire** (☎ 01433-651261) in the Derwent Valley, and **Parsley Hay** (☎ 01298-84493) and **Middleton Top** (☎ 01629-823204) for the Tissington and High Peak Trails. Tourist offices have a leaflet detailing all other hire centres. Charges hover around £12 to £17 per day for adults' bikes (deposit and ID required), and kids' bikes and trailers are also available.

WALKING

The Peak District is one of the most popular walking areas in England, crossed by a vast network of footpaths and tracks – especially in the White Peak – and you can easily find

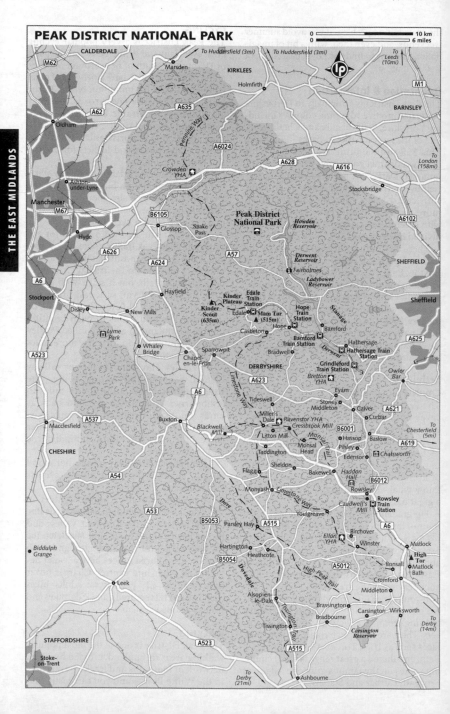

THE KINDER TRESPASS

Now passed into rambling folklore, the Kinder Trespass was a key turning point in the campaign for better-quality access to the countryside.

On Sunday 24 April 1932, some 400 ramblers descended onto Kinder Scout, the highest point in the Peak District, to exercise their right to free access to the region's open hills and moorland. The ramblers were mostly British working men, including many members of the Communist-inspired British Workers Sport Foundation, frustrated that little progress had been made through official channels toward the right to roam.

Before they reached the Kinder plateau they came across gamekeepers working for the local landowner, the Duke of Devonshire, who tried to stop them in their tracks, and fighting broke out, during which one keeper was injured. The ramblers continued undeterred to the plateau where they met up with a group of ramblers from Sheffield who had come across Kinder from Edale.

When they came back down again, six of the ramblers were arrested and eventually five were found guilty of unlawful assembly and breach of the peace; in July of that year they were handed out sentences of between two and six months.

The sentences caused public outcry: a few weeks later, a record 10,000 ramblers joined a Right to Roam rally in Winnats Pass near Castleton and pressure for greater access to the countryside increased.

It would take 17 more years, but in 1949 the ramblers finally received welcome news when the post-war Labour Government set in motion the creation of National Parks. The Peak District was the first to be designated, and almost immediately ramblers were allowed access to Kinder Scout, the former 'battlefields' of the 1930s.

Even so, the public remained barred from huge swathes of moorland for another 50 years until the Countryside and Rights of Way (CROW) Act was passed in 2000, and finally implemented in 2005.

a walk of a few miles or longer, depending on your energy and interests. If you want to explore the higher realms of the Dark Peak, which often involves the local art of 'bog trotting', make sure your boots are waterproof and be prepared for wind and rain – even if the sun is shining when you set off.

The Peak's most famous walking trail is the **Pennine Way**, with its southern end at Edale and its northern end over 250 miles away in Scotland. If you don't have a spare three weeks, from Edale you can follow the trail north across wild hills and moors for just a day or two, or even less. An excellent three-day option is to Hebden Bridge, a delightful little town in Yorkshire.

The 46-mile **Limestone Way** winds through the Derbyshire countryside from Castleton to Rocester in Staffordshire on a mix of footpaths, tracks and quiet lanes. The northern section of this route, through the White Peak between Castleton and Matlock, is 26 miles and hardy folk can do it over a long summer day, but two days is better. The route goes via Miller's Dale, Monyash, Youlgreave and Bonsall, with Youth Hostel Association (YHA) hostels and B&Bs along the way and ample pubs and cafes. Tourist offices have a detailed leaflet.

Various shorter walks are described throughout this section. All the villages make good bases for exploring the surrounding area, and Fairholmes at the Derwent Reservoirs is great for getting deep into the hills. The High Peak and Tissington Trails described in the previous Cycling section are equally popular with walkers.

Sleeping

Tourist offices have lists of accommodation for every budget. Perhaps the best budget options are the various camping barns (beds per person from £6.50) dotted around the Peak. Usually owned by farmers, they can be booked centrally through the **YHA** (☎ 0870 770 8868; www.yha.org.uk).

Getting There & Around

The Peak District authorities are trying hard to wean visitors off their cars, and tourist offices stock all kinds of timetables covering local buses and trains. For more details, see (p507).

BUXTON

pop 24,112

With its grand Georgian architecture, central crescent, flourishing parks and thermal waters, Buxton invites comparisons to Bath. It's smaller in scale, however, and lodged a little less up its own backside. It was the Romans who discovered the area's natural warm-water springs, but the town's glory days came in the 18th century when 'taking the waters' was highly fashionable. After years of relative obscurity, ambitious restoration projects recovered the town's sparkle, especially the resurrection of the Opera House, which had fallen into disuse in the 1970s.

Every Tuesday and Saturday, colourful stalls light up Market Pl. The town itself is full of book, antique and craft shops and quirky cafes, and is perfect for idle browsing.

Situated just outside the border of the Peak District National Park, Buxton is an excellent, picturesque base to get to the northern and western areas.

Orientation & Information

Buxton effectively has two centres: the historical area, with the Crescent, Opera House and Pavilion; and Market Pl, surrounded by pubs and restaurants. There are several banks with ATMs on the Quadrant.

Cyber@Emporium (☎ 01298-214455; 28 High St; ☺ noon-9pm Tue-Fri, 11am-9pm Sat, 11am-7pm Sun; per hr £3)

Post office (Spring Gdns; ☺ 8.30am-6pm Mon-Fri, to 3pm Sat) Inside the Co-operative.

Tourist office (☎ 01298-25106; www.peakdistrict -tourism.gov.uk; Pavilion Gardens; ☺ 9.30-5pm daily Oct-Mar, 10am-4pm Apr-Sep)

Sights & Activities

Buxton's gorgeously restored **Opera House** (☎ 0845 127 2190; www.buxtonoperahouse.org.uk; Water St) enjoys a full program of drama, dance, concerts and comedy as well as staging some renowned festivals and events (see right). Tours (£2.50) of the auditorium and backstage areas are available at 11am most Saturday mornings.

Next to the Opera House is the **Pavilion**, an impressive palace of glass and cast iron built in 1871 and overlooking the impeccably manicured **Pavilion Gardens**. Skirting the gardens, the grand, pedestrian **Broad Walk** is the perfect place for a gentle evening stroll.

Another impressive Buxton construction, the graceful curved terrace of the **Crescent**, is reminiscent of the Royal Crescent in Bath and is being transformed into a luxury hotel, due for completion in 2010. Just east of here is **Cavendish Arcade**, formerly a thermal bathhouse (you can still see the chair used for lowering the infirm into the restorative waters) with several craft and book shops and a striking coloured-glass ceiling.

Opposite the Crescent, the **Pump Room**, which dispensed Buxton's spring water for nearly a century, now hosts temporary art exhibitions. Just outside is **St Ann's Well**, a fountain from which Buxton's famous thermal waters still flow – and where a regular procession of tourists queue to fill plastic bottles and slake their thirst with the liquid's 'curative' power.

Behind the Pump Room, a small park called the **Slopes** rises steeply in a series of grassy terraces. From the top there are views over the centre and across to the grand old **Palace Hotel**, which has been welcoming guests since 1868, and the former **Devonshire Hospital**, with its magnificent dome (it's now part of the University of Derby).

Poole's Cavern (☎ 01298-26978; www.poolescavern .co.uk; adult/child £7/4; ☺ 10am-5pm Mar-Nov) is a magnificent natural limestone cavern, located about a mile from central Buxton. Guides take you deep underground to see an impressive formation of stalactites (the ones that hang down), including one of England's longest, and distinctive 'poached egg' formation stalagmites.

From the cave car park, a 20-minute walk leads up through Grin Low Wood to **Solomon's Temple**, a small tower with fine views over the town and surrounding Peak District.

A longer walk is the **Monsal Trail**, beginning 3 miles east of the town, which leads all the way to Bakewell (see p524).

Parsley Cycle Hire (☎ 01298-84493), at the junction of the High Peak and Tissington Trails, is the nearest place to rent bicycles (half-/full day £11/14).

Festivals & Events

All the big events in Buxton revolve around its beautifully restored Opera House.

Four Four Time An annual live-music festival staged each February, featuring a medley of jazz, blues, folk and world-music acts.

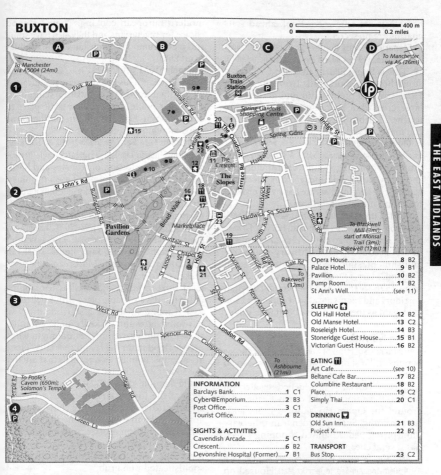

BUXTON

THE EAST MIDLANDS

INFORMATION	
Barclays Bank	1 C1
Cyber@Emporium	2 B3
Post Office	3 C1
Tourist Office	4 B2

SIGHTS & ACTIVITIES	
Cavendish Arcade	5 C1
Crescent	6 B2
Devonshire Hospital (Former)	7 B1
Opera House	8 B2
Palace Hotel	9 B1
Pavilion	10 B2
Pump Room	11 B2
St Ann's Well	(see 11)

SLEEPING	
Old Hall Hotel	12 B2
Old Manse Hotel	13 C2
Roseleigh Hotel	14 B3
Stoneridge Guest House	15 B1
Victorian Guest House	16 B2

EATING	
Art Cafe	(see 10)
Beltane Cafe Bar	17 B2
Columbine Restaurant	18 B2
Place	19 C2
Simply Thai	20 C1

DRINKING	
Old Sun Inn	21 B3
Project X	22 B2

TRANSPORT	
Bus Stop	23 C2

Buxton Festival (www.buxtonfestival.co.uk) This renowned festival takes place in July and is one of the largest of its kind in the country. As well as opera, literary notables such as Tariq Ali hold sway.

Buxton Fringe (www.buxtonfringe.com) Also in July, this more contemporary festival is gathering popularity.

International Gilbert & Sullivan Festival (www.gs-festival.co.uk) This very popular festival is held at the end of July/beginning of August.

Sleeping

Buxton is awash with good-value, elegant guesthouses – many dating from Victorian times – that are steeped in atmosphere. You'll find the pick of the bunch located on Broad Walk.

our pick **Roseleigh Hotel** (☎ 01298-24904; www.roseleighhotel.co.uk; 19 Broad Walk; s/d incl breakfast from £33/70; P ☐ wi-fi) This gorgeous family-run B&B in a spacious old terraced house has lovingly decorated rooms, many with fine views out onto the ducks paddling in the picturesque Pavilion Gardens lake. The owners are a welcoming couple, both seasoned travellers, with plenty of interesting tales to tell. There's a large guest lounge full of travel guides and maps for browsing, and a large Paddington bear if you get lonely.

Victorian Guest House (☎ 01298-78759; www.buxtonvictorian.co.uk; 3A Broad Walk; d incl breakfast from £72; P) This elegant house has eight individually decorated bedrooms furnished with Victorian and Edwardian antiques. The home-cooked breakfasts are renowned. Book ahead – its charms are no secret.

Stoneridge Guest House (☎ 01298-26120; www .stoneridge.co.uk; 9 Park Rd; s/d incl breakfast from £40/63; P 🖳 wi-fi) Bright B&B in an elegant Victorian stone house a short walk from the Opera House, with a pretty patio and garden and large, crisp white bedrooms with a few tartan touches. The breakfasts are delicious and they can make packed lunches.

Old Manse Hotel (☎ 01298-25638; www.oldmanse .co.uk; 6 Clifton Rd; s/d from £30/54) A Victorian stone building sheltering simple, cream-coloured rooms, a short walk away from the town centre. The helpful hosts are happy to provide maps and info about the area.

Old Hall Hotel (☎ 01298-22841; www.oldhallhotel buxton.co.uk; the Square; s/d incl breakfast £65/100; 🖳 wi-fi) There is a tale to go with every creak of the floorboards at this genial, history-soaked establishment, supposedly the oldest hotel in England. Mary, Queen of Scots, was held here from 1576 to 1578, and the wood-panelled corridors and rooms are as well appointed and as elegant as they must have been in her day.

Eating & Drinking

The Market Sq/High St area has a good choice of pubs and restaurants and is the place to go in the evenings – although the strip sometimes spills over with lairy, alco-fuelled revellers on weekend evenings. Head down to the area around the Opera House for a more laid-back evening. Spring Gardens, an otherwise uninspiring pedestrianised shopping street, has several cheap cafes.

Art Cafe (☎ 01298-23114; sandwiches & snacks £3-7; 🕙 9.30am-5pm Apr-Sep, to 3pm Oct-Mar) Housed on the 2nd floor of the Pavilion, with beautiful views over the gardens, this little spot is a great place to enjoy a coffee and some homemade cakes while perusing the works by local artists that are splashed across the walls.

Columbine Restaurant (☎ 01298-78752; Hall Bank; mains £11-13; 🕙 dinner 7-10pm Mon & Wed-Sat) Perched on the slope leading down to the Crescent, this excellent understated restaurant is top choice among Buxtonites in the know. It delivers large portions of excellent local produce including some good vegetarian choices.

The Place (☎ 01298-214565; www.theplacebuxton .co.uk; 9-11 Market St; mains £11-14; 🕙 dinner Tue & Wed, lunch & dinner Thu-Sat, lunch Sun) Lively, trendy modern restaurant serving light lunches and sandwiches as well as more expensive

modern European cooking. There's a good choice for vegetarians and they also have some smart accommodation upstairs (with doubles from £60).

Simply Thai (☎ 01298-24471; 2-3 Cavendish Circus; 🕙 lunch & dinner) This lovely serene restaurant – all polished wood floors, intricate sculptures, and super-polite staff – is a fantastic place to enjoy vibrant Thai flavours including some unusual regional specialities.

Beltane Cafe Bar (☎ 01298-26010; 8A Hall Bank; 🕙 10am-11pm, to 1am Sat) The laid-back atmosphere, good selection of real ales and hard-to-find lagers and evenings of live jazz, blues, soul and folk make this funky cafe-bar a popular spot. The food's not bad either and it's particularly known for its delectable crepes.

our pick **Project X** (☎ 01298-77079; The Old Court House, George St; 🕙 8am-midnight) The lavender walls, bright artwork, fairy lights, stacks of cookbooks and separate Moroccan-style nook make for an eclectic, cosy space that attracts local Buxton hipsters as well as tea-sipping grannies. It's a sociable place with a delicious, varied menu including a startling array of flavoured lattes and wickedly indulgent milkshakes. Things get more hectic at night when people flood in for beers and cocktails. There are a couple of internet terminals that are free for 30 minutes for customers.

Old Sun Inn (☎ 01298-23452; 33 High St) The pick of the town's straight pubs, retaining an Edwardian-era ambience. Low ceilings, antique light fittings, flagstone floors and a different crowd in every cranny of this warren-like ale-house make it *the* place to head for a pint – not to mention the surprisingly sophisticated pub grub.

Getting There & Away

Buxton is well served by public transport. The best place to get the bus is Market Sq, where services go to Derby (1½ hours, twice hourly), Chesterfield (1¼ hours, several daily) and Sheffield (65 minutes, every 30 minutes). Trains run to and from Manchester (50 minutes, hourly).

AROUND BUXTON
Tideswell

About 8 miles east of Buxton, deep in lovely White Peak countryside, the village of Tideswell makes a good base for walking.

Tideswell's centrepiece is the massive parish church – known as the **Cathedral of the**

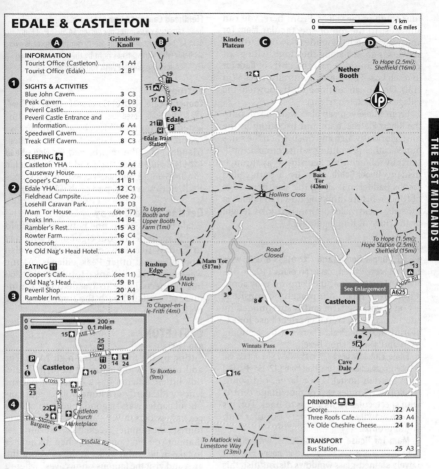

EDALE & CASTLETON

0	1 km
0	0.6 miles

INFORMATION
Tourist Office (Castleton)............1 A4
Tourist Office (Edale)................2 B1

SIGHTS & ACTIVITIES
Blue John Cavern.....................3 C3
Peak Cavern..........................4 D3
Peveril Castle.......................5 D3
Peveril Castle Entrance and
   Information........................6 A4
Speedwell Cavern.....................7 C3
Treak Cliff Cavern...................8 C3

SLEEPING
Castleton YHA 9 A4
Causeway House......................10 A4
Cooper's Camp.......................11 B1
Edale YHA...........................12 C1
Fieldhead Campsite..............(see 2)
Losehill Caravan Park...............13 D3
Mam Tor House..................(see 17)
Peaks Inn...........................14 B4
Rambler's Rest......................15 A3
Rowter Farm.........................16 C4
Stonecroft..........................17 B1
Ye Old Nag's Head Hotel.............18 A4

EATING
Cooper's Cafe..................(see 11)
Old Nag's Head......................19 B1
Peveril Shop........................20 A4
Rambler Inn.........................21 B1

Grindslow Knoll

Kinder Plateau

To Hope (2.5mi);
Sheffield (16mi)

Nether Booth

Edale

Edale Train Station

Back Tor (426m)

Hollins Cross

To Upper Booth and Upper Booth Farm (1mi)

To Hope (1.5mi);
Hope Station (2.5mi);
Sheffield (15mi)

Road Closed

Rushup Edge

Mam Tor (517m)

Mam Nick

See Enlargement

Castleton

A625

Hope Rd

To Chapel-en-le-Frith (4mi)

Winnats Pass

Cave Dale

To Buxton (9mi)

To Matlock via Limestone Way (23mi)

DRINKING
George..............................22 A4
Three Roofs Cafe....................23 A4
Ye Olde Cheshire Cheese.............24 B4

TRANSPORT
Bus Station.........................25 A3

0 | 200 m
0 | 0.1 miles

Mill La

Castleton

How La

Cross St

Castleton Church

Castle St

Back St

The Stones
Bargate

Castleton Marketplace

Pindale Rd

Peak – which has stood here virtually unchanged for 600 years. Look out for the old box pews, shiplike oak ceiling and huge panels inscribed with the Ten Commandments.

For accommodation, **Poppies** (☎ 01298-871083; www.poppiesbandb.co.uk; poptidza@dialstart.net; Bank Sq; s/d from £24/48) is frequently recommended by walkers, and with its hearty excellent evening meals, no wonder.

Bus 65 and 66 run between Buxton and Calver, via Tideswell, and with connections to Sheffield and Chesterfield.

EDALE

Surrounded by sweeping Peak District countryside at its most majestic, this tiny cluster of imposing stone houses and a parish church is

an enchanting place to pass the time. Edale lies between the White and Dark Peak areas, and is the southern terminus of the Pennine Way and a popular departure point for ramblers and mountain bikers. Its train station makes this seemingly remote enclave very accessible – and highly popular.

Information

All the leaflets, maps and guides you will need can be found at the **tourist office** (☎ 01433-670207; www.edale-valley.co.uk; Grindsbrook; ⏰ 10am-5pm).

Activities

Heading south, a great walk from Edale takes you up to **Hollins Cross**, a point on the ridge that runs south of the valley. From here, you can aim west to the top of spectacular **Mam Tor** and watch the hang-gliders swoop around above. Or go east along the ridge, with great views on both sides, past the cliffs of **Back Tor** to reach Lose Hill (which, naturally, faces Win Hill). Or you can continue south, down to the village of Castleton (right).

From Edale you can also walk north onto the **Kinder Plateau**, dark and brooding in the mist, gloriously high and open when the sun's out. Weather permitting, a fine circular walk starts by following the Pennine Way through fields to **Upper Booth**, then up a path called Jacobs Ladder and along the southern edge of Kinder, before dropping down to Edale via the steep rocky valley of Grindsbrook Clough, or the ridge of Ringing Roger.

Sleeping

our pick **Upper Booth Farm** (☎ 01433-670250; www .upperboothcamping.co.uk; sites per person/car £4/2; ☼ Feb–Nov; **P**) Located along the Pennine Way about a mile from Edale, this peaceful campsite is set on a working farm and is surrounded by spectacular scenery. It's a perfect base for exploring the High Peak. There's also a camping barn and a small shop here.

Edale YHA (☎ 0845 371 9515; www.yha.org.uk; dm members/nonmembers incl breakfast from £12/15; **P** **☐**) This Spartan hostel is in a large, old country house 1.5 miles east of the village centre, with spectacular views across to Back Tor. It's also an activity centre and very popular with youth groups.

Mam Tor House (☎ 01433-670253; www.mamtor house.co.uk; Grindsbrook; B&B per person around £25; **P**) Lovely stained-glass windows distinguish this charming lodging in an Edwardian house right next to the church.

Stonecroft (☎ 01433-670262; www.stonecroftguest house.co.uk; Grindsbrook; B&B from £70; **P**) This handsomely fitted-out home, built at the turn of the 1900s in the large stone typical of the area has two comfortable bedrooms. Vegetarians and vegans are well catered for – the organic breakfast is excellent. The owner also runs landscape-photography courses.

Other options for campers:

Cooper's Camp (☎ 01433-670372; pitch from £7, per car £2; **P**) At the far end of the village on a farm. There's great walking from the site; facilities are basic but fine for a short stay and hot showers run year-round. Caravans are also welcome and there is a shop, post office and cafe by the entrance.

Fieldhead Campsite (☎ 01433-670386; www.field head-campsite.co.uk; sites per person £4.50; **P**) Right next to the tourist office, this pretty campsite spreads over six fields with some pitches right by the river. With good facilities, it is also popular with youth groups.

Eating

Cooper's Cafe (☎ 01433-670401; Cooper's Camp; ☼ 8.30am-5pm, closed Tue) To stock up on cholesterol energy for hiking, head to this greasy spoon. Otherwise, Edale has two walker-friendly pubs, the refurbished **Old Nag's Head** (☎ 01433-670291; Grindsbrook) and the **Rambler Inn** (☎ 01433-670268; Grindsbrook), which also does B&B. Both serve OK pub grub (£5 to £10).

Getting There & Away

Edale is on the train line between Sheffield and Manchester (about eight daily Monday to Friday, five at weekends). Trains also stop at several other Peak villages. At the weekends and on Bank Holidays, the 260 bus connects Edale to Castleton (25 minutes, seven daily) with the final bus going on to Buxton.

CASTLETON
pop 1200

Sitting by the foot of 517m-high Mam Tor and topped by the ruins of Peveril Castle, tidy little Castleton has a couple of narrow lanes with sturdy gritstone houses and colourful gardens, and a good collection of cosy country pubs. Oh yes – and about a million tourists on summer weekends. But don't let that put you off. Come here when it's quieter to take in beautiful walks in the surrounding area and visit the famous 'showcaves', where a semiprecious stone called Blue John has been mined for centuries.

Orientation & Information

Castleton stands at the western end of the Hope Valley. The main road from the village goes up the narrow, spectacular gorge of Winnats Pass toward Edale (the A625 route used to cut across Mam Tor, but the peak's brittle shale led to a landslip in 1977 that destroyed the road).

Cross St is the main street, and most of the pubs, shops, cafes, B&Bs, the YHA hostel and the modern **tourist office** (☎ 01433-620679; ☼ 9.30am-5.30pm Mar-Oct, 10am-5pm Nov-Feb) are here or just nearby. There's also an interesting museum covering local Peak District information from Blue John geology to hang-gliding history.

Sights

Perched high on a hill to the south of Castleton is ruined **Peveril Castle** (EH; ☎ 01433-620613; adult/child £4/2; ☺ 10am-6pm May-Aug, to 5pm Sep, Oct & Apr, to 4pm Thu-Mon Nov-Mar), well worth the steep walk up from the village. William Peveril, son of William the Conqueror, built it originally, and Henry II added the central keep in 1176. The ruins are full of atmosphere, made even more special by stunning views over the Hope Valley, straight down to Castleton's medieval street grid and north to Mam Tor and beyond.

The area around Castleton is riddled with underground limestone caves, and four are open to the public. Although mostly natural, they have expanded from extensive lead, silver and Blue John mining over the centuries.

The most convenient, **Peak Cavern** (☎ 01433-620285; www.devilsarse.com; adult/child £7/5; ☺ 10am-5pm daily Apr-Oct, Sat & Sun Nov-Mar, last tour 4pm), is easily reached by a pretty streamside walk from the village centre. It has the largest natural cave entrance in England, known (not so prettily) as the Devil's Arse. Visits are by hourly guided tour only.

Claustrophobics should steer clear of **Speedwell Cavern** (☎ 01433-620512; www.speedwell cavern.co.uk; adult/child £8/6; ☺ 10am-5pm daily, last tour 4pm), which includes a unique boat trip through a flooded mineshaft, where visitors glide in eerie silence (save for the garrulous guides) to reach a huge underground lake called the Bottomless Pit.

Treak Cliff Cavern (☎ 01433-620571; adult/child £7/4; ☺ 10am-5pm daily, last tour 4.15pm) is a short walk from Castleton, with colourful exposed seams of Blue John and great limestone stalactites including the much-photographed 'stork'.

Blue John Cavern (☎ 01433-620638; adult/child £8/4; ☺ 9.30am-5.30pm summer, to dusk winter) is an impressive set of natural caverns, where the rich veins of the Blue John mineral are dazzling. You can get here on foot up the closed section of the Mam Tor road.

Activities

Castleton is the northern terminus of the Limestone Way (p515), which includes narrow, rocky Cave Dale, far below the east wall of the castle.

If you feel like a shorter walk, you can follow the Limestone Way up Cave Dale for a few miles, then loop round on paths and tracks to the west of Rowter Farm (p522) to meet the Buxton Rd. Go straight (north) on a path crossing fields and another road to eventually reach Mam Nick, where the road to Edale passes through a gap in the ridge. Go up steps here to reach the summit of Mam Tor for stunning views along the Hope Valley. (You can also see the fractured remains of the old main road.) The path then aims northwest along the ridge to another gap called Hollins Cross, from where paths and tracks lead back down to Castleton. This 6-mile circuit takes three to four hours.

A shorter option from Castleton is to take the path direct to Hollins Cross, then go to Mam Tor, and return by the same route (about 4 miles, two to three hours). From Hollins Cross, you can extend any walk by dropping down to Edale, or you can walk directly from Castleton to Edale via Hollins Cross. Maps are available at the tourist office, and its *Walks around Castleton* leaflet (30p) has plenty of alternative routes.

Sleeping

Prices listed are peak weekend rates, but almost all Castleton options have good weekday deals.

Castleton YHA (☎ 0845 371 9628; www.yha.org.uk; Castle St; dm members/non-members from £14/17; ⓟ ⬜) Rambling, old building with an abundance of rooms, this hostel is a great pit stop with knowledgeable staff who also conduct guided walks. There's a licensed bar too.

Rambler's Rest (☎ 01433-620125; www.ramblers rest-castleton.co.uk; Mill Bridge; s/d from £25/40; ⓟ) This well-appointed, attractively restored 17th-century stone cottage has five comfortable rooms, three of them en suite, and one big enough to accommodate a family or small group.

Causeway House (☎ 01433-623921; www.causeway house.co.uk; Back St; s/d £29/60) The floors within this ancient character-soaked gritstone building are gnarled with age, but the quaint bedrooms are bright and welcoming, as are the owners.

Ye Olde Nag's Head Hotel (☎ 01433-620248; Cross St; d from £50) This cosy, traditional 17th-century coaching house has comfy B&B rooms, some with antique four-posters including one with a Jacuzzi; get the ones on the top floor with a view and away from the noise of the pub. There's also a decent restaurant.

For campers, the nearest place is well-organised **Losehill Caravan Park** (☎ 01433-620636; Hope Rd; per site £8 plus per person £6). **Rowter Farm** (☎ 01433-620271; sites per person £4, ✆ Easter-Sep) is a simple campsite about 1 mile west of Castleton in a stunning location up in the hills. Drivers should approach via Winnats Pass; if you're on foot you can follow paths from the Castleton village centre as described in the Activities section earlier.

Eating & Drinking

Peaks Inn (☎ 01433-620247; www.peaks-inn.co.uk; How Lane; main £5-10) Large buzzing pub with gleaming wooden floors, leather sofas, fires in winter and a selection of hearty meals including good Sunday roasts and a number of daily specials.

George (☎ 01433-620238; Castle St; mains around £7) Flagstone floors, and the tankards dangling from the ceiling give this ageing local a measure of 'olde worlde' charm. But it's very much on the beaten tourist track – and the food, though it comes in big portions, isn't up to much.

Ye Olde Cheshire Cheese Inn (☎ 01433-620330; How Lane; mains £7-9) Tradition is everything at this well-known alehouse. The home cooking needs a little attention but go for the peaceful, snug atmosphere.

Peveril Shop (☎ 01433-620928; How Lane; ✆ 6.30am-5pm daily) Near the bus stop, this place sells food and groceries and does sandwiches to take away, ideal for a day on the hills or a long bus ride.

Teashops abound in Castleton. Most convenient is the **Three Roofs Cafe** (☎ 01433-620533; The Island; ✆ 10am-5pm Mon-Fri, to 5.30pm Sat & Sun), where muddy boots are welcome. At busy times, this can be packed, so just meander the streets in search of a cream-tea joint with chairs – it's all part of the fun in Castleton.

Getting There & Away

You can get to Castleton from Bakewell on bus 173 (45 minutes, five daily Monday to Friday, three daily at weekends) via Hope and Tideswell. The 68 goes to Buxton every afternoon from Monday to Saturday.

The nearest train station is Hope, about 1 mile east of Hope village (a total of 3 miles east of Castleton) on the line between Sheffield and Manchester. On summer weekends, a bus runs between Hope station and Castleton tying in with the trains, although it's not a bad walk in good weather.

DERWENT RESERVOIRS

Toward the north of the Peak District, three huge artificial lakes – Ladybower, Upper Derwent and Howden, known as the Derwent Reservoirs – collect water for nearby cities. They are also prime walking and mountain-biking territory.

The place to aim for is national park centre **Fairholmes**, near the Derwent Dam, which has a **tourist office** (☎ 01433-650953), a car park, a snack bar and **Derwent Cycle Hire** (☎ 01433-651261).

Numerous walks start here, from gentle strolls along the lakeside to more serious outings on the moors above the valley. For cycling, a lane leads up the west side of Derwent and Howden reservoirs (it's closed to car traffic at weekends), and a dirt track comes down the east side, making a good 12-mile circuit. Challenging off-road routes lead deeper into the hills. The tourist office stocks a very good range of maps and guidebooks.

Fairholmes is 2 miles north of the A57, the main road between Sheffield and Manchester. Bus 274 and 51A run to Fairholmes from Sheffield Interchange.

EYAM
pop 900

Quaint little Eyam (ee-em), a former lead-mining village, has a morbid and touching history. In 1665 a consignment of cloth from London delivered to a local tailor carried the dreaded Black Death plague. Thanks to the noble village inhabitants, what could have become a widespread disaster remained a localised tragedy: as the plague spread, the rector, William Mompesson, and his predecessor, Thomas Stanley, convinced villagers to quarantine themselves rather than transmit the disease further. Selflessly, they did so; by the time the plague ended in late 1666, it had wiped out whole families, killing around 270 of the village's 800 inhabitants. People in surrounding villages remained relatively unscathed. Even independently of this poignant story, Eyam, with its sloping streets of old cottages backed by rolling green hills, forms a classic postcard view of the Peak District and a well worth a visit.

Sights
Eyam Parish Church (☎ 01433-630930; ✆ 9am-6pm Apr-Sep, to 4pm Oct-Mar) dates from Saxon times

and carries a moving display on the plague and its devastating effect on the village. Look out for the plague register, recording those who died, name by name, day by day, and the stained-glass window telling the story of the plague, installed in 1985. Perhaps most touching is the extract from a letter the rector wrote to his children about his wife, Catherine Mompesson, who succumbed to the disease. Her headstone lies in the churchyard. In the same grounds is an 8th-century **Celtic cross**, one of the finest in England. Before leaving, you could also check your watch against the **sundial** on the church wall.

Around the village, many buildings have information plaques attached including the **plague cottages**, where the tailor lived, next to the church.

Eyam Hall (☎ 01433-631976; adult/child £6/4; ☒ noon-4pm Wed, Thu, Sun & Bank Holidays, Mon Jun-Aug, first three Sun in Dec) is a fine, old 17th-century manor house. The courtyard has a craft centre and a couple of eateries and there's a traditional English walled garden.

Eyam Museum (☎ 01433-631371; www.eyam.org.uk; Hawkhill Rd; adult/child £2/1; ☒ 10am-4.30pm Tue-Sun Easter-Oct) has some vivid displays on the tragic effect of the plague on Eyam's population, but also has exhibits on the village's Saxon past and its time as a lead-mining and silk-weaving centre.

Look out for the **stocks** on the village green – somewhere handy to leave the kids, perhaps, while you look at the church.

Activities
Eyam makes a great base for **walking** and **cycling** in the White Peak area. A short walk leads up Water Lane from the village square, then up through fields and a patch of woodland to meet another lane running between Eyam and Grindleford; turn right here and keep going uphill, past another junction to **Mompesson's Well**, where food and other supplies were left during the plague time for Eyam folk by friends from other villages. The Eyam people paid for the goods using coins sterilised in vinegar. You can retrace your steps back down the lane, then take a path which leads directly to the church. This 2-mile circuit takes about 1½ hours at a gentle pace.

Sleeping & Eating
Bretton YHA (☎ 0845 371 9626; www.yha.org.uk; Bretton, Hope Valley; dm members/non-members £14/15) If the

Eyam YHA is full, this basic place, the smallest hostel in the Peaks, is only 1.5 miles away.

Eyam YHA (☎ 0845 371 9738; www.yha.org.uk; Hawkhill Rd; dm members/nonmembers from £15/18) Simple place in a fine, old Victorian house with a folly, perched up a hill overlooking the village.

Miner's Arms (☎ 01433-630853; Water Lane; s/d £45/60) This grand old 17th-century inn, built just before the plague hit Eyam, has beamed ceilings, affable staff, a cosy stone fireplace and decent food. Comfortable rooms with en suite bathrooms are just a short climb upstairs for the weary limbed or the bleary eyed.

Crown Cottage (☎ 01433-630858; www.crown-cottage.co.uk; Main Rd; d £60) Bright and walker- and cyclist-friendly – plus it's full to the rafters most weekends. Book ahead to be sure of a spot.

Peak Pantry (☎ 01433-631293; cakes & tea £3-5; ☒ 9am-5pm Mon-Sat, 10am-5pm Sun) This unpretentious place on the village square has a mouthwatering array of slices and coffee.

Eyam Tea Rooms (☎ 01433-631274; cake & tea £4) There's more chintz at this place just up the road, but it serves delicious homemade cakes and pastries as well as hearty lunches.

Getting There & Away
Eyam is 7 miles north of Bakewell and 12 miles east of Buxton. The 175 from Bakewell goes to Eyam (three daily Monday to Saturday, no Sunday service). From Buxton, buses 65 and 66 run to and from Chesterfield, stopping at Eyam (40 minutes, about six daily).

BAKEWELL
pop 3979
The largest town in the Peak District after Buxton (though it's hardly a metropolis), Bakewell isn't as pretty or atmospheric as its graceful spa-town neighbour, but it's a useful base for cyclists and walkers. It has a famous pudding (the Bakewell Pudding – it's not a tart you know), a couple of fine country houses within ambling distance and a reputation as a notorious traffic bottleneck during the summer months.

Orientation & Information
The centre of town is Rutland Sq. From here, roads radiate to Matlock, Buxton and Sheffield. The helpful **tourist office** (☎ 01629-813227; Bridge St; ☒ 10am-5pm) in the old Market Hall has racks of leaflets and books about Bakewell and the national park.

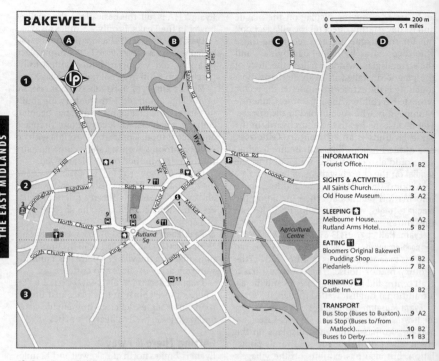

BAKEWELL

INFORMATION
Tourist Office..................................1 B2

SIGHTS & ACTIVITIES
All Saints Church...........................2 A2
Old House Museum.......................3 A2

SLEEPING
Melbourne House..........................4 A2
Rutland Arms Hotel.......................5 B2

EATING
Bloomers Original Bakewell
      Pudding Shop..........................6 B2
Piedaniels.......................................7 B2

DRINKING
Castle Inn.......................................8 B2

TRANSPORT
Bus Stop (Buses to Buxton).....9 A2
Bus Stop (Buses to/from
      Matlock)..............................10 B2
Buses to Derby.............................11 B3

Sights & Activities

Bakewell's weekly market is on Monday, when the square behind the tourist office is very lively. Up on the hill above Rutland Sq, **All Saints Church** has some ancient Norman features, and even older Saxon stonework remains including a tall cross in the churchyard, which sadly has suffered at the hands of time.

Near the church, the **Old House Museum** (☎ 01629-813642, Cunningham Pl; adult/child £3/1.50; 11am-4pm Apr-Oct) displays a Tudor loo and, also on a scatological theme, shows how early Peakland houses used to be made with materials including cow dung.

A stroll from Rutland Sq down Bridge St brings you – not surprisingly – to the pretty **medieval bridge** over the River Wye, from where riverside walks lead in both directions. Go upstream through the water meadows, and then along Holme Lane to reach **Holme Bridge**, an ancient stone structure used by Peak District packhorses for centuries.

On the northern edge of Bakewell, a former railway line has been converted to a walking and cycling track called the **Monsal Trail**. From Bakewell you can cycle about 3 miles north and 1 mile south on the old railway itself, and there are numerous other tracks and country lanes nearby. The nearest bike hire is near Buxton (see p516). Walkers on the Monsal Trail follow alternate sections of the old railway and pretty footpaths through fields and beside rivers. From Bakewell, an excellent out-and-back walk (3 miles each way) goes to the dramatic viewpoint at Monsal Head, where a good pub, Stables Bar at the Monsal Head Hotel, provides welcome refreshment. Allow three hours for the round trip.

If you're out for the day, from Monsal Head you can keep following the Monsal Trail northwest towards Buxton. A good point to aim for is Miller's Dale, where viaducts give a spectacular vista across the steep-sided valley, or you can go all the way to Blackwell Mill (3 miles east of Buxton) – a total distance of about 9 miles – and get a bus back. Alternatively, get a bus to Buxton, and walk back to Bakewell. The tourist offices at Bakewell and Buxton have a *Monsal Trail* leaflet with all the details.

Other walking routes go to the stately homes of Haddon Hall and Chatsworth House (right). You could take a bus or taxi there and walk back, so you don't muddy the duke's carpet.

Sleeping

Melbourne House (☎ 01629-815357; Buxton Rd; s/d £35/50; **P**) Located in a picturesque, listed building dating back more than three centuries, this is an inviting B&B in the very best Peak District tradition. It is situated on the main road leading to Buxton.

Rutland Arms Hotel (☎ 01629-812812; www.rutlandarmsbakewell.com; The Square; s/d £65/120; **P**) Aristocratic but slightly careworn, this hotel is the most refined of Bakewell's accommodation. Get a higher room if traffic noise keeps you up at night.

Eating & Drinking

Bakewell's streets are lined with cute teashops and bakeries, most with 'pudding' in the name, selling the town's eponymous cake. It would be bad manners not to try the local speciality when in town.

Bloomers Original Bakewell Puddings (☎ 01629-814844; Water St) Piled high with local cheeses, pies, meats and breads, this is the place to come to stock up for some alfresco dining. The eponymous puddings are among the best in town and come in three different sizes.

Piedaniels (☎ 01629-812687; Bath St; mains £12; ☻ lunch & dinner Tue-Sat) The toast of the local restaurant scene, Piedaniels is smart and slickly presented, from the crisp, white-and-cream colour scheme to the sumptuous, modern-French cuisine. Weekday lunch menus are fantastic value (three courses for £12).

Castle Inn (☎ 01629-812103; Bridge St) The ivy-draped Castle Inn is one of the better pubs in Bakewell, with four centuries' practice in warming the cockles of hamstrung hikers.

Getting There & Away

Buses serve Bakewell from Derby via Matlock (most 90 minutes but there are some faster buses, twice hourly) and Chesterfield (45 minutes, hourly). The TransPeak service goes on to Nottingham (one hour 50 minutes, hourly).

AROUND BAKEWELL
Haddon Hall

One of the finest medieval houses you will find anywhere, exquisite **Haddon Hall** (☎ 01629-812855; www.haddonhall.co.uk; adult/child £9/5; ☻ noon-5pm, last admission 4pm Sat-Mon Apr & Oct, daily May-Sep), is quick to weave its spell. Its charms are no secret to movie-makers – most recently, the producers of *Pride and Prejudice*, starring Dame Judi Dench and Keira Knightley, chose the magnificent turreted house and its fragrant terraced gardens as their shooting location. The hall dates back to the 12th century, and what you see today dates mainly from the 14th to 16th centuries. Haddon Hall was abandoned in the 18th and 19th centuries, so it escaped the 'modernisation' experienced by many other country houses. Highlights include the **Chapel**; the **Long Gallery**, stunningly bathed by natural light; and the vast **Banqueting Hall**, virtually unchanged since the days of Henry VIII.

The house is 2 miles south of Bakewell on the A6. You can get there on any bus heading for Matlock (every 30 minutes) or walk along the footpath through the fields, mostly on the east side of the river.

Chatsworth

The great stately home, manicured gardens and perfectly landscaped park of Chatsworth together form a major highlight for many visitors to England.

The main draw is sumptuous **Chatsworth House** (☎ 01246-582204; www.chatsworth.org; adult/child house & garden £12.50/6.50, garden only £7.50/4.50; ☻ 11am-5.30pm Mar-Dec). Known as the 'Palace of the Peak', this vast edifice has been occupied by the dukes of Devonshire for centuries. The original house was started in 1551 by the inimitable Bess of Hardwick; a little later came Chatsworth's most famous guest, Mary, Queen of Scots. She was imprisoned here on and off between 1570 and 1581 at the behest of Elizabeth I, under the guard of Bess's fourth husband, the earl of Shrewsbury. The **Scots bedrooms**, nine Regency rooms named after the imprisoned queen, are sometimes open to the public.

The house was extensively altered between 1686 and 1707, and again enlarged and improved in the 1820s; much of what you see dates from these periods. Among the prime attractions are the painted and decorated ceilings, although the 30 or so rooms are all treasure troves of splendid furniture and magnificent artworks.

The house sits in 25 sq miles of **gardens** (adult/child £7/4), home to a fountain so high it can be seen from miles away in the hills of the Dark Peak, and several bold, modern sculptures, of which the Duke and Duchess of Devonshire are keen collectors. For the kids, an **adventure playground** (admission £5.25) provides hours of fun.

Beyond that is another 400 hectares of parkland, originally landscaped by Lancelot 'Capability' Brown, open to the public for walking and picnicking.

Chatsworth is 3 miles northeast of Bakewell. If you're driving, it's £2 to park. Bus 170 and 218 go direct from Bakewell to Chatsworth (15 minutes, several daily). On Sunday, bus 215 also runs to Chatsworth.

Another option is to walk or cycle from Bakewell. Start out on the quiet lane that leads uphill from the old train station; walkers can take footpaths through Chatsworth park via the mock-Venetian village of Edensor (ensor), and cyclists can pedal via Pilsley.

The West Midlands & the Marches

The West Midlands has more than its fair share of bleak urban landscapes here – this is, after all, the area that gave birth to the Industrial Revolution. Lucky, then, that it's also home to gentle countryside, stately homes, leisurely canals and two of the country's best-known attractions: Warwick Castle, one of the finest medieval buildings in England, and Stratford-upon-Avon, a pilgrimage site for Shakespeare-lovers from around the world. What's more, the once derided city of Birmingham has reinvented itself as a dynamic, cultured city, bubbling over with influences from many different nations.

Hugging the Welsh borders to the west of Birmingham, the country pleasures of the Marches are a world away from big-city action and overrun tourist towns. The main joy here is in wandering around rippling hills and farmland and exploring sleepy, time-warp villages.

Beautiful Shropshire is home to an incredible World Heritage site at Ironbridge Gorge, an epicurean enclave at historic Ludlow, beguiling Tudor capital Shrewsbury and the sublime Shropshire hills. To the south, the canoe-friendly River Wye meanders through laid-back Herefordshire's lovely landscape, dotted with fairy-tale black-and-white villages, while Worcestershire is home to a historic capital, handsome Victorian hill resorts and the dramatic Malvern peaks.

HIGHLIGHTS

- Losing yourself amongst the second-hand bookshelves at **Hay-on-Wye** (p565)
- Wandering through fairy-tale villages on Hereford's **Black-and-white-village Trail** (p565)
- Enjoying first-rate shopping then taking in a Pakistani balti in the vibrant city of **Birmingham** (p530)
- Eating up a storm at the foodie mecca that is **Ludlow** (p582)
- Watching Shakespeare's stories come to life at **Stratford-upon-Avon** (p546)
- Wandering the haunting terracotta ruins of **Kenilworth Castle** (p545)

★ Birmingham
★ Ludlow   ★ Kenilworth Castle
★ Black-and-white-village Trail
★ Hay-on-Wye   ★ Stratford-upon-Avon

■ POPULATION: 5.57 MILLION	■ AREA: 4560 SQ MILES	■ GALLONS OF CIDER PRODUCED YEARLY IN HEREFORDSHIRE: 63 MILLION

History

This region has seen its share of action over the centuries. In the Marches, territorial scuffles and all-out battles took place between feuding kingdoms along what is today the border separating England and Wales. In the 8th century the Anglo-Saxon king Offa of Mercia built an earthwork barricade along the border in an attempt to quell the ongoing tension. It became known as Offa's Dyke Path, and much of it is still traceable as a very popular walking route today.

In an effort to subdue the Welsh and secure his new kingdom, William the Conqueror set up powerful, feudal barons – called Lords Marcher after the Anglo-Saxon word *mearc*, meaning 'boundary' – along the border, from where they repeatedly raided Wales, taking as much territory as possible under their control.

Meanwhile Birmingham, Staffordshire and Shropshire were making a name for themselves as centres of industry, from the wool trade to the metal, iron and coal industries. The region gradually became the most intensely industrialised in the country, giving birth to the Industrial Revolution in Shropshire in the 18th century.

Orientation

It is perhaps easiest to orientate yourself here by motorways. The M40 winds north from London, passing Stratford-upon-Avon and Warwick on its way to the M42 and Birmingham in the west of the Midlands. Routes spider out from Birmingham: the M6 runs east towards Coventry and the M1, and northwest up towards Wolverhampton, Stafford and Stoke-on-Trent; the M5 splits off at West Bromwich and heads down towards Worcester and Hereford; the M54 splits off at Wolverhampton to head over to Telford and Shrewsbury.

Information

The **Heart of England Tourist Board** (☎ 01905-761100; www.visitheartofengland.com) has centralised tourist information for the region and is a good place to start your planning.

Activities

There are beautiful walking and cycling routes everywhere in the Marches – through pastoral idylls, wooded valleys and gentle hills. But not all the action is situated on terra firma – lots of fun can be had in the water and in the sky too. See the county-specific Activities sections in this chapter for more information.

CYCLING

Shropshire in particular is ideal for touring, and you can rent bicycles in Shrewsbury, Church Stretton, Ludlow, Ironbridge and Ledbury.

Areas apt for off-road biking include the woods of Hopton near Ludlow, as well as Eastridge near Shrewsbury. High-level riding on the Long Mynd above Church Stretton is also rewarding.

In Herefordshire, you'll find the **Ledbury Loop** – a 17-mile rural circuit based around the town of Ledbury.

A pack of route maps and notes called *Cycling for Pleasure in the Marches* is available from the tourist offices for £6. Tourist offices also stock many free route leaflets, and you can find them on stretches of National Cycle Route 45 through Shropshire and Worcestershire through the **National Cycle Network** (NCN; www.sustrans.org) or you can download leaflets from www.shropshire.gov.uk.

WALKING

One of many great walks on which to get muddy, the glorious **Offa's Dyke Path** is a 177-mile national trail following an ancient earthen border defence. Running south–north from Chepstow to Prestatyn, it passes through some of the most spectacular scenery in Britain, but it's not for the inexperienced or unfit.

Less exhausting is the gentle 107-mile **Wye Valley Walk**, which follows the course of the River Wye from Chepstow upstream to Rhayader in Wales. Another popular route is the beautiful 100-mile **Three Choirs Way** linking the cathedral cities of Hereford, Worcester and Gloucester.

Shorter walks include the famous ridges of Wenlock Edge (p578) and the lovely Long Mynd (p580). These are in turn swallowed by the circular 136-mile **Shropshire Way**, which loops from Shrewsbury south to Ludlow.

One of the most beautiful places to walk is the **Malvern Hills** (p560), offering straightforward paths and breathtaking views on the boundary between Worcestershire and Herefordshire.

For more ideas, see the Activities sections of each county in this chapter.

OTHER ACTIVITIES

Symonds Yat (p568) on the River Wye is a great place for both easy-grade canoeing and white-water fun, while the river gorge's rocky buttresses are also a popular rock-climbing spot. The Long Mynd is renowned for its gliding and paragliding, with facilities in Church Stretton. For something completely different,

tourist offices can point you towards hot spots for mountain boarding.

A canal boat is one of the most fun ways to get active, with the metropolis of Birmingham the unlikely epicentre. Hire a boat and take some bikes with you, and you can enjoy the canalside paths by wheel or by foot at your leisure, as you gently chug your way through the country's massive network of artificial waterways.

Getting Around

Birmingham is a major rail interchange for the whole of England. **National Express** (☎ 08718 818181; www.nationalexpress.com) is the main coach service in the region and throughout the country. For general route information you can consult **Traveline** (☎ 0871 200 2233; www.travelinemidlands.co.uk).

The main bus operators:

Arriva (☎ 0844 800 4411; www.arrivabus.co.uk) An Arriva Go Anywhere ticket gives one day of unlimited travel.

First Travel (☎ 0800 587 7381; www.firstgroup.com) A FirstDay Wyvern ticket (adult/child £5.50/3.80) offers unlimited day travel on the First network in Worcestershire, Herefordshire and adjoining counties.

Stagecoach (☎ 01788-535555; Dayrider Gold tickets adult/child £6.50/4.50)

Travel West Midlands (www.travelwm.co.uk)

Rail networks are extensive in the West Midlands, but less so in the rural Marches, where they're only useful for major towns. Useful train operators include:

London Midland (www.londonmidland.com) Operates a train service throughout the Midlands and excellent connections with London.

Wrexham and Shropshire (www.wrexhamandshropshire.co.uk) Operates a direct train service from Shropshire to London Marylebone.

Public transport can be a hit-and-miss affair in the largely rural Marches. Without your own wheels, getting to countryside attractions takes time, planning and patience.

BIRMINGHAM

pop 977,087

Once the butt of many a joke, England's second-largest city – nicknamed 'Brum' – has spectacularly redefined its image from aesthetically challenged urban basket case to vibrant, cultural hot spot. Huge regeneration projects have revitalised the industrial landscapes and canals that criss-cross the city; now there are more glamorous shops, swanky bars and hectic nightclubs than you can shake a bargepole at.

Lookswise, though, it's still not a pretty picture. The unfortunate combination of WWII bombs and woeful town planning left a legacy of concrete and ring roads that may never be completely disguised. But, no

matter: Birmingham is making the most of what it's got. Established cultural and architectural gems dot the city centre and planners keep coming up with ever more innovative makeovers, such as the striking postindustrial Bullring shopping centre. Although the manufacturing industry that defined the city as the 'workhorse of the world' is declining, Birmingham will no doubt adapt. More self-assured than it has been in ages, it is hampered by only one thing – its inhabitants' accent, which is consistently voted England's least attractive.

HISTORY

Birmingham's first mention of any note was in the Domesday Book of 1086, where it was described as a small village. Over the next few centuries Birmingham established itself in the field of industry, starting off with the wool trade in the 13th century, and becoming an important centre for the metal and iron industries from the 16th century onwards.

It was also here that, in the mid-18th century, the pioneers of the Industrial Revolution formed the Lunar Society, which brought together geologists, chemists, scientists, engineers and theorists, including Erasmus Darwin, Matthew Boulton, James Watt, Joseph Priestly and Josiah Wedgwood, all of whom contributed to the ideas and vision of the times.

By this time, Birmingham had become the largest town in Warwickshire, and the world's first true industrial town, its population tripling by the end of the century. It had also become polluted, dirty and unsanitary.

In the mid-1800s, under enlightened mayors such as Joseph Chamberlain (1836–1914), Birmingham became a trendsetter in civic regeneration, but WWII air raids and postwar town planning were later to give the city an unattractive face.

ORIENTATION

The one aspect of Birmingham that's still indisputably a nightmare is driving in it. The endless ring roads, roundabouts and underpasses make it particularly confusing for motorists to navigate. It's wise to park somewhere and explore the city on foot until you get your bearings.

Taking the huge Council House as the centre, to the west is Centenary Sq, the

BIRMINGHAM

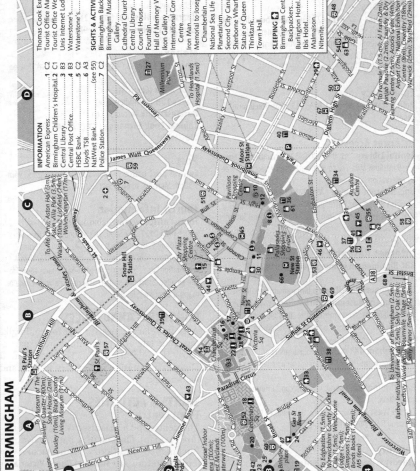

International Convention Centre and Symphony Hall, and the development at Gas St Basin and Brindleyplace.

Southeast of the Council House, most of Birmingham's shops can be found along pedestrianised New St and in the modern City Plaza, Pallasades and Pavilions shopping centres. The Arcadian Centre is further south but still in the centre, and marks the beginning of Chinatown. Between New St station and Digbeth coach station is the Bullring, a sleek, architecturally striking shopping complex (see www.bullring.co.uk).

INFORMATION
Bookshops

Bonds Books (☎ 0121-427 9343; www.bondsbooks.co .uk; 97A High St, Harborne) Well-known independent bookstore, about 10 miutes' bus journey from the centre.
Waterstone's High St (☎ 0121-633 4353; 24 High St); New St (☎ 0121-631 4333; 128 New St)

Emergency

Police station (☎ 0121-0845 113 5000; Steelhouse Lane)

Internet Access

Central Library (☎ 0121-303 4511; Chamberlain Sq; ⏱ 9am-8pm Mon-Fri, to 5pm Sat) Internet access is free by reservation.
Unis Internet Lounge (☎ 0121-632 6172; loft level, Pavilions Shopping Centre; per hr £2; ⏱ 9.30am-6pm Mon-Wed, Fri & Sat, to 7pm Thu, 11am-5pm Sun) Internet lounge and coffee bar.

Internet Resources

BBC Birmingham home page (www.bbc.co.uk /birmingham)
Birmingham Council (www.birmingham.gov.uk)
Birmingham Museums & Art Gallery (www.bmag .org.uk) Information on most of the city's museums and galleries, including opening hours, admission costs and forthcoming exhibitions.
Birmingham UK (www.birminghamuk.com)
icBirmingham (http://icbirmingham.icnetwork.co.uk) The local newspaper's website.
Gay Birmingham (www.gaybrum.com) Information for gay visitors.
Travel West Midlands (www.travelwm.co.uk) Travel planning from the main bus company.

Laundry

Laundry & Dry Cleaning Centre (☎ 0121-771 3659; 236 Warwick Rd, Sparkhill)

Left Luggage

New Street Station (☎ 0121-632 6884; station forecourt; locker hire per day £6; ⏱ 7am-11pm Mon-Sat, 8am-10pm Sun)

Media

The numerous free magazines available in hotel lobbies, bars and restaurants, will let you know what's hot on the Birmingham scene. The pick of the bunch is the fortnightly *What's On* magazine, available for free at some bars and the tourist office.

Medical Services

Birmingham Children's Hospital (☎ 0121-333 9999; Steelhouse Lane)
Heartlands Hospital (☎ 0121-424 2000; Bordesley Green E) Catch bus 15, 17, 97 or 97A.

Money

American Express (☎ 0121-644 5555; Bank House, 8 Cherry St)
HSBC Bank (Cherry St)
Lloyds TSB (2 Brindleyplace)
NatWest Bank (Arcadian Centre)
Thomas Cook Exchange (☎ 0121-643 5057; 130 New St)

Post

Central post office (1 Pinfold St, Victoria Sq; ⏱ 9am-5.30pm Mon-Fri, to 6pm Sat)

Tourist Information

Tourist office (www.visitbirmingham.com) Main branch (☎ 0121-202 5099; The Rotunda, 150 New St; ⏱ 9.30am-5.30pm Mon & Wed-Sat, 10am-5.30pm Tue, 10.30am-4.30pm Sun); Welcome Centre (cnr New & Corporation Sts; ⏱ 9am-5pm Mon-Sat, 10am-4pm Sun) The smaller, brochure-stuffed branch has a wide range of maps and themed leaflets.

DANGERS & ANNOYANCES

As in most large cities, it's wise to avoid walking alone late at night in unlit areas, particularly if you're a woman. The area around Digbeth bus station in not very well lit, and has an edge to it.

SIGHTS & ACTIVITIES
Town Centre

The central pedestrianised Victoria Sq features a giant **fountain** of a bathing woman (nicknamed 'the floozy in the Jacuzzi' by locals), and a drab **statue of Queen Victoria**. It adjoins Chamberlain Sq, with its **memorial**

BIRMINGHAM IN...

Two Days

Shopping is one of Birmingham's major attractions these days. Work out your credit cards as you browse the series of exceptional commercial redevelopments that have rejuvenated the city. Take in the quirkily original **Custard Factory** (p540) before heading up to the more mainstream **Bullring** (p540) with its space-age Selfridges building and hundreds of outlets. Dip south to the chic designer stores of the **Mailbox** (p540) and then take the trek up to the historical **Jewellery Quarter** (p534). Even if you're all out of cash, it's well worth a look. Worshipping at the altar of consumerism can work up an appetite; head back towards the Custard Factory and soothe your conscience with some wholesome vegie nourishment at the **Warehouse Cafe** (p538). Then head to the nearby **Factory Club** (p539) for a rocking night out. Gently does it on day two. Nourish the soul with the free, pre-Raphaelite-studded **Birmingham Museum & Art Gallery** (below). Then, to get up close and personal with the city's history, check out the restored courtyard of 19th-century working people's houses at the **Birmingham Back to Backs** (below). Culture fix satisfied, catch a bus or taxi to the famous **Balti Triangle** (p538) to sample the curry dish that was born in Birmingham.

Four Days

Follow the two-day itinerary, but add a **cruise** (p537) along Birmingham's extraordinary canal network. A show at the world-class **Repertory** (p540) should be next on the cards. Next morning, make a pilgrimage to the **Barber Institute of Fine Art** (p535) and **Aston Hall** (p535) to see the region's most outstanding art collections. For a sweet interlude, make your way down to the chocolate paradise of **Cadbury World** (p535) for a seriously sugary experience. In the evening, take in an art-house film at the **Electric Cinema** (p540), the oldest working cinema in the country.

to Joseph Chamberlain, one of Birmingham's more enlightened mayors. These squares share some eye-catching architecture. The imposing **Council House** forms the northeastern face of the precinct. Its northwestern corner is formed by the modernist **Central Library**, whose brutal design looks like an upturned ziggurat, with the Paradise Forum shop and cafe complex underneath it.

To the south stands the **Town Hall**, opened in 1834. Designed to look like the Temple of Castor and Pollux in Rome and featuring a 70ft-high organ, recent refurbishment has restored it to its former glory and reinvented it as a performing-arts venue. For those who won't make it to Gateshead to see Antony Gormley's *Angel of the North* statue (p757), his wingless **Iron Man** (1993), on Victoria Sq, is a step in the same direction.

West of the precinct, Centenary Sq is another pedestrian square closed off at the western end by the **International Convention Centre** and the Symphony Hall (p539), and overlooked by the Repertory Theatre (p540). Inside Centenary Sq is the **Hall of Memory War Memorial**, and there are often temporary exhibitions in the square.

The striking **Birmingham Museum & Art Gallery** (☎ 0121-303 2834; www.bmag.org.uk; Chamberlain Sq; admission free; ☼ 10am-5pm Mon-Thu & Sat, 10.30am-5pm Fri, 12.30-5pm Sun) houses an impressive collection of Victorian art including a selection of major Pre-Raphaelite works. There are also fascinating displays on local and natural history, archaeology, world cultures, and a number of interactive exhibits for kids. Other highlights include a fine porcelain collection, and works by Degas, Braque, Renoir and Canaletto. You can indulge in a cream tea in the elegant Edwardian tearoom.

One of England's smallest cathedrals, the impressive **Cathedral Church of St Philip** (☎ 0121-262 1840; Colmore Row; donations requested; ☼ 7.30am-6.30pm Mon-Fri, 8.30am-5pm Sat & Sun) was constructed in a neoclassical style between 1709 and 1715. The Pre-Raphaelite artist Edward Burne-Jones was responsible for the magnificent stained-glass windows: the *Last Judgement*, which can be seen at the western end, and *Nativity*, *Crucifixion* and *Ascension* at the eastern end.

The **Birmingham Back to Backs** (NT; ☎ 0121-666 7671; 55-63 Hurst St; adult/child £5.40/2.70; ☼ 10am-5pm Tue-Sun, guided tour only) is a cluster of restored working people's houses: the only survivor

---

THE PRE-RAPHAELITES & THE ARTS AND CRAFTS MOVEMENT

In a classic case of artists romanticising the 'good old days' they never experienced, the Pre-Raphaelite Brotherhood shunned the art of their time in favour of the directness of art prior to the High Renaissance, especially the work preceding that of Raphael. Three young Brits, Dante Gabriel Rossetti, William Holman Hunt and John Everett Millais led the movement in 1848; four others soon joined them. Their work was characterised by almost photographic attention to detail, a combination of hyper-realism and brilliant colours. The themes and methods attracted criticism at the time but ensured the movement's popularity to this day.

Birmingham Museum & Art Gallery (p533) has one of the best collections of works by the Pre-Raphaelites. If you get the bug, there are more fine paintings in the Lady Lever Art Gallery (p689) at Port Sunlight near Liverpool.

The Arts and Crafts Movement followed Pre-Raphaelitism in yearning for a pure, idealised mode. The socialist William Morris, the movement's leading light, was a close friend of Pre-Raphaelite Edward Burne-Jones and projected the same ideals into tapestries, jewellery, stained glass and textile prints, following the principles of medieval guilds, in which the same artists designed and produced the work.

---

of some 20,000 courts of back-to-back houses built during the 19th century for the city's expanding working-class population. The tour takes you through four homes, where you learn the stories of the people who lived here during different periods, from the 1840s to the 1970s.

Should you wish to stay longer, the National Trust has even turned part of the court into self-catering accommodation.

Gas St, Brindleyplace & the Mailbox

Birmingham sits on the hub of England's canal network (the city actually has more miles of canals than Venice), and visiting narrowboats can moor in the Gas St Basin right in the heart of the city. Nearby Brindleyplace, a waterfront development of shops, restaurants and bars created during the 1990s, has transformed the area west of Centenary Sq into a lively night-time destination. A similar development to the southeast, the buzzing Mailbox has a mixture of designer boutiques, smart restaurants, chain bars and upmarket fast-food joints.

The **Ikon Gallery** (☎ 0121-248 0708; www.ikon -gallery.co.uk; 1 Oozells Sq, Brindleyplace; admission free; ☯ 11am-6pm Tue-Sun) is a stylishly converted Gothic schoolhouse divided into smallish rooms. It has changing exhibitions of contemporary visual art. The adjoining cafe serves great tapas and sandwiches to refuel between cultural hot spots.

The **National Sea Life Centre** (☎ 0121-643 6777; www.sealifeeurope.com; 3A Brindleyplace; adult/child £12.50/8.50; ☯ 10am-4pm Mon-Fri, to 5pm Sat & Sun),

a state-of-the-art facility designed by Sir Norman Foster, is the largest inland aquarium in England and is flooded with exotic marine life. There's a sea-horse breeding facility, and the otter and turtle sanctuaries are a hit with kids. Arrive early in the school holidays – the queues can be enormous.

Jewellery Quarter

Birmingham has been a major player on the jewellery production scene for some 200 years, and the Jewellery Quarter is the place to go for a piece of the action. The tourist office provides a free booklet *Jewellery Quarter: The Essential Guide,* which includes background information about the industry and details of walking trails around the district's manufacturers and showrooms.

In the **Museum of the Jewellery Quarter** (☎ 0121-554 3598; 75-79 Vyse St; admission free; ☯ 11.30am-4pm Tue-Sun), the Smith & Pepper jewellery factory is preserved as it was on the day it closed in 1981 after 80 years of operation. You can explore the long history of the trade in Birmingham and watch jewellery-making demonstrations.

The Jewellery Quarter is three-quarters of a mile northwest of the centre; catch one of a host of buses (101 is the easiest), or take the metro from Snow Hill or the train from Moor St to Jewellery Quarter station.

About 1.5 miles from the Jewellery Quarter is **Soho House** (☎ 0121-554 9122; Soho Ave, Handsworth; admission free; ☯ 11.30am-4pm Tue-Sun Apr-Oct), where the industrialist Matthew Boulton lived from 1766 to 1809. It successfully recreates the styles of the 1700s, and includes the dining room where Boulton and the members of the Lunar Society would meet to discuss their world-changing ideas (see p530). Buses 74 and 79 pass nearby, or take the metro to Benson Rd station from Snow Hill.

Outlying Areas

Chocoholic magnet **Cadbury World** (☎ 0845 450 3599; www.cadburyworld.co.uk; Linden Rd; adult/child £13/9.95) takes you on a mouth-watering journey through the origins, manufacture and consumption of the ever popular cocoa-based confectionery, seen through the eyes of one of the world's largest chocolate-makers. Kids – and sweet-toothed grown-ups – will love it. Ride a beanmobile, take a wander down Cocoa Rd, paved with 'talking chocolate splodges', or try your hand at chocolate-making. Book ahead – it's very popular in July and August. Opening hours vary: it's closed for some of December and most of January, but open from 10am to 3pm or 10am to 4pm for most of the rest of the year (phone or check the website for details).

Cadbury World is part of pretty **Bournville Village**, designed for early-20th-century factory workers by the Cadbury family. Large houses, each unique, are set around a green. **Selly Manor** (☎ 0121-472 0199; Maple Rd; adult/child £3.50/1.50; ⊙ 10am-5pm Tue-Fri year-round, plus 2-5pm Sat & Sun Apr-Sep), dating from 1327 or earlier, was carefully taken apart and reconstructed by George Cadbury in order to save it from destruction. It has 18th century furnishings and a Tudor garden.

The easiest way to get to Bournville is by train from Birmingham New St (11 minutes).

East of the centre, the Millennium Point development is designed to help people understand science and technology. The focal point is **Thinktank** (☎ 0121-202 2222; www.thinktank .ac; Curzon St; adult/child £9.25/7.25; ⊙ 10am-5pm, last admission 4pm), an ambitious attempt to make science accessible (primarily to kids). Interactive displays cover topics such as the body and medicine, science in everyday life, nature, future technology, and industrial history. There's also an IMAX cinema (see p540) and a **Planetarium** (admission £2, advance booking required). A visit to the **Barber Institute of Fine Art** (☎ 0121-414 7333; www.barber.org.uk; admission free; ⊙ 10am-5pm Mon-Sat, noon-5pm Sun) is, for art-lovers, a highlight of a trip to Birmingham. The collection takes in Renaissance masterpieces, paintings by old masters such as Rubens and Van Dyck, British greats including Gainsborough, Reynolds and Turner, an array of Impressionist pieces and modern classics by the likes of Picasso and Schiele.

The Barber Institute is at the University of Birmingham, 2.5 miles south of the city centre. Take the train from New St to University station, or catch bus 61, 62 or 63 from Corporation St.

Aston Hall (☎ 0121-327 0062; Trinity Rd, Aston), a mansion built in the extravagant Jacobean style between 1618 and 1635, boasts some impressive friezes, ceilings and tapestries. To get there, take a train to Aston station from New St station. The Hall and grounds were closed for a major makeover at the time of writing and were due to reopen in summer 2009.

BRUM NIGHTLIFE WALKING TOUR

Birmingham by night is one of the liveliest city centres in the UK. This tour, about 2 miles long, will take you through some of the town's most memorable nightspots. Put aside two to three hours if you're pressed for time, otherwise just go with the flow…

Start off at the magnificent **Old Joint Stock** (1; p539) pub where you can share the suits' relief as they spill out of the nearby offices. Skirt by the old cathedral, ease your way through Victoria and Chamberlain Squares and on to the cluster of bars at Summer Row for a swift cocktail at trendy **Mechu** (2; p539). Next, wander through Centenary Sq, mingling with the theatre fans and concertgoers. Hungry yet? Just a little bit further and Brindleyplace has several swanky options – take in some tapas and fine sherry at the airy, arty Spanish cafe at the **Ikon Gallery** (3; opposite). Appetite sated? Now creep out to Broad St. Dodge the screeching hen and lairy stag parties and duck into the one oasis of sanity in this part of town, the **Tap and Spile** (4; p538). Fine ales on tap in a nooks-and-crannies pub are your reward. Now take the downstairs exit by the canal and stroll south by the water to join Birmingham's bright young things in the stylish bars of the flashy **Mailbox** development (5; opposite). There are plenty of other sleek places to be seen in this well-heeled part of town, which could easily distract you from the final leg of our tour, the Arcadian Centre, chock-a-block with night-time options. Depending on your energy levels, have a few drinks at the buzzing **So Bar** (6; p539) or the laid-back

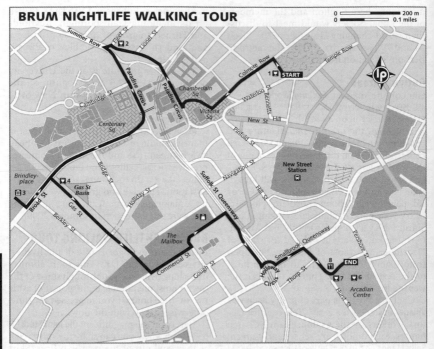

BRUM NIGHTLIFE WALKING TOUR

WALK FACTS

Start Old Joint Stock
Finish Mr Egg
Distance 2 miles
Duration two hours or more

Green Room (**7**; p539), perhaps stopping for a late-night grease fest at the legendary **Mr Egg** (**8**; p538). You've got this far, the rest of the night is up to you…

BIRMINGHAM FOR CHILDREN

The most obvious place to keep the kids entertained is Cadbury World (p535), where kids will learn about the history of chocolate as well as gorge themselves on it. Ease away the sugar high with a family cruise (opposite) down one of Birmingham's many narrow canals; a crucial part of the kids' education on why the city really mattered in the UK's development.

Just away from the Brindleyplace section of the canal, the National Sea Life Centre (p534) has water creatures aplenty. Playful

otters will appeal to everyone, but especially to the little ones. There's also plenty to explore at the Thinktank (p535), a gigantic attraction where the goal is to make science exciting and accessible, in particular for children. And you can keep them quiet under the vast domed ceiling of the Planetarium (p535) in the same complex.

QUIRKY BIRMINGHAM

There's always something unusual going on at the Custard Factory (p540). The old industrial complex – built by Sir Alfred Bird, the inventor of instant custard – has been inventively converted into a hive of galleries, bars, exhibition rooms, studios, shops and performance spaces. If it's off the wall you're looking for, this is your best bet.

Brindleyplace's Ikon Gallery (p534) also plays host to unconventional modernist exhibits. Mainstream is not the word – be sure to take an open mind. For those whose fetishes go beyond the realm of handcuffs, there's the adults-only Birmingham Bizarre Bazaar, held the third Sunday of every month at the Nightingale Club (p539). Entrance is

£5. For details, check out www.brumbazaar
.co.uk or phone ☎ 0121-602 1316.

TOURS

Second City Canal Cruises (☎ 0121-236 9811; www
.secondcityboats.co.uk; adult/child £5/3) Hour-long tours
leave by arrangement from the Canalside Souvenir Shop
in Gas St Basin.

Sherborne Wharf (☎ 0121-455 6163; www.sherborne
wharf.co.uk; Sherborne St; ⏱ 11.30am, 1pm, 2.30pm
& 4pm daily mid-Apr–Oct, Sat & Sun all year; adult/child
£6.50/5) Canal cruises leave from the International Convention Centre quayside.

West Midlands Waterways (☎ 0121-200 7400;
www.waterscape.com; Cambrian House, 2 Canalside;
⏱ 9am-5pm Mon-Fri, 10am-5pm Sat & Sun Apr-Oct)
Has leaflets, advice on days out by the water and details on
how and where to hire canal boats. It's off King Edward Rd.

FESTIVALS & EVENTS

Birmingham has a number of interesting
cultural festivals. Here are some of the
highlights.

Crufts Dog Show (www.crufts.org.uk) The world's
largest dog show, in March, with more than 20,000 canines
on parade.

Gay Pride (www.birminghamgaypride.co.uk) One of the
largest and most colourful celebrations of gay and lesbian
culture in the country, held in May.

Latin American Festival (www.abslatin.co.uk) This
annual festival in June/July celebrates the Latin American
community and culture in Birmingham.

Artsfest (www.artsfest.org.uk) The UK's largest free arts
festival features visual arts, dance and musical performances in various venues across the city in September.

Horse of the Year Show (www.hoys.co.uk) Top show-
jumping equestrian event in October.

SLEEPING

Most of Birmingham's central hotels are
aimed at business travellers and are usually
fairly expensive, although rates are sometimes
reduced at weekends. Check online or ask
about specials at the tourist office, which also
makes accommodation bookings. Few B&Bs
are central, but many lie within a 3-mile radius
of the city centre, especially in Acocks Green
(to the southeast) and the area that stretches
from Edgbaston to Selly Oak (southwest).

Budget

ourpick Birmingham Central Backpackers (☎ 0121-
643 0033; www.birminghamcentralbackpackers.com; 58
Coventry St; dm from £16; 🖴 wi-fi) Fun, friendly laid-
back backpackers spread across two buildings

a short walk from Digbeth bus station. Staff go
to a lot of effort to make guests feel welcome,
and there's a comfortable lounge with huge
projector screen and collection of DVDs (free
popcorn on movie nights), a little plant-filled
garden, and a bar. There are some manically
bright four- to eight-bed dorms, including
a pod room – with enclosed beds based on
Japanese capsule hotels.

Formule 1 (☎ 0121-773 9583; www.hotelformule1
.com; 3 Bordesley Park Rd, Small Heath Highway; r £25; 🅿)
Cheap, soulless, modern and clean: this place
uses the same formula here as it does elsewhere. Rooms fit up to three people and it's
about 1.5 miles from the centre.

Nitenite (☎ 0121-236 9000; www.nitenite.com; 18
Holliday St; r £45; 🅿 🖴 wi-fi) The rooms are inspired
by luxury yacht cabins, and they are suitably
pint-sized. They're strangely comfortable,
however, with full-size double beds, leather
headboards, cherry-wood furniture and giant
plasma TV screens with live Birmingham web-
cam images instead of windows. Parking is £14
per 24 hours. Wheelchair access is available.

Midrange

The better midrange options tend to be out of
town – character-challenged chains dominate
the centre, although they are convenient.

Ibis Hotel (☎ 0121-622 6010; fax 0121-622 6020;
Arcadian Centre, Ladywell Walk; d £65; 🅿 🖴 wi-fi) You
know exactly what you're getting here: a spotless identikit room with the same furnishings that you'll get in the same hotel chain
in Marrakesh. Within the Arcadian Centre
by Chinatown, it's in a convenient location
for a night out. Parking is £12 for a night.
Wheelchair access is available.

Westbourne Lodge (☎ 0121-429 1003; www.west
bournelodge.co.uk; Fountain Rd; s/d from £49/69; 🅿 🖴 wi-fi)
Removed from the bustle of the city centre,
this is still conveniently located just off the
main road in southwest Edgbaston. Rooms
are a little chintzy but spacious, and there's a
lovely terrace to enjoy in the summer.

Top End

Burlington Hotel (☎ 0844 879 9019; www.burlingtonhotel
.com; Burlington Arcade, 126 New St; s/d Sun-Thu £175/195, Fri
& Sat £83/107; 🅿 🖴 wi-fi) The venerable old gentleman of Birmingham hotels, the Burlington
is lavishly and conservatively furnished with
wood panelling, marble, classical columns
and expensive glass lampshades. Rooms range
from classic Victorian in style to the bland and

modern. The restaurant is a fine option for sophisticated Continental cuisine.

Malmaison (☎ 0121-246 5000; www.malmaison -birmingham.com; 1 Wharfside St; d from £160; **P** **□**) This boutique hotel in the Mailbox shopping centre is certainly style-conscious. Trendy music plays in the black-wood, minimalist lobby and the rooms, done out in crisp white and green, have floor-to-ceiling windows looking out onto the street. There's an equally smart bistro specialising in French classics as well as home-grown, local food, a great wine and champagne bar, and a spa. Wheelchair access is available.

EATING

Birmingham's most famous contribution to cuisine is the balti, a Pakistani dish that has been adopted by curry houses across the country. The heartland is the Birmingham **Balti Triangle** in Sparkbrook, 2 miles south of the centre. Pick up a complete listings leaflet in the tourist office (or see the website www .thebaltiguide.com) and head out on bus 4, 5, 6, 12, 31 or 37 from Corporation St.

Mount Fuji (☎ 0121-633 9853; Bullring; ☽ 11.30am-10pm Mon-Sat, to 9pm Sun) Come to this minimalist Japanese cafe to fill up on cheap, delicious sushi, bento boxes and sake when you're all worn out from shopping.

Mr Egg (☎ 0121-622 4344; 22 Hurst St; chips £1.50) A Birmingham institution, this greasy spoon is the place to go for a 3am lard fest when you're feeling a bit worse for wear. Look out for the picture of a dapper egg with breeches and a walking stick.

Punjab Paradise (☎ 0121-449 4110; 377-379 Ladypool Rd, Sparkbrook; mains £4.50-10; ☽ 5pm-1am Sun-Thu, to 2am Fri & Sat) Don't be put off by the faux Roman decor – the food here is good and authentic and the service very friendly.

Al Frash (☎ 0121-753 3120; www.alfrash.com; 186 Ladypool Rd, Sparkbrook; mains £5.20-7.90; ☽ 5pm-1am Sun-Thu, to 2am Fri & Sat) This is the best place in Birmingham to experience the legendary balti. Don't go expecting flourishes or fancy decor – you won't find it here; just huge, tasty, great-value portions, and warm service. If you're getting the bus ask the driver to stop by Ladypool Rd.

Oriental (☎ 0121-633 9988; 4 The Mailbox; mains £6.20-19; ☽ noon-11pm) Supersleek pan-Asian place that is easily the Mailbox's most stylish restaurant. Eat Malaysian, Thai and Chinese food while sitting on quirky silver chairs adorned

with silk-screen faces in a moody red, brown and black space, topped off with the odd chandelier and bursts of gilt wallpaper.

Cafe Soya (☎ 0121-622 3888; Upper Dean St; mains £6.50-8.90; ☽ noon-11pm) Excellent cafe dishing up rich, flavoursome plates of Chinese and Vietnamese food – try the huge bowls of noodle soup, or fragrant spicy rice dishes. There's a great selection of vegetarian dishes and it also does a nice line in soya-based deserts and soya and bean shakes.

Warehouse Cafe (☎ 0121-633 0261; 54-57 Allison St; mains £10-14; ☽ 11am-10pm, to 6pm Sun) Low-key little vegie and vegan cafe serving a good selection of vegie snacks, curries, meze and salad, as well as tasty homemade cakes. It also has a small shop selling organic products.

Chez Jules (☎ 0121-633 4664; www.chezjules.co.uk; 5A Ethel St; mains £10.50-15.50, 2-course lunch £8; ☽ noon-4pm & 5-11pm Mon-Sat, noon-4pm Sun) French finesse defines the hearty, classic dishes served up at this excellent bistro. Burgundy walls, a spacious dining area, long benches – perfect for group dining – and reasonable house-wine prices add a certain *je ne sais quoi*.

our pick Purnells (☎ 0121-212 9799; www.purnells restaurant.com; 55 Cornwall St; 3-course lunch/dinner £19/39; ☽ noon-4.30pm & 7pm-1am Tue-Fri, 7pm-1am Sat) Run by celebrated chef Glynn Purnell. Exquisite, inventive dishes (such as monkfish with liquorice charcoal) are served in an airy Victorian red-brick building with striking modern interior.

Simpsons (☎ 0121-454 3434; www.simpsonsrestaurant .co.uk; 20 Highfield Rd, Edgbaston; 3-course set lunch/dinner £25/30; ☽ lunch & dinner Mon-Sat, lunch Sun) Far out of the centre in a glorious Victorian house, it's worth making the journey for the top-quality modern cooking, served in an elegant dining room or conservatory overlooking the gardens. Reservations are recommended. If you fancy staying the night, there are four luxurious themed bedrooms upstairs.

DRINKING

Chain pubs litter the city centre, especially on the deeply unappealing main Broad St drag. There are, however, more than a few gems if you know where to look.

Tap and Spile (☎ 0121-632 5602; Gas St; ☽ 11am-11pm Sun-Thu, 11am-4am Fri & Sat) Overlooking the canal, this traditional pub is full of hidden alcoves and corners, especially once you move away from the minuscule top bar. There's a good selection of ales on tap here too.

Malt House (☎ 0121-633 4171; 75 King Edward Rd) The food is probably best avoided at this pub, but it has a decent selection of beers and the real draw is the expanse of outside space overlooking the canal. Apparently Bill Clinton had a drink here during the G8 Summit.

Old Joint Stock (☎ 0121-200 1892; 4 Temple Row West; ☽ closed Sun) This vast, high-ceilinged temple of beer, a former bank, serves good ales to a cheerful crowd. There's also an 80-seat theatre upstairs that puts on plays and regular comedy shows.

Sunflower Lounge (☎ 0121-472 0138; 76 Smallbrook Queensway; ☽ noon-11pm Mon-Wed, noon-1am Thu & Fri, 1pm-2am Sat, 5-10.30pm Sun) A quirky little mod bar in an unlikely setting by a dual carriageway near the New St rail station, this is a relatively undiscovered gem favoured by the indie crowd, and with a great alternative soundtrack. Live gigs occur regularly in the tiny underground basement venue.

So Bar (☎ 0121-693 5084; Arcadian Centre, Hurst St; ☽ 11am-2am Mon-Sat, 12.30pm-12.30am Sun) A glammed-up, shirted and booted crowd packs out this black-and-red bar to the strains of commercial dance and house.

Green Room (☎ 0121-605 4343; www.greenroom cafebar.co.uk; Arcadian Centre, Hurst St; ☽ 11am-11pm Mon-Wed, to midnight Thu, to 2am Fri & Sat, to 10.30pm Sun) This place has a mellow vibe. Sink into a leather sofa and drink a coffee or a beer, or head for the outside tables to watch the street action. There's good food here too.

Mechu (☎ 0121-710 4222; 47-59 Summer Row; ☽ noon-1am Mon-Wed, noon-3am Fri, 5pm-3am Sat) The natty grey suede interior, streetside tables and strong cocktails attract an after-work crowd to drink, eat and dance in the late-night bar.

ENTERTAINMENT

Tickets for most Birmingham events can be purchased through the national **TicketWeb** (☎ 08700 600100; www.ticketweb.co.uk). It is cheaper to book online than on the phone. Also check the listings (see p532) for what's going on.

Nightclubs

Birmingham's nightlife is fast-paced and exuberant. Discover how fun the city's after-hours life can be at any of the following venues.

Factory Club (☎ 0121-224 7502; www.factoryclub .co.uk; Custard Factory, Gibb St; ☽ from 10pm) The crew working this joint know only too well they are mixing it in the coolest club in town with a truly eclectic range of nights,

from Asian dub to breakbeat to electro pop. A blast.

Air (☎ 0845 009 8888; www.airbirmingham.com; Heath Mill Lane; ☽ from 10pm) This supersleek superclub is home to the renowned Godskitchen night (www.godskitchen.com), where some of the country's top DJs whip the crowd into a frenzy with trance mixes.

Q Club (☎ 0121-212 1212; www.queclub.co.uk; 212 Corporation St; ☽ from 8.30 or 10pm) The legendary Q Club has been brought back to life after an absence of six years. Electro, house, jungle and old-school club classics reverberate in a huge Grade II–listed building.

Nightingale Club (☎ 0121-622 1718; www.nightingale club.co.uk; Kent St; ☽ from 9pm) Birmingham's most established gay nightclub, the Nightingale rocks on three levels, with pop on the bottom floor and techno upstairs. Even after some 30 years of action it's still the region's top gay club and is known as a starting place for top-name DJs, with regular live acts.

Glee Club (☎ 0871 472 0400; www.glee.co.uk; Arcadian Centre; tickets £8-15; ☽ from 7 or 8pm Thu-Sat) One of the city's best-known comedy clubs, this place regularly attracts big-name comedians as well as live-music acts.

Live Music

Jam House (☎ 0121-200 3030; www.thejamhouse.com; 1 St Paul's Sq; ☽ noon-midnight Mon & Tue, noon-2am Wed-Fri, 6pm-2am Sat) This legendary live-music bar is all class. Presided over by pianist Jools Holland, it features live swing, jazz, R&B and rock and roll, mixed in with the occasional reggae and ska. Drinks are pricey, but the vibe is worth it. The global cuisine of the top-floor restaurant isn't bad either.

Birmingham Academy (☎ 0121-262 3000; www .birmingham-academy.co.uk; 52-54 Dale End) The best rock and pop venue in town, regularly attracting big-name acts such as Macy Gray and the Strokes. It also has regular nights showcasing local bands.

Barfly (☎ 0121-633 8311; www.barflyclub.com; 78 Digbeth High St) This place is a grooming stable for up-and-coming indie bands, spawned by the success of a London-based night. The entrance is on Milk St.

Symphony Hall (☎ 0121-780 3333; www.sym phonyhall.co.uk; Broad St; tickets from £8) For classical music, including performances by the City of Birmingham Symphony Orchestra, seek out the ultramodern Symphony Hall, which is known for its superb acoustics. World-music

THE WEST MIDLANDS & THE MARCHES

and jazz acts also feature. The recently renovated Town Hall (contact as Symphony Hall) also serves as a concert venue.

The giant **National Exhibition Centre Arena** (☎ 0121-767 2937), near Birmingham International Airport, hosts major rock and pop acts, as does its sister venue, the **National Indoor Arena** (☎ 0121-767 2937; King Edwards Rd) behind Brindleyplace.

Theatre & Cinemas

Birmingham Repertory Theatre (☎ 0121-236 4455; www.birmingham-rep.co.uk; Centenary Sq, Broad St) In two venues, the Main House and the more experimental Door, 'the Rep' presents top-notch drama and musicals, with an emphasis on contemporary work.

Hippodrome (☎ 0844 338 5000; www.birminghamhippo drome.co.uk; Hurst St) This is the venue for musical extravaganzas from *Mary Poppins* to *West Side Story*.

Alexandra Theatre (☎ 0870 607 7533; Suffolk St Queensway) This established venue stages everything from West End musicals to opera.

Electric Cinema (☎ 0121-643 7879; www.theelec tric.co.uk; 47-49 Station St; adult/child £6/4, £12 per sofa) Projectors have been rolling here for nigh 100 years, making it the oldest working cinema in the UK. It has an interesting art-house line-up as well as two-seater sofas from where you can text in an order and have food and drink (including champagne) brought to your seat.

IMAX (☎ 0121-202 2222; www.imax.ac; Curzon St; adult/child £8.25/6.25) Birmingham's first IMAX cinema, with a five-storey screen, is housed in the same building as the Thinktank (p535).

Sport

Villa Park (☎ 0800 612 0970; www.avfc.co.uk; tickets adult/child from £25/15) Aston Villa football club, one of the Midlands' most enduring teams, play in this arena north of the city centre.

Warwickshire County Cricket Club (☎ 0121-446 5506; www.edgbaston.com; County Ground, Edgbaston; tickets from £15) Tickets for international test matches sell out early, but local matches are usually available. The Twenty20 games are pulsating, even for the uninitiated.

SHOPPING

Custard Factory (☎ 0121-224 7777; www.custardfactory .com; Gibb St, Digbeth) One of the quirkiest places to shop in Birmingham, full of original, independent shops. So named because the building was constructed a century ago by custard magnate Sir Alfred Bird, this eye-catching development is a memorable place to buy things you never knew you wanted. Funky niche shops are dotted between an arts and media centre.

Jewellery Quarter (www.the-quarter.com) The obvious place for unique local shopping in Birmingham. Much of the jewellery manufactured in England comes from this region and there are more than a hundred shops selling traditionally handcrafted gold and silver jewellery, watches and more. The Museum of the Jewellery Quarter (p534) has leaflets detailing notable retail outlets and artisans.

Other options for serious retail therapy:

Bullring (☎ 0121-632 1500) This hellhole-turned-gleaming mall boasts '26 football pitches worth of shops, boutiques and restaurants'. The curved, silver Selfridges department store is worth a visit for the architecture alone.

Clone Zone (☎ 0121-666 6640; 84 Hurst St; ☒ 11am-9pm Mon-Sat, noon-7pm Sun) A branch of the world's largest gay retail chain, this place sells sex toys, clothes, accessories and adult novelties.

Mailbox (☎ 0121-632 1000; www.mailboxlife.com; Wharfside St) Label-hungry fashion victims head here for chic designer boutiques, including swish department store Harvey Nichols. They are on various levels in the unlikely setting of a converted mail-sorting factory, along with a raft of restaurants and bars.

GETTING THERE & AWAY

Air

Birmingham has a busy **international airport** (☎ 0870 733 5511; www.bhx.co.uk) with flights mainly to European destinations and New York. It's about 8 miles east of the centre of Birmingham.

Bus

Most intercity buses are running from a temporary bus station in Digbeth while the old coach station is being rebuilt. **National Express** (☎ 08717 818181, www.nationalexpress.com) runs coaches between Birmingham and destinations around England including London (£15.70 single, 2¾ hours, every 30 minutes), Oxford (£11.60 single, 1½ to two hours, five daily) and Manchester (£12.60 single, 2½ hours, 12 daily). Bus X20 runs to Stratford-upon-Avon hourly on weekdays and every two hours on weekends (1¼ hours) from Birmingham Moor St.

THE BLACK COUNTRY

The industrial region west of Birmingham is known as the Black Country, a 19th-century nickname given because pollution from local industries covered the area in black soot. Now cleaned up, it's still not a tourist hot spot, but is a fascinating stop for anyone interested in how industry shapes a country. Don't mistake the locals for Brummies; as anyone round here will tell you, the 'yam yams' (so called because of a Black Country–dialect habit of saying 'you am' instead of 'you are') have a very distinct identity of their own.

The extensive, lively **Black Country Living Museum** (☎ 0121-557 9643; www.bclm.co.uk; Tipton Rd, Dudley; adult/child £12.50/6.75; ☑ 10am-5pm daily Mar-Oct, 10am-4pm Wed-Sun Nov-Feb) features a coal mine, village and fairground, all restored to resemble the industrial heyday of the 19th century. Costumed characters recreate the living conditions of the time. It's entertaining, enlightening and kid-friendly, with a full program of mine trips, Charlie Chaplin films and opportunities to watch glass-cutters and sweet-makers in action.

Train

Most of the longer-distance trains are operated by Virgin Trains from New St station, beneath the Pallasades shopping centre, including those to/from London Euston (£10.50 value advance single, 1½ hours, every 30 minutes) and Manchester (£9 value advance single, 1¾ hours, every 15 minutes). Trains to London Marylebone run from Birmingham Snow Hill (two hours 20 minutes, two hourly). Other services, such as those to Stratford-upon-Avon (£5.90 single, 50 minutes, hourly), run from Snow Hill and Moor St stations.

In July and August, the **Shakespeare Express steam train** (☎ 0121-708 4960; www.vintagetrains.co.uk; standard return £20) operates between Birmingham Snow Hill and Stratford-upon-Avon twice each Sunday. Journeys take one hour.

GETTING AROUND
To/From the Airport

Trains are the easiest option for getting to the airport. They run frequently between New St and Birmingham International station (20 minutes, every 10 minutes). Buses 58 and 900 run to the airport (45 minutes, every 20 minutes) from Moor St Queensway. A **taxi** (☎ 0121-427 8888) from the airport to the centre costs about £20.

Car

easyCar (☎ 0906 333 3333; www.easycar.co.uk; 17 Horse Fair, Birmingham)
Hertz (☎ 0121-782 5158; 7 Suffolk St Queensway)

Public Transport

Network West Midlands (☎ 0121-214 7214; www.networkwestmidlands.com) provides general travel advice for getting around the West Midlands, including for those with mobility difficulties. The Daytripper ticket (adult/child £4.90/3.10) gives all-day travel on buses and trains after 9.30am; if you need to start earlier, buy the network one-day ticket (£6.10). Tickets are available from the **Central Travel Information Centre** (New St Station). **Traveline** (☎ 0871 200 22 33) has comprehensive travel information.

Local trains operate from Moor St station, which is only a few minutes' walk from New St; follow the red line on the pavement.

Birmingham's tram system, the **Metro** (www.travelmetro.co.uk), runs from Snow Hill to Wolverhampton via the Jewellery Quarter, West Bromwich and Dudley. Fares start at £1.10 and rise to £2.50 for the full length. A day pass covering both Metro and bus costs adult/child £4.60/3.05.

TOA black cabs taxis (☎ 0121-427 8888) are a good, reliable taxi firm.

WARWICKSHIRE

Warwickshire could have been just another picturesque English county of rolling hills and market towns were it not for the birth of a rather well-known wordsmith. Stratford-upon-Avon is one of the country's most visited areas outside London, attracting Shakespeare-hungry tourists from around the world. Also popular is magnificent Warwick Castle, rich in history and theme-park atmosphere.

Other, lesser-known attractions can be just as rewarding, however: try the russet ruins of Kenilworth Castle or visit the cathedrals (yes, plural) that shaped Coventry's past.

THE WEST MIDLANDS & THE MARCHES

Orientation & Information

Coventry sits to the north of the county. Kenilworth, Warwick and Stratford-upon-Avon run in a line southwest from Coventry along the A46.

The Shakespeare Country tourism website (www.shakespeare-country.co.uk) has information on the whole region.

Getting Around

The Warwickshire transport site (www.warwickshire.gov.uk/transport) has details of local bus and train services, as well as news on roads. Coventry is a major transport hub, with rail connections to London Euston and Birmingham New St.

A good ticket option is the Chiltern Rover (adult three days £39), which allows return train travel from London Marylebone or Paddington to Stratford-upon-Avon, Warwick or Leamington Spa on three chosen days within a seven-day period. It also includes unlimited travel in areas between, including Oxfordshire and Buckinghamshire, and free travel on Warwickshire's Stagecoach bus network. You can only buy the ticket from London's Marylebone Station.

COVENTRY

pop 300,848

The city was blitzed so badly in WWII that the Nazis coined a new verb 'Coventrieren', meaning 'to flatten'; postwar planning then capped off the aesthetic crimes. Today, Coventry's city centre is for the most part an unattractive mass of concrete, but is worth visiting for its striking modern cathedral, which was built alongside the haunting bombed-out ruins of the old one. The city also has an interesting industrial history as a prolific car-maker, the product of which can be seen in an absorbing transport museum.

Orientation & Information

Central Coventry is surrounded by a stark concrete ring road; most of the city's sights lie within. The main Pool Meadow bus station is central, while the train station is just outside of the ring road to the south. The **tourist office** (☎ 024-7623 4297; www.visitcoventry.co.uk; Millennium Pl; ☒ 9.30am-5.30pm Mon-Fri, 9am-5pm Sat, 10am-3pm Sun) is in the Coventry Transport Museum. There's another tourist office in St Michael's Tower, Coventry Cathedral (☎ 024-7622 5616).

Sights

The pretty **cathedral quarter** is historically the richest part of the city. The wonderfully evocative **cathedral ruins** of St Michael's Cathedral, destroyed by Nazi incendiary bombs in the blitz of 14 November 1940, still stand as a permanent memorial. You can climb the 180 steps of its **Gothic spire** for some panoramic views (£2.50). Symbolically adjoining the old cathedral's sandstone walls is the Sir Basil Spence–designed **cathedral** (☎ 024-7622 7597; www.coventrycathedral.org.uk; Priory Row; suggested donation £3; ☒ 9am-5pm), a modern, almost Gothic, architectural masterpiece. It includes a giant Graham Sutherland tapestry of Christ, glorious stained-glass nave windows (best seen from the altar), and a towering etched glass front. Look out for the Jacob Epstein statue of St Michael's conquest over the devil outside the main entrance. The story of Coventry's original cathedral, the Benedictine priory of **St Mary's** which was dismantled following the Reformation, is told through interactive computer displays and archaeological finds at the small but excellent **Priory Visitor Centre** (☎ 024-7655 2242; Priory Row; admission free; ☒ 10am-5pm Mon-Sat, noon-4pm Sun). In the same area is **St Mary's Guildhall** (☎ 024-7683 3328; Bayley Lane; admission free; ☒ 10am-4pm), one of the country's finest medieval guildhalls, where Mary Queen of Scots was briefly held. Look out for the centuries-old tapestry depicting Henry VI.

Further north, the extensive **Coventry Transport Museum** (☎ 024-7623 4270; www.transport-museum.com; Hales St; admission free; ☒ 10am-5pm) boasts the biggest collection of British-built vehicles in the world, most of them assembled in Coventry, ranging from early bicycles to vintage fire engines. There's interactive fun in the shape of the 'Coventry Blitz Experience' and the Thrust SSC land speed record simulator.

Sleeping & Eating

Spire View Guest House (☎ 024-7625 1602; 36 Park Rd; s/d £27/45; ℗) Crisp, clean rooms in a quiet residential street a few minutes' walk from the train station. The hosts are eager to help and there's a nice guest lounge with plenty of books for browsing.

Ramada Coventry (☎ 0870 890 3722; www.ramadacoventry.co.uk; The Butts; d incl breakfast from £85; ℗ ☐) Located just outside the ring road and a 10-minute walk into the town centre, the rooms are surprisingly nice for a chain hotel. They're bright and spotless and many have great views over the city. Wheelchair access available.

Playwrights (☎ 024-7623 1441; 4-6 Hay Lane; ☻ 10am-10pm Mon-Thu, 9am-10.30pm Fri & Sat) On a cobbled street leading to the cathedral, this friendly little cafe does big breakfasts, light lunches, sandwiches and burgers as well as a more substantial dinner menu.

Tin Angel (☎ 024-7655 9958; Medieval Spon St; ☻ closed Mon & Tue) This minuscule bar, with a laid-back atmosphere, alternative sound-track, and a little shop at the back selling obscure CDs and books, is the coolest place in town. There are occasional acoustic music and poetry nights and a light snack menu of soups and sandwiches. Don't expect speedy service though.

Getting There & Away

Coventry is a convenient transport hub. Trains go south to London Euston (every 20 minutes, one hour 10 minutes) and Bournemouth (hourly, three hours), and you will rarely have to wait more than 10 minutes for a train to Birmingham. From the main bus station, there is a constant flow of National Express

buses to most parts of the country. Bus X17 goes to Kenilworth, Leamington Spa and Warwick (every 20 minutes).

WARWICK
pop 25,434

Most visitors come to this quiet county town drawn by its magnificent turreted castle. It's an overwhelming sight – as are the queues in summer. Several other sights are less over-run, but also well worth stopping for. A quick stroll round the centre reveals well-preserved historic buildings – survivors of a fire in 1694 that destroyed much of the town – as well as absorbing museums and fine riverside views.

Orientation & Information

Warwick is simple to navigate; the A429 runs right through the centre with Westgate at one end and Eastgate at the other. The town centre lies just north of this axis. The castle, which looms over the River Avon, is just south.

The **tourist office** (☎ 01926-492212; www.warwick-uk .co.uk; Court House, Jury St; ☻ 9.30am-4.30pm), near the junction with Castle St, sells the informative *Warwick Town Trail* leaflet (50p).

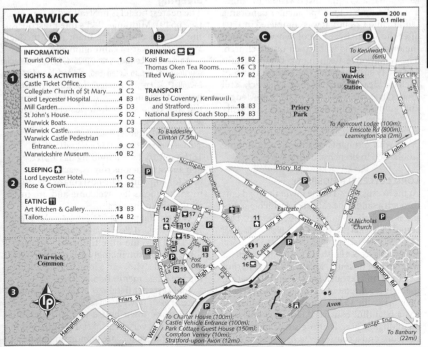

WARWICK

| | | 0 ——————— 200 m |
| | | 0 ——————— 0.1 miles |

INFORMATION	
Tourist Office.....................1	C3

SIGHTS & ACTIVITIES	
Castle Ticket Office...................2	C3
Collegiate Church of St Mary......3	C2
Lord Leycester Hospital...............4	B3
Mill Garden...............................5	D3
St John's House.........................6	D2
Warwick Boats...........................7	D3
Warwick Castle..........................8	C3
Warwick Castle Pedestrian	
Entrance.............................9	C2
Warwickshire Museum..............10	B2

SLEEPING	
Lord Leycester Hotel.................11	C2
Rose & Crown.........................12	B2

EATING	
Art Kitchen & Gallery...............13	B3
Tailors....................................14	B2

DRINKING	
Kozi Bar.................................15	B2
Thomas Oken Tea Rooms.........16	C3
Tilted Wig..............................17	B2

TRANSPORT	
Buses to Coventry, Kenilworth	
and Stratford....................18	B3
National Express Coach Stop.....19	B3

Sights & Activities

WARWICK CASTLE

Incredibly well-preserved medieval **Warwick Castle** (☎ 0870 442 2000; www.warwick-castle.co.uk; adult/child £18/11; ☼ 10am-6pm Apr-Sep, to 5pm Oct-Mar; 🅿) is an absolute stunner. Part of the Tussauds Group, it is prone to commercialism, crowds and cheesiness, of which the deeply naff Warwick Ghosts 'Alive' experience (entry £2.75) is a prime example. However, its grandeur and a palpable sense of history, including displays on influential historical figures such as 'kingmaker' Earl of Warwick Richard Neville, make it a must-see.

Plan on spending a full day if time permits. With eerily lifelike waxwork-populated private apartments, sumptuous interiors, ramparts, armour displays, dungeons (with torture chamber), gorgeous landscaped gardens and a 19th-century power-generating mill house, there's more than enough to see.

COLLEGIATE CHURCH OF ST MARY

Originally built in 1123, the magnificent **Collegiate Church of St Mary** (☎ 01926-492909; Old Sq; suggested donation £2; ☼ 10am-6pm Apr-Oct, to 4.30pm Nov-Mar) has a soaring tower, visible for miles around. Climb it for a spectacular panorama (adult/child £2/50p). It was completed in 1704 after the 1694 Great Fire of Warwick gutted the original along with much of the church. The remarkable Beauchamp Chapel (built 1442–64) survived and the bronze tomb of Richard Beauchamp, Earl of Warwick, still graces its centre. Ask one of the knowledgeable guides to point out 'the angel', a ghostly outline barely visible on the wall that was only recently spotted. Don't miss the 12th-century crypt with remnants of a medieval dunking stool, used to drench scolding wives.

LORD LEYCESTER HOSPITAL

At the Westgate end of the town, the road cuts through a sandstone cliff, above which perches the improbably leaning, timber-framed **Lord Leycester Hospital** (☎ 01926-491422; High St; adult/child £4.90/3.90, garden only £2; ☼ 10am-5pm Tue-Sun Apr-Sep, 10am-4.30pm Tue-Sun Oct-Mar). Despite its name, it was never a hospital. Robert Dudley, Earl of Leicester and favourite of Queen Elizabeth I, made it a retirement home for soldiers and their wives in 1571 – and it still is today. It has a beautiful courtyard, a fine chapel and a guildhall. There is also a small regimental museum and a cafe.

OTHER SIGHTS & ACTIVITIES

For a fragrant perspective of the castle, head for the **Mill Garden** (☎ 01926-492877; 55 Mill St; admission £1.50; ☼ 9am-6pm Apr-Oct), an explosion of flowers and plants within splashing distance of the weir that powered the castle mill. Money raised from this captivating little corner goes to charity. A fine alternative view of the castle is offered on the river itself. Head to **Warwick Boats** (☎ 01926-494743; www.warwick boats.co.uk; St Nicholas Park; rowing boat hire 30/60min £6/9; ☼ 10am-6.30pm daily Jun-Aug, 10am-6.30pm Sat & Sun Mar-May & Sep-Oct).

Other interesting sights include the **Warwickshire Museum** (☎ 01926-412501; Market Pl; admission free; ☼ 10am-5pm Tue-Sat year-round, plus 11.30am-5pm Sun Apr-Sep), in the 17th-century market building. It displays the Sheldon's Tapestry Map, a woven map of Warwickshire stretching 5m across, which dates from 1647. **St John's House** (☎ 01926-412132; St John's; admission free; ☼ 10am-5pm Tue-Sat year-round, plus 2.30-5pm Sun Apr-Sep) is a striking Jacobean mansion with an antique doll and toy display, reconstructed Victorian rooms and a regimental museum.

Sleeping

The nearest hostel is in Stratford-upon-Avon (see p549). Midrange B&Bs line Emscote Rd, the eastern end of the main road through Warwick toward Leamington Spa.

Agincourt Lodge (☎ 01926-499399; www.agin courtlodge.co.uk; 36 Coten End; s/d incl breakfast from £40/60 🅿). In an austere-looking Victorian house 10 minutes from the castle, some of the cosy rooms have four posters and there's a charming garden.

Park Cottage Guest House (☎ 01926-410319; www .parkcottagewarwick.co.uk; 113 West St; s/d £50/65 🅿) This 16th-century listed building has a pretty garden and six spacious rooms, each with a teddy bear for company. The hosts make a real effort to make guests feel welcome and are full of advice about the area.

Charter House (☎ 01926-496965; sheila@penon .gotadsl.co.uk; 87-91 West St; s/d incl breakfast from £56/85; 🅿 🖳) This cute little timbered cottage has three rooms convincingly decorated in medieval period styles, and a long list of choices on the breakfast menu. Book early.

Lord Leycester Hotel (☎ 01926-491481; www.lord -leycester.co.uk; 17 Jury St; s/d £62/83; 🅿) This rambling stone town house-turned-hotel, built in 1726, has very helpful staff but the rooms, while comfortable, are bland and dated.

Rose & Crown (☎ 01926-411117; www.roseand crownwarwick.co.uk; 30 Market Pl; r incl breakfast from £70; P 🖵 wi-fi) Most of the smart modern rooms look out onto Warwick's main square. They lie above a chic gastropub, which serves excellent food. There are only five rooms, so call in advance.

Eating & Drinking

Art Kitchen & Gallery (☎ 01926-494303; 7 Swan St; mains £7-13; 🕒 lunch & dinner daily) This place serves fresh, tasty Thai food with an emphasis on local produce and is very popular. All of the art on display, from bold prints on the walls to photos of celebs in the loos, is for sale.

Tailors (☎ 01926-410590; 22 Market Pl; 3-course dinner £27.50 🕒 6-10pm Mon-Sat) Warwick's newest restaurant, set in a former gentleman's tailors, serves fine modern English cuisine such as roasted wood pigeon and braised pork belly, in a small, simple dining room.

Tilted Wig (☎ 01926-411534; 11 Market Pl; 🕒 9.30am-5pm Mon-Sat) This large, lively pub on the main square spills out onto the streets in summer, provides a cosy haven in winter and serves some great beers – try the Slaughterhouse.

Kozi Bar (☎ 01926-493318; 62 Market Pl; 🕒 10am-11pm Mon-Thu, till 2am Fri & Sat) The dark orange walls, leather sofas and deep rattan armchairs create a warm ambience at this coffee shop, restaurant and cocktail bar. There's a sunny garden at the back for the summer and on the weekend it turns into Warwick's only late-night bar playing mainstream house and club classics.

Thomas Oken Tea Rooms (☎ 01926-499307; 20 Castle St; 🕒 10am-6pm) Just an arrow's flight away from the castle, this tearoom in a medieval house is pricey and usually packed – but it does have bags of atmosphere.

Getting There & Away

National Express coaches operate from Puckerings Lane. Stagecoach X17 runs to Coventry (55 minutes). Stagecoach bus 16 goes to Stratford-upon-Avon (40 minutes, hourly) in one direction, and Leamington Spa (15 minutes) the other. The main bus stops are on Market Sq.

Trains run to Birmingham (30 minutes, every half-hour), Stratford-upon-Avon (30 minutes, hourly) and London (1½ hours, every 20 minutes).

AROUND WARWICK
Baddesley Clinton

Boasting Elizabethan interiors that have barely changed since the 17th century, **Baddesley Clinton** (NT; ☎ 01564-783294; adult/child £8.40/4.20, grounds only £4.20/2.10; 🕒 11am-5pm Wed-Sun Oct-Feb, 1.30-5.30pm Wed-Sun May-Sep) is a beguiling 15th-century moated house. It was a haven for persecuted Catholics in the 16th century, as three cramped priest-holes show. It also has a murderous history: a priest was killed here after the owner, Nicholas Broom, found his wife in the man of God's arms.

Baddesley Clinton is 7.5 miles northwest of Warwick, just off the A4141. It is a pleasant 2-mile walk from Lapworth train station. Trains run direct from Warwick (15 minutes) and Birmingham (30 minutes).

Compton Verney

The once-decrepit 18th-century mansion of **Compton Verney** (☎ 01926-645500; adult/child £7.70/2; 🕒 10am-5pm Tue-Sun mid-Mar to mid-Dec) opened to the public in 2004 after a multimillion-pound overhaul. It now houses an art gallery, which includes a permanent exhibition on British folk art, Neapolitan masterpieces, Germanic medieval art, and bronze artefacts from China. There are regular high-profile exhibitions too. Word has spread fast – the small galleries quickly get crowded. If it gets too packed, the lovely grounds, landscaped by Lancelot 'Capability' Brown are perfect for a picnic. Bus 269 runs directly here from Stratford-upon-Avon (not on Sundays).

KENILWORTH
pop 23,219

The only thing that makes a visit to this unremarkable middle-England town truly worthwhile are the hauntingly atmospheric ruins of its castle. With crumbling walls and vivid history, it inspired Walter Scott to use it as a setting for his novel, called…*Kenilworth*.

Information

Contact the **tourist office** (☎ 01926-852595; Library, 11 Smalley Pl; 🕒 9am-7pm Mon & Thu, 9am-5.30pm Tue & Fri, 10.30am-5.30pm Wed, 9.30am-4pm Sat) for local tourist information.

Sights & Activities

Red-sandstone **Kenilworth Castle** (EH; ☎ 01926-852078; adult/child £6.20/3.10; 🕒 10am-5pm Mar-Oct, 10am-4pm Nov-Feb) isn't as popular as its commercial neighbour in Warwick, but is arguably more rewarding, and the dramatic ruins are brought to life through an excellent audio tour. It was founded around 1120 and enlarged in the 14th and 16th centuries. A number of powerful men, including John of Gaunt, Simon de Montfort and Robert Dudley (favourite of Elizabeth I), held sway here. Following the Civil War siege, the castle's vast lake was drained in 1644, and it fell into disrepair.

You can learn about the relationship between Dudley and the 'Virgin Queen', who visited the castle to tremendous fanfare, in an exhibition in the recently restored Leicester's Gatehouse. At the time of writing work was underway to recreate the magnificent gardens Dudley had built for Elizabeth in 1575, and they were due to open in late spring 2009.

Jane Austen and King Charles I are among the famous former guests in the 850-year history of **Stoneleigh Abbey** (☎ 01926-858535; www.stoneleighabbey.org; adult/child £6.50/3; ☹ tours 11am, 1pm & 3pm Tue-Thu & Sun Easter-Oct). Founded by Cistercian monks in 1154, it became the home of the wealthy Leigh family in the 16th century. The splendid Palladian west wing, completed in 1726, contains richly detailed plasterwork ceilings and panelled rooms. Don't miss the medieval gatehouse, dating from 1346. The landscaped grounds are fine picnic territory. Stoneleigh is 2 miles east of Kenilworth, off the B4115.

Sleeping & Eating

Castle Laurels Hotel (☎ 01926-856179; www.castlelaurels.co.uk; 22 Castle Rd; s/d incl breakfast £45/75; **P** **▣**) A stately guest house opposite the castle, where the owners pride themselves on the spotless rooms and the warmth of the welcome. The home-cooked breakfasts (with free-range eggs) are lovely.

Loweridge Guest House (☎ 01926-859522; www.loweridgeguesthouse.co.uk; Hawkesworth Dr; s/d incl breakfast £70/95; **P** **▣**) This handsome Victorian house has a grand staircase and elegant guest lounge straight out of *Country Life*. There are four huge rooms with swish, modern bathrooms, and three have their own private sun-trap patio. It's a 10-minute walk from the town centre, off Coventry road.

Virgins & Castle (☎ 01926-853737; 7 High St; pub food £4-6, mains £9-11) This worn, homely old pub is a real local favourite, full of nooks and crannies to lose yourself in. It has a decent menu of Filipino specialities.

Clarendon Arms (☎ 01926-852017; 44 Castle Hill; mains £6-12.95) Right opposite the castle, this atmospheric pub has home-cooked food, a warm ambience and a cosy little beer garden.

Getting There & Away

Bus X17 runs to and from Warwick (20 minutes), Coventry (25 minutes) and Leamington Spa (15 minutes).

STRATFORD-UPON-AVON
pop 22,187

Few towns are so dominated by one man's legacy as Stratford is by William Shakespeare, who was born here in 1564. Be prepared to fight the tourist masses for breathing space in the historic buildings associated with England's most famous wordsmith – especially during summer and on most weekends. But if you choose your time, this pretty, historic market town should definitely be on your 'to visit' list: be sure to take in a play if you're hitting the Shakespeare trail. It is also a handy base for exploring the mighty Warwick and Kenilworth Castles and the northern part of the picturesque Cotswold Hills.

Orientation

Arriving by coach or train, you'll find yourself within walking distance of the town centre, which is easy to explore on foot. Transport is only really essential for visiting Mary Arden's House.

Information

Cyber Junction (☎ 01789-263400; www.cyberjunction.co.uk; 28 Greenhill St; per hr £4; ☹ 10am-6pm Mon-Fri, 10.30am-5.30pm Sat) Internet access and game play.
Sparklean Laundrette (☎ 01789-269075; 74 Bull St; ☹ 8am-9pm)
Tourist office (☎ 0870 160 7930; www.shakespeare-country.co.uk; Bridgefoot; ☹ 9am-5.30pm Mon-Sat, 10am-4pm Sun Apr-Oct, 9am-5pm Mon-Sat, 10am-3pm Sun Nov-Mar) Helpful, but frantically busy in summer.

Sights & Activities
THE SHAKESPEARE HOUSES

The **Shakespeare Birthplace Trust** (☎ 01789-204016; www.shakespeare.org.uk; adult/child all 5 properties £15/7.50, 3 in-town houses £9/4.50; ☹ generally 9am-5pm Mon-Sat, 10am-5pm Sun Jun-Aug, hours vary rest of year) manages five buildings associated with Shakespeare. Three of the houses are central, one is an easy walk away, and the fifth a drive or bike ride

THE WEST MIDLANDS & THE MARCHES

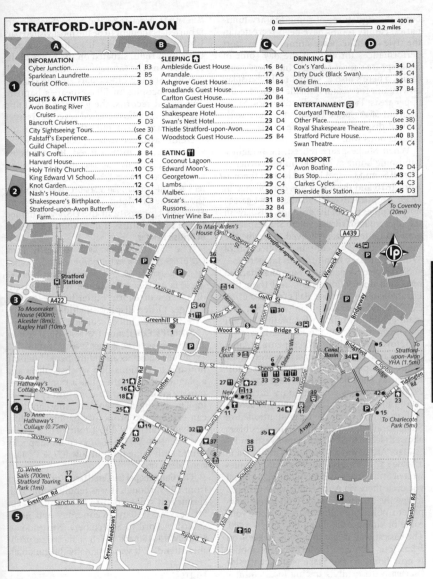

STRATFORD-UPON-AVON

0		400 m
0		0.2 miles

INFORMATION
Cyber Junction...............................**1** B3
Sparklean Laundrette.....................**2** B5
Tourist Office................................**3** D3

SIGHTS & ACTIVITIES
Avon Boating River
  Cruises **4** D4
Bancroft Cruisers...........................**5** D3
City Sightseeing Tours................(see 3)
Falstaff's Experience......................**6** C4
Guild Chapel.................................**7** C4
Hall's Croft...................................**8** C4
Harvard House...............................**9** C4
Holy Trinity Church......................**10** C5
King Edward VI School..................**11** C4
Knot Garden................................**12** C4
Nash's House................................**13** C4
Shakespeare's Birthplace..............**14** C3
Stratford-upon-Avon Butterfly
  Farm..**15** D4

SLEEPING 🛏
Ambleside Guest House..................**16** B4
Arrandale....................................**17** A5
Ashgrove Guest House...................**18** B4
Broadlands Guest House................**19** B4
Carlton Guest House.....................**20** B4
Salamander Guest House...............**21** B4
Shakespeare Hotel.......................**22** C4
Swan's Nest Hotel........................**23** D4
Thistle Stratford-upon-Avon.........**24** C4
Woodstock Guest House................**25** B4

EATING 🍴
Coconut Lagoon...........................**26** C4
Edward Moon's.............................**27** C4
Georgetown.................................**28** C4
Lambs..**29** C4
Malbec.......................................**30** C3
Oscar's.......................................**31** B3
Russons......................................**32** C4
Vintner Wine Bar.........................**33** C4

DRINKING 🍷
Cox's Yard...................................**34** D4
Dirty Duck (Black Swan)...............**35** C4
One Elm......................................**36** B3
Windmill Inn...............................**37** B4

ENTERTAINMENT 🎭
Courtyard Theatre........................**38** C4
Other Place.............................(see 38)
Royal Shakespeare Theatre...........**39** C4
Stratford Picture House.................**40** B3
Swan Theatre..............................**41** C4

TRANSPORT
Avon Boating...............................**42** D4
Bus Stop.....................................**43** C3
Clarkes Cycles.............................**44** C3
Riverside Bus Station....................**45** D3

**THE WEST MIDLANDS &
THE MARCHES**

out; a combination ticket costs about half as much as the individual admission fees combined. Opening times are complicated and vary during the low season (check the website for details). In summer, enormous crowds pack the small Tudor houses; a visit out of season is much more enjoyable. Note that wheelchair access to the properties is restricted.

The number one Shakespeare attraction, **Shakespeare's Birthplace** (Henley St), has 'olde worlde' charm hidden behind a modern exterior. It's been a tourist hot spot for three centuries (though there's no conclusive evidence Will was born here). Famous 19th-century visitor-vandals have scratched their names on a window, and the guest book bears the signatures of some literary luminaries. Family rooms have been recreated in the style of Shakespeare's time, and in short performances throughout the day some of Shakespeare's most famous characters come to life. There's also a 'virtual reality' display downstairs for visitors unable to access the upper areas. Tickets include admission to the adjacent **Shakespeare Exhibition**, where well-devised displays chart the life of Stratford's most famous son.

When Shakespeare retired, he bought a handsome home at New Pl on the corner of Chapel St and Chapel Lane. He died there in April 1616 and the house was demolished in 1759. An attractive Elizabethan **knot garden** now occupies part of the grounds. Displays in the adjacent **Nash's House**, where Shakespeare's granddaughter Elizabeth lived, describe the town's history and contain a collection of 17th-century oak furniture and tapestries.

Shakespeare's daughter Susanna married respected doctor John Hall, and their fine Elizabethan town house, **Hall's Croft** (☎ 01789-292107), stands near Holy Trinity Church. The main exhibition offers a fascinating insight into medicine back in the 16th century.

Before marrying Shakespeare, Anne Hathaway lived in Shottery, a mile west of the centre, in a pretty thatched farmhouse now known as **Anne Hathaway's Cottage** (☎ 01789-292100). As well as contemporary furniture, there's an orchard and **Shakespeare Tree Garden**, with examples of all the trees mentioned in Shakespeare's plays. A footpath (no bikes allowed) leads to Shottery from Evesham Pl.

Mary Arden was Shakespeare's mother, and a **house** (☎ 01789-293455) at Wilmcote, 3 miles west of Stratford, was her childhood home. If you cycle there via Anne Hathaway's Cottage, follow the Stratford-upon-Avon Canal towpath to Wilmcote rather than retracing your route or riding back along the busy A3400. The easiest way to get there otherwise is on a bus tour (see right). Mary Arden's house is now home to the **Shakespeare Countryside Museum**, with exhibits tracing local country life over the past four centuries. There's a collection of rare-breed farm animals here, as well as regular falconry displays.

OTHER SIGHTS

Holy Trinity Church (☎ 01789-266316; Old Town; admission to church free, Shakespeare's grave adult/child £1.50/50p; 8.30am-6pm Mon-Sat & 12.30-5pm Sun Apr-Oct, 9am-4pm Mon-Sat & 12.30-5pm Sun Nov-Mar), where Shakespeare is buried, is thought to be the most visited parish church in England. It's a lovely building in its own right, situated on the banks of the River Avon. The transepts from the mid-13th century are the oldest part. In the chancel are photocopies of Shakespeare's baptism and burial records, the graves of Will and his wife, and a bust created seven years after Shakespeare's death but before his wife's and therefore assumed to be a good likeness.

The exuberantly carved **Harvard House** (☎ 01789-204507; High St; adult/child £3.50/free, free with Shakespeare Houses ticket; noon-5pm Wed-Sun Jul & Aug, Fri-Sun May, Jun & Sep-Oct) was home to the mother of John Harvard, after whom Harvard University in the USA was named in the 17th century. It now houses a **Museum of British Pewter**.

The **Stratford-upon-Avon Butterfly Farm** (☎ 01789-299288; www.butterflyfarm.co.uk; Swan's Nest Lane; adult/child £5/3.60; 10am-6pm summer, 10am-dusk winter) is a large greenhouse with hundreds of species of exotic butterflies in tropical foliage. Other displays include the creepy 'Arachnoland', full of scorpions and spiders.

Falstaff's Experience (☎ 0870 350 2770; www.falstaffsexperience.co.uk; 40 Sheep St; adult/child £4.80/1.30; 10.30am-5.30pm) is an old timbered building housing recreations of a witches' glade and a plague cottage; rather like a rambling, stationary ghost train with some history thrown in. Those with an even more mordant bent can explore the property's paranormal history on adult-only ghost tours (£7.50; tours 6pm, 7pm, 8pm & 9pm Thu-Fri) or even more spooky jaunts with a medium in tow (£17.50; 10pm most Friday nights).

The **Guild Chapel** (cnr Chapel Lane & Church St) dates from 1269, though it was rebuilt in the 15th century. It's not open to the public except for services (10am Wednesday and noon Saturday April to September). Next door is **King Edward VI School**, which Shakespeare probably attended; it was originally the guildhall.

Tours

Two-hour **guided walks** (☎ 01789-292478; adult/child £5/2; 11am Mon-Wed, 2pm Thu-Sun) depart from Waterside, opposite Sheep St. Chill-seekers can go to the same starting point for the **Stratford Town Ghost Walk** (adult/child £5/3; 7.30pm Mon, Thu & Fri).

Open-top buses of **City Sightseeing** (☎ 01789-299123; www.city-sightseeing.com; adult/child £11/5.50;

SHAKESPEARE'S WORDS?

One of literature's greatest conspiracy theories questions whether Shakespeare actually wrote the plays attributed to him. Despite the Bard's prolific output of plays, no letters or other personal writing have survived. What little we know about him has been found in birth, death and marriage files and other official documents, and what's more, none of these official records list Will as a writer, only as an actor or a money lender. This lack of information has led to theories that Shakespeare didn't actually write the plays. Since none have survived in manuscript form, there's no handwritten evidence to conclusively prove that they're his. Some 'anti-Stratfordians' speculate that Shakespeare was simply not educated or worldly enough to have provided the background, experience and knowledge to write the plays. Favourites for the 'real' Shakespeare include Will's compatriot Christopher Marlowe, Edward de Vere, the Earl of Oxford or a combined business venture by a group of writers.

---

every 20 min Apr-Sep, fewer in winter) leave from the tourist office and go to each of the Shakespeare properties. They operate on a hop-on, hop-off basis, and are a convenient way of getting to the out-of-town houses.

Avon Boating (☎ 01789-267073; www.avon-boating .co.uk) runs river cruises (adult/child £4/2.50 per hour), which depart from either side of the tramway bridge. **Bancroft Cruisers** (☎ 01789-269669; www.bancroftcruisers.co.uk) runs 45-minute trips (adult/child £4.50/3, daily April to October) leaving from Clopton Bridge, opposite Cox's Yard.

Sleeping

Stratford's big hotels tend to be geared towards group travel, so they're often out of the price range of many independent travellers, and they fill up fast. B&Bs are plentiful though, and offer good-quality rooms in attractive Victorian houses. Vacancies can be hard to find, especially during summer. If there's no room at any of the following, the tourist office charges £3 plus 10% deposit to find something.

BUDGET

Stratford-upon-Avon YHA (☎ 0845 371 9661; www .yha.org.uk; Hemmingford House, Alveston; dm incl breakfast members/nonmembers £20/23; P ❑) This four-star youth hostel is situated in a large, 200-year-old mansion 1.5 miles east of the town centre along Tiddington Rd. Buses 18 and 18A operate to Alveston from Bridge St.

Other good budget options:

Stratford Touring Park (☎ 01789-201063; www .stratfordtouringpark.com; Luddington Rd; 2-person pitches £11, showers 50p; Easter-Sep; P) Camp site just off Evesham Rd a mile west of town.

Salamander Guest House (☎ 01789-205728; www .salamanderguesthouse.co.uk; 40 Grove Rd; s/d incl

breakfast from £20/40; P ❑ wi-fi) Comfortable rooms and friendly, informative hosts.

Arrandale (☎ 01789-267112; www.arrandale.netfirms .com; 208 Evesham Rd; s/d incl breakfast £23-46; P) Neatly kept lodgings, 10 minutes' walk from the centre.

Carlton Guest House (☎ 01789-293548; 22 Evesham Pl; s/d incl breakfast £20/52; P) The jolly proprietor has several reasonable en suite rooms available.

MIDRANGE

Ambleside Guest House (☎ 01789-297239; www .amblesideguesthouse.co.uk; 41 Grove Rd; s/d from £30/50; P ❑) Lovely, nonfrilly B&B, with spotless, homely rooms, amiable hosts who know everything that's going on around town, and great big organic breakfasts.

Moonraker House (☎ 01789-268774; www.moon rakerhouse.com; 40 Alcester Rd; s/d incl breakfast from £47/70; P ❑) Pristine to the point of fussy, the rooms behind the whitewashed facade of this memorable B&B are frilly, almost feminine affairs, and have a Shakespeare theme. Impeccably attentive owners provide healthy organic and vegetarian options for breakfast.

our pick **WhiteSails**(☎ 01789-264326;www.white-sails .co.uk; 85 Evesham Rd; r from £95; P ❑ wi-fi) This gorgeous, intimate guest house has four plush, individually furnished rooms with flat-screen TVs, climate control and glamorous modern bathrooms. The service is fantastic – breakfast features goodies such as freshly baked bread and muffins, homemade muesli and fresh fruit, and there are plenty of other of nice touches such as complementary sherry in the cosy guests lounge and teddy bears in the bathrooms. There's a lovely large garden to soak up the rays in the summer.

Other recommended midrange options:

Ashgrove Guest House (☎ 01789-297278; www.ash groveguesthousestratford.co.uk; 37 Grove Rd; s/d from

THE WEST MIDLANDS & THE MARCHES

£35/55; **P**) Tidy, airy rooms decked out in varying degrees of burgundy. Look for the funky wooden bear outside.

Woodstock Guest House (☎ 01789-299881; www .woodstock-house.co.uk; 30 Grove Rd; s/d from £30/56; **P**) Pastel, floral-themed rooms; deep, soft carpets; and a warm welcome.

Broadlands Guest House (☎ 01789-299181; www .broadlandsguesthouse.co.uk; 23 Evesham Pl; s/d from £45/80; **P**) Fancy, individually decorated rooms and filling breakfasts served in a pretty breakfast room.

TOP END

Swan's Nest Hotel (☎ 0844 879 9140; www.macdonald hotels.co.uk/SwansNest; Swan's Nest Lane; d with breakfast from £120; **P** 🖳) In a 17th-century red-brick house near the banks of the Avon, this hotel has airy rooms in shades of brown and cream, with many overlooking the hotel gardens. There's a nice wood-panelled bar and a terrace for summer evenings.

Shakespeare Hotel (☎ 0870 400 8182; www.mercure .com; Chapel St; s/d £135/150; **P** 🖳) A labyrinth of rooms enchants guests at this classic Tudor hotel. The pick of the rooms are those named after Shakespeare's plays. Some you have to stoop to get into, but with their wood-panelled headboards complemented by luxury bathrooms, they are a great base for soaking up the town's rich Elizabethan heritage. Discounts are usually available; check the website for deals.

Thistle Stratford-upon-Avon (☎ 01789-294949; stratford.uponavon@thistle.co.uk; Waterside; r incl breakfast from £140; **P** 🖳) Superbly located across the road from the Swan Theatre, the Thistle overlooks the River Avon and pretty bankside parkland. Brass reading lights brighten the corridors, and the fragrant, comfortable rooms are everything you would expect from a top-end chain. There's a terrace for summer dining. Large discounts are available in low season.

Eating

Shakespeare pilgrimages clearly work up an appetite: there's certainly no shortage of good restaurants. Sheep St is clustered with refined but relaxed eating options, mostly aimed at theatregoers.

Vintner Wine Bar (☎ 01789-297259; 5 Sheep St; mains £7-13; 🕒 9.30am-10pm Mon-Fri, to 9.30pm Sun) This quirky space is full of beams, exposed brick, tucked-away spaces and low ceilings to bang your head on. There's a relaxed atmosphere and a tasty menu of burgers, grills and pastas, with some good vegetarian options.

Coconut Lagoon (☎ 01789-293546; 21 Sheep St; mains £7.50-13; 🕒 noon-2.30pm & 5-11pm Tue-Sun) Fusing culinary influences as diverse as Dutch, Portuguese and South Indian, this elegantly decorated restaurant has the tastiest curry around. Highlights include pork cooked in nutmeg and vinegar and coconut milk–bathed Kerala chicken stew.

Edward Moon's (☎ 01789-267069; 9 Chapel St; mains £11-17; 🕒 lunch & dinner) Edward Moon was an itinerant cook who worked in the colonial service and loved English food spiced with local ingredients. His philosophy inspires the food at this charming, glass-fronted brasserie.

Lambs (☎ 01789-292554; 12 Sheep St; mains £11-18; 🕒 noon-2pm Mon-Sun, plus 5-10pm Mon-Sat, 6-9.30pm Sun) The classiest joint in town – from the imposing manor-house door to the aristocratic interior, to the delectable cuisine (pan-fried calves liver £16) and a fancy wine list.

Other recommendations:

Oscar's (☎ 01789-292202; 13/14 Meer St; sandwiches £3.50-4.30; 🕒 11.30am-late) This small cafe does appetising breakfasts, lunches and afternoon tea, and has live music or DJs in the evening.

Georgetown (☎ 01789-204445; 23 Sheep St; mains £8.50-15; 🕒 noon-2.30pm & 5-11pm Mon-Sat) Fresh daisies on each table, chandeliers: there is more than a hint of Raffles at this classy vegetarian-friendly Malaysian restaurant.

Russons (☎ 01789-268822; 8 Church St; mains £9-17.50 🕒 noon-2pm & 5-9pm Tue- Sat) Quaint, beam-laden dining rooms have a regularly changing menu of seasonal food, from hefty meat dishes to vegetarian specials.

Malbec (☎ 01789-269106; 6 Union St; mains £13.50-17.50; 🕒 noon-2pm Tue-Sat, plus 7-9.30pm Tue-Thu, 6-9.30pm Fri & Sat) Very swish but relaxed restaurant with a delicious, á la carte menu and personable service. The whitewashed lower level is particularly atmospheric.

Drinking

Dirty Duck (☎ 01789-297312; Waterside) Officially called the 'Black Swan', this enchanting riverside alehouse should be on your list of must-visit pubs in Stratford. It's a favourite postperformance thespian watering hole, and has a roll-call of former regulars (Olivier, Attenborough etc) that reads like an actors' *Who's Who*. The adjoining restaurant (11am to 10pm) is good value.

Windmill Inn (☎ 01789-297687; Church St) Ale was flowing here at the same time as rhyming couplets flowed from Shakespeare's quill – it's been around a while. Despite its age it's still one of the liveliest places in town.

One Elm (☎ 01789-404919; 1 Guild St) This modern gastropub, smart with leather chairs, trendy wallpaper and a courtyard garden makes a change from all the 'olde worlde' charm. There's a tempting menu of free-range, sustainable goodies.

Cox's Yard (☎ 01789-404600; Bridgefoot) Large riverside complex with a pub, cafe and music venue. It's a lovely place to enjoy a coffee, drink or a full-blown meal while watching the swans glide past.

Entertainment

Royal Shakespeare Company (RSC; ☎ 0844 800 1110; www.rsc.org.uk; tickets £8-38; ☒ 9.30am-8pm Mon-Sat) Seeing a RSC production is a must. Major stars have trod the boards here and productions are of very high standard. At the time of writing, the main Royal Shakespeare Theatre was closed for extensive renovations and was due to reopen in 2010. The adjoining Swan Theatre is also closed during this time. In the meantime, performances take place in the striking temporary Courtyard Theatre by the Other Place. The box office is in the foyer of the Courtyard Theatre until the main theatre reopens. Ticket prices depend on the performance and venue, but there are offers for under 25-year-olds, students, seniors and other groups, plus discounts for previews. Call or check the website for details – and book ahead for good seats. There are usually a few tickets sold on the day of performance.

Stratford Picture House (☎ 0870 7551 229; www .picturehouses.co.uk; Windsor St; adult/child £7/5) This cinema, tucked away just off the main drag, shows Hollywood blockbusters as well as art-house films.

Getting There & Away

The train station is a few minutes' walk west of the centre. Chiltern Railways offers direct services to London Marylebone (2¼ hours). Cheap returns (£16.90) are often available after 11am.

National Express destinations from Stratford's Riverside bus station include Birmingham (£7.20, one hour, twice daily), Oxford (£9.20, one hour, daily) and London Victoria (£16.00, 3½ hours, five daily).

In July and August, the **Shakespeare Express steam train** (☎ 0121-708 4960; www.vintagetrains.co.uk) operates between Birmingham Snow Hill and Stratford stations (adult/child £10/5, return £20/10, one hour, twice Sundays only).

Getting Around

BICYCLE

Stratford is small enough to explore on foot, but a bicycle is good for getting out to the surrounding countryside or the rural Shakespeare properties. The canal towpath offers a fine route to Wilmcote.

Clarkes Cycles (☎ 01789-205057; Guild St; per half/ full day from £6/10; ☒ 9.15am-5pm Tue-Sat) rents out bikes. It's most easily reached down a little alley off Henley St.

BOAT

Punts, canoes and rowing boats are available for hire from Avon Boating (p549) by Clopton Bridge – it's under the Thai Boathouse restaurant.

AROUND STRATFORD-UPON-AVON

If you're tired of looking at historic landmarks and greenery from the ground, **Heart of England Balloons** (☎ 01789-488219; www.ukballoons.com; Cross Lanes Farm, Walcote; 1hr-flight per person £145) based near Alcester, offers the chance to soar above it all in a hot-air balloon. Alcester is about 8 miles west of Stratford-upon-Avon along the A46.

Charlecote Park

A youthful Shakespeare is said to have poached deer in the grounds of **Charlecote Park** (NT; ☎ 01789-470277; charlecote.park@nationaltrust.org .uk; adult/child £8.20/4.10; ☒ noon-5pm Fri-Tue Mar-Oct, noon-4pm Sat & Sun Dec). Deer still roam the park, which was skilfully landscaped by Capability Brown. The house, built around 1551, has an interior redesigned in Elizabethan style in the early 19th century; the Victorian kitchen and Tudor gatehouse are particularly interesting. Charlecote is in Wellesbourne, around 5 miles east of Stratford-upon-Avon. Bus 18 runs from Stratford at quarter past every hour.

Ragley Hall

The family home of the Marquess and Marchioness of Hertford, **Ragley Hall** (☎ 01789-762090; www.ragleyhall.com; adult/child £8.50/5; ☒ 10am-6pm Sun-Fri mid-Jul–Aug; hours vary rest of year) is a grand Palladian mansion built between 1679 and 1683, with a later baroque plasterwork ceiling and some good modern paintings. The intriguing South Staircase Hall with its murals and ceiling painting was restored between 1969 and 1983. Youngsters weary of behaving themselves indoors can be turned loose in Ragley Adventure Wood, a forest playground.

THE WEST MIDLANDS & THE MARCHES

Taking in a play or concert in the beautiful landscaped gardens is a real summer pleasure, weather permitting. Ragley is 2 miles south-west of Alcester off the A435/A46, or about 10 miles west of Stratford-upon-Avon.

STAFFORDSHIRE

Stoke-born novelist Arnold Bennett once wrote that Staffordshire was 'unsung by searchers after the extreme', but that doesn't mean that it's boring. Wedged between the urban sprawls of Birmingham and Manchester, the county is surprisingly beautiful, from rolling Cannock Chase, a magnet for walkers and cyclists, to the jagged backbone of the Peak District known as the Roaches. The stern might of Lichfield's cathedral, the wild rides at Alton Towers, and the neoclassical mansion of Shugborough are among the county's other charms.

Orientation

Staffordshire's attractions are spread fairly evenly around the county: Stoke to the north-west; the Peak District and Leek northeast, with Alton Towers just south; Lichfield to the southeast; and Stafford just southwest of the centre.

Information

Staffordshire Tourism (☎ 01889-880151; www.stafford shire.gov.uk/tourism) has general information on where to stay and what to do in the county.

Getting There & Around

London Midland (☎ 0844 811 0133; www.london midland.com)

Travel Line (☎ 0871 200 2233; www.traveline midlands.co.uk)

Virgin Trains (☎ 0845 722 2333; www.virgintrains .co.uk)

LICHFIELD

pop 27,900

This pretty market town, full of cobbled streets and courtyard gardens, is home to one of the country's most beautiful cathedrals, a monumental three-spired Gothic masterpiece that is visible from miles away. It's also been something of a thinktank in its time: famed wit and lexicographer Samuel Johnson was born here, and Erasmus Darwin, Charles' grandfather and an important man in his own right, lived and studied here for years.

Information

The **tourist office** (☎ 01543-412121; www.visitlichfield .com; Lichfield Garrick, Castle Dyke; ☺ 9am-5pm Mon-Sat) doubles as the box office for the Lichfield Garrick theatre.

Sights & Activities
LICHFIELD CATHEDRAL

The magnificent **Lichfield Cathedral** (☎ 01543-306120; free, but donation requested; ☺ 7.30am-6.15pm) boasts a fine Gothic west front adorned with exquisitely carved statues of the kings of England from Edgar to Henry I, and the major saints. Approach the blackened facade from town by Minster Pond and you won't be the first to get goosebumps as you look up to the cathedral's hallmark three spires – especially when they are floodlit by night. Most of what you see dates from the various rebuildings of the Norman cathedral between 1200 and 1350.

A superb illuminated manuscript from 730, the *Lichfield Gospels,* is displayed in the beautifully vaulted mid-13th-century chapterhouse, while the Lady Chapel to the east boasts 16th-century Flemish stained glass. Following archaeological work in 2003, a Saxon statue of the Archangel Gabriel was uncovered beneath the nave, and was on display for a month in 2006. At the time of writing it was expected to be on permanent display from around 2009, if the restoration work was successful.

A stroll round the tranquil **Cathedral Close,** which is ringed with imposing 17th- and 18th-century houses, is also rewarding.

OTHER SIGHTS & ACTIVITIES

The amateurish but absorbing **Samuel Johnson Birthplace Museum** (☎ 01543-264972; www.samuel johnsonbirthplace.org; Breadmarket St; admission free; ☺ 10.30am-4.30pm Apr-Sep, 11am-3.30pm Oct-Mar) charts the life of one of the most remarkable figures in the history of the English language. Samuel Johnson, the pioneering lexicographer, was born here in 1709 and spent his formative years in this ramshackle, five-floored property that belonged to his bookseller father. Credited with inventing the dictionary, Samuel Johnson was immortalised in the famous biography *The Life of Samuel Johnson,* written by his close friend James Boswell. On the ground floor is a bookshop containing several of Johnson's works.

Grandfather of the more famous Charles, Erasmus Darwin was himself a remarkable autodidact, doctor, inventor, philosopher and poet, influencing the Romantics. The **Erasmus Darwin House** (☎ 01543-306260; Beacon St; adult/child £3/2; ☽ noon-5pm Tue-Sun, last admission 4.15pm), where he lived from 1758 to 1781, commemorates his life with a video, pictures and personal items. Exhibits and displays illustrate his varied work and association with luminaries such as Wedgwood, Boulton and Watt.

The **Lichfield Heritage Centre** (☎ 01543-256611; Market Sq; adult/child £3.50/1; ☽ 9.30am-4pm Mon-Sat, from 10am Sun) is a nicely presented series of exhibits covering 1300 years of Lichfield history in a former church. Climb the tower (adult/child £2/1) for fine views of the city.

Sleeping

32 Beacon St (☎ 01543-262378; r incl breakfast from £48) An unmarked gem, this is in a lovely centuries-old town house and the friendly proprietors have furnished the rooms impeccably.

No 8 The Close (☎ 01543-418483; www.ldb.co.uk /accommodation.htm; 8 The Close; s/d incl breakfast from £28/48) Sitting in the shadow of the cathedral, No 8 The Close is a listed 19th-century town house that's also a family home. There are three comfortable B&B rooms here but there's no sign outside the house; you should call in advance to make arrangements.

George Hotel (☎ 01543-414822; www.thegeorge lichfield.co.uk; 12-14 Bird St; s/d Fri-Sun £50/63, Mon-Thu from £80; ℗ ▫) A maze of rooms winds through this 18th-century coaching inn in the heart of the city. It's well located and comfortable but some of the rooms could do with a revamp.

Eating & Drinking

Tudor of Lichfield (☎ 01543-263951; Bore St; sandwiches £3-5; ☽ 9am-5.30pm Mon-Sat, 11am-4.30pm Sun) This cafe scores points over its local rivals in terms of age – the half-timbered building it is housed in was built in 1510. The signs are still there, with a suit of armour glowering over punters as they sip their morning coffee. They also sell a tempting array of hand-made chocolates.

Chapters Cathedral Coffee Shop (☎ 01543-306125; 19 The Close; sandwiches & salads £4-5; ☽ 9am-4.30pm Mon-Sat, 11am-4pm Sun) In a charming 18th-century house with a view onto a 13th-century walled garden, this cafe is ideal for afternoon tea, or even Sunday lunch.

Eastern Eye (☎ 01543-415047; 19 Bird St; mains £6-12; ☽ 5pm-midnight) An award-winning chef inhabits the kitchen of this smart Indian restaurant –

he earned a place in the *Guinness Book of World Records* in 2005 for producing the biggest curry ever made (at the time).

Chandlers (☎ 01543-416688; www.chandlersrestaurant .co.uk; Conduit St; 2-/3-course dinner £14/17.50; ☽ noon-3pm & 6-10pm) With its gleaming brass fittings, shiny wood floors, large, open dining area, and refined Mediterranean-style food, Chandlers is one of the best places to eat out in town. It is on the 1st floor of the old Corn Exchange.

King's Head (☎ 01543-256822; 4 Queen St) Samuel Johnson described Lichfield folk as 'the most sober, decent people in England' – but that was 250 years ago, and there are plenty of pubs to go round these days. The King's Head has a welcoming vibe, is a great place to sample real ales and it puts on regular live music.

Getting There & Away

Buses 112 and 7 run to Birmingham, while the 825 serves Stafford (1¼ hours, hourly). The bus station is opposite the central Lichfield City train station, with trains to Birmingham New St station (30 minutes, every 15 minutes). Direct trains to London Euston (from one hour 15 minutes, around eight daily) depart from Lichfield Trent Valley station, about 1.5 miles from town.

STOKE-ON-TRENT
pop 240,636

Stoke-on-Trent is Staffordshire's industrial heart, and is famed for its pottery production. There's not too much of interest here for the visitor, however, unless you happen to be a fan of porcelain. For a preview of Stoke, check out Arnold Bennett's memorable descriptions of the area in its industrial heyday in his novel *Anna of the Five Towns* (something of a misnomer as Stoke actually consists of six suburbs).

Orientation

Stoke-on-Trent is made up of Tunstall, Burslem, Hanley, Stoke, Fenton and Longton, together often called 'the Potteries'. Hanley is the official 'city centre'. Stoke-on-Trent train station is south of Hanley, but buses from outside the main entrance run there in minutes. The bus station is in the centre of Hanley.

Information

Ask at the helpful **tourist office** (☎ 01782-236000; www.visitstoke.co.uk; Victoria Hall, Bagnall St,

Hanley; ⏰ 9.15am-5.15pm Mon-Sat), adjacent to the bus station, for a map with the locations of the various showrooms, factory shops and visitors centres.

Sights & Activities

The recently expanded **Wedgwood Visitor Centre** (☎ 0870 606 1759; www.thewedgwoodvisitorcentre.com; Barlaston; Mon-Fri £8.25, Sat & Sun £6.25; ⏰ 9am-5pm Mon-Fri, 10am-5pm Sat & Sun), set in 81 hectares of attractive parkland, offers an absorbing look at the bone-china production process. Tours take in an extensive collection of historic pieces, and you can watch artisans calmly painting their designs onto china. Best of all, a troupe of Star Wars–esque anthropomorphic robots churn out perfect plates and mugs. Equally interesting are the film and displays on the life of founder Josiah Wedgwood (1730–95). An innovative potter, he was also a driving force behind the construction of England's canal system and the abolition of slavery. Wedgewood celebrates its 250th anniversary in 2009.

The **Potteries Museum & Art Gallery** (☎ 01782-232323; Bethesda St, Hanley; admission free; ⏰ 10am-5pm Mon-Sat & 2-5pm Sun Mar-Oct, 10am-4pm Mon-Sat & 1-4pm Sun Nov-Feb) covers the history of the Potteries and houses an impressively extensive ceramics display as well as a fine-art collection (Picasso, Degas).

Constructed around Stoke's last remaining bottle kiln, the **Gladstone Pottery Museum** (☎ 01782-319232; Uttoxeter Rd, Longton; adult/child £6/4.50; ⏰ 10am-5pm) presents a taste of what life was like for people working in the Victorian potteries. Those of a scatological bent will enjoy the Flushed With Pride exhibition, which charts the story of the toilet from chamber pots and shared privy holes (with smell effects!) to modern hi-tech conveniences. Buses 6 and 6A go to the museum from Hanley.

Sleeping & Eating

Verdon Guest House (☎ 01782-264244; www.verdon guesthouse.co.uk; 44 Charles St, Hanley; s/d from £25/40; P 🖵 wi-fi) A large, lovingly kept B&B in a grand Victorian house near the main bus station. The rooms have recently had a modern makeover and the no-nonsense owners are a mine of local travel advice.

The **Ivy House Restaurant** (☎ 0870 606 1759; www .thewedgwoodvisitorcentre.com; Barlaston; ⏰ 9am-5pm Mon-Fri, 10am-5pm Sat & Sun) is a large buffet-style restaurant and cafe in the Wedgwood Visitor Centre – all dishes are, of course, served on fine Wedgwood bone china.

Getting There & Away

National Express coaches run to/from London (four hours, five daily) and Manchester (1½ hours, eight daily). Trains run to Stafford (20 minutes, every 30 minutes) and London (1¾ hours, hourly).

AROUND STOKE-ON-TRENT
Biddulph Grange Gardens

The superbly landscaped Victorian **Biddulph Grange Gardens** (NT; ☎ 01782-517999; adult/child £6.40/3.20; ⏰ 11am-5pm Wed-Sun late Mar-Oct, 11am-3pm Sat & Sun Nov & Dec) present an exotic botanical-world tour, including a Chinese pagoda garden, an Egyptian courtyard, and Italian formal gardens. A highlight is the Rainbow, a huge bank of rhododendrons that flower simultaneously in spring. The gardens are 7 miles north of Stoke; take bus 6A from Hanley bus station (40 minutes, every 20 minutes). The gardens are a short walk from the bus stop.

Little Moreton Hall

Spectacular black-and-white, timber-framed moated manor house, **Little Moreton Hall** (NT; ☎ 01260-272018; adult/child £6.40/3.20; ⏰ 11.30am-5pm Wed-Sun late Mar-Oct, 11.30am-4pm Sat & Sun Nov-late Dec) dates back to the 16th century; within its over-the-top exterior there are a series of important wall paintings and an indefinable sense of romance. Little Moreton is off the A34 south of Congleton.

Alton Towers

The most popular theme park in England, **Alton Towers** (☎ 0870 444 4455; www.altontowers .com; adult/under 12yr £35/26; ⏰ 9.30am-5pm Oct–mid-Mar, longer hours mid-Mar–Sep) is a great option for thrill-seekers. There are more than 100 rides, including upside-down roller coasters and log flumes, and new thrills are introduced with relative frequency. Entry prices are almost as steep as the rides and are highest during school holidays.

There's a hotel within the park, but most visitors opt to stay in nearby villages. Alton itself is an attractive village with several B&Bs. The **Dimmingsdale YHA** (☎ 0845 371 9513; www.yha.org.uk; Oakamoor; dm members/nonmembers £14/17) is 2 miles northwest of the park. There are plenty of good rambles around the hostel too.

THE WEST MIDLANDS &
THE MARCHES

Alton Towers is east of Cheadle off the B5032. Public transport is sketchy, but various train companies offer all-in-one packages from London and other cities; check the website for current details.

Drayton Manor

Southern Staffordshire's answer to Alton Towers, **Drayton Manor** (☎ 08708 725252; www .draytonmanor.co.uk; adult/child £23/19; ☿ 10.30am-5pm Easter-Oct, longer hours May-Sep) is another massive theme park. Rides include the Apocalypse, a 54m 'stand up' drop from a tower, and the Pandemonium, in which two rotating gondolas swing with 64 screaming passengers. The park is near junctions 9 and 10 of the M42 on the A4091. Bus 110 leaves from Birmingham Bull St just off Corporation St and goes to Bonehill, just outside Tamworth, from where it is another 15 minutes' walk.

LEEK

pop 18,768

The attractive market town of Leek serves as a gateway to the Staffordshire moorlands, including the impressive Roaches, making it a convenient base for visiting the Potteries and the Peak District.

The **tourist office** (☎ 01538-483741; tourism.smdc@ staffordshire.gov.uk; 1 Market Pl; ☿ 9.30am-5pm Mon-Fri, 10am-4pm Sat) will book rooms for a £3 fee.

St Edward's Church (☎ 01538-388134; Church St; ☿ 10am-3pm), completed in 1306, has a beautiful rose window by William Morris' decorative-arts makers.

Described by John Betjeman as 'one of the finest churches in Britain', **All Saints Church** (☎ 01538-382588; Compton; ☿ 11am-4pm Wed & Sat) features Morris & Co stained-glass windows at the eastern end (from designs by Edward Burne-Jones), and ornate Arts and Crafts Movement wall-painting.

Brindley Mill (www.brindleymill.net; Mill St; adult/child £2/1.50; ☿ 2-5pm Mon-Wed mid-Jul–Aug, 2-5pm Sat & Sun Easter-Sep) was built in 1752 by canal pioneer James Brindley. It's been beautifully restored and once again mills corn; inside is a small museum dedicated to Brindley and the art of millwrighting.

Peak Weavers Hotel (☎ 01538-383729; www .peakweavershotel.co.uk; 21 King St; s/d incl breakfast from £35/80; P ☐) is a lovingly restored former mill owner's property (once also a convent). Its bedrooms are light and airy and there is

a great restaurant with a delicious, regularly changing menu.

Bus 18 runs to Leek from Hanley (Stoke-on-Trent, 45 minutes).

STAFFORD

pop 63,681

The county town of Stafford was once a major crossroads for travellers. It still has a couple of attractions that are worth a look if you happen to be passing by.

The **tourist office** (☎ 01785-619619; Market St; ☿ 9.30am-5pm Mon-Fri, 10am-4pm Sat) is behind the town hall and can give you the low-down on mountain biking and walking in nearby Cannock Chase.

The **Ancient High House** (☎ 01785-619131; Greengate St; admission free; ☿ 10am-4pm Tue-Sat) is the largest timber-framed town house in the country and has period rooms containing displays on the history of the house since its construction in 1595.

The remains of **Stafford Castle** (☎ 01785-257698; Newport Rd; admission free; ☿ visitor centre 10am-5pm Tue-Sun Apr-Oct, 10am-4pm Nov-Mar), which was built by the Normans, sit romantically on a hilltop with sweeping views over the landscape. The castle grounds play host to historical re-enactments throughout the summer. There's a small visitors centre and a 'medieval herb garden', as well as a network of forested trails for postpicnic wanders. It's about a mile from the town centre.

Bus X1 runs between Stafford and Stoke-on-Trent (1¼ hours, every 30 minutes).

AROUND STAFFORD

The regal, neoclassical mansion of **Shugborough** (☎ 01889-881388; adult/child £12/7, parking £3; ☿ 11am-5pm Tue-Sun Mar-Oct) is the ancestral home of renowned photographer Lord Lichfield (there's an exhibition of his work here). Started in 1693 and considerably extended during the 18th and 19th centuries, Shugborough has marvellous state rooms and a fine collection of Louis XV and XVI furniture. Shugborough is set on a 'working historic' estate and with the aid of costumed actors you can see what life was like for those living there in the 19th century, including the servants, the farm workers, and a lady in the Mansion House.

Shugborough is 6 miles east of Stafford on the A513; bus 825 runs nearby.

WORCESTERSHIRE

Serene Worcestershire's southern and western fringes burst with lush countryside, stunning walking trails and attractive riverside market towns, though the northern and eastern plains blend into the West Midlands, and have little to offer to visitors. Plump at the county's core is the capital Worcester, with its magnificent cathedral and world-renowned Royal Worcester Porcelain Works. Just south, the hillside Victorian resort of Great Malvern sits regally at the heart of the rolling Malvern Hills (the Malverns).

Information

For online information check out www.visitworcestershire.org, and for news try www.worcesternews.co.uk.

Activities

The longest riverside walk in the UK, the **Severn Way** winds its way through Worcestershire via Worcester and Upton-upon-Severn, while the **Three Choirs Way** links Worcester to Hereford and Gloucester.

Cyclists can pick up the handy *Elgar Ride Variations* leaflet from tourist offices detailing routes around the Malverns.

Getting Around

There are a few regular rail links from Worcester, and Kidderminster is the southern railhead of the popular Severn Valley Railway. Buses to rural areas can be frustratingly infrequent.

WORCESTER

pop 94,029

An ancient cathedral city on the banks of the River Severn, Worcester's (*woos*-ter) postwar architectural clangers and soulless shopping centre tend to eclipse the architectural gems that sprinkle the city. Scratch beneath the surface, however, and you'll be rewarded with a magnificent cathedral, pockets of timber-framed Tudor and elegant Georgian architecture, riverside walks, and tales of the Civil War, which finished here.

Information

The **tourist office** (☎ 01905-726311; www.visitworcester.com; Guildhall, High St; ☼ 9.30am-5pm Mon-Sat) will organise 1½-hour **walking tours** (☎ 01905-222117; www.worcesterwalks.co.uk; adult £4; ☼ 11am Mon-Fri). Internet access is available at **Coffee Republic** (☎ 01905-25069; 31 High St; per 20 min/1hr £1/3; ☼ 7am-6pm), opposite the Guildhall.

Sights

WORCESTER CATHEDRAL

Dominating the centre of the city, the majestic edifice of **Worcester Cathedral** (☎ 01905-732900; www.worcestercathedral.org.uk; suggested donation £3; ☼ 7.30am-6pm) encapsulates an assortment of styles and eras, and is full of the stories and symbols of England's violent past.

The atmospheric Norman crypt is the largest in England and dates back to when St Wulfstan, the only Saxon bishop to hang on to his see under the Normans, started building the cathedral in 1084. Other highlights include a striking 13th-century Lady Chapel and a lovely 12th-century circular chapterhouse.

You'll find the cathedral's most notorious inhabitant, King John, buried in the choir. Famous for his treachery towards older brother Richard Lionheart, and squabbles with the barons that forced him to sign the Magna Carta, John left England in chaos. In a somewhat fitting break from tradition, the stone lion under his feet is biting back. To boost his slim chances of passing the pearly gates, the dying king asked to be buried disguised as a monk.

The strong-legged can tackle the 249 steps up the **tower** (admission adult/child £3/1; ☼ 11am-5pm Sat & school holidays Easter-Sep); once up top, spare a thought for the unhappy Charles II, who surveyed his troops from here during the Battle of Worcester.

One-hour long **cathedral tours** (adult/child £3/free; ☼ 11am & 2.30pm daily Mon-Sat Apr-Sep, Sat only rest of year) run from the gift shop. Evensong is a splendid affair; it's held at 5.30pm Monday to Wednesday, Friday and Saturday, and at 4pm Sunday.

COMMANDERY

Recently reopened after a major refurbishment, the town's history museum, the **Commandery** (☎ 01905-361821; www.worcestercitymuseums.org.uk; College St; adult/child £5.25/2.25; ☼ 10am-5pm Mon-Sat, 1.30-5pm Sun) is housed in a splendid Tudor building that has been used, among other things, as a monastic hospital, a family home, and King Charles II's Civil War Headquarters during the battle of Worcester in 1651. Engaging audio guides and interactive

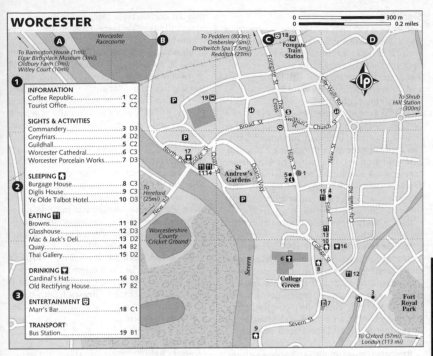

WORCESTER

INFORMATION		
Coffee Republic	**1**	C2
Tourist Office	**2**	C2
SIGHTS & ACTIVITIES		
Commandery	**3**	D3
Greyfriars	**4**	D2
Guildhall	**5**	C2
Worcester Cathedral	**6**	C3
Worcester Porcelain Works	**7**	D3
SLEEPING		
Burgage House	**8**	C3
Diglis House	**9**	C3
Ye Olde Talbot Hotel	**10**	D3
EATING		
Browns	**11**	B2
Glasshouse	**12**	D3
Mac & Jack's Deli	**13**	D2
Quay	**14**	D2
Thai Gallery	**15**	D2
DRINKING		
Cardinal's Hat	**16**	D3
Old Rectifying House	**17**	B2
ENTERTAINMENT		
Marr's Bar	**18**	C1
TRANSPORT		
Bus Station	**19**	B1

exhibits tell the story of the Commandery and of Worcester during key periods in its history. A highlight is the fascinating 'painted chamber', covered with intriguing 15th-century religious frescos.

ROYAL WORCESTER PORCELAIN WORKS
The king of British porcelain manufacture has come a long way since founder Dr John Wall started making ornate bone china as a hobby in 1751. Granted a royal warrant in 1789, the factory still supplies Her Royal Highness (HRH) with some of her preferred crockery, and now runs an entire visitor complex to promote its wares.

Worth visiting even for those that aren't ceramic-crazy, the **Worcester Porcelain Museum** (☎ 01905-746000; www.worcesterporcelainmuseum.org .uk; Severn St; adult/concession £5/4.25; ☒ 9am-5.30pm Mon-Sat, 11am-5pm Sun) enlivens its exhaustive collection of works with quirky asides detailing everything from the china's use by British Royals to the factory's sidelines in porcelain dentures and 'portable fonts' designed for cholera outbreaks. Entry includes an audio tour.

The enjoyable **Visitor Experience Tour** (adult/concession £5/4.25; ☒ 10am-5.30pm Mon-Sat, 11am-5pm Sun) walks visitors through the porcelain's design and manufacture. Combined tickets for the museum and tour cost £9/8 per adult/child.

You can browse the bewildering array of porcelain goodies in the on-site **shops**, from the daintiest traditional dinnerware sets to bonnet-shaped candle snuffers.

HISTORICAL PROPERTIES
For more of Worcester's bulldozer-dodging buildings of old, stroll through the idyllic cathedral-side College Green, then amble down Friar St and New St, both lined with lovely Tudor and Elizabethan buildings.

You can duck inside a 1480 timber-framed merchant's house, full of atmospheric wood-panelled rooms and backed by a pretty walled garden, at **Greyfriars** (NT; ☎ 01905-23571; Friar St; adult/child £4.20/2.10; ☒ 1-5pm Wed-Sat Mar-Dec, also Sun Jul-Aug). Also peek into the pompous 18th-century **Guildhall** (High St; admission free; ☒ 8.30am-4.30pm Mon-Sat), the creation of a pupil of Sir Christopher Wren who died in poverty after the city dragged its heels on paying him his dues.

THE WEST MIDLANDS &
THE MARCHES

Sleeping

Oldbury Farm (☎ 01905-421357; Lower Broadheath; s/d £35/55; P) This blissfully quiet Georgian farmhouse is next to Elgar Birthplace Museum (see opposite), and has airy, country-style rooms. The house comes complete with fishing rights and stables, beautiful views and easy access to local walking routes.

our pick Burgage House (☎ 01905-25396; www .burgagehouse.co.uk; 4 College Precincts; s/d £36/65) A well-camouflaged little gem, hidden on a narrow cobbled street overlooking the cathedral. The four huge rooms (three of which are accessed up a beautiful curved stone staircase) are decked out with paintings and tapestries and are elegant yet incredibly homely; those at the front have stunning views. It's run in a warm, unobtrusive manner and is family-friendly.

Ye Olde Talbot Hotel (☎ 01905-23573; www.old english.co.uk; Friar St; s/d £70/90) Attached to a popular bar and bistro right in the centre of town, this pleasantly decorated inn dates back to the 13th century and is pretty good value. Rooms sport rich fabrics, deep colours, modern gadgets and an occasional smattering of antique features. Discounted parking is available nearby.

Barrington House (☎ 01905-422965; www.barrington house.eu; 204 Henwick Rd; r £85; P ▯ wi-fi) Lovely Georgian house by the river with wonderful views, pretty walled garden, three plush bedrooms and hearty breakfasts served with eggs from the owners' hens.

Diglis House (☎ 01905-353518; www.diglishousehotel .co.uk; Severn St; P) This handsome Georgian house has an idyllic setting, right by the water, with town a short stroll along the river. At the time of writing the bedrooms and public areas were undergoing thorough refurbishment and were due to reopen in late 2008. Call or see website for price details. Wheelchair access available.

Eating

Quay (☎ 01905-745792; The Quay; mains £7-14; ☼ lunch & dinner) This place has an informal setting right next to the river with plenty of outside tables to soak up the atmosphere. Come for light lunches, afternoon tea or more substantial dinners served in a candlelit dining room.

Thai Gallery (☎ 01905-745902; 26-32 Friar St; mains £8-14; ☼ lunch & dinner Mon-Sun) In a half-timbered building, carved elephants and Thai paint-ings sit comfortably with heavy beams and low ceilings. The tasty Thai cuisine packs a punch.

Glasshouse (☎ 01905-611120; Danesbury House, College St; mains £13-19, 2-/3-course set lunch £10-14; ☼ lunch & dinner Mon-Sat, lunch Sun). This shiny, trendy, designer restaurant – all slate floors, grey leather banquettes, and ubermodern fireplaces – may look snooty but the service is friendly and the food delicious, well presented and unpretentious.

Browns (☎ 01905-26263; The Old Cornmill, South Quay; mains £14-24; ☼ lunch & dinner Mon-Sat, lunch Sun) Housed in a converted Victorian corn mill adjacent to the river, this top-class restaurant was renovated after flooding in 2007 and now has a mezzanine cocktail bar in addition to its stylish but low-key dining room. Classic British cooking with a few French flavours sneaked in is the order of the day here.

Mac & Jack's Deli (☎ 01905-731331; 44 Friar St; ☼ 9.30am-5.30pm Tue-Thu, 9am-6pm Fri & Sat) Bright little deli and cafe serving perfect picnic fodder such as local meats, cheeses, freshly baked bread and cakes; as well as soups, sandwiches and tarts to eat in.

Drinking

Cardinal's Hat (☎ 01905-22066; 31 Friar St) Despite its traditional old-English pub appearance, this atmospheric Worcester institution has a decidedly Austrian flavour. It sells Austrian beers in traditional steins and flutes and a choice of Austrian food at lunchtime.

Old Rectifying House (☎ 01905-619622; www .theoldrec.co.uk; North Pde; ☼ noon-1am) This multi-gabled riverside pile has a laid-back lounge bar over a chic restaurant. There's a good selection of real ales and lagers and solid English food such as bangers and mash, fish and chips, and all-day breakfasts. DJs play chill-out music on the weekends.

Entertainment

Marr's Bar (☎ 01905-613336; www.marrsbar.co.uk; 12 Pierpoint St; ☼ from 8pm) The best live-music venue for miles around, Marr's still has its original sprung dance floors from its days as a dance studio and you can bounce on them to your heart's content most nights thanks to packed listings. Gigs range from acoustic sessions to comedy.

If sport is your thing you can catch spring and summer racing at **Worcester Racecourse** (☎ 0870 220 2772; www.worcester-racecourse.co.uk), while the central **Worcestershire County Cricket Ground** (☎ 01905-337921; www.wccc.co.uk) is a lovely spot to cheer on the chaps.

Getting There & Around
Worcester has two stations but most trains run to Worcester Foregate (the other is Worcester Shrub Hill). Trains run hourly to London Paddington (£32.30, 2¼ to three hours) and Hereford (£6.80, 43 to 50 minutes).

National Express has two direct daily services to London Victoria (£21.10, four hours). Bus 44 runs to Great Malvern (30 minutes, twice-hourly), bus 363 goes to Upton-upon-Severn (30 minutes, hourly), and bus 417 goes to Ledbury (50 minutes, five daily Monday to Saturday).

Bikes can be hired from **Peddlers** (☎ 01905-24238; 46 Barbourne Rd; per day from £8).

AROUND WORCESTER
Elgar Birthplace Museum
England's greatest classical composer receives due pomp and circumstance at the **Elgar Birthplace Museum** (☎ 01905-333224; www .elgarmuseum.org; Lower Broadheath; adult/child £6/2; ⏰ 11am-5pm), partly housed in the humble cottage in which he was born in 1857, 3 miles west of Worcester. You can browse through an engrossing collection of the walrus-mustachioed composer's possessions, which range from his gramophone and musical manuscripts to endearing doodlings in the morning paper. Admission includes an audio tour with musical interludes so you can appreciate what all the fuss is really about.

Bus 308 goes from Worcester to Broadheath Common, a short walk from the museum (15 minutes, three times daily Monday to Saturday).

Witley Court
One of the country's most romantic ruins, **Witley Court** (EH; ☎ 01299-896636; Great Witley; adult/5-15yr/under 5yr £5.20/2.60/free; ⏰ 10am-5pm Mar-Oct, 10am-4pm Thu-Mon Nov-Feb) was a lavish Italianate mid-19th-century home left to rot after a disastrous fire in 1937. It now acts as a stunning folly crowning the Victorian splendour of its restored landscaped grounds. The spectacular Perseus and Andromeda fountain is one of Europe's biggest.

A COTTAGE OF YOUR OWN

To tour the countryside from your own base, try these websites for self-catering properties:

Eco Cabin (www.ecocabin.co.uk)
Farm Stay Worcs (www.farmstayworcs.co.uk)
Lunnon Farm (www.lunnoncottages.co.uk)
Shropshire Cottages (www.shropshire cottages.com)
Sykes Cottages (www.sykescottages.co.uk)

Don't miss the glittering gilded-plaster interior at the neighbouring **Great Witley Church** (www.greatwitleychurch.org.uk), the most magnificent baroque church in England. It's home to paintings by Bellucci and a glorious organ that composer Handel once played.

Bus 758 from Worcester to Tenbury Wells passes eight times daily (55 minutes).

Droitwich Spa & Around
The centre of England's salt industry since the Iron Age, thanks to brine springs that are 10 times stronger than sea water, Droitwich transformed itself into a fashionable spa town in the 19th century when the industry began to decline. Today there are still public baths and several elaborate medieval buildings worth seeing.

Housed in the former brine baths, the **tourist office** doubles as the town's **Heritage Centre** (☎ 01905-774312; Victoria Sq; ⏰ 10am-4pm Mon-Sat).

The area's biggest attraction is stately home **Hanbury Hall** (NT; ☎ 01527-821214; School Rd; adult/child £7.20/3.60; ⏰ 1-5pm Sat-Wed Mar-Oct), 4 miles east of Droitwich Spa. Built in 1701, the house is famed for its painted ceilings, elaborate staircase and stunning grounds.

To Droitwich Spa's west, **Ombersley** is so perfect a medieval village it looks like it was created by a Hollywood film crew. Its magpie black-and-white main road is studded with excellent pubs and eateries that include the wonderful **Venture Inn** (☎ 01905-620552; Main Rd; 3-course lunch/dinner £21.50/34; ⏰ lunch & dinner Tue-Sat, lunch Sun), serving modern British cuisine in a supposedly haunted building dating from 1430.

Bus 303 runs to Worcester (25 minutes) hourly.

Redditch

Stuck in a featureless commuter belt to big-city Birmingham, Victorian Redditch once dominated the world's needle trade, and the often-grisly tale is told in the lively **Forge Mill Needle Museum & Bordesley Abbey Visitor Centre** (☎ 01527-62509; www.forgemill.org.uk; Needle Mill Lane; adult/child £3.90/1; ☯ 11am-4.30pm Mon-Fri & 2-5pm Sat & Sun Easter-Sep, 11am-4pm Mon-Thu & 2-5pm Sun Oct-Nov & Feb-Easter), where the original water-powered machinery still runs on weekends. The museum sits on the riverside grounds of ruined 12th-century Bordesley Abbey.

Bus 350 goes direct to Worcester (55 minutes) three times daily; at other times change in Bromsgrove (15 minutes).

GREAT MALVERN
pop 35,558

This well-to-do Victorian spa town tumbles prettily down the slopes of the gorgeous **Malvern Hills**, which soar upwards from the flat Worcestershire plains. The place positively glows with health and well-being courtesy of its lush hill views, wide tree-lined avenues, booted hikers and pure spring waters that bubble up in unexpected places. Today the medicinal waters that first attracted overindulgent Victorians are harnessed for a successful bottled-water business.

The **tourist office** (☎ 01684-892289; www.malvernhills.gov.uk; 21 Church St; ☯ 10am-5pm) is brimming with walking and cycling information. The **Library** (☎ 01684-566553; Graham Rd; ☯ 9.30am-5.30pm Mon, Fri & Sat, 9.30am-8pm Tue-Thu) has free internet access; bring ID.

In June the town goes music-mad in the biannual **Elgar Festival** (☎ 01684-892277; www.elgar-festival.com) to celebrate the life and works of the composer who lived nearby at Malvern Link.

Sights & Activities
GREAT MALVERN PRIORY

The 11th-century **Great Malvern Priory** (☎ 01684-561020; www.greatmalvernpriory.org.uk; Church St; suggested donation £3; ☯ 9am-6.30pm Apr-Oct, 9am-4.30pm Nov-Mar) is packed with remarkable features: it's lined with clumsy Norman pillars and hides a delightfully bizarre collection of 14th-century misericords under the tip-up seats of the monks' stalls. Every one a delight, they depict everything from three rats hanging a cat to the mythological basilisk, and run through domestic labours of the months from the 15th century.

MALVERN MUSEUM OF LOCAL HISTORY

Straddling the pathway in the grand Priory Gatehouse (1470), the **Malvern Museum of Local History** (☎ 01684-567811; Abbey Rd; adult/child £2/50p; ☯ 10.30am-5pm Easter-Oct, except Wed during school term) offers a small but thorough exploration of the things for which Great Malvern is renowned, from hills geology to Victorian water cures.

MALVERN THEATRES

One of the country's best provincial theatres, **Malvern Theatre** (☎ 01684-892277; www.malvern-theatres.co.uk; Grange Rd) packs in a lively program of classical music, dance, comedy, drama and cinema.

The quirkly little **Theatre of Small Convenience** (☎ 01684-568933; www.wctheatre.co.uk; Edith Walk) is set in a converted Victorian men's lavatory decked out in theatrical Italianate flourishes. It's one of the world's smallest theatres, seating just 12 people for acts that range from puppetry to opera.

WALKING

The jack-in-the-box Malvern Hills, which pop up dramatically out of the innocently low Severn plains on the boundary between Worcestershire and Herefordshire, are made up of 18 named peaks; highest of the bunch being Worcester Beacon at 419m. The hills are criss-crossed by more than 100 miles of paths; trail guides (£1.75) are available at the tourist office. More than 70 springs and fountains pouring out the famous medicinal waters are dotted around the hills, and the tourist office has a map guide (£3.95) to all of them.

Sleeping

Como House (☎ 01684-561486; www.comohouse.co.uk; Como Rd; s/d £40/60; P □ wi-fi) This handsome Malvern-stone converted schoolhouse has three tastefully furnished, south-facing rooms, a self-catering apartment and a large garden, complete with a bridged pond and numerous statues. The owner picks guests up from the station and drops them off at walking points.

Bredon House Hotel (☎ 01684-566990; www.bredonhouse.co.uk; 34 Worcester Rd; s/d from £45/70; P □) A short saunter from the centre, this genteel family- and pet-friendly Victorian hotel has superb views and courteous service. Rooms are decorated in a quirky but tasteful mix of new and old, and the books, magazines and family photographs dotted around the communal areas give it a homely feel.

Cottage in the Wood Hotel (☎ 01684-575859; www
.cottageinthewood.co.uk; Holywell Rd, Malvern Wells; s/d from
£92/135; P ▣) This grand old traditional hotel
is a Malverns institution. Rooms are somewhat frumpy but its position – swaddled by
woodland, with sweeping views over the hills –
is marvellous. There's a popular fine-dining
restaurant here and a 600-strong wine list.

Other possibilities:

Copper Beech (☎ 01684-565013; www.copper
beechhouse.co.uk; 32 Avenue Rd; s/d from £43/70; P)
Wonderful guest house in a dignified late-Victorian building, about 1 mile from the town centre.

Treherne House (☎ 01684-572445; www.treherne
house.co.uk; 53 Guarlford Rd; r from £90; P) This fine
old gentleman's residence-turned-boutique B&B has
sumptuous bedrooms with a hint of French reproduction
styling and to-die-for food. It's on the outskirts of town.

Eating

St Ann's Well Cafe (☎ 01684-560285; St Ann's Well; piece
of cake £2; ☽ lunch daily Apr-Sep, Sat & Sun only Oct-Mar)
The best of Malvern's many cafes is in a handsome early-19th-century villa, a steep 99-step
ascent from town. It rewards the climb with
great vegetarian and vegan food, wholesome
salads and sinful cakes, which you can wash
down with fresh spring water that bubbles
into a carved basin by the door.

Pepper and Oz (☎ 01684-562676; 23 Abbey Rd; mains
£7-18.50; ☽ lunch & dinner Tue-Sat) Right by the museum, this brasserie has a lovely alfresco terrace and photography gallery, and serves solid
classics such as butch Herefordshire steaks.
There's a decent wine list and it also does
good-value pretheatre menus.

Anupam (☎ 01684-573814; 85 Church St; mains £8-13;
☽ lunch & dinner) This stylish and passionate
Indian restaurant is just off the main road.
Walls coated in primary colours and bubbly
service put guests in a cheerful mood, and
superb dishes such as duck with lemon and
garam masala keep them that way.

Leaf Coffee and Food House (☎ 01684-574989; 1
Edith Walk; mains £9-13; ☽ 8am-3pm Mon-Fri, 9am-4pm
Sun) Big wooden tables and fresh flowers welcome visitors to this wholesome cafe. They use
locally sourced and fair-trade produce to make
great salads, sandwiches, burgers and cakes.

Getting There & Around

There are twice-hourly trains to Worcester
(12 to 18 minutes) and every half-hour to
Hereford (£6.50, 30 minutes). Trains also go
regularly to Ledbury (13 minutes).

National Express runs one bus daily to
London (£21.10, 3½ hours) via Worcester
(20 minutes). Bus 44 connects Worcester (30
minutes, hourly) with Great Malvern.

Handy for walkers, the 244 – otherwise
known as the 'Malvern Hills Hopper' – runs
a hop-on, hop-off service (five daily weekends
and Bank Holidays mid-April to October)
through the hills to Upton-upon-Severn and
Eastnor Castle.

UPTON-UPON-SEVERN
pop 1789

A sweet little town with a random mix of
Tudor and Georgian buildings lining its narrow meandering streets, Upton makes for a
pleasant stop or a visit for the **Oliver Cromwell
jazz festival** (☎ 01684-593254; www.uptonjazz.co.uk) at
the end of June.

The **tourist office** (☎ 01684-594200; upton.tic@
malvernhills.gov.uk; 4 High St; ☽ 10am-5pm Mon-Sat) has
details. Walkers and map enthusiasts should
head for the **Map Shop** (☎ 01684-593146; www
.themapshop.co.uk; 15 High St), which has the best
selection in the county.

The town's oldest building, a stunted tower
nicknamed the 'Pepperpot' for its round-
topped shape, now houses the **Heritage Centre**
(☎ 01684-592679; Church St; admission free; ☽ 1.30-
4.30pm mid-April–Sep), where displays detail
the town's history. Opposite is **Tudor House**
(☎ 01684-592447; 16 Church St; adult/concession £1/50p;
☽ 2-5pm Apr-Oct), with a haphazard collection
of local life and history – some decidedly on
the quirky side.

Sleeping & Eating

Tiltridge Vineyard (☎ 01684-592906; www.tiltridge.com;
Upper Hook Rd; s/d £40/65; P) A homey farmhouse
B&B connected to a thriving vineyard 1 mile
west of town, Tiltridge offers little treats such
as sampling its award-winning wines on the
south-facing terrace, and a terrific breakfast
made with freshly laid eggs, local apple juice
and homemade jams. There are three simple country-style rooms, and packed lunches
are available.

White Lion (☎ 01684-592551; www.whitelionhotel
.biz; 21 High St; s/d £70/99; P) This 16th-century
coaching inn, famous for the Civil War connections and its place in Henry Fielding's
Tom Jones, is now known just as well for its
richly furnished classic rooms and romantic
oak-beamed and candlelit restaurant (mains
£10.50 to £19) serving excellent modern
British food. Wheelchair access is available.

Getting There & Away

Bus 363 runs between Upton and Worcester (30 minutes) at least nine times daily from Monday to Saturday (less frequently on Sunday).

HEREFORDSHIRE

Sleepy, rural Herefordshire is well off the mainstream tourist track. It can be difficult to negotiate, especially without a car, but your efforts will be rewarded by a tapestry of lush fields, black-and-white timbered villages, twisting lanes and more then enough leafy orchards to give you a taste for the county's famous ciders. The scenic River Wye ambles through the county, tempting canoeists and other water babies. County capital Hereford is home to a small cathedral, where you'll find the superb medieval Mappa Mundi; and perched on the border with Wales is renowned bookshop king, Hay-on-Wye.

Information

For online county-wide information on attractions, accommodation and events:
Visit Heart of England (www.visitheartofengland.com)
Visit Herefordshire (www.visitherefordshire.co.uk)

Activities

Herefordshire is a haven for walkers, with several established long-distance paths meandering through it (see p528). **Offa's Dyke Path** hugs the Welsh border, while the 107-mile Wye Valley Walk begins in Chepstow (Wales) and follows the river upstream into Herefordshire and then on to Rhayader in Wales. The **Three Choirs Way** is a 100-mile route connecting the cathedrals of Hereford, Worcester and Gloucester, where the music festival of the same name has been celebrated for more than three centuries.

The **Herefordshire Trail** (www.herefordshiretrail .com) is a 150-mile circular loop linking Leominster, Ledbury, Ross-on-Wye and Kington.

Getting Around

Busy railway stations with nationwide links can be found at Hereford, Leominster and Ledbury. To plan your way about, pick up a free *Public Transport Map & Guide* from tourist offices and bus stations, or go online through **Hereford Bus** (www.hereford bus.info) and **National Traveline** (☎ 0870 200 2233; www.traveline midlands.co.uk).

HEREFORD

pop 56,353

Straddling the River Wye at the heart of the county, agricultural capital Hereford is known for its cattle, cider and relationship with the composer Elgar. Even though it's the county capital it has a sluggish, provincial feel, although there are some youthful pockets in the centre and along its riverside. Hereford's most cherished possession is the extraordinary medieval map, the Mappa Mundi, housed in its dignified cathedral.

Orientation & Information

The triangular, pedestrianised High Town is the city's heart, just north of the River Wye. The cathedral is close to the river, while the bus and train stations lie to the northeast, on Commercial Rd.

The **tourist office** (☎ 01432-268430; www.visit herefordshire.co.uk; 1 King St; 🕑 9am-5pm Mon-Sat) is opposite the cathedral. **Guided walks** (£3; 🕑 11am Mon-Sat, 2.30pm Sun May-Sep) start from here. There's free internet access at the **library** (Broad St; 🕑 9.30am-7.30pm Tue-Wed & Fri, 9.30am-5.30pm Thu, 9.30am-4pm Sat), in the same building as the Hereford Museum & Art Gallery.

Sights
HEREFORD CATHEDRAL

After the Welsh torched the town's original cathedral, the new **Hereford Cathedral** (☎ 01432-374200; www.herefordcathedral.org; 5 College Cloisters; suggested donation £4; 🕑 7.30am-Evensong) began life on the same site in the 11th century. The building has evolved into a well-packaged lesson on the entire history of English architecture: the sturdy south transept is Norman but holds a 16th-century triptych; the exquisite north transept with its soaring windows dates from the 13th century; the choir and the tower date from the 14th century; and the Victorian influence is visible almost everywhere.

But the cathedral is best known for two ancient treasures housed here. The magnificent 13th-century **Mappa Mundi** (adult/child £4.50/3.50; 🕑 10am-5pm Mon-Sat & 11am-3pm Sun May-Sep, 10am-4pm Mon-Sat Oct-Apr) is a large calfskin vellum map intricately painted with the vivid world vision of the era's scholars, and an enthralling pictorial encyclopedia of the times. It is the largest

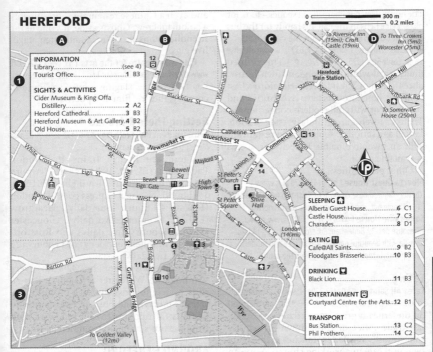

HEREFORD

0 — 300 m
0 — 0.2 miles

INFORMATION
Library.......................................(see 4)
Tourist Office...............................1 B3

SIGHTS & ACTIVITIES
Cider Museum & King Offa
  Distillery.................................2 A2
Hereford Cathedral.......................3 B3
Hereford Museum & Art Gallery.....4 B2
Old House..................................5 B2

SLEEPING
Alberta Guest House..................6 C1
Castle House.............................7 C3
Charades..................................8 D1

EATING
Cafe@All Saints.........................9 B2
Floodgates Brasserie..................10 B3

DRINKING
Black Lion.................................11 B3

ENTERTAINMENT
Courtyard Centre for the Arts...12 B1

TRANSPORT
Bus Station...............................13 C2
Phil Prothero.............................14 C2

To Riverside Inn (15mi); Croft Castle (19mi)
To Three Crowns Inn (5mi); Worcester (25mi)
Hereford Train Station
To Somerville House (250m)
To London (140mi)
To Golden Valley (12mi)

THE WEST MIDLANDS & THE MARCHES

and best-preserved example of this type of cartography anywhere, but more than that it's a bewitching journey through the world as then envisioned, roamed by basilisks and mythological monsters. Navigate your way through the barely recognisable mash of continents and you can even find Hereford itself.

The same wing contains the world's largest surviving **chained library**, hooked to its shelves by a cascade of long thin shackles. The unique collection of rare books and manuscripts includes a 1217 copy of the revised Magna Carta and the 8th-century *Hereford Gospels*, although the gospels' fragility means they aren't always on display.

The cathedral comes alive with Evensong at 5.30pm Monday to Saturday and 3.30pm on Sunday, and every three years in August it holds the famous **Three Choirs Festival** (www.3choirs.org), shared with Gloucester and Worcester Cathedrals.

OTHER SIGHTS

Marooned in a sea of bustling shops, the **Old House** (☎ 01432-260694; admission free; 10am-5pm Tue-Sat year-round, plus 10am-4pm Sun Apr-Sep) is a

wonderfully creaky black-and-white, three-storey wooden house, built in 1621, panelled and furnished in exquisitely carved wood.

The quirky collection at **Hereford Museum & Art Gallery** (☎ 01432-260692; Broad St; admission free; 10am-5pm Tue-Sat year-round, plus 10am-4pm Sun Apr-Sep) includes just about everything from 19th-century witches' curses to Roman antiquities. There's also some dressing-up gear to keep kids entertained.

Don't forget to claim your free samples in the **Cider Museum & King Offa Distillery** (☎ 01432-354207; www.cidermuseum.co.uk; Pomona Pl; adult/child £3.50/2; 10am-5pm Tue-Sat Apr-Oct, 11am-3pm Tue-Sat Nov-Mar), which explores cider-making history. Look for the fine costrels (minibarrels) and horn mugs used by agricultural workers to carry and quaff their wages, which were partially paid in cider.

Sleeping

Charades (☎ 01432-269444; www.charadeshereford.co .uk; 34 Southbank Rd; s/d £45/65; P) This imposing Georgian house built around 1870 has five recently revamped, comfortable rooms, some with soul-restoring views over the countryside.

The house itself has character in spades – look for old service bells in the hall. It's handy for the bus station, but a 1km walk from the cathedral.

Castle House (☎ 01432-356321; www.castlehse.co.uk; Castle St; s £120, d £175-220; P) This refined multiaward-winning Georgian town house, once the bishop's residence, is Hereford's best boutique hotel. Rooms have rich fabrics and classic decor with full modern conveniences. There's a lovely garden and riverside seating, as well as a seriously sophisticated restaurant with an inventive menu. Wheelchair access is available.

Other possibilities:

Alberta Guest House (☎ 01432-270313; www.thealbertaguesthouse.co.uk; 5-13 Newtown Rd; s/d £30/55; P) Simple but warm welcome in the town's north.

Somerville House (☎ 01432-273991; www.somervillehouse.net; 12 Bodenham Rd; s/d £50/79; P) Victorian villa with beautiful gardens and terrace and modern boutique-style rooms, 250m away from the centre.

Eating

Cafe@All Saints (☎ 01432-370414; www.cafeatallsaints.co.uk; High St; mains £3.60-8.75; 9am-5pm Mon-Sat) Sit underneath great stone arches as you sip fair-trade coffee or chow down on wholesome (mostly vegetarian) lunches in this natty two-level cafe in a working church. You can even enjoy a glass of wine – just remember, God's watching.

Floodgates Brasserie (☎ 01432-349000; Left Bank Village, Bridge St; mains £12.50-18; lunch & dinner) Part of the Left Bank Village complex, in a prime riverside spot, this sleek modern restaurant is slightly lacking in character but it has a lovely terrace overlooking the river, a sunny interior and a fine modern European menu.

our pick **Three Crowns Inn** (☎ 01432-820279; www.threecrownsinn.com; Ullingswick; mains £15; lunch & dinner Tue-Sun) Burrow into the countryside, 5 miles northeast of Hereford, to find this gorgeous 16th-century half-timbered gastropub. It's worth seeking out for its delicious organic food, rare-breed meats and homemade cheese. It also has classy rooms (singles/doubles £80/95).

Drinking & Entertainment

Black Lion (☎ 01432-343535; 31 Bridge St) The more real ales and local ciders you knock back in this traditional pub, the more you may believe the tales of resident ghosts from the site's history as a monastery, an orphanage, a brothel and even a Chinese restaurant – presumably a colourful crew. Ghosts aside, it's one of the friendliest inns in the area and often stages live gigs.

Courtyard Centre for the Arts (☎ 0870 112 2330; www.courtyard.org.uk; Edgar St) This lively arts centre has two venues staging a busy schedule of comedy, theatre, film and poetry.

Getting There & Around

Hire bikes at **Phil Prothero** (☎ 01432-359478; Bastion Mews) for £12 per day.

There are hourly trains to London Paddington (£37.20, 3¼ hours) via Newport, South Wales; and to Birmingham (£12.90, 1½ hours). National Express goes to London (£20.40, 4¼ hours, four daily), Heathrow (£21.10, 4¼ hours, two daily), Gloucester (£5.90, 1¼ hours, five daily) and Ross-on-Wye (30 minutes, four daily) or Ledbury (25 minutes, two daily).

From the bus station, bus 420 runs every two hours to Worcester (1¼ hours). Bus 38 runs hourly to Ross-on-Wye (40 minutes, six on Sunday), and bus 476 goes hourly to Ledbury (30 minutes, five on Sunday) – both from the bus station on Commercial Rd.

AROUND HEREFORD

Golden Valley

Nudging the foot of the Black Mountains, this lush valley was made famous by children's author CS Lewis (of *Narnia* acclaim) and the film that sought to portray him, *Shadowlands*. It follows the meandering River Dore (hence the name) and boasts gently undulating vistas peppered with historical ruins.

For more details or accommodation ideas, see www.golden-valley.co.uk.

Aymestrey & Around

our pick **Riverside Inn** (☎ 01568-708440; www.theriversideinn.org; Aymestrey; s/d £50/75; P) is a classic 16th-century black-and-white coaching inn resting alongside the River Lugg in the diminutive village of Aymestrey. There are terraced gardens behind the inn as well as tables right down by the river from where to enjoy bewitching views of the gurgling waters. Hop-strewn beams and red lamps mellow the bar and restaurant, and there are a handful of rustic bedrooms containing sturdy wooden furniture and rough walls. The modern British menu (mains £12 to £16) uses overwhelmingly local produce, much of it freshly plucked from the

---

BLACK-AND-WHITE VILLAGES

A triangle of Tudor England survives almost untouched in northwest Herefordshire, where higgledy-piggledy black-and-white villages cluster round idyllic greens, seemingly oblivious to the modern world. A wonderful 40-mile circular drive follows the **Black-and-white-village Trail**, meandering past the most handsome timber-framed buildings, old churches and tranquil villages. You can pick up a guide from any tourist office for 75p (there are also CD versions and an accommodation pamphlet available).

The route starts at **Leominster** and climaxes at **Eardisland**, one of the prettiest of all the villages. Also memorable is chocolate-box **Pembridge**, with its gaggle of classic houses; it makes a good base for touring the area, with lots of circular walks radiating from the village and the Mortimer Trail just to the north.

For stunning food and cosy accommodation head for the award-winning **Stagg Inn** (☎ 01544-230221; www.thestagg.co.uk; Titley; s £50-60, d £70-90; ☯ closed Sun evening & Mon). The first pub to be awarded a Michelin star, this is a wonderfully welcoming place that combines culinary excellence with a laid-back approach (mains £13 to £17). Roaring fires and antiques complement the warm ambience, and there are a handful of lovely rooms, making the roll home with a full and happy belly all the easier.

The 3-mile Titley Loop Walk begins here and winds through gorgeous countryside, making it a good way to work up an appetite.

---

inn's own herb and vegetable garden. Walkers should note that this place is about midway along the Mortimer Trail; it makes a wonderful stopover or a thirst-quenching pause to indulge in the real local ale. Aymestrey is on the A4110, 15 miles north of Hereford.

Two miles east of Aymestrey, and well beyond reach of a bus, is castellated country house **Croft Castle** (NT; ☎ 01568-780246; off the B4362; adult/child £6.50/3.25; ☯ 1-5pm Wed-Sun Apr-Sep, 1-4pm Sat & Sun Mar & Oct), worth the trip if you're turned on by flamboyant 18th century interiors.

Kilpeck Church

Deep in the Herefordshire countryside is the tiny hamlet of Kilpeck, home to a beguiling little Norman **church** that has barely changed since the 12th century. Original carvings encircle the building, from cartoon like pigs and bunnies, mythical monsters, grimacing heads, to a famous spread-legged *sheila-na-gig* (Celtic fertility figure). It's an extraordinary sight, well worth the 1-mile trip south of the main A465 road that comes from Hereford. Kilpeck is 9 miles south of Hereford, off the A465.

HAY-ON-WYE
pop 1450

Your inner bookworm will wriggle with joy upon discovery of Hay-on-Wye: this tiny border town has totally submitted itself to the second-hand book trade and is a point of pilgrimage for idle browsers, eagle-eyed collectors, and serious academics from around the world. That said, it's not just for book nuts but for anyone who enjoys a flick through everything from murder mysteries to classic children's stories to fascinating antique travel tomes.

The town straddles the border with Wales and on 1 April 1977 it famously declared itself independent from Britain, inviting a storm of publicity from around the world (see boxed text, p567). Every year for a week in May/June, the town becomes the centre of the literary universe for the **Hay Festival of Literature** (www.hayfestival.com), attracting big shots from the worlds of literature, art and politics, from Salman Rushdie to Jimmy Carter. For further information contact the **Hay Festival Office** (☎ 0870 727 2848; Drill Hall, 25 Lion St).

The **tourist office** (☎ 01497-820144; www.hay-on-wye.co.uk; Oxford Rd; ☯ 10am-1pm & 2-5pm Easter-Oct, 11am-1pm & 2-4pm Nov-Easter) is by the main car park. It has a couple of internet terminals.

Activities

Hay sits on the northeastern corner of Brecon Beacons National Park and makes an excellent base to explore western Herefordshire and the Welsh Black Mountains. The **Offa's Dyke Path** walking route (see p528) passes nearby. The Offa's Dyke Flyer circular minibus runs three times on summer Sundays and Bank Holidays

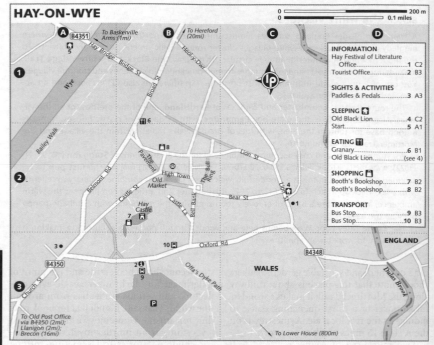

HAY-ON-WYE

INFORMATION
Hay Festival of Literature
Office.............................1 C2
Tourist Office.....................2 B3

SIGHTS & ACTIVITIES
Paddles & Pedals.................3 A3

SLEEPING
Old Black Lion...................4 C2
Start............................5 A1

EATING
Granary..........................6 B1
Old Black Lion.............(see 4)

SHOPPING
Booth's Bookshop................7 B2
Booth's Bookshop................8 B2

TRANSPORT
Bus Stop.........................9 B3
Bus Stop........................10 B3

to help you along the way. The tourist office has schedules.

For fun on the River Wye, hire kayaks and Canadian canoes from **Paddles & Pedals** (☎ 01497-820604; www.canoehire.co.uk; 15 Castle St; canoes per half-/full day £25/35; ☼ Easter-Oct), which, despite the name, doesn't 'do bikes. Rental prices include return transport to points along the Wye, depending on which route you're taking.

Sleeping

Don't bet on a bed *anywhere* nearby while the festival is on.

Start (☎ 01497-821391; www.the-start.net; Hay Bridge; s/d £35/60; **P**) This 18th-century stone cottage stands alone on a grassy bank on the opposite side of the river, giving it a blissful feeling of space and solitude despite it being only a short scenic walk across the bridge. Patchwork quilts adorn the pleasant country-style rooms – some of which have a view of the river – and there are good lock-up and drying facilities for hikers and bikers. Packed lunches and afternoon teas are also available.

Old Black Lion (☎ 01497-820841; www.oldblacklion .co.uk; Lion St; s/d £42.50/95; **P**) Atmospheric 17th-century inn full of blackened oak beams and moody lighting. The 10 spacious bedrooms are full of sturdy county furniture and rich fabrics, and each has its own show-stealing teddy bear.

Old Post Office (☎ 01497-820008; www.oldpost-office .co.uk; Llanigon; d from £60; **P**) If you've got your own wheels, this gorgeous converted village post office, 2 miles southwest of Hay off the B4350, is a fantastic option – all polished-oak floors, exposed beams, earthy colours and rural Welsh furniture. Breakfast is vegetarian: no artery-clogging meat feasts here.

our pick Lower House (☎ 01497-820773; www .lowerhousegardenhay.co.uk; Cusop Dingle; s/d £65/85; **P**) Wonderful guest house in a luscious self-contained valley of woods, orchard, fields and a stream. The two pretty guest rooms have wooden floors, window seats, retro radios and awesome views; one has wood-panelled walls and its own private sitting room, and, this being Hay-on-Wye, both rooms come with a healthy selection of books. The rooms share a heavily beamed

---

KING OF HAY-ON-WYE

King of the world's first book town, Richard Booth opened his first bookshop in Hay in 1961, but was dismayed by the falling fortunes and declining populations of rural areas. Not content to sit back and watch, he hatched a wacky plan to regenerate the town.

By 1977 he had persuaded a clutch of other booksellers to join him, and on April Fools' Day that year declared the border town independent from Britain. The town celebrated with a giant party as Booth was crowned in royal robes, orb and a sceptre made from an old ball cock and copper piping. As weird as the idea was, it had the desired effect and Hay hit the headlines all over the country.

Over 30 years on, Hay has more bookshops than even the most dedicated bibliophile can handle, and a host of thriving local businesses catering to the five million visitors a year. It has also been the inspiration for roughly 20 other international book towns, often in rural areas facing similar decline.

Aspiring lords and ladies can even apply for Hay Peerage, awarded by the king himself. See www.richardbooth.demon.co.uk/haypeerage/ for information.

---

guest drawing room complete with fireplace and grand piano. The house is about a 800 south of town along Offa's Dyke Path, which runs behind the house; or follow the B4348 east to Cusop Dingle.

Eating

Granary (☎ 01497-820790; Broad St; mains £6-10; ⦾ 10am-5pm) Housed in a converted grain store, this rustic cafe and restaurant serves wholesome home-cooked meals with plenty of vegetarian and vegan choices, tummy-rumbling cakes, fine cheeses and other local delicacies. If you have to disturb the peace and get online, they have free wi-fi.

Baskerville Arms (☎ 01497-821609; www.basker villearms.co.uk; Clyro; mains £7 12; ⦾ lunch & dinner) This country hotel, just over a mile northwest of Hay, has a good French chef, welcoming staff and lovely views of the countryside. It lights up a log fire in winter and the dining room is candlelit at night.

Old Black Lion (☎ 01497-820841; Lion St; mains £12-18; ⦾ lunch & dinner) This famous old inn's candlelit dining room has hops hanging from its low-beamed ceiling, stripped-pine tables, and is thick with romance and atmosphere. There are robust local ales on offer and a memorable menu including wonderful locally sourced lamb.

Shopping

The tourist office and most shops stock the handy pamphlet guide to the town's three dozen bookshops, from 'Murder and Mayhem' to the Cinema Bookshop. The most famous is **Booth's Bookshop** (☎ 01497-

820322; www.richardbooth.demon.co.uk; 44 Lion St; ⦾ 9am-8pm Mon-Sat, 11.30am-5.30pm Sun Apr-Oct, 9am-8pm Mon, Fri & Sat, 11.30am-5.30pm Sun, 9am-5.30pm Tue-Thu Nov-Mar), which supposedly has the highest turnover of second-hand books of any bookshop in the world. A smaller specialist arm is housed in a Jacobean mansion built into the walls of the battered 13th-century town castle.

Getting There & Away

If you're driving, allow time to cruise because the countryside is spellbinding.

Bus 39 from Hereford (55 minutes) and from Brecon (45 minutes) runs roughly every two hours Monday to Saturday.

ROSS-ON-WYE
pop 10,085

Snoozy little Ross-on-Wye, which perches prettily on a red sandstone bluff over a kink in the River Wye, is a gentle place to rest before or after exertions in the beautiful countryside that surrounds it. The town sparks to life in mid-August, when the **International Festival** brings fireworks, raft races, music and street theatre.

The salmon-pink 17th-century Market House sits atop its weathered sandstone columns in the Market Place. It contains a **Heritage Centre** (☎ 01989-260675; ⦾ 10am-5pm Mon-Sat, 10.30am-4pm Sun Apr-Oct, 10.30am-4pm Mon-Sat Nov-Mar) with local-history displays. The **tourist office** (☎ 01989-562768; tic-ross@herefordshire .gov.uk; Edde Cross St; ⦾ 9am-5pm Mon-Sat) has information on activities and walks.

Sleeping & Eating

White House Guest House (☎ 01989-763572; www
.whitehouseross.com; Wye St; s/d £45/65; **P** **□** wi-fi)
This 18th-century stone house has a great
location across the road from the River Wye.
Vivid window boxes give it a splash of colour and the rooms, decorated in rich shades
of burgundy and crisp white, are peaceful
and comfortable.

Bridge at Wilton (☎ 01989-562655; www.bridge
-house-hotel.com; Wilton; s/d from £80/98; **P**) A distinguished Georgian country house, a riverside
setting a short tumble down from town, and
a highly praised modern British restaurant
dedicated to local produce make this a wonderful spot to linger. Eight classically styled
rooms overlook the gardens and river.

Pots and Pieces (☎ 01989-566123; 40 High St; mains
£4.50-6; ⊙ 9am-5pm Mon-Fri, from 10am Sat) You can
browse all manner of ceramics, ironwork, jewellery and glassware before relaxing with a
postbrowse cream tea or frothy hot chocolate
at this cafe-cum-gallery. Savoury lunchtime
goodies are also available.

The closest hostel is 6 miles south at Welsh
Bicknor (see below).

Drinking

Hope & Anchor (☎ 01989-563003; Wye St) This
friendly riverside pub is a great place to
while away the time, especially in the summer, when tables spread right down the grassy
bank to the water's' edge and overflow with
happy customers.

Getting There & Around

Buses 38 and 33 run hourly Monday to
Saturday to and from Hereford and Gloucester
respectively (40 minutes each way).

You can hire bikes from **Revolutions**
(☎ 01989-562639; 48 Broad St; per day from £10).

AROUND ROSS-ON-WYE
Goodrich

Seemingly part of its craggy bedrock, **Goodrich
Castle** (EH; ☎ 01600-890538; adult/child £5/2.50; ⊙ 10am-
6pm daily Jun-Aug, 10am-5pm daily Mar-May & Sep-Oct,
10am-4pm Wed-Sun Nov-Feb) is an exceptionally
complete medieval castle, topped by a superb 12th-century keep that rewards the trek
up tight winding staircases with spectacular
views. A small exhibition tells the story of
the castle from its 11th-century origins to its
demise in the 1600s.

TOP PUBS FOR SUNDAY LUNCH

- Riverside Inn (p564; Aymestrey)
- Stagg Inn (p565; Titley)
- Three Crowns Inn (p564; Ullingswick)
- Waterdine Inn (p584; Llanfair Water-
  dine)

Welsh Bicknor YHA (☎ 0845 371 9666; www.yha
.org.uk; dm £18; ⊙ Apr-Oct; **P**) is well worth the
thigh-pumping 1½-mile climb to reach it
from Goodrich village. This austere-looking
former Victorian rectory surveys the glorious
countryside from 10 hectares of lovely riverside grounds. The Wye Valley Walk passes
the hostel.

Goodrich is 5 miles south of Ross off
the A40. Bus 34 stops here every two hours
on its way between Ross (15 minutes) and
Monmouth (20 minutes).

Symonds Yat

A remote little nook, huddled against the
River Wye, Symonds Yat is well worth a visit
for water babies, bird enthusiasts and those
fond of a relaxed riverside pint. An ancient
hand-hauled ferry (adult/child 80/40p) joins
two separate hill-backed villages on either
bank, usually with a few ducks hitching a
ride on the back. There's an abrupt change
of mood in upper Symonds Yat West, where
you'll find a big tacky fairground jingling to
the sound of pocket change, slot machines
and carousels.

ACTIVITIES

This area is renowned for canoeing and rock
climbing and there's also good hiking in the
nearby Forest of Dean. The **Wyedean Canoe
Centre** (☎ 01594-833238; www.wyedean.co.uk) hires
out canoes/kayaks from £20/16 for half-day,
and also organises multiday kayaking trips,
white-water trips, caving and climbing. Note
that the river has a strong current and is not
suitable for swimming.

From Symonds Yat East, it's a steep but
easy walk (at least on a dry day) up 504m
to the crown of the region, **Symonds Yat Rock**,
from where you'll get a fabulous view of the
river and valley. You can catch a rare glimpse
of the world's fastest creature doing aerial
acrobatics here, as peregrine falcons nest in
the cliffs opposite.

If that all sounds like too much hard work, **Kingfisher Cruises** (☎ 01600-891063) runs sedate 35-minute gorge cruises from beside the ferry crossing.

SLEEPING & EATING

Garth Cottage (☎ 01600-890364; www.garthcottage -symondsyat.com; Symonds Yat East; d £72; ☻ Apr-Oct; **P**) The pick of accommodation on the east side, this friendly, family-run B&B sits demurely by the riverside near the ferry crossing, and has spotlessly maintained, bright rooms with river views. Breakfast is served in the conservatory or on the terrace, both overlooking the water.

Saracen's Head (☎ 01600-890435; www.saracens headinn.co.uk; Symonds Yat East; mains £10-20; **P**) This black-and-white traditional inn is Symonds Yat's focal point, next to the ferry crossing. It has some river-view rooms (doubles from £74) sporting pine furniture and polished wood floors, and two luxury suites in the boathouse. It's a popular spot to enjoy a meal while waiting for the moment when the ferryman topples into the river.

Old Court Hotel (☎ 01600-890367; www.oldcourt hotel.co.uk; Symonds Yat West; r £80-200; **P**) This striking 16th-century manor house enchants history buffs without stinting on up-to-the-minute modern comforts. It's set in lovely gardens, complete with heated pool, and some rooms have characterful beams and four-posters, others crisp modern interiors. Children over 12 are welcome. Old Court is on the northern entrance to Symonds Yat West, across the river and roughly a 1-mile walk from the ferry crossing.

GETTING THERE & AWAY

Bus 34 can drop you off on the main road 1.5 miles from the village. Bikes are available for hire from the Royal Hotel (Symonds Yat East) for £13 per day.

LEDBURY
pop 8491

An atmospheric little town abundant with history and antique shops, Ledbury is a favourite destination for day trippers. The best way to pass the time is to simply wander its dense core of crooked black-and-white streets, which zero in on a delightfully leggy market house.

The helpful **tourist office** (☎ 01531-636147; tic -ledbury@herefordshire.gov.uk; 3 The Homend; ☻ 10am-5pm

Mon-Sat Apr-Oct, to 4pm Nov-Mar) has details about a lovely 17-mile cycle route called the Ledbury Loop (50p). To get online visit part ice-cream parlour, part internet cafe **Ice Bytes** (☎ 01531-634700; 38 The Homend; per 15min £1).

Sights

Ledbury's centrepiece is the delicate black-and-white **Market House**, a 17th-century timber-framed structure precariously balanced atop 16 narrow wooden posts supposedly gleaned from the defeated Spanish Armada. From here, wander up the narrow cobbled **Church Lane**, crowded with tilted timber-framed buildings, including the **Painted Room** (admission free; ☻ 11am-1pm & 2-4pm Mon-Fri Easter-Sep), with jigsaw-puzzle 16th-century floral frescos.

Here too are several small museums, including **Butcher's Row House** (☎ 01531-632942; Church Lane; admission free; ☻ 11am-5pm Easter-Sep), a pocket-sized folk museum stuffed with curios from 19th-century school clothing to an 18th-century communal 'boot' bath that used to be carted from door to door for the poor to scrub in. The **Heritage Centre** (☎ 01531-260692; admission free; ☻ 10.30am-4.30pm Easter-Oct) sits in another half-timbered treasure opposite and has more displays of the town.

At the top of the lane lies the 12th-century church of **St Michael and All Angels**, with a splendid 18th-century spire and tower separate from the church.

Sleeping & Eating

Budget travellers may struggle to find accommodation in Ledbury.

Talbot Hotel (☎ 01531-632963; www.visitledbury .co.uk/talbot; New St; s/d £55/80; **P**) A black-and-white, late-16th-century coaching inn with a lively little bar and dark oak-panelled restaurant, the Talbot also has a handful of simple, compact rooms in what used to be the hay loft. It can get a little noisy on weekends and breakfast costs extra.

Feathers Hotel (☎ 01531-635266; www.feathers -ledbury.co.uk; High St; s/d from £85/125; **P**) This charming black-and-white Tudor hotel looms over the main road. It has a mixture of rooms – ask for one in the oldest part of the building, which come with slanting floorboards and painted beams. Most of the modern rooms lack character. There's also a swimming pool.

The Verzon (☎ 01531-670381; www.verzonhouse .com; A438, Trumpet; s £90-105, d £155-175; **P** ☐) The ultimate country-chic retreat, 3 miles west of Ledbury, this lovely Georgian farmhouse has undergone a rather debonair makeover without sacrificing its rustic charm. Its eight rooms are luxuriously appointed with tactile tweeds, stand-alone baths, goose down pillows, and plush wool carpets. The brasserie's classic menu ranges from scrumptious roast rabbit in mustard sauce to Cornish lobster (mains £10 to £17).

Cameron & Swan (☎ 01531-636791; www.cameron andswan.co.uk; 15 The Homend; mains £6-7; ☷ lunch) New, bustling deli-cafe serving tasty deli platters, homemade tarts, cakes and bakes in a bright, airy dining room.

The Malthouse (☎ 01531-634443; www.malthouse -ledbury.co.uk; Church Lane; mains £13-20; ☷ dinner Tue-Sat, lunch Sat only) Walk through a pretty walled garden to find an elegant restaurant in an ivy-covered converted barn. Modern British food is on offer, locally sourced and with good choice of vegie options.

Getting There & Around

There are roughly hourly trains to Hereford (15 minutes), less often to Great Malvern (11 minutes), Worcester (23 to 27 minutes) and Birmingham (£11.50, 1¼ hours).

Bus 476 runs to Hereford hourly (30 minutes, every two hours on Sunday); bus 132 runs hourly to Gloucester (one hour).

You can hire mountain bikes at **Saddle Bound Cycles** (☎ 633433; 3 The Southend; per day £12).

AROUND LEDBURY
Eastnor Castle

Built more for fancy than fortification, the extravagant 19th-century medieval-revival folly of **Eastnor Castle** (☎ 01531-633160; www.eastnor castle.com; adult/child £8/5, grounds only £4/2) seems to have leapt out of the pages of a bedtime story. The opulent interior continues the romantic veneer, decorated in Gothic and Italianate features, tapestries and antiques. Even when the castle is closed – call or check the website, as the opening days are quite complicated – its maze, adventure playground and lakeside walks are worth a look. Its beautiful deer park is also stage to the **Big Chill** (☎ 020-7684 2020; www.bigchill.net; ☷ Aug), when campers, musicians, performers and artists round off the summer festival season in relaxed fashion.

The castle is just over 2 miles east of Ledbury on the A438. The Malvern Hills

Hopper bus runs here from Upton-upon-Severn and Great Malvern on summer weekends and Bank Holidays.

Much Marcle

The tiny village of Much Marcle isn't much more than a blip on the map, but it's home to one of England's oldest and most fascinating houses – **Hellens** (☎ 01531-660504; www .hellensmanor.com; adult/child £5/2.50; ☷ tours 2pm, 3pm & 4pm Wed, Thu, Sun & Bank Holidays Apr-Sep), a time capsule of English history dating right back to the 11th century. The superb 17th-century interiors echo the gallantry of that age, and there are heirlooms of Ann Boleyn, Mary Tudor, King Charles and more. The descendents of its 13th-century masters still own the house and admit visitors on guided tours only. Outside, the restored Tudor and Jacobean gardens and charming octagonal dovecote are wonderful.

Afterwards, you can celebrate the fact that you're deep in cider country by raising a glass at **Westons Cider Mills** (☎ 01531-660233; www.westons-cider.co.uk; The Bounds; ☷ 9am-4.30pm Mon-Fri, 10am-4pm Sat & Sun), just under a mile west of Hellens over the A449. Henry Weston started dabbling with cider and perry here in the 1870s; soon the local MP got Weston's cider put on tap in the parliament bar, and the rest is history. Tours (adult/child £5/3, 1¼ hours) are at 11am, 12.30pm and 2.30pm, and include the all-important tasting session.

Bus 45 from Ledbury (40 minutes) goes to Much Marcle four times per day Monday to Friday and five times on Saturday.

SHROPSHIRE

Dreamily beautiful and sparsely populated, Shropshire ripples over the River Severn from the Welsh border to Birmingham. The surroundings are most beautiful in the south, where the land is ripe with stunning moorland, gurgling rivers and pretty villages; and its undulating, heather-tickled hills make for awesome walking territory. The lovely Tudor town of Shrewsbury is the county capital, and nestled nearby is the remarkable World Heritage site of Ironbridge Gorge. At the county's base you'll find foodie magnet Ludlow, with its handsome castle and epicurean ways.

Information

For online county information:

North Shropshire (www.northshropshire.co.uk)
Secret Shropshire (www.secretshropshire.org.uk)
Shropshire Tourism (www.shropshiretourism.info)
Virtual Shropshire (www.virtual-shropshire.co.uk)
Visit South Shropshire (www.visitsouthshropshire
.co.uk)

Getting Around

Handy rail services from Shrewsbury go to
Church Stretton, Craven Arms and Ludlow.
The invaluable *Shropshire Bus & Train Map*,
available free from tourist offices, shows public transport routes. **Shropshire Hills Shuttle Buses**
(www.shropshirehillsshuttles.co.uk) also drops off walkers along popular hiking routes on weekends
and Bank Holidays. Call **Traveline** (☎ 0870 200
2233; www.traveline.org.uk) with any queries.

SHREWSBURY

pop 67,126

The higgledy-piggledy mass of medieval
streets in the heart of Shropshire's most picturesque town don't take long to work their
magic. Ancient passageways wind their way
between crooked Tudor buildings; dusky-
red sandstone warms an ancient abbey and
castle, and elegant parks tumble down to the
River Severn.

Nudging a horseshoe loop in the river,
Shrewsbury's defensive potential was crucial
in keeping the Welsh in line for many centuries. Then in medieval times the town grew
fat on the wool trade. It is also the birthplace
of Charles Darwin (1809–82), who rocked the
world with his theory of evolution.

Orientation

Shrewsbury's near-island status helps preserve
the Tudor and Jacobean streetscapes of its
centre and protects it from unattractive urban
sprawl. The train station is a five-minute walk
northeast of the centre and is as far as you'll
need to venture.

Information

Library (☎ 01743-255300; Castle Gates; ⏰ 9.30am-
5pm Mon, Wed, Fri & Sat, 9.30am-8pm Tue & Thu, 1-4pm
Sun) Free internet access.
Royal Shrewsbury Hospital (☎ 01743-261000;
Mytton Oak Rd)
Tourist office (☎ 01743-281200; www.visitshrewsbury
.com; Music Hall, The Square; ⏰ 9.30am-5.30pm Mon-

Sat, 10am-4pm Sun May-Sep; 10am-5pm Mon-Sat Oct-
Apr) Guided walking tours (adult/child £3.50/1.50 1½hr)
leave the tourist office at 2.30pm Monday to Saturday,
and 11am Sunday from May to September and at 2.30pm
Saturday only from November to April.

Sights

SHREWSBURY ABBEY

Most famous as a setting for monastic who-
dunits the *Chronicles of Brother Cadfael*
by Ellis Peters, the lovely red-sandstone
Shrewsbury Abbey (☎ 01743-232723; www.shrewsbury
abbey.com; Abbey Foregate; donation adult/child £2/1;
⏰ 10am-4.30pm Mon-Sat, 11.30am-2.30pm Sun) is what
remains of a large Benedictine monastery
founded in 1083, its outbuildings mostly lost
and its flanks unceremoniously chopped. It's
graced by a mix of Norman, Early English and
Victorian features and there's an exceptional
14th-century west window of heraldic glass.
The abbey is renowned for its fine acoustics
and a noticeboard provides information on
upcoming recitals.

SHREWSBURY MUSEUM & ART GALLERY

Rowley's House, the stunning timber-framed
Tudor merchant's mansion and warehouse in
which **Shrewsbury Museum & Art Gallery** (☎ 01743-
361196; www.shrewsburymuseums.com; Barker St; admission
free; ⏰ 10am-5pm Mon-Sat, to 4pm Sun Jun-Sep, 10am-4pm
Oct-May) is housed, is as much of an attraction
as its exhibits, which range from Roman finds
to Darwin's times. At the time of writing, the
museum was due to move to the Music Hall
in 2011, forming a part of a new museum
and tourist office. It will be closed for several
months a year until then.

Walking Tour

Begin your tour at the town's tourist office.
The mellow-stone building balancing on
chunky legs opposite you is Shrewsbury's
16th-century **Market Hall**, hub of the historic
wool trade. Look out for the holes in the pillars, which were used to count how many
fleeces were sold.

The most impressive of Shrewsbury's black-
and-white beauties, the stern timber-framed
Ireland's Mansion grabs attention to your left as
you step up to High St. Turn right and cross
over into charmingly named, narrow little
Grope Lane with its overhanging buildings, and
you'll emerge into atmospheric **Fish Street** and
see some steps leading to the 14th-century
Bear Steps Hall (⏰ 10am-4pm), now home to a

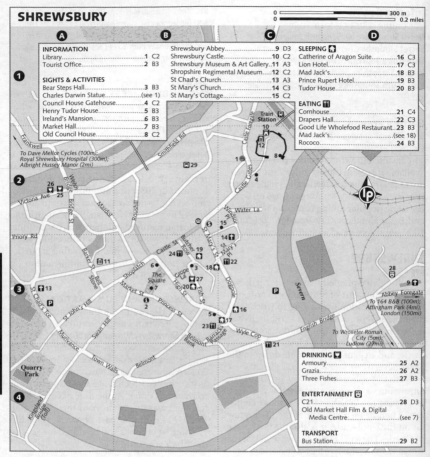

SHREWSBURY

0 ——— 300 m
0 ——— 0.2 miles

INFORMATION
Library......................................1 C2
Tourist Office..........................2 B3

SIGHTS & ACTIVITIES
Bear Steps Hall.......................3 B3
Charles Darwin Statue...........(see 1)
Council House Gatehouse.......4 C2
Henry Tudor House..................5 B3
Ireland's Mansion...................6 B3
Market Hall.............................7 B3
Old Council House..................8 C2

Shrewsbury Abbey..................9 D3
Shrewsbury Castle................10 C2
Shrewsbury Museum & Art Gallery..11 A3
Shropshire Regimental Museum..12 C2
St Chad's Church...................13 A3
St Mary's Church...................14 C3
St Mary's Cottage.................15 C2

SLEEPING 🏠
Catherine of Aragon Suite.......16 C3
Lion Hotel.............................17 C3
Mad Jack's............................18 B3
Prince Rupert Hotel................19 B3
Tudor House..........................20 B3

EATING 🍴
Cornhouse.............................21 C4
Drapers Hall..........................22 C3
Good Life Wholefood Restaurant..23 B3
Mad Jack's............................(see 18)
Rococo..................................24 B3

DRINKING 🍸
Armoury................................25 A2
Grazia...................................26 A2
Three Fishes.........................27 B3

ENTERTAINMENT 🎭
C21......................................28 D3
Old Market Hall Film & Digital
   Media Centre.....................(see 7)

TRANSPORT
Bus Station............................29 B2

small exhibition space. On the hall's other side is **Butcher Row**, home to more atmospheric black-and-white lovelies.

Head another street north to check out the magnificent spire of medieval **St Mary's Church** (St Mary's St; 11am-4pm Fri-Sun May-Sep), one of the highest in England. Duck inside for a peek at the astonishingly vivid Jesse window made from rare mid-14th-century glass.

Turn left into Windsor Place, before taking the second right into Castle St. You can't miss the entrance to russet **Shrewsbury Castle**, home to the stiff-upper-lip **Shropshire Regimental Museum** (☎ 01743-358516; adult/child £2.50/1.50; 10am-5pm Mon-Sat, to 4pm Sun May-Sep, 10am-4pm Tue-Sat Feb-Apr). It also has wonderful views.

Back near the entrance is the Jacobean-style **Council House Gatehouse**, dating from 1620, and the **Old Council House**, where the Council of the Welsh Marches used to meet.

Opposite the castle is an unusually grand **library**, with a severe-looking **statue** of Shrewsbury's most famous son, Charles Darwin. Returning to St Mary's St, follow it into Dogpole and turn right into Wyle Cop, Welsh for 'hilltop'. Henry VII stayed in the seriously overhanging **Henry Tudor House** before the Battle of Bosworth. At the bottom of Wyle Cop is the graceful 18th-century **English Bridge**, which takes you across to **Shrewsbury Abbey**.

If your feet aren't yet aching, double back over the bridge and stroll left along the riverside to enjoy an ice cream in sweeping gardens of **Quarry Park**, and listen to the cacophonous bells of odd 18th-century round church **St Chad's**, which surveys the park and the river.

Sleeping

164 (☎ 01743-367750; www.164bedandbreakfast.co.uk; 164 Abbey Foregate; s/d £35/54, with bathroom £45/58; P ☐ wi-fi) Despite the age of the building you won't find any chintz or faux Tudor interiors here. This B&B celebrates its lovely 16th-century timber frame with bright colours, contemporary fabrics and a quirky mix of artwork. As an extra treat, breakfast is served in bed.

Mad Jack's (☎ 01743-358870; www.madjacksuk.com; 15 St Mary's St; s/d from £65/75) The foot-sinking cream carpets, leather furniture and soft fur throws of this guest house's four smart rooms blend in perfectly with the quirks of the old building. There's a good restaurant downstairs.

Tudor House (☎ 01743-351735; www.tudorhouseshrewsbury.com; 2 Fish St; s/d from £69/79; ☐ wi-fi) If you're feeling nostalgic, this creaky medieval house has old-world charm by the bucketload. The building is festooned with floral window boxes and its handful of traditional oak-beamed rooms are turned out in high-shine fabrics, some with spindly metal-framed headboards entwined with flowers. Not all rooms have an en suite.

Lion Hotel (☎ 01753 353107; www.thelionhotelshrewsbury.co.uk; Wyle Cop; s/d from £76/92; P) A cowardly lion presides over the doorway of this grand old coaching inn. The most famous hotel in town, it has hosted many a luminary through its 400-year history. At the time of writing the hotel was undergoing a major refurbishment.

Prince Rupert Hotel (☎ 01743-499955; www.prince-rupert-hotel.co.uk; Butcher Row; s/d from £85/105; P ☐ wi-fi) King James' grandson Prince Rupert once lived at this oak-panelled hotel. Though most rooms are modern, tapestries, armour and heraldry haphazardly push the theme, and a few 15th- and 12th-century suites have all the quirky angles, beams and wood panelling you could ask for.

There are plenty more B&Bs huddled around Abbey Foregate.

Other options for bedding down:

Albright Hussey Manor (☎ 01743-290571; www.albrighthussey.co.uk; Ellesmere Rd; s/d from £79/95; P ☐ wi-fi) Romantic manor with excellent restaurant, surrounded by a moat, 2 miles north of town.

Catherine of Aragon Suite (☎ 01743-271092; www.aragonsuite.co.uk; the Old House, Dogpole; s/d £85/125 P ☐) Hugely atmospheric wood-panelled bedroom with its own sitting room in an old Tudor mansion.

Eating

Good Life Wholefood Restaurant (☎ 01743-350455; Barracks Passage; mains £3.50-7; ☉ lunch Mon-Sat) Healthy, freshly prepared vegetarian food is the name of the game in this cute little refuge off Wyle Cop. Favourites include quiches, nut loaf and slightly less health-conscious cakes and desserts.

Cornhouse (☎ 01743-231991; www.cornhouse.co.uk; 59A Wyle Cop; mains £8-14; ☉ lunch & dinner) This cosy corner holds a relaxed wine bar and restaurant, successfully mixing contemporary style with period features from its working cornhouse days. Its consistently good British food is served up in the shadow of a superb cast-iron spiral staircase.

Rococo (☎ 01743-363633; 18 Butcher Row; sandwiches £6-9, mains £9-17; ☉ 10am-midnight) Modern, bustling bar and brasserie with streetside seating serving everything from sandwiches and deli plates to full-on grills, fish and pasta dishes. It doubles up as a cocktail and wine bar.

Mad Jack's (☎ 01743-358870; www.madjacksuk.com; 15 St Mary's St; mains £11-16; ☉ 10am-10pm) Posh cafe, restaurant and bar that's passionate about local produce. Breakfasts, light lunches, afternoon tea and dinners are served in a bright, elegant dining room or a lovely plant-filled courtyard. Highlights include pistachio-crusted local lamb and chocolate torte with fennel ice cream.

Drapers Hall (☎ 01743-344679; St Mary's Pl; mains £12-17.50; ☉ lunch & dinner) The sense of history is palpable in this well-fossilised 16th-century hall, fronted by an elegant Elizabethan facade. Award-wining, Anglo-French haute cuisine is divided between dark oak-panelled rooms decked out in sumptuous fabrics and antique screens. The connoisseur's wine list is also well worthy of a special occasion.

Drinking

Armoury (☎ 01743-340525; www.armoury-shrewsbury.co.uk; Victoria Ave) There's a great warmth and conviviality to this converted riverside warehouse. Towering bookshelves, old pictures and curios help straddle the divide between posh restaurant (mains £9-17) and informal pub; large, curved windows invite in sheds of light, while a plethora of blackboard menus invite you to sample wines, guest ales and hearty British dishes.

Three Fishes (☎ 01743-344793; 4 Fish St) The quintessential creaky Tudor alehouse, with a jolly owner, mellow regulars and hops hanging from the 15th-century beamed ceiling. No music here, just plenty of good-value real ales on tap and solid bar food.

Grazia (☎ 01743-233222; www.gograzia.com; Victoria Ave) This cavernous, two-storey place has huge windows overlooking the river, a cocktail lounge decked out with low leather seating and plush cushions, and a glam restaurant done up in stark black and white. It puts on regular live music and wine-tasting evenings.

Entertainment

C21 (☎ 01743-271821; 21 Abbey Foregate; admission after 10pm £3-7; ☻ 8.30pm-3am) A polished city-chic club for over-25-year-olds to indulge in late-night cocktails and dance-floor acrobatics. On Mondays it's home to Shrewsbury's main gay and lesbian night.

For mainstream and art-house movies in an Elizabethan setting, try the **Old Market Hall Film & Digital Media Centre** (☎ 01743-281281; www .oldmarkethall.co.uk).

At the time of research, a massive new riverside theatre and music venue, Theatre Severn, was due to open in early 2009 on Frankwell Quay.

Getting There & Around
BIKE

You can hire bikes at **Dave Mellor Cycles** (☎ 01743-366662; www.thecycleshop.co.uk; 9 New St).

BUS

National Express has two direct buses to London (£17.80, 4½ hours) and two to Birmingham (£5.70, 1½ hours). Bus 96 serves Ironbridge (30 minutes) every two hours Monday to Saturday. Bus 435 travels to Ludlow (1¼ hours) via Church Stretton (45 minutes) eight times daily, and bus 553 heads to Bishop's Castle (one hour) 10 times daily.

TRAIN

There are five direct daily services between Shrewsbury and London Marylebone (£33, 3½ hours) on the Wrexham and Shropshire line. Otherwise you must change at Wolverhampton (£42.40, 2½ to three hours). Trains run twice-hourly to Ludlow (£8.40, 30 minutes) during the week and hourly at weekends.

Shrewsbury is a popular starting point for two scenic routes into Wales: one loop takes in Shrewsbury, northern Wales and Chester; the other, **Heart of Wales Line** (☎ 0870 9000 772; www.heart-of-wales.co.uk), runs southwest to Swansea (£19, 3¾ hours, four daily).

AROUND SHREWSBURY
Attingham Park

The most impressive of Shropshire's stately homes is late 18th-century mansion **Attingham Park** (NT; ☎ 01743-708123; house & grounds adult/child £7.40/3.70, grounds only £4.20/2.20; ☻ house 1-5pm Thu-Tue mid-Mar–Oct, grounds 10am-dusk Thu-Tue mid-Mar–Oct). Built in imposing neoclassical style, it's reminiscent of many a bodice-ripping drama. Behind the high-and-mighty facade, you'll find a picture gallery by John Nash, two wings respectively decorated into staunch masculine and delicate feminine Regency interiors. A herd of deer roam the landscaped grounds and there are pleasant walks along the River Tern.

Attingham Park is 4 miles southeast of Shrewsbury at Atcham. Buses 81 and 96 (18 minutes) run six times per day Monday to Friday, less frequently on weekends.

Wroxeter Roman City

The crumbled foundations of one of Roman Britain's largest cities, Viroconium, can be seen at **Wroxeter** (EH; ☎ 01743-761330; adult/child £4.20/2.10; ☻ 10am-5pm Mar-Oct, 10am-4pm Wed-Sun Nov-Feb). Geophysical work has revealed a Roman city as large as Pompeii lying underneath the lush farmland, but the costs of excavating the whole lot are, for now, too great. You'll have to make do with exploring the remains of the public baths and marketplace.

Wroxeter is 6 miles southeast of Shrewsbury, off the B4380. Bus 96 stops nearby, and runs six times per day Monday to Friday, less frequently on weekends.

IRONBRIDGE GORGE

Winding your way through the woods, hills and villages of this peaceful river gorge, it can be hard to imagine the trailblazing events that took place here some 300 years ago. But it was this sleepy enclave that gave birth to the Industrial Revolution, when three generations of the pioneering Darby family set about transforming their indus-

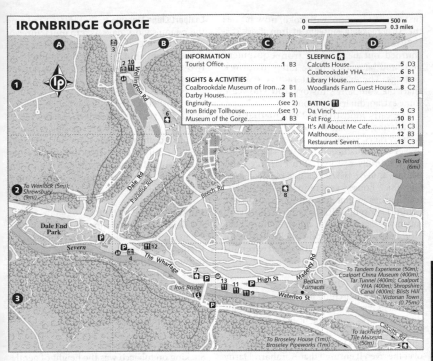

IRONBRIDGE GORGE

0 — 500 m
0 — 0.3 miles

INFORMATION	
Tourist Office...........................**1** B3	

SIGHTS & ACTIVITIES	
Coalbrookdale Museum of Iron...**2** B1	
Darby Houses..........................**3** B1	
Enginuity................................(see 2)	
Iron Bridge Tollhouse...............(see 1)	
Museum of the Gorge...............**4** B3	

SLEEPING	
Calcutts House.........................**5** D3	
Coalbrookdale YHA...................**6** B1	
Library House..........................**7** B3	
Woodlands Farm Guest House....**8** C2	

EATING	
Da Vinci's..............................**9** C3	
Fat Frog...............................**10** B1	
It's All About Me Cafe............**11** C3	
Malthouse............................**12** B3	
Restaurant Severn..................**13** C3	

To Telford (6mi)

To Wenlock (5mi); Shrewsbury (9mi)

Dale End Park

To Tandem Experience (50m); Coalport China Museum (400m); Tar Tunnel (400m); Coalport YHA (400m); Shropshire Canal (400m); Blists Hill Victorian Town (0.75mi)

Bedlam Furnaces

Iron Bridge

To Broseley House (1mi); Broseley Pipeworks (1mi)

To Jackfield Tile Museum (50m)

trial processes and in so doing irreversibly changed the world.

The story began quietly in 1709, when Abraham Darby determinedly set about restoring an old furnace to prove it was possible to smelt iron ore with coke, eventually paving the way for local factories to mass-produce the first iron wheels, rails and steam locomotives. Abraham Darby II's innovative forging process then enabled the production of single beams of iron, allowing Abraham Darby III to astound the world with the first ever iron bridge, constructed here in 1779. The bridge remains the valley's showpiece and dominates the main village, a jumble of cottages slithering down the gorge's steep bank.

Now written into history books as the birthplace of the Industrial Revolution, Ironbridge is a World Heritage Site and the Marches' top attraction. Ten very different museums now tell the story in the very buildings where it took place.

Orientation & Information

Driving or cycling can make life easier, as the museums are peppered throughout the long gorge. See p578 for public transport options.

The **tourist office** (☎ 01952-884391; www.visit ironbridge.co.uk; Tollhouse; ☷ 10am-5pm) is by the bridge.

Sights & Activities

The great-value **passport ticket** (adult/child £15/10) that allows year-round entry to all of the sites can be bought at any of the museums or the tourist office. The museums open from 10am to 5pm unless stated otherwise.

MUSEUM OF THE GORGE

A good way to begin your visit is the **Museum of the Gorge** (The Wharfage; adult/child £3/2.50), which offers an overview of the site. Housed in a Gothic warehouse by the river, it's filled with touch screens, fun exhibits and details of the horrific consequences of pollution and environmental hazards at the cutting edge of industry (Abraham I and III both died at 39). An absorbing video sets the museum in its historical context.

MUSEUM OF IRON & DARBY HOUSES

What was once the Coalbrookdale iron foundry, where pioneering Abraham Darby first smelted iron ore with coke, now houses the **Coalbrookdale Museum of Iron** (adult/child £5.95/4.25). An army of men and boys once churned out heavy-duty iron equipment here, and later, ever more fancy ironwork castings. The excellent interactive exhibits chart the company's history and showcase some extraordinary creations.

The early industrial settlement that surrounds the site has also happily survived, with workers' cottages, chapels, church and graveyard undisturbed. Just up the hill are the beautifully restored 18th-century **Darby Houses** (☎ 01952-433522; adult/child £4/2.50; ☼ Apr-Oct), which housed generations of the industrial bigwigs in gracious but modest Quaker comfort. Rosehill House is furnished with much original furniture, and next-door Dale House includes the wood-panelled office in which Abraham Darby III pored over his bridge designs.

IRON BRIDGE & TOLLHOUSE

The flamboyant arching **Iron Bridge** that gives the area its name was a symbol of the iron industry's success; a triumph of engineering that left contemporaries flabbergasted by its apparent flimsiness. As well as providing a crossing over the river, it ensured that Abraham Darby III and his village would be given a prominent place in the history books. The **tollhouse** (admission free; ☼ 10am-5pm) houses a small exhibition on the bridge's history.

BLISTS HILL VICTORIAN TOWN

To travel back to 19th-century Britain, hear the pounding of steam hammers and the clip-clop of horse hooves, or tip your hat to a cycling bobby, head to the vast open-air Victorian theme park, **Blists Hill** (☎ 01952-433522; Legges Way, Madeley; adult/child £10.50/7.50; ☼ 10am-5pm). This ambitious project does a remarkably good job of reconstructing an entire village, encompassing everything from a working foundry to a chemist to a bank, where you can exchange your cash for shillings to use on site. Costumed staff explain displays, craftspeople demonstrate skills, and you can even join in an old-fashioned knees-up round the piano at the Victorian pub.

COALPORT CHINA MUSEUM & TAR TUNNEL

When ironmaking moved elsewhere, Coalport china slowed the region's decline and the restored works now house an absorbing

Coalport China Museum (adult/child £6/4.25) tracing the region's glory days as a manufacturer of elaborate pottery and crockery. Craftspeople demonstrate china-making techniques and two enormous bottle kilns are guaranteed to awe even if the gaudily glazed chinaware leaves you cold.

A short stroll along the canal brings you to the 200-year-old **Tar Tunnel** (adult/child £2/1.50; ☼ Apr-Sep), dug as a water-supply channel but halted abruptly when natural bitumen unexpectedly started trickling treacle-like from its walls. You can still don a hard hat and stoop in deep enough to see the black stuff ooze.

JACKFIELD TILE MUSEUM

A kaleidoscopic collection of Victorian tiles, faience and ceramics can be found at the **Jackfield Tile Museum** (adult/child £6/4.25), displayed through a series of gas-lit period-style galleries reconstructing lustrous tiled interiors of everything from pubs to churches, tube stations and remarkably fancy toilets. Kids especially love the fairy-tale friezes for children's hospital wards.

BROSELEY PIPEWORKS

Sucking on tobacco was the height of gentlemanly fashion in the late 17th and early 18th centuries, and the **Broseley Pipeworks** (adult/child £4/2.50; ☼ 1-5pm mid-May–Sep), once Britain's most prolific pipe manufacturer, charts the history of the industry. A vast range of clay pipes from short-stemmed 'pipsqueaks' to arm-length 'church wardens' were produced here, until the factory finally closed in 1957; now visitors can explore its time-capsule contents, which are largely unchanged since the last worker turned out the lights. It's a mile-long walk to get here, signposted from the bridge.

ENGINUITY

Championing Ironbridge's spirit of brains before brawn, the fabulous interactive design and technology centre **Enginuity** (adult/child £6.25/5.25) invites you to move a steam engine with the flick of a wrist, X-ray everyday objects, power up a vacuum cleaner with self-generated electricity and basically dive head first into a vast range of hands-on, brains-on challenges, games and gadgets that explore design and engineering in modern life. If you have kids with you, allow at least two hours.

Sleeping

Coalbrookdale YHA (☎ 0845 371 9325; www.yha
.org.uk; 1 Paradise Rd, Coalbrookdale; dm £17; **P**) The austere former Literary and Scientific Institute,
a grand blue-grey building from 1859 sitting
high on the hillside behind sturdy iron gates,
now houses a newly refurbished hostel within
easy walking distance of the Museum of Iron.
It has a few en suite family rooms.

Coalport YHA (☎ 0845 371 9325; www.yha.org
.uk; High St, Coalport; dm £17; **P**) This historic
former china factory, a big bluff industrial-
looking building mere paces from the China
Museum and the canal, and close to pleasant countryside walks, now houses an 83-
bed hostel. The plain, modern rooms betray
little of their long history, however. It has
family-friendly rooms.

Calcutts House (☎ 01952-882631; www.calcuttshouse
.co.uk; Calcutts Rd; s/d/f from £45/66/95; **P**) This
former ironmaster's pad built in the 18th
century is tucked away a few strides from
the Jackfield Tile Museum. Its traditionally
decorated rooms have bags of character, some
have four-posters, and each is named after
a celebrated former owner of or visitor to
the house.

our pick Library House (☎ 01952-432299; www
.libraryhouse.com; 11 Severn Bank; s/d from £65/75;
P wi-fi) This lovingly restored Georgian
library building is hugged by vines, backed
by a beautiful garden and elegantly decorated
with light colours, deep cream sofas, rows
of vintage books, and the odd African arte-
fact. There are three charming, individually
decorated rooms, with seriously comfortable
beds, each named after a famous writer, and
the welcome from hosts and family dog is
exceedingly friendly.

Other options include the **Woodlands Farm
Guest House** (☎ 01952-432741; www.woodlandsfarm
guesthouse.co.uk; Beech Rd; d from £60; **P**), which
has five elegant rooms (including three suites),
most with lovely views of the gardens and
fields beyond.

Eating

Malthouse (☎ 01952-433712; www.themalthouseiron
bridge.com; The Wharfage; mains £8-17; lunch & dinner) This former malting house would be
worth visiting for the enormous plates of
good English cooking alone, but the vibrant
atmosphere, regular live jazz and riverfront
terrace are an added bonus. Stylish contemporary rooms (£63) are also available.

Fat Frog (☎ 01952-432240; www.fat-frog.co.uk;
Coalbrookdale; mains £10-16; lunch & dinner Mon-Sat,
lunch Sun) This quirky French bar-bistro is
cluttered with toy frogs and showbiz memorabilia, has a rustic candlelit basement and
plays nostalgic music from the ebullient Gallic
proprietor's prime. The food is excellent, and
as you'd expect, there's a great wine list with
plenty of half-bottles.

Restaurant Severn (☎ 01952-432233; 33 High St; 2-/
3-course dinner £25/27; dinner Wed-Sat, lunch Sun) The
highly-praised food is a hybrid of English and
French at this exciting fine-dining waterfront
restaurant. The simple decor and laid-back
service attests to the fact that the real star
here is the food – a delectable, locally sourced
menu that changes weekly.

Other spots to consider:

Da Vinci's (☎ 01952-432250; www.davincisironbridge
.co.uk; 26 High St; mains £12-18; dinner Tue-Sat)
Gourmet Italian food served in a classy wood-panelled
dining room.

It's All About Me Cafe (☎ 01952-432716; 29 High St;
main from £10; Tue-Sun 10am-11pm) The Mediterranean-inspired food isn't great, but the views of the gorge
from the sun terrace are. There are also good cocktails and
regular live music.

THE WEST MIDLANDS &
THE MARCHES

SOMETHING FOR THE WEEKEND

Kick off your weekend with a night of loved-up escapism and fine food at the barmy **Hundred
House Hotel** (p580) at Norton. Next morning, nip over to **Ironbridge Gorge** (p574) for a stroll
across the world's first iron bridge, then roll down to the beautiful **Long Mynd** (p580) to build
up an appetite on its stunning walking trails. Hold onto your hunger pangs just long enough
to put them to good use in the region's gourmet capital, **Ludlow** (p582), where **La Bécasse**
(p583) and **Mr Underhill's** (p583) are just two of the superb restaurants to choose between.
Sleep off your excesses in the stunning timber-framed **Feathers Hotel** (p582), then on Sunday
morning head south for a quick tour through the picture-postcard **black-and-white villages**
(see boxed text, p565). For a final fling, linger over an indulgent Sunday lunch at the **Stagg Inn**
(see boxed text, p565) and book yourself a trip to the gym on Monday.

Getting There & Away

The nearest train station is 6 miles away at Telford. Bus 96 runs every two hours (Monday to Saturday) between Shrewsbury (40 minutes) and Telford (15 to 20 minutes) via Ironbridge, stopping near the Museum of the Gorge. Bus 9 runs from Bridgnorth (30 minutes, four daily).

Getting Around

The Gorge Connect bus connects nine of the museums every half-hour on weekends and Bank Holidays only. It costs 50p per journey, or there's a Day Rover pass (£2.50/1.50 per adult/child). The service is free to museum-passport holders.

Midweek your only options are to walk or hire a bike from **Broseley House** (☎ 01952-882043; www.broseleyhouse.co.uk; 1 The Square, Broseley; per day £15), a mile and a half south of the bridge; booking is advised. You may also like to look into **Tandem Experience** (☎ 0845 60 66 456; www.tandeming.co.uk; tandem per day £50), located next to the Tile Museum; the price includes tuition for tandem riding.

MUCH WENLOCK
pop 1959

A tangle of narrow winding streets and historical buildings from the Tudor, Jacobean and Georgian eras, an arresting timbered guildhall and the enchanting remains of a 12th-century priory make this little town a real gem. It also claims to have jump-started the modern Olympics (see boxed text, opposite).

The **tourist office** (☎ 01952-727679; muchwenlock .tourism@shropshire-cc.gov.uk; The Square; ✆ 10.30am-1pm & 2-5pm Mon-Sat Apr-Oct, plus Sun Jun-Aug) shares a 19th-century building and opening hours with the local **museum** (admission free).

Sights & Activities

The tourist office provides a map to the town's sights of historical interest, as well as copies of *The Olympian Trail*, a pleasant 1½-mile walking tour of the town exploring the link between the village and the modern Olympics.

Otherwise, you can skip straight to the town's main highlight, the atmospheric 12th-century ruins of **Wenlock Priory** (EH; ☎ 01952-727466; adult/child £3.50/1.80; ✆ 10am-5pm daily; May-Aug, 10am-5pm Wed-Sun Apr & Sep-Oct, 10am-4pm Thu-Sun Nov-Feb) which rise up from vivid green lawns, sprinkled with quirky topiaries of bears, cats and rabbits. The remains include part of a finely decorated chapterhouse and an unusual carved lavabo, and there's a particularly entertaining audio tour.

Sleeping & Eating

The closest hostel is Wilderhope Manor YHA (opposite).

Talbot Inn (☎ 01952-727077; www.the-talbot-inn .com; High St; s/d £40/80; Ⓟ) A wonderfully atmospheric old place with colossal beams, cavernous fireplaces and good home-style fare (mains £10 to £15). There are some simple rooms in a converted 18th-century malthouse, with whitewashed walls, exposed beams and pine furniture.

Raven Hotel (☎ 01952-727251; www.ravenhotel.com; Barrow St; s/d £85/120; Ⓟ) Much Wenlock's finest, this 17th-century coaching inn and converted stables has thick oak beams, open fires and rich country-chic styling throughout. The excellent restaurant (two-/three-course meal £25/30) overlooks a flowery courtyard and serves up classic British and Mediterranean fare.

Fox (☎ 01952-727292; www.the-fox-inn.co.uk; 46 High St; lunch £3-5; dinner mains £14-17) Warm yourself by the massive fireplace, then settle down in the simple black-and-cream dining room to enjoy solid local produce such as venison, pheasant and Shropshire beef. When you're done you can sample some real ales at the bar.

Getting There & Away

Bus 436 runs from Shrewsbury (35 minutes) to Bridgnorth (20 minutes) hourly (five on Sunday).

AROUND MUCH WENLOCK

The spectacular limestone escarpment of **Wenlock Edge** swells up like an immense petrified wave, its ancient oceanic rock rich in fossils and its flanks frothy with woodland. It stretches for 15 miles from Much Wenlock to Craven Arms and makes for wonderful walking and dramatic views. The National Trust (NT) owns much of the ridge, and there are many waymarked trails starting from car parks dotted along the B4371. There are no convenient buses along this route.

For a bite, a beer or a bed, the 17th-century **Wenlock Edge Inn** (☎ 01746-785678; B4371, Hilltop; s/d £50/70; Ⓟ) is a good choice for hikers en route. It's a down-to-earth place with a recently revamped lively restaurant and bar with a fine choice of ales and Belgian beers. The food is a notch up from standard pub grub and provides

GRANDDADDY OF THE MODERN OLYMPICS

All eyes will be on London when the Olympic Games arrive in 2012, but they will not be the only Olympics taking place in England at that time. The altogether more modest annual games at tiny Much Wenlock were instrumental in the rebirth of their big fat Greek brother.

Local doctor and sports enthusiast William Penny Brookes fused his knowledge of the ancient Olympics and rural British pastimes to launch the Much Wenlock Olympic Games in 1850. Begun as a distraction for the beer-swilling local youth, the games soon pricked the interest of Baron Pierre Coubertin, who visited Much Wenlock in 1890 to see them for himself.

He and Brookes became firm friends, with the shared dream of reviving the ancient Olympics. Coubertin went on to launch the modern Olympics in Athens in 1896; the games featured many of the events he had seen in Much Wenlock (although wheelbarrow racing and chasing a greased pig around town never really caught on). Brookes was invited to the event but he died, aged 86, before the games opened.

The good doctor never really got his share of the Olympic limelight until almost a century later, when International Olympic Committee President Juan Antonio Samaranch visited his grave to 'pay tribute and homage to Dr Brookes, who really was the founder of the Modern Olympic Games'.

The Much Wenlock Olympics are still held every July, with events that range from the triathlon to bowls. You can find details at www.wenlock-olympian-society.org.uk.

hearty sustenance for the road ahead (mains £9 to £15). There are also some country-style rooms available. The pub is about 4.5 miles southwest of Much Wenlock on the B4371.

For top-value budget accommodation, ramble out to the remote **Wilderhope Manor YHA** (☎ 0845 371 9149; www.yha.org.uk; Longville-in-the-Dale; dm £17; ☒ Fri, Sat & school holidays; ℗), a gloriously atmospheric gabled Elizabethan manor, with oak spiral staircases, heavy beams, wood-panelled walls, an impressive stone-floored dining hall and surprisingly spacious rooms. The hostel is set deep in lush countryside and adjoins a picturesque if stinky farmyard.

You can catch buses from Ludlow and Bridgnorth to Shipton, a half-mile walk from Wilderhope.

BRIDGNORTH & AROUND
pop 11,891

Cleaved into two by a dramatic sandstone bluff that tumbles down to the River Severn, Bridgnorth's upper head and lower body are joined by means of the steepest inland railway in Britain, **Bridgnorth Cliff Railway** (☎ 01746-762052; www.bridgnorthcliffrailway.co.uk; return 90p; ☒ 8am-8pm Mon-Sat & noon-8pm Sun May-Sep, to dusk Oct-Apr), which has been trundling its way up the cliff since 1892. The town also boasts a cute colonnaded mid-17th-century town hall, and two interesting churches.

Bridgnorth is also the northern terminus of the **Severn Valley Railway** (☎ 01299-403816; www.svr

.co.uk; adult/child £13/6.50; ☒ daily May-Sep, Sat & Sun Oct-Apr), whose trains chug down the picturesque valley to Kidderminster.

There's something for cyclists here too: a beautiful 20-mile section of National Cycle Route 45, the **Mercian Way**, runs alongside the Severn Valley Railway from here to the Wyre Forest.

Organic, free-range, fair-trade and vegetarian is the name of the game in wholefood cafe **Cinnamon** (☎ 01746-762944; Waterloo House, Cartway; mains £5-8; ☒ 9am-6pm Mon-Fri, 10am-5pm Sat, 10am-4pm Sun), where you can munch on savoury bakes, quiches and homemade cakes on squashy sofas inside or while enjoying the views from the terrace. There's a wide selection of books and papers to browse and the owners put on frequent evenings of music, poetry and storytelling.

Getting There & Away

Buses 436 and 437 run from Shrewsbury to Bridgnorth 10 times daily (one hour, five times on Sunday), via Much Wenlock (25 minutes). You can catch the steam train from any of the stations in the Severn Valley.

CHURCH STRETTON & AROUND
pop 3841

Set deep in a valley formed by the Long Mynd and the Caradoc Hills, this scenic if restrained little town is the ideal base from which to venture into the glorious surroundings. It

---

SHROPSHIRE'S MOST ECCENTRIC HOTEL

Hundred House Hotel (☎ 01746-730353; www
.hundredhouse.co.uk; A442, Norton; s/d £90/105;
P ⬜) offers a taste of escapism at its
barmiest and best. Unashamedly romantic
bedrooms are crammed with flamboyant
decor, heart-shaped cushions and mirrors,
antique beds, and seven out of 10 rooms
sport suggestive velvet-covered swings
entwined with ribbons. Shampoo comes in
carafes and pillows are sprinkled with lavender water. The quirky herb gardens are
another adventure, full of hidden corners
and pathways, including a trail to a teddy
bears' picnic sculpture. The owners devote
just as much passion to their food; the excellent menu (mains £15 to £19) uses local
produce to perfection. Hundred House is 6
miles north of Bridgnorth.

---

also shelters some interesting old buildings,
including a 12th-century Norman church
most famous for its weather-beaten but still
undauntedly exhibitionist *sheila-na-gig* (Celtic
fertility figure) over its north door.

The **tourist office** (☎ 01694-723133; www.church
stretton.co.uk; Church St; ☉ 9.30am-1pm & 2-5pm Mon-Sat),
adjoining the library, has abundant walking
information as well as free internet access.

Activities

WALKING

The splendid hogback hill of **Long Mynd**,
Shropshire's most famous mountain, heaves
its bulk up above Church Stretton and is one
of the best walking areas in the Marches.
The area was dubbed 'Little Switzerland' by
the Victorians, who came in droves for its
healthy climes and spring waters. The entire area is riddled with walking trails with
memorable views.

You could begin with the **Carding Mill
Valley Trail**, which starts just outside Church
Stretton and leads up to the 517m summit of
the Long Mynd. This trail can get very busy
at weekends and in summer, so you might
prefer to pick your own peak or cross the
A49 and climb towards the 459m summit of
Caer Caradoc.

You can drive part of the way up the
Carding Mill Valley, although the NT
would rather you took the **Long Mynd shuttle**

bus (☉ weekends & Bank Holidays only Apr-Oct) from
Beaumont Rd or the station.

OTHER ACTIVITIES

The tourist office has maps of local mountain-
biking circuits and details of riding stables.
Daredevils can also look up **Beyond Extreme**
(☎ 01694-682640; www.beyondextreme.co.uk; 2 Burway
Rd) to organise hill-launch paragliding lessons
and tandem flights.

Sleeping

Bridges Long Mynd YHA (☎ 01588-650656; www
.yha.org.uk; Ratlinghope; dm £16; P) Once the village school, this old stone pile is one of the
country's longest-running YHA hostels, with
a handful of basic but comfortable dorms.
Hidden away in the Shropshire hills, it's a
perfect base for exploring the county's walking trails – it's right on the doorstep of the
Shropshire Way and walks to Long Mynd
and Stiperstones. Boulton's bus 551 comes
here from Shrewsbury on Tuesday only. On
weekends and Bank Holidays from April to
October the Long Mynd shuttle runs hourly
to Church Stretton.

Mynd House (☎ 01694-722212; www.myndhouse.com;
Ludlow Rd, Little Stretton; s/d/f from £37/70/120; P ⬜ wi-
fi). Set right at the foot of the Long Mynd, this
welcoming, family-friendly guest house has
splendid views out over the hills and makes
an excellent base for cycling, hiking or strolling. Rooms are clean and airy, and there's a
small bar and cosy lounge stocked with local
books. There are maps for guests to borrow,
and lots of advice on where to go hiking in the
surrounding area.

Jinlye Guest House (☎ 01694-723243; www.jinlye
.co.uk; Castle Hill, All Stretton; s/d £50/80; P) The Long
Mynd is literally your back garden, so you'll
have sheep as your neighbours at this beautifully restored crofter's cottage perched on the
hilltop, and graced by old beams, log fires and
leaded windows. Bedrooms are bright and
elegantly furnished with antiques and the off
floral frill. Expect a good old-fashioned welcome. Wheelchair access is available.

Other options include:
Willowfield (☎ 01694-751471; www.willowfieldguest
house.co.uk; Lower Wood; s/d £50/70; P) A 17th-century
farmhouse in an idyllic isolated location.
Longmynd Hotel (☎ 01694-722244; www.longmynd
.co.uk; Cunnery Rd; s/d £70/125; P ⬜ wi-fi) Hilltop
pile with airy rooms, a swimming pool, stunning vistas,
sculpture trail and excellent food.

Eating

Berry's Coffee House (☎ 01694-724452; www.berrys coffeehouse.co.uk; 17 High St; meals £6-8; ☺ 10am-5pm daily) A sociable cafe in an 18th-century building with little conservatory just off the main street. Berry's is proud of its organic, free-range, fair-trade, wholesome offerings, but makes up for all that goodness with wicked desserts.

Studio (☎ 01694-722672; 59 High St; set menus £22.50-27.50; ☺ dinner only Wed-Sat) A former artist's studio, still littered with interesting works, sets the scene for the town's best and most intimate restaurant. The award-winning menu jumps confidently between modern English and traditional French food, and uses plenty of local game and fish.

Van Doesburg's (☎ 01694-722867; 3 High St) You'll find everything you need for a classy picnic at this excellent patisserie-delicatessen. Highlights are posh sandwiches, flapjacks and quiches.

Getting There & Around

There are hourly trains to Shrewsbury (20 minutes), and bus 435, which runs between Shrewsbury (45 minutes) and Ludlow (40 minutes) six times daily, stops here.

You can hire 24-speed mountain bikes with front or full suspension and cheaper, simpler bikes from **Shropshire Hills Bike Hire** (☎ 723302; 6 Castle Hill, All Stretton; per day from £10).

BISHOP'S CASTLE
pop 1630

Home to a bewitching mixture of breweries, half-timbered buildings, second-hand book-shops and eclectic boutiques, this languid little border town makes stress seem like an alien concept. At the top of High St sits the adorable Georgian **town hall** and delightfully crooked 16th-century **House on Crutches** (☎ 630007; admission free; ☺ 1-5pm Sat & Sun), which also houses the town **museum**.

The pleasingly potty **Old Time** (☎ 01588-638467; www.bishopscastle.co.uk; 29 High St; ☺ 10am-6pm Mon-Sat, 10am-2pm Sun) offers limited tourist information.

Activities

Walk along the **Shropshire Way**, which runs through the town and joins up with **Offa's Dyke Path** to the south; the **Kerry Ridgeway** to the south; or head north and risk the forbidding

ridges of the **Stiperstones**, where Satan is said to hold court.

Sleeping & Eating

Poppy House (☎ 01588-638443; www.poppyhouse .co.uk; 20 Market Sq; s/d £40/70) Sweet little beamed rooms with dark burgundy bedspreads and lots of little extras, such as books and magazines and a complimentary breakfast-in-bed service win this B&B much praise. The downstairs restaurant has an interesting menu, featuring the likes of eel wrapped in prosciutto and sea bass on caramelised pineapple (mains £9 to £18; open 10am to 5pm and 6.30pm to 11pm).

Castle Hotel (☎ 01588-638403; www.thecastle hotelbishopscastle.co.uk; The Square; s/d £45/90; P) Occupying a regal position in an elevated square, this handsome 18th-century coaching inn has lovely terraced gardens and seven relaxing beamed rooms, many with soul-restoring views over the town and the valley. The oak-panelled restaurant dishes up classic English food and the bar serves a good choice of local brews.

Other possibilities:

Porch House (☎ 01588-638854; www.theporchhouse .com; High St; s/d £40/70; P 🖵 wi-fi) This stunning porch house dating back to 1564 has chic, contemporary rooms and plenty of extra touches to make you feel special.

Yarborough House (☎ 01588-638318; The Square) Excellent coffee and cakes in a classical music shop and second-hand bookshop.

Drinking

Three Tuns (☎ 01588-638797; Salop St) One of Shropshire's most famous alehouses is a surprisingly ordinary place but for the fact that it is next door to a Victorian brewery, close enough to smell the roasting malt. Though they're no longer run by the same folk, you can still sample the brewery's best at the Three Tuns bar.

Six Bells Inn (☎ 01588-630144; Church St; mains £7.50-13; ☺ lunch & dinner Tue-Sat, lunch Sun) This historic 17th-century coaching inn is alive with loyal locals and ramblers who come to sample ales from its adjoining brewery. The pub also has a reputation for traditional English comfort food such as homemade pies and Big Nev's bangers made with local ale.

Getting There & Away

Buses 435 runs to and from Shrewsbury (one hour) seven times daily.

LUDLOW

pop 9548

Fanning out from the rambling ruins of a fine Norman castle, beautiful Ludlow's muddle of narrow streets, flanked by half-timbered Jacobean and elegant Georgian buildings, are a magnet for foodies from miles around. This picturesque town is a temple to gastronomy, hosting independent butchers, bakers, grocers, cheesemongers and a handful of exceptional restaurants. Our advice: book ahead and punch a few extra holes in your belt – you can always work it all off in the nearby Shropshire hills afterwards.

Ludlow's helpful **tourist office** (☎ 01584-875053; www.ludlow.org.uk; Castle Sq; 10am-5pm) is in the 19th-century assembly rooms. There's also a small back-to-front **museum** (☎ 01584-813666; admission free; 10.30am-1pm & 2-5pm Easter-Oct) on the town and surrounding area here.

Internet can be tracked down at the **library** (☎ 01584-813600; 7-9 Parkway; 9.30am-5pm Mon-Wed & Sat, 9.30am-7.30pm Fri) and clothes can be washed, dried and pressed at **Ludlow Laundry** (Tower St; per bag £5; 9am-6pm Mon-Sat).

Sights & Activities

With seductive delicatessens and distracting antique dealers around every corner, the best way to explore Ludlow is to simply surrender to getting pleasurably lost on foot.

The town's finest attraction is its **castle** (☎ 01584-873355; www.ludlowcastle.com; Castle Sq; adult/child/senior & student £4.50/2.50/4; 10am-7pm Aug, to 5pm Apr-Jul & Sep, 10am-4pm Oct-Mar, weekends only Dec & Jan), which sits in an ideal defensive location atop a cliff above a crook in the river. One of a line of fortifications built along the Marches to ward off the marauding Welsh, it is full of secret passageways, ruined rooms, tucked-away nooks and mysterious stairwells. The sturdy Norman keep was built around 1090 and has wonderful views over the surrounding hills and the river below.

The castle was transformed into a 14th-century palace by the notorious Roger Mortimer, who was instrumental in the grisly death of Edward II, but its chequered history is reflected in different architectural styles. The round chapel in the inner bailey was built in 1120 and is one of few surviving in England.

The waymarked 30-mile **Mortimer Trail** to Kington starts just outside the castle entrance. The tourist office can provide a free leaflet on en route services, or a more thorough booklet for £1.50. Also see www.mortimercountry.co.uk.

Some delightfully cheeky medieval misericords lurk in the choir of **Church of St Laurence** (☎ 01584-872073; www.stlaurences.org.uk; King St; requested donation £2; 10am-5.30pm Apr-Sep, 11am-4pm Oct-Mar), one of the largest parish churches in Britain. These painstakingly carved 'mercy seats' show scenes of domestic 15th-century life both pious and profane, including a beer-swilling chap raiding his barrel.

Guided walks (£2) run from April to October, leaving the Cannon in Castle Sq at 2.30pm on Saturday and Sunday. You can also take the **ghost walk** (www.shropshireghostwalks.co.uk; adult/child £4/3; 8pm Fri) from outside the Church Inn on the Buttercross.

Festivals & Events

Markets are held in Castle Sq every Monday, Wednesday, Friday and Saturday. The town's busy calendar peaks with the **Ludlow Festival** (☎ 872150; www.ludlowfestival.co.uk), a fortnight of theatre and music in June and July that uses the castle as its dramatic backdrop. No surprise that most of the other events are foodie affairs. The renowned **Ludlow Marches Food & Drink Festival** (☎ 01584-873957; www.foodfestival.co.uk) is one of Britain's best, and takes place over a long weekend in September.

Sleeping

Mount (☎ 01584-874084; www.themountludlow.co.uk; 61 Gravel Hill; s/d from £30/55; P) The glorious sunset views from this good-looking Victorian house are worth the modest price tag alone. Walkers and cyclists are well catered to, despite unforgivingly crisp white bed linen and cream carpets, and the welcoming hostess offers lifts from the railway station.

Feathers Hotel (☎ 01584-875261; www.feathersatludlow.co.uk; Bull Ring; s/d from £75/95; P) Three storeys of stunning black-and-white timber-framed facade serve to introduce this famous Jacobean inn. Not all rooms are in the wonderfully atmospheric original building, so make sure you're getting the real deal when booking. Newer rooms follow the usual bland template with antique-styled trimmings. The deeply atmospheric restaurant (set lunch/dinner £15/25) is recommended.

Degreys (☎ 01584-872764; www.degreys.co.uk; 73 Lower Broad St; r £75-140) Set in an Elizabethan townhouse at Ludlow's heart, this classy B&B

THE WEST MIDLANDS & THE MARCHES

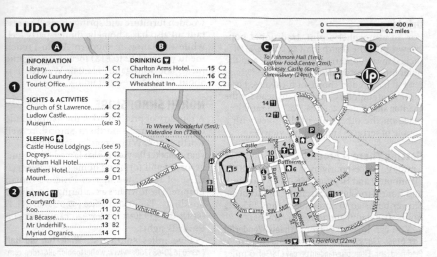

has nine luxurious rooms with low ceilings, beams, leaded windows and solid oak beds. The balance of period features and modern luxury is spot on and there's a fantastic traditional English tearoom downstairs.

Other options include:

Dinham Hall Hotel (☎ 01584-876464; www.dinham hall.co.uk; s £95, d £140-240; P) Resplendent 18th-century country manor with superb traditional restaurant, opposite the castle.

Castle House Lodgings (☎ 01584-874465; www.castle -accomodation.com; Ludlow Castle; an apt sleeping 4 for 3 nights £545-825; P) Glorious self-catering apartments in Castle House, within Ludlow Castle grounds.

Eating

If you can afford to splurge on food, this is unquestionably the place to do it. While we've picked our favourites, you needn't go far for more epicurean delights.

Ludlow Food Centre (☎ 01584-856000; Bromfield; mains £5-8; 9.30am-5.30pm Mon-Sat, 10.30am-4.30pm Sun) Wonderful food shop selling fresh baked bread and cakes, cheese, local meats, ciders, fresh pies and quiches ripe for a picnic. There's also a bright cafe selling similarly scrumptious produce in a converted barn next door. Two miles north west of Ludlow, just off the A49.

Courtyard (☎ 01584-878080; www.thecourtyard-lud low.co.uk; 2 Quality Sq; mains £5.50-10; lunch Mon-Sat, dinner Thu-Sat) Light relief from too much gastronomic extravagance, this simple cafe, tucked away in a tranquil courtyard, has a faithful local following for its lightning service and tasty seasonal food.

La Bécasse (☎ 01584-872325; www.labecasse.co.uk; 17 Corve St; 2-course lunch/6-course gourmand menu £20/55; dinner Tue-Sat, lunch Wed-Sun) Artfully presented modern French cuisine bursting with inventive flavour fusions – the spectacular tasting menu is enough to make you weak at the knees. The serious business of eating is conducted within the oak-panelled and exposed brick walls of a 17th-century coach house.

Koo (☎ 01584-878462; 127 Old St; 3-course set menu £22-26; dinner Tue-Sat) Three- and four-course Japanese menus are served up in this bright green cubby hole, overseen by its friendly Japanese owner who's always eager to chat with diners about Japanese culture and etiquette. During the festival, takeaway bento boxes are available for impromptu picnics.

Mr Underhill's (☎ 01584-874431; www.mr-underhills .co.uk; Dinham Weir; 6-course set menu £45-55; dinner Wed-Sun) Ludlow's only Michelin-starred restaurant is set in a converted corn mill that dips its toes in the river. Expect exquisite modern British food, though there's little choice before dessert, so make any dietary requests beforehand. It also offers stylish rooms (singles £120, doubles £140 to £235, suites £235 to £290). Reserve well in advance.

Some other options:

Myriad Organics (☎ 01584-872665; 22 Corve St; 8.30am-6pm Mon-Sat) Excellent all-organic deli opposite arch rival supermarket Tesco.

Fishmore Hall (☎ 01584-875148; Fishmore Rd; 2-course dinner £38.50; lunch & dinner) Imposing whitewashed Georgian hotel in a beautiful rural location with first-class food about a mile north of town.

Drinking

For an atmospheric pint, traditional hop-strewn pub the **Church Inn** (☎ 01584-872174) is tucked away on narrow Buttercross, and the quiet little **Wheatsheaf Inn** (☎ 01584-872980; Lower Broad St) has a good choice of local ales. For a more contemporary atmosphere head for the **Charlton Arms Hotel** (☎ 01584-872813), a rambling place on the other side of the river with a couple of terraces and sublime views.

Getting There & Around

Trains go twice-hourly to Shrewsbury (£8.40, 30 minutes) and Hereford (£6.40, 25 minutes), and hourly to Church Stretton (16 minutes). Slower buses go to Shrewsbury (bus 435, 1½ hours, five daily) and to nearby towns.

You can hire bikes from **Wheely Wonderful** (☎ 01568-770755; www.wheelywonderfulcycling.co.uk; Petchfield Farm, Elton; bike/tandem per day £18/36), 5 miles west of Ludlow.

AROUND LUDLOW

The wonky timber-framed tops and stunning Jacobean gatehouse of **Stokesay Castle** (EH; ☎ 01588-672544; adult/5-15yr/under 5yr £5/2.50/free; ☺ 10am-5pm daily Apr-Sep, 10am-5pm Wed-Sun Oct & Mar, 10am-4pm Thu-Sun Nov-Feb) give this fortified 13th-century manor house a fairy-tale glow that is hard to shake off. Built by Britain's most successful wool merchant, Lawrence of Ludlow, it has changed little since it was completed in 1291 and boasts a cavernous Great Hall, original timber staircase and gabled windows, and an enchanting garden that's hardly been touched since the original owners first pitched their medieval forks.

Stokesay Castle is 6 miles northwest of Ludlow, just off the A49. Bus 435 runs five times daily between Shrewsbury and Ludlow. Alternatively, catch the train from Ludlow Station to Craven Arms, just over a mile away.

our pick **Waterdine Inn** (☎ 01547-528214; www .waterdine.com; Llanfair Waterdine; s/d incl dinner & breakfast £80/160; **P**), a timbered and ivy-clad 16th-century longhouse, is well and truly in the middle of nowhere, with the River Teme border with Wales the only reminder of an outside world. Expect a warm welcome and simple cottage-style rooms with low ceilings,

wooden furniture and springy beds. The restaurant also has a homely, dinner-party feel, while the fantastic modern Anglo-French menu (mains £12 to £18) focuses on organic meats and wild game. Llanfair Waterdine is about 12 miles west of Ludlow.

NORTH SHROPSHIRE

A tapestry of pretty market towns and fertile countryside make northern Shropshire well worth a look. With a market dating back 750 years, **Market Drayton** is also famed for its gingerbread and for being home to terrible teen Clive of India, founder of Britain's Indian Empire. The town has a scattering of medieval buildings. The **tourist office** (☎ 01584-653114; 49 Cheshire St; ☺ 9.30am-4pm Mon-Sat) can point you towards sights.

Five miles southwest, **Wollerton Old Hall** (☎ 01630-685760; www.wollertonoldhallgarden.com; Wollerton; adult/child £5/1; ☺ Fri, Sun & Bank Holidays noon-5pm) is a treat for gardeners, with its beautifully manicured lawns and flowers surrounding a 16th-century house.

Another 4 miles west is the ideal energy-burning spot for kids, **Hawkstone Park** (☎ 01939-200611; www.hawkstone.co.uk; Weston-under-Redcastle; adult/child £6/4; ☺ 10am-4pm Mar-Sep, 10am-3pm Oct, 10am-2pm weekends only Jan & Feb), an 18th-century magical land of cliffs, spooky rock-hewn caves, deep woods and underground grottos.

Another leap westwards will bring you to the beautiful mere-drizzled countryside around **Ellesmere**. The six glacial lakes surrounding the town are ideal for gentle walking, with well-signposted circular routes to guide you.

The wonderfully remote **Pen-y-Dyffryn Hotel** (☎ 01691-653700; www.peny.co.uk; Rhydycroesau, Oswestry; s/d from £57/114; **P**) is a real treat, where the birdsong is the prevalent noise and sheep roam the steep valley sides. Serving award-winning organic food (three-course set menu £35) and offering 12 traditional rooms, the hotel is in a remote Georgian rectory with gorgeous views of the Welsh mountains. The lovely 16th-century **Top Farm House** (☎ 01691-682582; www.topfarmknockin.co.uk; Knockin; s/d/f £35/60/65; **P**) is criss-crossed with an elaborately painted black-and-white timber facade, has just three old-maidish floral rooms and serves the best breakfast around.

Yorkshire

With a population as big as Scotland's, and an area half the size of Belgium, Yorkshire is almost a country in itself. It even has its own flag (a white rose on a blue background), its own distinctive dialect (known as 'Tyke') and its own official celebration (Yorkshire Day, 1 August). Needless to say, while Yorkshire folk are proud to be English, they're even prouder to be natives of 'God's Own Country', as they (only half-jokingly) refer to their home patch.

The region's roots are in 9th-century Danelaw, a Viking-governed area that roughly coincides with the boundaries of today's Yorkshire. It was originally divided into three parts – the North, West and East Ridings. Today it's split into four separate counties: South Yorkshire, West Yorkshire, North Yorkshire and the East Riding of Yorkshire.

So what is it that make Yorkshire so special? First there's the landscape – from the dark, brooding moors and lush, green dales that roll their way to the dramatic cliffs of the coast, Yorkshire has some of England's most beautiful scenery; more than a third of the county's area lies in the Yorkshire Dales and North York Moors national parks.

Second, there's the sheer breadth of history – here you can explore virtually every facet of the English experience, from the Middle Ages to the 20th century, in abbeys, castles, historic houses, medieval cities, industrial monuments and urban playgrounds.

But ultimately, Yorkshire's greatest appeal lies in its people. Proud, industrious and opinionated, with a wry wit always ready to puncture the first signs of pomposity, they have a warmth and friendliness that breaks through any initial gruffness. Stay here for any length of time and you'll come away believing, like the locals, that God is indeed a Yorkshirewoman.

YORKSHIRE

HIGHLIGHTS

- Exploring the medieval streets of **York** (p621) and its awe-inspiring cathedral
- Pulling on your hiking boots and striding out across the moors of the **Yorkshire Dales** (p605)
- Chilling out in **Leeds** (p593): shopping, eating, drinking, dancing
- Being beside the seaside at **Scarborough** (p638) with its traditional bucket-and-spade atmosphere
- Riding on the **North Yorkshire Moors Railway** (p645), one of England's most scenic railway lines
- Discovering mining's dark side at the **National Coal Mining Museum for England** (p601)

■ POPULATION: 4.96 MILLION	■ AREA: 5958 SQ MILES	■ CALORIES IN A YORKSHIRE 'FAT RASCAL' : 350

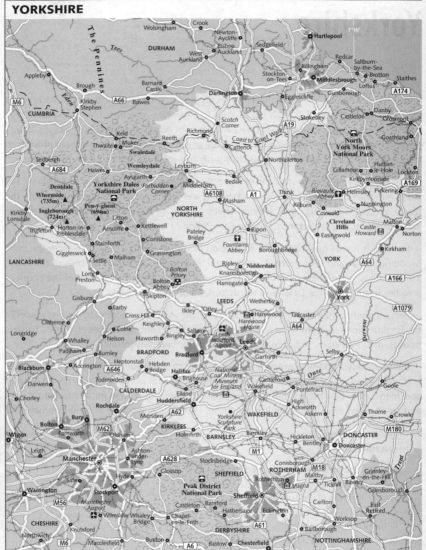

YORKSHIRE

History

As you drive through Yorkshire on the main A1 road, you're following in the footsteps of the Roman legions who conquered northern Britain in the 1st century AD. In fact, many Yorkshire towns – including York, Catterick and Malton – were founded by the Romans, and many modern roads (eg the

A1, A59, A166 and A1079) follow the lines of Roman roads.

When the Romans departed in the 5th century, native Britons battled for supremacy with invading Angles and, for a while, Yorkshire was part of the Kingdom of Northumbria. In the 9th century the Vikings arrived and conquered most of northern Britain. They

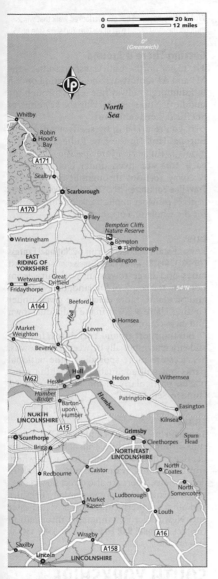

Battle of Stamford Bridge, before returning south to meet his appointment with William the Conqueror - and a fatal arrow - at the Battle of Hastings.

The inhabitants of northern England did not take the subsequent Norman invasion lying down. The Norman nobles built a chain of formidable castles throughout Yorkshire, including those at York, Richmond, Scarborough, Pickering and Helmsley. They also oversaw the establishment of the great abbeys of Rievaulx, Fountains and Whitby.

The Norman land grab formed the basis of the great estates that supported England's medieval aristocrats. By the 15th century, the duchies of York and Lancaster had become so wealthy and powerful that they ended up battling for the English throne – known as the Wars of the Roses (1455–87), it was a recurring conflict between the supporters of King Henry VI of the House of Lancaster (the red rose) and Richard, Duke of York (the white rose). They ended with the defeat of the Yorkist king Richard III by the earl of Richmond, Henry Tudor, at the Battle of Bosworth Field.

Yorkshire prospered quietly, with fertile farms in the north and the cutlery business of Sheffield in the south, until the big bang of the Industrial Revolution transformed the landscape – south Yorkshire became a centre of coal mining and steel works, while west Yorkshire was home to a massive textile industry, and the cities of Leeds, Bradford, Sheffield and Rotherham flourished. By the late 20th century another revolution was taking place. The heavy industries had died out, and the cities of Yorkshire were re-inventing themselves as shiny, high-tech centres of finance, higher education and tourism.

Information

The **Yorkshire Tourist Board** (www.yorkshire.com; 312 Tadcaster Rd, York, YO24 1GS) – postal and email enquiries only – has plenty of general leaflets and brochures. For more detailed information contact the local tourist offices listed throughout this chapter.

Activities

Yorkshire's varied landscape of wild hills, tranquil valleys, high moors and spectacular coastline offers plenty of opportunities for outdoor activities. See www.outdooryork shire.com for more details.

divided the territory that is now Yorkshire into *thridings* (thirds), which all met at Jorvik (York), their thriving commercial capital.

In 1066 Yorkshire was the scene of a pivotal showdown in the struggle for the English crown, when the Anglo-Saxon king Harold II rode north to defeat the forces of the Norwegian king Harold Hardrada at the

CYCLING

Yorkshire has a vast network of country lanes, although the most scenic areas also attract lots of motorists so even minor roads can be busy at weekends. Options include:

North York Moors Off-road bikers can avail themselves of the networks of bridle paths, former railways and disused mining tracks now converted to two-wheel use.

Whitby to Scarborough A 20-mile traffic-free route that follows a disused railway line, providing an effortless way to tour this rugged coast.

White Rose Cycle Route (NCN route 65) A 120-mile cruise from Hull to York and on to Middlesbrough, via the rolling Yorkshire Wolds and the dramatic western scarp of the North York Moors, with a traffic-free section on the old railway between Selby and York. It is part of the National Cycle Network (p792).

Yorkshire Dales Great cycling in the quieter areas in the north around Swaledale and Wensleydale, and the west around Dentdale. There's an excellent network of old drove roads (formerly used for driving cattle to market) which wind across lonely hillsides and tie in neatly with the country lanes in the valleys.

WALKING

For shorter walks and rambles the best area is the **Yorkshire Dales**, with a great selection of walks through scenic valleys or over wild hilltops, with a few higher summits thrown in for good measure. The **Yorkshire Wolds** hold hidden delights, while the quiet valleys and dramatic coast of the **North York Moors** also have many good opportunities.

All tourist offices stock a mountain of leaflets on local walks (free or up to £1.50), and sell more detailed guidebooks and maps. At train stations and tourist offices, it's worth looking out for leaflets detailing walks from train stations. Some tie in with train times, so you can walk one way and ride back.

Long-distance Walks

Cleveland Way A venerable moor-and-coast classic (details in the North York Moors section, p642).

Coast to Coast Walk England's No 1 walk, 190 miles across northern England from the Lake District across the Yorkshire Dales and North York Moors. The Yorkshire section takes a week to 10 days and offers some of the finest walking of its kind in England.

Dales Way Charming and not-too-strenuous amble from the Yorkshire Dales to the Lake District (details in the Yorkshire Dales section, p605).

Pennine Way The Yorkshire section of England's most famous walk runs for over 100 miles via Hebden Bridge, Malham, Horton-in-Ribblesdale and Hawes, passing near Haworth and Skipton.

Wolds Way Beautiful but oft-overlooked walk that winds through the most scenic part of eastern Yorkshire (see p615).

Getting There & Around

The major north–south transport routes – the M1 and A1 motorways and the main London to Edinburgh railway line – run through the middle of Yorkshire, serving the key cities of Sheffield, Leeds and York.

If you're arriving by sea from northern Europe, Hull (in the East Riding) is the region's main port. More specific details for each area are given under Getting There & Away sections throughout this chapter. **Traveline Yorkshire** (☎ 0871 200 2233; www.yorkshire travel.net) provides public transport information for the whole of Yorkshire.

BUS

Long-distances coaches run by **National Express** (☎ 08717 818181; www.nationalexpress.com) serve most cities and large towns in Yorkshire from London, the south of England, the Midlands and Scotland. More details are given under Getting There & Away in the individual town and city sections.

Bus transport around Yorkshire is frequent and efficient, especially between major towns. Services are more sporadic in the national parks but still adequate for reaching most places, particularly in the summer months (June to September).

TRAIN

The main line between London and Edinburgh runs through Yorkshire, with at least 10 trains per day calling at York and Doncaster, where you can change trains for other Yorkshire destinations. There are also direct services between the major towns and cities of Yorkshire and other northern cities such as Manchester and Newcastle. For timetable information contact **National Rail Enquiries** (☎ 08457 484950; www.nationalrail.co.uk).

SOUTH YORKSHIRE

As in the valleys of South Wales, it was a confluence of natural resources – coal, iron ore and ample water – that made South Yorkshire a crucible of the British iron, steel and mining industries. From the 18th century to the 20th, the region was the industrial powerhouse of northern England.

The blast furnaces of Sheffield and Rotherham and the coal pits of Barnsley and Doncaster may have closed long ago, but the hulking reminders of that irrepressible Victorian dynamism remain, not only in the old steel works and pit-heads – some of which have been converted into enthralling museums and exhibition spaces – but also in the grand civic buildings that grace Sheffield's city centre, fitting testaments to the untrammelled ambitions of their 19th-century patrons.

SHEFFIELD
pop 525,800

Steel is everywhere in Sheffield. Today, however, it's not the steel of the foundries, mills and forges that made the city's fortune, or the canteens of cutlery that made 'Sheffield steel' a household name, but the steel of scaffolding and cranes, of modern sculptures and supertrams, and of new steel-framed buildings rising against the skyline.

The steel industry that made the city famous is long since gone, but after many years of decline Sheffield is on the up again – like many of northern England's cities it has grabbed the opportunities presented by urban renewal with both hands and is working hard to reinvent itself. The new economy is based on services, shopping and the 'knowledge industry' that flows from the city's universities.

This renaissance got off to a shaky start in 2000 when the city's signature millennium

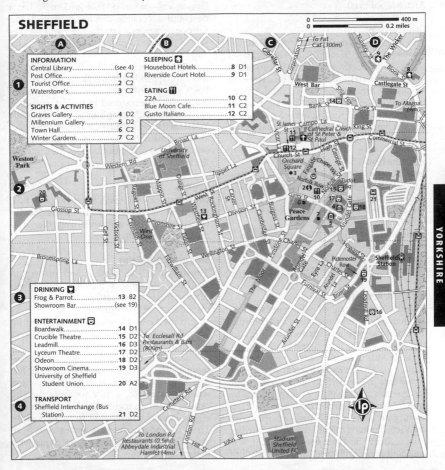

SHEFFIELD

INFORMATION	
Central Library	(see 4)
Post Office	1 C2
Tourist Office	2 C2
Waterstone's	3 C2

SIGHTS & ACTIVITIES	
Graves Gallery	4 D2
Millennium Gallery	5 C2
Town Hall	6 C2
Winter Gardens	7 C2

SLEEPING	
Houseboat Hotels	8 D1
Riverside Court Hotel	9 D1

EATING	
22A	10 C2
Blue Moon Cafe	11 C2
Gusto Italiano	12 C2

DRINKING	
Frog & Parrot	13 B2
Showroom Bar	(see 19)

ENTERTAINMENT	
Boardwalk	14 D1
Crucible Theatre	15 D2
Leadmill	16 D3
Lyceum Theatre	17 D2
Odeon	18 D2
Showroom Cinema	19 D3
University of Sheffield Student Union	20 A2

TRANSPORT	
Sheffield Interchange (Bus Station)	21 D2

YORKSHIRE

project, the National Centre for Popular Music, closed down due to lack of visitors only 15 months after it opened. An eye-catching and controversial piece of modern architecture shaped like four giant, stainless steel kettles, it now houses Sheffield Hallam University's student union.

But the city's redevelopment seems to be hitting its stride now, with attractive new public spaces and a clutch of interesting museums and galleries. And there's a lively nightlife fuelled by the large student population – the city's two universities support around 24,000 potential pubbers and clubbers – and Sheffield's long-standing reputation as a top spot for music (what do you mean, you've never heard of the Arctic Monkeys?).

Orientation

The most interesting parts of Sheffield are clustered in the 'Heart of the City' district about 300m northwest of the train station (and immediately west of the bus station), a compact area outlined by Arundel Gate, Furnival St, Carver St, West St, Church St and High St. Stretching west from here, Division St and Devonshire St have hip clothes and record shops, popular restaurants and trendy bars.

Information

Central Library (☎ 0114-273 4711; Surrey St; 10am-8pm Mon, 9.30am-5.30pm Tue & Thu-Sat, 9.30am-5pm Wed) Internet access.

Post office (Norfolk Row; 8.30am-5.30pm Mon-Fri, to 3pm Sat)

Tourist office (☎ 0114-221 1900; www.sheffieldcity centre.com; 14 Norfolk Row; 10am-5pm Mon-Sat)

Waterstone's (☎ 0114-272 8971; 24-26 Orchard Sq; 9am-6pm Mon-Sat, 10.30am-5pm Sun) Books & maps.

Sights & Activities

Since 2000 the city centre has been in the throes of a massive redevelopment that will continue into 2020 and beyond, so expect building sites and roadworks for several years to come.

Of the parts that are already complete, pride of place goes to the **Winter Gardens** (admission free; 8am-6pm), a wonderfully ambitious public space with a soaring glass roof supported by graceful arches of laminated timber. The 21st-century architecture contrasts sharply with the Victorian **town hall** nearby, and is further enhanced by the **Peace Gardens** – complete with fountains, sculptures and lawns full of

lunching office workers whenever there's a bit of sun.

Sheffield's cultural revival is spearheaded by the **Millennium Gallery** (☎ 0114-278 2600; www .museums-sheffield.org.uk; Arundel Gate; admission free, special exhibitions £6; 10am-5pm Mon-Sat, 11am-5pm Sun), a collection of four galleries under one roof. The **Ruskin Gallery** houses an eclectic collection of paintings, drawings and manuscripts established and inspired by Victorian artist, writer, critic and philosopher John Ruskin, while the **Metalwork Gallery** charts the transformation of Sheffield's steel industry into craft and design – the 'Sheffield steel' stamp on locally made cutlery and tableware now has the cachet of designer chic.

The nearby **Graves Gallery** (☎ 0114-278 2600; Surrey St; admission free; 10am-5pm Mon-Sat) has a neat and accessible display of British and European modern art; the big names represented include Cézanne, Gaugin, Miró, Klee and Picasso.

In the days before steel mills, metalworking was a cottage industry just like wool or cotton. For a glimpse of that earlier, more innocent era, explore the restored 18th-century forges, workshops and machines at the **Abbeydale Industrial Hamlet** (☎ 0114-236 7731; adult/child £3/2; 10am-4pm Mon-Thu, 11am-4.45pm Sun Easter-early Oct, closed Fri & Sat), 4 miles southwest of the centre on the A621 (towards the Peak District).

Events

Each year around April, Sheffield plays host to the immensely popular **World Snooker Championship** (www.worldsnooker.com), staged at the Crucible Theatre.

Sleeping & Eating

Tourism has not quite taken off yet in Sheffield, and most of the city centre hotels cater primarily to business travellers. New restaurants are springing up – there are several in the Leopold Square development on Leopold St – but the main restaurant areas are outside the centre.

There's a mile-long strip of bars, restaurants, cafes and take-aways on Ecclesall Rd, a mile to the southwest of the city centre, while London Rd, a mile south of the city centre, has a concentration of good-value ethnic restaurants ranging from Turkish to Thai. To find student bars and eateries head along Division St and Devonshire St just west of the city centre.

Riverside Court Hotel (☎ 0114-273 1962; www .riversidecourt.co.uk; 4 Nursery St; s/d/tr from £37/47/65) The riverside location and relative proximity to the city centre make this hotel a pretty good choice if you don't want to get stung for a midweek business rate; the rooms were undergoing a facelift at the time of research.

Houseboat Hotels (☎ 0114-232 6556; www.house boathotels.com; Victoria Quays, Wharfe St; d/q from £75/95) Here's something a bit different – kick off your shoes and relax on board your very own permanently moored houseboat, complete with self-catering kitchen and patio area. Guests are entitled to use the gym facilities at the Hilton across the road.

ourpick Gusto Italiano (☎ 0114-275 1117; 18 Church St; mains £3-6; ⏰ 7am-6.30pm Mon-Fri, 8am-6pm Sat) A *real* Italian cafe, from the Italian owners serving homemade Italian food to the genuine Italian coffee being enjoyed by Italian customers reading the Italian newspapers… you get the idea – Gusto Italiano is a great place for a hot lunch, or just cake and coffee.

22A (☎ 0114-276 7462; 22A Norfolk Row; mains £5-8; ⏰ 8am-5pm Mon-Sat) Nice music, nice people, nice place – this homely cafe serves hearty breakfasts and offers a mean wrap at lunchtime – hummus and roasted vegie is our favourite – and serves it with a decent cup of java.

Blue Moon Cafe (☎ 0114-276 3443; 2 St James St; mains £5-7; ⏰ 8am-8pm Mon-Sat) Tasty vegie and vegan creations, soups and other good-for-you dishes, all served with the ubiquitous salad, in a very pleasant atmosphere – perfect for a spot of Saturday afternoon lounging.

Drinking

Lots of bars in a relatively small area plus 24,000 students equals… a wild night out – a pretty straightforward formula, really. The main concentrations of bars are around Division/Devonshire St and West St in the city centre, and Ecclesall Rd to the southwest. Virtually every bar does pub grub until about 7pm.

Fat Cat (☎ 0114-249 4801; 23 Alma St) One of Sheffield's finest pubs, the Fat Cat serves a wide range of real ales (some brewed on the premises) in a wonderfully unreconstructed interior. There are three bars, good pub grub, a roaring fire in winter and – in the men's toilets – a fascinating exhibit on local sanitation.

Frog & Parrot (☎ 0114-272 1280; 94 Division St) Home to the world's strongest beer (allegedly), the 12% ABV 'Roger & Out'. Unsuspecting ale-heads saunter in looking to down a pint of something as strong as your average wine, which is why they only serve this particular brew in half-pint glasses – so that you have at least a 50/50 chance of walking out under your own steam.

Showroom Bar (☎ 0114-249 5479; 7 Paternoster Row) Originally aimed at film fans, this stylish bar with its arty, hip clientele is one of the best night-time destinations in town. The ambience is good, and so is the food, and Sunday afternoons have live jazz.

Entertainment

Sheffield has a good selection of nightclubs, a couple of top-notch theatres, and venues that attract the big names in music – both classical and popular. The weekly *Sheffield Telegraph* (out on Friday) has the lowdown on Sheffield's entertainment scene, as does the freebie *Exposed*, available almost everywhere.

CLUBS & LIVE MUSIC

Boardwalk (☎ 0114-279 9090; www.theboardwalklive .co.uk; 39 Snig Hill) A Sheffield institution, the Boardwalk provides a stage for local bands, old rockers, up-and-coming stars, world music, the obscure, the novel and the downright weird – they all play here. No real music fan should miss the chance to catch a gig here.

Leadmill (☎ 0114-221 2828; www.leadmill.co.uk; 6-7 Leadmill Rd) Every touring band has played the dark and dingy Leadmill on the way up (or on the way down), and it remains the best place in town to hear live rock and alternative music. There are club nights too, but they tend to be cheesy rubbish.

University of Sheffield Student Union (☎ 0114-222 8500; www.sheffieldunion.com; Western Bank) A varied and generally good program of rock gigs and club nights – including appearances by some pretty classy DJs – make this a good spot to spend an evening, plus there's the Last Laugh Comedy Club on Sunday nights. The Union is about a mile west of the city centre.

THEATRE & CINEMAS

The **Crucible Theatre** and **Lyceum Theatre** on Tudor Sq share the same **box office** (☎ 0114-249 6000; www.sheffieldtheatres.co.uk). Both are home to excellent regional drama; the Crucible was undergoing a major renovation at the time of research and will reopen in 2009.

YORKSHIRE

The **Showroom Cinema** (☎ 0114-275 7727; www .showroom.org.uk; Paternoster Row) is the largest independent cinema in England, screening a great mix of art-house, off-beat and not-quite-mainstream films. For everything else, there's the **Odeon** (☎ 0114-224 2007; www.odeon.co.uk; 45-47 Arundel Gate).

Getting There & Away

For all travel-related info in Sheffield and South Yorkshire, call ☎ 01709-515151 or consult www.travelsouthyorkshire.com.

BUS

The bus station – called the Interchange – is just east of the centre, about 250m north of the train station. National Express services link Sheffield with most major centres in the north; there are frequent buses linking Sheffield with Leeds (£5.20, 50 to 75 minutes, hourly), Manchester (£7.60, 1½ hours, three daily) and London (£16.50, 4½ hours, eight daily).

TRAIN

Sheffield is served by trains from all directions: Leeds (£8.20, 40 to 75 minutes, twice hourly); London St Pancras (£81, two to three hours, hourly) via Derby or Nottingham; Manchester Piccadilly (£13.80, one hour, twice hourly); and York (£14.50, 1¼ hours, twice hourly).

Getting Around

Buses run every 10 minutes during the day (Monday to Saturday, less frequently on Sundays). Sheffield also boasts a modern **Supertram** (www.supertram.com, tickets £1.20-2.70) that links the train station to the city centre and outer suburbs.

For a day of sightseeing, a **South Yorkshire Peak Explorer Pass** (adult/concession £8/5.25) is valid for one day on all bus and tram services in South Yorkshire and the northern Peak District. Buy a pass at the **transport information centre** (✆ 8am-6pm Mon-Fri, 8.30am-5pm Sat, 9am-5pm Sun) in Sheffield bus station, or at tourist offices in the Peak District.

AROUND SHEFFIELD

At its peak, the Templeborough steelworks was the world's most productive steel melter, with six 3000°C, electric-arc furnaces producing 1.8 million tonnes of metal a year. The mile-long works, which once had a 10,000-strong workforce, is now a 'science adventure centre' called **Magna** (☎ 01709-720002; www.visit

magna.co.uk; Sheffield Rd, Rotherham; adult/child £9.95/7.95 Apr-Oct, £9.95/7.95 Nov-Mar; ✆ 10am-5pm daily Mar–mid-Sep, 10am-5pm Tue-Sat mid-Sep–Feb).

An unashamed celebration of heavy industry, this vast, dimly lit shed smelling vaguely of machine oil, hot metal and past glory, is a hands-on paradise for kids of all ages, with a huge range of science and technology exhibits based around the themes of earth, air, water and fire. The latter section is especially impressive, with a towering tornado of flame as a centrepiece and the chance to use a real electric arc to create your own tiny puddle of molten steel, if only for a moment or two. The hourly 'Big Melt' – a massive sound, light and fireworks show – re-enacts the firing up of one of the original arc furnaces.

Magna is 4 miles northeast of Sheffield, just off the M1 motorway near Rotherham. Takes bus 69 from Sheffield bus station (30 minutes, every 20 minutes Monday to Friday, half-hourly Saturday, hourly Sunday) towards Rotherham; it'll drop you at the door.

WEST YORKSHIRE

What steel was to South Yorkshire, so wool was to West Yorkshire. It was the tough and unforgiving textile industry that drove the county's economy from the 18th century on, and the woollen mills and factories – and the canals that were built to transport raw materials and finished products – that defined much of its landscape. But that's all in the past, and recent years have seen the transformation of a once hard-bitten area into quite the picture postcard.

Leeds and Bradford, two adjoining cities so big that they've virtually become one, are the perfect case in point. Though both were founded amid the dark, satanic mills of the Industrial Revolution, both are undergoing radical redevelopment and reinvention, prettifying their town centres and trying to tempt the more adventurous tourist with a slew of new museums, galleries, restaurants and bars.

Beyond the cities, West Yorkshire is a landscape of bleak moorland dissected by deep valleys dotted with old mill towns and villages. The relics of the wool and cloth industries are still visible in the rows of weavers' cottages and workers' houses built along ridges overlooking the towering chimneys of the mills in the valleys – landscapes that were so vividly described by the Brontë sisters, West Yorkshire's most renowned literary export and biggest tourist draw.

Activities

The valleys and moors of West Yorkshire make good walking country. The tourist offices all have leaflets and guidebooks on local walks. Hebden Bridge and Haworth make ideal bases for circular walks, with opportunities for several long and short hikes. The **Haworth to Hebden Bridge Path** is a popular trail that links the two towns through quiet farmland and scenic wooded valleys.

The **Pennine Way** (p588), England's longest trail, follows the watershed through the area; some good walks are possible by following it for just a day or two.

Getting Around

The Metro is West Yorkshire's highly efficient train and bus network, centred on Leeds and Bradford – which are also the main gateways to the county. For transport information call **Metroline** (☎ 0113-245 7676; www.wymetro.com). The excellent Day Rover (£5 for train or bus, £6 train and bus) tickets are good for travel on buses and trains after 9.30am on weekdays and all day at weekends. There's a range of additional Rovers covering buses and/or trains, plus heaps of useful Metro maps and timetables, available from bus and train stations and most tourist offices in West Yorkshire.

LEEDS

pop 750,200

One of the fastest growing cities in the UK, Leeds is the glitzy, glamorous embodiment of newly rediscovered northern self-confidence. More than a decade of redevelopment has seen the city centre transform from near-derelict mill town into a vision of 21st-century urban chic, with skyscraping office blocks, glass and steel waterfront apartment complexes and renovated Victorian shopping arcades.

Known as the 'Knightsbridge of the North', Leeds has made itself into a shopping mecca, its streets lined with bustling malls sporting the top names in fashion. And when you've shopped till you drop there's a plethora of pubs, clubs and excellent restaurants to relax

in. From cutting-edge couture to contemporary cuisine, Leeds will serve it to you on a plate... or more likely in a stylishly designed bag. Amid all this cutting-edge style, it seems fitting that the network of city bus routes includes peach, mauve and magenta lines as well as the more humdrum red, orange and blue.

Orientation

Easily managed on foot, most of the action in Leeds' city centre is concentrated between Boar Lane to the south and The Headrow – the main drag – to the north, all within 10 to 15 minutes' walk from the train station. Briggate, which runs north–south between the two, is the focus of most of the shopping, while the best nightlife is concentrated in the warren of small streets at the eastern end of Boar Lane. In recent years there has been substantial waterfront development along the River Aire at The Calls and around Brewery Wharf.

Information

Central Library (☎ 0113-247 6016; Calverley St; ✆ 9am-8pm Mon-Wed, 9am-5pm Thu & Fri, 10am-5pm Sat, 1-5pm Sun) Internet access.
Gateway Yorkshire/Leeds Visitor Centre (☎ 0113-242 5242; www.visitleeds.co.uk; The Arcade, Leeds City Train Station; ✆ 9am-5.30pm Mon-Sat, 10am-4pm Sun)
Leeds General Infirmary (☎ 0113-243 2799; Great George St)
Post office (St John's Centre, 116 Albion St; ✆ 9am-5.30pm Mon-Sat)
Waterstone's (☎ 0113-244 4588; 93-97 Albion St; 9am-6.30pm Mon-Sat, 10.30am-4.30pm Sun) Maps and books.

Sights & Activities

Leeds' most interesting museum is undoubtedly the **Royal Armouries** (☎ 0113-220 1940; www .armouries.org.uk; Armouries Dr; admission free; ✆ 10am-5pm), beside the snazzy Clarence Dock residential development. It was originally built to house the armour and weapons from the Tower of London but was subsequently expanded to cover 3000 years' worth of fighting and self-defence. It all sounds a bit macho, but the exhibits are as varied as they are fascinating: films, live-action demonstrations and hands-on technology can awaken interests you never thought you had, from jousting to Indian elephant armour – we dare you not to learn something. Catch bus 95, or take the Waterbus (adult/child £2/1, 15 minutes, two to four daily) along the river from The Embankment at the Neville St bridge.

LEEDS

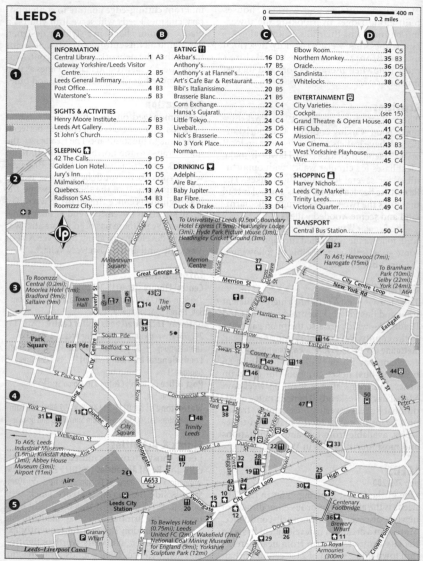

One of the world's largest textile mills has been transformed into the **Leeds Industrial Museum** (☎ 0113-263 7861; www.leeds.gov.uk/arm leymills; Canal Rd; adult/child £3/1; ⏰ 10am-5pm Tue-Sat, 1-5pm Sun), telling the story of Leeds' industrial past, both glorious and ignominious. The city became rich off the sheep's back but at some cost in human terms – working conditions were, well, Dickensian. As well as a selection of working machinery, there's a particularly informative display on how cloth is actually made. Take bus 5 from the train station.

If all this industrial stuff makes you feel starved of a bit of high culture, get yourself to the **Leeds Art Gallery** (☎ 0113-247 8256; www.leeds .gov.uk/artgallery; The Headrow; admission free; ⏰ 10am-

8pm Mon & Tue, noon-8pm Wed, 10am-5pm Thu-Sat, 1-5pm Sun). It's packed with 19th- and 20th-century British heavyweights – Turner, Constable, Stanley Spencer, Wyndham Lewis et al – along with contemporary pieces by more recent arrivals such as Antony Gormley, sculptor of the *Angel of the North* (p757). Pride of place, however, goes to the outstanding genius of Henry Moore (1898–1986), who graduated from the Leeds School of Art. The adjoining **Henry Moore Institute** (☎ 0113-246 7467; www.henry-moore-fdn.co.uk; The Headrow; admission free; ☙ 10am-5.30pm Thu-Mon, 10am-9pm Wed), in a converted Victorian warehouse, showcases the work of 20th-century sculptors but not, despite the name, anything by Moore; for more of Moore, head to the Yorkshire Sculpture Park (p601).

Tucked away off northern Briggate is the redundant but lovingly nurtured **St John's Church** (☎ 0113-244 1689; ☙ 9.30am-5.30pm Tue-Sat), a one-off masterpiece consecrated in 1634 – the first in the north of England following the Reformation. The gorgeous (and original) oak box pews are certainly eye-catching, but they're only a temporary distraction from the intricate medieval design of the magnificent Jacobean screen that is without parallel in all of England.

Leeds' most impressive medieval structure is the beautiful **Kirkstall Abbey** (☎ 0113-274 8041; Abbey Rd; admission free; ☙ 11am-4pm Tue-Sun Apr-Sep, to 3pm Oct-Mar), founded in 1152 by Cistercian monks from Fountains Abbey in North Yorkshire, and one of the best-preserved medieval abbeys in Britain.

Across the road, the **Abbey House Museum** (☎ 0113-230 5492; www.leeds.gov.uk/abbeyhouse; Abbey Rd; adult/child £3.50/1.50; ☙ 10am-5pm Tue-Fri & Sun, noon-5pm Sat), once the Great Gate House to the abbey, contains meticulously reconstructed shops and houses that evoke Victorian Leeds, and displays that give an interesting insight into monastic life. Children will enjoy it.

The abbey and museum are off the A65, three miles northwest of the centre; take bus 33, 33A or 757.

Festivals & Events

The August Bank Holiday (the weekend preceding the last Monday in August) sees 50,000-plus music fans converge on Bramham Park, 10 miles outside the city centre, for the **Leeds Festival** (☎ 0871 231 0821; www.leedsfestival.com), one of England's biggest rock music extravaganzas, spread across four separate stages.

Sleeping

There are no budget options in the city centre and the midrange choices are between absolute fleapits and chain hotels. If you want somewhere cheapish you're forced to head for the 'burbs, where there are plenty of decent B&Bs and smallish hotels.

MIDRANGE

Golden Lion Hotel (☎ 0113-243 6454; www.thegoldenlion-leeds.co.uk; 2 Lower Briggate; s/d from £85/99; P) They don't come much more central than Leeds' oldest hotel which, after a much-needed makeover, can now compete with the rest. The rooms are tidy and modern, if a little small, while the public areas retain a comfortably old-fashioned atmosphere.

Jury's Inn (☎ 0113-283 8800; www.jurysinns.com; Kendell St, Brewery Pl; r from £60-103; P ⌨) The successful Irish hotel chain has another hit with its Leeds hotel; large, functional rooms, plenty of personal charm and few complaints. If you're walking, it's just across the Centenary footbridge from the city centre, in the heart of the fashionable Brewery Wharf district.

Bewleys Hotel (☎ 0113-234 2340; www.bewleyshotels.com; City Walk, Sweet St; r £69; P ⌨) Bewleys is super-convenient for motorists, just off Junction 3 on the M621 but also just 10 minutes' walk from the city centre, and with secure basement parking. Rooms are stylish and well appointed, with soundproofed walls and windows; the flat rate accommodates up to two adults plus three kids under 16.

Roomzzz Central (☎ 0113-233 0400; www.roomzzz.co.uk; 2 Burley Rd; r from £79; P ⌨) This outfit offers bright and modern luxury apartments complete with fitted kitchen, with the added advantage of a 24-hour hotel reception. Roomzzz Central is half a mile west of the city centre; by 2009 there will also be **Roomzzz City** (12 Swinegate), right in the city centre.

The following places outside the city centre are also recommended:
Moorlea Hotel (☎ 0113-243 2653; www.moorleahotel.co.uk; 146 Woodsley Rd; s/d from £36/48) Family-friendly hotel northwest of the centre, near the University of Leeds.
Boundary Hotel Express (☎ 0113-275 7700; www.boundaryhotel.co.uk; 42 Cardigan Rd; s/d £40/50; ⌨) Basic but welcoming; 1.5 miles northwest of centre, near Headingley cricket ground.
Headingley Lodge (☎ 0113-278 5323; www.headingleylodge.co.uk; Headingley Stadium, St Michael's Lane; d/f £50/60; P ⌨) Smart, comfortable rooms with views of Headingley cricket ground; part of the stadium complex.

TOP END

Radisson SAS (☎ 0113-236 6000; www.leeds.radissonsas .com; 1 The Light, Cookridge St; r £100-130; P □) An extraordinary conversion of the former HQ of the Leeds Permanent Building Society, a listed building dating from 1930, with 'standard' rooms that are anything but – you have a choice of three styles: hi-tech, art deco and Italian, while the business-class rooms are truly luxurious.

Malmaison (☎ 0113-398 1000; www.malmaison.com; 1 Swinegate; s/d/ste from £130/160/275) Self-consciously stylish, this typical Malmaison property is set in a former bus and tram company HQ with a fabulous waterfront location and all of the trademark touches – huge comfy beds, sexy lighting and all the latest designer gear.

42 The Calls (☎ 0113-244 0099; www.42thecalls.co.uk; 42 The Calls; r/ste from £150/199; □) This snazzy boutique hotel in what was once a 19th-century grain mill is a big hit with the trendy business crowd, who love its sharp, polished lines and designer aesthetic. The smaller studio rooms are pretty compact, and breakfast is not included; it'll cost you an extra £15 for the full English.

our pick Quebecs (☎ 0113-244 8989; www.theeton collection.com; 9 Quebec St; s/d/ste from £160/170/280; □) Victorian grace at its opulent best is the theme of our favourite hotel in town, a conversion of the former Leeds and County Liberal Club. The elaborate wood panelling and heraldic stained-glass windows in the public areas are matched by the contemporary design of the bedrooms. Two of the deluxe split-level suites – the cutely named Sherbert and Liquorice suites – have dramatic spiral staircases.

Eating

The Leeds restaurant scene is constantly evolving, with new places springing up in the wake of new shopping and residential developments. The latest scheme is the **Corn Exchange** (www.cornx.net), a beautiful Victorian building with a spectacular domed roof. At the time of research it was being converted to house a collection of food and drink retailers, with a new branch of Anthony's (see opposite) in the central piazza.

BUDGET

Akbar's (☎ 0113-245 6566; www.akbars.co.uk; 15 Eastgate; mains £5.50-7; ☾ dinner only) Bit of an Egyptian theme going on at this exceptionally popular Indian restaurant – sarcophagi and cat-gods watch over the cutting-edge decor beneath a 'night in the desert' ceiling. The traditional curry dishes come in pyramid-size portions, and they don't take bookings – expect to wait half an hour for a table on weekend nights.

Art's Cafe-Bar & Restaurant (☎ 0113-243 8243; www.artscafebar.co.uk; 42 Call Lane; mains lunch £5-7, dinner £10-14; ☾ noon-11pm Mon-Fri, noon-2am Sat, 10.30am-11pm Sun) Local art on the walls and a Bohemian vibe throughout make this a popular place for quiet reflection, a chat and a really good cup of coffee. The dinner menu offers half a dozen old favourites, including beer-battered haddock (sustainably sourced, of course) with chips and peas.

Hansa's Gujarati (☎ 0113-244 4408; www.hansas restaurant.com; 72-74 North St; mains £5-7; ☾ 5-10pm Mon-Thu, 5-11pm Fri, 6-11pm Sat, noon-2pm Sun) A Leeds institution, Hansa's has been dishing up wholesome Gujarati vegetarian cuisine for 20 years. The restaurant is plain and unassuming, save for a Hindu shrine, but the food is exquisite – specialities of the house include *samosa chaat*, a mix of spiced potato and chickpea samosas with a yogurt and tamarind sauce.

Norman (☎ 0872 080 8000; www.normanbar.co.uk; 36 Call Lane; mains £7-9; ☾ noon-2am Mon-Sat, noon-midnight Sun) One of the city's hippest bars – a touch of tongue-in-cheek kitsch (think fringed lampshades and a cuckoo clock) spice up the stylish modern lines here – offers a tempting Asian noodle-bar menu with dishes ranging from squid tempura and edamame beans to seafood ramen and Vietnamese beef salad.

MIDRANGE

Little Tokyo (☎ 0113-243 9090; 24 Central Rd; mains £7-15; ☾ 11.30am-10pm Mon-Thu, 11.30am-11pm Fri & Sat) Fans of genuine Japanese food should go no further than this superb restaurant, which serves a wide array of quality sushi and sashimi (including half-portions) and Bento boxes – those handy trays that serve the Japanese equivalent of a four-course meal.

Nick's Brasserie (☎ 0113-246 9444; www.nicks brasserie.com; 20 Dock St; mains £10-14; ☾ noon-10pm Tue-Sat, noon-3pm Sun) Housed in a converted red-brick warehouse on up-and-coming Dock St, Nick's offers an intriguing menu that sees crab linguini with chilli and lime, and leek and ricotta cannelloni, alongside stalwarts such as devilled whitebait and steak-frites with pepper sauce. Weekend brunch (served noon to 4pm) ranges from a traditional fry-up or bacon sandwich to eggs Benedict or scrambled egg with smoked salmon.

Bibi's Italianissimo (☎ 0113-243 0905; www.bibis restaurant.com; Criterion Pl, Swinegate; mains £10-16; ✆ noon-10.30pm Mon & Tue, noon-11.30pm Wed-Sat, noon-10pm Sun) The mamma of Leeds' Italian eateries is a blast from the past, a glamorous, 1920s art deco–style palace – all mirrored pillars, crisp linen and waistcoated waiters – but with age comes experience and the food remains the best Italian in town. Live jazz Wednesday nights.

Livebait (☎ 0113-244 4144; 11-15 Wharf St, High Court; mains £10-17; ✆ noon-3pm & 5-10.30pm) Quality seafood – from Whitby crab and Canadian lobster to fresh oysters and langoustines – is the order of the day in this friendly and welcoming restaurant. Classic fish and chips is done with a light and crispy batter and served with homemade tartare sauce and deliciously minty mushy peas.

Brasserie Blanc (☎ 0113-220 6060; www.brasserie blanc.com; Victoria Mill, Sovereign St; mains £11-17; ✆ noon-2.45pm & 5.30-10.30pm Mon-Fri, noon-11pm Sat, noon-10pm Sun) The latest offering from Raymond Blanc manages to create a surprisingly intimate and romantic space amid the cast-iron pillars and red brick of an old Victorian warehouse. The menu is unerringly French, from escargots to Toulouse sausage, and there's a lovely outdoor terrace overlooking the river.

No 3 York Place (☎ 0113-245 9922; www.no3york place.co.uk; 3 York Pl; mains £12-17; ✆ lunch & dinner Mon-Fri, dinner Sat) Any debate over which is the best restaurant in town will include this superb French eatery, with its designer dining area and regularly changing menu of Gallic delicacies – how about roast duck with endive tarte tatin, or wood pigeon with caramelised apple and thyme jus?

Anthony's at Flannel's (☎ 0113-242 8732; www .anthonysatflannels.co.uk; 3rd fl, Flannel's Fashion Centre, 68-78 Vicar Lane; 2-/3-course lunch £15/18; ✆ 9am-6pm Tue-Thu, 9am-11pm Fri & Sat, 11am-5pm Sun) The brasserie-style brother of the award-winning Anthony's (see right), this bright and cheerful modern restaurant set amid white walls and timber beams features much of Anthony's style stuffed into its excellent sandwiches, salads, lunches and luxurious afternoon teas (£12). If you want to see and be seen, there's also **Anthony's Patisserie** in the classy setting of the Victoria Quarter arcade across the street.

TOP END

Anthony's (☎ 0113-245 5922; www.anthonysrestaurant .co.uk; 19 Boar Lane; 2-/3-course dinner £34/42; ✆ noon-2pm Tue-Sat, 7-9pm Tue-Thu, 7-10pm Fri & Sat) Probably the most talked about restaurant in town, Anthony's serves superb British cuisine to a clientele so eager that they'll think nothing of booking a month in advance. If you go at any other time except Saturday evening, you'll get away with making your reservations a day or so earlier.

Drinking

Leeds is justifiably renowned for its selection of pubs and bars. Glammed-up hordes of party animals crawl the cluster of venues around Boar Lane and Call Lane, where bars are opening (and closing) all the time. Most bars open till 2am; many turn into clubs after 11pm or midnight, with an admission charge.

Baby Jupiter (☎ 0113-242 1202; 11 York Pl) A retro gem with lots of purple velvet, hanging fishbowls and images from old sci-fi films, the basement bar sports a cool soundtrack that ranges from indie, funk and soul to punk, new wave and electro.

Bar Fibre (☎ 08701 200888; 168 Lower Briggate) Leeds' most popular gay bar, which spills out onto the cleverly named Queen's Court, is where the beautiful congregate to congratulate themselves on being so lucky. There's another cluster of gay bars downhill at the junction of Lower Briggate and The Calls.

Duck & Drake (☎ 0113-246 5806; 43 Kirkgate) A down-to-earth traditional boozer with a well-worn atmosphere, a cast of regular pub characters, and no fewer than 16, hand-pulled real ales to choose from.

Northern Monkey (☎ 0113-242 6630; 115 The Headrow) An attractive bare-floorboards-and-leather-sofas kind of bar catering to a youngish crowd – Becks and vodkas behind the bar, and an indie soundtrack with guest DJs on Friday and Saturday nights.

Oracle (☎ 0113-246 9912; 3 Brewery Pl) *The* place to be seen on a summer afternoon, Oracle has a huge outdoor terrace overlooking the River Aire. It serves gourmet burgers and a great selection of international beers just made to be served cold, from Guinness to Grolsch to Tsingtao. Upstairs there's a very chic cocktail and champagne bar that also sells spirits by the bottle, including Remy Martin at £300 a pop.

Sandinista (☎ 0113-305 0372; 5/5A Cross Belgrave St) This laid-back bar has a Latin look but a unifying theme, attracting an eclectic clientele with its mixed bag of music and unpretentious atmosphere. If you're not too fussed about looking glam, this is the spot for you.

Whitelocks (☎ 0113-245 3950; Turk's Head Yard) There's lots of polished wood, gleaming brass and colourful stained glass in this popular traditional pub dating from 1715. Theakstons, Deuchars IPA and several other real ales are on tap, and in summer the crowds spill out into the courtyard.

Other tips for a tipple:

Adelphi (☎ 0113-245 6377; 3-5 Hunslet Rd) Built in 1898 and hardly changed since.

Aire Bar (☎ 0113-245 5500; 32 The Calls) Red-brick vaults, leather sofas, Timothy Taylor's Landlord real ale, and a terrace overhanging the river.

Elbow Room (☎ 0113-245 7011; 64 Call Lane) Pop art, purple pool tables and laid-back music.

Entertainment

In order to make sense of the ever-evolving scene, get your hands on the fortnightly *Leeds Guide* (£1.90; www.leedsguide.co.uk) or *Absolute Leeds* (£1.50; www.absoluteleeds .co.uk).

CLUBS

The tremendous Leeds club scene attracts people from miles around. In true northern tradition people brave the cold wearing next to nothing, even in winter, which is a spectacle in itself. Clubs charge a variety of admission prices, ranging from as little as £1 on a slow weeknight to £10 or more on Saturday.

HiFi Club (☎ 0113-242 7353; www.thehificlub.co.uk; 2 Central Rd) This intimate club is a good break from the hardcore sound of four to the floor: if it's Tamla Motown or the percussive beats of dance-floor jazz that shake your booty, this is the spot for you.

Cockpit (☎ 0113-244 1573; www.thecockpit.co.uk; Swinegate) Snugly ensconced in a series of railway arches, the legendary Cockpit is the antidote to dance clubs. A live music venue of note – Coldplay, White Stripes, Flaming Lips and Amy Winehouse have all cut their teeth here – it also hosts The Session on Friday nights, a superb indie/electro/guitar club night.

Mission (☎ 0870 122 0114; www.clubmission.com; 8-13 Heaton's Ct) A massive club that redefines the term 'up-for-it'. Thursday night is gay go-go dancers bopping to commercial pop, while Saturdays are for the signature Glasshouse house session.

Wire (☎ 0113-234 0980; www.wireclub.co.uk; 2-8 Call Lane) This small, atmospheric basement club, set in a forest of Victorian cast-iron pillars, throbs to a different beat every night, from rock 'n' roll to drum 'n' bass. Popular with local students.

THEATRE & OPERA

City Varieties (☎ 0113-243 0808; www.cityvarieties.co.uk; Swan St) This old-fashioned music hall features anything from clairvoyants to comedy acts to country music.

Grand Theatre & Opera House (☎ 0113-222 6222; www.leedsgrandtheatre.com; 46 New Briggate) Hosts musicals, plays and opera, including performances by the acclaimed **Opera North** (☎ 0113-244 5326; www.operanorth.co.uk).

West Yorkshire Playhouse (☎ 0113-213 7700; www.wyplayhouse.com; Quarry Hill Mount) The Playhouse has a reputation for excellent live drama, from the classics to cutting-edge new writing.

CINEMA

Hyde Park Picture House (☎ 0113-275 2045; www.hydeparkpicturehouse.co.uk; Brudenell Rd) This Edwardian cinema shows a meaty range of art-house and mainstream choices. Take bus 56 from the city centre.

Vue Cinema (☎ 08712 240240; www.myvue.com; 22 The Light, The Headrow) For mainstream first-run films, head for the Vue on the second floor of The Light entertainment complex.

SPORT

Leeds United Football Club (☎ 0113-226 1000; www.leedsunited.com; Elland Rd) Leeds supporters know all about pain: relegation from the Premiership in 2004 to the relative wilderness of the Championship was bad enough, but in 2007 they dropped another rung down the ladder to League One. All the same, loyal fans continue to pack the Elland Rd stadium in their masses. Take bus 93 or 96 from City Sq.

Headingley has been hosting cricket matches since 1890. It is still used for test matches and is the home ground of the **Yorkshire County Cricket Club** (☎ tickets 0113-278 7394; www.yorkshireccc.org.uk). Take bus 18 or 56 from the city centre.

Shopping

Leeds' city centre has so many shopping arcades that they all seem to blend into one giant mall. The latest development – **Trinity Leeds**, between Commercial St and Boar Lane, scheduled to open in 2010 – will be the city's biggest.

The mosaic-paved, stained-glass-roofed Victorian arcades of **Victoria Quarter** (☎ 0113-245 5333; www.v-q.co.uk), between Briggate and Vicar Lane, are well worth visiting for aesthetic reasons alone; dedicated shoppers can join the footballers' wives browsing boutiques by Louis Vuitton, Vivienne Westwood and Swarovski. The flagship store here, of course, is **Harvey Nichols** (☎ 0113-204 8000; 107-111 Briggate).

Just across the street to the east you'll find the opposite end of the retail spectrum in **Leeds City Market** (☎ 0113-214 5162; www.leedsmarket.com; Kirkgate; 🕑 9am-5pm Mon-Sat, to 1pm Wed, open-air market Thu-Tue). Once the home of Michael Marks, who later joined Spencer, this is Britain's largest covered market, selling fresh meat, fish, fruit and vegetables, as well as household goods.

Getting There & Away

AIR

Eleven miles northwest of the city via the A65, **Leeds Bradford International airport** (☎ 0113-250 9696; www.lbia.co.uk) offers flights to a range of domestic and international destinations. The Metroconnect 757 bus (£2, 40 minutes, every 30 minutes, hourly on Sunday) runs between Leeds bus station and the airport. A taxi costs about £18.

BUS

National Express (☎ 08717 818181; www.nationalexpress.com) serves most major cities, including hourly services from London (£20, 4½ hours) and half-hourly services from Manchester (£8.40, 1¼ hours).

Yorkshire Coastliner (☎ 01653-692556; www.yorkshirecoastliner.co.uk) has useful services from Leeds to York, Castle Howard, Goathland and Whitby (840 and 842), and to York, Scarborough (843), Filey and Bridlington (845 and X45). A Freedom Ticket (£12) gives unlimited bus travel for a day.

TRAIN

Leeds City Station has hourly services from London King's Cross (£103, 2½ hours), Sheffield (£11, 45 minutes), Manchester (£15, one hour) and York (£10, 30 minutes).

Leeds is also the starting point for services on the famous Settle–Carlisle Line. For more details see p609.

Getting Around

Metro's **FreeCityBus** service runs every few minutes from 6.30am to 7.30pm Monday to Saturday, linking the bus and train stations to all the main shopping areas in the city centre.

The various **Day Rover** passes (see p593) covering trains and/or buses are good for reaching Bradford, Haworth and Hebden Bridge.

AROUND LEEDS

A day trip from Leeds opens up a fascinating range of options: stately splendour at Harewood, dust and darkness at the National Coal Mining Museum for England, or technology and poppadums at Bradford, to name but a few. Places are listed roughly in order of distance from Leeds, first to the west and north, then to the south.

Bradford

pop 293,700

Their suburbs may have merged into one sprawling urban conurbation, but Bradford remains far removed from its much more glamorous neighbour, Leeds. Or so Loiners (people from Leeds) would have you believe. But even Bradford is getting a facial: much of the drab city centre is undergoing a revamp which, according to town planners, will see it recast as an urban park with its very own lake in front of city hall. It sounds promising, and a far cry from the kind of 'ugliness that could not only be tolerated but often enjoyed,' as the city's favourite son, the cantankerous JB Priestley (1894–1984), once described it.

Thanks to its role as a major player in the wool trade, Bradford attracted large numbers of Bangladeshis and Pakistanis throughout the 20th century, who – despite occasional racial tensions – have helped reinvigorate the city and give it new energy. A high point of the year is the colourful Mela (see p600).

SIGHTS

Bradford's top attraction is the **National Media Museum** (☎ 01274-202030; www.nationalmediamuseum.org.uk; admission free, special events & cinemas adult/child £5.50/3.70, IMAX adult/child £6.95/4.95; 🕑 10am-6pm Tue-Sun), an impressive, glass-fronted building that chronicles the story of photography, film, TV, radio and the web from 19th-century cameras and early animation to digital technology and the psychology of advertising. There's lots of hands-on stuff too; you can film yourself in a bedroom scene or play at being a TV newsreader. The IMAX screen shows the usual combination of in-your-face nature films and space documentaries.

The other big draw is the **Alhambra Theatre** (☎ 01274-432375; www.bradford-theatres.co.uk; Morley St), a magnificent art-deco building dating from 1914 that is a monument to the Edwardian era of music hall entertainment. It is still in use, and regularly stages shows ranging from musicals to Shakespeare to ballet.

Bradford Industrial Museum (☎ 01274-435900; www.bradfordmuseums.org; Moorside Rd, Eccleshill; admission free; ☺ 10am-5pm Tue-Sat, noon-5pm Sun), 3 miles out of the centre, gives a hint of what a Yorkshire textile mill was like in the late 19th century. Other exhibits include various steam engines (sometimes working), and transport from the last 100 years, and a horse-drawn tram to give a quick 'step back in history' round the car park.

Another monument to Bradford's glorious past is the **Wool Exchange** (Hustlergate), a magnificent Victorian Gothic building that was once home to crowds of wool traders; today it must rank as the most impressive branch of Waterstone's bookshops in the country.

FESTIVALS & EVENTS

The **Bradford Mela** (www.visitbradford.com/events) – from the Sanskrit word 'to meet' – is a two-day celebration of Asian music, dance, arts, crafts and food. It's held in mid-June.

EATING

Bradford is famous for its curries, so if you're still here in the evening don't miss trying one of the city's hundred or so restaurants. A great help is the **Bradford Curry Guide** (http://website.lineone.net/~bradfordcurryguide), which sorts out the rogan josh from the rotten nosh.

Kashmir (☎ 01274-726513; 27 Morley St; mains £4-5; ☺ evenings to 3am) Bradford's oldest curry house has top Asian tucker, served with no frills or booze (it's BYO). Whatever you do, go for a table upstairs, as the soul-destroying, windowless basement has all the character of a public toilet. It's just along the street from the Alhambra Theatre.

GETTING THERE & AWAY

Bradford is on the Metro train line from Leeds (£2.65, 20 minutes), with very frequent services every day.

Saltaire

A Victorian-era landmark, Saltaire was a model industrial village built in 1851 by philanthropic wool-baron and teetotaller Titus Salt. The rows of neat honey-coloured cottages – now a Unesco World Heritage site – overlook what was once the largest factory in the world.

The factory is now **Salt's Mill** (☎ 01274-531163; www.saltsmill.org.uk; admission free; ☺ 10am-5.30pm Mon-Fri, 10am-6pm Sat & Sun), a splendidly bright and airy building where the main draw is a permanent exhibition of art by local boy David Hockney (1937–). In a fitting metaphor for the shift in the British economy from making things to selling them, this former engine of industry is now a shrine to retail therapy, housing shops selling books, crafts and outdoor equipment, and a cafe.

Saltaire's **tourist office** (☎ 01274-774993; www.visitsaltaire.com; 2 Victoria Rd; ☺ 10am-5pm) has maps of the village and runs hour-long guided walks (adult/child £3.50/2.50) through the town throughout the year.

Saltaire is 9 miles west of Leeds centre, and 3 miles north of Bradford centre. It's easily reached by Metro rail from either.

Harewood

The great park, sumptuous gardens and mighty edifice of **Harewood House** (☎ 0113-218 1010; www.harewood.org; adult/child £13.50/8.50; ☺ grounds 10am-6pm, house 11am-4.30pm mid-Mar–Oct, house & grounds 10am-4pm Sat & Sun Nov–mid-Mar) could easily fill an entire day trip from Leeds, and also makes a good port of call on the way to Harrogate.

A classic example of a stately English pile, the house was built between 1759 and 1772 by the era's superstar designers – John Carr designed the exterior, Lancelot 'Capability' Brown laid out the grounds, Thomas Chippendale supplied the furniture (the largest commission he ever received, costing the unheard of amount of £10,000), Robert Adams designed the interior, and Italy was raided to create an appropriate art collection. The superb terrace was added 100 years later by yet another top name, Sir Charles Barry – he of the Houses of Parliament.

Many locals come to Harewood just to relax or saunter through the grounds, without even thinking of going inside the house. Hours of entertainment can be had in the **Bird Garden**, with many exotic species including penguins (feeding time at 2pm is a highlight), and there's also a boating lake, cafe and adventure playground. For more activity, there's a network of walking trails around the lake or through the parkland.

Harewood is about 7 miles north of Leeds on the A61. Take bus 36 (20 minutes; at least half-hourly Monday to Saturday, hourly on Sunday) which continues to Harrogate. Visitors coming by bus get half-price admission, so hang on to your ticket. From the main gate, it's a 2-mile walk through the grounds to the house and gardens, or you can use the free shuttle service.

National Coal Mining Museum for England

For close to three centuries, West and South Yorkshire was synonymous with coal production; the collieries shaped and scarred the landscape, while entire villages grew up around the pits, each male inhabitant and their descendants destined to spend their working lives underground. The industry came to a shuddering halt in the 1980s, but the imprint of coal is still very much in evidence, even if there's only a handful of collieries left. One of these, at Claphouse, is now the **National Coal Mining Museum for England** (☎ 01924-848806; www.ncm.org.uk; Overton, near Wakefield; admission free; ☿ 10am-5pm, last tour 3.15pm), a superb testament to the inner workings of a coal mine.

The highlight of a visit is the underground tour – equipped with helmet and head-torch you descend almost 150m in the 'cage' then follow subterranean passages to the coal seam where massive drilling machines now stand idle. Former miners work as guides, and explain the details – sometimes with a suitably authentic and almost impenetrable mix of local dialect (known in Yorkshire as Tyke) and technical terminology.

Up on top, there are audiovisual displays, some fascinating memorabilia (including sketches by Henry Moore) and exhibits about trade unions, strikes and the wider mining communities – only a bit over-romanticised in parts. You can also stroll round the pit-pony stables (their equine inhabitants also now retired) or the slightly eerie bathhouse,

unchanged since the miners scrubbed off the coal dust for the last time and emptied their lockers. There are also nature trails in the surrounding fields and woods.

The museum is about 10 miles south of Leeds on the A642 between Wakefield and Huddersfield, which drivers can reach via Junction 40 on the M1. By public transport, take a train from Leeds to Wakefield (15 minutes, at least hourly), and then bus 232 towards Huddersfield (25 minutes, hourly).

Yorkshire Sculpture Park

One of England's most impressive collections of sculpture is scattered across the formidable 18th-century estate of Bretton Park, 200-odd hectares of lawns, fields and trees. A bit like the art world's equivalent of a safari park, the **Yorkshire Sculpture Park** (☎ 01924-830302; www.ysp .co.uk; Bretton, near Wakefield; admission free, parking £4; ☿ 10am-6pm Apr-Sep, to 5pm Oct-Mar) showcases the work of dozens of sculptors both national and international, but the main focus of this outdoor gallery is the work of local kids Barbara Hepworth (1903–75), who was born in nearby Wakefield, and Henry Moore.

The rural setting is especially fitting for Moore's work, as the artist was hugely influenced by the outdoors and preferred his art to be sited in the landscape rather than indoors. Other highlights include pieces by Andy Goldsworthy and Eduardo Paolozzi. There's also a program of temporary exhibitions and installations by visiting artists, plus a bookshop and cafe.

The park is 12 miles south of Leeds and 18 miles north of Sheffield, just off Junction 38 on the M1 motorway. If you're on public transport, take a train from Leeds to Wakefield (15 minutes, at least hourly), or from Sheffield to Barnsley (20 minutes, at least hourly); then take bus 444 which runs between Wakefield and Barnsley via Bretton Park (30 minutes, hourly Monday to Saturday).

HEBDEN BRIDGE
pop 4086

Tucked tightly into the fold of a steep-sided valley, Yorkshire's funkiest little town is a former mill town that refused to go gently into that good night with the dying of industry's light; it raged a bit and then morphed into an attractive little tourist trap with a distinctly bohemian atmosphere. Besides the honest-to-God Yorkshire folk who have lived here for years, the town is home to university academics, artists, die-hard hippies and a substantial gay community – all of which explains the abundance of craft shops, organic cafes and secondhand bookstores.

The **Hebden Bridge Visitor & Canal Centre** (☎ 01422-843831; www.calderdale.gov.uk; Butlers Wharf, New Rd; ❀ 9.30am-5.30pm Mon-Fri, 10.30am-5pm Sat & Sun mid-Mar–mid-Oct, 10am-5pm Mon-Fri, 10.30am-4.15pm Sat & Sun rest of year) has a good stock of maps and leaflets on local walks, including a saunter to **Hardcastle Crags**, the local beauty spot, and nearby **Gibson Mill** (NT; ☎ 01422-844518; adult/child £3.60/1.80; ❀ 11am-4pm Wed, Sat & Sun Mar-Oct, 11am-3pm Sat & Sun Nov-Feb), a renovated 19th-century cotton mill.

From the centre, a short stroll along the attractive waterfront of the Rochdale Canal leads to the **Alternative Technology Centre** (☎ 01422-842121; www.alternativetechnology.org.uk; Hebble End Mill; admission free; ❀ 10am-5pm Mon-Fri, noon-5pm Sat, noon-4pm Sun), which promotes renewable energy, recycling and sustainable lifestyles through a series of intriguing exhibits and workshops.

Above the town is the much older village of **Heptonstall**, its narrow cobbled street lined with 500-year-old cottages and the ruins of a beautiful 13th-century church. But it is the churchyard of the newer St Thomas' Church that draws literary pilgrims, for here is buried the poet Sylvia Plath (1932–63), wife of another famous poet, Ted Hughes (1930–98), who was born in nearby Mytholmroyd.

Sleeping & Eating

Pennine Camp & Caravan Site (☎ 01422-842287; High Greenwood House, Heptonstall; sites per person £4; closed Nov-Mar) A large, sloping field with a block of facilities in a converted barn, this campsite is about 3 miles northwest of town, on the minor road beyond Heptonstall that leads towards Widdop Reservoir.

Mankinholes YHA (☎ 0845 371 9751; www.yha.org .uk; Todmorden; dm £16) A converted 17th-century manor house 4 miles southwest of Hebden Bridge, this hostel has limited facilities (no TV room) but it is very popular with walkers; the Pennine Way passes only half a mile away.

White Lion Hotel (☎ 01422-842197; www.white lionhotel.net; Bridge Gate; s/d from £50/70) The choicest accommodation in town is this large 400-year-old coaching inn smack in the middle of it; the rooms in the converted coach house are that little bit more comfortable than the ones in the main house.

Downstairs is an excellent real-ale pub and a restaurant (mains £7 to £10) with a standard pub grub menu.

Crown Fisheries (☎ 01422-842599; 8 Crown St; mains £4-5; ❀ 10am-6.30pm) A terrific chip shop that serves up a great fish supper (fish, chips, bread and butter, and tea), and also does takeaways.

There are several appealing **cafes** along pedestrianised Bridge Gate in a peaceful setting beside the river and the old packhorse bridge that gave the town its name.

Getting There & Away

Hebden Bridge is on the Leeds–Manchester train line (£3.75, 50 minutes, every 20 minutes Monday to Saturday, hourly on Sunday). Get off at Todmorden for the Mankinholes YHA.

HAWORTH
pop 6100

It seems that only Shakespeare himself is held in higher esteem than the beloved Brontë sisters – Emily, Anne and Charlotte – at least, judging by the 8 million visitors a year who trudge up the hill from the train station to pay their respects at the handsome parsonage where the literary classics *Jane Eyre* and *Wuthering Heights* were born.

Not surprisingly, the whole village is given over to Brontë-linked tourism, but even without the literary associations Haworth is still worth a visit, though you'll be hard pushed not to be overwhelmed by the cottage industry that has grown up around the Brontës and their wonderful creations.

Information

The **tourist office** (☎ 01535-642329; www.haworth -village.org.uk; 2-4 West Lane; ❀ 9am-5.30pm Apr-Sep, to 5pm Oct-Mar) has an excellent supply of information on the village, the surrounding area and, of course, the Brontës.

Main St is lined with cafes, tearooms, pubs and shops selling everything imaginable bearing the Brontë name. Handy stops might include: the **post office** (98 Main St; ❀ 9am-5.30pm Mon-Fri, to 12.30pm Sat); **Venables & Bainbridge** (☎ 01535-640300; 111 Main St; ❀ 11am-5pm daily), selling used books including many vintage Brontë volumes; and **Rose & Co Apothecary** (☎ 01535-646830; 84 Main St; ❀ 10.30am-5.30pm daily), the beautifully restored chemist shop so favoured by Branwell Brontë.

BAD LUCK BRONTËS

The Rev Patrick Brontë, his wife Maria and six children moved to Haworth Parsonage in 1820. Within four years Maria and the two eldest daughters had died from cancer and tuberculosis. The treble tragedy led the good reverend to keep his remaining family close to him, and for the next few years the children were home-schooled in a highly creative environment.

The children conjured up mythical heroes and fantasy lands, and produced miniature home-made books. It was an auspicious start, at least for the three girls, Charlotte, Emily and Anne; the lone boy, Branwell, was more of a painter but lacked his sisters' drive and discipline. After a short stint as a professional artist, he ended up spending most of his days in the Black Bull pub, drunk and stoned on laudanum obtained across the street at Rose & Co Apothecary.

While the three sisters were setting the London literary world alight with the publication of three superb novels – *Jane Eyre, Wuthering Heights* and *Agnes Grey* – in one extraordinary year (1847), Branwell was fading quickly and died of tuberculosis in 1848. The family was devastated, but things quickly got worse. Emily fell ill with tuberculosis soon after her brother's funeral; she never left the house again and died on 19 December. Anne, who had also been sick, was next; Charlotte took her to Scarborough to seek a sea cure but she died on 28 May 1849.

The remaining family never recovered. Despite her growing fame, Charlotte struggled with depression and never quite adapted to her high position in literary society. Despite her misgivings she eventually married, but she too died, in the early stages of pregnancy, on 31 March 1855. All things considered, it's hardly surprising that poor old Patrick Brontë spent the remaining years of his life going increasingly insane.

Sights

Your first stop should be **Haworth Parish Church** (admission free), a lovely old place of worship built in the late 19th century on the site of the 'old' church that the Brontë sisters knew, which was demolished in 1879. In the surrounding churchyard, gravestones are covered in moss or thrust to one side by gnarled tree roots, giving the place a tremendous feeling of age.

Set in a pretty garden overlooking the church and graveyard, the **Brontë Parsonage Museum** (☎ 01535-642323; www.bronte.info; admission £6; ☺ 10am-5.30pm Apr-Sep, 11am-5pm Oct-Mar) is where the Brontë family lived from 1820 till 1861. The rooms are meticulously furnished and decorated exactly as they were in the Brontë era, with many personal possessions on display. There's also a neat and informative exhibition, which includes the fascinating miniature books the Brontës wrote as children.

Activities

Above Haworth stretch the bleak moors of the South Pennines – immediately familiar to Brontë fans – and the tourist office has leaflets on local **walks** to endless Brontë-related places. A 6.5-mile favourite leads to Top Withins, a ruined farm thought to have inspired *Wuthering Heights*, even though a plaque clearly states that the farm-

house bore no resemblance to the one Emily wrote about.

Other walks can be worked around the **Brontë Way**, a longer route linking Bradford and Colne via Haworth. Alternatively, you can walk or cycle the 8 miles south to Hebden Bridge via the scenic valley of Hardcastle Crags.

Sleeping & Eating

Virtually every second house on Main St offers B&B; they're mostly indistinguishable from each other but some are just that little bit cuter. There are a couple of good restaurants in town and many of the B&Bs also have small cafes that are good for a spot of lunch – mediocre servings of local dishes and nice safe bets such as sandwiches.

Haworth House (☎ 01535-643374; 6 Church St; s/d from £25/50) Tucked along the alley beside the church, this place has mostly spacious rooms with a New Age vibe, though the smaller, cheaper rooms are pretty cramped. Breakfast (£3 to £4 extra) is served in your bedroom.

Aitches (☎ 01535-642501; www.aitches.co.uk; 11 West Lane; s/d from £37/52) A very classy, stone-built Victorian house with four en suite rooms, each differently decorated with a pleasantly olde-worlde atmosphere. There's a residents' dining room where a three-course meal will cost £16 (prebooked, minimum four persons).

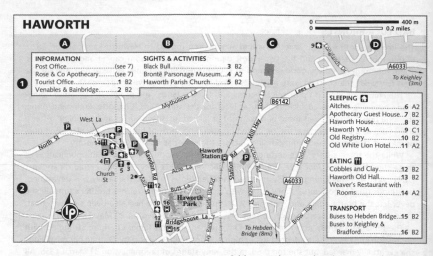

HAWORTH

INFORMATION	
Post Office	(see 7)
Rose & Co Apothecary	(see 7)
Tourist Office	1 B2
Venables & Bainbridge	2 B2

SIGHTS & ACTIVITIES	
Black Bull	3 B2
Brontë Parsonage Museum	4 A2
Haworth Parish Church	5 B2

SLEEPING	
Aitches	6 A2
Apothecary Guest House	7 B2
Haworth House	8 B2
Haworth YHA	9 C1
Old Registry	10 B2
Old White Lion Hotel	11 A2

EATING	
Cobbles and Clay	12 B2
Haworth Old Hall	13 B2
Weaver's Restaurant with Rooms	14 A2

TRANSPORT	
Buses to Hebden Bridge	15 B2
Buses to Keighley & Bradford	16 B2

Weaver's Restaurant with Rooms (☎ 01535-643822; www.weaversmallhotel.co.uk; 15 West Lane; s/d £60/100, mains £12-18; ☿ lunch Wed-Fri & Sun, dinner Tue-Sat) A stylish and atmospheric restaurant, Weaver's offers a menu featuring local specialities such as black pudding with corned beef hash, and sausage and mash with caramelised onion. Upstairs are three comfy bedrooms, two of which have views towards the moors.

Old Registry (☎ 01535-646503; www.theoldregistry haworth.co.uk; 2-4 Main St; r £75-100) This place is a bit special. It's an elegantly rustic hotel where each of the carefully themed rooms has a four-poster bed, whirlpool bath or valley view. The Blue Heaven room is just that – at least for fans of Laura Ashley's delphinium blue.

Other options:

Haworth YHA (☎ 0845 371 9520; www.yha.org.uk; Longlands Dr; dm £14; ℗ ▯) A big old house with a games room, lounge, cycle store and laundry. It's on the northeastern edge of town, off Lees Lane.

Apothecary Guest House (☎ 01535-643642; www .theapothecaryguesthouse.co.uk; 86 Main St; s/d £35/55)

Oak beams and narrow, slanted passageways lead to smallish rooms with cheerful decor.

Old White Lion Hotel (☎ 01535-642313; www.old whitelionhotel.com; West Lane; s/d from £57/80) Pub-style accommodation – comfortable if not spectacular – above an oak-panelled bar and highly rated restaurant (mains £10 to £16).

Cobbles and Clay (☎ 01535-644218; 60 Main St; mains £3-7; ☿ 9am-5pm) Attractive, child-friendly cafe offering Fairtrade coffee and healthy salads and snacks.

Haworth Old Hall (☎ 01535-642709; www.haworth oldhall.co.uk; Sun St; mains £8-12) Sixteenth-century pub serving real ale and decent food. If you want to linger longer, two comfortable doubles cost £65.

Getting There & Away

From Leeds, the easiest approach to Haworth is via Keighley, which is on the Metro rail network. Bus 500 runs from Keighley bus station to Haworth (15 minutes, hourly) and continues to Todmorden and Hebden Bridge. However, the most interesting way to get from Keighley to Haworth is via the Keighley & Worth Valley Railway (see boxed text, below).

STEAM ENGINES & RAILWAY CHILDREN

Haworth is on the **Keighley & Worth Valley Railway** (KWVR; ☎ 01535-645214; www.kwvr.co.uk; adult/ child return £9/4.50, adult/child Day Rover £14/7), which runs steam and classic diesel engines between Keighley and Oxenhope. It was here, in 1969, that the classic movie *The Railway Children* was shot; Mr Perks was stationmaster at Oakworth, where the Edwardian look has been meticulously maintained. Trains operate about hourly at weekends all year; in holiday periods they run hourly every day.

YORKSHIRE DALES NATIONAL PARK

The Yorkshire Dales – named from the old Norse word *dalr,* meaning 'valleys' – is the central jewel in the necklace of three national parks strung across the neck of northern England, with the dramatic fells of the Lake District to the west and the brooding heaths of the North York Moors to the east.

From well-known names such as Wensleydale and Ribblesdale, to obscure and evocative Langstrothdale and Arkengarthdale, these glacial valleys are characterised by a distinctive landscape of high heather moorland, stepped skylines and flat-topped hills rising above green valley floors patchworked with drystone dykes and dotted with picture-postcard towns and hamlets, where sheep and cattle still graze on village greens. And in the limestone country in the southern dales you'll find England's best examples of karst scenery.

The Dales have been protected as a national park since the 1950s, assuring their status as a walker's and cyclist's paradise. But there's plenty for non-walkers as well, from exploring the legacy of literary vet James Herriot of *All Creatures Great And Small* fame, to sampling Wallace and Gromit's favourite teatime snack at the Wensleydale Creamery.

Orientation & Information

The Yorkshire Dales National Park divides into two parts: in the north, two main valleys run west to east – broad expansive Wensleydale (home of the famous cheese) and narrow secretive Swaledale. In the busier, southern part, the main valleys – Ribblesdale, Malhamdale, Littondale and Wharfedale – run north to south.

The main Dales gateways are Skipton in the south and Richmond in the northeast. Good bases in the park itself include Settle, Grassington and Hawes. All have excellent tourist offices, stocking a mountain of local guidebooks and maps, and providing accommodation details.

To the northwest and west, the towns of Kirkby Stephen and Kirkby Lonsdale also make handy jumping-off points, although both are actually in the county of Cumbria (despite definite Dales affiliations).

The *Visitor* newspaper, available from tourist offices, lists local events and walks guided by park rangers, as well as many places to stay and eat. The official park website at www .yorkshiredales.org.uk is also useful.

Activities

CYCLING

Other than on busy summer weekends, this is excellent cycling country. Most roads follow the rivers along the bottom of the Dales so, although there are some steep climbs, there's also plenty on the flat. Tourist offices stock maps and leaflets with suggested routes (on-road and off-road) for a day or longer.

One example is the **Yorkshire Dales Cycle Way**, an exhilarating 130-mile loop, taking in the best of the park. Skipton is a convenient starting point, from where you ride up Wharfedale, then steeply over Fleet Moss to Hawes. From here turn east along Wensleydale to Aysgarth, then north over the wild hills to Reeth. The roads are steep but the scenery is breathtaking. Follow Swaledale westwards, through remote Keld and down to the market town of Kirkby Stephen. Then it's south to Sedbergh, and up beautiful Dentdale to pop out at Ribblehead. It's plain sailing now, through Horton-in-Ribblesdale to Stainforth, one more climb over to Malham, and finally back to Skipton for tea and medals.

There's also lots of scope for off-road riding, with around 500 miles of bridleways and trails – check out www.mtbthedales.org.uk for inspiration.

WALKING

The Yorkshire Dales has a vast footpath network, offering everything from easy strolls to challenging hikes; we suggest a few options throughout this section. Look out at tourist offices for leaflets describing walks from train stations, notably on the Settle–Carlisle Line. Serious walkers should equip themselves with 1:25,000 OS Explorer Maps Nos 2 and 30.

Two of England's most famous long-distance routes cross the Dales. The **Pennine Way** goes through the rugged western half of the park. If you haven't got three weeks to cover all 259 miles, a few days hiking between Malham and Hawes, for example, is well worth the effort. The **Coast to Coast Walk** (p588) passes through Swaledale in the

YORKSHIRE

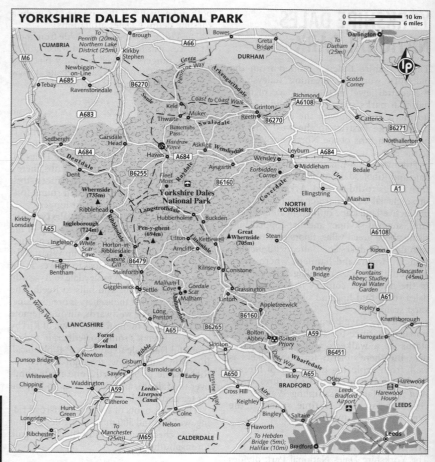

YORKSHIRE DALES NATIONAL PARK

northern Dales. Following the route for a day or two is highly recommended; see p612.

Another long-distance possibility is the **Dales Way** (www.dalesway.org.uk), which begins in Ilkley, follows the River Wharfe through the heart of the Dales, and finishes at Bowness-on-Windermere in the Lake District. If you start at Grassington, it's an easy five-day journey (60 miles). A handy companion is *Dales Way Route Guide* by Arthur Gemmell and Colin Speakman (£5.99), available at most bookshops.

Getting There & Around

The main gateway towns of Skipton and Richmond are well served by public transport, and local bus services radiate from there. Pick up the useful *Dales Explorer Travel Guide,* a free map available from tourist offices that covers bus and train services in the region, or consult the comprehensive **Traveldales website** (www.traveldales.org.uk).

Going by train, the best and most interesting access to the Dales is via the famous **Settle–Carlisle Line** (p609). From the south, trains start in Leeds and pass through Skipton, Settle, and numerous small villages, offering unrivalled access to the hills straight from the station platform. Of course, if you're coming from the north, Carlisle is the place to get on board.

Around 90% of visitors to the park arrive by car, and the narrow roads can be extremely crowded in summer; parking can also be a serious problem. If you can, try to use public transport as much as possible.

SKIPTON
pop 14,300

This busy market town on the southern edge of the Dales takes its name from the Anglo-Saxon *sceape ton* (sheep town) – no prizes for guessing how it made its money. Monday, Wednesday, Friday and Saturday are market days on High St, bringing crowds from all over and giving the town something of a festive atmosphere. The **tourist office** (☎ 01756-792809; www.skiptononline.co.uk; 35 Coach St; 10am-5pm Mon-Fri, 9am-5pm Sat) is on the northern edge of the town centre.

Sights & Activities

A pleasant stroll from the tourist office along the canal path leads to **Skipton Castle** (☎ 01756-792442; www.skiptoncastle.co.uk; High St; admission £5.80; 10am-6pm Mon-Sat, noon-6pm Sun Mar-Sep, to 4pm Oct-Feb), one of the best-preserved medieval castles in England – a fascinating contrast to the ruins you'll see elsewhere.

From the castle, wander along Skipton's pride and joy – the broad and bustling **High St**, one of the most attractive shopping streets in Yorkshire. On the first Sunday of the month it hosts the Northern Dales farmers market.

No trip to Skipton is complete without a cruise along the Leeds–Liverpool Canal that runs through the middle of town. **Pennine Boat Trips** (☎ 01756-790829; www.canaltrips.co.uk; The Wharf, Coach St; adult/child £6/3) runs hour-long trips daily from April to October; call for departure times.

Sleeping & Eating

There's a strip of B&Bs just outside the centre on Keighley Rd. All those between Nos 46 and 57 are worth trying.

Carlton House (☎ 01756-700921; www.carltonhouse.rapidial.co.uk; 46 Keighley Rd; s/d from £28/55) A handsome house with five pretty, comfortable rooms – no frills but lots of floral prints. The house is deservedly popular on account of the friendly welcome.

Bizzie Lizzies (☎ 01756-793189; 36 Swadford St; mains £5-8; 11.30am-9pm, takeaway till 11.30pm) This sit-down fish-and-chip restaurant overlooking the canal has won several awards for quality, a rare thing for what is essentially deep-fried fast food. There's also a takeaway counter.

Canalside (☎ 01756-795678; www.canalsideskipton.co.uk; Waterside Ct, Coach St; mains lunch £7-9, dinner £13-17; noon-9.30pm Wed-Mon) Set in a converted warehouse overlooking the canal basin, this brisk modern restaurant enjoys the best location in town. The menu runs from game pie and confit duck to Dales beef and pan-fried sea bass.

Also recommended:

Bojangles (☎ 01756-709333; 20 Newmarket St; mains £3-4) Best coffee in town, American-style breakfasts and burgers.

Narrow Boat (☎ 01756-797922; 38 Victoria St) Traditionally styled pub with a great selection of local ales and foreign beers, friendly service and bar food.

Getting There & Away

Skipton is the last stop on the Metro rail network from Leeds and Bradford (£7.10, 40 minutes, half-hourly, hourly on Sunday). For heading into the Dales, see the boxed text on p609.

For Grassington, take bus 72 (30 minutes, hourly Monday to Saturday, no Sunday service) from Skipton train station, or 66A (hourly, Sunday) from the Market Pl.

BOLTON ABBEY

The tiny village and country estate of **Bolton Abbey** (www.boltonabbey.com), owned by the duke of Devonshire, is about 5 miles east of Skipton. The big draw here is the ruined church of **Bolton Priory** (admission free, parking £5.50; 8.30am-5pm Apr-Oct, to 4pm Nov-Mar), an evocative and beautiful 12th-century ruin. Its soaring arches and huge windows silhouetted against the sky have inspired artists such as Wordsworth and Turner; part of the building is still used as a church today.

Apart from the priory ruins, the main attraction is the scenic **River Wharfe** which flows through the grounds – there's a network of walking trails beside the river and through the surrounding area. It's very popular with families (part of the riverbank looks like a beach at weekends); you can buy teas and ice creams in the **Cavendish Pavilion**, a short walk from the priory. Other highlights include the stepping stones – a large gap between stones in the middle of the river frequently forces faint-hearted walkers to turn around and use the bridge – and **The Strid**, a picturesque wooded gorge just upstream from the pavilion.

The **Devonshire Arms Country House Hotel** (☎ 01756 718111; www.thedevonshirearms.co.uk; s/d from £180/225; (P 🖵) – also owned by the duke of Devonshire – is actually more like a stately home hotel. The decoration of each bedroom was designed by the duchess herself, and while her tastes might not be everyone's cup of tea, there's no arguing with the quality and beauty of the furnishings; almost all of them were permanently borrowed from another of their properties, Chatsworth in Derbyshire.

There are half-hourly buses from Skipton and Grassington Monday to Saturday; on Sunday there's only an hourly service from Skipton.

GRASSINGTON
pop 1120

The perfect base for jaunts around the south Dales, Grassington's handsome Georgian centre teems with walkers and visitors throughout the summer months, soaking up an atmosphere that – despite the odd touch of faux rusticity – is as attractive and traditional as you'll find in these parts.

The **tourist office** (☎ 01756-751690; Hebden Rd; 🕙 9.30am-5pm daily Apr-Oct; Fri, Sat & Sun Nov-Mar) is beside the big car park on the edge of town. There's a good stock of maps and guides, and a nice little display that puts the surrounding scenery in context.

Sleeping & Eating

There are several B&Bs along and just off Main St.

Devonshire Fell (☎ 01756-718111; www.devon shirefell.co.uk; Burnsall; s/d from £85/135; P 🖵) A sister property to Bolton Abbey's Devonshire Arms Country House Hotel (p607), this former gentleman's club for mill owners has a much more contemporary feel, with beautiful modern furnishings crafted by local experts. The breakfast room/restaurant (dinner mains £16) has a stunning view over the valley. It's 3 miles southeast of Grassington on the B6160.

Ashfield House (☎ 01756-752584; www.ashfield house.co.uk; Summers Fold; r from £91; P 🖵) A secluded 17th-century country house behind a walled garden with exposed stone walls, open fireplaces and an all-round cosy feel. It's just off the main square.

Dales Kitchen (☎ 01756-753208; 51 Main St; mains £5-7; 🕙 9am-6pm) Classic Yorkshire munchies – rarebits, local sausage and, of course, Wensleydale – in a lovely tearoom in the middle of town.

Getting There & Away

Grassington is 6 miles north of Skipton; see p607 for buses from there. For onward travel, bus 72 continues up the valley to the villages of Kettlewell and Buckden.

AROUND GRASSINGTON

From Grassington narrow roads lead north up the beautiful valley of Wharfedale. If you're cycling, take the quieter road on the east side of the river; on foot, you can follow a charming stretch of the Dales Way to Kettlewell.

About 7 and 11 miles respectively from Grassington, the villages of **Kettlewell** and **Buckden** are good places to aim for, offering a good choice of camp sites, B&Bs, teashops and pubs offering food and accommodation. Favourite hostelries include the **Racehorses Hotel** (☎ 01756-760233; www.racehorseshotel.co.uk; s/d from £40/70) in Kettlewell, which has a nice riverside garden, and the **Buck Inn** (☎ 01756-760228; www.thebuckinnbuckden.co.uk; r from £75) in Buckden.

Check at Grassington tourist office about the local buses that trundle up and down Wharfedale daily in the summer months (weekends in winter) – ideal for bringing home weary walkers.

MALHAM
pop 120

Stretching west from Grassington to Ingleton is the largest area of limestone country in England, which has created a distinctive landscape dotted with dry valleys, potholes, limestone pavements and gorges. Two of the most spectacular features – Malham Cove and Gordale Scar – lie near the pretty village of Malham.

The **national park centre** (☎ 01969-652380; mal ham@yorkshiredales.org.uk; 🕙 10am-5pm daily Apr-Oct, 10am-4pm Sat & Sun Nov-Mar) at the southern edge of the village has the usual wealth of information. Note that Malham can only be reached via narrow roads that can be very congested in summer; leave your car at the national park centre and walk into the village.

Sights & Activities

A half-mile walk north from Malham village leads to **Malham Cove**, a huge rock amphitheatre lined with 80m-high vertical cliffs. You can hike steeply up the left-hand end of the cove (on the Pennine Way footpath) to see the extensive limestone pavement above the cliffs.

Another 1.5 miles further north is **Malham Tarn**, a glacial lake and nature reserve.

A mile east of Malham along a narrow road (very limited parking) is spectacular **Gordale Scar**, a deep limestone canyon with scenic cascades and the remains of an Iron Age settlement. The national park centre has a leaflet describing the **Malham Landscape Trail**, a 5-mile circular walk that takes in Malham Cove, Gordale Scar and the Janet's Foss waterfall.

The **Pennine Way** passes through Malham; Horton-in-Ribblesdale (p610) lies a day's hike away to the northwest.

Sleeping & Eating

Malham YHA (☎ 0845 371 9529; www.yha.org.uk; dm £14; Ⓟ) In the village centre you will find this purpose-built hostel; the facilities are top-notch and young children are well catered for.

Beck Hall (☎ 01729-830332; www.beckhallmalham .com; s/d from £25/50; Ⓟ Ⓛ) This rambling 17th-century country house on the edge of the village has 15 individually decorated rooms – we recommend the Green Room, with its old-style furnishings and four-poster bed. There's a rustling stream flowing through the garden and a nice tearoom (snacks about £4).

RIBBLESDALE & THE THREE PEAKS

Scenic Ribblesdale cuts through the southwestern corner of the Yorkshire Dales National Park, where the skyline is dominated by a trio of distinctive hills known as the **Three Peaks** – Whernside (735m), Ingleborough (724m) and Pen-y-ghent (694m). Easily accessible via the Settle–Carlisle railway line, this is one of England's most popular areas for outdoor activities, attracting thousands of hikers, cyclists and cavers each weekend.

Settle
pop 3621

The busy market town of Settle, dominated by its grand neo-Gothic town hall, is the gateway to Ribblesdale. Narrow cobbled streets lined with shops and pubs lead out from the central market square (Tuesday is market day), and the town offers plenty of accommodation options.

The **tourist office** (☎ 01729-825192; settle@ytbtic .co.uk; Town Hall, Cheapside; ☺ 9.30am-4.30pm Apr-Oct, to 4pm Nov-Mar) has maps and guidebooks, and an excellent range of local walks leaflets.

SLEEPING & EATING

Golden Lion Hotel (☎ 01729-822203; info@goldenlion .yorks.net; Duke St; s/d £43/75; lunch mains £8, dinner £9-14) This handsome 17th-century coaching inn has 12 warm and comfortable rooms, a traditional pub and a pleasant restaurant that is one of the most popular in town.

Ye Olde Naked Man (☎ 01729-823230; Market Pl; mains £3-7) Formerly an undertakers – look for the 'naked man' on the outside wall, dated

---

THE SETTLE–CARLISLE LINE

The Settle–Carlisle Line (SCL), built between 1869 and 1875, offers one of England's most scenic railway journeys. The 72-mile line's construction was one of the great engineering achievements of the Victorian era – 5000 navvies armed with picks and shovels built 325 bridges, 21 viaducts and blasted 14 tunnels in horrific conditions – nearly 200 of them died in the process.

Trains run between Leeds and Carlisle via Settle about eight times per day. The first section of the journey from Leeds is along the Aire Valley, stopping at **Keighley**, where the Keighley & Worth Valley Railway branches off to **Haworth** (p602); **Skipton** – gateway to the southern Dales; and **Settle**. The train then labours up the valley beside the River Ribble, through **Horton-in-Ribblesdale**, across the spectacular **Ribblehead Viaduct** and then through Blea Moor Tunnel to reach remote **Dent** station, at 350m the highest main-line station in the country.

The line reaches its highest point (356m) at Ais Gill where it leaves the Dales behind before easing down to **Kirkby Stephen**. The last halts are **Appleby** and **Langwathby,** just northwest of Penrith (a jumping-off point for the Lake District), before the train finally pulls into **Carlisle**.

The entire journey from Leeds to Carlisle takes two hours and 40 minutes and costs £22/27 for a single/day return; from Settle to Carlisle is 1¾ hours and £16/18. Various hop-on-hop-off passes for one or three days are also available. You can pick up a free SCL timetable – which includes a colour map of the line and brief details about places of interest – from most Yorkshire stations; for more information contact **National Rail Enquiries** (☎ 08457 484950) or click on to www.settle-carlisle.co.uk.

THREE PEAKS CHALLENGES

Since 1968 more than 200,000 hikers have taken up the challenge of climbing Yorkshire's Three Peaks in less than 12 hours. The circular 25-mile route begins and ends at the Pen-y-ghent Cafe in Horton-in-Ribblesdale – where you clock in and clock out to verify your time – and takes in the summits of Pen-y-ghent, Whernside and Ingleborough. Succeed, and you're a member of the cafe's Three Peaks of Yorkshire Club. You can find details of the route at www.merseyventure .com/yorks and download a guide (£3) at www.walkingworld.com (walk ID 4228 and 4229).

Fancy a more gruelling test of your endurance? Then join the fell-runners in the annual **Three Peaks Race** (www.threepeaksrace.org.uk) on the last Saturday in April, and run the route instead of walking it. First held in 1954 when six people competed, it now attracts around 900 entries; the course record is two hours, 43 minutes and three seconds

Cyclists get their chance too in the **Three Peaks Cyclo-Cross** (www.3peakscyclocross.org.uk; last week of Sep) which covers 38 miles of rough country and 1524m of ascent.

1663 – and now a bakery and cafe selling coffee, tea and scones with clotted cream.

Around Market Pl there are several other cafes, including the excellent **Shambles** (☎ 01729-822652; Market Pl; fish & chips £5-7).

GETTING THERE & AWAY

The easiest access is by train. Trains from Leeds or Skipton heading to Carlisle stop at the station near the town centre; those heading for Morecambe (on the west coast) stop at Giggleswick, about 1.5 miles outside town.

Horton-in-Ribblesdale
☎ 01729 / pop 560

A favourite with outdoor enthusiasts, the little village of Horton and its railway station is 5 miles north of Settle. Everything centres on the Pen-y-ghent Cafe which acts as the village **tourist office** (☎ 01729-860333; horton@ytbtic.co.uk), wet-weather retreat and hikers' information centre.

Horton is the starting point for climbing Pen-y-ghent and for doing the **Three Peaks Walk** (see boxed text above); it's also a stop on the Pennine Way. At the head of the valley, 5 miles north of Horton, is the spectacular **Ribblehead Viaduct**, built in 1874 and the longest on the Settle–Carlisle line – more than 30m high and 400m long. You can hike there along the Pennine Way and travel back by train from Ribblehead station.

SLEEPING & EATING

Horton is popular, so it's wise to book accommodation in advance.

Dub-Cote Farm Camping Barn (☎ 01729-860238; www.threepeaksbarn.co.uk; per person £10) This 17th-century stone barn enjoys a lovely hillside setting a mile southeast of the village, and is equipped with self-catering facilities (BYO sleeping bag and pillow case).

Golden Lion (☎ 01729-860206; www.goldenlion hotel.co.uk; s/d from £40/60, bunkhouse per person £10) The Golden Lion is a lively pub that offers comfortable B&B rooms and a basic, 15-bed bunkroom upstairs, and three public bars downstairs where you can tuck into a bit of grub washed down with a pint of hand-pulled ale.

Crown Hotel (☎ 01729-860209; www.crown-hotel .co.uk; s/d from £30/60; P) Another popular rest stop with walkers, the Crown has a variety of basic rooms (with slightly over-the-top floral decoration) and a cosy bar that serves a range of meals.

Pen-y-ghent Cafe (☎ 01729-860333; mains £3-7; ⏰ 9am-6pm Mon & Wed-Fri, 8am-6pm Sat & Sun) A traditional caff run by the same family since 1965, the Pen-y-ghent fills walkers' fuel tanks with fried egg and chips, homemade scones and pint-sized mugs of tea. It also sells maps, guidebooks and walking gear.

Ingleton
pop 2000

The village of Ingleton, perched precariously above a river gorge, is the caving capital of England. It sits at the foot of one of the country's most extensive areas of limestone upland, crowned by the dominating peak of Ingleborough and riddled with countless potholes and cave systems.

The **tourist office** (☎ 01524-241049; www.visiting leton.co.uk; ⏰ 10am-4pm Apr-Sep) is beside the main car park, while **Bernie's Cafe** (☎ 01524-241802; 4 Main St) is the centre of the local caving scene.

Ingleton is the starting point for two famous Dales hikes. The shorter and easier of the two is the circular, 4.5-mile **Waterfalls Walk** (www.ingletonwaterfallswalk.co.uk), which passes through native oak woodland on its way past a series of spectacular waterfalls on the Rivers Twiss and Doe. Around 120,000 people climb **Ingleborough** (724m) every year, but that doesn't make the 6-mile round trip any less of an effort; this is a proper hill walk, so pack waterproofs, food, water, and a map and compass.

Although most of the local caves are accessible only to experienced potholers, some are open to the general public. **White Scar Cave** (☎ 01524-241244; www.whitescarcave.co.uk; adult/child £7.50/4.50; ⏰ 10am-4.30pm daily Feb-Oct, Sat & Sun only Nov-Jan) is the longest show cave in England, with a series of underground waterfalls and impressive dripstone formations leading to the 100m-long Battlefield Cavern, one of the largest cave chambers in the country. The cave is 1.5 miles northeast of the village on the B6255 road.

Gaping Gill, on the southeastern flank of Ingleborough, is one of the most famous caves in England. A huge vertical pothole 105m deep, it was the largest known cave shaft in the UK until the discovery of Titan in Derbyshire in 1999. Gaping Gill is normally off-limits to non-cavers but, twice a year on the May and August bank holiday weekends, local caving clubs set up a winch so that members of the public can descend into the depths in a special chair (£10 per person). For details see www.bpc-cave.org .uk and www.cravenpotholeclub.org, and click on the Gaping Gill link.

Ingleton is 10 miles northwest of Settle; take bus 581 from Settle train station (25 minutes, two daily).

HAWES
pop 700

Hawes is the beating heart of Wensleydale, a thriving and picturesque market town (market day is Tuesday) with the added attraction of its own waterfall in the village centre. On busy summer weekends, however, Hawes' narrow arteries can get seriously clogged with traffic – leave the car in the parking area beside the **national park centre** (☎ 01969-666210; hawes@yorkshiredales.org.uk; Station Yard; ⏰ 10am-5pm year round) at the eastern entrance to the village.

Sights & Activities
Sharing a building with the park centre is the **Dales Countryside Museum** (adult/child £3/free), a beautifully presented social history of the area that explains the forces that shaped the landscape, from geology to lead mining to land enclosure.

At the other end of the village lies the **Wensleydale Creamery Visitor Centre** (☎ 01969-667664; www.wensleydale.co.uk; admission £2; ⏰ 9.30am-5pm Mon-Sat, 10am-4.30pm Sun), devoted to the production of Wallace and Gromit's favourite crumbly, white cheese. You can visit the cheese museum and then try before you buy in the shop, which is free to enter. There are one-hour tours of the creamery between 10am and 3pm.

About 1.5 miles north of Hawes is 30m-high **Hardraw Force**, the highest unbroken waterfall in England. By international standards it's not that impressive (except after heavy rain); access is through the Green Dragon pub, which levies a £2 admission fee.

Sleeping & Eating
Bainbridge Ings Caravan & Camp Site (☎ 01969-667354; www.bainbridge-ings.co.uk; tent, car & 2 adults £10.50, hikers & cyclists per person £4) An attractive site set in stone-walled fields around a spacious farmhouse about half a mile east of town. Gas, milk and eggs are sold on site.

Hawes YHA (☎ 0845 371 9120; www.yha.org.uk; Lancaster Tce; dm £16; ℗) A modern place on the western edge of town, at the junction of the main A684 (Aysgarth Rd) and B6255, this is a family-friendly hostel with great views of Wensleydale.

Green Dragon Inn (☎ 01969-667392; www.green dragonhardraw.co.uk; Hardraw; s/d from £24/45) A fine old pub with flagstone floors, low timber beams, ancient oak furniture and Theakstons on draught, the Dragon serves up a tasty steak and ale pie and offers B&B accommodation in plain but adequate rooms.

Herriot's Guest House (☎ 01969-667536; www.herriots inhawes.co.uk; Main St; r per person from £36) A delightful guest house set in an old stone building close to the bridge by the waterfall, Herriot's has seven comfy, en suite bedrooms set above an art gallery and coffee shop.

Cart House (☎ 01969-667691; www.hardrawforce .co.uk; Hardraw; mains £6; ⏰ 10am-5.30pm Mar-Nov) Across the bridge from the Green Dragon, this craft shop and tearoom offers a healthier diet of homemade soup, organic bread, and a 'Fellman's Lunch' of Wensleydale cheese, pickle and salad. There's a basic campsite at the back (£10 for two adults, tent and car).

Chaste (☎ 01969-667145; Market Pl; mains £13) An unusual name for a bistro, but this place is far from coy when it comes to promoting Yorkshire produce – almost everything on the menu, from the all-day breakfast to the vegetable hotpot to the black pudding and mashed potato is either homemade or locally sourced.

Getting There & Away

Dales & District buses 156 and 157 run from Bedale to Hawes (1¼ hours, eight daily Monday to Saturday, four on Sunday) via Leyburn, where you can connect with transport to/from Richmond. To get to Bedale from Northallerton train station on the main York–Newcastle line, take bus 73 (25 minutes, half-hourly Monday to Saturday, every two hours Sunday).

From Garsdale station on the Settle–Carlisle line, bus 113 runs to Hawes (20 minutes, three daily Monday to Saturday); on Sundays and bank holidays bus 808 goes to Hawes from Ribblehead station (50 minutes, two daily). Check the bus times at www.yorkshiretravel.net or a tourist office before using these routes.

RICHMOND
pop 8200

The handsome market town of Richmond is one of England's best-kept secrets, perched on a rocky outcrop overlooking the River Swale and guarded by the ruins of a massive castle. A maze of cobbled streets radiates from the broad, sloping market square, lined with elegant Georgian buildings and photogenic stone cottages, with glimpses of the surrounding hills and dales peeking through the gaps.

Orientation & Information

Richmond lies east of the Yorkshire Dales National Park but makes a good gateway for the northern part. The centre of everything is Market Pl (market day is Saturday). The **tourist office** (☎ 01748-828742; www.richmond.org; Friary Gardens, Victoria Rd; 9.30am-5.30pm Apr-Oct, to 4.30pm Nov-Mar) has the usual maps and guides, plus several leaflets showing walks in town and the surrounding countryside.

Sights

Top of the pile is the impressive heap that is **Richmond Castle** (EH; ☎ 01748-822493; admission £4; 10am-6pm Apr-Sep, to 4pm Oct-Mar), founded in 1070 and one of the first castles in England since Roman times to be built of stone. It's had many uses through the years, including a stint as a prison for conscientious objectors during WWI (there's a small and sobering exhibition about their part in the castle's history). The best part is the view from the top of the remarkably well-preserved 30m-high keep which towers over the River Swale.

Military buffs will enjoy the **Green Howards Museum** (☎ 01748-822133; www.greenhowards.org.uk; Trinity Church Sq; adult/child £3.50/free; 10am-4.30pm Mon-Sat, closed 24 Dec-31 Jan), which pays tribute to the famous Yorkshire regiment. In a different vein, the **Richmondshire Museum** (☎ 01748-825611; Ryder's Wynd; adult/child £2.50/1.50; 10.30am-4.30pm Apr-Oct) is a delight, with local history exhibits including an early Yorkshire cave-dweller and displays on lead mining, which forever altered the Swaledale landscape a century ago; you can also see the original set that served as James Herriot's surgery in the TV series *All Creatures Great and Small*.

Built in 1788, the **Georgian Theatre Royal** (☎ 01748-823710; www.georgiantheatreroyal.co.uk; Victoria Rd; tours per person £3.50; tours hourly 10am-4pm Mon-Sat mid-Feb–mid-Dec) is the most complete Georgian playhouse in Britain. Tours include a look at the country's oldest surviving stage scenery, painted between 1818 and 1836.

Activities

Walkers can follow paths along the River Swale, both upstream and downstream from the town. A longer option is to follow part of the famous long-distance **Coast to Coast Walk** (p588) all the way to Reeth (11 miles) and take the bus back (see www.dalesbus.info/richmond).

In September/October the town hosts the **Richmond Walking & Book Festival** (www.richmondwalking.com), 10 days of guided walks, talks, films and other events.

Cyclists can also follow Swaledale – as far as Reeth may be enough, while a trip to Keld and then over the high wild moors to Kirkby Stephen is a more serious but very rewarding 33-mile undertaking.

Sleeping

Willance House (☎ 01748-824467; www.willancehouse.com; 24 Frenchgate; s/d £40/65) This is an oak-

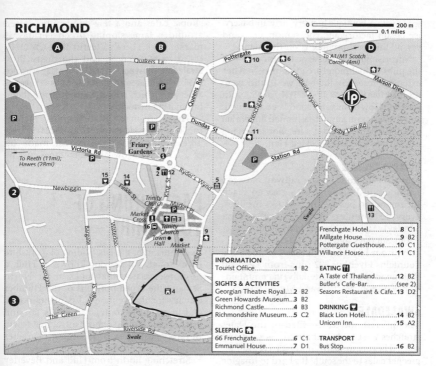

RICHMOND

INFORMATION	
Tourist Office	1 B2

SIGHTS & ACTIVITIES	
Georgian Theatre Royal	2 B2
Green Howards Museum	3 B2
Richmond Castle	4 B3
Richmondshire Museum	5 C2

SLEEPING	
66 Frenchgate	6 C1
Emmanuel House	7 D1
Frenchgate Hotel	8 C1
Millgate House	9 B2
Pottergate Guesthouse	10 C1
Willance House	11 C1

EATING	
A Taste of Thailand	12 B2
Butler's Cafe-Bar	(see 2)
Seasons Restaurant & Cafe	13 D2

DRINKING	
Black Lion Hotel	14 B2
Unicorn Inn	15 A2

TRANSPORT	
Bus Stop	16 B2

beamed house, built in 1600, with three immaculate rooms (one with a four-poster bed) that combine old-fashioned charm and all mod cons.

Frenchgate Hotel (☎ 01748-822087; www.thefrench gate.co.uk; 59-61 Frenchgate; s/d from £58/98; P) Eight elegant bedrooms occupy the upper floors of this converted Georgian town house, now a boutique guest house decorated with local art. The rooms have cool designer fittings that set off a period fireplace here, a Victorian roll-top bath there; downstairs there's an excellent **restaurant** (three-course dinner £29) and a hospitable lounge with oak beams and an open fire.

our pick Millgate House (☎ 01748-823571; www .millgatehouse.com; Market Pl; r £95-125; P) Behind an unassuming green door lies the unexpected pleasure of one of the most attractive guest houses in England. While the house itself is a Georgian gem crammed with period details, it is overshadowed by the multi-award-winning garden at the back, which has superb views over the River Swale and the Cleveland Hills – if possible, book the Garden Suite.

There's a batch of pleasant places along Frenchgate, and several more on Maison Dieu

and Pottergate (the road into town from the east). These include **66 Frenchgate** (☎ 01748-823421; www.66frenchgate.co.uk; 66 Frenchgate; s/d from £40/60;), where one of the three rooms has a superb river view, **Pottergate Guesthouse** (☎ 01748-823826; 4 Pottergate; d from £44) and **Emmanuel House** (☎ 01748-823584; 41 Maison Dieu; d from £40).

Eating & Drinking

Butler's Cafe-Bar (☎ 01748-825252; Victoria Rd; mains £2-5; 10am-2pm Mon & Tue, 10am-3pm Wed-Sat) Tucked away at the top of the Georgian Theatre Royal building, this little place serves fair-trade coffee, speciality teas and delicious hot, buttered muffins – try to get the one table with a view over Friary Gardens.

A Taste of Thailand (☎ 01748-829696; 15 King St; mains £6-8; 5-11pm) Does exactly what it says on the tin – an extensive menu of Thai favourites and a convenient BYO policy (corkage £2).

Seasons Restaurant & Cafe (☎ 01748-825340; Richmond Station, Station Rd; mains restaurant £14-17, cafe £6-10; restaurant 5.30-10pm, cafe 9am-11pm) Housed in the newly restored Victorian station building, this attractive, open-plan eatery shares space with a boutique brewery, artisan bakery, ice cream factory and cheesemonger – and yes, all this local produce is on the menu.

Surprisingly, despite a vast choice, few of the pubs in Richmond are up to much. After extensive research, the best we found were the **Black Lion Hotel** (☎ 01748-823121; Finkle St), with cosy bars, low beams and good beer and food, and the determinedly old-fashioned **Unicorn Inn** (☎ 01748-823719; 2 Newbiggin), a free house serving Theakstons and Old Speckled Hen.

Getting There & Away

From Darlington (on the railway between London and Edinburgh) it's easy to reach Richmond on bus X26 or X27 (35 minutes, every 15 minutes, every 30 minutes on Sunday). All buses stop in Market Pl.

On Sundays and bank holiday Mondays only, from late May to late September, the Fountains Flyer bus 802 runs from Leeds to Richmond (3½ hours, one daily) via Fountains Abbey, Ripon, Masham and Middleham.

SWALEDALE

The quietest and least-visited of the Dales stretches west from Richmond, its wild and rugged beauty in sharp contrast to the softer, greener dales to the south. It's hard to imagine that only a century ago this was a major lead mining area. When the price of ore fell in the 19th century, many people left to find work in England's burgeoning industrial cities, while others emigrated – especially to Wisconsin in the USA – leaving the valley almost empty, with just a few lonely villages scattered along its length.

In the heart of Swaledale is the pretty village of **Reeth**, home to some art and craft

shops, cafes and a few good pubs dotted around a large sloping green (Friday is market day). There's a **tourist office** (☎ 01748-884059; reeth@ytbtic.co.uk) and the dusty little **Swaledale Museum** (☎ 01748-884118; admission £1.50; ⏲ 10.30am-5pm Wed-Fri & Sun Easter-Oct, Sun only Nov-Easter), which tells the story of the dale's fascinating history.

There are many B&B options, including the **Arkleside Hotel** (☎ 01748-884418; www.arklesidehotel.co.uk; s/d from £60/100), made up of a converted row of old cottages just by the green.

EAST RIDING OF YORKSHIRE

In command of the East Riding of Yorkshire is the tough old sea dog known as Hull, a no-nonsense port that looks to the North Sea and the broad horizons of the Humber estuary for its livelihood. Just to its north, and in complete contrast to Hull's salt and grit, is East Riding's most attractive town, Beverley, with lots of Georgian character and one of England's finest churches.

Stretching north from Hull and Beverley are the Yorkshire Wolds, an area of gently rolling chalky hills that reaches the coast in a splash of white sea cliffs at Flamborough Head. Close by there are some classic seaside towns – bucket-and-spade Bridlington and the rather more upmarket Filey – while further south the coastline tapers away into the strange and otherwordly landscape of sand dunes and tussock grass that is Spurn Head.

DETOUR: FORBIDDEN CORNER

Hidden away in the eastern foothills of the Yorkshire Dales, 2 miles west of the village of Middleham, is one of Yorkshire's most bizarre tourist attractions. Built around 20 years ago as a private 'folly' for a local landowner, the **Forbidden Corner** (☎ 01969-640638; www.theforbidden corner.co.uk; Tupgill Park, Middleham; adult/child/family £8.50/6.50/29; ⏲ noon-6pm Mon-Sat, 10am-6pm Sun late Mar-Oct) is a labyrinth of miniature castles, caves, temples and gardens decorated with all manner of weird and wonderful sculptures. You enter through a gateway in the shape of a fanged mouth and follow a series of 'clues' in the form of rhyming couplets to reach a 'temple of the underworld'. It's great fun for kids, and some of the jokes will bring a smile to adult lips. And watch out for the sign 'cave aquae' – beware of the water.

Admission is through bookings only – by phone at the number above, or in person at the **tourist office** (☎ 01748-828747) in Leyburn, or at the **Central Stores** (☎ 01969-623224) in Middleham.

Activities
The area's main long-distance walk is the 79-mile **Wolds Way** (www.nationaltrail.co.uk /YorkshireWoldsWay), which starts at Hessle near the Humber Bridge and leads northwards through farmland, hills and quiet villages to end at the tip of Filey Brigg, a peninsula on the east coast just north of the town of Filey. Billed as 'Yorkshire's best-kept secret', it takes five days, and is an excellent beginners' walk.

The **Cleveland Way** (p588) also ends (or begins) at Filey; you can make an easy one-day walk by following the Cleveland Way along the scenic stretch of coast from Filey to Scarborough.

Getting There & Around
Hull is easily reached by rail from Leeds, York, Beverley, Filey and Scarborough, and is also the hub for regional bus services. The website at www.gettingaround.eastriding.gov.uk lists local transport operators.

HULL
pop 256,200

Tough and uncompromising, Hull is a curmudgeonly English seaport with a proud seafaring tradition. It has long been the principal cargo port of England's east coast, with an economy that grew up around carrying wool out and bringing wine in. It was also a major whaling and fishing port until the trawling industry died out, but it remains a busy cargo terminal and departure point for ferries to the Continent.

Hull too has climbed aboard the regeneration bandwagon, and the next few years from 2009 will see major redevelopment around the train station, at the marina and along the east bank of the River Hull. Meanwhile, the city's attractions include a fine collection of Victorian and Edwardian architecture, several good museums and a world-class aquarium. It's also home to the famous Hull Truck Theatre company, and counts among its famous former residents William Wilberforce (1759–1833), the Yorkshire politician who led the movement to abolish the slave trade; and the quintessentially English poet Philip Larkin (1922–85), who presided over Hull's university library for many years.

A distinctive feature of the city and surrounding area is its old-fashioned telephone boxes, which are cream-coloured rather than red. Hull was the only place in the UK to retain its own municipal phone system after all others were taken over by the Post Office in 1913; the company, now known as Kingston Communications, still provides the local phone service independently of British Telecom.

Orientation
The train and bus stations – collectively known as Hull Paragon Interchange – sit on the western edge of the city centre; all the main sights are within 20 minutes' walk from here. Arriving by car, head for the multi-storey car park at Princes Quay Shopping Centre, or the car park at The Deep.

Information
Central Library (☎ 01482-223344; Albion St; ⊙ 9.30am-8pm Mon-Thu, to 5.30pm Fri, 9am-4.30pm Sun) Internet access.
Post office (63 Market Pl; ⊙ 9am-5.30pm Mon-Sat)
Tourist office (☎ 01482-223559; www.hullcc.gov.uk; 1 Paragon St; ⊙ 10am-5pm Mon-Sat, 11am-3pm Sun)
Waterstone's (☎ 01482-580234; 19-21 Jameson St; ⊙ 9am-6pm Mon-Sat, 10.30am-4.30pm Sun)) Books and maps.

Sights
THE DEEP
Hull's biggest tourist attraction is **The Deep** (☎ 01482-381000; www.thedeep.co.uk; Tower St; adult/child £8.75/6.75; ⊙ 10am-6pm, last entry 5pm), a vast aquarium housed in a colossal, angular building that appears to lunge above the muddy waters of the Humber like a giant shark's head. Inside it's just as dramatic, with echoing commentaries and computer-generated interactive displays that guide you through the formation of the oceans and the evolution of sea life. The largest aquarium is 10m deep, filled with sharks, stingrays and colourful coral fishes, with moray eels draped over rocks like scarves of iridescent slime. A glass elevator plies up and down inside the tank, though you'll get a better view by taking the stairs. Don't miss the cafe on the very top floor, which has a great view of the Humber estuary.

MUSEUM QUARTER
Hull has several city-run **museums** (☎ 01482-300300; 36 High St; www.hullcc.gov.uk/museums; admission free; ⊙ 10am-5pm Mon-Sat, 1.30-4.30pm Sun) concentrated in an area promoted as the Museum

YORKSHIRE

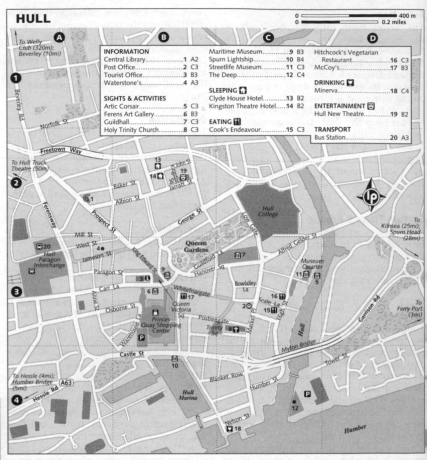

HULL

0 — 400 m
0 — 0.2 miles

INFORMATION
Central Library.....................1 A2
Post Office.........................2 C3
Tourist Office......................3 B3
Waterstone's.......................4 A3

SIGHTS & ACTIVITIES
Artic Corsair.......................5 C3
Ferens Art Gallery................6 B3
Guildhall...........................7 C3
Holy Trinity Church..............8 C3

Maritime Museum................9 B3
Spurn Lightship..................10 B4
Streetlife Museum...............11 C3
The Deep..........................12 C4

SLEEPING
Clyde House Hotel.............13 B2
Kingston Theatre Hotel......14 B2

EATING
Cook's Endeavour..............15 C3

Hitchcock's Vegetarian
  Restaurant.....................16 C3
McCoy's...........................17 B3

DRINKING
Minerva...........................18 C4

ENTERTAINMENT
Hull New Theatre..............19 B2

TRANSPORT
Bus Station.......................20 A3

Quarter. All share the same contact details, admission and opening hours.

The fascinating **Streetlife Museum** contains re-created street scenes from Georgian and Victorian times and from the 1930s, with all sorts of historic vehicles to explore, from stagecoaches to bicycles to buses and trams. Behind the museum, marooned in the mud of the River Hull, is the **Arctic Corsair** (tours 10am-4.30pm Wed & Sat, 1.30-4.30pm Sun). Tours of this Atlantic trawler, a veteran of the 1970s 'Cod Wars', demonstrate the hardships of fishing north of the Arctic Circle.

OLD TOWN

Hull's Old Town, whose grand public buildings retain a sense of the prosperity the town once knew, occupies the thumb of land between the River Hull to the east and Princes Quay to the west. The most impressive legacy is the **Guildhall** (☎ 01482-300300; Low Gate; admission free; ⌚ 8.30am-4.30pm Mon-Thu, to 3.30pm Fri), a huge neoclassical building that dates from 1916 and houses acres of polished marble, and oak and walnut panelling, plus a small collection of sculpture and art; phone to arrange a free guided tour.

The **Ferens Art Gallery** (☎ 01482-300300; Queen Victoria Sq; admission free; ⌚ 10am-5pm Mon-Sat, 1.30-4.30pm Sun), built in 1927, has a decent collection that includes works by Stanley Spencer and Peter Blake; across the square is the interesting **Maritime Museum** (same details as Ferens Art Gallery), housed in the former dock offices

(1871) and celebrating Hull's long association with the sea.

At the heart of the Old Town is **Holy Trinity Church** (☎ 01482-324835; Market Pl; 11am-2pm Tue-Fri Oct-Mar, 11am-3pm Mon-Fri, 9.30am-noon Sat Apr-Sep, services Sun year round), a magnificent 15th-century building with a striking central tower and a long, tall, unified interior worthy of a cathedral. It features huge areas of windows, built to keep the weight of the walls down as the soil here is unstable.

Built in 1927, the **Spurn Lightship** (☎ 01482-300300; Castle St; admission free; Apr-Sep, call for opening hrs) once served as a navigation mark for ships entering the notorious Humber estuary; she is now safely retired in the marina.

Festivals

Hull Literature Festival (www.humbermouth.org.uk) Last two weeks of June. A celebration of Hull's rich literary heritage: besides the Larkin connection, poets Andrew Marvell, Stevie Smith and playwrights Alan Plater and John Godber all hail from here.

Hull Jazz Festival (www.hulljazzfestival.co.uk) July. Week-long festival brings an impressive line-up of great jazz musicians to the city.

Hull Fair (☎ 01482-300300; www.hullcc.gov.uk) Second week in October. Europe's largest travelling funfair, with 250 different attractions including all kinds of stalls selling everything from palm reading to candy floss and all manner of rides, from the gentle, traditional kind to more modern white-knucklers.

Sleeping & Eating

Good accommodation in the city centre is pretty thin on the ground – mostly business-oriented chain hotels and a few mediocre guest houses. The tourist office will help book accommodation for free.

Clyde House Hotel (☎ 01482-214981; www.clyde househotel.co.uk; 13 John St; s/d £30/50) Overlooking leafy Kingston Sq, and close to the New Theatre, this is one of the best B&B options in the city centre; the rooms are nothing fancy, but are tidy and comfortable, and the owners are friendly and helpful.

Kingston Theatre Hotel (☎ 01482-225828; www .kingstontheatrehotel.com; 1-2 Kingston Sq; s/d/ste from £45/65/80) A slightly more formal hotel sharing the same central location, this place offers charming if not quite memorable rooms; upgrade to a suite if you're looking for a little leg room.

McCoy's (☎ 01482-327757; Colonial Chambers, Princes Dock St; mains £3-5; 8am-6pm Mon-Sat) This home-grown alternative to Starbucks serves excellent coffee, and a breakfast menu that ranges from porridge to a vegetarian fry-up to scrambled egg with smoked salmon. There are freshly baked cakes and pastries through the day, with salads and sarnies at lunch.

Hitchcock's Vegetarian Restaurant (☎ 01482-320233; 1 Bishop Lane, High St; per person £15; 8-9pm Tue-Sat) The word 'quirky' could have been invented to describe this place – an atmospheric maze of small rooms, an all-you-can-eat vegetarian buffet whose theme – Thai, Indian, Spanish, whatever – is chosen by the first person to book that evening, BYO alcohol, and no credit cards. But hey – the food is excellent and the welcome is warm. Bookings necessary.

Cook's Endeavour (☎ 01482-213844; 5 Scale Lane; 2-/3-course dinner £25/30; dinner Mon-Sat) Set in a quaint 15th-century building – the oldest surviving house in Hull – this wittily named place specialises in local produce, including Yorkshire beef and Whitby crab, prepared in traditional English style.

Drinking & Entertainment

Come nightfall – especially at weekends – Hull can be raucous and often rowdy, especially in the streets around Trinity Sq in the Old Town, and on the strip of pubs along Beverley Rd to the north of the city centre.

Hull Truck Theatre (☎ 01482-323638; www.hulltruck .co.uk; Spring St) Home to acclaimed playwright John Godber, who made his name with gritty comedies *Bouncers* and *Up'n'Under* – he is one of the most-performed playwrights in the English-speaking world – Hull Truck presents a lively program of drama, comedy and Sunday jazz. It's just northwest of the Old Town.

Hull New Theatre (☎ 01482-226655; www.hull cc.gov.uk; Kingston Sq) A traditional regional theatre hosting popular drama, concerts and musicals.

Welly Club (☎ 01482-326131, 221676; www.giveit somewelly.com; 105-107 Beverley Rd; admission free-£5; to 2am, closed Wed & Sun) The Welly is best known these days for the regular Saturday house night Déjà Vu (www.clubdejavu .co.uk), which was voted the best club night in Yorkshire in 2007. Choose Thursday if indie rock appeals more than house and trance.

YORKSHIRE

Minerva (☎ 01482-326909; Nelson St) If you're more into pubbing than clubbing, try a pint of Timothy Taylors at this lovely, 200-year-old pub down by the waterfront; on a sunny day you can sit outdoors and watch the ships go by.

Getting There & Away

National Express operates coaches direct from London (£24, 6½ hours, two daily) and Manchester (£15, 3¼ hours, one daily). Both National Express and bus X46 run to/from York (£7.60, 1¾ hours, one daily).

Hull has good rail links north and south to Newcastle (£43, 1½ hours, hourly, change at York) and London King's Cross (£61, 2½ hours, every two hours), and west to York (£17, 1¼ hours, every two hours) and Leeds (£16, one hour, hourly).

The ferry port is 3 miles east of the centre at King George Dock; a bus connects the train station with the ferries. For details of ferry services to Zeebrugge and Rotterdam see p805.

AROUND HULL
Humber Bridge

Opened in 1981, the **Humber Bridge** (www .humberbridge.co.uk) swoops gracefully across the broad estuary of the River Humber, its 1410m span made it the world's longest single-span suspension bridge – until 1998. It links Yorkshire to Lincolnshire (p490), opening up what was once an often-overlooked corner of the country.

The best way to appreciate the scale of the bridge, and the vastness of the estuary, is to walk or cycle out along the footway from the **Humber Bridge tourist office** (☎ 01482-640852; ⊙ 9am-5pm Mon-Fri, 9am-6pm Sat & Sun May-Sep, 10am-3pm Nov-Feb, 9am-4pm Mar, Apr & Oct) at the north end of the bridge (follow road signs for Humber Bridge Country Park). The car park here hosts a popular farmers market on the first Sunday in the month.

The bridge is a mile west of the small riverside town of **Hessle**, about 4 miles west of Hull. Bus 350 runs from Hull Paragon Interchange to Ferriby Rd in Hessle (15 minutes, every two hours), from where it's a 300m walk to the tourist office.

Spurn Head

Three and half miles long and less than 100m wide, Spurn Head (also called Spurn Point) is the front line in a constant battle between the River Humber and the North Sea. A series of sand and shingle banks tenuously held together by tussocks of marram grass, this fragile and unusual environment is a paradise for bird watchers and fossil hunters. It is also under threat – as the fastest-eroding stretch of coastline in Britain, it is only ever a storm away from destruction.

Most of the land is now part of the **Spurn National Nature Reserve** (☎ 01964-650533; www.ywt .org.uk; admission per car £3) which is managed by the Yorkshire Wildlife Trust; the tidal mud flats on the west side of the headland are a haven for wading birds and migrating water fowl. You can park for free at the **Blue Bell Tea Room & Visitor Centre** (☎ 01964-650139; ⊙ 11am-4.30pm Sat, 11am-5pm Sun Easter-Oct) and walk out along the Spurn Footpath to the tip of the headland (7 miles round trip), or pay the admission fee and drive along the very narrow road to a parking area at the old lighthouse. There are sandy beaches on either side, where the shingle is littered with fossil ammonites, and the very end of the headland is home to a remote community of lifeboat personnel and harbour pilots.

In 1804 gun batteries were built here to repel a possible French invasion, and during WWII guns of all sizes mounted in heavy concrete emplacements were added – the shattered concrete blocks and sandy scarps near the Blue Bell are a graphic illustration of how fast this coast is being lost to the sea.

There are a couple of pubs and tearooms in **Kilnsea**, the last village before the Blue Bell, and at **Easington**, two miles to the north.

Spurn Head is about 28 miles southeast of Hull city centre, on mostly minor roads – it's about an hour's drive. There is no public transport.

BEVERLEY
pop 29,110

Handsome, unspoilt Beverley is one of the most attractive of Yorkshire towns largely on account of its magnificent minster – a rival to any cathedral in England – and the tangle of streets that lie beneath it, each brimming with exquisite Georgian and Victorian buildings.

Orientation & Information

All the sights are a short walk from either train or bus station. There's a large mar-

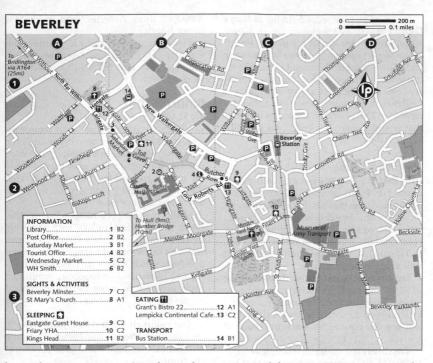

BEVERLEY

INFORMATION	
Library...................................1	B2
Post Office............................2	B2
Saturday Market...................3	B1
Tourist Office........................4	B2
Wednesday Market................5	C2
WH Smith..............................6	B2

SIGHTS & ACTIVITIES	
Beverley Minster....................7	C2
St Mary's Church...................8	A1

SLEEPING	
Eastgate Guest House...........9	C2
Friary YHA..........................10	C2
Kings Head.........................11	B2

EATING	
Grant's Bistro 22.................12	A1
Lempicka Continental Cafe..13	C2

TRANSPORT	
Bus Station.........................14	B1

ket in the main square on Saturday, and a smaller one on Wednesday on the square called – Wednesday Market.

Library (☎ 01482-885355; Champney Rd; ⏱ 9.30am-5pm Mon & Wed, 9.30am-7pm Tue, Thu & Fri, 9am-1pm Sat) Internet access and a small art gallery with changing exhibitions.

Post office (Register Sq; ⏱ 9am-5.30pm Mon-Fri, to 12.30pm Sat)

Tourist office (☎ 01482-391672; www.beverley.gov .uk; 34 Butcher Row; ⏱ 9.30am-5.15pm Mon-Fri, 10am-4.45pm Sat year round, 11am-3pm Sun Jul & Aug)

WH Smith (☎ 01482-870494; 39-41 Toll Gavel; ⏱ 8.45am-5.30pm Mon-Sat, 10am-4pm Sun) Books and maps.

Sights
One of the great glories of English religious architecture, **Beverley Minster** (☎ 01482-868540; www.beverleyminster.org; admission by donation; ⏱ 9am-5.30pm Mon-Sat May-Aug, 9am-5pm Sep-Oct & Mar-Apr, 9am-4pm Nov-Feb, also noon-4pm Sun year round) is the most impressive church in the country that is not a cathedral. Construction began in 1220 – it was the third church to be built on this site, the first dating from the 7th century and

continued for two centuries, spanning the Early English, Decorated and Perpendicular periods of the Gothic style.

The soaring lines of the exterior are imposing, but it is inside that the charm and beauty lie. The 14th-century **north aisle** is lined with original stone carvings, mostly of musicians – indeed, much of our knowledge of early musical instruments comes from these images – but also of goblins, devils and grotesque figures. Look out for the bagpipe player.

Close to the altar, the elaborate and intricate **Percy Canopy** (1340), a decorative frill above the tomb of local aristocrat Lady Eleanor Percy, is a testament to the skill of the sculptor, and the finest example of Gothic stone carving in England. In complete contrast, in the nearby chancel, is the 10th-century Saxon **frith stool**, a plain and polished stone chair that once gave sanctuary to anyone escaping the law.

In the roof of the tower is a restored **tread-wheel crane** (guided tours £4; ⏱ 11.15am & 2.15pm Mon-Sat), where workers ground around like hapless hamsters to lift the huge loads necessary to build a medieval church; access is by guided tour only.

YORKSHIRE

Doomed to play second fiddle, **St Mary's Church** (☎ 01482-865709; admission free; ⏰ 9.30am-4.30pm Mon-Fri, 10am-4pm Sat & 2-4pm Sun Apr-Sep, 9.30am-noon & 1-4pm Mon Fri Oct-Mar) at the other end of town was built between 1120 and 1530; the west front (early 15th century) is considered one of the finest of any parish church in England. In the north choir aisle there is a **carving** (c 1330) of a rabbit dressed as a pilgrim that is said to have inspired Lewis Carroll's White Rabbit.

Sleeping & Eating

Friary YHA (☎ 0845 371 9004; www.yha.org.uk; Friar's Lane; dm from £14; ℗) In Beverley, it's the cheapest accommodation that has the best setting and location – this hostel is housed in a beautifully restored 14th-century Dominican friary mentioned in Chaucer's *The Canterbury Tales*, and is only 100m from the minster and a short walk from the train station.

Eastgate Guest House (☎ 01482-868464; 7 Eastgate; s/d £45/60) This red-brick Victorian town house offers 15 very comfortable rooms in a central location, and the sort of hearty breakfast that will see you passing up lunch in favour of a snack.

Kings Head (☎ 01482-868103; 38 Saturday Market; s/d £50/65; 🖥) A Georgian coaching inn that has been given a modern makeover, the Kings Head is a lively, family-friendly pub with 12 bright and cheerful rooms above the bar – the pub opens late on weekend nights, but earplugs are supplied for those who don't want to join the revelry!

Lempicka Continental Cafe (☎ 01482-866960; 13 Wednesday Market; mains £5-7) Named and themed after Polish artist Tamara de Lempicka, this stylish and sepia-toned little cafe has a 1930s art-deco atmosphere and serves good fairtrade coffee and tea, wicked hot chocolate, homemade cakes and daily lunch specials.

Grant's Bistro 22 (☎ 01482-887624; 22 North Bar Within; 2-course lunch/dinner £13/25; ⏰ lunch Tue-Sat, dinner Mon-Sat) The top place in town is a great place for a romantic dinner *à deux*, with dark wood tables, fresh flowers and candlelight. The menu makes the most of fresh local beef, game and especially seafood.

Getting There & Away

There are frequent bus services from Hull including numbers 121, 122, 246 and X46/X47 (30 minutes, every 20 minutes). Bus X46/X47 links Beverley with York (1¼ hours, hourly).

There are regular trains to Scarborough via Filey (£11, 1½ hours, every two hours); trains to/from Hull (£4.90, 15 minutes) run twice an hour.

BRIDLINGTON
pop 33,600

Bridlington is one of those sleepy seaside resorts that seems to have been bypassed by the 21st century, pulling in a crowd of contented regulars who return year after year to enjoy the neatly groomed beaches of golden sand, the mini-golf and paddling pool, the deckchairs and donkey rides.

So the reopening of **Bridlington Spa** (☎ 01262-401400; South Marine Drive) in 2007 with a rock gig by Yorkshire indie band the Pigeon Detectives was a bit of a shot in the arm. The renovated building, which retains its Edwardian theatre and 1930s art-deco ballroom, promises a lively program of music and entertainment events that will liven things up down by the South Beach.

The **tourist office** (☎ 01262-673474; 25 Prince St; ⏰ 9.30am-5.30pm Mon-Sat, 11am-3pm Sun) is near the North Beach and has short-term parking at the front.

Food wise, Bridlington is famous for **Audrey's Fish and Chips** (☎ 01262-671920; 2 Queen St; mains £5-6; ⏰ 11.30am-6pm daily), an old-school fish and chip restaurant that serves superbly crisp battered haddock fried in beef dripping – the real deal.

For something more contemporary try **Rags Hotel** (☎ 01262-400355; www.ragshotel.co.uk; South Pier; mains £8-17; s/d from £60/85; ℗), a boutique-style place where you can enjoy a dish of *moules mariniére* with a view over the harbour.

Bridlington is on the railway line between Hull (£9.60, 45 minutes, every 30 minutes) and Scarborough (£6, 40 minutes, every two hours).

AROUND BRIDLINGTON

Northeast of Bridlington, the 120m-high chalk cliffs of **Flamborough Head** thrust out into the North Sea, providing nesting sites for England's largest seabird colony. The headland is also home to the country's oldest surviving **lighthouse tower**, dating from around 1670 – it stands in the golf course about 300m before the car park beside the modern lighthouse.

On the northern side of the headland, about 4 miles north of Bridlington, is the RSPB's **Bempton Cliffs Nature Reserve** (☎ 01262-851179; pedestrian/car free/£3.50; ☯ visitor centre 10am-5pm Mar-Oct, 9.30am-4pm Nov-Feb). From April to August these cliffs are home to more than 200,000 nesting sea birds, including guillemots, razorbills, fulmars, a rare colony of gannets, and those supermodels of the seagull world, the delicate and elegant kittiwakes, with their fat and fluffy chicks. The big crowd-pullers, though, are the comical and colourful puffins. There is a good visitor centre at the car park and the reserve has 3 miles of well-maintained paths along the cliffs. Binoculars can be rented for £3 and there are helpful volunteers on hand to offer guidance.

You can take a train from Bridlington to Bempton village (7 minutes, every 1½ hours), from where it's a 1½-mile walk to the reserve.

NORTH YORKSHIRE

The largest of Yorkshire's four counties – and the largest county in England – is also the most beautiful; unlike the rest of northern England, it has survived almost unscarred by the Industrial Revolution. On the contrary, North Yorkshire has always, since the Middle Ages, been about sheep and the woolly wealth that they produce.

Instead of closed-down factories, mills and mines, the man-made monuments that dot the landscape round these parts are of the magnificent variety – the great houses and wealthy abbeys that sit ruined or restored, a reminder that there was plenty of money to be made off the sheep's back.

All the same, North Yorkshire's biggest attraction is an urban one. Sure, the genteel spa town of Harrogate and the bright and breezy seaside resorts of Scarborough and Whitby have many fans, but nothing compares to the unparalleled splendour of York, England's most-visited city outside London.

Getting There & Around

The main gateway town is York, which has excellent road and rail links to the rest of the country (see p631). For countywide public transport information, call **Traveline Yorkshire** (☎ 0871 200 2233; www.yorkshiretravel.net). There are various Explorer passes, and individual bus and train companies also offer their own saver schemes, so it's worth asking for advice on the best deal when you buy your ticket.

YORK
pop 181,100

Nowhere in northern England says 'medieval' quite like York, a city of extraordinary cultural and historical wealth that has lost little of its preindustrial lustre. Its medieval spider's web of narrow streets is enclosed by a magnificent circuit of 13th-century walls. At the heart of the city lies the immense, awe-inspiring minster, one of the most beautiful Gothic cathedrals in the world. The city's long history and rich heritage is woven into virtually every brick and beam, and modern, tourist-oriented York – with its myriad museums, restaurants, cafes and traditional pubs – is a carefully maintained heir to that heritage.

Orientation

Compact and eminently walkable, York has five major landmarks to take note of: the wall enclosing the old city centre; the minster at the northern corner; Clifford's Tower at the southern end; the River Ouse, which divides the centre in two; and the train station to the west. Just to avoid the inevitable confusion, remember that round these parts *gate* means street and *bar* means gate.

Information

American Express (Amex; ☎ 01904-676501; 6 Stonegate; ☯ 9am-5.30pm Mon-Fri, 9am-5pm Sat) With foreign exchange service.

Borders (☎ 01904-653300; 1-5 Davygate; ☯ 9am-9pm Mon-Sat, 11am-5pm Sun) Well-stocked bookshop.

City Library (☎ 01904-552815; Museum St; ☯ 9am-8pm Mon-Wed & Fri, to 5.30pm Thu, to 4pm Sat; per 30min £1) Internet access.

Post office (22 Lendal; ☯ 8.30am-5.30pm Mon & Tue, 9am-5.30pm Wed-Sat)

Thomas Cook (☎ 01904-653626; 4 Nessgate) Full service travel agent and currency exchange.

York District Hospital (☎ 01904-631313; Wiggington Rd) A mile north of the centre.

York Visitor Centre (☎ 01904-550099; www.visityork .org; De Grey Rooms, Exhibition Sq; ☯ 9am-6pm Mon-Sat, 10am-5pm Sun Apr-Sep, 9am-5pm Mon-Sat, 10am-4pm Sun Oct-Mar) There's another branch at the train station (same hours).

YORK: FROM THE BEGINNING

York – or the marshy area that preceded the first settlement – has been coveted by pretty much everyone that has ever set foot on this island. In the beginning there were the Brigantes, a local tribe that minded their own business. In AD 71 the Romans – who were spectacularly successful at minding everyone else's business – built their first garrison here for the troops fighting the poor old Brigantes. They called it Eboracum, and in time a civilian settlement prospered around what became a large fort. Hadrian used it as the base for his northern campaign, while Constantine the Great was proclaimed emperor here in AD 306 after the death of his father. After the collapse of the Roman Empire, the town was taken by the Anglo-Saxons who renamed it Eoforwic and made it the capital of the independent kingdom of Northumbria.

Enter the Christians. In 625 a Roman priest, Paulinus, arrived and managed to convert King Edwin and all his nobles. Two years later, they built the first wooden church; for most of the next century the city was a major centre of learning, attracting students from all over Europe.

The student party lasted until 866, when the next wave of invaders arrived. This time it was those marauding Vikings, who chucked everybody out and gave the town a more tongue-friendly name, Jorvik. It was to be their capital for the next 100 years, and during that time they put a rest to their pillaging ways and turned the city into an important trading port.

The next arrival was King Eadred of Wessex, who drove out the last Viking ruler in 954 and reunited Danelaw with the south, but trouble quickly followed. In 1066 King Harold II managed to fend off a Norwegian invasion-rebellion at Stamford Bridge, east of York, but his turn came at the hands of William the Conqueror a few months later at the Battle of Hastings.

Sights

YORK MINSTER

Not content with being Yorkshire's most important historic building, the awe-inspiring **York Minster** (☎ 01904-557200; www.yorkminster.org; adult/child minster only £5.50/free, all areas £9.50/3; ✢ minster 9am-5pm Mon-Sat, noon-3.45pm Sun Apr-Oct, 9.30am-5pm Mon-Sat, noon-3.45pm Sun Nov-Mar) is also the largest medieval cathedral in all of Northern Europe. Seat of the archbishop of York, primate of England, it is second in importance only to Canterbury, home of the primate of *all* England – the separate titles were created to settle a debate over whether York or Canterbury was the true centre of the English church. But that's where Canterbury's superiority ends, for this is without doubt one of the world's most beautiful Gothic buildings. If this is the only cathedral you visit in England, you'll still walk away satisfied – so long as you have the patience to deal with the constant flow of school groups and organised tours that will invariably clog up your camera's viewfinder.

The first church on this spot was a wooden chapel built for the baptism of King Edwin of Northumbria on Easter Day 627; its location is marked in the crypt. It was replaced with a stone church that was built on the site of a Roman basilica, parts of which can be seen in the foundations. The first Norman minster was built in the 11th century; again, you can see surviving fragments in the foundations and crypt.

The present minster, built mainly between 1220 and 1480, manages to encompass all the major stages of Gothic architectural development. The transepts (1220–1255) were built in Early English style; the octagonal chapter house (1260–1290) and the nave (1291–1340) in the Decorated style; and the west towers, west front and central, or lantern, tower (1470–1472) in Perpendicular style.

You enter via the south transept, which was badly damaged by fire in 1984 but has now been fully restored. To your right is the 15th-century **choir screen** depicting the 15 kings from William I to Henry VI. Facing you is the magnificent **Five Sisters Window**, with five lancets over 15m high. This is the minster's oldest complete window; most of its tangle of coloured glass dates from around 1250. Just beyond it to the right is the 13th-century **chapter house**, a fine example of the Decorated style. Sinuous and intricately carved stonework – there are more than 200 expressive carved heads and figures – surrounds an airy, uninterrupted space.

Back in the main church, take note of the unusually tall and wide **nave**, the aisles of which (to the sides) are roofed in stone in contrast to the central roof, which is wood painted to

Willie exercised his own brand of tough love in York. After his two wooden castles were captured by an Anglo-Scandinavian army, he torched the whole city (and Durham) and the surrounding countryside so that the rebels knew who was boss – the 'harrying of the north'. The Normans then set about rebuilding the city, including a new minster. From that moment, everything in York was rosy – except for a blip in 1137 when the whole city caught fire – and over the next 300 years it prospered through royal patronage, textiles, trade and the church.

No sooner did the church finally get built, though, than the city went into full recession. In the 15th century Hull took over as the region's main port and the textile industry moved elsewhere. Henry VIII's inability to keep a wife and the ensuing brouhaha with the church that resulted in the Reformation also hit York pretty hard. Henry did establish a branch of the King's Council here to help govern the north, and this contributed to the city's recovery under Elizabeth I and James I.

The council was abolished during Charles I's reign, but the king established his court here during the Civil War, which drew the devastating attentions of the Parliamentarians. They besieged the rabidly promonarchist York for three months in 1644, but by a fortunate accident of history their leader was a local chap called Sir Thomas Fairfax, who prevented his troops from setting York alight, thereby preserving the city and the minster.

Not much happened after that. Throughout the 18th century the city was a fashionable social centre dominated by the aristocracy, who were drawn by its culture and new racecourse. When the railway was built in 1839 thousands of people were employed in the new industries that sprung up around it, such as confectionery. These industries went into decline in the latter half of the 20th century, but by then a new invader was asking for directions at the city gates, armed only with a guidebook.

look like stone. On both sides of the nave are painted stone shields of the nobles who met with Edward II at a parliament in York. Also note the **dragon's head** projecting from the gallery – it's a crane believed to have been used to lift a font cover. There are several fine windows dating from the early 14th century, but the most impressive is the **Great West Window** (1338), with its beautiful stone tracery.

Beyond the screen and the choir is the **lady chapel** and, behind it, the **high altar**, which is dominated by the huge **Great East Window** (1405). At 23.7m by 9.4m – roughly the size of a tennis court – it is the world's largest medieval stained-glass window and the cathedral's single most important treasure. Needless to say, its epic size matches the epic theme depicted within: the beginning and end of the world as described in Genesis and the Book of Revelations.

At the heart of the minster is the massive **tower** (adult/child £4/2; 9.30am-5pm Mon-Sat, 12.30-5pm Sun Apr-Oct, from 10am Nov-Mar), which is well worth climbing for the unparalleled views of York. You'll have to tackle a fairly claustrophobic climb of 275 steps and, most probably, a queue of people with cameras in hand. Access to the tower is near the entrance in the south transept, dominated by the exquisite **Rose Window** commemorating the union of the royal houses of Lancaster

and York, through the marriage of Henry VII and Elizabeth of York, which ended the Wars of the Roses and began the Tudor dynasty (see p40).

Another set of stairs in the south transept leads down to the **undercroft** (adult/child £4/2; 9.30am-5pm Mon-Sat, 12.30-5pm Sun), where you'll also find the **treasury** and **crypt** – these should on no account be missed. In 1967 the foundations were shored up when the central tower threatened to collapse; while engineers worked frantically to save the building, archaeologists uncovered Roman and Norman remains that attest to the site's ancient history – one of the most extraordinary finds is a Roman culvert, still carrying water to the Ouse. The treasury houses 11th-century artefacts including relics from the graves of medieval archbishops. The crypt contains fragments from the Norman cathedral, including the font showing King Edwin's baptism that also marks the site of the original wooden chapel.

AROUND THE MINSTER

Owned by the minster since the 15th century, **St William's College** (01904-637134; College St) is an attractive half-timbered Tudor building with elegant oriel windows built for the minster's chantry priests.

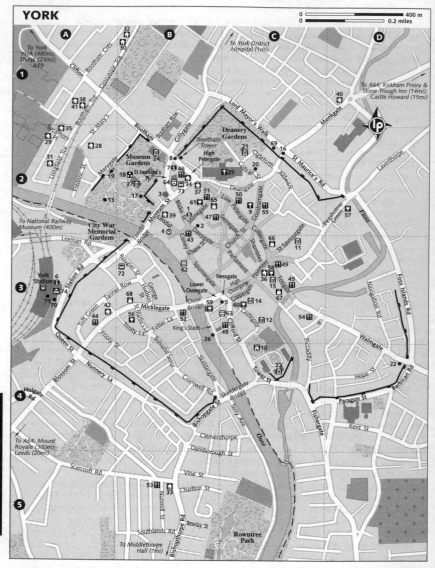

YORK

The **Treasurer's House** (NT; ☎ 01904-624247; Minster Yard; admission £5.80, house & basement £8; ☼ 11am-4.30pm Sat-Thu Apr-Oct, 11am-3pm Sat-Thu Nov) was home to the minster's medieval treasurers. Substantially rebuilt in the 17th and 18th centuries, the 13 rooms house a fine collection of furniture and provide a good insight into 18th-century life. The house is also the setting

for one of the city's most enduring ghost stories: during the 1950s a plumber working in the basement swore he saw a band of Roman soldiers walking *through* the walls; his story remains popular if unproven – but you can explore the cellar to find out.

Tucked away behind an inconspicuous gate and seemingly cut off from the rest of the

INFORMATION
Amex....1 B2
Borders....2 B2
City Library....3 B2
Post Office....4 B2
Thomas Cook....5 C3
York Visitor Centre (Branch)....6 A3
York Visitor Centre (Main Office)....7 B2

SIGHTS & ACTIVITIES
Bootham Bar....8 B2
Church of the Holy Trinity....9 C2
Clifford's Tower....10 C4
Dig....11 C3
Fairfax House....12 C3
Gatehall....13 A2
Hospitium....(see 13)
Jorvik....14 C3
Merchant Adventurers' Hall....15 C3
Monk Bar....16 C2
Multangular Tower....17 B2
Richard III Museum....(see 16)
St Mary's Abbey....18 B2
St Mary's Lodge....19 A2
St William's College....20 C2
Steps to City Walls....(see 16)
Steps to City Walls....(see 8)
Treasurer's House....21 C2
Walmgate Bar....22 D4
York Castle Museum....23 C4
York City Art Gallery....24 B2
York Minster....25 C2
YorkBoat River Trips....26 B3
Yorkshire Museum....27 B2

SLEEPING
23 St Mary's....28 A2
Alcuin Lodge....29 A2
Arnot House....30 B1
Briar Lea Guest House....31 A2
Brontë House....32 B1
Dairy Guesthouse....33 B5
Dean Court Hotel....34 B2
Elliotts B&B....35 A2
Golden Fleece....36 C3
Guy Fawkes....37 B2
Hedley House Hotel....38 A1
Judges Lodging Hotel....39 B2
Monkgate Guesthouse....40 D1
St Raphael....41 A1
York Backpackers....42 A3

EATING
Betty's....43 B3
Blake Head Vegetarian Cafe....44 A3
Blue Bicycle....45 C3
Cafe Concerto....46 B2
El Piano....47 B2
Fiesta Mexicana....48 C3
J Baker's....49 C3
La Vecchia Scuola....50 C2
Little Betty's....51 B2
Living Room....52 B3
Melton's....53 B5
Melton's Too....54 C3
Siam House....55 C2

DRINKING
Ackhorne....56 B3
Black Swan....57 D2
Blue Bell....58 C3
King's Arms....59 B3
Little John....60 C3
Ye Olde Starre....61 B2

ENTERTAINMENT
City Screen....62 B3
Grand Opera House....63 C3
York Theatre Royal....64 B2

SHOPPING
Antiques Centre....65 B2
Azendi....66 C3
Barbican Books....67 C3
Ken Spellman Booksellers....68 B3

TRANSPORT
Bob Trotter Bike Hire....69 C2
Europcar....70 A3
Hertz....71 A3
Local Bus Stops....72 B3
Road Train Stop....73 B2
Station Taxis....74 A3

town, the **Church of the Holy Trinity** (☎ 01904-613451; Goodramgate; 10am-5pm Tue-Sat May-Sep, 10am-4pm Oct-Apr) is a fantastically atmospheric old building, having survived almost unchanged for the last 200 years, with rare 17th- to 18th-century box pews, 15th-century stained glass, and wonky walls that seem to have been built without plumb line or spirit level.

CITY WALLS

If the weather's good, don't miss the chance to walk the **City Walls** (admission free; 8am-dusk), which follow the line of the original Roman walls – it gives a whole new perspective on the city. The full circuit is 4.5 miles (allow 1½ to two hours); if you're pushed for time, the short stretch from Bootham Bar to Monk Bar is worth doing for the views of the minster.

Start and finish in the Museum Gardens or at **Bootham Bar** (on the site of a Roman gate), where a multimedia exhibit provides some historical context, and go clockwise. Highlights include **Monk Bar**, the best-preserved medieval gate, which still has a working portcullis, and **Walmgate Bar**, England's only city gate with an intact barbican (an extended gateway to ward off uninvited guests).

At Monk Bar you'll find the **Richard III Museum** (☎ 01904-634191; www.richardiiimuseum.co.uk; admission £2.50; 9am-5pm Mar-Oct, 9.30am-4pm Nov-Feb). The museum sets out the case of the murdered 'Princes in the Tower' and invites visitors to judge whether their uncle, Richard III, killed them (see Dark Deeds in the Tower, p39).

You can download a free guide to the wall walk at www.visityork.org/explore.

SHAMBLES

The narrow, cobbled lane known as the **Shambles** (www.yorkshambles.com), lined with 15th-century Tudor buildings that overhang so

THE YORK PASS

If you plan on visiting a lot of sights, you can save yourself some money by using a **York Pass** (www.yorkpass.com; 1/2/3 days adult £24/32/36, child £14/18/22); it grants you free access to most pay-to-visit sights in town, as well as free passage on a handful of tours and discounts at a range of eateries. It's available at the tourist offices, or you can buy online.

much they seem to meet above your head, is the most visited street in Europe. Quaint and picturesque it most certainly is, and it hints at what a medieval street may have looked like – if it was overrun with people told they have to buy a tacky souvenir and be back on the tour bus in 15 minutes. It takes its name from the Saxon word *shamel*, meaning 'slaughterhouse' – in 1862 there were 26 butcher shops on this one street.

JORVIK

Interactive multimedia exhibits aimed at 'bringing history to life' often achieve just the opposite, but the much-hyped **Jorvik** (☎ 01904-543403; www.vikingjorvik.com; Coppergate; adult/child £8.50/6, Jorvik & Dig combined £11.25/8.50; ☼ 10am-5pm Apr-Oct, to 4pm Nov-Mar) – the most visited attraction in town after the minster – manages to pull it off with admirable aplomb. It's a smells-and-all reconstruction of the Viking settlement that was unearthed here during excavations in the late 1970s, brought to you courtesy of a 'time-car' monorail that transports you through 9th-century Jorvik (the Viking name for York). While some of the 'you will now travel back in time' malarkey is a bit naff, it's all done with a sense of humour tied to a historical authenticity that will leave you with a pretty good idea of what life must have been like in Viking-era York. In the exhibition at the end of the monorail, look out for the **Lloyds Bank Turd** – a fossilised human stool that measures an eye-watering nine inches long and half a pound in weight, and must be the only jobbie in the world to have its own Wikipedia entry.

You can cut time spent waiting in the queue by booking your tickets online and choosing the time you want to visit – it only costs £1 extra.

DIG

Under the same management as Jorvik, **Dig** (☎ 01904-543403; www.digyork.co.uk; St Saviour's Church, St Saviourgate; adult/child £5.50/5, Dig & Jorvik £11.25/8.50; ☼ 10am-5pm) cashes in on the popularity of archaeology programs on TV by giving you the chance to be an 'archaeological detective', unearthing the 'secrets' of York's distant past as well as learning something of the archaeologist's world – what they do, how they do it and so on. Aimed mainly at kids, it's much more hands-on than Jorvik, and a lot depends on how good – and entertaining – your guide is.

CLIFFORD'S TOWER

There's precious little left of York Castle except for this evocative stone **tower** (EH; ☎ 01904-646940; admission £3; ☼ 10am-6pm Apr-Sep, to 5pm Oct, to 4pm Nov-Mar), a highly unusual figure-of-eight design built into the castle's keep after the original one was destroyed in 1190 during anti-Jewish riots. An angry mob forced 150 Jews to be locked inside the tower and the hapless victims took their own lives rather than be killed. There's not much to see inside but the views over the city are excellent.

YORK CASTLE MUSEUM

Opposite Clifford's Tower, this excellent **museum** (☎ 01904-653611; www.yorkcastlemuseum .org.uk; adult/child £7.50/4, with Yorkshire Museum £9.50/6; ☼ 9.30am-5pm) contains displays of everyday life through the centuries, with reconstructed domestic interiors and a less-than-homely prison cell where you can try out the condemned man's bed – in this case the highwayman Dick Turpin's (he was imprisoned here before being hanged in 1739). There's a bewildering array of evocative objects from the past 400 years, gathered together by a certain Dr Kirk from the 1920s onwards for fear that the items would become obsolete and disappear completely. He wasn't far wrong, which makes this place all the more interesting.

NATIONAL RAILWAY MUSEUM

Many railway museums are the sole preserve of lone men in anoraks comparing dog-eared notebooks and getting high on the smell of machine oil, coal smoke and nostalgia. But this place is different. York's **National Railway Museum** (☎ 0844 815 3139; www.nrm.org.uk; Leeman Rd; admission free; ☼ 10am-6pm daily, closed 24-26 Dec) – the biggest in the world, with more than 100 locomotives – is so well presented and full of fascinating stuff that it's interesting even to folk whose eyes don't mist over at the thought of a 4-6-2 A1 Pacific class chuffing into a tunnel.

Highlights for the trainspotters among us include a replica of George Stephenson's *Rocket* of 1829, the world's first 'modern' steam locomotive; the sleek and streamlined *Mallard*, which set the world speed record for a steam locomotive in 1938 (126mph); a 1960s Japanese *Shinkansen* bullet train; and the world-famous *Flying Scotsman*, the first steam engine to break the 100mph barrier (still in bits in the workshop at time of research – should be on display by early 2009). There's also a massive 4-6-2 loco from 1949 that's been cut in half so you can see how it works.

But even if you're not a rail nerd you'll enjoy looking around the gleaming, silk-lined carriages of the royal trains used by Queen Victoria and Edward VII, or having a *Brief Encounter* moment over tea and scones at the museum's station platform cafe called, erm, Brief Encounter. Allow at least two hours to do the museum justice.

The museum is about 400m west of the train station; if you don't fancy walking you can ride the road train (adult/child £2/1) that runs every 30 minutes from 11am to 4pm between the minster and the museum.

OTHER SIGHTS

Most of York's Roman archaeology is hidden beneath the medieval city, so the displays in the **Yorkshire Museum** (☎ 01904-629745; www .yorkshiremuseum.org.uk; adult/child £5/3.50, with York Castle Museum £9.50/6; ☼ 10am-5pm) are invaluable if you want to get an idea of what Eboracum was like. There are excellent exhibits on Viking and medieval York too, including priceless artefacts such as the 8th-century Coppergate helmet, a 9th-century Anglian sword decorated with silver, and the 15th-century Middleham Jewel, an engraved gold pendant adorned with a giant sapphire.

In the peaceful **Museum Gardens** (☼ dawn-dusk) you can see the **Multangular Tower**, a part of the city walls that was once the western tower of the Roman garrison's defensive ramparts; the Roman stonework at the base has been built over with 13th-century additions.

On the other side of the Museum Gardens are the ruins of **St Mary's Abbey** (founded 1089), dating from 1270–1294. The ruined **Gatehall** was its main entrance, providing access from the abbey to the river. The adjacent **Hospitium** dates from the 14th century, although the timber-framed upper storey is a much-restored survivor from the 15th century; it was used as the abbey guest house. **St Mary's Lodge** was built around 1470 to provide VIP accommodation.

Adjacent to Museum Gardens on Exhibition Sq is the 19th-century **York City Art Gallery** (☎ 01904-551861; www.yorkartgallery.org.uk; Exhibition Sq; admission free; ☼ 10am-5pm), which includes works by Reynolds, Nash, Boudin. LS Lowry and controversial York artist William Etty, the first major British artist to specialise in nude painting back in the 1820s.

Built between 1357 and 1361, the **Merchant Adventurers' Hall** (☎ 01904-654818; www.theyork company.co.uk; Fossgate; admission £2.50; ☼ 9am-5pm Mon-Thu, 9am-3.30pm Fri & Sat, noon-4pm Sun Apr-Sep, 9.30am-3.30pm Mon-Sat Oct-Mar) is one of the most handsome timber-framed buildings in Europe, and testifies to the power of the medieval guilds that controlled all foreign trade into and out of York until 1830 – a handy little monopoly. There are displays of oil paintings and antique silver, but the building itself is the star.

If you're a fan of the Georgian style, then a visit to **Fairfax House** (☎ 01904-655543; www.fair faxhouse.co.uk; Castlegate; adult/child £5/free; ☼ 11am-4.30pm Mon-Thu & Sat, 1.30-5pm Sun, guided tours 11am & 2pm Fri) should be on your itinerary. Built in 1762 by John Carr (of Harewood House fame; see p600), this exquisitely restored town house features the best example of rococo stucco work to be found in the north of England, and houses a superb collection of Georgian furniture.

Tours

There's a bewildering range of tours on offer, from historic walking tours to a host of ever more competitive night-time ghost tours – York is reputed to be England's most haunted city. For starters, check the tourist office's own suggestions for walking itineraries at www.visityork.org/explore.

BOAT

YorkBoat (☎ 01904-628324; www.yorkboat.co.uk; 1hr daytime cruises adult/child £7/3.30, evening cruises adult/child £9/5.50) Runs one-hour cruises on the River Ouse departing from King's Staith at 10.30am, noon, 1.30pm & 3pm (and Lendal Bridge 10 minutes later) February to November. The evening 'ghost cruise' departs from King's Staith at 6.30pm April to October.

BUS

York Citysightseeing (☎ 01904-655585; www.city -sightseeing.com; day tickets adult/child £9/4; ☼ 9am-5pm) Two hop-on hop-off routes calling at all the main sights; buses leave every 15 minutes from Exhibition Sq outside the main tourist office.

WALKING

Association of Voluntary Guides (☎ 01904-640780; www.york.touristguides.btinternet.co.uk; ☼ tours 10.15am, also 2.15pm Apr-Sep & 6.45pm Jun-Aug) Free two-hour walking tours of the city starting from Exhibition Sq in front of York City Art Gallery.

Breadcrumbs Trail (☎ 01904-610676; www.end papers.co.uk; Collage Corner, 2 Norman Ct; book £9.95) Explore York by following the Hansel-and-Gretel-type trails laid out in the book – a novel and excellent way to keep the kids entertained. The book is available from bookshops and El Piano restaurant (see p630).

Ghost Hunt of York (☎ 01904-608700; www.ghost hunt.co.uk; adult/child £5/3; ⏱ tours 7.30pm) Award-winning and highly entertaining 75-minute tour laced with authentic ghost stories; the kids just love this one. Begins at the Shambles, no need to book.

Original Ghost Walk of York (☎ 01904-764222; www.theoriginalghostwalkofyork.co.uk; adult/child £4/2.50; ⏱ tours 8pm) An evening of ghouls, ghosts, mystery and history courtesy of a well-established group departing from the King's Arms pub by Ouse Bridge.

Roam'in Tours of York (☎ 07931 668935; www .roamintours.co.uk) Two-hour history and specialist tours (adult/child £4/2) with a guide, or you can take a DIY audio tour (£4.50).

Yorkwalk (☎ 01904-622303; www.yorkwalk.co.uk; adult/child £5.50/2.50) Offers a series of two-hour themed walks on an ever-growing list of themes, from the classics – Roman York, the snickelways (alleys) and City Walls – to specialised walks on chocolates and sweets, women in York, secret York and the inevitable graveyard, coffin and plague tour. Walks depart from Museum Gardens Gate on Museum St.

Festivals & Events

For a week in mid-February, York is invaded by Vikings once again as part of the **Jorvik Viking Festival** (☎ 01904-643211; www.vikingjorvik.com; Coppergate), which features battle re-enactments, themed walks, markets and other bits of Viking-themed fun.

Sleeping

Beds are tough to find midsummer, even with the inflated prices of the high season. The tourist office's accommodation booking service charges £4, which might be the best four quid you spend if you arrive without a booking.

Needless to say, prices get higher the closer to the city centre you are. However, there are plenty of decent B&Bs on the streets north and south of Bootham. Southwest of the town centre, there are B&Bs clustered around Scarcroft Rd, Southlands Rd and Bishopthorpe Rd.

It's also worth looking at serviced apartments if you're planning to stay two or three nights. **City Lets** (☎ 01904-652729; www.cityletsyork .co.uk) offers a good selection of places from around £90 a night for a two-person apart-

ment – we particularly like the stylish, modern flats in the peaceful courtyard at Talbot Court on Low Petergate.

BUDGET

York Backpackers (☎ 01904-627720; www.yorkback packers.co.uk; 88-90 Micklegate; dm/d from £14/35; 🖳) Housed in a Grade I Georgian building that was once home to the High Sheriff of Yorkshire, this large and well-equipped hostel was closed for refurbishment at the time of research, but should be open for 2009.

York YHA (☎ 0845 371 9051; www.yha.org.uk; 42 Water End, Clifton; dm £18.50; 🅿 🖳) Originally the Rowntree (Quaker confectioners) mansion, this handsome Victorian house makes a spacious and child-friendly youth hostel, with most of the rooms being four-bed dorms. It's about a mile northwest of the city centre; there's a riverside footpath from Lendal Bridge (poorly lit so avoid after dark). Alternatively, take bus 2 from Station Ave or Museum St.

Golden Fleece (☎ 01904-625171; www.goldenfleece .yorkwebsites.co.uk; 16 Pavement; per person from £45) Four distinctive, Gothic-themed rooms (including the Shambles Room, with views over York's most famous street) above the bar in what claims to be York's most haunted pub – we've yet to see a ghost, but we liked what we did see: nice furnishings, comfortable beds and great hospitality.

MIDRANGE

Elliotts B&B (☎ 01904-623333; www.elliottshotel.co.uk; 2 Sycamore Pl; s/d from £38/75; 🅿 🖳) A beautifully converted 'gentleman's residence', Elliotts leans towards the boutique end of the guest house market with stylish and elegant rooms, and hi-tech touches such as flat-screen TVs and free wi-fi. Excellent location, both quiet and central.

23 St Mary's (☎ 01904-622738; www.23stmarys .co.uk; 23 St Mary's; s £45-55, d £70-90; 🅿 🖳) A smart and stately town house with nine chintzy, country house-style rooms, some with hand-painted furniture for that rustic look, while others are decorated with antiques, lace and polished mahogany.

Brontë House (☎ 01904-621066; http://bronteguest house.yorkwebsites.co.uk; 22 Grosvenor Tce; s/d from £40/76; 🖳) The Brontë offers five homely en suite rooms, each decorated differently; our favourite is the double with a carved, 19th-century sleigh bed, William Morris wallpaper and assorted bits and bobs from another era.

Dairy Guesthouse (☎ 01904-639367; www.dairy guesthouse.co.uk; 3 Scarcroft Rd; s/d from £55/75; P) A lovely Victorian home that has retained many of its original features, including pine doors, stained glass and cast-iron fireplaces, but the real treat is the flower- and plant-filled courtyard that leads to the cottage-style rooms. Minimum two-night stay at weekends.

Hedley House Hotel (☎ 01904-637404; www.hedley house.com; 3 Bootham Tce; s/d/f from £50/80/90; P 💻) Run by a couple with young children, this smart red-brick terrace-house hotel could hardly be more family-friendly – plus it has private parking at the back, and is barely five minutes' walk from the city centre through the Museum Gardens.

Guy Fawkes (☎ 0845 460 2020; www.theguyfawkes hotel.com; 25 High Petergate; s/d/ste from £65/90/200; 💻) Directly opposite the minster is this comfortable hotel whose premises include a cottage that is reputed to be the birthplace of Guy Fawkes himself. We're not convinced, but the cottage is still the handsomest room in the building, complete with a four-poster and lots of red velvet.

Arnot House (☎ 01904-641966; www.arnothouse york.co.uk; 17 Grosvenor Tce; r £75-80; P) With three beautifully decorated rooms (provided you're a fan of Victorian floral patterns), including one with an impressive four-poster bed and curtain-draped bath, Arnot House sports an authentically old-fashioned look that appeals to a more mature clientele – and there are no children allowed.

Judges Lodging Hotel (☎ 01904-638733; www .judgeslodgings.com; 9 Lendal; s/d from £85/100) Despite being housed in an elegant Georgian mansion that was built for a wealthy physician, this is really a place for the party crowd to crash – it's within easy reach of city centre pubs, and the hotel's own lively courtyard bar rocks late into the night.

Also recommended:

Alcuin Lodge (☎ 01904-632222; www.alcuinlodge.com; 15 Sycamore Pl; s/d from £35/60; 💻) Elegant rooms in a beautiful Edwardian house, with fair-trade coffee and healthy breakfasts.

Briar Lea Guest House (☎ 01904-635061; www .briarlea.co.uk; 8 Longfield Tce; s/d from £35/60) Clean, simple rooms and a friendly welcome in a central location.

St Raphael (☎ 01904-645028; www.straphaelguest house.co.uk; 44 Queen Annes Rd; s/d from £59/68; 💻) Historic house with that half-timbered look, great central location and home-baked bread at breakfast.

Monkgate Guesthouse (☎ 01904-655947; www .monkgateguesthouse.com; 65 Monkgate; s/d from £40/76; P) Attractive and very child-friendly guest house with special family 'suite' with separate bedroom for two kids.

TOP END

Mount Royale (☎ 01904-628856; www.mountroyale .co.uk; The Mount; r £100-210; P) A grand, early 19th-century listed building that has been converted into a superb luxury hotel, complete with a solarium, beauty spa and outdoor heated tub and swimming pool. The rooms in the main house are gorgeous, but the best of the lot are the open-plan garden suites, reached via a corridor of tropical fruit trees and bougainvillea.

Dean Court Hotel (☎ 01904-625082; www.deancourt -york.co.uk; Duncombe Pl; s/d from £104/135; P 💻) Don't be put off by the Best Western sign this is no charmless chain hotel, but a gracious Victorian building that once housed the York Minster clergy. You won't find a better location – right across the street from the minster (though you only get a church view from the superior rooms).

Middlethorpe Hall (☎ 01904-641241; www.middle thorpe.com; Bishopsthorpe Rd; s/d from £130/190; P 💻) York's top spot is this breathtaking 17th-century country house set in 20 acres of parkland that was once the home of diarist Lady Mary Wortley Montagu. The rooms are spread between the main house, the restored courtyard buildings and three cottage suites. Although we preferred the grandeur of the rooms in the main house, every room is beautifully decorated with original antiques and oil paintings carefully collected so as to best reflect the period.

Eating

Eating well in York is not a problem – there are plenty of fine options throughout the city centre; most pubs also serve food.

BUDGET

Blake Head Vegetarian Cafe (☎ 01904-623767; 104 Micklegate; mains £4-6; ⏰ 9.30am-5pm Mon-Sat, 10am-5pm Sun) A bright and airy space at the back of a bookshop, filled with modern oak furniture and funky art, the Blake Head offers a tempting menu of daily lunch specials such as crispy bean burger with corn relish or hummus and roast red pepper open sandwich; great ginger and lemon cake too.

El Piano (☎ 01904-610676; www.elpiano.co.uk; 15 Grape Lane; mains £7; ☷ 11am-11pm Mon-Sat) With a menu that is 100% vegan, nut-free and gluten-free, this colourful, Hispanic-style spot is a vegetarian haven with a lovely cafe downstairs and three themed rooms upstairs: check out the Moroccan room, complete with floor cushions. They sell takeaways too.

Cafe Concerto (☎ 01904-610478; 21 High Petergate; snacks £2-6, mains £9-14; ☷ 10am-10pm) Walls papered with sheet music, chilled jazz on the stereo and battered, mismatched tables and chairs set the bohemian tone in this comforting coffee shop that serves breakfasts, bagels and cappuccinos big enough to float a boat in during the day, and a sophisticated bistro menu in the evening.

MIDRANGE

Betty's (☎ 01904-659142; www.bettys.co.uk; St Helen's Sq; mains £6-11, afternoon tea £15; ☷ 9am-9pm) Afternoon tea, old-school style, with white-aproned waitresses, linen tablecloths and a teapot collection ranged along the walls. House speciality is the Yorkshire Fat Rascal – a huge fruit scone smothered in melted butter.

Little Betty's (☎ 01904-622865; 46 Stonegate; mains £8-10; ☷ 10am-5.30pm) Betty's younger sister is more demure and less frequented, but just as good; you head upstairs and back in time to what feels like the interwar years – on any given day you are bound to spot a couple of Agatha Christie lookalikes nibbling crumpets in a corner.

Siam House (☎ 01904-624677; 63a Goodramgate; mains £8-14; ☷ dinner Mon-Sat) Delicious, authentic Thai food in about as authentic an atmosphere as you could muster up 6000km from Bangkok. The early bird, three-course special (£12, order before 6.30pm) is an absolute steal.

La Vecchia Scuola (☎ 01904-644600; 62 Low Petergate; mains £8-15; ☷ lunch & dinner) Housed in the former York College for Girls, the faux elegant dining room – complete with self-playing grand piano – is straight out of *Growing Up Gotti*, but there's nothing fake about the food: authentic Italian cuisine served in suitably snooty style by proper Italian waiters.

Fiesta Mexicana (☎ 01904-610243; 14 Clifford St; mains £9-12; ☷ dinner) Chimichangas, tostadas and burritos served in a relentlessly cheerful atmosphere, while students and party groups on the rip add to the fiesta; it's neither subtle nor subdued, but when is Mexican food ever so?

Melton's Too (☎ 01904-629222; 25 Walmgate; mains £9-13; ☷ 10.30am-10.30pm Mon-Sat, to 9.30pm Sun) A comfortable, chilled out, booth-lined cafebar and bistro, Melton's younger brother serves everything from cake and cappuccino to tapas-style snacks to a three-course dinner of Whitby crab, braised beef with Yorkshire pudding, and local strawberries with clotted cream.

Living Room (☎ 01904-461000; www.thelivingroom .co.uk; 1 Bridge St; mains £9-15; ☷ 10am-midnight Sun-Wed, till 1am Thu-Sat) The Living Room snapped up a hot location when it opened back in 2004, and has been making the most of its balcony tables overlooking the river ever since. The menu focuses on quality versions of classic dishes from around the world, from fish and chips and steak and ale pie to Thai fish cakes and Peking duck. Sunday brunch served noon to 6pm.

TOP END

Melton's (☎ 01904-634341; www.meltonsrestaurant .co.uk; 7 Scarcroft Rd; mains £15-18; ☷ lunch Tue-Sat, dinner Mon-Sat) Foodies come from far and wide to dine in one of Yorkshire's best restaurants. It tends to specialise in fish dishes but doesn't go far wrong with practically everything else, from sea trout with sorrel to marinaded wild boar. There's a good value lunch and early dinner set menu (£18.50 for two courses).

Blue Bicycle (☎ 01904-673990; www.theblue bicycle.com; 34 Fossgate; mains £15-22; ☷ lunch & dinner) Once upon a time, this building was a well-frequented brothel; these days it serves up a different kind of fare to an equally enthusiastic crowd. French food at its finest – the occasional anti-*foie gras* protester outside the door gives a clue as to the menu – served in a romantic, candlelit room, makes for a top-notch dining experience.

our pick J Baker's (☎ 01904-622688; www.jbakers .co.uk; 7 Fossgate; 2-/3-course dinner £23/27.50; ☷ lunch & dinner) Superstar chef Jeff Baker left Leeds' Pool Court and his Michelin star to pursue his own vision of Modern British cuisine here. The ironic 70s-style colour scheme (think chocolate/oatmeal/tango) with moo-cow paintings is echoed in the unusual menu, which offers witty, gourmet interpretations of retro classics, from macaroni cheese to Bakewell tart – the 'sausage roll and beans' is actually more like French *cassoulet*, and the Crunchie bar dessert is superb.

Drinking

With only a couple of exceptions, the best drinking holes in town are the older, traditional pubs. In recent years, the area around Ousegate and Micklegate has gone from moribund to mental, especially at weekends.

Ackhorne (☎ 01904-671421; 9 St Martin's Lane) Tucked away from beery, sloppy Micklegate, this locals' inn is as comfortable as old slippers; some of the old guys here look like they've merged with the bar. There's a pleasant beer garden at the back.

Black Swan (☎ 01904-686911; Peasholme Green) A classic black-and-white Tudor building where you'll find decent beer, friendly people and live jazz on Sundays.

our pick **Blue Bell** (☎ 01904-654904; 53 Fossgate) This is what a real English pub looks like – a tiny, wood-panelled room with a smouldering fireplace, decor (and beer and smoke stains) dating from c 1798, a pile of ancient board games in the corner, friendly and efficient bar staff, and Timothy Taylor and Black Sheep ales on tap. Bliss, with froth on top.

Little John (☎ 01904-658242; 5 Castlegate) This historic pub – the third oldest in York – is the city's top gay venue, with regular club nights and other events. In 1739 the corpse of executed highwayman Dick Turpin was laid out in the cellar here for the public to view at a penny a head; the pub is said to be haunted by his ghost. Not sure what's scarier though – the ghost story, or the Thursday night karaoke session…

King's Arms (☎ 01904-659435; King's Staith; lunch about £6) York's best-known pub is a creaky old place with a fabulous riverside location, with tables spilling out onto the quayside – a perfect spot for a summer's evening.

Ye Olde Starre (☎ 01904-623063; 40 Stonegate) Licensed since 1644, this is York's oldest pub – a warren of small rooms and a small beer garden, with half a dozen real ales on tap. It was used as a morgue by the Roundheads during the Civil War, but the atmosphere's improved a lot since then.

Entertainment

There are a couple of good theatres in York, and an interesting art-house cinema, but as far as clubs are concerned, forget it: historic York is best enjoyed without them anyway.

York Theatre Royal (☎ 01904-623568; www.york theatreroyal.co.uk; St Leonard's Pl) Stages well-regarded productions of theatre, opera and dance.

Grand Opera House (☎ 01904-671818; www.grand operahouseyork.org.uk; Clifford St) Despite the name there's no opera here, but a wide range of productions from live bands and popular musicals to stand-up comics and pantomime.

City Screen (☎ 0871 704 2054; www.picturehouses .co.uk; 13-17 Coney St) Appealing modern building in a converted printing works, screening both mainstream and art-house films; nice cafe-bar on the terrace overlooking the river.

Shopping

Coney St, Davygate and the adjoining streets are the hub of York's high-street shopping scene, but the real treat for visitors are the antique, bric-a-brac and secondhand book shops, which are concentrated in Micklegate and Fossgate.

Antiques Centre (☎ 01904-635888; www.antiques centreyorkeshop.co.uk; 41 Stonegate) A Georgian town house with a veritable maze of rooms and corridors, showcasing the wares of around 120 dealers; everything from lapel pins and snuff boxes to oil paintings and longcase clocks. And the house is haunted, too…

Azendi (☎ 01904-672822; www.azendi.com; 20 Colliergate) This jewellery boutique sells a range of beautiful contemporary designs in silver, white gold and platinum.

Barbican Books (☎ 01904-652643; www.barbicanbook shop.co.uk; 24 Fossgate) Wide range of secondhand titles, with special subjects that include railways, aviation, and walking and mountaineering.

Ken Spelman Booksellers (☎ 01904-624414; www .kenspelman.com; 70 Micklegate) This fascinating shop has been selling rare, antiquarian and secondhand books since 1910; with an open fire crackling in the grate in winter, it's a browser's paradise.

Getting There & Away
BUS

For timetable information call **Traveline Yorkshire** (☎ 0871 200 2233; www.yorkshiretravel .net), or check the computerised 24-hour information points at the train station and Rougier St. All local and regional buses stop on Rougier St, about 200m northeast of the train station.

There are National Express coaches to London (£24, 5¼ hours, four daily), Birmingham (£25, 3¼ hours, one daily) and Newcastle (£14, 2¾ hours, four daily).

CAR

A car is more of a hindrance than a help in the city centre; use one of the park and ride car parks on the edge of the city. If you want to explore the surrounding area, rental options include **Europcar** (☎ 01904-656161), by platform 1 in the train station (which also rents bicycles and stores luggage for £4 per bag); and **Hertz** (☎ 01904-612586) near platform 3 in the train station.

TRAIN

York is a major railway hub with frequent direct services to Birmingham (£40, 2¼ hours), Newcastle (£25, one hour), Leeds (£10, 25 minutes), London's King's Cross (£103, two hours), Manchester (£20, 1½ hours) and Scarborough (£12, 50 minutes).

There are also trains to Cambridge (£67, 2¾ hours), changing at Peterborough.

Getting Around

York is easy to get around on foot – you're never really more than 20 minutes from any of the major sights.

BICYCLE

The tourist offices have a useful free map showing York's cycle routes. If you're energetic you could pedal out to Castle Howard (15 miles), Helmsley and Rievaulx Abbey (12 miles) and Thirsk (a further 12 miles), and then catch a train back to York. There's also a section of the Trans-Pennine Trail cycle path from Bishopthorpe in York to Selby (15 miles) along the old railway line.

You can rent bikes from **Bob Trotter** (☎ 01904-622868; 13 Lord Mayor's Walk; ☯ 9am-5.30pm Mon-Sat, 10am-4pm Sun), outside Monk Bar; and **Europcar** (☎ 01904-656161; ☯ 8am-8.30pm Mon-Sat,

9am-8.30pm Sun), by platform 1 in the train station; both charge around £10 per day.

BUS

Local bus services are operated by **First York** (☎ 01904-622992; www.firstgroup.com); single fares range from £1 to £2.50, and a day pass valid on all local buses is £3.50 (available at park and ride car parks).

TAXI

Station Taxis (☎ 01904-623332) has a kiosk outside the train station.

AROUND YORK

Castle Howard

Stately homes may be two a penny in England, but you'll have to try pretty damn hard to find one as breathtakingly stately as **Castle Howard** (☎ 01653-648333; www.castlehoward.co.uk; adult/child house & grounds £10.50/6.50, grounds only £8/5; ☯ house 11am-4.30pm, grounds 10am-4.30pm Mar-Oct & 1st three weeks of Dec), a work of theatrical grandeur and audacity set in the rolling Howardian Hills. This is one of the world's most beautiful buildings, instantly recognisable from its starring role in *Brideshead Revisited* – which has done its popularity no end of good since the TV series first aired in the early 1980s.

When the earl of Carlisle hired his pal Sir John Vanbrugh to design his new home in 1699, he was hiring a bloke who had no formal training and was best known as a playwright; luckily Vanbrugh hired Nicholas Hawksmoor, who had worked for Christopher Wren, as his clerk of works – not only would Hawksmoor have a big part to play in the house's design but the two would later work wonders with Blenheim Palace (p236).

If you can, try to visit on a weekday, when it's easier to find the space to appreciate this

---

DETOUR: KIRKHAM PRIORY & STONE TROUGH INN

While the crowds queue up to get into Castle Howard, you could turn off on the other side of the A64 along the minor road to the hamlet of Kirkham. Here, the picturesque ruins of **Kirkham Priory** (EH; ☎ 01653-619768; admission £3; ☯ 10am-5pm Thu-Mon Apr-Sep, daily in Aug, Sat & Sun only in Oct) rise gracefully above the banks of the River Derwent, sporting an impressive 13th-century gatehouse encrusted with heraldic symbols.

After a stroll by the river, head up the hill on the far side to the **Stone Trough Inn** (☎ 01653-618713; www.stonetroughinn.co.uk; mains £9-17; ☯ noon-2pm & 6.30-9.30pm Tue-Sun) for a spot of lunch; this traditional country inn serves gourmet-style pub grub – try pork and herb sausages with thyme-scented mashed potato and real ale gravy – and has an outdoor terrace with a great view over the valley.

hedonistic marriage of art, architecture, landscaping and natural beauty. As you wander about the peacock-haunted grounds, views open up over the hills, Vanbrugh's playful Temple of the Four Winds and Hawksmoor's stately mausoleum, but the great baroque house with its magnificent central cupola is an irresistible visual magnet. Inside, it is full of treasures, such as the chapel's Pre-Raphaelite stained glass.

Castle Howard is 15 miles northeast of York, off the A64. There are several organised tours from York – check with the tourist office for up-to-date schedules. Yorkshire Coastliner bus 840 (40 minutes from York, one daily) links Leeds, York, Castle Howard, Pickering and Whitby.

THIRSK
pop 9100

Monday and Saturday are market days in handsome Thirsk, which has been trading on its tidy, attractive streets and cobbled square since the Middle Ages. Thirsk's brisk business was always helped by its key position on two medieval trading routes: the old drove road between Scotland and York, and the route linking the Yorkshire Dales with the coast. That's all in the past, though: today, the town is all about the legacy of James Herriot, the wry Yorkshire vet adored by millions of fans of *All Creatures Great and Small*.

Thirsk does a good job as the real-life Darrowby of the books and TV series, and it should, as the real-life Herriot was in fact local vet Alf Wight, whose house and surgery has been dipped in 1940s aspic and turned into the incredibly popular **World of James Herriot** (☎ 01845-524234; www.worldofjamesherriot .org; 23 Kirkgate; adult/child £5.50/3.90; ❧ 10am-5pm Easter-Oct, 11am-4pm Nov-Easter), an excellent museum full of Wight-related artefacts, a video documentary of his life and a re-creation of the TV show sets.

Thirsk's **tourist office** (☎ 01845-522755; thirsk@ ytbtic.co.uk; 49 Market Pl; ❧ 10am-5pm Easter-Oct, 11am-4pm Nov-Easter) is on the main square.

If you arrive in time for breakfast or just fancy a quick snack, head for the **Arabica Coffee Shop** (☎ 01845-523869; 87 Market Pl; mains £2-3) on the main square; this smart chrome and black diner is the opposite of chintz, and serves excellent freshly ground coffee, croissants, fry-ups, panini and wraps.

Thirsk is well served by trains on the line between York and Middlesbrough; however, the train station is a mile west of town and the only way to cover that distance is on foot or by **taxi** (☎ 01845-522473). There are also frequent daily buses from York (45 minutes).

RIPON
pop 16,468

Small town, huge cathedral: Ripon – all winding streets and a broad, symmetrical marketplace lined with Georgian houses – is mostly about its elegant church, but tourists also seem quite taken by the **Ripon Hornblower**, who 'sets the watch' every evening at 9pm in a tradition that supposedly dates back to 886, when Alfred the Great gave the locals a horn to sound the changing of the guard.

The **tourist office** (☎ 01765-604625; Minster Rd; ❧ 10am-1pm & 1.30-5.30pm Mon-Sat, 1-4pm Sun) is near the cathedral and has information on local walks, and will book accommodation. Market day is Thursday.

Ripon Cathedral (☎ 01765-602072; www.ripon cathedral.org.uk; suggested donation £3, treasury £1; ❧ 7.30am-6.15pm, Evensong 5.30pm) is well worth exploring. The first church on this site was built in 660 by St Wilfred, and its rough, humble crypt lies intact beneath today's soaring edifice. Above ground, the building was begun in the 11th century, with its harmonious Early English west front clocking in at 1220. Medieval additions have resulted in a medley of Gothic styles throughout, culminating in the rebuilding of the central tower – work that was never completed. It was not until 1836 that this impressive parish church got cathedral status. Look out for the fantastical creatures decorating the animated medieval misericords, believed to have inspired Lewis Carroll – his father was canon here from 1852 to 1868.

Until 1888 Ripon was responsible for its own law enforcement, and this has resulted in a grand array of punishing attractions. The **Law & Order Museums** (☎ 01765-690799; www .riponmuseums.co.uk; adult/child £6/free; ❧ 1-4pm Apr-Oct, 11am-4pm during school holidays, closed Nov-Mar) include the **Courthouse Museum**, a 19th-century courthouse (recognisable from sappy TV series *Heartbeat*), the **Prison & Police Museum**, which includes the medieval punishment yard and the clammy cells where no-good Victorians were banged up, and the **Workhouse Museum**, which shows the grim treatment meted out to poor vagrants from the 19th century to WWII.

Bus 36 runs from Leeds via Harrogate to Ripon (one hour 20 minutes, every 20 minutes). From York, take the train to Harrogate, then bus 36 to Ripon. Bus 159 runs between Ripon and Richmond (1½ hours, every two hours Monday to Saturday) via Masham and Middleham.

AROUND RIPON

Nestled in the secluded valley of the River Skell lie two of Yorkshire's most beautiful attractions – an absolute must on any northern itinerary. The beautiful and strangely obsessive water gardens of the **Studley Royal** estate were built in the 19th century to enhance the picturesque ruins of 12th-century **Fountains Abbey** (NT; ☎ 01765-608888; www.fountainsabbey.org.uk; adult/child £7.90/4.20; ✆ 10am-5pm Mar-Oct, to 4pm Nov-Feb). Together they present a breathtaking picture of pastoral elegance and tranquillity that have made them a Unesco World Heritage Site, and the most visited of all the National Trust's pay-in properties.

After falling out with the Benedictines of York in 1132, a band of rebel monks came here to what was then a desolate and unyielding patch of land to establish their own monastery. Struggling to make it on their own, they were formally adopted by the Cistercians in 1135; by the middle of the 13th century the new abbey had become the most successful Cistercian venture in the country. It was during this time that most of the abbey was built, including the church's nave, transepts and eastern end, and the outlying buildings (the church tower was added in the late 15th century).

After the Dissolution (p40) the abbey's estate was sold into private hands and between 1598 and 1611 Fountains Hall was built using stone from the abbey ruins. The hall and ruins were united with the Studley Royal estate in 1768.

Studley Royal was owned by John Aislabie (once Chancellor of the Exchequer), who dedicated his life to creating the park after a financial scandal saw him expelled from parliament. The main house of Studley Royal burnt down in 1946 but the superb landscaping, with its serene artificial lakes, survives almost unchanged from the 18th century.

Fountains Abbey is 4 miles west of Ripon off the B6265. Public transport is limited to shuttle bus 139 from Ripon on Sunday and bank holidays only (10 minutes, hourly), from mid-May to October.

BLACK SHEEP OF THE BREWING FAMILY

The village of Masham is a place of pilgrimage for connoisseurs of real ale – it's the frothing fountainhead of Theakston's beers, which have been brewed here since 1827. The company's most famous brew, Old Peculier, takes its name from the Peculier of Masham, a parish court established in medieval times to deal with religious offences, including drunkenness, brawling, and 'taking a skull from the churchyard and placing it under a person's head to charm them to sleep'. The court seal is used as the emblem of Theakston Ales.

To the horror of real ale fans, and after much falling out among members of the Theakston family, the Theakston Brewery was taken over by much-hated megabrewer Scottish and Newcastle in 1987. Five years later, Paul Theakston – who had refused to go and work for S&N, and was determined to keep small-scale, artisan brewing alive – bought an old maltings building in Masham and set up his own brewery, which he called Black Sheep. He managed to salvage all kinds of traditional brewing equipment, including six Yorkshire 'stone square' brewing vessels, and was soon running a successful enterprise.

History came full circle in 2004 when Paul's four brothers took the Theakston brewery back into family ownership. Both breweries now have visitor centres – the **Black Sheep Brewery** (☎ 01765-680100; ✆ 10.30am-4.30pm Sun-Thu, 10.30am-11pm Fri & Sat) and the **Theakston Brewery** (☎ 01765-680000; www.theakstons.co.uk; ✆ 10.30am-5.30pm Jul & Aug, to 4.30pm May, Jun, Sep & Oct); both offer guided tours (best booked in advance).

Masham (pronounced 'massam') is 9 miles northwest of Ripon on the A6108 to Leyburn. Bus 159 from Ripon (25 minutes, every two hours Monday to Saturday) and the Fountains Flyer bus 802 from Leeds (2¾ hours, one daily, Sunday and bank holidays only, late May to late September) stop at Masham.

HARROGATE

pop 85,128

The quintessential Victorian spa town, prim, pretty Harrogate has long been associated with a certain kind of old-fashioned Englishness, the kind that seems to be the preserve of retired army chaps and formidable dowagers who, inevitably, will always vote Tory. They come to Harrogate to enjoy the formidable flower shows and gardens that fill the town with magnificent display of colour, especially in spring and autumn. It is fitting that the town's most famous visitor was Agatha Christie, who fled here incognito in 1926 to escape her broken marriage.

Yet this picture of Victoriana redux is not quite complete. While it's undoubtedly true that Harrogate remains a firm favourite of visitors in their golden years, the New Britain makeover has left its mark in the shape of smart new hotels and trendy eateries catering to the boom in Harrogate's newest trade – conferences. All those dynamic young sales and marketing guns have to eat and sleep somewhere…

Orientation & Information

Harrogate is almost surrounded by parks and gardens, notably the 80-hectare **Stray** in the south. The train and bus stations are right in the centre of town, a few minutes' walk from the main sights.

The **tourist office** (☎ 0845 389 3223; www.harro gate.gov.uk/tourism; Crescent Rd; ✆ 9am-6pm Mon-Sat, 10am-1pm Sun Apr-Sep, 9am-5pm Mon-Fri, 9am-4pm Sat Oct-Mar) is in the Royal Baths Assembly Rooms; staff can tell you about free historical walking tours offered daily from Easter to October.

Sights & Activities

THE WATERS

The ritual of 'taking the waters' as a health cure became fashionable in the 19th century and peaked during the Edwardian era in the years before WWI. Charles Dickens visited Harrogate in 1858 and described it as 'the queerest place, with the strangest people in it, leading the oddest lives of dancing, newspaper reading and dining'; sounds quite pleasant, really.

You can learn all about the history of Harrogate as a spa town in the ornate **Royal Pump Room Museum** (☎ 01423-556188; Crown Pl; admission £3; ✆ 10am-5pm Mon-Sat, 2-5pm Sun Apr-Oct, to 4pm Nov-Mar), built in 1842 over the most famous of the sulphur springs. It gives an insight into how the phenomenon shaped the town and records the illustrious visitors that it attracted; at the end you get the chance to sample the spa water, if you dare.

If drinking the water isn't enough, you can immerse yourself in it at the fabulously tiled **Turkish Baths** (☎ 01423-556746; www.harrogate .co.uk/turkishbaths; Parliament St; admission £11.50-17.20; ✆ 9am-9pm) nearby. This mock Moorish facility is gloriously Victorian and offers a range of watery delights – hot rooms, steam rooms, plunge pools and so on; a visit should last around an hour and a half. There's a complicated schedule of opening hours that are by turns single sex and mixed pairs – call or check online for details.

MERCER ART GALLERY

Another surviving spa building, the Promenade Room, is now home to this elegant **gallery** (☎ 01423-556188; Swan Rd; admission free; ✆ 10am-5pm Tue-Sat, 2-5pm Sun), a stately space that hosts constantly changing exhibitions of visual art.

GARDENS

A huge green thumbs-up to Harrogate's gardeners; the town has some of the most beautiful public gardens in England. The **Valley Gardens** are overlooked by the vast, glass-domed **Sun Pavilion**, built in 1933. The nearby bandstand houses concerts on Sunday afternoons from June to August. Flower-fanatics should make for the **Harlow Carr Botanical Gardens** (☎ 01423-565418; www.rhs.org.uk; Crag Lane, Beckwithshaw; adult/child £6.50/2.20; ✆ 9.30am-6pm Mar-Oct, to 4pm Nov-Feb), the northern showpiece of the Royal Horticultural Society. The gardens are 1.5 miles southwest of town; to get here, take the B6162 Otley Rd or walk through the Pine Woods southwest of the Valley Gardens.

Festivals & Events

The year's main event is the immense **Spring Flower Show** (☎ 0870 758 3333; www.flower show.org.uk), held in late April, followed in late September by the **Autumn Flower Show**. Both take place at the Great Yorkshire Showground; admission prices range from £10 to £14.

If prize delphiniums aren't your thing, there's a lot more fun to be had at the **Great Yorkshire Show** (☎ 01423-541000; www.greatyorkshire show.org; adult/child £18/8), an exhibition staged

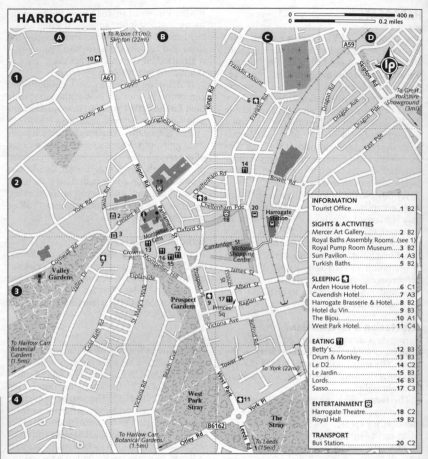

HARROGATE

INFORMATION
Tourist Office	1 B2

SIGHTS & ACTIVITIES
Mercer Art Gallery	2 B2
Royal Baths Assembly Rooms	(see 1)
Royal Pump Room Museum	3 B2
Sun Pavilion	4 A3
Turkish Baths	5 B2

SLEEPING
Arden House Hotel	6 C1
Cavendish Hotel	7 A3
Harrogate Brasserie & Hotel	8 B2
Hotel du Vin	9 B3
The Bijou	10 A1
West Park Hotel	11 C4

EATING
Betty's	12 B3
Drum & Monkey	13 B3
Le D2	14 C2
Le Jardin	15 B3
Lords	16 B3
Sasso	17 C3

ENTERTAINMENT
Harrogate Theatre	18 C2
Royal Hall	19 B2

TRANSPORT
Bus Station	20 C2

over three days in mid-July by the Yorkshire Agricultural Society (also held at the showground). It's a real treat, with all manner of primped and prettified farm animals competing for prizes, and entertainment ranging from show-jumping and falconry to cookery demonstrations and hot-air balloon rides.

Sleeping

MIDRANGE

Cavendish Hotel (☎ 01423-509637; cavendishhotel@gmail.com; 3 Valley Dr; s/d from £55/65, 4-poster £90) There are several guest houses ranged along tree-lined Valley Dr, a quiet and peaceful corner of town that is only a short walk from the centre. The Cavendish is one of

the best – the rooms are homely but show a touch of style, and many have a view over Valley Gardens.

Arden House Hotel (☎ 01423-509224; www.ardenhousehotel.co.uk; 69-71 Franklin Rd; s/d from £45/75; P Q) This grand old Edwardian house has been given a modern makeover with stylish contemporary furniture, Egyptian cotton bed linen and posh toiletries, but still retains some lovely period details including tiled, cast-iron fireplaces. Attentive service, good breakfasts and a central location are the icing on the cake.

West Park Hotel (☎ 01423-524471; www.westparkhotel.co.uk; 19 West Park; d from £75; P) Not quite sure what's going on with the decor here – oldstyle Harrogate having a go at contemporary but not quite pulling it off; a bit like your dad trying to dance to house music. Still, the location is lovely – the best rooms have views over the park – and the staff are really friendly and helpful.

The Bijou (☎ 01423-567974; www.thebijou.co.uk; 17 Ripon Rd; s/d from £75/85; P ☑) Bijou by name and bijou by nature, this Victorian villa sits firmly at the boutique end of the B&B spectrum – you can tell that a lot of thought and care has gone into the design of the place. The husband and wife team who own the place make fantastic hosts, warm and helpful but unobtrusive.

Harrogate Brasserie & Hotel (☎ 01423-505041; www.harrogatebrasserie.co.uk; 28-30 Cheltenham Pde; s/d from £60/90) Stripped pine, leather armchairs and subtle colour combinations make this one of Harrogate's most appealing places to stay. The cheerful cosy accommodation is complemented by an excellent restaurant and bar, with live jazz Wednesday to Sunday evenings.

TOP END

Hotel Du Vin (☎ 01423-856800; www.hotelduvin.com; Prospect Pl; r/ste from £125/165; P ☑) An extremely stylish boutique hotel that has made the other lodgings in town sit up and take notice. The loft suites with their exposed oak beams, hardwood floors and designer bathrooms are the nicest rooms we've seen in town, but even the standard rooms are spacious and very comfortable, each with a trademark huge bed draped in soft Egyptian cotton.

Eating

Le Jardin (☎ 01423-507323; www.lejardin-harrogate.com; 7 Montpellier Parade; mains £8; ☙ lunch & dinner Tue-Fri, 10am-8pm Sat, noon-3pm Sun) This cool little bistro has a snug, intimate atmosphere, especially in the evening when candlelight adds a romantic glow. During the day locals throng the tables to enjoy great salads, sandwiches and homemade ice cream.

Betty's (☎ 01423-502746; www.bettys.co.uk; 1 Parliament St; mains £8-10, afternoon tea £15; ☙ 9am-9pm) A classic tearoom in a classic location with views across the park, Betty's is a local institution. It was established in 1919 by a Swiss immigrant confectioner who took the wrong train, ended up in Yorkshire and decided to stay. Exquisite home-baked breads, scones and cakes, quality tea and coffee, and a downstairs gallery lined with Art Nouveau

marquetry designs of Yorkshire scenes commissioned by the founder in the 1930s.

Drum & Monkey (☎ 01423-502650; 5 Montpellier Gardens; mains £8-12; ☙ lunch & dinner Mon-Sat) This is a classic seafood restaurant of the old school, with traditional decor of mahogany and polished brass buffed up like the medals on a retired major's blazer, and a menu that would not have looked out of place in the 1930s, ranging from lobster bisque and asparagus with hollandaise, to Dover sole *bonne femme* and hearty seafood pie.

Le D2 (☎ 01423-502700; 7 Bower Rd; 2-course lunch/ dinner £9/15; ☙ lunch & dinner Tue-Sat) This bright and airy bistro is always busy, with diners drawn back again and again by the relaxed atmosphere, warm and friendly service, and a menu that takes fresh local produce and adds a twist of French sophistication.

Lords (☎ 01423-508762; 8 Montpellier St; mains lunch £10, dinner £15-18; ☙ lunch & dinner Tue-Sat, noon-8.30pm Sun) An elegant little place with a cosy, clubbish atmosphere enhanced by prints of cricket scenes and a collection of autographed cricket bats. The menu runs to Harrogate versions of classic comfort food – this not just any burger, this is a Yorkshire venison and Ribblesdale cheese burger…

Sasso (☎ 01423-508838; 8-10 Princes Sq; mains £14-21; ☙ lunch & dinner Tue-Sat, dinner Mon) A top-class basement trattoria where homemade pasta is served in a variety of traditional and authentic ways, along with a host of other Italian specialties.

Entertainment

There are two main entertainment venues in Harrogate. **Harrogate Theatre** (☎ 01423-502116; www.harrogatetheatre.com; Oxford St) is a historic Victorian building that dates from 1900, while the **Royal Hall** (☎ 0845 130 8840; www.royal hall.co.uk; Ripon Rd) is a gorgeous Edwardian theatre that is now a part of the Harrogate International conference centre. Both venues stage a varying program of drama, comedy and popular musicals.

Getting There & Away

Trains run to Harrogate from Leeds (£6.20, 40 minutes, about half-hourly) and York (£6.20, 45 minutes, hourly).

National Express coaches 561 and 381 run from Leeds (£3.40, 40 minutes, five daily). Bus 36 comes from Ripon (30 minutes, every 20 minutes), continuing to Leeds.

YORKSHIRE

SCARBOROUGH

pop 57,649

Scarborough is where the whole tradition of English seaside holidays began. And it began earlier than you might think – it was in the 1660s that a book promoting the medicinal properties of a local spring (now the site of Scarborough Spa) pulled in the first flood of visitors. A belief in the health-giving effects of sea-bathing saw wheeled bathing carriages appear on the beach in the 1730s, and with the arrival of the railway in 1845 Scarborough's fate was sealed. By the time the 20th century rolled in it was all donkey rides, fish and chips, seaside rock and boat trips round the bay, with saucy postcards, kiss-me-quick hats and blokes from Leeds with knotted hankies on their heads just a decade or two away.

Like all British seaside towns, Scarborough has suffered a downturn in recent decades as people jetted off to the Costa Blanca on newly affordable foreign holidays, but things are looking up again. The town retains all the trappings of the classic seaside resort, but is in the process of reinventing itself as a centre for the creative arts and digital industries – the Victorian spa is being redeveloped as a conference and entertainment centre, a former museum has been converted into studio space for artists, and there's free, open-access wi-fi along the promenade beside the harbour – an area being developed as the town's bar, cafe and restaurant quarter.

As well as the usual seaside attractions, Scarborough offers excellent coastal walking, a new geology museum, one of Yorkshire's most impressively sited castles, and a renowned theatre that is the home base of popular playwright Alan Ayckbourn, whose plays always premier here.

Orientation

Scarborough is built around a high headland with the castle perched on top, and beaches to its north and south. The train station and town centre are on a plateau above the South Beach, which has the harbour at its north end.

Most of the resort activity – bars, restaurants, amusements, funfair – are concentrated on Sandside, beside the harbour; the North Beach is less frantic. The walk from train station to harbour is about 15 minutes.

Information

Laundrette (☎ 01723-375763; 48 North Marine Rd)
Post office (11-15 Aberdeen Walk; ☽ 9am-5.30pm Mon-Fri, to 12.30pm Sat)
Scarborough Library (☎ 01723-383400; Vernon Rd; ☽ 9.30am-5.30pm Mon-Fri, 9.30am-noon Sat; per 30min £1) Internet access.
Tourist office (☎ 01723-383637; www.discoveryork shirecoast.com; Brunswick Shopping Centre, Westborough; ☽ 9.30am-5.30pm daily Easter-Oct, 10am-4.30pm Mon-Sat Nov-Easter)
Waterstone's (☎ 01723-500414; 97-98 Westborough; ☽ 9am-5.30pm Mon-Sat, 10am-4pm Sun) Books & maps.

Sights & Activities

Scarborough is not exclusively about sandcastles, seaside rock and walks along the prom. The massive medieval keep of **Scarborough Castle** (EH; ☎ 01723-372451; admission £4; ☽ 10am-6pm Apr-Sep, 10am-5pm Thu-Mon Oct, 10am-4pm Thu-Mon Nov-Mar) occupies a commanding position atop its headland – legend has it that Richard I loved the views so much his ghost just keeps coming back. Take a walk out to the edge of the cliffs where you can see the 2000-year-old remains of a **Roman signal station** – the Romans appreciated this viewpoint too.

Below the castle is **St Mary's Church** (☎ 01723-500541; Castle Rd; ☽ 10am-4pm Mon-Fri, 1-4pm Sun May-Sep), dating from 1180; in the little cemetery across the lane from the church is the grave of Anne Brontë.

The newly restored **Rotunda Museum** (☎ 01723-374839; www.rotundamuseum.co.uk; Vernon Rd; adult/child £4.50/free; ☽ 10am-5pm Tue-Sun) is dedicated to seaside rock of a different kind – the coastal geology of northeast Yorkshire, which has yielded many of Britain's most important dinosaur fossils. There's also a gallery illustrating how geology has shaped Scarborough's history and landscape.

Of all the family-oriented attractions on the waterfront, the best of the lot is the **Sea Life Centre & Marine Sanctuary** (☎ 01723-373414; www .sealife.co.uk; Scalby Mills; adult/child £12.95/9.50; ☽ 10am-6pm) overlooking North Bay. You can see coral reefs, turtles, octopuses, sea horses and many other fascinating sea creatures, though the biggest draw is the seal rescue centre. It's at the far north end of North Beach; a **miniature railway** (☎ 01723-260004; www.nbr.org.uk; ☽ 10.30am-4.45pm Apr-Sep) runs the 0.75-mile route (return fare £2.80).

There are some decent waves on England's northeast coast, which support a growing

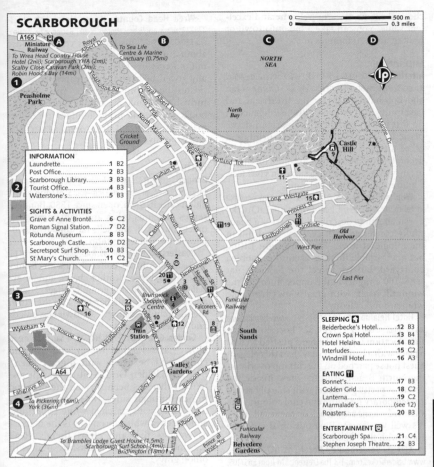

SCARBOROUGH

INFORMATION
Laundrette................................1 B2
Post Office................................2 B3
Scarborough Library..............3 B3
Tourist Office..........................4 B3
Waterstone's...........................5 B3

SIGHTS & ACTIVITIES
Grave of Anne Brontë.............6 C2
Roman Signal Station.............7 D2
Rotunda Museum.....................8 B3
Scarborough Castle..................9 D2
Secretspot Surf Shop............10 B3
St Mary's Church...................11 C2

SLEEPING
Beiderbecke's Hotel...............12 B3
Crown Spa Hotel....................13 B4
Hotel Helaina.........................14 B2
Interludes...............................15 C2
Windmill Hotel.......................16 A3

EATING
Bonnet's.................................17 B3
Golden Grid...........................18 C2
Lanterna.................................19 C2
Marmalade's.....................(see 12)
Roasters.................................20 B3

ENTERTAINMENT
Scarborough Spa....................21 C4
Stephen Joseph Theatre.......22 B3

---

surfing scene. **Scarborough Surf School** (☎ 01723-585585; www.scarboroughsurfschool.co.uk; Cayton Bay) is based 4 miles south of town, but you can get information and advice from the **Secretspot Surf Shop** (☎ 01723-500467; 4 Pavilion Tce) near the train station.

Sleeping

In Scarborough, if a house has four walls and a roof it'll offer B&B; competition is intense and in such a tough market multinight-stay special offers are two a penny, which means that single-night rates are the highest of all.

BUDGET

Scalby Close Caravan Park (☎ 01723-366212; www.scalbyclosepark.co.uk; Burniston Rd; sites £18; ☺ Easter-Oct)

A small park about 2 miles north of town with plenty of pitches for vans and tents (rate includes car and up to four people) as well as fixed holiday caravans for rent (£160 to £350 per week). Take bus 12 or 21.

Scarborough YHA (☎ 0845 371 9657; www.yha.org .uk; Burniston Rd; dm £18; ℗) This idyllic hostel set in a converted 17th-century water mill has comfortable four- and six-bed dorms and family-friendly facilities. It's 2 miles north of town along the A166 to Whitby; take bus 3, 12 or 21.

Brambles Lodge Guest House (☎ 01723-374613; www.brambleslodgeguesthouse.co.uk; 156-158 Filey Rd; s/d from £30/50; ℗ ▣) Set in a modern house on the A165 to Filey about 1.5 miles south of the town centre, this B&B offers bright and cheerful rooms, a warm welcome and excellent value. You can take a bus into town or walk there in 20 minutes or so.

MIDRANGE

Interludes (☎ 01723-360513; www.interludeshotel .co.uk; 32 Princess St; s/d from £30/54; 🖳) Owners Ian and Bob have a flair for the theatrical and have brought it to bear with visible success on this lovely, gay-friendly Georgian home plastered with old theatre posters, prints and other thespian mementos. The individually decorated rooms are given to colourful flights of fancy that can't but put a smile on your face. Children, alas, are not welcome.

Windmill Hotel (☎ 01723-372735; www.windmill -hotel.co.uk; Mill St; s/d from £32/64; P) Quirky doesn't begin to describe this place – a beautifully converted 18th-century windmill in the middle of town. There are tight-fitting but comfortable doubles around a cobbled courtyard, but try to get the balcony flat (£85–100 a night) in the upper floors of the windmill itself, with great views from the wrap-around balcony.

Hotel Helaina (☎ 01723-375191; www.hotelhelaina .co.uk; 14 Blenheim Tce; r £54-84; 🖳) Location, location, location – you'd be hard pushed to find a place with a better sea view than this elegant guest house perched on the cliff top overlooking North Beach. And the view inside the rooms is pretty good too, with sharply styled contemporary furniture and cool colours. The standard rooms are a touch on the small side – it's well worth splashing out on the deluxe room with the bay window.

our pick **Beiderbecke's Hotel** (☎ 01723-365766; www.beiderbeckes.com; 1-3 The Crescent; s/d from £65/105; P 🖳) Set in an elegant Georgian terrace in the middle of town, on a quiet street overlooking gardens, this hotel combines stylish and spacious rooms with attentive but friendly and informal service. It's not quite boutique, but with its intriguing modern art on the walls and snazzily coloured toilet seats it's heading in that direction.

TOP END

Crown Spa Hotel (☎ 0800 072 6134; www.crown spahotel.com; Esplanade; s/d from £75/130; P 🖳) This grand old hotel opened its doors in 1845 and has been going strong ever since, changing constantly with the times. After a recent refurbishment it's more opulent than ever, offering superb sea views and a luxurious spa.

Wrea Head Country House Hotel (☎ 01723-378211; www.englishrosehotels.co.uk; Barmoor La, Scalby; s/d £80/135; P) This fabulous country house about 2 miles north of the centre is straight out of *Remains of the Day*. The 20 individually styled bedrooms have canopied, four-poster beds, plush fabrics and delicate furnishings, while the leather couches in the bookcased, wood-heavy lounges are tailor-made for important discussions over cigars and expensive brandy.

Eating

Bonnet's (☎ 01723-361033; 38-40 Huntriss Row; mains £4-7; 🕓 9am-5pm Mon-Sat, 11am-4pm Sun) One of the oldest cafes in town, open since 1880, Bonnet's serves delicious cakes and light meals in a quiet courtyard, and sells handmade chocolates in the adjoining shop.

Roasters (☎ 07971 808549; 8 Aberdeen Walk; mains £5; 🕓 9am-5pm) A funky coffee shop with chunky pine tables, brown leather chairs, and an excellent range of freshly ground coffees. There's a juice and smoothie bar too, and the lunch menu includes ciabatta sandwiches, salads and jacket potatoes.

Golden Grid (☎ 01723-360922; 4 Sandside; mains £7-12; 🕓 11am-11pm) Whoever said fish and chips can't be eaten with dignity hasn't tried the Golden Grid, a sit-down fish restaurant that has been serving the best cod in Scarborough since 1883. It's staunchly traditional, with starched white tablecloths and starched white aprons, as is the menu – as well as fish and chips there's steak pie, mushy peas and Yorkshire pud with onion gravy.

Marmalade's (☎ 01723-365766; 1-3 The Crescent; mains £12-16; 🕓 noon-9.30pm) The stylish brasserie in Beiderbecke's Hotel – cream and chocolate colours, art with a musical theme, and cool jazz in the background – has a menu that adds a gourmet twist to traditional dishes – steak and ale pie with pease pudding, roast rack of lamb with forest berries, sea bass stuffed with lemon and herbs.

Lanterna (☎ 01723-363616; 33 Queen St; mains £13-19; 🕓 dinner Mon-Sat) A snug, old-fashioned Italian trattoria that specialises in fresh local seafood and classic dishes from the old country – as well as sourcing Yorkshire produce, the chef imports delicacies direct from Italy, including truffles, olive oil, prosciutto and a range of cheeses.

Entertainment

Stephen Joseph Theatre (☎ 01723-370541; www
.sjt.uk.com; Westborough) Stages a good range of
drama – renowned chronicler of middle-
class mores Alan Ayckbourn premieres his
plays here.

Scarborough Spa (☎ 01723-376774; www.scar
boroughspa.co.uk; South Bay) The revitalised spa
complex stages a wide range of entertainment, especially in the summer months –
orchestral performances, variety shows, popular musicals and old-fashioned afternoon
tea dances.

Getting There & Away

Bus 128 goes along the A170 from Helmsley to
Scarborough (1½ hours, hourly) via Pickering,
while buses 93 and X93 come from Whitby
(one hour, every 30 minutes) via Robin
Hood's Bay (hourly). Bus 843 arrives from
Leeds (£16, 2¾ hours, hourly) via York.

There are regular trains from Hull (£12,
1½ hours, hourly), Leeds (£20, one hour
20 minutes, hourly) and York (£15, 50
minutes, hourly).

Getting Around

Tiny, Victorian-era funicular railways rattle
up and down Scarborough's steep cliffs between town and beach daily from February
till the end of October (60p). Local buses leave
from the western end of Westborough and
outside the train station.

For a taxi call ☎ 361009; £5 should get you
to most places in town.

FILEY
pop 6468

None of yer nudge-nudge, saucy-postcard-
style seaside tat here, thank you very much.
Filey has a prim and proper prom – even
the miniature golf is designer mini-golf, all
bronze, hemp and limestone with a sea-
creature theme – and looks upon its brasher
neighbours in Bridlington and Scarborough
with a vaguely superior air.

A former fishing village – there are still a
handful of traditional Yorkshire cobles working nets from the beach – Filey is a popular hiking centre, being a hub for both the
Cleveland Way (p588), and the Wolds Way
(p588), while five miles of sandy Blue Flag
beach offer ample scope for cooling off weary
feet with a paddle in the sea.

Filey's **tourist office** (☎ 01723-518000; www.discover
yorkshirecoast.com; John St; ☎ 10am-6pm May-Sep, 10am-
12.30pm & 1-4.30pm Oct-Apr) is on the way down hill
from train station to beach.

Filey is 7 miles south of Scarborough on the
A165, and is served by trains on the line between Hull and Bridlington to the south and
Scarborough to the north (every two hours);
the bare-bones station is about a mile west
of the beach. Buses 120 and 121 run from
Scarborough (30 minutes, hourly).

NORTH YORK MOORS NATIONAL PARK

Inland from the north Yorkshire coast, the
wild and windswept North York Moors rise
in isolated splendour. Three-quarters of all
the world's heather moorland is to be found
in Britain, and this is the largest expanse in
all of England. Ridge-top roads climb up from
lush green valleys to the bleak open moors
where weatherbeaten stone crosses mark the
line of ancient drove roads, and where in summer the heather blooms in billowing drifts of
purple haze.

This is classic walking country, and the
moors are criss-crossed with footpaths old
and new, and dotted with pretty, flower-
bedecked villages. The national park is also
home to one of England's most picturesque
steam railways.

Orientation & Information

The main gateway towns are Helmsley and
Pickering in the south, and Whitby in the
northeast – all have good tourist offices. The
national park also has visitor centres at Sutton
Bank, Danby and Robin Hood's Bay; see also
www.visithemoors.co.uk.

The park produces the very useful *Moors
& Coast* visitor guide, available at tourist
offices, hotels etc, with information on
things to see and do. The OS Landranger
1:50,000 map, sheet 94, covers most of the
national park.

Activities

Tourist offices stock an excellent range of
walking leaflets (around 60p to 75p), as
well as more comprehensive walking and
cycling guidebooks.

YORKSHIRE

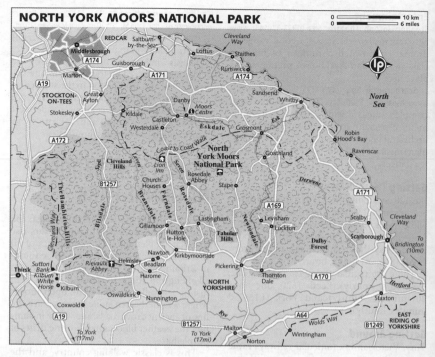

NORTH YORK MOORS NATIONAL PARK

YORKSHIRE

WALKING

There are more than 1400 miles of foot-paths criss-crossing the moors. The most scenic walking areas are along the western escarpment and the cliff tops on the coast, while the green and tranquil valleys offer relaxed rambling.

The famous **Coast to Coast walk** (p588) passes through the park, and the **Cleveland Way** covers three sides of the moors' outer rim on its 109-mile, nine-day route from Helmsley to Filey.

The **Cook Country Walk**, named after explorer Captain Cook who was born and raised in this area, links several monuments commemorating his life. This 40-mile, three-day route follows the flanks of the Cleveland Hills from Marton (near Middlesbrough) to Staithes, then south along the coast to Whitby.

CYCLING

Once you've climbed up onto the escarpment, the North York Moors make fine cycling country, with quiet lanes through the valleys and scenic roads over the hills.

There's also a great selection of off-road tracks for mountain bikes (see www.mtb-routes.co.uk/northyorkmoors).

Getting There & Around

From the south, there are regular buses from York (17 miles outside the park) to Helmsley, Pickering, Scarborough and Whitby. From the north, head for Middlesbrough then take the Esk Valley railway line, which stops at Danby, Grosmont and several other villages in the park. The **North Yorkshire Moors Railway** (NYMR, see p645) runs north–south across the park from Pickering to Grosmont. Using these two railway lines, much of the moors area is easily accessible for those without wheels. Call **Traveline Yorkshire** (☎ 0871 200 2233; www.yorkshiretravel.net) for all public bus and train information.

The **Moorsbus** (☎ 01845-597000) operates on Sunday from May to October, daily from mid-July to early September, and is ideal for reaching out-of-the-way spots. Pick up a timetable and route map from tourist offices, or go to www.visitthemoors.co.uk and click on 'Discover the Place' then 'Public

Transport'. A standard day pass costs £4, and for £12 the pass is valid on the Esk Valley railway too. Family tickets and one-off fares for short journeys are also available.

There's also a free public transport map, the *Moors Explorer Travel Guide,* available from tourist offices.

Note – if you're planning to drive on the minor roads over the moors, beware of wandering sheep and lambs – hundreds are killed by careless drivers every year.

HELMSLEY
pop 1620

Helmsley is a classic North Yorkshire market town, a handsome place full of old houses, historic coaching inns and – inevitably – a cobbled market square, all basking under the watchful gaze of a sturdy Norman castle. Nearby are the romantic ruins of Rievaulx Abbey and a fistful of country walks.

Orientation & Information
The centre of everything is Market Pl (market day is Friday); all four sides are lined with specialty shops, cosy pubs and cafes. The **tourist office** (☎ 01439-770173; 🕑 9.30am-5.30pm Mar-Oct, 10am-4pm Fri-Sun Nov-Feb) sells maps and books, and helps with accommodation.

Sights & Activities
The impressive ruins of 12th-century **Helmsley Castle** (EH; ☎ 01439-770442; admission £4; 🕑 10am-6pm Apr-Sep, 10am-5pm Mar & Oct, 10am-4pm Thu-Mon Nov-Mar) are defended by a striking series of deep ditches and banks to which later rulers added the thick stone walls and defensive towers – only one tooth-shaped tower survives today following the dismantling of the fortress by Sir Thomas Fairfax after the Civil War. The castle's tumultuous history is well explained in the visitor centre.

Just outside the castle, **Helmsley Walled Garden** (☎ 01439-771427; admission £4; 🕑 10.30am-5pm daily Easter-Oct, Mon-Fri Nov-Easter) would be just another plant and produce centre were it not for its dramatic position and fabulous selection of flowers, fruits and vegetables – some of which are quite rare – not to mention the herbs, including 40 varieties of mint. If you're into horticulture with a historical twist, this is Eden.

South of the castle stretches the superb landscape of **Duncombe Park** estate with the stately home of **Duncombe Park House** (☎ 01439-770213; www.duncombepark.com; house & gardens £7.25,

gardens only £4; 🕑 house by guided tour only, hourly 12.30-3.30pm, gardens 11am-5.30pm Sun-Thu Easter-Oct) at its heart. From the house and formal gardens, wide grassy walkways and terraces lead through woodland to mock-classical temples, while longer walking trails are set out in the parkland – now protected as a nature reserve. The house, ticket office and information centre are 1.5 miles south of town, an easy walk through the park.

You could easily spend a day here, especially if you take in one of the many **walks** in Duncombe Park. Cream of the crop is the 3.5-mile route to **Rievaulx Abbey** (p644) – the tourist office can provide route leaflets and advise on buses if you don't want to walk both ways. This route is also the opening section of the **Cleveland Way** (p588).

Sleeping
Wrens of Rydale (☎ 01439-771260; www.wrensofryedale .co.uk; Gale Lane, Nawton; tent & 2 adults £8, with car £14; 🕑 Apr-Oct) This excellent, sheltered camp site with three acres of pristine parkland is 3 miles east of Helmsley, just south of Beadlam.

Helmsley YHA (☎ 0845 371 9638; www.yha.org.uk; Carlton Lane; dm £16; **P**) This family-friendly hostel 0.25 miles east of the market square looks a bit like an ordinary suburban home; its location at the start of the Cleveland Way means that it's almost always full, so book in advance.

There are a number of old coaching inns on Market Pl that offer B&B, half-decent grub and a pint of hand-pumped real ale. The **Feathers Hotel** (☎ 01439-770275; www.feathershotelhelmsley .co.uk; Market Pl; s/d from £44/80) has four-poster beds in some rooms and historical trimmings throughout. For something plusher head for the **Feversham Arms** (☎ 01439-770766; www.fever shamarms.com; s/d from £130/140; **P**), where country charm meets boutique chic.

Eating
Star Inn (☎ 01439-770397; www.thestarathome.co.uk; Harome; mains £15-20; 🕑 dinner Mon-Sat, lunch Tue-Sat, noon-6pm Sun) This thatch-roofed country pub is home to one of Yorkshire's best restaurants, with a Michelin-starred menu that revels in top quality produce from the surrounding farms – slow roast belly pork with black pudding and apple salad, or wood pigeon with roast hazelnut pesto. It's the sort of place you won't want to leave, and the good news is you don't have to: the adjacent lodge has eight

YORKSHIRE

magnificent bedrooms (£130 to £150), each decorated in classic but luxurious country style. It's about 2 miles south of Helmsley just off the A170.

Helmsley is a bit of a foodie town, sporting a couple of quality delicatessens on the main square. There's **Perns** (☎ 01439-770249; 18 Market Pl), a butcher, deli and wine merchant under the same ownership as the Star at Harome; and flower-bedecked **Hunters of Helmsley** (☎ 01439-771307; www.huntersofhelmsley .com; 13 Market Pl), a cornucopia of locally made chutneys, jams, beers, cheeses, bacon, humbugs and ice cream – a great place to stock up for a gourmet picnic.

Getting There & Away
All buses stop in the main square. Bus 31X runs from York to Helmsley (1¼ hours, two daily Monday to Saturday. From Scarborough take bus 128 (£7, 1½ hours, hourly Monday to Saturday, four on Sunday) via Pickering.

AROUND HELMSLEY
Rievaulx
In the secluded valley of the River Rye, amid fields and woods loud with birdsong, stand the magnificent ruins of **Rievaulx Abbey** (EH; ☎ 01439-798228; admission £5; ☾ 10am-6pm Apr-Sep, to 5pm Thu-Mon Oct, to 4pm Thu-Mon Nov-Mar). This idyllic spot was chosen by Cistercian monks in 1132 as a base for missionary activity in northern Britain. St Aelred, the third abbot, famously described the abbey's setting as 'everywhere peace, everywhere serenity, and a marvellous freedom from the tumult of the world.' But the monks of Rievaulx (pronounced ree-voh) were far from unworldly, and soon created a network of commercial interests ranging from sheep farms to lead mines that formed the backbone of the local economy. The extensive ruins give a wonderful feel for the size and complexity of the community that once lived here – their story is fleshed out in a series of fascinating exhibits in the neighbouring visitor centre.

In the 1750s landscape-gardening fashion favoured a Gothic look, and many aristocrats had mock ruins built in their parks. The Duncombe family went one better, as their lands contained a real medieval ruin – Rievaulx Abbey. They built **Rievaulx Terrace & Temples** (NT; ☎ 01439-798340; admission £4.80;

☾ 11am-6pm Apr-Sep, to 5pm Oct & Nov) (p643) so that lords and ladies could stroll effortlessly in the 'wilderness' and admire the abbey in the valley below. Today, we can do the same, with views over Ryedale and the Hambleton Hills forming a perfect backdrop.

Rievaulx is about 3 miles west of Helmsley. Note that there's no direct access between the abbey and the terrace – their entrance gates are about a mile apart, though easily reached along a lane – steeply uphill if you're going from abbey to the terrace.

Sutton Bank & Kilburn White Horse
Sutton Bank is a steep escarpment 8 miles west of Helmsley, where the A170 to Thirsk drops down a very steep and winding hill (caravans not allowed!). From the top, where you'll find a car park and **tourist office** (☎ 01845-597426; ☾ 10am-5pm Apr-Oct, 11am-4pm Nov, Dec & Mar, 11am-4pm Sat & Sun Jan & Feb), there are magnificent views westwards to the Pennines and Yorkshire Dales.

From the car park, you can follow the Cleveland Way footpath south for 1.5 miles along the crest of the escarpment to the **Kilburn White Horse**, a chalk figure cut into the hillside in 1857. Said to be the largest white horse in England, it's best seen from the village of Kilburn, reached via a minor road off the A170 about a half mile east of the car park.

Coxwold
pop 190
Coxwold is a neatly symmetrical village of golden stone – just two rows of cottages perched atop grassy banks on either side of the single street – that nestles in beautiful countryside about 7 miles southwest of Helmsley.

Apart from the picture-postcard beauty of the place, the main attraction is 15th-century **Shandy Hall** (☎ 01347-868465; www.shandean.org; admission gardens/house £4.50/2.50; ☾ house 2-4.30pm Wed, 2.30-4.30pm Sun May-Sep, gardens 11am-4.30pm May-Sep), the former home of ebullient eccentric Laurence Sterne (1713–68), author of *Tristram Shandy*. The house is full of 'Sterneana', with lots of information on this entertaining character who was seemingly the first to use the expression 'sick as a horse'.

Nearby is **Byland Abbey** (EH; ☎ 01347-868614; admission £3.50; ☾ 11am-6pm daily Jul & Aug, Wed-Sun Apr-Jun & Sep), the elegant remains of a fine Cistercian creation, now a series of lofty arches surrounded by open green slopes.

A decent option for a good night's sleep is **Fauconberg Arms** (☎ 01347-868214; www.fauconbergarms.com; Main St; s/d £75/85, mains £11-16; **P**), a cosy local in the heart of the village that also offers a fine Continental-style menu in its elegant restaurant.

HUTTON-LE-HOLE
pop 210

With a scatter of gorgeous stone cottages, a gurgling brook and a flock of sheep grazing contentedly on the village green, Hutton-le-Hole must be a contender for the best-looking village in Yorkshire. The dips and hollows on the green may have given the place its name – it was once called simply Hutton Hole but wannabe posh Victorians added the Frenchified 'le', which the locals defiantly pronounce 'lee'.

The **tourist office** (☎ 01751-417367; ⏱ 10am-5.30pm mid-Mar–early Nov) has leaflets on walks in the area, including a 5-mile circuit to the nearby village of Lastingham.

Attached to the tourist office is the largely open-air **Ryedale Folk Museum** (☎ 01751-417367; www.ryedalefolkmuseum.co.uk; adult/child £5/3.50; ⏱ 10am-5.30pm mid-Mar–Oct, 10am-dusk Nov–mid-Mar, closed 21 Dec-20 Jan), a constantly expanding collection of North York Moors buildings from different eras, including a medieval manor house, simple farmers' houses, a blacksmith's forge and a row of 1930s village shops. Demonstrations and displays throughout the season give a pretty fascinating insight into local life as it was in the past.

The **Daffodil Walk** is a 2½-mile circular walk following the banks of the River Dove. As the name suggests, the main draws are the daffs, usually at their best in the last couple of weeks in April.

Sleeping & Eating
Lion Inn (☎ 01751-417320; www.lionblakey.co.uk; Blakey Ridge; s/d from £35/54; mains £9-16; **P**) From Hutton, the Blakey Ridge road climbs over the moors to Danby and, after 6 miles passes one of the highest and most remote pubs in England (altitude 404m). With its low-beamed ceilings and cosy fireplaces, hearty grub and range of real ales, the Lion is a firm favourite with hikers and bikers.

Burnley House (☎ 01751-417548; www.burnleyhouse.co.uk; d £70-90; **P**) This elegant Georgian home offers comfortable bedrooms and a hearty breakfast, but the best features are the lovely sitting room and garden where you can relax with a cup of tea and a book.

Getting There & Away
Hutton-le-Hole is 2.5 miles north of the main A170 road, about halfway between Helmsley and Pickering. Moorsbus services (p642) through Hutton-le-Hole include the M3 between Helmsley and Danby (seven per day) and the M1 and M2 between Pickering and Danby (eight per day) via the Lion Inn. Outside times when the Moorsbus runs, you'll need your own transport to get here.

PICKERING
pop 6600

Pickering is a lively market town with an imposing Norman castle that advertises itself as 'the gateway to the North York Moors'. That gateway is the terminus of the wonderful North Yorkshire Moors Railway, a picturesque survivor from the great days of steam.

The **tourist office** (☎ 01751-473791; www.ryedale.gov.uk; The Ropery; ⏱ 9.30am-5.30pm Mon-Sat, to 4pm Sun Mar-Oct, 10am-4pm Mon-Sat Nov-Feb) has the usual details as well as plenty of NYMR-related info.

Sights & Activities
The privately owned **North Yorkshire Moors Railway** (NYMR; ☎ Pickering Station 01751-472508, timetable 473535; www.nymr.co.uk; Pickering–Grosmont Day Rover ticket adult/child £14.50/7.30, Pickering–Whitby £20/12) runs for 18 miles through beautiful countryside to the village of Grosmont. Lovingly restored steam locos pull period carriages, resplendent in polished brass and bright paintwork. For visitors without wheels, it's ideal for reaching out-of-the-way villages in the middle of the moors. Grosmont is also on the main railway line between Middlesbrough and Whitby, opening up yet more possibilities for walking and sightseeing.

Dating mostly from the 13th and 14th centuries, **Pickering Castle** (EH; ☎ 01751-474989; admission £3.50; ⏱ 10am-6pm Apr-Sep, 10am-4pm Thu-Mon Oct) is a lot like the castles we drew as kids: thick stone walls around a central keep, perched atop a high motte (mound) with great views of the surrounding countryside.

Sleeping & Eating
White Swan Hotel (☎ 01751-472288; www.white-swan.co.uk; Market Pl; s/d from £110/145, mains £9-15; **P** 💻) The top spot in town successfully combines a

YORKSHIRE

smart pub, a superb restaurant serving local dishes with a Continental twist, and a luxurious boutique hotel all in one. Nine modern rooms in the converted coach house up the ante with flat-screen TVs and other stylish paraphernalia that add to the luxury found throughout the hotel.

There's a strip of B&Bs on tree-lined Eastgate (the A170 to Scarborough), and a few more on Westgate (heading towards Helmsley). Decent options include the flower-clad **Rose Folly** (☎ 01751-475057; www.rosefolly.freeserve.co.uk; 112 Eastgate; s/d £30/55; **P**), with lovely rooms and a beautiful breakfast conservatory; and **Eleven Westgate** (☎ 01751-475111; www.elevenwestgate.co.uk; 11 Westgate; d £60-68), a pretty house with patio and garden.

There are several cafes and teashops on Market Pl, but don't overlook the **tearoom** (mains £2-6) at Pickering station, which serves excellent home-baked goodies and does a tasty roast pork roll with apple sauce, crackling and stuffing.

Getting There & Away

In addition to the NYMR trains, bus 128 between Helmsley (40 minutes) and Scarborough (50 minutes) runs hourly via Pickering. Yorkshire Coastliner services 840 and 842 between Leeds and Whitby link Pickering with York (£11, 70 minutes, hourly).

DANBY
pop 290

The Blakey Ridge road from Hutton-le-Hole swoops steeply down to Danby, a compact, stone-built village set deep amid the moors at the head of Eskdale. It's home to the **Moors Centre** (☎ 01439-772737; www.visitthemoors .co.uk; ☉ 10am-5pm Apr-Oct, 10.30am-3.30pm Nov, Dec & Mar, 10.30am-3.30pm Sat & Sun Jan-Feb), the national park's HQ, which has interesting exhibits on the natural history of the moors as well as a cafe, an accommodation booking service and a huge range of local guidebooks, maps and leaflets.

There are several short circular walks from the centre, but a more challenging objective is **Danby Beacon**, a stiff 2 miles uphill to a stunning 360-degree panorama across the moors. Or you can cheat, and just drive up.

The **Duke of Wellington** (☎ 01287-660351; www .danby-dukeofwellington.co.uk; s/d from £45/70, mains £7-8) is a fine traditional pub that was used as a recruitment centre during the Napoleonic

Wars; it serves good beer and food and has nine well-appointed bedrooms.

You can reach Danby on the delightful **Esk Valley Railway** (☎ 08457 484950; www.eskval leyrailway.co.uk) – Whitby is 20 minutes east, Middlesbrough 45 minutes west. There are four departures daily Monday to Saturday, and two on Sunday.

WHITBY
pop 13,600

Whitby is a town of two halves, split down the middle by the mouth of the River Esk. It's also a town with two personalities – on the one hand a busy commercial and fishing port, with a bustling quayside fishmarket; on the other a traditional seaside resort, complete with sandy beach, amusement arcades and promenading holidaymakers slurping ice cream cones in the sun.

It's the combination of these two facets that makes Whitby more interesting than your average resort. The town has managed to retain much of its 18th-century character, recalling the time when James Cook – Whitby's most famous adopted son – was making his first forays at sea on his way towards becoming one of the best-known explorers in history. The narrow streets and alleys of the old town hug the riverside, now lined with restaurants, pubs and cute little shops, all with views across the handsome harbour where colourful fishing boats ply to and fro. Keeping a watchful eye over the whole scene is the atmospheric ruined abbey atop the East Cliff.

But Whitby also has a darker side. Most famously, it was the inspiration and setting for part of Bram Stoker's Gothic horror story *Dracula* (see the boxed text, p648). Less well known is the fact that Whitby is famous for the jet (fossilised wood) that has been mined from the local sea cliffs for centuries; this smooth, black substance was popularised in the 19th century when Queen Victoria took to wearing mourning jewellery made from Whitby jet. In recent years these morbid associations have seen the rise of a series of hugely popular Goth festivals (p648).

Orientation

Whitby is cut in half by the River Esk, with only one very busy bridge linking the two sides. The east side (East Cliff) is the older part of town; the newer (19th-century) town

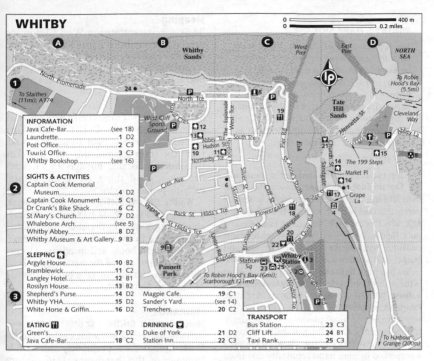

WHITBY

INFORMATION
Java Cafe-Bar.......................(see 18)
Laundrette................................**1** D2
Post Office................................**2** C3
Tourist Office...........................**3** C3
Whitby Bookshop.................(see 16)

SIGHTS & ACTIVITIES
Captain Cook Memorial
  Museum...............................**4** D2
Captain Cook Monument....**5** C1
Dr Crank's Bike Shack...........**6** C2
St Mary's Church....................**7** D2
Whalebone Arch...................(see 5)
Whitby Abbey..........................**8** D2
Whitby Museum & Art Gallery..**9** B3

SLEEPING
Argyle House..........................**10** B2
Bramblewick...........................**11** C2
Langley Hotel..........................**12** B1
Rosslyn House.........................**13** B2
Shepherd's Purse....................**14** D2
Whitby YHA.............................**15** D2
White Horse & Griffin............**16** D2

EATING
Green's.....................................**17** D2
Java Cafe-Bar..........................**18** C2

Magpie Cafe............................**19** C1
Sander's Yard......................(see 14)
Trenchers.................................**20** C2

DRINKING
Duke of York...........................**21** D2
Station Inn...............................**22** C3

TRANSPORT
Bus Station..............................**23** C3
Cliff Lift...................................**24** B1
Taxi Rank.................................**25** C3

grew up on the West Cliff. The bus and train stations are in the town centre on the west side of the river.

Note that many streets have two names – for example, Abbey Tce and Hudson St are opposite sides of the same street, as are West Tce and The Esplanade.

Information

Java Cafe-Bar (☎ 01947-820832; 2 Flowergate; per 10 min £1) Internet access.

Laundrette (72 Church St)

Post office (🕒 8.30am-5.30pm Mon-Sat) Inside the Co-op supermarket.

Tourist office (☎ 01947-602674; www.visitwhitby.com; Langborne Rd; 🕒 9.30am-6pm May-Sep, 10am-4.30pm Oct-Apr)

Whitby Bookshop (☎ 01947-606202; 88 Church St; 🕒 9.30am-5pm daily) Local history and secondhand books.

Sights

There are ruined abbeys and there are picturesque ruined abbeys, and then there's **Whitby Abbey** (EH; ☎ 01947-603568; admission £5; 🕒 10am-6pm Apr-Sep, 10am-4pm Thu-Mon Oct-Mar), dominat-

ing the skyline above the East Cliff like a great Gothic tombstone silhouetted against the sky. Looking more like it was built as an atmospheric film set than as a monastic establishment, it is hardly surprising that this medieval hulk inspired the Victorian novelist Bram Stoker – who holidayed in Whitby – to make it the setting for Count Dracula's dramatic landfall.

The 199 steps of **Church Stairs** lead steeply up to the abbey from the end of Church St, passing the equally atmospheric **St Mary's Church** (🕒 10am-5pm Apr-Oct, to 4pm Nov-Mar) and its spooky graveyard, a favourite haunt of Goth courting couples.

The fascinating **Captain Cook Memorial Museum** (☎ 01947-601900; www.cookmuseumwhitby .co.uk; Grape Lane; adult/child £4/3; 🕒 9.45am-5pm Apr-Oct, 11am-3pm Sat & Sun Mar) occupies the house of the ship owner with whom Cook began his seafaring career. Highlights include the attic where Cook lodged as a young apprentice, Cook's own maps and letters, etchings from the South Seas and a wonderful model of the *Endeavour*, with all the crew and stores laid out for inspection.

YORKSHIRE

WHITBY'S DARK SIDE

The famous story of *Dracula*, inspiration for a thousand lurid movies, was written by Bram Stoker while staying at a B&B in Whitby in 1897. Although most Hollywood versions of the tale concentrate on deepest, darkest Transylvania, much of the original book was set in Whitby, and many sites can still be seen today. The tourist office sells an excellent *Dracula Trail* leaflet (80p).

Atop the cliff on the harbour's west side, the **Captain Cook Monument** shows the great man looking out to sea, often with a seagull perched on his head. Nearby is the **Whalebone Arch**, which recalls Whitby's days as a whaling port. Below, Whitby's days as a seaside resort continue with donkey rides, ice cream and bucket-and-spade escapades on **Whitby Sands**.

Set in a park to the west of the town centre is the wonderfully eclectic **Whitby Museum & Art Gallery** (☎ 01947-602908; www.whitbymuseum.org.uk; Pannett Park; adult/child £3/1; ☼ 9.30am-4.30pm Tue-Sun), with displays of fossil plesiosaurs and dinosaur footprints, Cook memorabilia, ships in bottles, jet jewellery and the 'Hand of Glory' – a preserved human hand reputedly cut from the corpse of an executed criminal.

Activities

For a cracking day out, take a bus to Robin Hood's Bay, explore the village, have lunch, then hike the 6-mile **cliff-top footpath** back to Whitby (allow three hours).

First choice for a bike ride is the excellent 20-mile Whitby to Scarborough **Coastal Cycle Trail**, which starts a mile south of the town centre and follows the route of an old railway line via Robin Hood's Bay. Bikes can be hired from **Dr Crank's Bike Shack** (☎ 01947-606661; 20 Skinner St; ☼ 10am-5pm, closed Wed & Sun).

Festivals & Events

Whitby Gothic Weekends (www.wgw.topmum.co.uk; tickets £45) Twice yearly, last weekend of April and October. Goth heaven, with gigs, events and the Bizarre Bazaar – dozens of traders selling Goth gear, jewellery, art and music.

Moor & Coast Festival (www.moorandcoast.co.uk; tickets £35) May Bank Holiday weekend. Beards, sandals and real ale galore at this traditional festival of folk music, dance and dubious Celtic art.

Musicport Festival (www.whitbymusicport.com; tickets £75) Mid-October. A weekend-long festival of world music.

Sleeping

B&Bs are concentrated in West Cliff in the streets to the south and east of Royal Crescent; if a house here ain't offering B&B, chances are it's derelict. Accommodation can be tough to find at festival times; it's wise to book ahead.

BUDGET

Harbour Grange (☎ 01947-600817; www.whitbybackpackers.co.uk; Spital Bridge; dm £15) Overlooking the harbour and less than 10 minutes' walk from the train station, this tidy hostel is conveniently located but has an 11.30pm curfew – good thing we're all teetotal early-to-bedders, right?

Whitby YHA (☎ 0845 371 9049; www.yha.org.uk; Church Lane; dm £22; P ▯) With an unbeatable position next to the abbey, this hostel doesn't have to try too hard, and it doesn't. You'll have to book well in advance to get your body into one of the basic bunks. Hike up from the station, or take bus 97 (hourly Monday to Saturday).

MIDRANGE

White Horse & Griffin (☎ 01947-604857; www.whitehorseandgriffin.co.uk; 87 Church St; s/d/f from £35/60/85) Walk through the appropriately olde-worlde frontage of this handsome 18th-century coaching inn and discover a boutique hotel with individually designed, superstylish rooms that manage to mix the best of tradition (antique panelling, restored period furniture, real flame fires) with the kind of sleek, contemporary lines and modern comforts you'd expect from a top-class guest house.

Shepherd's Purse (☎ 01947-820228; www.theshepherdspurse.com; 95 Church St; r £45-60) This place combines a beads-and-baubles boutique with a wholefood shop and guest house accommodation in the courtyard at the back. The plainer rooms that share a bathroom are perfectly adequate, but we recommend the rustic en suite bedrooms situated around the courtyard; the four-poster beds feel a bit like they've been shoehorned in, but the atmosphere is cute rather than cramped.

Langley Hotel (☎ 01947-604250; www.langleyhotel.com; 16 Royal Cres; s/d from £70/90; P) With a cream and crimson colour scheme, and a gilt four-poster bed in one room, this grand old hotel exudes a whiff of Victorian splendour. Go for room 1 or 2, if possible, to make the most of the panoramic views from West Cliff.

CAPTAIN COOK – WHITBY'S ADOPTED SON

Although he was born in Marton (now a suburb of Middlesbrough), Whitby has adopted the famous explorer Captain James Cook, and ever since the first tourists got off the train in Victorian times local entrepreneurs have mercilessly cashed in on his memory, as endless 'Endeavour Cafes' and 'Captain Cook Chip Shops' testify.

Still, Whitby played a key role in Cook's eventual success as a world-famous explorer. It was here that he first went to sea, serving his apprenticeship with local ship owners, and the design of the ships used for his voyages of discovery – including the famous *Endeavour* – were based on the design of Whitby 'cats', flat-bottomed ships that carried coal from Newcastle to London.

Other recommendations:

Rosslyn House (☎ 01947-604086; rosslynhouse@ googlemail.com; 11 Abbey Tce; s/d from £29/50) Bright and cheerful with a friendly welcome.

Bramblewick (☎ 01947-604504; www.bramblewick .co.uk; 3 Havelock Pl; s/d from £27/60; **P**) Friendly owners, hearty breakfasts, abbey views from top floor room.

Argyle House (☎ 01947-602733; www.argyle-house .co.uk; 18 Hudson St; s/d £32/60) Comfortable as old slippers, and kippers for breakfast.

Eating & Drinking

Java Cafe-Bar (☎ 01947-820832; 2 Flowergate; mains £4-6) A cool little diner with stainless steel counters and retro decor, with internet access, music vids on the flat screen and a menu of healthy salads, sandwiches and wraps washed down with excellent coffee.

Sander's Yard (☎ 01947-820228; 95 Church St; mains £6-8) A vegie place in a pleasant courtyard behind the Shepherd's Purse wholefood shop, Sander's serves a great range of healthy, interesting snacks, sandwiches and home-baked cakes.

Magpie Cafe (☎ 01947-602058; 14 Pier Rd; mains £8-15; ☺ lunch & dinner) Flaunts its reputation for serving the 'world's best fish and chips'; damn fine they are too, but the world and his dog knows about it, and summertime queues can stretch along the street.

Trenchers (☎ 01947-603212; New Quay Rd; mains £9-15; ☺ lunch & dinner) Top-notch fish and chips minus the 'world's best' tagline – this place is your best bet if you want to avoid the queues at the Magpie (don't be put off by the modern look).

Green's (☎ 01947-600284; www.greensofwhitby.com; 13 Bridge St; bistro mains £10-18, restaurant 2-/3-course dinner £34/40; ☺ lunch & dinner Fri-Sun, dinner Mon-Thu) The classiest eatery in town is ideally situated to take its pick of the fish and shellfish freshly landed at the harbour, which makes its way onto the menu as crab with linguini, scallops with parmesan, pesto and prosciutto, and langoustine tempura.

Most of Whitby's pubs serve food, including the popular **Duke of York** (Church St) at the bottom of the Church Stairs, which has great views over the harbour and serves Timothy Taylor ales. But the best place in town for atmosphere and real ale is the **Station Inn** (New Quay Rd), which offers an impressive range of cask-conditioned beers including Theakston's Black Bull and Black Dog Abbey Ale.

Getting There & Away

Buses 93 and X93 run south to Scarborough (one hour, every 30 minutes) via Robin Hood's Bay (15 minutes, hourly), and north to Middlesbrough (hourly), with fewer services on Sunday. See p599 for details of the Yorkshire Coastliner service from Leeds to Whitby.

Coming from the north, you can get to Whitby by train along the Esk Valley Railway from Middlesbrough (£4.40, 1½ hours, four per day), with connections from Durham and Newcastle. From the south, it's easier to get a train from York to Scarborough, then a bus from Scarborough to Whitby.

Getting Around

Whitby is a compact place and hiking up and down the steep hills helps to burn off the fish and chips. But if you need one, there's a **taxi rank** outside the train station. Whitby Sands can be reached from West Cliff via the **cliff lift** (75p; ☺ May-Sep only), an elevator that has been running since 1931.

AROUND WHITBY
Robin Hood's Bay

Picturesque Robin Hood's Bay (www.robin -hoods-bay.co.uk) has nothing to do with the hero of Sherwood Forest – the origin of the name is a mystery, and the locals call it Bay Town, or just Bay. But there's no denying that

YORKSHIRE

this fishing village is one of the prettiest spots on the Yorkshire coast.

Leave your car at the parking area in the upper village, where 19th-century ship's captains built comfortable Victorian villas, and walk downhill to **Old Bay**, the oldest part of the village (don't even think about driving down). This maze of narrow lanes and passages is dotted with tearooms, pubs, craft shops and artists' studios – there's even a tiny cinema – and at low tide you can go down onto the beach and fossick around in the rock pools.

There are several pubs and cafes – best pub for ambience and real ale is **Ye Dolphin** (☎ 01947-880337; King St), while the **Swell Cafe** (☎ 01947-880180; Chapel St) does great coffee and has a terrace with a view over the beach.

Robin Hood's Bay is 6 miles south of Whitby; you can walk here along the coastal path in two or three hours, or bike it along the cycle trail in 40 minutes. Also, bus 93 runs hourly between Whitby and Scarborough via Robin Hood's Bay – the bus stop is at the top of the hill, in the new part of town.

Staithes

Tucked beneath high cliffs at the mouth of a small river, the fishing village of Staithes seems to hide away from the modern world. It's a lot less touristy than Robin Hood's Bay; the houses are less prettified – you can see fishermen's oilskins drying on washing lines – and seagulls the size of vultures swoop down the narrow alleys leading off the steep, narrow main street.

Captain James Cook worked for a grocer here when he was a boy; legend says that fishermen's tales of the high seas, and poor treatment from his master, led him to steal a shilling and run away to Whitby. The rest of the tale is told in detail in the fascinating **Captain Cook & Staithes Heritage Centre** (admission £3; ☸ 10am-5.30pm), packed to the gunwales with nautical relics.

Staithes is 11 miles northwest of Whitby; buses from Whitby to Middlesbrough can drop you at the top of the hill. If you're feeling fit, walking one way and bussing the other makes for a great day out

The Northwest

A city-lover's nirvana, the northwest is crammed with some of the country's coolest conurbations, a concrete jungle that was once England's mighty industrial heartland.

Sounds sexy, right? Oh, but it is. Within the relatively tight confines of the region you'll find life, music, history and hedonism all clamouring for your undivided attention. There's Manchester, a genuine contender for England's hippest city, only a short hop from Liverpool, whose cultural credentials are a match for anyone. Just down the road is picture-postcard Chester, its rich historical layers revealed in its architecture, while on the coast resides the grand dame of British seaside resorts, Blackpool – home to the most eye-popping, stomach-churning roller coaster on which we've ever been dizzy.

And when you need respite from the concrete paw-print of humankind, you're only a short ride from some of England's most beautiful countryside, including the ever-enticing Isle of Man. All of this from a region that once changed the world.

Born just down the road in Shropshire, the Industrial Revolution was raised in the mill towns of Lancashire into the overwhelming force of capitalism; where, in Manchester, the world's first modern city was conceived; and where the endless possibilities of the Age of Reason were put through their original paces.

These days, however, the northwest is all about looking forward, about being the region that leaves its imprint on the 21st century in the way that it has for the last couple of centuries. A tall order, no doubt, but the region knows a thing or two about mighty achievements, urban redesign and bloody good music: look and listen for yourself.

HIGHLIGHTS

- Learning exactly what kind of hell war is in the **Imperial War Museum** (p659) in Manchester
- Getting to the root of the game at Preston's **National Football Museum** (p692)
- Having your insides churned and twisted at Blackpool's **Pleasure Beach** (p690)
- Getting to grips with the **Isle of Man** (p696) – about as exotic as England gets
- Walking in Frodo's footsteps in and around **Hurst Green** (p695)
- Learning a valuable history lesson at the outstanding **International Slavery Museum** in Liverpool (p681)

★ Isle of Man

Blackpool ★   ★ Hurst Green
★ Preston

Liverpool ★   ★ Manchester

■ POPULATION: 6.7 MILLION	■ AREA: 5473 SQ MILES	■ ENGLAND'S LAST TEMPERANCE (NO ALCHOHOL) BAR: FITZPATRICK'S (RASTENSTALL, LANCASHIRE)

THE NORTHWEST

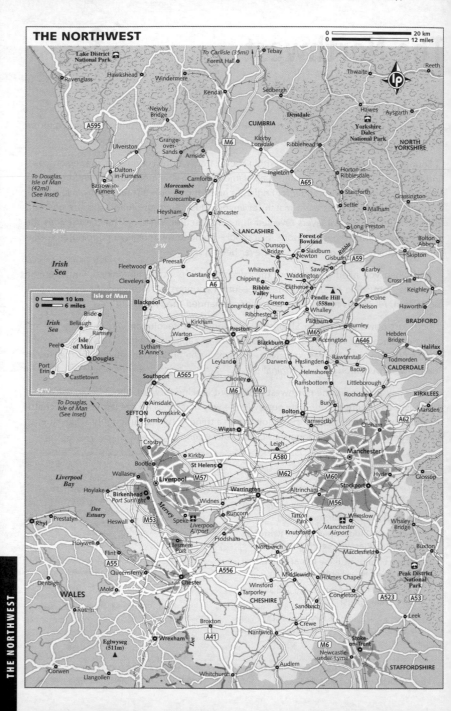

THE NORTHWEST

Information

Discover England's Northwest (www.visitnorthwest.com) is the centralised tourist authority that covers the whole of the northwest.

Activities

The northwest is predominantly an urban area, and there are few walking and cycling options. One main exception is the Ribble Valley, which has plenty of good walks including the 70-mile **Ribble Way**, and is also well covered by the northern loop of the **Lancashire Cycle Way**.

The Isle of Man has top-notch walking and cycling opportunities. Regional tourism websites contain walking and cycling information, and tourist offices stock free leaflets as well as maps and guides (usually £1 to £5) that cover walking, cycling and other activities.

Getting Around

The towns and cities covered in this chapter are all within easy reach of each other, and are well linked by public transport. The two main cities, Manchester and Liverpool, are only 34 miles apart and are linked by hourly bus and train services. Chester is 18 miles south of Liverpool, but is also easily accessible from Manchester by train or via the M56 motorway. Blackpool is 50 miles to the north of both cities, and is also well connected. Try the following for transport information:

Greater Manchester Passenger Transport Authority (www.gmpte.com) For extensive info on Manchester and its environs.

Merseytravel (☎ 0161-236 7676; www.merseytravel.gov.uk) Taking care of all travel in Merseyside.

National Express (☎ 08717 81 81 81; www.nationalexpress.com) Extensive coach services in the northwest; Manchester and Liverpool are major hubs.

MANCHESTER

pop 394,270

If London were to have a rival, Manchester would be it. Birmingham is big, but no city outside the capital has the kind of history, style and urban aplomb to match the uncrowned capital of the north. You don't have to take our word for it: in 2007 the BBC announced that five of its major departments – Sports, Children's, Five Live, New Media and Research – would be relocated to a pur-

pose-built complex called Media City in the Manchester suburb of Salford.

The move will be completed by 2011, but the city is more than ready, with its major-metropolis credentials being long established. This is, after all, the world's first modern city, where capitalism was born; where the Industrial Revolution blossomed; where communism and feminism were given theoretical legs; and where the first computer beeped into life. And it didn't stop there.

The change and influence of the last decade and a half has been nearly as dramatic. It began with a musical revolution, was interrupted by a bomb, and has climaxed in the transformation of Manchester into, arguably, Britain's most exciting 21st-century city – the envy of any urban centre in Europe. It is surely indicative of more than just northern one-upmanship over London that Manchester looks to Barcelona as its main rival and inspiration.

There are museums and enough heritage to satisfy even the most demanding historian, but what makes Manchester so inviting is that it has managed to weave the mementoes of its past with a forward-looking, ambitious program of urban development that has already offered a vision of what the future might hold.

The future, according to Manchester, is to ensure that form follows function, and that cities are first and foremost human dwellings. Testament to this belief is the remarkable life on show at street level, from the trendy bars and boutiques of the bohemian Northern Quarter to the loud-and-proud attitude of the Gay Village and the chic, self-possessed stylings of the Castlefield area. Spend enough time here and you too will be infected with the palpable confidence of a city that knows it's onto a good thing.

HISTORY

Canals and steam-powered cotton mills were what transformed Manchester from a small disease-infested provincial town into a big disease-infested industrial city. It all happened in the 1760s, with the opening of the Bridgewater Canal between Manchester and the coal mines at Worsley in 1763, and with Richard Arkwright patenting his super cotton mill in 1769. Thereafter, Manchester and the world would never be the same again. When the canal was extended to Liverpool and the open sea in

MANCHESTER

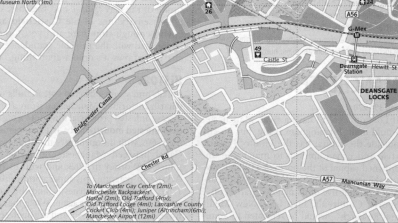

INFORMATION
Cameolord Chemist	1 F4
Central Library	(see 9)
Cornerhouse	2 F5
L2K Internet Gaming Cafe	3 F4
Lesbian & Gay Foundation	(see 61)
Police Station	4 E3
Post Office	5 E3
Tourist Office	6 F3
Waterstone's	7 E2
Waterstone's	8 E2

SIGHTS & ACTIVITIES
Central Library	9 E4
Chetham's Library & School of Music	10 F1
Early Years & Play	11 D4
Godlee Observatory	12 G4
Greater Manchester Police Museum	13 H2
John Rylands Library	14 E3
Manchester Art Gallery	15 F3
Museum of Science & Industry	16 C4
People's History Museum	17 D3
Town Hall	18 E3
Urbis	19 F1

SLEEPING
Abode	20 H3
Castlefield	21 C4
Great John Street Hotel	22 C4
Hatters	23 H2
Hilton Manchester Deansgate	24 D4
Jury's Inn	25 E5
Manchester YHA	26 C5
Midland	27 E4
New Union Hotel	28 G4
Ox	29 C4
Palace Hotel	30 F5
Premier Travel Inn	31 E4
Premier Travel Inn	32 F4
Radisson Edwardian	33 E4
Rembrandt Hotel	34 G4
Yang Sing Oriental Hotel	(see 43)

EATING 🍽
Bluu	35 G1
Brasserie Blanc	36 E3
Earth Cafe	37 G2
Eighth Day	38 G6
Ithaca	39 E3
Love Saves the Day	40 G2
Market Restaurant	41 G1
Modern	(see 19)
Trof	42 G2
Yang Sing	43 F4

DRINKING 🍷
A Place Called Common	44 G2
AXM	45 G4
Bar Centro	46 H2
Bluu	(see 35)
Britons Protection	47 E5
Dry Bar	48 G2
Dukes 92	49 C5
Lass O'Gowrie	50 G5
Mr Thomas Chop House	51 E3
Odd	52 G2
Old Wellington Inn	53 F1
Peveril of the Peak	54 E5
Taurus	55 G4
Temple of Convenience	56 F5

ENTERTAINMENT 🎭
AMC Cinemas	57 D4
Attic	58 F5
Band on the Wall	59 H1
Bridgewater Hall	60 E5
Club Alter Ego	61 G4
Cornerhouse	(see 2)
Essential Nightclub	62 G3
Green Room	63 F5
Library Theatre	(see 9)
Manchester Cathedral	64 E1
Manchester Central	65 E4
Manchester Opera House	66 D3
Moho Live	67 G2
Music Box	68 F5
Odeon Cinema	69 F1
Royal Exchange	70 E2
Ruby Lounge	71 G2
South	72 E3

SHOPPING 🛍
Affleck's Palace	73 G2
Harvey Nichols	74 E2
Oi Polloi	75 H2
Oxfam Original	76 G2

TRANSPORT
Bus Station	77 G3
Coach Station	78 G4
Travelshop	79 G3

To Salford Quays (1mi); Lowry & Imperial War Museum North (1mi)

Blackfriars St

Trinity Way

Irwell

Salford Station

Bridge St

Wood St

Irwell St

Spinningfields

Hardman St

Water St

Quay St

Great Northern St

Lower Byrom St

Castlefield Urban Heritage Park

Longworth St

CASTLEFIELD

Liverpool Rd

A56

G-Mex

Deansgate Station

Hewitt St

DEANSGATE LOCKS

Great Northern

Bridgewater Canal

Castle St

Chester Rd

To Manchester Gay Centre (2mi); Manchester Backpackers' Hostel (2mi); Old Trafford (4mi); Old Trafford Lodge (4mi); Lancashire County Cricket Club (4mi); Juniper (Altrincham)(6mi); Manchester Airport (12mi)

A57 Mancunian Way

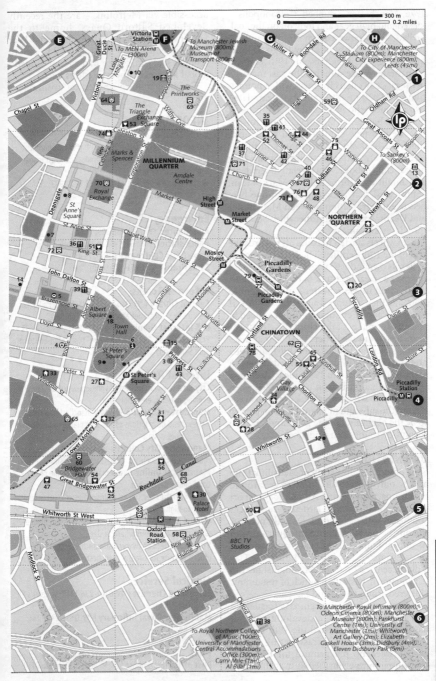

1776, Manchester – dubbed 'Cottonopolis' – kicked into high gear and took off on the coal-fuelled, steam-powered gravy train.

There was plenty of gravy to go around, but the good burghers of 19th-century Manchester made sure that the vast majority of the city's swollen citizenry (with a population of 90,000 in 1801, and 100 years later, two million) who produced most of it never got their hands on any of it. Their reward was life in a new kind of urban settlement: the industrial slum. Working conditions were scarcely better, with impossibly long hours, child labour, work-related accidents and fatalities commonplace. Mark Twain commented that he would like to live here because the 'transition between Manchester and Death would be unnoticeable'. So much for Victorian values.

The wheels started to come off towards the end of the 19th century. The USA had begun to flex its own industrial muscles and was taking over a sizeable chunk of the textile trade; production in Manchester's mills began to slow, and then it stopped altogether. By WWII there was hardly enough cotton produced in the city to make a tablecloth. The postwar years weren't much better: 150,000 manufacturing jobs were lost between 1961 and 1983 and the port – still the UK's third largest in 1963 – finally closed in 1982 due to declining traffic. The nadir came on 15 June 1996, when an IRA bomb wrecked a chunk of the city centre, but the subsequent reconstruction proved to be the beginning of the glass-and-chrome revolution so much in evidence today.

ORIENTATION

Shoe power and the excellent Metrolink tram are the only things you'll need to get around the compact city centre. All public transport converges at Piccadilly Gardens, a few blocks southeast of the cathedral. Directly north is the on-the-up boho Northern Quarter, with its offbeat boutiques, hip cafes and fabulous record shops. A few blocks south is the Gay Village, centred on Canal St and, just next to it, Chinatown, basically a bunch of restaurants clustered around Portland St.

Southwest of the city centre is Castlefield and Deansgate Locks, a development that has successfully converted the 19th-century canalside industrial infrastructure into a groovy weekend playground for the city's fine young things. Further west again – and

accessible via Metrolink – are the recently developed Salford Quays, home to the fab Lowry complex and the Imperial War Museum North. Not far away is Old Trafford football stadium, where Manchester United's global stars earn their fabulous keep.

For information on getting around, see p669.

INFORMATION
Bookshops
Cornerhouse (☎ 0161-200 1514; www.cornerhouse .org; 70 Oxford St) Art and film books, specialist magazines and kitschy cards.
Waterstone's Deansgate (☎ 0161-832 1992); St Anne's Sq (☎ 0161-837 3000)

Emergency
Ambulance (☎ 0161-436 3999)
Police station (☎ 0161-872 5050; Bootle St)
Rape Crisis Centre (☎ 0161-273 4500)
Samaritans (☎ 0161-236 8000)

Internet Access
Central Library (☎ 0161-234 1982; St Peter's Sq; per 30min £1; ☿ internet access 1-6pm Mon-Sat)
L2K Internet Gaming Cafe (☎ 0161-244 5566; 32 Princess St; per 30min £2; ☿ 9am-10pm Mon-Fri, 9am-9pm Sat & Sun)

Internet Resources
City Life (www.manchestereveningnews.co.uk) The city's evening paper in electronic form.
Manchester After Dark (www.manchesterad.com) Reviews and descriptions of the best places to be when the sun goes down.
Manchester City Council (www.manchester.gov.uk) The council's official website, which includes a visitors' section.
Manchester Online (www.manchesteronline.co.uk) Local online newspaper.
Real Manchester (www.realmanchester.com) Online guide to nightlife.
Virtual Manchester (www.manchester.com) Restaurants, pubs, clubs and where to sleep.
Visit Manchester (www.visitmanchester.com) The official website for Greater Manchester.

Medical Services
Cameolord Chemist (☎ 0161-236 1445; St Peter's Sq; ☿ 10am-10pm)
Manchester Royal Infirmary (☎ 0161-276 1234; Oxford Rd)

Post
Post office (Brazennose St; ☿ 9am-5.30pm Mon-Fri)

THE WARS OF THE ROSES

The Wars of the Roses was nothing more than a protracted quarrel between two factions – the House of Lancaster (whose symbol was a red rose) and the House of York (represented by a white rose) – over who would rule England.

It began with Lancastrian Henry VI (r 1422–61 and 1470–71), who was terrific as a patron of culture and learning, but totally inept as a ruler, and prone to bouts of insanity. During the worst of these episodes he had to hand over power to Richard, Duke of York, who served as protector but acted as king. Henry may have been nutty but his wife Margaret of Anjou, however, was anything but, and in 1460 she put an end to Richard's political ambitions by raising an army to defeat and kill him at the Battle of Wakefield. Round one to Lancaster.

Next it was the turn of Richard's son Edward. In 1461 he avenged his father's defeat by inflicting a defeat of his own on Henry and Margaret, declaring himself Edward IV (r 1461–70 and 1471–83) as a result. One all.

But Edward's victory owed much to the political machinations of Richard Neville, Earl of Warwick – appropriately nicknamed 'the kingmaker' – but the throne proved an amnesiac and in time Eddie forgot his friends. In 1470 Warwick jumped ship and sided with the Lancastrians. Edward was exiled and Henry, Margaret and the earl were all smiles. Half-time and the score was two–one to Lancaster.

Edward came back strongly a year later. He first defeated and killed the earl at the Battle of Barnet before crushing Henry and Margaret at Tewkesbury. Henry was executed in the Tower of London and Margaret was ransomed back to France, where she died in poverty. Just to make sure, Edward also killed their son.

The Yorkists were back in the game, and Edward proved to be a good and popular king. When he died in 1483 (apparently worn out by his sexual excesses), power passed to his brother Richard, who was to rule as regent until Edward's 12-year-old son came of age. Two months after the king's death, Richard arranged for the 'disappearance' of his nephew and he was crowned Richard III. But when rumours of Dickie's dastardly deed became known, he became as popular as a bad smell. In 1485, the Lancastrians, led by the young Henry Tudor, defeated Richard at the Battle of Bosworth, leaving the fallen king to offer his kingdom in exchange for a horse. Final result: victory to Lancaster.

The coronation of Henry VII, and his subsequent marriage to Edward IV's daughter Elizabeth, put an end to the fighting and ushered in the Tudor dynasty, but it didn't end the rivalry.

The two sides may not be fighting with swords and lances, but one of the great enmities in English football today exists between Lancashire's Manchester United – who wear red – and Yorkshire's Leeds United, who wear all-white.

Tourist Information

Tourist office (☎ 0871 222 8223; www.visitmanchester .com; Town Hall Extension, St Peter's Sq; ⊗ 10am-5.15pm Mon-Sat, 10am-4.30pm Sun)

SIGHTS & ACTIVITIES

There's so much to see in the city centre and in the surrounding suburbs – from Salford Quays towards the west (across the River Irwell) to the museums and galleries of the University of Manchester (located south of the city centre along and off Oxford Rd). Pretty much everywhere in Manchester can be reached easily by public transport.

City Centre

The city's main administrative centre is the superb Victorian Gothic **town hall** (admission free; tours adult/child £5/4; ⊗ tours 2pm Sat Mar-Sep) that dominates Albert Sq. The interior is rich in sculpture and ornate decoration, while the exterior is crowned by an impressive 85m-high tower. You can visit the building on your own, but because it's the city's main administrative centre you won't get the same access as you would by taking an organised tour, which departs from the tourist office.

Just behind the town hall, the elegant Roman Pantheon lookalike **Central Library** (☎ 0161-234 1900; St Peter's Sq; admission free; ⊗ 10am-8pm Mon-Thu, 10am-6pm Fri & Sat) was built in 1934.

MANCHESTER IN...

Two Days

Two days? It's hardly enough, but here's a good sample menu to get you started. After exploring the **Museum of Science and Industry** (opposite), take a peek inside the **John Rylands Library** (below) before hopping on the Metrolink for the Salford Quays and its trio of top attractions: the **Imperial War Museum North** (opposite), the **Lowry** (p660) and the **Manchester United Museum** (p660). If you'd rather eat glass than set foot in, or give money to, Man U PLC, skip across town to visit Manchester City's ground at the **City of Manchester Stadium** (p668). Pick a restaurant such as **Yang Sing** (p664) to kick off the evening, then try **A Place Called Common** (p665) and round off the night in **Music Box** (p666).

The next day, make a visit to **Urbis** (below) before indulging your retail chi in either the **Millennium Quarter** (p669) or the boutiques and offbeat shops of the **Northern Quarter** (p669). Finish your day with a jaunt to the suburb of West Didsbury and its selection of fantastic restaurants (see boxed text, p665).

Four Days

Congratulations. You've seen sense and have added a few days to really appreciate the city. Follow the two-day itinerary and also tackle some of the city's lesser-known museums – the **People's History Museum** (opposite), **Chetham's Library** (see boxed text, p660) and the **Manchester Jewish Museum** (see boxed text, p660). Get an insider's take on the city's rich musical heritage by going on a **Manchester Music Tour** (p483). Go south and explore the **Manchester Museum** (p661) and **Whitworth Art Gallery** (p661). If the weather is decent, visit the **Godlee Observatory** (see boxed text, p661) before examining the riches of the **Manchester Art Gallery** (below).

It is the country's largest municipal library, with more than 20 miles of shelves.

MANCHESTER ART GALLERY

A superb collection of British art and a hefty number of European masters are on display at the city's top **gallery** (☎ 0161-235 8888; www .manchestergalleries.org; Mosley St; admission free; ☷ 10am-5pm Tue-Sun). The older wing, designed by Charles Barry (of Houses of Parliament fame) in 1834, has an impressive collection that includes 37 Turner watercolours, as well as the country's best collection of Pre-Raphaelite art. The newer gallery features a permanent collection of 20th-century British art starring Lucien Freud, Francis Bacon, Stanley Spencer, Henry Moore and David Hockney. Finally, the Gallery of Craft & Design, in the Athenaeum, houses a permanent collection of pre-17th-century art, with works predominantly from the Dutch and early Renaissance masters.

JOHN RYLANDS LIBRARY

An easy candidate for top building in town, this marvellous Victorian Gothic **library** (☎ 0161-834 5343; www.library.manchester.ac.uk; 35 Deansgate; admission free; ☷ 10am-5pm Mon & Wed-Sat, noon-5pm Tue & Sun) was one hell of a way for Rylands' widow to remember her husband, John. Less a library and more a cathedral to books, Basil Champneys' stunning building is arguably the most beautiful library in Britain – although there's not much argument when you're standing in the simply exquisite Gothic 'Reading Room', complete with high-vaulted ceilings and stained-glass windows. It's such a breathtaking building that you could easily ignore the magnificent collection of early printed books and rare manuscripts. A £16 million refit has resulted in the addition of a surprisingly tasteful modern annexe with a cafe and a bookshop.

URBIS

The stunning glass triangle that is **Urbis** (☎ 0161-907 9099; www.urbis.org.uk; Cathedral Gardens, Corporation St; levels 2-4 admission free, charge for temporary exhibits; ☷ 10am-6pm Sun-Wed, 10am-8pm Thu-Sat) is a museum about how a city works and – often – doesn't work. The walls of the three floors are covered in compelling photographs, interesting statistics and informative timelines, but the best parts are the interactive videos, each of which tell stories about real people from radically different backgrounds and how they fare in Manchester.

It's all well and good to theorise, but there's nothing like a real story to hammer home the truth. Homelessness, rootlessness and dislocation are major themes of urban living, and Urbis doesn't shy away from encouraging visitors to consider what it's like to sleep on a park bench.

MUSEUM OF SCIENCE & INDUSTRY

The city's largest **museum** (MOSI; ☎ 0161-832 1830; www.msim.org.uk; Liverpool Rd; admission free, charge for special exhibitions; ☿ 10am 5pm) comprises 2.8 hectares in the heart of 19th-century industrial Manchester. It's in a landscape of enormous, weather-stained brick buildings and rusting cast-iron relics of canals, viaducts, bridges, warehouses and market buildings that makes up Castlefield, now deemed an 'urban heritage park'.

If there's anything you want to know about the Industrial (and post-Industrial) Revolution and Manchester's key role in it, you'll find the answers among the collection of steam engines and locomotives, factory machinery from the mills, and the excellent exhibition telling the story of Manchester from the sewers up.

With more than a dozen permanent exhibits, you could spend a whole day poking about the place, testing early electric-shock machines here and trying out a printing press there. A unifying theme (besides the fact that science and industry were pretty handy to the development of society) is that Manchester and Mancunians had a key role to play: did you know that Manchester was home to the world's first computer (a giant contraption called 'the baby'), in 1948, or that the world's first submarine was built to the designs of local curate Reverend George Garrett, in 1880? Nope, neither did we.

GREATER MANCHESTER POLICE MUSEUM

One of the city's best-kept secrets is this superb **museum** (☎ 0161-856 3287; www.gmp.police.uk; 57A Newton St; admission free; ☿ 10.30am-3.30pm Tue) housed within a former Victorian police station. The original building has been magnificently – if a little creepily – brought back to life, and you can wander in and out of 19th-century cells where prisoners rested their heads on wooden (!!) pillows; visit a restored magistrates' court from 1895; and examine the case histories (complete with mugshots and photos of weapons) of some of the more notorious names to have passed through its doors.

PEOPLE'S HISTORY MUSEUM

Social history and the labour movement are the themes at this **museum** (☎ 0161-839 6061; www.phm.org.uk; Left Bank, Bridge St). It's housed in an old Edwardian pumping station, which is currently undergoing a major refit. You'll have to wait until the end of 2009 to see displays like the desk at which Thomas Paine (1737–1809) wrote *Rights of Man* (1791).

Salford Quays

It seems that no 21st-century urban plan is complete without a docklands development; in Manchester's case, the docks are the Salford Quays, west of the city centre along the Ship Canal. Three major attractions draw in the punters, and a shopping centre makes sure they have outlets at which to spend their money. It's a cinch to get here from the city centre via Metrolink (£2); for the Imperial War Museum North and the Lowry, look for the Harbour City stop; get off at Old Trafford for the eponymous stadium.

IMPERIAL WAR MUSEUM NORTH

War museums generally appeal to those with a fascination for military hardware and battle strategy (toy soldiers optional), but Daniel Libeskind's visually stunning **Imperial War Museum North** (☎ 0161-836 4000; www.iwm.org.uk /north; Trafford Wharf Rd; admission free; ☿ 10am-6pm Mar-Oct, 10am-5pm Nov-Feb) takes a radically different approach. War is hell, it tells us, but it's a hell we revisit with tragic regularity.

The exhibits cover the main conflicts of the 20th century through a broad selection of displays, but the really effective bit comes every half-hour when the entire exhibition hall goes dark and one of three 15-minute films *(Children and War, Why War?* or *Weapons of War)* is projected throughout. Visitors are encouraged to walk around the darkened room so as to get the most out of the sensory bombardment.

Although the audiovisuals and displays are quite compelling, the extraordinary aluminium-clad building itself is a huge part of the attraction, and the exhibition spaces are genuinely breathtaking. Libeskind designed three distinct structures (or shards) that represent the three main theatres of war: air, land and sea.

MORE MUSEUMS

If you can't get enough of annotated exhibits, Manchester has a number of other museums worth checking out.

The **Manchester Jewish Museum** (☎ 0161-834 9879; www.manchesterjewishmuseum.com; 190 Cheetham Hill Rd; adult/child £4/3; 🕙 10.30am-4pm Mon-Thu, to 5pm Sun), in a Moorish-style former synagogue, tells the story of the city's Jewish community in fascinating detail, including the story of Polish refugee Michael Marks, who opened his first shop with partner Tom Spencer at 20 Cheetham Hill Rd in 1894. From Piccadilly Gardens, take bus 59, 89, 135 or 167.

Nearby, the wonderful **Museum of Transport** (☎ 0161-205 2122; www.gmts.co.uk; Boyle St, Cheetham Hill; admission £4/2; 🕙 10am-5pm Wed, Sat & Sun Mar-Oct, to 4pm Nov-Feb) is packed with old buses, fire engines and lorries built in the last 100 years.

Beautiful **Chetham's Library & School of Music** (☎ 0161-834 7861; www.chethams.org.uk; Long Millgate; admission free; 🕙 9am-12.30pm & 1.30-4.30pm Mon-Fri), built in 1421, is the city's oldest structure that's still completely intact – and was where Messrs Marx and Engels used to study (by the big bay window in the main reading room). It is only open by prearranged visit, as it is part of a national school for young musicians.

The **Pankhurst Centre** (☎ 0161-273 5673; www.thepankhurstcentre.org.uk; 60-62 Nelson St; admission free; 🕙 10am-4pm Mon-Fri) is the converted childhood home of Emmeline Pankhurst (1858–1928), a leading light of the British suffragette movement. It has displays on her remarkable life and political struggles.

LOWRY

Looking more like a shiny steel ship than an arts centre, the **Lowry** (☎ 0161-876 2020; www.the lowry.com; Pier 8, Salford Quays; 🕙 11am-8pm Tue-Fri, 10am-8pm Sat, 11am-6pm Sun & Mon) is the quays' most notable success. It attracts more than one million visitors a year to its myriad functions, which include everything from art exhibits and performances (see Classical Music, p668) to bars, restaurants and, inevitably, shops. You can even get married in the place.

The complex is home to more than 300 paintings and drawings by northern England's favourite artist, LS Lowry (1887–1976), who was born in nearby Stretford. He became famous for his humanistic depictions of industrial landscapes and northern towns, and gave his name to the complex.

OLD TRAFFORD (MANCHESTER UNITED MUSEUM & TOUR)

Here's a paradox: the world's most famous and supported football club, beloved of fans from Bangkok to Buenos Aires, is the most hated club in England and has a smaller fan base in Manchester than its far less successful cross-town rival, Manchester City (see boxed text, above). United fans snigger and dismiss this as small-minded jealousy, while treating the **Old Trafford stadium** (www.manutd.com; Sir Matt Busby Way; 🕙 9.30am-5pm) like holy ground and the stars who play there like minor deities.

Those stars return the compliment by winning everything – most recently a league and Champions' League double in 2008.

But there's no denying that a visit to the stadium is one of the more memorable things you'll do here. We strongly recommend that you take the **tour** (☎ 0870 442 1994; adult/child £12/8; 🕙 every 10min 9.40am-4.30pm except match days), which includes a seat in the stands, a stop in the changing rooms, a peek at the players' lounge (from which the manager is banned unless invited by the players) and a walk down the tunnel to the pitchside dugout, which is as close to ecstasy as many of the club's fans will ever get. It's pretty impressive stuff. The **museum** (adult/child £8.50/6.75; 🕙 9.30am-5pm), which is part of the tour but can be visited independently, has a comprehensive history of the club, and a state-of-the-art call-up system that means you can view your favourite goals – as well as a holographic 'chat' with Sir Alex Ferguson.

University of Manchester

About a mile south of the city, the University of Manchester is one of England's most extraordinary institutions, and not just because it is a top-class university with a remarkable academic pedigree and a great place to party. It is also home to a world-class museum and a superb art gallery.

THE SKY'S THE LIMIT

Maybe it's the vertiginous spiral staircase, but hardly anyone ever visits the fabulous **Godlee Observatory** (☎ 0161-200 4977; www.manastro.co.uk; fl G, Sackville Bldg, UMIST, Sackville St; admission free; ☾ by appointment only), one of the most interesting places in town. Built in 1902, it is a fully functioning observatory with its original Grubb telescope in place; even the rope and wheels that move the telescope are original. Not only can you glimpse the heavens (if the weather allows), but the views of the city from the balcony are exceptional. It's located at the University of Manchester Institute of Science and Technology (UMIST).

Alternatively, you'll get great views of the city from the Hilton bar atop the city's tallest skyscraper, the Beetham Tower (see Hilton Manchester Deansgate, p663).

MANCHESTER MUSEUM

If you're into natural history and social science, this extraordinary **museum** (☎ 0161-275 2634; www.museum.manchester.ac.uk; University of Manchester, Oxford Rd; admission free; ☾ 10am-5pm Tue-Sat, 11am-4pm Sun & Mon) is the place for you. It has galleries devoted to archaeology, archery, botany, ethnology, geology, numismatics and zoology. The real treat here, though, is the Egyptology section and its collection of mummies. One particularly interesting section is devoted to the work of Dr Richard Neave, who has rebuilt faces of people who have been dead for more than 3000 years; his pioneering techniques are now used in criminal forensics.

Take bus 11, 16, 41 or 42 from Piccadilly Gardens or bus 47, 190 or 191 from Victoria station.

WHITWORTH ART GALLERY

Manchester's second most important **art gallery** (☎ 0161-275 7450; www.whitworth.manchester.ac.uk; University of Manchester, Oxford Rd; admission free; ☾ 10am-5pm Mon-Sat, noon-4pm Sun) has a wonderful collection of British watercolours. It also houses the best selection of historic textiles outside London, and has a number of galleries devoted to the work of artists from Dürer and Rembrandt to Lucien Freud and David Hockney.

All this high art aside, you may find that the most interesting part of the gallery is the group of rooms dedicated to wallpaper – proof that bland pastels and horrible flowery patterns are not the final word in home decoration.

MANCHESTER FOR CHILDREN

Urbis (p658) is always full of kids who find the interactive displays quite engaging, and the **Museum of Science and Industry** (p659) is the perfect all-day destination, offering a host of different activities and exhibits suited to younger visitors. Nearby, the canalside parks and walkways of Castlefield are pleasantly distracting. Manchester United's ground, **Old Trafford** (opposite), is always popular with fans, who are getting younger and younger (kids seem to lose interest in Manchester City when they ask 'but what have they won?'). The **Imperial War Museum North** (p659) is designed to engage the interest of kids barely into double figures, despite its war-based themes not being a bunch of laughs.

If you're looking for some free time away from the kids, **Early Years & Play** (☎ 0161-234 7117; Overseas House, Quay St) is a city-centre crèche.

QUIRKY MANCHESTER

You don't have to work too hard to find oddity in Manchester: spend enough time in Piccadilly Gardens and you'll know what we mean. However, for a different (and altogether fabulous) view of the city, climb to the parapet of the **Godlee Observatory** (see boxed text, above), a place virtually nobody goes to. You can then do some (pretend) stir in the one of the Victorian prison cells of the **Greater Manchester Police Museum** (p659) before trawling through the marvellous collection of eclectic shops in the **Northern Quarter** (p669).

When you're done, you'll have to unwind with a pint in the **Temple of Convenience** (p665), a tiny basement pub with a terrific atmosphere located in...a former public toilet.

TOURS

The tourist office (see Information, p657) sells tickets for all sorts of guided walks, which operate almost daily year round and cost £5/4 per adult/child.

DETOUR: ELIZABETH GASKELL HOUSE

About three miles south of the city centre is **Elizabeth Gaskell House** (☎ 0161-225 1922; www
.elizabethgaskellhouse.org; 84 Plymouth Grove, Ardwick; admission free; ☺ noon-4pm 1st Sun of month Mar-Dec), a
Grade II detached Regency-style villa that was the home of novelist Elizabeth Gaskell, who lived
here from 1850–65 (and whose family continued to live here until 1913). It is a rare property:
besides its unique literary associations (Charlotte Brontë and Charles Dickens were regular visitors), it is one of the few homes in Manchester whose interior has been carefully maintained and
restored to its original elegance. The house has limited opening hours; to get here, take bus 50,
113, 130, 147, 191 or 197 from Piccadilly Gardens, or take the train to Ardwick.

FESTIVALS & EVENTS

Manchester Irish Festival (www.manchesterirish
festival.co.uk) Manchester's huge Irish community goes
bonkers for a week in mid-March.

Manchester International Festival (www.manchester
internationalfestival.com) With its exciting showcasing of
only new, commissioned work, this largely musical biennial
festival (held in July) is already the city's most popular.

Manchester Jazz Festival (www.manchesterjazz.com)
Takes place in 50 venues throughout the city in late July.

Futuresonic (www.futuresonic.com) Superb electronic
music and media arts festival that takes place in various
venues over a week in summer.

Manchester Pride (☎ 0871 230 2624; www.manchester
pride.com) One of England's biggest celebrations of gay,
bisexual and transgender life, held in late August.

Manchester International Film Festival (www
.kinofilm.org.uk) A biennial late-October film festival that
was launched in 2007.

SLEEPING

Although Manchester's beds cater mostly to
the business traveller – who can be trusted
to provide the steadiest flow of business –
the city's reputation as a capital of cool
has seen the standards of style go up, and
Manchester is now awash with all manner
of designer digs. Remember that during the
football season (August to May), rooms can
be almost impossible to find if Manchester
United is playing at home. If you are having
difficulty finding a bed, the tourist office's
accommodation service (£4) can help.

City Centre
BUDGET

Manchester YHA (☎ 0845 371 9647; www.yha.org
.uk; Potato Wharf; dm incl breakfast from £14; ℗ ⌨)
This purpose-built canalside hostel in the
Castlefield area is one of the best in the country. It's a top-class option with four- and six-
bed dorms, all with bathroom, as well as a host
of good facilities.

Hatters (☎ 0161-236 9500; www.hattersgroup.com;
50 Newton St; dm/s/d/tr from £17/28/50/70; ℗ ⌨) The
old-style lift and porcelain sinks are the only
leftovers of this former milliner's factory, now
one of the best hostels in town, with location
to boot – smack in the heart of the Northern
Quarter, you won't have to go far to get the
best of alternative Manchester.

Rembrandt Hotel (☎ 0161-236 1311; www.rem
brandtmanchester.com; 33 Sackville St; s/d/tr from £35/40/45)
Grande dame of the Gay Village; spartan
rooms but a very friendly welcome. Another
good option.

New Union Hotel (☎ 0161-228 1492; www.new
unionhotel.com; 111 Princess St; s/d/tr from £40/50/60) In
the heart of the Gay Village but not exclusively
pink, this terrific little hotel is all about affordable fun – the rooms are functional, but the
karaoke machine downstairs works just fine.
Not recommended for a quiet layover.

MIDRANGE

Ox (☎ 0161-839 7740; www.theox.co.uk; 71 Liverpool Rd;
d/tr from £55/75) Not quite your traditional B&B
(breakfast is extra), but an excellent choice,
nonetheless: nine ox-blood-red rooms with
tidy amenities above a fine gastropub in the
heart of Castlefield. It's the best deal in town
for the location.

Castlefield (☎ 0161-832 7073; www.castlefield-hotel
.co.uk; 3 Liverpool Rd; s/d from £70/99; ℗) This is another successful warehouse conversion that
has resulted in a thoroughly modern business hotel. Overlooking the canal basin, it has
spacious, comfortable rooms and excellent
amenities, including a fitness centre and pool
that are free to guests.

Palace Hotel (☎ 0161-288 1111; www.principal-hotels
.com; Oxford St; r from £80) An elegant refurbishment of one of Manchester's most magnificent
Victorian palaces resulted in a special boutique
hotel, combining the grandeur of the public
areas with the modern look of the bedrooms.

Abode (☎ 0161-247 7744; www.abodehotels.co.uk; 107 Piccadilly St; r from £80; ☐) Modern British style is the catchphrase at this converted textile factory. The original fittings have been combined successfully with 61 spanking-new bedrooms divided into four categories of ever-increasing luxury: Comfortable, Desirable, Enviable and Fabulous, the latter being five seriously swanky top-floor suites. Vi-Spring beds, Monsoon showers, LCD-screen TVs and stacks of Aqua Sulis toiletries are standard throughout. In the basement, star chef Michael Caines has a champagne and cocktail bar adjacent to his very own restaurant.

Radisson Edwardian (☎ 0161-835 9929; www.radisson edwardian.com/manchester; Peter St; r from £110; **P**) The Free Trade Hall saw it all, from Emmeline Pankhurst's suffragette campaign to the Sex Pistols' legendary 1976 gig. Today, those rabble-rousing noisemakers wouldn't be allowed to set foot in the door of what is now a sumptuous five-star hotel, all minimalist Zen and luxury. Unless, of course, they were *famous* rabble-rousing noisemakers, and then they would probably be headed straight for one of the four penthouse suites, one of which is named after Bob Dylan, who went electric at the Free Trade Hall in 1965.

Other options worth considering:

Jury's Inn (☎ 0161-953 8888; www.jurysdoyle.com; 56 Great Bridgewater St; r from £55) Comfortable Irish chain hotel a few doors down from the Bridgewater Hall.

Premier Travel Inn (☎ 0870 990 6444; www .premiertravelinn.com; r from £65) G-Max (Bishopsgate, 11 Lower Mosley St); Portland St (The Circus, 112 Portland St) Two convenient city-centre locations for this tidy chain.

Midland (☎ 0161-236 3333; www.themidland.co.uk; Peter St; r from £104; ☐) Mr Rolls and Mr Royce sealed the deal in the elegant lobby of this fancy business hotel.

TOP END

Hilton Manchester Deansgate (☎ 0161-870 1600; www .hilton.co.uk; 303 Deansgate; r from £114) A no-surprises Hilton occupying the lower 23 floors of the city's newest – and tallest – landmark, the Beetham Tower.

ourpick **Yang Sing Oriental Hotel** (☎ 0161-920 9651; www.yangsingoriental.com; 36 Princess St; r/ste from £179/239; ☐) The city's most famous Chinese restaurant (see p664) got into the hospitality business in 2008 with arguably the northwest's most luxurious small hotel. Japanese silk duvets and pillows; beautiful bespoke Asian furnishings; a complimentary minibar; and your choice of five separate room aromas (which

you can select when booking) – just some of the extravagant offerings at this exquisitely elegant new hotel, which has already raised the hospitality bar by several notches.

Great John Street Hotel (☎ 0161-831 3211; www .greatjohnstreet.co.uk; Great John St; r £235-395; ☐) Elegant, designer luxury? Present. Fabulous rooms with all the usual delights (Egyptian cotton sheets, fabulous toiletries, free-standing baths and lots of high-tech electronics)? Present. A butler to run your bath in the Opus Grand Suite? Present. This former schoolhouse (ah, now you get it) is small and sumptuous – and just across the street from Granada TV studios. A rare treat: the rooftop garden has a hot tub and views of the *Coronation Street* set. Now that's something you don't see every day.

Salford Quays
MIDRANGE

Old Trafford Lodge (☎ 0161-874 3333; www.lccc.co.uk; Talbot Rd; d Mon-Fri £64, d Sat & Sun £54; ☐) Cricket fans will salivate at the thought of watching a first-class match from the comfort of their bedroom balcony; for the rest of us, this is a pretty good business hotel with decent amenities.

TOP END

Lowry (☎ 0161-827 4000; www.rfhotels.com; 50 Dearman's Pl, Chapel Wharf; s/d from £350/385) Simply dripping with designer luxury and five-star comfort, Manchester's top hotel has fabulous rooms with enormous beds, ergonomically designed furniture, walk-in wardrobes, and bathrooms finished with Italian porcelain tiles and glass mosaic. You can soothe yourself with a skin-brightening treatment or an aromatherapy head-massage at the health spa.

Other Areas
BUDGET

Manchester Backpackers' Hostel (☎ 0161-865 9296; 64 Cromwell Rd; dm £15) A very pleasant private hostel in Stretford, 2 miles south of the city centre, with cooking facilities, a TV lounge and some doubles. It's a cinch to get to from the city centre via Metrolink (Stretford stop).

TOP END

Eleven Didsbury Park (☎ 0161-448 7711; www.eleven didsburypark.com; 11 Didsbury Pk, Didsbury; r £140-260) Tucked away in fashionably bohemian Didsbury, this utterly wonderful boutique hotel (part of the Eclectic group) is as romantic and stylish a place as you'll find in the city. Avoid, if you can, the smaller doubles. Although it's about 5 miles south of the city centre, it's easily reached by train from Piccadilly (to East Didsbury station).

EATING

Only London can outdo Manchester for the choice of cafes and restaurants. There's something for every palate, from the ubiquitous-but-excellent selections in Chinatown to Wilmslow Rd (the extension of Oxford St/Rd), aka the Curry Mile, with its unsurpassed concentration of Indian and Pakistani eateries. Organic is the order of the day throughout the Northern Quarter (where you'll also find some excellent vegie spots), while the city's fanciest fare is to be found in the suburbs, especially West Didsbury. Following is but a small starter course.

Budget

Trof (☎ 0161-832 1870; 5-8 Thomas St; sandwiches £4, mains around £8; ☷ 9.30am-midnight) Great music, top staff and a fab selection of sandwiches, roasts and other dishes (the huge breakfast is a proper hangover cure), as well as a broad selection of beers and tunes (Tuesday night is acoustic night), have made this new opening a firm favourite with students.

Eighth Day (☎ 0161-273 4878; 111 Oxford Rd; mains around £5; ☷ 9.30am-5pm Mon-Sat) New and most definitely improved after a major clean-up, this environmentally friendly hang-out is a favourite with students. It sells everything to make you feel good about your place in the world, from fair-trade teas to homeopathic remedies. The vegetarian- and vegan-friendly menu is substantial.

Earth Cafe (☎ 0161-834 1996; www.earthcafe.co.uk; 16-20 Turner St; chef's special £5.80; ☷ 10am-5pm Tue-Sat) Below the Manchester Buddhist Centre, this gourmet vegetarian cafe is working hard at becoming the first 100% organic spot in town. The chef's special – a main dish, side and two salad portions – is generally excellent and always filling.

Love Saves the Day (☎ 0161-832 0777; Tib St; lunch £6; ☷ 8am-7pm Mon-Wed, to 9pm Thu, to 8pm Fri, 10-6pm Sat, 10am-4pm Sun) The Northern Quarter's most popular cafe is a New York–style deli, small supermarket and sit-down eatery in one large, airy room. Everybody comes here – from crusties to corporate types – to sit around over a spot of lunch and discuss the day's goings-on. A wonderful spot. The house salad is £5.50.

Midrange

Al Bilal (☎ 0161-257 0006; 87-81 Wilmslow Rd; mains £7-14; ☷ lunch & dinner Sun-Fri) It's a given that you cannot leave Manchester without tucking into a curry along Wilmslow Rd, which is as famous as Bradford or Birmingham for its Indian cuisine. There are so many great restaurants to pick from – and some pretty awful ones, too – but Al Bilal will treat you and your tummy just right with its excellent dishes.

Yang Sing (☎ 0161-236 2200; 34 Princess St; mains £9-16; ☷ lunch & dinner) A serious contender for best Chinese restaurant in England, Yang Sing attracts diners from all over with its exceptional Cantonese cuisine. From a dim-sum lunch to a full evening banquet, the food is superb, and the waiters will patiently explain the intricacies of each item to punters who can barely pronounce the dishes' names.

Brasserie Blanc (☎ 0161-832 1000; www.brasserieblanc.com; 55 King St; mains £9-17; ☷ lunch & dinner Mon-Sat) Top chef Raymond Blanc brings his winning formula of French cuisine with world influences (Asian primarily, but lots of English touches) to Manchester with some style and plenty of success. The dining room is elegant enough - crisp, white linen on the tables and fancy art work on the walls - but the atmosphere is hardly stuffy: everyone comes to eat well and have fun doing it.

Bluu (☎ 0161-839 7740; www.bluu.co.uk; Unit 1, Smithfield Market, Thomas St; 3-course lunch £15, dinner mains £10-15; ☷ lunch & dinner) It's a chain cafe-bar, but Manchester's version has retained its kudos thanks to its location, look and clientele – a steady stream of hipsters who appreciate its aforementioned strengths and menu, which offers an inventive choice of British and Continental dishes using only the freshest ingredients.

Market Restaurant (☎ 0161-834 3743; www.market-restaurant.com; 104 High St; mains £11-16; ☷ lunch & dinner Wed-Fri, dinner Sat) It's a sorry-looking kind of place, but don't judge a restaurant by its shabby exterior: inside you'll find excellent British cuisine on a menu that changes monthly to take account of the season's best.

our pick **Modern** (☎ 0161-605 8282; Urbis, Cathedral Gardens, Corporation Street; 2-/3-course lunch £13/16, dinner mains £11-21; ☷ lunch & dinner) Top fare on top of the world, or an excellent meal atop Manchester's most distinctive landmark, Urbis, is one of the city's most enjoyable dining experiences. The food – mostly new British cuisine – will not disappoint, but being

---

EATING IN THE 'BURBS

If you want some truly fine meals, you'll need to venture out to the suburbs, where you'll be in good company. Top of the heap is the Michelin-starred **Juniper** (☎ 0161-929 4008; www.juniper-restaurant .co.uk; 21 The Downs, Altrincham; dinner around £30; ☺ lunch & dinner Fri & Sat, dinner Tue-Thu; ☒ Metrolink to Altrincham), but you'll also eat very well on one gourmet street (Lapwing Lane) in West Didsbury, home to French-influenced **Lime Tree** (☎ 0161-445 1217; www.thelimetreerestaurant.co.uk; 8 Lapwing Lane, West Didsbury; mains £14-20; ☺ lunch & dinner Tue-Fri & Sun, dinner Mon & Sat; ☒ East Didsbury); high-end gastropub **Metropolitan** (☎ 0161-374 9559; www.the-metropolitan.co.uk; 2 Lapwing Lane, West Didsbury; mains around £15; ☺ lunch & dinner; ☒ East Didsbury); and vegie **Greens** (☎ 0161-434 4259; 8 Lapwing Lane, West Didsbury; mains around £15; ☺ lunch & dinner Tue-Sun, dinner Mon; ☒ East Didsbury).

---

able to sit at a table close to the floor-to-ceiling windows make this place worthwhile.

Ithaca (☎ 0870 740 4000; www.ithacamanchester .com; 36 John Dalton St; mains £12-20; ☺ lunch & dinner) A new Asian experience spread over four floors, you'll find well-made Japanese (including excellent sushi) on the first two floors, and a Bangkok-style cocktail lounge on the 3rd floor, with an eye-catching solid, black-glass oval bar. The top floor is a members' club.

DRINKING

There's every kind of drinking hole in Manchester, from the really grungy ones that smell but have plenty of character to the ones that were designed by a team of architects but have the atmosphere of a freezer. Every neighbourhood in town has its favourites; here's a few to get you going.

Bars

A Place Called Common (☎ 0161-832 9245; www .aplacecalledcommon.co.uk; 39-41 Edge St; ☺ noon-midnight Mon-Wed, to 1am Thu, to 2am Fri & Sat, 2pm-midnight Sun) Common by name but great by nature, this is a terrific boozer favoured by an unpretentious crowd who like the changing artwork on the walls and the DJs who play nightly.

Bar Centro (☎ 0161-835 2863; 72-74 Tib St; mains £6-9; ☺ noon-midnight Mon-Wed, to 1am Thu, to 2am Fri & Sat, 2pm-midnight Sun) A Northern Quarter stalwart, very popular with the bohemian crowd precisely because it doesn't try to be. Great beer, nice staff and a better-than-average bar menu make this one of the choice spots in the area.

Bluu (☎ 0161-839 7740; www.bluu.co.uk; Unit 1, Smithfield Market, Thomas St; ☺ noon-midnight Sun-Mon, to 1am Tue-Thu, to 2am Fri & Sat) Our favourite of the Northern Quarter's collection of great bars. Bluu is cool, comfortable and comes with a great terrace on which to enjoy a pint and listen to music selected by folks with really good taste.

Dry Bar (☎ 0161-236 9840; 28-30 Oldham Rd; ☺ noon-midnight Mon-Wed, noon-2am Thu-Sat, 6pm-midnight Sun) The former HQ of Madchester's maddest protagonists (legend has it Shaun Ryder once pulled a gun on Tony Wilson here), Dry has remained cool long after the scene froze over, and it's still one of the best bars in the Northern Quarter.

Odd (☎ 0161-833 0070; www.oddbar.co.uk; 30-32 Thomas St; ☺ 11am-11pm Mon-Sat, to 10.30pm Sun) This eclectic little bar – with its oddball furnishings, wacky tunes and anti-establishment crew of customers – is the perfect antidote to the increasingly similar look of so many modern bars. A slice of Mancuniana to be treasured.

Temple of Convenience (☎ 0161-288 9834; Great Bridgewater St; ☺ noon-midnight Mon-Thu, to 1am Fri & Sat, noon-11pm Sun) This tiny basement bar with a capacity of about 30 has a great jukebox and a fine selection of spirits, all crammed into a converted public toilet. Hardly your bog-standard pub.

Pubs

ourpick **Britons Protection** (☎ 0161-236 5895; 50 Great Bridgewater St; mains around £7) Whisky – 200 different kinds of it – is the beverage of choice at

---

TOP FIVE PUBS FOR PINT IN THE NORTHWEST

- Philharmonic (p686; Liverpool)
- Temple of Convenience (above; Manchester)
- Britons Protection (above; Manchester)
- Albion (p674; Chester)
- Baby Cream (p686; Liverpool)

this liver-threatening, proper English pub that also does Tudor-style meals (boar, venison and the like). An old-fashioned boozer; no fancy stuff.

Dukes 92 (☎ 0161-839 8646; 2 Castle St) Castlefield's best pub, housed in converted stables that once belonged to the duke of Bridgewater, has comfy, deep sofas inside and plenty of seating outside, overlooking lock 92 of the Rochdale Canal – hence the name. If it's sunny, there's no better spot to enjoy a pint of ale.

Lass O'Gowrie (☎ 0161-273 6932; 36 Charles St; mains around £6) A Victorian classic off Princess St that brews its own beer in the basement. It's a favourite with students, old-timers and a clique of BBC employees who work just across the street in the Beeb's Manchester HQ. It also does good-value bar meals.

Other decent boozers:

Mr Thomas' Chop House (☎ 0161-832 2245; 52 Cross St; mains around £10) An old-style boozer that is very popular for a pint as well as for food.

Old Wellington Inn (☎ 0161-830 1440; 4 Cathedral Gates) One of the oldest buildings in the city and a lovely spot for a pint of genuine ale.

Peveril of the Peak (☎ 0161-236 6364; 127 Great Bridgewater St) An unpretentious pub with wonderful Victorian glazed tilework outside.

ENTERTAINMENT
Nightclubs

A handy tip: if you want to thrive in Manchester's excellent nightlife, drop all mention of Madchester (see boxed text, opposite) and keep talk of being 'up for it' to strict irony. Otherwise, you'll risk being labelled a saddo nostalgic or, worse, someone who should have gone home and grown up a decade ago. But fear not: there is still a terrific club scene and Manchester remains at the vanguard of dance-floor culture. There's a constantly changing mixture of club nights, so check the *Manchester Evening News* for details of what's on. Following are our favourite places.

Music Box (☎ 0161-236 9971; www.musicbox manchester.com; 65 Oxford St; admission £6-12; ☺ 8pm-midnight Wed & Thu, 10pm-3am Fri & Sat) Deep in Jilly's Rockworld complex you'll find our favourite club in town and – judging by the queues – almost everyone else's, too. The punters come for the superb monthly club nights, such as Mr Scruff's Keep It Unreal, as well a host of terrific one-offs.

Attic (☎ 0161-236 6071; www.thirstyscholar.co.uk; New Wakefield St; admission free; ☺ 11pm-2am Thu & Fri, to 3am Sat) This superb venue is at the top of a flight of stairs, in a building beneath a railway arch. Northern Soul nights share space with techno, alt grunge and live music nights. A student favourite and a great night out.

Sankey's (☎ 0161-950 4201; www.sankeys.info; Radium St, Ancoats; admission free-£12; ☺ 10pm-3am Thu & Fri, 10pm-4am Sat) With regulars like Danny Tenaglia, Sasha, and Layo & Bushwacka in the box, hard-core clubbers are in good hands when they trek out to the middle of Ancoats. Techno, breakbeats, tribal and progressive house.

South (☎ 0161-831 7756; www.south-club.co.uk; 4A South King St; admission £5-8; ☺ 10pm-3am Fri & Sat) An excellent basement club to kick off the weekend: Friday night is Rock 'n' Roll Bar, featuring everything from Ibrahim Ferrer to Northern Soul, and Saturday is Disco Rescue, which is more of the same eclectic mix of alternative and dance.

Cinemas

Cornerhouse (☎ 0161-228 2463; www.cornerhouse.org; 70 Oxford St) Your only destination for good art-house releases; also has a gallery, bookshop and cafe.

Odeon Cinema (☎ 0870 224 4007; www.odeon .co.uk; The Printworks, Exchange Sq) An ultramodern 20-screen complex in the middle of the Printworks centre.

AMC Cinemas (☎ 0161-817 3000; www.amccinemas .co.uk; The Great Northern, 235 Deansgate) A new 16-screen multiplex in a retail centre that was formerly a goods warehouse for the Northern Railway Company.

Theatre

Green Room (☎ 0161-236 1677; 54 Whitworth St W) The premiere fringe venue in town.

Manchester Opera House (☎ 0161-242 2509; www .manchestertheatres.co.uk; Quay St) West End shows and lavish musicals make up the bulk of the program.

Library Theatre (☎ 0161-236 7110; Central Library, St Peter's Sq) Old plays and new work in a small theatre beneath the Central Library.

Royal Exchange (☎ 0161-833 9833; St Anne's Sq) Interesting contemporary plays are standard at this magnificent, modern theatre-in-the-round.

Live Music
ROCK MUSIC

Band on the Wall (☎ 0161-834 1786; www.bandon thewall.org; 25 Swan St) A top-notch venue that

THE MADCHESTER SOUND

It is often claimed that Manchester is the engine room of British pop. If this is indeed the case, then the chief engineer was TV presenter and music impresario Tony Wilson (1950–2007), founder of Factory Records. This is the label that in 1983 released New Order's ground-breaking 'Blue Monday', to this day the best-selling 12" in British history, which successfully fused the guitar-driven sound of punk with a pulsating dance beat.

When the money started pouring in, Wilson took the next, all-important step: he opened his own nightclub that would provide a platform for local bands to perform. The Haçienda opened its doors with plenty of fanfare but just wouldn't take off. Things started to turn around when the club embraced a brand new sound coming out of Chicago and Detroit: house. DJs Mike Pickering, Graeme Park and Jon Da Silva were the music's most important apostles, and when ecstasy hit the scene late in the decade, it seemed that every kid in town was 'mad for it'.

Heavily influenced by these new arrivals, the city's guitar bands took notice and began shaping their sounds to suit the clubbers' needs. The most successful was the Stone Roses, who in 1989 released 'Fools Gold', a pulsating hit with the rapid shuffle of James Brown's 'Funky Drummer' and a druggie guitar sound that drove dancers wild. Around the same time, Happy Mondays, fronted by the laddish Shaun Ryder and the wacked-out Bez (whose only job was to lead the dancing from the stage), hit the scene with the infectious 'Hallelujah'. The other big anthems of the day were 'The One I Love' by the Charlatans, 'Voodoo Ray' by A Guy Called Gerald, and 'Pacific' by 808 State – all local bands and producers. The party known as Madchester was officially opened.

The party ended in 1992. Overdanced and overdrugged, the city woke up with a terrible hangover. The Haçienda went bust, Shaun Ryder's legendary drug intake stymied his musical creativity and the Stone Roses withdrew in a haze of postparty depression. The latter were not to be heard of again until 1994 when they released *Second Coming*, which just couldn't match their eponymous debut album. They lasted another two years before breaking up. The fertile crossover scene, which had seen clubbers go mad at rock gigs, and rock bands play the kind of dance sounds that kept the floor thumping until the early hours, virtually disappeared and the two genres withdrew into a more familiar isolation.

The next five years saw the rise of Manchester's most successful band, Oasis, whose *(What's the Story) Morning Glory* hit the shelves in 1995, selling more copies than all of the Manchester bands that preceded them. Despite their success and the in-your-face posturing of the Gallagher brothers, they were doomed to a limited run because they relied too much on the chord structures and infectious melodic lines created by the Beatles 25 years earlier. They're still going, but their one-time claim of being the most famous band in the world is sadly out of date.

Today, there is no such thing as Madchester. Eager to transcend the clichés that their success engendered, most of the city's musical talents refuse to be labelled as having any particular sound: jazzy house giant Mr Scruff (whose excellent Keep It Unreal nights are yours for the dancing at Music Box; see opposite), for instance, doesn't sound anything like the folksy guitar style of About a Boy or the funky hip-hop beats of Rae & Christian.

Madchester is legendary precisely because it is no more, but it was a lot of fun. If you missed the party, you can get a terrific sense of what it was like by watching Michael Winterbottom's *24-Hour Party People* (2002), which captures the hedonism, extravagance and genius of Madchester's cast of characters, particularly Tony Wilson, played with uncanny accuracy by Steve Coogan.

---

hosts everything from rock to world music, with splashes of jazz, blues and folk thrown in for good measure.

Manchester Central (☎ 0161-834 2700; www.manchestercentral.co.uk; Windmill St) A midsized venue southwest of St Peter's Sq, hosting rock concerts by not-quite-supersuccessful bands as well as exhibitions and indoor sporting events.

MEN Arena (☎ 0161-950 5000; Great Ducie St) A giant arena north of the centre that hosts large-scale rock concerts (as well as being the home of the city's ice-hockey and basketball teams).

Moho Live (☎ 0161-834 8188; www.moholive.com; 21-31 Oldham St) A new 500-capacity live music venue that has already proven incredibly popular with its line-up of live music and club nights.

THE NORTHWEST

GAY & LESBIAN MANCHESTER

The city's gay scene is unrivalled outside London, and caters to every taste. Its healthy heart beats loudest in the Gay Village, centred on handsome Canal St. Here you'll find bars, clubs, restaurants and – crucially – karaoke joints that cater almost exclusively to the pink pound.

The country's biggest gay and lesbian arts festival, **Queer Up North** (☎ 0161-833 2288; www .queerupnorth.com), takes place every two years – the next in spring 2009. **Manchester Pride** (☎ 0161- 236 7474; www.manchesterpride.com) is a 10-day festival in the middle of August each year and attracts over 500,000 people.

There are bars to suit every taste, but you won't go far wrong in **AXM** (☎ 0161-236 6005; www .axm-bar.co.uk; 10 Canal St), which is more of a cocktail lounge for the city's flash crowd; or **Taurus** (☎ 0161-236 4593; www.taurus-bar.co.uk; 1 Canal St), which is a little shabbier but equally good fun.

For your clubbing needs, look no further than **Club Alter Ego** (☎ 0161-236 9266; www.club alterego.co.uk; 105-107 Princess St; admission £5-9; ☯ 11pm-5am Thu-Sat), home to the fabulous Poptastic, and **Essential Nightclub** (☎ 0161-236 0077; www.essentialmanchester.com; 8 Minshull St; admission £5-9; ☯ 11pm-5am Thu-Sat), which is just as popular.

And then there's karaoke, the ultimate choice for midweek fun. The best of the lot is at the **New Union Hotel** (☎ 0161-228 1492; www.newunionhotel.com; 111 Princess St; ☯ 9pm-2am), where you can find your inner Madonna and Cyndi Lauper every Tuesday and Thursday – for a top prize of £50.

For more information, check with the **Manchester Gay Centre** (☎ 0161-274 3814; Sydney St, Salford) and the **Lesbian & Gay Foundation** (☎ 0161-235 8035; www.lgf.org.uk; 105-107 Princess St; ☯ 4-10pm). The city's best pink website is www.visitgaymanchester.co.uk.

Ruby Lounge (☎ 0161-834 1392; 26-28 High St) Terrific new live music venue in the Northern Quarter that features mostly rock bands.

CLASSICAL MUSIC

Bridgewater Hall (☎ 0161-907 9000; www.bridgewater -hall.co.uk; Lower Mosley St) The world-renowned Hallé Orchestra has its home at this enormous and impressive concert hall, which hosts up to 250 concerts and events a year. It has a widespread program that includes opera, folk music, children's shows, comedy and contemporary music.

Lowry (☎ 0161-876 2000; www.thelowry.com; Pier 8, Salford Quays) The Lowry has two theatres – the 1750-capacity Lyric and 460-capacity Quays – hosting a diverse range of performances, from dance to comedy.

Manchester Cathedral (☎ 0161-833 2220; Victoria St) Hosts a summer season of concerts by the Cantata Choir and ensemble groups.

Royal Northern College of Music (☎ 0161-907 5555; www.rncm.ac.uk; 124 Oxford Rd) Presents a full program of extremely high-quality classical music and other contemporary offerings.

Sport

For most people, Manchester plus sport equals football, and football means Manchester United. That may be true for outsiders (which is why United is covered in the Sights & Activities section, p660), but not for most Mancunians. Like all good northerners, they're more comfortable supporting the scrappy underdog with the huge heart, rather than the well-oiled football machine.

MANCHESTER CITY

Manchester's best-loved team is the perennial underachiever, Manchester City. But following a short-lived ownership by Thailand's ex-PM Thaksin Shinawatra, the club was bought by an Abu Dhabi-based investment group whose stated aim is to make the club the biggest in the world. City fans reeled at the news; some even allowed themselves to believe when Brazilian magician Robinho was snatched from mighty Chelsea's waiting

---

TOP FIVE MANCHESTER ALBUMS

- *Some Friendly* Charlatans
- *Pills 'n' Thrills & Bellyaches* Happy Mondays
- *Stone Roses* The Stone Roses
- *Strangeways Here We Come* The Smiths
- *Permanent* Joy Division

THE NORTHWEST

hands for a paltry £32.5 million. Although it's too soon to tell, these could be interesting times at the **Manchester City Experience** (☎ 0870 062 1894; www.mcfc.co.uk; tours adult/child £9.50/6; ☼ tours 10.30am, 2pm & 3.15pm Mon-Sat, 11.45am & 1.45pm Sun except match days) – a tour of the ground, dressing rooms and museum before the inevitable steer into the kit shop. Tours must be booked in advance. Take bus 216, 217, 230, X36 or X37 from Piccadilly Gardens.

LANCASHIRE COUNTY CRICKET CLUB

Cricket is a big deal here, and the **Lancashire club** (☎ 0161-282 4000; Warwick Rd), founded in 1816 as the Aurora before changing its name in 1864, is one of the most beloved of England's county teams. This is despite the fact that it hasn't won the county championship since 1930. The really big match in Lancashire's calendar is the Roses match against Yorkshire, but if you're not around for that, the other games in the county season (admission £11 to £17) are a great day out. The season runs throughout the summer.

International test matches, recently starring local hero Andrew 'Freddie' Flintoff, are also played here occasionally.

SHOPPING

The huge selection of shops here will send a shopper's pulse into orbit; every taste and budget is catered for. By the time you read this, the new Spinningfields retail centre on Deansgate will have opened, and the city will have yet *another* convenient, enclosed space for you to part with your money.

Millennium Quarter

The area around New Cathedral St, Exchange Sq and the impressive Triangle shopping arcade is the hot new shopping district, full of chichi boutiques and the king of all department stores, **Harvey Nichols** (☎ 0161-828 8888; 21 New Cathedral St).

Northern Quarter

Rag-trade wholesalers have given way to independent retailers stocking all manner of hip urban wear, retro fashions and other left-of-centre threads. Of the myriad shops, we like **Oi Polloi** (☎ 0161-831 7870; 70 Tib St), which specialises in trendy outdoor clothing and footwear; and the marvellous **Oxfam Original** (☎ 0161-839 3160; Unit 8, Smithfield Bldg, Oldham St), which has terrific retro gear from the 1960s and '70s.

West End

Everything needs a catchy name, so the traditionally upmarket shopping area around St Anne's Sq, King St and Bridge St – full of attractive boutiques for designers, both homegrown and international – is now called the West End.

GETTING THERE & AWAY
Air

Manchester Airport (☎ 0161-489 3000; www.manchester airport.co.uk), south of the city, is the largest airport outside London and is served by 17 locations throughout Britain.

Bus

National Express (☎ 08717 81 81 81; www.nationalexpress .com) serves most major cities almost hourly from Chorlton St coach station in the city centre. Destinations include Liverpool (£5, 1¼ hours, hourly), Leeds (£7.60, one hour, hourly) and London (£23, 3¾ hours, hourly).

Train

Manchester Piccadilly (east of the Gay Village) is the main station for trains to and from the rest of the country, although Victoria station (north of Urbis) serves Halifax and Bradford. The two stations are linked by Metrolink. Trains head to Blackpool (£12.20, 1¼ hours, half-hourly), Liverpool Lime St (£8.80, 45 minutes, half-hourly), Newcastle (£41.20, three hours, six daily) and London (£115, three hours, seven daily).

GETTING AROUND
To/From the Airport

The airport is 12 miles south of the city. A train to or from Victoria station costs £3.80, and a coach is £3.20. A taxi is nearly four times as much in light traffic.

Public Transport

The excellent public transport system can be used with a variety of **Day saver tickets** (bus £3, bus & train £3.80, bus & Metrolink £4.50, train & Metrolink £5, bus, train & Metrolink £6). For inquiries about local transport, including night buses, contact **Travelshop** (☎ 0161-228 7811; www.gmpte.com; 9 Portland St, Piccadilly Gardens; ☼ 8am-8pm).

BUS

Centreline bus 4 provides a free service around the heart of Manchester every 10 minutes. Pick up a route map from the tourist office. Most local buses start from Piccadilly Gardens.

METROLINK

There are frequent **Metrolink** (☎ 0161-205 2000; www.metrolink.co.uk) trams between Victoria and Piccadilly train stations and G-Mex (for Castlefield) as well as further afield to Salford Quays. Buy your tickets from the platform machine.

TRAIN

Castlefield is served by Deansgate station with rail links to Piccadilly, Oxford Rd and Salford stations.

CHESHIRE

Quiet and genteel, pastoral Cheshire is a very black-and-white kind of place, full of half-timbered Tudor farmhouses (surrounded by fields populated by Friesian cows) that are more than just a little reminiscent of ye olde England. Which is exactly why so many of the soccerati millionaires plying their overpaid trades in nearby Manchester and Liverpool choose to live here, usually in OTT mansions carefully guarded by tall security gates (nothing gives the illusion of good taste like a bit of bling and tradition). For the rest of us mere mortals, however, Cheshire is really just about Chester.

CHESTER
pop 80,130

Marvellous Chester is one of English history's greatest gifts to the contemporary visitor. Its red-sandstone wall, which today gift-wraps a tidy collection of Tudor and Victorian buildings, was built during Roman times. The town was then called Castra Devana, and was the largest Roman fortress in Britain.

It's hard to believe today, but throughout the Middle Ages Chester made its money as the most important port in the northwest. However, the River Dee silted up over time and Chester fell behind Liverpool in importance.

Besides its obvious elegance and grace, Chester ekes out a fairly substantial living as a major retail centre and tourist hot spot: visitors come, see and shop.

Orientation

Most places of interest are inside the walls where the Roman street pattern is relatively intact. From the Cross (the stone pillar that marks the town centre), four roads fan out to the four principal gates.

Information

Cheshire Constabulary (☎ 01244-350000; Town Hall, Northgate St)
Chester Visitors' Centre (☎ 01244-351609; www .visitchester.com; Vicar's Lane; ☽ 9.30am-5.30pm Mon-Sat & 10am-4pm Sun May-Oct, 10am-5pm Mon-Sat Nov-Apr)
Countess of Chester Hospital (☎ 01244-365000; Health Park, Liverpool Rd)
Post office (2 St John St; ☽ 9am-5.30pm Mon-Sat)
Tourist office (☎ 01244-402111; www.chester.gov.uk; Town Hall, Northgate St; ☽ 9am-5.30pm Mon-Sat & 10am-4pm Sun May-Oct, 10am-5pm Mon-Sat Nov-Apr)

Sights & Activities
CITY WALLS

A good way to get a sense of Chester's unique character is to walk the 2-mile circuit along the walls that surround the historic centre. Originally built by the Romans around AD 70, the walls were altered substantially over the following centuries but have retained their current position since around 1200. The tourist office's *Walk Around Chester Walls* leaflet (£2) is an excellent guide.

Of the many features along the walls, the most eye-catching is the prominent **Eastgate**, where you can see the most famous **clock** in England after London's Big Ben, built for Queen Victoria's Diamond Jubilee in 1897.

At the southeastern corner of the walls are the **wishing steps**, added in 1785; local legend claims that if you can run up and down these uneven steps while holding your breath your wish will come true. We question the veracity of this claim because our wish was not to twist an ankle.

Just inside Southgate, known here as **Bridgegate** (as it's at the northern end of the Old Dee Bridge), is the 1664 **Bear & Billet** pub, Chester's oldest timber-framed building and once a tollgate into the city.

ROWS

Chester's other great draw is the **Rows**, a series of two-level galleried arcades along the four streets that fan out in each direction from the central Cross. The architecture is a handsome mix of Victorian and Tudor (original

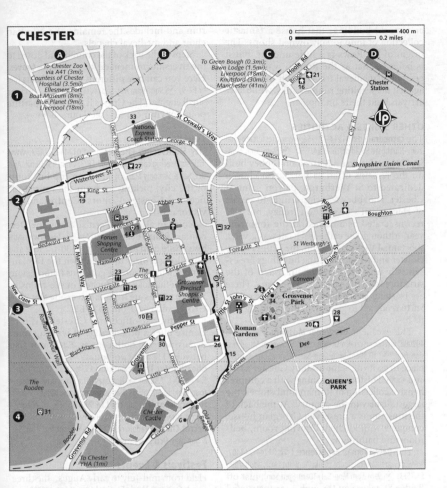

CHESTER

and mock) buildings that house a fantastic collection of individually owned shops. The origin of the Rows is a little unclear, but it is believed that as the Roman walls slowly crumbled, medieval traders built their shops against the resulting rubble banks, while later arrivals built theirs on top.

OTHER SIGHTS & ACTIVITIES

The **cathedral** (☎ 01244-324756; www.chestercathedral .com; Northgate St; adult/child £4/1.50; ☺ 9am-5pm Mon-Sat, 12.30-5pm Sun) was a Benedictine abbey built on the remains of an earlier Saxon church dedicated to St Werburgh, patron saint of Chester. The abbey was closed in 1540 as part of Henry VIII's dissolution frenzy, but was reconsecrated as a cathedral the following year. Although the cathedral itself was given a substantial Victorian facelift, the 12th-century cloister and its surrounding buildings are essentially unaltered and retain much of the structure from the early monastic years. There are 1¼-hour **guided tours** (free; ☺ 9.30am-4pm Mon-Sat) to really get to grips with the building and its history.

The excellent **Grosvenor Museum** (☎ 01244-402008; www.grosvenormuseum.co.uk; Grosvenor St; admission free; ☺ 10.30am-5pm Mon-Sat, 2-5pm Sun) is the place to go if you want to study Chester's rich and varied history, beginning with a comprehensive collection of Roman tombstones, the largest display in the country. At the back of the museum is a preserved Georgian house, complete with kitchen, drawing room, bedroom and bathroom.

The **Dewa Roman Experience** (☎ 01244-343407; www.dewaromanexperience.co.uk; Pierpoint Lane; adult/child £4.75/3; ☺ 9am-5pm Mon-Sat, 10am-5pm Sun), just off Bridge St, takes you through a reconstructed Roman street to reveal what Roman life was like.

Chester's most complete set of genuine Roman remains is opposite the visitors centre, outside the city walls. Here you'll find what's left of the **Roman amphitheatre** (admission free); once an arena that seated 7000 spectators (making it the country's largest), now it's little more than steps buried in grass.

Adjacent to the amphitheatre is **St John the Baptist Church** (Vicar's Lane; ☺ 9.15am-6pm), built on the site of an older Saxon church in 1075. It started out as a cathedral of Mercia before being rebuilt by the Normans. The eastern end of the church, abandoned in 1581 when St John's became a parish, now lies in peaceful

ruin and includes the remains of a Norman choir and medieval chapels.

Steps at the back of the church lead down to the riverside promenade known as the **Groves**. Here you can hire different kinds of **boats** (per hr £7-9; ☺ 9am-6pm Apr-Sep) with pedals, oars or small engines. The Groves is also the departure point for river cruises (see Tours, below).

Tours

City Sightseeing Chester (☎ 01244-347452; www .city-sightseeing.com; adult/child £8/3; every 15-30min Apr-Oct, Sat & Sun only Mar) offers open-top bus tours of the city, picking up from the tourist office and Chester Visitors' Centre and the visitor centre.

You can also take a cruise along the Dee; contact **Bithell Boats** (☎ 01244-325394; www.show boatsofchester.co.uk) for details of its 30-minute and hour-long cruises up and down the Dee, including a foray into the gorgeous Eaton Estate, home of the duke and duchess of Westminster. All departures are from the riverside along the Groves and cost from £6 to £12.

The tourist office and Chester Visitors' Centre offer a broad range of walking tours departing from both centres. Each tour lasts between 1½ and two hours.

Ghosthunter Trail (adult/child £5/4; ☺ 7.30pm Thu-Sat Jun-Oct, 7.30pm Sat Nov-May) The ubiquitous ghost tour, looking for things that go bump in the night.

History Hunter (adult/child £4.50/3.50; ☺ 10.30am) Two thousand years of Chester history.

Secret Chester (adult/child £5/4; ☺ 2pm Tue, Thu, Sat & Sun May-Oct) Exactly what it says on the tin.

Festivals & Events

Held from mid-July to early August, the three-week **Summer Music Festival** (☎ 01244-320700; www .chesterfestivals.co.uk) is a season highlight, featuring performances by all manner of stars both big and small. The **Chester Jazz Festival** (☎ 01244-340005; www.chesterjazz.co.uk; admission free-£12) is a two-week showcase from late August to early September.

Sleeping

If you're visiting between Easter and September, you'd better book early if you want to avoid going over budget or settling for far less than you bargained for. Except for a handful of options – including the city's best – most of the accommodation is outside the city walls but within easy walking distance of the centre. Hoole Rd, a just under a mile's walk from the centre and leading beyond the railway tracks to the M53/M56, is lined with budget to midrange B&Bs.

BUDGET

Chester Backpackers (☎ 01244-400185; www.chester backpackers.co.uk; 67 Boughton; dm from £14) Comfortable dorm rooms with nice pine beds in a typically Tudor white-and-black building. It's just a short walk from the city walls and there's also a pleasant garden.

Chester YHA (☎ 0845 371 9357; www.yha.org.uk; 40 Hough Green; dm £20) Located in an elegant Victorian home about a mile from the city centre, this hostel has a variety of dorms that sleep from two to 10 people; there's also a cafeteria, a kitchen and a shop on the premises.

Brook St, near the train station, has a couple of good-value B&Bs from around £24 per person. The friendly and accommodating **Ormonde** (☎ 01244-328816; 126 Brook St) and the comfortable **Aplas Guest House** (☎ 01244-312401; 106 Brook St) are both less than five minutes' walk from the train station.

MIDRANGE

Chester Townhouse (☎ 01244-350021; www.chester townhouse.co.uk; 23 King St; s/d £45/75; P) Five beautifully decorated rooms in a handsome 17th-century house within the city walls make Chester Townhouse a terrific option – you're close to the action and you'll sleep in relative luxury.

Grove Villa (☎ 01244-349713; www.grovevillachester .com; 18 The Groves; r from £60) You won't find a more tranquil spot in town than this wonderfully positioned Victorian home overlooking the Dee. The rooms have antique beds and great river views.

Bawn Lodge (☎ 01244-324971; www.bawnlodge .co.uk; 10 Hoole Rd; r from £75) Spotless rooms with plenty of colour make this charming guest house a very pleasant option. It's like staying with a favourite relative: no fuss but plenty of friendliness (and a delicious breakfast). Rates go up during the Chester Races.

TOP END

our pick **Green Bough** (☎ 01244-326241; www.green bough.co.uk; 60 Hoole Rd; r £175-345; P ✕ 🖵) The epitome of the boutique hotel, this exclusive, award-winning Victorian town house (winner of Small Hotel of the Year for 2006) has individually styled rooms dressed in the best Italian fabrics. The rooms come adorned with wall coverings, superb antique furniture and period cast-iron and wooden beds, including a handful of elegant four-posters. Modern touches include plasma-screen TVs, mini stereos and a range of fancy toiletries.

Chester Grosvenor Hotel & Spa (☎ 01244-324024; www.chestergrosvenor.com; 58 Eastgate St; r from £195; P ✕ 🖵) The best hotel in town, with the best location. The huge, sprawling rooms have exquisite period furnishings and all mod cons; the spa (which is open to nonguests) offers a range of body treatments, including reiki, LaStone therapy, Indian head massage and four-handed massage. There's also Arkle, a Michelin-starred restaurant, downstairs (see Eating, below).

Eating

Chester has great food – it's just not in any of the tourist-oriented restaurants that line the Rows. Besides the better restaurants, you'll find the best grub in some of the pubs (see p674).

Katie's Tea Rooms (☎ 01244-400322; 38 Watergate St; tea & scones £3.80, restaurant 2-course dinner £13; ☺ tearoom 9am-5pm Tue-Sat, restaurant dinner Tue-Sat) This stone-walled tearoom located inside an historic building is the place to go for a light lunch. After 5pm it turns into MD's Restaurant, a Continental eatery with a pretty tasty menu.

Boulevard de la Bastille (Bridge St; sandwiches £4, meals £5-9; ☺ 9am-6pm) Our favourite cafe in town is also one of the most handsome: a very French place on the top tier of the Rows that is perfect for a *cafe au lait* and *pain au chocolat* (a flat, chocolate-filled croissant).

Old Harker's Arms (☎ 01244-344525; www.harkers arms-chester.co.uk; 1 Russell St; mains £9-14; ☺ 11am-late) An old-style boozer with a gourmet kitchen, this is the perfect place to tuck into Cumberland sausages or a Creole rice salad with sweet potatoes, and then rinse your palate with a pint of Waddies (as Wadworth Ale is know round here). It also serves bars snacks and sandwiches.

Upstairs at the Grill (☎ 01244-344883; www.upstairs atthegrill.co.uk; 70 Watergate St; mains £15-25; ☺ dinner) A superb steakhouse almost hidden on the 2nd floor, this is the place to devour every cut of meat from American-style porterhouse to a sauce-sodden chateaubriand.

Arkle (☎ 01244-895618; www.chestergrosvenor.com; Chester Grosvenor Hotel & Spa, 58 Eastgate St; 3-course dinner £59; ☺ dinner Tue-Sat) Named after the famous Irish champion racehorse, Simon Radley's

THE NORTHWEST

Arkle serves up a sumptuous feast of French-inspired classics such as tranche of monkfish with air-dried ham, and braised turbot with baby squid. It's elegant (gentlemen in jackets, please) and sophisticated and has a Michelin star to prove it.

Drinking

Falcon (☎ 01244-314555; Lower Bridge St; mains from £5.50) This is an old-fashioned boozer with a lovely atmosphere; the surprisingly adventurous menu offers up dishes such as Jamaican peppered beef or spicy Italian sausage casserole. Great for both a pint and a bite.

Albion (☎ 01244-340345; 4 Albion St; mains £8-11) No children, no music, and no machines or big screens (but plenty of Union Jacks). This 'family hostile' Edwardian classic pub is a throwback to a time when ale-drinking still had its own *rituals* – another word for ingrained prejudices. Still, this is one of the finest pubs in northwest England precisely because it doggedly refuses to modernise.

Other good pubs include the **Boat House** (The Groves), with great views overlooking the river, and the **Boot Inn** (Eastgate St), where 14 Roundheads were killed. **Alexander's Jazz Theatre** (☎ 01244-340005; Rufus Ct; admission after 10pm £3-10; 🕑 8pm-2am Mon-Sat, 7.30pm-12.30am Sun) is a combination wine bar, coffee bar and tapas bar.

Entertainment
SPORT
Horse Racing

Chester's ancient and very beautiful racetrack is the **Roodee** (☎ 01244-304600; www.chester-races.co.uk; 🕑 May-Sep), on the western side of the walls, which has been hosting races since the 16th century. Highlights of the summer flat season include the two-day July Festival and the August equivalent.

Getting There & Away
BUS

National Express (☎ 08717 81 81 81; www.nationalexpress.com) coaches stop on Vicar's Lane, just opposite the tourist office by the Roman amphitheatre. Destinations include Birmingham (£10.70, 2½ hours, four daily), Liverpool (£6.90, one hour, three daily), London (£22.40, 5½ hours, three daily) and Manchester (£6.10, 1¼ hours, three daily).

For information on local bus services, ring the **Cheshire Bus Line** (☎ 01244-602666). Local buses leave from the Town Hall bus exchange

on Princess St. On Sundays and bank holidays a **Sunday adventurer ticket** (adult/child £4/3) gives you unlimited travel in Cheshire.

TRAIN

The train station is about a mile from the city centre via Foregate St and City Rd, or Brook St. City-Rail Link buses are free for people with rail tickets, and operate between the station and Bus Stop A on Frodsham St. Trains travel to Liverpool (£4.45, 45 minutes, hourly), London Euston (£61.60, 2½ hours, hourly) and Manchester (£11.20, one hour, hourly).

Getting Around

Much of the city centre is closed to traffic from 10.30am to 4.30pm, so a car is likely to be a hindrance. Anyway, the city is easy to walk around and most places of interest are close to the wall.

City buses depart from the **Town Hall Bus Exchange** (☎ 01244-602666).

Davies Bros Cycles (☎ 01244-371341; 5 Delamere St) has mountain bikes for hire at £14 per day.

AROUND CHESTER
Chester Zoo

The largest of its kind in the country, **Chester Zoo** (☎ 01244-380280; www.chesterzoo.org.uk; adult/child £15/11; 🕑 10am-dusk, last admission 4pm Mon-Fri, 5pm Sat & Sun Apr-Oct & 3pm Mon-Fri & 4pm Sat & Sun Nov-Mar) is about as pleasant a place as caged animals in artificial renditions of their natural habitats could ever expect to live. It's so big that there's even a **monorail** (adult/child £2/1.50) and a **waterbus** (adult/child £2/1.50) on which to get around. The zoo is on the A41, 3 miles north of the city centre. Buses 11C and 12C (£2.50 return, every 15 minutes Monday to Saturday, half-hourly Sunday) run between Chester's Town Hall bus exchange and the zoo.

Blue Planet Aquarium

Things aren't done by halves around Chester: you'll also find the country's largest aquarium, **Blue Planet** (☎ 0151-357 8804; www.blueplanetaquarium.com; adult/child £14/10; 🕑 10am-5pm Mon-Fri, 10am-6pm Sat & Sun). It's home to 10 different kinds of shark, which able to be viewed from a 70m-long moving walkway that lets you eye them up close. It's 9 miles north of Chester at junction 10 of the M53 near Liverpool. Buses 1 and 4 run there every half-hour from the Town Hall Bus Exchange in Chester.

Ellesmere Port Boat Museum

Near the aquarium, on the Shropshire Union Canal about 8 miles north of Chester, is the superb **Ellesmere Port Boat Museum** (☎ 0151-355 5017; www.boatmuseum.org.uk; South Pier Rd; adult/child £5.50/3.50; ♥ 10am-5pm Apr-Oct, 11am-4pm Sat-Wed Nov-Mar), which has a large collection of canal boats as well as indoor exhibits. Take Bus 4 from the Town Hall Bus Exchange in Chester, or it's a 10-minute walk from Ellesmere Port train station.

KNUTSFORD

pop 12,660

Fascinating Knutsford would be a typical lowland English market town if it wasn't for the eccentric philanthropy of Richard Watt (1842–1913), a millionaire glove manufacturer with his own personal vision of Mediterranean architecture. The weird and wonderful buildings that he commissioned for the town make it one of the most interesting places in Cheshire.

Although Watt's influence was certainly greater, Knutsford makes the biggest deal of its links with Elizabeth Cleghorn Gaskell (1810–65), who spent her childhood here and used the town as the model for *Cranford* (1853), her most noteworthy novel. It was made into a BBC series starring Dame Judi Dench following the successful 2004 serialisation of another of her novels, *North And South* (1855). Gaskell, however, left Knutsford and spend her most productive years in the Manchester suburb of Ardwick, where you can visit her former home (see boxed text, p662).

The **tourist office** (☎ 01565-632611; Toft Rd; ♥ 9am-5pm Mon-Fri, 9am-1pm Sat) is in the council offices opposite the train station.

The **Knutsford Heritage Centre** (☎ 01565-650506; 90A King St; admission free; ♥ 1.30-4pm Mon-Fri, noon-4pm Sat, 2-4.30pm Sun) is a reconstructed former smithy that has plenty of information on Gaskell, including the *Cranford Walk Around Knutsford* (£1), a leaflet about her local haunts. The most interesting displays, though, are on Watt and his quirky contributions to English architecture.

You can see the best of these along King St, which is a fine example of the splendidly haphazard harmony of English urban architecture. See in particular the **King's Coffee House** (meant to lure the men from the pubs) and the **Ruskin Reading Room** (Drury Lane).

The eye-catching **Gaskell Memorial Tower** incorporates the swanky **Belle Epoque Brasserie** (☎ 01565-633060; www.thebelleepoque.com; 60 King St; mains £9-16, s/d £95/110; ♥ lunch & dinner Mon-Sat), a *fin-de-siècle*-style restaurant that Oscar Wilde would look perfectly at home in. Upstairs are seven gorgeous rooms styled in accordance with the overall late-19th-century theme of the building.

Getting There & Away

Knutsford is 15 miles southwest of Manchester and is on the Manchester–Chester train line (Chester £8.80, 45 minutes, hourly; Manchester £5.10, 30 minutes, hourly). The train station is on Adams Hill, at the southern end of King St.

AROUND KNUTSFORD

The southern end of King St in Knutsford marks the entrance to the 400-hectare **Tatton Park** (NT; ☎ 01625-534400; www.tattonpark.org.uk; admission free, individual attractions adult/child £4/2; ♥ 10am-7pm). At the heart is a Regency **mansion** (♥ 1-5pm Tue-Sun Mar-Oct); a wonderful Tudor **Old Hall** (♥ noon-4pm Sat & Sun Apr-Oct); a 1930s-style **working farm** (♥ noon-5pm Tue-Sun Mar-Oct, Sat & Sun Nov-Feb); and a series of superb Victorian **gardens** (♥ 10am-6pm Tue-Sun Apr-Sep, 11am-4pm Oct-Mar). The **Totally Tatton Ticket** (adult/child £6/3) allows you entry to all attractions over two days. Car admission to the park costs £4.50.

On Sundays bus X2 links Tatton Park with Chester (one hour). At other times you'll need your own wheels.

NANTWICH

pop 13,450

Cheshire's second-best example of black-and-white Tudor architecture after Chester is the elegant town of Nantwich. After a devastating fire in 1583, the town was rebuilt thanks to a nationwide appeal by Elizabeth I, who deemed the town's salt production so important that she had to intercede to help. The queen personally donated £1000, and her generosity is proudly commemorated with a plaque on the aptly named **Queen's Aid House** (High St), itself a striking Tudor building.

The rest of the largely pedestrianised centre has plenty of fine examples of the black-and-white style, although it's a wonder how so many of them stay standing, such is their off-kilter shape and design.

Very few buildings survived the fire; the most important of those that did is the 14th-century **Church of St Mary** (☎ 01565-625268; ⏰ 9am-5pm), a fine example of medieval architecture.

Apart from salt, the town grew up around the production of cheese and leather, and all three are depicted in the **Nantwich Museum** (☎ 01565-627104; Pillory St; admission free; ⏰ 10am-4.30pm Mon-Sat Apr-Sep, Tue-Sat Oct-Mar).

The helpful **tourist office** (☎ 01565-610983; fax 01565-610880; Church Walk; ⏰ 9.30am-5pm Mon-Fri, 10am-4pm Sat, 11am-3pm Sun) is near the main square.

Sleeping & Eating

Crown Hotel (☎ 01565-625283; www.crownhotelnantwich.com; High St; s/d from £68/84) There is barely a straight line in the place, but this gorgeous Tudor half-timbered hotel is easily top choice in town. The ground-floor Casa Italiana restaurant is a decent and popular spot that has every possible Italian dish on its menu, with mains priced from £9 to £13.

Pillory House & Coffee Shop (☎ 01565-623524; Pillory St; sandwiches £4-5) An old-style tearoom that serves sandwiches and inexpensive hot dishes – perfect for that quick lunch.

Getting There & Away

The **bus station** (Beam St) is 300m north of the tourist office; there is an hourly bus from Chester (£5.40, one hour).

To get to Manchester, Chester or Liverpool, you'll have to change trains in Crewe (15 minutes, half-hourly). The train station is about half a mile south of the centre.

LIVERPOOL

pop 469, 020

Like the impatient belle who just couldn't wait to get to the ball, Liverpool took to its role as European Capital of Culture in 2008 with the kind of fervour that could only be mustered up by a city desperate for international recognition. Which is no bad thing, considering that for decades Liverpool was a bit of a mess, a perennial victim of an economic lashing that left much of the city centre an unattractive mix of ugly retail outlets and dereliction.

It's all changing, though, as a seemingly never-ending program of urban regeneration is restoring the city's architectural treasures and building some pretty swanky new ones, all in the hope of creating a 21st-century version of Liverpool's 19th-century greatness. At the heart of it is the new Liverpool ONE, a gigantic, ultraswish retail centre that occupies an almighty chunk of the city centre. It opened its (literally) hundreds of doors in the summer of 2008, and it's likely to be the financial backbone of Liverpool's efforts to return to the status of major city.

What have never been in question, however, are the city's cultural credentials. The city's store of superb museums and top-class art galleries – all free – have put paid to the scurrilous rumour that Liverpool peaked with the Beatles. In 2004 the whole of the waterfront and docks was declared a Unesco World Heritage Site because there are more listed buildings here than in any other city in England, except London. Oh, and the nightlife: as rich and varied as you'd expect from a good northern city.

Then there are the Scousers themselves, a proud and resilient bunch that have weathered every storm with great character and humour. Most people are familiar with the concept of hometown pride, but in Liverpool they're just that little bit more in love with their city. They'll slag it off, all right – slagging has always been an Olympic sport around here – but it's a critique born of a deep pride that these days is extremely well placed.

HISTORY

Liverpool grew wealthy on the back of the triangular trading of slaves, raw materials and finished goods. From 1700 ships carried cotton goods and hardware from Liverpool to West Africa, where they were exchanged

LIVERPOOL IN...

Two Days

Head to the waterfront and explore the Albert Dock museums – the **Tate Liverpool** (p681), the **Merseyside Maritime Museum** (p681) and the unmissable **International Slavery Museum** (p681) – before paying tribute to the Fab Four at the **Beatles Story** (p681). Keep to the Beatles theme and head north towards the Cavern Quarter around Mathew St before surrendering to the retail giant that is **Liverpool ONE** (p688), with its hundreds of shops. Round off your evening with dinner at **London Carriage Works** (p685) and a pint at the marvellous **Philharmonic** (p686), and wrap yourself in the crisp linen sheets of the **Hope Street Hotel** (p684). Night hawks can tear it up in the bars (see City Centre, p686) and clubs (see Nightclubs, p686) of the hip **Ropewalks** area. The next day, explore the city's two **cathedrals** (p680) and check out the twin delights of the **World Museum Liverpool** (p680) and the **Walker Art Gallery** (p679).

Four Days

Follow the two-day itinerary but add in a **Yellow Duckmarine tour** (p683) to experience the docks from the water. Make a couple of pilgrimages to suit your interests: visit **Mendips** (see boxed text, p682) and **20 Forthlin Rd** (see boxed text, p682), the childhood homes of John Lennon and Paul McCartney, respectively; or walk on holy ground at Anfield, home of **Liverpool Football Club** (p688). Race junkies can head out to the visitor centre at **Aintree racecourse** (see boxed text, p687), which hosts England's most beloved race, the Grand National.

for slaves, who in turn were carried to the West Indies and Virginia, where they were exchanged for sugar, rum, tobacco and raw cotton.

As a great port, the city drew thousands of Irish and Scottish immigrants, and its Celtic influences are still apparent. However, between 1830 and 1930 nine million emigrants – mainly English, Scots and Irish, but also Swedes, Norwegians and Russian Jews – sailed from here for the New World.

The start of WWII led to a resurgence of Liverpool's importance. More than one million American GIs disembarked here before D-Day and the port was, once again, hugely important as the western gateway for transatlantic supplies. The GIs brought with them the latest American records, and Liverpool was thus the first European port of call for the new rhythm and blues that would eventually become rock 'n' roll. Within 20 years, the Mersey Beat was *the* sound of British pop, and four mop-topped Scousers had formed a skiffle band…

ORIENTATION

Liverpool is a cinch to get around. The main attractions are Albert Dock (west of the city centre), and the trendy Ropewalks area (south of Hanover St and west of the two cathedrals). Lime St station, the Paradise St bus station,

the 08 Place tourist office and the Cavern Quarter – a mecca for Beatles fans – lie just to the north.

The tourist office and many of the city's hotels have an excellent map with all of the city's attractions clearly outlined.

INFORMATION
Bookshops

Waterstone's (☎ 0151-708 6861; 14 16 Bold St)

Emergency

Merseyside police headquarters (☎ 0151-709 6010; Canning Pl) Opposite Albert Dock.

Internet Access

CafeLatte.net (☎ 0151-709 9683; 4 South Hunter St; per 30min £1.50; 🕙 9am-6pm)
Planet Electra (☎ 0151-708 0303; 36 London Rd; per 30min £1.50; 🕙 9am-5pm)

Internet Resources

Clubs in Liverpool (www.clubsinliverpool.co.uk) Everything you need to know about what goes on when the sun goes down.
Liverpool Magazine (www.liverpool.com) Insiders' guide to the city, including lots of great recommendations for food and nights out.
Mersey Guide (www.merseyguide.co.uk) Guide to the Greater Mersey area.

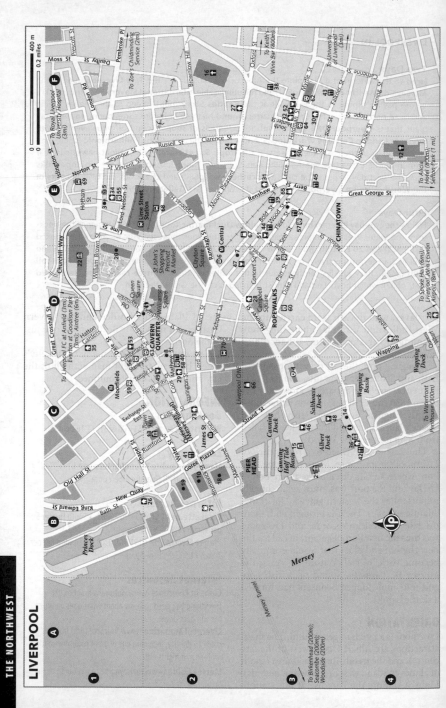

LIVERPOOL

Merseyside Today (www.merseysidetoday.co.uk) Guide to the city and surrounding area.

Tourist office (www.visitliverpool.com)

Medical Services

Mars Pharmacy (☎ 0151-709 5271; 68 London Rd) Open until 10pm every night.

Royal Liverpool University Hospital (☎ 0151-706 2000; Prescot St)

Post

Post office (Ranelagh St; ⏰ 9am-5.30pm Mon-Sat)

Tourist Information

Liverpool's tourist office has three branches in the city. It also offers an **accommodation hotline** (☎ 0845 601 1125; ⏰ 9am-5.30pm Mon-Fri, 10am-4pm Sat).

08 Place tourist office (☎ 0151-233 2008; Whitechapel; ⏰ 9am-8pm Mon-Sat, 11am-4pm Sun Apr-Sep, 9am-6pm Mon-Sat, 11am-4pm Sun Oct-Mar) The main branch of the tourist office.

Albert Dock tourist office (☎ 0151-478 4599) Anchor Courtyard (⏰ 10am-6pm) Merseyside Maritime Museum (⏰ 10am-6pm)

SIGHTS

The wonderful Albert Dock is the city's biggest tourist attraction, and the key to understanding the city's history, but the city centre is where you'll find most of Liverpool's real day-to-day life.

City Centre

ST GEORGE'S HALL

Arguably Liverpool's most impressive building, **St George's Hall** (☎ 0151-707 2391; William Brown St; admission free; ⏰ Tue-Sat 10am-5pm, 1-5pm Sun) was built in 1854 and restored in recent years to the tune of £27 million – it finally reopened in 2007. Curiously, it was built as law courts *and* a concert hall – presumably a judge could pass sentence and then relax to a string quartet. Tours (£5) of the hall are run in conjunction with the tourist office; check for times.

WALKER ART GALLERY

Touted as the 'National Gallery of the North', the city's foremost **gallery** (☎ 0151-478 4199; www.liverpoolmuseums.org.uk/walker; William Brown St; admission free; ⏰ 10am-5pm) is the national gallery for northern England, housing an outstanding collection of art dating from the 14th century. Its strong suits are Pre-Raphaelite art, modern British art, and sculpture – not to mention the rotating exhibits of contemporary expression.

WORLD MUSEUM LIVERPOOL

Natural history, science and technology are the themes of this sprawling **museum** (☎ 0151-478 4399; www.liverpoolmuseums.org.uk/wml; William Brown St; admission free; 🕑 10am-5pm), whose exhibits range from birds of prey to space exploration. It also includes the country's only free planetarium. This vastly entertaining and educational museum is divided into four major sections: the Human World, one of the top anthropological collections in the country; the Natural World, which includes a new aquarium as well as live insect colonies; Earth, a geological treasure trove; and Space & Time, which includes the planetarium. Highly recommended.

NATIONAL CONSERVATION CENTRE

Ever wonder how art actually gets restored? Find out at this terrific **conservation centre** (☎ 0151-478 4999; www.liverpoolmuseums.org.uk/conservation; Whitechapel; admission free; 🕑 10am-5pm), housed in a converted railway goods depot. Handheld audio wands help tell the story, but the real fun is actually attempting a restoration technique with your own hands. Sadly, our trembling paws weren't allowed near anything of value – that was left to the real experts, whose skills are pretty amazing.

FACT

Proof that Ropewalks isn't all about booze and bars, this **media centre** (Foundation for Art & Creative Technology; ☎ 0151-707 4450; www.fact.co.uk; 88 Wood St; 🕑 galleries 11am-6pm Tue & Wed, 11am-8pm Thu-Sat, noon-5pm Sun, cinemas noon-10pm) is all about film and new media such as digital art. Two galleries feature constantly changing exhibitions and three screens show the latest art-house releases, although we've noticed that the odd mainstream release has crept into the schedule – financial pressures overriding creative intent? There's also a bar and cafe.

LIVERPOOL WAR MUSEUM

The secret command centre for the Battle of the Atlantic, the **Western Approaches** (☎ 0151-227 2008; www.liverpoolwarmuseum.co.uk; 1 Rumford St; adult/child £5.25/4; 🕑 10.30am-4.30pm Mon-Thu & Sat Mar-Oct), was abandoned at the end of the war with virtually everything left intact. You can get a good glimpse of the labyrinthine nerve centre of Allied operations.

THE CATHEDRALS

The city's two cathedrals are separated by the length of Hope St.

Metropolitan Cathedral of Christ the King

At the northern end of Hope St, off Mt Pleasant, you'll find the Roman Catholic **Metropolitan Cathedral of Christ the King** (☎ 0151-709 9222; 🕑 8am-6pm Mon-Sat, 8am-5pm Sun Oct-Mar). It was completed in 1967 according to the design of Sir Frederick Gibberd, and after the original plans by Sir Edwin Lutyens, whose crypt is inside. It's a mightily impressive modern building that looks like a soaring concrete tepee, hence its nickname – Paddy's Wigwam.

Liverpool Cathedral

At Hope St's southern end stands the life work of Sir Giles Gilbert Scott (1880–1960), the neo-Gothic **Liverpool Cathedral** (☎ 0151-709 6271; www.liverpoolcathedral.org.uk; Hope St; 🕑 8am-6pm). Sir Scott's other contributions to the world were the red telephone box, and the power station in London that is now home to the Tate Modern. Size is a big deal here: this is the largest church in England and the largest Anglican cathedral in the world. The central bell is the world's third-largest (with the world's highest and heaviest peal), while the organ, with its 9765 pipes, is likely the world's largest operational model.

A new visitor centre features the **Great Space Film & Audio Tour** (☎ 0151-702 7255; adult/child £4.25/3.50; 🕑 9am-4pm Mon-Sat, noon-2.30pm Sun), a 10-minute, panoramic high-definition movie about the history of the cathedral. It's followed by your own audiovisual tour, courtesy of a snazzy headset.

There are terrific views of Liverpool from the top of the cathedral's 101m **tower** (☎ 0151-702 7217; adult/child £4.25/3, combined tower & Great Space tour adult/child £6.75/5; 🕑 10am-5pm Mon-Sat, noon-2.30pm Sun).

Albert Dock

Liverpool's biggest tourist attraction is **Albert Dock** (☎ 0151-708 8854; www.albertdock.com; admission free), 2¾ hectares of water ringed by enormous cast-iron columns and impressive five-storey warehouses; these make up the country's largest collection of protected buildings and are a World Heritage Site. A fabulous development program has really brought the dock to life; here you'll find several outstanding museums and an extension of London's Tate Gallery, as well as a couple of top-class restaurants and bars.

MERSEYSIDE MARITIME MUSEUM

The story of one of the world's great ports is the theme of this excellent **museum** (☎ 0151-478 4499; www.liverpoolmuseums.org.uk/maritime; Albert Dock; admission free; ☺ 10am-5pm) and, believe us, it's a graphic and compelling page-turner. One of the many great exhibits is Emigration to a New World, which tells the story of nine million emigrants and their efforts to get to North America and Australia; the walk-through model of a typical ship shows just how tough conditions on board really were.

INTERNATIONAL SLAVERY MUSEUM

Museums are, by their very nature, like a still of the past, but the extraordinary **International Slavery Museum** (☎ 0151-478 4499; www.liverpool museums.org.uk/ism; Albert Dock; admission free; ☺ 10am-5pm) resonates very much in the present. It reveals slavery's unimaginable horrors – including Liverpool's own role in the triangular slave trade – in a clear and uncompromising manner. It does this through a remarkable series of multimedia and other displays, and it doesn't baulk at confronting racism, slavery's shadowy ideological justification for this inhumane practice.

The history of slavery is made real through a series of personal experiences, including a carefully kept ship's log and captain's diary. These tell the story of one slaver's experience on a typical trip, departing Liverpool for West Africa. The ship then purchased or captured as many slaves as it could carry before embarking on the gruesome 'middle passage' across the Atlantic to the West Indies. The slaves that survived the torturous journey were sold for sugar, rum and molasses, which were then brought back to England for profit. Exhibits include original shackles, chains and instruments used to punish rebellious slaves – each piece of metal is more horrendous than the next.

It's heady, disturbing stuff, but as well as providing an insightful history lesson, we are reminded of our own obligations to humanity and justice throughout the museum, not least by the displayed words of Gee Barton, whose son Anthony was murdered in a racially motivated attack in the Liverpool suburb of Huyton on 30 July 2005: 'Do not let my son's death be in vain.' A visit to this magnificent museum is a good place to start.

TATE LIVERPOOL

Touted as the home of modern art in the north, this **gallery** (☎ 0151-702 7400; www.tate.org.uk /liverpool; Albert Dock; admission free, special exhibitions adult/ child from £5/4; ☺ 10am-5.50pm Jun-Aug, 10am-5.50pm Tue-Sun May-May) features a substantial checklist of 20th-century artists across its four floors, as well as touring exhibitions from the mother ship on London's Bankside. But it's all a little sparse, with none of the energy we'd expect from the world-famous Tate.

BEATLES STORY

Liverpool's most popular **museum** (☎ 0151-709 1963; www.beatlesstory.com; Albert Dock; adult/child £12.50/6.50; ☺ 9am-7pm) won't illuminate any dark, juicy corners in the turbulent history of the world's most famous foursome – there's ne'er a mention of internal discord, drugs or Yoko Ono – but there's plenty of genuine memorabilia to keep a Beatles fan happy. Particularly impressive is the full-size replica Cavern Club (which was actually tiny) and the Abbey Rd studio where the lads recorded their first singles, while George Harrison's crappy first guitar (now worth half a million quid) should inspire budding, penniless musicians to keep the faith. The museum is also the departure point for the Yellow Duckmarine tour (see p683).

North of Albert Dock

The area to the north of Albert Dock is known as **Pier Head**, after a stone pier built in the 1760s. This is still the departure point for ferries across the River Mersey (see Boat, p689), and was, for millions of migrants, their final contact with European soil.

Their story – and that of the city in general – will be told in the enormous **Museum of Liverpool**, currently being built on an area known as Mann Island and not slated to open until 2010 or 2011. Until its opening, this part of the dock will continue to be dominated by a trio of Edwardian buildings known as the 'Three Graces', dating from the days when Liverpool's star was still ascending. The southernmost, with the dome mimicking St Paul's Cathedral, is the **Port of Liverpool Building**, completed in 1907. Next to it is the **Cunard Building**,

---

DOING THE BEATLES TO DEATH

Although it's kind of hard to stomach anyone banging on about the Beatles being the best band in the world – they broke up in 1970! That's nearly 40 years ago! – it is easy to understand how Liverpool is still making as much as it can out of the phenomenon that was the Fab Four.

It doesn't matter that two of them are dead, that the much-visited Cavern Club is an unfaithful reconstruction of the original club that was the scene of their earliest gigs, or that, if he were alive, John Lennon would have devoted much of his cynical energy to mocking the 'Cavern Quarter' that has grown up around Mathew St. No, it doesn't matter at all, because the phenomenon lives on and a huge chunk of the city's visitors come to visit, see and touch anything – and we mean anything – even vaguely associated with the Beatles.

Which isn't to say that a wander around Mathew St isn't fun: from shucking oysters in the Rubber Soul Oyster Bar to buying a Ringo pillowcase in the From Me to You shop, virtually all of your Beatles needs can be taken care of. For decent memorabilia, check out the **Beatles Shop** (0151-236 8066; www.thebeatleshop.co.uk; 31 Mathew St).

True fans will undoubtedly want to visit the National Trust–owned **Mendips**, the home where John lived with his Aunt Mimi from 1945 to 1963, and **20 Forthlin Rd**, the plain terraced home where Paul grew up; you can only do so by prebooked **tour** (0151-427 7231; adult/child £15/3; 10.30am & 11.20am Wed-Sun, Easter-Oct) from outside the National Conservation Centre (p680). Visitors to Speke Hall (see p690) can also visit both from there.

If you'd rather do it yourself, the tourist offices stock the *Discover Lennon's Liverpool* guide and map, and *Robin Jones' Beatles Liverpool*.

---

in the style of an Italian palazzo, once HQ to the Cunard Steamship Line. Finally, the **Royal Liver Building** (pronounced *lie*-ver) was opened in 1911 as the head office of the Royal Liver Friendly Society. It's crowned by Liverpool's symbol, the famous 5.5m copper Liver Bird.

LIVERPOOL FOR CHILDREN

The museums on Albert Dock are extremely popular with kids, especially the **Merseyside Maritime Museum** (p681) – which has a couple of boats for kids to mess about on – and the **Beatles Story** (p681). The **Yellow Duckmarine Tour** (opposite) is a sure-fire winner, as is the **National Conservation Centre** (p680), which gets everyone involved in the drama of restoration. Slightly older (and very old) kids – especially those into football – will enjoy the tour of Anfield Stadium, home to **Liverpool Football Club** (p688), as it means getting your feet on the sacred turf.

Need a break from the tots? Drop them off at **Zoe's Childminding Service** (0151-228 2685; 15 Woodbourne Rd), about 2 miles east of the city centre.

QUIRKY LIVERPOOL

When a working public toilet is a tourist attraction, you know you have something special, and the men's loo at the **Philharmonic** (p686) is just that. The **Yellow Duckmarine Tour** (opposite),

an amphibious exploration of Albert Dock, is a bit silly but the guides are hilarious, and the **ferry across the Mersey** (see River Explorer Cruise, opposite) is something special – the tired commuters will give you more than a stare if you sing the song too loudly. The **Grand National Experience** (see boxed text, p687) at Aintree is proof that the English really do love their horses, and the concerts at the **Philharmonic Hall** (p687) often throw up something avant-garde, instead of the Beethoven concerto you might expect.

TOURS

Beatles Fab Four Taxi Tour (0151-601 2111; www .thebeatlesfabfourtaxitour.co.uk; per tour £45) Get your own personalised 2½-hr tour of the city's moptop landmarks. Pick-ups arranged when booking. Up to five people)

Liverpool Beatles Tour (0151-281 7738; www .beatlestours.co.uk; tours £45-80) Your own personalised tour of every bit of minutiae associated with the Beatles, from cradle to grave. Tour range from the two-hour Helter Skelter excursion to There Are Places I Remember, by the end of which, presumably, you'll be convinced you were actually in the band. Pick-ups are arranged upon booking.

Magical Mystery Tour (0151-709 3285; www .cavernclub.org; per person £13; 2.30pm year round, plus noon Sat Jul & Aug) This two-hour tour takes in all Beatles-related landmarks – their birthplaces, childhood homes, schools and places such as Penny Lane and Strawberry Field – before finishing up in the Cavern Club (which isn't the original). Departs from outside the tourist office at the 08 Place.

River Explorer Cruise (☎ 0151-639 0609; www .merseyferries.co.uk; adult/child return £5.30/3; ☺ hourly 10am-3pm Mon-Fri, 10am-5pm Sat & Sun) Do as Gerry & the Pacemakers wanted and take a ferry 'cross the Mersey, exploring the bay and all its attractions as you go. Departs from Pier Head.

Yellow Duckmarine Tour (☎ 0151-708 7799; www .theyellowduckmarine.co.uk; adult/child/family £12/10/34; ☺ from 11am) Take to the dock waters in a WWII amphibious vehicle after a quickie tour of the city centre's main points of interest. It's not especially educational, but it is a bit of fun. Departs from Albert Dock, near the Beatles Story.

FESTIVALS & EVENTS

Aintree Festival (☎ 0151-522 2929; www.aintree .co.uk) A three-day race meeting culminating in the world-famous Grand National steeplechase, held on the first Saturday in April.

Africa Oye (www.africaoye.com) The UK's largest free festival celebrating African music and culture takes place in the suburb of Sefton Park in the second half of June.

Liverpool Comedy Festival (☎ 0870 787 1866; www .liverpoolcomedyfestival.co.uk) A fortnight of comedy, both local and international, in venues throughout the city. Usually kicks off in mid-July.

Merseyside International Street Festival (www .brouhaha.uk.com) A three-week extravaganza of world culture beginning in mid-July and featuring indoor and outdoor performances by artists and musicians from pretty much everywhere.

Eclectica Music Festival (☎ 01744-755150; www .visitsthelens.com) A free festival of folk, alternative and roots music in nearby St Helen's town centre, held on one day in mid-August.

Creamfields (☎ 0208-969 4477; www.cream.co.uk) An alfresco dance-fest that brings together some of the world's best DJs and dance acts during the last weekend in August. It takes place at the Daresbury Estate near Halton, Cheshire.

Mathew St Festival (☎ 0151-239 9091; www .mathewstreetfestival.com) The world's biggest tribute to the Beatles features six days of music, a convention and a memorabilia auction during the last week of August.

SLEEPING

There have been some stylish new arrivals on the scene, but lean towards the boutique and luxury end of the scale. For the rest, standardised business hotels and midrange chains dominate the city centre's hotel lists. Beds are extremely tough to find when Liverpool FC are playing at home (it's less of a problem with

Everton) and during the Beatles convention in the last week of August.

City Centre
BUDGET
International Inn (☎ 0151-709 8135; www.inter nationalinn.co.uk; 4 South Hunter St; dm/d from £15/36) A superb converted warehouse in the middle of uni-land: heated rooms with tidy wooden beds and bunks,, accommodate from two to 10 people. Facilities include a lounge, baggage storage, laundry and 24-hour front desk. The staff is terrific and CafeLatte.net (see p677) internet cafe is next door.

University of Liverpool (☎ 0151-794 6440; www.liv .ac.uk; Greenbank Lane; r from £17.50) Accommodation in comfortable, modern rooms is provided out of term at the Roscoe and Gladstone Residence Hall, located at one end of Penny Lane. Besides its Beatles connections, this is a beautiful part of the city, with nice parks and a duck-filled lake nearby.

MIDRANGE
Aachen Hotel (☎ 0151-709 3477; www.aachenhotel.co.uk; 89-91 Mt Pleasant; s/d from £50/70) This funky listed building is a perennial favourite, with a mix of rooms (some with attached bathroom, some shared). The decor is strictly late '70s to early '80s – lots of flower patterns and crazy colour schemes – but it's all part of the welcoming, offbeat atmosphere.

Feathers Hotel (☎ 0151-709 9655; www.feathers .uk.com; 119-125 Mt Pleasant; s/d from £55/80) A better choice than most of the similar-priced chain hotels, this rambling place spreads itself across a terrace of Georgian houses close to the Metropolitan Cathedral. The rooms are all comfortable (except for the wardrobe-sized singles at the top of the building) and all feature nice touches such as full-package satellite TV. The all-you-can-eat buffet breakfast is a welcome morning treat.

Alicia Hotel (☎ 0151-727 4411; www.feathers.uk.com; 3 Aigburth Dr, Sefton Park; r from £65) Once a wealthy cotton merchant's home, Alicia is a sister hotel to Feathers (see above), but it's a far more handsome place. Most of the rooms have extra luxuries, such as CD players and PlayStations. There's also a nice park on the grounds.

Other midrange options in town:
Lord Nelson Hotel (☎ 0151-709 5161; Hotham St; s/d from £40/55) Modern rooms and contemporary style in the middle of town.

THE NORTHWEST

Hanover Hotel (☎ 0151-709 6223; www.hanover
-hotel.co.uk; 62 Hanover St; s/d from £48/75) Older breed
of hotel-over-a-pub, with decent if unspectacular rooms.

TOP END

our pick **Hope Street Hotel** (☎ 0151-709 3000; www
.hopestreethotel.co.uk; 40 Hope St; r/ste from £115/180)
Luxurious Liverpool's pre-eminent flag-
waver is this stunning boutique hotel, on
the city's most elegant street. The building's
original features – heavy wooden beams,
cast-iron columns and plenty of exposed
brickwork – have been incorporated into a
contemporary design inspired by the style
of a 16th-century Venetian palazzo. King-
sized beds draped in Egyptian cotton; oak
floors with underfloor heating; LCD wide-
screen TVs; and sleek modern bathrooms
(with REN bath and beauty products) are
but the most obvious touches of class at this
supremely cool address. Breakfast, taken in
the marvellous London Carriage Works (opposite), is not included.

Hard Days Night Hotel (☎ 0151-236 1964; www
.harddaysnighthotel.com; Central Bldgs, North John St; r £120-
160, ste from £180) You don't have to be a fan to
stay here, but it helps: unquestionably luxurious, the 110 ultramodern, fully equipped
rooms come with a specially commissioned
piece of artwork by Shannon, who has made
a career out of drawing John, Paul, George
and Ringo. And if you opt for one of the
suites, named after Lennon and McCartney
(even the hotel acknowledges the band's
pecking order) you'll get a white baby grand
piano in the style of 'Imagine'.

62 Castle St (☎ 0151-702 7898; www.62castlest.com;
62 Castle St; s/d from £150/180; P ▯) As exclusive
a boutique hotel as you'll find anywhere,
this wonderful new property successfully
blends the traditional Victorian features of
the building with a sexy, contemporary style.
The 20 fabulously different suites come with
plasma screen TVs, drench showers and
Elemis toiletries as standard.

Around Albert Dock

BUDGET

Liverpool YHA (☎ 0845 371 9527; www.yha.org.uk;
25 Tabley St; dm £16) It may have the look of an
Eastern European apartment complex, but
this award-winning hostel, adorned with
plenty of Beatles memorabilia, is one of the
most comfortable you'll find anywhere in
the country. The dorms with attached bathroom even have heated towel rails, and rates
include breakfast.

MIDRANGE

Campanile Hotel (☎ 0151-709 8104; www.campanile
-liverpool-queens-dock.co.uk; Chaloner St, Queen's Dock; r £49;
P) Functional, motel-style rooms in a purpose-built hotel. Great location and perfect for
families – children under 12 stay for free.

Premier Inn (☎ 0870 990 6432; www.premierinn.
co.uk; Albert Dock; r from £55; P) As chain hotels
go, this is perfectly fine; what makes us include it is its location, which is about two
steps away from the Beatles Story museum
on Albert Dock.

Crowne Plaza Liverpool (☎ 0151-243 8000; www
.cpliverpool.com; St Nicholas Pl, Princes Dock, Pier Head;
r from £82; P) The paragon of the modern and
luxurious business hotel, the Crowne Plaza
has a marvellous waterfront location and
plenty of facilities including a health club and
swimming pool.

EATING

Liverpool's dining scene is getting better
all the time. There are plenty of choices in
Ropewalks, along Hardman St and Hope St,
along Nelson St in the heart of Chinatown or
slightly further afield in Lark Lane, near Sefton
Park, which is packed with restaurants.

Budget

Lucy in the Sky with Diamonds (☎ 0151-236 0096;
8 Cavern Walks, Mathew St; mains about £4; ☿ 8am-5pm
Mon-Sat) It's hard to imagine that a cafe with
this name, in a shopping arcade in a touristy area of town, should be authentic in any
way. But this cluttered caff (with a vaguely
Mediterranean feel) is a great place for a sandwich or a greasy fry.

Keith's Wine Bar (☎ 0151-728 7688; 107 Lark Lane;
mains around £5; ☿ 11am-11pm) This friendly,
bohemian and mostly vegetarian hang-out
(that happens to have a sensational wine cellar) is the favourite resting place of the city's
alternative-lifestyle crowd.

Everyman Bistro (☎ 0151-708 9545; www.every
man.co.uk; 13 Hope St; mains £5-8; ☿ noon-2am Mon-Fri,
11am-2am Sat, 7-10.30pm Sun) Out-of-work actors
and other creative types on a budget make
this great cafe-restaurant (located beneath
the Everyman Theatre) their second home –
with good reason. Great tucker and a
terrific atmosphere.

> **APARTMENT LUXURY**
>
> If you want to live it up in self-catering style, you can opt for a luxury apartment that's along the waterfront or in the heart of town. Apartments are available on a per-night basis; the price includes gas and electricity.
>
> **Imagine Apartments** (☎ 0844 870 0123; www.imagineapartments.com; Renshaw St; apt from £105) Beautiful one- and two-bedroom apartments perfectly situated in the middle of the city and furnished to four-star standard.
>
> **Premier Apartments** (☎ 0151-487 7440; www.premierapartments.com; 23 Hatton Gardens; apt from £79) Award-winning apartments with interiors designed by Irish fashion star John Rocha.
>
> **Waterfront Penthouse** (☎ 01695-727877; www.stayinginliverpool.com; Clippers Quay; apt from £120) One luxury pad with sensational views and all the trimmings.

Italian Club (☎ 0151-708 5508; 85 Bold St; mains £6-10; ☻ 9.30am-9pm) The Picinisco family must have been homesick for southern Italy, so they opened this fabulous spot, adorned it with family pictures and began serving the kind of food relatives visiting from the home country would be glad to tuck into.

Midrange

Tea Factory (☎ 0151-708 7008; 79 Wood St; mains £7-12; ☻ 11am-late) Who knew that cod 'n' chips could be so…cool? The wide-ranging menu covers all bases from typical Brit to funky finger food such as international tapas, but it's the room, darling, that makes this place so popular. Rock stars and the impossibly beautiful have found a home here.

Tokyou (☎ 0151-445 1023; 7 Berry St; mains £8-13; ☻ 5 11.30pm) Cheap, healthy Asian cuisine from Japan, China, Taiwan and Korea reminds us of a larger chain like Wagamama, but this place is friendlier and more intimate. Whether takeaway or eat-in (at long picnic-style benches), the food is terrific.

Quarter (☎ 0151-707 1965; 7-11 Falkner St; mains £9-13; ☻ lunch & dinner) A gorgeous little wine bar and bistro with outdoor seating for that elusive summer's day. It's perfect for a lunchtime plate of pasta or just a coffee and a slice of mouth-watering cake.

Top End

Pan-American Club (☎ 0151-709 7097; Britannia Pavilion, Albert Dock; mains £13-24; ☻ 11am-2am) A truly beautiful warehouse conversion has created this top-class restaurant and bar, easily one of the best dining addresses in town. Fancy steak dinners and other American classics can be washed down with drinks from the Champagne Lounge.

Meet Argentinean (☎ 0151-258 1816; 2 Brunswick St; mains lunch £9-26, dinner £15-21; ☻ noon-11pm) Liverpool's first Argentinean restaurant is really an elegant tribute to grilled beef served the size of a small wheel – just as any self-respecting gaucho would demand. Thankfully, there are some cuts that are smaller but just as good; the 16oz grilled fillet steak was plenty for us.

Alma de Cuba (☎ 0151-709 7097; www.alma-de-cuba.com; St Peter's Church, Seel St; mains £16-24; ☻ lunch & dinner) This extraordinary venture has seen the transformation of a Polish church into a Miami-style Cuban extravaganza, a bar and restaurant where you can feast on a suckling pig (the menu heavily favours meat) or clink a perfectly made mojito at the long bar. ¡Salud!

London Carriage Works (☎ 0151-705 2222; www.tlcw.co.uk; 40 Hope St; 2-/3-course meals £35/45; ☻ 8am-10pm Mon-Sat, 8am-8pm Sun) Liverpool's dining revolution is being led by Paul Askew's award-winning restaurant. Its followers are the fashionistas, socceristas and other members of the style brigade who share the large, open space that is the dining room – actually more of a bright glass box divided only by a series of sculpted glass shards. They indulge in the marvellous, eclectic ethnic menu, which reveals influences from every corner of the world.

DRINKING

Put mildly, Scousers like a good night out. Health officials may despair, but Liverpool's wealth of pubs and bars of every hue only exist to satisfy a seemingly inexhaustible desire to get loaded, especially in the 'party zone' that is Ropewalks. Unless specified, all the bars included here open 11am until 2am Monday to Saturday, although most have a nominal entry charge after 11pm.

City Centre

Bar Ça Va (☎ 0151-709 9300; 4A Wood St) Our favourite of the Ropewalks bars, this place has more of an indie vibe than the others that surround it. You can still get coloured jello shots and cheap bottles of alcopops, but the crowd here is a little more discerning, meaning it takes a lot more booze than usual to start a conga line.

Hannah's (☎ 0151-708 5959; 2 Leece St) One of the top student bars in town. Try to land yourself a table on the outdoor patio, which is covered in the event of rain. Staying open late, a friendly, easygoing crowd and some pretty decent music make this one of the better places in which to have a drink.

Magnet (☎ 0151-709 6969; 39 Hardman St) Red leather booths, plenty of velvet and a suitably seedy New York–dive atmosphere where Iggy Pop or Tom Waits would feel right at home. The upstairs bar is very cool but totally chilled out, while downstairs the dance-floor shakes to the best music in town, spun by up-and-comers and supported with guest slots by some of England's most established DJs.

Philharmonic (☎ 0151-707 2837; 36 Hope St; ☺ to 11.30pm) This extraordinary bar, designed by the shipwrights who built the *Lusitania*, is one of the most beautiful bars in all of England. The interior is resplendent with etched and stained glass, wrought iron, mosaics and ceramic tiling – and if you think that's good, just wait until you see inside the marble men's toilets, the only heritage-listed lav in the country.

Jacaranda (☎ 0151-708 9424; 21-23 Slater St) The Beatles used to play in this cellar bar – the clue is in the pictures on the walls and the constant

playing of their albums – but this is a great, no-nonsense boozer in its own right.

Albert Dock

Blue Bar (☎ 0151-709 7097; Edward Pavilion) You don't need a premiership contract to guarantee entry anymore, which means that mere mortals can finally enjoy the relaxed ambience of this elegant waterside lounge. So where have all the footballers gone? Downstairs, to the far more glam Baby Blue, a private members' bar.

Baby Cream (☎ 0151-702 5823; www.babycream .co.uk; Atlantic Pavilion) This supertrendy bar, run by the same crowd that created Liverpool's now-defunct-but-still-legendary Cream nightclub, is gorgeous and pretentious in almost equal measure. One pretty cool feature, though, is Creamselector – a set of touch screens where you can make your own compilation CD from a databank of more than 4000 tracks (for a price) – it's like taking a piece of the famous nightclub home with you.

ENTERTAINMENT

The schedule is pretty full these days, whether it's excellent fringe theatre, a performance by the superb Philharmonic or an all-day rock concert. And then there's the constant backbeat provided by the city's club scene, which pulses and throbs to the wee hours, six nights out of seven. For all information, consult the *Liverpool Echo*.

Nightclubs

Most of the city's clubs are concentrated in Ropewalks, where they compete for customers with a ton of late-night bars; considering the number of punters in the area on a Friday or Saturday night, we're guessing there's plenty of business for everyone. Most clubs open at 11pm and turf everyone out by 3am.

Barfly (☎ 0870 907 0999; 90 Seel St; admission £4-11; ☾ Mon-Sat) This converted theatre is home to our favourite club in town. The fortnightly Saturday Chibuku Shake Shake (www.chibuku.com) is one of the best club nights in all of England, led by a mix of superb DJs including Yousef (formerly of Cream nightclub) and superstars such as Dmitri from Paris and Gilles Peterson. The music ranges from hip-hop to deep house – if you're in town, get in line. Other nights feature a superb mixed bag of music, from trash to techno.

Le Bateau (☎ 0151-709 6508; 62 Duke St; admission £2-5; ☾ Thu-Sat) This oddly named club – there's nothing boatlike about this building – is home to a superb indie club, where 500 punters cram the dance-floor and shake it to sounds that have nothing to do with the charts – you'll hear everything from techno to hard rock.

Nation (☎ 0151-709 1693; 40 Slater St, Wolstenholme Sq; admission £4-13) It looks like an air-raid shelter, but it's the big-name DJs dropping the bombs at the city's premier dance club, formerly the home of Cream. These days, it also hosts live bands as well as pumping techno nights.

Theatre

Most of Liverpool's theatres feature a mixed bag of revues, musicals and stage successes that are as easy on the eye as they are on the mind, but there is also more interesting work on offer.

Everyman Theatre (☎ 0151-709 4776; 13 Hope St) This is one of England's most famous repertory theatres, and it's an avid supporter of local talent, which has included the likes of Alan Bleasdale.

Unity Theatre (☎ 0151-709 4988; Hope Pl) Fringe theatre for those keen on the unusual and challenging. There's also a great bar on the premises.

Live Music
ROCK MUSIC

Academy (☎ 0151-794 6868; Liverpool University, 11-13 Hotham St) This is the best venue to see major touring bands.

Cavern Club (☎ 0151-236 1965; 8-10 Mathew St) The 'world's most famous club' is not the original basement venue where the Fab Four began their careers, but it's a fairly faithful reconstruction. There's usually a good selection of local bands, and look out for all-day gigs.

CLASSICAL MUSIC

Philharmonic Hall (☎ 0151-709 3789; Hope St) One of Liverpool's most beautiful buildings, the art-deco Phil is home to the city's main classical orchestra, but it also stages the work of avant-garde musicians such as John Cage and Nick Cave.

Sport

Liverpool's two football teams – the reds of Liverpool FC and the blues of Everton – are

---

THE GRAND NATIONAL

England loves the gee-gees, but never more so than on the first Saturday in April, when 40-odd veteran stalwarts of the jumps line up at Aintree to race across 4.5 miles and over the most difficult fences in world racing. Since the first running of the Grand National in 1839 – won by the aptly named Lottery – the country has taken the race to heart. There's hardly a household that doesn't tune in, with betting slips nervously in hand.

The race has captured the national imagination because its protagonists aren't the pedigreed racing machines that line up for the season's other big fixtures, the Derby and the Gold Cup: they're ageing bruisers full of the oh-so-English qualities of grit and derring-do. They need these in abundance to get over tough jumps like the Chair, Canal Turn and Becher's Brook, named after a Captain Becher who fell into it in 1839 and later commented that he had no idea water could taste so awful without whisky in it.

You can book **tickets** (☎ 0151-522 2929; www.aintree.co.uk) for the Grand National, or visit the **Grand National Experience** (☎ 0151-523 2600; adult/child with tour £8/5, without tour £4/3), a visitor centre that includes a race simulator – those jumps are very steep indeed. We recommend the racecourse tour, which takes in the stableyard and the grave of three-time winner Red Rum, the most loved of all Grand National winners.

pretty much the alpha and the omega of sporting interest in the city. There is no other city in England where the fortunes of its home football clubs are so inextricably linked with those of its inhabitants. It's almost easy to forget Liverpool is also home to the Grand National – the world's most famous steeplechase event – which is run on the first weekend in April at Aintree, north of the city (see boxed text, p687).

LIVERPOOL FC

Doff o' the cap to Evertonians and Beatlemaniacs, but no single institution represents the Mersey spirit and strong sense of identity more powerfully than **Liverpool FC** (☎ 0151-263 9199, ticket office 220 2345; www.liverpoolfc.tv; Anfield Rd), England's most successful football club. Virtually unbeatable for much of the 1970s and '80s, they haven't won the league championship since 1990, but their fortunes have improved dramatically under Spanish manager Rafa Benitez and a pair of billionaire American owners. They pay local boy and legend Steve Gerrard the huge salary commensurate with his talent.

The club's home is the marvellous Anfield, but plans relocate to a new 60,000-capacity stadium a stone's throw away in Stanley Park are still pending at the time of writing; construction on the new ground may well have begun by the time you read this. The experience of a live match is a memorable one, especially the sound of 40,000 fans singing 'You'll Never Walk Alone', but tickets are pretty tricky to come by. You may have to settle for a **tour** (☎ 0151-260 6677; combined ticket with museum adult/child £10/6; ☼ every 2hrs except match days), which includes the home dressing room, a walk down the famous tunnel and a seat in the dugout, or you could just head to the **museum** (admission £5), which features plenty of memorabilia.

EVERTON FC

Liverpool's 'other' team are the blues of **Everton FC** (☎ 0151-330 2400, ticket office 330 2300; www.evertonfc.com; Goodison Park), who may not have their rivals' winning pedigree but are just as popular locally.

Tours (☎ 0151-330 2277; adult/child £8.50/5; ☼ 11am & 2pm Sun-Wed & Fri) of Goodison Park run throughout the year, except on the Friday before home matches.

SHOPPING

Frankly, Liverpool's shopping scene was pretty paltry – the most interesting shops were along Bold St – but the opening of the simply ginormous **Liverpool ONE** shopping district ('centre' just feels too small) has changed all that. There are over 160 high street stores and trendy boutiques under one huge roof: you need never go anywhere else again.

Alternative shoppers should still venture along Bold St, home to **Hairy Records** (☎ 0151-709 3121; 124 Bold St; ☼ 11am-5.30pm Mon-Sat), the best record shop in the city, and **Resurrection** (☎ 0151-709 2676; 25 Bold St; ☼ 10am-6pm Mon-Wed & Fri-Sat, to 8pm Thu, 11am-5pm Sun), where you can find individualistic styles far removed from the similar brands sold by high street retailers.

GETTING THERE & AWAY
Air
Liverpool John Lennon Airport (☎ 0870 750 8484; www.liverpooljohnlennonairport.co.uk) serves a variety of international destinations including Amsterdam, Barcelona, Dublin and Paris, as well as destinations in the UK (Belfast, London and the Isle of Man).

Bus
The **National Express Coach Station** (☎ 08705 808080; Norton St) is situated 300m north of Lime St station. There are services to/from most major towns, including Manchester (£5, 1¼ hours, hourly), London (£24, five to six hours, seven daily), Birmingham (£10.20, 2¾ hours, five daily) and Newcastle (£20.50, 6½ hours, three daily).

Train
Liverpool's main station is Lime St. It has hourly services to almost everywhere, including Chester (£4.45, 45 minutes), London (£61.60, 3¼ hours), Manchester (£8.80, 45 minutes) and Wigan (£4.60, 50 minutes).

GETTING AROUND
To/From the Airport
The airport is 8 miles south of the centre. **Arriva Airlink** (per person £1.70; ☼ 6am-11pm) buses 80A and 180 depart from Paradise St station, and **Airportxpress 500** (per person £2.50; ☼ 5.15am-12.15am) buses leave from outside Lime St station. Buses from both stations take half an hour and run every 20 minutes. A taxi to the city centre should cost no more than £15.

THE NORTHWEST

SOMETHING FOR THE WEEKEND

Let's get a little greedy and do a two-for-one weekend, making the most of the fact that, despite their huge historic rivalries, Manchester and Liverpool are only 37 miles apart. Spend the first night in Liverpool – check in to the **Hope Street Hotel** (p684) to really do it in style. It's Friday night, so dinner downstairs in the **London Carriage Works** (p685) or down the street at **Alma de Cuba** (p685), should be followed by a pint in the **Philharmonic** (p686) or a spot of dancing at one of the many clubs in and around Ropewalks. Saturday is all about the museums of the city centre and Albert Dock, which should leave you plenty of time to make your train to Manchester (a trip that's less than an hour).

Claim your room at Manchester's **Great John Street Hotel** (p663) – yup, we're still stylin', but if you're looking for something a little more demure, the **Ox** (p662) offers affordable cool. Then do a little window shopping before grabbing a bite. Pick a bar, any bar, and keep going: there's an unhealthy choice of clubs if you're not that keen on a Sunday morning start.

You have your choice of things to visit, but we recommend **Urbis** (p658) and the **Imperial War Museum North** (p659) for a mere taste of the city's cool culture.

But, if dreams could come true, this would be our ideal way to spend the weekend: we'd have tickets to see Liverpool play (and beat) Chelsea on Saturday afternoon at **Anfield** (opposite), while Sunday afternoon would see us make the trek to **Old Trafford** (p660) to see United struggle to get a draw against Manchester City in the derby. Ah, to sleep, perchance to dream…

Boat

The famous cross-Mersey **ferry** (adult/child £1.35/1.05) for Woodside and Seacombe departs from Pier Head Ferry Terminal, next to the Royal Liver Building (to the north of Albert Dock).

Car & Motorcycle

You won't really have much use for a car in Liverpool, and it'll no doubt end up costing you plenty in parking fees. If you have to drive, there are parking meters around the city and a number of open and sheltered car parks. Car break-ins are a significant problem, so leave absolutely nothing of value in the car.

Public Transport

Local public transport is coordinated by **Merseytravel** (☎ 0151-236 7676; www.merseytravel .gov.uk). Highly recommended is the **Saveaway ticket** (adult/child £3.70/1.90), which allows for one day's off-peak travel on all bus, train and ferry services throughout Merseyside. Tickets are available at shops and post offices throughout the city. Paradise St bus station is in the city centre.

MERSEYRAIL
Merseyrail (☎ 0151-702 2071; www.merseyrail.org) is an extensive suburban rail service linking Liverpool with the Greater Merseyside area. There are four stops in the city centre: Lime St, Central (handy for Ropewalks), James St (close to Albert Dock) and Moorfields (for the Liverpool War Museum).

Taxi

Mersey Cabs (☎ 0151-298 2222) operates tourist taxi services and also has some wheelchair-accessible cabs.

AROUND LIVERPOOL

PORT SUNLIGHT

Southwest of Liverpool, across the River Mersey on the Wirral Peninsula, picturesque Port Sunlight is a 19th-century village created by the philanthropic Lever family to house workers from their soap factory. The main reason to come here is the wonderful **Lady Lever Art Gallery** (☎ 0151-478 4136; www.liverpoolmuseums.org.uk/ladylever; admission free; ☯ 10am-5pm), off Greendale Rd, where you can see some of the greatest works of the Pre-Raphaelite Brotherhood (see boxed text, p534), as well as some fine Wedgwood pottery.

Take the Merseyrail to Bebington on the Wirral line; the gallery is a five-minute walk from the station. Alternatively, bus 51 from Woodside will get you here.

SPEKE

A marvellous example of a black-and-white half-timbered hall can be visited at **Speke Hall** (NT; ☎ 0151-427 7231; www.nationaltrust.org.uk; house & gardens adult/child £7.50/3.80, gardens only adult/child £4.50/2.50; ⊗ 1-5.30pm Wed-Sun Apr-Oct, 1-4.30pm Sat & Sun Nov-Mar), six miles south of Liverpool in the plain suburb of Speke. It contains several priest's holes where 16th-century Roman Catholic priests could hide when they were forbidden to hold Masses. Any airport bus from Paradise St will drop you within a half-mile of the entrance. Speke Hall can also be combined with a National Trust 1½-hour **tour** (☎ 0151-486 4006; with Speke Hall adult/child £15/3) to the childhood homes of both Lennon and McCartney (see boxed text, p682) – you can book at Speke Hall or at the tourist offices in Liverpool.

LANCASHIRE

As industrious as it is isolated, Lancashire has a bit of everything. The southern half is just a teeny bit urban – indeed, there's no part of England so heavily urbanised – and it includes mighty Manchester, so big that it's administered separately (and given its own section in this chapter). But once you go north, past Blackpool – the empress of the traditional British seaside resort – you arrive at the undulating rolls of the Ribble Valley, a gentle and beautiful warm-up for the Lake District that lies just beyond Lancashire's northern border. Head north of the Ribble Valley you'll come across a the handsome Georgian county town of Lancaster.

BLACKPOOL

pop 142,290

The queen bee of England's fun-by-the-sea-type resorts is unquestionably Blackpool. It's bold and brazen in its efforts to cement its position as the country's second-most-visited town after London. Tacky, trashy and, in recent years, a little bit tawdry, Blackpool doesn't care because 16 million annual visitors don't either.

Blackpool works so well because it has mastered the time-tested, traditional British holiday-by-the-sea formula with high-tech, 21st-century amusements that thrill even the most cynical observer. Basically, a holiday here is all about pure, unadulterated fun.

The town is famous for its tower, its three piers, its Pleasure Beach and its Illuminations, the latter being a successful ploy to extend the brief summer holiday season. From early September to early November, 5 miles of The Promenade are illuminated with thousands of electric and neon lights.

Orientation & Information

Blackpool is surprisingly spread out, but can still be managed easily without a car; trams run the entire 7-mile length of the seafront Promenade.

Tourist office (www.visitblackpool.com) Clifton St (☎ 01253-478222; 1 Clifton St; ⊗ 9am-5pm Mon-Sat); Central Promenade (☎ 01253-403223; ⊗ 9am-5pm Mon-Sat, 10am-4pm Sun Apr-Sep)

Sights

PLEASURE BEACH

The main reason for Blackpool's immense popularity is the simply fantastic **Pleasure Beach** (☎ 0870 444 5566; www.blackpoolpleasurebeach .com; Freedom Pass £5; ⊗ from 10.30am Apr-early Nov), a 16-hectare collection of more than 145 rides. It attracts some seven million visitors annually, and, as amusement parks go, this is the best you'll find anywhere in Europe.

The park's major rides include the Big One, the tallest and fastest roller coaster in Europe, reaching a top speed of 85mph before hitting a near-vertical descent of 75m; the Ice Blast, which delivers you up a 65m steel tower before returning to earth at 80mph; and the vertiginous Infusion, which features five loops, a double-line twist and a suspended looping coaster – which should help bring up that lunch just nicely.

The hi-tech, modern rides draw the biggest queues, but spare a moment to check out the marvellous collection of old-style wooden roller coasters, known as 'woodies'. You can see the world's first Big Dipper (1923), but be sure to have a go on the Grand National

(1935), whose carriages trundle along a 1½-mile track in an experience that is typically Blackpool – complete with riders waving their hands (despite the sombre-toned announcement not to).

Rides are divided into categories, and once you've gained entry to the park with your Freedom Ticket you can buy tickets for individual categories or for a mixture of them all. Alternatively, an Unlimited Ride **wristband** (1-day adult/child £26/17, 2-day £45) includes the £5 entrance fee; there are good discounts to be had if you book your tickets online.

There are no set times for closing; it depends how busy it is.

OTHER SIGHTS

Blackpool's most recognisable landmark is the 150m-high **Blackpool Tower** (☎ 01253-622242; www.theblackpooltower.co.uk; adult/child £17/13; ☥ 10am-6pm), built in 1894. Inside is a vast entertainment complex that should keep the kids happy, including a dinosaur ride, Europe's largest indoor jungle gym and a Moorish circus.

The highlight is the magnificent rococo **ballroom** (☥ 10am-6pm Mon-Fri & Sun, to 11pm Sat), with extraordinary sculptured and gilded plasterwork, murals, chandeliers and couples gliding across the beautifully polished wooden floor to the melodramatic tones of a huge Wurlitzer organ.

Across from Pleasure Beach is **Sandcastle Waterpark** (☎ 01253-343602; www.sandcastle-waterpark.co.uk; adult/child £12.60/11; ☥ from 10am May-Oct, from 10am Sat & Sun Nov-Feb), an indoor water complex. It has 15 different slides and rides, including the Master Blaster, the world's largest indoor waterslide. Forget the beach – this is the most pleasant place to have a swim.

Of the three Victorian piers, the most famous – and the longest – is the **North Pier**, built in 1862 and opening a year later, charging a penny for admission. Today admission to its plethora of assorted rides and attractions is free.

Near the Central Pier is the state-of-the-art **Sealife Centre** (☎ 01253-622445; www.sealifeeurope .com; New Bonny St; adult/child £12.50/9.50; ☥ 10am-8pm), which features 2½m-long sharks and a giant octopus.

Sleeping

With more than 2500 hotels, B&Bs and self-catering units, Blackpool knows how to put

visitors up for the night. Whatever you do, though, book ahead if you want a decent room during the Illuminations. If you want to stay close to the waterfront, prepare for a noisy, boisterous night; accommodation along Albert and Hornby Rds, 300m back from the sea, is that little bit quieter. The tourist offices will assist you in finding a bed.

our pick **Number One** (☎ 01253-343901; www.numberoneblackpool.com; 1 St Lukes Rd; s/d from £70/120; ℗) Far fancier than anything else around, this stunning boutique guesthouse is all luxury and contemporary style. Everything exudes a kind of discreet elegance, from the dark-wood furniture and high-end mod cons to the top-notch breakfast. It's on a quiet road just set back from the South Promenade near Pleasure Beach.

Big Blue Hotel (☎ 0845 367 3333; www.bigbluehotel.com; Blackpool Pleasure Beach; s/d/ste from £75/90/160; ℗ ▣) Cool, minimalist and very much a look into Blackpool's future, this hotel caters to 21st-century demands: smartly kitted-out rooms come with DVD players and computer games, while its location at the southern entrance to Pleasure Beach should ensure that everyone has something to do.

Other options you can try:

Dutchman (☎ 01253-404812; www.dutchmanhotel .co.uk; 269 The Promenade; s/d from £20/45) Harsh blue neon out the front invites you into a self-styled party hotel whose prices double at weekends.

New President Hotel (☎ 01253-624460; www.thepresidenthotel.co.uk; 320-324 North Promenade; s/d from £45/70; ℗) Newly renovated with 65 comfortable rooms. Also serves meals (£8 to £13) in the fancy-ish Atlanta restaurant.

Ruskin Hotel (☎ 01253-624063; www.ruskinhotel .com; Albert Rd; s/d £45/80) Victorian-style hotel at the prom end of Albert Rd, near Blackpool Tower.

Eating

Forget gourmet meals – the Blackpool experience is all about stuffing your face with burgers, doughnuts, and fish and chips. Most people eat at their hotels, where roast and three vegetables often costs just £5 per head.

There are a few restaurants around Talbot Sq (near the tourist office) on Queen St, Talbot Rd and Clifton St. Our favourite meal in town is at the Mediterranean **Kwizeen** (☎ 01253-290045; www.kwizeenrestaurant.co.uk; 49 King St; mains £13; ☥ lunch & dinner), which serves a delicious suckling pig in a Sardinian style, topped with a bacon roulade.

THE NORTHWEST

DETOUR: NATIONAL FOOTBALL MUSEUM

It is fitting that this **museum** (☎ 01772-908442; Sir Tom Finney Way, Preston; admission free; ⌚ 10am-5pm Tue-Sat, 11am-5pm Sun), dedicated to the world's most popular game, should have its home in the stand of Preston North End FC. Although the game originated in the public schools of southern England, it was the Lancashire mill towns, led by Preston, that first began employing professionals in the 1870s and 1880s – basically because the working-class players couldn't afford to take the time off work to play. The towns helped launch the first professional league in 1888 (Preston North End were its first champions but they haven't won it since 1889). Besides outlining the history of the game, the museum is home to a number of fascinating (for football fans, anyway) exhibits, including a shirt worn in the world's first international match (30 November 1872: a thrilling 0-0 draw between England and Scotland); the oldest FA Cup trophy (from 1896); and jerseys worn by some of the game's true greats, including Sir Stanley Matthews and Diego Maradona. Oh, and just so you don't think that football is strictly a man's game, you'll find out that the world's first organised women's team were the Dick Kerrs Ladies from Preston. Preston is easily reached by train from Blackpool (£6.30, 30 minutes, half-hourly).

Getting There & Away

BUS

The central coach station is on Talbot Rd, near the town centre. Destinations include Liverpool (£8.60, 1½ hours, one daily), London (£27, 6½ hours, five daily) and Manchester (£6.90, 1¾ hours, five daily).

TRAIN

The main train station is Blackpool North, about five blocks east of the North Pier on Talbot Rd. There is a direct service from Manchester (£12.20, 1¼ hours, half-hourly) and Liverpool (£13.80, 1½ hours, seven daily), but most other arrivals change in Preston (£6.30, 30 minutes, half-hourly).

Getting Around

A host of travel-card options for trams and buses ranging from one day to a week are available at the tourist offices and most newsagents. With more than 14,000 car-parking spaces in Blackpool, you'll have no problem parking. In 2008 a new **land train service** (one way/ return £2/3; ⌚ from 10.30am Apr-Oct) began. It shuttles funsters between the central corridor car parks and the main entrance to Pleasure Beach every five minutes or so throughout the day.

LANCASTER

pop 45,960

Lancashire's county seat is handsome Lancaster, lined with Georgian buildings that lend the place an air of austere gentility. Folks have done business here since Roman times, but none more successfully than during the 18th century, when Lancaster was an important port in the slave trade (see International Slavery Museum, p681).

Information

Post office (85 Market St; ⌚ 9am-5.30pm Mon-Fri, 9am-12.30pm Sat)

Tourist office (☎ 01524-841656; www.citycoastcountry side.co.uk; 29 Castle Hill; ⌚ 9am-5pm Mon-Sat)

Sights

LANCASTER CASTLE & PRIORY

Lancaster's imposing **castle** (☎ 01524-64998; www .lancastercastle.com; adult/child £5/4; ⌚ 10am-5pm) was originally built in 1150. Later additions include the **Well Tower**, more commonly known as the Witches' Tower because it was used to incarcerate the accused of the famous Pendle Witches Trial of 1612 (see Pendle Hill, p695), and the impressive twin-towered **gatehouse**, both of which were added in the 14th century. However, most of what you see today dates from the 18th and 19th centuries, when the castle was substantially altered to suit its new, and still current, role as a prison. Consequently, you can only visit the castle as part of a 45-minute **guided tour** (⌚ every 30min 10.30am-4pm), but you do get a chance to experience what it was like to be locked up in the dungeon.

Immediately next to the castle is the equally fine **priory church** (☎ 01524-65338; admission free; ⌚ 9.30am-5pm), founded in 1094 but extensively remodelled in the Middle Ages.

OTHER SIGHTS

The steps between the castle and the church lead down to the 17th-century **Judges' Lodgings**

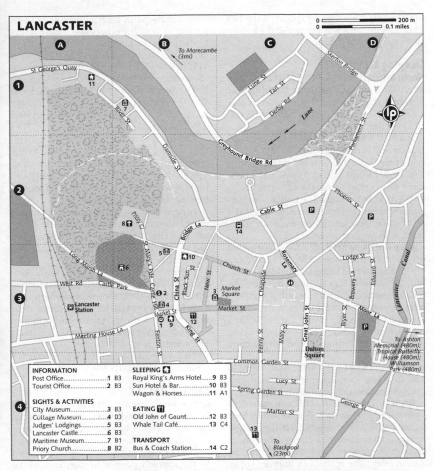

LANCASTER

INFORMATION		SLEEPING	
Post Office	**1** B3	Royal King's Arms Hotel	**9** B3
Tourist Office	**2** B3	Sun Hotel & Bar	**10** B3
		Wagon & Horses	**11** A1
SIGHTS & ACTIVITIES			
City Museum	**3** B3	**EATING**	
Cottage Museum	**4** D3	Old John of Gaunt	**12** B3
Judges' Lodgings	**5** B3	Whale Tail Café	**13** C4
Lancaster Castle	**6** B3		
Maritime Museum	**7** B1	**TRANSPORT**	
Priory Church	**8** B2	Bus & Coach Station	**14** C2

(☎ 01524-32808; adult/child £3/2; ☾ 10.30am-1pm & 2-5pm Mon-Fri, 2-5pm Sat Jul-Sep, 2-5pm Mon-Sat Oct-Jun). Once the home of witch-hunter Thomas Covell (he who 'caught' the poor Pendle women), it is now home to a Museum of Furnishings by master builders Gillows of Lancaster, whose work graces the Houses of Parliament. It also houses a Museum of Childhood, which has memorabilia from the turn of the 20th century.

A trio of other museums complete the picture: the **Maritime Museum** (☎ 01524-64637; St George's Quay; adult/child £3/2; ☾ 11am-5pm Easter-Oct, 12.30-4pm Nov-Easter), in the 18th-century Custom House, recalls the days when Lancaster was a flourishing port at the centre of the slave trade; the **Cottage Museum** (☎ 01524-64637; 15 Castle Hill; adult/child £1/free; ☾ 2-5pm Easter-Sep) gives us a peep into life in early Victorian times; and the **City Museum** (☎ 01524-64637; Market Sq; admission free; ☾ 10am-5pm Mon-Sat) has a mixed bag of local historical and archaeological exhibits.

Lancaster's highest point is the 22-hectare spread of **Williamson Park** (www.williamsonpark.com; admission free; ☾ 10am-5pm Easter-Oct, 11am-4pm Nov-Easter), from which there are great views of the town, Morecambe Bay and the Cumbrian fells to the north. In the middle of the park is the **Ashton Memorial**, a 67m-high baroque folly built by Lord Ashton (the son of the park's founder, James Williamson) for his wife. More beautiful, however, is the Edwardian Palm House, now the **Tropical Butterfly House** (adult/child £4.50/3.50; ☾ 10am-5pm Easter-Oct, 11am-4pm Nov-Easter), full of exotic and stunning species. Take bus 25 or 25A from the station, or else it's a steep short walk up Moor Lane.

Sleeping & Eating

Wagon & Horses (☎ 01524-846094; 27 St George's Quay; s/d £35/48) A pleasant pub near the Maritime Museum with five comfortable rooms upstairs; only one has attached bathroom, but all have river views.

Sun Hotel & Bar (☎ 01524-66006; www.thesunhotel andbar.co.uk; 63 Church St; s/d from £45/65; P) An excellent hotel in a 300-year-old building with a rustic, old world look that stops at the bedroom door; a recent renovation has resulted in 16 pretty snazzy rooms. The pub downstairs is one of the best in town and a top spot for a bit of grub; there are three menus to choose from, with meals from £8 to £15.

Royal King's Arms Hotel (☎ 01524-32451; www.best western.com; Market St; s/d from £50/70; P) Lancaster's top hotel is a period house with modern, comfortable rooms and an all-round businesslike interior. Look out for the beautiful stained-glass windows, one of the only leftovers from the mid-19th century when Charles Dickens frequented the place. The hotel restaurant is an excellent dining choice, with mains around £11.

Old John of Gaunt (☎ 01524-32358; 53 Market St; mains £5-6) Your one stop for traditional pub grub, decent ale and live music.

Whale Tail Cafe (☎ 01524-845133; www.whaletailcafe .co.uk; 78A Penny St; mains £6-7; dinner Mon-Fri, lunch & dinner Sat & Sun) This gorgeous 1st-floor vegie restaurant has an elegant dining room and a more informal plant-filled yard for lunch on a sunny day. The spicy bean burger (£6) is particularly good.

Getting There & Away

Lancaster is on the main west-coast railway line and on the Cumbrian coast line. Destinations include Carlisle (£23, one hour, hourly), Manchester (£12.60, one hour, hourly) and Morecambe (£1.80, 15 minutes, half-hourly).

MORECAMBE
pop 49,570

Blackpool is tough enough competition for traditional seaside resorts in *other* parts of England, so imagine what it must be like for Morecambe. It was a minding-its-own-business fishing village until the middle of the

19th century, when the railway brought trains packed with mill workers and their families to its shores. Its popularity with the bucket-and-spade brigade fell away dramatically after WWII, when bolder and brasher Blackpool to the south really began to flex its muscles.

The **tourist office** (☎ 01524-582808; Old Station Bldgs; 9.30am-5pm Mon-Sat year round, plus 10am-4pm Sun Jun-Sep) is on Central Promenade and runs a free accommodation service.

The town is in the middle of a regeneration project that will bring new life to the crumbling arcades that line the glorious bay. The bay is considered the country's most important wintering site for birds, and sunsets here can be quite spectacular.

Further down the promenade is the town's most famous statue: Graham Ibbeson's tribute to Ernie Bartholomew, better known as Eric Morecambe, one half of comic duo Morecambe and Wise.

There are plenty of hotels in the town, none more inviting than the newly restored **Midland Hotel** (☎ 01524-424000; www.midlandmorecambe.co.uk; Marine Rd West; s/d from £60/90; P), an art-deco masterpiece with 44 thoroughly modern rooms that have retained the essence of their 1930s style.

Trains run half-hourly from Lancaster (15 minutes), only 5 miles to the southeast.

RIBBLE VALLEY

Lancashire's most attractive landscapes lie east of the brash tackiness of Blackpool and north of the sprawling conurbations of Preston and Blackburn.

The northern half of the valley is dominated by the sparsely populated moorland of the Forest of Bowland, which is a fantastic place for walks, while the southern half features rolling hills, attractive market towns and ruins, with the River Ribble flowing between them.

Activities
WALKING & CYCLING

The **Ribble Way**, a 70-mile footpath that follows the River Ribble from its source at Ribblehead (in the Yorkshire Dales) to the estuary at Preston, is one of the more popular walks in the area and passes through Clitheroe. For online information check out www.visitlancashire.com.

The valley is also well covered by the northern loop of the **Lancashire Cycle Way**; for more information about routes, safety and so on

---

DETOUR: HELMSHORE MILLS TEXTILE MUSEUM

If you're on your way to the Ribble Valley from Manchester, or if, like us, you have an insatiable curiosity about the Industrial Revolution's early years, then a visit to this **textile museum** (☎ 01706-226459; Holcombe Rd, Helmshore, Rossendale; adult/child £4/free; ☀ noon-4pm Mon-Fri, noon-5pm Sat & Sun Jan-Oct) will go a long way towards quenching your thirst for knowledge. The museum is made up of two of Lancashire's original textile mills – Higher Mill and Whitaker's Mill – beautifully situated at the bottom of the Rossendale Valley. The museum exhibits, including a version of Richard Arkwright's Water Frame and a working water wheel, tell the story of how cotton and wool became cloth. These fabrics made the fortunes of many an 18th-century industrialist, and helped determine the course of human history, which is no mean boast. There's the ubiquitous gift shop and coffee shop. The museum is in Helmshore (on the outskirts of Haslingden), about 16 miles north of Manchester.

---

contact **Blazing Saddles** (☎ 01442-844435; www.blazing saddles.co.uk), a Yorkshire-based bike store.

The tourist office in Clitheroe (below) has three useful publications: *Bowlands by Bike* (£1), *Mountain Bike Ribble Valley Circular Routes* (£2.50) and *Mountain Bike Rides in Gisburn Forest* (£2).

Clitheroe
pop 14,700

Located northeast of Preston, the Ribble Valley's largest market town is best known for its impressive **Norman keep** (admission free; ☀ dawn-dusk), built in the 12th century and now, sadly, standing empty; there are great views of the river valley below. The extensive grounds are home to the mildly interesting **castle museum** (☎ 01200-424635), currently closed for repairs – it should reopen in the summer of 2009.

The **tourist office** (☎ 01200-425566; www.ribble valley.gov.uk; 14 Market Place; ☀ 9am-5pm Mon-Sat, 10am-4pm Sun) has information on the town and surrounding area. **Pedal Power** (☎ 01200-422066; Waddington Rd) has bikes for rent.

Decent accommodation options include **Brooklyn Guesthouse** (☎ 01200-428268; 32 Pimlico Rd; s/d from £26/44), a handsome Georgian house with comfy flower-print rooms, and **Swan & Royal Hotel** (☎ 01200-423130; www.swanandroyal .co.uk; 26 Castle St; s/d from £35/55), a family-run, half-timbered hotel with six rooms. **Halpenny's of Clitheroe** (☎ 01200-424478; Old Toll House, 1-5 Parson Lane; mains around £5) is a traditional teashop that serves sandwiches, and dishes such as Lancashire hotpot.

Pendle Hill

The Valley's top attraction is Pendle Hill (558m), made famous in 1612 as the stomping ground of the Pendle Witches. These were 10 women who, allegedly, practised all kinds of malefic doings until they were convicted on the sole testimony of a child, and hanged. The tourist authority makes a big deal of the mythology surrounding the unfortunate women, and every Halloween a pseudomystical ceremony is performed here to commemorate their 'activities'.

If that isn't enough, the hill is also renowned as the spot where George Fox had a vision in 1652 that led him to found the Quakers. Whatever your thoughts on witchcraft and religious visions, the hill, a couple of miles east of Clitheroe, is a great spot to walk to.

A WALK THROUGH MIDDLE EARTH

Ever wondered what it would be like to walk in Frodo Baggins' beloved Shire…without the aid of hallucinogens? JRR Tolkien's descriptions of Hobbiton and the Shire in *The Lord of the Rings* were inspired by the countryside around Hurst Green, about 5 miles southwest of Clitheroe. Tolkien was a regular guest in the grounds of Stonyhurst College during the years in which he wrote the epic novel, a favourite of fantasy nerds all over the world (including this author).

A 5.5-mile circular walk has been created, following Tolkien's own footsteps – it begins at Shireburn Arms (where he was partial to the ale) and includes the crossing of the Rivers Ribble and Hodder (Rivers Shirebourne and Brandywine in the book). The Ribble Valley official website (www .ribblevalley.gov.uk) has details of the walk; Hurst Green is on the Clitheroe–Preston bus line.

Forest of Bowland
☎ 01200

This vast, grouse-ridden moorland is somewhat of a misnomer. The use of 'forest' is a throwback to an earlier definition, when it served as a royal hunting ground. Today it is an Area of Outstanding Natural Beauty (AONB), which makes for good walking and cycling. The **Pendle Witch Way**, a 45-mile walk from Pendle Hill to northeast of Lancaster, cuts right through the area, and the **Lancashire Cycle Way** runs along the eastern border. The forest's main town is Slaidburn, about 9 miles north of Clitheroe on the B6478.

Other villages worth exploring are Newton, Whitewell and Dunsop Bridge.

SLEEPING & EATING

The popular **Slaidburn YHA** (☎ 0845 371 9343; www.yha.org.uk; King's House, Slaidburn; dm £12; ◷ Apr-Oct), a converted 17th-century village inn, is especially popular with walkers and cyclists.

More-luxurious accommodation is limited. In Slaidburn, the wonderful 13th-century **Hark to Bounty Inn** (☎ 01200-446246; www.harktobounty .co.uk; s/d £43/85) has atmospheric rooms with exposed oak beams. An excellent restaurant (mains £8 to £13) downstairs specialises in homemade herb breads.

Elsewhere, the stunning **Inn at Whitewell** (☎ 01200-448222; www.innatwhitewell.com; Whitewell Village; s/d from £70/96) is a remarkable place set amid 1½ hectares of grounds. Once the home of Bowland's forest keeper, it is now a superb guest house with a wonderfully eccentric feel. The gorgeous rooms have antique furniture, peat fires and Victorian claw-foot baths. The restaurant (mains £10 to £16) specialises in traditional English game dishes.

Getting There & Around

Clitheroe is served by regular buses from Preston and Blackburn as well as by hourly train from Manchester (£8.30, 75 minutes) and Preston (£5.60, 50 minutes). Once here, you're better off if you have your own transport, as there is only a Sunday bus service between Clitheroe and the rest of the valley villages. If you need a rental, go to **Castle Car Hire** (☎ 01200-426000; 6 St Anne's Sq, Clitheroe).

ISLE OF MAN

Beloved of tax dodgers, petrol-heads and folks who like tailless cats, the Isle of Man (Ellan Vannin in Manx, the Gaelic language of the island) has long had to endure notions about being populated by odd folk with even odder ways. This unfounded prejudice is hard to fathom, but a clue is perhaps in the islanders' dogged refusal to relinquish their quasi-independent status and become fully fledged Englanders, which invariably makes mainlanders suspicious.

But chances are that those same mainlanders have never actually seen the lush valleys, barren hills and rugged coastlines of what is a beautiful island. Perfect for walking, cycling, driving or just relaxing, this is a place that refuses to sell itself down the river of crass commercialism and mass tourism. Except, of course, for the world-famous summer season of Tourist Trophy (TT) motorbike racing, which attracts around 50,000 punters and bike freaks every May and June. Needless to say, if you want a slice of silence, be sure to avoid the high-rev bike fest.

Home to the world's oldest continuous parliament, the Isle of Man enjoys special status in Britain, and its annual parliamentary ceremony honours the thousand-year history of the Tynwald (a Scandinavian word meaning 'meeting field'). Douglas, the capital, is a run-down relic of Victorian tourism with fading B&Bs.

Orientation & Information

Situated in the Irish Sea, equidistant from Liverpool, Dublin and Belfast, the Isle of Man is about 33 miles long by 13 miles wide. Ferries arrive at Douglas, the port and main town on the southeast coast. Flights come in to Ronaldsway airport, 10 miles south of Douglas. Most of the island's historic sites are operated by Manx Heritage, which offers free admission for National Trust or English Heritage members. Unless otherwise indicated, **Manx Heritage** (MH; ☎ 01624-648000; www.gov.im/mnh) sites are open 10am to 5pm daily, from Easter to October. The Manx Heritage **4 Site Pass** (adult/child £11/5.50) grants you entry into four of the island's heritage attractions; pick it up at any of the tourist offices.

ISLE OF MAN

0 — 10 km
0 — 6 miles

To Belfast (85mi);
Stranraer (100mi);
(Summer Only)

Point of
Ayre

Raad ny Foillan

A10

Bride

Jurby

Andreas

*Irish
Sea*

Sulby

Ramsey

*Ramsey
Bay*

A3

Churchtown

Bellaugh

Maughold

Kirk Michael

TT Circuit

A3

Snaefell
(621m)

A2

*Isle
of Man*

Peel

Tynwald
Hill

Laxey

St John's

Patrick

Cregny
Baa

Baldrine

Heritage Walk

Foxdale

Crosby

Lonan
Old
Church

Dalby

A1

Millennium Way

Douglas

To
Heysham
(65mi)

A5

St Marks

Ballasalla

Port Erin

A5

To
Liverpool
(75mi)

Cregneash

Chapel
Hill

Castletown

Port
St Mary

Isle of Man
(Ronaldsway)
Airport

*Calf
of Man*

To Dublin (90mi);
(Summer Only)

Activities
WALKING & CYCLING
With plenty of great marked trails, the Isle of Man is a firm favourite with walkers and is regularly voted one of the best walking destinations in Britain. Ordnance Survey (OS) Landranger Map 95 (£6.99) covers the whole island, while the free *Walks on the Isle of Man* is available from the tourist office in Douglas. The **Millennium Way** is a walking path that runs the length of the island amid some spectacular scenery. The most demanding of all the island's walks is the 95-mile **Raad ny Foillan** (Road of the Gull), a well-marked path that makes a complete circuit of the island and normally takes about five days to complete. The **Isle of Man**

Walking Festival (www.isleofmanwalking.com) takes place over five days in June and has proven such a success that a three-day **autumn festival** was added in 2007.

There are six designated off-road cycling trails on the island, each with varying ranges of difficulty. See www.gov.im/tourism/activities/events/mountainbiking.xml for details.

Besides some great cycling trails, the Isle of Man is also the birthplace of the UK's top cyclist of the moment, Mark Cavendish, who won an unprecedented four stages in the 2008 Tour de France. He withdrew from the remainder of the tour in order to prepare for the Beijing Olympics, but failed to win a medal...

Getting There & Away

AIR

Ronaldsway Airport (☎ 01624-821600; www.iom-airport
.com; Ballasalla) is 10 miles south of Douglas near
Castletown.

Airline contacts:

Aer Arann (☎ 0800 587 2324; www.aerarann.com; one
way £45) From Dublin.

Blue Islands (☎ 0845 620 2122; www.blueislands.com;
one way £170) From Guernsey & Jersey.

British Airways (☎ 0870 850 9850; www.ba.com; one
way £113) From Glasgow Prestwick and Edinburgh; linked
with Loganair.

Eastern Airways (☎ 01652-681099; www.easternairways
.com; one way £90) From Newcastle and Birmingham.

Flybe (☎ 0871 700 0535; www.flybe.com) From
Birmingham (£30), London Gatwick (£60), Luton (£50),
Manchester (£27), Southampton (£35), Liverpool (£27) and
Newquay (£61).

Manx2 (☎ 0871 200 0440; www.manx2.com; from £49)
From Belfast, Blackpool, Leeds-Bradford, Gloucester M5
and East Midlands.

VLM Airlines (☎ 0870 850 5400; www.flyvlm.com;
from £120) From London, Amsterdam, Antwerp, Rotterdam, Brussels and Luxembourg.

BOAT

Isle of Man Steam Packet (☎ 0870 552 3523; www
.steam-packet.com; foot passenger single/return £30/32, car
& 2 passengers single/return £122/94) is a car ferry and
high-speed catamaran service from Liverpool
and Heysham to Douglas. There is also a summer service (mid-April to mid-September)
to Dublin (three hours) and Belfast (three
hours). It's often cheaper to buy a return ticket
than to pay the single fare.

Getting Around

Buses link the airport with Douglas every 30
minutes between 7am and 11pm; a taxi should
cost you no more than £18.

The island has a comprehensive **bus service** (www.iombusandrail.info); the tourist office
in Douglas has timetables and sells tickets.
It also sells the **Island Explorer** (1-day adult/child
£13/6.50, 3-day £26/13), which gives you free rides
on all public transport, including the tram to
Snaefell and Douglas' horse-trams.

Bikes can be hired from **Eurocycles** (☎ 01624-
624909; 8A Victoria Rd; per day £15-18; ✆ Mon-Sat).

Petrol-heads will love the scenic, sweeping
bends that make for some exciting driving
– and the fact that outside of Douglas town
there's no speed limit. Naturally, the most
popular drive is along the TT route. Car-hire

operators have desks at the airport, and charge
from around £35 per day.

The 19th-century electric and steam **rail
services** (☎ 01624-663366; ✆ Easter-Sep) are a thoroughly satisfying way of getting from A to B:

Douglas–Castletown–Port Erin Steam Train
(return £9.40)

Douglas–Laxey–Ramsey Electric Tramway
(return £5.80)

Laxey–Summit Snaefell Mountain Railway
(return £8)

DOUGLAS

pop 26,218

All roads lead to Douglas, which is still recovering from the faded glories of its Victorian
seaside past. Back then, the town was an exotic
getaway for businessmen and their families
during the 19th century. Still, it has the best
of the island's hotels and restaurants – as well
as the bulk of the finance houses that are frequented so regularly by tax-allergic Brits. The
tourist office (☎ 01624-686766; www.visitisleofman.com;
Sea Terminal Bldg; ✆ 9.15am-7pm May-Sep, 9am-5pm Apr
& Oct, 9am-5.30pm Mon-Fri, 9am-12.30pm Sat Nov-Mar)
makes accommodation bookings for free.

The **Manx Museum** (MH; admission free; ✆ 10am-
5pm Mon-Sat) gives an introduction to everything
from the island's prehistoric past to the latest
TT race winners.

Sleeping

The seafront promenade is crammed with
B&Bs. Unless you booked back in the 1990s,
however, there's little chance of finding accommodation during TT week and the weeks
either side of it. The tourist office's camping information sheet lists sites all around
the island.

Ascot Hotel (☎ 01624-675081; www.hotel-ascot.co.uk;
7 Empire Tce; s/d from £40/80; P) If you can ignore
the fact that it's just a little bit worn around
the edges (the beds are in dire need of replacement, for instance), this hotel is one of the
friendliest hotels on the island. It has first-rate
service and an excellent English breakfast,
and it's a short walk uphill from the harbour.
Make sure to get a room with a harbour view,
otherwise you'll be stuck staring at a yard.

Hilton Hotel (☎ 01624-662662; www.hilton.co.uk
/isleofman; Central Promenade; r from £70; P ▣) The
Hilton's brand of business hotel has come to
Douglas and made a very good first impression; the rooms are modern and functional
(high-speed internet is standard throughout),

if a little lacking in decorative imagination. There's also a small gym and a casino on the premises, but don't bother with the awfully bland Colours Bar and Atlantis restaurant.

Sefton Hotel (☎ 01624-645500; www.seftonhotel .co.im; Harris Promenade; r from £95; P ⊠) Douglas' best hotel is an upmarket oasis with its own indoor water garden and rooms that range from plain and comfy to elegant and very luxurious. The rooms overlooking the water garden are superb, even better than the ones with sea views. You save up to 10% if you book online.

Admiral House (☎ 01624-629551; www.admiralhouse .com; Loch Promenade; s/d from £95/110; P) This elegant guest house overlooks the harbour near the ferry port. The 23 spotless and modern rooms are a cheerful alternative to the worn look of a lot of other seafront B&Bs. In the basement, the smart Ciapelli's is a top-notch Italian restaurant that is probably the best eatery in town, serving mains for around £9 to £12.

Eating & Drinking

Spill the Beans (☎ 01624-614167; 1 Market Hill; snacks £3-5; ☷ 9.30am-6pm Mon-Sat) The most pleasant coffee shop in Douglas delivers proper caffeine kicks – who says you can't have coffee in a bowl? – as well as cakes, buns and other freshly made pastries.

Tanroagan (☎ 01624-472411; www.tanroagan.co.uk; 9 Ridgeway St; mains £9-18; ☷ lunch & dinner Tue-Fri, dinner Sat) The place for all things from the sea, this elegant eatery is the trendiest in Douglas. It serves fresh fish straight off the boats, giving them the merest of Continental twists or just a spell on the hot grill. Reservations are recommended.

There are a few good pubs around, including the trendy **Bar George** (☎ 01624-617799; St George's Chambers, 3 Hill St), and **Rover's Return** (☎ 01624-676459; 11 Church St), which specialises in the local brew, Bushy Ales.

AROUND DOUGLAS

You can follow the TT circuit up and over the mountain or wind around the coast. The mountain route goes close to the summit of **Snaefell** (621m), the island's highest point. It's an easy walk up to the summit, or you can take the electric tram from Laxey, near the coast.

On the edge of Ramsey, on the north of the island, is the **Grove Rural Life Museum** (MH; admission £3.30; ☷ 10am-5pm Apr-Oct). The church in the small village of **Maughold** is on the site of

an ancient monastery; a small shelter houses quite a good selection of stone crosses and ancient inscriptions.

It's no exaggeration to describe the **Lady Isabella Laxey Wheel** (MH; admission £3.30), built in 1854 to pump water from a mine, as a 'great' wheel; it measures 22m across and can draw 1140L of water per minute from a depth of 550m. It is named after the wife of the then lieutenant-governor and is the largest wheel of its kind in the world.

The wheel-headed cross at **Lonan Old Church**, just north of Douglas, is the island's most impressive early Christian cross.

CASTLETOWN & AROUND

At the southern end of the island is Castletown, a quiet harbour town that was originally the capital of the Isle of Man. The town is dominated by the impressive 13th-century **Castle Rushen** (MH; admission £4.80). The flag tower affords fine views of the town and coast. There's also a small **Nautical Museum** (MH; admission £3.30) displaying, among other things, its pride and joy, *Peggy*, a boat built in 1791 and still housed in its original boathouse. There is a school dating back to 1570 in **St Mary's church** (MH; admission free), behind the castle.

Between Castletown and Cregneash, the Iron Age hillfort at **Chapel Hill** encloses a Viking ship burial site.

On the southern tip of the island, the **Cregneash Village Folk Museum** (MH; admission £3) recalls traditional Manx rural life. The **Calf of Man**, the small island just off Cregneash, is a bird sanctuary. **Calf Island Cruises** (☎ 01624-832339; adult/child £10/5; ☷ 10.15am, 11.30am & 1.30pm Apr-Oct, weather permitting) run between Port Erin and the island.

For a decent bit of grub, the **Garrison Tapas Bar** (☎ 01624-824885; 5 Castle St; tapas £4-6; ☷ lunch & dinner Mon-Sat, lunch Sun) brings Iberian flavour to a handsome 17th-century building in the centre of town. The paella (£20) is fantastic, but it feeds four. A new terrace upstairs will keep smokers happy.

Port Erin & Port St Mary

Port Erin, another Victorian seaside resort, plays host to the small **Railway Museum** (admission £1; ☷ 9.30am-5.30pm Apr-Oct), which reveals the history of steam railway on the island.

Port Erin has a good range of accommodation, as does Port St Mary, across the headland and linked by steam train.

Our Port Erin choice would be the Victorian **Falcon's Nest Hotel** (☎ 01624-834077; falconsnest@enter prise.net; Station Rd; s/d from £35/70), once supremely elegant, now just handsome in a nostalgic sort of way. The rooms are nothing special, but the views over the water are superb.

The slightly more splendid Victorian-style **Aaron House** (☎ 01624-835702; www.aaronhouse.co.uk; The Promenade, Port St Mary; s/d from £35/70) is a B&B that has fussed over every detail, from the gorgeous brass beds and claw-foot baths to the old-fashioned photographs on the walls; it's like stepping back in time, minus the inconvenience of cold and discomfort. The sea views are also sensational.

PEEL & AROUND

The west coast's most appealing town, Peel has a fine sandy beach, but its real attraction is the 11th-century **Peel Castle** (MH; admission £3.30), stunningly positioned atop St Patrick's Island and joined to Peel by a causeway.

The excellent **House of Manannan** (MH; admission £5.50; ☉ 10am-5pm) museum uses interactive displays to explain Manx history and its seafaring traditions. A combined ticket for both the castle and museum costs £7.70.

Three miles east of Peel is **Tynwald Hill** at St John's, where the annual parliamentary ceremony takes place on 5 July.

Peel has several B&Bs, including the **Fernleigh Hotel** (☎ 01624-842435; www.isleofman.com /accommodation/fernleigh; Marine Pde; r per person incl breakfast from £24; ☉ Feb-Nov), which has 12 decent bedrooms. For a better-than-average bite, head for the **Creek Inn** (☎ 01624-842216; jeanmcaleer@manx .net; East Quay; mains around £8), opposite the House of Manannan, which serves Manx queenies (scallops served with white cheese sauce) and has self-catering rooms from £38.

Cumbria & the Lake District

If it's grandstand views you're looking for, nowhere in England can measure up to the dumbfounding drama of Cumbria and the Lake District. Wedged against the Scottish border, trammelled by the Yorkshire Dales and the grey rollers of the Irish Sea, it's a place where the superlatives run dry – home to the nation's longest and deepest lakes, as well as the smallest church, steepest road, highest town and loftiest peak in England. The great glaciers which carved out this landscape during the last ice age have long since melted, leaving behind a spectacular string of razor crags, scree-strewn fells and sparkling tarns that form the heart of one of England's original national parks – the stunning Lake District, founded in 1951 and still the spiritual heartland of English hiking.

With so much natural splendour on show, it's hardly surprising that Cumbria and the Lake District is one of northern England's busiest corners. Over 14 million visitors flock to the national park every year to explore its hilltop trails, literary landmarks and lakeside towns, and on summer weekends that cloudlike feeling can feel frustratingly elusive. But even on the busiest days it's possible to find some solitude in the county's lesser-known corners – the lush and little-visited Eden Valley, the seaside ports and wind-battered sands of the umbrian coast, or the bleakly beautiful moorland of eastern Cumbria. And if all else fails you can always take refuge in a solid old Lakeland inn for a pint of homebrewed ale and a hearty plate of tattie hotpot, Cumberland sausage or Herdwick lamb. Reet grand, as they'd say round these 'ere parts...

HIGHLIGHTS

- Conquering William Wordsworth's favourite mountain, **Helvellyn** (p732) or England's highest peak, **Scaféll Pike** (p729)

- Plumbing the gloomy depths of the **Honister Slate Mine** (p730)

- Escaping the outside world in the remote valleys of **Wastwater** (p723) and **Eskdale** (p722)

- Chowing down on some first-class Cumbrian cooking at Hawkshead's **Drunken Duck** (p718) or Penrith's **Yanwath Gate Inn** (p741)

- Watching the wild ospreys at **Bassenthwaite Lake** (p725)

- Cruising Coniston Water aboard the steam yacht **Gondola** (p720)

Bassenthwaite Lake ★   ★ Penrith
Honister Slate Mine ★   ★ Helvellyn
Wastwater ★
Scaféll Pike ★
★ Eskdale   ★ Hawkshead
Coniston Water ★

| POPULATION: 496,200 | AREA: 2629 SQ MILES | NUMBER OF LAKE DISTRICT PEAKS OVER 900M: 5 |

History

The earliest settlers arrived in the Lake District 5000 years ago, building stone circles like Castlerigg (p727) and quarrying flint and stone around Stonethwaite and Seatoller. The region was subsequently occupied by Celts, Angles, Vikings and Romans, and during the Dark Ages marked the centre of the kingdom of Rheged, which extended across much of modern Cumbria, Dumfries and Galloway, and was annexed by neighbouring Northumbria sometime in the 8th century.

During the Middle Ages Cumbria marked the start of 'The Debatable Lands', the wild frontier between England and Scotland. Bands of Scottish raiders known as Border Reivers regularly plundered the area, prompting the construction of distinctive *pele* towers, built to protect the inhabitants from border raiders, and the stout fortresses at Carlisle, Penrith and Kendal.

The area was a centre for the Romantic movement during the 19th century, and writers including Coleridge, de Quincey and William Wordsworth were among the first to champion the area's natural beauty above its potential for industrial resources (a cause taken up by other literary luminaries including John Ruskin and Beatrix Potter). The Lake District became one of the nation's first national parks in 1951, and the modern county of Cumbria was formed from the old districts of Cumberland and Westmorland in 1974.

Activities

CYCLING

Cycling is popular in Cumbria, especially mountain biking on the fells, but you'll need nerves (and legs) of steel on the more challenging routes. Cycle-hire shops are widespread, and tourist offices stock a cycling map showing traffic-free routes; bike hire starts at around £15 to £18 per day.

Long-distance bikers can follow the 72-mile **Cumbria Way** (www.cumbriawaycycleroute.co.uk) between Ulverston, Keswick and Carlisle, and the Cumbrian section of the 140-mile **Sea to Sea Cycle Route** (C2C; www.c2c-guide.co.uk) from Whitehaven via the northern Lake District en route to the North Pennines and Newcastle.

WALKING

For many people, hiking on the fells is the main reason for a Lake District visit. Trails range from low-level rambles to full-blown mountain ascents; most tourist offices sell maps and guidebooks, including the Collins *Lakeland Fellranger* and Ordance Survey's *Pathfinder Guides*, as well as Alfred Wainwright's classic hand-drawn, seven-volume set, *A Pictorial Guide to the Lakeland Fells*. If you're planning on anything more than a low-level stroll in the Lakes – especially if you're heading into the high fells – a decent quality map is absolutely essential. Walkers have a choice of two map publishers – traditionalists generally opt for the Ordnance Survey 1:25000 *Landranger* series, which are renowned for their clarity and accuracy and are used for reference by most official bodies. But many hikers prefer Harvey *Superwalker* 1:25000 maps, which are specifically made for walkers and clearly mark major trail routes (as well as all 214 fells detailed by Alfred Wainwright in his classic walking guides).

Wainwright also dreamt up the **Coast to Coast Walk** (www.golakes.co.uk/map/walks.asp), which cuts west to east from St Bees to Robin Hood's Bay in North Yorkshire, a distance of 191 miles. The Cumbrian section passes through Honister Pass, Grasmere, Patterdale, Kirkby Stephen and Shap en route to the Yorkshire Dales, a five- to seven-day hike of 82 miles. Walkers also attempt the Cumbria way (see Cycling).

Door-to-door baggage services can be useful if you don't want to lug your pack along the whole route. Contact **Coast to Coast Packhorse** (☎ 017683-71777; www.cumbria.com/packhorse), **Sherpa Van** (☎ 020-8569 4101; www.sherpavan.com) or the YHA Shuttle Bus (see p704).

OTHER ACTIVITIES

Cumbria is a haven for adrenalin-fuelled activities ranging from rock climbing and orienteering to quad biking, fell running and ghyll scrambling (a cross between coasteering and river canyoning). Sailing, kayaking and windsurfing are obviously popular too, especially around Windermere, Derwent Water and Coniston.

Check out www.lakedistrictoutdoors.co.uk for the lowdown.

Getting There & Away

TRAIN

Carlisle is on the main Virgin West Coast line from London Euston–Manchester–Glasgow, with trains running roughly hourly from both north and south.

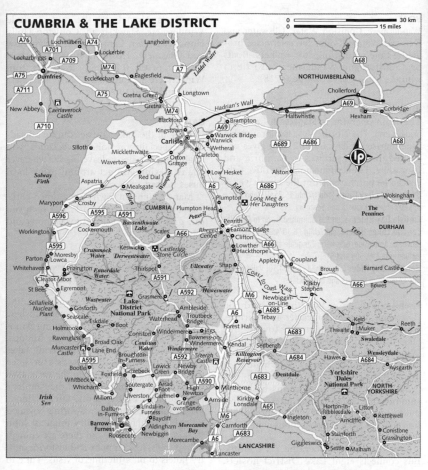

To get to the Lake District, you need to change at Oxenholme, from where regular trains travel west into Kendal and Windermere. There are at least three direct trains from Windermere and Kendal south to Lancaster, Manchester and Manchester Airport.

For something more soulful, Carlisle sits along two of the UK's most scenic railways: the Cumbrian Coast line via Ulverston and Ravenglass (see Getting Around, p732), and the Settle–Carlisle Railway across the Yorkshire Dales (see p609).

In the Lakes, you can hop aboard chuffing steam trains on the Ravenglass & Eskdale Railway (p736) or the Lakeside & Haverthwaite Steam Railway (p710) from Bowness/Ambleside to Windermere.

Call ☎ 08457 484950 for information on Day Ranger passes covering the Cumbrian rail network.

BUS

National Express coaches run direct from London and Glasgow to Windermere, Carlisle and Kendal; count on seven hours between London Victoria and Windermere.

Getting Around

Traveline (☎ 0871 200 22 33; www.travelinenortheast .info) provides travel information. Tourist offices stock the free *Getting Around Cumbria* booklet, with timetables for buses, trains and ferries.

BOAT

Windermere, Coniston Water, Ullswater and Derwent Water all offer ferry services, providing time-saving links for walkers. Boats on Coniston and Windermere also tie in with the Cross-Lakes Shuttle (p718).

BUS

The main operator is **Stagecoach** (www.stage coachbus.com). The North West Explorer ticket (one/four/seven days £9.50/21/30) gives unlimited travel on services in Cumbria and Lancashire. Twenty-four-hour Dayrider tickets can be purchased from the bus driver.

Borrowdale Day Rider (adult/child £5.25/4) Valid on Bus 79 between Keswick and Seatoller.

Carlisle Day Rider (adult £3) Unlimited travel in Carlisle.

Central Lakes Rider (adult/child £6.30/4.70) Covers Bowness, Ambleside, Grasmere, Langdale and Coniston; includes the 599, 505 and 516.

Honister Day Rider (adult/child £6.25/4.50) Valid on Bus 77 between Keswick and Borrowdale.

Useful bus routes include the 555 and 556 (Lakeslink) between Lancaster and Carlisle, which stop at all the main towns; bus 505 (Coniston Rambler), linking Kendal, Windermere, Ambleside and Coniston; and the X4/X5 from Penrith to Workington via Troutbeck, Keswick and Cockermouth.

We've given bus suggestions based on summer timetables; most routes run a reduced winter service. You can download timetables at www.stagecoachbus.com/north west/timetables.php.

From Easter to October, the YHA Shuttle Bus connects eight Lake District hostels, and provides a baggage transport service for guests. Hostels on the route include Windermere, Hawkshead, Coniston Holly How, Elterwater, Langdale, Butharlyp How and Grasmere. Hostel-to-hostel transport costs £3, or £2.50 for bags; transport from Windermere Station costs £2 to Windermere YHA, and £2.50 to Ambleside YHA.

CAR

Driving in the Lake District can be a headache, especially on holiday weekends; you might find it easier to leave the car wherever you're staying and get around using local buses instead.

Many Cumbrian towns use a timed parking permit for on-street parking, which you can pick up for free from local shops and tourist offices.

THE LAKE DISTRICT

If you're a lover of the great outdoors, the Lake District is one corner of England where you'll want to linger. This sweeping panorama of slate-capped fells, craggy hilltops, misty mountain tarns and glittering lakes has been pulling in the crowds ever since the Romantics pitched up in the early 19th century, and it remains one of the country's most popular beauty spots. Literary landmarks abound, from Wordsworth's boyhood school to the lavish country estate of John Ruskin at Brantwood, and there are enough hilltop trails, hidden pubs and historic country hotels to fill a lifetime of visits. Time to get inspired.

CUMBRIA ON A SHOESTRING

The Lake District has plenty of lavish country-house hotels and boutique B&Bs, but you don't have to break the bank to visit. There are several fantastic hostels, housed in everything from shepherds' huts to converted mansions; the flagship YHA establishments in Ambleside, Windermere and Keswick are superb. Reservations can be made at www.yhabooking.org.uk or by calling ☎ 01629 592700.

Camping is also hugely popular in the Lakes, with lots of excellent sites dotted around the national park. The National Trust runs three sites at Low Wray, Wasdale and Great Langdale (the last two also offer funky wooden 'camping pods' for £20 to £35 per night); tourist offices publish an annual *Caravan and Camping Guide*, or you can visit www.lakedistrictcamping.co.uk.

The Lake District also has several camping barns (sometimes called 'stone tents'). Facilities are basic; you'll need the usual camping gear apart from a tent, although some places provide breakfast. Contact **Lakeland Camping Barns** (☎ 01946-758198; www.lakelandcampingbarns.co.uk).

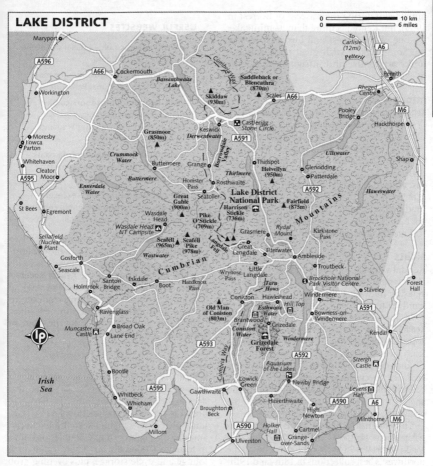

Orientation

The Lake District is shaped in a rough star formation, with valleys, ridges and lakes radiating out from the high ground around Scaféll Pike. The busiest bases are Keswick, Ambleside, and Windermere and Bowness; Coniston and Ullswater make less hectic alternatives. Wasdale is the wildest and least accessible valley.

Information

The Lake District's tourist offices are among the best in England, crammed with information on local hikes, activities and accommodation, and stocked with trail books, maps and hiking supplies. The main offices are in Windermere, Ambleside, Keswick and Carlisle, and there's a fantastic visitor centre at Brockhole (p708). It's worth noting that Ullswater, Coniston and Derwent Water lakes have a speed restriction of 10mph, and powerboats are banned on Grasmere, Crummock Water and Buttermere.

KENDAL
pop 28,398

Technically Kendal isn't in the Lake District, but it's a major gateway, so we've put it here. Mention Kendal to any seasoned hillwalker and they'll mumble a single word – 'mintcake'. The town has been famous for its peppermint treat since the mid-19th century, and it's been a staple item in England's backpacks ever since Edmund Hillary and Tensing Norgay munched it during their ascent of Everest in 1953). But Kendal is more than its mintcake: it's one of the largest and busiest towns in the South Lakes, with great restaurants, a funky arts centre and intriguing museums to explore.

Information

Kendal Laundrette (☎ 01539-733754; Blackhall Rd; ☿ 8am-6pm Mon-Fri, to 5pm Sat & Sun)

Library (☎ 01539-773520; 75 Stricklandgate; per hr £2; ☿ 9.30am-5.30pm Mon & Tue, 9.30am-7pm Wed & Fri, 9.30am-1pm Thu, 9am-4pm Sat, noon-4pm Sun) Internet access.

Post office (75 Stricklandgate; ☿ 9am-5.30pm Mon-Fri, to 12.30pm Sat)

Tourist office (☎ 01539-725758; kendaltic@southlake land.gov.uk; Highgate; ☿ 9am-5pm Mon-Sat, 10am-4pm Sun Easter-Oct, closed Sun Nov-Easter) Inside the town hall.

Sights

Kendal's most famous resident is Alfred Wainwright, the accountant, writer and in- veterate hillwalker who penned the classic handwritten *Pictorial Guides*. From 1945 to 1974, Wainwright was honorary curator at the **Kendal Museum** (☎ 01539-721374; www.kendalmuseum .org.uk; Station Rd; adult/child £2.80/free; ☿ noon-5pm Thu-Sat), where you can visit a reconstruction of his old office, complete with the great man's rucksack, spectacles and well-chewed pipe. An eclectic collection of archaeological finds and spooky stuffed animals are dotted around the rest of the museum.

The **Abbot Hall Art Gallery** (☎ 01539-722464; www .abbothall.org.uk; admission £4.75; ☿ 10.30am-5pm Mon-Sat Apr-Oct, to 4pm Mon-Sat Nov-Mar) houses one of the northwest's best collections of 18th- and 19th- century art, especially strong on portraiture and Lakeland landscapes. Look out for works by Constable, Varley and Turner, as well as portraits by John Ruskin and local boy George Romney, born in Dalton-in-Furness in 1734, and a key figure in the 'Kendal School'.

Opposite Abbot Hall is the **Museum of Lakeland Life** (☎ 01539-722464; www.lakelandmuseum .org.uk; adult/child £3.20; ☿ 10.30am-5pm Mon-Sat Apr-Oct, to 4pm Mon-Sat Nov-Mar) which re-creates various scenes from Lakeland life during the 18th and 19th centuries, including spinning, mining, weaving and bobbin-making. There's also a reconstruction of the study of Arthur Ransome, author of *Swallows and Amazons*.

Kendal's old brewery is now **Brewery Arts Centre** (☎ 01539-725133; Highgate; www.brewery

arts.co.uk), an excellent arts complex with two cinemas, gallery space, cafe and a theatre host- ing dance, performance and live music. It's also the main venue for the **Kendal Mountain Festival** (☎ 01539 738669; www.mountainfilm.co.uk), an annual celebration of all things mountain- themed, with prizes for the top new films, books and documentaries in the field of adventure travel.

Sleeping

Kendal YHA (☎ 0845 371 9641; www.yha.org.uk; 118 Highgate; dm from £18; ☿ Easter-Oct; ▣) Bang next door to the Brewery Arts Centre, this Georgian hostel is kitted out in functional YHA fash- ion. Bold colour schemes keep things cheery, and there's a choice of five doubles or bunks in four- to 10-bed dorms. There's a kitchen, lounge and cycle storage, plus evening grub on request.

Heaves Hotel (☎ 01539-560396; www.heaveshotel .com; Heaves; s from £40, d £62-72; ℗) Play lord of the manor at this mansion, surrounded by 4 hectares of grounds and woodland 4 miles south of Kendal along the A591. It's a true- blue country house, owned by the same family for the last half-century. The old-fashioned rooms are cluttered with antiques, old rugs and gilded mirrors, and most have bucolic views à la *Gosford Park*.

Balcony House (☎ 01539-731402; www.balconyhouse .co.uk; 82 Shap Rd; s/d £45/60) A cut above Kendal's other guesthouses, it's traditional but comfy nonetheless. Despite the name, there's only one balcony room; all are finished in rosy tones or smart stripy wallpaper, and big comfy beds, DVD players and bathrobes are standard issue.

Beech House (☎ 01539-720385; www.beechhouse -kendal.co.uk; 40 Greenside; s £45-75, d £70-90; P) Another spiffing B&B with a dash of designer style, inside a creeper-clad house in central Kendal. Some rooms boast velour bedspreads and fluffy cushions, others LCD TVs, chequerboard bathrooms with rolltop tubs and drink-stocked minifridges; go for the larger Greenside or Penthouse rooms for maximum space.

Eating
CAFES
our pick **1657 Chocolate House** (☎ 01539-740702; 54 Branthwaite Brow; lunches £2-6) Got a sweet tooth? Then dip into this chocaholic honeypot, brimming with homemade candies and umpteen varieties of mintcake. Upstairs, waitresses in bonnets serve up 18 types of hot chocolate, including almondy 'Old Noll's Potion' and the bitter-choc 'Dungeon'. Take that, Willy Wonka...

Waterside Wholefoods (☎ 01539-729743; Kent View, Waterside; lunches £4-10; 8.30am-4.30pm Mon-Sat) Organic bread, vegie chillis, piping-hot soups and fair-trade coffee at a much-loved riverside cafe. Even committed carnivores won't be able to resist the wonderfully sticky homebaked cakes.

RESTAURANTS
New Moon (☎ 01539-729254; 129 Highgate; mains £9.50-15; lunch & dinner Tue-Sat) Kendal's fooderati flock here for Med flavours mixed with the best of English ingredients. The decor's contemporary – think clean lines and funky cutlery – while the menu ranges from lamb meatballs with couscous to a stonking great 'Cumberland skillet'. The two-course pretheatre menu, served before 7pm, is great value at £9.95.

Grain Store (pizzas £6.50-8, mains £10-16.50; from 10am Mon-Sat) The Brewery Arts brasserie has recently had a decorative overhaul, but it's as buzzy and busy as ever. The gourmet pizzas are still in evidence, plus hefty club sandwiches and chargrilled wraps; things get more sophisticated by night, with enticing mains of Barbary duck and 'Cloonacool' char.

Drinking & Entertainment
Kendal's arty crowd shoot the breeze over cappuccinos and real ales at the Vats Bar at the

Brewery Arts Centre, while hipsters head for metro-chic **Mint** (☎ 01539-734473; 48/50 Highgate; to 2am Fri & Sat), with club nights and DJs at the weekend.

If all you're after is a pint and a pie, try the **Black Swan** (☎ 01539-724278; 8 Allhallows Lane), or the **Ring O' Bells** (☎ 01539-720326; Kirkland Ave), where even the beer is blessed – the pub stands on consecrated ground next to the parish church.

Getting There & Around
BUS
Kendal's handiest bus is the Lakeslink 555/556 (hourly Monday to Saturday, 10 on Sunday), which leaves Kendal en route to Windermere (30 minutes), Ambleside (40 minutes) and Grasmere (one hour), or Lancaster (one hour) in the opposite direction.

There are two daily buses from Kendal to Coniston (bus 505; one hour) via Windermere, Ambleside and Hawkshead, while the X35 travels south to Grange before returning via Haverthwaite Station, Ulverston and Barrow (hourly Monday to Saturday, four on Sunday).

TRAIN
Kendal is on the Windermere (£3.40, 15 minutes, hourly) line from Oxenholme, 2 miles south of town, which has hourly trains from Carlisle (£16.50, 1¼ hours) and London Euston (£121, 3¾ hours).

AROUND KENDAL
Three and half miles south of Kendal along the A591 is **Sizergh Castle** (☎ 015395-60070; adult/child £6.40/3.20, gardens only £4.70/2.40; gardens 11am-5pm Sun-Thu mid-Mar–Nov, castle 1-5pm Sun-Thu mid-Mar–Nov), the feudal seat of the Strickland family. The castle is renowned for its *pele* tower and for the lavish wood panelling on display in the Great Hall.

Nearby, the farm shop at **Low Sizergh Barn** (☎ 015395-60426; www.lowsizerghbarn.co.uk) stocks some of Lakeland's finest home-grown produce – chutneys, honeys, jams, Cumbrian puddings and organic cheeses.

Two miles further south along the A6 is **Levens Hall** (☎ 015395-60321; www.levenshall.co.uk; house & gardens adult/child £10/4.50, gardens only £7/3.50; gardens 10am-5pm, house noon-5pm Sun-Thu mid-Mar–mid-Oct), another Elizabethan manor built around a mid-13th-century *pele* tower. Fine Jacobean furniture is on display throughout

STAVELEY

This little village near Newby Bridge has become a hotbed of culinary creativity, with some of the Lake District's top foodie outlets dotted around the village's higgledy-piggledy streets. Start with doorstop sandwiches at **Wilf's Cafe** (☎ 01539-822329; Staveley Mill Yard) before sampling local brews at the **Hawkshead Brewery** (☎ 01539-822644; Staveley Mill Yard) beer hall. Try a hand-made cornet at **Scoop** (☎ 01539-822866; Unit 5a, Staveley Mill Yard), owned by the Windermere Ice Cream Co; pick up fresh-baked bread at **Le Pain de Paris** (☎ 01539-822102; Units 9-11 Mill Yard); and local sausages and picnic supplies at **Lakes Speciality Food** (☎ 01539-822713; 5 Bankside Barn, Crook Rd); then stop for culinary tips at **LucyCooks** (☎ 01539-432288; www.lucycooks.co.uk; Mill Yard) cookery school.

the house, but the real draw is the 17th-century topiary garden, a surreal riot of pyramids, swirls, curls, pom-poms and pea-cocks straight out of *Alice in Wonderland*.

The 555/556 bus (hourly Monday to Saturday) from Grasmere, Ambleside, Windermere and Kendal runs past the castle gates.

WINDERMERE & BOWNESS
pop 8432

Of all England's lakes, none carries quite the cachet of regal Windermere. Stretching for 10.5 silvery miles from Ambleside to Newby Bridge, it's one of the classic Lake District vistas, and has been a centre for Lakeland tourism since the first steam trains chugged into town in 1847 (much to the chagrin of the local gentry, including William Wordsworth). The town itself is split between Windermere, 1.5 miles uphill from the lake, and bus-tling Bowness – officially 'Bowness-on-Windermere' – where a bevy of boat trips, ice-cream booths and frilly teashops jostle for space around the shoreline. It's busy, brash and a touch tatty in places, but the lake itself is still a stunner, especially viewed from one of Windermere's historic cruise boats.

Orientation

The A592 travels into Bowness from southern Cumbria, tracking the lakeshore before join-ing the A591 northwest of town. The train and bus stations are in Windermere town. Most of the hotels and B&Bs are dotted around Lake Rd, which leads downhill to Bowness and the lakeshore.

Information
Brockhole National Park Visitor Centre
(☎ 015394-46601; www.lake-district.gov.uk; ☀ 10am-5pm Easter-Oct) The Lake District's flagship visitor centre is 3 miles north of Windermere on the A591, with a teashop, adventure playground and gardens.

Library (☎ 015394-62400; Broad St; ☀ 9am-7pm Mon, to 5pm Tue, Thu & Fri, to 1pm Sat, closed Wed & Sun) Internet access (£1 per half-hour).

Post office (21 Crescent Rd; ☀ 9am-5.30pm Mon-Fri, to 12.30pm Sat)

Tourist office – Bowness (☎ 015394-42895; bownesstic@lake-district.gov.uk; Glebe Rd; ☀ 9.30am-5.30pm Easter-Oct, 10am-4pm Fri-Sun Nov-Mar)

Tourist office – Windermere (☎ 015394-46499; windermeretic@southlakeland.gov.uk; Victoria St; ☀ 9am-5.30pm Mon-Sat, 9.30am-5.30pm Sun Apr-Oct, shorter hours in winter) In a chalet opposite Natwest bank.

THE LAKELESS LAKES

This may come as something of a shock (except to pub quiz enthusiasts), but the Lake District only has one lake – Bassenthwaite Lake, just northwest of Keswick. All the other lakes are actu-ally **meres** (eg Buttermere, Thirlmere, Windermere), **waters** (Coniston Water, Derwent Water, Wastwater) or **tarns** (Sprinkling Tarn, Stickle Tarn, Blea Tarn).

Strictly speaking, a *mere* refers to a lake which has a large surface area relative to its depth; a *tarn* usually denotes a smaller pool of water left behind a retreating glacier; while a 'water' is simply the traditional local word for a pool or area of water. But you'll find the terms used pretty much interchangeably – and after all, Winderwater and Butterwater just don't have quite the same ring.

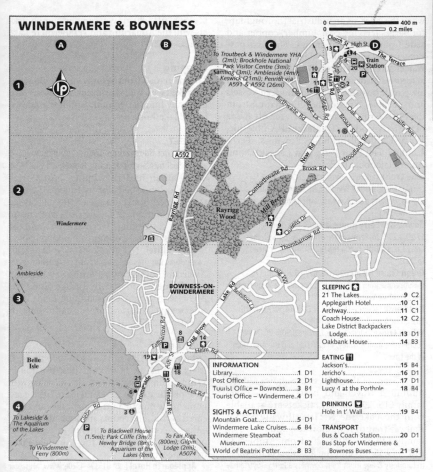

WINDERMERE & BOWNESS

0 — 400 m
0 — 0.2 miles

To Troutbeck & Windermere YHA (2mi); Brockhole National Park Visitor Centre (3mi); Samling (3mi); Ambleside (4mi); Keswick (21mi); Penrith via A591 & A592 (26mi)

A592

Windermere

Rayrigg Wood

Mill Beck

BOWNESS-ON-WINDERMERE

Belle Isle

To Ambleside

To Lakeside & The Aquarium of the Lakes

To Windermere Ferry (800m)

To Blackwell House (1.5mi); Park Cliffe (3mi); Newby Bridge (8mi); Aquarium of the Lakes (8mi)

To Fair Rigg (800m); Gilpin Lodge (2mi); A5074

Church St High St
The Terrace
Train Station
Oak St
Cliffe Ave
Woodland Rd
Broad St
Main Rd
College Rd
Old College La
Birthwaite Rd
New Rd
Brook Rd
Queens Dr
Thornbarrow Rd
Craig Wk
Lake Rd
Beresford Rd
Rayrigg Rd
Combthwaite Rd
Helm Rd
Crag Brow
Rahtfell Rd
Kendal Rd
Promenade
Ash St
Fallbarrow Rd
Cliffe Rd
Glebe Rd

SLEEPING	
21 The Lakes	9 C2
Applegarth Hotel	10 C1
Archway	11 C1
Coach House	12 C2
Lake District Backpackers Lodge	13 D1
Oakbank House	14 B3

INFORMATION	
Library	1 D1
Post Office	2 D1
Tourist Office – Bowness	3 B4
Tourist Office – Windermere	4 D1

SIGHTS & ACTIVITIES	
Mountain Goat	5 D1
Windermere Lake Cruises	6 B4
Windermere Steamboat Museum	7 B2
World of Beatrix Potter	8 B3

EATING	
Jackson's	15 B4
Jericho's	16 D1
Lighthouse	17 D1
Lucy 4 at the Porthole	18 B4

DRINKING	
Hole in t' Wall	19 B4

TRANSPORT	
Bus & Coach Station	20 D1
Bus Stop for Windermere & Bowness Buses	21 B4

Sights

Most attractions are dotted around the Bowness lakeshore. Top draw for Tiggywinkle fans is the **World of Beatrix Potter** (☎ 015394-88444; www.hop-skip-jump.com; adult/child £6/3; ☺ 10am-5.30pm Apr-Sep, 10am-4.30pm Oct-Mar), which brings to life scenes from the author's books (including Peter Rabbit's garden and Mr McGregor's greenhouse). The displays are unashamedly aimed at the younger crowd; seek refuge in the Tailor of Gloucester tearoom if it all gets a bit too button-cute.

The **Aquarium of the Lakes** (☎ 015395-30153; www. aquariumofthelakes.co.uk; Lakeside, Newby Bridge; adult/3-15yr £8.50/5.50; ☺ 9am-6pm Apr-Oct, to 5pm Nov-Mar), located at the southern end of the lake near Newby Bridge, explores underwater habitats

from tropical Africa through to Morecambe Bay. Highlights include a simulated diving bell and an underwater tunnel beneath Windermere's lakebed, complete with pike, char and diving ducks. You could arrive by ferry from Bowness or Ambleside (see below), aboard the Lakeside & Haverthwaite Railway (p710), or via bus 618 from Windermere.

The **Windermere Steamboat Museum** is closed while plans for a revamped national boating museum gather steam. Check www.steam boat.co.uk for the latest news.

Activities

BOAT TRIPS

Windermere is officially a public highway (the same as a motorway), a bizzare hangover from when the lake was an industrial thoroughfare for barges ferrying coal, lumber, copper and slate from the nearby mines. The first passenger ferry was launched back in 1845, and **Windermere Lake Cruises** (☎ 015395-31188; www .windermere-lakecruises.co.uk) keeps the tradition alive with boat trips aboard modern vessels and a couple of period beauties dating from the 1930s. Cruises allow you to jump off at one of the ferry landings (Waterhead/Ambleside, Wray Castle, Brockhole, Bowness, Ferry Landing, Fell Foot Ferry and Lakeside) and catch a later boat back.

Blue Cruise (adult/5-15yr/family £6.20/3.10/17) Circular cruise around Windermere's shoreline and islands. Departs from Bowness with an optional stop at Ferry Landing.

Bowness to Ferry House (adult/5-15yr/family/ £2.20/1.20/6.20) Ferry service which links up with the Cross-Lakes shuttle to Hill Top (p718) and Hawkshead (p717).

Green Cruise (adult/5-15yr/family £6.20/3.10/17) 45-minute cruise from Waterhead/Ambleside via Wray Castle and Brockhole Visitor Centre.

Red Cruise (adult/5-15yr/family £8.25/4.50/23) North lake cruise from Bowness to Ambleside.

Yellow Cruise (adult/5-15yr/family £8.50/4.70/24) South cruise from Bowness to Lakeside and the Aquarium of the Lakes.

A Freedom of the Lake ticket allows a day's unlimited travel and costs adult/5-15yr/ family £15/7.50/40. Joint tickets are available with the Lakeside & Haverthwaite Steam Railway (return from Bowness adult/5-15yr/ family £13.50/7.20/37.20, from Ambleside £18.70/9.35/52) and the **Aquarium of the Lakes** (return ferry & aquarium from Bowness adult/5-15yr/family £15.25/8.70/45.50, from Ambleside £21.75/11.50/61.50).

If you'd rather explore under your own steam, from April to October rowing boats can be hired for £5/2.50 per adult/child. Open-top motorboats cost £15 per hour, or there's a closed-cabin version for £18. There's a 10mph speed limit on Windermere.

LAKESIDE & HAVERTHWAITE RAILWAY
Classic standard-gauge steam trains puff their way along this vintage **railway** (☎ 015395-31594; www.lakesiderailway.co.uk; Haverthwaite Station; ☺ mid-Mar–Oct) from Haverthwaite, near Ulverston, to Newby Bridge and Lakeside. There are five to seven daily trains in season, timed to correspond with the Windermere cruise boats. Standard returns are adult/5-15yr/family

£5.40/2.70/14.80, or you can buy combo tickets with the Aquarium and Windermere Lake Cruises (p709).

Sleeping
The main road from Windermere to Bowness is stacked with wall-to-wall guesthouses; you'll generally find better value uphill than down by the lakeshore.

BUDGET
Lake District Backpackers Lodge (☎ 015394-46374; www.lakedistrictbackpackers.co.uk; High St; dm £10-12.50; ▣) Rather underwhelming hostel with cramped bunk-bed dorms squeezed into a slate-roofed house down a little cul-de-sac near the station. Still, the beds are cheap, there's a cosy lounge (with Sky TV) and the managers organise biking and hiking trips.

Park Cliffe (☎ 015395-31344; www.parkcliffe .co.uk; Birks Rd; sites for 2 adults incl car & tent £19-25) Award-winning campsite midway between Windermere and Newby Bridge along the A592, with a choice of camping fields (fellside or ghyll-side) and private bathrooms for an extra £12.50.

MIDRANGE
Archway (☎ 015394-45613; www.the-archway.com; 13 College Rd; d £46-60) Is this the best brekkie in Windermere? We think so – it's bursting with local produce from Lakeland tea to fresh eggs, homemade muesli, buttery pancakes and dry-cured bacon. The rooms are none too shabby, either – cool and uncluttered in white and pine, with hill views to the Langdale Pikes from the front.

Applegarth Hotel (☎ 015394-43206; www.lakesapple garth.co.uk; College Rd; s £55-60, d £96-156; ℗) This fine mansion, built by the 19th-century industrial bigwig John Riggs, is one of Windermere's most dashing guesthouses. Polished wood panels, antique lamps and stained glass conjure a staid Victorian vibe; cheaper rooms are disappointingly bland, but the pricier ones feature four-posters and fell views.

Coach House (☎ 015394-44494; www.lakedistrict bandb.com; Lake Rd; d £60-80; ℗) Citrus yellows meet candy pinks and sky blues at this off-the-wall number, converted from a Victorian stables. The five rooms have cast-iron beds, bespoke decor and black-and-white en suite showers, and there's a cosy sitting room for guests' use. Ask nicely and they'll pack you a picnic for lunch on the fells.

Fair Rigg (☎ 015394-43941; www.fairrigg.co.uk; Ferry View; d £66-84; P) Pastel blues, country creams and checked duvets keep things fresh at this conventional B&B, set back from the touristy fizz of downtown Windermere. It's hardly groundbreaking, but a decent option for simple, spick-and-span rooms.

21 The Lakes (☎ 015394-45052; www.21thelakes .co.uk; Lake Rd; d £70-180; P) This place gives the English B&B a well-deserved boot into the 21st century. There's a dazzling choice of camped-up rooms: suites range from the wood-beamed Grasmere (with flouncy four-poster and outdoor hot tub) to the chic Contemporary, with stripped pine, floating bed, sunken TV and 'aqua-air' bath. Glitzy, gaudy and great fun.

Oakbank House (☎ 015394-43386; www.oakbank househotel.co.uk; Helm Rd; d £82-88; P) The pick of the Bowness B&Bs, inside a slate-topped house along Helm Rd. Rich reds, peaches and regal blues meet hefty wardrobes, wrought-iron bedsteads, plush sofas and rugs; the four superior rooms offer a smidgen more comfort. Lake views throughout, plus access to a nearby country club.

TOP END

Gilpin Lodge (☎ 015394-88818; www.gilpinlodge.co.uk; Crook Rd; r £135-155, ste £170-195; P) This much-lauded country-house hotel languishes in 8 private hectares 2 miles from the lakeshore. The feel is formal (plenty of Audis and Mercedes in the driveway), but it's far from snooty. Rooms are classic, all with moorland views, Molton Brown bath goodies and upmarket furniture; top of the heap are the spanking-new garden suites, with cedarwood hot tubs, adventurous wallpapers and glass-fronted lounges leading onto private gardens. Mmm.

Samling (☎ 015394-31922; www.thesamling.com; Dove Nest; r Mon-Fri £200-490, Sat & Sun £230-520; P) Three miles north of Bowness, the Samling estate has been a local feature since the days of Wordsworth, and it remains one of Windermere's most posh addresses. These days the property, spread over 27 hectares, is a super-indulgent pamper-pad that's much favoured by the style mags and sojourning celebs. Ten rustic-chic rooms and self-contained cottages drip with designer trappings: split-level mezzanines and slate bathrooms in some, clawfoot tubs, rain showers and private lounges in others.

Eating & Drinking

Lighthouse (☎ 88260; Main Rd; mains £8-20; ☺ breakfast, lunch & dinner) Continental cafe-bar at the top of Windermere, ideal for pastries and coffee, or something more substantial at lunchtime. Plate-glass windows keep things light and bright; opt for a streetside table if the outlook's sunny.

Lucy 4 at the Porthole (☎ 42793; 3 Ash St; mains £10-20; ☺ dinner Wed-Mon) The homely old Porthole has been overhauled courtesy of the Lake District's culinary trendsetter, Lucy's of Ambleside. It boasts the same laidback atmosphere, pick-and-mix menu and wine-bar feel as the original Lucy 4, only this time steps from the Windermere shoreline.

Jackson's (☎ 015394-46264; St Martin's Sq; mains £12-18) An old staple on the Bowness dining scene, Jackson's is small and unpretentious, with a dining room dotted with potted plants and wooden furniture. Straightforward bistro food – duck breast, pan-fried fish, hefty steaks – keep the local clientele well fed.

Jericho's (☎ 015394-42522; www.jerichos.co.uk; Waverly Hotel, College Rd; mains from £14-18; ☺ dinner Tue-Sun) Windermere's top table excels at modern British cooking, which makes it a fave with the foodie guides. Tuck into sophisticated dishes – Gressingham duck, Scotch beef and baked portobello mushroom – in refined new surroundings on the ground floor of the Waverley Hotel.

Hole in t' Wall (☎ 015394-43488; Fallbarrow Rd) Polish off pub grub and ales at this venerable boozer, with the all-essential flagstones and fireplaces, plus a beer garden in case the Lakeland weather plays ball.

Getting There & Away
BUS

There's a daily National Express coach from London (£32.50, 8½ hours) via Lancaster and Kendal.

The Lakeslink Bus (No 555/556) runs hourly to Kendal (30 minutes) and on to Lancaster, and to Brockhole Visitor Centre (seven minutes), Ambleside (15 minutes) and Grasmere (30 minutes).

The Coniston Rambler (Bus 505) travels from Windermere to Coniston (50 minutes, eight daily Monday to Saturday, six on Sunday) via Ambleside.

The open-topped Lakes Rider (Bus 599) travels half-hourly (including Sundays) between Bowness, Windermere, Troutbeck,

Brockhole, Rydal Church (for Rydal Mount, p715), Dove Cottage and Grasmere in summer.

TRAIN
Windermere is the only town inside the national park accessible by train. It's on the branch line to Kendal and Oxenholme (£4, 30 minutes, 14 to 16 Monday to Saturday, 10 on Sunday), with regular connections to Manchester (£25.50, two hours, hourly) and London Euston (£123.50, four hours, eight to 10 daily Monday to Saturday, six on Sunday), and north to Glasgow or Edinburgh.

AROUND BOWNESS
Blackwell Arts & Crafts House
Two miles south of Bowness on the B5360, **Blackwell House** (☎ 015394-46139; www.blackwell .org.uk; adult/child £6.60/3.85; ☻ 10.30am-5pm Apr-Oct, to 4pm Feb-Mar & Nov-Dec) is one of the finest examples of the 19th-century Arts and Crafts Movement. Inspired by the aesthetic principles of John Ruskin and William Morris, Arts and Crafts was a reaction against the machine-driven mentality of the Industrial Revolution, placing emphasis on simple architecture, high-quality craftsmanship and natural light. Designed by Mackay Hugh Baillie Scott, the house has all the hallmarks of classic Arts and Crafts: light, airy rooms, serene decor, and bespoke craftwork ranging from Delft tiles to handmade doorknobs and wood panelling. There's a tearoom and gift shop for when you've finished moseying round the house.

Troutbeck
The titchy hamlet of Troutbeck nestles on a hilltop a mile from Windermere. The main draw is **Townend** (NT; ☎ 015394-32628; adult/child £3.80/1.90; ☻ 1-5pm Wed-Sun Mar-Oct, to 4pm Wed-Sun Nov & late Mar), a beautifully preserved Lakeland farmhouse built for a wealthy yeoman farmer in the 17th century. Topped by cylindrical chimneys and grey slate tiles, the house contains rustic artefacts, books and vintage farming tools, plus original wooden furniture carved by the Browne family who owned the house until 1943.

Windermere YHA (☎ 0845 371 9352; www.yha.org .uk; Bridge Lane, Troutbeck; dm £12-14; ☻ mid-Feb–Nov; ℗ 🖳) This YHA hostel occupies a whitewashed house with panoramic lake views.

The facilities are top-notch, with shipshape modern dorms, a well-stocked shop, a canteen and a gear-drying room. Buses stop at Troutbeck Bridge, a mile from the hostel; minibus pickups can be arranged between April and October.

our pick Queen's Head (☎ 015394-32174; www .queensheadhotel.com; d £95-120; ℗) is like a Lakeland Tardis. Outside, a solid old coaching inn; inside a bang up-to-date gastropub, where traditional slate and popping fires mix with offbeat decor and modern English cooking (braised lamb shank, celeriac pork, pan-fried pigeon). The upstairs rooms have bags of charm, with a mix of checks, stripes or flowery prints; space is tight in the 'La'al Doubles'; the 'Reet Grand' bedrooms and Four Poster suites offer more elbow room.

The village's oldest pub is the **Mortal Man** (☎ 33193; www.themortalman.co.uk; mains £8-14), overlooking the Troutbeck Valley. Hearty pub lunches are served in the battered bar or the outside terrace, but the old-fashioned rooms are overpriced.

Four miles north of Troutbeck along the A592 is Kirkstone Pass, where you can stop for sustenance and drink in the views at the **Kirkstone Pass Inn** (☎ 015394-33888), before plunging down the valley towards Ullswater (p730).

The Kirkstone Rambler (bus 517; three daily mid-July to August, weekends only mid-March to July and September to November) travels through Troutbeck to Bowness and Glenridding.

AMBLESIDE
pop 3382
Sheltering among a dramatic cluster of fells at the northerly end of Windermere, Ambleside is one of the Lake District's main walking bases. Hill trekkers descend upon the town to stock up on hiking gear and supplies before tackling the classic trails nearby, and it can get uncomfortably crowded in the summer months. But despite its popularity, Ambleside feels a good deal less commercialised than neighbouring Windermere and Bowness, and, with a selection of top-notch B&Bs and restaurants dotted around its slate-grey streets, it makes an ideal launching pad for exploring the central Lakes.

Information

Laundromat (☎ 015394-32231; Kelsick Rd; 🕑 10am-6pm)

Library (☎ 015394-32507; Kelsick Rd; per hr £3; 🕑 10am-5pm Mon & Wed, to 7pm Tue & Fri, to 1pm Sat) Internet access.

Post office (Market Cross; 🕑 9am-5pm Mon-Sat)

Tourist office (☎ 015394-32582; tic@thehubof ambleside.com; Central Buildings, Market Cross; 🕑 9am-5pm) Sells fishing permits, guidebooks and bus passes.

Sights & Activities

Ambleside's best-known landmark is **Bridge House**, which spans the tumbling brook of **Stock Ghyll** downhill from Market Cross. Nearby at the **Armitt Museum** (☎ 015394-31212; www.armitt.com; Rydal Rd; adult £2.50; 🕑 10am-5pm), artefacts include a lock of John Ruskin's hair, a collection of botanical watercolours by Beatrix Potter, and prints by the pharmacist-turned-photographer Herbert Bell.

Footy fans should check out **Homes of Football** (☎ 015394-34440; 100 Lake Rd; admission free; 🕑 10am-5pm Wed-Sun), displaying footy-themed photos amassed over two decades by the local photographer Stuart Clarke.

Down by the lakeshore, **cruise boats** set out from the Waterhead dock for Bowness (see p710). Self-powered vessels can be hired from **Low Wood Watersports & Activity Centre** (☎ 015394-39441; watersports@elhmail.co.uk), including row boats (one/four hours £10/25), kayaks (two/four hours £14/21), canoes (two/four hours £20/26), dinghies (two/four hours £35/53) and motor boats (one/four hours £18/45).

If you're feeling energetic, Ambleside marks the start of several well-known walks, including the wooded trail up to the 60ft waterfall of **Stock Ghyll Force**, or the three-hour round trip via **Wansfell** and **Jenkins Crag**, with views across to Coniston and the Langdale Pikes. Serious hikers can tackle the 10-mile **Fairfield Horseshoe** via Nab Scar, Heron Pike, Fairfield and Dove Crag.

Sleeping

BUDGET

Low Wray (☎ 015394-32810; lowwraycampsite@ nationaltrust.org.uk; adult £4.50-5.50, 5-15yr £2-2.50, car £3-3.50; 🕑 Easter-Oct) Quiet and spacious lakeside campsite run by the National Trust, with a supplies shop, bike rental and fab views. Advance bookings aren't taken, so pitch up early. It's 3 miles along the B5286; bus 505 stops nearby.

Ambleside Backpackers (☎ 015394-32340; www .englishlakesbackpackers.co.uk; Old Lake Rd; dm £16; **P** 🖥) This popular indie hostel occupies a converted Lakeland cottage a short walk south from Ambleside's centre. It's clean, smart and tidy, but the bunks are rammed in tight; thankfully there's room to spare in the cosy common room and huge stainless-steel kitchen.

Ambleside YHA (☎ 0845 371 9620; www.yha.org .uk; Windermere Rd; dm from £18; **P** 🖥 wi-fi) Further along Lake Rd, this is another supremely well-organised YHA hostel, popular for its activity breaks (which run the gamut from water sports to ghyll scrambling). Clean dorms, plenty of beds and top facilities (kitchen, bike rental, boat jetty and on-site bar) mean it's heavily subscribed in high season. At the time of writing, Ambleside YHA was due to close for a refurb and planning to reopen April 2009.

MIDRANGE

Compston House Hotel (☎ 015394-32305; www.compston house.co.uk; Compston Rd; d from £56) Take your pick of the Yankee-themed bedrooms at this entertaining B&B, run by an Anglicised New York couple. Choices include sunny Florida, chic Manhattan, cowboy-style Texas and maritime Maine (complete with Cape Cod bedspread), and even the breakfast has Stateside touches, including fresh-baked blueberry muffins and maple pancakes.

Easedale Lodge (☎ 015394-32112; www.easedaleamble side.co.uk; Compston Rd; d £70-96) Twisted willow, zingy cushions and wrought-iron bed frames decorate this immaculate guesthouse on the corner of Compston Rd. Some rooms are finished in cappuccino and creams, others in stripes, florals or cool greys; all have private bathrooms, although not necessarily en suite.

Riverside (☎ 015394-32395; www.riverside-at -ambleside.co.uk; Under Loughrigg; d £82-98; **P**) Lodged beside the clattering River Rothay half a mile from town, this detached Victorian villa is a cut above. It's the little luxuries that make it special: a lounge stocked with walking guides, bathrooms furnished with ethical bath products, fresh chutneys from the Hawkshead Relish Company on the brekkie table. Two rooms have spa baths, one a pine four-poster.

Lakes Lodge (☎ 015394-33240; www.lakeslodge.co.uk; Lake Rd; r from £90; 🖥) Don't be fooled by the stern slate exterior: inside this place is modern and minimal, all cool colours, funky furniture and razor-sharp lines. Slate-floored bathrooms mix with stark white walls in the rooms, all with flat screens and DVDs. Local bangers and fresh fruit salad are served up for breakfast in the puce-and-lilac dining room.

Cote How Organic Guest House (☎ 015394-32765; www.bedbreakfastlakedistrict.com; Rydal, near Ambleside; single £98-£108, d £110-120; P 🖵 wi-fi) You won't find a greener place in the Lakes than this ecofriendly cottage. Food is 100% local and organic, power's sourced from a green supplier, and they'll even lend you wind-up torches and candles (5% discount if you hang up your car keys, too). The three rooms are elegantly Edwardian, with cast-iron beds, roll-top baths and fireplaces; sophisticates will want the top-end Rydal Suite, once used by ex-president Woodrow Wilson. The house is in Rydal, 1.5 miles north of Ambleside.

TOP END
Waterhead Hotel (☎ 08458-504503; waterhead@elhmail .co.uk; r £106-256; P 🖵) City slickers will feel right at home at this quietly swish townhouse hotel, revamped with all the boutique trappings: ice white walls, wall-mounted TVs, mountain-size beds, contemporary fabrics and a liberal smattering of leather, stripped wood and slate. The patio-bar is a beauty, nestled beside the lakeshore, and there's a similarly sophisticated vibe in the Bay Restaurant.

Eating
Lucy 4 (☎ 015394-34666; 2 St Mary's Lane; tapas £4-8; 🕙 5-11pm Mon-Sat, to 10.30pm Sun) A snazzy wine-bar offshoot of Lucy's on a Plate down the street. There's a massive list of wines and beers, plus an eclectic 'sharing' giving Lucy's spin on traditional tapas.

Apple Pie (☎ 015394-33679; Rydal Rd; lunches £4-12; 🕙 breakfast & lunch) This sunny cafe on Ambleside's main street is perennially popular for lunchtime sarnies, jacket spuds and afternoon cakes, not to mention its trademark pies (available in sweet and savoury concoctions).

Zeffirelli's (☎ 015394-33845; Compston Rd; pizza £5.50-7.45; 🕙 lunch & dinner) Zeff's is a buzzy pizza and pasta joint which doubles as Ambleside's jazz club after dark. The owners also run Ambleside's cinema; book ahead for the popular £16.95 'Double Feature' menu, which includes a main meal and a ticket to the flicks.

Lucy's on a Plate (☎ 015394-31191; www.lucys ofambleside.co.uk; Church St; lunch £6-12, dinner £15-25; 🕙 10am-9pm) Lucy's started life in 1989 as a specialist grocery, but over the last decade it's mushroomed into a full-blown gastronomic empire, with premises dotted all over Ambleside, as well as a Windermere outpost and a cookery school near Newby Bridge. This hugger-mugger bistro is still the best of the bunch. It's laidback and informal, with a handwritten intro courtesy of the great lady and offbeat dishes veering from 'fruity porker' to 'fell-walker filler'. The only drawback? It gets very, very busy, so plan ahead.

Glass House (☎ 015394-32137; Rydal Rd; lunch £8-14, dinner £13-19; 🕙 lunch & dinner) Housed in a converted watermill (with the original millwheel and machinery still in situ), this ritzy restaurant is the town's top table. Asian, Med and French flavours are underpinned by top-quality local ingredients – Herdwick lamb, Lakeland chicken, and fish from the north coast ports. Eagle-eyed diners might remember the restaurant from Gordon Ramsay's *Kitchen Nightmares*.

Drinking & Entertainment
Ambleside has plenty of pubs: locals favour the **Golden Rule** (☎ 015394-33363; Smithy Brow) for its ale selection, while the **Royal Oak** (☎ 015394-33382; Market Pl) packs in the posthike punters.

Ambleside's two-screen **Zeffirelli's Cinema** (☎ 015394-33100; Compston Rd) is next to Zeff's, with extra screens in a converted church down the road.

Shopping
Compston Rd has enough equipment shops to launch an assault on Everest, with branches of **Rohan** (☎ 015394-32946) and **Gaymer Sports** (☎ 015394-33305) on Market Cross. **Black's** (☎ 015394-33197; 42 Compston Rd) is a favourite with hikers, and the **Climber's Shop** (☎ 015394-33297; Compston Rd) specialises in rock-climbing gear.

Getting There & Around
Lots of buses run through Ambleside, including the 555 to Grasmere and Windermere (hourly, 10 on Sunday), the 505 to Hawkshead and Coniston (10 Monday to Saturday, six on Sunday mid-March to October), and the 516 (six daily, five on Sunday) to Elterwater and Langdale.

Ghyllside Cycles (☎ 015394-33592; www.ghyllside .co.uk; The Slack; per day £16) and **Bike Treks** (☎ 015394-

---

CHAT LIKE A CUMBRIAN

Like many corners of England, Cumbria has its own rich regional dialect. Celtic, Norse, Anglo-Saxon and the ancient Cumbric language have contributed to a wonderful repository of local words, many of which you're bound to hear on your travels. As well as the commonly-used *beck* (river), *ghyll* (ravine) and *force* (waterfall), keep your ears peeled for *la'al* (little), *lowp* (jump), *gander* (look), *yat* (gate), *cowie* (thing), *yam* (home), *lewer* (money), *blether* (gossip) and our personal favourites, *jinnyspinner* (daddy-long-legs) and *snotter-geggin* (miserable person).

Cumbria even had its own system of counting, sometimes called 'sheep counting numerals' since they were once widely used by shepherds throughout northern England. The exact words vary according across the county, but nearly all start with *yan* (one), *tyan* (two), *tethera* (three) and climb up to *dick* (ten), *bumfit* (fifteen) and *giggot* (twenty). Only in England...

31505; www.biketreks.net; Compston Rd; per half-/full day £14/18) both rent mountain bikes, including maps, pump, helmet and lock.

AROUND AMBLESIDE

While most people flock to poky Dove Cottage (right) in search of William Wordsworth, those in the know head for **Rydal Mount** (☎ 015394-33002; www.rydalmount.co.uk; adult/5-15yr £5.50/2, gardens only £3; ☒ 9.30am-5pm Mar-Oct, 10am-4pm Wed-Mon Nov & Feb), the Wordsworth family home from 1813 until his death in 1850.

Still owned by the poet's descendants, the house is a treasure trove of Wordsworth memorabilia. Downstairs you can wander around the book-lined drawing room (look out for William's pen, inkstand and picnic box, and a celebrated portrait of the poet by the American painter Henry Inman). Upstairs you can nose around the family bedrooms (including one belonging to Wordsworth's sister Dorothy, who never married and remained with the family until her death in 1855). On the top floor is Wordsworth's attic study, containing his encyclopedia and a sword belonging to his younger brother John, killed in a shipwreck in 1805.

Most of the gardens around the house were laid out according to Wordsworth's own designs; you can even rest your legs in the little summerhouse where the poet liked to sound out his latest verse. Below the house is **Dora's Field**, which Wordsworth planted with daffodils in memory of his eldest daughter, who succumbed to tuberculosis in 1847.

The house is 1.5 miles northwest of Ambleside, off the A591. Bus 555 (and bus 599 from April to October), between Grasmere, Ambleside, Windermere and Kendal, stops at the end of the drive.

GRASMERE
pop 1458

Even without its Romantic connections, gorgeous Grasmere would still be one of the Lakes' biggest draws. It's one of the prettiest of the Lakeland hamlets, huddled at the base of a sweeping valley dotted with woods, pastures and slate-coloured hills, but most of the thousands of trippers come in search of its famous former residents: opium-eating Thomas de Quincey, unruly Coleridge and grand old man William Wordsworth. With such a rich literary heritage, Grasmere unsurprisingly gets crammed; avoid high summer if you can.

Sights

First stop is **Dove Cottage** (☎ 015394-35544; www .wordsworth.org.uk; adult/child £7.50/4.50; ☒ 9.30am-5.30pm), where Wordsworth penned some of his great early poems and kick-started the Romantic movement. Originally an inn called The Dove and Olive, the house became Wordsworth's first Lake District base; William and his sister Dorothy arrived in 1799, joined in 1802 by William's new wife Mary and the three eldest Wordsworth children – John, Dora and Thomas – born in 1803, 1804 and 1806. The tiny cottage was a cramped but happy home for the growing family – a time memorably recounted in Dorothy's diary, later published as the *Grasmere Journal* – and after they were eventually forced to seek more space at nearby Allan House in 1808, the cottage was leased by Wordsworth's young friend Thomas de Quincey.

Covered with climbing roses, honeysuckle and tiny latticed windows, the cottage contains some fascinating artefacts – keep your eyes peeled for a pair of William's ice skates and a set of scales used by de Quincey to weigh out his opium. Entry is by timed

---

GRASMERE WALKS

Wordsworth did some of his best composing while tramping around Grasmere, and it's worth following in the poet's footsteps. The most popular walk is the 4-mile circuit around Grasmere and the base of Loughrigg Fell. Redbank Rd leads from the village along the western shore: you can hire rowboats from the **Faeryland Tea Garden** (☎ 015394-35060; ✆ 10am-6pm Mar-Oct) or continue though Redbank Woods to **Loughrigg Terrace,** with views of the lake and **Loughrigg Fell**. The trail continues past **Rydal Water** before crossing the A591 near Rydal Mount. To get back to Grasmere, follow the old **Coffin Trail** (used by pallbearers bearing coffins to St Oswald's Church) for another hour back to Dove Cottage.

Hardier hikers could follow the two-hour trek to **Easedale Tarn**, or the tougher ascents up **Loughrigg Fell** (335m) or **Helm Crag** (405m), locally known as 'the Lion and the Lamb'. Wainwright described Helm Crag as 'the best known hill in the country': you can download an MP3 version of his guide to the route from www.golakes.co.uk; it's read by the narrator of the BBC series *Wainwright Walks*.

---

ticket to prevent overcrowding, and includes a half-hour tour.

Next door is the **Wordsworth Museum & Art Gallery,** which houses a fascinating collection of letters, portraits and manuscripts relating to the Romantic movement, and regularly hosts events and poetry readings.

You'll find several illustrious graves under the spreading yews of **St Oswald's churchyard** in the centre of Grasmere. William, Mary and Dorothy are all buried here, as well as the Wordsworth children Dora, Catherine and Thomas, and Coleridge's son Hartley.

Near the church, the village school where Wordsworth taught is now a famous gingerbread shop (opposite).

Sleeping

BUDGET

Thorney How YHA (☎ 0845 371 9319; www.yha.org .uk; Easedale Rd; dm £13; ✆ Apr-Oct) Tucked away on a back lane 15 minutes from Grasmere, this rustic farmhouse is popular with families and walkers (the C2C route runs right outside the front door). The rooms are spartan, but you'll be staying in a historic spot – Thorney How was the first hostel purchased by the YHA, way back in 1931.

Butharlyp How YHA (☎ 0845 371 9319; www.yha .org.uk; Easedale Rd; dm £15.50; ✆ daily Feb-Nov, weekends Dec-Jan; P 💻) You'll find more comfort at this Victorian house a mile nearer the village. Bright, modernish dorms (including plenty of doubles and quads), lovely grounds and a decent bar-restaurant (serving everything from puddings to Perry cider) make this another superior YHA.

Grasmere Hostel (☎ 015394-35055; www.grasmere hostel.co.uk; Broadrayne Farm; dm £17.50; P) Quaint farmhouse turned excellent indie hostel, just off the A591 near the Traveller's Rest pub. It's brimming with backpacker spoils (en suite bathrooms for each dorm, two stainless steel kitchens, even a Nordic sauna), although it feels cramped when it's full. Bus 555 stops nearby.

MIDRANGE & TOP END

Raise View House (☎ 015394-35215; www.raiseview house.co.uk; White Bridge; s/d £48/96; P 💻 wi-fi) Look no further for fantastic fell views. Rolling hills and green fields unfurl from every window, especially from 'Helm Crag' and the double-aspect 'Stone Arthur'. The finish is elegantly English: Farrow and Ball paints, plumped-up cushions, puffy bedspreads and starchy linen.

Beck Allans (☎ 015394-35563; www.beckallans.com; College St; d £62-81; P) Blending in seamlessly with the rest of the village, this grey-stone B&B is actually a modern build, so all the rooms are spacious, light and thoroughly up-to-date. Crisp whites and pine furniture predominate, all with gleaming bathrooms, some with power showers; self-catering apartments are available for longer stays.

How Foot Lodge (☎ 015394-35366; www.howfoot .co.uk; Town End; d £66-76; P) Wordsworth groupies will adore this stone cottage just a stroll from William's digs at Dove Cottage. The six rooms are light and contemporary, finished in fawns and beiges; ask for the one with the private sun lounge for that indulgent edge.

Lancrigg (☎ 015394-35317; www.lancrigg.co.uk; Easedale; r £140-210; P) Originally the home of

Arctic adventurer John Richardson, Lancrigg now touts itself as the Lakes' only 100% vegetarian hotel. All the rooms have individual quirks: Whittington is lodged in the attic and reached via a private staircase, Franklin has Middle Eastern rugs and a four-poster, while Richardson has a plasterwork ceiling and claw-foot bath screened by lace curtains. It's half a mile along Easedale Rd.

our pick **Moss Grove Hotel · Organic** (☎ 015394-35251; www.mossgrove.com; r £225-325; **P** **⌂** wi-fi) Green credentials are second to none at this ecofriendly beauty: sheep-fleece insulation, natural-ink wallpapers and organic paints grace the walls, while the beds are made from reclaimed timber. This Victorian villa is sexy, too: bedrooms are massive and minimal, with bespoke wallpapers, duck-down duvets, Bose hi-fis and fantastic underfloor-heated bathrooms, and the buffet breakfast overflows with organic and fair-trade treats. Pricey, yes, but worth every penny.

Eating

Sarah Nelson's Gingerbread Shop (☎ 015394-35428; www.grasmeregingerbread.co.uk; Church Stile; 12 pieces of gingerbread £3.50; ⌂ 9.15am-5.30pm Mon-Sat, 12.30-5pm Sun) Don't think about leaving Grasmere without sampling Sarah Nelson's legendary gingerbread, produced to the same secret recipe for the last 150 years, and still served by ladies in frilly pinnies and starched bonnets.

Rowan Tree (☎ 015394-435528; Stocks Lane; mains £3-10, pizzas £6-9; ⌂ lunch & dinner) Riverside cafe with an outside terrace above the brook. Lunch is mainly sandwiches, baguettes and pizzas, but supper also offers fishy dishes and vegie mains.

Villa Colombina (☎ 015394-35268; Townend; lunch mains €4-10, dinner mains from £12) The old Dove Cottage tearooms have had a rebrand: salads, sarnies and sticky cakes by day, with Italianate flavours after dark, including Tuscan chicken, steaks, pizzas and risottos.

Miller Howe Cafe (☎ 015394-35234; Red Lion Sq; mains £5-12; ⌂ breakfast & lunch) This chrome-tinged cafe-cum-art gallery serves up crusty sandwiches, baked spuds and handmade pies, plus the frothiest of cappuccinos and creamiest of cream teas.

our pick **Jumble Room** (☎ 015394-35188; Langdale Rd; mains £13-23; ⌂ lunch & dinner Wed-Sun) You won't find a warmer welcome anywhere in Cumbria than at this boho bistro, run by an energetic husband-and-wife team with a died-in-the-

wool dedication to Lakeland produce. It's a bit like having a gourmet feast in your front room: the informal atmosphere (colourful cushions, local artwork, jumble-sale furniture) is matched by the down-to-earth menu, stuffed with local fare, from haddock in beer batter to handmade game pie.

Getting There & Away

The hourly 555 runs from Windermere to Grasmere (15 minutes), via Ambleside, Rydal Church and Dove Cottage. The open-top 599 (two or three per hour March to August) runs from Grasmere south via Ambleside, Troutbeck Bridge, Windermere and Bowness.

HAWKSHEAD
pop 1640

Wordsworth and Beatrix Potter both have connections to Hawkshead, an enticing muddle of rickety streets, whitewashed houses and country pubs halfway between Coniston and Ambleside. The village made its name as a medieval wool centre, overseen by the industrious monks from Furness Abbey (p735), but these days tourism is the main trade. Cars are banned in the village, so even on its busiest days it still feels fairly tranquil.

Sights

Well-to-do young Lakeland gentleman from across the Lakes were sent for schoolin' at the **Hawkshead Grammar School** (admission £2; ⌂ 10am-1pm & 2-5pm Mon-Sat, 1-5pm Sun Apr-Sep, 10am-1pm & 2-3.30pm Mon-Sat, 1-3.30pm Sun Oct), including a young William Wordsworth, who attended the school from 1779 to 1787. Pupils studied a punishing curriculum of Latin, Greek, mathematics, science and literature for up to 10 hours a day; no wonder naughty young Willie carved his name in one of the desks.

Beatrix Potter's husband, the solicitor William Heelis, was based in Hawkshead. His former office is now the **Beatrix Potter Gallery** (NT; ☎ 015394-36355; Red Lion Sq; adult/child £4/2; ⌂ 10.30am-4.30pm Sat-Thu mid-Mar–Oct), displaying a selection of watercolours from the National Trust's Beatrix Potter collection.

The **Hawkshead Relish Company** (☎ 015394-36614; www.hawksheadrelish.com; The Square; ⌂ 9.30am-5pm Mon-Fri, from 10am Sun) sells award-winning chutneys, relishes and mustards, from the superfruity Westmorland Chutney to beetroot-and-horseradish and classic piccalilli.

THE CROSS-LAKES SHUTTLE

To help cut down on the hideous summer traffic jams, the **Cross-Lakes Shuttle** (which runs from mid-March to October) allows you to cross from Windermere to Coniston without setting foot inside an automobile.

Boats operate from Bowness to Ferry House, from where a minibus travels to Hill Top and Hawkshead. From Hawkshead, you can catch the X30 bus to Moor Top, Grizedale and Haverthwaite, or catch another minibus to High Cross and Coniston Water.

Current singles from Bowness: to Ferry House (adult/child £2.20/1.70), to Hill Top (£4.70/2.50), to Hawkshead (£5.60/2.90), to Coniston (£9.70/5.10) and to Grizedale (£7/3.80). A return from Bowness to Coniston and back costs £16.60/9. The route operates 10 times daily from Bowness to Coniston, and nine times in the opposite direction (roughly hourly from 10am to 5pm).

The only drawback is that the buses get very crowded in summer, and if all they're full you'll have no choice but to wait for the next one (you can't prebook). Cyclists should note there's only space for five bikes on the minibuses.

For info and timetables, contact **Mountain Goat** (☎ 015394-45161; Victoria Rd, Windermere) or so a search on www.lake-district.gov.uk.

Sleeping & Eating

Hawkshead YHA (☎ 0845 371 9321; www.yha.org.uk; dm from £16; 🖳) Hawkshead's hostel is a wonder, set inside a Regency house a mile along the Newby Bridge road. Grand features – cornicing, panelled doors, a veranda – make this feel closer to a country hotel than a hostel. Dorms are roomy, there's bike rental, and buses stop outside the door.

Ann Tyson's Cottage (☎ 015394-36405; www.anntysons.co.uk; Wordsworth St; s £29-55, d £58-78) In the middle of Hawkshead, this geranium-covered cottage once provided room and board for the Wordsworth boys, but it's now a pleasant olde-worlde B&B. Rooms are snug and chintzy; one has an antique bed once owned by John Ruskin.

Yewfield (☎ 015394-36765; www.yewfield.co.uk; Hawkshead Hill; d £78-120; 🅿) Run by the owners of Zeff's in Ambleside, this swanky Victorian getaway reinvents the B&B experience. Ditch the doilies and tea-trays: here it's all Oriental fabrics, wool-rich carpets, DVD players and oak panelling (although the Tower Room has a more classic feel). Breakfast is 100% vegie (sourced from the kitchen garden), and the house is buried in orchards and wildflower meadows. It's 2 miles west of Hawkshead on the B5285.

our pick Drunken Duck (☎ 015394-36347; www.drunkenduckinn.co.uk; Barngates; r £120-250; 🅿) The deluxe Duck, two miles from Hawkshead on the B5285, takes the gastropub concept to new heights. It's a design mag's dream, blending the 400-year-old architecture of a Lakeland inn with the bespoke feel of a boutique hotel.

Flagstones and fireplaces mix with rich leather and slate in the bar (stocked with home-brewed beers from the on-site brewery), and the same antique-modern vibe runs into the restaurant (mains £18 to £25), renowned for its inventive English flavours. The rooms are bright and inviting, livened up by spoils such as Roberts radios, enamel baths and antique chairs; some overlook a private tarn. Golly.

Getting There & Away

Hawkshead is linked with Windermere, Ambleside and Coniston by bus 505 (10 Monday to Saturday, six on Sunday mid-March to October), and to Hill Top and Coniston by the Cross-Lakes Shuttle (above).

AROUND HAWKSHEAD
Grizedale Forest

Stretching across the hills between Coniston Water and Esthwaite Water is Grizedale, a dense woodland of oak, larch and pine, the name of which derives from the Old Norse for 'wild boar'. The forest has been mostly replanted over the last hundred years; by the 19th century, the original woodland practically disappeared thanks to the local logging industry.

Over 40km of trails criss-cross the forest, but Grizedale is best known for its outlandish **artwork**. Since 1977, artists have created over 90 outdoor sculptures around the forest, including a wooden xylophone, a wave of carved ferns and a huge Tolkienesque 'man of the forest'.

For information on the forest's trails, head for **Grizedale Visitors Centre** (☎ 01229-860010; www .forestry.gov.uk/grizedaleforestpark; ⓨ 10am-4pm Easter-Oct), where you'll also find **Grizedale Mountain Bike Hire** (☎ 01229-860369; www.grizedalemountainbikes .co.uk; per day adult £20-30, child £15; ⓨ 9am-5.30pm Mar-Oct, last hire 2pm).

Budding Tarzans can test their skills at nearby **Go Ape** (☎ 0870 458 9189; www.goape.co.uk; adult/child £25/20; ⓨ 9-5pm Mar-Oct, plus winter weekends), a gravity-defying assault course through the Grizedale trees along rope ladders, bridges, platforms and hair-raising zip-slides.

The X30 Grizedale Wanderer (four daily March to November) runs from Haverthwaite to Grizedale via Hawkshead and Moor Top, meeting the Cross-Lakes Shuttle (opposite).

Hill Top

Ground zero for Potterites is the picture-postcard farmhouse of **Hill Top** (NT; ☎ 015394-36269; adult/child £5.80/2.90; ⓨ 10.30am-4.30pm Sat-Thu, garden 10.30am-5pm mid-Mar–Oct, 10am-4pm Nov-Feb, weekends only early Mar), where Beatrix wrote and illustrated many of her famous tales.

Purchased in 1905 (largely on the proceeds of her first few books), Hill Top is crammed with decorative details which fans will recognise from the author's illustrations. The house features in *Samuel Whiskers*, *Tom Kitten* and *Jemima Puddleduck*, while the garden and vegetable patch appeared in *Peter Rabbit*, and the cast-iron kitchen range graced many of Potter's underground burrows. Despite Hill Top's considerable charms, after 1909 Beatrix lived almost exclusively at nearby Castle Farm; Hill Top was mainly used as an administrative base for her expanding property portfolio.

Thanks to its worldwide fame (helped along by the 2006 biopic *Miss Potter*), Hill Top is one of the Lakes' most popular spots. Entry is by timed ticket, and the queues can be seriously daunting during the summer holidays.

Hill Top is 2 miles south of Hawkshead. Bus 505 travels through the village on its between Coniston and Windermere, or you can catch the Cross-Lakes Shuttle (opposite).

CONISTON
pop 1948

Above the tranquil surface of Coniston Water, with its gliding steam yachts and quiet boats, looms the pockmarked peak known as the Old Man of Coniston (803m). The village grew up around the copper-mining industry; these days, Coniston makes a fine place for relaxing by the quiet lakeside.

The lake is famous for the world-record speed attempts made here by Sir Malcolm Campbell and his son, Donald, between the 1930s and 1960s. Tragically, after smashing the record several times, Donald was killed during an attempt in 1967, when his futuristic jet-boat *Bluebird* flipped at around 320mph. The boat and its pilot were recovered in 2001; Campbell was buried in the cemetery near St Andrew's church.

The lake also famously inspired Arthur Ransome's classic children's tale *Swallows & Amazons*. Peel Island, towards the southern end of Coniston Water, doubles in the book as 'Wild Cat Island', while the Gondola steam yacht (p720) apparently gave Ransome the idea for Captain Flint's houseboat.

Information

Coniston Tourist Office (☎ 015394-41533; www .conistontic.org; Ruskin Ave; ⓨ 9.30am-5.30pm Easter-Oct, till 4pm Nov-Mar) The Coniston Loyalty Card (£2) offers local discounts, and there's wi-fi for a small donation.
Hollands Cafe (☎ 015394-41303; Tilberthwaite Ave; per hr £5) Internet access.
Post office (Yewdale Rd; ⓨ 9am-5.30pm Mon-Fri, to 12.30pm Sat)

Sights
RUSKIN MUSEUM

Coniston's **museum** (☎ 015394-41164; www.ruskin museum.com; adult/child £4.25/2, ⓨ 10am-5.30pm Easter–mid-Nov, 10.30am-3.30pm Wed-Sun mid-Nov–Easter) explores Coniston's history, touching on copper mining, Arthur Ransome and the Campbell story – the museum's latest acquisitions are the tail fin and the air-intake from Donald Campbell's fated *Bluebird* boat. There's also an extensive section on John Ruskin, with displays of his writings, watercolours and sketchbooks.

BRANTWOOD

John Ruskin (1819–1900), the Victorian polymath, philosopher and critic, was one of the great thinkers of 19th-century society, expounding views on everything from Venetian architecture to the finer points of traditional lace-making. In 1871 he purchased **Brantwood** (☎ 015394-41396; www.brantwood.org.uk; adult/5-15yr £6/1.20; gardens only £4/1.20; ⓨ 11am-5.30pm mid-Mar–mid-Nov, 11am-4.30pm Wed-Sun mid-Nov–mid-Mar) and spent the next 20 years expanding and modifying the house and grounds, championing his concept of 'organic architecture' and the value of traditional 'Arts and Crafts' over soulless factory-made materials.

The result is a living monument to Ruskin's aesthetic principles: every inch of the house, from the handmade furniture through to the formal gardens, was designed according to his painstaking instructions (he even dreamt up some of the wallpaper designs). Upstairs you can view a collection of his watercolours, before stopping for tea at the nearby **Jumping Jenny** (☎ 015394-41715; lunches £4-8) cafe and catching a leisurely boat back to Coniston (see below).

Activities
BOAT TRIPS
For a dash of Victorian elegance, you can't top the puffing steam-yacht **Gondola** (☎ 015394-63850; adult/5-15yr £6.50/3.30), built in 1859 and restored to its former glory in the 1980s by the National Trust. Looking like a cross between a Venetian *vaporetto* and an English houseboat, complete with cushioned saloons and polished wood seats, it's a stately way of seeing the lake, especially if you're visiting Brantwood (p719). She makes five trips daily from mid-March to October. And you don't need to fret about carbon emissions from the Gondola's steam-plume; she's switched from mucky coal to ecofriendly waste-wood logs, cutting her carbon footprint by 90%.

Not to be outdone by the Gondola, the two **Coniston Launches** (☎ 015394-36216; www .conistonlaunch.co.uk) were converted to run on solar panels in 2005, making them just about the greenest ferries in England. The Northern route (adult/three to 16 years return £6.20/3.10) calls at the Waterhead Hotel, Torver and Brantwood, while the Southern route (adult/three to 16 years return £8.60/4.80) sails to the jetties at Torver, Water Park, Lake Bank, Sunny Bank and Brantwood via Peel Island. You can break your journey and walk to the next jetty; trail leaflets are sold on board for £1.80. Extra cruises available are the Campbells on Coniston (adult/five to 15 years £8/5; departing 1pm Tuesday mid-March to October) and Swallows and Amazons (adult/five to 15 years £9/5.50; 12.35pm Wednesday mid-March to October).

Coniston Boating Centre (☎ 015394-41366; Coniston Jetty) hires out rowing boats, Canadian canoes and motorboats.

WALKING
If you're in Coniston to hike, chances are you've come to conquer the **Old Man** (7.5 miles, four to five hours). It's a steep but rewarding climb past Coniston's abandoned copper mines to the summit, from where the views stretch to the Cumbrian Coast on a clear day.

Another popular trail leads to **Tarn Hows**, a man-made lake backed by woods and mountains, donated to the National Trust by Beatrix Potter in 1930, and now a favourite hang-out for red squirrels. It's a 5-mile round-trip of around three hours. The tourist office has leaflets on more walks and the annual **Coniston Walking Festival** (www.conistonwalkingfestival.org), held in September.

Summitreks (☎ 015394-41212; www.summitreks .co.uk; 14 Yewdale Rd) arranges outdoor activities in the Coniston area.

Sleeping
Coniston Hall Campsite (☎ 015394-41223; sites from £12; ☯ Easter-Oct) Busy lakeside campsite a mile from town, with plenty of showers, a laundry room and a small shop – although it can be tough to find a peak-season pitch.

Coppermines YHA (☎ 0845 371 9630; www.yha .org.uk; dm £14; ☯ Easter-Oct) Hikers tackling the Old Man get a head start at this former mine-manager's house, huddled a couple of miles into the mountains along an unmetalled road. The small dorms, battered furniture and cosy kitchen are all part of the backcountry charm.

Holly How YHA (☎ 0845 371 9511; www.yha.org.uk; Far End; dm £16) Coniston's main hostel occupies a slate-fronted period house along the road towards Ambleside, and offers the usual YHA facilities: kitchens, evening meals and bike hire, with a choice of four-, eight- or 10-bed dorms. It's a school-trip favourite, so book ahead.

Crown Inn Coniston (☎ 015394-41243; Tilberthwaite Ave; www.crowninnconiston.com; s £50, d £80-95; **P**) The bedrooms at this solid old inn have been given a spicy overhaul, and they're now spacious and comfortably equipped, with large beds and decent hot tubs for a posthike soak.

our pick **Yew Tree Farm** (☎ 015394-41433; www .yewtree-farm.com; s £70, d £100-114) Farmhouses don't come finer than this whitewashed, slate-roofed beauty, which doubled for Hill Top in *Miss Potter* (fittingly, since Beatrix Potter owned Yew Tree in the 1930s). It's still a working

---

SOMETHING FOR THE WEEKEND

Start your weekend in Keswick with a romantic twilight cruise across **Derwent Water** (p727) before checking into the swish rooms at **Howe Keld** (p727).

On Saturday head south via Wordsworth's former houses at **Rydal Mount** (p715) and **Dove Cottage** (p715). After lunch at the **Jumble Room** (p717) energetic types could tackle the trail to **Helm Crag** (p716) or follow the easier stroll around the lake via the **Coffin Trail** (p716). Overnight in serious style at **Moss Grove** (p717) or the **Waterhead** (p714) in Ambleside, with an evening meal courtesy of **Lucy's** (p714).

On Sunday morning travel via the pretty village of **Hawkshead** (p717) and Beatrix Potter's house at **Hill Top** (p719), followed by a fantastic Sunday lunch at the **Drunken Duck** (p718), and an afternoon cruising on board the **Coniston Launches** (opposite) to John Ruskin's country estate, **Brantwood** (p719). If there's time, late afternoon tea at **Yew Tree Farm** (opposite) is a must. Finish things off with some culinary fireworks and boutique rooms at **L'Enclume** (p734) in Cartmel or at the **Queen's Head** (p712) in Troutbeck.

---

farm, but these days offers luxurious lodgings alongside the cowsheds. Cream of the crop is 'Tarn Hows' with its wood-frame rafters, slate-floored bathroom and regal four-poster bed. If it's fully booked, console yourself with a nutty flapjack or a Hot Herdwick sandwich at the delightful Yew Tree Tea Room next door.

Wheelgate Country Guest House (☎ 015394-41418; www.wheelgate.co.uk; Little Arrow; d £74-84) As long as you don't mind florals and frills, you'll be happy at this creeper-covered cottage in the centre of Coniston. The rooms are named after local lakes: try Derwent if you like oak-beamed character, Buttermere if you're a sucker for four-posters, and Coniston for countryside views.

Eating

Bluebird Cafe (☎ 015394-41649; Lake Rd; lunches £4-8; ❧ breakfast & lunch) Beside the Coniston jetty, the busy Bluebird is a fine spot for tea and cakes or a quick ice cream before hopping aboard the cross-lake launch.

Black Bull (☎ 015394-41335; www.conistonbrewery .com; Yewdale Rd; mains £6-14; ❧ lunch & dinner) Local punters and visiting hikers alike swing by the Old Bull for the best home-brewed ale in the Lakes, especially the trademark Bluebird Bitter and Old Man Ale. Pub grub is served in front of the log-fuelled fire: try the fantastic Cumberland Sausage platter, or tuck into locally hooked Esthwaite trout.

Sun Hotel (☎ 015394-41248; www.thesunconiston .com; mains £12-20; ❧ lunch & dinner) Squatting on the hillside, this old coaching inn has been whetting Coniston's whistles for centuries, but it's best known for its association with Donald Campbell, who was headquartered

here during his fateful campaign. Campbell memorabilia litters the inn, and you'll find solid, uncomplicated fare in the bar (which still boasts its original range and 16th-century flagstoned floor).

Getting There & Around

Bus 505 runs from Windermere (10 Monday to Saturday, six on Sunday mid-March to October), via Ambleside, with a couple of daily connections to Kendal (1¼ hours).

The Ruskin Explorer ticket (adult/child £14.95/6.50) includes the Windermere bus fare, a Coniston launch ticket and entrance to Brantwood; pick it up from the tourist office or the bus driver.

LANGDALE

Travelling north from Coniston, the road passes into increasingly wild, empty countryside. Barren hilltops loom as you travel north past the old Viking settlement of Elterwater en route to Great Langdale, where the main road comes to an end and many of the Lakes' greatest trails begin – including the stomp up the Langdale Pikes past Harrison Stickle (736m) and Pike o' Stickle (709m), and the spectacular ascent of Crinkle Crags (819m). An old road (now sealed with tarmac, although still one of the steepest and windiest in the entire country) leads through Little Langdale over Wrynose and Hardknott Passes to the coast, passing a ruined Roman fort en route.

Getting There & Away

Bus 516 (the Langdale Rambler, six daily, five on Sunday) is the only scheduled bus service to the valley, with stops at Ambleside, Skelwith

Bridge, Elterwater, and the Old Dungeon Ghyll Hotel in Great Langdale.

Elterwater

Ringed by trees and fields, the small, charming lake of Elterwater derives its name from the Old Norse for 'swan', after the colonies of whooper swans that winter here. With its maple-shaded village green and quiet country setting, it's a popular base for exploring the Langdale fells.

Langdale YHA (☎ 0845 371 9748; www.yha.org .uk; High Close, Loughrigg; dm £12; ✆ Mar-Oct; P ☐), halfway between Grasmere and Elterwater, has an impressive Victorian facade, but the rooms are standard YHA. Lots of dorm-size choice though, and good amenities including laundry, shop and games room.

Elterwater YHA (☎ 0845 371 9017; www.yha.org.uk; dm £14; ✆ Easter-Oct; ☐) is lodged inside an old barn and farmhouse opposite the village pub. It's institutional – easy-clean fabrics, boarding-school bunk beds and a functional kitchen – but dead handy for local trails.

The smart **Eltermere Country House Hotel** (☎ 015394-37207; www.eltermere.co.uk; d from £90; P) near the village YHA has 15 pleasant, modern rooms and lovely lakeside grounds, and a private jetty onto Elterwater.

The lovely old **Britannia Inn** (☎ 015394-37210; www.britinn.net; d £94-114; P) is a longstanding walkers' favourite. All the rooms have been redone with fresh fabrics and shiny en suites, and hikers cram into the downstairs bar for hearty steaks, pints and pies (mains £8 to £16). The Sunday roast is rather fine, too.

Great Langdale

Hemmed in by towering hills, this little hamlet is one of the Lake District's classic walking centres. Some of the most famous (and challenging) Lakeland fells are within reach, including Pike o' Blisco (705m), Crinkle Crags (859m) and the chain of peaks known as the 'Langdale Pikes': Pike O' Stickle (709m), Loft Crag (682m), Harrison Stickle (736m) and Pavey Ark (700m).

Many hikers choose to kip at the **Great Langdale Campsite** (☎ 37668; langdalecamp@national trust.org.uk; adult £4.50-5.50, child £2-2.50, car £3-3.50), a typically well-run NT campground a mile up the valley.

The classic stay in Great Langdale is the **Old Dungeon Ghyll** (☎ 015394-37272; www.odg.co.uk; d £100-110; P), backed by soaring fells and built from sturdy Lakeland stone. It's been the getaway of choice for many well-known walkers and it's still endearingly old-fashioned: country chintz, battered armchairs and venerable furniture in the rooms; oak beams, wood tables and a crackling fire in the walker's bar; and more history per square inch than practically anywhere in the Lakes.

For more contemporary trappings, try the ivy-clad **New Dungeon Ghyll** (☎ 015394-37213; www .dungeon-ghyll.co.uk; d £108-120; P) next door.

The **Stickle Barn** (☎ 015394-37356; Great Langdale; mains £4-12) is a popular choice for a posthike dinner, with curries, casseroles and stews to warm those weary bones. There's basic dorm accommodation in the bunkhouse out back.

Little Langdale

Separated from Great Langdale by Lingmoor Fell (459m), Little Langdale is a quiet village on the road to Wrynose Pass. There are many little-known walks nearby, and at the head of the valley is the **Three Shire Stone**, marking the traditional meeting point of Cumberland, Westmoreland and Lancashire.

The only place to stay is the **Three Shires Inn** (☎ 015394-37215; www.threeshiresinn.co.uk; d £76-106; P), ideally placed for walkers on the route to Lingmoor Fell via Blea Tarn. There are lunch mains for £7.25 to £8.75, and dinner mains from £14.

ESKDALE

Strap yourself in: the road west from Little Langdale into the Eskdale Valley is a rollercoaster, snaking across glacial valleys and empty hills all the way to the Cumbrian coast, traversing two of the country's steepest roads, Wrynose Pass (1 in 4 – 1m up for every 4m forward) and Hardknott Pass (1 in 3) en route. If you don't feel up the challenge of the twin passes (a seriously wise decision on busy summer weekends and icy winter days), you can also reach Eskdale from the west via the turn-off near Gosforth, or via bus or the Ravenglass & Eskdale Railway (p736).

Perched above Eskdale are the ruins of **Hardknott Roman Fort**, which once guarded the old pack route from the Roman harbour at Ravenglass (p736). You can still make out the foundations of the commandant's house, watchtowers and parade ground, and the views are eye-popping, but you can't help feeling sympathy for the legionaries stationed here – it's hard to think of a lonelier spot in the entire Roman Empire.

Three miles further down the valley is shoebox-sized **Boot**, which hosts a hearty **beer festival** (www.bootbeer.co.uk) every June. It's also handy for **Dalegarth**, the eastern terminus of the Ravenglass & Eskdale Railway (p736).

Hunkering under the hills, the purpose-built **Eskdale YHA** (☎ 0845 371 9317; www.yha.org.uk; Boot; dm £16; ☻ Easter-Oct) is a favourite waypoint for walkers and Ravenglass railway travellers. Zingy pinks, yellows and tangerines liven up the dorms and TV lounge, there's bike rental and a decent kitchen, and endless walks start right outside the front door.

Boot Inn (☎ 0845 130 6224; www.bootinn.co.uk; Boot; mains £7-12; **P**) Boot's boozer is a beauty, offering hale and hearty Lakeland food and local ales served at the green-slate bar. The beer garden's particularly nice, with great views and play-areas to keep the nippers happy. There are also single rooms available for £50, doubles £100.

Just east of Boot, the **Woolpack Inn** (☎ 019467-23230; **P**) has its own microbrewery concocting homemade ales for the two hugger-mugger 'baas', both covered in sporting prints and country memorabilia. The grub's good and there's often live music (think fiddles and guitars), but the upstairs rooms are overpriced (£65 to £120).

Apart from the Ravenglass steam railway and Shanks' pony, there's no public transport to Eskdale.

WASDALE

Hunched at the end of a twisting road, the valley of Wasdale is as close as you'll get to true wilderness in the Lake District. Surrounded by a brooding circle of scree-scattered peaks, including the summits of Scaféll Pike and Great Gable, it's a world away from the bustling quays of Windermere: the only signs of human habitation are a couple of cottages and a sturdy inn, dwarfed by the green-grey arc of **Wastwater**, England's deepest lake. For many walkers this is the quintessential location for Lakeland hiking – classic routes to the summits of Great Gable, Lingmell and Scaféll Pike all start off from the Wasdale Head area. Little wonder that Wasdale recently topped a television poll to find Britain's favourite view: you won't find a grander spot this side of the Scottish highlands.

WASDALE'S WHITE LIES

Cumbrians are renowned for their tall tales, but Will Ritson, a popular 19th-century publican, took the propensity and finessed it into an art, telling porkies about giant turnips and a cross between a foxhound and a golden eagle (it could leap of drystone walls, see). In honour of Ritson, the Bridge Inn at Santon Bridge holds the **World's Biggest Liar Contest** (www.santonbridgeinn .com/liar) every November.

The only place for supplies is the **Barn Door Shop** (☎ 019467-26384; www.wasdaleweb.com) at Wasdale Head, right next to the Wasdale Head Inn.

Sleeping
Wasdale Head Campsite (☎ 019467-26220; www .wasdalecampsite.org.uk; adult £4.50-5.50, child £2-2.50, car £3-3.50) This NT campsite is in a fantastically wild spot, nestled beneath the Scaféll range a mile from Wastwater. Facilities are basic (laundry room, showers and not much else), but the views are fine.

Wastwater YHA (☎ 0845 371 9350; www.yha.org.uk; Wasdale Hall, Nether Wasdale; dm £12; ☻ year-round by advance booking) Another stunning Lakeland hostel in a half-timbered 19th-century Gothic mansion in Nether Wasdale, at the lake's western end. There's a restaurant serving Cumbrian nosh and real ales, and many dorms have outlooks across the water.

Rainors Farm (☎ 019467-25934; www.rainorsfarm .co.uk; s £30-40, d £55-65) Three sweet rooms in a whitewashed farmhouse cottage, prettied up with checks, crimson spreads and country views. There's a choice of traditional or vegie breakfasts, and campers can bunk down in a back-garden yurt (£550 per week). It's in Gosforth, about 5 miles west of Nether Wasdale.

Strands Inn (☎ 019467-26237; www.strandshotel.com; Nether Wasdale; s/d £50/75) This unpretentious inn does a decent supper (pigeon breast, braised rabbit pâté, black pudding stack) and brews its own ale, but the white and pine rooms are on the simple side.

Lingmell House (☎ 019467-26261; www.lingmell house.co.uk; Wasdale Head; d £60; **P**) If you're really looking to escape, this stern granite house is the place, perched at the end of the valley's road. The rooms are sparse – don't expect creature comforts, or even much furniture – but at least traffic noise won't be a problem.

our pick **Wasdale Head Inn** (☎ 019467-26229; www .wasdale.com; d £108-118; P) This historic inn can stake a claim as the spiritual home of English mountain climbing: one of the inn's early owners, Will Ritson, was among the adventurous gaggle of Victorian gents who pioneered the techniques of early mountaineering in the late 19th century. Dog-eared photos and climbing memorabilia are dotted around the inn, and upstairs you'll find simple, snug rooms crammed with character: for more space, ask for one of the barn-conversion rooms across the way. Home-brewed ales, hearty food and a genuine slice of Lakeland history – what more could you ask for?

Getting There & Away

The **Wasdale Taxibus** (☎ 019467-25308) runs between Gosforth and Wasdale twice daily on Thursday, Saturday and Sunday; ring to book a seat.

COCKERMOUTH

pop 8225

Plonked in flat fields beyond the northerly fells, Cockermouth is best known as the birthplace of William Wordsworth and the home base of one of Cumbria's largest beer makers, Jenning's Brewery. It's a quiet, workaday kind of town; Georgian houses and old coaching inns line the main street, and the valleys of Borrowdale and Buttermere are within easy reach.

Information

Cockermouth (www.cockermouth.org.uk) Useful town guide.

Library (☎ 01900-325990; Main St; per 30 min £1; ⏰ 10am-7pm Mon-Wed & Fri, 9am-noon Thu & Sat) Internet access.

Post office (South St; ⏰ 9am-5.30pm Mon-Fri, 9.30am-12.30pm Sat) Inside Lowther Went shopping centre.

Tourist office (☎ 01900-822634; cockermouthtic@ co-net.com; ⏰ 9.30am-5pm Mon-Sat, 10am-2pm Sun Jul-Aug, 9.30am-4.30pm Mon-Sat Apr-June & Sep-Oct, 9.30am-4pm Mon-Fri & 10-2pm Sat Jan-Mar & Nov-Dec) Inside the grand town hall.

Sights

Cockermouth boasts two famous sons. Fletcher Christian, lead mutineer on the *Bounty*, was born outside town in 1764, but the town is better known as the birthplace of William

Wordsworth. Cockermouth's main attraction is **Wordsworth House** (NT; ☎ 01900-824805; Main St; adult/ child £5.60/2.80; ⏰ 11am-4.30pm Mon-Sat mid-Mar–Oct), where all five Wordsworth children were born (William was the second to arrive, born on 7 April 1770, followed a year later by Dorothy). Built around 1745, the elegant Georgian mansion has been painstakingly restored based on family accounts from the Wordsworth archive. Highlights include the flagstoned kitchen, the grand 1st-floor drawing room and the beautiful walled garden, immortalised in Wordsworth's epic poem *The Prelude*.

For something less cerebral, head for **Jenning's Brewery** (☎ 01900-821011; www.jennings brewery.co.uk; adult/over 12yr £5.50/2.50), which has been plying Cumbria's pubs with traditional ales and bitters since 1874. Tours of the brewery include a tasting session in the Old Cooperage bar; try the golden Cocker Hoop, malty Cumberland Ale or the extravagantly named Sneck Lifter.

Castlegate House Gallery (☎ 01900-822149; www .castlegatehouse.co.uk; ⏰ 10.30am-5pm Fri, Sat & Mon, 2.30-4.30pm Sun) exhibits local artwork in a Georgian house opposite the 12th-century Cockermouth Castle, now a private residence.

Sleeping

Cockermouth YHA (☎ 0845 371 9313; www.yha.org.uk; Double Mills; dm £14; ⏰ Apr-Oct) There are just three dorms inside this converted 17th-century watermill, so it's much quieter than many Lakeland hostels. Camping space and cycle storage are available, but there's no cafe, so you'll be cooking your own meals.

Six Castlegate (☎ 01900-826749; www.sixcastlegate .co.uk; 6 Castlegate; s £35-45, d £60-75; 🖳 wi-fi) Grade-II listed mansion that's had a comprehensive facelift, retaining its Georgian interiors while bringing the rooms bang up to date. Feather pillows, flat-screen TVs (all with Freeview), lofty ceilings and sparkling showers make this Central Cockermouth's choicest sleep.

Croft House (☎ 01900-827533; www.croft-guesthouse .com; 6/8 Challoner St; s/d £38/65; P 🖳 wi-fi) This fancy number boasts chicly styled rooms in creams and purples, reclaimed timber floors and wall-mounted LCD TVs (one room has funky bunk beds for the kids). Vegie options and locally sourced bangers grace the morning table.

our pick **Old Homestead** (☎ 01900-822223; www .byresteads.co.uk; Byresteads Farm; d £70-90; P) If you've got wheels, this posh farm conversion 2 miles west of Cockermouth is an utter delight.

THE BASSENTHWAITE OSPREYS

In 2001 the first wild ospreys to breed in England for 150 years set up home at Bassenthwaite Lake, near Keswick. These magnificent birds of prey were once widespread, but were driven to extinction by hunting, environmental degradation and egg collectors. The last wild breeding pair was destroyed in Scotland in 1916, but following years of careful conservation the ospreys have slowly recolonised several areas of the British Isles.

Over the last few years, the birds have usually arrived at Bassenthwaite in April, spending the summer at the lake before heading for Africa in late August or early September. There are two official viewpoints, both in **Dodd Wood**, about 3 miles north of Keswick on the A591 (follow signs for Dodd Wood and Cattle Inn). The **lower hide** (10am-5pm) is about 15 minutes' walk from the car park at Mirehouse, and the new **upper hide** (10.30am-4.30pm) is half an hour further. There's an informative osprey display and live video feed at the **Whinlatter Forest Park visitor centre** (017687-78469; Braithwaite, near Keswick; 10am-5pm Apr-Aug).

A special Osprey Bus (six on weekends April to mid-July, daily mid-July to August) runs from Keswick; alternatively catch the X4 from Penrith or Cockermouth, or the X5 or 77 from Keswick. Disabled visitors can arrange for access to the lower hide by calling the Whinlatter Visitor Centre. Find out more at www.ospreywatch.co.uk.

The farmhouse clutter has been cleared to leave light, airy rooms with just a few rustic touches for character (a wood rafter here, a stone tile or hardwood mirror there). Top choices are the Cruck rooms (with burnished leather sofas) and the Master's Room (with handcrafted four-poster bed), both with vistas across 73-odd hectares of working sheep farm.

Eating & Drinking

Merienda (01900-822790; 7a Station St; mains £4-8; breakfast & lunch, to 10pm Fri) Savour light bites, authentic tapas and open-faced sandwiches at this sunny Med-style diner, with an admirable penchant for fair-trade goods, local producers and specialist coffees.

Quince & Medlar (01900-823579; 13 Castlegate; www.quinceandmedlar.co.uk; mains from around £14; dinner Tue-Sat) Who ever said vegie food had to be bland? Forget your clichéd quiches and nut roasts, here at the Quince things are rather spicier. Depending on the season, you could find yourself tucking into Indian spinach globes, Cumberland cheese roulade or butternut-and-bean bakes wrapped in vine leaves, all served in the august surroundings of a Georgian dining room. Take that, you carnivores...

Bitter End (01900-828993; Kirkgate) From the sublime to the ridiculous; alongside king-size Jennings is this miniature microbrewery and village pub, where the beers are brewed in time-honoured fashion using barley, wheat, hops and Cumbrian spring water (pint o' Cuddy Lugs, anyone?)

Getting There & Away

The X4/X5 (13 Monday to Saturday, six on Sunday) travels from Workington via Cockermouth on to Keswick (35 minutes) and Penrith (1¼ hours).

KESWICK

pop 5257

Ask many people for their picture-perfect image of a Lakeland town, and chances are they'll come up with something close to Keswick. This sturdy slate town is nestled alongside one of the region's most idyllic lakes, Derwent Water, a silvery curve studded by wooded islands and criss-crossed by puttering cruise boats. Keswick makes a less frantic Lakeland base than Ambleside or Windermere, but there's plenty to keep you occupied: classic trails rove the surrounding hilltops, and the town is home to a clutch of oddball attractions including an original Batmobile and the world's largest pencil.

Information

Keswick Laundrette (017687-75448; Main St; 7.30am-7pm)

Keswick & the North Lakes (www.keswick.org) Comprehensive guide to all things Keswick.

Post office (017687-72269; 48 Main St; 9am-5.30pm Mon-Fri, to 12.30pm Sat)

Tourist office (017687-72645; keswicktic@lake-district.gov.uk; Moot Hall, Market Pl; 9.30am-5.30pm Apr-Oct, to 4.30pm Nov-Mar) Sells discounted launch tickets.

U-Compute (017687-72269; 48 Main St; 9am-5.30pm; per hr £3) Internet access above the post office.

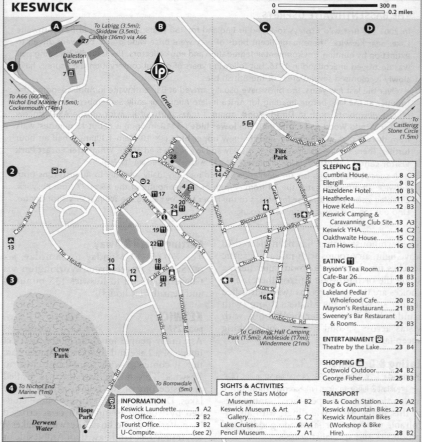

KESWICK

SLEEPING		
Cumbria House................8	C3
Ellergill.........................9	B2
Hazeldene Hotel............10	B3
Heatherlea....................11	C2
Howe Keld....................12	B3
Keswick Camping &	
Caravanning Club Site.13	A3
Keswick YHA.................14	C2
Oakthwaite House..........15	C2
Tarn Hows....................16	C3

EATING		
Bryson's Tea Room........17	B2
Cafe-Bar 26..................18	B3
Dog & Gun...................19	B3
Lakeland Pedlar	
Wholefood Cafe........20	B2
Mayson's Restaurant......21	B3
Sweeney's Bar Restaurant	
& Rooms....................22	B3

ENTERTAINMENT		
Theatre by the Lake........23	B4

SHOPPING		
Cotswold Outdoor..........24	B2
George Fisher................25	B3

INFORMATION		
Keswick Laundrette..........1	A2
Post Office......................2	B2
Tourist Office..................3	B2
U-Compute..............(see 2)	

SIGHTS & ACTIVITIES		
Cars of the Stars Motor	
Museum.......................4	B2
Keswick Museum & Art	
Gallery.........................5	C2
Lake Cruises...................6	A4
Pencil Museum................7	A1

TRANSPORT		
Bus & Coach Station........26	A2
Keswick Mountain Bikes...27	A1
Keswick Mountain Bikes	
(Workshop & Bike	
Hire)..........................28	B2

Sights

The heart of Keswick is the old Market Pl, in the shadow of the town's former prison and meeting rooms at the **Moot Hall** (now occupied by the tourist office).

The River Greta runs parallel to Main St, overlooked by the green expanse of **Fitz Park**. Nearby is the **Keswick Museum & Art Gallery** (☎ 017687-73263; Station Rd; admission free; ☺ 10am-4pm Tue-Sat Feb-Oct), which has hardly changed since its opening in 1898. Dusty cases fill the halls: exhibits on display include a Napoleonic teacup, a centuries-old stuffed cat and a set of musical stones once played for Queen Victoria.

Back across the river, the equally odd **Cars of the Stars Motor Museum** (☎ 017687-73757; www

.carsofthestars.com; Standish St; adult/child £5/3; ☺ 10am-5pm) houses a fleet of celebrity vehicles: Chitty Chitty Bang Bang, Mr Bean's Mini, a Batmobile, KITT from *Knightrider*, the A-Team van and the Delorean from *Back to the Future*, as well as lots of Bond cars.

At the southern end of Main St is the old Cumberland Pencil Factory, now the **Pencil Museum** (☎ 017687-73626; www.pencilmuseum.co.uk; Southy Works; adult/child £3/1.50; ☺ 9.30am-5pm). Keswick was once a centre for graphite mining; the museum's exhibits include a reconstruction of the old Borrowdale slate mine and the world's longest pencil (measuring 8m end to end). The factory still produces luxury colouring pencils under the 'Derwent' brand.

A mile east of Keswick stands **Castlerigg Stone Circle**, a group of 48 stones between 3000 and 4000 years old, set on a hilltop surrounded by a brooding amphitheatre of mountains. The purpose of the circle is uncertain (current opinion is divided between a Bronze Age meeting place and a celestial timepiece), but one thing's for certain – those prehistoric builders knew a good site when they saw one.

Activities

Keswick has plenty of outdoor shops. There's a huge branch of **Cotswolds Outdoor** (☎ 017687-81030; 16 Main St), but the traditionalists' choice is **George Fisher** (☎ 017687-72178; 2 Borrowdale Rd).

BOAT TRIPS

Lake Rd leads west past Crow Park to the lovely lake of Derwent Water, where you can catch a cruise with **Keswick Launch Company** (☎ 017687-72263; www.keswick-launch.co.uk). Boats call at seven landing stages: Ashness Gate, Lodore Falls, High Brandlehow, Low Brandlehow, Hawse End, Nichol End and back to Keswick. Boats leave every hour (adult/child £8.50/4.25, 50 minutes); single fares to each jetty are also available. There are at least six daily boats from mid-March to mid-November, with extra sailings in summer, plus a twilight cruise at 7.30pm (adult/child £9/4.50, one hour, July and August). Only two boats run from mid-November to mid-March.

Nichol End Marine (☎ 017687-73082; Nichol End; ☼ 9am-5pm) hires out kayaks, rowboats and motorboats.

WALKING

Keswick has enough hikes to fill a lifetime of tramping. The most popular walk is the ascent of **Lattrigg Fell**, along an old railway path that's now part of the C2C cycle trail. Other possible routes climb **Walla Crag** (379m), **Skiddaw** (931m) and **Blencathra** (868m), or you can catch the boat to Hawse End for the supremely scenic hike up **Catbells** (451m).

Festivals & Events

Keswick needs no excuse for a shindig.
Keswick Mountain Festival (www.keswickmountain festival.co.uk) May
Keswick Beer Festival (www.keswickbeerfestival .co.uk) June
Keswick Agricultural Show (www.keswickshow.co.uk) August Bank Holiday; held every year since 1860.

Sleeping
BUDGET

Keswick YHA (☎ 0845 371 9746; www.yha.org .uk; Station Rd; dm £23; ☐) Fresh from a refit, this former woollen mill is now one of Lakeland's top YHAs. Some of the dorms, doubles and triples have balconies over the river and Fitz Park, and the hostel has all the facilities a discerning backpacker could wish for.

Tent-pitchers can try **Castlerigg Hall Camping Park** (☎ 017687-74499; www.castlerigg.co.uk; Rakefoot Lane, off A591; sites £14.50-16.50) and **Keswick Camping & Caravanning Club Site** (☎ 017687-72392; Crow Park Rd; adult £6.60-8.60, child £2.25-2.35, tent £2.90; ☼ Feb-Nov), down beside the lake.

MIDRANGE

our pick Howe Keld (☎ 017687-72417; www.howekeld .co.uk; 5-7 The Heads; s £45, d £80-90) On the edge of Hope Park, this old workhorse has had a glamorous makeover and now boasts some of Keswick's most impressive rooms. Gone are the chintzy wallpapers; in come luxury pocket-sprung beds, Egyptian cotton sheets and goose-down duvets, plus designer wall hangings and handmade furniture courtesy of a local joiner. Bathrooms sparkle, the clutter's minimal, the key-fobs are made of local slate, and the brekkie's up for a national award. Seriously good.

Cumbria House (☎ 017687-73171; www.cumbria house.co.uk; 1 Derwent Water Pl; r £52 64) Charming Georgian surroundings and an admirable eco-policy (fair-trade coffee, local produce, and a 5% discount for car-free guests) make this another smart option. Families can rent the top three rooms as a single suite, with views all the way to Blencathra.

Heatherlea (☎ 017687-72430; www.heatherlea -keswick.co.uk; 26 Blencathra St; d £54) One of the best choices in the B&B-heavy area around Blencathra St. Tasteful decor (pine beds, crimson-striped cushions, beige throws) distinguishes the rooms; it's worth bumping up to superior for the sparkling shower and gargantuan flat-screen TV.

Ellergill (☎ 017687-73347; www.ellergill.co.uk; 22 Stanger St; d £56-64) Velour bedspreads, plumped-up cushions and either regal purples or fiery reds give this B&B an opulent edge, marrying well with the house's Victorian features (including tiled hearths and a lovely hallway floor).

Oakthwaite House (☎ 017687-72398; www.oak thwaite-keswick.co.uk; 35 Helvellyn St; d £58-68) Just four rooms at this upper-crust guesthouse, but all scream achingly good taste. Digital TVs, power showers, white linen and cool shades throughout, with a cosy dormer room for that attic hideaway feel, or two swanky king-size rooms if you're a sucker for fell views.

Also recommended:

Tarn Hows (☎ 017687-73217; www.tarnhows.co.uk; 3-5 Eskin St; s £33, d £58-70) Cast-iron bedsteads and fancy quilts in a traditional Eskin St guesthouse.

Hazeldene Hotel (☎ 017687-72106; www.hazeldene -hotel.co.uk; The Heads; d £75-95) Pick of the Victorian villas opposite Hope Park, with cheery doubles and a spacious suite with stone fireplace. Ask for park views.

TOP END

Lyzzick Hall Hotel (☎ 017687-72277; www.lyzzickhall .co.uk; Underskiddaw; r £120-144; P ♨) Lyzzick (meaning 'little oak') is pricey, but you're really paying for the setting, wedged on lower Skiddaw 3 miles from Keswick, with jaw-dropping views to the Eden Valley. Rooms are simple, unfussy and just a smidge old-fashioned (the Garden and Derwent suites are the most spacious); the panoramic patio and the sexy indoor pool are tailor-made for basking.

Eating
CAFES

Bryson's Tea Room (☎ 017687-72257; 42 Main St; cakes £2-5) A historic Lakeland bakery turning out fruit cakes, Battenburgs, plum breads and florentines. Bag 'em up and take 'em home, or stop for afternoon tea at the upstairs caff.

Lakeland Pedlar Wholefood Cafe (☎ 017687-74492; www.lakelandpedlar.co.uk; Hendersons Yard; mains £3-10; ☽ 9am-5pm) Bikers and vegies are both well catered for at this homely cafe, noted for doorstep sandwiches, homemade soups, vegie chillis and ultracrumbly cakes. If you need to work off the calories, bikes are hired upstairs.

Cafe-Bar 26 (☎ 017687-80863; 26 Lake Rd; mains £3.25-7.50) Big-city style in little-town Keswick. Bag a streetside table for authentic cappuccinos, wines and beers from across the globe, or bistro burgers, bruschetta and Cajun chicken tortillas.

RESTAURANTS

Mayson's Restaurant (☎ 01768 774104; 33 Lake Rd; mains £6-10; ☽ lunch & dinner) If you're looking for a quick sit-down meal, this relaxed little buffet diner takes some beating. Choose your meal from the woks lined up on the bar (anything from Cajun chicken to chow mein), pick a drink and a table, and your meal will be dished up in double time. Potted plants and posters on the walls keep things cosy.

Sweeney's Bar Restaurant & Rooms (☎ 017687-772990; 18-20 Lake Rd; mains £7-12) Count on decent Brit cooking in comfortable surrounds at Sweeney's. It's half chic wine bar, half restaurant-with-rooms: leather sofas and polished tables spread over two floors, with a beer garden for soaking up the rays.

Dog & Gun (☎ 017687-73463; 2 Lake Rd; mains around £8) Russet-faced farmers rub shoulders with trail-weary hikers at Keswick's top pub, a wonderful place dotted with hunting prints, faded carpets and well-worn wood. The grub's honest and uncomplicated – mainly goulash, stews, steaks and pies – and there are Cumbrian ales to wash everything down.

Entertainment

Theatre by the Lake (☎ 017687-74411; www.theatreby thelake.com; Lakeside) Drama both new and classic is performed here, on the shores of Derwent Water.

Getting There & Away

The Lakeslink bus (555/556) runs hourly to Ambleside (40 minutes), Windermere (50 minutes) and Kendal (1½ hours), or the hourly X4/X5 travels from Penrith to Workington via Keswick (eight on Sunday). For buses to Borrowdale, see p730.

Getting Around

Hire full-suspension bikes, hardtails and hybrids at **Keswick Mountain Bikes** (☎ 017687-75202; 1 Daleston Ct) for £15 to £20 per day. They have a second branch on Otley Rd.

BORROWDALE & BUTTERMERE

Views don't get any more breathtaking than the one from the B5289 into Borrowdale. Historically, the valley was an important centre for two crucial local industries – farming and slate-mining – but these days Borrowdale is walkers' country, with countless paths crossing the surrounding fells, including landmark routes up to the summits of Great

---

THE ROOF OF ENGLAND

In Scotland it's Ben Nevis (1344m), in Wales it's Snowdon (1085m), and in England it's **Scaféll Pike** (978m): collectively the three highest peaks of the British mainland. While they might not be on quite the same scale as the French Alps or the Canadian Rockies, many a hiker has set out to conquer this sky-topping trio, the ultimate goal for British peak-baggers (especially for hardy souls attempting the Three Peaks Challenge, in which all three mountains are conquered in 24 hours).

The classic ascent up Scaféll Pike is from Wasdale Head (p723), but the more scenic route starts near Seathwaite Farm. The trail travels past Styhead Tarn before cutting along the Corridor Route towards the summit, descending via the neighbouring peaks of Broad Crag, Ill Crag and Great End, or the easier route past Esk Hause. It's a challenging 8-mile, six-hour round trip, and not for inexperienced hikers; don't even think about tackling it without proper supplies (rucksack, OS map, compass, food and water, and decent hiking boots) and a favourable weather forecast.

Gable and Scaféll Pike, and an idyllic panorama of tree-clad fells, patchwork pastures and rickety barns.

Borrowdale

The B5289 tracks Derwent Water into the heart of Borrowdale Valley, overlooked by the impressive peaks of Scaféll and Scaféll Pike. Past the small village of **Grange-in-Borrowdale**, the valley winds into the jagged ravine of the **Jaws of Borrowdale**, a well-known hiking spot with wonderful views, notably from the summit of **Castle Crag** (290m).

From here, the road curls into the stout hamlet of **Rosthwaithe**, which marks the starting point for the annual **Borrowdale Fell Race**. Held on the first Saturday in August, this muscle-shredding 17-mile slog makes the Iron Man Challenge look like child's play; you can see a list of previous winners in the bar at the Scaféll Hotel.

SLEEPING & EATING

Borrowdale YHA (☎ 0845 371 9624; www.yha.org.uk; Longthwaite; dm £15.50; ☷ Feb-Dec) Purpose-built chalet-style hostel further up the valley, specialising in walking and activity trips. The facilities are great, but it's often booked out throughout the summer.

Derwentwater YHA (☎ 0845 371 9314; www.yha.org .uk; Barrow House; dm £16; ☷ Feb-Nov, weekends Nov-Jan; **P** 💻) Originally built for the 19th-century notable Joseph Pocklington, this lakeside mansion 2 miles south of Keswick boasts high-ceilinged dorms, a billiard room, playgrounds and a man-made waterfall that runs the hostel's hydrogenerator.

Yew Tree Farm (☎ 017687-77675; http://www.borrow daleherdwick.co.uk; Rosthwaite; d from £60; **P**) Not to be confused with the *other* Yew Tree Farm (p720), this fine old farmhouse is a sanctuary of chintz. Floral motifs run riot in the three rooms, all snuggled under low ceilings; bathrooms are titchy, and there are no TVs, so you'll have to make do with the views. For brekkie, there's Cumbrian bacon and Herdwick bangers, and you'll find homebaked cakes across the road at the Flock Inn tearoom.

Scaféll Hotel (☎ 017687-77208; www.scafell.co.uk; Rosthwaite; d £124-175; **P**) Rosthwaite's former coaching inn makes for a cosy stay. Period furniture and musty rugs conjure up an antique air (the newer annexe is more contemporary). En suite bathrooms and country views are (nearly) universal, and the fire-lit Riverside Bar makes the ideal place to sink a brew.

Borrowdale Gates Hotel (☎ 017687-77204; www .borrowdale-gates.com; Grange; d £150-210; **P**) There's no arguing with the spacious rooms, gourmet restaurant (mains £16 to £22) or sweeping 0.8-hecatre grounds at this country retreat, but if you can't stand country clutter and Laura Ashley furnishings, you'll be better off elsewhere.

Hazel Bank (☎ 017687-77248; www.hazelbankhotel .co.uk; Rosthwaite; r £170-190; **P**) Oozing English luxury from every corniced corner, this Lakeland mansion is another fancy getaway, reached via its own humpbacked bridge and ensconced in private gardens, with upmarket boudoirs stuffed with swags, drapes, ruffled curtains and half-tester beds.

Seatoller

The last stop before Honister, Seatoller was originally a settlement for workers employed in the local slate quarries, and still feels one step removed from the outside world.

Rooms at the family-run **Langstrath Inn** (☎ 017687-77239; www.thelangstrath.com; Stonethwaite; d £75-90, tr £75-79; **P** **□** wi-fi) have been stripped to the essentials. Forget net curtains and geranium-print wallpaper, here it's crisp white sheets and neutral tones set off by slate grey blankets, crimson cushions or chrome fixtures. The bar is more olde-worlde, but the food is reassuringly modern – Herdwick lamb on olive oil mash, or Cumberland tattie pot with local steak (mains £10.75 to £15.50).

A charmingly Potteresque hidey-hole beneath Honister Pass, the 17th-century **Seatoller House** (☎ 017687-77218; www.seatollerhouse.co.uk; s/d £55/110; **P**) brims with period features, and the rooms have their own decorative tics. Ground-floor Badger has a massive hearth and garden views, while Osprey is jammed into the rafters with a Velux skylight. Rates include a four-course dinner and hearty breakfast.

Just before the upward climb to Honister, take a break at the **Yew Tree** (☎ 017687-77634; mains £8-18; ☽ lunch Tue-Sun) and fortify yourself with a ploughman's lunch or a gravy-filled pie. Pitch up after dark and you'll find rather more sophisticated fare – ostrich steak, perhaps?

Honister Pass

This bleak, wind-battered mountain pass into Buttermere was once the most productive quarrying area in the Lake District, and still produces much of the region's grey-green Westmorland slate.

Claustrophobes should steer well clear of the **Honister Slate Mine** (☎ 017687-77230; www .honister-slate-mine.co.uk; adult/child £9.75/4.75; ☽ tours 10.30am, 12.30pm & 3.30pm Mar-Oct), where tours venture deep into the bowels of the old 'Edge' and 'Kimberley' mines (a tour into the 'Cathedral' mine runs on Friday by request, but you'll need eight people).

Honister's latest attraction is the UK's first **Via Ferrata** (Iron Way; adult/under 16yr/16-18yr £19.50/9.50/15). Modelled on the century-old routes across the Italian Dolomites, this vertiginous clamber follows the cliff trail once used by the Honister slate miners, using a system of fixed ropes and iron ladders. It's exhilarating and great fun, but unsurprisingly you'll need a head for heights.

Black Sail YHA (☎ 07711-108450; www.yha.org.uk; Ennerdale, Cleator; dm £14; ☽ Easter-Oct) This gloriously isolated shepherd's bothy is the place to

escape the madding crowd. It's only accessible on foot 2.5 miles west of Honister Pass, and the facilities are scarily spartan: the hostel's solar-powered, there's no electricity in the kitchen, and only a very basic shower-loo – but the mountain setting is unforgettable. Bring a torch...

Honister Hause YHA (☎ 0845 371 9522; www.yha .org.uk; Seatoller; dm from £14; ☽ Easter-Oct, weekends Nov) Next to Honister, these former quarry-workers' lodgings have been turned into another bare-bones walkers' hostel, with functional cooking facilities and a lounge that doubles as a drying room (expect stinky socks).

Buttermere

From the high point of Honister, the road drops sharply into the deep bowl of Buttermere, skirting the lakeshore to Buttermere village, 4 miles from Honister and 9 miles from Keswick. From here, the B5289 cuts past Crummock Water (once joined with its neighbour) before exiting the valley's northern edge.

Buttermere marks the start of Alfred Wainwright's all-time favourite circuit: up **Red Pike** (755m), and along **High Stile**, **High Crag** and **Haystacks** (597m). In fact, the great man liked it so much he decided to stay here for good: after his death in 1991, his ashes were scattered across the top of Haystacks as requested in his will.

Buttermere has limited accommodation. Walkers bunk down at the **Buttermere YHA** (☎ 0845 371 9508; www.yha.org.uk; dm £17.50), a slate-stone house above Buttermere Lake, while those looking for more luxury try the upmarket **Bridge Hotel** (☎ 017687-70252; www.bridge-hotel .com; r incl dinner £148-210; **P**) or the historic Fish Hotel (see opposite).

Getting There & Away

Bus 79 (the Borrowdale Rambler) runs hourly (eight times on Sunday) between Keswick and Seatoller, while the 77/77A (Honister Rambler) makes the round trip from Keswick to Buttermere via Borrowdale and Honister Pass four times daily March to November. For day tickets, see p704.

ULLSWATER & AROUND
☎ 017684

Second only to Windermere in terms of stature, stately Ullswater, in the east of the Lake District, stretches for 7.5 miles between Pooley

THE MAID OF BUTTERMERE

The **Fish Hotel** (☎ 017687-70253; www.fish-hotel.co.uk; 2-night minimum stay d £190; P) in Buttermere is famous as the home of the legendary beauty Mary Robinson, the so-called 'Maid of Buttermere'. A visiting hiker named Joseph Palmer spied this 15-year-old glamour puss during a stopover in 1792; he later wrote about her in his book *A Fortnight's Ramble in the Lake District*, and soon visitors were trekking from across the Lakes to see if Mary's beauty lived up to its reputation. Wordsworth was suitably impressed, devoting several lines to her in *The Prelude*, although the rakish Coleridge was apparently rather underwhelmed.

Mary later became doubly notorious for being duped by the unscrupulous conman John Hatfield, who passed himself off as an army colonel and MP in order to win her hand; within a year Hatfield had been exposed as a bankrupt and a bigamist, arrested by the Bow Street Runners in Swansea, and sentenced to death by hanging. Despite her terribly public embarrassment, Mary soldiered on and married again, this time to a more reliable type from Caldbeck; together they ran the inn until Mary's death in 1837. The local author Melvyn Bragg relates the tale in his novel *The Maid Of Buttermere*.

Bridge, and Glenridding and Patterdale in the south. Carved out by a long-extinct glacier, the deep valley in which the lake sits is flanked by an impressive string of fells, most notably the razor ridge of Helvellyn (p732), Cumbria's third-highest mountain. Historic steamers have sputtered around the lake since 1859, and there are lovely woods and gardens to explore nearby if the summer crowds are too much.

Pooley Bridge
elevation 301m

Sitting along a pebble-strewn shore at the northern corner of Ullswater, the pocket-sized village of Pooley Bridge makes a useful base, with a couple of country pubs and a village shop where you can stock up on supplies.

Ullswater 'Steamers' (☎ 017684-82229; www .ullswater-steamers.co.uk) set out from the Pooley Bridge jetty for the southern reaches of the lake, stopping at Howtown and Glenridding before looping back to Pooley Bridge. The company's two oldest vessels have worked on Ullswater for over a century: *Lady of the Lake* was launched in 1887, followed by *Raven* in 1889. These two grand old girls have been joined by a couple of younger fillies: the *Lady Dorothy* (transported from Guernsey in 2001) and the *Totnes Castle* (launched in 2007, and rechristened the *Lady Wakefield*).

Up to 12 daily ferries run in summer, dropping to three in winter. Current returns from Pooley Bridge are £4.80 to Howtown, or £11.30 to Glenridding and back. Children travel half price.

Campers are spoilt for choice. **Hillcroft Park** (☎ 017684-486363; Roe Head Lane; sites £11-20) is closest to the village, while **Park Foot** (☎ 86309; www.park footullswater.co.uk; Howtown Rd; sites incl 2 adults, tent & car £12-24) has the best facilities (including tennis courts, bike hire and pony trekking).

Break out the lederhosen, the weird **Pooley Bridge Inn** (☎ 017684-86215; www.pooleybridgeinn .co.uk; d £75-100; P) looks like it's upped sticks from the Alsatian Alps and set up shop in Pooley Bridge. Hanging baskets, cartwheels and wooden balconies decorate the exterior, and inside you'll find dinky rooms heavy on the florals and oak beams. The stable restaurant is worth a look for baked trout and solid sausage-and-mash.

You'll need deep pockets to stay at **Sharrow Bay Country House Hotel** (☎ 017684-86301; www .sharrowbay.co.uk; d £185-400; P ▣ wi-fi), but if you can afford it you'll be treated to the last word in luxury: 5 hectares of woods and lakeside gardens; king-sized rooms crammed with antiques, chaise-longues, canopied beds and gilded mirrors; and a Michelin-rated restaurant worthy of a French chateau.

For something less lavish, there's always the homely **Sun Inn** (☎ 486205; mains £5-12) with the usual range of ales and a beautiful beer garden.

Glenridding & Patterdale
elevation 253m

Seven miles south as the crow flies from Pooley Bridge are the neighbouring villages of Patterdale and Glenridding, the favoured starting point for the challenging ascent of Helvellyn (p732). If your legs won't stretch

THE HIKE TO HELVELLYN

Alongside Scaféll Pike, the hike up **Helvellyn** (950m) is the most famous (and challenging) Lake District trail. Wainwright adored it, and Helvellyn exercised a peculiarly powerful hold over William Wordsworth: the mountain crops up frequently in his work, and he continued to climb the mountain well into his seventies. One of the most famous portraits of the poet, completed by the painter Benjamin Haydon in 1842, depicts Wordsworth deep in thought with Helvellyn as a broodingly Romantic backdrop.

The classic route up Helvellyn is the gravity-defying ridge scramble along **Striding Edge,** a challenging route for even experienced walkers, with dizzying drops to either side and a fair amount of hand-and-knee scrambling (don't consider it if you're even slightly wary of heights). Beyond the summit and its glorious 360-degree views, the usual descent is via **Swirral Edge** and **Red Tarn.** Count on at least 7 miles and six hours on the mountain, and, as usual, come suitably prepared unless you fancy coming down in the rescue chopper.

to the main event, you can tackle lower-level trails nearby: the easy amble to **Lanty's Tarn** starts just south of Glenridding, while the popular walks up to **High Force** and **Aira Force** start in the wooded surroundings of **Gowbarrow Park,** 3 miles north.

The **Ullswater Information Centre** (☎ 017684-82414; ullswatertic@lake-district.gov.uk; Beckside car park; ☼ 9am-5.30pm Apr-Oct) details local hikes, hotels and events.

The high-altitude **Helvellyn YHA** (☎ 0845 371 9742; www.yha.org.uk; Greenside; dm £12; ☼ Easter-Oct, phone ahead at other times) is perched 274m above Glenridding along a mountain track, and is mainly used by Helvellyn hikers; guided walks can be arranged through the hostel staff.

Cream walls and pinewood beds grace the smallish rooms at **Mosscrag** (☎ 017684-82500; www.mosscrag.co.uk; Glenridding; s £42.50-47.50, d £64-80; P) B&B, but you'll have to pay extra for an en suite.

Apart from the Glenridding Hotel (now owned by Best Western), **Inn on the Lake** (☎ 017684-82444; www.innonthelakeullswater.co.uk; d £128-184; P ☐) is the only passable hotel in the village. It feels corporate, but as long as you can look past the generic decor, you'll be treated to top-notch facilities: Jacuzzi baths, tennis courts, sauna and gym, plus a choice of mountain or lake views from the rooms.

Traveller's Rest (☎ 017684-82298; mains £5.50-15) is a typically friendly Cumbrian pub with fire-lit lounges, a lovely fell-view patio and a hearty bar menu. Hungry hikers come from miles around for the 'Traveller's Mixed Grill' (£14.70) of rump steak, lamb chop, gammon, black pudding and Cumberland sausage, all crowned with a fried egg.

Getting There & Around

Bus 108 runs from Penrith to Patterdale via Pooley Bridge and Glenridding (six Monday to Friday, five on Saturday, four on Sunday). The 517 (Kirkstone Rambler; three daily July and August, otherwise weekends only) travels over the Kirkstone Pass from Bowness and Troutbeck, stopping at Glenridding and Patterdale.

The **Ullswater Bus-and-Boat** ticket (£13.60) combines a day's travel on the 108 with a return tip on an Ullswater Steamer.

CUMBRIAN COAST

While the central lakes and fells pull in a never-ending stream of visitors, surprisingly few ever make the trek west to explore Cumbria's coastline. And that's a shame: while it might not compare to the wild grandeur of Northumberland or the rugged splendour of Scotland's shores, Cumbria's coast is well worth exploring, with a cluster of sandy bays and a gaggle of seaside towns including the old port of Whitehaven, the Edwardian resort of Grange-over-Sands and the Roman harbour at Ravenglass, starting point for the La'al Ratty steam railway. Less attractive is the nuclear plant of Sellafield, still stirring up controversy some 50 years after its construction.

Getting Around

The Cumbrian Coast railway line loops 120 miles from Lancaster to Carlisle, stopping at the coastal resorts of Grange, Ulverston, Ravenglass, Whitehaven and Workington.

THE MORECAMBE BAY CROSSING

Before the coming of the railway, the sandy expanse of **Morecambe Bay** provided the quickest route into the Lake District from the south of England. The traditional crossing is made from Arnside on the eastern side of the bay over to Kent Bank in the west, but it's always been a risky journey. Morecambe Bay is notorious for its fast-rising tide and treacherous sands; even experienced locals have been known to lose carts, horses and tractors, and there have been numerous strandings, most recently in 2004, when 18 Chinese cockle pickers were caught by the tide and drowned (an incident that inspired Nick Broomfield's 2006 film *Ghosts*).

It's possible to walk across the flats at low tide, but only in the company of the official **Queen's Guide**, a role established in 1536. Cedric Robinson, a local fisherman, is the 25th official Queen's Guide, and leads walks across the sands throughout the year. You'll need to register a fortnight in advance; ask at the Grange tourist office for details of the next crossing. The 8-mile crossing takes around 3½ hours. You get back to your start point by train on the Cumbria Coast Line.

Find out more about this unique waterway at www.morecambebay.org.uk.

GRANGE-OVER-SANDS
pop 4098

Teashops, manicured gardens and Victorian villas line the winding streets of Grange, which established itself as a seaside getaway for Edwardian day-trippers following the 19th-century arrival of the railway. The town's heyday has long since faded, but as long as you don't mind your sea air stiff and bracing, Grange makes a fine spot to sample the peculiar charms of the English seaside, stroll the elegant seafront and drink in the sweeping views over Morecambe Bay.

Information
Library (☎ 015395 32749; Grange Fell Rd; ☷ 9am-5pm Mon-Fri, 9.30am-12.30pm Sat)
Post office (☎ 015395-34713; Main St; ☷ 9am-5pm Mon-Fri, to 12.30pm Sat)
Tourist office (☎ 015395-34026; grangetic@south lakeland.gov.uk; Victoria Hall, Main St; ☷ 10am-5pm Easter-Oct)

Sleeping & Eating
Lymehurst Hotel (☎ 015395-33076; www.lymehurst .co.uk; Kents Bank Rd; s £35-38, d £76-90; ☒) Splendid guesthouse harking back to Grange's good old days. The rooms are mostly modern, with light colours, contemporary furniture and white bed linen, although the top-of-the range Premier room is more Victorian in style. Breakfast is a wonder, prepared by renowned chef Kevin Wyper, who also oversees things at the Lymestone Restaurant.

Thornfield House (☎ 015395-32512; www.grange guesthouse.co.uk; Kents Bank Rd; d £58-70; ☒) Nothing ground-breaking, but if you're happy with rooms in lemon yellows and peachy pas-

tels, plus a decent fry-up for breakfast, then you'll be comfy enough. On-site parking is a bonus.

Graythwaite Manor (☎ 015395-32001; www .graythwaitemanor.co.uk; Fernhill Rd; s/d £126/139; ☒) A chimney-topped pile brimming with polished wood panels, leather armchairs, ticking grandfather clocks and antiquey knick-knacks. Rooms are stately and stuffy: expect huge beds topped with flowery quilts, and latticed windows overlooking trimmed lawns.

Hazelmere Cafe (☎ 015395-32972; 1-2 Yewbarrow Tce; sandwiches £4-6, mains £6-10; ☷ 10am-5pm summer, to 4.30pm winter) This delightful cafe doubles as the town's top bakery, and offers Cumbrian delicacies such as potted Morecambe Bay shrimps, rabbit pie and crumbly cheese toasties.

Getting There & Away
Both the train station and bus stop are downhill from the tourist office.

Bus X35 from Kendal stops at Grange (30 minutes, hourly) on its way to Ulverston (one hour).

Grange is on the Cumbria Coast Line, with frequent connections to Lancaster (30 minutes, hourly) and Carlisle (£24.50, 1½ hours, hourly).

AROUND GRANGE
Cartmel
pop 1798

Tucked away in the countryside above Grange, tiny Cartmel is known for three things: its 12th-century priory, its miniature racecourse and its world-famous sticky toffee pudding, on sale at the **Cartmel Village**

LIVING THE GOOD LIFE

Howbarrow Organic Farm (☎ 015395-36330; www.howbarroworganic.co.uk; d £57.50; ☺ farm shop 10am-5pm Wed-Sat; ℗) If you've ever fantasised about growing your own, you'll want to pick up tips at this wonderful 100% organic farm outside Cartmel. The farm shop is stocked with organic goodies straight from the fields; self-caterers can pick up a Howbarrow vegetable box, or choose from damson jams, marmalades, fruit and fairtrade choccies. If you fancy staying, there are two simple but sweet farmhouse rooms (with a shared bathroom).

Shop (☎ 015395-36201; www.stickytoffeepudding.co.uk; The Square; ☺ 9am-5pm Mon-Sat, 10am-4.30pm Sun).

The heart of the village is the medieval market square, from where a winding lane leads to **Cartmel Priory** (☎ 015395-36261; ☺ 9am-5.30pm May-Oct, to 3.30pm Nov-Apr), one of the few priories to escape demolition during the dissolution. Light pours in through the 15th-century **east window**, illuminating the tombs set into the flagstoned floor; note the memento mori of skulls and hourglasses, intended to remind the pious of their own inescapable mortality.

SLEEPING & EATING

Prior's Yeat (☎ 015395-35178; priorsyeat@hotmail.com; Aynsome Rd; s/d £32/64; ℗) Cartmel's B&Bs are on the flouncy side, but the three rooms at this redbrick Edwardian house are smarter than most. One's sky blue with twin beds, the other two are doubles with flower prints and pine. Vegie options are available for breakfast, and the owners will make packed lunches if you ask the day before.

Cavendish Arms (☎ 015395-36240; www.thecavendish arms.co.uk; mains £10-15) The pick of Cartmel's pubs, a venerable coaching inn plonked on the village square. The 10 rooms (doubles £60) are plainly furnished, but full of atmosphere, and the bar menu is crammed with lip-smacking mains such as venison steak and roast guinea fowl.

L'Enclume (☎ 015395-36362; www.lenclume.co.uk; Cavendish St; lunch 2/3 courses £18/25, dinner menu £65; ☺ lunch Thu-Sun, dinner Tue-Sun) Gird your gastronomic loins – this Michelin-starred wonder is an assault on your senses. The foodie critics have gone ga-ga for its boundary-pushing cooking, dreamt up by one of the nation's most adventurous chefs, Simon Rogan, but you might need an interpreter to make sense of the menu (unless you're already au fait with egg drop hot and sour soup or eel-veal ragout). Rooms (£98 to £188) are surprisingly understated, mostly in cool whites and beiges, mixed up with the odd Toile de Jouy fabric or wet-room bathroom.

GETTING THERE & AWAY

Bus 530/532 travels from Cartmel to Grange (40 minutes) 10 to 12 times from Monday to Saturday.

Holker Hall & Lakeland Motor Museum

Arguably the finest stately home in Cumbria, **Holker Hall** (☎ 015395-58328; www.holker-hall.co.uk; admission house & grounds £8.80, grounds only £5.70; ☺ house 10.30am-4.30pm Sun-Fri, grounds 10am-6pm Mar-Oct) has been the family seat of the Cavendish family for nigh on 400 years. Though parts of Holker Hall date from the 16th century, the house was almost entirely rebuilt following a devastating fire in 1871. It's a typically ostentatious Victorian affair, covered with mullioned windows, gables and copper-topped turrets, and filled with historic portraits, wood-panelled rooms and an elaborate central staircase. But Holker's real attraction is its wonderful grounds, stretching for 10 hectares and encompassing a rose garden, woodland, ornamental fountains and a 72ft-high lime tree.

The **Lakeland Motor Museum** (☎ 015395-58509; adult/6-15yr £7/4.50; ☺ 10.30am-4.45pm), inside the old stables, contains a collection of classic cars (from Jaguars to Bentleys) and a replica of Donald Campbell's boat, *Bluebird*. There's also a fantastic **food hall** (☎ 015395-59084) stocking Lakeland produce.

ULVERSTON
pop 11,670

It's not the prettiest town in Cumbria, but at least Ulverston has an excuse for its workmanlike appearance – the town was once an important industrial centre for leather, copper and iron ore. Ulverston makes a cheap, quiet base for exploring the surrounding coastline, especially for those setting out for the long-distance Cumbria Way (p702), which has its official starting point in the town.

Information

Library (☎ 01229-894151; Kings Rd; per 30 min £1) Internet access.

Tourist office (☎ 01229-587120; ulverstontic@south lakeland.gov.uk; County Sq; ☺ 9am-5pm Mon-Sat)
Ulverston Online (www.ulverston.net) Town website.

Sights

Silent film fans will already know Ulverston's main claim to fame: Stan Laurel, the spindlier half of Laurel and Hardy, was born here in 1890. The **Laurel & Hardy Museum** (☎ 01229-582292; www.laurel-and-hardy.co.uk; 4c Upper Brook St; adult/child £3/2; ☺ 10am-4.30pm Feb-Dec) was founded by an avid Laurel & Hardy collector in 1983, and now houses floor-to-ceiling memorabilia relating to the bumbling duo, and a little cinema where you can view some slapstick flicks. At the time of writing there were plans to relocate the museum; check the website for info.

The tower on **Hoad Hill** commemorates Ulverston's other famous son, the explorer, author and Secretary to the Admiralty Sir John Barrow (1764–1848). It's usually open on summer weekends.

Ulverston's lively **market** fills the town's streets every Thursday, with a smaller market on Saturday and a local **food fair** every third Saturday of the month.

Sleeping

Walkers Hostel (☎ 01229-585588; www.walkers hostel.co.uk; Oubas Hill; dm £20) New owners are in charge, but this friendly townhouse hostel remains a hikers' haven, run on ecofriendly lines with clean dorms, a good sized kitchen and corridor bathrooms. The hostel's 10 minutes' walk from town on the A590 to Kendal.

St Mary's Mount Manor House (☎ 01229-849005; www.stmarysmount.co.uk; Belmont; s £35, d £45-75; P) Brass beds, half-tester canopies and original fireplaces distinguish this slate-roofed manor house on the hill above town.

Lonsdale House Hotel (☎ 01229-581260; www .lonsdalehousehotel.co.uk; 11 Daltongate; r £85-110; P) Georgian townhouse with 20 bright rooms furnished in checks and rosy drapes. Top rooms have four-poster beds and Jacuzzis, and the quietest ones overlook the lovely back garden, enclosed by a Gothic wall.

Bay Horse Hotel (☎ 01229-583972; www.thebay horsehotel.co.uk Canal Foot; d £85-120; P 🖳 wi-fi) Our top Ulverston tip is this riverside restaurant-with-rooms, beautifully positioned beside the Levens estuary (follow signs to Canal Foot from the A590). There's a choice of garden or river-view rooms, and the restaurant is

known for its upmarket nosh: venison, ostrich and saltmarsh lamb shank.

Eating & Drinking

Hot Mango (☎ 01229-584866; 27 King St; lunch £5-8; ☺ lunch Tue-Sat) Lively bistro-cafe with zesty lunchtime mains – try a saddleback pork burger or a Mediterranean sea-bass fillet, accompanied by homemade salsa and hand-cut chips.

Farmer's Arms (☎ 01229-584469; 3 Market Place; mains £6-14) Ulverston's best pub is on the market square. The trappings are traditional (white-washed frontage, wood beams, beer-stocked bar), but the menu's bold, encompassing Greek meze, Morecambe Bay shrimps and stir-fried Cajun chicken.

World Peace Cafe (☎ 01229-587793; www.world peacecafe.org; 5 Cavendish St; mains £3-6; ☺ 10am-4.30pm Tue-Sat) If you need to knock your *chi* into shape, this holistic cafe (an offshoot of the Conishead Priory, below) is ideal. Organic lunches, fair-trade coffee and lunchtime meditation sessions make it popular with Ulverston's alternative crowd.

Getting There & Away

Regular trains from Carlisle (£27.50, two hours) and Lancaster (£6, 40 minutes) stop at Ulverston station, five minutes' walk south of the centre.

The hourly X35 travels from Ulverston via Haverthwaite, Newby Bridge, Grange and Kendal from Monday to Saturday (three times on Sunday).

AROUND ULVERSTON
Conishead Priory

Two miles south of Ulverston, **Conishead Priory** (☎ 01229-584029; www.manjushri.org.uk; admission free; ☺ 2-5pm weekdays, noon-5pm weekends & bank holidays Easter-Oct, 2-4pm Nov-Easter) is one of the UK's main Manjushri Buddhist Centres, and the site of Europe's only Kadampa Temple. There are weekend tours at 2.15pm and 3.30pm, and meditation retreats are available if you're bitten by the Buddhist bug.

Furness Abbey

Eight and a half miles southwest of Ulverston, the rosy ruins of **Furness Abbey** (EH; ☎ 823420; admission £3.40; ☺ 10am-6pm Apr-Sep, to 5pm Oct, to 4pm Wed-Sun Nov-Mar) are all that remains of one of northern England's most powerful monasteries. Founded in the 12th century, the abbey's lands and properties once stretched across southern Cumbria and the Lakes, but like many of England's monasteries, it met an ignominious end in 1537 during the dissolution. You can still make out the abbey's basic footprint; various arches, windows and the north and south transept walls are still standing, alongside the remains of the abbey bell tower. An informative audio guide is included in the admission price.

Several buses, including the hourly X35 from Ulverston, stop nearby.

RAVENGLASS & AROUND

Halfway along the coast road toward Whitehaven is Ravenglass, a tiny seaside port established by the Romans in the 4th century (you can see the remains of a Roman bathhouse half a mile from the train station). Ravenglass is also the start of the steam enthusiast's dream come true, the **Ravenglass & Eskdale Railway** (☎ 01229-717171; www.ravenglass-railway.co.uk), built in 1875 to ferry iron ore from the Eskdale mines to the coast. Affectionately known as La'al Ratty, the pocket-sized choo-choos chug for 7 miles into Eskdale and the Lake District foothills, terminating at Dalegarth Station, near Boot (p723). There are up to 17 trips daily in summer, dropping to two in winter; single fares are adult/five to 15 years £6/3, or day tickets cost £10.20/5.10.

There's an interesting **museum** exploring the railway's history, and you can find good pub grub at the sepia-tinted **Ratty Arms** (☎ 01229-717676; mains £8-15), covered with railway memorabilia and black-and-white photos plucked from the railway's heyday.

A mile south of Ravenglass is **Muncaster Castle** (☎ 01229-717614; www.muncaster.co.uk; adult/5-15yr incl owl centre, gardens & maze £7.50/5.50, castle extra £2.50/1.50; ☑ gardens 10.30am-6pm/dusk, castle noon-4.30pm Sun-Fri Feb-Nov), built around a 14th-century *pele* tower, and home to the Pennington family for the last seven centuries. Highlights include the dining room, great hall and an extraordinary octagonal library, but the house is most renowned for its spooks – countless spectres stalk the castle's corridors, including a malevolent jester known as Tom Fool (you can arrange for your own overnight 'ghost sit' for £405 to £475). The castle's gardens contain an ornamental maze and an owl centre.

North of Ravenglass, the coast sweeps past the gloomy chimney stacks of **Sellafield**, Britain's largest nuclear reprocessing plant, to-

wards **St Bees Head**, site of an RSPB bird reserve and official starting point for Wainwright's C2C route, which ends 190 miles east at Robin Hood's Bay (p649).

Ravenglass is on the Cumbrian Coast Line, with frequent links north and south. Bus 6 from Whitehaven stops at Ravenglass and terminates at Muncaster (70 minutes, five daily). Bus X6 travels the same route on Sunday (four daily).

WHITEHAVEN
pop 23,795

During the 18th century the pretty port of Whitehaven was the third largest in England, with a fortune founded on the lucrative trade in coal, iron and slaves. These days it's a sleepy pleasure marina, with refurbished Georgian houses and smart yachts lined up along the polished-up harbourside. The town is at its liveliest during the biennial **maritime festival**, the next on at the time of writing scheduled for 2009.

The main **tourist office** (☎ 01946-598914; tic@copelandbc.gov.uk; Market Pl; ☑ 9.30am-5pm Mon-Sat Apr-Oct, 10am-4.30pm Nov-Mar) is in Market Hall in the town centre.

Whitehaven's most notorious incident occurred during the American War of Independence, when the town was attacked by the American naval commander John Paul Jones (actually a Scot, born in Arbigland in 1747). Jones convinced his reluctant crew to mount a daring night raid on Whitehaven, hoping to strike a fearsome blow against one of Britain's key ports. Unfortunately, strong winds and tides, coupled with a shortage of ammunition, a semi-mutinous crew and the troublesome distractions of Whitehaven's taverns, meant the raid was a total flop; of the 200-odd ships stationed in Whitehaven's harbour, Jones sank just a single lowly coal barge.

You can find out more about Jones' bungled raid at the **Beacon** (☎ 01946-592302; www.thebeacon-whitehaven.co.uk; West Strand; adult/under 16yr £5/free; ☑ 10am-4.30pm Tue-Sun), fresh from a £2.2 million refit, with lots of displays on local history, smuggling and the sugar, rum and slave trades.

Rum Story (☎ 01946-592933; www.rumstory.co.uk; Lowther St; adult/child £5.45/3.45; ☑ 10am-4.30pm) explores Whitehaven's rum-running history using waxwork models. It's fun, if slightly tacky – look out for an 18th-century sugar workshop, a debauched 'punch tavern' and a weird exhibit showing Nelson's body being pickled in brandy following the Battle of Trafalgar.

Sleeping & Eating

Glenfield (☎ 01946-691911; www.glenfield-whitehaven .co.uk; Back Corkickle; s £35, d £55-65; P) In the middle of Whitehaven's conservation area, the six rooms of this trad-brick B&B ooze Victorian atmosphere. Our favourites are maritime St Bees, with power shower and town views, and Corkickle, with period fireplace, DVD player and bay window.

Georgian House Hotel (☎ 01946-696611; 9-11 Church St; www.thegeorgianhousehotel.net; s £79, d £89-99; P 🖳 wi-fi) Georgian by name, Georgian by nature, this converted merchant's house offers elegant hotel accommodation, decked out in shipshape fashion with wooden bedsteads, designer-print wallpapers and flat-screen TVs.

Moresby Hall (☎ 01946-696317; www.moresbyhall .co.uk; Moresby; s £80-100, d £100-140; P) For aristocratic atmosphere, head 2 miles north along the A595 to this stunning manor house, Grade I–listed and overflowing with historic curiosities. A lavish oak staircase leads to traditionally styled B&B rooms, all with huge beds, hydromassage showers and Gilchrist & Soames bath stuffs; 'De Asby' and 'Copeland' have four-posters and views across walled grounds.

Zest (☎ 01946-66981; 8 West Strand; mains £8-12 🕑 breakfast, lunch & dinner) Fresh harbourside brasserie with a nice line in lunchtime wraps, panini and salads.

For more complicated British cooking, head to its sister establishment on **Low Rd** (☎ 01946-692848; mains £14-20; 🕑 dinner Wed-Sat).

Getting There & Away

Whitehaven is on the Cumbrian Coast Line with hourly trains in each direction. Bus 6/X6 travels to Ravenglass (one hour, four daily).

NORTHERN CUMBRIA

Many visitors speed through the northern and eastern reaches of Cumbria in a headlong dash for the Lake District, but this is an area that's worth exploring – a bleakly beautiful landscape of isolated farms, barren

heaths and solid hilltop towns, cut through by the Roman barrier of Hadrian's Wall.

CARLISLE
pop 69,527

Precariously perched on the tempestuous border between England and Scotland, in the area once ominously dubbed the 'Debatable Lands', Carlisle is a city with a notoriously stormy past. Sacked by the Vikings, pillaged by the Scots, and plundered by the Border Reivers, Carlisle has stood in the frontline of England's defences for the last 1000 years. The battlements and keeps of the stout medieval castle still stand watch, built from the same rosy red sandstone as the city's cathedral and terraced houses; but Cumbria's only city is a more peaceful place these days, with a buzzy student population that keeps this old city young at heart.

History

A Celtic camp (or *caer*) provided an early military station for the Romans, and Carlisle became the northwest's main administrative centre following the construction of Hadrian's Wall. After centuries of intermittent conflict between Picts, Saxons and Viking raiders, the Normans seized Carlisle from the Scots in 1092.

The English developed Carlisle as a military stronghold throughout the Middle Ages, enlarging the walls, citadels and the great gates, and the city became an important strategic base for Royalist forces during the Civil War.

Peace came to the city with the Restoration, and the city developed as an industrial centre for cotton and textiles after the arrival of the railway in the mid 19th century.

Orientation

From the M6, the main routes into town are London Rd and Warwick Rd. The train station is south of the city centre, a 10-minute walk from Town Hall Sq (also known as Greenmarket) and the tourist office. The bus station is on Lonsdale St, about 250m east. Most of the town's B&Bs are dotted along Victoria Pl and Warwick Rd.

Information

@Cybercafe (☎ 01228-512308; www.atcybercafe.co.uk; 8-10 Devonshire St; 🕑 10am-10pm Mon-Sat, 1-10pm Sun; per hr £3)

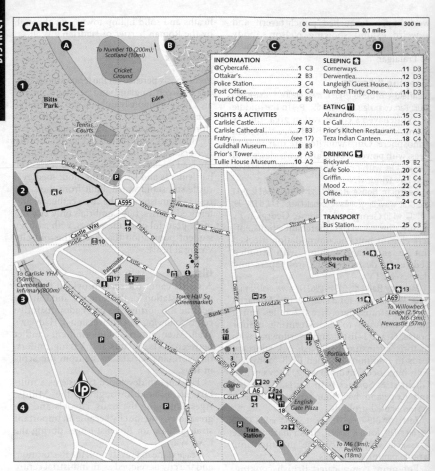

CARLISLE

INFORMATION	
@Cybercafé	1 C3
Ottakar's	2 B3
Police Station	3 C4
Post Office	4 C4
Tourist Office	5 B3

SIGHTS & ACTIVITIES	
Carlisle Castle	6 A2
Carlisle Cathedral	7 B3
Fratry	(see 17)
Guildhall Museum	8 B3
Prior's Tower	9 A3
Tullie House Museum	10 A2

SLEEPING	
Cornerways	11 D3
Derwentlea	12 D3
Langleigh Guest House	13 D3
Number Thirty One	14 D3

EATING	
Alexandros	15 C3
Le Gall	16 C3
Prior's Kitchen Restaurant	17 A3
Teza Indian Canteen	18 C4

DRINKING	
Brickyard	19 B2
Cafe Solo	20 C4
Griffin	21 C4
Mood 2	22 C4
Office	23 C4
Unit	24 C4

TRANSPORT	
Bus Station	25 C3

Cumberland Infirmary (☎ 01228-523444; Newtown Rd) Half a mile west of the city centre.

Ottakar's (☎ 01228-542300; 66 Scotch St; 9am-5.30pm Mon-Sat, 10am-4pm Sun) Large chain bookshop stocking new titles and local books.

Police station (☎ 0845 33 00 247; English St; 8am-midnight)

Post office (20-34 Warwick Rd)

Tourist office (☎ 01228-625600; www.historic-carlisle .org.uk; Greenmarket; per 15min £1; ⏰ 9.30am-5pm Mon-Sat, 10.30am-4pm Sun) Offers internet access.

Sights & Activities

CARLISLE CASTLE

The brooding, rust-red **Carlisle Castle** (☎ 01228-591922; adult/child £4.50/2.30; ⏰ 9.30am-5pm Apr-Sep, 10am-4pm Oct-Mar) was founded around a Celtic and Roman stronghold, with a Norman keep added in 1092 by William Rufus, and later enlargements (which included the supposedly cannon-proof towers) added by Henry VIII. The castle has witnessed some dramatic events over the centuries: Mary Queen of Scots was imprisoned here in 1568, and the castle was the site of a notorious eight-month siege during the English Civil War, when the Royalist garrison survived by eating rats, mice and the castle dogs before finally surrendering in 1645. Look out for the 'licking stones' in the dungeon, which Jacobite prisoners supposedly lapped for moisture.

Admission includes entry to the Kings Own Royal Border Regiment Museum, which explores the history of Cumbria's

Infantry Regiment. There are guided tours from April to September.

CARLISLE CATHEDRAL

Carlisle's scarlet **cathedral** (☎ 01228-548151; www.carlislecathedral.org.uk; 7 The Abbey; donation £2; ⊙ 7.30am-6.15pm Mon-Sat, to 5pm Sun) was founded as a priory church in 1122. During the 1644–45 siege by Parliamentarian troops, two-thirds of the nave was torn down to repair the city walls. Serious restoration didn't begin until 1853, but a surprising amount survives, including the 14th-century east window and part of the Norman nave. Other features include the 15th-century misericords, the lovely Brougham Triptych and some ornate choir carvings.

Surrounding the cathedral are other priory relics, including the 16th-century Fratry (see Prior's Kitchen Restaurant, p740) and the **Prior's Tower**.

TULLIE HOUSE MUSEUM

Carlisle's main **museum** (☎ 01228-534781; Castle St; www.tulliehouse.co.uk; adult/under 18yr £5.20/free; ⊙ 10am-5pm Mon-Sat, 11am-5pm Sun July-Aug, 10am-5pm Mon-Sat, noon-5pm Sun Apr-June & Sep-Oct, 10am-4pm Mon-Sat, noon-4pm Sun Nov-Mar) is a treat for history buffs, with exhibits exploring the foundation of the city, life under Roman rule and the development of modern Carlisle. The museum has a strong archaeology collection, including a Bronze Age spear-mould, Roman tablets collected from Hadrian's Wall, and artefacts recovered from Viking burial sites in nearby Ormside and Hesket.

GUILDHALL MUSEUM

This tiny **museum** (☎ 01228-532781; Greenmarket; admission free; ⊙ noon-4.30pm Tue-Sun Apr-Oct) is housed in a wonky 15th-century townhouse built for Carlisle's trade guilds. Among the modest exhibits are a ceremonial mace, the city's stocks and a section of exposed wall showing the building's wattle-and-daub construction.

Tours

Open Book Visitor Guiding (☎ 01228-670578; www.greatguidedtours.co.uk) offers tours of Carlisle and the surrounding area from April to September, including visits to Carlisle Castle and Hadrian's Wall. Tours leave from the tourist office.

Sleeping

BUDGET

Carlisle YHA (☎ 0870 770 5752; www.yha.org.uk; Bridge Lane; dm £21; ⊙ Jul-Sep) Lodgings at the old Theakston brewery now provide student digs for Carlisle University; rooms are usually available during the summer hols. It's just west of the centre.

MIDRANGE & TOP END

Cornerways (☎ 01228-521733; www.cornerwaysguesthouse.co.uk; 107 Warwick Rd; s £30-35, d £55-65; P ⬛ wifi) In the heart of Carlisle's conservation district, this cheery corner guesthouse offers reliable B&B rooms (not all are en suite). Period touches (including a tiled Victorian hallway) keep it a cut above Carlisle's bog-standard B&Bs.

Langleigh Guest House (☎ 01228-530440; www.langleighhouse.co.uk; 6 Howard Pl; s/d £35/70; P) Gilded mirrors, armchairs and porcelain knick-knacks cover every inch of this terrific-value guesthouse. All rooms are decorated in well-to-do Edwardian fashion – think brass bedside lamps, marble fireplaces and watercolour prints.

Derwentlea (☎ 01228-409706; www.derwentlea.co.uk; 14 Howard Pl; s/d £35/70; P) Red leather armchairs and ticking mantle clocks set the period vibe at this small, trad-brick B&B. Big, soft beds, full-length mirrors and dressing tables distinguish the smartest rooms, and there's a ground-floor room for mobility-restricted guests. Storage is available for bikes.

Number Thirty One (☎ 01228-597080; www.number31.freeservers.com; 31 Howard Pl; s/d from £65/95; P) Dig out the glad rags – Number 31 oozes opulence from every nook and cranny. The three colour-coded rooms all have keynote decor: Blue is classically old-fashioned with polished wooden bed frame and upmarket wallpaper; Yellow is cosily countrified, with flower-print quilt and half-tester bed; Red has a touch of Zen sophistication thanks to its Japanese-print bedspread and decorative dragon headboard.

Willowbeck Lodge (☎ 01228-513607; www.willowbeck-lodge.com; Lambley Bank, Scotby; d £100-120; P ⬛ wi-fi) The architects have gone doolally at this palatial B&B, 3 miles east of the city centre. It's a modernist marvel, boasting six deluxe rooms furnished in creams and taupes, with luxury spoils including corner tubs, broadband and LCD TVs. The centrepiece is the 7m-high gabled lounge, which overlooks a private pond frequented by kingfishers and herons. Fabulous.

Eating

Alexandros (☎ 01228-592227; 68 Warwick Rd; meze £3-6, mains £10-16; ☺ dinner Mon-Sat) Go Greek with authentic meze, grilled kebabs and calamari at this ever-popular restaurant on Warwick Rd – just remember that smashing your plates is reserved for special occasions...

Prior's Kitchen Restaurant (☎ 01228-543251; Carlisle Cathedral; lunches £4-6; ☺ 9.45am-4pm Mon-Sat) Hidden in the old monk's mess hall, this cosy little cafe is always a favourite stop for jacket spuds, club sandwiches and homemade quiches – and it does a mean cream tea, too.

Le Gall (☎ 01228-818388; 7 Devonshire St; mains £5-12; ☺ lunch & dinner) Despite the Gallic name, this town-centre bistro brims with world flavours. Italian panini and pastas, Mexican wraps and Cumbrian standards fill the specials board.

our pick **Teza Indian Canteen** (☎ 01228-525111; 4a English Gate Plaza; mains £8-14; ☺ lunch & dinner Mon-Sat) Wave goodbye to those tired old vindaloos – this 21st-century Indian stands out from Carlisle's other curry houses like a Bollywood superstar in a crowd of extras. It shimmers with chrome, plate glass and modern art, and champions a new breed of Indian cuisine – Keralan fish curry, tiger prawns with coriander and cloves, and slow-cooked lamb in pickled ginger.

Number 10 (☎ 01228-524183; 10 Eden Mount; mains £13-21; ☺ dinner Tue-Sat) Arguably the city's top spot, this classy Brit brasserie north of the centre takes its cue from the culinary produce it finds on its doorstep, from Thornby Moor goat's cheese to farm-bred lamb and Morecambe Bay shrimps. Tables are limited, and it gets busy.

Drinking

Botchergate's the place for late-night action, but it gets notoriously rowdy after kicking-out time, so watch your step.

Office (☎ 01228-404303; Botchergate) Industrial pipes, cube lights and stripped style define this hipster hang-out, with DJs spinning breakbeat, chunky house and hip-hop.

Unit (☎ 01228-514823; Botchergate) Another metro-style bar decked out in retro garb, with DJs and deep leather sofas to pull in Carlisle's trendy set.

Griffin (☎ 01228-598941; Court Sq) The pick of the town centre pubs, housed in a converted bank. Jennings ales on tap, street tables for when the sun shines, and a half-decent Sunday roast to boot.

Cafe Solo (☎ 01228-631600; 1 Botchergate) Sink lattes by day, chased down with Sol beers, margaritas and late-night tapas after dark at this Balearic corner bar.

Mood 2 (☎ 01228-520383; 70 Botchergate) Concept club fresh from a £1m refurbishment. Charty choons in the main room, hip-hop and R&B in the annexe, plus a cocktail chill-out bar when you're done shaking your booty.

Brickyard (☎ 01228-512220; www.brick-yard.com; 14 Fisher St) Carlisle's main gig venue, housed in the former Memorial Hall.

Getting There & Away

BUS

Carlisle is Cumbria's main transport hub. National Express coaches travel from the bus station on Lonsdale St to London (£33, 7½ hours, three direct daily, with extra buses via Birmingham), Glasgow (£17.20, two hours, 14 daily) and Manchester (£24, 3¼ hours, seven daily).

The most useful services to the Lakes are the 600 (one hour, seven Monday to Saturday) to Cockermouth and the 554 to Keswick (70 minutes, three daily), connecting with the 555/556 LakesLink to Windermere and Ambleside.

The 104 operates to Penrith (40 minutes, hourly Monday to Saturday, nine on Sunday), and Bus AD122 (the Hadrian's Wall bus; six daily late May to late September) connects Hexham and Carlisle.

TRAIN

Carlisle is on the London Euston (£123.50, 3¼ to 4¼ hours) to Glasgow (£43.20, 1¼ to 1½ hours) line, with hourly connections in either direction. It's also the terminus for several regional railways:

Cumbrian Coast Line Follows the coastline to Lancaster (£23, three to four hours).

Lakes Line Branches at Oxenholme near Kendal for Windermere (£19.50, one to two hours depending on connections).

Settle-Carlisle Line Cuts southeast across the Yorkshire Dales (£15.80, 1½ hours).

Tyne Valley Line Follows Hadrian's Wall to Newcastle-upon-Tyne (£12.10, 1½ hours).

Getting Around

To book a taxi, call **Radio Taxis** (☎ 01228-527575), **Citadel Station Taxis** (☎ 01228-523971) or **County Cabs** (☎ 01228-596789).

PENRITH

pop 14,882

Traditional butchers, greengrocers and quaint little teashops line the streets of Penrith, a stout, redbrick town which feels closer to the no-nonsense villages of the Yorkshire Dales than to the chocolate-box villages of the Central Lakes. Once the region's capital, Penrith remains a busy commercial centre for eastern Cumbria; life still revolves around the centuries-old market square, from where a tight warren of colonnaded alleyways and cobbled streets radiate out towards Beacon Fell, where warning fires were once lit to warn of impending border raids.

The **tourist office** (☎ 01768-867466; pen.tic@eden .gov.uk; Middlegate; ☺ 9.30am-5pm Mon-Sat, 1-4.45pm Sun) houses a small town museum displaying archaeological finds.

Opposite the station is the ruined 14th-century **Penrith Castle** (☺ 7.30am-9pm Easter-Oct, to 4.30pm Oct-Easter), built by William Strickland (later Bishop of Carlisle and Archbishop of Canterbury) and expanded by Richard III to resist Scottish raids, one of which razed the town in 1345.

Penrith's name derives from an old Celtic word meaning 'red fell', and the area's crimson sandstone can be seen in many town buildings, including the 18th-century **St Andrew's Church**. A legendary giant (the 'rightful king of all Cumbria') is said to be buried in the churchyard, but the stone pillars supposedly marking his grave are actually the weathered remains of Celtic crosses.

Sleeping

Brooklands (☎ 01768-863395; www.brooklandsguest house.com; 2 Portland Pl; s £30-35, d £65-75) This topnotch Victorian guesthouse distinguished by its richly furnished rooms and thoughtful decor. Some feature huge pine fourposters and rich purples, while others go for soothing magnolias and flower prints. For the full swank-factor you'll want the fluffy-pillowed suite, with brass bedstead and wall-mounted TV.

Brandelhow (☎ 01768-864470; www.brandelhow guesthouse.co.uk; 1 Portland Pl; s £32.50, d & tw £65) Next door to Brooklands, there are plain, uncom-

plicated rooms at this Portland Pl staple, all in pine and neutral beige, with lots of little luxuries (minifridges, bickies, bath-robes). Tuck into a sit-down tea on arrival, topped off with a slice of Grandma's Courting Cake or Lanie's Expedition Flapjack.

Bank House (☎ 01768-868714; www.bankhouse penrith.co.uk; Graham St; s £38, d £68-76; 🖳 wi-fi) Unpretentious Cumbrian guesthouse which does all the basics right (including a kingly breakfast of coiled Cumberland sausage and fresh-baked granary loaf). The rosy pink twin room might be too lacy for some, but the other doubles are more neutral, with DVD players and wooden bed frames.

Hornby Hall (☎ 01768-891114; www.hornbyhall .co.uk; Brougham; d £50-84; P) Aspiring aristocrats should head for this amber-stone manorhouse, 3 miles south of Penrith in Brougham. The five sunny rooms overlook the manicured grounds; two are reached via a Hogwartsesque spiral staircase, and breakfast is served in the 16th-century dining hall with its original stone hearth and Victorian range.

Eating

No 15 (☎ 01768-867453; 15 Victoria Rd; lunches £6-10; ☺ daily) Look no further for lunch in Penrith than this zingy little cafe-cum-gallery. There are 15 specials to choose from behind the counter, plus a bevy of artisan teas, cakes and sarnies, and you can check out local art and photography in the gallery annexe.

ᴏᴜʀ ᴘɪᴄᴋ **Yanwath Gate Inn** (☎ 01768-862886; Yanwath; mains £16-19) Two miles south of town, this award-winning inn has scooped a clutch of culinary prizes for its gastro-grub. Wood panels and A-frame beams conjure a convincingly rural atmosphere, and the menu ranges the fells in search of local smoked venison, salt lamb and crispy pork belly, chased down by a delicious selection of Cumbrian cheeses.

Getting There & Away

BUS

The bus station is northeast of the centre, off Sandgate. Bus 104 runs between Penrith and Carlisle (45 minutes, hourly Monday to Saturday, nine on Sunday).

Bus X4/X5 (13 Monday to Saturday, six on Sunday) travels via Rheged, Keswick and Cockermouth en route to the Cumbrian Coast.

CUMBRIA & THE LAKE DISTRICT

TRAIN

Penrith has frequent connections to Carlisle (£6.70, 20 minutes, hourly) and Lancaster (£12.50, 50 to 60 minutes, hourly).

AROUND PENRITH

Cunningly disguised as a Lakeland hill 2 miles west of Penrith, **Rheged** (☎ 01768-686000; www .rheged.com; ☿ 10am-6pm) houses a large-screen IMAX cinema and an exhibition on the history and geology of Cumbria, as well as an excellent retail hall selling Cumbrian goods from handmade paper to chocolate and chutneys.

There's a revolving line-up of movies show. A new film starts hourly; one film costs £4.95/3 per adult/child, with each extra one costing £3/2.

The frequent X4/X5 bus between Penrith and Workington stops at the centre.

ALSTON

pop 2227

Surrounded by the bleak hilltops of the Pennines, isolated Alston's main claim to fame is its elevation: at 305m above sea level, it's thought to be the highest market town in England (despite no longer having a market). It feels much closer to the stout market towns of the Pennines than the cosy rural settlements of the Lake District, and the views in all directions are sublime. It's also famous among steam enthusiasts thanks to the **South Tynedale Railway** (☎ 01434-381696, talking timetable 01434-382828; www.strps.org.uk; adult/3-15yr return £5.50/2.50; ☿ Apr-Oct), which puffs and clatters through the hilly country between Alston and Kirkhaugh, along a route that originally operated from 1852 to 1976. The return trip takes about an hour; there are up to five daily trains in midsummer.

Alston's **tourist office** (☎ 01434-382244; alston.tic@ eden.gov.uk; Town Hall, Front St; ☿ 10am-5.30pm Mon-Sat, to 4pm Sun Apr-Oct) is south of the town square.

Sleeping & Eating

Alston YHA (☎ 0845 371 9301; The Firs; dm £12; ☿ Easter-Oct) Basic hostel with three dorms overlooking the South Tyne Valley. It's popular with walkers and cyclists on the C2C route, so book ahead.

Lowbyer Manor (☎ 01434-381230; www.lowbyer.com; Alston; s £33, d £66-90) Handmade quilts (woven by the owner's relatives) and an endearing mix-and-match decor make this lovely manorhouse Alston's cosiest B&B. The nine rooms range from a titchy single to a king-size four-poster suite overlooking Alston Moor. It's especially handy for the steam train – the station's just a stroll away.

Yew Tree Chapel (☎ 01434-382525; www.yewtree chapel.co.uk; Slaggerby; s/d £39/68; **P**) Funky B&B in a converted church, overflowing with wit and style – the original organ and stained-glass windows feature alongside flea-market furniture and globe lights in the lounge. The style is boho-chic – colourful furnishings, bric-a-brac and scatter cushions, plus fresh-baked bread, cinnamon toast and gourmet muesli for brekkie. It's in Slaggerby, 3 miles north of Alston.

Lovelady Shield (☎ 0871 288 1345; www.lovelady .co.uk; Nenthead Rd; d £100-170; **P**) The country hideaway par excellence, overflowing with swag-draped beds, flouncy curtains and posh wallpapers in white and gold. All rooms have sofa suites, widescreen TVs and wonderful views across the grounds, but it might be a bit too stuffy for some.

Getting There & Away

Bus 888 travels twice daily to Newcastle (£8, 80 minutes), and once to Penrith (£6, 1¼ hours) and Keswick (£7, 1¾ hours). Bus 680 runs from Nenthead to Carlisle via Alston (four Monday to Saturday).

The Northeast

Northeast England knows a thing or two about hard living. Perched atop of England along the border with Scotland, this has always been frontier country – inhabited by a people who are passionate, independent, and historically not afraid to get into a scrap over territory.

And what a territory it is. You only need take a glance at the vast, almost epic countryside to get a sense of its brooding, menacing beauty – from the wind-lashed stretch of coast through the heather-carpeted Cheviot Hills and on into the wilderness of Northumberland National Park before arriving at the feet of the dark slopes of the North Pennines. Beyond them is Scotland, the other actor in an 800-year-old historical drama of war, bloodshed and conquest: no wonder the folks up here have a reputation for being hardy.

It has taken the best efforts of Man to make a dent on this indomitable landscape. The Romans did their bit, leaving us the magnificent Hadrian's Wall, which served as their empire's northern border for nearly 300 years. The Normans acquitted themselves equally well: their legacy was in splendid castles and, in Durham, a magnificent cathedral. Against their splendid backdrops, these marvellous constructions serve only to reinforce an impression of a landscape that hasn't changed much since the region was part of the ancient kingdom of Northumbria.

If you look closely, however, you will see that the landscape is run through with dark, menacing scars: dotted throughout are the rusting hulks of an industry that drove this region for nearly 700 years. Mining is all but defunct now, yet the cities it built are still very much alive, none more so than Newcastle, the biggest in the region and one of the most dynamic urban centres in England.

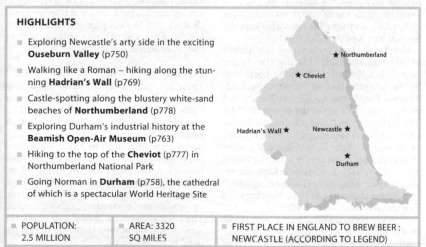

HIGHLIGHTS

- Exploring Newcastle's arty side in the exciting **Ouseburn Valley** (p750)
- Walking like a Roman – hiking along the stunning **Hadrian's Wall** (p769)
- Castle-spotting along the blustery white-sand beaches of **Northumberland** (p778)
- Exploring Durham's industrial history at the **Beamish Open-Air Museum** (p763)
- Hiking to the top of the **Cheviot** (p777) in Northumberland National Park
- Going Norman in **Durham** (p758), the cathedral of which is a spectacular World Heritage Site

★ Northumberland
★ Cheviot
Hadrian's Wall ★   Newcastle ★
★ Durham

| POPULATION: 2.5 MILLION | AREA: 3320 SQ MILES | FIRST PLACE IN ENGLAND TO BREW BEER : NEWCASTLE (ACCORDING TO LEGEND) |

History

Violent history has shaped the region more than any other in England, primarily because of its frontier position. Although Hadrian's Wall was not quite the defensive barrier some believe it to be, it nevertheless marked the northern frontier of Roman Britain and was the Empire's most heavily fortified line. Following the Romans' departure, the region became part of the Anglian kingdom of Bernicia, which united with the southern kingdom of Deira (which stretched across much of modern-day Yorkshire) to form Northumbria in 604.

The kingdom changed hands and had its borders (which extended up into present-day Scotland) altered several times over the next 500 years as various Anglo-Saxon lords and, later, Danes struggled to get their hands on it. The land north of the River Tweed was finally ceded to the emerging kingdom of Scotland in 1018, while the nascent kingdom of England kept its hands on everything below it…and so the fun really began.

The arrival of the Normans in 1066 added a new spice to the mix, as William I was eager to secure his northern borders against the Scots, but he also had to contend with local tribes who weren't too happy about the Norman presence. He ordered the construction of most of the castles you can see along the coast, and cut deals with the prince bishops of Durham to ensure their loyalty. It worked, but only up to a point: the new lords of Northumberland became very powerful because, as Marcher Lords (from the use of 'march' as a synonym of 'border'), they were the ones who kept the Scots at bay. And they did, regularly.

Northumberland's reputation as a hotbed of rebellion intensified during the Tudor years, when the largely Catholic north, led by the seventh duke of Northumberland, Thomas Percy, rose up against Elizabeth I in the defeated Rising of the North in 1569. The region's refusal to fully submit to national authority is perhaps best exemplified in the actions of the Border Reivers, raiders from both sides of the border who rose to real power in the 16th century and kept the region in a perpetual state of lawlessness, which only subsided after the Act of Union between England and Scotland in 1707.

Northumberland also played a central role in the Industrial Revolution. The region's coalmines were key to the development of industry and the development of the railway, which transported coal to the Tyne and the shipbuilding and armament works that grew up around Newcastle.

Orientation & Information

The Pennine hills are the dominant geological feature, forming a north–south spine that divides the region from Cumbria and Lancashire in the west and provides the source of major rivers such as the Tees and the Tyne.

The major transport routes are east of this spine, from Durham northwards to Newcastle and Edinburgh. Newcastle is an important ferry port for Scandinavia (see p756 for details). There's a northeast region website at www.thenortheast.com.

Activities

With the rugged moors of the Pennines and stunning seascape of the Northumberland coast, there's some good walking and cycling in this region. The scenery is beautiful in a wild and untouched way – quite different from the picture-postcard landscape of areas such as Devon or the Cotswolds. If you're out in the open, be prepared for wind and rain at any time of year. But when the sun shines, you can't go wrong. More details on walking and cycling are given in the Outdoor England chapter (p141), and suggestions for shorter routes are given throughout this chapter. Regional tourism websites all contain walking and cycling information, and tourist information centres (TICs; referred to throughout this book simply as tourist offices) all stock free leaflets plus maps and guides (usually £1 to £5) covering walking, cycling and other activities.

CYCLING

There are some excellent cycling routes in this part of the world. Part of the National Cycle Network (see the boxed text, p792), a long-time favourite is the **Coast & Castles Cycle Route** (NCN route 1), which runs south–north along the glorious Northumberland coast between Newcastle-upon-Tyne and Berwick-upon-Tweed, before swinging inland into Scotland to finish at Edinburgh. Of course you can also do it north–south, or just do the northeast England section. The coast is exposed, though, so check the weather and try to time your ride so that the wind is behind you.

THE NORTHEAST

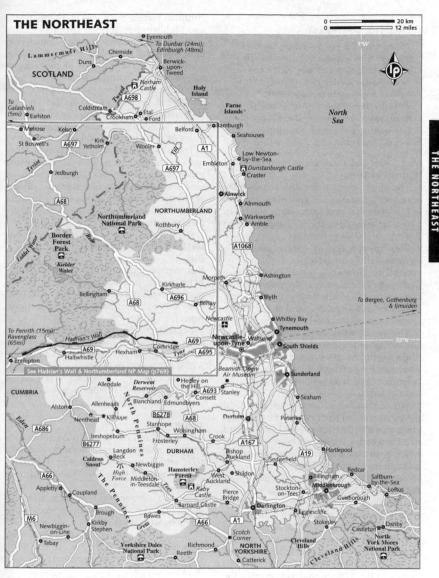

See Hadrian's Wall & Northumberland NP Map (p769)

The 140-mile **Sea to Sea Cycle Route** (C2C; www.c2c-guide.co.uk) runs across northern England from Whitehaven or Workington on the Cumbrian coast, through the northern part of the Lake District, and then over the wild hills of the North Pennines to finish at Newcastle-upon-Tyne or Sunderland. This popular route is fast becoming a classic, and most people go west–east to take advantage of prevailing winds. You'll need five days to complete the whole route; the northeast England section, from Penrith (in Cumbria) to the east coast is a good three-day trip. If you wanted to cut the urban sections, Penrith to Consett is perfect in a weekend. The C2C is aimed at

THE NORTHEAST

CALL THE NORTHEAST

The northeast is the call-centre capital of England, mostly because the area desperately needed to attract jobs to the region following the demise of traditional industry. But another reason might have to do with the distinctive accent, which polls have shown to be the friendliest and most trustworthy of all English accents!

road bikes, but there are several optional off-road sections.

The other option is the **Hadrian's Cycleway** (www.cycleroutes.org.uk), a 172-mile route opened in July 2006 that runs from South Shields in Tyneside, west along the wall and down to Ravenglass (p736) in Cumbria.

Most people riding along Hadrian's Cycleway also go west–east to take advantage of the prevailing wind (ie, it's more likely to be behind you), and a long-distance trans-England circuit combining Hadrian's Cycleway and the C2C (and a bit of the Cumbrian coast) is growing in popularity.

The newish **Wheels to the Wild** is a 70-mile circular cycle route that explores the dales of the North Pennines. From Wolsingham, it weaves a paved route through Weardale, Allendale and Teesdale on mostly quiet country lanes.

For dedicated off-road riding, good places to aim for in northeast England include Kielder Forest in Northumberland and Hamsterley Forest in County Durham, which both have a network of sylvan tracks and options for all abilities.

WALKING

The North Pennines are billed as 'England's last wilderness', and if you like to walk in quiet and fairly remote areas, these hills – along with the Cheviots further north – are the best in England. Long routes through this area include the famous **Pennine Way**, which keeps mainly to the high ground as it crosses the region between the Yorkshire Dales and the Scottish border, but also goes through sections of river valley and some tedious patches of plantation. The whole route is over 250 miles, but the 70-mile section between Bowes and Hadrian's Wall would be a fine four-day taster. If you prefer to go walking just for the day, good bases for circular walks in the North

Pennines include the towns of Alston (p742) and Middleton-in-Teesdale (p766).

Elsewhere in the area, the great Roman ruin of **Hadrian's Wall** is an ideal focus for walking. There's a huge range of easy loops taking in forts and other historical highlights. A very popular walk is the long-distance route from end to end, providing good options for anything from one to four days (see p770).

The Northumberland coast has endless miles of open beaches, and little in the way of resort towns (the frequently misty weather has seen to that), so walkers can often enjoy this wild, windswept shore in virtual solitude. One of the finest walks is between the villages of Craster and Bamburgh via Dunstanburgh, which includes two of the area's most spectacular castles.

Getting There & Around
BUS

Bus transport around the region can be difficult, particularly around the more remote parts of Northumbria in the west. Call ☎ 0870 608 2608 for information on connections, timetables and prices.

Several one-day Explorer tickets are available; always ask if one might be appropriate. The Explorer North East (adult/child £5.75/4.75), available on buses, covers from Berwick down to Scarborough, and allows unlimited travel for one day, as well as numerous admission discounts.

TRAIN

The main lines run north to Edinburgh via Durham, Newcastle and Berwick, and west to Carlisle roughly following Hadrian's Wall. Phone ☎ 0845 748 4950 for all train inquiries.

There are numerous Rover tickets for single-day travel and longer periods, so ask if one might be worthwhile. For example, the North Country Rover (adult/child £61.50/30.75) allows unlimited travel throughout the north (not including Northumberland) any four days out of eight.

NEWCASTLE-UPON-TYNE

pop 189,863

Of all of England's cities, Newcastle is perhaps the most surprising to the first-time visitor, especially if they come armed with the preconceived notions that have dogged the city's reputation since, well, always. A sooty, industrial wasteland for salt-of-the-earth toughies whose favourite hobby is drinking and braving the elements with a T-shirt on. Coal slags and cold slags? You're in for a pleasant surprise.

Welcome to the hipster capital of the northeast, a cool urban centre that knows how to take care of itself and anyone else who comes to visit with an enticing mix of culture, heritage and sophistication, best exemplified not just by its excellent new art galleries and magnificent concert hall, but by its growing number of fine restaurants, choice hotels and interesting bars. It's not just about the Tyne bridges – although the eclectic, cluttered array of Newcastle's most recognisable feature is pretty impressive.

Thankfully, Newcastle's hip rep is built on a set of deep-rooted traditions and mores embodied by the city's greatest strength: the locals. Raised and subsequently abandoned by coal and steel, Geordies (see the boxed text, p749) are a fiercely independent bunch, tied together by history, adversity and that impenetrable dialect, the closest language to 1500-year-old Anglo-Saxon left in England. They are also proud, hard-working and indefatigably positive – perhaps their greatest quality considering how tough life has been.

And then of course there's the nightlife, source of so many of the city's most brazen stereotypes. Of course you can go mad here – there's an irrepressible energy that borders on the irresponsible – but you don't have to, and there are plenty of options that don't involve draining blue-coloured vodka or running bare-chested through the streets.

ORIENTATION

The River Tyne marks the boundary between Newcastle to the north and Gateshead to the south; it is also one of the focal points for visitors to the city. Newcastle's attractive Victorian centre – which the local council has called Grainger Town to the uncertain shrugs of the locals – is only a short, uphill walk from the river. The up-and-coming Ouseburn is less than a mile east of here, while genteel Jesmond is north of the city and easily reached by bus or with the excellent Metro underground. The Tyne's southern bank – home to the impressive Baltic gallery and stunning Sage entertainment venue – is as far into Gateshead as you'll likely need to venture.

Central Station (train) is between the river and the city centre; the coach station is on Gallowgate, while local and regional buses leave from Eldon Sq and Haymarket bus stations.

Maps

All tourist offices have handy, free tearaway maps of Newcastle and Gateshead. The Ordnance Survey's *Mini-Map* (£2) is a handy foldaway pocket map of Newcastle, but not Gateshead.

The **Newcastle Map Centre** (☎ 0191-261 5622; 1st fl, 55 Grey St) supplies copious maps and guides.

INFORMATION

Blackwell's Bookshop (☎ 0191-232 6421; 141 Percy St) A comprehensive range of titles.
Clayton Road Laundrette (☎ 0191-281 5055; 4 Clayton Rd, Jesmond)
Main post office (35 Mosley St; ⏲ 9am-5.30pm Mon-Fri, to 12.30pm Sat) In the city centre.
McNulty's Internet Cafe (☎ 0191-232 0922; 26-30 Market St; per hr £5 ⏲ 8am-6.30pm Mon-Sat) About 14 terminals to fix all of your online needs.
Newcastle General Hospital (☎ 0191-273 8811; Westgate Rd) Half a mile northwest of the city centre, off Queen Victoria St.
Police station (☎ 0191-214 6555; cnr Pilgrim & Market Sts)
Thomas Cook (☎ 0191-219 8000; 6 Northumberland St) Has a bureau de change; it's just east of Monument.
Tourist offices (www.visitnewcastlegateshead.com) Main branch (☎ 0191-277 8000; Central Arcade, Market St; ⏲ 9.30am-5.30pm Mon-Wed, Fri & Sat, to 7.30pm Thu year-round, plus 10am-4pm Sun Jun-Sep); Gateshead Library (☎ 0191-433 8420; Prince Consort Rd; ⏲ 9am-7pm Mon, Tue, Thu & Fri, to 5pm Wed, to 1pm Sat); Guildhall (☎ 0191-277 8000; Newcastle Quayside; ⏲ 11am-6pm Mon-Fri, 9am-6pm Sat, 9am-4pm Sun); Sage Gateshead (☎ 0191-478 4222; Gateshead Quays; ⏲ 9am-5pm Mon-Fri, 10am-5pm Sat, 11am-5pm Sun) All offices listed here provide a booking service (☎ 0191-277 8042) as well as other assorted tourist sundries.
Waterstone's (☎ 0191-261 7757; Emerson Chambers, Blackett St) Four floors of books to satisfy most of your needs.

SIGHTS
Quayside

Newcastle's most recognisable attractions are the seven bridges that span the Tyne and some of the striking buildings that line it. Along Quayside, on the river's northern side, is a handsome boardwalk that makes

NEWCASTLE-UPON-TYNE

for a pleasant stroll during the day but really comes to life at night, when the bars, clubs and restaurants that line it are full to bursting. A really great way of experiencing the river and its sights is by cruise (see Tours, p752).

TYNE BRIDGES
The most famous view in Newcastle is the cluster of Tyne bridges, and the most famous of these is the **Tyne Bridge** (1925–28), built at about the same time as (and very reminiscent of) Australia's Sydney Harbour Bridge. The quaint little **Swing Bridge** pivots in the middle to let ships through. Nearby, **High Level Bridge**, designed by Robert Stephenson, was the world's first road and railway bridge

(1849). The most recent addition is the multiple-award-winning **Millennium Bridge** (aka Blinking Bridge; 2002), which opens like an eyelid to let ships pass.

OTHER SIGHTS
The Tyne's northern bank was the hub of commercial Newcastle in the 16th century. On Sandhill is **Bessie Surtee's House** (☎ 0191-261 1585; 41-44 Sandhill; admission free; ☽ 10am-4pm Mon-Fri), a combination of two 16th- and 17th-century merchant houses – all dark wood and sloping angles. Three rooms are open to the public. The daughter of a wealthy banker, feisty Bessie annoyed Daddy by falling in love with John Scott (1751–1838), a pauper. It all ended in smiles because John went on to become Lord

THE NORTHEAST

Chancellor. Today it is run in conjunction with English Heritage (EH; for details see p801).

Just across the street is the rounded **Guildhall**, built in 1658. It now houses a branch of the tourist office.

City Centre

Newcastle's Victorian centre, a compact area bordered roughly by Grainger St to the west and Pilgrim St to the east, is supremely elegant and one of the most compelling examples of urban rejuvenation in England. At the heart of it is the extraordinarily handsome Grey St, lined with fine classical buildings – undoubtedly one of the country's finest thoroughfares: in 2005 BBC Radio 4 listeners voted it Britain's most beautiful street.

CENTRE FOR LIFE

This excellent **science village** (☎ 0191-243 8210; www.life.org.uk; Scotswood Rd; adult/child £8/5.85; ☽ 10am-6pm Mon-Sat, 11am-6pm Sun, last admission 4pm), part of the sober-minded complex of institutes devoted to the study of genetic science, is one of the more interesting attractions in town. Through a series of hands-on exhibits and the latest technology you (or your kids) can discover the incredible secrets of life. The highlight is the Motion Ride, a motion simulator that, among other things, lets you 'feel' what it's like to score a goal at St James' Park and bungee jump from the Tyne Bridge. There's lots of thought-provoking arcade-style games, and if the information sometimes gets lost on the way, never mind, kids will love it.

LAING ART GALLERY

The exceptional collection at the **Laing** (☎ 0191-232 7734; www.twmuseums.org.uk; New Bridge St; admission free; ☽ 10am-5pm Mon-Sat, 2-5pm Sun) includes works by Kitaj, Frank Auerbach and Henry Moore, and an important collection of paintings by Northumberland-born artist John Martin (1789–1854).

Outside the gallery is Thomas Heatherwick's famous **Blue Carpet** (2002) with shimmering blue tiles made from crushed glass and resin.

DISCOVERY MUSEUM

Newcastle's rich history is uncovered through a fascinating series of exhibits at this excellent **museum** (☎ 0191-232 6789; www.twmuseums.org.uk; Blandford Sq; admission free; ☽ 10am-5pm Mon-Sat,

WHY A GEORDIE?

Truth is, no one really knows for sure, not even the Geordies themselves. The most attractive explanation, at least here, is that the name was coined to disparage the townspeople who chose to side with the German Protestant George I ('Geordie' being a diminutive of George) against the 'Old Pretender', the Catholic James Stuart, during the Jacobite Rebellion of 1715. But a whole other school contends that the origins are a little less dramatic, and stem from Northumberland miners opting to use a lamp pioneered by George 'Geordie' Stephenson over one invented by Sir Humphrey Davy.

NEWCASTLE IN...

Two Days

You'll invariably want to start on Quayside, where you'll find the famous **Tyne bridges** (p748). A good walk is to cross the Millennium Bridge into Gateshead and check out **Baltic** (opposite) and the **Sage** (p755), where you can grab a scenic coffee. Wander back across the bridge and hop on a Quayside Q2 bus out to the Ouseburn Valley to visit the **Biscuit Factory** (opposite), stopping for a bite to eat in the **Brasserie Black Door** (p754). If you're with the kids, stop into **Seven Stories** (opposite). Otherwise, have a pint in one of the area's selection of fabulous pubs – we love the **Free Trade Inn** (p755).

Back in the elegant Victorian centre, visit **Laing Art Gallery** (p749) and the science village **Centre for Life** (p749). Stop off in **Blake's Coffee House** (p754) for a pick-me-up. Work your way up to the **Trent House Soul Bar** (p755) and find that song you love but haven't heard in years on the incredible jukebox. And just keep going; everyone else is, so why shouldn't you?

The next day, devote the morning to the **Great North Museum** (below) before hopping on a bus south through Gateshead to the **Angel of the North** (p757) statue. Unfortunately, there's not much else going on here, so you'll have to head back into town. If you're looking for an alternative end to your day, take in an art film at the Star And Shadow (p755).

Four Days

Follow the two-day itinerary and then explore further afield, beginning with a side trip to **Bede's World** (p758) in the eastern suburb of Jarrow. In the afternoon, head to the seaside suburb of **Tynemouth** (p757), where you can ride the waves if you choose. The next day, head for the Roman fort at **Segedunum** (p758), at the start of Hadrian's Wall. All the while, be sure to fuel your efforts; the other bars in Ouseburn should not go undiscovered, especially the **Ship Inn** (p755) and **Cumberland Arms** (p755). Round off your stay with a gig at the Cluny (p755) or a play at the Northern Stage (p756).

2-5pm Sun). The exhibits, spread across three floors of the former Co-operative Wholesale Society building, surround the mightily impressive 30m-long *Turbinia,* the fastest ship in the world in 1897. The different sections are all worth a look; our favourites were the self-explanatory Story of the Tyne and the interactive Science Maze.

CASTLE GARTH KEEP

The 'New Castle' that gave its name to the city has been largely swallowed up by the railway station, leaving only the square Norman **keep** (adult/child £2/1; ⏲ 9.30am-5.30pm Apr-Sep, to 4.30pm Oct-Mar) as one of the few remaining fragments. It has a fine chevron-covered chapel and great views across the Tyne bridges from its rooftop.

GREAT NORTH MUSEUM

The **Great North Museum** (☎ 0191-222 8996; www .greatnorthmuseum.org), which at the time of writing was expected to open in spring 2009, will be the north's foremost museum of the natural sciences, archaeology, history and culture. The

main exhibition hall will be in the neoclassical building that once was home to the natural history exhibits of the prestigious Hancock Museum, where new additions include a life-size model of a *Tyrannosaurus rex.* Besides the expanded contents of the Hancock, the 11 galleries will also combine the contents of Newcastle University's other museums: the Greek art and archaeology of the Shefton Museum and the magnificent Museum of Antiquities, the Roman exhibits of which will now include an interactive model of Hadrian's Wall.

The museum will also include a new planetarium and a space to host the major touring exhibitions of the world, both of which are being added to the back of the building. Across the street, the well-known Hatton Gallery and its permanent collection of West African art have been absorbed into the new project. Take the Metro to Haymarket.

Ouseburn Valley

About a mile east of the city centre is the Ouseburn Valley, the 19th-century industrial heartland of Newcastle and now one of the city's hippest districts, full of potteries, glass-blowing studios and other skilled craftspeople, as well as a handful of great bars, clubs and our favourite cinema in town. To get there, jump onto the yellow Quayside Q2 bus that runs a loop through the valley from the city centre. For more info on the area, check out www.ouseburntrust.org.uk.

BISCUIT FACTORY

No prizes for guessing what this brand-new public **art gallery** (☎ 0191-261 1103; www.the biscuitfactory.com; Stoddart St; admission free; ☼ 10am-8pm Tue-Sat, 11am-5pm Sun) used to be. What it is now, though, is the country's biggest art shop, where you can peruse and buy work by artists from near and far in a variety of mediums, including painting, sculpture, glassware and furniture. Prices are thoroughly democratic, ranging from £30 to £30,000, but even if you don't buy, the art is excellent and there's a top-class restaurant too (see Brasserie Black Door, p754).

SEVEN STORIES – THE CENTRE FOR CHILDREN'S BOOKS

A marvellous conversion of a handsome Victorian mill has resulted in **Seven Stories** (☎ 0845 271 0777; www.sevenstories.org.uk; 30 Lime St; adult/child £5.50/4.50; ☼ 10am-5pm Mon-Wed, Fri & Sat, to 6pm Thu, 11am-5pm Sun), a very hands-on museum dedicated to the wondrous world of children's literature. Across the seven floors you'll find original manuscripts, a growing collection of artwork from the 1930s onwards, and a constantly changing program of exhibitions, activities and events designed to encourage the AA Milnes of the new millennium.

36 LIME STREET

The artistic, independent spirit of Ouseburn is particularly well represented in this **artists cooperative** (☎ 0191-261 5666; www.36limestreet.co.uk; Ouseburn Warehouse, 36 Lime St; admission free), the largest of its kind in the northeast, featuring an interesting mix of artists, performers, designers and musicians. They all share a historic building designed by Newcastle's most important architect, John Dobson (1787–1865), who also designed Grey St and Central Station in the neoclassical style. As it's a working studio you can't just wander in, but there are regular exhibitions and open days; check the website for details. It is attached to the popular Cluny bar (see p755).

LET THERE BE LIGHT

Mosley St – which runs on an east–west axis across the bottom of Grey St – was the first street in the world to be lit by electricity, all thanks to the genius of Sir Joseph Wilson Swan (1828–1914), the inventor of the incandescent light bulb, for which he received a patent in 1878 – a year before Thomas Edison got his. Swan, who had a business on Mosley St, hung the first light outside his shop in February 1879.

The two inventors worked in tandem to improve on Swan's original design, and in 1883 the two formed the Edison & Swan Electric Light Company (better known as Ediswan, the forerunner to US giant General Electric), changing the world forever.

Gateshead

You probably didn't realise that that bit of Newcastle south of the Tyne is the 'town' of Gateshead, but local authorities are going to great lengths to put it right, even promoting the whole kit-and-caboodle-on-Tyne as 'NewcastleGateshead'. A bit clumsy, but we get the point. To date, the ambitious program of development has seen the impressive transformation of the southern banks of the Tyne, but as yet there's little to make you travel further afield than the water's edge.

BALTIC – THE CENTRE FOR CONTEMPORARY ART

Once a huge, dirty, yellow grain store overlooking the Tyne, **Baltic** (☎ 0191-478 1810; www.balticmill.com; admission free; ☼ 10am-6pm Mon-Tue & Thu-Sun, to 8pm Wed) is now a huge, dirty, yellow art gallery to rival London's Tate Modern. Unlike the Tate, there are no permanent exhibitions here, but the constantly rotating shows feature the work and installations of some of contemporary art's biggest show stoppers. The complex has artists in residence, a performance space, a cinema, a bar, a spectacular rooftop restaurant (you'll need to book) and a ground-floor restaurant with riverside tables. There's also a viewing box for a fine Tyne vista.

NEWCASTLE FOR CHILDREN

Newcastle is friendly, full stop. Although at first glance the bonhomie mightn't seem to extend past buying rounds in the pub, on closer inspection there's plenty to keep the young 'uns entertained.

The utterly wonderful **Seven Stories** (p751) is the perfect destination for any kid who has an imagination, while virtually next door, the **Round** (☎ 0191-260 5605; www.the-round.com; 34 Lime St) is the Northeast's only theatre devoted exclusively to kids.

Closer to the centre the **Centre for Life** (p749) and the **Discovery Museum** (p749) are brilliant and should keep the kids busy for the guts of a day. The most popular park in town is **Leazes Park**, just north of St James' Park, which has a rowing lake, but the nicest of all is **Saltwell Park** (☽ dawn-dusk), an elegant Victorian space behind Gateshead College and easily accessible by bus 53 and 54 from the Gateshead Interchange. Pedestrians can get in through entrances on East Park Rd, West Rd, Saltwell Rd South, Saltwell View and Joicey Rd.

QUIRKY NEWCASTLE

Take in the David Lynch vibe at **Blackie Boy** (p754), where it's not all it appears to be. Pop your coins into the world's best jukebox at the **Trent House Soul Bar** (p755) for the stomping sound of northern soul and pretend that James Blunt had stayed in the army. Attend a 'happening' at **36 Lime Street** (p751) before taking in an old art-house movie at the excellent **Star And Shadow** (p755) and then going to a late gig at the **Head of Steam@The Cluny** (p755). Take a rowing boat onto the lake at **Leazes Park** (above) – watch out for those fishing rods. Cross one of the **Tyne bridges** (p748) on foot.

TOURS

There are a handful of tour options:
Newcastle City Tours (☎ 07780 958679; www.new castlecitytours.co.uk; per tour from £40) Tailored tours of the city as well as heritage tours of the surrounding region.
River Tyne Cruises (☎ 0191-296 6740/1; www.tyne leisureline.co.uk; adult/child £12/7; noon Sat & Sun May–early Sep) Three-hour river cruises departing from Quayside pier at Millennium Bridge, opposite Baltic.
Tom Keating Tours (☎ 0191-488 5115; www.tom keating.net) Expert, tailor-made tours of the city by a well-respected blue-badge guide. Tours of surrounding region also available.
Walking Tours (adult/child £3/2; 2pm Wed & Sat Jun & Sep, Mon-Sat Jul-Aug) Ninety-minute walking tours of the main sites of interest, run by and departing from the main branch of the tourist office.

SLEEPING

Although the number of city-centre options is on the increase, they are still generally restricted to the chain variety – either budget or business – that caters conveniently to the party people and business folk that make up the majority of Newcastle's overnight guests. Most of the other accommodations are in the handsome northern suburb of Jesmond, where the forces of gentrification and student power fight it out for territory; Jesmond's main drag, Osborne Rd, is lined with all kinds of bed types as well as bars and restaurants – making it a strong rival with the city centre for the late-night party scene. As the city is a major business destination, weekend arrivals will find that most places drop their prices for Friday and Saturday nights.

City Centre

As you'd expect, bedrooms in the city centre are pricier than most anywhere else, but there are some good budget and midrange options that don't involve too much of a hike.

BUDGET

Euro-Hostel Newcastle (☎ 0845 490 0371; www.euro -hostel.co.uk; Garth Heads St; dm/d £17/60; ⓟ 🖳) This hostel offers a broader range of options than any hostel and most hotels, from a bed in a dorm to a private room or self-catering apartment suitable for families of up to seven people. The building is part of a new development perfectly situated halfway between the city centre and Ouseburn Valley.

Albatross Inn! (☎ 0191-233 1330; www.albatrossnew castle.com; 51 Grainger St; dm/d from £17.50/45; ⓟ 🖳) Clean, fully equipped hostel with decent-sized dorms, a self-catering kitchen, top-notch bathroom facilities, CCTV, electronic key cards and an internet station. There's even a small car park.

MIDRANGE

Premier Lodge (☎ 0870 990 6530; www.premierlodge .com; Quayside; r from £59) With a superb location in the old Exchange Building, this budget chain is right in the heart of the action. If you're here for the party, you shouldn't care that your room has about as much flavour as day-old chewing gum – if all goes according to plan, you won't be spending much time here anyway!

Jury's Inn (☎ 0191-201 4400; www.jurysinn.com/newcastle; St James' Gate, Scotswood Rd; r from £63) A short walk from Central Station, this edition of the popular Irish chain has rooms, a restaurant, and a bar best described as big, bland and absolutely inoffensive. And at these prices, who cares? The difference here is the friendliness of the staff, which is genuine.

Waterside Hotel (☎ 0191-230 0111; www.watersidehotel.com; 48-52 Sandhill, Quayside; s/d £75/80) The rooms are a tad small, but they're among the most elegant in town: lavish furnishings and heavy velvet drapes in a heritage-listed building. The location is excellent.

Copthorne (☎ 0191-222 0333; www.millenniumhotels.com; The Close, Quayside; s/d from £75/85; P 🖳 wi-fi) A superb waterside location makes this modern hotel a perfect choice – especially if you pick a room overlooking the water (the Connoisseur rooms, for instance). The bathrooms could do with some freshening, but that's only a minor complaint. Whatever you do, book online – the rack rate can be three times more expensive.

TOP END

Vermont (☎ 0191-233 1010; www.vermont-hotel.com; Castle Garth; s/d/ste from £110/130/250; P 🖳 wi-fi) Mid-1930s Manhattan with new-millennium facilities, the Vermont was the top dog in town, until the arrival of the Mal and Greystreet. The location is good, but a view of the castle keep just isn't enough of a sales pitch; the iPod docking stations are a decent contemporary touch.

our pick **Greystreethotel** (☎ 0191-230 6777; www.greystreethotel.com; 2-12 Grey St; d/ste from £145/165; P) A bit of designer class along the classiest street in the city centre has been long overdue: the rooms are gorgeous if a tad poky, all cluttered up with flat-screen TVs, big beds and handsome modern furnishings.

Malmaison (☎ 0191-245 5000; www.malmaison.com; Quayside; r from £125; ste £225-350; P 🖳 wi-fi) The affectedly stylish Malmaison touch has been applied to this former warehouse with considerable success, even down to the French-speaking lifts. Big beds, sleek lighting and designer furniture flesh out the Rooms of Many Pillows. Breakfast is £13.

Jesmond

The northeastern suburb of Jesmond is packed with budget and midrange accommodation to cater to the thousands that throng the area's bars and restaurants. There's a big party atmosphere around here that is easily a match for the city centre.

Catch the Metro to Jesmond or West Jesmond, or bus 80 from near Central Station, or bus 30, 30B, 31B or 36 from Westgate Rd.

BUDGET

Newcastle YHA (☎ 0845 371 9335; www.yha.org.uk; 107 Jesmond Rd; dm/d £16.50/40; 🖰 end Jan-end Dec) This nice, rambling place has small dorms that are generally full, so book in advance. It's close to the Jesmond Metro stop.

MIDRANGE

Adelphi Hotel (☎ 0191-281 3109; www.adelphihotelnewcastle.co.uk; 63 Fern Ave; s/d £39/60) Just off Osborne Rd, this attractive hotel has nice floral rooms that are clean and very neat – a rare thing around here for this price range.

Whites Hotel (☎ 0191-281 5126; www.whiteshotel.com; 38-42 Osborne Rd; s/d £45/75) First impressions don't promise a great deal, as the public areas are a bit tatty, but don't let that put you off; this is our favourite of the Osborne Rd hotels, with uniformly modern rooms and first-rate service.

New Northumbria Hotel (☎ 0191-281 4961; www.newnorthumbriahotel.co.uk; 61-73 Osborne Rd; s/d incl breakfast from £85/95) Trendy, clean and fairly pleasant, the New Northumbria likes to parade its five-star qualification, but that's just from the tourist office – this is a fine hotel with decent rooms and a good breakfast. Not more.

TOP END

Jesmond Dene House (☎ 0191-212 3000; www.jesmonddenehouse.co.uk; Jesmond Dene Rd; s £135, d £160-200, ste £225-275; P 🖳 wi-fi) As elegant a hotel as you'll find anywhere, this exquisite property is the perfect marriage between traditional styles and modern luxury. The large, gorgeous bedrooms are furnished in a modern interpretation of the Arts and Crafts style and are bedecked with all manner of technological goodies (flat-screen digital TVs, digital radios, wi-fi) and wonderful bathrooms complete with underfloor heating. It also has an outstanding restaurant; see p754.

EATING

The Geordie palate is pretty refined these days and there are a host of fine dining options in all price categories that make their mark. Conversely, if all you're looking for is stomach-lining crappy fast food and dodgy ethnic cuisine, well there's plenty of that too.

City Centre

BUDGET

Blake's Coffee House (☎ 0191-261 5463; 53 Grey St; breakfast £3-4.50, sandwiches £3-4; ⊗ 9am-6pm) There is nowhere better than this high-ceilinged cafe for a Sunday-morning cure on any day of the week. It's friendly, relaxed and serves up the biggest selection of coffees in town, from the gentle push of a Colombian blend to the toxic shove of Old Brown Java. We love it.

MIDRANGE

Cafe Royal (☎ 0191-231 3000; 8 Nelson St; cafe mains £4-5, restaurant mains £8-12; ⊗ lunch & dinner Mon-Sat, to 7pm Sun) Dowstairs is a pleasant cafe that serves sandwiches and decent cakes, upstairs is a dining room with a Mediterranean menu with vaguely Pacific Rim influences.

Big Mussel (☎ 0191-232 1057; www.bigmussel.co.uk; 15 The Side; mains £6-12; ⊗ lunch & dinner) Mussels and other shellfish – all served with chips – are a very popular choice at this informal diner. There are pasta and vegetarian options as well, and students get 15% off everything. There's another branch (☎ 261 8927) on Leazes Park Rd, close to St James' Park, that does a roaring trade on match days.

TOP END

Secco Ristorante Salentino (☎ 0191-230 0444; www .seccouk.com; 86 Pilgrim St; mains £12-20; ⊗ lunch & dinner) Top-notch food from Salento in the Italian heel of Puglia makes this place an easy contender for best Italian restaurant in town. Some punters have been disappointed with the slowish service, which, for the price, should probably be a little snappier.

Cafe 21 (☎ 0191-222 0755; Trinity Gardens, Quayside; mains £14.50-22; ⊗ lunch & dinner Mon-Sat) Simple but hardly plain, this elegant restaurant – all white tablecloths and smart seating – offers new interpretations of England's culinary backbone: pork and cabbage, liver and onions and a sensational Angus beef and chips.

Ouseburn Valley

MIDRANGE

Brasserie Black Door (☎ 0191-260 5411; Biscuit Factory, 16 Stoddard St; mains £10-16; ⊗ lunch & dinner Mon-Sat) Less a museum restaurant and more a restaurant in a museum, the Black Door serves up excellent modern English fare – which generally involves a twist from pretty much any other part of the world – in a bright, elegant room. Even if you're not visiting the museum this is a great spot for lunch.

Jesmond

MIDRANGE

Pizzeria Francesca (☎ 0191-281 6586; 134 Manor House Rd, Jesmond; mains £4-12; ⊗ lunch & dinner Mon-Sat) This is how all Italian restaurants should be: chaotic, noisy, friendly, packed cheek-to-jowl and absolutely worth making the effort for. Excitable, happy waiters and huge portions of pizza and pasta keep them queuing at the door – get in line and wait because you can't book in advance.

TOP END

ourpick Jesmond Dene House (☎ 0191-212 3000; www.jesmonddenehouse.co.uk; Jesmond Dene Rd; mains £18-22) Chef Terry Laybourne is the architect of an exquisite menu heavily influenced by the northeast: venison from County Durham, oysters from Lindisfarne and the freshest herbs plucked straight from the garden. The result is a gourmet delight and one of the best dining experiences in the city.

DRINKING

There are no prizes for guessing that Geordies like a good night out – but you may be surprised to know that not only is there nightlife beyond the coloured cocktails of the Bigg Market, but that it is infinitely more interesting and satisfying than the sloppy boozefest that defines the stereotype. The Ouseburn is our area of choice, but also worth checking out is the western end of Neville St, which has a decent mix of great bars and is also home to the best of the gay scene.

We daren't even begin to list the pubs and bars in town, but here's a handful to start with. Get a bottle of dog and get doon.

City Centre

Blackie Boy (☎ 0191-232 0730; 11 Groat Market) At first glance, this darkened old boozer looks like any old traditional pub. Look closer. The overly red lighting. The single bookcase. The large leather armchair that is rarely occupied. The signage on the toilets: 'Dick' and 'Fanny'. This place could have featured in *Twin Peaks*, which is why it's so damn popular with everyone.

Crown Posada (☎ 0191-232 1269; 31 The Side) An unspoilt, real-ale pub that is a favourite with more seasoned drinkers, be they the after-work or instead-of-work crowd.

Forth (☎ 0191-232 6478; Pink Lane) It's in the heart of the gay district, but this great old pub draws all kinds with its mix of music, chat and unpretentious atmosphere.

Tokyo (☎ 0191-232 1122; 17 Westgate Rd) Tokyo has a suitably darkened atmosphere for what the cognoscenti consider the best cocktail bar in town, but we loved the upstairs garden bar where you can drink, smoke and chat with a view.

Trent House Soul Bar (☎ 0191-261 2154; 1-2 Leazes Lane) The wall has a simple message: 'Drink Beer. Be Sincere.' This simply unique place is the best bar in town because it is all about an ethos rather than a look. Totally relaxed and utterly devoid of pretentiousness, it is an old-school boozer that out-cools every other bar because it isn't trying to. And because it has the best jukebox in all of England – you could spend years listening to the extraordinary collection of songs it contains. It is run by the same folks behind the superb World Headquarters (p756).

Ouseburn Valley

Free Trade Inn (☎ 0191-265 5764; St Lawrence Rd) Our favourite bar in the Ouseburn is a no-nonsense boozer overlooking the Tyne that is frequented by students and long-standing patrons; it doesn't look like much but it's one of the coolest pubs in town (and the jukebox is brilliant). It's a short walk from the Quayside.

Ship Inn (☎ 0191-232 4030; Stepney Bank) The Ouseburn's oldest extant bar (early 19th century) has recently had a facelift, but not so that its traditional look and feel has disappeared, thereby ensuring that it continues to be a firm fixture on the valley's authentic pub crawl.

Cumberland Arms (☎ 0191-265 6151; off Byker Bank, Ouseburn) Sitting on a hill at the top of the Ouseburn, this 19th-century bar has a sensational selection of ales as well as a range of Northumberland meads. There's a terrace outside, where you can read a book from the Bring One, Borrow One library inside.

Cluny (☎ 0191-230 4474; 36 Lime St) Cool bar by day, superb musical venue by night, this superpopular spot defines the independent spirit of the Ouseburn Valley.

Jesmond

Mr Lynch (☎ 0191-281 3010; Archbold Tce) Newcastle goes shabby chic with this '60s-style bar at the southernmost edge of Jesmond, in truth only a short stroll from Newcastle University. Ignore the appearance and focus on the crowd, which is a knowledgeable mix of students and local trendies. There's live music on Sunday.

TOP FIVE PUBS FOR A PINT

- Trent House Soul Bar (left; Newcastle)
- Free Trade Inn (opposite; Newcastle)
- Ship Inn (p781; Low-Newton-by-the-Sea, Embleton Bay)
- Ye Old Cross (p779; Alnwick)
- Ship Inn (p783; Holy Island)

ENTERTAINMENT

Are you up for it? You'd better be, because Newcastle's nightlife doesn't mess about. There is nightlife beyond the club scene – you'll just have to wade through a sea of staggering, glassy-eyed clubbers to get to it. For current listings go online to www.thecrack magazine.com. Club admissions range from £4 to £15.

Cinema

Star And Shadow (☎ 0191-261 0066; www.starand shadow.org.uk; Stepney Bank, Ouseburn Valley; membership £1, admission £4) This unlikely looking cine-club in an old warehouse once used to store props for Tyne-Tees TV. It is the best movie experience in town, and the place to go for your art-house, cult, black & white and gay & lesbian film needs. Asylum seekers get in free.

Live Music

Head of Steam@The Cluny (☎ 0191-230 4474; www .headofsteam.co.uk; 36 Lime St, Ouseburn Valley) This is one of the best spots in town to hear live music, attracting all kinds of performers, from experimental prog-rock heads to up-and-coming pop goddesses. Touring acts and local talent fill the bill every night of the week. Take the Metro to Byker.

Sage Gateshead (☎ 0191-443 4666; www.thesage gateshead.org; Gateshead Quays) Norman Foster's magnificent chrome-and-glass horizontal bottle is not just worth gaping at and wandering about in – it is also a superb venue to hear live music, from folk to classical orchestras. It is the home of the Northern Sinfonia and Folkworks.

Nightclubs

Digital (☎ 0191-261 9755; www.yourfutureisdigital.com; Times Sq) A two-floored cathedral to dance music, this megaclub was voted in the top 20 clubs in the world by DJ Magazine – thanks to the best sound system we've ever heard.

THE NORTHEAST

A MONUMENT TO ROCK

Newcastle has produced a fair number of musical celebrities, from 1960s rockers The Animals to The Police's Sting. These days the best-known are punk revivalists Maxïmo Park, who formed in the city in 2000. Their 2007 album, *Our Earthly Pleasures*, features a song called 'By the Monument', which refers to Grey's Monument at the top of Grey St. And when the lads played a homecoming gig in December 2007 at the Newcastle Metro Radio Arena, they were afforded the ultimate accolade: local brewers Newcastle Brown Ale created a limited edition Maximo Brown Ale in their honour.

Our favourite night is Thursday's Stonelove (£6), a journey through 40 years of alternative rock and funk. Saturday's Shindig (£12 before 11pm, £15 after) brings the world's best house DJs to town.

Foundation (☎ 0191-261 8985; www.foundation-club .com; 57-59 Melbourne St) This warehouse-style club features a massive sound system, fantastic lighting rig and regular guest slots of heavyweight DJs from all over. If you want a night of hard-core clubbing, this is the place for you.

World Headquarters (☎ 0191-261 7007; www.trent house.com; Curtis Mayfield House, Carliol Sq) Dedicated to the genius of black music in all its guises – funk, rare groove, dance-floor jazz, northern soul, genuine R&B, lush disco, proper house and reggae – this fabulous club is strictly for true believers, and judging from the numbers, there are thousands of them.

Theatre
Northern Stage (☎ 0191-230 5151; www.northern stage.co.uk; Barras Bridge, Haymarket) The original Newcastle Playhouse has been transformed

into this marvellous new performance space (three stages and a high-tech, movable acoustic wall) that attracts touring international and national shows.

Theatre Royal (☎ 0191-232 2061; www.theatre -royal-newcastle.co.uk; 100 Grey St) The winter home of the Royal Shakespeare Company is full of Victorian splendour and has an excellent program of drama.

Sport
Newcastle United Football Club (☎ 0191-201 8400; www.nufc.premiumtv.co.uk) is more than just a football team: it is the collective expression of Geordie hope and pride as well as the release for decades of economic, social and sporting frustration. Its fabulous ground, **St James' Park** (Strawberry Pl), is always packed, and you can get a **stadium tour** (☎ 0191-261 1571; adult/child £10/7; ☺ 11am, noon, 1.30pm daily & 4hr before kick-off on match days) of the place, including the dugout and changing rooms. Match tickets go on public sale about two weeks before a game or you can try the stadium on the day, but there's no chance for big matches, such as those against arch-rivals Sunderland.

GETTING THERE & AWAY
Air
Newcastle International Airport (☎ 0191-286 0966; www.newcastleairport.com) is 7 miles north of the city off the A696. It has direct services to a host of UK and European cities as well as long-haul flights to Dubai. Tour operators fly charters out of Newcastle to the Americas and Africa.

Boat
Norway's **Fjord Line** (☎ 0191-296 1313; www.fjordline .com) operates ferries between Newcastle, Stavanger and Bergen. **DFDS Seaways** (☎ 0870

GAY & LESBIAN NEWCASTLE

Newcastle's gay scene is pretty dynamic, with its hub at the 'Pink Triangle' formed by Waterloo, Neville and Collingwood Sts, but stretching as far south as Scotswood Rd. There are plenty of gay bars in the area and a few great clubs.

Camp David (8-10 Westmorland Rd) An excellent mixed bar that is as trendy with straights as it is with the gay community.

Loft (☎ 0191-261 5348; 10A Scotswood Rd) Loud, proud and completely cheesy, this 1st-floor club above the equally cheesy Switch bar is open seven nights a week with nights like Monday's Shag Tag and Saturday's Passion.

Powerhouse Nightclub (☎ 0191-261 4507; 9-19 Westmorland Rd) Newcastle's brashest queer nightclub, with flashing lights, video screens and lots of suggestive posing.

---

533 3000; www.dfdsseaways.co.uk) operates ferries to Newcastle from Kristiansand in Norway, the Swedish port of Gothenburg and the Dutch port of Ijmuiden, near Amsterdam. For online ferry bookings, check out www.newcastleferry.co.uk.

Bus

National Express buses arrive and depart from the Gallowgate coach station. You can get to most anywhere, including London (£27, seven hours, six daily) and Manchester (£17.50, five hours, six daily). For Berwick-upon-Tweed (two hours, five daily) take bus 505, 515 or 525 from Haymarket bus station.

Local and regional buses leave from Haymarket or Eldon Sq bus stations. For local buses around the northeast, don't forget the excellent-value Explorer North East ticket, valid on most services for £7.

Train

Newcastle is on the main rail line between London and Edinburgh. Services go to Alnmouth (for connections to Alnwick; £8.40, 30 minutes, four daily), Berwick (£23.80, 45 minutes, every two hours), Edinburgh (£42, 1½ hours, half-hourly), London King's Cross (£124.50, three hours, half-hourly) and York (£21.40, 45 minutes, every 20 minutes). There's also the scenic Tyne Valley Line west to Carlisle. See p771 for details.

GETTING AROUND
To/From the Airport & Ferry Terminal

The airport is linked to town by the Metro (£2.80, 20 minutes, every 15 minutes).

Bus 327 links the ferry (at Tyne Commission Quay, 8.5 miles east), Central Station and Jesmond Rd. It leaves the train station 2½ hours and 1¼ hours before each sailing.

There's a taxi rank at the terminal; it costs about £18 to the city centre.

Car

Driving around Newcastle isn't fun thanks to the web of roads, bridges and one-way systems, but there are plenty of car parks.

Public Transport

There's a large bus network, but the best means of getting around is the excellent underground Metro, with fares from £1.30. There are also several saver passes. The tourist office can supply you with route plans for the bus and Metro networks.

The DaySaver (£4.50, £3.70 after 9am) gives unlimited Metro travel for one day, and the DayRover (adult/child £5.80/3) gives unlimited travel on all modes of transport in Tyne & Wear for one day.

Taxi

On weekend nights taxis can be rare; try **Noda Taxis** (☎ 0191-222 1888), which has a kiosk outside the entrance to Central Station.

AROUND NEWCASTLE

ANGEL OF THE NORTH

In 2008 the world's most viewed work of art celebrated its 10th birthday; we are, of course, referring to the Gateshead Flasher, an extraordinary 200-tonne, rust-coloured human frame with wings that is more soberly known as the *Angel of the North*. It is the most viewed due to its location, towering over the A1 (M) about 5 miles south of Newcastle – you just can't miss it. At 20m high and with a wingspan wider than a Boeing 767, Antony Gormley's most successful work is the country's largest sculpture. Buses 723 and 724 from Eldon Sq, or 21, 21A and 21B from Pilgrim St, will take you there.

TYNEMOUTH

One of the most popular Geordie days out is to this handsome seaside resort 6 miles east of the city centre. Besides being the mouth of the Tyne, this is one of the best surf spots in all of England, with great all-year breaks off the immense, crescent-shaped Blue Flag beach. In October, it hosts the **National Surfing Championships** (www.bpsauktour.com).

For all your surfing needs including lessons, call into the **Tynemouth Surf Company** (☎ 0191-258 2496; www.tynemouthsurf.co.uk; Grand Parade), which provides two-hour group lessons for £25 or one-hour individual lesson for the same price.

Front St runs perpendicular to the beach, and is where you'll find pubs, restaurant and cafes, as well as **Razzberry Bazaar** (☎ 0191-296 3133; www.razzberrybazaar.co.uk; 14 Front St), the most interesting curio shop we've seen, with gee-gaws of all shapes and sizes from through the world.

Tynemouth is on the Metro line.

DETOUR: BEDE'S WORLD

The fairly grim southeastern suburb of Jarrow is embedded in labour history for the 1936 Jarrow Crusade, when 200 men walked from here to London to protest against the appalling conditions brought about by unemployment.

But it is also famous as the home of the Venerable Bede, author of the *Ecclesiastical History of the English People* (see also opposite). **Bede's World** (☎ 0191-489 2106; www.bedes world.co.uk; admission £4.50; ⏰ 10am-5.30pm Mon-Sat, noon-5.30pm Sun Apr-Oct, noon-4.30pm Nov-Mar) comprises St Paul's Church, which dates back to the 7th century; a museum; and many reconstructed medieval buildings. It's accessible via the Metro.

SEGEDUNUM

The last strong post of Hadrian's Wall was the fort of **Segedunum** (☎ 0191-295 5757; www .twmuseums.org.uk; adult/child/concession £4/free/2.25; ⏰ 9.30am-5.30pm Apr-Aug, 10am-5pm Sep, 10am-3.30pm Nov-Mar), 6 miles east of Newcastle at Wallsend. Beneath the 35m tower, which you can climb for some terrific views, is an absorbing site that includes a reconstructed Roman bathhouse (with steaming pools and frescoes) and a fascinating museum that gives visitors a well-rounded picture of life during Roman times.

Take the Metro to Wallsend.

COUNTY DURHAM

Best known for its strikingly beautiful capital that is one of England's star attractions, County Durham spreads itself across the lonely, rabbit-inhabited North Pennines and the gentle ochre hills of Teesdale, each dotted with picturesque, peaceful villages and traditional market towns.

Ironically, this pastoral image, so resonant of its rich medieval history, has only been reclaimed in recent years; it took the final demise of the coal industry, all-pervasive for the guts of 300 years, to render the county back to some kind of pre-industrial look. A brutal and dangerous business, coal mining was the lifeblood of entire communities and its sudden end in 1984 by the stroke of a Conservative pen has left some pur-

poseless towns and an evocatively scarred landscape.

Durham has had a turbulent history, though it pales in comparison with its troublesome northern neighbour. To keep the Scots and local Saxon tribes quiet, William the Conqueror created the title of prince bishop in 1081 and gave them vice-regal power over an area known as the Palatinate of Durham, which became almost a separate country. It raised its own armies, collected taxes and administered a separate legal system that – incredibly – wasn't fully incorporated into the greater English structure until 1971.

Getting Around

The Explorer North East ticket (see p746) is valid on many services in the county.

DURHAM

pop 42,940

The sheer magnificence of Durham is best appreciated if arriving by train on a clear morning: emerging from the train station, the view across the River Wear to the hilltop peninsula will confirm your reason for coming. England's most beautiful Romanesque cathedral, a masterpiece of Norman architecture and a resplendent monument to the country's ecclesiastical history, rates pretty highly in our Best of Britain list. Consider the setting: a huge castle, the aforementioned cathedral and, surrounding them both, a cobweb of cobbled streets usually full of upper-crust students attending Durham's other big pull, the university. It's all so…English.

OK, so the university may not have the hallowed prestige of Oxbridge – it was only founded in 1832 – but its terrific academic reputation and competitive rowing team make the disappointment of not getting into Oxford or Cambridge that bit easier to bear.

Durham is unquestionably beautiful, but once you've visited the cathedral and walked the old town looking for the best views there isn't much to do; we recommend that you either visit it as a day trip from Newcastle or as an overnight stop on your way to explore the rest of the county.

Orientation

Market Pl, the tourist office, castle and cathedral are all on the peninsula surrounded by the River Wear. The train and bus sta-

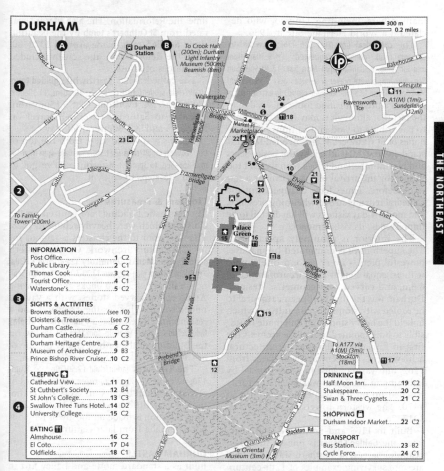

DURHAM

INFORMATION	
Post Office...................................1	C2
Public Library..............................2	C1
Thomas Cook...............................3	C2
Tourist Office...............................4	C1
Waterstone's...............................5	C2

SIGHTS & ACTIVITIES	
Browns Boathouse.............(see 10)	
Cloisters & Treasures...........(see 7)	
Durham Castle.............................6	C2
Durham Cathedral.......................7	C3
Durham Heritage Centre.............8	C3
Museum of Archaeology.............9	B3
Prince Bishop River Cruiser...10	C2

SLEEPING	
Cathedral View.........................11	D1
St Cuthbert's Society...............12	B4
St John's College......................13	C3
Swallow Three Tuns Hotel......14	D2
University College....................15	C3

EATING	
Almshouse.................................16	C2
El Coto.......................................17	D4
Oldfields...................................18	C1

DRINKING	
Half Moon Inn...........................19	C2
Shakespeare...............................20	C2
Swan & Three Cygnets.............21	C2

SHOPPING	
Durham Indoor Market............22	C2

TRANSPORT	
Bus Station................................23	B2
Cycle Force...............................24	C1

tions are to the west, on the other side of the river. Using the cathedral as your landmark, you can't really go wrong. The main sites are within easy walking distance of each other.

Information

Post office (Silver St; ⏰ 9am-5.30pm Mon-Sat)
Public library (Millennium Pl; ⏰ 9.30am-5pm Mon-Sat) The only place in town to check email.
Thomas Cook (☎ 0191-382 6600; 24-25 Market Pl) Near the tourist office.
Tourist Office (☎ 0191-384 3720; www.durhamtourism.co.uk; 2 Millennium Pl; ⏰ 9.30am-5.30pm Mon-Sat, 10am-4pm Sun) In the Gala complex, which includes a theatre and cinema.
Waterstone's (☎ 0191-383 1488; 69 Saddler St) A good selection of books.

Sights

DURHAM CATHEDRAL

Durham's most famous building – and the main reason for visiting unless someone you know is at university here – has earned superlative praise for so long that to add more would be redundant; how can you do better than the 19th-century novelist Nathaniel Hawthorne, who wrote fawningly: 'I never saw so lovely a magnificent a scene, nor (being content with this) do I care to see better.' Let's not go nuts here. No building is *that* beautiful, but the definitive structure of the Anglo-Norman Romanesque style is still pretty amazing. We would definitely put it in our top-church-in-England list – as do many others, including Unesco, who declared it a World Heritage Site in 1986.

The **cathedral** (☎ 0191-386 4266; www.durham cathedral.co.uk; donation requested; ☯ 9.30am-8pm mid-Jun–Aug, 9.30am-6.15pm Mon-Sat, 12.30-5pm Sun Sep–mid-Jun, private prayer & services only 7.30-9.30am Mon-Sat, 7.45am-12.30pm Sun year-round) is enormous and has a pretty fortified look; this is due to the fact that although it may have been built to pay tribute to God and to house the holy bones of St Cuthbert, it also needed to withstand any potential attack by the pesky Scots and Northumberland tribes who weren't too thrilled by the arrival of the Normans a few years before. Times have changed, but the cathedral remains an overwhelming presence, and modern-day visitors will hardly fail to be impressed by its visual impact.

The interior is genuinely spectacular. The superb nave is dominated by massive, powerful piers – every second one round, with an equal height and circumference of 6.6m, and carved with geometric designs. Durham was the first European cathedral to be roofed with stone-ribbed vaulting, which upheld the heavy stone roof and made it possible to build pointed transverse arches – the first in England, and a great architectural achievement. The central tower dates from 1262, but was damaged in a fire caused by lightning in 1429, and was unsatisfactorily patched up until it was entirely rebuilt in 1470. The western towers were added in 1217–26.

Built in 1175 and renovated 300 years later, the **Galilee Chapel** is one of the most beautiful parts. The northern side's **paintings** are rare surviving examples of 12th-century wall painting and are thought to feature Sts Cuthbert and Oswald. The chapel also contains the **Venerable Bede's tomb**. Bede was an 8th-century Northumbrian monk, a great historian and polymath whose work *The Ecclesiastical History of the English People* is still the prime source of information on the development of early Christian Britain. Among other things, he introduced the numbering of years from the birth of Jesus. He was first buried at Jarrow (see boxed text, p758), but in 1022 a miscreant monk stole his remains and brought them here.

The **Bishop's Throne**, built over the tomb of Bishop Thomas Hatfield, dates from the mid-14th century. Hatfield's effigy is the only one to have survived another turbulent

time: the Reformation. The **high altar** is separated from **St Cuthbert's tomb** by the beautiful stone **Neville Screen**, made around 1372–80. Until the Reformation, the screen included 107 statues of saints.

The cathedral has worthwhile **guided tours** (adult/child/student £4/free/3; ☯ 10.30am, 11.30am & 2.30pm Mon & Sat). Evensong is at 5.15pm from Tuesday to Saturday (Evening Prayer on Monday) and at 3.30pm on Sunday.

There's a splendid view from the top of the **tower** (adult/child £3/1.50; ☯ 10am-4pm Mon-Sat mid-Apr–Sep, to 3pm Oct-Mar), but you've got to climb 325 steps to enjoy it.

Cloisters & Treasures

The monastic buildings are centred on the cloisters, which were heavily rebuilt in 1828. The west door to the cloisters is famous for its 12th-century ironwork. On the western side is the **Monks' Dormitory** (adult/child £1/30p; ☯ 10am-3.30pm Mon-Sat, plus 12.30-3.15pm Sun Apr-Sep), now a library of 30,000 books and displaying Anglo-Saxon carved stones, with a vaulted undercroft that houses the Treasures and a restaurant. There is also an **audiovisual display** (adult/child £1/30p; ☯ 10am-3pm Mon-Sat Apr-Nov) on the building of the cathedral and the life of St Cuthbert.

The **Treasures** (adult/child £2.50/70p; ☯ 10am-4.30pm Mon-Sat, 2-4.30pm Sun) refer to the relics of St Cuthbert, but besides his cross and coffin, there's very little here related to the saint. The collection is made up mostly of religious paraphernalia from later centuries.

DURHAM CASTLE

Built as a standard motte-and-bailey fort in 1072, **Durham Castle** (☎ 0191-374 3800; www.durham castle.com; adult/concession £5/3.50; ☯ tours 10am, 11am noon, 12.30pm & 2-4pm Jun-Oct, 2-4pm Mon, Wed, Sat & Sun Nov-May) was the prince bishops' home until 1837, when it became the first college of the new university. It remains a university hall, and you can stay here (see p762).

The castle has been much altered over the centuries, as each successive prince bishop sought to put his particular imprint on the place, but heavy restoration and reconstruction were necessary anyway as the castle is built of soft stone on soft ground. Highlights of the 45-minute tour include the groaning 17th-century Black Staircase, the 16th-century chapel and the beautifully preserved Norman chapel (1080).

ENGLAND'S WONDER WORKER

St Cuthbert (c 634–687) is one of Britain's most venerated saints as much for an eventful afterlife as for a pious life. A kick-ass monk who fought under arms, nurtured the poor and succeeded in the thankless task of bringing the independent monastic settlements of the northeast to Roman heel following the Synod of Whitby (664), which laid down the law on when exactly Easter should be observed, Cuthbert spent the last years of his life in contemplative solitude on Inner Farne, dying on 20 March 687. And then things got really interesting.

According to legend, his burial casket was opened a few years after his death and his body was found to be perfectly preserved, or incorrupt, which quickly made him the most popular British saint in the country. When the Vikings invaded LIndisfarne in 875, a group of monks took his body on a seven-year journey across the northeast, but another Danish invasion in 995 led to another prolonged period of wandering. He eventually found a permanent home in a stone church that preceded the current cathedral. In 1104 his body and relics were transferred to a shrine inside the new cathedral, which itself was desecrated during the Reformation, although his relics surprisingly survived.

OTHER SIGHTS

Near the cathedral, in what was the St Mary-le-Bow Church, is the **Durham Heritage Centre** (☎ 0191-386 8719; www.durhamheritagecentre.org.uk; St Mary le Bow, North Bailey; admission £2; ⏰ 2-4.30pm Jun, 11am-4.30pm Jul-Sep, 11am-4.30pm Sat & Sun Apr, May & Oct), with a pretty crowded collection of displays on Durham's history from the Middle Ages to mining. It's all suitably grim, especially the reconstructed prison cells.

Durham and its environs have other museums that may be of interest, including the small **Museum of Archaeology** (☎ 0191-334 1823; Old Fulling Mill, Prebend's Walk; admission £1; ⏰ 11am-4pm Apr-Oct, 11.30am-3.30pm Fri-Mon Nov-Mar), located in a converted riverside mill building; and the **Oriental Museum** (☎ 0191-334 5694; Elvet Hill; admission £1.50; ⏰ 10am-5pm Mon-Fri, noon-5pm Sat & Sun), 3 miles south of the city centre in the university campus. It has a good collection that ranges from fine Egyptian artefacts to a monster of a Chinese bed. Take either bus 5 or 6.

Crook Hall (☎ 0191-384 8028; www.crookhallgardens.co.uk; Sidegate; adult/child £5.50/4.50; ⏰ 11am-5pm Sun-Thur Apr-Sep, seasonal variations) is a medieval hall with 1.6 hectares of charming small gardens, about 200m north of the city centre.

Finally, if you really can't get enough of war and the uniforms people wear to fight them, you won't want to miss the **Durham Light Infantry Museum** (☎ 0191-384 2214; Aykley Heads; admission £3.25; ⏰ 10am-5pm Jun-Sep, to 4pm rest of year), 500m northwest of town. The history of Durham's County Regiment and its part in various wars from 1758 to 1968

is brought to life through anecdotes and poignant artefacts; there's a small art gallery with changing exhibitions.

Activities
BOATING

The **Prince Bishop River Cruiser** (☎ 0191-386 9525; www.princebishoprc.co.uk; Elvet Bridge; adult £5.50; ⏰ cruises 2pm & 3pm Jun-Sep) offers one-hour cruises.

You can hire a rowing boat from **Browns Boathouse** (☎ 0191-386 3779; per hr per person £5), below Elvet Bridge.

WALKING

There are superb views back to the cathedral and castle from the riverbanks; walk around the bend between Elvet and Framwellgate Bridges, or hire a boat at Elvet Bridge.

Guided walks (adult/child £3.50/free; ⏰ 2pm Wed, Sat & Sun May-Sep) of 1½ hours leave from Millennium Place; contact the tourist office for details. **Ghost walks** (☎ 0191-386 1500; adult/child £4/2; ⏰ 6.30pm Mon Jun-Sep, 8.30pm Jul & Aug) lasting 1½ hours also drift around town.

Sleeping

There's only one view that counts – a cathedral view. But when you consider that it's visible from pretty much everywhere, it's quality, not quantity, that counts. The tourist office makes local bookings free of charge, which is a good thing considering that Durham is always busy with visitors: graduation week in late June results in accommodation gridlock.

Swallow Three Tuns Hotel (☎ 0191-386 4326; www.swallowhotels.com; New Elvet; s/d from £55/90) A

THE NORTHEAST

UNIVERSITY ACCOMMODATION

Several colleges rent their rooms during the holidays (Easter and July to September). The rooms are generally modern and comfortable, like most contemporary student halls. Phone ☎ 0191-374 7360 for more information.

St Cuthbert's Society (☎ 0191-374 3364; 12 South Bailey; s/d £26/48) A few doors down from St John's College, with similar student-style rooms.

St John's College (☎ 0191-334 3877; 3 South Bailey; s/d £27/50) This college is right next to the cathedral; none of the rooms are en suite.

University College (☎ 0191-374 3863; s/d with bathroom £39/70, without bathroom £27/50) Smack on the Palace Green, this has the best location. Some rooms are available year-round, such as the bishop's suite (per person £90), decked out with 17th-century tapestries.

---

converted 16th-century coaching inn, the Three Tuns has plenty of olde-worlde feel – in the low-hanging ceilings, creaking passageways and heavy wooden beams throughout – until you get to the bedrooms, which are comfortable, modern and, well, a little bland. The rooms in the older section are larger than those in the new wing.

Cathedral View (☎ 0191-386 9566; www.cathedral view.com; 212 Gilesgate; s/d from £60/80) This plain-fronted Georgian house has no sign, but inside it does exactly what it says on the tin. Six large rooms decorated with lots of cushions and coordinated bed linen and window dressings make up the numbers, but it's the three at the back that are worth the fuss: the views of the cathedral are superb. A small breakfast terrace with the same splendid vista is an added touch of real class.

Farnley Tower (☎ 0191-375 0011; www.farnley-tower.co.uk; The Ave; s/d from £65/85; ℗) A beautiful Victorian stone building that looks more like a small manor house than a family-run B&B, this place has 13 large rooms, none better than the superior rooms, which are not just spacious but have excellent views of the cathedral and castle. The service is impeccable.

Eating

Cheap eats aren't a problem in Durham thanks to the students, but quality is a little thin on the ground. Some pubs do good bar food; see Drinking (right).

Almshouse (☎ 0191-386 1054; Palace Green; dishes £5-9; ☻ 9am-8pm) Fancy imaginative and satisfying snacks (how about spicy beef with red-bean casserole and rice?) served in a genuine 17th-century house right on Palace Green? It's a shame about the interior, which has been restored to look like any old museum cafe.

El Coto (☎ 0191-384 4007; 17 Hallgarth St; lunch about £12, dinner mains £8-11; ☻ lunch & dinner Mon-Sat, closed dinner Sun) A full range of inviting Spanish tapas fills the menu at this terrific restaurant – such as sweet and spicy peppers stuffed with black pudding or the perennial favourite *albondigas* (lamb meatballs). The atmosphere is lovely, as are the staff.

our pick **Oldfields** (☎ 0191-370 9595; 18 Claypath; 2-/3-course menu £10/13; ☻ lunch & dinner Mon-Sat, closed dinner Sun) A couple of years ago, Oldfields won the restaurant of the year award with its strictly seasonal menus that use only local or organic ingredients sourced within a 60-mile radius of Durham, and it's just gone from strength to strength ever since. Why not start with warmed mushroom and sage paste, followed by braised shin of Neasham Farm beef and finish off with a gorgeous raspberry *cranachan* (oatmeal and whisky cream)? The best meal in town, in the old boardroom of the former HQ of the Durham Gas Company (1881).

Drinking

Durham may be a big student town, but most students seem to take the whole study thing really seriously, because the nightlife here isn't as boisterous as you might expect from a university town. There is, however, a fistful of lovely old bars. The tourist office has a bimonthly *What's On* guide.

Half Moon Inn (New Elvet) Sports fans love this old-style bar for its devotion to the mixed pleasures of Sky Sports; we like it for its wonderful collection of whiskies and ales. There's a summer beer garden if you want to avoid the whoops and hollers of the armchair jocks.

Shakespeare (63 Saddler St) As authentic a traditional bar as you're likely to find in these parts, this is the perfect locals' boozer, complete with nicotine-stained walls, cosy snugs and a small corner TV to show the racing. Needless to say, the selection of beers and spirits is terrific. Not surprisingly, students love it too.

Swan & Three Cygnets (☎ 384 0242; Elvet Bridge) This high-ceilinged riverside pub with courtyard tables overlooks the river. It also serves some pretty good food (mains around £8) – usually fancy versions of standard bar fare such as bangers and mash.

Shopping

Durham Indoor Market (☎ 0191-384 6153; Market Pl; ☽ 9am-6pm Mon-Sat) It's less about what you might buy and more about the place itself, but this Victorian market is worth a browse, if only for the motley collection of wares on sale, from fruit and veg to garden gnomes.

Getting There & Away

BUS

The bus station is west of the river on North Rd. All National Express buses arrive here, while bus 352 links Newcastle and Blackpool via Durham, Barnard Castle, Raby Castle and Kirkby Stephen. Destinations include Edinburgh (£23.50, four hours, one daily), Leeds (£15.30, 2½ hours, four daily) and London (£27, 6½ hours, four daily). There are three daily National Express buses to Newcastle (£2.80, 30 minutes); bus 21 provides a half-hourly service but takes twice as long because it makes plenty of stops along the way.

TRAIN

There are services at least hourly to London (£124.50, three hours), Newcastle (£6.80 single, 20 minutes) and York (£23.50, one hour).

Getting Around

Pratt's Taxis (☎ 0191-386 0700) charges a minimum of £2.80. **Cycle Force** (☎ 0191-384 0319; 29 Claypath) charges £10/16 per half-/full day for mountain-bike hire.

AROUND DURHAM
Beamish Open-Air Museum

County Durham's greatest attraction is **Beamish** (☎ 0191-370 4000; www.beamish.org.uk; admission Nov-Mar £6, Apr Oct adult/child £16/10; ☽ 10am-5pm Apr-Oct, to 4pm Tue-Thu, Sat & Sun Nov-Mar, last entry 3pm year-round), a living, breathing, working museum that offers a fabulous, warts-and-

all portrait of industrial life in the northeast during the 19th and 20th centuries. Instructive and lots of fun to boot, this huge museum spread over 121 hectares will appeal to all ages.

You can go underground, explore mine heads, a working farm, a school, a dentist and a pub, and marvel at how every cramped pit cottage seemed to find room for a piano. Don't miss a ride behind an 1815 Steam Elephant locomotive or a replica of Stephenson's *Locomotion No 1*.

Allow at least three hours to do the place justice. Many elements (such as the railway) aren't open in the winter (when the admission price is cheaper); call for details.

Beamish is about 8 miles northwest of Durham; it's signposted from the A1(M) – take the A693 west at junction 63. Buses 709 from Newcastle (50 minutes, hourly) and 720 from Durham (30 minutes, hourly) operate to the museum.

Bishop Auckland

The name's a giveaway, but this friendly, midsized market town 11 miles southwest of Durham has been the country residence of the bishops of Durham since the 12th century and their official home for over 100 years. The castle is just next to the large, attractive market square; leading off it are small-town streets lined with high-street shops and a sense that anything exciting is happening elsewhere.

The **tourist office** (☎ 01388-604922; Market Pl; ☽ 10am-5pm Mon-Fri, 9am-4pm Sat year-round, plus 1-4pm Sun Apr-Sep) is in the town hall on Market Pl.

The imposing gates of **Auckland Castle** (☎ 01388-601627; www.auckland-castle.co.uk; adult/child £4/free; ☽ 2-5pm Sun-Mon Easter-Jul & Sep, plus Wed Aug), just off Market Pl behind the town hall, lead to the official home of the bishop of Durham. It's palatial – each successive bishop extended the building. Underneath the spiky Restoration Gothic exterior, the buildings are mainly medieval. The outstanding attraction of the castle is the striking 17th-century chapel, which thrusts up into the sky. It has a remarkable partially 12th-century interior, converted from the former great hall. Admission is by guided tour only.

Around the castle is a hilly and wooded 324-hectare **deer park** (admission free; ☽ 7am-sunset) with an 18th-century deer shelter.

THE NORTHEAST

DETOUR: LOCOMOTION

If you or your kids can't get enough of steam trains, then a half-day trip to the National Railway Museum at Shildon, now known as **Locomotion** (☎ 01388-777999; www.locomotion.uk.com; Shildon; admission free; ☉ 10am-5pm mid-Mar–Sep, to 4pm Wed-Sun Oct–mid-Mar) is a must. Shildon is best known as the starting point for Stephenson's *No 1 Locomotion* in 1825, finishing up in Stockton-on-Tees (for more on the train, see Head of Steam, below). Less museum and more hands-on experience, this regional extension of the National Railway Museum in York (see p626) has all manner of railway paraphernalia spread out over a half-mile area (and linked by free bio-bus) that all leads to a huge hanger that is home to 70-odd locomotives from all eras. Railway buffs will love it. It's 5 miles southeast of Bishop Auckland. Shildon is on the Darlington to Bishop Auckland rail line; buses 1 & 1B run every half hour from Darlington and stop here on the way to Crook and Tow Law.

Bus 352 running from Newcastle to Blackpool passes through Bishop Auckland (daily March to November, Saturday and Sunday December to February), as does bus X85 from Durham to Kendal (one on Saturday June to September).

You need to change at Darlington for regular trains to Bishop Auckland.

Binchester Roman Fort

One and a half miles north of Bishop Auckland are the ruins of **Binchester Roman Fort** (☎ 01388-663089; www.durham.gov.uk/binchester; admission £3; ☉ excavations 11am-5pm Easter-Sep), or Vinovia as it was originally called. The fort, first built in wood around AD 80 and rebuilt in stone early in the 2nd century, was the largest in County Durham, covering 4 hectares. Excavations show the remains of Dere St, the main high road from York to Hadrian's Wall, and the best-preserved example of a heating system in the country – part of the commandant's private bath suite. Findings from the site are displayed at the Bowes Museum in Barnard Castle (opposite).

Escomb Church

The stones of the abandoned Binchester Fort were often reused, and Roman inscriptions can be spotted in the walls of the hauntingly beautiful **Escomb Church** (☎ 01388-602861; admission free; ☉ 9am-8pm Apr-Sep, to 4pm Oct-Mar). The church dates from the 7th century – it's one of only three complete surviving Saxon churches in Britain. It's a whitewashed cell, striking and moving in its simplicity, incongruously encircled by a 20th-century cul-de-sac. If no-one's about, collect the keys from a hook outside a nearby house. Escomb is 3 miles west of

Bishop Auckland (bus 86, 87 or 87A; 15 per day Monday to Saturday, 10 on Sunday).

DARLINGTON
pop 97,838

Darlington might be best known these days for its retail opportunities, but its main claim to fame came in 1825, when it served as the arrival point for the world's first passenger train, George Stephenson's *No 1 Locomotion*, which chugged along the new rail link to Stockton at the breakneck speed of 10mph to 13mph, carrying 600 people – mostly in coal trucks.

The event – and the subsequent effect of transport history – is the subject of the city's top attraction, the recently reopened (and rebranded) **Head of Steam** (☎ 01325-460532; www .darlington.gov.uk; North Rd; adult/child £5/3; ☉ 10am-4pm Tue-Sun Apr-Sep, 11am-3.30pm Tue-Sun Oct-Mar), also known as the Darlington Railway Museum, which is actually situated on the original 1825 route, in Stockton & Darlington railway buildings attached to the North Rd Station and dating from the mid-19th century. Pride of place goes to the surprisingly small *Locomotion*, but railway buffs will also enjoy a close look at other engines, such as the *Derwent*, which is the earliest surviving Darlington-built locomotive. The original displays have been complemented by an impressive range of audiovisuals that tell the story of the railway and its impact on Darlington. The museum is about a mile north of the centre.

There aren't many other reasons to linger, but you should definitely pop your head into Our Lady of the North, better known as **St Cuthbert's Church** (Market Pl), founded in 1183 and one of the finest examples of the Early

English Perpendicular style. It is topped by a 14th-century tower. The **tourist office** (☎ 01325-388666; www.visitdarlington.com; Dolphin Centre, 13 Horsemarket; ☼ 9am-5pm Mon-Fri, to 3pm Sat) is on the south side of Market Place.

The town has some decent restaurants around the centre; best of them is **Oven** (☎ 01325-466668; 30 Duke St; mains £8-16; ☼ lunch & dinner Mon-Sat, noon-8pm Sun), a classy French spot that was voted the best Sunday lunch in the northeast by readers of the *Observer*.

Getting There & Away

Darlington is 13 miles southwest of Durham on the A167. Buses 13 and 723 run between Darlington and Durham (£3.40, 35 minutes, every 30 minutes Monday to Saturday, hourly Sunday). Bus 723 also runs half-hourly to Newcastle (£5.70, 1¾ hours). Most buses go and arrive opposite the Town Hall on Feethams, just off Market Place.

Darlington is also on the York (£17, 30 minutes) to Newcastle (£7.10, 40 minutes) line, with a service every 20 minutes or so.

AROUND DARLINGTON
Barnard Castle
pop 6720

Barnard Castle, or just plain Barney, is anything but: this thoroughly charming market town is a traditionalist's dream, full of antiquarian shops and atmospheric old pubs that serve as a wonderful setting for the town's twin-starred attractions, a daunting ruined castle at its edge and an extraordinary French chateau on its outskirts. If you can drag yourself away, it is also a terrific base for exploring Teesdale and the North Pennines. The **tourist office** (☎ 01833-690909; www.teesdalediscovery.com; Woodleigh, Flatts Rd; ☼ 9.30am-5.30pm Easter-Oct, 11am-4pm Mon-Sat Nov-Mar) has information on all the sights.

SIGHTS

Once one of northern England's largest castles, **Barnard Castle** (EH; ☎ 01833-638212; www .english-heritage.org.uk; admission £4; ☼ 10am-6pm Easter-Sep, to 4pm Oct, Thu-Mon only Nov-Mar) was partly dismantled during the 16th century, but its huge bulk, on a cliff above the Tees, still manages to cover more than two very impressive hectares. Founded by Guy de Bailleul and rebuilt around 1150, its occupants spent their time suppressing the locals

and fighting off the Scots – on their days off they sat around enjoying the wonderful views of the river.

If the beautifully atmospheric ruins of one castle aren't enough, then about half a mile east of town is the extraordinary, Louvre-inspired French chateau that is the **Bowes Museum** (☎ 01833-690606; www.bowesmuseum.org .uk; adult/child £7/free; ☼ 10am-5pm Mar-Oct, to 4pm Nov-Feb). The museum was the brainchild of 19th-century industrialist and art fanatic John Bowes; he commissioned French architect Jules Pellechet to build a new museum to show off his terrific collection, which could give the Victoria & Albert Museum a run for its money. Opened in 1892, the museum has lavish furniture and paintings by Canaletto, El Greco and Goya. The museum's most beloved exhibit, however, is the marvellous mechanical silver swan, which operates at 12.30pm and 3.30pm.

SLEEPING & EATING

Marwood House (☎ 01833-637493; www.marwoodhouse .co.uk; 98 Galgate; s/d £29/58) A handsome Victorian property with tastefully appointed rooms (the owner's tapestries feature in the decor and her homemade biscuits sit on a tray), Marwood House's standout feature is the small fitness room in the basement, complete with a sauna that fits up to four people.

Greta House (☎ 01833-631193; www.gretahouse .co.uk; 89 Galgate; s/d £40/60) This lovely Victorian home stands out for the little touches that show that extra bit of class – fluffy bathrobes, face cloths and posh toiletries. What really did it for us though was the stay-in service: a tray of lovely homemade sandwiches and a superb cheeseboard to nibble at from the comfort of bed.

Old Well Inn (☎ 01833-690130; www.oldwellinn .info; 21 The Bank; r from £69) You won't find larger bedrooms in town than at this old coaching inn, which makes it an excellent option for families – it even takes pets. It has a reputation for excellent, filling pub grub and a decent Italian restaurant that does good pizzas and pastas (mains £8 to £11).

GETTING THERE & AWAY

Bus 352 runs daily between Newcastle and Blackpool via Durham, Bishop Auckland, Barnard Castle, Raby Castle and Kirkby

THE NORTHEAST

DETOUR: MIDDLESBROUGH INSTITUTE OF MODERN ART

Middlesbrough, 15 miles east of Darlington and Teeside's largest town, is something of a postin-dustrial mess, an unattractive urban centre that does little to entice the interested visitor. It might all change with the opening of the boldly modern **Middlesbrough Inistitute of Modern Art** (☎ 01642-726720; www.visitmima.com; Centre Sq, Middlesbrough; admission free; ☒ 10am-5pm Tue, Wed, Fri & Sat, 10am-8pm Thu, noon-4pm Sun), which has gathered the city's municipal art collections under one impressive roof. The 1500 or so pieces includes work by some of Britain's most impor-tant 20th-century artists, including Duncan Grant, Vanessa Bell (sister of Virginia Woolf), Henri Gaudier-Brzeska and Frank Auerbach. Also exhibited is a good collection of ceramics and jewel-lery. Middlesbrough is served by hourly buses from Darlington (£4.90, 30 minutes). Buses arrive at Gilke St, about 500m from MIMA.

Stephen. Buses 75 and 76 runs almost hourly from Darlington (40 minutes).

Egglestone Abbey

The ransacked, spectral ruins of **Egglestone Abbey** (☒ dawn-dusk), dating from the 1190s, overlook a lovely bend of the Tees. You can envisage the abbey's one-time grandeur de-spite the gaunt remains. They're a pleasant mile-long walk south of Barnard Castle.

Raby Castle

About 7 miles northeast of Barnard Castle is the sprawling, romantic **Raby Castle** (☎ 01833-660202; www.rabycastle.com; adult/child £9.50/4, park & gardens only adult/child £4/3; ☒ castle 1-5pm, grounds 11am-5.30pm Sun-Fri Jun-Aug, Wed & Sun May & Sep), a stronghold of the Catholic Neville family until it engaged in some ill-judged plotting (the 'Rising of the North') against the oh-so Protestant Queen Elizabeth in 1569. Most of the interior dates from the 18th and 19th centuries, but the exterior remains true to the original design, built around a courtyard and surrounded by a moat. There are beau-tiful formal gardens and a deer park. Buses 8 and 352 zip between Barnard Castle and Raby (20 minutes, eight daily).

NORTH PENNINES

The North Pennines stretch from western Durham to just short of Hadrian's Wall in the north. In the south is Teesdale, the gently undulating valley of the River Tees; to the north is the much wilder Weardale, carved through by the River Wear. Both dales are marked by ancient quarries and mines – industries that date back to Roman times. The wilds of the North Pennines are also home to the picturesque Derwent and Allen Valleys, north of Weardale.

For online information, check out www .northpennines.org.uk.

TEESDALE

Scattered unspoilt villages, waterfalls and sinuous moorland define Teesdale, which stretches from the confluence of the Rivers Greta and Tees to a waterfall, Caldron Snout, at the eastern end of Cow Green Reservoir, the source of the Tees. The landscapes get wilder as you travel northward into the Pennines; the Pennine Way snakes along the dale.

Middleton-in-Teesdale

This tranquil, pretty village of white and stone houses among soft green hills was from 1753 a 'company town', the entire kit and caboo-dle being the property of the London Lead Company, a Quaker concern. The upshot was that the lead miners worked the same hours in the same appalling conditions as everyone else, but couldn't benefit from a Sunday pint to let off steam.

For information on local walks, go to the **tourist office** (☎ 01833-641001; ☒ 10am-1pm & 2-5pm Apr-Oct, 10am-4pm Nov-Mar).

Middleton to Langdon Beck

As you travel up the valley past Middleton towards Langdon Beck, you'll find **Bowlees Visitor Centre** (☎ 01833-622292; ☒ 10.30am-5pm Apr-Oct, 10.30am-4pm Sat & Sun Nov-Feb) 3 miles on, with plenty of walking and wildlife leaflets and a small natural-history dis-play. A number of easy-going trails spread out from here, including one to the tum-bling rapids of **Low Force**, a number of metre-high steps along a scenic stretch of river. One mile further on is the much more compelling **High Force** (adult/child £1.50/1, car park £2), England's largest waterfall – 21m of almighty roar that shatters the general tranquillity of the surroundings. It's a sight best appreciated after a rainfall, when the torrent is really powerful.

The B6277 leaves the River Tees at High Force and continues up to **Langdon Beck**, where the scenery quickly turns from green rounded hills to the lonely landscape of the North Pennines, dotted with small chapels. You can either continue on the B6277 over the Pennines to Alston and Cumbria or turn right and take a minor road over the moors to St John's Chapel in Weardale.

Bus 73 connects Middleton and Langdon Beck, via Bowlees and High Force, at least once a day Tuesday, Wednesday, Friday and Saturday. Buses 75 and 76 serve Middleton from Barnard Castle almost hourly.

Sleeping & Eating

Brunswick House (☎ 01833-640393; www.brunswick house.net; 55 Market Pl, Middleton-in-Teesdale; s/d £40/60) This pretty Georgian house has a floral, fluffy theme: nice quilted duvets and big pillows with flowers all over them. Everything else is painted white.

High Force Hotel & Brewery (☎ 01833-622222; www.highforcehotel.com; Forest-in-Teesdale; s/d £40/80) This former hunting lodge by the High Force waterfall is best known for the award-winning beers brewed on the premises: Teesdale Bitter, Forest XB and Cauldron Snout – at 5.6% it has a kick like a mule. Upstairs are six decent enough bedrooms, while the bar also serves food.

Langdon Beck YHA (☎ 0845 371 9027; www.yha.org .uk; Forest-in-Teesdale; dm £14; 🕑 Mon-Sat Apr-Sep, Fri & Sat Nov, Tue-Sat early Feb-Mar, Sep-Oct) Walkers on the Pennine Way are avid fans of this hostel between High Force and Langdon Beck. The hostel is also a good base for short walks into the dales and the Pennines, in particular to Cow Green Reservoir, the source of the Tees.

WEARDALE

A one-time hunting ground of the prince bishops, Weardale's 19th-century legacy as a lead-mining centre has left rust- and olive-coloured patchwork moors pitted with mining scars. Mining relics notwithstanding, there are some splendid walks in and around

the surrounding valley, which is sheltered by the Pennines.

Stanhope & Ireshopburn

Peaceful Stanhope is a honey-coloured town with a cobbled marketplace – a good base for windswept walks across the moors. Its interesting church is Norman at the base, but mostly dates from the 12th century. There's a great farmers market on the last Saturday of every month.

The **tourist office** (☎ 01388-527650; www.durham dalescentre.co.uk; Market Pl; 🕑 10am-5pm Apr-Oct, to 4pm Nov-Mar) has lots of information on walks in the area, and there's a small tearoom.

In Ireshopeburn, 8 miles west of Stanhope, the **Weardale Museum** (☎ 01388-537417; www.weardale museum.co.uk; adult/child £2/50p; 🕑 2-5pm Wed-Sun May-Jul & Sep, daily Aug) allows a glimpse into local history, including a spotless lead-mining family kitchen and information on preacher John Wesley. It's next to **High House Chapel**, a Methodist chapel (1760) that was one of Wesley's old stomping grounds.

SLEEPING & EATING

Belle Vue Farm Cottages (☎ 01388-526225; www .tranquil-life.info; Hall Rd, Stanhope; s/d £38/62) This beautiful farmhouse about a mile northwest of Stanhope has great views of the dale and comfortable, rustic-style rooms, some with four-poster beds. It's very popular with cyclists (the town is the last stop on the C2C route before cyclists push on to Sunderland), who can avail of the workshop for repairs. There's also a coarse fishing pond on the grounds.

Queen's Head (☎ 01388-528160; 89 Front St, Stanhope; mains £5-8) This handsome pub in the middle of Stanhope is a good spot for hearty pub grub.

Killhope

At the top of the valley, about 13 miles from Stanhope, is a good example of just how bleak miners' lives really were. In the **Killhope Lead Mining Centre** (☎ 01388-537505; www.durham.gov.uk /killhope; adult/child £4.50/1.50, with mine trip £6.50/3.50; 🕑 10.30am-5pm Apr-Oct), the blackened machinery of the old works is dominated by an imposing 10m-high water wheel that drove a crushing mechanism.

In one of those unfortunate linguistic ironies, 'hope' actually means 'side valley', but once you get a look inside the place you'll understand the miners' black humour about the name. An absorbing exhibition explains what life was like: poor pay, poorer living conditions and the constant threat of the 'Black Spit' (coal dust in the lungs) that killed so many of its sufferers. The most poignant records are those of the washer boys – children employed in freezing, back-breaking work. The mine closed in 1910 but you can visit its atmospheric underground network as it was in 1878, on an hour-long guided tour; wear warm clothes.

It's possible to buy a combined ticket for the mine and the South Tynedale Railway (p742). From the mining centre it's another 7 miles up over the highest main road in England (617m) and the North Pennines and down into Alston.

Bus 101 makes the regular trip up the valley from Bishop Auckland to Stanhope (10 daily). If you ring ahead, it will go on to Killhope midmorning and pick you up in the afternoon. Call **Wearhead Motor Services** (☎ 01388-528235) to arrange the service.

DERWENT VALLEY

Pretty Blanchland and Edmundbyers, two small, remote villages, are south of the denim expanse of the **Derwent Reservoir**, surrounded by wild moorland and forests. The 3.5-mile-long reservoir has been here since 1967, and the county border separating Durham and Northumberland runs right through it. The valley's a good spot for walking and cycling, as well as sailing, which can be arranged through the **Derwent Reservoir Sailing Club** (☎ 01434-675258).

Nestling among trees, and surrounded by wild mauve and mustard moors, **Blanchland** is an unexpected surprise. It's a charming, golden-stoned grouping of small cottages arranged around an L-shaped square, framed by a medieval gateway. The village was named after the white cassocks of local monks – there was a Premonstratensian abbey here from the 12th century. Around 1721 the prince bishop of the time, Lord Crewe, seeing the village and abbey falling into disrepair, bequeathed the buildings to trustees on the condition that they be protected and looked after.

Another inviting, quiet village, **Edmundbyers** is 4 miles east of Blanchland on the B6306 along the southern edge of Derwent Reservoir.

Edmundbyers is 12 miles north of Stanhope and 10 miles south of Hexham on the B6306. Bus 773 runs from Consett to Townfield via Blanchland and Edmundbyers three times a day, Monday to Saturday.

Sleeping & Eating

Edmundbyers YHA (☎ 0845 371 9633; www.yha.org.uk; Low House, Edmundbyers; dm £14; ☻ daily Jul-Aug, Wed-Sun Apr-Jun & Sep-Oct) This beautiful hostel is in a converted 17th-century former inn. The hostel helps to serve walkers in the area and cyclists on the C2C route.

Lord Crewe Arms Hotel (☎ 01434-675251; www .lordcrewehotel.co.uk; Blanchland; s/d from £60/100) This glorious hotel was built as the abbot's lodge. It's a mainly 17th-century building, with a 12th-century crypt that makes a cosy bar. If you're looking for a bit of atmosphere – open fires, hidden corners, tall windows and superb food (lunch £6 to £12) – you won't find better, but make sure to ask for a garden room, which has its own sitting room.

ALLEN VALLEY

The Allen Valley is in the heart of the North Pennines, with individual, remote villages huddled high up, surrounded by bumpy hills and heather- and gorse-covered moors. It's fantastic walking country, speckled with the legacy of the lead-mining industry.

Tiny **Allendale** is a hamlet around a big open square. The quiet rural community hots up on New Year's Eve when the distinctly pagan and magical 'Tar Barrels' ceremony is performed (see the boxed text, p770). It's 7 miles from Hexham on the B6295.

Four miles further south towards the Wear Valley is England's highest village, **Allenheads**, nestled at the head of Allen Valley. It really just consists of a few houses and a marvellously eccentric hotel. There's a small **heritage centre** (☎ 01434-685395; admission £1; ☻ 9am-5pm Apr-Oct) with some displays on the history of the village and surrounding area and access to a blacksmith's cottage, and a small nature walk.

An attraction in its own right, **Allenheads Inn** (☎ 01434-685200; www.theallenheadsinn.co.uk; Allenheads; s/d £35/60), an 18th-century low-beamed pub, has a quite extraordinary and bizarre collection of assorted bric-a-brac and ephemera, from mounted stag heads to Queen Mum plates. It's a friendly, creaky place to stay, and serves up hearty, tasty food (mains around £8) as well.

Bus 688 runs up and down the Allen Valley from Hexham to Allenheads (stopping at Allendale town; 25 minutes, 11 daily).

HADRIAN'S WALL

What exactly have the Romans ever done for us? The aqueducts. Law and order. And this enormous wall, built between AD 122 and 128 to keep 'us' (Romans, subdued Brits) in and 'them' (hairy Pictish barbarians from Scotland) out. Or so the story goes. Hadrian's Wall, named in honour of the emperor who ordered it built, was one of Rome's greatest engineering projects, a spectacular 73-mile testament to ambition and the practical Roman mind. Even today, almost 2000 years after the first stone was laid, the sections that are still standing remain an awe-inspiring sight, proof that when the Romans wanted something done, they just knuckled down and did it.

It wasn't easy. When completed, the mammoth structure ran across the narrow neck of the island, from the Solway Firth in the west almost to the mouth of the Tyne in the east. Every Roman mile (1.62 miles) there was a gateway guarded by a small fort (milecastle) and between each milecastle were two observation turrets. Milecastles are numbered right across the country, starting with Milecastle 0 at Wallsend and ending with Milecastle 80 at Bowness-on-Solway.

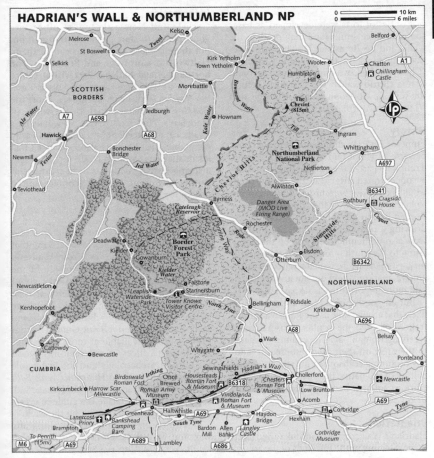

FLAMING ALLENDALE

Thought to be Viking or pagan in origin, the **Baal Fire** (aka Tar Barrels) on New Year's Eve – a procession of flaming whisky barrels through Allendale – has certainly been taking place for centuries. The 45 barrels are filled with tar and carried on the heads of a team of 'guisers' with blackened or painted faces – this hot and hereditary honour gets passed from generation to generation. The mesmerising procession, accompanied by pounding music, leads to a pile of branches, where the guisers chuck the scorching barrels to fire up an enormous pyre at midnight, doing their best not to set themselves alight.

A series of forts were developed as bases some distance south (and may predate the wall), and 16 lie astride it. The prime remaining forts on the wall are Cilurnum (Chesters), Vercovicium (Housesteads) and Banna (Birdoswald). The best forts behind the wall are Corstopitum at Corbridge, and Vindolanda, north of Bardon Mill.

History

Emperor Hadrian didn't order the wall built because he was afraid of northern invasion. Truth is no part of the wall was impenetrable – a concentrated attack at any single point would have surely breached it – but was meant to mark the border as though to say that the Roman Empire would extend no further. By drawing a physical boundary, the Romans were also tightening their grip on the population to the south – for the first time in history, passports were issued to citizens of the empire, marking them out not just as citizens but, more importantly, as taxpayers.

But all good things come to an end. It's likely that around 409, as the Roman administration collapsed, the frontier garrisons ceased receiving Roman pay. The communities had to then rely on their own resources, gradually becoming reabsorbed into the war-band culture of the native Britons – for some generations soldiers had been recruited locally in any case.

Orientation

Hadrian's Wall crosses beautiful, varied landscape. Starting in the lowlands of the Solway coast, it crosses the lush hills east of Carlisle to the bleak, windy ridge of basalt rock known as Whin Sill overlooking Northumberland National Park, and ends in the urban sprawl of Newcastle. The most spectacular section lies between Brampton and Corbridge.

Carlisle, in the west, and Newcastle, in the east, are good starting points, but Brampton, Haltwhistle, Hexham and Corbridge all make good bases.

The B6318 follows the course of the wall from the outskirts of Newcastle to Birdoswald; from Birdoswald to Carlisle it pays to have a detailed map. The main A69 road and the railway line follow 3 or 4 miles to the south. This section follows the wall from east to west.

Information

Carlisle and Newcastle tourist offices are good places to start gathering information, but there are also tourist offices in Hexham, Haltwhistle, Corbridge and Brampton. The **Northumberland National Park Visitor Centre** (☎ 01434-344396; Once Brewed; ☑ 10am-5pm mid-Mar–May, Sep & Oct, 9.30am-6pm Jun-Aug) is off the B6318. The official portal for the whole of Hadrian's Wall Country is www.hadrians-wall.org, an excellent, attractive and easily navigable site. There is also a **Hadrian's Wall information line** (☎ 01434-322002) too. May sees a spring festival, with lots of re-creations of Roman life along the wall (contact tourist offices for details).

Activities

The **Hadrian's Wall Path** (www.nationaltrail.co.uk /hadrianswall) is an 84-mile National Trail that runs the length of the wall from Wallsend in the east to Bowness-on-Solway in the west. The entire route should take about seven days on foot, giving plenty of time to explore the rich archaeological heritage along the way. Anthony Burton's *Hadrian's Wall Path – National Trail Guide* (Aurum Press, £12.95) available at most bookshops and tourist offices in the region, is good for history, archaeology and the like, while the *Essential Guide to Hadrian's Wall Path National Trail* (Hadrian's Wall Heritage Ltd, £3.95) by David McGlade is a guide to everyday facilities and services along the walk.

If you're planning to cycle along the wall, tourist offices sell the *Hadrian's Wall Country Cycle Map* (£3.50); you'll be cycling along part of Hadrian's Cycleway (see p746).

Getting There & Around

BUS

The AD 122 Hadrian's Wall bus (three hours, six daily June to September) is a hail-and-ride guided service that runs between Hexham (the 9.15am service starts in Wallsend) and Bowness-on-Solway. Bus 185 covers the route the rest of the year (Monday to Saturday only).

West of Hexham the wall runs parallel to the A69, which connects Carlisle and Newcastle. Bus 685 runs along the A69 hourly, passing near the YHA hostels and 2 miles to 3 miles south of the main sites throughout the year.

The Hadrian's Wall Rover ticket (adult/child one-day £7.50/4.80, three-day £15/9.60) is available from the driver or the tourist offices, where you can also get timetables.

TRAIN

The railway line between Newcastle and Carlisle (Tyne Valley Line) has stations at Corbridge, Hexham, Haydon Bridge, Bardon Mill, Haltwhistle and Brampton. This service runs daily, but not all trains stop at all stations.

CORBRIDGE

pop 2800

The mellow commuter town of Corbridge is a handsome spot above a green-banked curve in the Tyne, its shady, cobbled streets lined with old-fashioned shops. Folks have lived here since Saxon times when there was a substantial monastery, while many of the buildings feature stones nicked from nearby Corstopitum.

The **tourist office** (☎ 01434-632815; www.thisiscorbridge.co.uk; Hill St; ⊙ 10am-6pm Mon-Sat, 1-5pm Sun mid-May–Sep, 10am-5pm Mon-Sat Easter–mid-May & Oct) is part of the library.

Corbridge Roman Site & Museum

What's left of the Roman garrison town of **Corstopitum** (EH; ☎ 01434-632349; admission incl museum £4.50; ⊙ 10am-6pm Apr-Sep, to 4pm Oct, Sat & Sun only Nov-Mar) lies about a half a mile west of Market Pl on Dere St, once the main road from York to Scotland. It is the oldest fortified site in the area, predating the wall itself by some 40

> ### HADRIAN'S WALL CIRCULAR WALK
>
> Starting at Once Brewed National Park Centre, this walk takes in the most complete stretch of Hadrian's Wall. The walk is 7.5 miles long and takes approximately 4½ hours. The wall follows the natural barrier created by steep dramatic cliffs, and the views north are stunning. Some parts of the wall are so well preserved that they have featured in films. You might recognise Sycamor Gap, which stole the screen from Kevin Costner in *Robin Hood – Prince of Thieves*. The trail returns to the YHA hostel across swaths of farmland. The centre has a good map.

years, when it was used by troops launching retaliation raids into Scotland. Most of what you see here, though, dates from around AD 200, when the fort had developed into a civilian settlement and was the main base along the wall.

You get a sense of the domestic heart of the town from the visible remains, and the Corbridge Museum displays Roman sculpture and carvings, including the amazing 3rd-century Corbridge Lion.

Sleeping & Eating

2 The Crofts (☎ 01434-633046; www.2thecrofts.co.uk; A695; s/d incl breakfast £35/58) A typical Victorian terraced home on the edge of town has only one room, a comfortable twin, which ensures that you'll get all of the owner's attention. The breakfast is excellent.

Errington Arms (☎ 01434-672250; Stagshaw, B6318 off A68 roundabout; mains £8-13; ⊙ 11am-11pm Mon-Sat, noon-3pm Sun) About 3 miles north of town is this marvellous 18th-century stone pub where delicious food is served up in suitably atmospheric surroundings. From the mouthwatering ploughman's lunch to more intricate delicacies such as loin of lamb with mushroom and chive risotto, Errington won't disappoint. Wash it all down with a pint of real ale.

Valley Restaurant (☎ 01434-633434; www.valleyrestaurants.co.uk; Station Rd; mains £9-12; ⊙ dinner Mon-Sat) This fine Indian restaurant in a lovely building above the station supplies a unique service as well as delicious food. A group of 10 or more diners from Newcastle can catch the 'Passage to India' train to Corbridge accompanied by a waiter, who will supply snacks

THE NORTHEAST

and phone ahead to have the meal ready when the train arrives!

Getting There & Away

Bus 685 between Newcastle and Carlisle comes through Corbridge, as does the half-hourly bus 602 from Newcastle to Hexham, where you can connect with the Hadrian's Wall bus AD 122. Corbridge is also on the Newcastle–Carlisle railway line.

HEXHAM
pop 10,690

Tynedale's administrative capital is a handsome market town long famed for its fine Augustinian abbey. Hexham is a bustling place, with more restaurants, hotels and high-street shops lining its cobbled alleyways than any other wall town between Carlisle and Newcastle. The **tourist office** (☎ 01434-652220; www.hadrianswallcountry.org; Wentworth Car Park; ☺ 9am-6pm Mon-Sat, 10am-5pm Sun mid-May–Oct, 10am-5pm Mon-Sat Oct–mid-May) is northeast of the town centre.

Sights

Stately **Hexham Abbey** (☎ 01434-602031; ☺ 9.30am-7pm May-Sep, to 5pm Oct-Apr) is a marvellous example of early English architecture. Inside, look out for the Saxon crypt, the only surviving element of St Wilifrid's Church, built with inscribed stones from Corstopitum in 674.

The **Old Gaol** (☎ 01434-652349; adult/child £4/2; ☺ 10am-4.30pm Apr-Oct, Mon, Tue & Sat Oct–mid-Nov), completed in 1333 as England's first purpose-built prison, was recently revamped and all four floors can be visited in all their gruesome glory. The history of the Border Reivers – a group of clans who fought, kidnapped, blackmailed and killed each other in an effort to exercise control over a lawless tract of land along the Anglo-Scottish border throughout the 16th century – is also retold, along with tales of the punishments handed out in the prison.

Sleeping & Eating

West Close House (☎ 01434-603307; Hextol Tce; s/d from £30/60) This immaculate 1920s house, in a leafy cul-de-sac off Allendale Rd (the B6305) and surrounded by a beautiful garden, is highly recommended for its friendliness and comfort.

Hallbank Guest House (☎ 01434-605567; www.hall bankguesthouse.com; Hallgate; s/d from £70/100) Behind

the old gaol is this fine Edwardian house with three extravagantly furnished rooms: leather furniture, flat-screen TVs and huge beds.

There are several bakeries on Fore St and, if you turn left into the quaintly named Priestpopple near the bus station, you'll find a selection of restaurants.

Dipton Mill (☎ 01434-606577; Dipton Mill Rd; mains around £6-10) For sheer atmosphere, you can't beat this superb country pub 2 miles out on the road to Blanchland, among woodland and by a river. It offers sought-after ploughman's lunches and real ale, not to mention a terrific selection of whiskies.

Getting There & Away

Bus 685 between Newcastle and Carlisle comes through Hexham hourly. The AD 122 and the winter-service bus 185 connect with other towns along the wall, and the town is on the Newcastle–Carlisle railway line (hourly).

CHESTERS ROMAN FORT & MUSEUM

The best-preserved remains of a Roman cavalry fort in England are at **Chesters** (EH; ☎ 01434-681379; admission £4.50; ☺ 9.30am-6pm Apr-Sep, 10am-4pm Oct-Mar), set among idyllic green woods and meadows and originally constructed to house a unit of troops from Asturias in northern Spain. They include part of a bridge (beautifully constructed and best appreciated from the eastern bank) across the River North Tyne, four well-preserved gatehouses, an extraordinary bathhouse and an underfloor heating system. The museum has a large collection of Roman sculpture. Take bus 880 or 882 from Hexham (5.5 miles away); it is also on the route of Hadrian's Wall bus AD 122.

HALTWHISTLE
pop 3810

It's one of the more important debates in contemporary Britain: where exactly is the centre of the country? The residents of Haltwhistle, basically one long street just north of the A69, claim that they're the ones. But then so do the folks in Dunsop Bridge, 71 miles to the south. Will we ever know the truth? In the meantime, Haltwhistle is the spot to get some cash and load up on gear and groceries. Thursday is market day.

The **tourist office** (☎ 01434-322002; ☺ 9.30am-1pm & 2-5.30pm Mon-Sat, 1-5pm Sun May-Sep, 9.30am-noon & 1-3.30pm Mon, Tue, & Thu-Sat Oct-Apr) is in the train station.

DETOUR: LANGLEY CASTLE

Langley Castle (☎ 01434-688888; www.langleycastle.com; s £110-200, d £135-255) This 14th-century castle in 4 hectares of woodland is the real deal minus the medieval privations. Live like one of the many nobles associated with the castle's history in one of the grand rooms, with pointy four-poster beds and window seats set in 2m-thick walls. Top of the heap is the fabulous Radcliffe Room, with a sunken circular bath and a sauna – modern guests are better off than the room's namesake, Sir Edward, who bought the Langley Estate in 1631 and pronounced himself the top aristocrat in Northumberland. The rooms in the recently converted gate lodge also have canopied beds but aren't nearly as grand. It's off the A686 (the road for Alston), which is off the A69 just before Haydon Bridge.

Ashcroft (☎ 01434-320213; www.ashcroftguesthouse .co.uk; Lanty's Lonnen; s/d from £36/72) is a marvellous Edwardian home surrounded by beautifully manicured, layered lawns and gardens from which there are stunning views (also enjoyed from the breakfast room). The owners like their flowers so much they decorated most of the house accordingly. Highly recommended.

Bus 685 comes from Newcastle (1½ hours) and Carlisle (45 minutes) 12 times daily. Hadrian's Wall bus AD 122 (June to September) or 185 (October to May) connects Haltwhistle with other places along the wall. Bus 681 heads south to Alston (55 minutes, three daily Monday to Saturday). The town is also on the Newcastle–Carlisle railway line (hourly).

AROUND HALTWHISTLE
Vindolanda Roman Fort & Museum
The extensive site of **Vindolanda** (☎ 01434-344277; www.vindolanda.com; admission £5.20, with Roman Army Museum £8; ☉ 10am-6pm Apr-Sep, to 5pm Feb-Mar & Oct-Nov) offers a fascinating glimpse into the daily life of a Roman garrison town. The time-capsule museum displays leather sandals, signature Roman toothbrush-flourish helmet decorations, and countless writing tablets such as a student's marked work ('sloppy'), and a parent's note with a present of socks and underpants (things haven't changed – in this climate you can never have too many).

The museum is just one part of this large, extensively excavated site, which includes impressive parts of the fort and town (excavations continue) and reconstructed turrets and temple.

It's 1.5 miles north of Bardon Mill between the A69 and B6318 and a mile from Once Brewed.

Housesteads Roman Fort & Museum
The wall's most dramatic site – and the best-preserved Roman fort in the whole country – is at **Housesteads** (EH; ☎ 01434-344363; admission £4.50; ☉ 10am-6pm Apr-Sep, to 4pm Oct-Mar). From here, high on a ridge and covering 2 hectares, you can survey the moors of Northumberland National Park, and the snaking wall, with a sense of awe at the landscape and the aura of the Roman lookouts.

The substantial foundations bring fort life alive. The remains include an impressive hospital, granaries with a carefully worked-out ventilation system and barrack blocks. Most memorable are the spectacularly situated communal flushable latrines, which summon up Romans at their most mundane.

Housesteads is 2.5 miles north of Bardon Mill on the B6318, and about 3 miles from Once Brewed. It's popular, so try to visit outside summer weekends, or late in the day when the site will be quiet and indescribably eerie.

Other Sights
A mile northwest of Greenhead, near Walltown Crags, the kid-pleasing **Roman Army Museum** (☎ 016977-47485; www.vindolanda.com; admission £4, with Vindolanda £7.50; ☉ 10am-6pm Apr-Sep, to 5pm Feb-Mar & Oct-Nov) provides lots of colourful background detail to wall life, such as how far soldiers had to march per day.

Technically it's in Cumbria (we won't tell if you don't), but the remains of the once-formidable **Birdoswald Roman Fort** (EH; ☎ 016977-47602; admission £4.50; ☉ 10am-5.30pm Mar-Oct), on an escarpment overlooking the beautiful Irthing Gorge, were part of the wall and so merit inclusion in this chapter on logical grounds. They're on a minor road off the B6318, about 3 miles west of Greenhead; a fine stretch of wall extends from here to Harrow Scar Milecastle. Across the impressive river footbridge, about half a mile away, is another good bit of wall, ending in two turrets and the meticulous structure of the **Willowford Bridge abutment**.

About 3 miles further west along the A69, are the peaceful raspberry coloured ruins of **Lanercost Priory** (EH; ☎ 016977-3030; admission £3; ☼ 10am-6pm Apr-Sep, to 4pm Thu-Mon Oct), founded in 1166 by Augustinian canons. Ransacked several times, after the dissolution it became a private house and a priory church was created from the Early English nave. The church contains some beautiful Pre-Raphaelite stained glass. The AD 122 bus drops off at the gate.

Sleeping

Once Brewed YHA (☎ 0845 371 9753; www.yha.org.uk; Military Rd, Bardon Mill; dm £12; ☼ year-round) This modern and well-equipped hostel is central for visiting both Housesteads Fort, 3 miles away, and Vindolanda, 1 mile away. Bus 685 (from Hexham or Haltwhistle train stations) will drop you at Henshaw, 2 miles south, or you could leave the train at Bardon Mill 2.5 miles southeast. The Hadrian's Wall bus can drop you at the door from June to September.

Greenhead YHA (☎ 016977-47401; www.yha.org.uk; dm £13; ☼ Jul-Aug, call to check other times) A converted Methodist chapel by a trickling stream and a pleasant garden, 3 miles west of Haltwhistle. The hostel is served by bus AD 122 or 685.

Birdoswald YHA (☎ 0845 371 9551; www.yha.org.uk; dm £14; ☼ Easter-Oct, call to check other times) This farmhouse within the grounds of the Birdoswald complex has recently been converted into a hostel with basic facilities, including a self-service kitchen and laundry. The price includes a visit to the fort.

Holmhead Guest House (☎ 016977-47402; www.bandbhadrianswall.com; Thirlwall Castle Farm, Greenhead; dm/s/d from £12.50/43/66) Four fairly compact rooms are available in this lovely remote old cottage; most of the space is taken up by the big beds. All the rooms have a shower rather than a bath. A barn was recently converted into a large dorm room, perfect for budget walkers and cyclists. It's about half a mile north of Greenhead.

NORTHUMBERLAND NATIONAL PARK

England's last great wilderness is the 398 sq miles of natural wonderland that make up Northumberland National Park, spread about the soft swells of the Cheviot Hills, the spiky

moors of autumn-coloured heather and gorse, and the endless acres of forest guarding the deep, colossal Kielder Water. Even the negligible human influence – even today, there are only about 2000 inhabitants here – has been benevolent: the finest sections of Hadrian's Wall run along the park's southern edge and the landscape is dotted with prehistoric remains and fortified houses – the thick-walled *peles* were the only solid buildings built here until the mid-18th century.

Orientation & Information

The park runs from Hadrian's Wall in the south, takes in the Simonside Hills in the east and runs into the Cheviot Hills along the Scottish border. There are few roads.

For information, contact **Northumberland National Park** (☎ 01434-605555; www.northumberland-national-park.org.uk; Eastburn, South Park, Hexham). Besides the tourist offices mentioned, there are relevant offices in **Once Brewed** (☎ 01434-344396; ☼ 10am-5pm mid-Mar–May, Sep & Oct, 9.30am-6pm Jun-Aug) as well as **Ingram** (☎ 01665-578890; ingram@nnpa.org.uk; ☼ 10am-5pm Easter-Oct). All the tourist offices handle accommodation bookings.

Activities

The most spectacular stretch of the Hadrian's Wall Path (p770) is between Sewingshields and Greenhead in the south of the park.

There are many fine walks through the Cheviots, frequently passing by prehistoric remnants; the towns of Ingram, Wooler and Rothbury make good bases, and their tourist offices can provide maps, guides and route information.

Though at times strenuous, cycling in the park is a pleasure; the roads are good and the traffic is light here. There's off-road cycling in Border Forest Park.

Getting There & Around

Public transport options are limited, aside from buses on the A69. See the Hadrian's Wall section (p771) for access to the south. Bus 808 (55 minutes, two daily Monday to Saturday) runs between Otterburn and Newcastle. Postbus 815 and bus 880 (45 minutes, eight daily Monday to Saturday, three on Sunday) run between Hexham and Bellingham. National Express bus 383 (three hours, four daily, £16.60) goes from Newcastle to Edinburgh via Otterburn, Byrness (by request), Jedburgh, Melrose and Galashiels.

BELLINGHAM

The small, remote village of Bellingham (bellin-*jum*) is a pleasant enough spot on the banks of the North Tyne, surrounded by beautiful, deserted countryside on all sides. It is an excellent base from which to kick off your exploration of the park.

The **tourist office** (☎ 01434-220616; Main St; ☺ 9.30am-1pm & 2-5pm Mon-Sat, 1-5pm Sun Apr-Oct, 2-5pm Mon-Sat Nov-Mar) handles visitor inquiries.

There's not a lot to see here save the 12th-century **St Cuthbert's Church**, unique because it retains its original stone roof, and **Cuddy's Well**, outside the churchyard wall, which is alleged to have healing powers on account of its blessing by the saint.

The **Hareshaw Linn Walk** passes through a wooded valley and over six bridges, leading to a 9m-high waterfall 2.5 miles north of Bellingham (*linn* is an Old English name for waterfall).

Bellingham is on the Pennine Way; book ahead for accommodation in summer. Most of the B&Bs are clustered around the village green.

Bellingham YHA (☎ 01434-220258; www.yha.org .uk; Woodburn Rd; dm £15; ☺ mid-Apr–Oct) is on the edge of the village. It is almost always busy, so be sure to book ahead. There are showers, a cycle store and a self-catering kitchen on the premises.

Lyndale Guest House (☎ 01434-220361; www.lyndale guesthouse.co.uk; s/d from £30/60) The bedrooms in this pleasant family home just off the village green are modern and extremely tidy; it's a bit like visiting a really neat relative.

Pub grub is about the extent of the village's dining; recommended is the Black Bull or the Rose & Crown.

ROTHBURY

pop 1960

The one-time prosperous Victorian resort of Rothbury is an attractive, restful market town on the River Coquet that makes a convenient base for the Cheviots.

There's a **tourist office & visitor centre** (☎ 01669-620887; Church St; ☺ 10am-5pm Apr-Oct, to 6pm Jun-Aug).

The biggest draw in the immediate vicinity is **Cragside House, Garden and Estate** (NT; ☎ 01669-620333; admission £11, gardens & estate only £7; ☺ house 1-5.30pm Tue-Sun mid-Mar–Sep, 1-4.30pm Tue-Sun Oct–mid-Mar, gardens 10.30am-5.30pm Tue-Sun mid-Mar–Sep, 11am-4pm Wed-Sun Oct–mid-Mar), the quite incredible country retreat of the first Lord Armstrong.

In the 1880s the house had hot and cold running water, a telephone and alarm system, and was the first in the world to be lit by electricity, generated through hydropower – the original system has been restored and can be observed in the Power House. The Victorian gardens are also well worth exploring: huge and remarkably varied, they feature lakes, moors and one of the world's largest rock gardens. Visit in May to see myriad rhododendrons.

The estate is 1 mile north of town on the B6341; there is no public transport to the front gates from Rothbury; try **Rothbury Motors** (☎ 01669-620516) if you need a taxi.

High St is a good area to look for a place to stay.

Beamed ceilings, stone fireplaces and canopied four-poster beds make **Katerina's Guest House** (☎ 01669-602334; Sun Buildings, High St; www .katerinasguesthouse.co.uk; s/d from £45/68) one of the nicer options in town, even though the rooms are a little small.

Alternatively, the **Haven** (☎ 01669-620577; Back Crofts; s/d/ste £40/80/130) is a beautiful Edwardian home up on a hill with six lovely bedrooms and one elegant suite.

Food options are limited to pub grub. For takeaway you could try the **Rothbury Bakery** (High St) for pies and sandwiches or **Tully's** (High St) for flapjacks.

Bus 416 from Morpeth (30 minutes) leaves every two hours from Monday to Saturday and three times on Sunday.

KIELDER WATER

The northeast was thirsty, so they built it a lake, and a bloody huge one it is: Europe's largest artificial lake holds 200,000 million litres and has a shoreline of 27 miles. Surrounding it is England's largest forest, 150 million spruce and pine trees growing in nice, tidy fashion. Besides being busy creating H_2O and O_2 for this part of the world, the lake and forest are the setting for one of England's largest outdoor-adventure playgrounds, with water parks, cycle trails, walking routes and plenty of bird-watching sites, but it's also a great place to escape humanity: you are often as much as 10 miles from the nearest village. In summer, however, your constant companion will be the insistent midge: bring strong repellent.

The **Tower Knowe Visitor Centre** (☎ 0870 240 3549; www.visitnorthumberland.com; ☺ 10am-5pm Jun & Sep, to 6pm Jul-Aug, to 4pm Oct-Apr), near the southeastern end of the lake, has plenty of information on the area, with lots of walking leaflets and maps, a cafe and a small exhibition on the history of the valley and lake. *Cycling at Kielder* and *Walking at Kielder* are useful leaflets available from any of the area's tourist offices (£2.70 each). They describe trails in and around the forest, their length and difficulty.

Sights & Activities

Most of the lake's activities are focused on **Leaplish Waterside Park** (☎ 0870-240 3549), located a few miles northwest of Tower Knowe. It is a purpose-built complex with a heated outdoor pool, sauna, fishing and other water sports as well as restaurants, cafes and accommodation.

The **Birds of Prey Centre** (☎ 01434-250400; www .discoverit.co.uk/falconry; admission £5; ⏰ 10.30am-5pm Mar-Oct) is also located here, with owls, falcons and hawks flapping about; the birds are flown twice daily from April to September.

The **Osprey** (☎ 01434-250312; adult/child £7/4.50) is a small cruiser that navigates the lake (four per day Easter to October) and is the best way to get a sense of its huge size.

At the lake's northern end, 6 miles on from Leaplish and 3 miles from the Scottish border, is the sleepy village of **Kielder**.

Kielder Castle (☎ 01434-250209; admission free; ⏰ 10am-5pm Apr-Oct, to 6pm Aug, 11am-4pm Sat & Sun Nov-Dec) was built in 1775 as a hunting lodge by the Duke of Northumberland. It now houses a Forestry Enterprise information centre, with countless maps and leaflets.

Sleeping & Eating

Leaplish Waterside Park (☎ 0870 240 3549; site per person £8, cabins £60; Reiver's Rest dm/d £17.50/38; ⏰ Apr-Oct) The water park offers three distinct types of accommodation. The small campsite (12 pitches) is set among trees; the Reiver's Rest (formerly a fishing lodge) has en suite doubles and two dorms that all share a kitchen and a laundry, while the fully self-contained log cabins offer a bit of waterside luxury, complete with TVs and videos. The catch is that the cabins can only be rented for a minimum of three nights.

Kielder YHA (☎ 0845 371 9126; www.yha.org.uk; Butteryhaugh, Kielder Village; dm £12; ⏰ Apr-Oct) This well-equipped, activities-based hostel on the lake's northern shore has small dorms and a couple of four-bed rooms (£15 per person).

Gowanburn (☎ 01434-250254; s/d £34/70) Probably the most remote B&B in England is Mrs

Scott's fabulous spot on the eastern side of the lake at Gowanburn, accessible by a narrow road from Kielder village. The iron-grey lake spreads out before the house, the welcome is warm and the breakfast fantastic.

Falstone Tea Rooms (☎ 01434-240459; Old School House, Falstone) This place has filling all-day breakfasts for around £4.

Getting There & Around

From Newcastle, bus 714 – the 'Kielder Bus' (1½ hours) – goes directly to Kielder on Sundays and bank holidays, May to October. The bus leaves in the morning, turns into a shuttle between the various lake attractions and returns in the afternoon. Bus 814 (one hour, two daily Monday to Friday in term time) arrives from Otterburn, calling at Bellingham, Stannersburn, Falstone, Tower Knowe Information Centre and Leaplish; the bus begins in Bellingham from June to September (Tuesday and Friday only). **Postbus 815** (☎ 01452-333447) runs between Hexham train station and Kielder (two daily Monday to Friday, one Saturday) on a similar route along the lake and makes a detour to Gowanburn and Deadwater in the morning.

Kielder Bikes (☎ 01434-250392; Castle Hill; bike hire adult/child £22/14; ⏰ 10am-6pm Easter-Sep) is opposite Kielder Castle. If no-one's around, there's an excellent long-distance doorbell.

WOOLER
pop 1860

A harmonious, stone-terraced town, Wooler owes its sense of unified design to a devastating fire in 1863, which resulted in an almost complete reconstruction. It is an excellent spot to catch your breath in, especially as it is surrounded by some excellent forays into the nearby Cheviots (including a clamber to the top of The Cheviot, at 815m the highest peak in the range) and is the midway point for the 65-mile St Cuthbert's Way, which runs from Melrose in Scotland to Holy Island on the coast.

The **tourist office** (☎ 01668-282123; www.wooler .org.uk; Cheviot Centre, 12 Padgepool Pl; ⏰ 10am-5pm Mon-Sat & 10am-4pm Sun Jul-Aug, to 4pm Mon-Sat Apr & Oct, to 5pm Sat & Sun only Nov-Mar) is a mine of information on walks in the hills.

Activities

A popular walk from Wooler takes in **Humbleton Hill**, the site of an Iron Age hill fort and the location of yet another battle (1402)

between the Scots and the English. It's immortalised in 'The Ballad of Chevy Chase' (no, not *that* Chevy Chase – see boxed text, right) and Shakespeare's *Henry IV*. There are great views of the wild Cheviot Hills to the south and plains to the north, merging into the horizon. The well-posted 4-mile trail starts and ends at the bus station. It takes approximately two hours. Alternatively, the yearly **Chevy Chase** (www.woolerrunningclub.co.uk) is a classic 20-mile fell run with over 4000ft of accumulated climb, run at the beginning of July.

A more arduous hike leads to the top of the **Cheviot**, 6 miles southeast. The top is barren and wild, but on a clear day you can see the castle at Bamburgh and as far out as Holy Island. It takes around four hours to reach the top from Wooler. Check with the tourist office for information before setting out.

Sleeping & Eating

Wooler YHA (☎ 0845 371 9668; www.yha.org.uk; 30 Cheviot St; dm £14; ☾ Mon-Sat Apr-Jun, Tue-Sat Sep, Fri & Sat Mar) This recently refurbished hostel has 44 beds in a variety of rooms, a modern lounge and a small cafe.

Black Bull (☎ 01668-281309; www.theblackbullhotel .co.uk; 2 High St; s/d from £25/50; ☐) A 17th-century coaching inn that has retained much of its traditional character, this is probably the best option in town; it also does decent pub grub (mains around £8).

Tilldale House (☎ 01668-281450; www.tilldalehouse .co.uk; 34-40 High St; s/d from £35/40) This place has comfortable, spacious rooms that work on the aesthetic premise that you can never have enough of a floral print.

Getting There & Around

Wooler has good bus connections to the major towns in Northumberland. Bus 464 comes in from Berwick (50 minutes, five daily Monday to Saturday). Buses 470 (six daily Monday to Saturday) or 473 (eight daily Monday to Saturday) come from Alnwick. Bus 710 makes the journey from Newcastle (1½ hours, Wednesday and Saturday).

Cycle hire is available at **Haugh Head Garage** (☎ 01668-281316; per day from £15) in Haugh Head, 1 mile south of Wooler on the A697.

AROUND WOOLER

One of England's most interesting medieval castles, **Chillingham** (☎ 01668-215359; www.chilling

---

> **WHICH CHEVY?**
>
> In 'The Ballad of Chevy Chase', the Chevy chase refers to a Cheviot hunt (ie hunting for deer). It was an English hunting party crossing into Scotland that caused the famous battle. Perhaps unexpectedly, there is a link between the American actor Chevy Chase and this Northumberland battle ballad – Mr Chase's grandmother was Scottish and gave him this nickname. His real name is Cornelius. Really.

ham-castle.com; adult/child £6.75/3; ☾ 1-5pm Sun-Fri Easter-Sep) is steeped in history, warfare, torture and ghosts: it is said to be one of the country's most haunted places, with ghostly clientele ranging from a phantom funeral to Lady Mary Berkeley in search of her errant husband.

The current owner, Sir Humphrey Wakefield, has gone to great lengths to restore the castle to its eccentric, noble best. This followed a 50-year fallow period when the Grey family (into which Sir Humphrey married) abandoned it, despite having owned it since 1245, because they couldn't afford the upkeep.

Well done, Sir H. Today's visitor is in for a real treat, from the extravagant medieval staterooms that have hosted a handful of kings in their day to the stone-flagged banquet halls, where many a turkey leg must surely have been hurled to the happy hounds. Belowground, Sir Humphrey has gleefully restored the grisly torture chambers, which have a polished rack and the none-too-happy face of an Iron Maiden. There's also a museum with a fantastically jumbled collection of objects – it's like stepping into the attic of a compulsive and well-travelled hoarder.

In 1220, 148 hectares of land were enclosed to protect the herd of **Chillingham Wild Cattle** (☎ 01668-215250; www.chillinghamwildcattle .com; adult/child £4.50/1.50; ☾ park 10am-noon & 2-5pm Mon & Wed-Sat, 2-5pm Sun Apr-Oct) from borderland raiders; this fierce breed is now the world's purest. They were difficult to steal, as they cannot herd and apparently make good guard animals. Around 40 to 60 make up the total population of these wild white cattle (a reserve herd is kept in a remote place in Scotland, in case of emergencies).

THE NORTHEAST

It's possible to stay at the medieval fortress in the seven apartments designed for guests, where the likes of Henry III and Edward I once snoozed. Prices vary depending on the luxury of the apartment; the **Grey Apartment** (£156) is the most expensive – it has a dining table to seat 12 – or there's the **Tower Apartment** (£120), in the Northwest Tower. All of the apartments are self-catering.

Chillingham is 6 miles southeast of Wooler. Bus 470 running between Alnwick and Wooler (six daily Monday to Saturday) stops at Chillingham.

NORTHUMBERLAND

The utterly wild and stunningly beautiful landscapes of Northumberland don't stop with the national park. Hard to imagine an undiscovered wilderness in a country so modern and populated, but as you cast your eye across the rugged interior you will see ne'er a trace of Man save the fortified houses and friendly villages that dot the horizon.

While the west is covered by the national park, the magnificent and pale sweeping coast to the east is the scene of long, stunning beaches, bookmarked by dramatic wind-worn castles and tiny islands offshore that really do have an air of magic about them. Hadrian's Wall emerges from the national park and slices through the south.

History

Northumberland takes its name from the Anglo-Saxon kingdom of Northumbria (north of the River Humber). For centuries it served as the battleground for the struggle between north and south. After the arrival of the Normans in the 11th century, large numbers of castles and *peles* (fortified buildings) were built and hundreds of these remain. All this turmoil made life a tad unsettled till the 18th century brought calm. Today the land's turbulent history has echoes all around the sparsely populated countryside.

Getting Around

The excellent *Northumberland Public Transport Guide* (£1.90) is available from local tourist offices. Transport options are good, with a train line running along the coast from Newcastle to Berwick and on to Edinburgh.

ALNWICK
pop 7770

Northumberland's historic ducal town, Alnwick (no tongue gymnastics: just say 'annick') is an elegant maze of narrow cobbled streets spread out beneath the watchful gaze of a colossal medieval castle. Not only will you find England's most perfect bookshop, but also the most visited attraction in the northeast at Alnwick Garden.

The castle is on the northern side of town and overlooks the River Aln. The **tourist office** (☎ 01665-510665; www.visitalnwick.org.uk; 2 The Shambles; ☼ 9am-5pm Mon-Sat, 10am-4pm Sun) is by the marketplace, in a handsome building that was once a butcher's shop.

There has been a market in Alnwick for over 800 years. Market days are Thursday and Saturday, with a farmers market on the last Friday of the month.

Sights

The outwardly imposing **Alnwick Castle** (☎ 01665-510777; www.alnwickcastle.com; adult/child/concession £10.50/4.50/9; ☼ 10am-6pm Apr-Oct), ancestral home of the Duke of Northumberland and a favourite set for film-makers (it was Hogwarts for the first couple of *Harry Potter* films) has changed little since the 14th century. The interior is sumptuous and extravagant; the six rooms open to the public – staterooms, dining room, guard chamber and library – have an incredible display of Italian paintings, including Titian's *Ecce Homo* and many Canalettos.

The castle is set in parklands designed by Lancelot 'Capability' Brown. The woodland walk offers some great aspects of the castle, or for a view looking up the River Aln, take the B1340 towards the coast.

As spectacular a bit of green-thumb artistry as you'll see in England, **Alnwick Garden** (☎ 01665-510777; www.alnwickgarden.com; adult/child/concession £10/free/7.50; ☼ 10am-7pm Jun-Sep, to 6pm Apr-May & Oct, to 4pm Nov-Jan, to 5pm Feb-Mar) is one of the northeast's great success stories. Since the project began in 2000, the 4.8-hectare walled garden has been transformed from a derelict site into a spectacle that easily exceeds the grandeur of the castle's 19th-century gardens, a series of magnificent green spaces surrounding the breathtaking Grand Cascade – 120 separate jets spurting over 30,000L of water down 21 weirs for everyone to marvel at and kids to splash around in.

SOMETHING FOR THE WEEKEND

Northumberland's historic ducal town of Alnwick is the perfect choice for a getaway weekend and the **White Swan Hotel** (below) in the middle of town is the perfect base. On Saturday, visit the **castle** and its spectacular **garden** (opposite) – but don't miss the market, which has been running since the early 13th century. Also not to be missed is a pilgrimage to **Barter Books** (below), arguably the best bookshop in the country and a browser's dream. Kick off the evening with a pint in **Ye Old Cross** (below) before dining in Edwardian splendour in the dining room of the **White Swan Hotel** (below), which has the original decor from the *Titanic's* sister ship, the *Olympic*.

Sunday should be about exploring the surrounding area. **Warkworth Castle** (p780) is only a few miles away, while further on up the coast (only 6 miles from Alnwick) is the little sea village of **Craster** (p780), famous for its kippers. A short walk from here is **Dunstanburgh Castle** (p780) and **Embleton Bay** (p780), a wonderfully idyllic spot that reveals the best of Northumberland's windswept coastline.

THE NORTHEAST

There are a half-dozen other gardens, including the Franco-Italian–influenced Ornamental Garden (with more than 15,000 plants), the Rose Garden and the particularly fascinating Poison Garden, home to some of the deadliest – and most illegal – plants in the world, including cannabis, magic mushrooms, belladonna and even tobacco.

Festivals
The **Alnwick Fair** is an annual costumed re-enactment of an original medieval *fayre*. It features arts and crafts stalls, hog roasts, street theatre and the ubiquitous Dunking of the Wenches (in icy cold water): surely no fair is complete without it? Festivities kick off the last Sunday in June.

Sleeping & Eating
White Swan Hotel (☎ 01665-602109; www.classiclodges .co.uk; Bondgate Within; s/d from £70/115; P 🖳 wi-fi) Alnwick's top address is this 300-year-old coaching inn right in the heart of town. Its rooms are all of a pretty good standard (LCD screen TVs, DVD players and free wi-fi), but this spot stands out for its dining room, which has elaborate original panelling, ceiling and stained-glass windows filched from the *Olympic*, sister ship to the *Titanic*.

A row of handsome Georgian houses along Bondgate Without offers several worthwhile options that all charge around £32 per person, including **Lindisfarne Guest House** (☎ 01665-603430; 6 Bondgate Without) and the **Teapot** (☎ 604473; 8 Bondgate Without), which has the largest teapot collection in town.

A number of atmospheric pubs do a good line in traditional food. The **Market Tavern**

(☎ 01665-602759; 7 Fenkle St; stottie £6), near Market Sq, is the place to go for a traditional giant beef stottie (bread roll), while **Ye Old Cross** (☎ 01665-602735; Narrowgate; mains £6) is good for a drink to go along with your stottie cake, and is known as 'Bottles', after the dusty bottles in the window: 150 years ago the owner collapsed and died while trying to move them and no-one's dared attempt it since.

Shopping
Barter Books (☎ 01665-604888; www.barterbooks.co.uk; Alnwick Station; 🕙 9am-7pm) One of the country's largest second-hand bookshops is the magnificent, sprawling Barter Books, housed in a Victorian railway station with coal fires, velvet ottomans and reading (once waiting) rooms. You could spend days in here.

Getting There & Away
There are regular buses from Newcastle (501, 505 and 518; one hour, 28 per day Monday to Saturday, 18 on Sunday). Bus 518 has 10 to 14 daily services to the attractive towns of Warkworth (25 minutes) and Alnmouth (15 minutes), which has the nearest train station. Buses 505 and 525 come from Berwick (45 minutes, 13 daily Monday to Saturday). The Arriva Day Pass (adult/child £6/5) is good value.

WARKWORTH
Biscuit-coloured Warkworth is little more than a cluster of houses around a loop in the River Coquet, but it makes for an impressive sight, especially if you arrive on the A1068 from Alnwick, when the village literally unfolds before you to reveal the craggy ruin of the enormous 14th-century castle.

A 'worm-eaten hold of ragged stone', **Warkworth Castle** (EH; ☎ 01665-711423; adult £4; ☺ 10am-5pm Apr-Sep, to 4pm Oct, Sat-Mon only Nov-Mar) features in Shakespeare's *Henry IV* Parts I and II and will not disappoint modern visitors. Yes, it is still pretty worm-eaten and ragged, but it crowns an imposing site, high above the gentle, twisting river. *Elizabeth* (1998), starring Cate Blanchett, was filmed here.

Tiny, mystical, 14th-century **Warkworth Hermitage** (EH; adult/child £3/free; ☺ 11am-5pm Wed & Sun Apr-Sep), carved into the rock, is a few hundred yards upriver. Follow the signs along the path, then take possibly the world's shortest ferry ride. It's a lovely stretch of water and you can hire a **rowing boat** (adult/child per 45 min £5/3; ☺ Sat & Sun May-Sep).

Fourteen huge, country-style bedrooms sit above a cosy bar at the **Sun Hotel** (☎ 01665-711259; www.rytonpark-sun.co.uk; 6 Castle Tce; s/d from £55/85, with dinner £69/112; **P**), and an elegant restaurant serves local dishes given the French treatment. There are excellent views of both the castle and the river.

Right in the centre of the village, the **Greenhouse** (☎ 01665-712322; 21 Dial Pl; mains £8-14; ☺ lunch & dinner Mon & Wed-Sat, lunch only Sun) is a cafe-bistro that serves great coffee, cakes and more substantial fish and meat dishes on large pine tables.

Bus 518 links Newcastle (1½ hours, hourly), Warkworth, Alnmouth and Alnwick. There's a train station on the main east-coast line, about 1.5 miles west of town.

CRASTER

Sandy, salty Craster is a small sheltered fishing village about 6 miles north of Alnwick that is famous for its kippers. In the early 20th century, 2500 herring were smoked here *daily;* these days, it's mostly cigarettes that are smoked, but the kippers they do produce are excellent.

The place to buy them is **Robson & Sons** (☎ 01665-576223; www.kipper.co.uk; 2 for around £8), which has been stoking oak-sawdust fires since 1865. For fish facts and other info, call into the **tourist office** (☎ 01665-576007; Quarry Car Park; ☺ 9.30am-5.30pm Apr-Oct, to 4.30pm Sat & Sun Nov-Mar).

You can also sample the day's catch – crab and kipper pâté are particularly good – and contemplate the splendid views at the **Jolly Fisherman** (☎ 01665-576218; sandwiches £3-5).

Bus 401 or 501 from Alnwick calls at Craster (30 minutes, around five daily). A pay-and-display car park is the only place in Craster where it's possible to park your car.

Dunstanburgh Castle

A dramatic 1-mile walk along the coast from Craster is the most scenic path to the striking, weather-beaten ruins of yet another atmospheric **castle** (EH & NT; ☎ 01665-576231; admission £3.50; ☺ 10am-5pm Apr-Sep, to 4pm Oct-Mar, Thu-Mon only Nov-Mar). The haunting sight of the ruins, high on a basalt outcrop famous for its sea birds, can be seen for miles along this exhilarating stretch of shoreline.

Dunstanburgh was once one of the largest border castles. Its construction began in 1314, it was strengthened during the Wars of the Roses, but then left to rot. Only parts of the original wall and gatehouse keep are still standing; it was already a ruin by 1550, so it's a tribute to its builders that so much is left today. It is jointly administered by English Heritage and the National Trust.

You can also reach the castle on foot from Embleton.

EMBLETON BAY

From Dunstanburgh, beautiful Embleton Bay, a pale wide arc of sand, stretches around to the endearing, sloping village of **Embleton**. The village is home to the stunning seaside **Dunstanburgh Castle Golf Club** (☎ 01665-576562; www .dunstanburgh.com; green fee weekday/weekend £25/30) – first laid out in 1900 and improved upon by golf legend and 'inventor' of the dogleg, James Braid (1870–1950), in 1922 – and a cluster of houses. Bus 401 or 501 from Alnwick calls here too.

Past Embleton, the broad vanilla-coloured strand curves around to end at **Low-Newton-by-the-Sea**, a tiny whitewashed, National Trust–preserved village with a fine pub. Behind the bay is a path leading to the **Newton Pool Nature Reserve**, an important spot for breeding and migrating birds such as black-headed gulls and grasshopper warblers. There are a couple of hides where you can peer out at them. You can continue walking along the headland beyond Low Newton, where you'll find **Football Hole**, a delightful hidden beach between headlands.

Sleeping & Eating

Sportsman (☎ 01665-576588; www.sportsmanhotel .co.uk; 6 Sea lane, Embleton; s/d from £36/64) This large, relaxed place set up from the bay has a wide deck out the front and a spacious, plain wooden bar that serves top nosh. Upstairs are 12 beautifully appointed rooms – nine of which look over the bay and golf course – but all have solid-oak beds and handsome pine furniture.

Ship Inn (☎ 01665-576262; www.shipinnnewton.co.uk; Low-Newton-by-the-Sea; bar food £4-8, mains £9) Our favourite pub in all of Embleton Bay is this wonderfully traditional ale house with a large open yard for fine weather, although it would take a real dose of sunshine to tear yourself away from the cosy interior. The menu puts a particular emphasis on local produce, so you can choose from local lobster (caught 50m away), Craster kippers or perhaps a good ploughman's lunch made with cheddar from a local dairy. A converted barn is a self-contained apartment that sleeps up to four people (double £70, per week £420).

Blink Bonny (☎ 01665-576595; Christon Bank; mains £6-9) Named after a famous racehorse, this typical stone country pub is a cut above the average. A huge open fireplace, oak panelling everywhere and a menu that puts a heavy accent on seafood (the lobster is particularly recommended), plus traditional music at weekends – what more could you want?

FARNE ISLANDS

One of England's most incredible seabird conventions is found on a rocky archipelago of islands about 3 miles offshore from the undistinguished fishing village of **Seahouses**. There's a **tourist office** (☎ 01655-720884; Seafield Rd; ❧ 10am-5pm Apr-Oct) near the harbour in Seahouses and a **National Trust Shop** (☎ 01665-721099; 16 Main St; ❧ 10am-5pm Apr-Oct) for all island-specific information.

The best time to visit the **Farne Islands** (NT; ☎ 01665-720651; admission £5.60, Apr & Aug-Sep £4.80; ❧ 10.30am-6pm Apr & Aug-Sep, Inner Farne also 1.30-5pm May-Jul, Staple also 10.30am-1.30pm May-Jul) is during breeding season (roughly May to July), when you can see feeding chicks of 20 species of seabird, including puffin, kittiwake, Arctic tern, eider duck, cormorant and gull. This is a quite extraordinary experience, for there are few places in the world where you can get so close to nesting seabirds. The islands are also home to England's only colony of grey seals.

To protect the islands from environmental damage, only two are accessible to the public: Inner Farne and Staple Island. Inner Farne is the more interesting of the two, as it is also

the site of a tiny chapel (1370, restored 1848) to the memory of St Cuthbert, who lived here for a spell and died here in 687.

Getting There & Away

There are various tours, from 1½-hour cruises to all-day specials, and they get going from 10am April to October. Crossings can be rough, and may be impossible in bad weather. Some of the boats have no proper cabin, so make sure you've got warm, waterproof clothing if there's a chance of rain. Also recommended is an old hat – those birds sure can ruin a head of hair!

Of the operators from the dock in Seahouses, **Billy Shiel** (☎ 01665-720308; www.farne-islands.com; 3hr tour adult/child £12/8, all-day tour with landing £25/15) is recommended – he even got an MBE for his troubles.

BAMBURGH

Bamburgh is all about the castle, a massive, imposing structure high up on a basalt crag and visible for miles around. The village itself – a tidy fist of houses around a pleasant green – isn't half bad, but it's really just about the castle, a solid contender for England's best.

Bamburgh Castle (☎ 01668-214515; www.bamburgh castle.com; adult/child £7/2.40; ❧ 10am-5pm Mar-Oct) is built around a powerful 11th-century Norman keep probably built by Henry II, although its name is a derivative of Bebbanburgh, after the wife of Anglo-Saxon ruler Aedelfrip, whose fortified home occupied this basalt outcrop 500 years earlier. The castle played a key role in the border wars of the 13th and 14th centuries, and in 1464 was the first English castle to fall as the result of a sustained artillery attack, by Richard Neville, Earl of Warwick, during the Wars of the Roses. It was restored in the 19th century by the great industrialist Lord Armstrong, who also turned his passion to Cragside (p775) and was the owner of Jesmond Dene House in Newcastle (p753). The great halls within are still home to the Armstrong family. It's just inland from long open stretches of empty white-sand beach, ideal for blustery walks.

The **Grace Darling Museum** (☎ 01668-214465; admission by donation £2; ❧ 10am-5pm) has displays on Bamburgh's most famous resident, lighthouse keepers in general and the small boats they rescued people in. Grace was a local lass who rowed out to the grounded, flailing SS *Forfarshire* in 1838 and saved its

THE NORTHEAST

TOP FIVE NORTHEAST ENGLAND CASTLES

- Chillingham Castle (p777; Wooler)
- Warkworth Castle (p780; Warkworth)
- Bamburgh Castle (p781; Bamburgh)
- Dunstanburgh Castle (p780; Embleton Bay)
- Lindisfarne Castle (opposite; Holy Island)

---

crew in the middle of a dreadful storm. She became the plucky heroine of her time – a real Victorian icon.

Sleeping & Eating

Bamburgh Hall Farm (☎ 01668-214230; www.bamburgh hallfarm.com; s/d incl breakfast £40/60; **P**) This magnificent farmhouse built in 1697 has only one room, but we highly recommend it for the sheer pleasure of the views, right down to the sea, and the huge breakfast, served in the very dining room where the Jacobite officers met during the rebellion of 1715.

Victoria Hotel (☎ 01668-214431; www.victoria hotel.net; Front St; s/d from £65/90; **P**) Overlooking the village green is this handsome hotel with bedrooms decorated with quality antiques and – in the superior rooms – handcrafted fourposters. Here you'll also find the best restaurant in town, with a surprisingly adventurous menu (mains £10 to £16) that matches local fare with exotic flavours – how about a fillet of beef with pak choi?

Greenhouse (☎ 01668-214513; www.thegreenhouse guesthouse.co.uk; 5-6 Front St; r from £65; **P**) With four large, modern rooms with power showers and a mix of views (rooms 1 and 2 overlooking the front are best), this is a decent option, although they are loath to sell a room as a single during the summer.

ourpick **Waren House Hotel** (☎ 01668-214581; www.warenhousehotel.co.uk; Waren Mill; d/ste £143/175; **P** 🖳) This most romantic of getaway hotels presents a delicious dilemma: whether to spend more time enjoying the superb setting, overlooking Budle Bay and Holy Island to the east and the Cheviot Hills to the west, or to lock yourself indoors and lose yourself in the luxurious trappings (try the three-course dinner, £27) of this magnificent house. The hotel is in the small hamlet of Waren Mill, 2 miles northwest of Bamburgh along the B1340.

You can stock up for a picnic at the **Pantry** (☎ 01668-214455; 13 Front St; sandwiches £2.50-4.50); the **Copper Kettle** (☎ 01668-214361; 22 Front St; afternoon tea £5-7) is a gift shop with a pleasant tearoom.

Getting There & Away

Bus 501 runs from Newcastle (2¼ hours, two daily Monday to Saturday, one Sunday) stopping at Alnwick and Seahouses. Bus 401 or 501 from Alnwick (four to six daily) takes one hour.

HOLY ISLAND (LINDISFARNE)

'A strange and mystical island,' a local might whisper solemnly in your ear, inferring even a hint of magic. Holy Island is often referred to as an unearthly place, and while a lot of this talk is just that (and a little bit of bring- 'em-in tourist bluster), there *is* something almost other-worldly about this small island (it's only 2 sq miles). It's tricky to get to, as it's connected to the mainland by a narrow, glinting causeway that only appears at low tide. It's also fiercely desolate and isolated, barely any different from when St Aidan came to what was then known as Lindisfarne to found a monastery in 635. As you cross the empty flats to get here, it's not difficult to imagine the marauding Vikings that repeatedly sacked the settlement between 793 and 875, when the monks finally took the hint and left. They carried with them the illuminated *Lindisfarne Gospels* (now in the British Library in London) and the miraculously preserved body of St Cuthbert (see boxed text, p761), who lived here for a couple of years but preferred the hermit's life on Inner Farne. A priory was re-established in the 11th century but didn't survive the dissolution in 1537.

It is this strange mix of magic and menace that attracts the pious and the curious; during summer weekends the tiny fishing village, built around the red-sandstone remains of the medieval priory, swarms with visitors. The island's peculiar isolation is best appreciated midweek or preferably out of season, when the wind-lashed, marram-covered dunes offer the same bleak existence as that taken on by St Aidan and his band of hardy monks.

Whatever you do, pay attention to the crossing-time information, available at tourist offices and on notice boards throughout the area. Every year there is a handful of go-it-alone fools who are caught midway by the incoming tide and have to abandon their cars.

Sights

Lindisfarne Priory (EH; ☎ 01289-389200; admission £4; ⏺ 9.30am-5pm Apr-Sep, to 4pm Oct & Feb-Mar, 10am-2pm Sat-Mon Nov-Jan) consists of elaborate red and grey ruins and the later 13th-century St Mary the Virgin Church. The museum next to these displays the remains of the first monastery and tells the story of the monastic community before and after the dissolution.

Twenty pages of the luminescent *Lindisfarne Gospels* are on view electronically at the **Lindisfarne Heritage Centre** (☎ 01289-389004; www .lindisfarne.org.uk; Marygate; adult/child £3.50/free; ⏺ 10am-5pm Apr-Oct, according to tides Nov-Mar), which also has displays on the locality.

Also in the village is **St Aidan's Winery** (☎ 01289-389230), where you can buy the sickly sweet Lindisfarne Mead, cleverly foisted upon unsuspecting pundits as an age-old aphrodisiac.

Half a mile from the village stands the tiny, storybook **Lindisfarne Castle** (NT; ☎ 01289-389244; adult £6; ⏺ 10.30am-3pm or noon-4.30pm Tue-Sun Apr-Oct), built in 1550, and extended and converted by Sir Edwin Lutyens from 1902 to 1910 for Mr Hudson, the owner of *Country Life* magazine. You can imagine some decadent parties have graced its alluring rooms – Jay Gatsby would have been proud. Its opening times may be extended depending on the tide. A **shuttle bus** (☎ 01289-389236) runs here from the car park.

Sleeping & Eating

It's possible to stay on the island, but you'll need to book in advance.

Open Gate (☎ 01289-389222; opengate@aidanand hilda.demon.co.uk; Marygate; s/d £32/58) This spacious Elizabethan stone farmhouse with comfortable rooms caters primarily to those looking for a contemplative experience – you're not as much charged a room rate as 'encouraged' to give the listed price as a donation. There is a small chapel in the basement and a room full of books on Celtic spirituality, and there are organised retreats throughout the year.

Ship Inn (☎ 01289-389311; www.theshipinn-holyisland .co.uk; Marygate; s/d/tr £72/94/112) Three exceptionally comfortable rooms – one with a four-poster – sit above an 18th-century public house known here as the Tavern. There's good local seafood in the bar.

Getting There & Around

Holy Island can be reached by bus 477 from Berwick (Wednesday and Saturday only, Monday to Saturday July and August). People taking cars across are requested to park in one of the signposted car parks (£5 per day). The sea covers the causeway and cuts the island off from the mainland for about five hours each day. Tide times are listed at tourist offices, in local papers and at each side of the crossing.

BERWICK-UPON-TWEED
pop 12,870

The northernmost city of England is a salt-encrusted fortress town that is the stubborn holder of two unique honours: it is the most fought-over settlement in European history (between 1174 and 1482 it changed hands 14 times between the Scots and the English); and its football team, Berwick Rangers, are the only English team to play in the Scottish League – albeit in lowly Division Two. (In fact, a 2008 poll showed most residents would like the town to become part of Scotland again.)

Although it has been firmly English since the 15th century, it retains its own peculiar identity, as though the vagaries of its seesaw history have forced it to look inwards and not trust anyone but its own – you need only walk its massive ramparts, built during Elizabethan times and still virtually complete, to understand the town's insularity.

Orientation & Information

The fortified town of Berwick is on the northern side of the Tweed; the three bridges link with the uninteresting suburbs of Tweedmouth, Spittal and Eastcliffe.

The **tourist office** (☎ 01289-330733; www.berwick -upon-tweed.gov.uk; 106 Marygate; ⏺ 10am-6pm Easter-Jun, to 5pm Jul-Sep, to 4pm Mon-Sat Oct-Easter) is helpful. Access the internet at **Berwick Backpackers** (☎ 01289-331481; 56-58 Bridge St; per 20 min £2).

Sights & Activities

Berwick's superb **walls** (EH; admission free) were begun in 1558 to reinforce an earlier set built during the reign of Edward II. They represented state-of-the-art military technology of the day and were designed both to house artillery (in arrowhead-shaped bastions) and to withstand it (the walls are low and massively thick, but it's still a long way to fall).

THE NORTHEAST

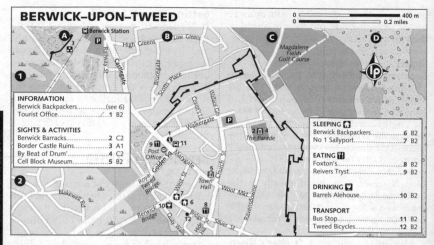

You can walk almost the entire length of the walls, a circuit of about a mile. It's a must, with wonderful, wide-open views. Only a small fragment remains of the once mighty **border castle**, by the train station. The tourist office has a brochure describing the main sights.

Designed by Nicholas Hawksmoor, **Berwick Barracks** (EH; ☎ 01289-304493; The Parade; admission £4; ⏲ 10am-5pm Apr-Oct, to 4pm Nov-Mar) is the oldest purpose-built barracks (1717) in Britain and now houses the By Beat of Drum Museum, chronicling the history of British soldiery from 1660 to 1900.

The original gaol cells in the upper floor of the town hall (1750–61) have been preserved to house the **Cell Block Museum** (☎ 01289-330900; Marygate; admission £2.50; ⏲ tours 10.30am & 2pm Mon-Fri Apr-Oct), devoted to crime and punishment, with tours taking in the public rooms, museum, gaol and belfry.

Recommended are the one-hour **guided walks** (adult/child £4/free; ⏲ 10am, 11.15am, 12.30pm & 2pm Mon-Fri Apr-Oct) starting from the tourist office.

Sleeping

There are plenty of B&Bs around the town, most of which offer fairly basic but comfortable rooms; the tourist office can assist in finding one.

Berwick Backpackers (☎ 01289-331481; www .berwickbackpackers.co.uk; 56-58 Bridge St; dm/s/d from £13/16/38; Ⓟ ▣) This excellent hostel, basically a series of rooms in the outhouses of a Georgian home around a central courtyard, has one large comfortable dorm, a single and two doubles, all en suite. Highly recommended.

ourpick No 1 Sallyport (☎ 01289-308827; www .1sallyport-bedandbreakfast.com; 1 Sallyport, off Bridge St; r £110-170) Not just the best in town, but one of the best B&Bs in England, No 1 Sallyport has only six suites – each carefully appointed to fit the theme. The Manhattan Loft, crammed into the attic, makes the minimalist most of the confined space; the Lowry Room is a country-style Georgian classic; the Smuggler's Suite has a separate sitting room complete with wide-screen TV, DVD players and plenty of space to lounge around in. Newer additions include the Tiffany Suite and the recently added attic Mulberry Suite, bathed in light.

Eating & Drinking

Good dining is a little thin on the ground, but there are a few exceptions.

Foxton's (☎ 01289-303939; 26 Hide Hill; mains £8-12; ⏲ lunch & dinner Mon-Sat) This decent brasserie-style restaurant has Continental dishes to complement the local fare, which means there's something for everyone.

Reivers Tryst (☎ 01289-332455; 119 Marygate; lunch mains £4-7, dinner mains £8-12; ⏲ lunch & dinner Mon-Sat) From the hearty breakfast through to home-made pies for lunch and the likes of lemon sole in the evening, this place specialises in classic English cuisine – nothing fancy, but very good.

Barrels Alehouse (☎ 01289-308013; 56 Bridge St) Elvis and Muhammad Ali grace the walls of this fine pub, where you'll also find real ale and vintage Space Invaders. There's regular live music in the atmospherically dingy basement bar.

Getting There & Away
BUS
Buses stop on Golden Sq (where Marygate becomes Castlegate); there are good links from Berwick into the Scottish Borders; there are buses west to Coldstream, Kelso and Galashiels. Buses 505, 515 and 525 go to Newcastle (2¼ hours, five daily) via Alnwick. Bus 253 goes to Edinburgh (two hours, six daily Monday to Saturday, two Sunday) via Dunbar.

TRAIN
Berwick is almost exactly halfway between Edinburgh (£18.20, one hour) and Newcastle (£17.50, 50 minutes) on the main east-coast London–Edinburgh line. Half-hourly trains between Edinburgh and Newcastle stop in Berwick.

Getting Around
The town centre is compact and walkable; if you're feeling lazy try **Berwick Taxis** (☎ 01289-307771). **Tweed Bicycles** (☎ 01289-331476; 17a Bridge St) hires out mountain bikes for £14 a day.

AROUND BERWICK-UPON-TWEED
Norham Castle
Once considered the most dangerous place in the country, the pinkish ruins of **Norham Castle** (EH; ☎ 01289-382329; admission £2.50; ☒ 10am-6pm Sat & Sun Mar-Sep) are quiet these days, but during the border wars it was besieged no less than 13 times, including a year-long siege by Robert the Bruce in 1318. The last attack came just three weeks before the Battle of Flodden (see Crookham & Around, right), and the castle was once again restored to the prince bishops of Durham, for whom it was originally built in 1160 to guard a swerving bend in the River Tweed.

The castle ruins are 6.5 miles southwest of Berwick on a minor road off the A698; bus 23 regularly passes Norham Castle from Berwick train station on its way to Kelso in Scotland (seven daily Monday to Saturday).

Etal & Ford
The pretty villages of Etal and Ford are part of a 23.45-sq-mile working rural estate set between the coast and the Cheviots, a lush and ordered landscape that belies its ferocious, bloody history.

Etal (*eet*-le) perches at the estate's northern end, and its main attraction is the roofless 14th-century **castle** (EH; ☎ 01890-820332; admission £3.50; ☒ 11am-4pm Apr-Oct). It was captured by the Scots just before the ferocious Battle of Flodden (see below), and has a striking border-warfare exhibition. It is 12 miles south of Berwick on the B6354.

About 1.5 miles southeast of here is Ford, where you can visit the extraordinary **Lady Waterford Hall** (☎ 01890-820524; adult/child £2/1.50; ☒ 10.30am-12.30pm & 1.30pm-5.30pm Apr-Oct, other times by appointment), a fine Victorian schoolhouse decorated with biblical murals and pictures by Louisa Anna, Marchioness of Waterford. The imposing 14th-century **Ford Castle** is closed to the public.

If you're travelling with kids, we recommend a spin on the toy-town **Heatherslaw Light Railway** (☎ 01890-820244; adult/child £6/4; ☒ hourly 11am-3pm Apr-Oct, to 4.30pm mid-Jul–Aug), which chugs from the Heatherslaw Corn Mill (about halfway between the two villages) to Etal Castle. The 3.5-mile return journey follows the river through pretty countryside.

SLEEPING & EATING
Estate House (☎ 01890-820668; www.theestatehouse .co.uk; Ford; s/d £45/70) This fine house near Lady Waterford Hall has three lovely bedrooms (all with handsome brass beds) overlooking a colourful, mature garden. An excellent choice – the owners have a plethora of local information.

Black Bull (☎ 01890-820200; Etal) This whitewashed, popular place is Northumberland's only thatched pub. It serves great pub food and pours a variety of well-kept ales.

GETTING THERE & AWAY
Bus 267 between Berwick and Wooler stops at both Etal and Ford (six daily, Monday to Saturday).

Crookham & Around
Unless you're a Scot or a historian, chances are you won't have heard of the Battle of Flodden, but this 1513 encounter between the Scots and the English – which left the English victorious and the Scots to count 10,000 dead, including James IV of Scotland and most of his nobles – was a watershed in the centuries-old scrap

between the two. A large stone cross, a monument 'to the brave of both nations', surmounts an innocuous hill overlooking the battlefield and is the only memorial to the thousands used as arrow fodder.

SLEEPING & EATING

our pick Coach House (☎ 01890-820293; www.coach housecrookham.com; Crookham; s/d incl breakfast from £52/74) This is an exquisite guesthouse spread about a 17th-century cottage, an old smithy and other outbuildings. There is a variety of rooms, from the traditional (with rare chestnut beams and country-style furniture) to contemporary layouts flavoured with Mediterranean and Indian touches. The food (dinner £19.50), beginning with an organic breakfast, is absolutely delicious and the equal of any restaurant around.

GETTING THERE & AWAY

The battlefield is 1.5 miles west of Crookham, on a minor road off the A697; Crookham itself is 3 miles west of Ford. Bus 710, which runs between Newcastle and Kelso serves these parts (two daily Monday to Friday).

Directory

CONTENTS

Country-wide practical information is given in this Directory. For details on specific areas, flip to the relevant regional chapter.

ACCOMMODATION

Accommodation in England is as varied as the sights you visit. From hip hotels to basic barns, the wide choice is all part of the attraction.

B&Bs & Guesthouses

The B&B ('bed and breakfast') is a great British institution. Basically, you get a room in somebody's house, and at smaller places you'll really feel part of the family. Larger B&Bs may have around 10 rooms and more facilities. 'Guesthouse' is sometimes just another name for a B&B, although they can be larger, with higher rates.

In country areas, your B&B might be in a village or isolated farm; in cities it's usually a suburban house. Facilities usually reflect price – for around £20 per person you get a simple bedroom and share the bathroom. For around £25 to £30 you get extras like TV or 'hospitality tray' (kettle, cups, tea, coffee) and a private bathroom – either down the hall or en suite.

B&B prices are usually quoted per person, based on two people sharing a room. Solo travellers have to search for single rooms and pay a 20% to 50% premium. Some B&Bs simply won't take single people (unless you pay the full double-room price), especially in summer.

Here are some more B&B tips:

- Advance reservations are always preferred at B&Bs, and are essential during popular periods. Many require a minimum two nights at weekends.
- If a B&B is full, owners may recommend another place nearby (possibly a private house taking occasional guests, not in tourist listings).
- In cities, some B&Bs are for long-term residents or people on welfare; they don't take passing tourists.
- In country areas, most B&Bs cater for walkers and cyclists, but some don't, so let them know if you'll be turning up with dirty boots or wheels.
- Some places reduce rates for longer stays (two or three nights).
- Most B&Bs serve enormous breakfasts; some offer packed lunches (around £5) and evening meals (around £12 to £15).
- If you're on a flexible itinerary and haven't booked in advance, most towns

---

BOOK YOUR STAY ONLINE

For more accommodation reviews and recommendations by Lonely Planet authors, check out the online booking service at www.lonelyplanet.com/hotels. You'll find the true, insider lowdown on the best places to stay. Reviews are thorough and independent. Best of all, you can book online.

have a main drag of B&Bs; those with spare rooms hang up a 'Vacancies' sign.

- When booking, check where your B&B actually is. In country areas, postal addresses include the nearest town, which may be 20 miles away – important if you're walking! Some B&B owners will pick you up by car for a small charge.

Bunkhouses & Camping Barns

A bunkhouse is a simple place to stay, handy for walkers, cyclists or anyone on a budget in the countryside. They usually have a communal sleeping area and bathroom, heating and cooking stoves, but you provide the sleeping bag and possibly cooking gear. Most charge around £10 per person per night.

Camping barns are even more basic: they're usually converted farm buildings, with sleeping platforms, a cooking area, and basic toilets outside. Take everything you'd need to camp except the tent. Charges are from around £5 per person.

Camping

The opportunities for camping in England are numerous – ideal if you're on a tight budget or simply enjoy the great outdoors. In rural areas, campsites range from farmers' fields with a tap and a basic toilet, costing as little as £3 per person per night, to smarter affairs with hot showers and many other facilities, charging up to £10.

ROOM RATES

Throughout this book, most Sleeping sections are divided into three price bands:
Budget – under £50 per double
Midrange – £50-120 per double
Top end – over £120 per double

These are high season rates for a double room with en suite bathroom; at quieter times of year prices drop. Single rooms are usually about 75% the double rate. The exception is accommodation in London, where 'budget' in this book means under £80 for a double room, midrange is £80-150, and top end is over £150.

Hostels

There are two types of hostel in England: those run by the **Youth Hostels Association** (YHA; ☎ 01629 592700; www.yha.org.uk) and independent hostels – most of which are listed in the **Independent Hostels** guidebook and website (www.independenthostelguide.co.uk). You'll find hostels in rural areas, towns and cities, and they're aimed at all types of traveller – whether you're a long-distance walker or touring by car – and you don't have to be young or single to use them. The YHA also handles bookings for many bunkhouses and camping barns around the country.

YHA HOSTELS

Many years ago, YHA hostels had a reputation for austerity, but today they're a great option for budget travellers. Some are purpose-built but many are converted cottages, country houses and even castles – often in wonderful locations. Facilities include showers, drying room, lounge and equipped self-catering kitchen. Sleeping is usually in dormitories, and many hostels also have twin or four-bed rooms, some with private bathroom.

You don't *have* to be a member of the YHA (or another Hostelling International organisation) to stay at YHA hostels, but nonmembers pay £3 extra per person per night (£1.50 for under-18s), so it's usually worth joining. Annual YHA membership costs £16; under-26s and families get discounts. Throughout this book we have generally quoted the member rates for YHA hostels.

Small basic hostels cost from £10, larger hostels with more facilities are £14 to £19. London's excellent YHA hostels cost £19 to £25. All plus £3 if you're not a member. Reservations and advance payments with credit card are usually possible.

It's important to note that YHA prices (just like train fares) vary according to demand and season. Book early for a Tuesday night in May and you'll get the best rate. Book late for a weekend in August and you'll pay top price – if there's space at all. Throughout this book, we have generally quoted the cheaper rates (in line with those listed on the YHA's website); you may find yourself paying more.

YHA hostels tend to have complicated opening times and days, especially in remote locations or out of tourist season, so check before turning up.

INDEPENDENT HOSTELS

England's independent and backpacker hostels offer a great welcome. In rural areas, some are little more than simple bunkhouses (charging around £6), while others are almost up to B&B standard, charging £15 or more. In cities, backpacker hostels are perfect for young budget travellers. Most are open 24/7, with a lively atmosphere, good range of rooms (doubles or dorms), bar, cafe, internet computer, wi-fi and laundry. Prices are around £15 for a dorm bed, or £20 to £35 for a bed in a private room.

Hotels

A hotel in England might be a small and simple place, perhaps a former farmhouse now stylishly converted, where peace and quiet – along with luxury – are guaranteed. Or it might be a huge country house with fancy facilities, grand staircases, acres of grounds and the requisite row of stag-heads on the wall. With such a great choice your only problem will be deciding where to stay.

How much is a hotel in England? It depends. Charges vary as much as quality and atmosphere. At the bargain end, you can find singles/doubles costing £30/40. Move up the scale and you can easily pay to £100/150 or beyond. More money doesn't always mean a better hotel though – whatever your budget, some are excellent value, while others overcharge.

If all you want is a place to put your head down, budget chain hotels can be a good option. Most are totally lacking in style or ambience, but who cares? You'll only be there for eight hours, and six of them you'll be asleep. **Travelodge** (www.travelodge .co.uk) offers rooms at variable prices based on demand; on a quiet night in November twin-bed rooms with private bathroom start at around £20, and at the height of the tourist season you'll pay £45 or more. Other chains with similar pricing structures include **Premier Inn** (www.premierinn.com), **Etap Hotels** (www.etaphotel.com) and **Hotel Formule 1** (www.hotelformule1.com).

REACH FOR THE STARS

Hotels and B&Bs (and even hostels) in England are awarded stars by the national tourist board and main motoring organisations, according to their levels of quality and service. Don't go by stars alone though. Some five-star hotels have loads of facilities but can feel a bit impersonal, whereas many one- or two-star places are small and owner-managed guests feel especially welcome. In addition, many smaller B&Bs prefer not to pay the necessary fees to register with the tourist board and so don't get any stars, even though their service is absolutely fine. The moral: if you use official accommodation lists as your only source, you might miss out on a real gem.

Pubs & Inns

As well as selling drinks, many pubs and inns offer lodging, particularly in country areas. Staying in a pub can be good fun – you're automatically at the centre of the community – although accommodation varies enormously, from stylish suites to threadbare rooms aimed at (and last used by) 1950s commercial salesmen. Expect to pay around £20 per person at the cheap end, and around £30 to £35 for something better. An advantage for solo tourists: pubs are more likely to have single rooms.

If a pub does B&B, it normally does evening meals, served in the bar or an adjoining restaurant. Breakfast may also be served in the bar next morning – not always enhanced by the smell of stale beer.

Rental Accommodation

If you want to slow down and get to know a place better, renting for a week or two can be ideal. Choose from neat flats (apartments) in towns and cities, or quaint old houses and farms (always called cottages, whatever the size) in country areas. Cottages for four people cost from around £200 to £300 per week in high season. Rates fall at quieter times, and you may be able to rent for a long weekend.

University Accommodation

Many universities offer student accommodation to visitors during vacations. You usually get a functional single bedroom with private bathroom, and self-catering flats are also available. Prices range from £15 to £30 per person.

ACTIVITIES

This section covers the practical side of outdoor activities. For more description and inspiration see the Outdoor England colour section, p141. In this book, we focus particularly on walking and cycling as these are the most popular, easy and straightforward. Some other activities, such as kitesurfing or mountaineering, are a bit more structured or need some advance preparation – but are still jolly good fun.

Walking

England has a 'right of way' network – public paths and tracks across private property – that is the envy of walkers from many other countries. Nearly all land (including in national parks) in England is privately owned, but if there's a right of way, you can follow it, as long as you keep to the route and do no damage.

The main types of rights of way for walkers are footpaths and bridleways (and open to horse riders and mountain bikers too). You'll also see 'byways', which, due to a quirk of history, are open to *all* traffic, so don't be surprised if you're disturbed by the antics of off-road driving fanatics as you're quietly strolling along enjoying the countryside.

Thanks to the landmark Countryside Act of 2004 – after more than 70 years of

---

ACCOMMODATION CONTACTS

Locally focused accommodation websites are listed in the regional chapters. For a country-wide view an excellent first stop is **Stilwell's** (www.stilwell.co.uk), a huge user-friendly database of accommodation for independent tourists, listing holiday cottages, B&Bs, hotels, campsites and hostels. Stilwell's is not an agency – once you've found what you want, you deal with the cottage or B&B owner direct. From the website you can also order a hard-copy brochure.

Good agencies include **Bed & Breakfast Nationwide** (☎ 01255-831235; www.bedandbreakfast nationwide.com) and **Hoseasons** (☎ 01502-502588; www.hoseasons.co.uk), the latter covering cottages and holiday parks.

For details on hostels, contact the **YHA** (☎ 01629-592700; www.yha.org.uk); the website also has information about bunkhouses, camping barns and YHA camp sites. The excellent **Independent Hostel Guide** (www.independenthostelguide.co.uk) covers hundreds of hostels in England and beyond – also available as an annually updated book.

If you're planning to tour England with a tent or campervan (motorhome) it's well worth joining the **Camping & Caravanning Club** (☎ 0845 130 7632; www.campingandcaravanningclub.co.uk), which owns almost 100 campsites and lists thousands more in the invaluable *Big Sites Book* (free to members). Annual membership costs £35 and includes discounted rates on club sites and various other services, including insurance and special rates for cars on ferries.

SOMETHING FOR THE WEEKEND?

England has a beguiling selection of accommodation options, and throughout this book we list many that stand out above the crowd. To widen the choice still further, and maybe discover a gem for yourself, contact the **Landmark Trust** (☎ 01628-825925; www.landmarktrust.org.uk), an architectural charity that rents historic buildings; your options include ancient cottages, medieval castles, Napoleonic forts and 18th-century follies.

Another option is **Distinctly Different** (☎ 01225-866842; www.distinctlydifferent.co.uk), specialising in unusual or even bizarre places to stay. Can't sleep at night? How about a former funeral parlour? Need to spice up your romance? Go for the converted brothel or the 'proudly phallic' lighthouse. Feeling brave? We have just the haunted inn for you.

Back safely down to earth with the final option. The **National Trust** (www.nationaltrust.org.uk) has over 300 holiday cottages and 80 B&Bs, many on the land of stately homes and working farms, in some of the finest locations in the country.

campaigning by the Ramblers Association and other groups – walkers (not bikes or other vehicles) can now move freely *beyond* rights of way in some mountain and moorland areas, but not in enclosed fields or cultivated areas. Where this is permitted it's clearly shown on maps, and by 'Access Land' or 'Open Access' notices on gates and signposts. The land is still privately owned, and occasionally Access Land is closed, for example if wild birds are nesting or if the farmer is rounding up sheep, but the 'right to roam' legislation opens up thousands of square miles of landscape previously off-limits to walkers. For more information see www.countrysideaccess.gov.uk.

While enjoying your walking, it's always worth remembering the fickle nature of English weather. The countryside can appear gentle and welcoming, and often is, but sometimes conditions can turn nasty – especially on the higher ground. At any time of year, if you're walking on the hills or open moors, it's vital to be well equipped. You should carry warm and waterproof clothing (even in summer), a map and compass (that you know how to use), some drink, food and high-energy stuff such as chocolate. If you're really going off the beaten track, leave details of your route with someone.

Cycling

Cycling is a cheap and enjoyable way of getting around, with a tiny carbon footprint. Legally, you can cycle on any public road except motorways, although main roads (A-roads) can be busy and should also be avoided. Many B-roads suffer heavy motor traffic too, so the best places for cycling are the small C-roads and unclassified roads (lanes) that cover rural England, where you can tour through quiet countryside relatively untroubled by infernal combustion engines.

Away from the roads, cycling is *not* allowed on footpaths, but mountain bikers can ride on bridleways (also called bridlepaths, originally for horses but now for bikes too), byways and other tracks as long as they're a right of way path.

For trouble-free mountain biking it's often worth seeking out forestry areas; among the vast plantations, signposted routes of varying difficulty have been opened up, ranging from delightful dirt roads ideal for families to precipitous drops and technical stretches for hardcore single-track fans.

Other Activities
COASTEERING

If edging along cliffs interspersed with dunks in the sea appeals, then coasteering is for you. It's not the thing to do on your own,

ROUTE OF ALL KNOWLEDGE

For comprehensive coverage of a selection of long and short walking routes, we (naturally) recommend Lonely Planet's very own *Walking in Britain*, which also covers getting there, and places to stay and eat along the way. If you're on two wheels, *Cycling in the UK* is an excellent handbook published by bike campaign group Sustrans, coving over 40 day-rides and a range of longer 'holiday routes'. For off-roading, the best book is *Where to Mountain Bike in Britain*, or see www.wheretomtb.com.

THE NATIONAL CYCLE NETWORK

Anyone riding a bike through England will almost certainly come across the National Cycle Network (NCN), a UK-wide 10,000-mile web of roads and traffic-free tracks. Strands of the network in busy cities are aimed at commuters or school kids (where the network follows city streets, cyclists normally have their own lane, separate from motor traffic), while other sections follow the most remote roads in the country and are perfect for touring.

The whole scheme is the brainchild of Sustrans (derived from 'sustainable transport'), a campaign group barely taken seriously way back in 1978 when the network idea was first announced. But the growth of cycling, coupled with near-terminal car congestion, has earned the scheme lots of attention – not to mention serious millions from government, regional authorities and (in early 2008) the national lottery.

Several long-distance touring routes use the most scenic sections of the NCN – plus a few less-than-scenic urban sections, it has to be said. Other features include a great selection of artworks to admire along the way. In fact, the network is billed as the country's largest outdoor-sculpture gallery. The whole scheme is a resounding success and a credit to the visionaries who persevered against inertia all those years ago. For more details see www.sustrans.org.uk.

---

but joining an organised group for a half- or full-day outing is easy enough. The outdoor centres provide wetsuits, helmets and buoyancy aids. You provide an old pair of training shoes and a sense of adventure. For more information see www.coasteering.org.

HORSE RIDING & PONY TREKKING

Exploring the English countryside on horseback is a great day out – even for total novices. You can find out about riding centres from tourist offices, and many advertise in national park newspapers (available free from hotels, tourist offices and local shops). A half-day pony trek starts from around £15, a full day around £35. Serious riders pay higher rates for superior mounts. The website of the **British Horse Society** (www.bhs.org.uk) lists approved riding centres and – if you fancy a few days in the saddle – outfits offering riding holidays.

ROCK CLIMBING & MOUNTAINEERING

If you want to try your hand (and feet) at rock climbing, local guides can be hired for one-on-one instruction in areas such as the Lake District, or you can join a group organised through an activity centre. As always, local tourist offices can provide contact details. For more info, the website of the **British Mountaineering Council** (www.thebmc.co.uk) includes access rules for outdoor locations (don't forget, all mountains and outcrops are privately owned), tips for beginners and much more.

SAILING & WINDSURFING

Your first port of call for any sailing or windsurfing matter should be the **Royal Yachting Association** (☎ 0845 345 0400; www.rya.org.uk). This organisation can provide all the details you need about training centres where you can improve your skills or simply charter a boat for pleasure.

SURFING & KITESURFING

England may not seem an obvious place for surfing, but conditions are surprisingly good, and the huge tidal range means often a completely different set of breaks at low and high tides. Apart from a board, your essential piece of equipment is a wetsuit – even in summer (when water temperatures are around 13°C). These can be easily hired from surf shops. For more information, the **British Surfing Association** (☎ 01637-876474; www.britsurf.co.uk) website has news on approved instruction centres, courses, competitions and so on. Combine this with comprehensive guidebook *Surf UK* by Wayne Alderson and you're sorted. For kitesurfing, there are several schools along the English coast that can show you the ropes. The **British Kite Surfing Association** (www.kitesurfing.org) has more information.

BEACHES

England has a great many beaches – from tiny hidden coves in Cornwall to vast neon-lined strands such as Brighton or Blackpool. Other great beaches can be found in Devon, Somerset and along the south coast, in Suffolk, Norfolk, Lancashire, Yorkshire and

Northumberland – each with their own distinct character. The best resort beaches earn the coveted international **Blue Flag** (www .blueflag.org) award, meaning sand and water are clean and unpolluted. Other parameters include the presence of lifeguards, litter bins and recycling facilities – meaning some wild beaches may not earn the award, but are still stunning nonetheless.

BUSINESS HOURS
Shops, Banks & Post Offices
Monday to Friday, most shops and post offices operate 9am to 5pm (possibly 5.30pm or 6pm in cities). Banks open at 9.30am. Saturday, shops open 9am to 5pm, and banks (main branches only) open 9.30am to 1pm. Post offices may open all or half-day Saturday. Sunday shopping hours are around 10am to 4pm or 11am to 5pm, but banks and post offices are closed.

London and other cities have 24/7 convenience stores, but in smaller towns shops often close at weekends and for lunch (normally 1pm to 2pm), and in country areas on Wednesday or Thursday afternoon too. In cities and large towns there's usually 'late-night' shopping on Thursday – up to about 7pm or 8pm.

Museums & Sights
Large museums and places of interest are usually open every day. Some smaller places open five or six days per week, usually including Saturday and Sunday and often closed on Monday and/or Tuesday. Much depends on the time of year, too; they'll open daily in high season but just at weekends (or shorter hours) in quieter periods.

Restaurants & Cafes
Restaurants in England open for lunch (about noon to 3pm) *and* dinner (about 6pm to 11pm – earlier in smaller towns, midnight or later in cities), or they might open for lunch *or* dinner – usually every day of the week, although some close on Sunday evening, or all day Monday.

Cafes and teashops vary according to location. In towns and cities, cafes may open from 7am, providing breakfast for people on their way to work. In country areas, teashops will open in time for lunch, and may stay open until 7pm or later in the summer, catering to tourists leaving stately homes or hikers

down from the hill. In winter months country cafe and restaurant hours are cut back, while some places close completely from October to Easter.

Throughout this book we indicate if restaurants and cafes are open for lunch or dinner or both, but precise opening times and days are given only if they differ markedly from the pattern outlined here.

Pubs, Bars & Clubs
Pubs in towns and country areas usually open daily from 11am to 11pm Sunday to Thursday, sometimes to midnight or 1am Friday and Saturday. Most open all day, although some may shut from 3pm to 6pm. Throughout this book, we don't list pub opening and closing times unless they vary significantly from these hours.

In cities some pubs open until midnight or later, but it's mostly bars and clubs that have taken advantage of relatively recent licensing laws ('the provision of late-night refreshment', as it's officially called) until stay open to 2am or beyond. As every place is different, we list opening hours for bars and clubs.

CHILDREN
Many national parks and resort towns organise activities for children, especially in the school holiday periods (see p796), and local tourist offices are a great source of information on kid-friendly attractions.

Some hotels welcome kids (with their parents) and provide cots, toys and babysitting services, while others prefer to maintain an adult atmosphere, so you need to check this in advance. Likewise restaurants: some will have crayons and highchairs, and not mind if the menu lands on the floor; others firmly say 'no children after 6pm'. Pubs and bars ban under-18s, unless they're specifically 'family-friendly' places – and many are, especially those serving food.

Breastfeeding in public remains mildly controversial, but if done modestly is usually considered OK. On the sticky topic of dealing with nappies while travelling, most museums and historical attractions have good baby-changing facilities (cue old joke: I swapped mine for a nice souvenir), as do department stores. Elsewhere, you'll find facilities in motorway service stations and city-centre toilets – although these can be a bit grimy.

For more advice see www.babygoes2.com – packed with tips and encouragement for parents on the move.

CLIMATE CHARTS

England's changeable weather is discussed on p20. The charts shown here give details for specific regions.

CUSTOMS

The UK has a two-tier customs system – one for goods bought in another European Union (EU) country where taxes and duties have already been paid, and the other for goods bought duty-free outside the EU. Below is a summary of the rules; for more details go to www.hmce.gov.uk and search for 'Customs Allowances'.

Duty Free

If you bring duty-free goods from *outside* the EU, the limits include 200 cigarettes, 2L of still wine, plus 1L of spirits or another 2L of wine, 60cc of perfume, and other duty-free goods (including beer) to the value of £145.

Tax & Duty Paid

There is no limit to the goods you can bring from *within* the EU (if taxes have been paid), but customs officials use the following guidelines to distinguish personal use from commercial imports: 3200 cigarettes, 200 cigars, 10L of spirits, 20L of fortified wine, 90L of wine and 110L of beer. Still enough to have one hell of a party.

DANGERS & ANNOYANCES

England is a remarkably safe country, considering the wealth disparities you'll see in many areas, but crime is certainly not unknown in London and other cities, so you should take care, especially at night. When travelling by tube, tram or urban train service, choose a carriage containing other people. It's also best to avoid some deserted suburban tube stations at night; a bus or taxi can be a safer choice.

As well as licensed taxis and minicabs (see p809), unlicensed minicabs – essentially a bloke with a car earning money on the side – operate in large cities, but these are worth avoiding unless you know what you're doing. Annoyances include driving round in circles, then charging an enormous fare. Dangers

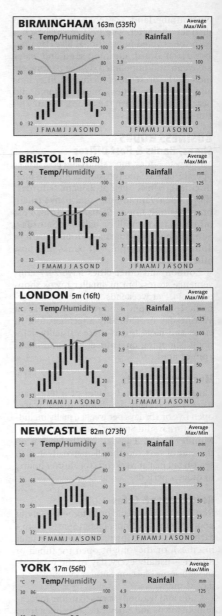

include driving to a remote location then robbery or rape. To avoid this, use a metered taxi or phone a reputable minicab company and get an up-front quote for the ride. London and other cities have websites and phone lines to help you find licensed cabs; details are in the relevant chapters of this book.

On the main streets of big cities, mugging or bag-snatching is rare, but money and important documents are best kept out of sight and out of reach. Pickpockets operate in crowded public places such as stations or bars (bags and jackets hanging on chair-backs are popular targets), so make sure your stuff is secure here too.

In large hotels, don't leave valuables lying around; put them in your bag or use the safe if there is one. Do the same at city B&Bs, although in rural areas there's far less risk. In hostel dorms, especially independent/backpacker hostels in cities, keep your stuff packed away and carry valuables with you. Many hostels provide lockers, but you need your own padlock.

If driving, remove luggage from the car when parking overnight in cities and towns. The same applies even in some apparently safe rural locations. While you're out walking in the countryside, someone may well be walking off with your belongings. Where possible, look for secure parking areas near tourist offices.

DISCOUNT CARDS

There's no specific discount card for visitors to England, although travel cards (see p807) are discounted for younger and older people. Membership of the YHA (see p789) can get you discounts in bookshops and outdoor gear shops, and on some public transport.

EMBASSIES & CONSULATES

This selection of embassies, consulates and high commissions in London will be useful if you're from overseas and, for example, lost your passport. But they won't be much help if you're in trouble for committing a crime; even as a foreigner, you're bound by English laws.

Australia (Map pp104-5; ☎ 020-7379 4334; www.australia .org.uk; The Strand, WC2B 4LA)
Canada (Map pp104-5; ☎ 020-7258 6600; www.canada .org.uk; 1 Grosvenor Sq, W1X 0AB)
China (Map pp104-5; ☎ 020-7299 4049; www.chinese -embassy.org.uk; 49-51 Portland Pl, London W1B 4JL)

> **TRACE THE ANCESTORS**
>
> If you're a visitor with ancestors from England, your trip could be a good chance to find out more about them – or simply find long-lost relatives. The best place to start is the website of the **Family Records Centre** (www.familyrecords.gov.uk), full of advice on tracing family history, covering topics such as records of births, deaths, marriages, immigration and adoption, and with links to numerous other handy resource sites. The Family Records Centre cannot search individual records for you, but the **Association of Genealogists & Researchers in Archives** (www.agra.org.uk) lists professional researchers who can.

France (☎ 020-7073 1000; www.ambafrance-uk.org; 58 Knightsbridge, SW1 7JT)
Germany (Map pp104-5; ☎ 020-7824 1300; www .london.diplo.de; 23 Belgrave Sq, SW1X 8PX)
Ireland (Map pp104-5; ☎ 020-7235 2171; www .embassyofireland.co.uk;17 Grosvenor Pl, SW1X 7HR)
Japan (Map pp104-5; ☎ 020-7465 6500; www.uk.emb -japan.go.jp; 101 Piccadilly, W1J 7JT)
Netherlands (☎ 020-7590 3200; www.netherlands -embassy.org.uk; 38 Hyde Park Gate, SW7 5DP)
New Zealand (☎ 020-7930 8422; www.nzembassy .com/uk; 80 Haymarket, SW1Y 4TQ)
Poland (☎ 0870 774 2700; www.polishembassy.org.uk; 47 Portland Pl, London W1B 1HQ)
USA (Map pp104-5; ☎ 020-7499 9000; www.usembassy .org.uk; 24 Grosvenor Sq, W1A 1AE)

For a complete list of foreign embassies in the UK, see the website of the **Foreign & Commonwealth Office** (www.fco.gov.uk), which also lists Britain's diplomatic missions overseas.

FOOD

For a flavour of England's cuisine, see the Food & Drink chapter (p73). Throughout this book, most Eating sections are divided into three price bands: budget (up to £8), midrange (£8-16) and top end (over £16).

GAY & LESBIAN TRAVELLERS

England is a generally tolerant place for gays and lesbians. London, Manchester and Brighton have flourishing gay scenes, and in other sizeable cities (even some small towns) you'll find communities not entirely in the closet. That said, you'll still find pockets of homophobic hostility in some areas.

For info, listings and contacts, see monthly magazines (and websites) **Gay Times** (www.gay times.co.uk) and **Diva** (www.divamag.co.uk), or the twice-monthly **Pink Paper** (www.pinkpaper.com). In the capital, a useful source of information is the **London Lesbian & Gay Switchboard** (☎ 020-7837 7324; www.llgs.org.uk); there are similar services in cities and regions across the country. See also the boxes of specific information in the major city sections throughout this book.

HOLIDAYS
Public Holidays
In England and Wales, most businesses and banks close on these official public holidays (hence the term 'bank holiday'):

New Year's Day 1 January
Easter March/April (Good Friday to Easter Monday inclusive)
May Day First Monday in May
Spring Bank Holiday Last Monday in May
Summer Bank Holiday Last Monday in August
Christmas Day 25 December
Boxing Day 26 December

If a public holiday falls on a weekend, the nearest Monday is usually taken instead.

On public holidays, some small museums and places of interest close, but larger attractions specifically gear up and have their busiest times, although nearly everything closes on Christmas Day. Generally speaking, if a place closes on Sunday, it'll probably be shut on bank holidays as well.

As well as attractions, virtually everything – shops, banks, offices – closes on Christmas Day, although pubs are open at lunchtime. There's usually no public transport on Christmas Day, and a very minimal service on Boxing Day.

School Holidays
Most schools have three main terms, interspersed with three main holidays (when roads get busy and hotel prices go up), although the exact dates vary from year to year and region to region:

Easter Holiday Week before and week after Easter
Summer Holiday Third week of July to first week of September
Christmas Holiday Mid-December to first week of January.

There are also three week-long 'half-term' school holidays – usually late February (or early March), late May and late October. Some regions are moving towards six terms (and six holidays) of more equal length

INSURANCE
Regardless of nationality, everyone receives free *emergency* treatment at accident and emergency (A&E) departments of state-run National Health Service (NHS) hospitals. For other medical treatment, many countries have reciprocal health agreements with the UK, meaning visitors from overseas get the same standard of care from hospitals and doctors as any British citizen. Travel insurance, however, is still highly recommended as it offers greater flexibility over where and how you're treated. It will usually cover medical consultation and treatment at a private clinics – which can be quicker than NHS places – and emergency dental care. Travel insurance will cover loss of baggage or valuable items (such as a camera) and, most important, the cost of any emergency flights home. For more medical information see the Health chapter (p812). Car insurance is covered on p807. Worldwide travel insurance is available at www.lonelyplanet.com/travel_services. You can buy, extend and claim online anytime – even if you're already on the road.

INTERNET ACCESS
Internet cafes are surprisingly rare in England, especially once you get away from tourist spots. Most charge from £1 per hour, and out in the sticks you can pay up to £5 per hour. Public libraries often have computers with free internet access, but only for 30-minute slots, and demand is high. All the usual warnings apply about keystroke-capturing software and other security risks – especially if you're using the internet to keep tabs on, say, your banking while on the move. For information on websites about England, see the Internet Resources section on p24.

If you'll be using your laptop to get online, your connection cable may not fit in English sockets, although adaptors are easy to buy at electrical stores in airports or city centres. Sockets are thankfully becoming a thing of the past as an increasing number of hotels, hostels, stations and coffee shops (even some trains) have wi-fi access, charging anything from nothing to £5 per hour. Throughout this book, we use an ⌨ icon to show if a place has PCs for public use and '□ wi-fi' if it has wi-fi.

LEGAL MATTERS
Driving Crimes & Transport Fines
Drink-driving is a serious offence. See the Transport chapter for more information and details about speed limits (p808) and parking rules (p808).

On buses and trains (including the London Underground), people without a valid ticket for their journey may be fined – usually around £20 – on the spot.

Antisocial Behaviour
On-the-spot fines, or immediate fines (as for driving offences), can be imposed by police for antisocial behaviour, which includes drinking in public and littering.

Drugs
Illegal drugs are widely available, especially in clubs. All the usual dangers apply and there have been much-publicised deaths associated with ecstasy. Cannabis possession is a criminal offence; punishment for carrying a small amount may be a warning – or a fine or imprisonment. Dealers face stiffer penalties, as do people caught with any other 'recreational' drugs.

Age Restrictions
You must be over 18 to buy alcohol, but over-16s may buy cigarettes. You usually have to be 18 to enter a pub or bar, although the rules are different if you have a meal. Some bars and clubs are over-21 only.

MAPS
For a map of the whole country, a road atlas is handy – especially if you're travelling by car. The main publishers are Ordnance Survey (OS) and Automobile Association (AA), with atlases in all sizes and scales. If you plan to use minor roads, you'll need a scale of about 1:200,000 (3 miles to 1in). Most road atlases cost £5 to £10 and are updated annually, which means old editions are sold off every January – look for bargains at motorway service stations.

For greater detail, the OS *Landrangers* (1:50,000) are ideal for walking and cycling. OS *Explorer* maps (1:25,000) are even better for walking in lowland areas, but can sometimes be hard to read in complex mountain

landscapes. Your best choice here is the excellent specialist series produced for ramblers, walkers, mountaineers and other outdoor types by **Harvey Maps** (www.harveymaps.co.uk), covering upland areas and national parks, plus routes for hikers and bikers.

If you're spending any length of time in London, iconic A-Z street maps (online and in book form) are incredibly detailed and invaluable. The books are sold at newsagents and souvenir shops – remember to pronounce it 'A to Zed'. Similar street maps are available for other cities and big towns across the country.

MONEY
The currency of England (and Britain) is the pound sterling. Paper money comes in £5, £10, £20 and £50 denominations, although £50s can be difficult to change because fakes circulate. Prices quoted in this book are in UK pounds (£), unless otherwise stated, although other currencies are very rarely accepted if you're buying goods and services, except for some places in the ferry ports of southern England, which take euros, and the smarter souvenir and gift shops in London, which may take euros, US dollars, yen and other major currencies. A guide to exchange rates is given on the inside front cover of this book, and there are some pointers on costs on p20.

ATMs
Debit or credit cards are perfect companions – the best invention for travellers since the backpack. You can use them in most shops, and withdraw cash from ATMs (often called 'cash machines') which are easy to find in cities and even small towns. But ATMs aren't fail-safe, and it's a major headache if your only card gets swallowed, so take a backup. And watch out for ATMs which might have been tampered with; a common ruse is to attach a card-reader to the slot; your card is scanned and the number used for fraud.

Credit & Debit Cards
Visa and MasterCard credit and debit cards are widely accepted in England, and are good for larger hotels, restaurants, shopping, flights, long-distance travel, car hire etc. Smaller businesses, such as pubs or B&Bs, prefer debit cards (or charge a fee for credit cards), and some take cash or cheque only.

Since early 2006, nearly all credit and debit cards use the 'Chip and PIN' system; instead of signing, you enter a PIN (personal identification number). If you're from overseas, and your card isn't Chip and PIN enabled, you should be able to sign in the usual way, but some places will not accept your card.

Moneychangers

Finding a place to change your money (cash or travellers cheques) into pounds is never a problem in cities, where banks and bureaus compete for business. Be careful using bureaus, however; some offer poor rates or levy outrageous commissions. You can also change money at some post offices – very handy in country areas, and exchange rates are fair (and usually commission free).

Tipping & Bargaining

In restaurants you're expected to leave a tip of around 10%, but at smarter restaurants in larger cities waiters can get a bit sniffy if the tip isn't nearer 12% or even 15%. Either way, it's important to remember that you're not obliged to tip if the service or food was unsatisfactory (even if it's been added to your bill as a 'service charge'). At smarter cafes and teashops with table service, around 10% is fine. If you're paying with a credit or debit card and you want to add the tip to the bill, it's worth asking the waiting staff if they'll actually receive it. Some prefer to receive tips in cash.

Taxi drivers also expect tips (about 10%, or rounded up to the nearest pound), especially in London. It's less usual to tip minicab drivers. Toilet attendants (if you see them loitering) may get tipped around 50p.

In pubs, when you order drinks at the bar, or order and pay for food at the bar, tips are not expected. If you order food at the table and your meal is brought to you, then a tip may be appropriate – if the food and service have been good, of course.

Bargaining is rare, although it's occasionally encountered at markets. It's fine to ask if there are student discounts on items such as theatre tickets, books or outdoor equipment.

Travellers Cheques

Travellers cheques offer protection from theft, so are safer than wads of cash, but are rarely used in England, as credit/debit cards and ATMs have become the method of choice. If you prefer travellers cheques, note that they are rarely accepted for purchases (except at large hotels), so for cash you'll still need to go to a bank or bureau.

POST

There are two classes of post within the UK: a standard letter costs 36p first-class (normally delivered next day) and 27p second-class (up to three days). The cost goes up if the letter is heavier than 100g, larger than 240x165mm or thicker than 5mm, and up again if heavier than 750g and bigger than 353x250x25mm. Stamps are available at post offices, and there's usually a handy device for checking the size of your letters before you buy. Stamps for straightforward 1st and 2nd class mail can also be bought at shops and newsagents. Letters by airmail start at 50p to EU countries and 56p to the rest of the world (up to 10g). For details on all prices, see www.postoffice.co.uk.

TELEPHONE

England's iconic red phone boxes can still be seen in city streets and especially in conservation areas, although many have been replaced by soulless glass cubicles. With the advent of mobile phones (cellphones), many phone booths have been removed and not replaced at all. Where they do exist, public phones usually accept coins and credit/debit cards. The minimum charge is 20p.

Area codes in Britain do not have a standard format and vary in length, which can be confusing for foreigners (and locals). For example ☎ 020 for London, ☎ 0161 for Manchester, ☎ 01225 for Bath, ☎ 015394 for Ambleside, followed as usual by the individual number. In this book, area codes and individual numbers are listed together, separated by a hyphen.

As well as the geographical area codes, other codes include: ☎ 0500 or ☎ 0800 for free calls and ☎ 0845 for calls at local rate, wherever you're dialling from within the UK. Numbers starting with ☎ 087 are charged at national-call rate, while numbers starting with ☎ 089 or ☎ 09 are premium rate, and should be specified by the company using the number (eg in their advertising literature), so you know the cost before you call. (These codes and numbers are not separated by hyphens, as you always have to dial the whole number.) Note that many numbers starting with 08 or 09 do not work if you're calling from outside the UK, or if they do you'll be charged for a full international call – and then some.

Codes for mobile phones usually start with ☎ 07 – more expensive than calling a landline.

International Calls

To call outside the UK dial ☎ 00, then the country code (☎ 1 for USA, ☎ 61 for Australia etc), the area code (you usually drop the initial zero) and the number.

Direct-dialled calls to most overseas countries can be made from most public telephones, and it's usually cheaper between 8pm and 8am Monday to Friday and at weekends. You can usually save money by buying a phonecard (usually denominated £5, £10 or £20) with a PIN that you use from any phone by dialling an access number (you don't insert it into the machine). There are dozens of cards, usually available from city newsagents, with rates of the various companies often vividly displayed.

To make reverse-charge (collect) calls, dial ☎ 155 for the international operator. It's expensive, but at least the person at the other end is paying.

To call England from abroad, dial your country's international access code, then ☎ 44 (the UK's country code), then the area code (dropping the first 0) and the phone number.

Most internet cafes now have Skype or some other sort of VOIP system, so you can make international calls for the price of your time online.

Local & National Calls

From public phones the weekday rate is about 5p per minute; evenings and weekends are cheaper, but still with a minimum charge of 20p. Local calls (within 35 miles) are cheaper than national calls. All calls are cheaper between 6pm and 8am Monday to Thursday, and from 6pm Friday to 8am Monday. From private phones, rates vary between telecom providers.

For the operator, call ☎ 100. For directory inquiries, a host of agencies compete for your business and charge from 10p to 40p; numbers include ☎ 118 192, ☎ 118 118, ☎ 118 500 and ☎ 118 811.

Mobile Phones

Around 50 million people in the UK have mobile phones, and thus the ability to tell their loved ones they're on the train. The terse medium of SMS is a national passion, with a billion text messages sent monthly.

Phones in the UK use GSM 900/1800, which is compatible with Europe and Australia but not with North America or Japan (although phones that work globally are increasingly common).

Even if your phone works in the UK, because it's registered overseas a call to someone just up the road will be routed internationally and charged accordingly. An option is to buy a local SIM card (around £30), which includes a UK number, and use that in your own handset (as long as your phone isn't locked by your home network).

A second option is to buy a pay-as-you-go phone (from around £50, including SIM and number); to stay in credit, you buy 'top-up' cards at newsagents.

TIME

Wherever you are in the world, time is measured in relation to Greenwich Mean Time (GMT, or Universal Time Coordinated, UTC as it's more accurately called), so a highlight for many visitors to London is a trip to Greenwich and its famous line dividing the western and eastern hemispheres.

To give you an idea, if it is noon in London, it is 4am on the same day in San Francisco, 7am in New York and 10pm in Sydney. British summer time (BST) is Britain's daylight saving; one hour ahead of GMT from late March to late October.

TOURIST INFORMATION

Before leaving home, check the informative, comprehensive and wide-ranging websites **VisitBritain** (www.visitbritain.com) and **EnjoyEngland** (www.enjoyengland.com), covering all the angles of national tourism, with links to numerous other sites. Details about local and regional websites and tourist organisations listed throughout this book.

Tourist Offices Abroad

In recent years, VisitBritain has moved away from physical offices in overseas capitals, and instead improved their web-based services. From the www.visitbritain.com portal you can follow links to a wealth of information on Britain aimed at visitors from many different countries and in many different languages. For specific questions, you can email your nearest VisitBritain office via the website, but only a few have public phone numbers. Main contacts include the following:

Australia (☎ 1300 85 85 89; www.visitbritain.com/au; 15 Blue St, North Sydney, NSW 2060)
Canada (☎ 1 888 847 4885; www.visitbritain.com/ca)
France (www.visitbritain.com/fr)
Germany (www.visitbritain.com/de)
Netherlands (www.visitbritain.com/nl)
New Zealand (☎ 0800 700741; www.visitbritain.com/nz)
USA (☎ 800 462 2748; www.visitbritain.com/us)

Local Tourist Offices

All English cities and towns (and some villages) have a tourist information centre (TIC). Some TICs are run by national parks and often have small exhibits about the area. You'll also see visitor welcome centres or visitor information centres, often run by chambers of commerce or civic trusts. For ease we've called all these places 'tourist offices' in this book. Whatever the name, these places have helpful staff, books and maps for sale, leaflets to give away and loads of advice on things to see or do. They can also assist with booking accommodation. Most tourist offices keep regular business hours; in quiet areas they close from October to March, while in popular areas they open daily year-round. For a list of all tourist offices around Britain see www.visitmap.info/tic.

Look out for tourist information points – usually a rack of leaflets about local attractions set up in a post office or shop in a village not big enough to have its own full-on tourist office.

TRAVELLERS WITH DISABILITIES

If you happen to be us wheelchair or crutches, or just find moving about a bit tricky, you'll find England a mixed bag. All new buildings have wheelchair access, and even hotels in grand old country houses often have lifts, ramps and other facilities added, although smaller B&Bs are often harder to adapt, so you'll have less choice here. In the same way, you might find a restaurant with ramps and excellent wheelchair-access loo, but tables so close you can't get past.

When getting around in cities, new buses have low floors for easy access, but few have conductors who can lend a hand when you're getting on or off. Many taxis take wheelchairs, or just have more room in the back, so that might be a better way to go.

For long-distance travel, coaches may present problems if you can't walk, but the main operator, **National Express** (www.nationalexpress.com) has wheelchair-friendly coaches on many routes, with plans for more. For details, ring their dedicated Disabled Passenger Travel Helpline on ☎ 0121-423 8479 or try the website. On most inter-city trains there's more room and better facilities, and usually station staff around; just have a word and they'll be happy to help.

Useful organisations and websites
All Go Here (www.allgohere.com) Comprehensive info on hotels and travel.
Disability UK (www.disabilityuk.com) Excellent information resource; shopping, benefits, diseases, drugs, and more.
Good Access Guide (www.goodaccessguide.co.uk) The name says it all.
Holiday Care Service (☎ 0845 124 9971; www.holidaycare.org.uk) Travel and holiday information; publisher of numerous booklets on UK travel.
Royal Association for Disability & Rehabilitation (RADAR; ☎ 020-7250 3222; www.radar.org.uk) Published titles include *Holidays in Britain and Ireland*. Through RADAR you can get a key for 7000 public disabled toilets across the UK.
Shopmobility (www.shopmobilityuk.org) Directory of cities and towns across Britain where manual or powered wheelchairs can be hired, often for free.

VISAS

If you're a European Economic Area (EEA) national, you don't need a visa to visit (or work in) England or any other part of the UK. Citizens of Australia, Canada, New Zealand, South Africa and the USA are given leave to enter the UK at their point of arrival for up to six months (three months for some nationalities), but are prohibited from working. If you intend to work, see opposite.

UK immigration authorities are tough, and if they suspect you're here for more than a holiday, you may need to prove that you have funds to support yourself, details of any hotels or local tours booked, or personal letters from people you'll be visiting. Having a return ticket helps.

Visa and entry regulations are always subject to change, so it's vital to check before leaving

HISTORY TIPS

For many visitors, a highlight of a journey through England is visiting the numerous castles and historic sites that pepper the country. Membership of the **National Trust** (NT; ☎ 0844 800 1895; www.nationaltrust.org.uk) and **English Heritage** (EH; ☎ 0870 333 1181; www.english-heritage.org.uk) gets you free admission (quite a saving when individual entry to NT sites can be around £5, while EH sites range from free to about £6), as well as reciprocal arrangements with other heritage organisations (in Wales, Scotland and beyond), information handbooks and so on. You can join at the first NT or EH site you visit. If you are a member of a similar organisation in your own country, this may get you free or discounted entry at NT and EH sites in England.

The NT protects hundreds of historic buildings plus vast tracts of land with scenic importance. Annual membership costs £46 (with discounts for under-26s and families), reduced by about 25% if you pay by direct debit. Alternatively, a Touring Pass allows free entry to NT properties for one/two weeks (£19/24 per person); families and couples get cheaper rates.

English Heritage is a state-funded organisation responsible for numerous historic sites. Annual membership costs £42 (couples and seniors get discounts). An Overseas Visitors Pass allows free entry to most sites for seven/14 days for £19/23 (with cheaper rates for couples and families).

We have included the relevant acronym (NT or EH) in the information brackets after properties listed throughout this book.

home. Your first stop should be www.ukvisas .gov.uk or www.ukba.homeoffice.gov.uk, and if you still have queries contact your local British embassy, high commission or consulate.

WEIGHTS & MEASURES

England is in transition when it comes to weights and measures, as it has been for the last 40 odd years – and probably will be for 40 more. For length and distance, most people still use the imperial units of inches, feet, yards and miles, although mountain heights on maps are given in metres.

For weight, many people use pounds and ounces, even though since January 2000 goods in shops must be measured in kilograms. And nobody knows their weight in pounds or kilograms; Brits weigh themselves in stones, an archaic unit of 14 pounds.

When it comes to volume, things are even worse: most liquids are sold in litres or half-litres, except milk and beer – which are available in pints. Garages sell petrol priced in pence per litre, but measure car performance in miles per gallon. Great, isn't it?

In this book we have reflected this wacky system of mixed measurements. Heights are given in metres (m) and distances in miles and metres. For conversion tables, see the inside front cover.

WOMEN TRAVELLERS

Occasional wolf whistles from building sites aside, solo women will find England fairly enlightened. There's nothing to stop women going into pubs alone, for example (although you may feel conspicuous in a few places). Restaurants may assume you're waiting for a date unless you specify a table for one, but it's no big deal once you've clarified.

Safety is not a major issue, although commonsensical caution should be observed when walking in big cities, especially at night. Hitching is always unwise, and see p794 for advice on travel by minicab. Unfortunately, women having their drinks spiked with 'date-rape drugs' can be a problem in some bars and clubs, so once again precautions (such as not leaving your drink unattended) should be taken.

The contraceptive pill is available free on prescription in England, as is the morning-after pill (also on sale at chemists/pharmacies). Most cities have Well Woman Clinics that can advise on general health issues; they're listed in the local phone book. Most cities and towns have a rape crisis centre, where information or counselling is free and confidential; see www.rapecrisis.org.uk.

WORK

Nationals of most European countries don't need a permit to work in England, but everyone else does. If you're a non-European and work is the main purpose of your visit, you must be sponsored by an English company.

Exceptions include most Commonwealth citizens with a UK-born parent; the 'Right of

DIRECTORY

Abode' allows you to live and work in England and the rest of the UK. Most Commonwealth citizens under 31 are eligible for a Working Holidaymaker Visa. It's valid for two years, you can work for a total of 12 months, and it must be obtained in advance, but you're not allowed to establish a business or work as a professional athlete.

Once you've got permission to work, the next step is finding some. Many bars, restaurants and shops in London seem to be staffed by Australasians, so that gives a clue to one option – and it's not restricted to London at all. Some visitors arrange work in small towns and villages in remote areas, and enjoy getting under the skin of a local community for a few months. Other options include teaching in language schools, nursing, nannying and general office temping. Obviously, you'll need to appropriate qualifications and other paperwork for some of these jobs.

Useful websites are listed below. Also very useful is the 'Living & Working Abroad' thread on the Thorntree forum at lonelyplanet.com.

BUNAC (www.bunac.org)

Go Work Go Travel (www.goworkgotravel.com) Working holidays worldwide, including the UK.

UK Border Agency (www.ukba.homeoffice.gov.uk)

UK Employment & Recruitment Agencies (www.employmentrecruitment.co.uk)

Working Holiday Guru (www.workingholidayguru.com) Aimed mainly at Australians coming to Europe.

Transport

CONTENTS

GETTING THERE & AWAY

London is a global transport hub, so you can easily fly to England from just about anywhere in the world. In recent years, the massive growth of budget ('no-frills') airlines has increased the number of routes – and reduced the fares – between England and other countries in Europe.

Your other main option for travel between England and mainland Europe is ferry, either port-to-port or combined with a long-distance bus trip – this type of travel has less environmental impact than flying, although journeys can be long and financial savings not huge compared with budget airfares. International trains are much more comfortable, and another 'green' option; the Channel Tunnel allows direct rail services between England, France and Belgium, with onward connections to many other European destinations.

THINGS CHANGE...

The information in this chapter is particularly vulnerable to change. Check directly with the airline or a travel agent to make sure you understand how a fare (and ticket you may buy) works and be aware of the security requirements for international travel. Shop carefully. The details given in this chapter should be regarded as pointers and are not a substitute for your own careful, up-to-date research.

Getting from England to Scotland and Wales is easy. The bus and train systems are fully integrated and in most cases you won't even know you've crossed the border. Passports are not required – although some Scots and Welsh may think they should be!

Flights, tours and rail tickets can be booked online by accessing www.lonely planet.com/travel_services.

AIR

Airports

London's main airports for international flights are Heathrow and Gatwick. Luton and Stansted deal largely with charter and budget European flights, and London City Airport specialises in business flights. For details on getting between these airports and central London, see p169.

Some planes on European and long-haul routes go direct to major regional airports including Manchester, while smaller regional airports such as Southampton and Birmingham are served by flights to and from continental Europe and Ireland.

HEATHROW

Some 15 miles west of central London, **Heathrow** (LHR; ☎ 0870 000 0123; www.heathrowairport .com) is the world's busiest airport, often chaotic and crowded, with five terminals. Check which terminal your flight departs from.

GATWICK

Smaller than Heathrow, but still the UK's number-two airport, **Gatwick** (LGW; ☎ 0870 000 2468; www.gatwickairport.com) is 30 miles south of central London.

STANSTED

London's third-busiest airport, **Stansted** (STN; ☎ 0870 000 0303; www.stanstedairport.com) is 35 miles northeast of central London, and one of Europe's fastest-growing airports.

LUTON

Some 35 miles north of central London, **Luton** (LTN; ☎ 01582-405100; www.london-luton.co.uk) is especially well-known as a holiday flight airport.

CLIMATE CHANGE & TRAVEL

Climate change is a serious threat to the ecosystems that humans rely upon, and air travel is the fastest-growing contributor to the problem. Lonely Planet regards travel, overall, as a global benefit, but believes we all have a responsibility to limit our personal impact on global warming.

Flying & Climate Change

Pretty much every form of motor travel generates CO_2 (the main cause of human-induced climate change) but planes are far and away the worst offenders, not just because of the sheer distances they allow us to travel, but because they release greenhouse gases high into the atmosphere. The statistics are frightening: two people taking a return flight between Europe and the US will contribute as much to climate change as an average household's gas and electricity consumption over a whole year.

Carbon Offset Schemes

Climatecare.org and other websites use 'carbon calculators' that allow jetsetters to offset the greenhouse gases they are responsible for with contributions to energy-saving projects and other climate-friendly initiatives in the developing world – including projects in India, Honduras, Kazakhstan and Uganda.

Lonely Planet, together with Rough Guides and other concerned partners in the travel industry, supports the carbon offset scheme run by climatecare.org. Lonely Planet offsets all of its staff and author travel.

For more information check out our website: lonelyplanet.com.

LONDON CITY

A few miles east of central London, **London City** (LCY; ☎ 020-7646 0088; www.londoncityairport.com) has flights to/from European and other UK airports.

MANCHESTER

In northern England, the airport for England's second city, **Manchester** (MAN; ☎ 08712 710711; www.manchesterairport.co.uk) is increasingly busy with direct flights to/from Europe, the Gulf states, South Asia and beyond.

Airlines

Most of the world's major airlines have services to England from many parts of the world, and budget airlines fly between England and other European countries. Charter flights are another option; you can buy seat-only deals on the planes that carry tourists between, for example, England and numerous Mediterranean resorts. The best deals are usually available online, and to save going to every airline's site individually, it's worth using an internet travel agency or price comparison site; these include the following:

Cheapflights.co.uk (www.cheapflights.co.uk)
Expedia (www.expedia.com)
Flightline.co.uk (www.flightline.co.uk)
LowCostAirlines.org (www.lowcostairlines.org)

skyscanner (www.skyscanner.com)
Travelocity Travel (www.travelocity.com)

Tickets

Because London is one of the world's main air travel hubs, there's coemption between the airlines, and that means competitive fares. You can purchase your airline ticket from a travel agency (in person, by telephone or on the internet), or direct from the airline (the best deals are often available online only). It always pays to shop around. Internet travel agencies work well if you're doing a straightforward trip, but for anything even slightly complex there's no substitute for a real-live travel agent who knows the system, the options, the special deals and so on.

Australia & New Zealand

The route to England from the southern hemisphere is very popular, with a wide range of fares from about AUD$1500 to AUD$3000 return. From New Zealand it's often best to go via Australia. Round-the-world tickets can sometimes work out cheaper than a straightforward return.

Continental Europe

You can fly between England and pretty much every capital city in Europe (and many other cities too), using national airlines such as Air France, Lufthansa and so on, or budget airlines such as Ryanair, easyJet and Virgin Express.

Ireland

There are numerous flights each day between the capitals Dublin and London, and many more between other cities in Ireland and England. If you book early and avoid the busy periods (such as Friday afternoon and evening), fares on budget airlines can be just a few pounds or euros.

Canada & the USA

There's a continuous price war on the world's busiest transcontinental route. Return fares from the east coast to London range from US$300 to US$600. From the west coast, fares are about US$100 higher.

LAND
Bus

You can easily get between England and other European countries via long-distance bus or coach. The international network **Eurolines** (www.eurolines.com) connects a huge number of destinations; the website is full of information on routes and options, and you can buy tickets online via one of the national operators. Services to/from England are operated by **National Express** (www.nationalexpress.com) and some sample journey times to/from London are: Amsterdam 12 hours; Paris eight or nine hours; Dublin 12 hours; Barcelona 24 hour. If you book early, and can be flexible with timings (ie travel when few other people want to) you can get some very good deals – some branded as 'fun fares' and 'promo fares'. For example, London to Paris or Amsterdam one-way starts at just £18, although paying nearer £25 is more usual. It's still worth checking the budget airlines, though. You may pay a similar fare and knock a large chunk off the journey time.

Train
CHANNEL TUNNEL SERVICES

The Channel Tunnel makes direct train travel between England and continental Europe a fast and enjoyable option. High-speed **Eurostar** (☎ 08705 186 186; www.eurostar.com) passenger services hurtle at least 10 times daily between London and Paris (the journey takes 2½ hours) or Brussels (two hours). You can buy tickets from travel agencies, major train

stations or direct from the Eurostar website. The normal single fare between London and Paris/Brussels is around £150, but if you buy in advance and travel at a less busy period, deals drop to around £90 return or less. You can also buy 'through fare' tickets from many cities in England – for example York to Paris, or Manchester to Brussels. You can also get very good train and hotel combination deals – bizarrely sometimes cheaper than train fare only.

If you've got a car, use **Eurotunnel** (☎ 08705 353535; www.eurotunnel.com). At Folkestone in England or Calais in France, you drive onto a train, go through the tunnel and drive off at the other end. The trains run about four times an hour from 6am to 10pm, then hourly. Loading and unloading is an hour; the journey takes 35 minutes. You can book in advance direct with Eurotunnel or pay on the spot (cash or credit card). The standard one-way cost for a car (and passengers) is £90 to £150 depending on the time of day (less busy times are cheaper). Promotional fares often bring the cost nearer to £50.

TRAIN & FERRY CONNECTIONS

As well as Eurostar, many 'normal' trains run between England and mainland Europe. You buy one ticket, but get off the train at the port, walk onto a ferry, then get another train on the other side. Routes include Amsterdam–London (via Hook of Holland and Harwich). Travelling between Ireland and England, the main train-ferry-train route is Dublin to London, via Dun Laoghaire and Holyhead. Ferries also run between Rosslare and Fishguard or Pembroke (Wales), with train connections on either side.

SEA

The main ferry routes between England and Ireland include Holyhead to Dun Laoghaire. Between England and mainland Europe, ferry routes include Dover to Calais or Boulogne (France), Harwich to Hook of Holland (Netherlands), Hull to Zeebrugge (Belgium) and Rotterdam (Netherlands), Portsmouth to Santander or Bilbao (Spain), and Newcastle to Bergen (Norway) or Gothenberg (Sweden). There are many more.

Competition from Eurotunnel and budget airlines has forced ferry operators to discount heavily and offer flexible fares, meaning great bargains at quiet times of day or year. For example, the short cross-channel routes such as Dover to Calais or Boulogne can be as low as £20 for a car plus up to five passengers, although around £50 is more likely. If you're a foot passenger, or cycling, there's often less need to book ahead, and cheap fares on the short crossings start from about £10 each way.

Some ferry operators take only online bookings; others charge a supplement (up to £20) for booking by phone. Main operators include the following.

Brittany Ferries (www.brittany-ferries.com)
DFDS Seaways (☎ 0871 522 9955; www.dfds.co.uk)
Irish Ferries (☎ 08705 17 17 17; www.irishferries.com)
Norfolkline (☎ 08701 450603; www.irishferries.com)
P&O Ferries (☎ 08716 645 645; www.poferries.com)
Speedferries (☎ 0871 222 7456; www.speedferries.com)
Stena Line (www.stenaline.com)
Transmanche (☎ 0800 917 1201; www.transmanche ferries.com)

Another very handy option is www.ferry booker.com, a single site covering all sea-ferry routes and operators, plus Eurotunnel.

GETTING AROUND

For getting around England your first main choice is going by car or public transport. While having your own car helps you make the best use of your time to reach remote places, rental and fuel costs can be expensive for budget travellers – while the trials of traffic jams and parking in major cities hit everyone – so public transport is often the better way to go.

Your main public transport options are train and long-distance bus (called coach in England). Services between major towns and cities are generally good, although at 'peak' (busy) times you must book in advance to be sure of getting a ticket. Conversely, if you book ahead early and/or travel at 'off-peak' periods, tickets can be very cheap.

As long as you have time, using a mix of train, coach, local bus, the odd taxi, walking and occasionally hiring a bike, you can get almost anywhere without having to drive. You'll certainly see more of the countryside than you might slogging along grey motorways, and in the serene knowledge that you're doing less environmental damage.

Traveline (☎ 0871 200 2233; www.traveline.org.uk) is a very useful information service covering bus, coach, taxi and train services nationwide, with numerous links to help plan your journey. By phone, you get transferred automatically to an advisor in the region you're phoning *from;* for details on another part of the country, you need to key in a code number (81 for London, 874 for Cumbria etc) – for a full list of codes, go to the Traveline website.

AIR

England's domestic air companies include British Airways, BMI, BMIbaby, EasyJet and Ryanair, but flights around the country aren't really necessary for tourists unless you're really pushed for time. Even if you're going from one end of the country to the other (eg London to Newcastle, or Manchester to Newquay) trains compare favourably with planes, once airport down-time is factored in. You might get a bargain air fare, but with advance planning trains can be cheaper.

BICYCLE

England is a compact country, and getting around by bicycle is perfectly feasible – and a great way to really see the country – if you've got time to spare. For more inspiration see Outdoor England, p141. For road rules and other hard facts see p791. For taking bikes on trains, see the boxed text on p811.

Renting a bike is easy in London (outlets include www.londonbicycle.com; see www .lcc.org.uk for a list) and at other tourist spots such as Oxford and Cambridge. Rates start at about £10 per day, but £20 per day is more usual for something half decent. Bike rental is also possible in country areas, especially at forestry sites and reservoirs now primarily used for leisure activities, for example Kielder Water in Northumberland (www.the bikeplace.co.uk), Grizedale Forest in the Lake District (www.forestry.gov.uk/grizedale), and the Peak District in Derbyshire, where disused railway lines are now bike routes (www.derby shire-peakdistrict.co.uk/cycling.htm).

Finally, mention must be made of Bristol – England's first 'cycling city'. From mid-2008 to mid-2011, around £11 million is planned to be invested in bike paths and other facilities, including a major rental network modelled on Paris's famous Vélib ('freedom bike') project. Other cities, such as York, Cambridge and Chester will also get similar schemes.

BUS & COACH

If you're on a tight budget, long-distance buses are nearly always the cheapest way to get around, although they're also the slowest – sometimes by a considerable margin.

In England, long-distance express buses are called coaches, and in many towns there are separate bus and coach stations. Make sure you go to the right place!

National Express (☎ 08717 818181; www.nationalexpress.com) is the main operator, with a wide network and frequent services between main centres. Fares vary: they're cheaper if you book in advance and travel at quieter times, and more expensive if you buy your ticket on the spot and it's Friday afternoon. As a guide, a 200-mile trip (eg London to York) will cost around £15 to £20 if you book a few days in advance.

Megabus (www.megabus.com) operates a budget airline–style coach service between about 30 destinations around the country. Go at a quiet time, book early, and your ticket will be very cheap. Book later, for a busy time and…you get the picture.

For information about short-distance and local bus services see p808.

Bus Passes & Discounts

National Express offers discount passes to full-time students and under-26s, called Young Persons Coachcards. They cost £10 and get you 30% off standard adult fares. Also available are coachcards for people over 60, families and disabled travellers.

For touring the country, National Express also offers Brit Xplorer passes, which allow unlimited travel for seven days (£79), 14 days (£139) and 28 days (£219). You don't need to book journeys in advance with this pass; if the coach has a spare seat, you can take it.

CAR & MOTORCYCLE

Travelling by private car or motorbike means you can be independent and flexible, and reach remote places. For solo budget travellers a downside of car travel is the expense, and in cities you'll need superhuman skills to negotiate heaving traffic and deep pockets for parking charges. But if there's two or more of you, car travel can work out cheaper than public transport.

> ### HOW MUCH TO…?
>
> When travelling long-distance by train or bus/coach in England, it's important to note that there's no such thing as a standard fare. Prices vary according to demand and how early you buy your ticket. Book long in advance and travel on Tuesday mid-morning, and it's cheap. Buy your ticket on the spot late Friday afternoon, and it'll be a lot more expensive. Ferries (eg to the Isles of Wight or Man) use similar systems. Throughout this book, to give you an idea, we have generally quoted sample fares somewhere in between the very cheapest and most expensive options. The price you pay will almost certainly be different.

Motorways and main A-roads are dual carriageways and deliver you quickly from one end of the country to another. Lesser A-roads, B-roads and minor roads are much more scenic and fun, as you wind through the countryside from village to village – ideal for car or motorcycle touring. You can't travel fast, but you won't care.

Hire

Compared to many countries (especially the USA), hire rates are expensive in England; you should expect to pay around £250 per week for a small car (unlimited mileage) but rates rise at busy times and drop at quiet times. Some main players:

1car1 (☎ 0113 263 6675; www.1car1.com)
Avis (☎ 0844 581 0147; www.avis.co.uk)
Budget (☎ 0844 581 9998; www.budget.co.uk)
Europcar (☎ 0870 607 5000; www.europcar.co.uk)
Sixt (☎ 08701 567567; www.sixt.co.uk)
Thrifty (☎ 01494-751540; www.thrifty.co.uk)

Many international websites have separate web pages for customers in different countries, and the prices for a car in England on the UK webpages can differ from the same car's prices on the USA or Australia pages. The moral is – you have to surf a lot of sites to find the best deals.

Another option is to look online for small local car-hire companies in England who can undercut the big boys. Generally those in cities are cheaper than in rural areas. See under Getting Around in the main city sections for more details, or see a rental-broker site such as **UK Car Hire** (www.ukcarhire.net).

Yet another option is to hire a motorhome or campervan. It's more expensive than hiring a car but it does help you save on accommodation costs, and gives almost unlimited freedom. Sites to check include these:

Cool Campervans (www.coolcampervans.com)

Just Go (www.justgo.uk.com)

Wild Horizon (www.wildhorizon.co.uk)

Motoring Organisations

Large motoring organisations include the **Automobile Association** (www.theaa.com) and the **Royal Automobile Club** (www.rac.co.uk); annual membership starts at around £35, including 24-hour roadside breakdown assistance. A greener alternative is the **Environmental Transport Association** (www.eta.co.uk); it provides all the usual services (breakdown assistance, roadside rescue, vehicle inspections etc) but doesn't campaign for more roads.

Parking

England is small, and people love their cars, so there's often not enough parking space to go round. Many cities have short-stay and long-stay car parks; the latter are cheaper though maybe less convenient. 'Park and Ride' systems allow you to park on the edge of the city then ride to the centre on regular buses provided for an all-in-one price.

Yellow lines (single or double) along the edge of the road indicate restrictions. Find the nearby sign that spells out when you can and can't park. In London and other big cities, traffic wardens operate with efficiency; if you park on the yellow lines at the wrong time, your car will be clamped or towed away, and it'll cost you £100 or more to get driving again. In some cities there are also red lines, which mean no stopping at all.

Road Rules

A foreign driving licence is valid in England for up to 12 months. If you plan to bring a car from Europe, it's illegal to drive without (at least) third-party insurance. Some other important rules:

- drive on the left (!)
- wear fitted seat belts in cars
- wear crash helmets on motorcycles

- give way to your right at junctions and roundabouts
- always use the left-side lane on motorways and dual-carriageways, unless overtaking (although so many people ignore this rule, you'd think it didn't exist)
- don't use a mobile phone while driving unless it's fully hands-free (another rule frequently flouted).

Speed limits are 30mph (48km/h) in built-up areas, 60mph (96km/h) on main roads and 70mph (112km/h) on motorways and most (but not all) dual carriageways. Drinking and driving is taken very seriously; you're allowed a minimum blood-alcohol level of 80mg/100mL (0.08%) – campaigners want it reduced to 50mg/100mL.

All drivers should read the *Highway Code*. It's available at main newsagents and some tourist offices, and online from www.direct.gov.uk.

HITCHING

Hitching is not as common as it used to be in England, maybe because more people have cars, maybe because few drivers give lifts any more. It's perfectly possible, however, if you don't mind long waits, although travellers should understand that they're taking a small but potentially serious risk, and we don't recommend it. If you decide to go by thumb, note that it's illegal to hitch on motorways; you must use approach roads or service stations.

LOCAL TRANSPORT

English cities usually have good local public transport systems, although buses are often run by a confusing number of separate companies. The larger cities have tram and underground rail services too. Tourist offices can provide information, and more details are given in the city sections throughout this book.

Bus

There are good local bus networks year-round in cities and towns. Buses also run in rural areas year-round, and in tourist spots (especially national parks) there are frequent services from Easter to September. Elsewhere in the countryside, bus timetables are designed to serve schools and industry, so there can be few midday and weekend services (and they may stop running during school holidays), or buses may link local villages to a market town on only one day each week. It's always worth double-checking at a tourist office before planning your day's activities around a bus that may not actually be running.

In this book, along with the local bus route number, frequency and duration, we have provided indicative prices if the fare is over a few pounds. If it's less than this, we have generally omitted the fare details.

BUS PASSES

If you're taking a few local bus rides in a day of energetic sightseeing, ask about day-passes (with names like Day Rover, Wayfarer or Explorer), which will be cheaper than buying several single tickets. If you plan to linger longer in one area, three-day passes are a great bargain. Often they can be bought on your first bus, and may include local rail services. Passes are mentioned in the regional chapters, and it's always worth asking ticket clerks or bus drivers about your options.

POSTBUS

A postbus is a van on usual mail service that also carries passengers. Postbuses operate in rural areas (and some of the most scenic and remote parts of the country), and are especially useful for walkers and backpackers. For information and timetables contact **Royal Mail Postbus** (☎ 08457 740 740; www.royalmail.com/postbus).

Taxi

There are two sorts of taxi in England: the famous black cabs (some with advertising livery in other colours), which have meters and can be hailed in the street; and minicabs, which are cheaper but can only be called by phone. (See p794 for information on the dangers of unlicensed minicabs.) In London and other big cities, taxis cost £2 to £3 per mile. In rural areas it's about half of this, which means when you find the next bus out of the charming village you've been staying in won't arrive for three days, a taxi can keep you moving. The best place to find the local taxi's phone number is the local pub. Alternatively, if you call **National Cabline** (☎ 0800 123444) from a landline phone, the service pinpoints your location and transfers you to an approved local taxi company. Also useful is www.traintaxi

.co.uk – designed to help you 'bridge the final gap' between the train station and your hotel or other final destination.

TRAIN

For long-distance travel around England, trains are generally faster and more comfortable than coaches but can be more expensive, although with discount tickets they're competitive – and often take you through beautiful countryside. In the 1990s, rail travel had a bad reputation for delays and cancellations. A decade later, the situation had improved markedly (so much so that passenger numbers have increased massively), with around 85% of trains running on or pretty close to schedule. The other 15% of journeys that get delayed or cancelled mostly impact commuters rather than long-distance leisure travellers. If your journey from London to Bath runs 30 minutes late, what's the problem? You're on holiday!

About 20 different companies operate train services in Britain (for example: First Great Western runs from London to Bristol, Cornwall and South Wales; National Express East Coast runs London to Leeds, York and Scotland; Virgin Trains run the 'west coast' route from London to Birmingham, Carlisle and Scotland), while Network Rail operates track and stations. For some passengers this system can be confusing at first, but information and ticket-buying services are mostly centralised. If you have to change trains, or use two or more train operators, you still buy one ticket – valid for the whole of your journey. The main railcards are also accepted by all operators.

Your first stop should be **National Rail Enquiries** (☎ 08457 484950; www.nationalrail.co.uk), the nationwide timetable and fare information service. This site also advertises special offers, and has real-time links to station departure boards, so you can see if your train is on time (or not). Once you've found the journey you need, links take you to the relevant train operator or to centralised ticketing services (www.thetrainline.com, www.qjump.co.uk, www.raileasy.co.uk) to buy the ticket. These websites can be confusing at first (you always have to state an approximate preferred time and day of travel, even if you don't mind when you go), but with a little delving around they can offer some real bargains.

You can also buy train tickets on the spot at stations, which is fine for short journeys, but discount tickets for longer trips are usually not available and must be bought in advance by phone or online.

For planning your trip, some very handy maps of the UK's rail network can be downloaded from the National Rail Enquiries website.

Classes

There are two classes of rail travel: first and standard. First class costs around 50% more than standard and, except on very crowded trains, is not really worth it. However, at weekends some train operators offer 'upgrades' for an extra £10 to £15 on top of your standard class fare, so you can enjoy more comfort and leg room.

Costs & Reservations

For short journeys (under about 50 miles) it's usually best to buy tickets on the spot at rail stations. You may get a choice of express or stopping service – the latter is obviously slower, but can be cheaper, and may take you through charming countryside or grotty suburbs.

For longer journeys, on-the-spot fares are always available, but tickets are much cheaper if bought in advance. Essentially, the earlier you book, the cheaper it gets. You can also save if you travel at 'off-peak' times, Fridays and Sundays. Advance purchase usually gets a reserved seat too. The cheapest fares are nonrefundable though, so if you miss your train you'll have to buy a new ticket.

If you buy by phone or website, you can have the ticket posted to you (UK addresses only), or collect it at the originating station on the day of travel, either at the ticket desk (leave time to spare, as queues can be long) or from automatic machines.

Whichever operator you travel with and wherever you buy tickets, these are the three main fare types:

Advance Buy ticket in advance, travel only on specific trains
Off-peak Buy ticket any time, travel off-peak
Anytime Buy anytime, travel anytime

Advance tickets are subject to availability, and usually available as singles only, but if you're making a return journey (ie coming back on the same route) you just buy two singles.

For an idea of the price difference, an Anytime single ticket from London to York will cost around £100, and an Off-peak around £80, while an Advance single can be less than £20, and even less than £10 if you book early enough or don't mind arriving at midnight.

Off-peak and Anytime tickets are available as returns and the price can vary from just under double the single fare to just a pound more than the single fare.

Children under five travel free on trains; those aged between five and 15 pay half price, except on tickets already heavily discounted. A Family & Friends Railcard is usually better value (see Train Passes, below).

If train doesn't get you all the way to your destination, a **PlusBus** supplement (usually around £2) validates your train ticket for onwards travel by bus – more convenient, and usually cheaper, than buying a separate bus ticket. For details see www.plusbus.info.

And finally, it's worth a look at **Megatrain** (www.megatrain.com) – from the people who brought you Megabus; ultra-low train fares on ultra off-peak services between London and a few destinations in southwest England and the East Midlands.

Train Passes

Local train passes usually cover rail networks around a city (many include bus travel too), and are mentioned in the individual city sections throughout this book. If you're staying in England for a while, passes known as 'railcards' are available:

16-25 Railcard – for those aged 16 to 25, or a full-time UK student
Senior Railcard – for anyone over 60
Family & Friends Railcard – covers up to four adults and four children travelling together.

These railcards cost around £25 (valid for one year, available from major stations or online) and get you a 33% discount on most train fares, except those already heavily discounted. With the Family card, adults get 33% and children get 60% discounts, so the fee is easily repaid in a couple of journeys. Proof of age and a passport photo may be required. For full details see www.railcard.co.uk.

A **Disabled Person's Railcard** costs £18. You can get an application from stations or from the railcard website. Call ☎ 0191-281 8103 for more details.

If you're concentrating your travels on southeast England (eg London to Dover, Weymouth, Cambridge or Oxford) a **Network**

TRANSPORT

BIKES ON TRAINS

Bicycles can be taken free of charge on most local urban trains (although they may not be allowed at peak times when the trains are too crowded with commuters) and on shorter trips in rural areas, on a first-come-first-served basis – though there may be space limits. Bike can be carried on long-distance train journeys free of charge as well, but advance-booking is required for most conventional bikes. (Folding bikes can be carried on pretty much any train at any time.) In theory, this shouldn't be too much trouble as most long-distance rail trips are best bought in advance anyway, but you have to go a long way down the path of booking your seat, before you start booking your bike – only to find space isn't available. A better course of action is to buy in advance at a major rail station, where the booking clerk can help you through the options, or phone the relevant operator's Customer Service department. Have a large cup of coffee and a stress-reliever handy. And a final warning: when railways are repaired, cancelled trains are replaced by buses – and they won't take bikes.

A very useful leaflet called 'Cycling by Train' is available at major stations or downloadable from www.nationalrail.co.uk/passenger_services/cyclists.html.

Railcard covers up to four adults and up to four children travelling together outside peak times. For details see p173.

For country-wide travel, **BritRail** (www .britrail.com) passes are good value, but they're only for visitors from overseas and not available in England. They must be bought in your country of origin from a specialist travel agency. There are many BritRail variants, each available in three different versions: for England only; for the whole of Britain (England, Wales and Scotland); and for the UK and Ireland. Below is an outline of the main options, quoting adult prices. Children's passes are usually half price (or free with some adult passes), and seniors get discounts too. For about 30% extra you can upgrade to first class. Other deals include a rail pass combined with the use of a hire car, or travel in Britain combined with one Eurostar journey. For more details see the BritRail website.

BritRail England Consecutive Unlimited travel on all trains in England for four, eight, 15, 22 or 30 days, for US$209/299/449/569/675. Anyone getting their money's worth out of the last pass should earn some sort of endurance award.

BritRail England Flexipass No need to get on a train every day to get full value. Your options are four days of unlimited travel in England within a 60-day period for US$265, eight in 60 days for US$385, or 15 in 60 days for US$579.

If you don't (or can't) buy a BritRail pass, an **All Line Rover** gives virtually unlimited travel for 14 days anywhere on the national rail network. You can travel at any time, but aren't guaranteed a seat (reservations cost extra), so it's best to travel at off-peak times if you can. The pass costs £565 and can be purchased in England, by anyone.

Of the other international passes, Eurail cards are not accepted in England, and InterRail cards are only valid if bought in another mainland European country.

Health Dr Caroline Evans

CONTENTS

England is a healthy place to travel, and the excellent National Health Service (NHS) is free on the point of delivery, which – although Brits may complain – is better than most other countries offer. Across the country, hygiene standards are high (despite what your nose tells you on a crowded tube train) and there are no unusual diseases to worry about. Your biggest risks will be from overdoing activities – physical, chemical or other.

BEFORE YOU GO

No immunisations are mandatory for visiting England or the rest of the UK. Travel insurance, however, is highly recommended, for the reasons outlined in the Insurance section on p796.

You should also check reciprocal medical arrangements between the UK and your own country. Everyone gets emergency treatment (see In England, right) and European Economic Area (EEA) nationals get free non-emergency treatment (ie the same service British citizens receive) with a European Health Insurance Card (EHIC) validated in their home country. Reciprocal arrangements between the UK and some other countries (including Australia) allow free medical treatment at hospitals and surgeries, and subsidised dental care. For details see the **Department of Health** (www.doh.gov.uk) website –

NATIONAL HEALTH WEBSITES

If you're visiting England from overseas, it's a good idea to consult your government's travel health website before departure. Try the following:
Australia (www.dfat.gov.au/travel)
Canada (www.travelhealth.gc.ca)
USA (www.cdc.gov/travel/)

---

follow links to 'Health care', 'Entitlements' and 'Overseas Visitors'.

Internet Resources

Useful sites include the following:
Age Concern (www.ageconcern.org.uk) Advice on travel (and much more) for the elderly.
Center for Disease Control and Prevention (www.cdc.gov)
Foreign & Commonwealth Office (www.fco.gov.uk) The Travelling & Living Overseas section is for Brits going abroad, but useful for incomers.
Marie Stopes International (www.mariestopes.org.uk) Sexual health and contraception.
MD Travel Health (www.mdtravelhealth.com) Worldwide recommendations, updated daily.
World Health Organization (www.who.int) Go to the International travel and health section.

IN TRANSIT
Deep Vein Thrombosis

Deep vein thrombosis (DVT) refers to blood clots that can form in the legs during plane flights, chiefly because of prolonged immobility. The longer the flight, the greater the risk. The chief symptom is swelling or pain in the foot, ankle or calf. When a blood clot travels to the lungs, it may cause chest pain and breathing difficulties. To prevent DVT on long flights you should walk about the cabin, contract and release leg muscles while sitting, drink plenty of fluids and avoid alcohol.

Jet Lag

To avoid jet lag (common when crossing more than five time zones), try drinking plenty of nonalcoholic fluids and eating light meals. Upon arrival, get exposure to natural sunlight and readjust to a local schedule (for meals, sleep etc) as soon as possible.

IN ENGLAND
Medical Services

Regardless of nationality, everyone receives free emergency treatment at accident and emergency (A&E) departments of state-run NHS hospitals.

If you don't need full-on hospital treatment, chemists (pharmacies) can advise on minor ailments such as sore throats and earaches. In large cities, there's always at least one 24/7 chemist.

Sunburn

In summer in England, you can get sunburnt quickly – even under cloud cover and especially on water. Use sunscreen, wear a hat and cover up with a shirt and trousers.

Water

Tap water in England is safe unless there's a sign to the contrary (eg on trains). Don't drink from streams in the countryside – you never know if there's a dead sheep upstream.

Women's Health

Emotional stress, exhaustion and travel through time zones can upset the menstrual pattern. If using oral contraceptives, remember some antibiotics, diarrhoea and vomiting can stop them from working.

If you're already pregnant, travel is usually possible, but you should consult your doctor. The most risky times are the first 12 weeks of pregnancy and after 30 weeks.

HEALTH

Glossary

almshouse – accommodation for the aged or needy

bailey – outermost wall of a castle
bairn – baby or child (northern England)
banger – old, cheap car (colloquial)
bap – bun
bar – gate (York, and some other northern cities)
beck – stream (northern England)
bent – not altogether legal (slang)
billion – the British billion is a million million (unlike the American billion – a thousand million)
bloke – man (colloquial)
bodge job – poor-quality repair (colloquial)
bonnet (of car) – hood
boot (of car) – trunk
bridleway – path that can be used by walkers, horse riders and cyclists
Brummie – native of Birmingham
bum – backside (not tramp, layabout etc as in American English)
bus – local bus; see also *coach*

cairn – pile of stones marking path, junction or peak
canny – good, great, wise (northern England)
cheers – goodbye; thanks; also a drinking toast
chemist – pharmacist
chine – valley-like fissure leading to the sea (southern England)
circus – junction of several streets, usually circular
coach – long-distance bus
coasteering – adventurous activity that involves making your way around a rocky coastline by climbing, scrambling, jumping or swimming
cob – mixture of mud and straw for building
cot – small bed for a baby ('crib' to Americans)
couchette – sleeping berth in a train or ferry
court – courtyard
crack – good conversation, or good times (anglicised version of Gaelic 'craic')
croft – plot of land with adjoining house worked by the occupiers

dear – expensive
DIY – do-it-yourself, ie home improvements
dosh – money, wealth (colloquial)
dough – money (colloquial)
downs – rolling upland, characterised by lack of trees
duvet – quilt replacing sheets and blankets ('doona' to Australians)

EH – English Heritage
en suite room – hotel room with private attached bathroom (ie shower, basin and toilet)
Essex – derogatory adjective (as in 'Essex girl'), meaning showy/tarty
EU – European Union
evensong – daily evening service (Church of England)

fag – cigarette; also boring task (colloquial)
fagged – exhausted (colloquial)
fanny – female genitals (offensive slang), not backside as in American English
fell race – tough running race through hills or moors
fen – drained or marshy low-lying flat land
fiver – five-pound note
flat – apartment
flip-flops – plastic sandals with a single strap over toes ('thongs' to Australians)
footpath – path through countryside and between houses, not beside a road (that's called a 'pavement')

gaffer – boss or foreman (colloquial)
gate – street (York, and some other northern cities)
ginnel – alleyway (Yorkshire)
graft – work (colloquial term; not corruption, as in American English)
grand – one thousand (colloquial)
grockle – tourist (colloquial)
gutted – very disappointed (colloquial)
guv, guvner – from governor, a respectful term of address for owner or boss; can sometimes be used ironically

hammered – drunk (colloquial)
hart – deer
HI – Hostelling International (organisation)
hire – rent
hosepipe – garden hose
hotel – accommodation with food and bar, not always open to passing trade
Huguenots – French Protestants

inn – pub with accommodation

jumper – woollen item of clothing worn on torso ('sweater' to Americans)

karst – landscape usually featuring limestone rock, caves, sinkholes and a lack of surface water
kirk – church (northern England)

lager lout – see *yob*

lass – young woman (northern England)

ley – clearing

lift – machine for carrying people up and down in large buildings ('elevator' to Americans)

lock – part of a canal or river that can be closed off and the water levels changed to raise or lower boats

lolly – money (colloquial); candy on a stick (possibly frozen)

lorry – truck

love – term of address, not necessarily to someone likeable

machair – grass- and wildflower-covered sand dunes

mad – insane (not angry, as in American English)

Marches – borderlands (ie between England and Wales or Scotland) after the Anglo-Saxon word *mearc,* meaning 'boundary'

Martello tower – small, circular tower used for coastal defence

mate – friend of any gender; also term of address, usually male-to-male

midge – mosquito-like insect

motorway – major road linking cities (equivalent to 'interstate' or 'freeway')

motte – mound on which a castle was built

naff – inferior, in poor taste (colloquial)

nappies – worn by babies before they're toilet trained ('diapers' to Americans)

NCN – National Cycle Network

NT – National Trust

oast house – building containing a kiln for drying hops

off-license ('offie') – carry-out alcoholic drinks shop (colloquial)

OS – Ordnance Survey

owlers – smugglers

p (pronounced 'pee') – pence (ie 2p is 'two p' not 'two pence' or 'tuppence')

pargeting – decorative stucco plasterwork

pele – fortified house

pissed – drunk (slang; not angry)

pissed off – angry (slang)

pitch – playing field

ponce – colloquial term for ostentatious or effeminate male; also to borrow (usually permanently)

pop – fizzy drink (northern England)

postbus – minibus delivering the mail, also carrying passengers

provost – mayor

punter – customer (colloquial)

quid – pound (colloquial)

ramble – short easy walk

red-tops – 'popular' newspapers such as the *Sun* and *Daily Mirror,* as opposed to 'serious' newspapers such as the *Times* and *Guardian*

reiver – warrior (historic term – northern England)

return ticket – round-trip ticket

roll-up – roll-your-own cigarette

RSPB – Royal Society for the Protection of Birds

RSPCA – Royal Society for the Prevention of Cruelty to Animals

rubber – eraser; also (and less commonly) condom

rubbish bin – what Americans call a 'garbage can'

rugger – rugby union

sarsen – boulder, a geological remnant usually found in chalky areas (sometimes used in neolithic constructions eg Stonehenge and Avebury)

shag – have sex (slang); also a tough or tiring task (colloquial)

shagged – tired (colloquial)

sheila-na-gig – Celtic fertility symbol of a woman with exaggerated genitalia, often carved in stone on churches and castles. Rare in England, found mainly in the Marches, along the border with Wales.

shout – to buy a group of people drinks, usually reciprocated (colloquial)

shut – partially covered passage

single ticket – one-way ticket

sixth-form college – further-education college

snicket/snickleway – narrow alley (York)

snog – long, drawn-out kiss (colloquial term; not just a peck on the cheek)

spondulicks – money (colloquial)

SSSI – Site of Special Scientific Interest

stone – unit of weight equivalent to 14lb or 6.35kg

subway – underpass (for pedestrians)

sweets – what Americans call 'candy' and Australians call 'lollies'

ta – thanks

tenner – £10 note

thwaite – clearing in a forest (northern England)

ton – one hundred (colloquial)

tor – pointed hill (Celtic)

torch – flashlight

Tory – Conservative (political party)

towpath – path running beside a river or canal, where horses once towed barges

trainers – running/tennis shoes

traveller – nomadic person (traditional and New Age hippy types)

twit – foolish (sometimes annoying) person (colloquial)

twitcher – obsessive birdwatcher

twitten – passage, small lane

Tube, the – London's underground railway system (colloquial)

Underground, the – London's underground railway system

VAT – value-added tax, levied on most goods and services, currently 17.5%
verderer – officer upholding law and order in the royal forests

wanker – stupid/worthless person (offensive slang)
wide boy – ostentatious go-getter, usually on the make (colloquial)
wolds – open, rolling countryside

YHA – Youth Hostels Association
yob – hooligan (colloquial)

GLOSSARY OF ENGLISH RELIGIOUS ARCHITECTURE

aisle – passageway or open space along either side of a church's *nave*
apse – area for clergy, traditionally at the east end of the church

barrel vault – semicircular arched roof
boss – covering for the meeting point of the ribs in a *vaulted* roof
brass – memorial consisting of a brass plate set into the floor or a tomb
buttress – vertical support for a wall; see also *flying buttress*

campanile – free-standing belfry or bell tower
chancel – eastern end of the church, usually reserved for choir and clergy
chantry – *chapel* established by a donor for use in their name after death
chapel – small church; shrine or area of worship off the main body of a cathedral
chapel of ease – *chapel* built for those who lived far away from the parish church
choir – area in the church where the choir is seated
cloister – covered walkway linking the church with adjacent monastic buildings

close – buildings grouped around a cathedral
corbel – stone or wooden projection from a wall supporting a beam or arch
crossing – intersection of the *nave* and *transepts* in a church

flying buttress – supporting *buttress* in the form of one side of an open arch
font – basin used for baptisms, often in a separate *baptistry*
frater – common or dining room in a medieval monastery

lady chapel – *chapel* dedicated to the Virgin Mary
lancet – pointed window in Early English style
lierne vault – *vault* containing many tertiary ribs

minster – church connected to a monastery
misericord – hinged choir seat with a bracket (often elaborately carved)

nave – main body of the church at the western end, where the congregation gather

presbytery – eastern area of *chancel* beyond the choir, where the clergy operate
precincts – see *close*
priory – religious house governed by a prior
pulpit – raised box where the priest gives sermons

quire – medieval term for *choir*

refectory – monastic dining room
reredos – literally 'behind the back'; backdrop to an altar
rood – archaic word for cross (in churches)
rood screen – screen carrying a *rood* or crucifix, separating *nave* from *chancel*

squint – angled opening in a wall or pillar to allow a view of a church's altar

transepts – north–south projections from a church's *nave*, giving church a cruciform (cross-shaped plan)

undercroft – vaulted underground room or cellar

vault – roof with arched ribs, usually in a decorative pattern
vestry – priest's robing room

The Authors

DAVID ELSE
Coordinating Author; History; Food & Drink; Environment; Directory; Transport; Glossary

As a full-time professional travel writer, David has authored more than 20 books, including Lonely Planet's guides to *Great Britain* and *Walking in Britain*. His knowledge of England comes from a lifetime of travel around the country (often on foot or by bike), a passion dating from university years, when heading for the hills was always more attractive than visiting the library. Originally from London, David has lived in Yorkshire and Derbyshire, and is currently based on the southern edge of the Cotswolds. For those interested in domestic matters: David is married with two young children, who already find themselves on the back of their dad's tandem whenever the sun shines.

OLIVER BERRY
Destination England; Getting Started; Itineraries; The Culture; Cumbria & the Lake District

A born and bred Brit, Oliver has been seeking out England's more eccentric corners for the last 30-odd years, and it was an absolute pleasure to do a bit more exploring for this book. Having worked on several previous editions of the *England* guide, for this book Oliver clambered down into the murky slate mines of Honister, tackled the trails of the Cumbrian fells, and stuffed himself silly with tattie hotpot, Grasmere gingerbread and Bluebird ale. When he's not out on the road, Oliver lives and works in Cornwall as a writer and photographer.

FIONN DAVENPORT
The Northwest; The Northeast

Dublin-based Fionn has been visiting and writing about northern England for about a decade, which is a good thing considering that it's his favourite bit of the country – mostly because the people remind him of the folks across the puddle in Ireland. When he's not traipsing around Newcastle or Manchester – or watching his beloved Liverpool FC at Anfield – he's juggling his commitments to Irish radio and TV, where he doles out travel advice and gives out about globalisation fatigue. And when he's not doing that, he spends most of his time wondering where he'd like to go next.

BELINDA DIXON
Wessex; Devon & Cornwall

Belinda was drawn to the southwest in the 1990s to do a postgrad (having been impressed there were palm trees on the campus) and, like the best west-country limpets, has proved hard to shift since. She spends as much time as possible in the sea, but can also be seen and heard writing and broadcasting in the region. Personal highlights for this latest Lonely Planet adventure are sitting in the stone circle at Avebury, rigorously testing the new wave of Cornish cuisine and exploring utterly exhilarating Exmoor.

PETER DRAGICEVICH
London

After a dozen years working for newspapers and magazines in New Zealand and Australia, London's bright lights and loud guitars could no longer be resisted. Like all good Kiwis, Peter got to know the city while surfing his way between friends' flats all over London. Now, living an even more nomadic life as a Lonely Planet writer, London is one of three cities that he likes to think of as home. He has contributed to nine Lonely Planet titles, including writing the Thames Path section of *Walking in Britain*.

NANA LUCKHAM
The Southeast; The East Midlands;
The West Midlands & the Marches

Nana spent most of her childhood in Brighton, aside from a few years in Tanzania, Ghana and Australia. After university, she worked as an editorial assistant in London and a UN press officer in New York and Geneva before becoming a full-time travel writer. Now based in London, she spends most of her time on research trips in exotic faraway climes, so she jumped at the chance to rediscover her home region of the southeast and relive her university days in the Midlands, during which she developed a new-found enthusiasm for the old country.

ETAIN O'CARROLL
Oxford, the Cotswolds & Around; East Anglia

Travel writer and photographer Etain O'Carroll grew up in small-town Ireland and regular childhood trips to England were tinged with the excitement of eating gammon and pineapple in motorway service stations, examining the countless sparkly pens in swanky Woolies and meeting all those cousins with funny accents. In between were the trips to the chocolate-box villages, stately homes, massive castles and ruined abbeys. Now living in Oxford, Etain's childish awe has become a long-term appreciation for the fine architecture, bucolic countryside and rich heritage of her adopted home. Work often takes her far away but she cherished the excuse to traipse around her own back yard searching for hidden treats.

Behind the Scenes

NEIL WILSON   Yorkshire

From rock-climbing trips to Yorkshire gritstone in his university days, to
weekend getaways in York and Whitby in more recent years, Neil has made
many cross-border forays into 'God's own country' from his home in Scotland. Whether hiking across the high tops of the Yorkshire Dales, savouring
Britain's best fish and chips on the Whitby waterfront, or worshipping at the
fountainhead of Theakston Ales in Masham, he's never short of an excuse
for yet another visit. Neil is a full-time travel writer based in Edinburgh, and
has written more than 40 guidebooks for various publishers.

Behind the Scenes

THIS BOOK

This 5th edition of *England* was researched and written by David Else (coordinating author), Oliver Berry, Peter Dragicevich, Fionn Davenport, Belinda Dixon, Nana Luckham, Etain O'Carroll and Neil Wilson. The previous edition was also researched by Jolyon Attwooll, Charlotte Beech and Laetitia Clapton. This guidebook was commissioned in Lonely Planet's London office and produced by the following people:

Commissioning Editor Clifton Wilkinson
Coordinating Editors Daniel Corbett, Branislava Vladisavljevic
Coordinating Cartographer Diana Duggan
Coordinating Layout Designer Tamsin Wilson
Managing Editor Bruce Evans
Managing Cartographer Mark Griffiths, Adrian Persoglia
Managing Layout Designer Laura Jane
Assisting Editors Michala Green, Charlotte Harrison, Margedd Heliosz, Helen Koehne, Joanne Newell, Charlotte Orr, Simon Sellars
Assisting Cartographers Joshua Geoghegan, Alex Leung, Joanne Luke, Anthony Phelan, James Reagan
Assisting Layout Designers Wibowo Rusli
Cover Designer Pepi Bluck
Project Manager Rachel Imeson

Thanks to Jennifer Garrett, Chris Girdler, Lisa Knights, Lyahna Spencer

THANKS
DAVID ELSE

As always, massive appreciation goes to my wife, Corinne, for joining me on many of my research trips around England, and for not minding when I locked myself away for 12 hours at a time to write this book – and for bringing coffee when it got nearer 16 hours.

Thanks also to the coauthors of this book; my name goes down as coordinating author, but I couldn't have done it without Belinda, Nana, Neil, Fionn, Oliver, Etain and Peter. And finally, thanks to Cliff Wilkinson, my commissioning editor at Lonely Planet London, and to all the friendly faces in the editorial, cartography, layout and design departments at Lonely Planet Melbourne who helped bring this book to final fruition.

OLIVER BERRY

As always a whole host of thank-yous. Back home a huge thanks as always to Susie Berry for keeping me fed and watered during long nights of typing, Jenks and the o-region boys for keeping things ticking over Kernowside while I was on the road, TSP for serial long-distance Skyping, and the Hobo

THE LONELY PLANET STORY

Fresh from an epic journey across Europe, Asia and Australia in 1972, Tony and Maureen Wheeler sat at their kitchen table stapling together notes. The first Lonely Planet guidebook, *Across Asia on the Cheap,* was born.

Travellers snapped up the guides. Inspired by their success, the Wheelers began publishing books to Southeast Asia, India and beyond. Demand was prodigious, and the Wheelers expanded the business rapidly to keep up. Over the years, Lonely Planet extended its coverage to every country and into the virtual world via lonelyplanet.com and the Thorn Tree message board.

As Lonely Planet became a globally loved brand, Tony and Maureen received several offers for the company. But it wasn't until 2007 that they found a partner whom they trusted to remain true to the company's principles of travelling widely, treading lightly and giving sustainably. In October of that year, BBC Worldwide acquired a 75% share in the company, pledging to uphold Lonely Planet's commitment to independent travel, trustworthy advice and editorial independence.

Today, Lonely Planet has offices in Melbourne, London and Oakland, with over 500 staff members and 300 authors. Tony and Maureen are still actively involved with Lonely Planet. They're travelling more often than ever, and they're devoting their spare time to charitable projects. And the company is still driven by the philosophy of *Across Asia on the Cheap*: 'All you've got to do is decide to go and the hardest part is over. So go!'

for constantly keeping my shadow company. Special thanks to the Cumbrian Tourist Board and the region's many excellent tourist offices, to Lucy's in Ambleside, to David Else and Cliff Wilkinson for casting an experienced eye over my front chapters, and especially to my coauthors for providing me with plenty of useful material to back up my own research. Here's to you Fionn, Neil, Belinda, Peter, Nana and Etain.

FIONN DAVENPORT

In the northwest, a big thank-you to Trevor Evers, Louise Latham and Marketing Manchester, who answered all my questions with great enthusiasm. Thanks also to Craig Gill for spending the afternoon with me and giving me the insider's guide to Madchester's days of glorious ignominy. In the northeast, I owe a debt of gratitude to Lisa Hadwin, Tina Snowball, Lisa Carroll, Pete Warne and, particularly, Pat, who guided me around her beloved Newcastle and made me understand how brilliant it really is. Thanks to Kevin Taylor for his help, and also to Jonathan Edwards – as friendly and charming an Olympic gold medallist as you're ever likely to meet! Thanks to everyone at Lonely Planet, especially Cliff and David for their leniency and understanding!

BELINDA DIXON

So many people to thank – so little time... Best limit it to Lonely Planet's fine team – from Cliff (thank you – again!), David Else (how you manage it amazes me) and fellow authors (OTB, how about that beer?), to the production elves, cartographers and editors who knock it all into shape, stitch it together and ship it out. Bravo! As ever sincere thanks to all who provided info and assistance along the way, official and unofficial; friends and family for reminding me what's important; and to the AD for calm, kindness and a broader view.

PETER DRAGICEVICH

Firstly, a huge thank-you to Sue Ostler and Ed Lee for their incredible hospitality and their assistance in 'researching' London's bars and restaurants. Special thanks are also due to Tim Benzie, Sarah Welch and Yvonne New, Suzannah and Oliver de Montford, Adrienne and Ben Preston, Kurt Crommelin, Laryssa Nyrvana and Vanessa Irvine.

NANA LUCKHAM

Thanks to Clifton Wilkinson and David Else at Lonely Planet. Also to Claire Young for putting me up in Birmingham and showing me many of the sights, and to all who helped me with research along the

way – Simon Macdonald, Linda Griggs, Shahrezad Razavi, Claire Bulmer, Chyono Flynn, Jill and Dennis Swift, Robin Luckham and Louise Gerber. Thanks also to Ben Swift for chauffeuring me around the Peak District with much patience as always.

ETAIN O'CARROLL

Huge thanks to the cheerful staff in tourist offices around my area for their help and advice. Sincere gratitude also to Ben Wong for the insight into life in an Oxford college; to Aimee O'Carroll for the low-down on Cambridge; to Liz Goold, Beccy Mullett and Juliette Strother for tips and help on travel in Essex; to Sandy and Norah Kennedy for a local's view of Stroud; to Monika, Toine and Adriana Roozen, and Sarah Burbridge for company, opinions and help in Norfolk. Thanks too to Cliff at Lonely Planet for cheerful assistance the whole way through the project, to Mark for coming along on a few trips and for patience and support as a deadline loomed, and to Osgur for the heart-melting smiles and for being more patient than I could ever have imagined on long days on the road.

NEIL WILSON

Thanks to the many Yorkshire folk who freely offered advice and recommendations, to the tourist office staff for answering dumb questions, to

SEND US YOUR FEEDBACK

We love to hear from travellers – your comments keep us on our toes and help make our books better. Our well-travelled team reads every word on what you loved or loathed about this book. Although we cannot reply individually to postal submissions, we always guarantee that your feedback goes straight to the appropriate authors, in time for the next edition. Each person who sends us information is thanked in the next edition – and the most useful submissions are rewarded with a free book.

To send us your updates – and find out about Lonely Planet events, newsletters and travel news – visit our award-winning website: lonelyplanet.com/contact.

Note: we may edit, reproduce and incorporate your comments in Lonely Planet products such as guidebooks, websites and digital products, so let us know if you don't want your comments reproduced or your name acknowledged. For a copy of our privacy policy visit lonelyplanet.com/privacy.

the friendly folk at Beiderbecke's in Scarborough, and to eerie Andy Dextrous in York for his help – much appreciated. Thanks also to Lonely Planet's editors and cartos, and to Carol for letting me borrow her car.

OUR READERS

Many thanks to the travellers who used the last edition and wrote to us with helpful hints, useful advice and interesting anecdotes:

James, Lucy Alexander, Paul Anderton, Peter Arcus, Pamela Ashby, John Baker, Sophie Bannister Martin, Molly Blackburn, Yves Blavet, Rosy Blockley, K Bridges, David Brooks, Francis Cagney, Jenny Connolly, Jim Conwell, Paul Costello, Bob Cromwell, Emma-Jane Crozier, Simon Curtis, Bill Darcy, Catherine Deleplace, James Dunn, Waltraud Englefield, Annalena Erlenbach, Elizabeth Fox, Liz Gammie, Richard Gammie, Ross Geach, Tom Griffiths, Bob Hart, Andy Hellis, Jenny Hinson, Kirsty Hughes, Ruth Hunt, James Irvine, Reka Kozalek, Wendy Lawrence, Anne Leroy, Robert Loaring,

Maria Luk, Glenys Lunt, Graham Lupp, Marilyn Marston, Trevor Mazzucchelli, William McCartney, Kim Moody, Anthony Moore, Sophie O'Donnell, Rob Olston, Saw Ai Ooi, Rita Packford, Suzanne Parry, Clare Power, Ana Ramos, Jen Randall, Frances Rein, Cynthia Rignanese, Walter Sassard, Greg Slade, Jo-Anne Smetherham, Judy Smith, Bas Van Der Maat, Jason Vaughan, Mitzi Waltz, Susan Weiss, Silvia Woodier, Ann Young, Summer Zeh

ACKNOWLEDGMENTS

Many thanks to the following for the use of their content:

London Underground Map © Transport for London 2006. Globe on title page ©Mountain High Maps 1993 Digital Wisdom, Inc.

All images are the copyright of the photographers unless otherwise indicated. Many of the images in this guide are available for licensing from Lonely Planet Images: www.lonelyplanetimages.com.

Index

INDEX

000 Map pages
000 Photograph pages

INDEX

INDEX

INDEX

GreenDex

GOING GREEN

Researching this guidebook we discovered many hotels, cafes, pubs, restaurants and attractions demonstrating a commitment to sustainability, and we take great pleasure in highlighting some of them here. We've selected places to eat that support local producers or champion 'slow food' – we've also highlighted some farmers markets and some local producers themselves. We've listed accommodation deemed to be environmentally friendly, demonstrating, for example, a commitment to recycling or energy conservation (and they've got to be a great place to stay, too). The range of 'green' attractions is especially broad, including places involved in conservation and environmental education, or winners of ecological awards. If you want to do your bit, see the Getting Started chapter (p20) for a few ideas on sustainable and responsible travel in England, or check www.lonelyplanet.com /responsibletravel for the bigger picture. And if you want to add to the list, or if you disagree with our choices, email talk2us@lonelyplanet.com.au and set us straight for next time.

MAP LEGEND

ROUTES

Tollway	Unsealed Road
Freeway	One-Way Street
Primary	Mall/Steps
Secondary	Tunnel
Tertiary	Pedestrian Overpass
Lane	Walking Tour
Under Construction	Walking Trail
	Walking Path

TRANSPORT

Ferry	Rail (Underground)
Metro	Tram
Tube Station	Cable Car, Funicular
Rail	

HYDROGRAPHY

River, Creek	Water
Canal	

BOUNDARIES

International	Ancient Wall
State, Provincial	Cliff

AREA FEATURES

Airport	Land
Area of Interest	Mall
Beach	Market
Building	Park
Campus	Rocks
Cemetery, Christian	Sports
Forest	Urban

POPULATION

✪ CAPITAL (NATIONAL)	◉ CAPITAL (STATE)
● Large City	● Medium City
● Small City	● Town, Village

SYMBOLS

Sights/Activities
- Beach
- Buddhist
- Castle, Fortress
- Christian
- Hindu
- Islamic
- Jain
- Jewish
- Monument
- Museum, Gallery
- Point of Interest
- Pool
- Ruin
- Sikh
- Surfing, Surf Beach
- Trail Head
- Winery, Vineyard
- Zoo, Bird Sanctuary

Eating
- Eating

Drinking
- Drinking
- Cafe

Entertainment
- Entertainment

Shopping
- Shopping

Sleeping
- Sleeping
- Camping

Transport
- Airport, Airfield
- Bus Station
- Cycling, Bicycle Path
- General Transport
- Parking Area
- Taxi Rank

Information
- Bank, ATM
- Embassy/Consulate
- Hospital, Medical
- Information
- Internet Facilities
- Police Station
- Post Office, GPO
- Telephone
- Toilets

Geographic
- Lighthouse
- Lookout
- Mountain
- National Park
- Pass, Canyon
- Picnic Area
- River Flow
- Waterfall

LONELY PLANET OFFICES

Australia
Head Office
Locked Bag 1, Footscray, Victoria 3011
☎ 03 8379 8000, fax 03 8379 8111
talk2us@lonelyplanet.com.au

USA
150 Linden St, Oakland, CA 94607
☎ 510 250 6400, toll free 800 275 8555
fax 510 893 8572
info@lonelyplanet.com

UK
2nd fl, 186 City Rd,
London EC1V 2NT
☎ 020 7106 2100, fax 020 7106 2101
go@lonelyplanet.co.uk

Published by Lonely Planet Publications Pty Ltd

ABN 36 005 607 983

© Lonely Planet Publications Pty Ltd 2009

© photographers as indicated 2009

Cover photograph: Castlerigg Stone Circle, Cumbria, England, Giovanni Simeone/SIME-4Corners I. Many of the images in this guide are available for licensing from Lonely Planet Images: www.lonelyplanetimages.com.

Printed through Hang Tai.
Printed in China.